W9-AEQ-984

Lourdes Library
Gwynedd Mercy College
P. O. Box 901
Gwynedd Valley, PA 19437-0901

LIBRARY
CURRICULUM COLLECTION

CUR
973
AV
1995

★ A HISTORY OF THE UNITED STATES ★

AMERICAN VOICES

Lourdes Library
Gwynedd Mercy College
P. O. Box 901
Gwynedd Valley, PA 19437-0901

LOURDES LIBRARY
CURRICULUM COLLECTION

One by one, sometimes bold, sometimes hesitant, sometimes demanding, sometimes faltering, they emerged—individuals. People, with voices, faces, eyes. People with hope. People without hope. People still fighting. People with all courage squeezed out of them. People with stories.

—Lorena Hickok, 1937

CUR
923
AV
1995

A HISTORY OF THE UNITED STATES

AMERICAN VOICES

LOURDES LIBRARY
CURRICULUM COLLECTION

AUTHORS

Carol Berkin
Baruch College
The City University of New York

Alan Brinkley
Columbia University

Clayborne Carson
Stanford University

Robert W. Cherny
San Francisco State University

Robert A. Divine
University of Texas at Austin

Eric Foner
Columbia University

Jeffrey B. Morris
Brooklyn Law School

The Reverend Arthur Wheeler, C.S.C.
University of Portland

Leonard Wood
Eastern Illinois University, *Emeritus*

![ScottForesman]
ScottForesman

A Division of HarperCollins*Publishers*

Editorial Offices: Glenview, Illinois
Regional Offices: Sunnyvale, California • Atlanta, Georgia • Glenview, Illinois • Oakland, New Jersey • Carrollton, Texas

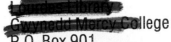
Lourdes Library
Gwynedd Mercy College
P. O. Box 901
Gwynedd Valley, PA 19437-0901

PROGRAM AUTHORS

Carol Berkin, professor of history at Baruch College, The City University of New York, specializes in American colonial history and women's history. She has written several books, including *Jonathan Sewell: Odyssey of an American Loyalist* (1974), which won the Bancroft Award.

Alan Brinkley, professor of history at Columbia University, specializes in 20th-century U.S. history. He is the author of *Voices of Protest: Huey Long, Father Coughlin, and the Great Depression* (1982).

Clayborne Carson, professor of history at Stanford University, specializes in African American history. He is the author of the award-winning *In Struggle: SNCC and the Black Awakening of the 1960s* (1981) and is the editor of the papers of the Rev. Dr. Martin Luther King, Jr.

Robert Cherny, professor of history at San Francisco State University, specializes in 19th-century and early 20th-century U.S. history. His books include *A Righteous Cause: The Life of William Jennings Bryan* (1985).

Robert A. Divine, George W. Littlefield Professor in American History at the University of Texas at Austin, specializes in American diplomatic history. Among his books is *Eisenhower and the Cold War* (1981).

Eric Foner, DeWitt Clinton Professor of History at Columbia University, specializes in the Civil War and Reconstruction. His books include the award-winning *Reconstruction: America's Unfinished Revolution* (1988). Dr. Foner is the author of the chapter on the Civil War and Reconstruction.

Jeffrey B. Morris, professor of law at the Brooklyn Law School, specializes in constitutional history. He is the co-editor of works that include *Great Presidential Decisions* and *Encyclopedia of American History*.

The Reverend Arthur Wheeler, C.S.C., professor of history at the University of Portland, specializes in modern European history, in particular, World War II.

Leonard Wood, professor emeritus at Eastern Illinois University, specializes in 19th-century and 20th-century U.S. history. He has also taught at secondary schools and has extensive experience developing high-school instructional materials.

Contributing Authors/Source Readings

Heidi Roupp, history teacher at Aspen High School, Aspen, Colorado, is Regional Director of the Colorado Council for the Social Studies.

David Pasquini, chairman, Social Studies department, at Glenbrook South High School, Glenview, Illinois, participates in Glenbrook's Academy Program, an intensive curriculum combining history, literature, and foreign language.

Academic Consultants

Hispanic History
Felix Almaráz, Jr.
University of Texas at San Antonio

American Colonial History
Jean Friedman
University of Georgia

20th-Century U.S. History
James Penick
University of Alabama at Birmingham

20th-Century and African American History
Christopher Reed
Roosevelt University

Achieving English Proficiency
Shahrzad Mahootian
Northwestern University

Critical Thinking
John Barell
Montclair State College

Reading Comprehension
Robert Pavlik
Lorraine Gerhart
Cardinal Stritch College

Teacher Consultants

William Bartelt
William Henry Harrison High School
Evansville, Indiana

Myrth Buckley
La Quinta High School
Westminster, California

Dr. Thomas Caughron
Upland High School
Upland, California

Armando Cunanon
Mt. Miguel High School
Spring Valley, California

Loyal Darr
Denver Public Schools
Denver, Colorado

Carol Ann Davis
Lowell High School
Lowell, Massachusetts

Dominick De Cecco
Bethlehem High School
Del Mar, New York

Frederick Dorsett
Northeast High School
St. Petersburg, Florida

John A. Jones, Jr.
New Orleans Public Schools
New Orleans, Louisiana

James R. Mullen
Del Mar High School
San Jose, California

Marilyn Washington
Jordan High School
Los Angeles, California

Copyright © 1995, 1992

Scott, Foresman and Company, A Division of Harper Collins *Publishers,* Glenview, Illinois. All Rights Reserved. Printed in the United States of America.

This publication is protected by Copyright and permission should be obtained from the publisher prior to any prohibited reproduction, storage in a retrieval system, or transmission in any form or by any means, electronic, mechanical, photocopying, recording, or otherwise. For information regarding permission, write to: Scott, Foresman, 1900 East Lake Avenue, Glenview, Illinois 60025.

ISBN: 0-673-35176-9
Acknowledgments for quoted matter and illustrations are included in the acknowledgments section on pages 1076–1078. The acknowledgments section is an extension of the copyright page.

345678910 DR 0201009998979695

C O N T E N T S

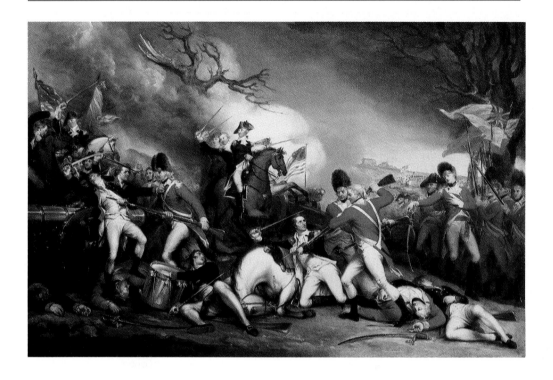

Prologue: Key Themes in American History / xlii

CONNECTING WITH PAST LEARNINGS: THE UNITED STATES TO 1900

Unit 2   America at Peace and at War / 342

Chapter 8   The Progressive Era 1900–1917 / 344

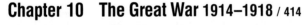

Unit 5   Troubled Times / 748

Special Features

Maps

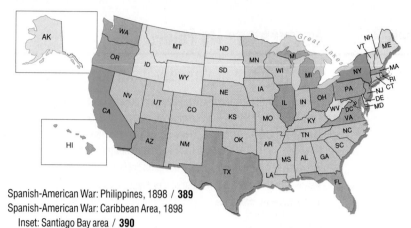

Geography in American History

Touring the Past

Key Documents in U.S. History

Charts, Tables, Diagrams

Highlights of American Life

Building Critical Thinking Strategies

Meet the Presidents

Point/Counterpoint

Voices from the Past

What is History?

What is history? As one noted historian has explained, historians have three definitions of history. First, there is what happened, which may or may not be open to investigation. Second, there is what the past left behind for historians to investigate, or what is referred to as the historical record. This includes not only written and printed sources — diaries, journals, memoirs, court records, newspapers, and the like — but physical and institutional artifacts as well, such as buildings, language, laws, and theories of government. Third, there is the interpretation of that historical evidence. This is the principal concern of the historian.

Because most historical facts are not questionable, historians seldom argue about what happened. For example, you will not find historians debating whether the Civil War occurred, but you will find them arguing about why it happened and debating its consequences. This is not to suggest that facts are irrelevant. However, historians do more than merely record events. Rather, they try to explain and interpret what happened. As the late E.H. Carr wrote, "The historian without his facts is rootless and futile; the facts without their historian are dead and meaningless."

In formulating an explanation of the past, historians refrain from looking at events in isolation. Instead, they consider events within their complex historical context, or as a part of a long chain of events. The task of the historian is to sort out the complexity of the past, to determine which events are most significant, and to explain why he or she believes so. Different historians will have different answers. Every historian has a bias that will influence how he or she interprets the past. Moreover, historical questions are often determined by present issues. The example of how historians have interpreted Reconstruction will demonstrate this point.

Writing in 1897, U.S. historian William A. Dunning argued that the experiment in extending civil liberties to African Americans had been a mistake. Like many people of his day, Dunning believed in the natural inferiority of blacks and was convinced that the two races were incapable of coexisting. Any attempt to legislate equality, therefore, was doomed to fail.

The Dunning interpretation remained the accepted view until the 1950s, when a new school of scholars, influenced by the civil rights movement, reevaluated Reconstruction. Led by Professor Kenneth Stampp, these historians accused Dunning of distorting and exaggerating Reconstruction's failures and of overlooking its accomplishments. The 14th and 15th amendments, they argued, were radical achievements that provided the legal basis for the civil rights movement.

Historian Eric Foner has provided the most recent interpretation of Reconstruction. Although he praises Stampp's challenge to Dunning, Foner criticizes Stampp for seeing African Americans as passive victims of the actions of others. Instead, Foner views African Americans as active participants.

As the example of Reconstruction illustrates, history is a dynamic discipline. Historians often see the same events differently. Facts can be marshalled to reach opposite conclusions and diametrically opposed interpretations. Moreover, you can see that each generation of historians reinterprets the past. The orthodox, or accepted, interpretation of a generation also has given way to a new orthodoxy. Today's accepted interpretations of the American past are not final.

For these reasons, you should approach all works of history, including your textbook, with a questioning mind. You should realize that what you are reading is not the definitive word on the past but only contemporary historians' interpretations of the past. It is up to you, the critical reader, to determine whether they are convincing.

> **H**uman history is in essence a history of ideas.
>
> H.G. Wells,
> *Outline of History, 1920*

Definitions of History

It is somewhat unfortunate that the word history *should be used in several different senses. In its origin (Greek . . .) it meant learning by inquiry. The historian . . . was a searcher after knowledge, an investigator. But by a subtle transformation the term came to be applied to the record or narrative of what had been learned by investigation; and in this sense it passed over into the Latin* historia *and into modern speech. . . . Meantime another ambiguity . . . caused confusion in thought. The word* history *is used to denote not only the record of what has been learned by inquiry, but also the course of events themselves.*

Allen Johnson,
The Historian and Historical Evidence, 1926

History is the witness of the times, the light of truth, the life of memory, the teacher of life, the messenger of antiquity.

**Marcus Tullius Cicero,
106–43 B.C., Roman statesman**

History is . . . the record of what one age finds worthy of note in another.

**Jakob Burckhardt, 1818–1897,
Swiss historian**

The history of the world is but the biography of great men.

Thomas Carlyle.
Heroes and Hero-Worship, 1841

History is made out of the failures and heroism of each insignificant moment.

**Franz Kafka, 1883–1924,
Czech novelist**

My image of History would have . . . at least two persons, talking, arguing, always listening to the other as they gestured at their books; and it would be a film, not a still picture, so that you could see that sometimes they wept, sometimes they were astonished, sometimes they were knowing, and sometimes they laughed with delight.

Natalie Zemon Davis, American historian, 1988, on the complexity and multiple vision of history

History . . . is indeed little more than the register of crimes, follies, and misfortunes of mankind.

**Edward Gibbon,
Decline and Fall of the Roman Empire, 1776–1788**

The history of all hitherto existing society is the history of class struggles.

**Karl Marx and Friedrich Engels,
The Communist Manifesto, 1848**

The history of the world is the record of [people] in quest of . . . daily bread and butter.

**Hendrik Van Loon,
The Story of Mankind, 1921**

The subject of history is the life of peoples and of humanity.

**Count Leo Tolstoy,
War and Peace, 1869**

The Role of the Historian

Historians ought to be precise, truthful, and quite unprejudiced, and neither interest or fear, hatred nor affection, should cause them to swerve from the path of truth, whose mother is history.

Miguel de Cervantes,
***Don Quixote*, 1605–1615**

The whole past . . . consists of the infinite number of things which each person who ever lived has said, thought, and done. . . . Historians select a few of these thoughts, words, and deeds that seem to have general significance, and these become history as we ordinarily think of it. Because . . . ideas of what is significant change from time to time and because new knowledge frequently becomes available[,] history is constantly being rewritten.

Bernard Norling,
***Towards a Better Understanding of History*, 1960**

H*istory repeats itself, says the proverb, but that is precisely what it never really does. It is the historians (of a sort) who repeat themselves.*

Clement F. Rogers, 1866–1949,
British theologian

I *teach kings the history of their ancestors so that the lives of the ancients might serve them as an example, for the world is old, but the future springs from the past.*

Djeli Mamoudou Kouyaté,
an African griot (historian), 1950s

Faithfulness to the truth of history involves far more than a research, however patient and scrupulous, into special facts. Such facts may be detailed with the most minute exactness, and yet the narrative, taken as a whole, may be unmeaning or untrue. The narrator must seek to imbue himself with the life and spirit of the time. He must study events in their bearings near and remote; in the character, habits, and manners of those who took part in them. He must himself be, as it were, a sharer or a spectator of the action he describes.

Francis Parkman,
***Pioneers of France in the New World*, 1865**

The Uses of History

To enable [people] *to understand the society of the past and to increase* [their] *mastery over the society of the present is the dual function of history.*

Edward H. Carr,
What Is History?, 1962

Study the past if you would divine the future.

Confucius,
Chinese philosopher, 500s B.C.

Those who cannot remember the past are condemned to repeat it.

George Santayana,
1863–1952, American philosopher

Our custom of taking records and preserving them is the main barrier that separates us from the scatter-brained races of monkey. For it is this extension of memory that permits us to draw upon experience and which allows us to establish a common pool of wisdom. . . . Knowledge of things said and done . . . is a knowledge which not merely sees us through the trivial decisions of the moment, but also stands by in the far more important time of personal or public crisis.

Sherman Kent,
Writing History, 1941

For policy making, history offers no blueprint, no specific solution to problems. One of its lessons is the folly of expecting such, for the essence of history is change. Still, history reveals much about human behavior; its possibilities and its limits, what may be expected under certain conditions, the danger signs to be considered, the aspirations to be taken into account, the scourges of pride and dogma, and the fruits of endurance and attention to detail.

Paul A. Gagnon,
American historian, 1988

The study of history is said to enlarge and enlighten the mind. Why? Because . . . it gives it a power of judging of passing events, and of all events, and a conscious superiority over them, which before it did not possess.

John Henry Cardinal Newman,
On the Scope and Nature of University Education,
1852

Using Critical Thinking Strategies

What is critical thinking? Why do you need to know how to think critically? What does critical thinking have to do with U.S. history? These questions may occur to you as you are asked to think critically while reading *American Voices*.

People who think critically demonstrate "reasoned judgment." People who don't think critically jump to conclusions or accept arguments without considering whether they are valid. The cartoon below, for example, illustrates what critical thinking is not.

Why do you need to know how to think critically? To be an effective, capable citizen, you must learn how to think critically. Will you vote for the candidate with the winning smile and personality, or will you vote for the one who spoke to issues and took positions that you believe are important? Will you believe everything you read in a newspaper or hear

on television? Will you be able to tell when the media are biased? Will you be able to make important decisions in life based on fact or on intuition? Dealing with such situations effectively requires you to think critically.

What does critical thinking have to do with U.S. history? *American Voices* is first and foremost a comprehensive course in the history of the United States. However, it also can be used to help you develop critical thinking problem-solving strategies that will serve you well in a wide range of subjects and situations. Critical thinking strategies are embedded throughout *American Voices*. Each chapter teaches or emphasizes one critical thinking skill, but you will find several opportunities to practice each skill throughout the book. The following 17 critical thinking skills are taught in *American Voices*.

Critical Thinking Skills for Problem-Solving Strategies

1. *Identifying central issues* is identifying the main ideas or points of, for example, a passage, argument, or political cartoon. It sometimes involves distinguishing real issues, which are often unstated, from stated issues. It requires separating crucial information from secondary or peripheral information. In Chapter 3, for example, you will identify the central issues of George Washington's Farewell Address.

2. *Making comparisons* is finding similarities and differences between or among two or more things, ideas, or situations. In Chapter 21, for example, you will compare the treatment returning Vietnam veterans received with that received by returning veterans of World War II.

3. *Determining relevant information* is making distinctions between essential and incidental information in, for example, an argument or passage. It also involves determining how important pieces of information are to an issue or question. This skill can help you analyze and understand different interpretations of the significance of information related to a single subject. In Chapter 12, for example, you will determine the relevant information in a magazine advertisement from the 1920s.

4. *Formulating appropriate questions* is developing relevant questions aimed at clarifying and increasing your understanding of an issue or situation. In Chapter 10, for example, you will formulate questions you might have asked President Woodrow Wilson about the Versailles Treaty and the League of Nations.

5. *Expressing problems* is stating issues or views clearly and concisely. It requires you first to recognize or isolate an issue or problem in a passage or situation and then to put it into words. In Chapter 17, for example, you will express problems that have prevented the United Nations in the past from becoming an organization that can effectively deal with international problems.

6. *Distinguishing fact from opinion* is separating verifiable statements from unverifiable ones. It further involves separating opinions from reasoned opinions (opinions based on facts). In Chapter 13, for example, you will analyze a political cartoon from the Great Depression to determine whether the images reflect facts or opinions.

"Well, so long. I'll see you at lunch at the Bankers Club."

7. *Checking consistency* is analyzing a passage or situation for cohesion. It involves checking statements and images to determine whether they are consistent with one another and with their context. In Chapter 20, for example, you will check the consistency of President Johnson's statements with his domestic policy decisions.

8. *Identifying assumptions* is finding the unstated beliefs (what is taken for granted) in an argument or passage. In Chapter 14, for example, you will identify the assumptions President Franklin Delano Roosevelt made about his power following his landslide election in 1936 and judge whether his assumptions were accurate.

9. *Recognizing bias* is identifying partialities or prejudice in graphic or verbal materials and judging the credibility of sources. It involves recognizing emotional factors, propaganda, stereotyping, and clichés. In Chapter 18, for example, you will recognize bias in a political cartoon depicting U.S. progress in the space race with the Soviet Union and you will convert biased or prejudicial statements into unbiased form.

10. *Recognizing values* is identifying statements based on deeply held beliefs or philosophies. It involves recognizing various value orientations and ideologies. In Chapter 7, for example, you will recognize the value that some parents place on religious instruction for their children in school.

11. *Distinguishing false from accurate images* is separating images that are misleading or oversimplified from images that fairly represent a person, institution, idea, or thing. In Chapter 21, for example, you will be asked to view one or more films produced about the Vietnam War and determine whether these accounts of the war are false or accurate representations.

12. *Analyzing cause and effect* is identifying contributing factors to particular outcomes. It also involves recognizing multiple causation and judging adequate and inadequate grounds for establishing cause and effect. In Chapter 19, for example, you will analyze the causes and effects of the Civil Rights Act of 1964.

13. *Drawing conclusions* is reaching or generating conclusions based upon available information. It may require making inferences or hypotheses in order to draw reasonable conclusions. In Chapter 15, for example, you will draw conclusions about the effectiveness of the Maginot Line in preventing a German attack on France.

14. *Identifying alternatives* is finding or proposing alternatives, especially alternative solutions to problems. It also involves evaluating the alternatives. In Chapter 23, for example, you will consider several alternatives President Jimmy Carter could have pursued in foreign policy.

15. *Testing conclusions* is determining the validity of conclusions by evaluating the quality and quantity of their supporting evidence or information. In Chapter 16, for example, you will test the conclusions President Truman used to defend the use of the atomic bomb on Japan.

16. *Predicting consequences* is predicting the probable consequences of an event or series of events. It also involves assessing the desirability or undesirability of predicted consequences. In Chapter 24, for example, you will predict the consequences to the human race of the abuse of the environment.

17. *Demonstrating reasoned judgment* is producing conclusions or arguments based on all available evidence. It involves recognition that the strength of an argument is directly related to the strength of the evidence. It requires you to detect faulty reasoning, make generalizations, and develop a line of reasoning that takes into account opposing points of view. In Chapter 22, for example, you will decide whether allowing the National Guard to fire into the crowd at Kent State University demonstrated reasoned judgment.

These 17 skills are an integral part of *American Voices*. When you have learned to use these critical thinking strategies, you will have mastered important analytical tools that will be of value to you for the rest of your life.

Geography : Background for American History

Geography Seeks a Global Perspective

A view of the earth from space reveals a new way to look at the Pacific Ocean as it edges toward the Americas.

When everything else has gone from my brain—the president's name, the state capitals, the neighborhoods where I lived, and then my own name and what it was on earth I sought, and then at length the faces of my friends, and finally the faces of my family— when all this has dissolved, what will be left, I believe, is topology: the dreaming memory of land as it lay this way and that.

Though geography may begin with the personal and local, it persistently pushes outward, pursuing the interactions within and between places, following networks of interaction that finally embrace its true and final subject—the earth itself. Geography may be thought of as the science of the living organism of earth, seeking to understand the anatomy of its landforms and water bodies, the respiratory systems of climate and weather, the circulatory systems of migration and trade, the mechanisms of growth and decay.

The globe is more than a tool for geographers. The globe is a symbol of the wholeness and unity of their subject. However tightly they focus on a particular locality, however closely they scrutinize a particular interaction, however narrowly they specialize, geographers always maintain a global perspective. Students of history should do the same.

Geography and history are interwoven. The strands of history and geography are closely knit. When we attempt to unravel them, we tend to produce generalizations such as "History describes human activity over time; geography describes the place in which that activity occurs." Or, "History asks 'who, what, when, how, and why' questions; geography asks 'where' questions." Or, "History provides the drama; geography provides the stage."

Before the first word was written, a map had been drawn. That mapmaking is an older art than writing tells us how fundamental and urgent is our need to know our earth and our place within it. Geography is a discipline that continues the ancient human quest to know the world and to understand the multitude of physical and human systems that make it work.

Geography is personal and global. Our understanding of geography might begin with the recognition that geography is first of all personal. We are individually shaped and influenced by the "where" of our lives. The writer Annie Dillard has vividly expressed the power of place in these words:

Such simplifications usually understate the significance of geography. Geography is more than the "where" of history. History's "how" and "why" questions often have geographic answers. Geography is more than history's passive background; geography is a dynamic influence on human activity—a cause of action as well as a place of action.

A city begins, develops, and thrives not alone by the decisions of its founders and the ambitions of its citizens, but also by the gifts of geography: a deep-water harbor, for example, a stable climate, rich mineral deposits, smooth avenues of transportation. An epic battle was fought at Gettysburg not by any general's choice, but because that Pennsylvania town was centered in a spider web of roads that drew the armies toward collision. The battle was won by the army that held the highest ground and the shortest lines of communication—the geographic advantage.

The interactions of geography's personal and global issues—and the interweaving of geography with history—may be explored in an incident involving one wilderness, two young men, and three rivers. In 1754 France and Britain competed for dominance in the North American wilderness. A geographic key to that wilderness was a union of rivers, the location where the Allegheny and the Monongahela meet to form the Ohio. The French built a fort

there, and alarmed colonists in Virginia responded by dispatching a small militia force led by a tall young officer of large ambition but little experience. A French scouting party, led by an equally young and untried officer, was sent to shadow the Virginians. On a drizzling morning in May, the two groups met in a brief explosion of violence.

The encounter was fatal to the French officer, Ensign Jumonville, and for a time it marred the reputation of the young Virginian, Lt. Colonel Washington, though he was physically unscathed. This tangle of personal fate, minor combat, and obscure location would hardly seem worthy of an historical footnote—except that it proved to be the opening action of the vast and lengthy French and Indian War, a conflict that affected hundreds of thousands of lives and determined the fate of a continent.

George Washington, it is known, proceeded to other accomplishments; so too did the region of the three rivers. As the United States developed, the meeting place of the Allegheny, Monongahela, and Ohio continued to flex its potent geographic influence, no longer in military advantage but in economic and industrial effects. The transporting powers of the rivers combined with the resources of iron ore, limestone, coal, and human energy to forge a great city of steel where the rivers meet. We call it Pittsburgh, Pennsylvania.

In Pittsburgh the Allegheny and Monongahela rivers converge to form the Ohio—creating a golden triangle that has influenced both the history and development of that city and the area surrounding it.

Two different images of climate—winter in Kalamazoo, Michigan, and a rainbow over North Park, Colorado—present a contrasting view of the physical geography of the United States.

Geography has two main branches. The tasks of geography can be divided into two distinct categories, physical and cultural. **Physical geography** focuses on the natural features and systems of the earth: waters and landforms, rocks and soils, weather and climate, plants and animals. **Cultural geography** focuses on human activities, studying the changes made on earth by human thought and effort and exploring the reasons for such change. Cultural geographers study such particulars as cities, languages, agriculture, architecture, religions, and social development.

We are accustomed to encountering most of these physical and cultural topics within the domains of specialized branches of science and scholarship—geology, botany, sociology, and anthropology, for example. Geographers do not compete with the specialists of these disciplines. Their task is to study these elements from geography's unique global perspective, to see them clearly in terms of earthly location and earthly interrelation.

A basic procedure of both physical and cultural geographers is to study patterns of distribution, to examine how a given something occurs on the surface of the earth—whether it be human population, oak trees, largemouth bass, rainfall, killer bees, iron ore, personal computers, or chicken pox. Distributions, or patterns of location, are readily shown on maps, and their graphic depiction stimulates questions about causes and interconnections.

For example, the distribution of certain diseases might be displayed on a world map. Some diseases would appear concentrated in some areas of the world and virtually nonexistent in other areas. These patterns would stimulate geographers (and medical researchers) to investigate possible reasons for the pattern. Is climate or latitude a factor? Diet? Genetics? Air or water quality? Cultural or religious practices?

Interaction between people and earth, that is, cultural geography, takes on new dimensions when viewed with Landsat, or heat-sensitive photography. The image of southern Florida, with Miami on the eastern coast, glows with deep blues (water) and reds (vegetation).

Five Themes Create a Geographical Perspective

Geographers have developed a framework of five themes to create a comprehensive understanding of geography: location, place, relationships within places, movement, and regions. Any thorough understanding of geography will encompass those five themes.

1. Location focuses on "where." The location theme examines one of geography's most basic questions: "Where on earth is it?" At a personal level we are attentive to nuances of location: it can be pleasant to live near a beach; it can be stressful to live on a floodplain. On a global level it is usually not difficult to appreciate the locational merits of a given point on the earth.

Location may be described in relative and absolute terms. **Relative location** establishes an approximate position in relation to a known, familiar place. "I live two blocks east of the post office." "New Orleans is at the mouth of the Mississippi River." Relative location is not exact enough to get your mail delivered, however. **Absolute location** establishes exactly where something is placed on the earth. Your postal address is one kind of absolute location. People frequently joke about mail delivery, taking for granted that a few jotted lines on a stamped envelope will routinely direct a letter to the one person out of earth's five billion for whom it was intended.

Geographers have developed an even more efficient system for pinpointing absolute location by imposing an imaginary grid system on the surface of the earth. **Latitude** lines (also called parallels) run parallel to the equator and measure distance north or south. Distance is expressed in degrees, from 0° at the equator to 90° at the North or South poles. Each degree is subdivided into 60 minutes; each minute is subdivided into 60 seconds; a part of a second can be shown as a decimal fraction. **Longitude** lines (also called meridians) measure distance east or west of the Prime Meridian, which passes through Greenwich, England. Distance again is measured in degrees east or west from the 0° line of Prime Meridian to the 180° line on the opposite side of the globe.

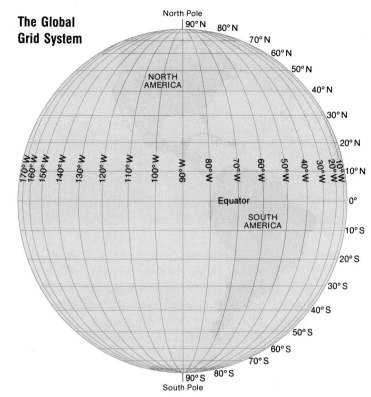

The Global Grid System

Any place on earth can be pinpointed with only a few numbered coordinates. For example, New Orleans is located at 90°W 30°N. No other location on earth has those coordinates.

2. Place examines unique characteristics. The theme of place explores the physical and human factors that create the unique identity of a particular location. Any place may be described in terms of its prominent natural features such as landforms, climate, vegetation, soil quality, and so on. We might speak of a certain place as "mountainous," "cool," "thickly forested," and "rich in mineral deposits."

The presence of people also defines a place: their number; their languages, religions, and cultures; the changes they have produced by their use and abuse of physical resources. The "human touch" pervades nature. A wild plant or animal may have been transplanted by human management. Even "untouched" areas of the earth wear human names and boundaries.

Physical and human characteristics combine to create the identity of a place. When a place

The grid system shown on the globe above indicates both lines of latitude—which run parallel to the equator and measure distance north or south—and longitude—which measure distance east or west of the Prime Meridian.

made by their footsteps to the furrows they scratched in fields for their first crops. Today people have a far greater degree of control over their environment. We can cool a hot room; we can irrigate a parched land. We can literally move mountains and reverse the course of rivers. Our cities tower into the sky; air and water are stained with our use; asphalt and concrete carpet a vast acreage of our world. How and why did people make these changes? What are the consequences? The interactions of people with their environments raise these vital questions for historians, geographers—and all the rest of us.

4. Movement examines links of transportation and communication. The theme of movement encompasses not only such obvious factors as the flow of people and goods in migration and trade; it includes the movements of language, culture, religion, technology— even the spread of microbes. The Pilgrims at Plymouth planted their first crops in fields left tragically vacant by an Indian people annihilated by disease. The spread of lethal illness had a darkly significant influence in the colonial settlement of North America.

A happier contagion was provided by the ideas of enlightenment and human freedom generated in Europe by thinkers such as Rousseau, Locke, and Montesquieu. These ideas spread through the North American colonies,

Environmental interaction takes many different forms. For example, the Amish, a religious group that lives primarily in Pennsylvania, Indiana, and Ohio, rely on simple farming techniques and low-energy forms of transportation.

is described in sufficient detail, its identity emerges with the distinctiveness and uniqueness of a signature or a fingerprint.

3. Relationships within places explores the interaction between people and their environments. Humans have been called the most adaptable creatures on earth. People live in virtually every environment earth offers, adapting their shelter, clothing, diet, and habits of life to survive and thrive even in the harshest circumstances.

As they adapt themselves to their environment, however, humans also alter their environment. People have been changing their world from earliest times, from the simple trails

Americans have found a variety of ways to harness the natural power of water—including irrigating the dry lands of Nevada, at left, and building dams such as the one at right on the Skagit River in Washington State.

dynamically shaping the American Revolution and the United States Constitution.

The theme of movement has special relevance in the Western Hemisphere, a domain once empty of human life. History in the New World necessarily begins with journey, and every person in the New World is a traveler or the descendant of travelers.

5. Regions emphasizes areas with shared characteristics. It's difficult to study the earth "all at once" in its totality and particularity. Geographers explore the earth in more manageable portions called regions. A **region** is any area of the world defined by a unifying characteristic. The unifying factor may be language or culture (the Arab World); physical terrain (the Great Plains); a dominant crop (the Corn Belt). A neighborhood is one kind of region; a school district is another. Political regions may be as large as Europe or as small as a voting precinct. Your own town or city has several regions: a residential area, an industrial area, a "downtown" business and commercial center.

There are countless ways of identifying regions, and they may assume an infinite variety of size and scope. Examining the earth in terms of regions helps geographers to highlight the similarities within an area and to sharpen the contrasts between different places.

Movement in the geographical sense can involve both people and objects. At left new immigrants to America land at Ellis Island in New York. At right goods are transported by ship to and from Seattle, Washington.

Regions may be formed by either cultural or physical features. For example, the New England village at left creates a distinct unit, as does the neighborhood group above in San Antonio, Texas.

Maps Are Tools of Geography and History

Mercator Projection

Today's modern maps far surpass the simple scratches in dirt, or clay, or stone that represent the first human attempts to map. No matter how complex and elaborate our maps become, each is a link to those first efforts to know and show the earth. Each map too is an interaction of geography and history—an attempt to picture a place and a time.

Geographers have a variety of maps to fit their purposes. **Physical maps** display landforms and bodies of water. **Political maps** focus on national, state, and city boundaries. **Thematic maps** are designed to show particular distributions, for example, population, rainfall, vegetation, or mineral resources. Mapmakers can show changes over time by including "before and after" details and dates on a single map, or by using a series of maps to show changes—the movement of troops in a battle for example, or the territorial growth of the United States. **General reference maps**, common to atlases and texts, usually combine physical and political features.

The understanding of any map is aided by certain elements and details. A **title** states what the map shows and sometimes explains its purpose. A **date** establishes the historical framework. **Grid lines** of latitude and longitude identify the global location of the map's details. In the absence of grid lines, a **compass symbol** or a simple, north-pointing arrow provides direction. **Labels** within the map identify specific features, most commonly, cities, states, major landforms, and bodies of water. A **scale** shows the relationship between the distances on the map and the actual distance of the earth's surface. For example, a centimeter or a fraction of an inch of a map might equal 500 miles of real distance. A **key** or **legend** explains the meaning of the symbols, lines, and colors used on the map. Some map symbols and conventions (using blue to represent water, for example) are so familiar they need no explanation.

Map projections. The most accurate picture of the surface of the earth is provided by a globe—a three-dimensional model. A globe gives a true picture of land shapes and sizes, and correctly shows distances and directions. This perfection, alas, is marred only by a globe's inconvenience. Even large globes fail to show useful details of particular areas of the earth, and even small globes fail to fit conveniently into pockets, glove compartments, and history books.

A **projection** is any system for representing the curved surface of the earth on the flat surface of a map. Any projection requires a certain amount of stretching and shrinking that affect a map's accuracy of distance, direction, shape, or area. No single map can be correct in all four properties, so mapmakers have produced a variety of projections and combination of projections, each with different advantages and distortions.

The Mercator projection depicts meridians as parallel lines, creating a neatly rectangular grid that shows true directions. First developed in the 16th century, Mercator maps were priceless tools of the Age of Exploration, for they enabled sailors to plot an accurate course as a simple straight line. Mercator maps are still valuable for ocean travel today.

The price of true direction is a distortion of area that grows progressively worse near the poles because Mercator meridians do not curve toward intersection. Mercator maps are notorious for a grossly inflated Greenland, which in actual area is only a fraction of the South American continent it seems to dwarf.

A number of projections are more attentive to accuracy of area. **Goode's Interrupted projection** is one of these equal-area maps. Shapes and sizes of land masses are shown with an excellent degree of accuracy, making the Goode projection valuable in the study of land areas. The ocean areas, however, are "interrupted"—cut apart—and directions and distances between places are not true.

Azimuthal Equidistant projections show true distance from a given central point on earth, usually the North or South poles. These projections are very accurate near their centers, but land shapes become increasingly distorted at the edges of the map. A distinction of equidistant projections is that the straight lines that pass through the center of the map represent great circles, the most direct paths over the surface of a sphere. Pilots of aircraft always seek these most efficient routes between locations, and polar equidistant projections are favored in the aviation industries.

The **Robinson projection** effectively shows how the continents compare in size. Ocean areas are not interrupted; there is some distortion of shape at the edges of the map. The North and South poles are shown as lines rather than points. The Robinson projection is gaining acceptance as an effective compromise of area, shape, and direction. Most of the world maps in this book are based on the Robinson projection.

Each of the map projections on these pages offers both strengths and weaknesses. Examine and analyze each one.

Goode's Interrupted Projection

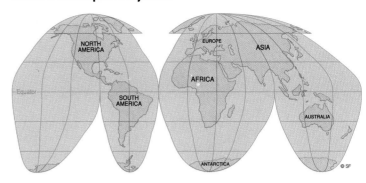

Azimuthal Equidistant Projection

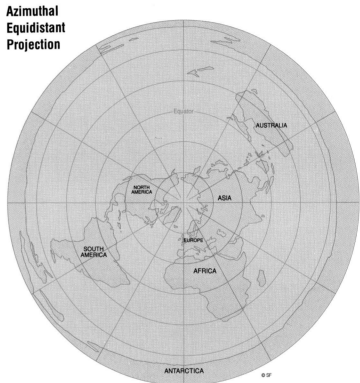

Robinson Projection

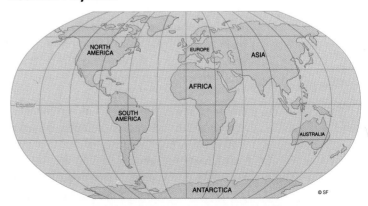

North America: A Cross-Section View

COAST RANGES
PACIFIC OCEAN
CENTRAL VALLEY
SIERRA NEVADA
DEATH VALLEY
GREAT BASIN
ROCKY MTNS.
FRONT RANGE
GREAT PLAINS

The basic terrain of North America is little changed from the 16th century, yet our scrutiny of the physical map of the continent (page 1004) fails to kindle the wide-eyed excitement of 16th-century explorers. For us the continent is no New World. To us it simply looks like home.

To find a new perspective on North America, consider the cross-section view of the land displayed above. If you were to start at the East Coast and travel west along the 37th parallel, you would encounter the land as follows:

On the Atlantic Coastal Plain, you would cross the sites of the oldest English colonies. As you reached the end of the tidewater area, a sharp rise would indicate the fall line (**G**), the place where the hard rock of the Appalachian system (**F**) begins. Waterfalls and rapids here provided good sites for factories in the age of water-driven machinery. The first bump of mountain is the Blue Ridge; behind it lies the Great Valley where Stonewall Jackson maneuvered in the early days of the Civil War.

The high, rounded peaks of the Smoky Mountains bring the elevations to over a mile before the plateau behind gradually slopes downward, a coasting space for the pioneers moving westward into the central plains. Note how the Mississippi River (**E**) lies at the lowest point in the interior. It reaches almost all the way to the Great Lakes without exceeding 500 feet in elevation, a low gradient that is the secret of the river's navigability.

As the pioneers pushed beyond the great river into the Great Plains (**D**), they were at times diverted by rugged terrain such as the Ozark Plateau, a distant reach of the Appalachian system. As the plains gain in elevation,

OZARK PLATEAU

N
W · E
S
Mississippi River

CENTRAL LOWLAND

APPALACHIAN MTNS.

FALL LINE

ATLANTIC COASTAL PLAIN

ATLANTIC OCEAN

40°
35°

about the 100th meridian, rainfall diminishes. Dry America lies westward. It is not surprising that settlements collapsed here in the Dust Bowl seasons of the 1890s and 1930s.

The Front Range of the Rocky Mountains **(C)** abruptly marks the end of the plains and the beginning of the Mountain West, a 1,000-mile stretch of plateaus and mountains, basins and ranges. Except on the western faces of upland areas, the land remains dry. By the time you reach the 110th meridian and cross the Colorado River, you're deep in desert conditions. Just after you enter California, in a fault that reaches below sea level, Death Valley **(B)** records the hottest, driest climate and the lowest elevation on the continent.

Abruptly mountains rise again, reaching nearly three miles above sea level at the top of Mount Whitney in the Sierra Nevada range.

Then the terrain plunges down into the Central Valley of California. These fertile lowlands have become an immense agricultural resource, partitioned from the Pacific Ocean by the low but very rugged Coast Ranges **(A)**. When these are crossed, you've arrived at the West Coast.

This cross-sectional, cross-country jaunt provided only a narrow view of some of North America's diverse terrain and climates. Yet even in this deliberately limited context, you encountered again and again the interconnection of geography and history (colonial sites, Stonewall Jackson, the pioneers traveling westward, Dust Bowls). You also encountered, surely you noticed, each of geography's five themes—location, place, relationships within places, movement, and regions. With this fresh recognition of geography's deep connection with history, listen to *American Voices*.

HOW TO USE **American Voices**

American Voices has been organized so that you will find it easy to use. The text is divided into six units and 24 chapters.

Unit Organization

Each of the six units in *American Voices* opens with a vivid photograph or painting depicting an event in the period covered. Accompanying it is a dramatic primary source description of what it was like to be at the scene when the event was taking place. This description is called "You Are There." Each unit also begins with a list of the chapters included in the unit, a list of the unit themes around which the unit is organized, and a time line of both U.S. and world events. World events are marked on all time lines by a globe. Each unit ends with a Unit Survey — a brief summary of key ideas for each chapter that you may use as a preview or review of the unit. Also at the end of the unit are two features, American Characteristics and Writing Strategies.

Unit 5

Chapter Organization

Each of the 24 chapters begins with two illustrations — one from the present, one from the past — showing you how the past is linked to the present. Each chapter also has a narrative introduction that sets the scene for the entire chapter's events, which are highlighted on a chapter time line. Each chapter ends with a variety of Chapter Source Readings and a helpful Chapter Review. In the Review are a Chapter Summary, Chapter Themes, Chapter Study Guide, Chapter Time Line, and Chapter Activities.

21

CHAPTER PREVIEW

Section Organization

Each chapter is further organized into three to five sections. A section begins with a Reading Preview that alerts you to the Key Terms you should know and your key learning objectives. You will find as you read that each of the key learning objectives focuses on a main idea that appears in full sentence form as a section head. In the Section Review are questions that ask you about each main idea. For example, in Section 3 of Chapter 18 on Vietnam, one of the learning objectives is to learn "how Americans reacted to the Tet Offensive." The main idea section head for that objective is "The Tet Offensive alarmed Americans." The relevant question in the Section Review is "Why were Americans shocked to hear about the Tet Offensive?" So, as you can see, the authors of this text have carefully written the text to make it easy for you to know what you are supposed to learn, organized the material of each section to reflect those learning goals, and then provided appropriate questions to help you test your new knowledge. You will note that as an additional aid to your learning, Key Terms, Key People, and Key Places are highlighted in dark type in the text and tested in the Section Review. Finally, to stretch your thinking, each Section Review also includes a question that will help you master important critical thinking strategies.

SECTION **1**

America gradually became involved in Vietnam.

Themes of American History

Woven throughout the chronological narrative of *American Voices* are themes to help you understand the overall pattern of U.S. history. You will find these themes highlighted in the Prologue, developed in special Theme Essays introduced at critical points in the narrative, explained in the Unit Introductions and in the Chapter Reviews, and finally summarized in the Epilogue. A careful study of these themes will help you remember what underlying ideas shaped American history and what is important to remember long after you leave the classroom.

Theme Essay: Watergate produced positive results.

Key Terms: CRP, Presidential Election Campaign Fund

Reading Preview
As you read this section, you will learn:

Literature and Primary Sources

Rich primary and secondary sources and excerpts from significant works of American literature are incorporated throughout *American Voices*. Each chapter includes several quotations called An American Speaks, which feature the words of an ordinary — or sometimes, extraordinary — American who participated in or witnessed a key moment in our history. Every chapter also includes Voices from the Past, which consists of excerpts of important documents in U.S. history as well as poems, speeches, diaries, and other writings. At the end of each chapter are several pages of Chapter Source Readings that provide in-depth selections of primary and secondary sources to heighten your understanding of events in the chapter. Each unit concludes with selections from significant works of American literature that reflect the period of history covered in the unit, including such outstanding classics as John Steinbeck's *The Grapes of Wrath*, Lorraine Hansberry's *A Raisin in the Sun*, and exciting works from new authors of interest — among them Amy Tan's *The Joy Luck Club* and Tomás Rivera's *And the Earth Did Not Devour Him.*

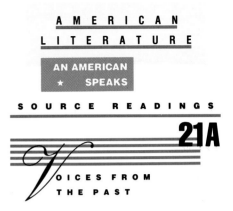

Special Features

Eight special features in *American Voices* add interesting sidelights to your study of history and provide study aids and skill development.

Highlights of American Life appears in each chapter. This feature focuses on various aspects of American culture in the broadest sense of the term, from serious culture to popular culture. Some of the Highlights that you will be reading about are blue jeans, barbed wire, the blues, modern art, and Vietnam-era protest music.

Building Critical Thinking Strategies appears in each chapter. This feature teaches you how to apply critical thinking strategies to issues you have read about in the chapter. Some of the strategies you will learn are Analyzing Cause and Effect, Distinguishing False from Accurate Images, and Demonstrating Reasoned Judgment.

Point/Counterpoint appears in each chapter. This feature highlights a controversial issue in U.S. history by presenting the key arguments on both sides. Some of the Point/Counterpoints that you will be reading about are the Japanese American internment, civil rights methods, the Penta- gon Papers, and the Iran-contra affair.

Meet the President appears in each chapter in which a president of the United States takes office. This feature highlights the personality of each president and his achievements.

Geography in American History appears in each unit. This feature shows how geography has affected the course of events in U.S. history. Some of the Geography features that you will be reading about are the Columbian Exchange, the Cold War, and the Persian Gulf Crisis.

Touring the Past appears in each unit except the last. This feature describes significant historical places that you may wish to visit. A first-person account of someone who visited this place is also included. Some of the Touring features that you will be reading about are Gettysburg, Oak Ridge, and Ellis Island.

American Characteristics appears at the end of each unit. This feature includes quotations illustrating some of the following characteristics Americans like to call their own: liberty, reform, religious freedom, equality, optimism, and ingenuity.

Writing Strategies appears at the end of each unit. This feature teaches process writing techniques and strategies using the quotations from American Characteristics.

The Reference Section

The Reference Section appears at the back of the book. This section includes the Atlas, a U.S. Data Bank, a Biographical Dictionary, Glossary, Gazetteer, Index, and Acknowledgments. The Atlas includes detailed political, physical, historical, and spe- cial purpose maps. The U.S. Data Bank includes charts, graphs, and time lines featuring important economic, political, and cultural information in U.S. history, a list of U.S. Presidents, Facts About the 50 States, Flag Etiquette, and other reference information. The Biographical Dictionary is an illustrated mini-dictionary of all the Key People in the book. The Glossary provides you with a handy detailed listing of all the Key Terms in the book, and the Gazetteer, with a listing of all the Key Places.

Prologue | Key Themes in American History

As a high-school student beginning a U.S. history class, you may be wondering how a text such as *American Voices* is put together. How do historians decide what to include and what to leave out? Whose history are the authors telling? Are historians ever critical of anything in our past?

You may be surprised to learn that these questions voice concerns common to many historians today. We historians expect more than politics and war to be included in the history of a nation. We want the experiences and contributions of women and children, African Americans, Hispanic Americans, Asian Americans, and Native Americans to have an equal place beside what one historian has called the history of "great white men." We also want to understand how the choices and opportunities we face today came to be. We therefore demand that the mirror held up to America's past reflect not only successes and achievements but also failures and mistakes.

As a result, *American Voices* includes accounts of family life and religious movements, popular culture and fine art, how people worked and played, and how change affected ordinary men, women, and children. The book also tells the stories of people from a rich diversity of ethnic and racial groups, the stories of men, women, and children who together make up the drama of our national history.

Aside from questions of content and point of view, you may have questions that focus on what historians today call *agency*—that is, who or what makes things happen the way they do? Are there forces greater than individuals that sweep over a nation, shaping its destiny? Do unique individuals create history through their genius or their madness? Are political, economic, and military choices based on rational considerations, conscious intellectual commitments, and sensible self-interest? Or do accident and chance, surprise and confusion play a role in molding the human past? The answer, frustrating but sound, is yes, all of these are agents of change. The historian's detective work therefore lies in discovering which, to what degree, and in what combination these agents operate in any particular historical case.

In *American Voices* you will find the question of agency running throughout the narrative.

To organize their research and study, historians often rely on broad themes that span large periods of history. Accordingly, eight major themes are emphasized throughout *American Voices*. Using these themes will help you to understand better the flow of U.S. history, to learn how events and movements are connected across time and with one another. Listed at the beginning of each unit, you will find the themes that are developed in that unit. Furthermore, each chapter review includes a discussion of the most important themes in that chapter—how they were developed, tested, or changed over time. The eight themes selected are listed here, followed by a brief discussion of each.

- ■ **Our society reflects racial, ethnic, and religious diversity.**
- ■ **Our economic system is organized around free enterprise and the protection of private property.**
- ■ **The American political system is built upon constitutional and representative government.**
- ■ **Conflict and cooperation have been essential elements in the development of the United States.**
- ■ **Americans have made choices based on geography as they interacted with the environment.**
- ■ **Americans express social and political concerns within a religious and ethical framework.**
- ■ **The American belief in a unique national destiny influences its relations with other nations.**
- ■ **Encouraging technological and scientific innovation has helped shape American society.**

Some people who have been part of American history include, clockwise from bottom left, cowboys in *Bronco Busting*, 1895 (Charles Russell); a colonial family, 1798 (Ralph Earl); a 19th-century Mexican American grinding corn in California; a contemporary Native American in New Mexico; and Cuban Americans in Miami.

Throughout American history cultural diversity has been a crucial fact of life. The United States is indeed a land of immigrants, enriched by people of different colors, faiths, and ethnic backgrounds. As *American Voices* will show you, sometimes Americans have found this diversity a strength, sometimes a stumbling block. We have faced its challenges and difficulties with both energy and genius, pessimism and violence.

Two conditions have combined to make America's multicultural experience unique among countries with diverse populations. First, new groups have joined the American community all throughout its history, enriching American life and expanding its culture. Second, the United States has struggled with contradictory ideals concerning immigrants: the wish to promote cultural diversity and tolerate differences and the desire to Americanize each new wave of immigrants.

The United States honors its diverse heritage in many ways. Students from Brentwood, California, at top, reflect America's multicultural mix. In Chicago, at bottom, Philippine Americans celebrate Philippines Independence Day. Historically as well, people of many ethnic and racial backgrounds have contributed to American society—including this Japanese immigrant family around 1900, center left, and Harriet Tubman, an African American abolitionist and humanitarian in the 1800s, center right.

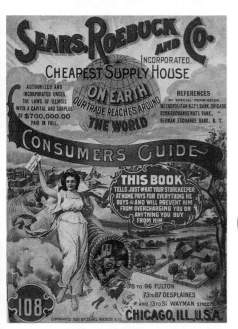

THEME: Our economic system is organized around free enterprise and the protection of private property.

The American economic system is rooted in a European tradition. As the first American colonies were being founded, England was undergoing a tremendous commercial and industrial revolution. Its effects spread to the colonies, shaping how Americans dealt with the economic issues of creating and distributing wealth.

From this European tradition, Americans acquired a commitment to capitalism. Capitalism emphasizes private property and individual freedom to generate and acquire wealth. It also places a premium on initiative and risk-taking in a competitive market. Americans have, from this country's earliest days, argued the benefits and costs of this economic system, noting the depressing poverty and uneven concentrations of wealth that the system generates. In periods of economic boom and of economic bust, Americans have challenged, altered, and reformed economic principles and policies. Yet the commitment to private property and free market exchange remains central to American economic life.

Americans have thrived on economic opportunity from the earliest times to the present. The Sears catalog, this one from the late 1800s, demonstrates early marketing efforts. Today this Navajo geologist, at top, works at the Black Mesa coal mine. Jolyn Robichaux, the African American woman pictured center right, displays products from the Chicago ice cream company she heads, and this Hispanic architect, bottom, designs a shopping mall in Texas.

THEME: The American political system is built upon constitutional and representative government.

From the Pilgrims' Mayflower Compact to recent Supreme Court rulings, American history gives evidence of men and women seeking the protection of basic freedoms and the stability of society through the rule of law. In almost every political crisis, the starting point for debate has been the rights and duties of citizens as stated in a written contract or constitution or as established by law and custom.

This tradition has allowed Americans to disagree over domestic and foreign policy or the personal leadership of the country, without a long or sustained resort to bloodshed and persecution. It has also inclined us to judge the breakdown of law and order as a fundamental failure in the history of the nation. It has shaped our judgment of the past—motivating us to see the Civil War as a tragedy, slavery as an evil, and each victory over discrimination based on political beliefs, religion, race, or sex as marks of integrity. It has also shaped our expectations for the future—motivating men and women to demand a voice in creating the laws by which they live.

American politics works on both a personal and national level—from individuals exercising their right to vote, center, to political protests such as the 1965 march from Selma, Alabama, to the state capitol in Montgomery, bottom, to large gatherings such as this 1988 Republican convention, shown at top.

Two patterns of human behavior occur again and again in American history—conflict between and co-operation among individuals and societies. Although they seem to be mutually exclusive, conflict and cooperation often work together. Cooperative efforts, if unsuccessful, frequently have resulted in conflict, and conflicts, if serious enough, at times have drawn people into co-operative efforts.

In the development of the United States, conflict and cooperation have played a special role. Many people first came to America as a way of escaping conflict in their native lands—religious persecution, political unrest, or social divisions. Over the years Americans have struggled to create a society in which democratic cooperation was an ideal—in forming and settling communities, in writing the U.S. Constitution, and in meeting the challenges of a multicultural nation. Still, conflict has been ever present, making itself known in wars both domestic and international, in the workings of a society in which racism and sexism have affected more than half the population, and in a myriad of political debates and struggles.

Americans express conflict and cooperation in many ways—from women working together for the right to vote, top, to people such as actor Meryl Streep testifying before Congress about concerns, center, to former President Jimmy Carter helping renovate housing for the poor.

5

Throughout history Americans' choices about where and how to live have been affected by such geographic concerns as climate, location, and the availability of natural resources such as fresh water and fertile soil. Environmental conditions have brought both rich benefits and serious challenges to Americans—from the Indians who adapted their cultures to the prairies or woodlands to today's urban dwellers who must deal with crowded freeways, polluted air and water, dwindling natural resources, and the management of human and industrial waste.

Geography has also affected the military and political development of the United States. Consider, for example, how geographic conditions such as location and place influenced America's role in the two world wars and the Vietnam War. Think also about the mass movements of people that have shaped American society—the waves of immigrants traveling from Europe, Africa, Asia, and Latin America, the large numbers of African Americans coming north around the time of World War I in search of both jobs and equality, and the many Americans flocking to the warm Sunbelt states.

Americans have made choices to exploit as well as to save their country's resources. In the 1800s, for example, the spread of the railroad, as shown at top in Robert Lindneux's painting *A Holdup on the Prairie* (1943), wiped out the buffalo of the Great Plains. Today recycling, such as in the Earth Day 1990 display above, has become big business, as has protecting the West Coast's ancient redwood trees, far right.

THEME: Americans express social and political concerns within a religious and ethical framework.

As you read *American Voices,* you will find that Americans often cast debates within a framework of religious and ethical concerns. Decisions about political, military, or social issues are very often tied to people's religious beliefs and moral principles.

As both famous and ordinary people speak to you from the past, you will often be struck by their search for solutions that are morally sound, that are guided by religious and ethical values, and that honor the ideal as well as the practical. A sensitivity to the pattern will help you understand the persistence of reform and the popularity of reform movements in the United States.

Religious groups in the United States, such as Catholics, center, and Shakers, bottom, have been a powerful force for social change and compassion—as demonstrated by this shelter for the homeless, top left, and William Lloyd Garrison's abolitionist newspaper, top right.

Americans of every era and in every region have exhibited an optimism about the future and a fierce belief in the special nature of their society that has amazed, puzzled, and sometimes annoyed other nations. Puritan settlers in 1630 spoke of their small colony as a "city upon a hill," a beacon and model for the rest of the world. The framers of the United States Constitution argued that the new nation and its constitution were the noblest experiment in self-government in the history of humankind. Later, as waves of white Americans moved west through the 1800s, they carried with them a belief in their country's "manifest destiny" to stretch from sea to sea. In the 20th century, Americans have continued to believe that the United States has a unique mission and special role as a leader in world affairs.

Throughout history Americans have led the way toward change and development. In the 1800s, for example, Americans such as this family portrayed in William Tylee Ranney's painting *Pioneers* set out west with a belief in manifest destiny. One hundred years later, Americans turned their attention to the skies, and in 1969 U.S. astronaut Neil Armstrong became the first person to set foot on the moon.

THEME: Encouraging technological and scientific innovation has helped shape American society.

Since the time of Benjamin Franklin, America has produced and encouraged men and women who are innovative, experimental, and committed to the application of theory to practical, material advancement. Americans have been particularly receptive to technological innovation and to the dramatic social changes that often follow.

No one can ignore the impact that technology has had on American society. From the cotton gin and the steamboat to the television and personal computer, our economy has been drastically altered by practical inventiveness. Our personal lives have been transformed by transportation and communications revolutions, by medical research, and by the machines and gadgets that fill our homes, schools, and workplaces. These products of technology help create the material world in which our history is made.

New technologies have played a key role in shaping American society. In the 1950s the television set, top, was just beginning to fascinate audiences young and old. By the 1990s Americans were using computers and robots both to help the movements of handicapped persons, center, and to build better cars more efficiently, a trend begun in 1908 with Henry Ford.

As you read *American Voices,* and as you look at the American past from your own perspective, these themes will help you see more clearly both the continuities and changes in our national history. Used as tools, rather than fixed truths, these themes can unlock for you the complex motivations, intentions, and accidents that generate our rich historical past.

Unit 1

You Are There

The way, the only way to stop this evil, is for the red men to unite in claiming a common and equal right in the land, as it was at first, and should be now—for it was never divided, but belongs to all. No tribe has the right to sell, even to each other, much less to strangers. . . .

Sell a country! Why not sell the air, the great sea, as well as the earth? Did not the Great Spirit make them all for the use of his children?
—*Shawnee chief Tecumseh speaking out against the loss of Indian lands, 1810*

Tecumseh addresses William Henry Harrison, seated at right, and others in this painting by Stanley Arthurs (Delaware Art Museum).

The New Nation

Unit Outline

Unit Themes

In this unit you will analyze the following themes of U.S. history:

▶ Our society reflects racial, ethnic, and religious diversity.

▶ Our economic system is organized around free enterprise and the protection of private property.

▶ The American political system is built upon constitutional and representative government.

▶ Encouraging technological and scientific innovation has helped American society.

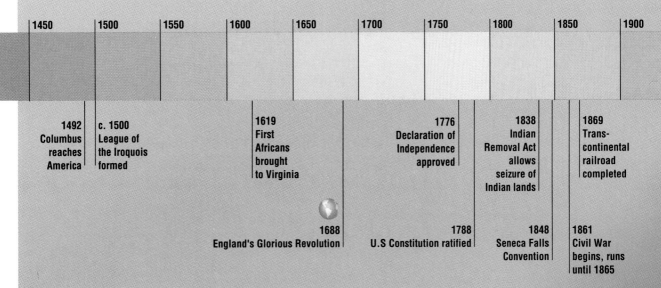

| 1450 | 1500 | 1550 | 1600 | 1650 | 1700 | 1750 | 1800 | 1850 | 1900 |

1492
Columbus reaches America

c. 1500
League of the Iroquois formed

1619
First Africans brought to Virginia

1776
Declaration of Independence approved

1838
Indian Removal Act allows seizure of Indian lands

1869
Trans-continental railroad completed

1688
England's Glorious Revolution

1788
U.S Constitution ratified

1848
Seneca Falls Convention

1861
Civil War begins, runs until 1865

Linking Past to Present

Moctezuma's Aztec people welcomed the Spanish explorer Hernán Cortés to the Americas in 1519 with this striking feather shield, inset. More than four centuries later, the influence of Spanish culture in the Americas remains visible in such structures as San Francisco's Everett Middle School.

The Meeting of Three Cultures

P r e - C o l u m b i a n   E r a — 1 6 2 4

Moctezuma, leader of the Aztec people, called magicians to interpret the omens. What explanation could they give of the report that "towers or small mountains" floated on the waves of the sea, carrying a strange people with "very light skin, . . . long beards, and . . . hair . . . only to their ears?" Was war coming?

The magicians gave no satisfactory answers, but Moctezuma knew what he must do. He called for some of the best artists in his capital city. He gave them careful instructions for the design of a magnificent turquoise mask, a cloak, golden armlets, fans, bracelets, throatbands, and medallions, each decorated with feathers and emeralds. When the work was done, Moctezuma ordered messengers to the coast, to carry these gifts to the strangers. The presents were fit for a god, and that is exactly what Moctezuma believed they would encounter.

Later, aboard his ship, the Spanish explorer Hernán Cortés allowed the Aztec messengers to place the mask and jewelry on him. The golden bells tinkled in the breeze. The feathers shone in the sunlight. "And is this all?" Cortés asked. "Is this your gift of welcome? Is this how you greet people?" Was this a sign of how European exploration would affect the Americas and the three cultures that met there—Native American, African, and European? Would these diverse peoples ever forge a common society?

CHAPTER PREVIEW

In this chapter you will learn how the meeting of three diverse cultures in the Western Hemisphere changed the world.

SECTIONS IN THIS CHAPTER:
1. **Diverse Native American cultures peopled the continent.**
2. **Africa and Europe had rich civilizations.**
3. **An exchange of cultures shaped the Americas.**
4. **England and France challenged Spain.**
5. **English settlers established Jamestown.**

1480	1500	1520	1540	1560	1580	1600	1620	1640

1492
Columbus lands in the Americas

c. 1500
League of the Iroquois founded

1607
The English settle Jamestown

1619
First Africans brought to Virginia

1521
Cortés conquers Aztec empire

13

Diverse Native American cultures peopled the continent.

Key Terms: Maya, Aztecs, Incas, matrilineal, polytheistic

Reading Preview
As you read this section, you will learn:

1. when groups of people first settled in the Americas.
2. what caused a diversity of North American cultures to develop.
3. what most Native Americans shared in common.

Families of hunters and gatherers crossed from Asia to North America by way of a land bridge that existed where the waters of the Bering Strait now flow.

As Europeans reckoned time, it was the 15th century. On the continents of North and South America, the divisions of time followed other rhythms and were called by different names. Yet here, as in Europe, the passage of centuries had given rise to a variety of societies, each with its own economic patterns, religious beliefs and institutions, political organizations, and family arrangements. Most of our written accounts of these cultures come to us through European eyes. In recent years, however, archaeologists and anthropologists, as well as historians, have recaptured some measure of the world as the Indians themselves saw it and shaped it.

People first settled in the Americas some 12,000 to 30,000 years ago.

Some 100,000 years ago, humans began to spread out from the grasslands of Africa. Traveling by way of Asia, these people reached the Western Hemisphere some time later. They came, anthropologists think, between 12,000 and 30,000 years ago, during the last Ice Age, a time when much of the earth's water was frozen in huge glaciers. The people, hunter-gatherers, were probably pursuing large game animals across a northern land bridge that connected Asia and North America. As you can see from the map on page 15, the land bridge formed where the waters of the **Bering Strait** now flow.

The prehistoric hunting bands fanned out and moved south and east across the continent of North America. Armed with flint-tipped weapons, they tracked the mammoths and mastodons that a warming climate would eventually make extinct. These early hunters were the ancestors of almost all the native peoples of North and South America. Much later, some

North American Indian Groups About 1500 to 1800

Language Families

- Inuit-Eskimo-Aleut
- Athapascan
- Algic-Algonquian
- Iroquois
- Caddoan
- Muskogean-Gulf
- Siouan
- Uto-Aztecan
- Mayan
- Other language families

Azimuthal Equal-Area Projection

© SF

Maya, Aztec, and Inca Empires

Not all Indian groups shown lived in the same time period. In the Great Plains some groups formed later than others, and some groups moved from one place to another. Within the same language family, ways of living varied widely.

map study

Regions On this map the colored areas represent major Indian language families. Which Indian groups lived in your region during this time? To what language families did these groups belong?

Critical Thinking As the map footnote explains, ways of living varied widely within the same language family. Note the extent of the Algic-Algonquian area. How might the way of life of the Narraganset have differed from that of the Cheyenne?

Aztec School Days

An Aztec woman recalls how young leaders were educated in the days before the Spanish conquest. How does their school day compare with your class schedule?

And when they had breakfasted, they (the adults) began teaching them how to live, how to obey, and how to honor people, to give themselves to the good. . . . And likewise at midday, when the sun was very hot, they sent them to the edge of the woods . . . They ran vigorously . . . and in a very short while they returned. And when they had eaten, right away they (the adults) began teaching them again . . . to some how to do battle, or how to hunt. . . . Others were taught song composition and oratory . . . also the science of the heavens. . . . And indeed some they took to the fields . . . to teach them how to sow seeds . . . and to cultivate and work the land. They taught them all it was needful for them to know by way of service, knowledge, wisdom, and prudent living.

4,000 years ago, another group of people reached the Americas. Eskimos and Aleuts came, traveling by kayaks, for by this time the land bridge was covered over by water.

Geographic conditions led to a diversity of Indian cultures.

By the time of Columbus, in the late 1400s, the descendants of these hunters had established themselves throughout the American landmass—from sunny California to the woodlands of Virginia, from glacier-gouged Alaska to the icy Tierra del Fuego at the southern tip of South America.

The continent north of the Rio Grande contained some four million people, of whom perhaps 500,000 lived in areas accessible to the early European settlers. The Indians, as the Europeans called all Native Americans, created a diverse range of civilizations, adapting to a va-

riety of geographic conditions. Some cultures were quite simple, others highly elaborate.

Agriculture helps explain some of the differences between cultures. Between 8000 and 5000 B.C., Indians in Central America began to cultivate plants for food, soon mastering the basics of agriculture. As people turned to farming, they began to settle down. With the insecurity of a hunting and gathering existence lessened, they established permanent villages. As the supply of food increased through farming, so did the Native American population. As a result, some Indians could be freed from the work of sustaining life in order to concentrate on art and architecture. Indians of Mexico and the Southwest were among the earliest farmers and thus tended to be more culturally advanced than the Indians of the Northeast, who knew nothing about the domestication of plants or learned of it relatively late.

Mexico, Central America, and South America. The most advanced Native American cultures arose in present-day Mexico and Central America. About 500 B.C. the **Maya** developed a civilization located chiefly in the tropical **Yucatán peninsula** (present-day southeastern Mexico, Guatemala, and Belize). For roughly 1,700 years, the Maya dominated the area, making many lasting intellectual achievements. They created a highly advanced system of writing, in which symbols stood for ideas. They also developed a very accurate calendar and a system of numbers that included the idea of zero, a new concept at the time.

In the 13th century, the **Aztecs**, a warlike people, swept into central Mexico from the northwest, possibly southern Utah or northern Arizona. By the time of Cortés' arrival, they had taken control of the area, governing an empire of at least five million people. Over the years the Aztecs developed an advanced form of government, in which they ruled over their conquered peoples by the sword and forced them to pay tribute.

Other mighty empires emerged in South America, notably the **Incas** of Peru. The Incas, settling in the Andes around the 11th century, eventually conquered the native peoples. By the 1500s they ruled an empire of more than

The Adena, a moundbuilding people, constructed the Great Serpent Mound near Hillsboro, Ohio. The mound measures about one-quarter mile in length. Many of the moundbuilders were skilled artisans, as this exquisite tortoise shell hair ornament or comb shows. It dates from the Hopewell culture of roughly A.D. 200.

12 million people who spoke 20 different languages and belonged to more than 100 different ethnic groups. Unlike the Aztecs, the Incas absorbed the people they conquered into their own culture. They kept their huge empire intact with highly organized systems of government, communication, and transportation.

Western North America. In western North America, Indians responded to differing environmental conditions. Along the Pacific coast, for example, the Chinook of present-day Washington and Oregon depended on fishing, in addition to growing crops and gathering seeds and berries. In the Southwest, hunters became farmers as early as 2000 B.C. They depended upon corn, beans, and squash. By the time the Spanish arrived in the 1500s, the Pueblo people, ancestors of present-day Hopi and Zuñi, were using irrigation canals, dams, and hillside terracing to bring water to their arid corn fields. Extending their talents to other ventures, the Pueblo constructed villages of multistoried buildings on terraces along the sides of cliffs or other easily defended sites. They also were skilled in ceramics and used woven textiles for clothing. In these and other areas, such as village life, Pueblo society resembled that of peasant communities in many parts of Europe and Asia.

Central North America. In the heartland region of North America, from the Rockies to the Appalachian Mountains, Native Americans adapted to prairies, plains, and dense forests. In general these peoples hunted large game animals while also cultivating fields of corn, squash, and beans. On the Great Plains, the bison provided food, clothing, and tools.

Some of the midcontinent's most impressive societies were those of the moundbuilders. When migrants reached the Ohio Valley around 800 B.C., they adapted their agricultural knowledge to the rich, fertile soils of the region. These people forged a culture distinct in its use of earthen mounds, some of them 70 feet high, for the burial of their dead. The ceremonial mounds were sculpted both in geometric designs and in the shapes of humans, birds, or serpents. Several moundbuilding societies followed one another, until their decline about 1,000 years before Europeans reached the continent. A few centuries later, another moundbuilding society emerged in the Mississippi Valley, with its center, a city of perhaps 40,000, located near Cahokia, Illinois. The Mississippi culture eventually declined, but not before its influence spread out to thousands of villages from Wisconsin to Louisiana and from Oklahoma to Tennessee.

Eastern North America. On the fringes of the moundbuilding empire, and influenced by its culture, a woodland society evolved. The English colonizers who settled in Virginia and New England met Indians of this woodland culture, which dominated the Atlantic coastal lands. These people were skilled farmers, growing corn, beans, and melons. Most of the eastern woodland peoples lived in waterside villages, planting their fields of corn near fishing grounds. This way they could take advantage of the water's natural benefits—fishing, trading, and communicating. These eastern Native Americans, generally coming late to the agricultural life, nonetheless had learned to use natural plants for food, medicine, dyes, and flavoring by the time Europeans arrived on their shores.

Animal faces display their strength and ferocity on the Grizzly Totem, located in Bight, Alaska. Totem poles were most common among the Pacific Northwest peoples.

Native Americans shared many beliefs and values.

Although the North American Indian societies differed in the ways they managed survival and the growth of their communities, most held several important beliefs and values in common. Many of these values contrasted directly with those held by Europeans, leading eventually to conflict.

First, their families were organized along kinship lines, meaning that family membership was defined by blood connection. In many Native American societies, family connections were **matrilineal**, that is, made through the female line. A typical family thus consisted of an old woman, her daughters with their husbands and children, and her unmarried granddaughters and grandsons. When a son or grandson married, he moved from this female-headed household to one headed by the female leader of his wife's family. Women also controlled divorce. If a woman wanted a divorce, she simply set her husband's possessions outside their dwelling door. Families were joined in clans, again defined by kinship ties.

Second, the division of labor within Indian societies most frequently set women in charge of child care and cultivation or agriculture. The men were responsible for activities in which child care would be a burden, such as hunting, trading, and fighting.

Politically, women's roles and status varied from culture to culture. Women were more likely to assume leadership roles among the agricultural peoples than among nomadic hunters. In addition, in many cases in which women did not become village chiefs, they still exercised substantial political power. For example, in Iroquois villages, when selected men sat in a circle to discuss and make decisions, the senior women of the village stood behind them, lobbying and instructing the men. In addition, the elder women named the male village chiefs to their positions.

Third, although religious beliefs varied widely among cultures, certain threads were common. One of these threads was that the Indians were **polytheistic**, that is, they believed in a multitude of gods. Another was the tie between the most important rituals of an Indian culture and that culture's way of life. For example, the major deities of agricultural Indians such as the Pueblo were associated with cultivation, and their primary festivals centered on planting and harvesting. By contrast, the most important deities of hunting Indians were associated with animals, and their major festivals revolved around hunting. Women's role in religion varied, with females holding the most prominent positions in those agricultural societies in which they also produced the food.

Fourth, Indians valued prestige more than the accumulation of wealth or possessions. Giving away riches added to a person's prestige, and thus in many Indian societies there were elaborate rituals and ceremonies of giving gifts. Trading and gift giving bound community members to one another and formed the basis of friendly relationships with neighboring Indian communities or groups. Among many Indian cultures, land was owned communally, although among many societies families were granted their own hunting territories, fishing spots, and gardens. Individuals owned the objects they produced, the food they grew, gathered or killed. Despite this pattern of private property, it is unlikely that the legal and social energies of Indians were as intensely focused as the Europeans were on defining and ensuring permanent private possession of land and other wealth.

SECTION 1 REVIEW

Identify Key People and Terms
Write a sentence to identify: Maya, Aztecs, Incas, matrilineal, polytheistic

Locate Key Places

1. Between what two continents does the Bering Strait lie?
2. What present-day countries lie on the Yucatán peninsula?

Master the Main Ideas

1. **Understanding Native American cultures:** How did the first settlers reach the Americas?
2. **Understanding Native American cultures:** How did geography contribute to differences among Native American cultures?
3. **Understanding Native American cultures: (a)** What values did many Native Americans share? **(b)** In what ways did some of these differ from values held by many Europeans?

Apply Critical Thinking Skills: Making Comparisons
Compare the ideas of polytheism and ownership of property held by many Native Americans to those held by most Americans in modern society. How might the differences affect the opinions of a modern American toward an Indian from the 14th or 15th century?

SECTION **2**

Africa and Europe had rich civilizations.

Key Terms: Islam, Renaissance, Christianity, Judaism, Protestant Reformation

Reading Preview
As you read this section, you will learn:

1. what influenced the development of African societies.
2. what many West Africans had in common.
3. what occurred in Europe in the 15th and 16th centuries.
4. which gender was dominant in European society.

Some 500 years before Hernán Cortés first sailed to the Americas, Europeans made their first known contacts with North America. Around the year 1000, Scandinavian sailors known as Vikings explored barren regions of the North Atlantic Ocean. Eric the Red and his son, Leif Erikson, both led voyages that resulted in settlements they named Greenland and Vinland (northern Newfoundland). These settlements ultimately failed, and the Vikings soon lost interest in North America. News of their travels did not likely reach the rest of Europe.

Interest in this distant land later resurfaced in another part of Europe, however. It came at a time when Europeans were better prepared for such exploration and colonization, and the effects reached far and wide. Directly affected were the peoples of America and Africa. The Africans, who had enjoyed a rich history of political and cultural development for centuries, would find their futures forever entangled with that of America.

Geography influenced African societies.

Fifteenth-century Africa, like 15th-century America, supported a variety of cultures

19

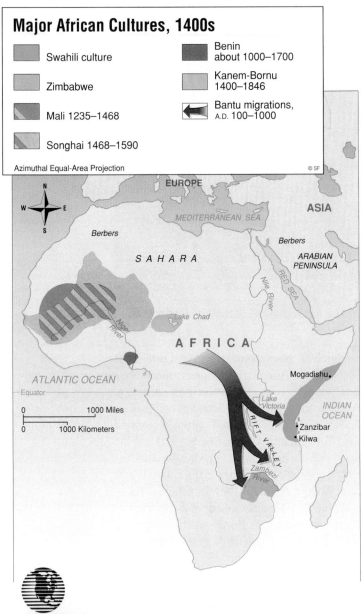

Major African Cultures, 1400s

- Swahili culture
- Zimbabwe
- Mali 1235–1468
- Songhai 1468–1590
- Benin about 1000–1700
- Kanem-Bornu 1400–1846
- Bantu migrations, A.D. 100–1000

Azimuthal Equal-Area Projection   © SF

EUROPE

ASIA

MEDITERRANEAN SEA

Berbers

SAHARA

Berbers

ARABIAN PENINSULA

RED SEA

Nile River

Niger River

Lake Chad

AFRICA

ATLANTIC OCEAN

Equator

0   1000 Miles
0   1000 Kilometers

Mogadishu

Lake Victoria

INDIAN OCEAN

Zanzibar
Kilwa

RIFT VALLEY

Zambezi River

map study

Place Geography influenced the growth of African cultures. People living along the Indian Ocean coast developed trade relations with Asia, giving birth to the Swahili culture. The grasslands of West Africa supported farming and trading cultures that eventually became powerful kingdoms. In the late 1400s, European explorers and traders traveled along Africa's west coast. Which African cultures shown on the map would the Europeans have come in contact with first?

Critical Thinking Which West African culture remained strong into the 1800s? Why might this culture have been less affected by the early Europeans than others?

adapted to different geographic conditions. Many of these cultures had long histories. In the north, along the **Mediterranean Sea**, lived the Berbers, a nomadic people who followed **Islam**, a religion founded by the prophet Muhammad in the 7th century. Islam's followers are known as Muslims. In the east, facing the Indian Ocean, city-states such as Kilwa and Zanzibar had evolved from their beginnings as coastal marketplaces. The Africans had been trading with India, China, and the Islamic Empire of Southwest Asia for many centuries by the time the Europeans arrived on the continent. Africans exported gold, ivory, and iron. Eventually a Swahili culture developed in the city-states, a unique blend of African, Islamic, and Asian cultures and languages.

In the African interior stood the Sahara. As you can see from the map at left, the huge desert served as a formidable barrier to trade and travel. South of the Sahara, much of Africa is divided between tropical rainforests and grassy plains. Here, Bantu-speaking peoples came to dominate. About 2,000 years ago, the Bantu-speaking peoples had left their homeland in present-day Nigeria and moved slowly southward across the continent. Along the way they conquered or absorbed other ethnic groups, eventually building a capital city at Zimbabwe in eastern Africa.

West Africa, south of the Sahara, was home to most of the Africans who would eventually be sent as slaves to the Americas. For at least 10,000 years before Europeans arrived there in the 1400s, this land of vast grasslands and tropical rainforests was inhabited largely by farmers and traders. Since the year 500, the northern portion was governed by a series of large empires, first the kingdom of Ghana (500–1235), then its successors, the empires of Mali (1235–1468) and Songhai (1468–1590). You can see from the map at left how far the influence of these empires reached. The West African empires controlled a lucrative trade with Muslims across the Sahara. The West Africans provided gold, ivory, and slaves in exchange for salt, dates, and such goods as silk and cotton cloth. In addition, the trade brought an Islamic influence to West Africa.

In the south and along the coast, Islam had less influence. Here, people practiced religions in which their rituals and festivals served to ensure good and plentiful harvests. Individual villages and small kingdoms took the place of the large empires of the West African interior. Along the coast, agricultural products and practices varied according to geographic conditions. Fishing, rice cultivation, and grain farming were all important.

West Africans shared social and religious practices.

Despite the different political arrangements found throughout West Africa, many of its inhabitants shared social and religious values and beliefs. For example, family relationships, which were central to West African society, were defined by kinship. In many West African societies, as in many Native American ones, the family was matrilineal, with property rights and political leadership coming through the mother.

West African cultures assigned essential tasks within their society by gender. In most West African cultures, men hunted, tended livestock, and fished. Women were responsible for childcare and the production of food and cloth. Women, however, were also the primary traders, developing and managing trade networks within their own communities and within the larger region. Both sexes created and controlled their own political and religious activities and organizations. Thus, male leaders ruled men and females ruled the women in parallel but separate governments. West African religions reinforced the belief that males and females had different roles and destinies.

Slavery was a part of these African societies. Notably, slavery in the African context was different from that which eventually developed in the Americas. African slavery did not completely destroy the legal and economic rights of the slave. Slaves, usually taken captive in war, could marry into the community and eventually become citizens. Until the colonization of the New World, the trade in slaves from Africa to Europe or the Muslim world was limited. However, once the slave trade began

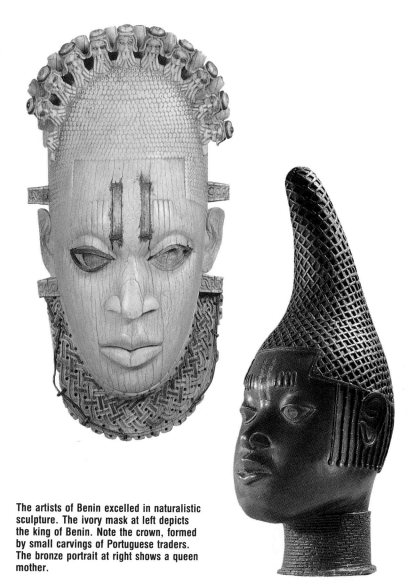

The artists of Benin excelled in naturalistic sculpture. The ivory mask at left depicts the king of Benin. Note the crown, formed by small carvings of Portuguese traders. The bronze portrait at right shows a queen mother.

to supply the plantations of the Americas, the effect on African societies was severe.

Europe experienced a revival in the 15th and 16th centuries.

The Europe that would eventually take up that slave trade in Africa underwent significant changes in the late 1400s and early 1500s—in culture, politics, religion, and technology. Before the mid-1400s, Europeans were quite unprepared to take a leading role in worldwide exploration. Politically, feudal nobles dominated small districts throughout Europe, their demands for local loyalty precluding any strong central government. Intellectually, most Europeans were ignorant of classical learning and

Europe About 1490

⊙ Capital city with same name as state

• Other major cities

Azimuthal Equal-Area Projection © SF

map study

Relationships within Places Until the late 1400s, Europe was dominated by the Roman Catholic Church. Gradually, however, nation-states emerged as separate political regions. Which present-day nation bordered the Holy Roman Empire on the west?

Critical Thinking Why was it natural for Portugal to be the leader in navigation and exploration?

unaware of the larger world. In addition, terrible plagues such as the bubonic plague or Black Death, which killed between one-fourth to one-half of Europe's population in the mid-1300s, had devastating effects. After the mid-1400s, however, changes occurred. Europe became more prosperous, and its population began to grow.

Cultural change. Much of Europe's economic growth centered in the trading city-states of the Mediterranean, where a lucrative Asian trade brought in silk, spices, and other exotic goods. The region's economic growth subsequently led to a rebirth in culture and learning. In city-states on the Italian peninsula, such as Genoa, Venice, and Florence, wealthy merchant families supported new work and scholarship in the arts, literature, and science. This revival, known as the **Renaissance**, gradually spread from the Italian peninsula to other parts of Europe. Leaders of other kingdoms looked with envy upon the commercial wealth of the Mediterranean cities. Throughout the 1300s and 1400s, they sought new routes to Asia in order to break the Italian monopoly.

Political change. At the same time, political forces were at work that would make that exploration more feasible. A group of strong-willed monarchs began to wrest control of their lands from the feudal lords who had dominated them for centuries. In England, France, and Spain, nation-states slowly emerged, with their own armies, revenues, and court systems. Thus, European countries began to have the financial and military resources necessary for worldwide exploration.

Religious change. Around the same time, a religious revolution also took place. Most Europeans followed **Christianity**, the religion based on the teachings of Jesus Christ. Others, known as Jews, practiced **Judaism**, a religion based on the teachings of Moses and the prophets in the Old Testament of the Bible. Throughout much of European history, the Jews experienced intolerance of their religious views and practices. During the 13th and 14th centuries, the intolerance reached a peak in violent persecution and anti-Jewish laws.

Until the late 1400s, the Roman Catholic Church was the strongest power in Europe, both religiously and politically. At that time, however, people began to question the authority and integrity of the Church. The rise of secular ideas (non-religious ideas), widespread corruption in the Church, and power politics all contributed to the challenges that led to the **Protestant Reformation**.

Led by the German monk **Martin Luther** and the French scholar **John Calvin**, the Reformation swept Europe. Although its primary goal was to reform the Roman Catholic Church, the Reformation resulted in the formation of new Protestant churches that urged people to form a more direct, personal relationship with God.

Technological change. Technological innovation was the final element in the rise of Europe and its role in exploration. Before the 15th century, the ships that sailed the Mediterranean were slow and clumsy. They were difficult to maneuver, especially into the wind, and often required large numbers of oarsmen. In addition, much of the knowledge of the physical world collected by ancient geographers, such as the Greek scientist Ptolemy in the 2nd century A.D., was lost to Europeans during the Middle Ages, making navigation of unknown waters both difficult and dangerous. During the Renaissance this knowledge resurfaced, aiding sailing efforts.

Portugal, a small, poor nation-state facing the Atlantic Ocean, took the lead in developing new technologies for ship design, navigation, and mapmaking. Like other rulers, Portugal's Prince Henry the Navigator was motivated by two things. First, he was aware of the vast wealth that awaited the first European nation to tap directly the riches of Africa and Asia. Second, he wanted to help spread Christianity to the non-Christian world.

In the 1400s Prince Henry encouraged and financed exploration along Africa's coast. He also set up a famous school to train navigators. Some of the innovations aiding the Portuguese sea ventures were the invention of the quadrant (used to more accurately gauge latitude) and the adaptation of a Moorish ship design to create the caravel. The triangular sails of the caravel permitted the ship to sail against the wind, an advantage required to sail southward along the African coast. By the mid-1400s, the Portuguese had reached the west coast of Africa, where they began a profitable trade in gold, ivory, and slaves. Later, in 1488 Bartolomeu Días rounded the tip of Africa, and in 1498 Vasco da Gama followed the same route and sailed on to India. The Portuguese threatened at last to break the Italian monopoly on Asian trade.

European societies were male-dominated.

In spite of such monumental cultural, religious, technological, and political change, the lives of most Europeans remained untouched for nearly a century. As in Africa and the Americas, most European commoners lived with their families in small agricultural villages. However, unlike Africa and America, European society was not based on kinship groups. The Roman Catholic Church, to which almost all Europeans belonged, insisted that people marry nonrelatives, discouraging strong kinship ties.

Another difference was the dominance of men in almost all aspects of European life. Whereas Native American and African women often played important roles in politics and religion, European women, with only a few exceptions (such as Elizabeth I of England), were

Developments in sailing technology helped promote Europe's leadership in world exploration. The astrolabe at left aided navigation by measuring the altitude of the sun or stars. The caravel surpassed existing ships in terms of sail design.

generally excluded from positions of power in either of these arenas. In the family as well, men controlled the lives of their wives, children, and servants. In agricultural families, men did most of the field work, with women helping at planting and harvest times. Women's work generally involved childcare and such household duties as food preparation and the milking of cows. If a woman's husband was an artisan or shopkeeper, she might help in the business.

Differences in gender roles among the Europeans, Native Americans, and Africans would ultimately lead to conflict in the Americas. Because each culture believed their division of labor to be natural and sensible, each was critical of the other.

SECTION **2** REVIEW

Identify Key People and Terms
Write a sentence to identify: Islam, Renaissance, Christianity, Judaism, Protestant Reformation, Martin Luther, John Calvin

Locate Key Places
Which body of water lies north of Africa?

Master the Main Ideas

1. **Recognizing the influence of physical features:** How was location important to the development of African societies?
2. **Respecting beliefs of other cultures:** What values and beliefs were shared by many West African societies?
3. **Understanding causes of exploration:** In what ways did Europe change in the 15th and 16th centuries?
4. **Recognizing societal values: (a)** In what ways was European society male-dominated? **(b)** What was the role of European women?

Apply Critical Thinking Skills: Predicting Consequences
Consider the different social values and practices of the Native Americans, Africans, and Europeans of the 15th century. What consequences would you predict would come from their interaction in the Americas?

SECTION **3**

An exchange of cultures shaped the Americas.

Key Term: conquistadores

Reading Preview
As you read this section, you will learn:

1. which country Christopher Columbus brought to world exploration.
2. what contributed to the European conquest of the Americas.
3. what was exchanged between the Old and New worlds.

The Portuguese route to Asia, by way of Africa, turned out to be a long and dangerous journey. Thus, it was not likely to be as profitable as the Mediterranean trade. Therefore, **Christopher Columbus**, a Genoese sailor born Cristoforo Colombo but known by the Latinized version of his name, pressed to continue the search for a western route across the Atlantic to Asia.

Columbus brought Spain into the age of exploration.

Having little schooling, Columbus taught himself what he needed to know to make his voyage. He learned Latin in order to read the geography books of the time, and he taught himself to read and write Spanish so that he could communicate when he traveled to Spain.

In 1484, when he was 33, Columbus presented his plan for sailing to China to the king of Portugal, then home to the most advanced navigators in the world. The Portuguese spurned his idea, calling it "vain, simply founded on imagination, or things like that." Columbus then turned to **Queen Isabella** of Castile. Her marriage to Ferdinand in 1469 had united the kingdoms of Castile and Aragon under Catholic rule. Their combined armies later defeated the Muslim states in southern Spain, thereby creating a unified, Christian Spain for the first time. Initially, the two were no more interested in Columbus' plan than the Portu-

BUILDING
CRITICAL THINKING STRATEGIES

COLUMBUS' ARRIVAL
Skill: Making Comparisons

Introducing the Skill. "We see the world in terms of our cultural heritage," writes Jamake Highwater, a Native American of Blackfoot and Cherokee descent. How might cultural backgrounds have led the Native Americans and Europeans each to view the arrival of Christopher Columbus differently?

Learning the Skill. By comparing and contrasting the experiences of both Native Americans and Europeans, you are **making comparisons**. This means determining how two or more things are alike and how they are different. For example, when comparing the members of your favorite baseball team, you might notice that they all have the same coach. Still, you would also notice their differences—in batting talent, fielding ability, or age. Use the following five steps to make a comparison:

1. Identify the main features of each item.
2. Select a feature in one item and determine whether it can be found in all the other items.
3. Classify as a similarity any feature found in all the given items.
4. Classify as a difference any feature not found in all the given items.
5. Repeat this process for each main feature.

Applying the Skill. Study the two illustrations on this page, both portraying Columbus' arrival in the Americas. The first is a 16th-century engraving by an anonymous artist, presumably European. The second is a drawing by Choctaw artist Asa Battles, commissioned by Highwater to show an Indian perspective for his book, *Many Smokes, Many Moons*.

1. Compare the two illustrations, listing any similarities and differences.
2. How do you account for the differences in the two illustrations?

Compare the illustrations at right. How does each artist portray the coming of Christopher Columbus to the Americas?

guese. However, the young sailor was stubborn and wore down the monarchs' opposition by playing on their rivalry with Portugal. With Spanish backing, Columbus thus set sail on August 3, 1492, with a fleet of three ships—two caravels, the *Niña* and the *Pinta*, and the square-rigged *Santa María*.

By October of the same year, land was spotted. Columbus had not reached Asia, of course, but when he planted the flag of Isabel's Castile in the soil of an island in the West Indies, he did indeed make history. Historians and geographers still debate where exactly Columbus landed, but many now believe that his first stop was **San Salvador**, an island in the Bahama chain. Columbus made several more voyages to the Americas before his death in 1506. By then Europeans were beginning to understand

Point

Benefits to Europe

- led to spread of Christianity
- brought new wealth
- introduced new foods and animals

Counterpoint

Problems for America

- destroyed native cultures
- caused much loss of life
- led to European domination

the nature of their experience. Here were vast continents unknown to their civilization—a New World.

Dreams of personal wealth and fame prompted a century of European exploration of this New World. Spanish expeditions to South and Central America brought Europeans and the Indian empires of the Incas and Aztecs into contact and conflict. The success of leaders such as **Hernán Cortés**, who destroyed Moctezuma's Aztec Empire in 1521, and **Francisco Pizarro**, who defeated the Incas in 1532, won these Europeans the title **conquistadores** [kon kē′stə dôr′ez]. On the ruins of the Aztec capital of Tenochtitlán, Cortés built a new city, Mexico City, which became the capital of New Spain. Massive hoards of gold and silver were gathered up and shipped to Spain. Some 50 or 60 years after Cortés arrived, an old Aztec noblewoman remembered:

Here in our home of Tetzcohco [Texcoco], your birthplace, things are also coming to an end. There

AN AMERICAN
★ SPEAKS

were innumerable rulers and nobles. . . . And how many noble houses there were, the palaces of the former nobles and rulers! It was like one big palace. . . . But now everywhere our Lord is destroying and reducing the land, we are coming to an end and disappearing. Why? For what reason? Perhaps we have incurred his wrath and offended Him with our sins and wrongdoing. But what are we to do?

Reports of vast riches inspired other Spaniards to strike out north of Mexico into land that is now part of the United States. Pánfilo de Narváez, Hernando de Soto, and Francisco Vásquez de Coronado all led large expeditions that without exception were disappointing. No gold was found, and thousands of Indians and Spaniards alike lost their lives. Indeed, as the Indians were to learn, the Europeans meant to conquer, not to live in peace.

Disease contributed to the European conquest of the Americas.

Why were the European military expeditions so often successful? Some Europeans of the time pointed to the justice of Christian forces overcoming societies of what they called heathens and savages. Others were satisfied to applaud the bravery and military genius of the conquistadores. Historians, too, have pondered the question of European success. At first, they assumed that the combination of European weaponry and a horse-mounted army gave the conquerors their advantage. Recently, however, historians have paid closer attention to the invisible world of pathogens, or disease-carrying bacteria and viruses. They have discovered that the invasion of America included the attack by deadly diseases unknown to the Indian immune system.

European disease killed many more Native Americans than sword or musket. Smallpox, carried by air, decimated the populations of the New World. The disease, which killed many in the 16th and 17th centuries, raged on through the 1800s and entered the myth and legend of

In the battles between Aztec warriors and Spanish conquistadores, the adversaries were well matched in valor.

the North American Indians. The Kiowa of the southern Great Plains told of the meeting between a stranger named Smallpox and Saynday, the mythic hero of their tribe. Smallpox says:

I come from far away, across the Eastern Ocean. I am one with the white men—they are my people as the Kiowas are yours. Sometimes I travel ahead of them, and sometimes I lurk behind. But I am always their companion.

Saynday asks: "What do you do?" and Smallpox answers, "I bring death . . . I bring destruction . . . No people who have looked at me will ever be the same."

The Kiowa's stranger told the truth. Historians now believe that, even before Columbus arrived, the early contact of the Scandinavians may have unleashed European diseases upon Native American civilizations.

Food and animals were exchanged between continents.

Death and disease were not the only forms of exchange between the Old and New worlds. Animal life and vegetation crossed the oceans with explorers and settlers. In this way foods, plants, and animals traveled from Europe to America and back to the rest of the world.

Vegetation. The Europeans' vegetation overtook much of the American landscape. As the conquistadores destroyed forests and grazed their animals, they carried with them many types of weeds, the most aggressive type of plant life. Many of the plants we think of as native to America were actually imported in the age of conquest. Thistles, plantain, rye, radishes, asparagus, beets, sugar, and peaches were brought by Europeans. Kentucky bluegrass, the pride of that state, is actually a Eurasian mixture of wild grasses.

American foods likewise survived the transatlantic voyage to Africa, Asia, and Europe. The cassava of South America became a staple food of the black peoples of Africa. The white potato, known popularly as the Irish potato, came from the New World as well. The transplanting of grains such as Indian corn also illustrates the positive side of the exchange.

Animals. Legend has it that the Indians were awed by the sight of Spanish soldiers on horseback. If so, however, awe quickly turned to mastery. The horse, reproducing rapidly on the grassy Argentinian pampas and in the American Southwest, became central to the cultures of Indian populations there. Europeans also brought pigs, chickens, cattle, sheep and goats, all of which contributed to the destruction of native ground cover, the extinction of some native animals, and a new protein diet for the Indians.

The sometimes invisible and sometimes unnoticed struggle and exchange between Old and New World diseases, foods, vegetation, and animals is a major piece of the story of conquest and colonization. The visible effects of trade, political and economic domination, intermarriage, and military alliance is another piece of the Columbian exchange.

SECTION 3 REVIEW

Identify Key People and Terms
Write a sentence to identify: Christopher Columbus, Queen Isabella, Hernán Cortés, Francisco Pizarro, conquistadores

Locate Key Places
On what Bahama island do many historians believe Columbus first landed?

Master the Main Ideas
1. **Understanding exploration:** How did Columbus involve Spain in exploration?
2. **Understanding exploration:** In what way did disease aid the European conquest of the Americas?
3. **Recognizing effects of exploration:** What foods and animals were involved in the Columbian exchange?

Apply Critical Thinking Skills: Recognizing Bias
Consider the different reasons given over time for the success of European conquest in the Americas, from moral superiority to disease. How might the interpretations of historians and other thinkers, in past and present times, reflect the bias of a particular society? Support your answer with evidence.

GEOGRAPHY IN AMERICAN HISTORY

Columbian Exchange

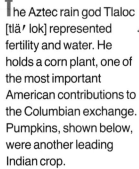

The Aztec rain god Tlaloc [tlä′ lok] represented fertility and water. He holds a corn plant, one of the most important American contributions to the Columbian exchange. Pumpkins, shown below, were another leading Indian crop.

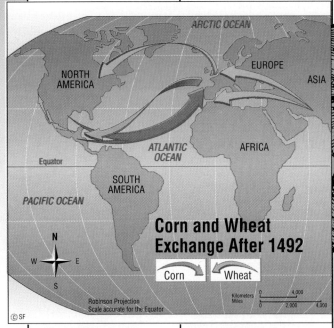

Corn and Wheat Exchange After 1492

Corn → Wheat →

Robinson Projection
Scale accurate for the Equator

Kilometers 0 4,000
Miles 0 2,000 4,000

© SF

Movement Until 1492 very different food plants were cultivated in the Old World and the Americas. The map shows the two most important food crops exchanged worldwide after 1492. What are the two crops? Which crop moved from the New World to Europe and Asia?

Critical Thinking What barriers isolated the Americas from the rest of the world? Why were European explorers important in the story of food crop exchange?

The movement of corn, from North America, and wheat, from Europe and Asia, shows how the Columbian exchange changed how people around the world ate and lived.

The Americas to Europe
corn, white potatoes, sweet potatoes/yams, cassava/manioc, turkey, guinea pigs

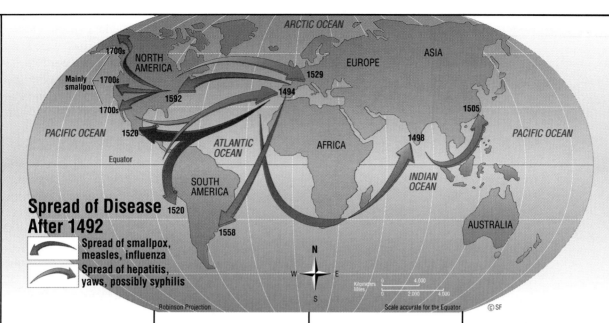

Spread of Disease After 1492

↰ Spread of smallpox, measles, influenza

↰ Spread of hepatitis, yaws, possibly syphilis

Robinson Projection

Scale accurate for the Equator

© SF

N
W — E
S

Kilometers 0 — 4,000
Miles 0 — 2,000 — 4,000

Movement As the map shows, disease carried by Europeans spread through all parts of the Americas after 1492. In the New World, revered Indian leaders as well as thousands of ordinary people died from imported Old World infections. Thus the deadly exchange disrupted both the political and social stability of the New World Indian empires. Which three major diseases came to the Americas from Europe?

Critical Thinking The dates on the map show that smallpox did not reach the west coast of the present-day United States until the 1700s. Why might that be so?

Europe to the Americas
wheat, rice, citrus fruits, sugar cane.
horses, pigs, cattle, sheep, goats, oxen.

© SF

European explorers devastated Native Americans with their deadly diseases. At right are Aztecs suffering from smallpox picked up during the Cortés invasion. The etching dates from a 16th-century book by Fray Bernardo de Sahagun.

England and France challenged Spain.

Key Terms: presidio, mission, sea dogs, Spanish Armada, League of the Iroquois, *coureurs de bois*

Reading Preview
As you read this section, you will learn:

1. where Spain established colonies.
2. who challenged the power of Spain.
3. where France concentrated its explorations.
4. what economic venture the French built in North America.

By the middle of the 16th century, Spanish conquest had given way to Spanish colonization of the New World, and the pioneer replaced the conquistador. As the Spaniards turned their attention to colonizing and governing the Americas, conflicts inevitably arose between the native peoples and their conquerors. At the same time, two other European powers, England and France, began taking notice of the rich promise of the Americas.

Spain established colonies in North and South America.

The Spaniards' mission in the Americas was twofold and often contradictory. On the one hand, the king hoped to baptize and convert these new Spanish subjects to the Roman Catholic faith. On the other hand, he demanded that the New World colonies enrich Spain financially. With these goals, the Spaniards set about colonizing the Americas.

Spain's southern colonies. Much of the Spanish system encouraged the subjugation of the Indians. First, the vast wealth of the Americas lay in rich silver mines and fertile fields of sugar cane. Both enterprises required intensive labor by many men and women, so the Spaniards forced the Indians to serve the Crown as laborers. Second, the Spanish land policy fur-

ther ensured that the Indians would work for the white colonists. The king granted trusteeships over Indian residents, which were known as *encomiendas*, to colonists as rewards for successful and loyal service. Frequently, the Spaniards treated the Indians like slaves, and many Indians lost their lives to the harsh working conditions.

The impact of conquest and colonization on the Indians troubled some Spaniards, especially within the Church. The Dominican bishop **Bartolomé de las Casas** was the most outspoken champion of Indian rights and critic of Spanish policy. His powerful account of the evils of the conquest was widely read by his countrymen and women. The very critical judgment of Spanish conquest formed by later generations was shaped by de las Casas.

The demand for forced labor in the cane fields and silver mines soon affected the lives of Africans as well as Indians. Thousands of Africans were brought to the Americas as slaves during the 16th century. The Africans who came were skilled at metal working, herding, horseback riding, fishing, and rice cultivation. Most were West Africans, sold along the 3,000 miles of coastline from present-day Senegal to Angola. Their labor in the sugar fields of the Caribbean generated a sizeable portion of the wealth that made European industrialization possible. In turn, the textiles produced in the early factories of England were used to purchase African slaves.

Spain's northern colonies. Spain's desire to protect its Central and South American colonies from invasion by rival nations explains much of the settlement made north of Mexico. Outposts in Florida, Texas, New Mexico, and California operated as buffers between New Spain and its European rivals.

Each Spanish outpost was organized around two institutions: the presidio and the mission. The **presidio** was the fortified area of the settlement. In case of enemy attack, all colonists took shelter within its walls. The **mission** was the religious center where churchmen devoted their lives to converting the local Indians to Christianity and teaching them Spanish customs, traditions, and ways of life.

Mexican religious art reflected its Spanish heritage. This *santos* shows Our Lady of Guadalupe framed by an arch and sending forth heavenly rays.

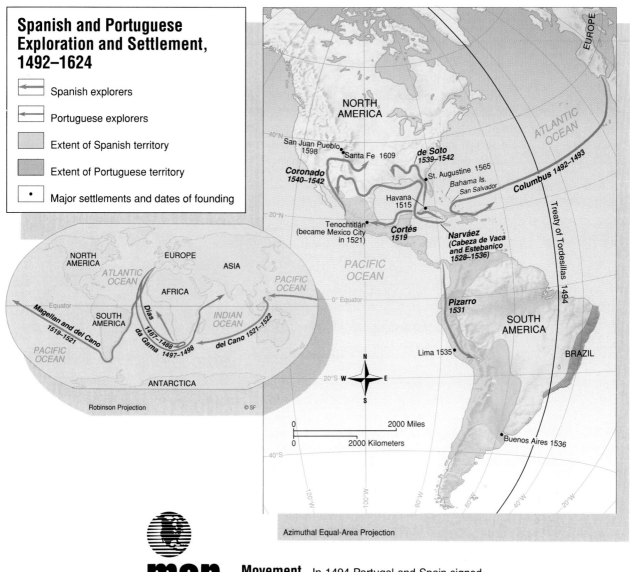

Spanish and Portuguese Exploration and Settlement, 1492–1624

← Spanish explorers

← Portuguese explorers

▨ Extent of Spanish territory

▨ Extent of Portuguese territory

• Major settlements and dates of founding

NORTH AMERICA

San Juan Pueblo 1598

Santa Fe 1609

Coronado 1540–1542

de Soto 1539–1542

St. Augustine 1565

Bahama Is. San Salvador

Columbus 1492–1493

ATLANTIC OCEAN

EUROPE

Havana 1515

Tenochtitlán (became Mexico City in 1521)

Cortés 1519

Narváez (Cabeza de Vaca and Estebanico 1528–1536)

Treaty of Tordesillas 1494

PACIFIC OCEAN

Pizarro 1531

SOUTH AMERICA

Lima 1535

BRAZIL

Buenos Aires 1536

0 2000 Miles
0 2000 Kilometers

Azimuthal Equal-Area Projection

NORTH AMERICA

EUROPE

ASIA

ATLANTIC OCEAN

AFRICA

PACIFIC OCEAN

Magellan and del Cano 1519–1521

Equator

SOUTH AMERICA

Dias 1487–1488

da Gama 1497–1498

del Cano 1521–1522

INDIAN OCEAN

PACIFIC OCEAN

ANTARCTICA

Robinson Projection   © SF

map study

Movement   In 1494 Portugal and Spain signed the Treaty of Tordesillas, dividing the world. Which nation settled the present-day United States?

Critical Thinking   Which nation came to control Central and South America? What evidence can you give?

Among the most important outpost settlements were Saint Augustine (San Agustín), San Juan Pueblo, and El Paso. **Saint Augustine**, founded in 1565 in Florida, is the oldest European town in the United States. There the Spanish navy organized its protection of the empire's treasure ships and rescued Spanish vessels that might be blown ashore.

As you can see from the map above, other settlements followed. In 1598 San Juan Pueblo (later called San Gabriel) was established by Juan de Oñate [hwän′ dā ō nyä′tä] as a Spanish outpost on the Rio Grande. In 1659 Spanish priests started a mission at El Paso, then a part of New Mexico. The first settlements in Spanish Texas were begun some

30 years later in 1690, designed to stop French encroachment in the Mississippi and Red River valleys.

Spain's weaknesses. Spain's New World empire made it the most powerful nation in Europe in the 16th century. Yet the Spanish empire had serious weaknesses. The size of the sprawling empire made it difficult to govern efficiently. In addition, the tight control the Spanish government exercised over all aspects of colonial life, from politics to economics, often created tension between Spain and her colonists. Finally, Spain simply did not have sufficient financial resources to accomplish all that it attempted.

These weaknesses meant that the enormous lead Spain enjoyed over its European rivals was less secure and permanent than it may have first appeared. As we shall see, England was ready to mount a challenge to Spanish power by the early 17th century. That challenge was destined to succeed.

Estebanico and the Lost Cities

Many people believe that a certain black kachina honored by the Pueblo peoples represents Estebanico, the first African they encountered.

The legend of seven lost treasure cities was a powerful magnet to Spanish explorers of the Southwest in the 16th century. Bound up with the legend is the true story of a remarkable man, Estebanico the Moor, the first African to explore North America.

In 1536 four gaunt survivors of a long-lost expedition reappeared in New Spain. Their reports of golden cities to the north—"the seven cities of Cibola"—ignited great excitement. Only one of the survivors, Estebanico, dared to return to the region, guiding the expedition of Friar Marcos de Nico in 1539. With his charismatic personality and his special knowledge of the land and languages, Estebanico came to dominate the expedition, and ranged far ahead of Marcos. When he arrived at the first of the "lost cities," Hawikuh (near present-day Gallup, New Mexico), he ignored the warnings of the Zuñi people and confidently told them he was the forerunner of a mighty force. The Zuñis promptly killed him. It was an ironic end for a man who had survived so much and lived so agreeably among the Indians.

Marcos fled back to Mexico, where he reported that he had seen one gleaming treasure city—Hawikuh—from a distance. Other expeditions followed. Coronado's party discovered the Grand Canyon and searched as far as present-day Kansas but found no treasure. The golden myth of the seven lost cities of Cibola finally dwindled to the adobe reality of seven Zuñi villages.

The legend of the lost cities died, but the memory of Estebanico lives on in the Southwest. Pueblo Indians still remember that "the first 'white man' our people ever saw was a black man." Some believe that Estebanico is recalled in ceremonial dances that include a dancer with a black-painted face, with a patch of black wool covering his head.

Highlights of American Life

English sailors challenged the might of Spain.

In 1497 King Henry VII sponsored the first English voyage of exploration to America. The captain of the expedition was not English, however, but Genoese. John Cabot burned with the desire to find the fabled Northwest Passage, a water route linking the Atlantic with the Pacific Ocean—and thus England with Asia. Cabot found no such passage. Nor did his son, Sebastian, who took up his father's quest in 1509. Still, their voyages established English claims to America.

Despite the Cabots' failures, England's fortunes improved in the 16th century. Under the leadership of Henry VIII and his remarkable daughter, Queen **Elizabeth I**, the island kingdom's wealth and influence increased steadily. The brilliant and forceful leadership of Elizabeth gave the English people a fierce sense of national pride. The creation of a well-equipped and well-commanded navy increased England's security and gave it a powerful potential weapon against rivals.

As English strength grew, the English desire to challenge Spanish political and economic power grew also. Spain's King Philip was devoutly Catholic, a champion and defender of the pope and the Church. England's Elizabeth was head of the nation's Protestant Church of England. Religious nationalism thus joined economic ambition as fuel for the competition between the two countries.

Elizabeth I was careful not to challenge directly the might of Spain too soon. Instead, the queen secretly gave money and support to a group of merchants and sailors willing, indeed eager, to steal Spanish treasure and sink Spanish ships at sea. Although these **sea dogs** were national heroes at home, to the Spanish they were pirates.

The most famous sea dog was a young naval captain, **Francis Drake**. Drake was dashing, handsome, and a favorite of Queen Elizabeth herself. In December 1577 Drake began his most spectacular adventure, sailing through the Strait of Magellan to the west coast of Central America. Because the Spanish sailors never suspected an attack in the Pacific Ocean, their

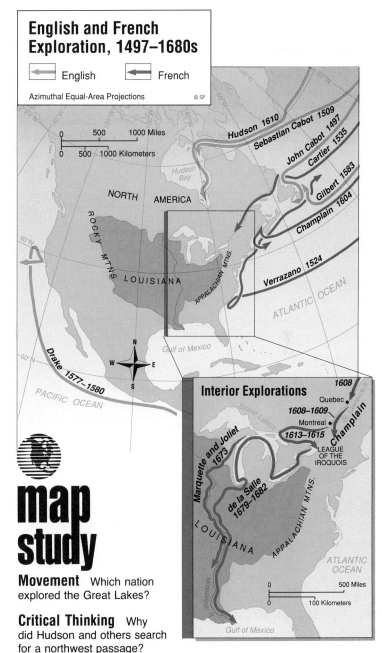

English and French Exploration, 1497–1680s

← English   ← French

Azimuthal Equal-Area Projections   © SF

map study

Movement Which nation explored the Great Lakes?

Critical Thinking Why did Hudson and others search for a northwest passage?

treasure ships were unarmed and unguarded. Drake's ship, the *Pelican*, was soon filled with gold, silver, and jewels taken from the defenseless Spaniards.

Drake's flight to safety took him on a three-year voyage around the world. When he returned to England, sailing the ship he had renamed the *Golden Hind*, all of England celebrated. Spain, of course, was less overjoyed.

The Spanish king demanded that Drake be executed for piracy.

Drake took the uproar in stride. He sailed boldly up the Thames River to London and cordially invited the queen to come aboard for a banquet. Elizabeth accepted. On the deck of the *Golden Hind*, the queen defied Spain. Laughingly, she said to Drake: "The king of Spain has demanded Drake's head of me, and here I have a gilded sword to strike it off." She ordered the sea dog to kneel before her. Touching him lightly on the shoulder, she declared "I bid thee rise, Sir Francis Drake."

Elizabeth's action was a virtual declaration of war. Spain responded by amassing a huge naval and military force to invade England. In 1588 the mighty fleet, the **Spanish Armada**, set sail with 30,000 troops on board 130 ships.

René-Robert Cavelier, Sieur de La Salle, claimed the entire Mississippi Valley for his native France. Here he brings the cross, a symbol of Christianity, among the Indians.

Once again Sir Francis Drake took charge. Under his command, the small, more maneuverable English fleet held its own against the large and slow-moving Armada ships. For ten days the two nations battled each other. When the Spanish ships withdrew to make repairs, Drake and a violent storm off the coast of Scotland destroyed them. Spain had met defeat.

France began exploring and colonizing North America.

In the early 1500s, France joined the European race to colonize North America. With discovery voyages by Giovanni da Verrazano [vä′rä tsä′nō] and Jacques Cartier [zhäk kär-tyä′], France claimed its role in North American history.

The first successful French settlements in North America were the work of a remarkable soldier-statesman, **Samuel de Champlain**. In 1608 he selected the Indian village of Stadacona, located on a mighty rock on the St. Lawrence River, as the site of **Quebec** (in present-day southeastern Canada). From his base at Quebec, Champlain explored southward into present-day New York State. He made friends with the area's Huron Indians and helped them defeat their enemies, the Mohawks. This alliance proved to be a costly mistake. The Mohawks belonged to a powerful confederation, the **League of the Iroquois**. From that day onward, until the English finally defeated the French in 1763, members of the Iroquois league always aided the enemies of France.

Champlain's work of nearly 30 years of explorations of the Great Lakes region and the North American coastlines was taken up by an equally dedicated and remarkable team of French explorers, the Jesuit missionary Father Jacques Marquette and the daring fur trader Louis Joliet. In 1673 the two set out by canoe from Lake Michigan and traveled the Mississippi River for hundreds of miles. A few years later, a third French exploration began with Robert de La Salle. He reached the mouth of the Mississippi River, claiming it for France and naming the river region "Louisiana" in honor of the French king, Louis XIV. France now claimed all the land extending from the mouth of the St. Lawrence River westward to the Rocky Mountains and south along the Mississippi to the Gulf of Mexico.

The French built a thriving fur trade in North America.

French success in the New World rested mainly on the fur trade, which grew rapidly and became well organized. The trade required a close working relationship with the Indians who supplied the furs, and with the fatal exception of the Iroquois, the French got along extremely well with the northern Indians. French missionaries and fur traders lived among the Indians, and many Frenchmen married Indian women and became members of their clans.

French fur traders in North America were known as *coureurs de bois* [kü rer′ də bwä′], or runners of the woods. Each fall they left Montreal and headed for the interior. Each spring they returned with fleets of Indian canoes piled high with pelts. For several weeks a rich carnival atmosphere prevailed along the banks of the St. Lawrence. The Indians traded their animal pelts for knives, axes, hatchets, hoes, kettles, woolen blankets, colored cotton cloth, guns, gunpowder, and brandy. When the trading was at last over, the Indians returned upstream in their canoes.

Despite the successful fur trade, New France suffered from several weaknesses. First, few colonists came to settle in the region. The young and ambitious Frenchmen who did journey to North America preferred the life of the *coureur de bois* to settler. The attempts of the French government to persuade farmers and artisans to settle in the area generally failed. In part, the French king's land policy was to

The French *coureurs de bois* adapted well to the North American environment, learning from the Indians and respecting their cultures.

Chapter Summary

Write supporting details under each of the following main ideas as you review the chapter.

Section 1
1. People first settled in the Americas between 12,000 and 30,000 years ago.
2. Different geographic conditions led to a diversity of Native American cultures.
3. Native Americans shared many beliefs and values.

Section 2
1. Geography influenced the development of African societies.
2. West Africans shared social and religious practices.
3. Europe experienced a revival in the 15th and 16th centuries.
4. European societies were male-dominated.

Section 3
1. Columbus brought Spain into the age of exploration.
2. Disease contributed to the European conquest of the Americas.
3. Food and animals were exchanged between the Old and New worlds.

Section 4
1. Spain established colonies in North and South America.
2. England challenged the might of Spain.
3. France began exploring and colonizing North America.
4. The French built a thriving fur trade in North America.

Section 5
1. The Virginia Company of London brought settlers to America.
2. John Smith helped the Jamestown settlement survive.
3. Tobacco saved the Virginia colony.
4. Self-government began to develop in the colony.

Chapter Themes

1. **Racial, ethnic, religious diversity:** Native Americans, Africans, and Europeans each brought different cultural values to America. Together, these three groups began to forge a common society, one in which each made significant and lasting contributions.

2. **Geography and environmental interaction:** Jamestown's settlers learned to farm corn and tobacco and to fish the waters around them to survive and, eventually, prosper. The French used northern rivers to explore and to trade with Indians who hunted and trapped in abundant northern forests. In addition, an exchange of cultures, foods, animals, and diseases resulted from the interaction of different peoples.

Chapter Study Guide

Identifying Key People and Terms

Name the key person or key term that describes the:
1. type of society in which family connections were made through the female line
2. people who believe in the existence of a multitude of gods
3. period of European revival that began in the 14th century
4. business organization owned by a number of investors, used to set up colonies

Locating Key Places

1. What body of water now covers the land over which America's first inhabitants crossed from Asia to North America?
2. On what island did Columbus probably make his first stop in the New World?

Mastering the Main Ideas

1. Describe the accomplishments of the following Native North American groups discussed in Section 1: Pueblo, Moundbuilders, and Woodland Indians.
2. How did the cultural, political, religious, and technological changes that occurred in Europe during the Renaissance lead to successful exploration?
3. Compare the exploration and settlement of the New World by Spain, England, and France.
4. Were the original goals of the Jamestown colony achieved? Explain.

Applying Critical Thinking Skills

1. **Identifying assumptions:** What beliefs led European explorers to take an active role in the spread of Christianity?

1480	1500	1520	1540	1560	1580	1600	1620	1640

1492
Columbus arrives in America

c. 1500
League of the Iroquois founded

1607
Jamestown founded by English

1619
First Africans brought to Virginia

1497
Cabot explores North America for England

1521
Cortés conquers Aztecs

1532
Pizarro defeats Incas

1565
Saint Augustine founded by Spanish

2. Distinguishing fact from opinion: Explain why the following statement is an opinion. Then rewrite it as a factual statement. "The use of horses and European weapons was the most important factor in Spain's conquest of the New World."

3. Making comparisons: Compare the different reasons why Spain, France, and England each succeeded in settling the New World.

4. Identifying central issues: How was the establishment of the House of Burgesses an early demonstration of American freedom?

Chapter Activities

Learning Geography Through History

1. What modern nations lie along the western coast of Africa, where Portuguese explorers passed on their way to southern Africa?

2. On a map, measure the approximate distance between Spain and San Salvador in the Bahamas. Calculate the average number of miles that Columbus and his men traveled in a month.

Relating the United States to the World

1. Explain how the differences between African culture and European culture in the 16th century would eventually lead to conflict.

2. In 1685 French absolute monarch Louis XIV revoked the Edict of Nantes that had given French Huguenots (Protestants) religious freedom. How did his act affect the French community in North America?

Using the Time Line

1. How many years elapsed between Columbus' arrival in the Americas and the defeat of the Aztecs?

2. How much time was there between John Cabot's first trip to the New World and the founding of Jamestown?

Linking Past to Present

1. What ethnic group probably shaped the early history of the following places: Joliet, IL; Marquette, MI; El Paso, TX; Jamestown, VA; and Raleigh, NC?

2. Compare the reasons that explorers and colonists came to the New World with the reasons immigrants come to America today.

Practicing Critical Thinking Strategies

Making Comparisons
Compare the role of women in Native American and European cultures. Consider such issues as family organization and the division of labor and power.

Learning More About The Meeting of Three Cultures

1. Using Source Readings: Read the Source Readings for this chapter and answer the questions.

2. Making a poster: Using books from your library, research and make a poster illustrating the accomplishments of one of the civilizations discussed in this chapter—such as the Maya or the Songhai.

3. Researching about explorers: Choose one of the explorers mentioned in this chapter. Research the explorer's life and write a biographical sketch.

Linking Past to Present

A little over a century after their humble beginnings, colonial cities such as New York City, viewed in inset from the Brooklyn shore in 1757, bustled with economic activity. The larger aerial view of New York today shows the effects of almost 370 years of continuous development.

The Enlightenment and the Revolutionary Era

1 6 0 0 – 1 7 8 8

William Pond's hand shook as he opened the letter dated March 15, 1630, for it contained news of his two sons in the distant colony of Massachusetts Bay. The letter offered the Englishman a bleak vision of his sons' life in America. The landscape was hilly and rocky and contained much marshy ground. Timber, acorns, fish, and wild fowl existed in abundance, but a lack of proper tools and poor health prevented the settlers from taking advantage of these natural riches. Disease had struck the colonists even before they reached Massachusetts Bay. "We were wonderfully sick as we came at sea, with the small pox," explained Pond's son, and "no man thought that I and my little child would have lived. My boy is lame [ill] and my girl too. . . ." The younger Pond envisioned a life of hardship in which he and his family would depend indefinitely upon England for supplies and aid.

Life for many in the English colonies proved to be less bleak than William Pond's sons predicted. By the early 1700s, the American colonies boasted prosperous farms, busy cities, and a thriving transatlantic trade. Yet, in the earliest years of most colonies, hardships were commonplace. What, then, prompted thousands of European men and women to risk a long, dangerous ocean voyage and the difficulties of starting a life in an unknown land? What did they hope to find in America?

CHAPTER PREVIEW

In this chapter you will learn how 13 British colonies in America were settled and how they grew and developed until they ultimately challenged Great Britain and won their independence.

SECTIONS IN THIS CHAPTER:
1. **Europeans founded the 13 American colonies.**
2. **Enlightenment ideas came to the colonies.**
3. **The colonies moved toward war.**
4. **The Americans won the War for Independence.**
5. **The nation devised a new government.**

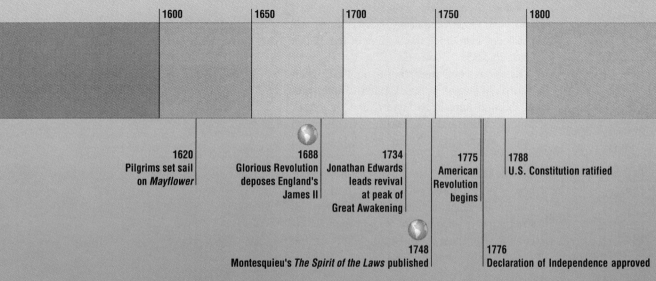

1600	1650	1700	1750	1800

1620
Pilgrims set sail
on *Mayflower*

1688
Glorious Revolution
deposes England's
James II

1734
Jonathan Edwards
leads revival
at peak of
Great Awakening

1775
American
Revolution
begins

1788
U.S. Constitution ratified

1748
Montesquieu's *The Spirit of the Laws* published

1776
Declaration of Independence approved

Europeans founded the 13 American colonies.

Key Terms: Puritans, Separatists, Pilgrims, Mayflower Compact, Quakers, middle passage

Reading Preview
As you read this section, you will learn:
1. what factors encouraged colonization in America.
2. what prompted New England's founding.
3. which colonies welcomed diversity.
4. what flourished in the Southern Colonies.

In a period of a century and a quarter—from the founding of Jamestown in 1607 to 1732— the English founded 13 colonies along the east coast of mainland North America. England's belated spurt of colonization resulted, in large part, from problems within England itself.

Problems in England encouraged colonization in America.

As English colonization in America was beginning, England was experiencing political and religious controversy and economic turmoil. The monarchs who followed Elizabeth I to the throne believed they should have absolute power over the country and its people. This belief set them at odds with Parliament, which had been slowly acquiring its own rights and privileges ever since the signing of the Magna Carta in 1215.

Religious controversy began in 1534, when Henry VIII left the Roman Catholic Church and established himself as head of the Protestant Church of England. Elizabeth's reign brought a degree of accommodation and tolerance to England. However, it also brought a growing radical Protestant movement called Puritanism. The **Puritans** wanted to "purify" the Church of England, or Anglican Church, by stripping it of all traces of Roman Catholic influence. The most radical of the Puritans, the

Separatists, believed that their only choice was to separate themselves totally from the Anglican Church.

During the time of Elizabeth's successors— James I (1603–1625) and Charles I (1625– 1649)— conflict between absolutist monarchs and a Puritan-controlled Parliament produced almost continuous political conflict. That conflict eventually led to civil war between the supporters of the monarchy and those who supported Parliament.

Added to this conflict were significant changes in the economy. The growing importance of England's wool textile industry resulted in the forcing of more than two million people off the land, with pastures converted for sheep. This event is called the enclosure movement. Many displaced farmers flocked to cities that could not employ them. A large group of restless, unemployable people with little hope and a widespread belief that England was overpopulated further encouraged overseas colonization.

Religion prompted New England's founding.

A group of English Separatists that had fled to Holland in search of religious freedom requested and received permission from the Virginia Company to colonize the northern part of its territory in North America. In the summer of 1620, about 30 of these **Pilgrims** set out, stopping first in England to pick up supplies and another group of colonists. In September

After their landing on Plymouth Rock, the Pilgrims developed small farm communities like they had left in England.

the Mayflower sailed with 101 passengers to start a new colony in America.

Rough seas prevented the captain of the Mayflower from sailing southward around Cape Cod. Since winter was approaching, the colonists decided to put ashore at what became their settlement at **Plymouth**. First, however, 41 adult male colonists signed the **Mayflower Compact**, an agreement that bound them together in a government modeled after the church covenants that Puritans made within their own church congregations.

The Pilgrims faced many hardships that winter, and half of them did not survive their first year in America. With the help of some local Indians, the Pilgrims at Plymouth learned to plant corn and other crops. Others arrived from England, and the settlement slowly grew.

In 1630 a more prosperous group of Puritans, facing increased religious persecution, set sail for New England. They were both well-financed and amply supplied. The group, led by **John Winthrop**, established the **Massachusetts Bay Colony** near Boston Bay, along the Charles River.

The Puritans came to Massachusetts with a mission: to build a model Puritan community for all of England to see. Winthrop told his fellow Puritans that "we shall be as a city upon a hill, the eyes of all people are upon us." Although they had come to America for their own religious freedom, the Puritans were not interested in allowing such freedom to others. Intensely religious and totally committed to their Calvinist theology, they had no tolerance for dissent or religious controversy. Nevertheless, dissent arose.

In 1631 **Roger Williams** came to the pulpit in the Massachusetts Bay town of Salem. He began to criticize the colony's policies and leadership and took issue with many of its religious beliefs. The colony's leadership determined to banish the troublemaker. Warned that he was to be sent back to England, Williams chose to flee Massachusetts in the dead of winter in 1635.

Williams took refuge with the Narragansett Indians, and the following spring he settled near Narragansett Bay, naming his new home

OICES FROM THE PAST

The Mayflower Compact

The Mayflower Compact is a confident early expression of the authority of people to govern themselves. In addition to life-sustaining kernels, the Plymouth colonists were planting irresistible seeds of democracy in the American soil. What reasons do the colonists give for creating the Mayflower Compact?

In the name of God, Amen. We, whose names are underwritten . . . having undertaken for the glory of God and advancement of the Christian faith, and honor of our king and country, a voyage to plant the first colony in the northern parts of Virginia, do . . . solemnly and mutually in the presence of God, and of one another, covenant and combine ourselves together into a civil body politic; for our better ordering and preservation . . . to enact . . . such just and equal laws, ordinances, acts, constitutions, and offices, from time to time, as shall be thought most meet and convenient for the general good of the colony, unto which we promise all due submission and obedience.

Early Puritans, shown at right, learned from the Pilgrims the value of a charter such as the Mayflower Compact, being signed above.

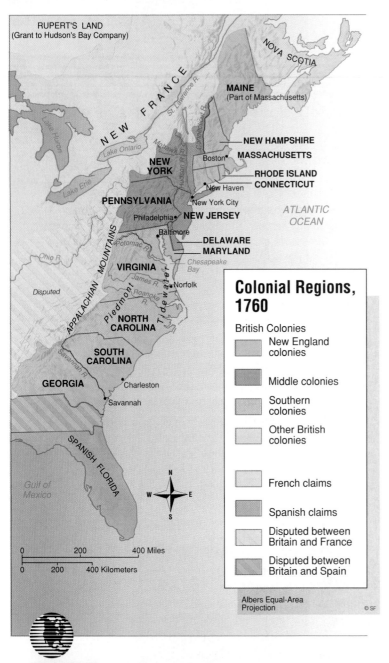

RUPERT'S LAND
(Grant to Hudson's Bay Company)

NOVA SCOTIA

NEW FRANCE

St. Lawrence R.

MAINE
(Part of Massachusetts)

Lake Huron

Lake Ontario

Mohawk R.

Connecticut R.

NEW HAMPSHIRE

MASSACHUSETTS

Boston

NEW YORK

Lake Erie

RHODE ISLAND

CONNECTICUT

New Haven

PENNSYLVANIA

New York City

Philadelphia

NEW JERSEY

ATLANTIC OCEAN

Baltimore

Potomac R.

DELAWARE

MARYLAND

Ohio R.

Chesapeake Bay

APPALACHIAN MOUNTAINS

VIRGINIA

James R.

Piedmont

Roanoke R.

Norfolk

Tidewater

Disputed

NORTH CAROLINA

SOUTH CAROLINA

Savannah R.

GEORGIA

Charleston

Savannah

SPANISH FLORIDA

Gulf of Mexico

N
W E
S

0   200   400 Miles
0   200   400 Kilometers

Colonial Regions, 1760

British Colonies

New England colonies

Middle colonies

Southern colonies

Other British colonies

French claims

Spanish claims

Disputed between Britain and France

Disputed between Britain and Spain

Albers Equal-Area Projection

© SF

map study

Regions In the 1700s France, Spain, and Great Britain competed for control of North America. By 1760 Britain had established colonies that stretched from present-day Canada to Florida. How many British colonies were there between Maine and Florida in 1760?

Critical Thinking Note the disputed areas shown on the map. What geographical advantage did Great Britain hold over Spain and France?

Providence. Faithful members of his Salem congregation and other men and women seeking religious freedom joined him in building a new colony that in 1644 became chartered by Parliament as Rhode Island.

A second major challenge to Puritan leadership arose in 1636. It came from an unlikely source, the wife of a merchant and the mother of a dozen children. **Anne Hutchinson** was no ordinary housewife, however, as she was well-educated, articulate, and a brilliant interpreter of the Scriptures. Had she been a man,,friends and enemies alike agreed, she would have been a minister. Instead, she became a fierce critic of the ministry itself.

Hutchinson insisted that no minister's sermon could assist a person in the search for salvation, and no church, not even a Puritan one, could help save a person's soul. Her suggestion that churches and ministers might be unnecessary was more than Puritan leaders could bear. The fact that she attracted a surprisingly large following troubled the church leaders even more, and they brought Hutchinson to trial in the winter of 1636.

The trial stretched on for weeks, despite the confusion over just how Hutchinson was guilty. Although Hutchinson was pregnant at the time, the court refused to allow her to sit down. Despite her obvious discomfort, she matched wits and words with her accusers until weariness and pride got the best of her. In a dramatic moment, she claimed that her views were based upon direct revelation from God. For the Puritans, such a claim was a clear act of heresy. Hutchinson, like Williams, was banished.

Others left the Massachusetts Bay Colony because they wanted land and an opportunity to improve their lives. A Puritan congregation led by Thomas Hooker left in 1636 for the Connecticut River Valley, where they founded the town of Hartford. Other land-hungry Puritans founded towns nearby. In 1662 Hartford and 14 other towns were chartered by Charles II of England as the Connecticut Colony. Some Puritans moved northward and settled in what later became New Hampshire and Maine. New Hampshire broke free of Massachusetts and won a charter in 1679.

The Quakers believed that the "Inner Light" of Christ was present in everyone. The belief was reflected in the Quaker meeting, shown at left, in which individuals rose to speak as the spirit moved them, without the formal guidance of a minister. The silver collar at right served as a token of peace from the Quaker William Penn to a group of Indians.

The Middle Colonies welcomed diversity.

As Puritans began settling New England in the 1620s, Dutch traders and farmers were starting to colonize **New Netherland**. The English were eager to drive the Dutch from North America. Not only did their colony block New England's expansion, but it also controlled the valuable fur trade with the Iroquois Indians. In 1664 Charles II offered New Netherland to his brother James, Duke of York, if he could take it away from the Dutch. James sent an English fleet to demand the surrender of the colony, took it over, and renamed it New York in honor of James.

When James took over New Netherland, he granted two friends of his, Lord Berkeley and Sir George Carteret, a large tract of land lying east and north of the Delaware River. The two nobles called their colony New Jersey. In 1681 **William Penn** received from Charles II a huge tract of land west of the Delaware River. There, Penn founded the colony of Pennsylvania as a haven for his fellow **Quakers**. The Quakers believed that each person could experience a direct revelation from God. Thus there was no need for priests, ministers, or preachers. Every Quaker—men and women alike—could speak with authority at their services. The Quakers, who disregarded social status and religious authority, were considered even more radical and dangerous than the Puritans, and they were harshly persecuted in England. Penn thus supported religious toleration in America.

A year later Penn purchased some additional land from the Duke of York. These "Three Lower Colonies" of Pennsylvania eventually became the independent colony of Delaware. This wise move assured that Pennsylvania would have access to the Atlantic and that Philadelphia would become a bustling port city.

The Middle Colonies had populations far more varied than those of New England or Virginia. Thousands of English Quakers flocked to Pennsylvania, but so did thousands of non-Quakers who were attracted by the freedom and opportunity Pennsylvania offered. By 1685 some 8,000 settlers had arrived from England, Scotland, Ireland, France, Holland, Germany, Sweden, and Denmark. New York's population was equally diverse. In addition to the original Dutch inhabitants, there were sizable numbers of English, Germans, and Scandinavians in the colony. The Dutch West India Company had imported slaves from Africa as well.

African slaves who reached the Southern Colonies used their agricultural skills to make rice the leading crop of such coastal areas as South Carolina. (Glenbow Museum, Calgary, Alberta, Canada)

Plantation agriculture flourished in the Southern Colonies.

In 1632 Sir George Calvert, Lord Baltimore, was given land in America by Charles I to create a haven for Catholics. Although he died before he could realize his dream, Calvert's eldest son, **Cecilius Calvert**, actively promoted the colonization of what became Maryland. Located just north of the Potomac River from Virginia, Maryland was well suited to the same kind of tobacco-growing plantations as the earlier colony. As settlement continued in Maryland, Lord Baltimore realized that Catholics would soon be outnumbered by Protestants. Consequently, he set up a government that separated church and state and for a time offered religious freedom to all Christians.

Another southern colony was planted in America after Charles II, between 1663 and 1665, gave eight of his friends a land grant south of Virginia. The proprietors named their colony Carolina. A small number of Virginians had already settled the northern tip of Carolina near Albemarle Sound. These families farmed tobacco and corn and drew tar from the local pine trees to produce naval stores—turpentine, pitch, and resin.

A second Carolina settlement evolved far to the south, separated from the Albemarle set-

tlement by vast swamplands. This settlement at Charles Towne (later called Charleston) had a fine harbor and fertile land that attracted planters from the West Indies, as well as some Scottish, French, and German settlers. They established large rice plantations worked by African slaves. Thus, two very different societies arose in Carolina, characterized by mostly small tobacco plantations and farms in the north and large rice plantations in the south. In 1729 the two regions separated into royal colonies of North Carolina and South Carolina.

The large southern plantations relied heavily on slave labor. The Atlantic crossing for these slaves was a **middle passage** between all that was familiar and all that was foreign. For Olaudah Equiano, also known as Gustavus Vassa, the experience evoked pure terror. Equiano, kidnapped from the kingdom of Benin (in West Africa) in the mid-1700s, wondered whether he had entered "a world of bad spirits" and was to be killed. Upon boarding the slave ship that would carry him to the West Indies, his doubts dissolved into fear:

> When I look round the ship too, and saw a large furnace of copper boiling, and a multitude of black people of every description chained together, every one of their countenances expressing dejection and sorrow, I no longer doubted of my fate; and, quite overpowered with horror and anguish, I fell motionless on the deck and fainted. . . . I was soon put down under the decks, and there I received such a salutation in my nostrils as I had never experienced in my life: so that, with the loathsomeness of the stench, and crying together, I became so sick and low that I was not able to eat, nor had I the least desire to taste anything. I now wished for the last friend, death, to relieve me.

AN AMERICAN ★ SPEAKS

As the ship set sail, the horrors multiplied. Confined so tightly within the dark holds of the ship that they could neither sit nor stand, the slaves suffered horribly inhumane conditions.

In 1732 King George II granted a group of men led by **James Oglethorpe** a charter for a new colony between South Carolina and Spanish Florida. The new colony, Georgia, was to serve as a buffer between the Spanish and South Carolina and as a place where English debtors could start a new life. Restrictions on the Georgia colonists, such as a limit of 500 acres of land for any one owner and a ban on slavery, slowed the growth of the colony. However, these restrictions were removed after Georgia became a royal colony in 1752.

SECTION 1 REVIEW

Identify Key People and Terms
Write a sentence to identify: Puritans, Separatists, Pilgrims, Mayflower Compact, John Winthrop, Roger Williams, Anne Hutchinson, William Penn, Quakers, Cecilius Calvert, middle passage, James Oglethorpe

Locate Key Places

1. Where did the Mayflower Pilgrims establish the first New England settlement?
2. What colony was founded by a large group of Puritans from England?
3. What town did Roger Williams found after leaving Massachusetts?
4. What colony did the English take over and rename New York?

Master the Main Ideas

1. **Understanding economic motivations:** How did economic changes in England encourage colonization in America?
2. **Understanding religious motivations:** Why did Pilgrims and Puritans move to America?
3. **Understanding colonial settlement:** How did the people of the Middle Colonies differ from those of New England?
4. **Understanding colonial settlement:** In what ways did the Southern Colonies differ from the New England colonies?

Apply Critical Thinking Skills: Identifying Central Issues
Consider the reasons that led people to leave 17th-century England for the American colonies. What reasons might people today have for immigrating to the United States? Support your response with specific examples.

SECTION 2

Enlightenment ideas came to the colonies.

Key Terms: indentured servant, Enlightenment, social contract, Great Awakening

Reading Preview
As you read this section, you will learn:

1. what kind of leadership emerged in the colonies.
2. what philosophical ideas influenced the colonial leaders.
3. what movement inspired feelings of equality.

As the American colonies grew and prospered, a talented group of leaders emerged to guide their development. These leaders were influenced by English and other European ideas, but they never forgot that they were Americans. Although they borrowed political and intellectual concepts from abroad, they freely adapted them to the American situation.

An educated leadership emerged in the colonies.

Nowhere in the colonies was education considered more important than in New England. The Puritans wanted to build a model society based on religious principles. Education was important to them because the Bible was to be the basis for their society, and every church member had to be able to read and study it.

In 1636, only 6 years after the founding of Massachusetts Bay, the colony's leaders established Harvard College in **Cambridge**, Massachusetts (just across the Charles River from Boston). Harvard, the oldest university in the country, was meant to educate a ministry for the Puritan congregations of New England.

By the time Harvard opened its doors, many New England towns had already established elementary and grammar schools. Elementary schools taught the basics of reading and writing, and grammar schools prepared students for college. In 1647 Massachusetts passed a law requiring every town with 50 or more households to provide a teacher of reading and writing and every town of 100 households to set up a grammar school. The other New England Colonies lagged only slightly behind Massachusetts in setting up public (government-supported) or private schools.

Since settlement in New England always centered around a town, it was far easier to establish schools there than in the Southern Colonies. The southern population was spread over large plantations and smaller, scattered frontier farms. Although many attempts were made to establish schools in the South, most of them failed because of the difficulty in bringing together enough students to justify the expense of a schoolmaster.

Nevertheless, some southern children did obtain an education. Wealthy planters often hired an educated indentured servant to teach their sons. An **indentured servant** was a person who pledged several years of service in return for passage to America. Less often, planters sent their sons to England to be educated, particularly to Oxford or Cambridge or to one of the London Inns of Court, which trained lawyers. William Byrd of Westover, one of Virginia's wealthiest planters in the early 1700s, sent both his son William (age 9) and his daughter Susan (age 6) to school in England.

The Middle Colonies, too, were lacking in public schools. The Dutch had set up schools in New Netherland, but New York failed twice to pass legislation to establish free schools. Many of the schools that did exist in New York were in towns settled by New Englanders. Pennsylvania's Quakers and some of the German communities in that colony were much more concerned with education.

Formal education for girls and young women was far more rare, but it did exist, especially for those from wealthier families. Many girls learned reading, writing, spinning, needlework, and perhaps a little music and dancing at dame schools, schools in which a woman taught students in her own home. Occasionally a young woman's desire to learn was indulged. Mercy Otis, of Massachusetts, read along with her brother as he studied. Even when James Otis went to college, he sent his reading assignments and class notes home to his sister. **Mercy Otis Warren** later became a noted poet and playwright, as well as the author of an early history of the American Revolution—the three-volume *History of the Rise, Progress, and Termination of the American Revolution* (1805).

The majority of the colonial population did not have access to the kind of education available to the wealthiest colonists. Nevertheless, in spite of the fact that throughout the colonial period the first necessity for most colonists was to scratch out a living in a mostly untamed

Hornbooks such as the one above, helped young children learn their alphabet. They are named for the transparent sheet of horn that protected the wooden paddles from dirty fingers. Colonial education often took place in one-room schools, which were often dark and cramped. Those who sat near the fire roasted, while those in the far corners suffered "blue noses, chattering jaws, and aching toes."

Mercy Otis Warren

land, America produced a large number of literate, politically aware citizens. More than that, by the 18th century the colonies had a body of highly intelligent and cultured leaders who could hold their own with the best minds of Europe.

Enlightenment ideas influenced colonial leaders.

Europe, by the 18th century, was teeming with new and revolutionary ideas that would strongly influence the American colonies' relationship with the British government. The period from about the mid-1600s through the 1700s is often called the Age of Reason. During that time, in a movement now called the **Enlightenment**, thinkers developed new ideas about nearly every aspect of human life, including government.

The person who perhaps most influenced ideas about government was the English thinker **John Locke** (1632–1704). In writing about government, Locke said that people possessed certain natural rights, chiefly the rights to life, liberty, and property. When the people established a government, they gave it the power to protect those rights. Locke called this agreement between the people and their government a **social contract**. He maintained that if a government failed to live up to its part of the social contract—if it failed to protect the people's natural rights—the people had the right to depose that government and set up a new one. This, obviously, was a revolutionary idea at a time when many European monarchs continued to believe in absolutism.

The French noble and judge, the Baron de **Montesquieu** (1689–1755) was another critic of absolute monarchy and defender of liberty against tyranny. Montesquieu concluded that individual freedom must be protected from royal absolutism. A rational society, he insisted, must include many layers of social structures and governing bodies. Moreover, he maintained that liberty required a separation and balance of powers in government. As an example of this principle, he pointed to the government of England, where the monarch and

Parliament balanced each other and were both controlled by an independent judiciary. Montesquieu's concept of separation of powers would later guide the men who created the United States Constitution.

Another Enlightenment thinker, the Swissborn Frenchman **Jean Jacques Rousseau** (1712–1778), went beyond Locke's idea of an agreement between ruler and people. In his book *Social Contract,* Rousseau stated that a community was based on an understanding among all its members. In such a community, all members felt that they were among people who shared common values and attitudes.

The Enlightenment extended beyond a group of individual philosophers and theorists. It included journalists, social critics, reformers, and popularizers who spread the ideas of the Enlightenment among the masses. Ideas were spread through letters, newspapers, pamphlets, journals, meetings, and public discussions of various kinds. Societies were formed to propagate knowledge and ideas. The Royal Society of London had among its members several Americans, including **Benjamin Franklin**, who sent a report on his experiments with electricity to be read at a society meeting.

The ideas of the Enlightenment were eagerly studied and discussed in the American colonies. They would come to play a great part not only in the American decision to declare independence from the British government, but also in the establishment of a government for the newly formed United States of America.

The Great Awakening inspired feelings of equality.

At the same time as educated Americans were discussing the ideas of the Enlightenment, a movement that was, in many ways, the opposite of the Enlightenment was sweeping through the colonies. The **Great Awakening**, unlike the Enlightenment, appealed to faith through purely emotional means. It was a revival of intense religious expression and flourished throughout the colonies from the 1720s through the 1740s.

The movement reached its peak with the work of **Jonathan Edwards**, a young Congregationalist pastor in Massachusetts, and **George Whitefield**, a traveling Methodist preacher from England. Edwards believed in predestination and delivered terrifying sermons on the fate of those who were not saved:

AN AMERICAN
★ SPEAKS

So that thus it is, that natural men are held in the hand of God over the pit of Hell; they have deserved the fiery pit, and are already sentenced to it; . . . the Devil is waiting for them, Hell is gaping for them, the flames gather and flash about them, and would fain lay hold on them and swallow them up.

With his preaching, Edwards revitalized Protestantism and brought forth intense religious experiences among his followers. Whitefield, though his sermons were different in content,

also left crowds of trembling sinners in his wake. Listeners to his preaching openly wept and proclaimed their sins.

Benjamin Franklin was so enthralled by Whitefield's preaching that he grew more and more generous as the collector's dish came toward him. "He finished so admirably that I emptied my pocket wholly into the collector's dish, gold and all."

Benjamin Franklin's Enlightened Spirit

If Americans who protested British rule seemed uncommonly well organized and well read, the "fault" was partly Benjamin Franklin's. Franklin started the first public library in America in 1731. He and a group of friends regularly met to discuss issues in science and philosophy. Since books were expensive and most were imported from England, the group decided to pool their collection and lend their books out to each other. In time they bought books as a group and opened the library to anyone who would pay a small monthly fee for the expansion of the collection. Soon other communities began public lending libraries. Franklin observed,

These libraries have improved the general conversation of the Americans [and] made the common tradesman and farmer as intelligent as most gentlemen from other countries.

Franklin's most important contribution to America, however, was his enlightened spirit. Inspired by European philosophers, Franklin always sought to improve his mind and to learn from everything around him. He wrote, "he who removes a Prejudice or Error from our Minds, contributes to their Beauty." This striving for truth led Franklin and others to embrace ideas that ultimately led to revolution.

Franklin, at right, invented bifocals, top left, and wrote *Poor Richard's Almanack*, below left.

Highlights of American Life

By the mid-1740s the revivalist movement began to fade, but its impact continued with increased church membership. The Great Awakening had other consequences as well. The intensity of religious interest inspired a sense of democracy and equality in its followers. The message that all people had the opportunity to win salvation implied that all people were equal before God. To many people this sense of equality applied not only to religion but to society as well. As revivalist ministers encouraged rebellion against conventional religious authority, they also fostered in the colonists a willingness to criticize established political authority—including the authority of monarch and Parliament.

SECTION 2 REVIEW

Identify Key People and Terms
Write a sentence to identify: indentured servant, Mercy Otis Warren, Enlightenment, John Locke, social contract, Montesquieu, Jean Jacques Rousseau, Benjamin Franklin, Great Awakening, Jonathan Edwards, George Whitefield

Locate Key Places
Where was the first college in the American colonies, Harvard, established?

Master the Main Ideas

1. **Analyzing information:** Which colonists were most likely to receive a good education in the colonies? How did they acquire it?
2. **Understanding political ideas:** How did the Enlightenment affect the colonists' ideas about government?
3. **Understanding religious movements:** How did the Great Awakening affect colonial society?

Apply Critical Thinking Skills: Recognizing Values
Consider the relationship between religion and government. With so many different religious beliefs and values—both in the colonies and in the United States today—how does this relationship work? In what ways might the acceptance of different religions be beneficial to a government? difficult? Support your answer.

SECTION 3

The colonies moved toward war.

Key Terms: French and Indian War, Stamp Act, Declaratory Act, Boston Massacre, Boston Tea Party, Coercive Acts, Continental Congress, *Common Sense*, Declaration of Independence

Reading Preview
As you read this section, you will learn:

1. why Great Britain fought France.
2. what resulted from the British victory.
3. what British policies the colonists protested.
4. what the American colonists moved toward.

During the first half of the 1700s, few American colonists gave any thought to breaking away from British rule. Great Britain and France had fought three major wars between 1689 and 1748, and each of them had involved the colonists. As the 1750s began, the fear of the French and their Indian allies was still strong in the British colonies, especially along the frontier.

Great Britain fought France in a war for empire.

Great Britain and France, long-standing rivals, were both attempting to build world empires. Each nation had extensive possessions in North America. Trouble arose in a region both countries claimed—the **Ohio Valley**, valuable for both its fertile land and the rich fur trade with the Indians.

A group of Virginia planters and land speculators formed the Ohio Company in 1747, intending to profit in the fur trade and to sell farmland in the Ohio Valley to new settlers willing to move west of the Appalachian Mountains. The French began building a line of forts to protect the region from British expansion.

In early 1754 the Ohio Company and the governor of Virginia sent a party of men to build a fort where the Allegheny and Monongahela rivers meet to form the Ohio River (where present-day Pittsburgh is). **George Washington**, a young Virginia militia officer, had identified the importance of this location in a expedition into the area the previous year:

I spent some time in reviewing the Rivers and the Land in the Fork; which I think extremely well suited for a Fort, as it has the absolute Command of both Rivers.

AN AMERICAN
★ SPEAKS

The French had the same idea. They forced the Virginians to leave their site and began to build their own fort: Fort Duquesne [dü kān′].

Unaware of the French action, the Virginia governor sent two companies of militia commanded by George Washington to protect Virginia's fort builders. Before reaching the Ohio forks, Washington learned of the French takeover and of a small party of French troops ahead of him. He led an attack on the party in which the French commander and nine troops were killed. He then fell back and quickly built a crude fort. On July 3, 1754, French and Indian forces attacked, forcing Washington to surrender and lead his militia back to Virginia.

Although no one realized it at the time, this military action was the first in what would become a long, worldwide war between France and Great Britain. The American phase of the war, which began two years before England formally declared war on France, is called the **French and Indian War** because of the important role played by France's Indian allies.

In 1755 the British made another attempt at capturing the strategic fork of the Ohio. A large force of British regulars led by General Edward Braddock and a group of Virginia militia struck out toward Fort Duquesne, but they were ambushed by French and Indian forces and humiliatingly defeated. The war continued to go badly for the British until a new prime minister, **William Pitt**, reorganized the army in 1758 and planned a strategy for defeating France in North America.

Committed to victory at any cost, Pitt's government levied heavy taxes on the British people to pay for ships, weapons, troops, and military supplies. The government also borrowed heavily to meet its war expenses. Pitt's strategy turned the war around. A series of British victories followed, capped in 1759 by the successful defeat of the French at Quebec,

In 1745 William Pepperrell led 90 ships and 4,000 soldiers in an attack to claim the French fortress at Louisbourg, on Cape Breton Island. Forty days later the siege ended, and the New England army won control.

the capital of French Canada, and the French surrender of Montreal in the following year. Although the war dragged on elsewhere, it was essentially over in North America.

In the peace treaty signed in Paris in 1763 France surrendered all of its North American claims east of the Mississippi River except for two small islands off Newfoundland. The British allowed France to give Louisiana to Spain, which gave up Florida to the British in return.

The British victory led to problems with the American colonists.

The terms of the peace treaty nearly doubled the size of British North America, but it also led to new problems. With the French eliminated, many American colonists wanted to strike out for the new lands in the West. The Indians of the region, however, resisted this threat of white settlement. Led by the Ottawa chief, **Pontiac**, they attacked British forts and trading posts throughout the region north of the Ohio River, killing more than 200 traders and settlers. After British troops finally crushed the Indian uprising, the British government tried to prevent further troubles with the Indians by forbidding settlement west of the Appalachian Mountains. Land-hungry colonists fumed, and many ignored the ban.

The costs of the war had left Britain with an enormous debt and had forced the government to increase taxes in England until people in some areas rioted. British leaders felt that the Americans ought to share at least part of the burden of defending the colonies with British troops.

In 1764 Parliament passed what colonists called the Sugar Act, which placed a duty on sugar and molasses imported into the colonies from the West Indies. A year later Parliament passed the **Stamp Act**, a measure that required the colonists to put stamps on newspapers, playing cards, legal documents, and many other items. The stamps were to be sold to merchants, who would paste them onto products and pass on the added cost to their customers.

Both measures, but especially the Stamp Act, brought vigorous protests in the colonies. American newspapers wrote angry editorials denouncing the Stamp Act, crowds demonstrated in the streets, and a Stamp Act Congress was formed to plan joint action. In Boston stamp agents were attacked and their property destroyed by angry colonists. In addition, American merchants refused to import British goods and many American families pledged not to use them. These agreements struck at British merchants, who pressured Parliament to drop the hated taxes.

Some Americans opposed the very idea that Great Britain had the power to impose taxes on them. The colonists could be taxed, they said, but only by their own colonial assemblies, which were made up of representatives they had elected. "No taxation without representation," became the cry of the colonists.

Pontiac, an Ottawa leader, formed an alliance with members of such other Indian nations as the Delaware, Miami, Shawnee, Potawatomi, and Chippewa.

When the British required revenue stamps, lower right, for everyday items such as newspapers and playing cards, the colonists protested with such symbols as the skull and crossbones shown at left.

The colonists eventually won their war against the Stamp Act. However, the British government did not accept the colonists' view of taxation. While repealing the Stamp Act in 1766, Parliament also passed the **Declaratory Act**, which asserted that Parliament had the right and the authority to make laws for "the colonies and people of America . . . in all cases whatsoever." It also said that any acts of the colonial assemblies that questioned the authority of Parliament were null and void. This struck directly at the colonists' concept of self-government.

Colonists protested British taxation policies.

In 1767 **Charles Townshend** assumed financial leadership in Parliament and tried again to place taxes on the Americans. The colonial response was increased protest. Customs agents were attacked in several port cities. Merchants again agreed to boycott British goods, and shopkeepers who were found selling them had their shops attacked and their lives threatened.

The protests were particularly violent in Boston, where the radical leader **Samuel Adams** did his best to encourage public anger against the Townshend taxes. British troops were sent to Boston in 1768 to try to contain the protests, but they had the opposite effect. As soldiers drilled in the town square, crowds taunted them and occasionally pelted them with stones.

The tension continued until, on March 5, 1770, a rowdy Boston crowd shouted insults and hurled rocks and snowballs at a troop of British soldiers. The soldiers fired into the crowd, killing five Bostonians in what the colonists soon called the **Boston Massacre**. On that same day, ironically, the Revenue Act was repealed. However, Parliament retained the Townshend tax on tea to show that it had the right to tax its colonies.

The next crisis occurred after a group of Bostonians, on December 16, 1773, disguised themselves as Mohawk Indians and threw 342 chests of tea into Boston Harbor to protest a new tax on tea. Parliament reacted to this **Boston Tea Party** by passing the **Coercive Acts** that the Americans renamed the Intolerable Acts. One of the acts closed the port of Boston until the destroyed tea was paid for. Another put Massachusetts under the control of a military governor and moved the colony's government out of Boston. Town meetings—a mainstay of New England political life—could take place only with the permission of the governor. Still another act provided that any royal official accused of a crime punishable by death would be tried in England.

American colonists moved toward independence.

Americans took quick and united action against the Coercive Acts. In September 1774 the First **Continental Congress**, with all the colonies except Georgia represented, met in Philadelphia. It soon became clear that the majority of the delegates no longer believed that Parliament had any right to govern the colonies. Rather, they saw the colonial assemblies

Both the Daughters of Liberty, shown above, and the Sons of Liberty led protests against British colonial rule in America.

The Boston Tea Party, at left, and Paul Revere's biased engravings of the Boston Massacre, at right, served to heighten colonial tension and protest.

This 1775 engraving by Amos Doolittle, who was on the scene, shows the attack on the British soldiers as they marched from Concord back to Boston. Colonial minutemen fired from cover.

and the British Parliament as equal governing bodies linked only by their shared loyalty to the king.

The Congress passed a resolution calling on the people of Massachusetts to arm themselves and to organize their militias. It also wrote an appeal to King George III, asking him to end the punishment of Boston and urging him to take an active role in restoring peace. King George, however, had already declared the New England colonies to be in rebellion.

While British troops paraded in Boston, colonial militias drilled all across Massachusetts. On April 18, 1775, colonists learned that British troops were planning a march on the town of **Concord**. The British were ordered to seize weapons and ammunition and to arrest Samuel Adams and John Hancock.

On their way to Concord, the British first passed through **Lexington**, where colonial militia were gathered on the village green. A British officer ordered the militia to disperse, but before they could do so, shots rang out, fired by someone nervous. Eight Americans were killed, and ten more fell wounded. The first shots of the Revolution had been fired.

Joseph Plumb Martin, 14 years old and large for his age, was plowing his grandfather's fields near Milford, Connecticut, in the spring of 1775 when bells began to ring and guns went off in the village. War had begun on Lexington Green, and soldiers were needed near Boston. By the next spring, young Martin had enlisted for six months—a short term that appealed to him. "I wished only to take a priming before I took upon me the whole coat of paint of a soldier."

A Second Continental Congress met in Philadelphia and began planning for war. The delegates called for a continental army and named George Washington as its commander in chief. While preparing for war, the Congress made still another attempt to avoid it. It sent a petition to the king proposing an end to violence and the lifting of the Coercive Acts. It did no good. In autumn 1775 Parliament issued an act ordering the British navy to seize American ships as enemy vessels. This was as good as a declaration of war.

By the end of 1775, each American had to choose: loyalty to king or revolution. The choice was not easy. The colonists had been raised to respect the king and to honor the British constitution. One radical, **Thomas Paine**, did much to help the colonists throw off their old affection for the mother country. In January 1776 Paine published a pamphlet called ***Common Sense*** in which he argued that the separation of the children (the colonies) from the parent (England) was a natural part

A contemporary illustration shows John Hancock signing the Declaration of Independence. (*Freedom Writes in a Big, Bold Hand*, by John Clymer)

of growth. The time for independence had, quite simply, come. Paine shocked many Americans by his open attack on King George III, but he also convinced them. Within three months of publication, Paine's pamphlet had sold some 120,000 copies, making it an instant best seller. Its furious, informal language electrified the colonists. *Common Sense* also stirred the debate on independence, putting intense pressure on moderates who continued to hope for a turnaround from England.

The following June Congress appointed a committee to draft a declaration of independence. After some debate over the wording of the document, mostly the work of Virginia's **Thomas Jefferson**, the Congress adopted the **Declaration of Independence** on July 4, 1776. This declaration was in reality an act of treason. The document presented revolutionary ideas that would stun the world. The American colonists were no longer struggling just to defend their rights. They were fighting for their independence and a completely new way of life.

Identify Key People and Terms

Write a sentence to identify: George Washington, French and Indian War, William Pitt, Pontiac, Stamp Act, Declaratory Act, Charles Townshend, Samuel Adams, Boston Massacre, Boston Tea Party, Coercive Acts, Continental Congress, Thomas Paine, *Common Sense*, Thomas Jefferson, Declaration of Independence

Locate Key Places

1. What region of North America was claimed by both France and Britain?
2. Where did British troops hope to capture arms and ammunition as well as two important colonial leaders?
3. Where were the first shots of the American Revolution fired?

Master the Main Ideas

1. **Understanding international conflicts: (a)** What was the initial cause of the French and Indian War? **(b)** What did Great Britain gain as a result of the war?
2. **Identifying the impact of wars:** What problems arose with the colonies as a result of the British victory over the French?
3. **Recognizing events leading to U.S. independence:** What caused and what were the results of the Boston Massacre and the Boston Tea Party?
4. **Recognizing events leading to U.S. independence:** What steps were taken by **(a)** the First Continental Congress and **(b)** the Second Continental Congress?

Apply Critical Thinking Skills: Identifying Central Issues

Read the Declaration of Independence, printed on pages 74–77. What central issues does the document address? Support your answer with evidence.

S E C T I O N **4**

The Americans won the War for Independence.

Key Terms: Patriots, Loyalists, Battle of Bunker Hill, Treaty of Paris of 1783

Reading Preview
As you read this section, you will learn:
1. what factor favored the Americans in the war.
2. where the war began.
3. what led to a peace treaty.

The fighting at Lexington and Concord occurred more than a year before the Americans declared their independence. Although radicals such as Samuel Adams were overjoyed when war broke out, other Americans were more cautious. They knew that Great Britain had great resources for waging war.

Geography favored the Americans in the war.

Great Britain had a strong central government under the king and Parliament. America's Continental Congress, however, had little authority over the 13 separate colonies. The British had a large, well-trained, and well-equipped professional army. Britain's navy had been weakened because of the nation's financial problems following the French and Indian War, but it still was powerful and capable of blockading the American coast. In contrast, the colonial militias, though eager, were untrained, undisciplined, and poorly equipped. These highly individualistic citizen-soldiers agreed to serve only for limited periods, after which the men returned home.

Another British advantage was the division of opinion about the war within America. Not all Americans were **Patriots**, those in favor of independence. About one-third of the population remained neutral, and about one-fifth stayed loyal to Great Britain. More than 30,000

Loyalists took up arms on the British side. In New York City, Philadelphia, and parts of the Carolinas and Georgia, Loyalists outnumbered the Patriots.

Geographic factors, on the other hand, favored the Americans. First, 3,000 miles of ocean lay between Great Britain and North America. The supply lines were long, and communications between London and the British armies in America were often delayed.

Second, the United States had no single strategic center for Britain to conquer. The continent was huge, settlements were widely scattered, colonial militias were everywhere, and the Continental Army, under General Washington, was able to continually evade capture by vastly superior British forces.

Third, the war was fought mostly over rugged terrain. The British, accustomed to European warfare where battles were fought on open fields, often found themselves fighting amid forests, hills, and swamps. The American terrain lent itself to surprise raids and ambushes, tactics the Americans often used.

The war began in the North.

In mid-1775 the British army under General Thomas Gage occupied Boston, supported by British warships in the harbor. American militias from throughout New England surrounded the city by land.

General Gage fortified Dorchester Heights, on a hilly peninsula southeast of Boston. As you can see on the map on page 66, this position commanded both the city and its harbor. On June 16 the Americans decided to counter by occupying Bunker Hill, across the

American Revolution

Point

Patriots

- disagreed with Parliament's right to govern colonies
- supported independence and revolution, as well as reforms
- made up of groups that had dominated colonial society

Counterpoint

Loyalists

- remained loyal to England
- opposed independence and revolution
- included English-appointed officials and merchants, as well as many black slaves and Indians

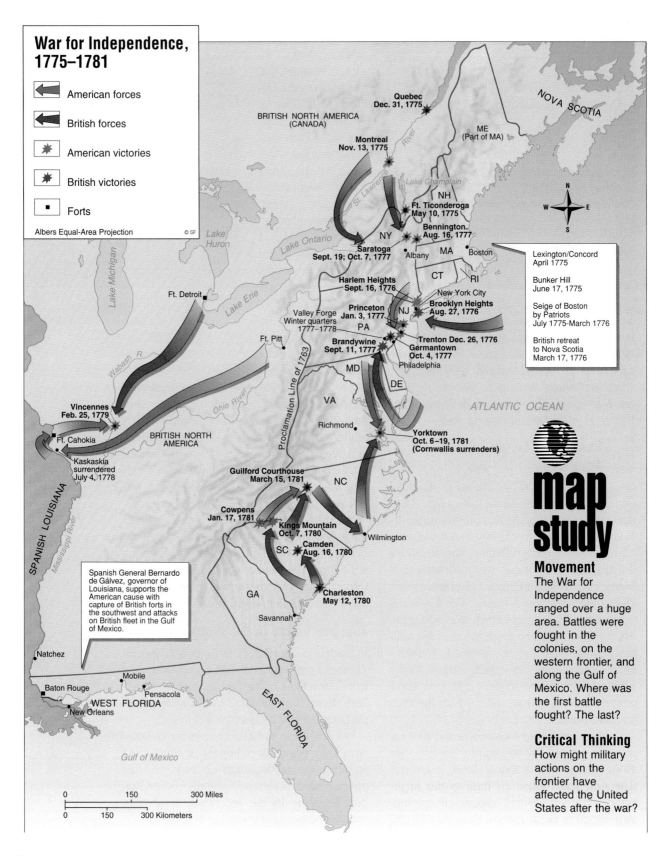

War for Independence, 1775–1781

← American forces

← British forces

✴ American victories

✴ British victories

■ Forts

Albers Equal-Area Projection   © SF

BRITISH NORTH AMERICA (CANADA)

NOVA SCOTIA

Quebec
Dec. 31, 1775

ME
(Part of MA)

Montreal
Nov. 13, 1775

St. Lawrence River

Lake Champlain

NH

Ft. Ticonderoga
May 10, 1775

Bennington
Aug. 16, 1777

Lake Ontario

Saratoga
Sept. 19; Oct. 7, 1777

Albany

MA

Boston

NY

CT

RI

Harlem Heights
Sept. 16, 1776

New York City

Brooklyn Heights
Aug. 27, 1776

Ft. Detroit

Lake Erie

Valley Forge
Winter quarters
1777–1778

Princeton
Jan. 3, 1777

NJ

Ft. Pitt

Wabash R.

Ohio River

Proclamation Line of 1763

PA

Brandywine
Sept. 11, 1777

Germantown
Oct. 4, 1777

Philadelphia

Trenton Dec. 26, 1776

MD

DE

Vincennes
Feb. 25, 1779

Ft. Cahokia

Kaskaskia
surrendered
July 4, 1778

BRITISH NORTH
AMERICA

VA

Richmond

ATLANTIC OCEAN

Yorktown
Oct. 6–19, 1781
(Cornwallis surrenders)

Guilford Courthouse
March 15, 1781

NC

Cowpens
Jan. 17, 1781

Kings Mountain
Oct. 7, 1780

Camden
Aug. 16, 1780

SC

Wilmington

SPANISH LOUISIANA

Mississippi River

Spanish General Bernardo
de Gálvez, governor of
Louisiana, supports the
American cause with
capture of British forts in
the southwest and attacks
on British fleet in the Gulf
of Mexico.

GA

Charleston
May 12, 1780

Savannah

Natchez

Mobile

Baton Rouge

Pensacola

WEST FLORIDA

New Orleans

EAST FLORIDA

Gulf of Mexico

Lake Huron

Lake Michigan

Lexington/Concord
April 1775

Bunker Hill
June 17, 1775

Seige of Boston
by Patriots
July 1775–March 1776

British retreat
to Nova Scotia
March 17, 1776

0   150   300 Miles

0   150   300 Kilometers

map study

Movement
The War for Independence ranged over a huge area. Battles were fought in the colonies, on the western frontier, and along the Gulf of Mexico. Where was the first battle fought? The last?

Critical Thinking
How might military actions on the frontier have affected the United States after the war?

bay from Boston in Charlestown. For some unknown reason, the Americans dug in on Breed's Hill instead, leading to the confusion that resulted in the battle there being called the **Battle of Bunker Hill**.

On June 17 General Howe led 2,500 men against the 2,200 Americans on Breed's Hill. The Redcoats, in full battle uniform and carrying heavy knapsacks, climbed uphill toward the American position. The Yankee sharpshooters waited until the enemy was almost upon them before firing, cutting the British down in droves. After beating back a second assault, the Americans ran out of gunpowder and were forced to retreat. The British took both Breed's and Bunker hills, but it was a costly victory.

When General Washington reached Boston, he took command of the militia there. These soldiers became the nucleus of the Continental Army and ultimately forced the British to evacuate Boston.

British General William Howe, who replaced the discredited Gage at Boston, took the British forces by sea to New York City. By mid-August 1776 he had been joined there by Generals Henry Clinton and Lord Charles Cornwallis with 32,000 new troops. Washington's army, which had moved to New York to face the British, had only 19,000 men. The British forced the Americans from their position at Brooklyn Heights to Manhattan, then northward to White Plains. Howe's overly cautious tactics, however, allowed Washington to evade a major pitched battle with the larger British force with a retreat to Pennsylvania.

Washington's dwindling army was soon strengthened with reinforcements. He decided on a daring and unexpected raid on the British garrison at **Trenton**, New Jersey. On the snowy night of December 25, 1776, he led his force across the Delaware River from Pennsylvania into New Jersey. At dawn the next day they swept into the Trenton garrison, surprising the still-sleepy German mercenaries—soldiers the British had hired to help them fight the war. The Americans killed 30 mercenaries in the attack and took 918 prisoners. Only three Americans were wounded.

On October 19, 1777, American troops won an important victory against the British near Saratoga, New York. News of the victory rocked Europe. Nations there, hesitant to openly support the American cause in the early months of the war, were now willing to do so. Both France and Spain had secretly provided money and supplies to the rebels since 1776. In 1778 France formally declared war on Great Britain. The following year, Spain entered the war on the side of France. Spain, which then claimed most of the present-day United States west of the Mississippi River, proved helpful to the Patriots even before its public declaration of war. The courageous governor of Louisiana, **Bernardo de Gálvez**, had opened the port of New Orleans to American privateers and harassed the British all along the Gulf of Mexico, capturing thousands of enemy soldiers.

Along with gaining support from foreign nations, American soldiers—both Patriot and Loyalist—counted on important contributions from colonial women. Almost immediately after the battle of Lexington Green, women began to collect money and supplies for their chosen cause. Many Patriot women also formed spinning clubs and sewing groups to provide clothing for Washington's army, which lacked almost every item needed to fight a war. Women also carried the burden of running America's farms, shops, and households as the men took to the battlefields.

Some women chose instead to join the troops at the front. Many packed up their children and joined their husbands in the army. These women performed vital services in the camps—typically sewing, cooking, and nursing the sick. A few women sought out more dramatic action, volunteering as soldiers and spies. The most famous of these women soldiers was a farm girl named Deborah Sampson. Disguised as a man, she served as Private Robert Shurtleff under Washington himself.

In dramatic acts, and in the more ordinary acts of survival and endurance, women demonstrated more than bravery and fortitude. They showed to themselves and to others that they were capable of, and chose to exercise, political commitments and convictions.

Many black Loyalists migrated to Canada during the War for Independence in search of freedom from slavery. (painting by Robert Petley, Canada Public Archives, Ottawa, Ontario)

Deborah Sampson, below at right, dressed in men's clothing and joined the Continental Army as a soldier.

vided, in all but two states, into two separate houses that could check each other's actions. The new constitutions also reflected the Americans' distrust of the kind of governmental authority their former British rulers had exercised.

The Confederation government. The Americans also created a constitutional government for their nation. In June 1776 the Continental Congress appointed a committee to draft a national constitution. The **Articles of Confederation**, mostly the work of **John Dickinson** of Pennsylvania, but greatly weakened by Congress, was sent to the state legislatures for ratification in 1777. Conflicts among the states over western lands held back ratification until 1781.

The Articles created a loose alliance of the 13 states while preserving the independence and most of the powers of each of them. Each state had one vote in the Confederation legislature, and no significant decision could be made without the approval of at least nine states. Any amendments to the Articles had to have the approval of all 13 states.

These restrictions on the national government were a reflection of the fear of a strong central authority that might conflict with the rights and powers of the individual states. It produced, however, a national government with severe restrictions, many of which became evident in the years of the American Revolution.

The Confederation government had the power to conduct foreign affairs and make treaties. It was given authority in Indian affairs and could settle disputes between states and conduct a postal service. It could not, however, coin money, which left the nation with the possibility of each state's issuing its own form of currency. Nor could Congress raise taxes except by requesting it from the states, a restriction that left the Continental Army unsupplied, unclothed, and unpaid for much of the war.

The Articles of Confederation created a government without an executive or judicial branch. Congress, therefore, acted as both lawmaker and executive. Wrangling in Congress often left the government powerless to carry out its laws, and quick action in a time of emergency usually proved impossible.

Nevertheless, the new government did succeed in taking some positive actions. Most significantly, it acted to provide for the expansion of the new nation.

Western lands. The opening of the western lands intensified debate over who should have the right to exploit these

map study

Northwest Territory, 1785

1 Mile

1 Mile

Half Section
320 Acres

Quarter Section
160 Acres

A Section
640 Acres

Quarter
Quarter
Section
40 Acres

Half Quarter
Section 80 Acres

A Township

6 Miles

6 Miles

6 Miles

Seventh Range
Sixth Range
Fifth Range
Fourth Range
Third Range
Second Range
First Range

First Base Line

Ohio River

VIRGINIA

PENNSYLVANIA

Area of
First Survey

CANADA

Great Lakes

MN
MI
WI
MI
MI
Mississippi R.
Area of first survey
NORTHWEST TERRITORY
IL   IN   OH
Missouri R.
Ohio R.

Map shows present-day boundaries

© SF

Location The U.S. government auctioned off the land in the Northwest Territory, setting aside the proceeds from the sale of one section in each township to create and support public schools. How many sections were in one township? How large was a section?

Critical Thinking The township system gave each piece of land an address. Why might that be necessary?

lands: speculators or individual settlers, the national government or individual states. The **Land Ordinance of 1785** attempted to resolve the issue by providing for the orderly sale and settlement of the **Northwest Territory**—the region defined by the Ohio River, the Great Lakes, and the Mississippi. The ordinance created a system of townships—areas of land six miles square.

To administer the Land Ordinance of 1785, the Confederation Congress enacted the **Northwest Ordinance of 1787**. Provision was made for the creation of three to five new states in the territory, in which slavery was forbidden. In the earliest stages, Congress would appoint a territorial governor. When a territory's population reached 60,000, it could write a constitution and apply for statehood. Thus, the Northwest Ordinance ensured that the new nation would not create colonies of its own.

The Confederation government led to a Constitutional Convention.

It soon became evident that the Confederation government was unable to deal with problems that arose in the new nation. The states took advantage of their right to regulate their own trade by taxing the goods crossing their borders from neighboring states. More than half the states exercised the right to issue their own money, and some states proved less responsible than others. By 1785 rivalries between and within the states were erupting in violence.

In the summer of 1786, angry farmers in western Massachusetts, hard hit by a postwar depression and increased taxes imposed by the state, rose in a rebellion led by Daniel Shays, a former captain in the Continental Army. The state's governor sent a well-armed militia against the rebels, and **Shays' Rebellion** was crushed. However, a legacy of fear remained. Many Americans believed that a stronger national government was needed to bring order to the country.

In September 1786 a small group of political leaders from five states gathered at Annapolis, Maryland. They had come together to discuss problems of interstate commerce, but the conversation moved quickly to the national crisis.

The delegates recommended that a convention be held to revise the Articles of Confederation, and the Confederation Congress consented.

Fifty-five men, representing 12 states, made their way to **Philadelphia** in the spring of 1787. Rhode Island refused to attend. The delegates were well-educated, wealthy men, members of that "natural aristocracy of talent" Thomas Jefferson believed to be the greatest resource of the new nation.

After electing George Washington as chairman of the convention, the delegates quickly settled the ground rules for debate and voting. Each state would have one vote regardless of the number of its delegates, and a simple majority would decide all questions. All meetings would be held in secrecy. This rule protected the delegates from criticism. It also allowed them to go beyond their instructions to amend the Articles and draft a new constitution.

The delegates accepted a number of points of major importance without debate. They all approved of a written constitution and assumed the continued existence of the states. They also wanted a republican form of government with some separation of powers.

Compromises aided the Constitutional Convention.

The Virginia delegation was the first to arrive at the convention, and **James Madison** had already drawn up a plan for a government. Madison's plan, which became known as the Virginia Plan, called for three branches of government— executive, judicial, and legislative—and provided for a two-house legislature, with the number of seats a state held in each house based on the state's population.

Delegates from the smaller, less populous states objected to a system of representation based on population. William Paterson of New Jersey proposed a single-house legislature in which each state would have equal representation regardless of population. His New Jersey Plan also called for an executive committee chosen by Congress rather than an independent executive branch. After weeks of heated debate, the delegates agreed to a compromise proposal from Roger Sherman. In the lower

Springtime marked a time for western settlers to burn up any fallen trees on their lands.

CONSTITUTIONAL CONVENTION
Skill: Identifying Alternatives

Introducing the Skill. The delegates who gathered in Philadelphia in the summer of 1787 were a disparate group of men. They were divided on a number of key issues. Benjamin Franklin, addressing the Convention, wondered:

> When you assemble a number of men, to have the advantage of their joint wisdom, you inevitably assemble with those men all their prejudices, their passions, their errors of opinion, their local interests and their selfish views. From such an assembly, can a perfect production be expected?

Learning the Skill. Arriving at a "perfect production" may not always be possible, but arriving at a workable compromise can often be reached by **identifying alternatives**. To do so, you need first to define your situation or problem clearly and completely. Then brainstorm to develop several possible solutions. If few or no solutions readily appear, list potential areas in which to conduct research or study. You might also wish to consult a variety of people in order to benefit from different experiences and points of view.

For example, consider the problem faced by Constitutional Convention delegates concerning representation in Congress. Two principle arguments arose. Delegates from large states wanted representation to be based on population levels of each state. Delegates from smaller states preferred a system in which each state had equal representation. After much discussion, an alternate solution was reached: representation in the House of Representatives would be based on population and representation in the Senate would be based on equal representation.

Applying the Skill. Consider the problem of how to count slaves. Then answer the following questions.
1. What were the different plans suggested by delegates?
2. What was the alternate solution eventually reached? What other solutions might have been possible?

house (the House of Representatives) each state's members would be in proportion to the state's population. In the upper house (the Senate) each state, regardless of size, would have two senators. This solution was called the **Great Compromise**.

Another dispute arose over the issue of slavery. Were slaves to be counted as people in determining congressional representation? The northern states argued that, since slaves were considered a form of wealth, they should not be counted as people but should be taxed as property. Southern delegates objected. Unless slaves were counted, their states would have fewer representatives in Congress. Again a compromise was reached. For purposes of both representation and taxation, five slaves would be counted as three people—the **Three-fifths Compromise**.

By September 10 all issues were settled and the convention voted to approve the Constitution. The document went to a Committee on Style, chaired by Pennsylvania's Gouverneur Morris. It was Morris who added the preamble, beginning "We, the people of the United States." This left no doubt that the new government was to be a government of the people.

Not all the delegates were totally satisfied with the final document. Some refused to sign it, but most doubters followed the advice of Benjamin Franklin:

I confess that there are several parts of the Constitution which I do not at present approve, but I am not sure that I shall never approve them. . . . Thus I consent, sir, to this Constitution because I expect no better, and because I am not sure that

AN AMERICAN ★ SPEAKS

it is not the best. . . . I cannot help expressing a wish that every member of the Convention who may still have objection to it, would with me, on this occasion, doubt a little of his own infallibility, and to make manifest our unanimity, put his name to this instrument.

Federalists and Anti-Federalists debated ratification.

The Constitution provided for special ratifying conventions to meet in each of the states. As soon as nine of these conventions approved the Constitution, the new government would go into effect in those states. Before that happened, those who approved of the Constitution and those who opposed it campaigned for their different views.

The proponents of the Constitution called themselves **Federalists**, taking a name that implied that they supported the strong national government the Constitution would establish. The Federalists turned to persuasive political writers to argue the virtues and advantages of the Constitution in the newspapers. Together **John Jay**, **Alexander Hamilton**, and James Madison published a series of 85 newspaper essays in New York. These brilliant and powerful discussions concerning the Constitution were published in book form as *The Federalist*.

Anti-Federalists, those who opposed ratification, believed that strong state governments embodied the goals of the Revolution. They argued that such governments were more democratic and more responsive to the people's wishes than a distant national government. What disturbed the Anti-Federalists most was the absence of a **Bill of Rights**, a statement of the fundamental rights of the people. Why, they asked in their essays and speeches, did the Constitutional Convention fail to affirm individual liberties?

The most dramatic fight took place in Virginia, where Federalists and Anti-Federalists were almost evenly divided. For 23 days the debate raged as delegates argued each aspect of the proposed Constitution.

By June 21, 1788, the required nine states had ratified the Constitution—Delaware, Pennsylvania, New Jersey, Georgia, Connecticut, Massachusetts, Maryland, South Carolina, and New Hampshire. Virginia and New York, two of the most populous states, had not yet voted. On June 25, the Federalists won in Virginia with a vote of 89 to 79. New York's approval came the following day with another narrow margin: 30 to 27. North Carolina and Rhode Island, the final holdouts, joined the fold in 1789 and 1790 respectively, after the new government had been installed.

Alexander Hamilton was a leading voice for the Federalists in the debate over the Constitution.

SECTION **5** REVIEW

Identify Key People and Terms
Write a sentence to identify: Articles of Confederation, John Dickinson, Land Ordinance of 1785, Northwest Ordinance of 1787, Shays' Rebellion, James Madison, Great Compromise, Three-fifths Compromise, Federalists, John Jay, Alexander Hamilton, Anti-Federalists, Bill of Rights

Locate Key Places

1. What bodies of water defined the boundaries of the Northwest Territory?
2. Where did the Constitutional Convention meet?

Master the Main Ideas

1. Understanding political development: (a) What features were common to most of the state governments? **(b)** What were the most important achievements of the Confederation government?
2. Understanding political development: What factors led to a call for the Constitutional Convention?
3. Recognizing the value of compromise: How were some major issues at the Constitutional Convention resolved?
4. Examining political issues: Why did the Anti-Federalists oppose the Constitution?

Apply Critical Thinking Skills: Demonstrating Reasoned Judgment
Some people have argued that the United States would have been better off under the Articles of Confederation. Explain why you agree or disagree.

73

Although the Declaration of Independence has no legal force today, it remains a hallowed statement of the American creed. Politically, its significance rests in the new theory of government put forth, that government derives its powers solely "from the consent of the governed." Socially, its significance lies in the recognition of the equality of people and that each has certain natural rights, among them "life, liberty, and the pursuit of happiness." Economically, this "pursuit of happiness" has meant an equality of economic opportunity in American life, a guiding philosophy that has permitted successive generations of Americans to pursue their view of the better life.

1. Why do you think the colonists felt obligated to tell the world that they had petitioned the King on several occasions to correct wrongs?

IN CONGRESS, JULY 4, 1776. THE UNANIMOUS DECLARATION OF THE THIRTEEN UNITED STATES OF AMERICA — When in the Course of human events, it becomes necessary for one people to dissolve the political bands which have connected them with another, and to assume among the powers of the earth, the separate and equal station to which the Laws of Nature and of Nature's God entitle them, a decent respect to the opinions of mankind requires that they should declare the causes which impel them to the separation.

We hold these truths to be self-evident, that all men are created equal, that they are endowed by their Creator with certain unalienable Rights, that among these are Life, Liberty and the pursuit of Happiness.

That to secure these rights, Governments are instituted among Men, deriving their just powers from the consent of the governed.

That whenever any Form of Government becomes destructive of these ends, it is the Right of the People to alter or to abolish it, and to institute new Government, laying its foundation on such principles and organizing its powers in such form, as to them shall seem most likely to effect their Safety and Happiness. Prudence, indeed, will dictate that Governments long established should not be changed for light and transient causes; and accordingly all experience hath shown, that mankind are more disposed to suffer, while evils are sufferable, than to right themselves by abolishing the forms to which they are accustomed. But when a long train of abuses and usurpations, pursuing invariably the same Object evinces a design to reduce them under absolute Despotism, it is their right, it is their duty, to throw off such Government, and to provide new Guards for their future security.

2. How does the Declaration of Independence describe the colonies? Do you agree or disagree with this description? Explain your answer.

Such has been the patient sufferance of these Colonies; and such is now the necessity which constrains them to alter their former Systems of Government.

The history of the present King of Great Britain is a history of repeated injuries and usurpations, all having in direct object the establishment of an absolute Tyranny over these States. To prove this, let Facts be submitted to a candid world.

Sometimes one group of people (the colonists) must break away from the country (England) that has been governing them to form their own country. When this happens, they should explain to the world the reasons why they are doing so.

We believe that all people have equal rights; that God has given people the right to life, liberty, and the chance to be happy, and that no one can give these rights away. People set up governments to protect these rights. If the government fails to do so, then the people have the right to do away with the government and set up another one that will do a better job.

Governments should be changed only when absolutely necessary. If fact, history shows that people will usually put up with a great deal rather than take such a drastic step. However, when a government continues to take away their rights and to use power unjustly, the people have a duty to change the government.

The colonies have reached the point where they must change their government. The British king has tried to take away the rights of the colonists and to use his power unjustly. Here is a list of his acts for the world to see:

3. The Declaration of Independence states that the King of Great Britain committed certain acts against the colonies. This document then lists the "Facts." Looking at the facts stated in the document, which would you classify as facts and which are really opinions?

He has refused his Assent to Laws, the most wholesome and necessary for the public good.

He has forbidden his Governors to pass Laws of immediate and pressing importance, unless suspended in their operation till his Assent should be obtained; and when so suspended, he has utterly neglected to attend to them.

He has refused to pass other Laws for the accommodation of large districts of people, unless those people would relinquish the right of Representation in the Legislature, a right inestimable to them and formidable to tyrants only.

He has called together legislative bodies at places unusual, uncomfortable, and distant from the depository of their public Records, for the sole purpose of fatiguing them into compliance with his measures.

He has dissolved Representative Houses repeatedly, for opposing with manly firmness his invasions on the rights of the people.

He has refused for a long time, after such dissolutions, to cause others to be elected; whereby the Legislative powers, incapable of Annihilation, have returned to the People at large for their exercise; the State remaining in the mean time exposed to all the dangers of invasion from without, and convulsions within.

He has endeavoured to prevent the population of these States; for that purpose obstructing the Laws for Naturalization of Foreigners; refusing to pass others to encourage their migration hither, and raising the conditions of new Appropriations of Lands.

He has obstructed the Administration of Justice, by refusing his Assent to Laws for establishing Judiciary powers.

He has made Judges dependent on his Will alone, for the tenure of their offices, and the amount and payment of their salaries.

He has erected a multitude of New Offices, and sent hither swarms of Officers to harass our people, and eat out their substance.

He has kept among us, in times of peace, Standing Armies, without the Consent of our legislatures.

He has affected to render the Military independent of and superior to the Civil power.

The king has refused to approve laws the colonies need.

He has refused to allow his governors to pass the laws the colonies need unless he approves them. Then, while the colonies wait for his approval, he won't even look at the laws.

He has refused to approve laws for cities and heavily populated areas unless the people give up the right to be represented in the legislature — a very important right that only an unjust ruler would try to take away from the people.

He has called meetings of the colonial legislatures at distant places so that the delegates are too tired when they arrive to argue against his policies.

He has canceled meetings of the colonial legislatures when the delegates oppose his actions.

He has refused to allow new legislators to be elected, thus leaving a colony unable to defend itself against enemies and riots.

He has tried to stop people from coming to the colonies by refusing to pass naturalization laws and by making it difficult to obtain new land.

He has refused to pass laws setting up a system of courts.

He has kept colonial judges under his control by deciding how long they can remain in office and what they will earn.

He has sent many new officers to the colonies to bother the people, live in their homes, and eat their food.

He has sent soldiers to the colonies in peacetime without the approval of colonial legislatures.

He has given the army its own rules to follow and given it authority over colonial legislatures.

4. The Declaration of Independence states that the King of Great Britain approved certain laws. Evaluate these laws. Which do you feel were the most harmful to the economic well-being of the colonies? Which do you feel were the most serious violations of the colonists' civil liberties?

He has combined with others to subject us to a jurisdiction foreign to our constitution, and unacknowledged by our laws; giving his Assent to their Acts of pretended Legislation:

For quartering large bodies of armed troops among us:

For protecting them, by a mock Trial, from punishment for any Murders which they should commit on the Inhabitants of these States:

For cutting off our Trade with all parts of the world:

For imposing Taxes on us without our Consent:

For depriving us in many cases, of the benefits of Trial by Jury:

For transporting us beyond Seas to be tried for pretended offences:

For abolishing the free System of English Laws in a neighbouring Province, establishing therein an Arbitrary government, and enlarging its Boundaries so as to render it at once an example and fit instrument for introducing the same absolute rule into these Colonies:

For taking away our Charters, abolishing our most valuable Laws, and altering fundamentally the Forms of our Governments:

For suspending our own Legislatures, and declaring themselves invested with power to legislate for us in all cases whatsoever.

5. What acts of war does the Declaration of Independence say the King of Great Britain committed against the colonies? To what specific acts of war were the colonists referring?

He has abdicated Government here, by declaring us out of his Protection and waging War against us.

He has plundered our seas, ravaged our Coasts, burnt our towns, and destroyed the lives of our people.

He is at this time transporting large Armies of foreign Mercenaries to compleat the works of death, desolation and tyranny, already begun with circumstances of Cruelty & perfidy scarcely paralleled in the most barbarous ages, and totally unworthy the Head of a civilized nation.

He has constrained our fellow Citizens taken Captive on the high Seas to bear Arms against their Country, to become the executioners of their friends and Brethren, or to fall themselves by their Hands.

He has excited domestic insurrections amongst us, and has endeavoured to bring on the inhabitants of our frontiers, the merciless Indian Savages, whose known rule of warfare, is an undistinguished destruction of all ages, sexes and conditions.

He has made laws that go against our constitution. He has approved the following laws:

He has forced us to house British soldiers.

He has prevented soldiers, who have killed colonists, from being punished by pretending to try them.

He has cut off our trade with other nations.

He has taxed us without the approval of our legislatures.

He has taken away our right to a jury trial.

He has forced us to go to England to stand trial for crimes we have not committed.

He has taken away the rights of the people in a nearby province, Canada, as an example of what he can do to the colonies if he so wishes.

He has tried to change our form of government, and put in its place one that is more suitable to him.

He has dissolved colonial legislatures and made laws for the colonies himself.

He has declared war against us instead of protecting us.

He has attacked us at sea and along our coasts, burned our towns, and killed our people.

He has hired foreign soldiers to bring death and destruction to Americans.

He has captured American sailors at sea and forced them to fight against their country, friends, and families.

He has caused riots in the colonies and encouraged the Indians to attack us.

In every stage of these Oppressions We have Petitioned for Redress in the most humble terms: Our repeated Petitions have been answered only by repeated injury. A Prince, whose character is thus marked by every act which may define a Tyrant, is unfit to be the ruler of a free people.

We have tried over and over again to petition the king to correct these wrongs. Each time, our petitions have been ignored and a new law has been passed to punish us. A king who would do such things is not fit to rule a free people.

6. Why do you think the colonists appealed to the British public for support? How were the colonists and British citizens in Great Britain alike? How were they different?

Nor have We been wanting in attention to our Brittish brethren. We have warned them from time to time of attempts by their legislature to extend an unwarrantable jurisdiction over us. We have reminded them of the circumstances of our emigration and settlement here. We have appealed to their native justice and magnanimity, and we have conjured them by the ties of our common kindred to disavow these usurpations, which, would inevitably interrupt our connections and correspondence. They too have been deaf to the voice of justice and of consanguinity. We must, therefore, acquiesce in the necessity, which denounces our Separation, and hold them, as we hold the rest of mankind, Enemies in War, in Peace Friends.

We have also appealed to the British people. We have tried to tell them how we feel about the unfair laws Parliament has passed. We have reminded them why we came to America. We have asked them, as fellow citizens, to support us. The people, like the king, have not listened. We, therefore, have no choice but to separate ourselves from Great Britain.

7. You Decide: Did the colonists commit treason by declaring their independence from Great Britain? Were there other choices available to them? Explain your answer.

WE, THEREFORE, THE REPRESENTATIVES OF THE UNITED STATES OF AMERICA, in General Congress, Assembled, appealing to the Supreme Judge of the world for the rectitude of our intentions, do, in the Name, and by Authority of the good People of these Colonies, solemnly publish and declare, That these United Colonies are, and of Right ought to be FREE AND INDEPENDENT STATES; that they are Absolved from all Allegiance to the British Crown, and that all political connection between them and the State of Great Britain, is and ought to be totally dissolved; and that as Free and Independent States, they have full Power to levy War, conclude Peace, contract Alliances, establish Commerce, and to do all other Acts and Things which Independent States may of right do. And for the support of this Declaration, with a firm reliance on the protection of Divine Providence, we mutually pledge to each other our Lives, our Fortunes and our sacred Honor.

Therefore, appealing to God who knows that our feelings are justified, we, as representatives of the colonists, do declare that the colonies are and have the right to be free and independent. We have the power to declare war, make peace, sign treaties, establish trade, and do everything an independent nation does. Relying on God's protection, we pledge our lives, our honor, and our property in support of this declaration of independence.

John Hancock
Button Gwinnett
Lyman Hall
George Walton
William Hooper
Joseph Hewes
John Penn
Edward Rutledge
Thomas Heyward, Junior

Thomas Lynch, Junior
Arthur Middleton
Samuel Chase
William Paca
Thomas Stone
Charles Carroll of Carrollton
George Wythe
Richard Henry Lee

Thomas Jefferson
Benjamin Harrison
Thomas Nelson, Junior
Francis Lightfoot Lee
Carter Braxton
Robert Morris
Benjamin Rush
Benjamin Franklin
John Morton

George Clymer
James Smith
George Taylor
James Wilson
George Ross
Caesar Rodney
George Read
Thomas McKean
William Floyd
Philip Livingston

Francis Lewis
Lewis Morris
Richard Stockton
John Witherspoon
Francis Hopkinson
John Hart
Abraham Clark
Josiah Bartlett
William Whipple
Samuel Adams

John Adams
Robert Treat Paine
Elbridge Gerry
Stephen Hopkins
William Ellery
Roger Sherman
Samuel Huntington
William Williams
Oliver Wolcott
Matthew Thornton

Anne Hutchinson Is Banished

2A

TIME FRAME
1637

GEOGRAPHIC SETTING
Massachusetts

Born in England, William and Anne Hutchinson (1591–1643) moved with their large family (different sources give them from 12 to 14 children) to Boston in 1634, where Anne served as a midwife. Her unorthodox and increasingly radical religious views, which stressed the importance of individual revelation (and thus diminished the importance of the organized church) brought her into conflict with the Puritan leaders. In 1637 she was tried and banished from Massachusetts Bay Colony as "a woman not fit for our society." She was eventually killed in an Indian raid. The following is an excerpt from the record of her trial. The first speaker is Anne Hutchinson.

T herefore take heed what ye go about to do unto me. You have power over my body, but the Lord Jesus hath power over my body and soul; neither can you do me
5 any harm, for I am in the hands of the eternal Jehovah, my Savior. I am at his appointment, for the bounds of my habitation are cast in Heaven, and no further do I esteem of any mortal man than creatures
10 in his hand. [She means that every person is subject to the will of God.] I fear none but the great Jehovah, which hath foretold me of these things, and I do verily believe that he will deliver me out of your hands.
15 Therefore take heed how you proceed against me; for I know that for this you go about to do to me, God will ruin you and your posterity [descendants], and this whole state.

20 MR. NOWELL. How do you know that it was God that did reveal these things to you, and not Satan?

MRS. HUTCHINSON. How did Abraham know that it was God that bid him offer
25 [sacrifice] his son, being a breach of the sixth commandment?

DEPUTY-GOVERNOR DUDLEY. By an immediate voice.

MRS. HUTCHINSON. So to me by an im-
30 mediate revelation.

DEPUTY-GOVERNOR. How! an immediate revelation?

MRS. HUTCHINSON. By the voice of his own spirit to my soul.

35 GOVERNOR WINTHROP. Daniel was delivered by miracle; do you think to be delivered so too?

MRS. HUTCHINSON. I do here speak it before the Court. I look that the Lord should
40 deliver me by his providence. . . .

GOVERNOR WINTHROP. The Court hath already declared themselves satisfied concerning the things you hear, and concerning the troublesomeness of her spirit, and
45 the danger of her course amongst us, which is not to be suffered. Therefore, if it be the mind of the Court that Mrs. Hutchinson, for these things that appear before us, is unfit for our society, and if it be the
50 mind of the Court that she shall be banished out of our liberties, and imprisoned till she be sent away, let them hold up their hands.

All but three held up their hands.

55 GOVERNOR WINTHROP. Those that are contrary minded, hold up yours.

Mr. Coddington and Mr. Colburn only.

MR. JENNISON. I cannot hold up my hand one way or the other, and I shall give my
60 reason if the Court require it.

GOVERNOR WINTHROP. Mrs. Hutchinson, you hear the sentence of the Court. It is that you are banished from out our jurisdiction as being a woman not fit for our
65 society. And you are to be imprisoned till the Court send you away.

MRS. HUTCHINSON. I desire to know wherefore I am banished. [The charges against her were, in fact, sedition and
70 contempt.]

GOVERNOR WINTHROP. Say no more. The Court knows wherefore, and is satisfied.

Several of the men listening to Anne Hutchinson preach in this painting by Howard Pyle (1853–1911) appear to be disturbed by what they are hearing.

Discussing the Reading

1. Why did Anne Hutchinson feel that the Court should "take heed what ye go about to do unto me" (lines 1–2)?

2. Why was Deputy-Governor Dudley so interested in Hutchinson's admission that God's will was made known to her "by an immediate revelation" (lines 29–30)?

3. What did Governor Winthrop mean when he mentioned "the danger of her course amongst us" (line 45)?

CRITICAL THINKING
Expressing Problems

If you had been Anne Hutchinson's lawyer, how would you have conducted her defense? Specifically, what points would you have made in your summation of the case for the defense?

Olaudah Equiano Endures the Middle Passage

TIME FRAME
Mid-1750s

GEOGRAPHIC SETTING
West Africa and
the Atlantic Ocean

Olaudah Equiano [ō lou′dä ā′kwē ä′nō] was born around 1745 in what is now Nigeria. The son of a chief, he was kidnapped by enemy tribesmen when he was about ten and sold into slavery. After enduring the horrors of the "middle passage," the voyage between West Africa and the Americas, Equiano was taken to Virginia, where he was purchased by an officer in the Royal Navy, who renamed him Gustavus Vassa (after a 16th-century Swedish king). Eventually he was sold to a Philadelphia Quaker, who enabled Equiano to purchase his freedom. In the following passage from Equiano's autobiography, written in 1791, he described the brutality and despair he suffered during the middle passage. (The spelling of the original has been retained.)

On the opposite page, the plan of the lower deck of a slave ship showed how to cram the maximum human cargo aboard. Below is the portrait of Olaudah Equiano that accompanied the 1791 edition of his autobiography.

The first object which saluted my eyes when I arrived on the coast was the sea, and a slave ship, which was then riding at anchor, and waiting for its cargo. These filled me with astonishment, which was soon connected with terror, when I was carried on board. I was immediately handled, and tossed up to see if I were sound, by some of the crew; and I was now persuaded that I had gotten into a world of bad spirits, and that they were going to kill me. Their complexions too differing so much from ours, their long hair, and the language they spoke (which was very different from any I had ever heard), united to confirm me in this belief.

Indeed, such were the horrors of my views and fears at the moment, that, if ten thousand worlds had been my own, I would have freely parted with them all to have exchanged my condition with that of the meanest slave in my own country. When I looked round the ship too and saw a large furnace or copper [pot] boiling, and a multitude of black people of every description chained together, every one of their countenances expressing dejection and sorrow, I no longer doubted of my fate; and, quite overpowered with horror and anguish, I fell motionless on the deck and fainted.

When I recovered a little, I found some black people about me, who I believed were some of those who had brought me on board, and had been receiving their pay; they talked to me in order to cheer me, but all in vain. I asked them if I were not to be eaten by those white men with horrible looks, red faces, and long hair. They told me I was not: and one of the crew brought me a small portion of spirituous liquor [alcoholic drink] in a wine glass; but being afraid of him, I would not take it out of his hand. . . .

Soon after this, the blacks who brought me on board went off, and left me abandoned to despair. I now saw myself deprived of all chance of returning to my native country. . . . I was not long suffered to indulge my grief; I was soon put down under the decks, and there I received such a salutation [greeting] in my nostrils as I had never experienced in my life: so that with the loathsomeness [nastiness] of the stench and crying together, I became so sick and low that I was not able to eat, nor had I the least desire to taste anything.

I now wished for the last friend, death, to relieve me; but soon, to my grief, two of the white men offered me eatables; and, on my refusing to eat, one of them held me fast by the hands, and laid me across,

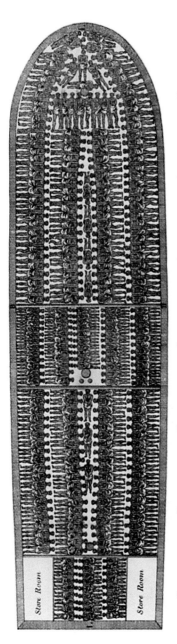

I think, the windlass [device used to raise a ship's anchor], and tied my feet, while the other flogged me severely.

I had never experienced anything of this kind before; and although, not being used to the water, I naturally feared that element the first time I saw it, yet nevertheless, could I have got over the nettings, I would have jumped over the side, but I could not; and, besides, the crew used to watch us very closely who were not chained down to the decks, lest we should leap into the water: and I have seen some of these poor African prisoners most severely cut for attempting to do so, and hourly whipped for not eating. . . .

The closeness of the place, and the heat of the climate, added to the number in the ship, which was so crowded that each had scarcely room to turn himself, almost suffocated us. . . . The shrieks of the women, and the groans of the dying, rendered the whole a scene of horror almost inconceivable.

Happily perhaps for myself I was soon reduced so low here that it was thought necessary to keep me almost always on deck; and from my extreme youth I was not put in fetters [chains]. In this situation I expected every hour to share the fate of my companions, some of whom were almost daily brought upon deck at the point of death, which I began to hope would soon put an end to my miseries. Often did I think many of the inhabitants of the deep much more happy than myself. I envied them the freedom they enjoyed, and as often wished I could change my condition for theirs. . . .

One day, when we had a smooth sea and moderate wind, two of my wearied countrymen who were chained together (I was near them at the time), preferring death to such a life of misery, somehow made through the nettings and jumped into the sea: immediately another quite dejected fellow, who on account of his illness was suffered to be out of irons, also

followed their example; and I believe many more would very soon have done the same if they had not been prevented by the ship's crew who were instantly alarmed.

Those of us that were the most active were in a moment put down under the deck, and there was such a noise and confusion amongst the people of the ship as I never heard before, to stop her, and get the boat out to go after the slaves. However two of the wretches were drowned, but they got the other, and afterwards flogged him unmercifully for thus attempting to prefer death to slavery.

In this manner we continued to undergo more hardships than I can now relate, hardships which are inseparable from this accursed trade. Many a time we were near suffocation from the want of fresh air, which we were often without for whole days together. . . .

Discussing the Reading

1. When young Olaudah Equiano first encountered white men, what aspects of their appearance and behavior impressed (and terrified) him?

2. For what "offenses" were the slaves punished? Why?

CRITICAL THINKING
Recognizing Values

Equiano was later baptized and, as a Christian, presumably regarded suicide as a sin. However, there is no indication of this in his account of the suicides of some of his fellow slaves. Which of the following reasons seems the most likely explanation of this omission?
  a. He regarded their suicides as justifiable.
  b. He was reluctant to condemn people who had suffered so much brutality.
  c. He would not apply Christian morality to non-Christians.

"As Poor Richard Says . . ."

TIME FRAME
1730s–1750s

GEOGRAPHIC SETTING
Philadelphia

Selling on the average more than 10,000 copies each year, Benjamin Franklin's *Poor Richard's Almanack* was one of the most popular publications in colonial America. "As Poor Richard says . . ." became a familiar catch phrase, used to give authority to any piece of prudent advice. The following are a sample of Poor Richard's maxims. The pictures on these pages, which are from an engraving called *Poor Richard Illustrated,* have mottoes taken from Franklin's *Almanack.*

Never leave that till tomorrow, which you can do today.

   He that riseth late must trot all day, and shall scarce overtake his business at night; while Laziness travels so slowly, that Poverty soon overtakes him.

   Sloth, like rust, consumes faster than labor wears; while the used key is always bright.

   The sleeping fox catches no poultry, and there will be sleeping enough in the grave.

   It would be thought a hard government that should tax its people one-tenth part of their time, to be employed in its service. But idleness taxes many of us much more.

   Help, hands, for I have no lands; or, if I have, they are smartly taxed.

20 ≈ At the workingman's house hunger looks in, but dares not enter.

≈ Then plough deep while sluggards sleep, and you shall have corn to sell and to keep.

25 ≈ Early to bed, and early to rise, makes a man healthy, wealthy, and wise.

≈ Handle your tools without mittens; remember, that the cat in gloves catches no mice.

30 ≈ It is true there is much to be done, and perhaps you are weak-handed; but stick to it steadily, and you will see great effects; for constant dropping wears away stones.

Discussing the Reading

1. Can you infer anything about Benjamin Franklin's religious views from these maxims? Why or why not?

2. What did Franklin mean when he said, "At the workingman's house hunger looks in, but dares not enter"? Is this always true? Explain.

CRITICAL THINKING
Identifying Central Issues

Indicate the principal qualities or behaviors that Franklin was recommending in these maxims. Do these seem the most valuable human traits to you? If not, what qualities are more important?

"And Pattern Be to Others Yet Unborn"

TIME FRAME
Early 17th–early
19th century

GEOGRAPHIC SETTING
America (particularly
New England)

In colonial America, even very young girls of seven and eight were expected to be already skillful at a variety of kinds of sewing. Most of these were routine do-
5 mestic tasks—mending and hemming their families' clothing, for example. A more artistic and personal demonstration of a girl's needlework was the "exampler," or "sampler," in which a variety of stitches
10 were used to create decorative patterns, from simple borders and alphabets to elaborate pictures and brief verses on moral living. For example, one sampler, dating from 1654, observed:

15 In prosperity friends will be plenty
But in adversity not one in twenty

Yet another, from the late 18th century, cautioned:

While God doth spare
20 For death prepare

A slightly more upbeat note about the future was struck in the concluding lines of a verse from a 1738 sampler:

This New Year's gift your sampler may
25   adorn
And pattern be to others yet unborn

The sampler shown opposite, which dates from 1795, reads:

If I am right oh teach my heart
30 Still in the right to stay
If I am wrong thy grace impart
To find the better way

The popularity of the sampler reached its height in the 18th century, and began to
35 decline early in the 19th century.

The silk sampler on the facing page was stitched in 1788 by Slowi Hays, the 9-year-old daughter of a rich Boston merchant. The sampler above, also of silk, was done around 1795.

Discussing the Samplers

1. Most of the figures decorating the sampler shown above appear to be courting couples. (To the left in the center panel are Venus, the Roman goddess of love, and her son Cupid, who is taking aim at one of the couples.) Does such romantic imagery seem inconsistent with the character of the verse on this sampler? Explain.

2. Are the sampler verses quoted here similar to the maxims in *Poor Richard's Almanac* (Source Reading 2C)? Why or why not?

CRITICAL THINKING
Recognizing Values

What inferences can you make about the cultural values of the American society that created and treasured samplers?

Jonathan Edwards Reflects on the Great Awakening

TIME FRAME
1740–1742

GEOGRAPHIC SETTING
Massachusetts

A bulky and impressive George Whitefield preaches from the pulpit, perhaps on one of his American tours, in this early engraving. Whitefield inspired the founding of nearly fifty colleges and universities throughout the United States.

Among the most eminent theologians that America has produced, Jonathan Edwards (1703–1758) was a Congregational minister in Northampton, Massachusetts. During 1734, he began a series of revivals among the young people in his community. The influence of these local revivals was spread widely as a result of the arrival in America in 1740 of the dynamic English preacher George Whitefield (1714–1770), creating the religious movement known as the Great Awakening. (The great English actor David Garrick, himself sometimes referred to as the "Whitefield of the stage," said that the preacher's voice was so powerful in impact that Whitefield "could make men either laugh or cry by pronouncing the word *Mesopotamia*.") In a letter dated December 12, 1743, Jonathan Edwards reflected on the Great Awakening.

In the year 1740, in the spring, before Mr. Whitefield came to this town, there was a visible alteration. There was more seriousness and religious conversation, especially among young people.... And thus it continued till Mr. Whitefield came to town, which was about the middle of October following. He preached here four sermons in the meetinghouse (besides a private lecture at my house)—one on Friday, another on Saturday, and two upon the Sabbath. The congregation was extraordinarily melted by every sermon; almost the whole assembly being in tears for a great part of sermon time. Mr. Whitefield's sermons were suitable to the circumstances of the town, containing just reproofs of our backslidings, and, in a most moving and affecting manner, making use of our great profession and great mercies as arguments with us to return to God, from whom we had departed.

Immediately after this, the minds of the people in general appeared more engaged in religion, showing a greater forwardness to make religion the subject of their conversation, and to meet frequently together for religious purposes, and to embrace all opportunities to hear the Word preached. . . .

In the month of May 1741, a sermon was preached to a company at a private house. Near the conclusion of the exercise, one or two persons that were professors were so greatly affected with a sense of the greatness and glory of divine things, and the infinite importance of the things of eternity, that they were not able to conceal it; the affection of their minds overcoming their strength, and having a very visible effect on their bodies. . . . And many others at the same time were overcome with distress about their sinful and miserable state and condition; so that the whole room was full of nothing but outcries, faintings, and suchlike. . . .

But in the latter part of [the revival], in the year 1742, it was otherwise. The work continued more pure, till we were infected from abroad. Our people, hearing and some of them seeing the work in other places where there was a greater visible commotion than here, and the outward appearances were more extraordinary, were ready to think that the work in those places far excelled what was among us; and their eyes were dazzled with the high profession and great show that some made who came hither [to there] from other places.

That those people went so far beyond them in raptures and violent emotions of the affections and a vehement zeal, and what they called boldness for Christ, our people were ready to think was owing to their far greater attainments in grace and intimacy with Heaven. They looked little in their own eyes in comparison of them, and were ready to submit themselves to them, and yield themselves up to their conduct, taking it for granted that everything was right that they said and did. These things had a strange influence on the people, and gave many of them a deep and unhappy tincture, that it was a hard and long labor to deliver them from and which some of them are not fully delivered from to this day.

The effects and consequences of things among us plainly shows the following things, viz.: that the degree of grace is by no means to be judged of by the degree of joy, or the degree of zeal; and that indeed we cannot at all determine by these things who are gracious and who are not; and that it is not the degree of religious affections but the nature of them that is chiefly to be looked at. Some that have had very great raptures of joy, and have been extraordinarily filled (as the vulgar phrase is), and have had their bodies overcome, and that very often have manifested far less of the temper of Christians in their conduct since than some others that have been still and have made no great outward show.

Discussing the Reading

1. What evidence did Jonathan Edwards offer of a spiritual change in the people of Northampton in 1740?

2. What happened to these people in 1742 when they got news of the impact of the Great Awakening in other towns?

CRITICAL THINKING
Drawing Conclusions

Did Edwards see any direct relationship between interior virtue and exterior signs of religious feeling, such as weeping in a penitent mood? Why or why not?

Deganawidah Establishes the League of the Iroquois

TIME FRAME
Late 16th century

GEOGRAPHIC SETTING
Upper New York State

The Native American peoples living east of the Mississippi often organized their tribal groups into confederacies. The most powerful of these was the League of the Iroquois, which ruled over the area that is now Upper New York State. The League was initially composed of five nations — the Mohawk, Oneida, Seneca, Cayuga, and Onondaga. It was at the height of its power in the 17th and 18th centuries, successfully ending fighting among the nations composing it and giving them unity in facing their enemies. The government of the League was in the hands of a ruling council composed of 50 principal chiefs, or sachems [sā'chemz]. The sachems, who met in council each fall, were themselves selected by the female clan leaders. The League had an important influence on the development of the institutions of American government. In 1754, when Benjamin Franklin was pleading the cause of political union of the American colonies at Albany, New York, he offered the League of the Iroquois as an example of a successful confederation. Later, Thomas Jefferson is said to have studied the Iroquois government when it came time to frame the U.S. Constitution. In the following reading, the traditional founder of the Iroquois League, Deganawidah [de'gä nä wē'dä], who lived in the latter part of the 16th century, describes the principles that were to guide the Iroquois sachems in council.

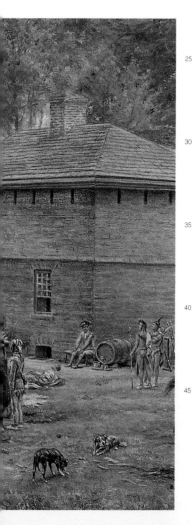

More than 150 years after Deganawidah established the League of the Iroquois, this Native American government remained a powerful unified force. Here, in the mid-1700s, a council meeting is shown conferring with Sir William Johnson, the British Superintendent of Indian Affairs in the North, in front of his estate near Schenectady, New York. Johnson married the daughter of the greatest Mohawk war chief and was so well respected that he was made a sachem. The scene was painted by E.L. Henry.

I am Deganawidah, and with the Five Nations confederate lords I plant the Tree of the Great Peace . . . I name the tree the Tree of the Great Long Leaves. Under the shade of this Tree of the Great Peace we spread the soft white feather down of the globe thistle as seats for you, Atotarho [traditional name for the premier chief of the Onondaga] and your cousin lords. There shall you sit and watch the council fire of the confederacy of the Five Nations. Roots have spread out from the Tree, and the name of these roots is the Great White Roots of Peace. If any man of any nation shall show a desire to obey the laws of the Great Peace, they shall trace the roots to their source, and they shall be welcomed to take shelter beneath the Tree of the Long Leaves. The smoke of the confederate council fire shall pierce the sky so that all nations may discover the central council fire of the Great Peace. I, Deganawidah, and the confederate lords now uproot the tallest pine tree and into the cavity thereby made we cast all weapons of war. Into the depth of the earth, down into the deep underearth currents of water flowing into unknown regions, we cast all weapons of war. We bury them from sight forever and plant again the Tree.

We do now crown you with the sacred emblem of the antlers, the sign of your lordship. You shall now become a mentor of the people of the Five Nations. The thickness of your skin will be seven spans, for you will be proof against anger, offensive action, and criticism. With endless patience you shall carry out your duty, and your firmness shall be tempered with compassion for your people. Neither anger nor fear shall find lodgment in your mind, and all your words and actions shall be tempered with calm deliberation. In all your official acts, self-interest shall be cast aside. You shall look and listen to the welfare of the whole people, and have always in view, not only the present but the coming generations — the unborn of the future Nation.

The Onondaga lords shall open each council by expressing their gratitude to their cousin lords, and greeting them, and they shall make an address and offer thanks to the earth where men dwell, to the streams of water, the pools, the springs, the lakes, to the maize and the fruits, to the medicinal herbs and the trees, to the forest trees for their usefulness, to the animals that serve as food and who offer their pelts as clothing, to the great winds and the lesser winds, to the Thunderers, and the Sun, the mighty warrior, to the moon, to the messengers of the Great Spirit who dwells in the skies above, who gives all things useful to men, who is the source and the ruler of health and life.

Then shall the Onondaga lords declare the council open.

Discussing the Reading

1. What standards of personal conduct did Deganawidah establish for the Iroquois sachems?

2. What attitudes toward the elements of the natural world were embodied in the ceremonies surrounding the Iroquois council?

CRITICAL THINKING
Distinguishing False from Accurate Images

In speaking of the institutions by which the League of the Iroquois was to be governed, Deganawidah compared them to a tree. Does this seem to be an appropriate image? Why or why not?

"If Men Were Angels, No Government Would Be Necessary"

TIME FRAME
1788

GEOGRAPHIC SETTING
New York City

In 1787 and 1788 there appeared in New York newspapers a series of 77 brilliant essays explaining and defending the new Constitution. The series was then published in two volumes as *The Federalist,* which Thomas Jefferson praised as "the best commentary on the principles of government which has ever been written." The series' three authors were Alexander Hamilton (1755–1804), John Jay (1745–1829) of New York, and James Madison (1751–1836) of Virginia. In the following excerpt from *Federalist* Number 51, Madison discusses the necessity for the system of checks and balances between the branches of the government proposed by the new Constitution.

I n order to lay a due foundation for that separate and distinct exercise of the different powers of government, which to a certain extent is admitted on all hands to

Shown at right, the title page of the first volume of *The Federalist.* Colonial printers were indispensible to the revolution and the young republic for the dissemination of news and opinion. Descendants of these opinion leaders include newspaper and broadcast journalists.

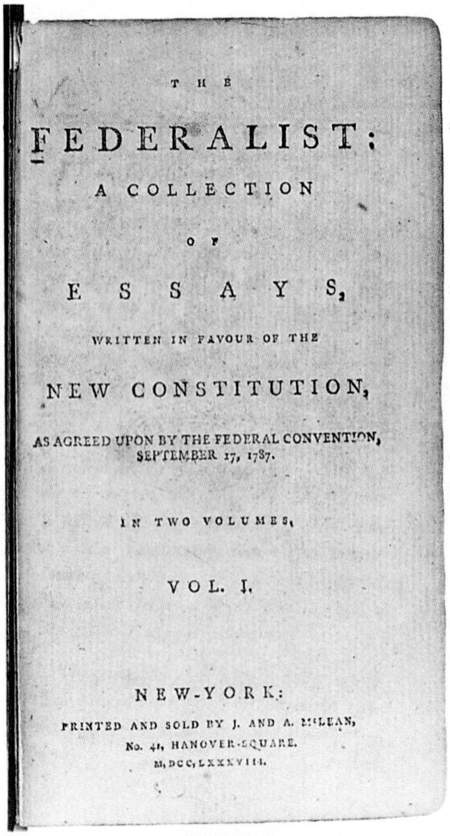

THE

FEDERALIST;

A COLLECTION

OF

E   S   S   A   Y   S,

WRITTEN IN FAVOUR OF THE

NEW CONSTITUTION,

AS AGREED UPON BY THE FEDERAL CONVENTION,
SEPTEMBER 17, 1787.

IN TWO VOLUMES,

VOL. I.

NEW-YORK:
PRINTED AND SOLD BY J. AND A. M^CLEAN,
No. 41, HANOVER-SQUARE.
M,DCC,LXXXVIII.

5 be essential to the preservation of liberty, it is evident that each department should have a will of its own; and consequently should be so constituted that the members of each should have as little agency 10 [power] as possible in the appointment of the members of the others. Were this principle rigorously adhered to [strictly followed], it would require that all the appointments for the supreme executive, 15 legislative, and judiciary magistracies [offices] should be drawn from the same foundation of authority, the people, through channels having no communication whatever with one another. Perhaps 20 such a plan of constructing the several departments would be less difficult in practice than it may in contemplation appear. Some difficulties, however, and some additional expense would attend the execu- 25 tion of it. Some deviations, therefore, from the principle must be admitted [allowed]. In the constitution of the judiciary department in particular, it might be inexpedient to insist rigorously on the principle: first, 30 because peculiar [special] qualifications being essential in the members, the primary consideration ought to be to select that mode of choice which best secures these qualifications; secondly, because 35 the permanent tenure by which the appointments are held in that department, must soon destroy all sense of dependence on the authority conferring them.

It is equally evident, that the members 40 of each department should be as little dependent as possible on those of the others, for the emoluments [salary] annexed to their offices. Were the executive magistrate, or the judges, not independent of 45 the legislature in this particular, their independence in every other would be merely nominal.

But the great security against a gradual concentration of the several powers in the same department, consists in giving to those who administer each department the necessary constitutional means and personal motives to resist encroachments of the others. The provision for defense must in this, as in all other cases, be made commensurate [equal] to the danger of attack. Ambition must be made to counteract ambition. The interest of the man must be connected with the constitutional rights of the place. It may be a reflection on human nature, that such devices should be necessary to control the abuses of government. But what is government itself, but the greatest of all reflections on human nature? If men were angels, no government would be necessary. If angels were to govern men, neither external nor internal controls on government would be necessary. In framing a government which is to be administered by men over men, the great difficulty lies in this: you must first enable the government to control the governed; and in the next place oblige it to control itself. A dependence on the people is, no doubt, the primary control on the government; but experience has taught mankind the necessity of auxiliary precautions.

This policy of supplying, by opposite and rival interests, the defect of better motives, might be traced through the whole system of human affairs, private as well as public. We see it particularly displayed in all the subordinate distributions of power, where the constant aim is to divide and arrange the several offices in such a manner as that each may be a check on the other—that the private interest of every individual may be a sentinel [guard] over the public rights. These inventions of prudence cannot be less requisite in the distribution of the supreme powers of the State.

But it is not possible to give to each department an equal power of self-defense.

In republican government, the legislative authority necessarily predominates. The remedy for this inconveniency is to divide the legislature into different branches; and to render them, by different modes of election and different principles of action, as little connected with each other as the nature of their common functions and their common dependence on the society will admit. . . .

Discussing the Reading

1. Madison argued that each branch of the government should have as little power as possible in the appointments of the members of the other branches. "Were this principle rigorously adhered to," what would be necessary in his view?

2. What special factors did Madison feel were involved in the selection of the members of the judicial branch? How do these factors affect the principle of checks and balances?

CRITICAL THINKING
Checking Consistency

Each of the following statements from *The Federalist* was written by Madison. Which of them is *not* consistent with his views here on the necessity for checks and balances in the conduct of public affairs? Defend your answer.

a. "No one is allowed to be a judge in his own cause, because his interest would certainly bias his judgment. . . . "

b. "The powers requisite for attaining [national security] must be effectually confined to the federal councils."

c. "The accumulation of all powers, legislative, executive, and judiciary, in the same hands . . . may justly be pronounced the very definition of tyranny."

Chapter Summary

Write supporting details under each of the following main ideas as you review the chapter.

Section 1

1. Problems in England encouraged colonization in America.
2. Religion prompted New England's founding.
3. The Middle Colonies welcomed diversity.
4. Plantation agriculture flourished in the Southern Colonies.

Section 2

1. An educated leadership emerged in the colonies.
2. Enlightenment ideas influenced colonial leaders.
3. The Great Awakening inspired feelings of equality.

Section 3

1. Great Britain fought France in a war for empire.
2. The British victory led to problems with the American colonists.
3. Colonists protested British taxation policies.
4. American colonists moved toward independence.

Section 4

1. Geography favored the Americans in the war.
2. The war began in the North.
3. Victory at Yorktown led to a peace treaty.

Section 5

1. Americans created new governments for the states and the nation.
2. The Confederation government led to a Constitutional Convention.
3. Compromises aided the Constitutional Convention.
4. Federalists and Anti-Federalists debated ratification.

Chapter Themes

1. **Racial, ethnic, and religious diversity:** The search for religious freedom and toleration led many Europeans to migrate to North America.
2. **Constitutional and representative government:** In the colonial period, Americans protested for their right to be represented in Parliament. After winning their independence, they struggled with creating their own constitutional government.
3. **Conflict and cooperation:** Most colonists hoped to resolve their differences with Great Britain peacefully, but the Revolutionary War broke out nonetheless. Conflicts between Native Americans and settlers also marked the colonial period.

Chapter Study Guide

Identifying Key People and Terms

Name the key person or key term that describes the:

1. Massachusetts woman banished for insisting that no minister or church was needed to assist a person in the search for salvation
2. the agreement between the people and their government that assures the protection of certain natural rights
3. writer of the Declaration of Independence
4. proponents of a constitution creating a strong national government
5. Age of Reason, a time in which revolutionary ideas swept Europe

Locating Key Places

1. Where did the Pilgrims first settle in America?
2. Where were the first shots of the American Revolution fired?
3. In which city was the Constitutional Convention held?

Mastering the Main Ideas

1. How did education of young people vary throughout the colonies?
2. Why did the British fight the French and their Indian allies from 1754 to 1763?
3. Discuss the advantages and disadvantages faced by the Americans in the War for Independence.
4. Describe the goals and compromises that led to the forging of a new constitution.

Applying Critical Thinking Skills

1. **Making comparisons:** Compare the reasons for founding the Massachusetts Bay Colony with those for founding the Carolinas.
2. **Predicting consequences:** How might the values of the Great Awakening have encouraged the belief in democracy and equality instilled in the Declaration of Independence and U.S. Constitution?

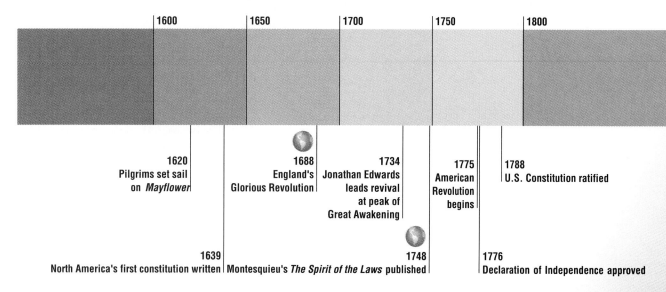

| 1600 | 1650 | 1700 | 1750 | 1800 |

1620
Pilgrims set sail on *Mayflower*

1688
England's Glorious Revolution

1734
Jonathan Edwards leads revival at peak of Great Awakening

1775
American Revolution begins

1788
U.S. Constitution ratified

1639
North America's first constitution written

1748
Montesquieu's *The Spirit of the Laws* published

1776
Declaration of Independence approved

3. Drawing conclusions: Some historians have said that the Revolutionary War was also a civil war. How might the Loyalist presence in the colonies have affected the course of the war? In what sense was the war between Americans?

4. Expressing problems: The farmers who rose up with Daniel Shays seemed ready to fight another revolution. What deeper crisis did Shays' Rebellion reveal?

Chapter Activities

Learning Geography Through History

1. Which of the 13 original states bordered on the Northwest Territory?

2. In what city were *The Federalist* essays first published?

Relating the United States to the World

1. What European nations competed with Great Britain for power in North America?

2. Why might one say that the French and Indian War was really only a part of a worldwide war?

Linking Past to Present

1. Thomas Jefferson and George Washington played key roles in the early days of the American Revolution. List ways in which Americans today have memorialized these two men. Think of specific monuments, schools, and names of states, cities, and streets.

2. Make a list of countries or territories that recently have questioned, challenged, or discarded the influence or control of the Soviet Union over their governments. How

have their struggles been similar or different from that of colonial Americans in 1776?

Using the Time Line

1. Which event on the time line has to do with religion?

2. How many years elapsed between the signing of the Declaration of Independence and the ratification of the U.S. Constitution?

Practicing Critical Thinking Strategies

Identifying Alternatives

The American Revolution was a long, violent struggle costing many lives. What alternatives might the Patriots have pursued? Do you think they should have tried other courses besides violence? Support your response with evidence from your text or research.

Learning More About the Enlightenment and the Revolutionary Era

1. Using Source Readings: Read the Source Readings for this chapter and answer the questions.

2. Analyzing Literature: The quest for independence inspired many writers of the time to express with eloquence the values that still define America. Read excerpts from the following works, or from others that you may find in your library, and write an essay in which you analyze the author's theme and purpose. What images and symbols does the author use? Begin with these sources: Paine, Thomas. *Common Sense*, Penguin American Library, New York, 1982. Washington, George. *The Diaries of George Washington*, University Press of Virginia, Charlottesville, VA, 1979.

Linking Past to Present

A million visitors a year view the nation's three most valuable documents at the National Archives in Washington, D.C.: the Declaration of Independence in the upper case and the Constitution and Bill of Rights below. In a painting in the Capitol, inset, by Howard Chandler Christy (1873–1919), George Washington presides over the signing of the Constitution.

Examining the Constitution

1 7 8 7 – 1 8 2 4

3

Great celebrations greeted the ratification of the Constitution. The "Federal Procession" in New York became an all-day parade. The party in Philadelphia attracted fully half the city, and the citizens proved to be as hungry as they were happy: they consumed 4,000 pounds of beef and 2,500 pounds of lamb. With full hearts and stomachs they rejoiced with doctor and patriot Benjamin Rush, "Tis done! We have become a nation!"

When Dr. Rush spoke, that nation clung to a single coastline and communicated at the speed of a trotting horse. Today the United States stretches beyond a continent and communicates at nearly the speed of light. For all its vastness and complexity, the United States remains governed by a system outlined in 1787 on four handwritten sheets of parchment. The durability of the Constitution is unmatched in history, but that is only one of its wonders. The first marvel is that the Constitution exists at all. A diverse people mutually recognized the weakness of their government and proceeded—without armies and blood, but with committees and ink—to quietly reinvent themselves as a nation. In that "invention," how did the framers balance the powers of state and national government? How did they balance the rights of individuals against the needs of society? How did they balance the needs of their own day against the unknown requirements of the future?

CHAPTER PREVIEW

In this chapter you will learn how government functions under the Constitution.

SECTIONS IN THIS CHAPTER:
1. **The framers created a federal system.**
2. **The framers balanced the roles of government.**
3. **The Constitution permits change.**
4. **The Federalists yielded to the Republicans.**
5. **War shaped a new American nationalism.**

NOTE: The complete Constitution is printed at the end of this chapter on pages 132–161, along with a section-by-section paraphrase.

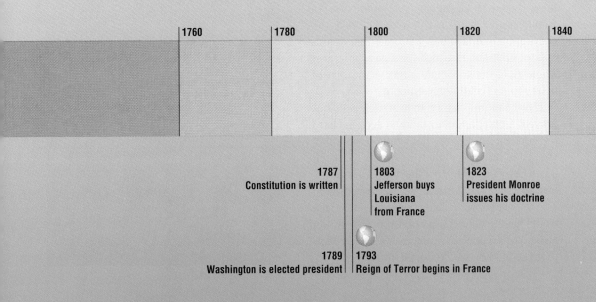

| 1760 | 1780 | 1800 | 1820 | 1840 |

1787
Constitution is written

1803
Jefferson buys Louisiana from France

1823
President Monroe issues his doctrine

1789
Washington is elected president

1793
Reign of Terror begins in France

SECTION **1**

The framers created a federal system.

Key Terms: federalism, supremacy clause, reserved powers, concurrent powers

Reading Preview
As you read this section, you will learn:

1. how the concept of federalism was created.
2. how federalism defined the roles of state and national governments.
3. what the economic impact of the Constitution was.

chart study

Under the federal system, powers are constitutionally divided and shared by the national government and the governments of the various states, as shown on the chart at right. What powers are shared concurrently by both the national and state governments?
Critical Thinking
Where do both national and state governments receive their power?

In describing the result of the Constitutional Convention, one delegate described the proposed government as "partly national, partly federal." His words have the careful tone of compromise. The Constitution itself is equally careful. The words *national* and *federal* never appear. In their place, the framers prudently used the expression *the United States*. Why?

Compromise created federalism.

Men such as James Madison and Alexander Hamilton came to Philadelphia envisioning a single efficient national government. States, if they existed at all, might have some use as administrative districts. However, others at the convention intended only a more effective federal government, in which the sovereign states would dole out a slightly larger allowance of power to the central government.

There was no chance that a "new and improved" Confederation would be acceptable to the convention. It was equally impossible that the states would volunteer to vanish. Between those two impossibilities the framers found a possible solution. A strong central government would coexist with state governments. Each would have separate areas of responsibility, but some of their powers would overlap. This compromise is known as **federalism**.

GOVERNMENT POWERS IN THE FEDERAL SYSTEM

Powers Delegated to the National Government

• Coin money
• Regulate interstate and foreign trade
• Conduct relations with foreign countries
• Establish post offices
• Govern territories and admit new states
• Grant patents and copyrights
• Maintain the armed forces
• Declare war and make peace
• Establish immigration and naturalization laws
• Fix standards of weights and measures
• Make all laws necessary and proper for carrying out the delegated powers

Powers Denied to the National Government

• Tax articles exported by the states
• Give preference to the trade of one state over another

Powers Reserved to the State Governments

• Provide for local governments
• Conduct elections
• Make laws about contracts, wills, and domestic relations
• Provide for and supervise schools
• Regulate commerce within the states
• Ratify constitutional amendments
• Assume power not granted to the United States nor prohibited to the states

Powers Denied to the State Governments

• Negotiate or sign separate treaties with other nations
• Coin money
• Impair the obligation of contracts
• Tax imports or exports without the consent of Congress
• Maintain troops or warships without the consent of Congress

Powers Shared by the National and State Governments Concurrently

• Tax
• Borrow money
• Charter banks
• Pass bankruptcy laws
• Establish courts
• Build roads
• Promote agriculture, industry, and science
• Protect the health, safety, and morals of the people
• Take property for public purposes
• Pay debts

The Constitution created the self-sufficient central government the nation needed. It also provided the assurances that the states required. The existence of the states and their laws were guaranteed, and each state would be treated equally under the law.

Federalism balanced national needs and states' rights.

The delegates at Philadelphia made sure that their new national government avoided the weaknesses of the old Confederation system. The national government was empowered to tax, to borrow and coin money, to regulate interstate and foreign trade, and to maintain an army and a navy. The ultimate authority of the national government was boldly expressed in the **supremacy clause** of Article VI: the Constitution and national laws and treaties are "the supreme law of the land."

In an age when communication was slow and travel was hazardous, the national government would be remote from most Americans. It was therefore natural for the "local" governments—the states—to keep their responsibilities for matters affecting the daily lives of citizens. Under the Constitution, states retained their powers to provide for the health, welfare, safety, and morals of those who lived within their borders. State governments supervised matters of education, marriage, divorce, inheritance, elections, and aspects of criminal law.

If the national government had the supremacy clause, the state governments also had a powerful constitutional support, the concept of **reserved powers**. The delegates at the convention clearly understood that any right or power not specifically assigned or denied by the Constitution was reserved to the states or the people. The Tenth Amendment later officially confirmed this doctrine of reserved powers.

Governments at any level have certain basic needs; money usually heads the list. The framers gave the states and the national government certain **concurrent powers**, or powers that they each exercise. Both the states and the national government have the power to tax and to borrow money, to establish courts and charter banks, to build roads and enforce laws.

VOICES FROM THE PAST

Revising the Preamble

The clarity and power of the Constitution's language is credited to Gouverneur Morris of Pennsylvania. In writing the final draft, Morris condensed 23 articles into seven and, more importantly, revised the preamble. What important change do you find in the first seven words?

First Draft

We the People of the States of New Hampshire, Massachusetts, Rhode Island and the Providence Plantations, Connecticut, New Jersey, Pennsylvania, Delaware, Maryland, Virginia, North Carolina, South Carolina, and Georgia, do ordain, declare and establish the following Constitution for the government of ourselves and our posterity.

Final Version

We the People of the United States, in Order to form a more perfect Union, establish Justice, insure domestic Tranquility, provide for the common defence, promote the general Welfare, and secure the Blessings of Liberty to ourselves and our Posterity, do ordain and establish this Constitution for the United States of America.

The chart on page 96 shows how the powers of national and state governments often overlap.

Disagreements about the powers of national government and the rights of states have been frequent, at times dangerous, and once—in the Civil War—disastrous. From minimum wages to maximum speed limits, the national government now plays a larger role in daily life than the framers ever imagined. The balance of federalism still holds, however. The complicated compromise continues into a third century.

Constitutional government released the nation's economic energies.

Shays' Rebellion in 1786 demonstrated to many Americans the urgent need for sound, strong government. In 1794 another uprising,

To raise money to pay its debts, the national government placed a high tax on whiskey in 1791. The whiskey tax imposed a heavy burden on backwoods farmers, who usually distilled their grain into whiskey because it was easy to ship to market. In the summer of 1794, the farmers of western Pennsylvania rioted to protest this use of governmental power. President George Washington raised against them a larger force than he had led against Cornwallis at Yorktown. The president is shown reviewing the troops at Fort Cumberland, Maryland, in this painting by James Peale (1749–1831).

this time in western Pennsylvania, gave the new national government a chance to flex its muscle. A militia army of 13,000 was raised against the so-called Whiskey Rebellion, and President Washington himself briefly joined their march. The contrast between this vigorous action and the feeble days of Confederation could not have been more obvious.

The effectiveness of the new government extended beyond military and political strength. Several provisions of the Constitution contributed to a revitalized economy. Alexander Hamilton's daring economic program took advantage of congressional powers to levy taxes, pay debts, and borrow money. The national government took responsibility for the outstanding wartime debts of the Confederation and the states. These actions soon firmly established the credit of the United States.

The Constitution prevented states from interfering with interstate trade; the national government was prohibited from taxing articles exported from the states. The national government created a standard system of currency and a uniform system of weights and measures; it also ensured that "the privileges and immunities of citizens" would be honored throughout all the states. Taken together, these provisions helped create a large common market for goods to be freely traded.

A free market and a sound economic environment brought prosperity to many. The Constitution's safeguards of private property protected that prosperity. Americans who grew rich through farming or trade could confidently invest their wealth in the United States. In the words of 20th-century chief justice Warren Burger,

This freedom created by the Constitution unleashed the **AN AMERICAN ★ SPEAKS** energies, abilities, and talents of every individual to develop as the individual's own ambitions . . . and industry allowed.

Samuel Slater was one young man "unleashed" by America's economic opportunities. He arrived in the United States the very year that the new federal government began operation—1789. Slater had little in his pocket, but a great deal in his head. He wrote his future partner, Moses Brown:

I was informed that you wanted a manager of cotton **AN AMERICAN ★ SPEAKS** spinning, etc. . . . I can give the greatest satisfaction, in making machinery, making good yarn, as any that is made in England.

In **Pawtucket, Rhode Island**, Slater quickly determined that the primitive American cotton machinery was virtually useless. England had a much more advanced cotton industry but carefully guarded its position by prohibiting the exportation of its machinery or the emigration of textile workers. Slater himself had left the country in disguise.

Brown challenged Slater to make new machinery. Imagine that a worker at a lawnmower factory agrees to build all the machinery needed to make lawnmowers. A similar challenge faced Slater in 1790. He was 21 years old. With the aid of Oziel Wilkinson, a skilled blacksmith (and his future father-in-law), Slater tried to recreate—without a single note or diagram—the intricate water-powered textile machines he had known in his youth.

> If I don't make as good yarn as they do in England, I will have nothing for my services, but will throw the whole of what I attempted over the bridge.

With time, tinkering, and his incredible memory, Slater produced machinery that worked. By December 1790 his automatic machinery was producing quality yarns—but at some personal cost. Slater spent hours each winter morning breaking the water wheel free

of ice. These frigid soakings would permanently affect his health.

Twenty years later, more than 160 cotton mills were clattering away in Rhode Island, Massachusetts, and Connecticut. Slater owned seven, on his way to becoming an early American millionaire. Slater's success was not merely personal, however; the ripples of his achievement touched many lives. The cost of cotton cloth was dramatically reduced. Several of his employees went on to found their own mills. Slater built schools for his workers and enlarged his investment in America by starting a bank and a textile machine factory, and by promoting several turnpikes.

SECTION 1 REVIEW

Identify Key People and Terms
Write a sentence to identify: federalism, supremacy clause, reserved powers, concurrent powers

Locate Key Places
Where did Samuel Slater create his first water-powered textile machines?

Master the Main Ideas

1. **Valuing compromise as a democratic process:** Describe how the framers made a compromise between a national and a local system of government.
2. **Understanding the development of the federal government:** Give two examples of concurrent powers held by the national and the state governments.
3. **Understanding the economic development of the United States:** What provisions in the Constitution helped promote free trade within the United States?

Apply Critical Thinking Skills: Predicting Consequences
As mentioned, the national government has developed a far stronger role in the lives of citizens than most framers probably intended. What if the nation decided to drop the complications of federalism altogether and gave all the governmental roles to the central government? List three specific ways your own life would be affected by such a change.

Men, women, and children worked in the New England cotton mills. Samuel Slater, founder of the American cotton industry, employed mostly children in his first factory because they were agile and their small hands could tend the machines easily. This lithograph of a textile factory was published in the early 19th century.

The framers balanced the roles of government.

Key terms: separation of powers, balance of powers, checks and balances, veto, bill of impeachment

Reading Preview
As you read this section, you will learn:

1. how many branches of government were created by the Constitution.
2. what the role of Congress is.
3. what the role of the president is.
4. what the role of the courts is.
5. how the Constitution protects diversity.

As they planned their national government, the framers were not writing on a blank page of history. Decades before, the French political philosopher Montesquieu had analyzed the English political system and identified three basic governmental powers: legislative, executive, and judicial. To protect liberty and prevent tyranny, Montesquieu believed that those powers should be separated and balanced among different departments or individuals.

Montesquieu's ideas were a powerful influence at the Philadelphia convention. The framers' challenge was to translate those ideas from the bookish realm of theory into the tumult of the real world.

The framers developed three interactive branches of government.

The framers readily adopted the principle of **separation of powers**. Each function of government was distributed to a separate branch of government. Congress makes the laws. The president, or chief executive, carries out those laws. The judiciary, or court system, interprets and applies the laws.

To ensure a **balance of powers** among the branches, the framers devised a system of **checks and balances**. Each branch of government is subject to checks or restraints by the other two branches. The branches of government must interact with and depend on one another to do their work.

Congress makes the laws.

Article I of the Constitution assigns to Congress the power to make the laws of the nation. It can do so only through a series of interactions. The first interaction is internal. Congress consists of two houses, each slightly different in character. For example, the Senate represents each state equally, and senators serve six-year terms. In the House of Representatives, states are represented by population, and its members serve two-year terms. A bill must be approved in both the House and the Senate before it is sent to the president.

The president interacts with Congress by signing the bill into law but also has the power to reject, or **veto**, a bill. Congress may override this veto, but a two-thirds vote of both houses is necessary. The president has power to call special sessions of Congress and possesses informal but significant powers of persuasion. Presidents have proven skilled at using public opinion and private conferences with members of Congress to influence and control the progress of legislation.

The Supreme Court has developed its own interaction with Congress. The Court can check the lawmaking power of Congress by ruling on the constitutionality of a law. If the Court finds an act unconstitutional, the law becomes invalid.

The president administers the laws.

Article II of the Constitution gives the president the power to administer, or carry out, the laws. Most of the framers at Philadelphia had a deep-seated fear of monarchy, and they took care to provide significant restraints against the abuse of executive power.

Congress may remove the president if the chief executive is found guilty of misusing power. This powerful restraint requires another internal interaction. The House must vote a bill of **impeachment**, a formal list of charges. The Senate then conducts the trial of the president. Andrew Johnson is the only president ever im-

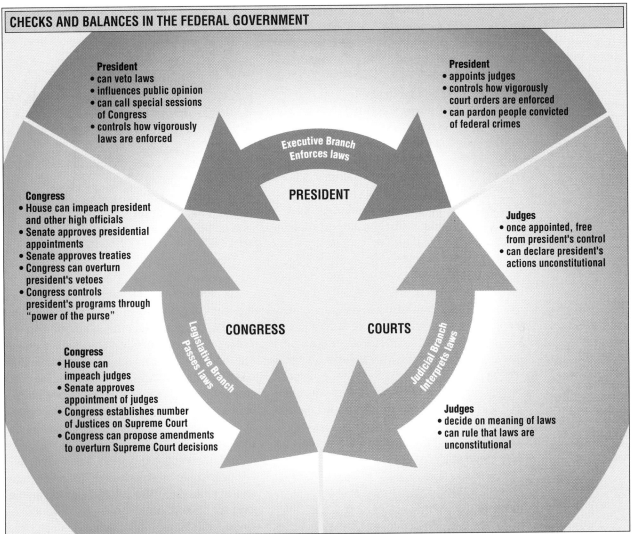

peached by the House. In 1868 the Senate found him not guilty by a single vote.

Other restraints on the president are less dramatic but more frequently used. The Senate has approval power over treaties the president makes with foreign governments and over the president's appointments to government posts and federal judgeships. With a two-thirds vote, as noted earlier, Congress can override a president's veto.

Over the years the presidency has developed powers of independent action far beyond the dreams (or nightmares) of the framers. One constitutional restraint, however, has remained particularly effective. Bold presidential actions cost money. Congress controls taxation and government spending. This "power of the purse" has frequently compelled even the most independent-minded presidents to seek congressional agreement.

The courts interpret the laws.

Article III of the Constitution gives the judiciary power to interpret the laws of the nation. Once appointed, federal judges are free to serve for life "during good behavior." The framers intended to keep judges free of presidential control, but several important checks on judicial power remain.

Congress has the power to impeach and remove judges, and has done so several times. It can also control the number of judges on the

chart study

How does the Constitution permit the judiciary to exercise control over Congress? **Critical Thinking** How does the system of checks and balances operate to resolve disagreements between the branches?

The Republican Congress is pictured as a domineering housewife and President Truman as the henpecked husband in this 1947 cartoon by Jacob Burck, right. Ohio Senator Robert A. Taft is the new maid. Congress had just passed the Taft-Hartley Act over Truman's veto.

Four judges preside over the York, Pennsylvania, courtroom pictured in this 1801 watercolor. The accused person was convicted and whipped for stealing a horse.

Supreme Court. (Though now fixed at nine members, the Court has had as few as five justices and as many as ten.) By proposing constitutional amendments for state ratification, Congress can seek to negate Supreme Court decisions it finds unfavorable. That process has succeeded four times. The 11th, 14th, 16th, and 26th Amendments have overturned decisions of the Supreme Court.

As many presidents have discovered to their regret, they cannot control a judge's actions after appointment. That power of appointment, however, has an important influence on the judiciary. By filling judicial vacancies with men and women who share the president's viewpoint, the chief executive can gradually change the character of the Supreme Court and the federal court system. The president's power to pardon people convicted of federal crimes is another restraint on the courts. A less formal but real power is the president's control over the effective enforcement of a Supreme Court decision. Andrew Jackson starkly demonstrated this power when he ignored a decision by Chief Justice John Marshall favoring Indians in Georgia. Jackson reportedly remarked, "John Marshall has made his opinion; now let him enforce it."

"NEVER MIND WHAT HE SAYS—YOU'RE HIRED!"

An illustration of the interplay of all three branches of government occurred in the 20th century during the Truman Administration. In 1947, concerned that labor unions were growing too powerful, Congress passed a bill that enabled the government to delay, and in some cases prevent, labor strikes by unions. President Truman strongly disagreed with Congress and vetoed the bill. Congress responded by passing the Taft-Hartley Act over his veto.

In 1952, during the Korean War, a crisis developed in the steel industry. The steel companies refused to grant pay hikes or to bargain with the unions. The workers went on strike. Under Taft-Hartley provisions, Truman was empowered to make the workers return to work. Demonstrating the presidential power to choose his action, Truman ignored Taft-Hartley and instead issued an executive order placing the steel companies under the control of the government. Here the Supreme Court played its restraining role. The Court declared that Truman's seizure of the steel mills was an unconstitutional use of his powers.

A balanced system protects American diversity.

The separation of powers, with its built-in system of checks and balances, was created to protect Americans against governmental tyranny. The people who drafted the Constitution also had another goal. They wanted to make

the nation's government a safe and level field of competition for opposing interests and viewpoints. The framers recognized that it was the nature of human beings to differ and to compete. As James Madison noted in *The Federalist* Essay Number Ten, society includes rich and poor, debtors and creditors, people in commerce and in agriculture, citizens with one religious belief or another. Their interests are often in direct conflict. How should government cope with the problem of "factions"?

Madison dismissed two possible responses:

AN AMERICAN
★ SPEAKS

There are again two methods of removing the causes of faction: the one, by destroying the liberty which is essential to its existence; the other, by giving to every citizen the same opinions, the same passions, and the same interests.

It could never be more truly said than of the first remedy that it was worse than the disease. . . . The second expedient is as impracticable as the first would be unwise. As long as the reason of man continues fallible, and he is at liberty to exercise it, different opinions will be formed.

The framers in Philadelphia avoided the twin tyrannies of oppression and uniformity. They had the courage to design a government that allows differing ideas and interests to exist and to compete under the rule of law. They relied on the separation of powers and the dynamic tensions of checks and balances to prevent a single person or a single interest group from dominating government for selfish purposes.

Consider the difficulties of winning full control of the U.S. government. A would-be dictator and his or her political party would have to win the presidency and win majorities in both houses of Congress. Laboriously, vacancy by vacancy, they might gain control of the Supreme Court—but all the while, every two years, citizens would have the opportunity of electing new representatives and senators. Every four years citizens might elect a new president; after eight years they must do so. Such a scenario highlights the vital role that the different lengths of office play in the system of checks and balances.

Should the federal government be dominated by a single interest group, there is yet another balancing force—the independent

Suffrage had not broadened to include women or African Americans when George Caleb Bingham painted *The County Election* in 1851–1852. Missouri politics was the hobby of Bingham (1811–1879), a noted American portrait and genre painter. (Genre paintings show scenes of everyday life.) Bingham was a state legislator when he painted this.

103

governors and legislatures of the states. Federalism itself is an essential ingredient in the American system of checks and balances.

The protections the Constitution offers against the tyranny of a minority and the tyranny of a majority do not contribute to the simplicity, speed, or efficiency of government operation. The framers who created this system, however, believed that efficiency was less important than safeguarding liberty. More than two hundred years of American history argue that they were right.

SECTION 2 REVIEW

Identify Key People and Terms
Write a sentence to identify: separation of powers, balance of powers, checks and balances, veto, impeachment

Master the Main Ideas

1. **Understanding the principles that underlie the Constitution:** What did the framers recognize as the three major functions of government?
2. **Understanding the development of the three branches of government:** Name two ways in which congressional power is checked by other branches of government.
3. **Understanding the development of the three branches of government:** What actions of the president must be approved by the Senate?
4. **Understanding the development of the three branches of government:** Explain how the courts interpret the laws.
5. **Understanding the principles that underlie the Constitution:** Explain how the separation of power and the system of checks and balances help protect citizens against tyranny.

Apply Critical Thinking Skills: Identifying Alternatives
Do you think the present balance between the three branches of government is effective? Is the president too powerful? Is the Supreme Court too independent? Is Congress too inefficient? What new check would strengthen the balance of powers? Write your suggestion in the form of a proposed amendment to the Constitution.

The Constitution permits change.

Key Terms: elastic clause, unwritten constitution, civil liberties, bill of attainder, *ex post facto* laws, writ of habeas corpus, Bill of Rights, due process of law

Reading Preview
As you read this section, you will learn:

1. how the wording of the Constitution helps make it flexible.
2. how the Constitution can be changed.
3. what liberties the Constitution protects.
4. what additions to the Constitution Americans demanded.
5. how the Constitution protects the rights of minority Americans.

Although the delegates in Philadelphia aimed for "a more perfect Union," they did not imagine their Constitution was perfect. Even as the ink was drying, some framers realized that the omission of a bill of rights was a huge mistake. Other shortcomings would soon appear. The framers did not foresee the development of political parties that would make their original system of presidential election unworkable. Bitter political opponents are not ideal partners as president and vice president, and the system would be revised within 15 years.

Some of the compromises embedded in the Constitution failed to hold. Unresolved issues regarding states' rights and slavery, for example, were to be settled only by a civil war. Despite flaws and failures of anticipation, however, the Constitution met the needs of the nation in the late 18th century—and in the 19th and 20th centuries. It is the oldest, still-functioning written constitution. The secret of the Constitution's vitality is not that the delegates in Philadelphia were smart enough to decide the future, but that they were wise enough to let the future make its own decisions.

The language of the Constitution permits interpretation.

Part of the Constitution's flexibility is derived from its style of language. The Constitution is a short, terse document with little room for detailed explanations, definitions, and lists. The framers expressed many of their intentions in broad statements that require interpretation rather than simple obedience. For example, in Article I Congress is given power "to regulate commerce." The framers deliberately did not define "commerce" or "regulate," giving Congress the ability to adjust as business has moved from the age of oxcarts and quill pens to an age of jet aircraft and laser printers.

The Supreme Court has been called a "constitutional convention in continuous session" because it frequently makes judgments about the meaning of the Constitution as it decides cases. For example, in the 1896 case *Plessy* v. *Ferguson*, the Supreme Court ruled that separate public facilities (such as schools, restaurants, and parks) for black Americans were legal so long as the facilities were equal to those provided for white citizens. In 1954 a different Supreme Court reversed this decision. In *Brown* v. *Board of Education of Topeka*, the Court found the separate-but-equal doctrine unconstitutional in regard to public schools. Court cases have traditionally been a way of redefining constitutional liberties.

Beyond the flexibility of its language, the Constitution created a specific means for Congress to respond to changing circumstances. The final clause of Section 8, Article I is known as the **elastic clause**. It empowers Congress

> *To make all laws which shall be necessary and proper for carrying into execution the foregoing powers, and all other powers vested by this Constitution in the government of the United States, or in any department or officer thereof.*

With three simple words, "necessary and proper," the framers saved a sea of ink and a perpetual series of amendments. Over the years, Congress has employed this elastic clause widely. In the 20th century, for example, laws governing the working conditions of em-

ployees have been judged "necessary and proper" to the regulation of interstate trade. There are few challenges to the wisdom of having the elastic clause, but there has been much debate over who should determine if a law is "necessary and proper." The Constitution is silent on the matter.

John Marshall, the forceful and brilliant chief justice of the Supreme Court between 1801 and 1835, claimed the power of the Court to rule on the application of the elastic clause. He also interpreted the clause to give Congress wide scope for action. In *McCulloch* v. *Maryland* (1819), Marshall stated

Let the end be legitimate, let it be within the scope of the **AN AMERICAN ★ SPEAKS** Constitution, and all means which are appropriate, which are plainly adapted to that end, which are not prohibited, but consist [agree] with the letter and spirit of the Constitution are constitutional.

Marshall's firmness did not end the debate, of course, and his reference to "letter and spirit" highlights a point of contention. Some Americans continue to emphasize the letter of the Constitution, insisting that interpretation closely follow the literal wording of the document and the original intent of the framers. Other Americans choose to emphasize the spirit of the Constitution, seeking a looser,

Individual courage made public school desegregation a reality. Within ten years after the 1954 Supreme Court ruling that held racial segregation must end, all public schools had accomplished desegregation. Ignoring racial slurs and rotten vegetables, U.S. marshals escort a youngster to school in this 1964 *Look* magazine picture celebrating that achievement. The artist was Norman Rockwell (1894–1978), one of the most popular 20th-century painters.

The 26th Amendment, the latest amendment to the Constitution, gave more than ten million people between the ages of eighteen and twenty-one the right to vote. These eighteen-year-olds were being registered in 1971. The Vietnam War had intensified support for the amendment because members of this age group were serving in the armed forces.

broader understanding that goes beyond the actual wording of the document.

What is beyond debate is the effectiveness of the elastic clause. Congress has functioned across two centuries of dynamic change with the aid of only 26 changes—the amendments, two of which cancel each other out.

The Constitution may be changed by amendment and tradition.

The clearest expression of the Constitution's openness to change is found in its amendment process. The framers provided two methods of proposing change and two methods of ratification, shown in the chart below. A national

convention has never been called to propose an amendment, and the state convention method of ratification has been used only once, to ratify Amendment 21, the repeal of Prohibition. As the framers intended, no combination of methods in the amending process is swift or easy.

The Constitution was designed to be completed by experience. Over the years, a considerable body of traditions and procedures has arisen that is essential to modern government but that is not even mentioned in the Constitution. These traditions and procedures form part of an **unwritten constitution**.

The Constitution makes no provision for political parties. Many framers hoped that such "factions" would not mar the lofty deliberations of government, but the give and take of party politics began almost immediately—possibly as soon as Alexander Hamilton and Thomas Jefferson entered the same room. The competition of political parties has become essential to the operation of modern government.

chart study

What are the two methods of proposing constitutional amendments? What are the two methods of ratification?
Critical Thinking Why have Congress and the states probably never called a national constitutional convention?

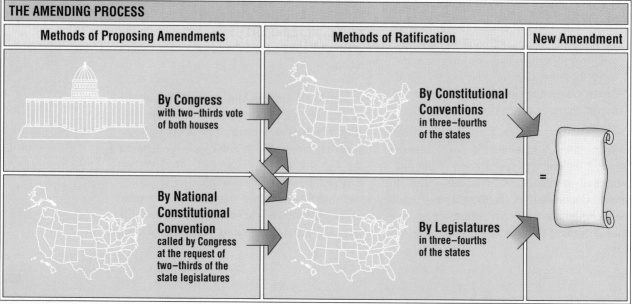

THE AMENDING PROCESS

Methods of Proposing Amendments	Methods of Ratification	New Amendment
By Congress with two-thirds vote of both houses	**By Constitutional Conventions** in three-fourths of the states	
By National Constitutional Convention called by Congress at the request of two-thirds of the state legislatures	**By Legislatures** in three-fourths of the states	

The unwritten constitution is not a monument to things the framers forgot or never imagined. Rather, it is a reminder that the framers created a living Constitution, a system capable of growing and changing according to need. The genius of the delegates in Philadelphia was not that they predicted the future but that they recognized the certainty of change.

The Constitution protects civil liberties.

Civil liberties are basic rights guaranteed by laws or by a constitution. They cannot easily be tampered with by a particular leader or government. Americans usually associate civil liberties with the Bill of Rights, but the body of the Constitution itself contains powerful safeguards against tyranny. It is perhaps because

of their very effectiveness that these protections are sometimes taken for granted.

Section 9 of Article I forbids Congress from passing bills of attainder and *ex post facto* laws. A **bill of attainder** is a law designed to punish a specific person or group without the bother of a trial. Attempts to pass bills of attainder have been rare in American history. One case occurred during World War II when Congress passed a provision that withheld the salaries to three government workers suspected of being "un-American." The Supreme Court later voided this provision as a bill of attainder.

Ex post facto is a Latin expression meaning "after the deed." An ***ex post facto law*** prescribes punishment for an action that took place before the law was passed. Such a law might punish a person's actions on Monday with a law passed on Tuesday, or increase the penalty for a crime already committed.

Section 9 also protects the ancient right of habeas corpus, which makes it impossible for a government to arrest and imprison people without stating the charges against them. If a citizen is arrested but not charged, he or she can demand a **writ of habeas corpus**; the government is then required to "produce the body" of the person being held as well as evidence of wrongdoing. The prisoner is released if the evidence is insufficient.

The right to a writ of habeas corpus is a powerful protection against a government's efforts to suppress dissent or criticism. The president can suspend the right of habeas corpus only in the most extreme cases of rebellion or invasion, and only with legal authorization from Congress.

During the Civil War, Abraham Lincoln became the first president to suspend the writ of habeas corpus. He did so at first in limited areas for military reasons but without authorization from Congress, which was not in session. Later, with the assent of Congress, he suspended the writ nationwide. Scholars are still debating the legality of these actions.

In Article VI the framers made a brief but powerful assertion of religious freedom. In the summer of 1787, Jonas Phillips, who described himself as "being one of the people called Jews

The elephant, left, the popular symbol of the Republican party, came from the pen of political cartoonist Thomas Nast (1840–1902) in the 1870s. The donkey was first used as the Democratic party symbol during Jackson's Administration, but Nast did much to popularize this symbol as well.

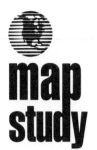

map study

Regions Compare slave populations among the states. Which state had the most slaves?

Critical Thinking Why did the Three-fifths Compromise on representation (five slaves equal three persons) appeal to the northern states?

of the City of Philadelphia, a people scattered and dispersed among all nations," wrote to the delegates at the Constitutional Convention. He reminded them that under the Pennsylvania Constitution anyone holding public office had to swear to his belief in God and acknowledge the Old and New Testaments to be divinely inspired. Phillips urged the delegates not to require an oath that the New Testament was divinely inspired. The delegates did better than that. They banned the use of any religious test as a qualification for public office.

Americans demanded a Bill of Rights.

The Constitution did not provide a list of guaranteed freedoms. Some delegates at the Convention objected to this lack, and during the ratification process, many insisted that the Constitution include a bill of rights, that is, a guarantee of the political, economic, religious, and civil rights that belong to the people.

Thomas Jefferson, on government business in Paris, wrote, "a bill of rights is what the people are entitled to . . . and what no just government should refuse." Amending the Constitution became an early task of the new Congress, and ratification of the first ten amendments, the **Bill of Rights**, occurred in just over two years. (See pages 152–161 for the Bill of Rights with an amendment-by-amendment paraphrase.)

Many of the rights preserved by the first ten amendments have their roots in the Magna Carta of 1215 and in the principles established as the "rights of Englishmen" during the 1600s. For example, the First Amendment grants to Americans freedom of religion, speech, the press, peaceable assembly, and petition.

The Bill of Rights devotes much of its attention to the **due process of law**. This includes the right of a citizen to know what crime he or she is charged with and the right to answer those charges before a jury. The Eighth

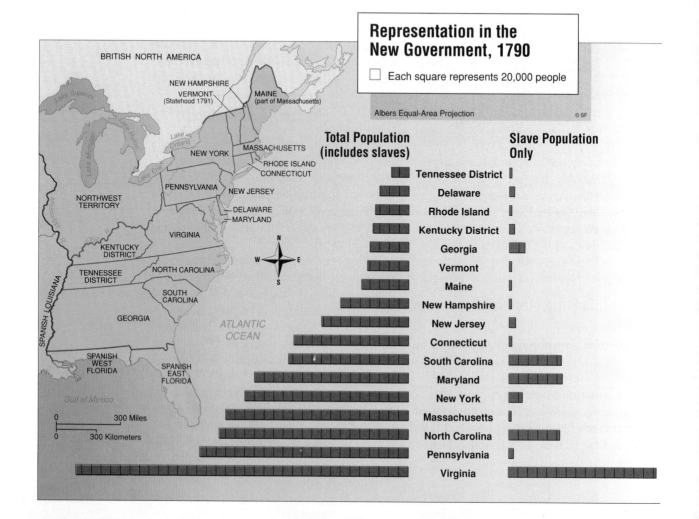

Representation in the New Government, 1790

☐ Each square represents 20,000 people

Albers Equal-Area Projection

Total Population (includes slaves) / **Slave Population Only**

Tennessee District
Delaware
Rhode Island
Kentucky District
Georgia
Vermont
Maine
New Hampshire
New Jersey
Connecticut
South Carolina
Maryland
New York
Massachusetts
North Carolina
Pennsylvania
Virginia

Amendment, for example, ensures a reasonable bail and protection from cruel and unusual punishments.

The writers of the Constitution realized that personal rights must be balanced against the rights of others and against the legitimate needs of society. The Constitution does not protect the right to persuade other people to overthrow the government by force, for example. In times of national crisis, certain rights, such as habeas corpus, can be suspended temporarily. However, the suspension of any right has always been highly controversial in the United States. For example, many Americans disagreed that the military emergencies of the Civil War were sufficient reasons to suspend habeas corpus.

Determining when a limit on civil liberties is proper is usually the responsibility of the judicial branch. In protecting and clarifying individual rights, the courts have also expanded the scope of those rights.

The rights of minorities and women were poorly protected.

As Supreme Court Justice Thurgood Marshall reminded Americans during the bicentennial of the Constitution, when the framers used the phrase "We the People," they did not have in mind the majority of America's citizens. "On a matter so basic as the right to vote, for example," Marshall noted, "Negro slaves were excluded, although they were counted for representational purposes—at three-fifths each. Women did not gain the right to vote for over a hundred and thirty years." Among those also neglected in 1787 were Indians and white men without property.

Slavery.   Patriots cried out against a king who threatened to reduce them to slavery, yet many Americans were slaveholders themselves. "How is it," mocked British writer Samuel Johnson, "that we hear the loudest yelps for liberty from the drivers of negroes?"

Simple self-interest was not the only reason that slaveholders hesitated to end slavery. Thomas Jefferson, for instance, agreed that slavery was morally wrong: "I tremble for my country when I reflect that God is just." Yet this great visionary thinker, himself a slaveholder, could imagine no alternative to slavery in the new nation. What role, Jefferson asked, would the tens of thousands of African Americans play in the United States if they were free? Surely, he wrote, former slaves could never be American citizens. In these views, Jefferson revealed himself as a man of his times.

The Constitution did not challenge slavery, it tiptoed around it. The actual words "slave" and "slavery" do not appear; "other persons" and "such persons" are the code-word substitutes. Many of the framers undoubtedly hoped that the institution would gradually disappear through state action. The actual effect of the Three-fifths Compromise and the extension of the slave trade, however, was to give a solid legal basis for the existence of slavery.

Indian rights.   The Constitution granted Congress the power "to regulate commerce . . . with the Indian Tribes." This single reference to Indians expressed a federal intention to treat Indian tribes as sovereign nations. Over the next eight decades, the relation between the government and the Indian tribes would produce 389 treaties. Congress constantly promised that Indian lands would not be taken without consent except in "lawful war."

Chiefs of five Plains Indian tribes and U.S. officials met in 1867 at Medicine Lodge, Kansas, a site regarded as sacred by the Indians. The treaty negotiated there opened the area to settlers and to the railroads.

Congress never once declared war on an Indian tribe; nor did Congress ever once succeed in keeping a treaty unbroken. The supremacy of treaty law and the force of Supreme Court decisions had little effect against the land hunger of settlers and state governments. The consistent effect of government action was to transfer Indian lands to non-Indians, and to transfer the Indians themselves, those that survived, to unwanted lands in the West.

Women's rights. No women participated in the Constitutional Convention or in any of the state ratifying conventions. Although women such as Abigail Adams urged their patriot husbands to "remember the ladies" and give women more legal rights, the revolutionary leaders probably did less thinking about sexual inequality than about any other social problem. Tradition prevailed, and tradition dictated that women were the dependents of their fathers or husbands, rather than independent adults.

Because men of the time—Thomas Jefferson, Alexander Hamilton, or even the worldly Benjamin Franklin—believed that American men protected and represented women, they saw no need for women to have a separate voice in the new governments. Neither the state constitutions nor the national Constitution reformed the colonial laws governing women's lives. Women continued to be represented in the society only by and through the males of the household. Single women were not represented politically at all.

The preceding details provide abundant evidence that the American Revolution was far from complete in 1787. In the years since then, constitutional amendments, Supreme Court decisions, federal laws, and executive actions have worked to reduce oppression and unfairness for African Americans, Indians, and women. It is worth noting that all these measures spring directly from the Constitution.

Key issues remain behind the words of the Constitution and the debates of the Constitutional Convention. Do these issues relate mostly to domestic or foreign affairs?
Critical Thinking How did the framers use conflict to guarantee freedom?

SECTION **3** REVIEW

Identify Key People and Terms
Write a sentence to identify: elastic clause, unwritten constitution, civil liberties, bill of attainder, *ex post facto* laws, writ of habeas corpus, Bill of Rights, due process of law

Master the Main Ideas

1. **Perceiving cause-effect relationships:** How does the language of the Constitution contribute to its flexibility?
2. **Understanding constitutional developments:** What is the more frequently used method of ratifying a constitutional amendment?
3. **Recognizing the rights of American citizens:** Describe three abuses of civil rights that are banned in the body of the Constitution.
4. **Understanding the principles that underlie the Constitution:** What were some of the historical roots of the Bill of Rights?
5. **Recognizing the influence of societal values:** Why did the framers of the Constitution neglect **(a)** African Americans, **(b)** Indians, and **(c)** women?

Apply Critical Thinking Skills: Identifying Alternatives
In your judgment, what groups in today's American society are neglected, oppressed, or deprived of rights? What do you think would be the best method of correcting these wrongs through constitutional means?

BASIC CONSTITUTIONAL PRINCIPLES–13 ENDURING ISSUES

1. National Power—limits and potentials
2. Federalism—the balance between nation and state
3. The Judiciary—interpreter of the Constitution or shaper of public policy
4. Civil liberties—the balance between government and the individual
5. Criminal liberties—rights of the accused and protection of the community
6. Equality—its definition as a constitutional value
7. The rights of women under the Constitution
8. The rights of ethnic and racial groups under the Constitution
9. Presidential power in wartime and in foreign affairs
10. The separation of powers and the capacity to govern
11. Avenues of representation
12. Property rights and economic policy
13. Constitutional change and flexibility

The Federalists yielded to the Republicans.

Key Terms: Judiciary Act of 1789, cabinet, Bank of the United States, Federalist party, Democratic Republican party, Alien and Sedition Acts, Kentucky and Virginia Resolutions

Reading Preview
As you read this section, you will learn:

1. who created a working government.
2. what resulted from disagreements within Washington's cabinet.
3. what led to party politics.

MEET THE PRESIDENT

He lost his father at age 11. He idolized his older brother. He yearned to join the Royal Navy (his mother forbade him). He started working at age 15. He could draw beautiful maps. He was a fine athlete and horseman. He liked to gamble and loved to dance. He found "something charming" in the sound of bullets. He would become, of all the talents that made the American Revolution, the one "essential man": George Washington.

Washington knew too well that he was the nation's precedent as well as president. Perhaps the most vital example he gave to democracy was the natural ease

GEORGE WASHINGTON

Born: February 22, 1732
Died: December 14, 1799
In office: 1789–1797

with which he relinquished his nation's greatest power. Neither Caesar nor Napoleon could do this at all. Washington did it twice.

Throughout the Constitutional Convention, there was little doubt in the minds of those present that George Washington would become the new nation's first president. He was elected unanimously and joined the newly elected Congress in **New York City**, which served as the seat of government until the capital was moved to **Philadelphia** in 1790.

The Constitution provided a blueprint for government. Now the new leaders must build that government. Washington was well aware of the importance of his presidency. He wrote:

I walk on untrodden ground. There is scarcely any part of my conduct [which] may not hereafter be drawn into precedent.

AN AMERICAN ★ SPEAKS

Washington and the Federalists created a working government.

Congress was already assembled and a president had been chosen, but there was no judicial branch. By passing the **Judiciary Act of 1789**, Congress created federal district courts and a circuit court of appeals. The Constitution established the Supreme Court with a chief justice and five associate justices. President Washington, with Senate approval, appointed **John Jay**, one of the authors of the Federalist papers, as the first chief justice.

Congress organized the executive branch by creating departments of state, treasury, and war as well as an attorney general and a postmaster general. Washington gave the post of secretary of state to his fellow Virginian Thomas Jefferson. Alexander Hamilton of New York, who had served under Washington in the Continental Army, became secretary of the treasury. Another veteran of the Revolution, Henry Knox, was appointed secretary of war. Washington began the practice of meeting regularly with these three top officers to get their advice. Thus the **cabinet**—a group of advisers chosen by the president—began.

Disagreements in Washington's cabinet brought political division.

In asking Jefferson and Hamilton to serve in his Administration, Washington chose two of the most brilliant and talented men in the

Hamilton envisioned an urban, commercial society. Government, he believed, should foster the economic success of individuals such as Elijah Boardman, the prosperous cloth merchant shown in a painting above left by Ralph Earl (1751–1801). Jefferson spoke for the independent farmers and for the preservation of a quiet agricultural world, as shown in the engraving of Bethlehem, Pennsylvania, just 16 years after its founding in 1741 by members of the Moravian church.

country. However, he couldn't possibly have chosen two people with such totally different ideas about what the role of the federal government should be.

Jefferson opposed a strong national government. "I own [admit] I am not a friend to a very energetic government," he said. "It is always oppressive." State governments, he thought, would be more responsive to the people than a national one. This philosophy put him at odds with Hamilton, who believed in the consolidation of power at the national level and who was suspicious of giving too much authority to the people. According to Hamilton:

AN AMERICAN ★ SPEAKS

The voice of the people has been said to be the voice of God; . . . [but] it is not true in fact. The people are turbulent and changing; they seldom judge or determine right.

Jefferson and Hamilton had other disagreements as well. In 1789 France had a revolution of its own. The French people deposed their king and set up a republic, but political conflicts among the rebels, followed by war with Britain and other nations in Europe, brought year after year of bloody conflict in France and eventually in much of Europe. Jefferson, who approved of revolution and said that "no country should be long without one," was a friend of France and regarded Britain with suspicion. Hamilton, on the other hand, saw only chaos in France. He wanted closer ties with Britain, whose trade would benefit American merchants and bring the government income from import duties as well.

Hamilton wanted to build the nation's economy by encouraging commerce, trade, and manufacturing. He was confident that an urban, commercial society would benefit every citizen living within it. Jefferson had no trust in commerce and industry. He dreamed of a nation of independent farmers who would transform the wilderness into cultivated farmlands. As for cities, he wrote:

AN AMERICAN ★ SPEAKS

I think our government will remain virtuous for many centuries as long as they [the people] are chiefly agricultural. . . . When they get piled upon one another in large cities, as in Europe, they will become as corrupt as in Europe.

Capable individual farmers, Jefferson claimed, would conduct their own affairs so well that government would be reduced to a minimum.

Again and again the two men clashed. Washington tried to maintain peace between his chief advisers, but the differences did not remain confined to his cabinet. Disputes arose in Congress as well, where James Madison, serving in the House, led those who sided with Jefferson. The opposition became especially strong when Hamilton's economic plans were debated in Congress.

Hamilton wanted the United States to pay not only its overseas war debts but also take on the debts of the states and those owed to its own citizens, including the Revolutionary officers and soldiers who had been paid with certificates of debt rather than hard currency. Most of the veterans and other debtors, however, had long since sold their certificates to speculators at greatly reduced prices. Hamilton proposed that all certificates be honored at their face value.

Madison and the other Jeffersonians in Congress argued that full face value should be paid only to the original holders of the debt certificates, not to speculators who hoped to profit from them. Their position reflected a regional split. Most of the speculators were New Englanders. Southerners also objected to having the national government assume the state debts. All of the southern states except South Carolina had already paid their debts. Under Hamilton's proposal their citizens would be taxed to pay the debts of other states.

A bargain was struck to settle the issue. The Jeffersonians accepted Hamilton's plan. In return Hamilton and northerners would support the construction of a "Federal City"—later named **Washington, D.C.**—in the South.

Controversy raged again over Hamilton's proposal to establish a national bank. The Jeffersonians feared that such a bank would favor northern commercial interests over the agricultural sector. Jefferson argued further that since the Constitution made no provision for a national bank, establishing one would be unconstitutional. Hamilton took the position that the "elastic clause" permitted the setting up of the bank.

The government moved from Philadelphia to Federal City (Washington, D.C.) in 1800, during John Adams' presidency. His wife, Abigail, described its swampy site on the Potomac River, idealized below in 1801, as the "very dirtiest hole I ever saw." A French army engineer who had served in the American Revolutionary War, Pierre Charles L'Enfant laid out the capital's broad avenues, as shown in an official engraving from 1792.

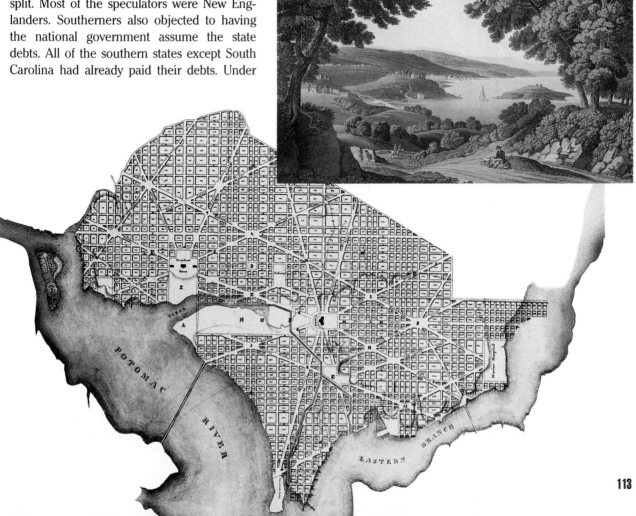

WASHINGTON'S FAREWELL ADDRESS
Skill: Identifying Central Issues

Introducing the Skill.
When President Washington published his Farewell Address in September of 1796, he did more than just detail the dangers he saw facing the young nation. He also outlined what he believed to be the issues central to good government and political success. What were these issues?

Learning the Skill.
To understand Washington's ideas, begin by **identifying central issues**, or main points, in his Farewell Address. First, define the situation at hand. In this instance that would mean Washington's advice concerning religion and morality in government. Next, look for words and phrases that support and give reasons for the president's position. Finally, use this analysis to list the central issues presented by Washington.

Applying the Skill.
Read the following excerpt from Washington's Farewell Address, in which the president discusses his views on religion and morality:

Of all the dispositions and habits which lead to political prosperity, religion and morality are indispensable supports. In vain would that man claim the tribute of patriotism, who should labor to subvert these great pillars of human happiness, these firmest props of the destinies of men and citizens. The mere politician, equally with the pious man, ought to respect and cherish them. Let it simply be asked, Where is the security for property, for reputation, for life, if the sense of religious obligation desert the oaths, which are instruments of investigations in the courts of law? And let us with caution indulge the supposition that morality can be maintained without religion. . . . Reason and experience both forbid us to expect that national morality can prevail in exclusion of religious principle.

1. What words or phrases demonstrate Washington's opinions about the role of religious and moral principle in government?
2. Identify the central issues that Washington presents in favor of religion.

Hamilton won. In 1791 Congress passed a bill establishing the **Bank of the United States** and Washington signed it into law. However, the battle of opposing opinions was not over.

Conflicting ideas about government led to party politics.

In spite of the differences between the Jeffersonians and the Hamiltonians, the members of Washington's first Administration did not, at first, think of themselves as members of opposing parties. Near the end of Washington's second term, in his so-called Farewell Address, the president warned of "factions," which he feared would divide Americans and make it impossible for them to cooperate in national affairs. Nevertheless, factions already existed by that time, and by the time of the election of 1796, two political parties ran candidates for the presidency.

The **Federalist party** was the party of Hamilton and those who believed in his policies. Washington's vice president, John Adams of Massachusetts, was their candidate for the presidency. Jefferson and Madison brought their followers together in the **Democratic Republican party**—often called the Jeffersonian Republicans or simply the Republicans.

The election of 1796 produced an unexpected result. Adams received the most votes in the electoral college and became president. Jefferson received the next highest number of votes and, under the terms of the Constitution, became vice president. Thus the nation had a president and a vice president from opposing political parties. As might be expected, it produced a stormy Administration.

Hamilton and his supporters in Congress pushed the **Alien and Sedition Acts** through Congress in 1798. Two of these acts lengthened the period of time necessary for immigrants to become eligible for citizenship and authorized the president to deport dangerous aliens. Since many recent immigrants had supported the Republicans, these acts were seen by them as political weapons of the Federalists. A third act also appeared to be aimed at Republicans. The Sedition Act imposed fines and prison terms for sedition—speech or acts meant to arouse discontent or rebellion against the government. Several Republican newspaper editors were convicted under this law.

In response Jefferson drafted a set of resolutions that were adopted by the Kentucky state legislature, and Madison wrote another set for the Virginia legislature. The **Kentucky and Virginia Resolutions** stated that the Alien and Sedition Acts violated the freedoms guaranteed by the Bill of Rights and were therefore unconstitutional. The Resolutions insisted that any state has the right to nullify, or void, such laws. The issues raised by these resolutions were not fully settled in the late 1700s, and they would return to create new tensions in the 1800s.

New popular concern over the Alien and Sedition Acts damaged the Federalists, as did a struggle for power within the party between Adams and Hamilton. In September 1800 Adams secured a treaty ending the undeclared naval war and restoring normal diplomatic relations with France. That accomplishment won Adams the Federalist party nomination but did not increase his popularity enough for him to win re-election in 1800.

The election once more produced unforeseen results. Jefferson and Aaron Burr of New York, the Republican candidates for president and vice president, each received the same number of electoral votes. The election went to the House of Representatives for a decision. For two days the House took vote after vote without a clear winner. One witness wrote:

JOHN ADAMS

John Adams made a career out of stubbornly doing the right thing for his country. The young lawyer who chose to defend the British troops on trial for the Boston Massacre became the president who made an unpopular but necessary peace with France and thus lost any chance for re-election.

Adams' term coincided with the nation's first painful lessons in party politics, and he faced those ill-tempered times without the wholehearted support of his own party or his own cabinet.

The end of his term brought the first transfer of executive power from one party to another as Thomas Jefferson took office. This national

Born: October 30, 1735
Died: July 4, 1826
In office: 1797–1801

milestone was one that Adams missed: he had left town at sunrise. He lived to age 90, long enough to learn of a more satisfying inauguration, that of John Quincy Adams, his son.

THOMAS JEFFERSON

Thomas Jefferson was a man of staggering talent, and in 40 years of public service he contributed simple gifts of ingenuity—and sweeping concepts of human freedom. Along the way he invented a plow, a money system, and a political party. Jefferson wished to be remembered for founding the University of Virginia and writing the Declaration of Independence and the Virginia statute on religious freedom. His presidency found no place on this self-written epitaph.

Despite his omission, Jefferson's two terms are worth remembering, if only for his wisdom in overcoming scruples and stretching the Constitution "till it cracked" to

Born: April 13, 1743
Died: July 4, 1826
In office: 1801–1809

acquire the Louisiana Territory. Jefferson doubled the nation's size and its opportunities, giving wider scope for Americans to pursue life, liberty, and happiness.

Many [members of the House] had sent home for night-caps and pillows, and wrapped in shawls and great-coats, lay about the floor of the committee rooms, or sat sleeping in their seats.

AN AMERICAN ★ SPEAKS

Hamilton finally broke the deadlock. Much as he disapproved of Jefferson, he thought Burr was worse. He threw his support behind Jefferson, who was elected president on the 36th ballot. The Republicans took charge, and they would hold on to the presidency for the next four decades.

SECTION 4 REVIEW

Identify Key People and Terms
Write a sentence to identify: Judiciary Act of 1789, John Jay, cabinet, Bank of the United States, Federalist party, Democratic Republican party, Alien and Sedition Acts, Kentucky and Virginia Resolutions

Locate Key Places

1. What were the first and second cities to serve as the capital of the new government?
2. What is the present-day name for the "Federal City" that Congress decided to build in the South?

Master the Main Ideas

1. **Understanding government:** What did Congress do to organize the executive and judicial branches of government?
2. **Understanding political controversy:** Contrast the views of Hamilton and Jefferson on the nature and function of the national government.
3. **Understanding political controversy:** How did party politics lead to the Alien and Sedition Acts, and how did those acts affect the election of 1800?

Apply Critical Thinking Skills: Demonstrating Reasoned Judgment
Consider Jefferson's and Hamilton's views of the new nation. Which of their ideas do you think more accurately reflected what the country needed in the late 1700s? Explain your position fully.

SECTION 5

War shaped a new American nationalism.

Key Terms: midnight judges, *Marbury* v. *Madison*, judicial review, Louisiana Purchase, impressment, embargo, War Hawk, Hartford Convention, Missouri Compromise, Monroe Doctrine

Reading Preview
As you read this section, you will learn:

1. what conflicts marked Jefferson's first term of office.
2. which countries caused problems for both Jefferson and Madison.
3. what achievements marked Monroe's administration.

In his inaugural address, Jefferson made a plea for unity, exclaiming that "We are all Republicans, we are all Federalists." He was unable, however, to avoid political conflict with a weakened but still functioning Federalist party that opposed many of his views.

Party conflict and territorial growth marked Jefferson's first term.

In keeping with his republican principles, Jefferson tried to keep the federal government small and out of the affairs of the people and the states. He hoped to avoid foreign entanglements and run a thrifty government.

At his urging, the Republican-controlled Congress repealed two unpopular taxes and the Alien and Sedition Acts that had not already expired. The new president also cut military spending. He did not, however, attempt to destroy all the Federalist programs. He honored the debt repayments arranged by Hamilton and allowed the Bank of the United States to continue to operate.

The Federalist Judiciary. The new president's first major political battle involved the federal court system. Just before a new Congress took over, while the Federalists were still in power, they passed the Judiciary Act of

1801, which increased the number of judges in the circuit and lower courts. Before leaving office, President Adams appointed loyal Federalists to judgeships, hoping to secure at least the judicial branch for his party. The Republicans called them **midnight judges**, suggesting that Adams had stayed up late on his last night in office to appoint them. One of those appointments was **John Marshall**, who as chief justice would dominate the Supreme Court through the Administrations of five presidents.

Jefferson got the Republican Congress to repeal the Judiciary Act of 1801. However, one of the midnight judges, William Marbury, asked the Supreme Court to force Secretary of State James Madison to deliver his commission. In *Marbury* v. *Madison*, Chief Justice John Marshall denied Marbury's request, ruling part of the Judiciary Act of 1789 invalid. In doing so, he asserted the Court's power of **judicial review**—the right to declare any law unconstitutional.

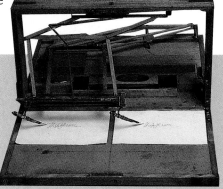

Jefferson's polygraph machine made a copy of each letter while he wrote the original.

Jefferson's Monticello

In 1961 President John F. Kennedy held a dinner party to honor America's Nobel Prize winners. He welcomed his guests by remarking, "This is the most

Jefferson said of his hilltop home in Virginia, "All my wishes end where I hope my days will end, at Monticello."

extraordinary collection of talent . . . that has ever been gathered together at the White House—with the possible exception of when

Thomas Jefferson dined alone." Indeed, Thomas Jefferson was among the most talented individuals America has ever produced. His home at Monticello, in Virginia, was a showcase for his many and varied talents.

Jefferson designed Monticello in the classical revival style, of which he was the first American exponent. Monticello's central dome was inspired by the elegant buildings Jefferson saw in France while he served as ambassador. Distributed throughout Jefferson's spacious house were his ingenious inventions. In the entrance hall was his large clock that not only told time, but also indicated the day of the week. In the dining room, concealed at the side of the fireplace, was his dumbwaiter used to bring bottles of wine up from the cellar. In the study was his polygraph machine, which copied his letters as he wrote them. In the bedroom was his swivel chair, of a

design still copied today.

Jefferson planned stately gardens for his estate, with beautiful plants from all over the world. Although the gardens remained unfinished, Jefferson used his land to experiment with new varieties of farm products. He developed a new strain of rice, suited to America's climate. This enabled our country to become a major rice producer.

Jefferson is quoted as saying, "Determine never to be idle. No person will have occasion to complain of want of time who never loses any. It is wonderful how much may be done if we are always doing." Jefferson's example and his home at Monticello prove how much one person can achieve if so determined.

Highlights of American Life

Louisiana. As Jefferson was struggling with the judiciary, a new problem was arising in the West. Farmers in the West relied on the Mississippi River and its tributaries to transport their goods to **New Orleans**. From there goods could be shipped to eastern ports or overseas markets. Whoever controlled New Orleans could control the economy of the West.

By 1801 Jefferson learned that Spain had secretly turned over Louisiana to France, which was now ruled by **Napoleon Bonaparte**. Jefferson instructed American representatives to France to offer Napoleon $10 million for the port of New Orleans and the Floridas. Napoleon astounded Jefferson's representatives with an offer to sell the Americans all 817,000 square miles of Louisiana. The Americans, although they had no authority to strike a deal, settled on a price of $15 million, hoping that the president and Congress would approve of the agreement.

The **Louisiana Purchase** presented a dilemma to Jefferson. In his strict view of the Constitution, he had no power to acquire new territory. He considered asking for a constitutional amendment to allow the purchase, but feared that Napoleon might change his mind before an amendment could be ratified. He put his constitutional scruples aside and approved

Louisiana Purchase

Point	Counterpoint
Strict construction	**Loose construction**
■ president does not have power to make the purchase ■ president has no authority to use a power not expressed in the Constitution	■ president has the power to make the purchase ■ president has the right to use implied powers to protect the nation

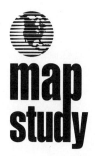

map study

Movement One of Lewis and Clark's goals was to find a water route to the Pacific. Does such a route exist?

Critical Thinking Why were such explorations important to the growth of the United States?

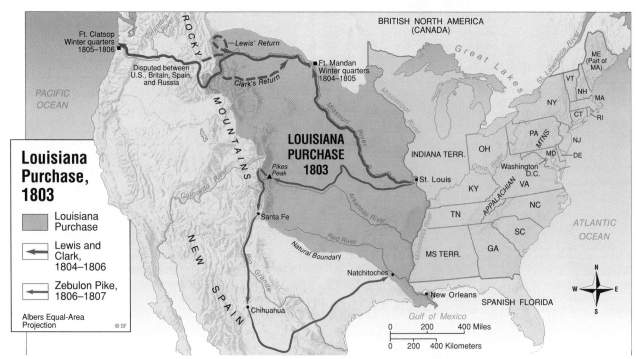

Louisiana Purchase, 1803

- Louisiana Purchase
- Lewis and Clark, 1804–1806
- Zebulon Pike, 1806–1807

Albers Equal-Area Projection © SF

the purchase, and Congress confirmed it by quickly voting the funds. With surprising ease, the United States nearly doubled its territory.

Months before the Louisiana Purchase, Jefferson had persuaded Congress to finance a western expedition. Jefferson's young secretary, Meriwether Lewis, headed the expedition and was joined by William Clark, a veteran of Indian wars. The Louisiana Purchase made the exploration urgent.

It took the Lewis and Clark expedition 18 months to travel from St. Louis, Missouri, to the Pacific, aided by a Shoshone Indian guide and interpreter, Sacajawea, who carried her infant son on her back. Lewis and Clark reached the Pacific in November 1805. When the explorers finally returned to St. Louis in September 1806, with maps and samples of plant, animal, and insect life from the Far West, they had been given up for lost.

Jefferson and Madison struggled with foreign powers.

Jefferson could be proud of the accomplishments of his first term of office. He was reelected by a landslide in 1804. Wars in Europe made his second term far more troubled.

Impressment and embargo. Napoleon was determined to conquer Europe, and the British were determined to stop him. By 1803 France and Britain were at war again and in a stalemate in which France's armies controlled Europe and the British navy controlled the seas. Each side tried to block its enemy's overseas trade.

At first American shippers used their country's neutrality to profit by trading with both countries. Opportunities for profit dried up when Britain began to blockade American ports and intercept ships carrying cargoes to France. In 1806 and 1807, both Britain and France enacted laws restricting the rights of neutral countries.

American ships were also the target of the British practice of **impressment**. Some British sailors, lured by better pay on American merchant ships, deserted. Britain's navy claimed the right to stop ships, search for deserters, and impress, or seize, sailors known to be British

subjects. British sea captains, desperate for sailors, often impressed able-bodied men whether they were British or not.

As American anger at the British grew, Jefferson tried to avoid American entanglement by getting Congress to impose an **embargo**— an order forbidding merchant ships from entering or leaving ports. The Embargo Act, passed in late 1807, would eliminate the possibility of impressment. Jefferson also thought that by denying both Britain and France any goods from the United States, he could force them to recognize America's freedom of the seas.

Sacajawea served as an interpreter for Meriwether Lewis, center, and William Clark, center left, as they explored the Louisiana Purchase.

Through the ill-fated Embargo Act, Jefferson meant to punish Great Britain for molesting U.S. merchant ships. The embargo's ruinous effect on American shipping made it unpopular.

OGRABME, or. The American Snapping-turtle.

JAMES MADISON

Born: March 16, 1751
Died: June 28, 1836
In office: 1809–1817

After completing college in only two years, James Madison returned in broken health to his family's Virginia plantation. There "Jemmy" tutored the younger children and gloomily predicted for himself a short and undistinguished life. He failed to foresee his great and happy distinctions as Father of the Constitution and husband of the dazzling Dolley.

The War of 1812, unwanted and mismanaged, clouded most of Madison's presidency. The tardy but spectacular triumph at New Orleans, however, renewed national pride and unity. Madison enjoyed two years of restored popularity before the election of his hand-picked successor.

The frail Madison proved surprisingly durable. In 1836, at age 85, he became the last of the nation's founders to pass into history.

The embargo, however, won no concessions from either European power, and it brought an economic depression at home. Merchants and shippers, particularly in New England, opposed the embargo, and many ignored it.

New Englanders showed their anger by electing several Federalist candidates to Congress in 1808, breathing new life into the party. James Madison, Jefferson's handpicked candidate who succeeded him as president, lost all but one state in New England. Some New Englanders even spoke of leaving the Union. In 1809, three days before leaving office, Jefferson signed the Non-Intercourse Act, which replaced the Embargo Act. The new act reopened overseas commerce with all nations except France and Britain. In leaving the presidency, the discouraged Jefferson commented, "Never did a prisoner, released from his chains, feel such relief as I shall on shaking off the shackles of power."

The War of 1812. The Non-Intercourse Act was no more effective than the Embargo Act had been. Other approaches to Britain by President Madison also failed to produce results. Meanwhile, a group of **War Hawks** in Congress felt that war was the only means left to defend American honor. An agricultural depression led farmers in the South and the West to favor war. Westerners also complained that the British were arming Indians and encouraging attacks on frontier settlements. Only New England, still dominated by Federalists, resisted the call for war. On June 18, 1812, Congress declared war on Britain.

In spite of a few notable victories, the War of 1812 was a disaster for the United States, which was unprepared for war. An American attempt to invade Canada ended in a humiliating failure. The British invaded Washington, D.C., and forced Madison to flee the capital to avoid capture, while Dolley Madison hurriedly saved what she could from the White House before British troops set fire to it, the Capitol, and other public buildings.

The Americans did achieve some naval victories, as on Lake Erie, where forces under Captain Oliver Hazard Perry defeated a British fleet and secured control of the lake. One of the notable American successes on land was at Fort McHenry, Maryland, where Americans withstood three days of bombardment by a British fleet and kept it from capturing the city

As British troops marched into the capital on August 24, 1814, the charming and effervescent Dolley Madison, right, slipped away with the presidential silver and the Gilbert Stuart portrait of George Washington. Her portrait is also by Stuart (1755–1828).

120

War of 1812

⬅ U.S. offensives,
1812–1814

⬅ British offensives,
1814

····· British naval
blockade

✸ U.S. victories

✸ British victories

✶ Indian
defeats

Albers Equal-Area Projection   © SF

map study

Regions In the War of 1812, the British and the Indians joined forces against the Americans. Where did two Indian defeats occur?

Critical Thinking Why might the western region have supported this war?

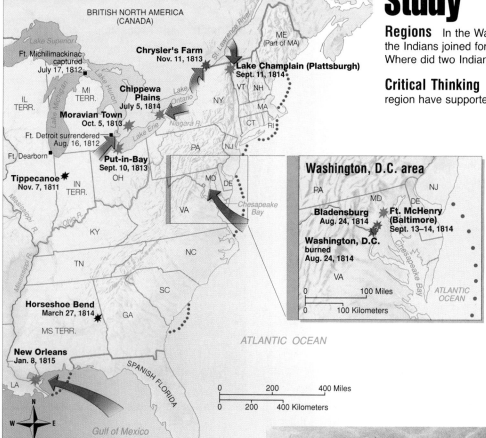

BRITISH NORTH AMERICA
(CANADA)

Lake Superior

Ft. Michilimackinac
captured
July 17, 1812

St. Lawrence River

ME
(Part of MA)

Chrysler's Farm
Nov. 11, 1813

Lake Champlain (Plattsburgh)
Sept. 11, 1814

MI
TERR.

**Chippewa
Plains**
July 5, 1814

Lake Huron

Lake Michigan

Lake Ontario

VT NH

IL
TERR.

Moravian Town
Oct. 5, 1813

Niagara R.

Lake Erie

NY

MA

Ft. Detroit surrendered
Aug. 16, 1812

CT RI

Ft. Dearborn

Put-in-Bay
Sept. 10, 1813

PA

NJ

Tippecanoe
Nov. 7, 1811

IN
TERR.

OH

MD DE

Mississippi R.

Ohio R.

KY

VA

Chesapeake
Bay

NC

TN

SC

MS TERR.

Horseshoe Bend
March 27, 1814

GA

New Orleans
Jan. 8, 1815

LA

SPANISH FLORIDA

ATLANTIC OCEAN

0   200   400 Miles

0   200   400 Kilometers

N
W   E
S

Gulf of Mexico

Washington, D.C. area

PA

MD

NJ

DE

Bladensburg
Aug. 24, 1814

**Ft. McHenry
(Baltimore)**
Sept. 13–14, 1814

Washington, D.C.
burned
Aug. 24, 1814

VA

Chesapeake Bay

ATLANTIC
OCEAN

0   100 Miles

0   100 Kilometers

Andrew Jackson, far right, led a mixed army of backwoods riflemen, Indians, African Americans, and Creole militiamen who decisively defeated the British regulars at New Orleans in January 1815. Soldiers who served under Jackson gave him the nickname Old Hickory because he was "tough as hickory"—a tough, hard wood.

of Baltimore. The sight of the American flag still flying over the fort after one night's shelling inspired Francis Scott Key to write the words to the "Star Spangled Banner."

The greatest American victory occurred in the last action in the war, on January 8, 1815, in New Orleans. General Andrew Jackson led about 5,000 hastily assembled militiamen, sailors, and local citizens to victory over a British invasion force of 8,000 seasoned troops. The British suffered 2,000 casualties, the Americans only 21. The battle was unnecessary, however, for a peace treaty had been signed in Ghent,

The last of the founders to serve as president, James Monroe was the only one who had shed blood in the Revolution. He had been one of the two Americans wounded at the Battle of Trenton.

Monroe's public career included 40 years service as soldier, governor, senator, and diplomat. He did double duty in Madison's cabinet as secretary of state and secretary of war.

Thriving in an "era of good feelings," Monroe negotiated a peaceful border with Canada and obtained Florida from Spain. Most famously, his Monroe Doctrine set the Americas off limits to European meddling.

JAMES MONROE

Born: April 28, 1758
Died: July 4, 1831
In office: 1817–1825

Monroe was the only president aside from Washington unopposed for re-election. The good fortune he enjoyed in the White House did not follow him into retirement, however. Monroe died in poverty on July 4, 1831.

Foreign affairs dominated Monroe's Administration.

With the Federalists discredited, James Monroe, the Republican candidate to succeed Madison as president, coasted to victory in 1816 and again in 1820. Political opposition seemed so feeble that one newspaper labeled the age an "era of good feelings."

Growth and expansion. With the war ended, America's economy revived as overseas trade resumed and increased. The national population climbed steadily as well—from 7 million in 1810 to 13 million by 1830. Many of these new Americans were immigrants from Ireland, Germany, and Great Britain.

As the population grew, it also expanded westward. By 1800 three new states—Vermont, Kentucky, and Tennessee—had joined the original 13. By 1819 statehood for Ohio, Louisiana, Indiana, Mississippi, Illinois, and Alabama brought the number of states to 22. Settlers already were moving into lands west of the Mississippi, especially into the territory of Missouri.

Missouri's application for statehood in 1819 created a crisis involving slavery. The 22 states were evenly divided into 11 that allowed slavery and 11 that did not. This produced a political balance in the Senate between southern slave states and northern free states. If Missouri entered the Union as a slave state, the balance

New settlers lived in crude cabins made of bark-covered logs in the valleys of the Appalachian Mountains and in the wooded lands to the west. Some settlers carved farms out of the wilderness. Others lived mainly by hunting and fishing rather than farming. Visitors were nearly always welcome because they broke the boredom and hard work of pioneer life. A French visitor to America in 1826, Daniel Collot, used this engraving to illustrate a book about his travels.

Belgium, two weeks earlier.

The Hartford Convention. Another casualty of the war was the Federalist party. In December 1814, unaware that peace talks in Europe were close to agreement, 26 Federalist antiwar delegates from New England met in Hartford, Connecticut. The **Hartford Convention** adopted proposals asserting the right of the individual states to reject national policies or laws they found objectionable. The Federalists were now preaching a states' rights doctrine that they had opposed when Jefferson and Madison had proposed them in the Kentucky and Virginia Resolutions.

News of peace caught the delegates by surprise, making them look foolish and unpatriotic. Republicans took advantage of the situation, accusing the Federalists of treason. The Hartford Convention became another nail in the coffin of the Federalist party.

would tip toward the South. The incident also raised the issue of the spread of slavery into other territories in the West. Debate raged in Congress and the nation. A New York newspaper editorial said:

AN AMERICAN ★ SPEAKS

This question involves not only the future character of our nation, but the future weight and influence of the free states. If now lost—it is lost forever.

The issue was settled by compromise after Maine applied for statehood in 1820. Congress agreed in the **Missouri Compromise** that Missouri would enter the Union as a slave state and Maine as a free state. In addition, slavery was banned north of 36°30′ north latitude, except in Missouri. The compromise retained the balance between free and slave states, but the conflict over slavery would continue in the years ahead.

Foreign affairs. Many problems remained between the United States and Britain after the War of 1812. Agreements that solved several of these problems were made under the leadership of John Quincy Adams, Monroe's secretary of state and the son of former President Adams. One agreement reduced the number of warships each nation would have on the Great Lakes and Lake Champlain. In another, the British and Americans agreed on the 49th parallel as the boundary between the United States and Canada. A treaty with Spain gave the United State legal title to all of Florida and established the western boundaries of the Louisiana Purchase territory.

Revolutions in Latin America set the scene for another foreign policy issue. By 1823 most of Spain's colonies in the Americas had successfully won their independence. The United States became concerned that other European powers might try to gain a foothold in the Western Hemisphere. At the same time, Russia was establishing settlements along the Pacific coast as far south as California.

Adams urged Monroe to issue a warning to potential European colonizers of North America. Monroe put the final touches on a statement drafted by Adams and made it part of his annual message to Congress in December 1823. This statement, which came to be called the **Monroe Doctrine**, said that the United States recognized the new republics of Latin America. Monroe said that "the American continents . . . are henceforth not to be considered as subjects for colonization by any European powers." Monroe promised that the United States, in turn, would not interfere in internal affairs in Europe.

The Doctrine was largely symbolic at the time, since the United States lacked the power to enforce it. However, the Monroe Doctrine would become an important part of American foreign policy later in the 19th century, when the United States would be ready and able to stand behind its words.

SECTION **5** REVIEW

Identify Key People and Terms
Write a sentence to identify: midnight judges, John Marshall, *Marbury* v. *Madison*, judicial review, Napoleon Bonaparte, Louisiana Purchase, impressment, embargo, War Hawk, Hartford Convention, Missouri Compromise, Monroe Doctrine

Locate Key Places
Where did the final battle of the War of 1812 take place?

Master the Main Ideas

1. **Examining political issues:** What political issues marked Jefferson's first term as president?
2. **Analyzing information:** How did Jefferson and Madison deal with foreign policy challenges during their presidencies?
3. **Drawing conclusions: (a)** In what way did growth and expansion bring on the threat of disunity? **(b)** How did the United States assert itself in foreign affairs under Monroe?

Apply Critical Thinking Skills: Identifying Alternatives
How would you evaluate Jefferson's judgment in suggesting the Embargo Act? What other alternatives do you think the president and Congress might have considered? What evidence exists to suggest that one of these alternatives might have been effective?

The Constitutional Convention Debates the Slave Trade

3A

TIME FRAME
1787

GEOGRAPHIC SETTING
Philadelphia

We know what happened during the secret deliberations of the Constitutional Convention because James Madison (1751–1836) of Virginia kept a detailed record of the debates that went on in secret behind the closed doors—and windows—of the State House at Philadelphia throughout the sweltering summer of 1787. As historian Richard Morris observes, "Not missing a single day, the diligent and meticulous Virginian took systematic notes, providing us with the principal record of the debates in the convention. The ordeal, he later said, 'almost killed' him; but having undertaken the task, he was 'determined to accomplish it.' " In the excerpt from Madison's record that follows, the delegates debate a proposal by the Southerners that Congress be forbidden from prohibiting or taxing the importation of slaves. Madison opposed slavery and objected to having any protection for the slave trade in the Constitution. Ultimately, however, he was overruled, and in the final draft of the Constitution, Congress was forbidden to outlaw the importation of slaves before 1808.

M R. MARTIN [Maryland] wanted to change Article VII, Section 4, to allow a prohibition [ban] or tax on the importation of slaves. As five slaves are to
5 be counted as three free men in the apportionment of representatives, [the Southern proposal] would encourage this traffic. It was inconsistent with the principles of the revolution and dishonorable to
10 the American character to have such a feature in the Constitution.

MR. ELLSWORTH [Connecticut] wanted to leave that section as it stands and let every state import what it pleases. The
15 morality or wisdom of slavery are considerations belonging to the states themselves. What enriches a part enriches the whole, and the states are the best judges of their particular interest. The old
20 confederation [the Articles of Confederation] had not meddled with this point, and he did not see any greater necessity for bringing it within the policy of the new one.

25 MR. CHARLES PINCKNEY [South Carolina]. South Carolina can never receive the plan if it prohibits the slave trade. In every proposed extension of the powers of the Congress, that state has expressly objected to
30 meddling with the importation of slaves. If the states be all left at liberty on this subject, South Carolina may perhaps by de-

grees do of herself what is wished, as Virginia and Maryland have already done.

MR. SHERMAN [Connecticut] wanted to leave the clause as it stands. He disapproved of the slave trade; yet as the states were now possessed of the right to import slaves, as the public good did not require it to be taken from them, and as it was expedient to have as few objections as possible to the proposed scheme of government, he thought it best to leave the matter as we find it. He observed that the abolition of slavery seemed to be going on in the United States and that the good sense of the several states would probably by degrees complete it. He urged on the Convention the necessity of dispatching its business.

MR. ELLSWORTH. As he had never owned a slave could not judge of the effects of slavery on character: He said however that if it was to be considered in a moral light we ought to go farther and free those already in the country. Slaves also multiply so fast in Virginia and Maryland that it is cheaper to raise than import them, while in the sickly rice swamps, foreign supplies are necessary. If we go no farther than is urged, we shall be unjust towards South Carolina and Georgia. Let us not meddle. As population increases, poor laborers will be so plentiful as to render slaves useless.

MR. SHERMAN said it was better to let the Southern states import slaves than to part with them [the Southern states]. He thought that a tax on the importation of slaves would make the matter worse, because it implied they were *property*.

MR. ELLSWORTH was for taking the plan as it is. This widening of opinions has a threatening aspect. If we do not agree on this middle and moderate ground, he was afraid we should lose two states, with such others as may be disposed to stand aloof, should fly into a variety of shapes and directions, and most probably into several confederations, and not without bloodshed.

The hold of the slave ship *Albatross,* as depicted in a watercolor by eyewitness Godfrey Meynall. This painting reflects typical conditions on the lower decks of ships engaged in the slave trade.

Discussing the Reading

1. What economic arguments did Oliver Ellsworth offer in support of the Southern proposal?

2. Roger Sherman opposed slavery, but argued against prohibiting the slave trade. What reasons did he give for his position?

CRITICAL THINKING
Identifying Assumptions

Based on the evidence of this passage, what was Ellsworth's attitude toward slavery? If he had lived in the 1830s, would he have been an Abolitionist?

John Marshall Lays the Foundation for Federalism

TIME FRAME
1821

GEOGRAPHIC SETTING
Washington

John Marshall (1755–1835) was not a delegate to the Constitutional Convention, but he argued for it forcefully in Virginia. As Chief Justice of the U.S. Supreme Court from 1801 to 1835, he wrote some of the most important legal opinions interpreting the federal system. All of these opinions extended the power of the federal government over the states. The excerpt that follows, from his opinion in the case of *Cohens* v. *Virginia* in 1821, expresses his view of the sovereign power of the federal government.

A constitution is framed for ages to come and is designed to approach immortality as nearly as human institutions can approach it. Its course cannot always
5 be tranquil [calm]. It is exposed to storms and tempests, and its framers must be unwise statesmen indeed if they have not provided it, so far as its nature will permit, with the means of self-preservation from
10 the perils it may be destined to encounter. No government ought to be so defective

This portrait of Chief Justice John Marshall by Rembrandt Peale, painted about 1832, currently hangs in the Supreme Court Building in Washington. Peale (1778–1860), a member of the Peale family of painters from Philadelphia, helped inaugurate American academic painting.

The Cohens of Virginia sold lottery tickets, like those shown above, which led to their conviction for having violated Virginia law.

20 one people. In all commercial regulations we are one and the same people. In many other respects the American people are one, and the Government which is alone capable of controlling and managing their 25 interests in all these respects is the government of the Union. . . .

America has chosen to be, in many respects, and to many purposes, a nation; and for all these purposes her government 30 is complete; to all these objects it is competent. The people have declared that in the exercise of all the powers for these objects it is supreme. It can, then, in effecting these objects, legitimately control all in- 35 dividuals or governments within the American territory. The constitution and laws of a State, so far as they are repugnant [offensive] to the Constitution and laws of the United States, are absolutely 40 void [not binding]. These States are constituent parts of the United States. They are members of one great empire—for some purposes sovereign, for some purposes subordinate.

in its organization as not to contain within itself the means of securing the execution of its own laws against other dangers than 15 those which occur every day. . . .

That the United States form, for many and for most important purposes, a single nation, has not yet been denied. In war we are one people. In making peace we are

Discussing the Reading

1. John Marshall mentioned three circumstances under which the separate states "form . . . a single nation." What were they? What other circumstances might he have mentioned?

2. According to Marshall, under what circumstances are the laws of a state not binding?

CRITICAL THINKING
Identifying Alternatives

One area in which the states do not "form a single nation" is public education, where state and local laws remain sovereign. What might some of the advantages and disadvantages be if there existed federal laws establishing, for example, a national curriculum?

Abigail Adams Urges Her Husband to "Remember the Ladies"

TIME FRAME
1776

GEOGRAPHIC SETTING
Massachusetts
and Pennsylvania

In the estimate of historian Daniel Boorstin, Abigail Adams (1744–1818) was "one of the brightest, most public-minded, and most sacrificing" of her brilliant and patriotic family. During the long separations from her husband John that resulted from his public service, she had the heavy burden of running the family farm in Braintree, Massachusetts, and raising their four children alone. Her eloquent letters display the vigor of her intelligence and the strength of her democratic ideals. While John Adams was at the Continental Congress in Philadelphia in the spring of 1776, Abigail and her husband exchanged views on the subject of what American political independence should mean for the freedom of American women. The following passage is an excerpt from Jack Shepherd's *The Adams Chronicles*. (The spelling and punctuation of the original letters have been retained.)

While John Adams was in Philadelphia working for independence, Abigail made declarations of her own for women's liberation. On March 31, 1776, she wrote John: "I have sometimes been ready to think that the passion for Liberty cannot be Eaquelly Strong in the Breasts of those who have been accustomed to deprive their fellow Creatures of theirs.... I am certain that it is not founded upon that generous and christian principle of doing to others as we would that others should do unto us....

"I long to hear that you have declared an independancy—and by the way in the new Code of Laws which I suppose it will be necessary for you to make I desire you would Remember the Ladies, and be

more generous and favorable to them than your ancestors. Do not put such unlimited power into the hands of the Husbands. Remember all Men would be tyrants if they could. If particular care and attention is not paid to the Ladies, we are determined to foment [stir up] a Rebelion, and will not hold ourselves bound by any Laws in which we have no voice, or Representation.

"That your Sex are Naturally Tyrannical is a Truth so thoroughly established as to admit of no dispute, but such of you as wish to be happy willingly give up the harsh title of Master for the more tender and endearing one of Friend. Why then, not put it out of the power of the vicious and the Lawless to use us with cruelty and indignity with impunity. Men of Sense in all Ages abhor [hate] those customs which treat us only as the vassals of your Sex. Regard us then as Beings placed by providence under your protection and in immitation of the Supreem Being make use of that power only for our happiness."

John Adams mulled this over in Philadelphia, and replied to Abigail on April 14: "As to your extraordinary Code of Laws, I cannot but laugh. We have been told that our Struggle has loosened the bands of Government every where. That Children and Apprentices were disobedient—that schools and Colledges were grown turbulent—that Indians slighted their Guardians, and Negroes grew insolent to their Masters. But your Letter was the first Intimation [hint] that another Tribe more numerous and powerful than all the rest were grown discontented.—This is rather too coarse a Compliment but you are so saucy [bold], I won't blot it out.

"Depend on it. We know better than to repeal our Masculine systems. Although they are in full Force, you know they are little more than Theory. We dare not exert our Power in its full Latitude. We are obliged to go fair, and softly, and in Practice you know We are the subjects. We have only the Name of Masters, and rather than give up this, which would compleatly subject Us to the Despotism of the Peticoat, I hope General Washington, and all our Heroes would fight. I am sure every good Politician would plot . . . as he would against Despotism, Empire, Monarchy, Aristocracy, Oligarchy or Ochlocracy [mob rule]."

Abigail, dissatisfied with John's reply, wrote back on May 7: "I can not say that I think you very generous to the Ladies, for whilst you are proclaiming peace and good will to Men, Emancipating all Nations, you insist upon retaining an absolute power over Wives. But you must remember that Arbitrary power is like most other things which are very hard, very liable to be broken—and notwithstanding all your wise Laws and Maxims, we have it in our power not only to free ourselves but to subdue our Masters, and without violence throw both your natural and legal authority at our feet." Adams was unmoved.

A maidservant drapes a sheet over a clothesline in the East Room of the White House as Abigail Adams looks on in this depiction of an early White House domestic scene. The inset shows a contemporary portrait of Abigail Adams.

Discussing the Reading

1. What was Abigail Adams' tone in these letters? Angry? Humorous? Pleading? What was her husband's tone? Cite lines in support of your answer.

2. Does it seem probable, as John Adams said had been claimed (lines 47–54), that the American Revolution unsettled all social relations in the colonies? Why or why not?

CRITICAL THINKING
Using Reasoned Judgment

What arguments did Abigail Adams use in support of women's rights? What argument did John Adams use to oppose the points his wife made? Whom do you find more convincing? Explain.

Chapter Summary

Write supporting details under each of the following main ideas as you review the chapter.

Section 1
1. Compromise created federalism.
2. Federalism balanced national needs and states' rights.
3. Constitutional government released the nation's economic energies.

Section 2
1. The framers developed three interactive branches of government.
2. Congress makes the laws.
3. The president administers the laws.
4. The courts interpret the laws.
5. A balanced system protects American diversity.

Section 3
1. The language of the Constitution permits interpretation.
2. The Constitution may be changed by amendment and tradition.
3. The Constitution protects civil liberties.
4. Americans demanded a Bill of Rights.
5. The rights of minorities and women were poorly protected.

Section 4
1. Washington and the Federalists created a working government.
2. Disagreements in Washington's cabinet brought about political division.
3. Conflicting ideas about government led to party politics.

Section 5
1. Party conflict and territorial growth marked Jefferson's first term.
2. Jefferson and Madison struggled with foreign powers.
3. Foreign affairs dominated Monroe's Administration.

Chapter Themes

1. **Constitutional and representative government:** The framers of the Constitution remembered the abuses of the past and constructed a constitution that would guard against tyranny. To do this, they established a federal system under which powers were shared between the states and the national government.

2. **Relations with other nations:** In foreign affairs both Washington and Adams struggled to establish credibility, gain respect, and maintain neutrality in the face of numerous threats to the sovereignty of the new nation.

Chapter Study Guide

Identifying Key People and Terms

Name the key person or key term that describes the:
1. sharing of powers between the states and the national government
2. idea that each branch of government had distinct functions
3. basic rights guaranteed by law or by a constitution
4. president's department heads and chief advisers
5. case in which the concept of judicial review was exercised at the national level

Locating Key Places

1. Where did Samuel Slater set up his first factory in the United States?
2. What are the three main cities that have served as the capital of the United States?

Mastering the Main Ideas

1. How did federalism balance the national needs with states' rights?
2. Describe the roles of each branch of the federal government.
3. Why did Americans demand a bill of rights?
4. What different philosophies of government divided Jefferson and Hamilton?
5. How might the Monroe Doctrine have set the stage for U.S. intervention in Latin America in the 20th century?

Applying Critical Thinking Skills

1. **Predicting consequences:** How might the government of the United States be different if political parties had not developed?
2. **Demonstrating reasoned judgment:** Do you think a government would ever be justified in passing an *ex post facto* law? Explain.
3. **Drawing conclusions:** In what way might the addition of the Bill of Rights be considered the first triumph of the United States Constitution?

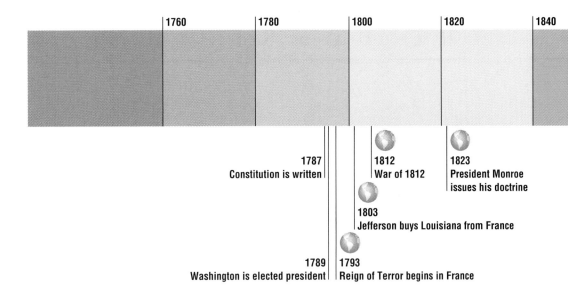

| 1760 | 1780 | 1800 | 1820 | 1840 |

1787
Constitution is written

1812
War of 1812

1823
President Monroe issues his doctrine

1803
Jefferson buys Louisiana from France

1789
Washington is elected president

1793
Reign of Terror begins in France

4. **Identifying assumptions:** Hamilton's plan for a bank started a lasting debate over the interpretation of the Constitution. What assumptions underlie the argument for a "loose" interpretation and the argument for a "strict" interpretation?

5. **Drawing conclusions:** America did not win the War of 1812, yet it entered into a new era of "good feelings" immediately following the war. What did the war teach the United States about itself?

Chapter Activities

Learning Geography Through History

1. How did geographical differences in Washington's original cabinet set the stage for the fundamental split that occurred among the Federalists?
2. What geographical divisions existed among the states in regard to support for the War of 1812?

Relating the United States to the World

1. How did the political and philosophical ideas from England and France influence the U.S. Constitution?
2. Which of Washington's advisers favored France? England? Why was this the case?
3. What European countries held territory in the Western Hemisphere in the early 19th century?

Linking Past to Present

1. How have the political rights of women, Native Americans, and African Americans changed since 1788?

2. What political parties dominate the U.S. political scene today? What major differences are there between these parties?
3. What recent U.S. interventions in Latin America might be considered extensions of the Monroe Doctrine?

Using the Time Line

1. How many years did it take for the Constitution to be written and the first president elected?
2. Which time line events concern U.S. relations with European nations?
3. During whose Administration was the Louisiana Purchase negotiated?

Practicing Critical Thinking Strategies

Identifying Central Issues
What positions did Thomas Jefferson and Alexander Hamilton take concerning two central issues on which they differed?

Learning More About the Constitution

1. **Using Source Readings:** Read the Source Readings for this chapter and answer the questions.
2. **Using Literature:** Read Chapter 24 of William Hosokawa's *Nisei*, a book about the Japanese internment during World War II. What constitutional issues were involved with the internment?
3. **Using Geography:** Create a map of the route that Lewis and Clark took as they explored the territory gained in the Louisiana Purchase. Determine how physical features such as rivers, mountains, and lakes forced Lewis and Clark to take certain routes.

P R E A M B L E

We the people of the United States, in order to form a more perfect Union, establish justice, ensure domestic tranquillity, provide for the common defense, promote the general welfare, and secure the blessings of liberty to ourselves and our posterity, do ordain and establish this Constitution for the United States of America.

We the People...

A R T I C L E I

LEGISLATIVE BRANCH

The Constitution created a government for the whole United States, which we call the federal government. It is divided into the legislative, executive, and judicial branches. Article I explains what the federal legislature is and what it can or cannot do. It also puts some limits on the state governments.

1. Who has the power to make laws?

SECTION 1 Congress

All legislative powers herein granted shall be vested in a Congress of the United States, which shall consist of a Senate and House of Representatives.

Legislative power is the power to make laws. All of the federal government's power to make laws is given to a group of people called *Congress*. Congress is divided into two parts, called *houses*. One house is called the Senate; the other, the House of Representatives.

2. Who chooses representatives, and how long is a representative's term?

SECTION 2 House of Representatives

Sec. 2, clause 1. The House of Representatives shall be composed of members chosen every second year by the people of the several states, and the electors in each state shall have the qualifications requisite for electors of the most numerous branch of the state legislature.

Representatives are chosen every two years by the voters of each state. People who are allowed to vote for state legislators are also qualified to vote for their representative in the national legislature. This clause gives each state the power to decide who is qualified to vote for members of Congress. Several amendments have put limitations on the voting laws states can make. Today, nearly every adult citizen is qualified to be a voter.

3. Who can be a representative?

Sec. 2, clause 2. No person shall be a representative who shall not have attained to the age of twenty-five years, and been seven years a citizen of the United States, and who shall not, when elected, be an inhabitant of that state in which he shall be chosen.

A representative must be at least twenty-five years old, must have been a United States citizen for at least seven years, and must live in the state from which he or she is chosen.

4. How many representatives are there?

Sec. 2, clause 3. Representatives and direct taxes shall be apportioned among the several states which may be included within this Union, according to their respective numbers, which shall be determined by adding to the whole number of free persons, including those bound to service for a term of years, and excluding Indians not taxed, three fifths of all other persons.

The actual enumeration shall be made within three years after the first meeting of the Congress of the United States, and within every subsequent term of ten years, in such manner as they shall by law direct. The number of representatives shall not exceed one for every thirty thousand, but each state shall have at least one representative; and until such enumeration shall be made, the state of New Hampshire shall be entitled to choose three, Massachusetts eight, Rhode Island and Providence Plantations one, Connecticut five, New York six, New Jersey four, Pennsylvania eight, Delaware one, Maryland six, Virginia ten, North Carolina five, South Carolina five, and Georgia three.

The number of representatives a state has is based on the number of people in the state. A *census*, or count of the people, must be taken every ten years. Congress decides how the count shall be made, and uses the census results to decide how many representatives each state shall have. Because of Amendments 13 and 14, the three-fifths clause is no longer in force. Since 1929, Congress has limited the number of representatives to 435. Since 1940, Indians have been included in the census.

5. How are vacancies filled?

Sec. 2, clause 4. When vacancies happen in the representation from any state, the executive authority thereof shall issue writs of election to fill such vacancies.

If a representative dies or leaves office, the governor (the *executive authority*) of the state calls an election to fill the vacancy.

6. Who organizes the House, and who has the power to impeach?

Sec. 2, clause 5. The House of Representatives shall choose their speaker and other officers; and shall have the sole power of impeachment.

Every two years, a new Congress meets. At that time, the House elects its presiding officer or *speaker,* as well as other officers.

Only the House of Representatives has the power to *impeach.* This is the power to decide whether or not high executive or judicial officers should go to trial for serious misbehavior in office.

SECTION 3 Senate

7. What is the Senate?

Sec. 3, clause 1. The Senate of the United States shall be composed of two senators from each state, chosen ~~by the legislature thereof,~~ for six years; and each senator shall have one vote.

The Senate is made up of two senators from each state. Each senator is elected for a six-year term and has one vote. Until 1913, senators were chosen by the state legislatures, but Amendment 17 changed this.

8. How long do senators serve?

Sec. 3, clause 2. Immediately after they shall be assembled in consequence of the first election, they shall be divided as equally as may be into three classes. The seats of the senators of the first class shall be vacated at the expiration of the second year, of the second class at the expiration of the fourth year, and of the third class at the expiration of the sixth year, so that one third may be chosen every second year; ~~and if vacancies happen by resignation, or otherwise, during the recess of the legislature of any state, the executive thereof may make temporary appointments until the next meeting of the legislature, which shall then fill such vacancies.~~

Only one-third of the senators are elected in any one election year. Unlike the House, which can change greatly after one election, the Senate changes slowly.

9. Who can be a senator?

Sec. 3, clause 3. No person shall be a senator who shall not have attained to the age of thirty years, and been nine years a citizen of the United States, and who shall not, when elected, be an inhabitant of that state for which he shall be chosen.

A senator must be at least thirty years old, a U.S. citizen for at least nine years, and must live in the state that he or she represents.

10. How is the Senate organized?

Sec. 3, clause 4. The Vice-President of the United States shall be president of the Senate, but shall have no vote, unless they be equally divided.

Sec. 3, clause 5. The Senate shall choose their other officers, and also a president pro tempore, in the absence of the Vice-President, or when he shall exercise the office of President of the United States.

The vice president presides at Senate meetings, but votes only if there is a tie.

The Senate chooses its other officers, including a person to preside at Senate meetings when the vice president is absent. This person is called the president pro tempore, or pro tem for short.

11. How does the Senate try impeachments?

Sec. 3, clause 6. The Senate shall have the sole power to try all impeachments. When sitting for that purpose, they shall be on oath or affirmation. When the President of the United States is tried, the Chief Justice shall preside; and no person shall be convicted without the concurrence of two-thirds of the members present.

Only the Senate has the power to try officials impeached by the House of Representatives. The Senate sits as a jury, and the senators must take an oath to try the case fairly. (The writers of the Constitution knew that some religions do not allow people to take oaths. So they provided that a senator could swear or affirm. *Affirm* means "to declare positively

We the People...

12. How are convicted officials punished?

Sec. 3, clause 7. Judgment in cases of impeachment shall not extend further than to removal from office and disqualification to hold and enjoy any office of honor, trust, or profit under the United States; but the party convicted shall nevertheless be liable and subject to indictment, trial, judgment, and punishment, according to law.

that something is true.") If the president is on trial, the Chief Justice of the United States presides over the trial. In other cases the vice president presides. To convict, two-thirds of the senators present must vote guilty.

Impeachment gives Congress a check on both the president and the judicial branch. However, this check is rarely used. In all, the House has impeached only fifteen individuals, including one president, Andrew Johnson. Only seven, all judges, were found guilty by the Senate.

The Senate's power to punish a convicted official is limited. All it can do is remove the official from office and keep him or her from ever holding another office in the U.S. government. However, the official may also be punished by the regular courts.

SECTION 4   Elections and Meetings

13. When is Congress elected?

Sec. 4, clause 1. The times, places, and manner of holding elections for senators and representatives shall be prescribed in each state by the legislature thereof; but the Congress may at any time by law make or alter such regulations, except as to the places of choosing senators.

Each state may decide when, where, and how elections for its senators and representatives are held, unless Congress disagrees.

14. When does Congress meet?

Sec. 4, clause 2. The Congress shall assemble at least once in every year, and such meeting shall be on the first Monday in December, unless they shall by law appoint a different day.

Congress must meet at least once a year. Amendment 20 set January 3 as the regular meeting date.

SECTION 5   Rules of Procedure

15. How many members make a quorum?

Sec. 5, clause 1. Each house shall be the judge of the elections, returns, and qualifications of its own members, and a majority of each shall constitute a quorum to do business; but a smaller number may adjourn from day to day, and may be authorized to compel the attendance of absent members, in such manner, and under such penalties as each house may provide.

The House of Representatives decides if members are entitled to be in the House. The Senate decides if senators are entitled to be in the Senate. This power is mainly used when an election is so close that the winner changes each time the ballots are recounted.

Neither the House nor the Senate can hold meetings for business unless it has a *quorum*. That is, more than half the members must be present. The Senate and the House of Representatives can each make rules and set penalties for not attending meetings.

16. Who makes the rules for Congress?

Sec. 5, clause 2. Each house may determine the rules of its proceedings, punish its members for disorderly behavior, and, with the concurrence of two-thirds, expel a member.

The House and the Senate may each make rules for conducting business and punish their members for not following these rules. In either the House or the Senate, two-thirds of the members must agree if they wish to expel a member.

SECTION 8 Powers of Congress

Section 8 of Article I describes the powers of Congress. It is, therefore, one of the most important parts of the Constitution, for the list of congressional powers is also a list of the major powers of the U.S. government.

24. What taxing power does Congress have?

Sec. 8, clause 1. The Congress shall have power to lay and collect taxes, duties, imposts, and excises, to pay the debts and provide for the common defense and general welfare of the United States; but all duties, imposts, and excises shall be uniform throughout the United States.

Congress has the power to raise money by taxing. Taxes can be used (1) to pay the debts of the national government, (2) to defend the country, and (3) to provide services for the good of all the people. Most federal taxes must be the same in all parts of the country.

25. How else can Congress raise money?

Sec. 8, clause 2. To borrow money on the credit of the United States;

Congress has the power to borrow money for the government to use. The Constitution sets no limit on the amount of money the government can borrow.

26. What controls does Congress have over commerce?

Sec. 8, clause 3. To regulate commerce with foreign nations, and among the several states, and with the Indian tribes;

Congress can pass laws to control trade with other countries, among the states, and with groups of Indians. The power to regulate commerce has been interpreted broadly. Among other things, it has been used to set up national banks and to regulate radio and television broadcasting.

27. What powers concerning naturalization and bankruptcy does Congress have?

Sec. 8, clause 4. To establish a uniform rule of naturalization, and uniform laws on the subject of bankruptcies throughout the United States;

Congress can pass laws that say how people born in other countries can become U.S. citizens. This is the process of *naturalization*. Congress can also pass a bankruptcy law that is the same in all the states. Bankruptcy laws set up rules for paying off debts when a person goes broke.

28. How are money and measurement systems provided?

Sec. 8, clause 5. To coin money, regulate the value thereof, and of foreign coin, and fix the standard of weights and measures;

Congress has the power to coin money and to say how much it is worth. It also has the power to say how much foreign money is worth in American money. Congress has the power to define weights and measures so that they will be the same throughout the nation.

We the People...

29. What control over counterfeiters does Congress have?

Sec. 8, clause 6. To provide for the punishment of counterfeiting the securities and current coin of the United States;

Congress has power to punish persons who make fake government bonds or money.

30. Who controls the postal services?

Sec. 8, clause 7. To establish post offices and post roads;

Congress can provide a postal service and roads to be used in delivering the mail.

31. Who issues copyrights and patents?

Sec. 8, clause 8. To promote the progress of science and useful arts, by securing for limited times to authors and inventors the exclusive rights to their respective writings and discoveries;

Congress can encourage science, industry, and the arts by passing patent and copyright laws. Such laws prevent others from profiting from the work of inventors and writers for a specified period.

32. Who sets up the court system?

Sec. 8, clause 9. To constitute tribunals inferior to the Supreme Court;

Congress has the power to set up courts that are lower in authority than the Supreme Court.

33. What powers does Congress have concerning piracy and international law?

Sec. 8, clause 10. To define and punish piracies and felonies committed on the high seas, and offenses against the law of nations;

Congress has power to make laws about crimes committed on the seas or oceans. Congress also has power to make laws to punish those who violate treaties or international customs (international law).

34. Who has power to declare war?

Sec. 8, clause 11. To declare war, grant letters of marque and reprisal, and make rules concerning captures on land and water;

Congress has the power to declare war. Congress was originally allowed to give persons permission to capture or destroy ships and goods of enemy nations without being guilty of piracy. This practice was given up in 1856 when Congress agreed to follow a rule of international law. Congress makes rules about seizing enemy property on land or sea.

35. What control over the military forces does Congress have?

Sec. 8, clause 12. To raise and support armies, but no appropriation of money to that use shall be for a longer term than two years;
Sec. 8, clause 13. To provide and maintain a navy;
Sec. 8, clause 14. To make rules for the government and regulation of the land and naval forces;

Congress has the power to raise an army and a navy and to give them supplies. But Congress may not provide money for the army for more than two years at a time. No time limit was put on appropriations for the navy. Congress also has the power to make rules for the organization and regulation of the armed services.

36. When can Congress use the state militias?

Sec. 8, clause 15. To provide for calling forth the militia to execute the laws of the Union, suppress insurrections and repel invasions;

The volunteer armed forces of the different states used to be called the *militia*. Since the National Defense Act of 1916, the militia have been called the National Guard. This clause gives Congress the power to call out the Guard (1) to enforce the national laws, (2) to put down rebellion, and (3) to drive out invading armies.

37. What control over the state militia does Congress have?

Sec. 8, clause 16. To provide for organizing, arming, and disciplining the militia, and for governing such part of them as may be employed in the service of the United States, reserving to the states respectively the appointment of the officers and the authority of training the militia according to the discipline prescribed by Congress;

Congress has the power to organize, arm, and discipline the National Guard. Each state has the power to appoint the officers of its Guard and to see that the soldiers are trained according to rules made by Congress.

38. What provisions are there for a national capital?

Sec. 8, clause 17. To exercise exclusive legislation in all cases whatsoever, over such district (not exceeding ten miles square) as may, by cession of particular states, and the acceptance of Congress, become the seat of the government of the United States, and to exercise like authority over all places purchased by the consent of the legislature of the state in which the same shall be, for the erection of forts, magazines, arsenals, dockyards, and other needful buildings;

This clause gives Congress the power to govern the District of Columbia, the national capital. In 1974, Congress gave the District a charter allowing a mayor and a 13-member city council. Still, Congress can overrule city council actions. Congress also governs all places bought from the states for forts, ammunition storage, navy yards, and other uses.

39. What other powers does Congress have?

Sec. 8, clause 18. And to make all laws which shall be necessary and proper for carrying into execution the foregoing powers, and all other powers vested by this Constitution in the government of the United States, or in any department or officer thereof.

Congress has the power to make all laws needed to carry out the power granted in clauses 1-17. Congress also has the power to make all laws needed to carry out powers that other clauses of the Constitution grant to Congress or to other federal officials. Clause 18 is called the "elastic clause" because it stretches Congress's powers. It does *not* give Congress power to do whatever it wants. However, this clause has been interpreted generously so that the federal government has a good deal more power than you might think from reading the first 17 clauses.

SECTION 9 Powers Denied to the Federal Government

Section 9 of Article I lists some of the things that Congress or other branches of the U.S. government may not do.

40. What can Congress do about the slave trade?

Sec. 9, clause 1. ~~The migration or importation of such persons as any of the states now existing shall think proper to admit, shall not be prohibited by the Congress prior to the year one thousand eight hundred and eight, but a tax or duty may be imposed on such importation, not exceeding ten dollars for each person.~~

This clause was part of the compromise over commerce. It said that Congress could make no law before 1808 to forbid the international sale of slaves. By agreeing that the foreign slave trade might possibly be ended 20 years later, those who favored slavery gained a more favorable wording of the commerce and treaty clauses. However, Congress was allowed to place a tax as high as $10 on each slave brought into the country. The writers did not use the word *"slave"* anywhere in the original Constitution. Even the expression "such persons" was part of a compromise.

41. When is habeas corpus guaranteed?

Sec. 9, clause 2. The privilege of the writ of habeas corpus shall not be suspended, unless when in cases of rebellion or invasion the public safety may require it.

The government cannot arrest and imprison people without reason to believe that they have broken the law. When a person is arrested, the friends or family can go into court and ask for a *writ of habeas corpus* [hā′bē əs kôr′pəs]. This order directs the jailer to bring the prisoner immediately into court. The arresting officials must then show that they have the right to hold the prisoner, or else he or she will be released. Clause 2 says that only when the country is in danger of rebellion or invasion can Congress remove this important guarantee of personal liberty.

42. What are some laws that Congress is forbidden to pass?	***Sec. 9, clause 3.*** No bill of attainder or ex post facto law shall be passed.	Congress cannot pass a *bill of attainder*—a law convicting or punishing a particular person. Congress cannot pass an *ex post facto* law—a law that makes unlawful something that was not illegal at the time it was done.
43. What restrictions are there for direct taxes?	***Sec. 9, clause 4.*** No capitation, or other direct, tax shall be laid, unless in proportion to the census or enumeration herein before directed to be taken.	If Congress is to levy "head" taxes or land taxes, they must be based upon population; the wealth or physical size of states cannot be considered. An income tax is a direct tax, but because of Amendment 16, it does not have to be based on population.
44. What taxes are forbidden?	***Sec. 9, clause 5.*** No tax or duty shall be laid on articles exported from any state.	Congress cannot tax goods or products being sent out of any state.
45. What treatment is guaranteed to state ports?	***Sec. 9, clause 6.*** No preference shall be given by any regulation of commerce or revenue to the ports of one state over those of another; nor shall vessels bound to, or from, one state, be obliged to enter, clear, or pay duties in another.	Congress cannot make laws that favor one state's harbors over another's. Ships from any state may enter the ports of other states without paying duties.
46. What rules affect spending?	***Sec. 9, clause 7.*** No money shall be drawn from the treasury, but in consequence of appropriations made by law; and a regular statement and account of the receipts and expenditures of all public money shall be published from time to time.	Government money can be spent only if Congress passes a law for that purpose. An account of how much money is collected and how it is spent must be made public.
47. What rules cover titles of nobility and gifts?	***Sec. 9, clause 8.*** No title of nobility shall be granted by the United States; and no person holding any office of profit or trust under them, shall, without the consent of the Congress, accept of any present, emolument, office, or title, of any kind whatever, from any king, prince, or foreign state.	The U.S. government cannot give a title of nobility (such as count, duchess, earl) to anyone. No one in the service of the United States can accept a title, a present, or a position from another country without permission of Congress. This clause was intended to prevent foreign governments from corrupting U.S. officials.

We the People...

We the People...

SECTION 10 Powers Denied to the States

48. What are some actions that the states are forbidden to take?

Sec. 10, clause 1. No state shall enter into any treaty, alliance, or confederation; grant letters of marque and reprisal; coin money; emit bills of credit; make anything but gold and silver coin a tender in payment of debts; pass any bill of attainder, ex post facto law, or law impairing the obligation of contracts, or grant any title of nobility.

This clause lists eight things states cannot do. (1) States cannot make treaties with other countries. Nor can they become a part of some other country. (2) States cannot give private citizens permission to fight other countries. (3) States cannot coin their own money or issue paper money. (4) States cannot pass laws that allow anything other than gold and silver to be used as money. (5) States cannot pass laws declaring a particular person guilty of an offense and describing the punishment. (6) States cannot pass laws that would punish a person for something that was not against the law when it was done. (7) States cannot pass laws that excuse people from carrying out lawful agreements. (8) States cannot give titles of nobility.

49. What actions by the states require congressional approval?

Sec. 10, clause 2. No state shall, without the consent of the Congress, lay any imposts or duties on imports or exports, except what may be absolutely necessary for executing its inspection laws; and the net produce of all duties and imposts, laid by any state on imports or exports, shall be for the use of the treasury of the United States; and all such laws shall be subject to the revision and control of the Congress.

Sec. 10, clause 3. No state shall, without the consent of Congress, lay any duty of tonnage, keep troops or ships of war in time of peace, enter into any agreement or compact with another state, or with a foreign power, or engage in war, unless actually invaded, or in such imminent danger as will not admit of delay.

These two clauses list actions that states may take only with the approval of Congress. States cannot tax goods coming from or going to other countries unless Congress agrees. However, states may charge an inspection fee if necessary. Any profit from state import or export taxes approved by Congress must go into the U.S. Treasury, and these state tax laws may be changed by Congress. Unless Congress provides otherwise, states may not tax ships, or keep troops (except the National Guard) or warships in time of peace. States cannot make agreements with other states or with foreign countries unless Congress agrees. For example, if three states want to form a compact to deal with a river that flows through their land, they must get the permission of Congress. States cannot go to war unless they have been invaded or are in such great danger that delay would be disastrous.

A R T I C L E   II
EXECUTIVE BRANCH

Article II outlines the powers of the president, says who can be president, and describes how the president is chosen.

SECTION 1 President and Vice President

50. Who has executive power and for how long?

Sec. 1, clause 1. The executive power shall be vested in a President of the United States of America. He shall hold his office during the term of four years, and, together with the Vice-President, chosen for the same term, be elected as follows:

Executive power is the power to carry out the laws. This power is given to the president, who is the chief executive of the U.S. government. The president serves a four-year term of office. The vice president is elected at the same time as the president and serves the same term.

51. Who elects the president?

Sec. 1, clause 2. Each state shall appoint, in such manner as the legislature thereof may direct, a number of electors, equal to the whole number of senators and representatives to which the state may be entitled in the Congress; but no senator or representative, or person holding an office of trust or profit under the United States, shall be appointed an elector.

The people do not elect the president directly, although they do have a great deal to say about who will be elected president. A group of electors known as the *electoral college* votes the president into office. Each state legislature decides on the way its electors are chosen. The number of electors from each state is equal to the total number of senators and representatives the state has in Congress. No senators or representatives and no one holding a position in the national government may be an elector.

52. How was the president formerly elected?

Sec. 1, clause 3. The electors shall meet in their respective states, and vote by ballot for two persons, of whom one at least shall not be an inhabitant of the same state with themselves. And they shall make a list of all the persons voted for, and of the number of votes for each; which list they shall sign and certify, and transmit sealed to the seat of the government of the United States, directed to the president of the Senate. The president of the Senate shall, in the presence of the Senate and House of Representatives, open all the certificates, and the votes shall then be counted. The person having the greatest number of votes shall be the President, if such number be a majority of the whole number of electors appointed; and if there be more than one who have such majority, and have an equal number of votes, then the House of Representatives shall immediately choose by ballot one of them for President; and if no person have a majority, then from the five highest on the list the said House shall in like manner choose the President. But in choosing the President, the votes shall be taken by states, the representation from each state having one vote; a quorum for this purpose shall consist of a member or members from two-thirds of the states, and a majority of all the states shall be necessary to a choice. In every case, after the choice of the

This clause describes the original way of electing the president and vice president. It was changed by Amendment 12.

We the People...

60. What temporary appointments may the president make?

Sec. 2, clause 3. The President shall have power to fill up all vacancies that may happen during the recess of the Senate, by granting commissions which shall expire at the end of their next session.

The president may temporarily appoint people to federal offices that become vacant while Congress is not in session. These appointments last until the end of the next meeting of the Senate.

SECTION 3 Duties of the President

He shall from time to time give to the Congress information of the state of the Union, and recommend to their consideration such measures as he shall judge necessary and expedient; he may, on extraordinary occasions, convene both houses, or either of them, and in case of disagreement between them, with respect to the time of adjournment, he may adjourn them to such time as he shall think proper; he shall receive ambassadors and other public ministers; he shall take care that the laws be faithfully executed, and shall commission all the officers of the United States.

This section is an important source of the president's role in the legislative process. It calls for the president to speak regularly to Congress about the nation's problems. This is the State of the Union message the president gives at the beginning of each session of Congress. Only Congress can make laws, but the president has power to suggest laws that Congress should pass. This power gives the president enormous influence.

In emergencies, the president may call a meeting of either or both houses of Congress. If the houses of Congress disagree about when to end their meeting, the president may decide when to end it.

The president is the official who meets with representatives of other countries. This power makes the president chief foreign-policy maker because the power to receive ambassadors is the power to recognize foreign governments.

It is the duty of the president to see that the laws of the country are followed. The president must sign the papers that give officers the right to hold their positions.

We the People...

SECTION 4 Impeachment

The President, Vice-President and all civil officers of the United States, shall be removed from office on impeachment for, and conviction of, treason, bribery, or other high crimes and misdemeanors.

The president, vice president, and other officers of the U.S. government (except congressmen and military officers) will lose their position in government if they are impeached and convicted of certain crimes. *Treason* is giving help to the nation's enemies. Nobody is sure exactly what *high crimes* and *misdemeanors* are, but the basic idea is that an officer can be removed if he or she has seriously abused his or her power.

A R T I C L E   III
JUDICIAL BRANCH

The writers of the Constitution gave Congress the job of creating most of the courts to be run by the U.S. government. They also listed the kinds of cases that might be heard in the federal courts.

SECTION 1   Federal Courts

61. What courts are there and how independent are the judges?

The judicial power of the United States shall be vested in one Supreme Court, and in such inferior courts as the Congress may from time to time ordain and establish. The judges, both of the supreme and inferior courts, shall hold their offices during good behavior, and shall, at stated times, receive for their services, a compensation, which shall not be diminished during their continuance in office.

Judicial power is the power to decide cases in a court of law. This power is given to the Supreme Court and to lower courts set up by Congress. Once appointed, judges hold office for life or until they have been impeached and found guilty of wrongful acts. The salary paid to a judge cannot be lowered so long as he or she holds office. The writers of the Constitution wanted judges to be free of political pressures. The provisions about judges' salaries and terms check both Congress and the president.

SECTION 2   Extent of Judicial Powers

62. What power do federal courts have?

Sec. 2, clause 1. The judicial power shall extend to all cases, in law and equity, arising under this Constitution, the laws of the United States, and treaties made, or which shall be made, under their authority; — to all cases affecting ambassadors, other public ministers and consuls; — to all cases of admiralty and maritime jurisdiction; — to controversies to which the United States shall be a party; — to controversies between two or more states; between a state and citizens of another state; — between citizens of different states; — between citizens of the same state claiming lands under grants of different states; and between a state, or the citizens thereof, and foreign states, citizens or subjects.

Federal courts hear cases that have to do with the Constitution, with laws of the United States, with treaties, and with ships and shipping. They hear any case in which the U.S. government is one of the two opposing sides. They settle disputes between two or more states. They originally heard cases involving a state and people from another state or from a foreign country. Amendment 11 took away this power except when the state is the one that takes the case to court. They settle disputes between citizens of different states; disputes about certain claims to grants of land; disputes between a state and a foreign country or its people; and disputes between an American and a foreign country or its people.

One power that the courts have that is not described in the Constitution is *judicial review*. It is the power to say that a law or executive action is unconstitutional. To be constitutional, a law must not violate or go beyond the powers given to the government by the Constitution.

63. What cases does the Supreme Court hear?

Sec. 2, clause 2. In all cases affecting ambassadors, other public ministers and consuls, and those in which a state shall be party, the Supreme Court shall have original jurisdiction. In all the other cases before mentioned, the Supreme Court shall have appellate jurisdiction, both as to law and fact, with such exceptions, and under such regulations as the Congress shall make.

Jurisdiction [jür′is dik′shən] is the right of a court to hear a particular kind of case. The Supreme Court has *original jurisdiction* in all cases involving a representative from a foreign country or involving a state. This means that it hears the facts of the case and decides which side wins the case. All other cases must be tried in the lower courts first. The decision of the lower courts can then be appealed to the Supreme Court, which has *appellate jurisdiction*. Congress decides which kinds of cases can be appealed.

64. What rules govern trials?

Sec. 2, clause 3. The trial of all crimes, except in cases of impeachment, shall be by jury; and such trial shall be held in the state where the said crimes shall have been committed; but when not committed within any state, the trial shall be at such place or places as the Congress may by law have directed.

Any person accused of committing a crime against the United States has the right to a trial by jury. The trial is held in a federal court in the state where the crime was committed. Congress describes by law where trials are held in places that are not states (in territories, for example). The only exceptions to these rules are impeachment trials, which are tried as described in Article I.

SECTION 3 Treason

65. What is treason?

Sec. 3, clause 1. Treason against the United States shall consist only in levying war against them, or in adhering to their enemies, giving them aid and comfort. No person shall be convicted of treason unless on the testimony of two witnesses to the same overt act, or on confession in open court.

Treason is defined as carrying on war against the United States or helping enemies of the United States. Convicting a person of treason is difficult. At least two witnesses must testify in court that the accused person committed the same act of treason. Any confession by the accused must be made in court. Confessions made elsewhere are not accepted as evidence.

66. How is treason punished?

Sec. 3, clause 2. The Congress shall have power to declare the punishment of treason, but no attainder of treason shall work corruption of blood or forfeiture except during the life of the person attainted.

Congress has the power to decide the punishment for treason. It can only punish the guilty person. No punishment can be set for heirs or family of the guilty person. *Corruption of blood* is punishment of the family of a wrongdoer. It involves taking away a wrongdoer's right to pass an estate or title on to the family. *Forfeiture* involves taking away the goods and honors of the wrongdoer during his or her lifetime.

A R T I C L E   IV
THE STATES

Article IV describes how the states are to deal with one another. It also sets out a procedure for the addition of territories and states.

SECTION 1 Recognition of Each Other's Acts

67. How shall one state treat the laws of other states?

Full faith and credit shall be given in each state to the public acts, records, and judicial proceedings of every other state. And the Congress may by general laws prescribe the manner in which such acts, records, and proceedings shall be proved, and the effect thereof.

All states must accept the laws, records, and court decisions of other states as legal and binding. Congress has the power to make laws that force the states to respect each other's laws, records, and court decisions.

SECTION 2 Citizens' Rights in Other States

68. How will each state treat citizens from other states?

Sec. 2, clause 1. The citizens of each state shall be entitled to all privileges and immunities of citizens in the several states.

A citizen from another state has basically the same rights as the citizens of the state where he or she happens to be. He or she is not to be treated as a foreigner.

69. What happens to accused criminals who escape to one state from another?

Sec. 2, clause 2. A person charged in any state with treason, felony, or other crime, who shall flee from justice, and be found in another state, shall on demand of the executive authority of the state from which he fled, be delivered up, to be removed to the state having jurisdiction of the crime.

People cannot escape justice by running out of state. Anyone accused of a crime in one state who flees to another state must be returned if the governor of the state where the crime was committed requests it. This process is called *extradition*.

70. What happened to escaping slaves?

Sec. 2, clause 3. No person held to service or labor in one state, under the laws thereof, escaping into another, shall, in consequence of any law or regulation therein, be discharged from such service or labor, but shall be delivered up on claim of the party to whom such service or labor may be due.

Persons held to service or labor were slaves, indentured servants, or apprentices. They could not become free by escaping to another state. They had to be sent back to their owners.

SECTION 3 New States and Territories

71. How shall new states enter the Union?

Sec. 3, clause 1. New states may be admitted by the Congress into this Union; but no new state shall be formed or erected within the jurisdiction of any other state; nor any state be formed by the junction of two or more states, or parts of states, without the consent of the legislatures of the states concerned as well as of the Congress.

Congress has power to add new states to the United States. (No way is provided for a state to leave the Union.) No state may be divided to make another state without the consent of the original state and Congress. The consent of Congress and the states involved is also needed for a new state to be made by putting parts of two or more states together.

72. How shall territories be treated?

Sec. 3, clause 2. The Congress shall have power to dispose of and make all needful rules and regulations respecting the territory or other property belonging to the United States; and nothing in this Constitution shall be so construed as to prejudice any claims of the United States, or of any particular state.

Congress can sell or give away government lands and property. It has power to make laws governing lands and property. This clause is the source of power for Congress to decide how territories are governed before they become states. Nothing in the Constitution is intended to favor one state over another, or over the United States, in disputes over land claims.

SECTION 4 Guarantees to the States

The United States shall guarantee to every state in this union a republican form of government, and shall protect each of them against invasion; and on application of the legislature, or of the executive (when the legislature cannot be convened) against domestic violence.

The federal government promises that every state in the Union shall have a government in which representatives are elected by the people. It promises to protect each state from invasion. It also promises to send help in putting down riots. The help must be requested by the state legislature or, if the state legislature cannot meet soon enough, by the governor.

We the People...

ARTICLE V

AMENDING THE CONSTITUTION

73. What is the amendment procedure, and what amendments are forbidden?

We the People…

The Congress, whenever two-thirds of both houses shall deem it necessary, shall propose amendments to this Constitution, or, on the application of the legislatures of two-thirds of the several states, shall call a convention for proposing amendments, which, in either case, shall be valid to all intents and purposes, as part of this Constitution, and when ratified by the legislatures of three-fourths of the several states, or by conventions in three-fourths thereof, as the one or the other mode of ratification may be proposed by the Congress; provided that no amendment which may be made prior to the year one thousand eight hundred and eight shall in any manner affect the first and fourth clauses in the ninth Section of the first Article; and that no state, without its consent, shall be deprived of its equal suffrage in the Senate.

The writers of the Constitution realized that if their work was to last, they would have to provide ways to adapt the Constitution to changes in society. Article V provides several ways.

There are two ways of proposing amendments to the Constitution. One way is for two-thirds of both the Senate and the House of Representatives to vote for a specific amendment. The other way is for the legislatures of two-thirds of the states to ask Congress to call a special convention to propose amendments. All proposed amendments must be ratified by the states. An amendment can be ratified in one of two ways. The legislatures of three-fourths of the states can approve the amendment, or conventions in three-fourths of the states can approve the amendment. Congress chooses the method of ratification at the time an amendment is proposed.

No amendment proposed before 1808 could stop the international slave trade or allow a different method of figuring direct taxes. No amendment can decrease the number of senators a state has unless the affected state agrees to the change.

ARTICLE VI

NATIONAL SUPREMACY

74. What happened to existing debts?

All debts contracted and engagements entered into, before the adoption of this Constitution, shall be as valid against the United States under this Constitution, as under the Confederation.

All debts and treaties that Congress made under the Articles of Confederation are binding on the United States under the Constitution.

75. Which laws are supreme?

This Constitution, and the laws of the United States which shall be made in pursuance thereof; and all treaties made, or which shall be made, under the authority of the United States, shall be the supreme law of the land; and the judges in every state shall be bound thereby, anything in the constitution or laws of any state to the contrary notwithstanding.

This Constitution and federal laws or treaties constitutionally made are the highest law of the land. State judges must follow this law, even if state laws or constitutions contradict it.

76. What do officials promise?

The senators and representatives before mentioned, and the members of the several state legislatures, and all executive and judicial officers, both of the United States and of the several states, shall be bound by oath or affirmation, to support this Constitution; but no religious test shall ever be required as a qualification to any office or public trust under the United States.

All federal and state officials must promise to support this Constitution. However, no officials or public employees can ever be required to take any kind of religious test in order to hold office.

A R T I C L E VII

RATIFICATION

77. How can the Constitution be ratified?

The ratification of the conventions of nine states shall be sufficient for the establishment of this Constitution between the states so ratifying the same. Done in convention by the unanimous consent of the states present the seventeenth day of September in the year of our Lord one thousand seven hundred and eighty seven and of the independence of the United States of America the twelfth. In witness whereof we have hereunto subscribed our names.

Article VII describes how the Constitution could be approved by the states.

Government under this Constitution could begin after nine states approved it at special conventions. (Nine states ratified the Constitution by June 21, 1788.) This Constitution was signed on September 17, 1787, in the twelfth year of the country's independence. These were the signers:

George Washington — President and deputy from Virginia

New Hampshire
John Langdon
Nicholas Gilman

Massachusetts
Nathaniel Gorham
Rufus King

Pennsylvania
Benjamin Franklin
Thomas Mifflin
Robert Morris
George Clymer
Thomas FitzSimons
Jared Ingersoll
James Wilson
Gouverneur Morris

Delaware
George Read
Gunning Bedford, Junior
John Dickinson
Richard Bassett
Jacob Broom

Maryland
James McHenry
Daniel of St. Thomas Jenifer
Daniel Carroll

Connecticut
William Samuel Johnson
Roger Sherman

New York
Alexander Hamilton

New Jersey
William Livingston
David Brearley
William Paterson
Jonathan Dayton

Virginia
John Blair
James Madison, Junior

North Carolina
William Blount
Richard Dobbs Spaight
Hugh Williamson

South Carolina
John Rutledge
Charles Cotesworth Pinckney
Charles Pinckney
Pierce Butler

Georgia
William Few
Abraham Baldwin

We the People...

AMENDMENT 9 (1791)
All Other Rights

The enumeration in the Constitution of certain rights shall not be construed to deny or disparage others retained by the people.

The mention of certain rights in the Constitution does not mean that these are the only rights that people have and does not make other rights less important.

AMENDMENT 10 (1791)
Rights of States and the People

The powers not delegated to the United States by the Constitution, nor prohibited by it to the states, are reserved to the states respectively, or to the people.

This is the "reserved powers amendment." The states or the people have all powers that have not been assigned to the federal government or prohibited to the states.

AMENDMENT 11 (1795)
Suits Against a State

The judicial power of the United States shall not be construed to extend to any suit in law or equity, commenced or prosecuted against one of the United States by citizens of another state, or by citizens or subjects of any foreign state.

Citizens of other states or foreign countries cannot sue a state in the federal courts without its consent.

AMENDMENT 12 (1804)
Election of President

The writers of the Constitution wanted the president and the vice president to be the two best qualified persons. For that reason, the original election method provided for the vice president to be the person who came in second in the election. This plan worked during the first three presidential elections.

The electors shall meet in their respective states and vote by ballot for President and Vice-President, one of whom, at least, shall not be an inhabitant of the same state with themselves; they shall name in their ballots the person voted for as President, and in distinct ballots the person voted for as Vice-President, and they shall make distinct lists of all persons voted for as President, and all persons voted for as Vice-President, and of the number of votes for each, which lists they shall sign and certify, and transmit sealed to the seat of the government of the United States, directed to the president of the Senate;

The president of the Senate shall, in the presence of the Senate and House of Representatives, open all the certificates and the votes shall then be counted;

The person having the greatest number of votes for President, shall be the President, if such number be a majority of the whole number of electors appointed; and if no person have such majority, then from the persons having the highest numbers not exceeding three on the list of those voted for as President, the House of Representatives shall choose immediately, by ballot, the President. But in choosing the President, the votes shall be taken by states, the representation from each state having one vote; a quorum for this purpose shall consist of a member or members from two-thirds of the states, and a majority of all the states shall be necessary to a choice.

In 1800, however, the vote was tied between the Republican candidates for president and vice president. The election had to be decided in the House of Representatives.

In the House, the tie was not broken until the 36th ballot. Soon after the election, this amendment was proposed and ratified. It says that the vice president is specifically elected to that office.

The electors meet in their own states, where they cast separate ballots for president and vice president. At least one of the candidates they vote for must live in another state. After the vote, the electors make a list of the persons voted for as president and another list of persons voted for as vice president. On each list they write the total votes cast for each person. Then they sign their names, seal the lists, and send them to the president of the Senate in Washington, D.C.

In a meeting attended by both houses of Congress, the president of the Senate opens the lists from all the states, and the votes are counted.

The person having the most votes for president is president. However, the number of votes received must be more than half of the total number of all electors (now 270 or more). If no person has this many votes, the House of Representatives selects the president from the three candidates who have the largest number of electoral votes. Each state has one vote, no matter how many representatives it has. Two-thirds of the states must be represented when this vote is cast. The can-

~~And if the House of Representatives shall not choose a President whenever the right of choice shall devolve upon them, before the fourth day of March next following, then the Vice-President shall act as President, as in the case of the death or other constitutional disability of the President.~~

The person having the greatest number of votes as Vice-President, shall be the Vice-President, if such number be a majority of the whole number of electors appointed, and if no person have a majority, then from the two highest numbers on the list, the Senate shall choose the Vice-President; a quorum for the purpose shall consist of two-thirds of the whole number of senators, and a majority of the whole number shall be necessary to a choice.

But no person constitutionally ineligible to the office of President shall be eligible to that of Vice-President of the United States.

didate who receives a majority of the votes of the states is president.

If the House of Representatives does not elect a president before the date set for the new president to take office, the vice president acts as president. (The date for this was changed by Amendment 20.)

The person who receives the most electoral votes for vice president becomes vice president. However, he or she must get more than half the electoral votes. If no person has more than half, the Senate chooses a vice president from the two candidates with the most votes. Two-thirds of all the senators must be present when the vote is taken. To be elected vice president, the candidate must receive the votes of more than half (now 51 or more) of all the senators.

A person who does not have the qualifications for president of the United States cannot be vice president.

AMENDMENT 13 (1865)
Abolition of Slavery

Sec. 1. Neither slavery nor involuntary servitude, except as a punishment for crime whereof the party shall have been duly convicted, shall exist within the United States, or any place subject to their jurisdiction.

Slavery is not allowed in the United States or in any lands under its control. No one may be forced to work unless a court has set that as punishment for committing a crime.

Sec. 2. Congress shall have power to enforce this article by appropriate legislation.

Congress has the power to make laws that will put this amendment into effect.

AMENDMENT 14 (1868)
Civil Rights in the States

Sec. 1. All persons born or naturalized in the United States, and subject to the jurisdiction thereof, are citizens of the United States and of the state wherein they reside. No state shall make or enforce any law which shall abridge the privileges or immunities of citizens of the United States; nor shall any state deprive any person of life, liberty, or property, without due process of law; nor deny to any person within its jurisdiction the equal protection of the laws.

Amendment 14 did several things. It gave citizenship to former slaves and their decendants, gave them equal rights, canceled the clause counting three-fifths of the slaves in deciding how many representatives a state would have, punished Confederate officers, and canceled Confederate debts.

Everyone who was born or naturalized in the United States and is subject to the country's laws is a citizen of the United States and also of the state in which he or she lives. States cannot make or enforce laws that prevent any citizen from enjoying rights given by federal law. This amendment also makes the due-process clause of the Fifth Amendment apply to the states as well as to the federal government. The Supreme Court has said that it makes other parts of the Bill of Rights, such as freedom of speech, apply to the states too. The "equal protection" clause is very important. One thing it does is to make it illegal for states to discriminate on unreasonable grounds, like the color of a person's skin. By defining state citizenship, the amendment made it impossible for states to have their own citizenship requirements that keep African Americans from being state citizens.

We the People...

We the People...

Sec. 2. Representatives shall be apportioned among the several states according to their respective numbers, counting the whole number of persons in each state, excluding Indians not taxed. But when the right to vote at any election for the choice of electors for President and Vice-President of the United States, representatives in Congress, the executive and judicial officers of a state, or the members of the legislature thereof, is denied to any of the male inhabitants of such state, being twenty-one years of age, and citizens of the United States, or in any way abridged, except for participation in rebellion, or other crime, the basis of representation therein shall be reduced in the proportion which the number of such male citizens shall bear to the whole number of male citizens twenty-one years of age in such state.

All people, except untaxed Indians, are counted in order to determine how many representatives in Congress each state is to have. This section amended Article I, Section 2, clause 3, in which slaves were counted as three-fifths of a free person. A state will lose representatives in proportion to the male citizens over twenty-one who have not committed crimes that it prevents from voting. This provision, intended to force states to allow African American men to vote, has never been enforced. However, Amendment 15 has been used to enforce African Americans' voting rights.

Sec. 3. No person shall be a senator or representative in Congress, or elector of President and Vice-President, or hold any office, civil or military, under the United States, or under any state, who, having previously taken an oath, as a member of Congress, or as an officer of the United States, or as a member of any state legislature, or as an executive or judicial officer of any state, to support the Constitution of the United States, shall have engaged in insurrection or rebellion against the same, or given aid or comfort to the enemies thereof. But Congress may by a vote of two-thirds of each house, remove such disability.

Congress worded section 3 so that Confederate leaders who had previously held national or state office were no longer able to vote or hold office. On June 6, 1898, Congress removed this barrier.

Sec. 4. The validity of the public debt of the United States, authorized by law, including debts incurred for payment of pensions and bounties for services in suppressing insurrection or rebellion, shall not be questioned. But neither the United States nor any state shall assume or pay any debt or obligation incurred in aid of insurrection or rebellion

The states or the federal government cannot pay any part of the Confederate debt. The payment of the Union debt cannot be questioned. No payment can be made for slaves who have been emancipated.

against the United States, or any claim for the loss or emancipation of any slave; but all such debts, obligations, and claims shall be held illegal and void.

Sec. 5. The Congress shall have power to enforce, by appropriate legislation the provisions of this article.

Congress has the power to make laws that will put this amendment into effect.

**AMENDMENT 15 (1870)
African American
Suffrage**

Sec. 1. The right of citizens of the United States to vote shall not be denied or abridged by the United States or by any state on account of race, color, or previous condition of servitude.

Neither the United States nor any state has the right to keep citizens from voting because of their race or color or because they were once slaves.

Sec. 2. The Congress shall have power to enforce this article by appropriate legislation.

Congress has the power to make laws that will put this amendment into effect.

**AMENDMENT 16 (1913)
Income Tax**

The Congress shall have power to lay and collect taxes on incomes, from whatever source derived, without apportionment among the several states, and without regard to any census or enumeration.

This amendment changes Article I, (Section 2, clause 3, and Section 9, clause 4) by saying that Congress has the power to put a tax on income *without* dividing the amount due among the states according to population.

**AMENDMENT 17 (1913)
Direct Election of
Senators**

Sec. 1. The Senate of the United States shall be composed of two senators from each state, elected by the people thereof, for six years; and each senator shall have one vote. The electors in each state shall have the qualifications requisite for electors of the most numerous branch of the state legislatures.

This amendment changed the method of selecting senators described in Article I, Section 3, clause 1 to say that senators would be elected by the people of each state, not by the state legislatures.

Sec. 2. When vacancies happen in the representation of any state in the Senate, the executive authority of such state shall issue writs of election to fill such vacancies: *Provided,* That the legislature of any state may empower the executive thereof to make temporary appointments until the people fill the vacancies by election as the legislature may direct.

We the People...

Sec. 3. This amendment shall not be so construed as to affect the election or term of any senator chosen before it becomes valid as part of the Constitution.

**AMENDMENT 18 (1919)
National Prohibition**

Sec. 1. ~~After one year from the ratification of this article the manufacture, sale, or transportation of intoxicating liquors within, the importation thereof into, or the exportation thereof from the United States and all territory subject to the jurisdiction thereof for beverage purposes is hereby prohibited.~~

One year after this amendment was ratified it became illegal in the United States and its territories to make, sell, or carry intoxicating liquors for drinking purposes. It became illegal to send such liquors out of the country and its territories or to bring such liquors into them.

Sec. 2. ~~The Congress and the several states shall have concurrent power to enforce this article by appropriate legislation.~~

The states and the federal government shared enforcement duties.

Sec. 3. ~~This article shall be inoperative unless it shall have been ratified as an amendment to the Constitution by the legislatures of the several states, as provided in the Constitution, within seven years from the date of the submission hereof to the states by the Congress.~~

This amendment would not have become a part of the Constitution if it had not been ratified by the legislatures of the states within seven years. The need for ratification within seven years was written into several amendments.

**AMENDMENT 19 (1920)
Women's Suffrage**

The right of citizens of the United States to vote shall not be denied or abridged by the United States or by any state on account of sex.

Congress shall have power to enforce this article by appropriate legislation.

Neither the United States nor any state can keep a citizen from voting because she is a woman. Congress has the power to make laws that will make this amendment effective.

**AMENDMENT 20 (1933)
"Lame-Duck" Amendment**

Sec. 1. The terms of the President and Vice-President shall end at noon on the twentieth day of January, and the terms of senators and representatives at noon on the third day of January, of the years in which such terms would have ended if this article had not been ratified; and the terms of their successors shall then begin.

Sec. 2. The Congress shall assemble at least once in every year, and such meeting shall begin at noon on the third day of January, unless they shall by law appoint a different day.

Sec. 3. If, at the time fixed for the beginning of the term of the President, the President-elect shall have died, the Vice-President-elect shall become President. If a President shall not have been chosen before the time fixed for the beginning of his term, or if the President-elect shall have failed to qualify, then the Vice-President-elect shall act as President until a President shall have qualified; and the Congress may by law provide for the case wherein neither a President-elect nor a Vice-President-elect shall have qualified, declaring who shall then act as President, or the manner in which one who is to act shall be selected, and such person, shall act accordingly until a President or Vice-President shall have qualified.

Sec. 4. The Congress may by law provide for the case of the death of any of the persons from whom the House of Representatives may choose a President whenever the right of choice shall have devolved upon them, and for the case of the death of any of the persons from whom the Senate may choose a Vice-President whenever the right of choice shall have devolved upon them.

Sec. 5. Sections 1 and 2 shall take effect on the fifteenth day of October following the ratification of this article.

A person who holds office after his or her replacement has been chosen does not have much influence, and so is known as a "lame duck." This amendment shortens the "lame duck" period. Formerly a president and vice president elected in November did not take office until March 4. Now they are sworn in in January. Formerly, new members of Congress waited 13 months to take their seats. Now they wait only about two. Sections 3 and 4 give procedures for the selection of president and vice president in situations not covered by Amendment 12. This amendment had to be approved within seven years of its being sent to the states.

We the People...

Sec. 6. This article shall be inoperative unless it shall have been ratified as an amendment to the Constitution by the legislatures of three-fourths of the several states within seven years from the date of its submission.

AMENDMENT 21 (1933)
Repeal of Prohibition

Sec. 1. The eighteenth article of amendment to the Constitution of the United States is hereby repealed.

We the People...

This amendment repeals Amendment 18. Prohibition is no longer a national law.

Sec. 2. The transportation or importation into any state, territory, or possession of the United States for delivery or use therein of intoxicating liquors, in violation of the laws thereof, is hereby prohibited.

A state can forbid liquor for drinking purposes. Carrying liquor across state boundaries for use in a "dry" state is a crime against the United States as well as against the state.

Sec. 3. This article shall be inoperative unless it shall have been ratified as an amendment to the Constitution by conventions in the several states, as provided in the Constitution, within seven years from the date of the submission hereof to the states by the Congress.

Amendment 21 had to be ratified by state conventions chosen specifically for their views on the issue. The conventions had to approve the amendment within seven years.

AMENDMENT 22 (1951)
Presidential Term of Office

Sec. 1. No person shall be elected to the office of the President more than twice, and no person who has held the office of President, or acted as President, for more than two years of a term to which some other person was elected President shall be elected to the office of the President more than once. But this article shall not apply to any person holding the office of President when this article was proposed by the Congress, and shall not prevent any person who may be holding the office of President, or acting as President, during the term within which this article becomes operative from holding the office of President or acting as President during the remainder of such term.

No person can have more than two terms as president. Holding the office of president or acting as president for more than two years will be considered as one full term. This amendment did not apply to Harry Truman, who was president at the time this amendment was both proposed by Congress and ratified by the states.

Sec. 2. This article shall be inoperative unless it shall have been ratified as an amendment to the Constitution by the legislatures of three-fourths of the several states within seven years from the date of its submission to the states by the Congress.

This amendment had to be ratified within seven years in order to take effect.

AMENDMENT 23 (1961)
Voting in the District of Columbia

Sec. 1. The district constituting the seat of government of the United States shall appoint in such manner as the Congress may direct:

A number of electors of President and Vice-President equal to the whole number of senators and representatives in Congress to which the District would be entitled if it were a state, but in no event more than the least populous state; they shall be in addition to those appointed by the states, but they shall be considered, for the purposes of the election of President and Vice-President, to be electors appointed by a state; and they shall meet in the district and perform such duties as provided by the twelfth article of amendment.

Sec. 2. The Congress shall have power to enforce this article by appropriate legislation.

This amendment gives people living in Washington, D.C., a voice in choosing the president and vice president. It says the District of Columbia may choose electors in the election of the president and vice president of the United States. The number of electors is limited to the number of electors from the state with the smallest population. The electors follow the rules for elections described in Amendment 12. Congress can pass laws to put this amendment into effect.

AMENDMENT 24 (1964)
Abolition of Poll Taxes

Sec. 1. The right of citizens of the United States to vote in any primary or other election for President or Vice-President, for electors for President or Vice-President, or for senator or representative in Congress, shall not be denied or abridged by the United States or any state by reason of failure to pay any poll tax or other tax.

Sec. 2. The Congress shall have power to enforce this article by appropriate legislation.

Neither the United States nor any state can make the payment of a poll tax or any other tax a requirement for voting in any election for national officers. This rule applies to the election of the president, vice president, electors of these, senators, and representatives in Congress. The amendment does not make poll taxes illegal in elections of state officials. However, it makes them unlikely and impractical because to require a poll tax in state elections but not in federal elections, a state would have to keep two different lists of voters and print two different kinds of ballots. Congress can make laws to enforce this amendment.

AMENDMENT 25 (1967)
Presidential Disability and Succession

Sec. 1. In case of the removal of the President from office or of his death or resignation, the Vice-President shall become President.

If the president dies or resigns, or is removed from office, the vice president becomes president.

Sec. 2. Whenever there is a vacancy in the office of the Vice-President, the President shall nominate a Vice-President who shall take office upon confirmation by a majority vote of both houses of Congress.

The president appoints a vice president if no one is serving in that office. The appointment must be approved by a majority vote in both houses of Congress.

Sec. 3. Whenever the President transmits to the president pro tempore of the Senate and the speaker of the House of Representatives his written declaration that he is unable to discharge the powers and duties of his office, and until he transmits to them a written declaration to the contrary, such powers and duties shall be discharged by the Vice-President as Acting President.

If the president notifies Congress in writing that he or she is unable to perform official duties, the vice president takes over as acting president until the president notifies Congress in writing that he or she is again able to serve.

Sec. 4. Whenever the Vice-President and a majority of either the principal officers of the executive departments or of such other body

If a disabled president is unable or unwilling to notify Congress of his or her disability, the vice president may. In such a case, a majority

as Congress may by law provide, transmit to the president pro tempore of the Senate and the speaker of the House of Representatives their written declaration that the President is unable to discharge the powers and duties of his office, the Vice-President shall immediately assume the powers and duties of the office as Acting President.

Thereafter, when the President transmits to the president pro tempore of the Senate and the speaker of the House of Representatives his written declaration that no inability exists, he shall resume the powers and duties of his office unless the Vice-President and a majority of either the principal officers of the executive departments or of such other body as Congress may by law provide, transmit within four days to the president pro tempore of the Senate and the speaker of the House of Representatives their written declaration that the President is unable to discharge the powers and duties of his office. Thereupon Congress shall decide the issue, assembling within forty-eight hours for that purpose if not in session. If the Congress, within twenty-one days after receipt of the latter written declaration, or, if Congress is not in session, within twenty-one days after Congress is required to assemble, determines by two-thirds vote of both houses that the President is unable to discharge the powers and duties of his office, the Vice-President shall continue to discharge the same as Acting President; otherwise, the President shall resume the powers and duties of his office.

of the cabinet, or some other group named by Congress in law, must agree. Then the vice president becomes acting president.

The president may notify Congress of a recovery and resume the powers and duties of office. However, if the vice president and a majority of the designated group do not agree that the president has recovered, they must notify Congress before four days have passed. Congress must meet within forty-eight hours. They have twenty-one days to discuss the issue. If two-thirds or more of each house votes against the president, the vice president continues to serve as acting president. Otherwise, the president resumes office.

We the People...

AMENDMENT 26 (1971)
Eighteen-Year-Old Vote

Sec. 1. The right of citizens of the United States, who are eighteen years of age or older, to vote shall not be denied or abridged by the United States or by any state on account of age.

Sec. 2. The Congress shall have the power to enforce this article by appropriate legislation.

The United States and the state governments cannot say that eighteen-year-olds are too young to vote. Congress can pass laws to enforce this amendment.

We the People...

Linking Past to Present

A sense of mission and adventure drove emigrants westward to Oregon. "I remember the water came rushing into the wagon box to my waist," young Jesse Applegate recalled of a river fording like that shown in the inset painting by Samuel Colman (1832–1920). With seed carried from Missouri, the Applegates planted the first of the lush orchards that dot Oregon's Willamette Valley today.

Expansion, Reform, and Constitutional Conflicts

1 8 2 4 – 1 8 6 0

4

The sense of being marked by a Provident God for a special mission was present from the beginning of American history. During the crucial years from 1824 to 1860, some Americans began to feel that it was also their destiny to expand into thinly settled lands across the "whole boundless continent." Prompted by success, by geographic factors, and by their own self-confidence, Americans ventured into Mexican lands in Texas, New Mexico, and a land of Eden, California. Others went into the Oregon Country, then claimed by both Great Britain and the United States. Among them was a seven-year-old boy, Jesse Applegate, whose family joined the first large company of Oregon emigrants in 1843.

In later life Applegate described a perilous passage near what is now Oregon's eastern border with a Biblical reference comparing it to the journey to Heaven.

AN AMERICAN ★ SPEAKS It is a very narrow ridge with a gorge a thousand feet deep on the left hand and a sheer precipice on the right down to the Snake River, which looked . . . like a ribbon not more than four inches wide. The danger was so great that no one rode in the wagons. . . . [At] many places there was not a foot to spare for the wagon wheels. . . . The Bible says: *"Strait is the gate, and narrow is the way, which leadeth unto life."*

Later generations of Americans have continued to use the concept of mission to give special meaning to their own lives and to that of their nation. Does this concept still define America's search for identity today?

CHAPTER PREVIEW

In this chapter you will learn about reform movements and about how westward expansion and constitutional crises led to the breakup of the Union.

SECTIONS IN THIS CHAPTER.
1. **Andrew Jackson gave his name to a new era.**
2. **An Age of Reform swept the nation.**
3. **Manifest Destiny became a national battle cry.**
4. **The United States acquired western lands from Mexico.**
5. **Sectional differences led to war.**

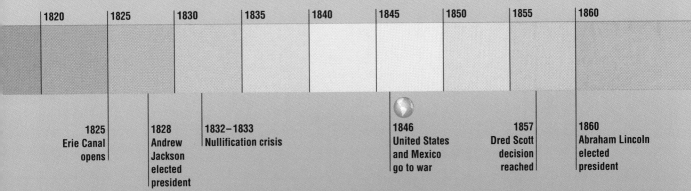

| 1820 | 1825 | 1830 | 1835 | 1840 | 1845 | 1850 | 1855 | 1860 |

1825
Erie Canal opens

1828
Andrew Jackson elected president

1832–1833
Nullification crisis

1846
United States and Mexico go to war

1857
Dred Scott decision reached

1860
Abraham Lincoln elected president

SECTION 1

Andrew Jackson gave his name to a new era.

Key Terms: Industrial Revolution, nominating conventions, Democratic party, Tariff of Abominations, nullify, Indian Removal Act, Whig party

Reading Preview
As you read this section, you will learn:

1. what new forces shaped American life in the early 1800s.
2. what developed politically in the early 1800s.
3. who dominated the Jackson Administration.
4. why the Whig party emerged.

Besides benefiting the areas now known as the Midwest, the Erie Canal made New York City the country's leading port. A horse and mule pull a canalboat alongside a towpath in this painting by William R. Miller.

Life in America changed dramatically in the first half of the 1800s. The nation's population grew from 5.3 million in 1800 to more than 23 million by 1850. During that same period, the United States gradually expanded its territory until it stretched from the Atlantic Ocean to the Pacific. The nation was also beginning to enjoy spectacular economic growth. Farm prof-

its from wheat, corn, and cotton soared. A factory system had been developed and was flourishing.

New economic forces shaped American life.

After 1815 a national system of transportation on roads and rivers began to link the nation's communities. Thousands of miles of new roads, turnpikes, and canals, together with such improvements as the steamboat, made travel cheaper and quicker than ever before. This transportation network also expanded markets and made industrial growth possible.

New York State provided the most striking example of the new geographic mobility when it completed the **Erie Canal** in 1825. The 363-mile-long canal connected Lake Erie at Buffalo with the Hudson River at Albany and, by way of the Hudson, with the port of New York. The canal became an important artery for settlement and trade, linking the Atlantic Coast with the Great Lakes region.

Competition from railroads eventually brought ruin to most canals, but the advent of the railroad signaled an even greater revolution in transportation. The Baltimore and Ohio Railroad, organized in 1827, carried its first passengers in horse-drawn cars over 15 miles of

track in 1830. Ten years later steam locomotives were operating over nearly 3,000 miles of track. By mid-century the country's rail network had grown to more than 9,000 miles.

Improved transportation, new technology, and new sources of capital made the growth of factories possible. Increased mechanization and new forms of power swelled into what is called the **Industrial Revolution**—the change from home industries to a factory system. In the United States this revolution got underway in New England's textile industry, with an increasing number of factories powered first by harnessing waterfalls and later by steam.

The invention of the cotton gin in 1793 by **Eli Whitney** aided the growth of the textile industry by making it possible to remove the seeds from raw cotton fast enough to supply the textile factories. In towns such as Lowell, Massachusetts, the nation's first communities of factory workers began to manufacture cotton textiles.

The factory towns relied heavily on women and children for long hours of labor—usually 12 or 13 hours a day, six days a week. In the 1820s and 1830s some men and women factory workers tried to gain improved working conditions and better pay. However, these early attempts at labor organization met with little success. With increasing numbers of immigrants desperately seeking work, factory owners had a plentiful supply of cheap labor.

A new system of party politics developed.

Americans gradually developed a more democratic political system in the early 1800s. They waged a steady campaign to remove the property qualification for voters. By the 1820s the vote had become the right of free, white, male citizens in almost every state. Women and most free African Americans, however, continued to be excluded. Native Americans, as members of sovereign Indian nations, and African American slaves were not considered citizens. Thus, although the electorate had been greatly increased, a majority of Americans did not yet participate directly in the nation's political life.

The young women who worked in the cotton mills at Lowell, Massachusetts, wrote and edited their own magazine, the *Lowell Offering*, from 1840 to 1845. The editors, Harriot F. Curtis and Harriet Farley, meant the cover "To represent the New England school-girl, of which our factories are made up, standing near a beehive, emblem of industry and intelligence, and in the background the Yankee schoolhouse, church, and factory."

Many states revised their constitutions to call for the popular election of officials who had traditionally been appointed. By 1824, 18 out of the 24 states chose presidential electors by popular vote. New ways of nominating candidates for the presidency also arose. Instead of relying on congressional leaders to caucus, or meet privately to select candidates, voters supported **nominating conventions.** These conventions opened the selection of party candidates to democratically elected delegates much like national party conventions do today.

With the demise of the Federalists after 1816, the Republican party remained the nation's only political party. Underneath the outward appearance of unity, however, a fierce competition for power had been brewing within the party for several years. The election of 1824 made that struggle public—and permanently divided the Republicans.

MEET THE PRESIDENT

JOHN QUINCY ADAMS

Son of a president, John Quincy Adams was a child of history. At seven, he watched the Battle of Bunker Hill. At ten, he accompanied his father on a mission to France. At fourteen, he was secretary to the American minister in Russia. By birth and experience, Adams was made for the White House.

The irony of Adams' life was that his presidency was not the pinnacle of his life, but rather a pinched, unhappy interval that separated his outstanding career as a diplomat and secretary of state from his distinguished career in Congress. As president he lacked political finesse and public support.

Born: July 11, 1767
Died: February 23, 1848
In office: 1825–1829

Adams served his country until he literally dropped. At 80, he collapsed on the floor of the House of Representatives and died in the Speaker's office two days later.

The election of 1824. Five candidates—all Republicans—began to campaign for the presidency in 1824. John C. Calhoun of South Carolina soon dropped out of the race to run unopposed for the vice presidency. Each of the remaining four represented a particular part of the United States. **John Quincy Adams**, President Monroe's secretary of state and the son of former President John Adams, had the backing of New England. William H. Crawford, a Georgian with strong support in the South, was the nominee of the party's congressional caucus. His nomination by what the other candidates called an "undemocratic caucus" and a serious stroke that left him half paralyzed dimmed Crawford's hopes. Henry Clay, a Virginian by birth, moved to Kentucky as a young man, and had been Speaker of the House for 14 years. He drew his support from the West. **Andrew Jackson**, the hero of the Battle of New Orleans and another westerner, drew his strength from both the West and the South.

With four candidates, the vote was badly split. The winner in both the popular vote and the electoral college was Jackson, with 99 electoral votes. Adams came in second with 84, Crawford had 41, and Clay 37. Since no candidate received a majority, the election went to the House of Representatives to make a choice from the top three candidates, as stated in the 12th Amendment to the Constitution. Clay, who had finished fourth and was out of the race, threw his influence behind Adams, who was elected by the House.

Adams had won the battle, but the war was far from over. When he announced that his secretary of state was to be Henry Clay, Jackson raged, certain that a "corrupt bargain" had been made between Adams and Clay to deny him the presidency. Jackson began his campaign to capture the office in 1828.

A new political party. Even before Adams' inauguration, Jackson's supporters began working to forge a new coalition, or alliance, between Jackson's West, the South, and such key northern states as New York and Pennsylvania. The political mastermind of this strategy was **Martin Van Buren** of New York. Van Buren was a brilliant organizer whose own New York State political machine controlled one wing of the state's Republican party. A political machine is a tightly run, organized political group with a successful record of winning public office. Van Buren created a similar machine at the national level for Andrew Jackson. Through the new **Democratic party** Van Buren created, Jackson's personal popularity was transformed into political power.

To help win support in the key states of New York, Pennsylvania, Missouri, Ohio, and Kentucky (states Jackson had lost in the 1824 election), Jackson's supporters in Congress passed a new protective tariff in 1828. The tariff priced imported pig iron, hemp, sailcloth, and wool out of the American market. All of these were raw materials needed by New England's shipbuilders and factories. The West, along with New York and Pennsylvania, supported the tariff. New England and the South opposed it.

New England, however, would vote solidly for Adams anyway, and the South was certain to support Jackson over Adams in spite of its feelings against the tariff.

The Democrats created political excitement to appeal to masses of voters. They held meetings in cities and towns all over the country. They established newspapers to support their candidate and distributed pamphlets praising Jackson and criticizing his opponent. Their million-dollar campaign added up to a spectacle of rallies, speeches, songs, cartoons, and slogans presenting Jackson as a man of the people. Jackson won a large majority in the popular vote and swept the electoral college by 178 votes to Adams' 83. Thus, a new political party was launched and a new style of campaigning established in American political life.

Andrew Jackson dominated his Administration.

Jackson clearly meant to run his own Administration. Unlike President Adams, he saw nothing wrong in using presidential patronage powers. He dismissed men who had served in Adams' Administration and appointed loyal Democratic party members in their place. Operating under the principle that "to the victor belong the spoils," Jackson initiated what became known as the spoils system into national politics. Also unlike earlier presidents, who relied heavily upon the judgment of their cabinet, Jackson appointed men he could dominate by the force of his own personality.

Nullification. Jackson's first serious challenge came from his own vice president, **John C. Calhoun**. By leading South Carolina's strong protest against the tariff of 1828, which southerners called the **Tariff of Abominations**, Calhoun raised anew the troubling question of state versus federal

M E E T   T H E   P R E S I D E N T

ANDREW JACKSON

Andrew Jackson carried on his face a British scar and in his chest a duelist's bullet. He was as tough, violent, and colorful as the frontier that made him. His ascent to the presidency reflected the rise of common people to full status in American life.

Though he entered the White House a worn-out 61, grieving for his wife, stiff with old wounds and plagued by headaches and tuberculosis, Jackson had plenty of fight left in him. He continued the combative pattern of his life in conflicts with Congress, with Washington wives, with the Bank, with foreign powers, with nullifiers, with the Cherokees. Jackson did not

Born: March 15, 1767
Died: June 8, 1845
In office: 1829–1837

always win, but his aggressiveness magnified the power of the presidency. The force of his character stamped his name on an era: The Age of Jackson.

power. Calhoun argued that the federal government's powers were limited and specific and that all powers not specifically delegated to the federal government by the Constitution

The southern states, which imported most of their manufactured goods, viewed high tariffs as a constant threat to their prosperity. In this cartoon protesting the Tariff of Abominations, the industrial North is growing fat at the South's expense. The South raised the issue of states' rights in its defense.

States' Rights

Point

States are supreme

- The states created the federal government as their agent and therefore possess the higher power.
- Within its own borders a state can nullify acts of the federal government.
- The Tenth Amendment reserves to the states or to the people "powers not delegated to the United States by the Constitution, nor prohibited by it to the States."

Counterpoint

Federal government is supreme

- Article I, Section 8 of the Constitution grants the federal government certain broad, fundamental powers such as the authority to "regulate Commerce with foreign Nations, and among the several States."
- Article I, Section 8 gives Congress the power to make all laws "which shall be necessary and proper" for carrying out its delegated powers.
- Article VI states that the Constitution and laws made by Congress shall be "the supreme law of the land."

were reserved to the states. He asserted that a state had the right to **nullify**, or cancel, any act of the federal government that went beyond these limited, specific powers.

The question of nullification reached the floor of the Senate in January 1830 in the midst of a debate over the government's policy restricting the sale of western lands. As South Carolina's Senator Robert Y. Hayne joined in opposing this exercise of federal power, the debate soon centered on the nature of the federal Union itself and the rights of the states against the national government.

Daniel Webster of Massachusetts argued against Hayne's states' rights challenge. Senator Webster painted a prophetic picture of what would come about 30 years later in the Civil War.

> When my eyes shall be turned to behold, for the last time, the sun shining in heaven, may I not see him shining on the broken and dishonored fragments of a once glorious Union; on States dissevered, discordant, belligerent; on a land rent with civil feuds, or drenched, it may be, in fraternal blood.

AN AMERICAN ★ SPEAKS

Webster closed with a plea for "Liberty *and* Union, now and forever, one and inseparable."

Tempers continued to rise over the next few years. In 1832 a special South Carolina convention nullified the tariff laws and declared that federal customs would no longer be collected in the state. Calhoun resigned as vice president to enter the Senate and lead the fight for nullification there. Jackson expressed his outrage to a South Carolina congressman:

> If one drop of blood be shed there in defiance of the laws of the United States, I will hang the first man of them I can get my hands on to the first tree I can find.

AN AMERICAN ★ SPEAKS

In December 1832 he issued a proclamation condemning nullification as "incompatible with the existence of the Constitution." In January 1833, at Jackson's request, Congress began debating a bill approving the use of federal troops to collect customs duties in South Carolina. Jackson sent a warship to Charleston and threatened to lead an army into the state. Finally, cooler heads prevailed. Henry Clay proposed a compromise tariff, and South Carolina accepted it.

Jackson and the bank. Jackson showed equal determination in his war on the Second Bank of the United States. Chartered by Congress in 1816, the Second Bank collected taxes, served as a depository for U.S. funds, controlled the issuance of paper money, and made loans to the government.

Bankers and business people, particularly in the West, resented the bank's power over credit and paper money. New York financiers and politicians opposed the bank because the customs duties collected in New York were sent to Philadelphia, where the bank's main branch was located. The greatest enemy of the bank was the president himself. His main objection was that Congress had granted the bank enormous economic power but had left it accountable to no one. When Congress approved the rechartering of the bank in 1832, Jackson vetoed the bill and killed the bank.

Jackson and the Indians. The War of 1812 had spelled defeat for the Indians between the Appalachian Mountains and the Mississippi River. During Jackson's presidency almost all these Indian groups were driven off their lands. They were forced to move to the **Indian Territory**, a part of the Great Plains that now mostly comprises the state of Oklahoma. The policy of removing the Indians from areas occupied by settlers started long before Jackson, but he readily supported it. Jackson held the conviction of the ordinary Americans of his time that Indian lands must be freed for economic development.

About 53,000 Creeks, Cherokees, Choctaws, Chickasaws, and Seminoles still lived in the South when Jackson took office in 1828. These groups had long lived in farming communities and had developed rich and complex cultures. Except for the Seminoles, who resisted attempts to change their culture, they had learned to blend European American and Native American cultures. The Cherokees of Georgia, for example, were a rich and literate farming community with books in their native

An unknown artist satirizes Andrew Jackson's Indian policies. As president, Jackson brutally removed some 100,000 peaceful Indians from desirable lands, including cultivated farms in the Southeast, to barren Indian Territory reservations west of the Mississippi. He is shown, however, as a protective, loving father.

Indian Removal from the South, 1830s

- ■ Ceded lands and dates of cession
- ■ Indian reservations
- ⬅ Cherokee's Trail of Tears
- ⬅ Other routes of Indian removal
- ▭ Boundaries of 1830

Albers Equal-Area Projection

© SF

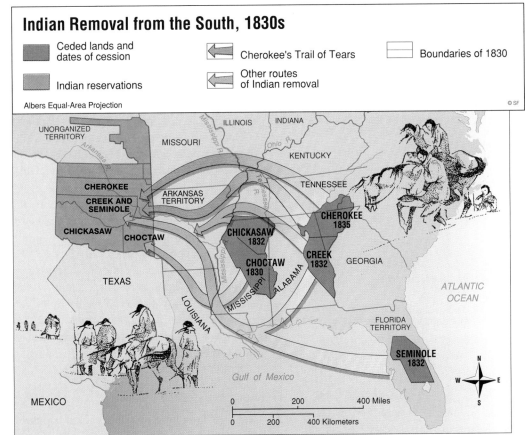

map study

Movement In the 1830s the U.S. government forced Indian groups in the Southeast to move permanently to reservations in present-day Oklahoma. The map shows five major Indian groups affected by the federal policy. What are those groups?

Critical Thinking Why were Indians forcibly removed from their lands in the Southeast?

language and a weekly newspaper. Some were wealthy slaveholders.

In 1828 the Georgia legislature denied the Cherokee nation's right to its farmlands, ordering them off the land and out of the state. In 1830 Congress passed an **Indian Removal Act** that allowed the federal government to seize most Indian lands so long as some compensation was paid. The Cherokees, under their leader John Ross, took their case to the Supreme Court, which ruled, in two separate cases in 1831 and 1832, that the Georgia action was unconstitutional. Like the state of Georgia, however, President Jackson ignored the Supreme Court ruling, reportedly saying, "John Marshall has made his opinion; now let him enforce it."

In 1838, 7,000 federal troops forced the Cherokees out of Georgia. About 15,000 men, women, and children were forced to move, mostly on foot, to Indian Territory. About 4,000 of them died on the brutal journey that came to be called the Trail of Tears.

Most other groups of Indians were also gradually forced from their homes. Some, such as the Winnebagos in Wisconsin, were moved repeatedly from one place to another until they virtually lost their tribal identity. Others, including the Seminoles in Florida, fought for their land until federal troops defeated them. By mid-century few Indians remained on the lands east of the Mississippi River.

The Whig party emerged to challenge the Democrats.

By 1834 elements of the shattered Republican party had re-formed into two distinct national parties, the Democratic party of Andrew Jackson, and the **Whig party** of his enemies. United by a dislike for Jackson, the Whigs took their name from the party in England that supported Parliament and opposed the king.

The Democratic party was led by wealthy southern planters and ambitious, rising businessmen. It attracted support from every section of the country and from every class of people, including the new urban immigrants. The Democrats favored a conservative government that gave citizens freedom to pursue prosperity with a minimum of interference.

The Whig party was led by the wealthiest Americans. Many southern planters, commercial farmers from all sections, businessmen, and nonimmigrant workers were supporters of the Whigs. The Whigs favored an active government that promoted national development.

Unable to agree on any one person in 1836, the Whig party ran three candidates for the presidency: William Henry Harrison of Ohio, Daniel Webster of Massachusetts, and Hugh White of Tennessee. Martin Van Buren, the Democratic nominee, won easily. (Profiles of Van Buren and the seven presidents who followed him appear on pages 190–191.)

A terrible financial panic in 1837 plagued Van Buren's presidency. The issue of slavery also proved troublesome. In his desire to hold southern voters in the Democratic party, Van Buren refused to interfere with slavery. Many northerners could not accept his position.

In 1840 the Whigs nominated a single candidate, William Henry Harrison, to oppose President Van Buren. Like Jackson, Harrison was a military hero who had gained popularity fighting Indians. He was called "Old Tippe-

The Whigs in 1840 avoided key issues and focused instead on William Henry Harrison's ties with the frontier. The newly minted term "OK," used as a jocular abbreviation for "all correct," became a popular campaign insignia.

canoe," after the 1811 battle in which he had defeated the Shawnees. Although he was actually wealthy, the Whigs presented him as a man of the frontier. With John Tyler of Virginia as Harrison's running mate, the Whigs adopted the slogan "Tippecanoe and Tyler too."

More than 2.4 million voters went to the polls in 1840, more than twice as many as in 1828. The Whig candidates won, but Harrison did not live long to enjoy his triumph. He died one month after his inauguration. As the Age of Jackson ended, John Tyler stepped into the presidency.

SECTION 1 REVIEW

Identify Key People and Terms
Write a sentence to identify: Industrial Revolution, Eli Whitney, nominating conventions, John Quincy Adams, Andrew Jackson, Martin Van Buren, Democratic party, John C. Calhoun, Tariff of Abominations, nullify, Daniel Webster, Indian Removal Act, Whig party

Locate Key Places
1. In what state is the Erie Canal?
2. In what present-day state was the Indian Territory mostly located?

Master the Main Ideas
1. **Analyzing economic growth:** How did developments in transportation and technology change American life in the early 1800s?
2. **Examining political issues:** What political changes occurred in the early decades of the 1800s?
3. **Analyzing political conflicts:** How did President Jackson deal with the major issues that arose during his Administration?
4. **Contrasting political parties:**
   (a) How did the philosophies of the Democrats and the Whigs differ?
   (b) What groups tended to support each party?

Apply Critical Thinking Skills: Recognizing Values
Decide whether the spoils system exists in American politics today, and explain why the system should or should not be a part of political life.

SECTION 2

An Age of Reform swept the nation.

Key Terms: temperance movement, normal school, abolitionists

Reading Preview
As you read this section, you will learn:
1. what helped inspire widespread reform in the United States.
2. what social crusaders tried to reform.
3. what reform movement dominated the era.

The Age of Jackson changed the political life of the United States. At the same time, reformers who sought to transform the social fabric of the nation increasingly questioned many aspects of American life. Religious revivalism fostered the belief that individuals could be reformed and human character perfected. Consequently, many Americans were confident that all social ills could be corrected and society could be improved. Their enthusiasm and dedication stimulated reform campaigns throughout the period between 1820 and 1860.

Religious movements inspired widespread reform.

The Second Great Awakening began on the southern frontier in Tennessee and Kentucky in the late 1790s. Like the earlier Great Awakening, this religious revival movement, with its fervent preaching and emotional camp meetings, strengthened personal morality and promoted a greater recognition of human imperfection.

In the 1820s a unique form of revivalism developed in the Northeast. In contrast to the South, where evangelists appealed to rural congregations, evangelists in the Northeast, such as **Lyman Beecher** in New England and **Charles G. Finney** in New York, gathered followers from cities and towns. Beecher and Finney brought many people to a greater

The preacher at a frontier camp meeting implored all listeners to accept instant conversion. Religious revivalism stimulated other reforms, including the temperance movement. *The Drunkard's Progress*, below, a popular 1846 lithograph by Nathaniel Currier (1813–1888), carried a powerful appeal to abstain from using intoxicating liquor.

THE DRUNKARDS PROGRESS.
FROM THE FIRST GLASS TO THE GRAVE.

awareness of the social problems that arose out of industrialization and the economic changes then sweeping through the Northeast.

The enthusiasm generated by the religious revival stimulated organized social reform in American society. Ministers encouraged their congregations not only to overcome their own bad habits and reshape their own characters, but also to spread the gospel of moral improvement to others. According to Finney, true Christians must commit themselves to "the universal reformation of the world."

The **temperance movement** sprang most directly from religious revivalism. (Temper-

ance is the practice of avoiding alcoholic drinks.) Founded in 1826 by Lyman Beecher, the American Society for the Promotion of Temperance used the methods of revivalism to achieve its ends. The society's members pointed to the broken homes, ruined lives, and criminal acts that resulted from drunkenness. Typical of the tone of the many tracts circulated by the society is this passage from one written by Charles P. McIlvaine, an Episcopalian bishop:

AN AMERICAN ★ SPEAKS

Ask the records of madhouses and they will answer that one-third of all their wretched inmates were sent there by intemperance. Ask the keepers of our prisons and they will testify that, with scarcely an exception, their horrible population is from the schools of intemperance. Ask the history of the 200,000 paupers now burdening the hands of public charity and you will find that two-thirds of them have been the victims, directly or indirectly, of intemperance. Inquire at the gates of death and you will learn that no less than 30,000 souls are annually passed for the judgment bar of God, driven there by intemperance.

By 1834 one million Americans, especially women, had joined 5,000 local branches of the movement. Most of them crusaded for total abstinence and for legal prohibition of the manufacture and sale of alcoholic beverages. The latter goal would not be reached nationwide for nearly a century, and then only briefly.

Social crusaders tried to reform American life.

In addition to working for temperance, Lyman Beecher also championed educational reform, arguing that economic growth was not enough to ensure the survival of democracy. "We must educate! We must educate!" he insisted, "or we shall perish by our own prosperity."

Education. Boston educator **Horace Mann** was one of the most outspoken and effective educational reformers of the period. As head of the Massachusetts Board of Education from 1837 to 1848, he transformed the state's educational system, creating a model of tax-supported schools other states would follow. Mann defended the use of tax dollars for education, arguing that schools were a debt that the rich owed to their country. He criticized the undereducated, unskilled, and temporary teaching staffs in public schools and fought for a trained, professional staff of teachers. To supply such a teaching staff, he proposed establishing **normal schools**, or teacher-training academies. Mann helped set up the first such institution in the United States.

The mentally ill and the handicapped. The champion of the mentally disturbed was **Dorothea Dix**, who traveled from state to state, inspecting mental institutions and publicizing their abuses. Typical of her condemnation of such institutions were the comments she addressed to the Massachusetts legislature in 1843:

I proceed, gentlemen, briefly to call your attention to the *present* state of insane persons confined within this Commonwealth, in *cages, closets, cellars, stalls, pens! Chained, naked, beaten with rods,* and *lashed* into obedience.

AN AMERICAN ★ SPEAKS

Although little was known at the time about how to deal with the mentally ill, the publicity Dix gave to the problem helped improve the living conditions for many of them.

Much more successful were the attempts to help the handicapped. **Thomas Hopkins Gallaudet** developed methods for teaching the deaf that were widely adopted. By 1851, 14 states had schools using the Gallaudet technique. **Samuel Gridley Howe** directed the first American institute for the blind. He won acclaim by educating Laura Bridgman, who had lost her sight and hearing at the age of two. She became the first visually, hearing, and speech-impaired person to be successfully taught.

Women's rights. The Age of Reform also saw the beginning of a women's rights movement. In 1848 **Elizabeth Cady Stanton** and **Lucretia Mott** helped organize a convention in Stanton's hometown, **Seneca Falls**, New York, "to discuss the social, civil, and religious rights of women." Stanton prepared a manifesto for the convention modeled after the Declaration of Independence. It began, "We hold these truths to be self-evident, that all men and women are created equal."

The efforts of Dorothea Dix, above, brought widespread reforms in the care of the mentally ill both in the United States and abroad. Mental patients were subjected to inhumane and bizarre methods of treatment such as this 1818 circulating swing that was supposed to correct mental imbalance.

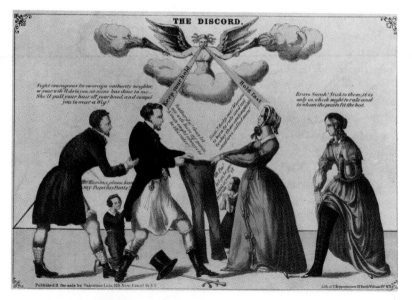

THE DISCORD.

In 1831 **William Lloyd Garrison** struck the determined and fearless note of abolition in the first issue of his newspaper, *Liberator*. "I will be as harsh as truth, and as uncompromising as justice. . . . I will not retreat a single inch— AND I WILL BE HEARD." Garrison, an effective writer and speaker who was filled with moral fervor, helped found the New England Anti-Slavery Society in 1831.

The most moving of the testimonials against slavery came from former slaves, who could tell of the horrors of the institution from personal experience. Some slaves who had fled north to freedom became leaders in the abolition movement. **Henry Highland Garnet** and **Frederick Douglass**, both born to slavery, were the most noted of those leaders.

Garnet and Douglass, who became rivals for black abolitionist leadership, also demonstrated the divisions within the movement. The more militant Garnet, in an 1843 speech at a convention of free African Americans in Buffalo, New York, called upon slaves to rebel against their owners:

Think [of the tears you have shed and] . . . go to your   **AN AMERICAN ★ SPEAKS**
lordly enslavers and tell them plainly, that you *are determined to be free.* . . . If they then commence the work of death, they, and not you, will be responsible for the consequences. You had better all die—*die immediately,* than live slaves. . . . If you would be free in this generation, here is your only hope . . . there is not

Women's demands at the Seneca Falls Convention in 1848 subjected them to ridicule and hostility. This 1855 cartoon implies that such demands would rob men of all authority.

The convention passed a number of resolutions dealing with such issues as the right of women to own property, to be allowed entrance into colleges and professional schools, and to vote. Few of these goals were achieved before the Civil War ended the Age of Reform. Only one woman who attended the Seneca Falls Convention lived long enough to vote in a presidential election—72 years later.

The abolition movement dominated the era.

The issue that dominated the Age of Reform was that of slavery. Beecher, Mann, Dix, Howe, Stanton, and Mott—most of the crusaders involved in other areas of reform—were also ardent and active **abolitionists**, people who worked to abolish, or do away with, slavery.

The abolitionists often used the methods of the revivalists—fervent preaching, lengthy meetings, and the call for individuals to come forth and announce their conversion to the cause. They also used the mass vote-gathering techniques of the political parties to wage their moral campaign. They held parades and rallies, gathered and sent petitions to local governments and Congress, and distributed millions of antislavery tracts and leaflets. By 1837 the abolitionists' mass campaign had resulted in the establishment of more than 1,000 antislavery societies in the nation.

Born into slavery, Henry Highland Garnet, above, and Frederick Douglass, right, later led the abolition movement.

much hope without the shedding of blood. If you must bleed, let it all come at once—rather *die freemen, than live to be slaves.*

Douglass, along with many other abolitionists, opposed such calls to violent rebellion. Abolitionists also differed over whether to work for gradual or immediate and complete abolition, whether to seek abolition through political channels or simply appeal to morality, and whether to allow women to participate in the movement. In spite of their differences, however, they became a powerful voice against the institution of slavery, a voice that would increasingly contribute to political crises in the growing nation.

S E C T I O N **2** R E V I E W

Identify Key People and Terms
Write a sentence to identify: Lyman Beecher, Charles G. Finney, temperance movement, Horace Mann, normal school, Dorothea Dix, Thomas Hopkins Gallaudet, Samuel Gridley Howe, Elizabeth Cady Stanton, Lucretia Mott, abolitionists, William Lloyd Garrison, Henry Highland Garnet, Frederick Douglass

Locate Key Places
Where did the first women's rights convention take place?

Master the Main Ideas

1. **Analyzing religious movements:** How did the Second Great Awakening differ from the earlier revivalist movement?
2. **Understanding social reform movements:** What were the goals of the various reform movements during the Age of Reform?
3. **Analyzing social reform movements:** What motivated the abolitionists?

Apply Critical Thinking Skills: Recognizing Values
Social reform movements such as the temperance movement often involve the attempt to impose one group's values and standards of behavior on other people. What justification can you offer for such an attempt? What criticisms of it can you suggest?

S E C T I O N **3**

Manifest Destiny became a national battle cry.

Key Terms: Manifest Destiny, Mountain Men, Forty-Niners

Reading Preview
As you read this section, you will learn:

1. why Texans fought a revolution.
2. how the United States acquired the Oregon Country.
3. what brought settlers to California and Utah.

Editor John L. O'Sullivan captured the popular imagination in 1845 with a new expression: **Manifest Destiny**. He editorialized in his *U.S. Magazine and Democratic Review:*

Away, away with all these cobweb tissues of rights of discovery, exploration, settlement. . . . [The American claim] is by the right of our manifest destiny to overspread and to possess the whole of the continent which Providence has given us for the development of the great experiment of liberty and federative self government entrusted to us.

AN AMERICAN ★ SPEAKS

Many people began to agree with O'Sullivan that it was America's destiny to expand.

Texans fought a revolution to achieve independence from Mexico.

Attention turned first to the great expanse of Texas, a province of Spanish-ruled Mexico. In 1820 Moses Austin, a Connecticut-born resident of Missouri, convinced the Spanish authorities to grant him 200,000 acres of Texas land for settlement. Moses Austin died the following year, but his son, **Stephen F. Austin**, led a small group of settlers to the fertile coastal plain between the Brazos and Colorado rivers of central Texas. After Mexico declared its independence, Americans received further

Free land drew Stephen F. Austin, left, to Texas in 1821 as well as many later migrants. Friedrich Richard Petri painted these German settlers in 1843.

couragement from the Mexican government. More settlers arrived, and by 1833 Texas was the home of more than 35,000 Americans.

The newcomers to Texas agreed to obey Mexican laws, pay Mexican taxes, and convert to Catholicism. The settlers failed to keep these promises. Moreover, many of them had brought their slaves with them, thus violating a Mexican law forbidding slavery. Because of these violations, Mexico decided in 1830 to forbid future American immigration to Texas.

For their part, the Americans who settled in Texas had some legitimate complaints against the Mexican government. The politicians in control in Mexico City believed in a strong central government and ignored Mexico's constitutional guarantees of local self-government. Austin tried unsuccessfully to negotiate with General **Antonio López de Santa Anna**, the dictator who seized control of the Mexican government in 1834. Santa Anna began to clamp down. He abolished the Mexican constitution of 1824 and threatened to use military force to make the Texans obey Mexican law. In addition, Texans began to hear rumors that he would expel all Americans from Texas. Fighting broke out between American Texans and Mexican troops.

In February 1836 Santa Anna led a force of several thousand troops to San Antonio. The town was defended by only a handful of Texans and volunteers from the United States. This small force of some 150 men took refuge behind the walls of the **Alamo**, a makeshift fort that had once been the Mission of San Antonio de Valero. Santa Anna's troops surrounded the compound and began shelling it with light cannon. The defenders could easily have escaped, but they chose to stay and fight. On March 6, Santa Anna's troops scaled the walls and massacred the defenders without mercy.

While the Alamo was undergoing siege, a convention of Texan delegates met and declared their independence from Mexico. They drew up a constitution for the Republic of Texas, formed a government, and appointed **Sam Houston** commander in chief of the republic's armed forces outside San Antonio.

The massacre at the Alamo was followed by another defeat, which resulted in the massacre of some 300 Texan prisoners at Goliad. Meanwhile Santa Anna went in pursuit of Houston and his army of some 700 Texans. The two forces met at San Jacinto, in southeastern Texas, near present-day Houston. On April 21, 1836, Houston assaulted the larger force in a surprise attack, winning a great victory. Santa Anna was captured but released and allowed to return to Mexico City after he signed a treaty acknowledging the independence of Texas.

Although Santa Anna repudiated the treaty, political turmoil within Mexico prevented further action against Texas. In the next few years Texas' population grew to such an extent that Mexico could hold out little hope of regaining it. Mexico did, however, refuse to accept the Rio Grande as its boundary with Texas, insisting on a border at the Nueces River. That dis-

American settlers rose in revolt against Mexico in 1835 and established the Republic of Texas in Spring 1836. At the Alamo, a fort in San Antonio, in March 1836, every American defender died, including the legendary rifleman Davy Crockett, shown in buckskins with his rifle raised. ''Remember the Alamo'' became the Texas war cry.

agreement, and the desire of most Texans to have their country annexed by the United States, would lead to war with Mexico in 1846. (See pages 180–184.) Through that war, the United States gained California and the New Mexico Territory (present-day Utah, Nevada, and parts of New Mexico, Arizona, Colorado, and Wyoming).

The United States acquired the Oregon Country by treaty.

For a time in the 1840s the Pacific Northwest, known then as the Oregon Country, was vying with Texas for the attention of adventurous, land-seeking Americans. Tales of the lush valleys, snow-capped mountains, and pristine rivers suggested that the Oregon Country was a pioneer's paradise. Claimed at one time by several European nations, the Oregon Country had been home for centuries to the Northwest Coast and Plateau Indians.

The United States and Great Britain could not agree on a boundary line, so in 1818 they accepted joint occupation of the disputed region. Then by 1825 Spain and Russia withdrew their claims. American interest grew as trappers and fur traders ventured into Oregon and challenged the British monopoly on the fur trade. These **Mountain Men**, as they were called, mapped out routes over the mountains to both Oregon and California.

Alfred Jacob Miller (1810–1874) captured the fierce independence of the Mountain Man in *Presenting Gifts to the Indians*. Miller traveled throughout the West in 1837 painting Indian life.

The Mountain Men were the vanguard of a huge westward migration. Between 1843 and 1846, some 10,000 Americans followed the Applegate family you read about earlier over the Oregon Trail to the Pacific Northwest. Jesse Applegate tells of a narrow escape on the trail that almost cost his life. Against his mother's warning, seven-year-old Jesse was riding on a provision wagon. As the driver drowsed, Jesse somehow got hold of the big ox whip:

AN AMERICAN
★ SPEAKS

Feeling now the importance of my position as teamster, I swung the whip around and then forward with all my strength to make it pop over the oxen's backs. But the effort to jerk it back pulled me forward and I slid off . . . between the oxen's heels and the front wheels of the wagon, one of which ran over the small of my back. I tried to escape the hind wheel, but it rolled over my legs.

One of the men scooped Jesse up in time to avoid the oncoming wagons. Although badly hurt, Jesse recovered to complete the journey over the snow-clad Rockies to the damp, green lands of western Oregon.

Jesse's brother Warren and cousin Edward were less fortunate. They perished when their small boat capsized as they shot the turbulent Columbia River rapids near the end of the journey westward.

As more and more Americans pushed westward, Oregon became an American community by sheer force of numbers. The Democratic candidate for president in 1844, **James K. Polk**, won the election after a loud popular campaign for annexing all of the Oregon Country.

American and British officials finally settled the thorny question in 1846 by dividing Oregon at the 49th parallel, which already separated their lands east of the Rocky Mountains. The American portion later became the states of Oregon, Washington, Idaho, and parts of Wyoming and Montana.

Blue Jeans

In July of 1872, Levi Strauss, the owner of a prosperous dry-goods business in San Francisco, received a package from a steady customer, Jacob Davis. Davis, a tailor in the mining town of Reno, had enclosed two sturdy pants and a letter of explanation.

The secratt of them Pents is the Rivits that I put in those Pockets and I found the demand so large that I cannot make them up fast enough. . . . My nabors are getting yealouse of these success and unless I secure it by Patent Papers it will soon become a general thing. . . . Tharefore Gentleman, I wish to make you a Proposition that you should take out the Latter Patent in my name. . . . I will give you half the right to sell all such clothing Revited according to the Patent, for all the Pacific States and Teroterious.

Levis Strauss, who had been in business in California since the early days of the gold rush, took the tailor up on his offer. Levi's pants, made of the strongest fabrics, became popular with miners, ranchers, lumberjacks, and other workmen in the West. With their narrow cuff, the pant legs could easily be tucked into workboots. Rivets, punched into the pocket corners, made the pockets sturdy enough to hold nails, bullets, and gold nuggets without tearing. A leather patch sewn to the back of the pants guaranteed that the owner would be given a new pair if seams ripped.

In 1873, Strauss and Davis agreed to work together in the profitable venture. Levi's jeans, as they came to be known, were

Riveted construction helped blue jeans withstand the harshest wear, as these California gold miners of the 1880s could attest.

Highlights of American Life

A Mormon poses with five wives and five children at Echo City, Utah Territory, in 1868. Persecuted for their religious beliefs and social customs, the Mormons were nonetheless described by emigrants passing through Utah as "a quiet, orderly, industrious, and well-organized society."

Pioneers sought gold in California and religious freedom in Utah.

The pioneeers who headed for Oregon were largely families who intended to settle there and farm. Those who flocked to California in the late 1840s were mostly men who left their families back home. Home could be nearly

soon distributed throughout the United States. Today they are a worldwide symbol of American culture.

every major nation on earth, including for the first time on a large scale, China. The lure of gold drew people to California after discovery of the precious metal at Sutter's Mill near the present city of Sacramento in 1848. These **Forty-Niners**—so called because most of them went to California in 1849—made the port of **San Francisco** into a boom town.

The gold excitement died down in the 1850s, but a growing base of non-Hispanic settlers remained. By 1860 more than 40 percent of California's residents were foreign born, including 35,000 Chinese.

While pioneers with the glint of gold in their eyes were heading for California, the Mormons under the leadership of **Brigham Young**, were trekking to the salt flats of Utah, where they hoped to practice their religious beliefs in peace. The Church of Jesus Christ of Latter-Day Saints, or Mormon church, was founded in New York State by Joseph Smith in the 1820s. The church grew rapidly through the 1830s, but opposition to it and distrust of it grew equally rapidly. Smith's followers were forced to move from New York to Ohio to Missouri and then to Nauvoo, Illinois.

In 1844 the prejudice against Mormonism erupted into violence. After Smith was murdered by a mob in Nauvoo, his followers decided to travel overland to the Great Salt Valley in Utah, which was then loosely governed by Mexico. Making this their base, they would develop a community free from the restrictive laws of the United States.

In 1847 Brigham Young led the first group of Mormons westward to the barren plain near the Great Salt Lake. By 1849 more than 6,000 Mormons had made the westward trek. The industrious community built irrigation ditches to bring life-giving waters from the mountains to their fields of grain and vegetables.

Mormon hopes of developing their new community in isolation were soon shattered. The gold strike in California brought more and more people through their settlement, and the Treaty of Guadalupe Hidalgo, which you will read about in the next section, made their land part of the United States. In 1849 the Mormons set up a civil government and developed plans to apply for statehood. They reasoned that their religious freedom and political rights might be best preserved by passing state laws.

SECTION **3** REVIEW

Identify Key People and Terms
Write a sentence to identify: Manifest Destiny, Stephen F. Austin, Antonio López de Santa Anna, Sam Houston, Mountain Men, James K. Polk, Forty-Niners, Brigham Young

Locate Key Places
1. In what Texas city is the Alamo located?
2. What city became the chief Pacific port after 1849?

Master the Main Ideas
1. **Supporting basic civic values:** Why did the Texans rebel against the Mexican government?
2. **Examining international cooperative efforts:** How did Britain and the United States settle the Oregon question?
3. **Studying the effects of natural resources on population patterns:** How were people who sought their fortunes in California different from those who settled in Oregon in the 1840s?

Applying Critical Thinking Skills: Predicting Consequences
Would Texas have remained a part of Mexico if the Mexican government had not abandoned the country's constitution of 1824? Explain your position.

SECTION **4**

The United States acquired western lands from Mexico.

Key Terms: Treaty of Guadalupe Hidalgo, Gadsden Purchase

Reading Preview
As you read this section, you will learn:
1. what triggered a war with Mexico.
2. how Americans and Mexicans viewed the war.
3. what helped delay an American victory in Mexico.

When the Texans won their independence from Mexico in 1836, many of them hoped and expected to become part of the United States. However, not everyone in the nation was sure they wanted Texas to join the Union. Most northern Whigs were opposed to annexation because they believed it would provoke a war with Mexico. More importantly, a growing number of northern abolitionists were opposed to annexation because they did not want to add any more slave territory to the Union. Those who favored annexation, many of them southern Democrats, insisted that the acquisition of Texas was part of the nation's Manifest Destiny.

The annexation of Texas triggered a war with Mexico.

Although the issue of the annexation of Texas was one of the most hotly debated topics of the day, initially little was done to resolve it. President Martin Van Buren, who served from 1837 to 1841, largely ignored the Texas question. Early in President **John Tyler's** Administration (1841–1845), however, overtures made by Britain to Texas began to worry some people. They believed the United States needed to act quickly on the Texas issue before Britain struck an agreement of its own with the Republic of Texas. Britain's interest in Texas was primarily in securing a supply of cotton and a low-tariff market for its manufactured

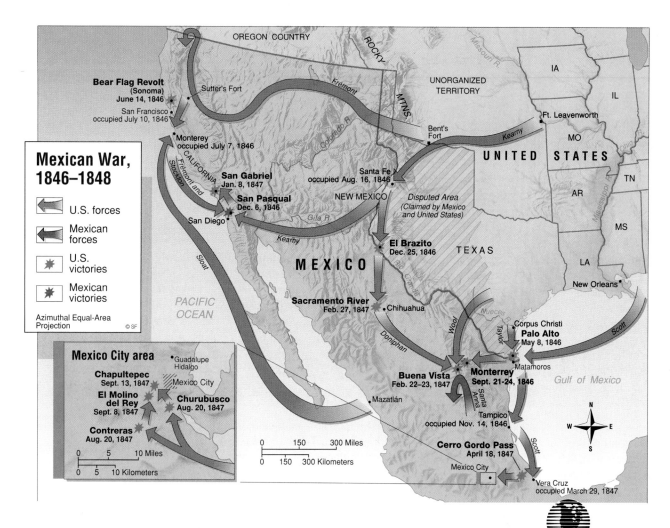

Mexican War, 1846–1848

← U.S. forces

← Mexican forces

✳ U.S. victories

✳ Mexican victories

Azimuthal Equal-Area Projection © SF

OREGON COUNTRY

ROCKY MTNS.

UNORGANIZED TERRITORY

IA

IL

Ft. Leavenworth

MO

UNITED STATES

TN

AR

MS

LA

New Orleans

Bear Flag Revolt (Sonoma) June 14, 1846

Sutter's Fort

Frémont

Bent's Fort

Kearny

San Francisco occupied July 10, 1846

Monterey occupied July 7, 1846

CALIFORNIA

Frémont and Stockton

San Gabriel Jan. 8, 1847

San Pasqual Dec. 6, 1846

San Diego

Gila R.

Kearny

Sloat

Colorado R.

Santa Fe occupied Aug. 16, 1846

NEW MEXICO

Disputed Area (Claimed by Mexico and United States)

TEXAS

El Brazito Dec. 25, 1846

MEXICO

Sacramento River Feb. 27, 1847

Chihuahua

Doniphan

Rio Grande

Nueces

Wool

Taylor

Corpus Christi

Palo Alto May 8, 1846

Scott

Matamoros

Buena Vista Feb. 22–23, 1847

Monterrey Sept. 21–24, 1846

Santa Anna

Gulf of Mexico

Mazatlán

Tampico occupied Nov. 14, 1846

Cerro Gordo Pass April 18, 1847

Mexico City

Vera Cruz occupied March 29, 1847

Scott

PACIFIC OCEAN

0   150   300 Miles
0   150   300 Kilometers

Mexico City area

Guadalupe Hidalgo

Chapultepec Sept. 13, 1847

Mexico City

El Molino del Rey Sept. 8, 1847

Churubusco Aug. 20, 1847

Contreras Aug. 20, 1847

0   5   10 Miles
0   5   10 Kilometers

N E S W

---

goods. Texas would benefit from such an agreement because Britain would guarantee its independence and provide protection from Mexico.

On March 1, 1845, after a long and heated battle in the Senate, President John Tyler finally succeeded in getting Congress to pass a joint resolution annexing Texas as a slave state. Consequently, Texas drew up a state constitution and had it approved by Congress. In December 1845 Texas became the 28th state in the Union.

When the United States annexed Texas, it assumed the republic's claim to a disputed area between the Nueces River and the Rio Grande. Locate this area on the map above. Mexico had begrudgingly accepted the loss of Texas, but it refused to give up its claim to the large tract of fertile land between the two rivers. Mexico

reacted to annexation by breaking off diplomatic relations with the United States and preparing for war.

President Polk, in response to the actions of the Mexican government, also began preparing for war. He sent General **Zachary Taylor** and a force of some 3,000 soldiers to Corpus Christi, at the mouth of the Nueces River to await further orders. However, the president made one last attempt to avert conflict. He sent a representative to Mexico to seek a resolution to the border problem and to try to persuade Mexico to sell New Mexico and California to the United States.

When word reached Washington in 1846 that Mexico had refused to receive his representative, President Polk concluded that force would probably be needed to achieve his goals. Thus he ordered General Zachary Taylor to ad-

map study

Location After the Mexican War, the United States gained California, New Mexico, and the disputed area. Were any battles of this war fought in the United States?

Critical Thinking Why might western settlers have supported the war?

WAR WITH MEXICO
Skill: Analyzing Cause and Effect

Introducing the Skill. With the election of James Polk as president in 1844, many Americans signaled their desire to add the territories of Texas and Oregon to the United States. In that same vein, John O'Sullivan of the *Democratic Review* wrote in 1845 that it was the nation's divine right and "manifest destiny to overspread the continent." These feelings eventually led the United States into a war with Mexico. What caused the conflict over Texas to erupt into war?

Learning the Skill. Identifying the causes of the war with Mexico is a part of the skill of **analyzing cause and effect**. A cause makes something happen, that is, it brings about an outcome or result known as an effect.

Complex events such as a war often have multiple causes of varying importance and immediacy. An underlying cause is a long-term condition that helps to make something happen. An immediate cause, by contrast, leads directly to an event. For example, an underlying cause of a swimmer winning an Olympic medal might be years of practice and dedication. An immediate cause would be the swimmer's superior time in the actual race.

Applying the Skill. Study the following list of possible causes for the war with Mexico. Then answer the questions below.

a. Congress passed a resolution in 1845 annexing Texas.

b. The Mexican government refused to discuss disputed Texas boundaries with U.S. negotiators.

c. Southern states wanted the added strength of another slave state in the Union.

d. Mexico wanted to regain the Texas territory lost in the Texas revolt.

e. President Polk sent Zachary Taylor's troops to the north bank of the Rio Grande.

f. On April 25, 1846, Mexican troops crossed the Rio Grande and captured an American scouting party, killing or wounding 16 American soldiers.

g. Many Americans supported the idea of manifest destiny.

1. Which of the listed causes are underlying causes of the war with Mexico?

2. Which of the causes are immediate causes of the war?

vance to the north bank of the Rio Grande near Matamoros. Meanwhile, about 8,000 Mexican soldiers had gathered across the river.

With the troops of the two countries facing each other, an incident leading to a clash of arms was highly likely. The clash came on April 25, when a force of about 1,600 Mexican troops engaged about 60 of Taylor's mounted soldiers. Several Americans were killed, and the rest were taken prisoner. On May 8, however, Taylor defeated the numerically superior Mexican army at Palo Alto.

In response to the fighting, President Polk successfully sought a declaration of war from Congress. He based his request on the grounds that Mexico had attacked the United States and shed American blood on American soil.

Not all Americans and Mexicans supported the war.

Now that war had been declared, Polk was determined to win by force of arms what he had failed to obtain by negotiations. In his war message to Congress he stated that the American aim was to "acquire California, New Mexico, and other further territory" as compensation for American expenses and losses.

Although most Americans supported the war, a sizable number opposed it, especially in New England. Whigs and abolitionists were against the war because they feared that the territory won from Mexico would become slave territory. Some Whigs accused Polk of conspiring to bring on the war in order to acquire new territory. Abraham Lincoln, then a new representative from Illinois, spoke in the House of Representatives, calling upon the president to prove that American soldiers had been killed on American soil. The essayist and philosopher **Henry David Thoreau** refused to pay his taxes as a protest against the war and spent a night in jail for his refusal (until a relative paid them for him). He later wrote the essay "Civil Disobedience" to justify his action:

|If the alternative is to keep all just men in prison, or give up **AN AMERICAN ★ SPEAKS** war and slavery, the State will not hesitate which to choose. If a thousand men were not to pay their tax-bills this year, that would not be a bloody measure, as it would be to pay them, and enable the State to commit violence and shed innocent blood.

More than a hundred years later, Thoreau's essay would influence the civil rights and antiwar movements in America.

In Mexico, as in the United States, some people did not support the war. Most Mexicans, however, saw the confrontation as a last-ditch effort to regain Texas. Although smaller in population and economically weaker than the United States, Mexico had a larger army and the advantage of fighting a defensive war.

Geography helped delay the American victory in Mexico.

The American campaign to win the war was carried forward in three areas—California, New Mexico, and Mexico itself. In California and New Mexico, victories were won with relative ease and with very little bloodshed. By January of 1847, California and New Mexico were totally under the control of U.S. forces. The major campaign was to be farther south, where the rugged terrain presented enormous difficulties and the Mexican forces proved a powerful adversary.

Fortunately for the United States, the American forces that fought in Mexico had an extremely talented military strategist to lead them—General **Winfield Scott**. Scott, who was almost 60 years old at the outset of the war, was a vain, pompous, and often quarrelsome man who earned the nickname "Old Fuss and

Feathers" from his troops. The nickname aptly referred to the general's insistence on strict discipline and his fondness for dazzling, heavily decorated uniforms.

On March 9, 1847, Scott and 10,000 well-prepared soldiers staged an amphibious assault on the important port of **Vera Cruz**, about 250 miles directly east of Mexico City. By March 29, Scott captured the city and immediately began to plan his army's trek to Mexico City.

By August the American troops were outside Mexico City and poised to attack. Despite the difficulties presented by the city's geography—it was surrounded by mountains, lakes, and marshland—General Scott's army moved steadily forward, engaging the Mexican army in bloody hand-to-hand combat. On September 14 the Americans finally gained control of the Mexican capital. The war that was not supposed to last long or cost very much was finally over. In the end the war had claimed more than 13,000 American lives, the majority from

General Winfield Scott landed an army at Vera Cruz, Mexico, in March 1847. The Mexicans failed to attack while the force approached in boats, and Scott forced the city's surrender with few losses. The U.S. 6th Infantry flag, crowded with battle names, is shown at right.

As cotton cultivation spread westward after the invention of the cotton gin, slavery spread as well. The census of 1850 showed that 3.5 million African Americans lived in the United States. Of that number about 3.2 million were slaves, most of whom worked at cotton production in the South.

Treatment of slaves varied widely—from paternal and benign to incredibly cruel—but in all cases slaves were considered to be pieces of property, not people. They had no civil rights and virtually no human rights. Family members could be sold and separated from their loved ones without notice. Slaves expressed their discontent in a number of ways. Some staged armed rebellion, some chose to run away, and others intentionally worked slowly and inefficiently. Knowing that there was no realistic alternative at the time, most slaves managed somehow to retain an inner sense of worth and human dignity.

Sources of conflict. Economic differences increasingly divided the North and the South.

Northerners, for example, as well as most westerners, favored government support for the building of roads, canals, and railroads, which helped connect factories with markets. The South, which had few factories and used the region's rivers to transport its agricultural products to markets, opposed the spending of federal money on internal improvements.

Tariffs, as you have seen, were another area of contention. The North saw them as a means of protecting its industries from the competition of cheap imported products. Southerners, often rich in land and slaves, but cash poor, preferred to have access to cheap finished goods from abroad rather than the more costly products of northern factories.

The slavery issue intensified after the Mexican War.

In 1846, when the Mexican War was just beginning, the House of Representatives passed a measure known as the **Wilmot Proviso**, which would have outlawed slavery in any territory acquired from Mexico. Bitterly opposed by southerners, the measure passed the House but was defeated in the Senate. The debate over the extension of slavery touched off by the Wilmot Proviso died down during the war but was revived with renewed bitterness with the coming of peace.

Southern commerce centered on individual plantations such as the cotton plantation on the Mississippi River below. Cotton shipped by steamboat met a growing world demand. However, slavery was the foundation of the plantation system. The slaves at right were photographed near their cabins on St. Helena Island, South Carolina.

In the presidential election of 1848 both the Democrats and the Whigs avoided the slavery issue so as not to offend voters. The evasive tactics of the major parties infuriated abolitionists. Many of them turned to a new party, the **Free Soil party**, which came out strongly against the extension of slavery in the territories. The Free Soilers took enough votes from the Democrats in New York to throw the election to the Whig candidate, Zachary Taylor, who had gained popularity as a general in the Mexican War.

By the time Taylor took office in March 1849, California had acquired sufficient population to qualify for statehood. This development produced a national crisis. Admitting California as a free state would upset the balance of free and slave states that had been maintained since the Missouri Compromise of 1820, when Missouri was admitted as a slave state and Maine, formerly part of Massachusetts, was admitted as a free state.

When Congress met in December 1849, three towering figures of American political history were on hand to lead the debate over the admission of California—John C. Calhoun of South Carolina, **Henry Clay** of Kentucky, and Daniel Webster of Massachusetts. Calhoun, a spokesman for states' rights and slavery, argued that the Constitution protected slavery. He demanded a constitutional amendment to restore and preserve the North-South balance and threatened that if that balance were not maintained the South would secede from the Union. Clay and Webster, although opposed to slavery, argued for a compromise that would save the Union.

The debate dragged on through the summer of 1850. The impasse was broken with the unexpected death of President Taylor, who had favored a pro-North settlement. His successor, **Millard Fillmore,** favored compromise, and with his support a solution was found. As finally passed, the **Compromise of 1850** carefully balanced sectional interests based on a proposal by Henry Clay. California came into the Union as a free state. The rest of the land won from Mexico was divided into the territories of New Mexico and Utah, with no restrictions on

VOICES FROM THE PAST

Ain't I a Woman?

Sojourner Truth was a former slave who became active in the abolitionist and feminist movements. Both causes blaze forth in her speech to a women's rights convention in Akron, Ohio. How does Sojourner Truth demonstrate her strength as a woman?

That man over there says that women need to be helped into carriages, and lifted over ditches, and to have the best place everywhere. . . . Look at me! Look at my arm! I have ploughed and planted, and gathered into barns, and no man could head me! And ain't I a woman? I could work as much and eat as much as a man—when I could get it—and bear the lash as well! And ain't I a woman? I have borne thirteen children, and seen them most all sold off to slavery, and when I cried out with my mother's grief, none but Jesus heard me! And ain't I a woman?

slavery. As a concession to the North, the slave trade—but not slavery—was abolished in the **District of Columbia.** Finally, a strong **Fugitive Slave Law,** as favored by the South, was passed.

The compromise was at best an uneasy truce. After a few years, the slavery issue began to heat up again as abolitionists protested enforcement of the Fugitive Slave Law. Northerners were incensed when federal marshals began issuing warrants for the arrest of runaways and free African Americans were forced back into slavery. Mobs in Boston and New York tried to rescue captives, and some state and local governments passed personal liberty laws meant to prevent slave owners from claiming runaways. Many people continued to help slaves escape to free territory. The North's hostility to the Fugitive Slave Law convinced southerners that they had been the losers in the Compromise of 1850, since that law had been the one real gain for the South.

map study

Regions As states and territories were formed in the early 1800s, the balance between slave and free regions became an issue. As shown on the top map, the Compromise of 1820 balanced the slave state of Missouri with the free state of Maine and set limits to slavery in the territories. However, as the middle map shows, the Compromise of 1850 opened two new territories to slavery. How did the Kansas-Nebraska Act affect the slavery issue and change the Missouri Compromise of 1820?

Critical Thinking

What two groups would likely come into conflict after passage of the Kansas-Nebraska Act of 1854? Why?

Slave and Free States and Territories, 1820–1854

Free or gradual abolition

Slave

Decision left to voters in territory

Albers Equal-Area Projections   © SF

Missouri Compromise, 1820

Compromise of 1850

Kansas-Nebraska Act, 1854

The Kansas-Nebraska Act heightened sectional conflict.

A new crisis arose over a measure introduced in Congress in 1854 by **Stephen A. Douglas** of Illinois. This measure, called the Kansas-Nebraska Act, proposed dividing the Nebraska Territory into two territories, Kansas and Nebraska. Douglas introduced the bill in the interest of establishing a transcontinental railroad through the Midwest.

The Nebraska Territory had been closed to slavery by the Missouri Compromise. Douglas proposed to remove the restriction and apply the principle of **popular sovereignty**, allowing the voters of a territory to decide for themselves whether to allow slavery there.

The bill set off a bitter debate, and one of the chief casualties in the struggle was the Whig party. Northern Whigs, unwilling to support the act, joined with anti-slavery Democrats and Free Soilers to form a new party they named the Republican party.

During the two years following passage of the Kansas-Nebraska Act, violence flared in Kansas. Rival groups of proslavery and anti-slavery Kansans called conventions and drafted constitutions, each group seeking recognition for statehood from Washington. President Pierce recognized the proslavery government, but this did not settle the issue. Bands roamed the countryside, raiding farms and villages. Acts of violence on the Kansas plains had their counterpart in the halls of Congress, where Representative Preston Brooks of South Carolina viciously attacked Senator Charles Sumner of Massachusetts with a cane. The congressional atmosphere became charged with hate.

With violence flaring in the West, the nation prepared for the presidential election of 1856. The Democrats nominated **James Buchanan** of Pennsylvania, a northerner who was acceptable to the South. The new Republican party nominated John C. Fremont, who had won fame in California during the Mexican War. The Republicans made a strong showing, but victory went to Buchanan.

President Buchanan had been in office only two days when the Supreme Court made a rul-

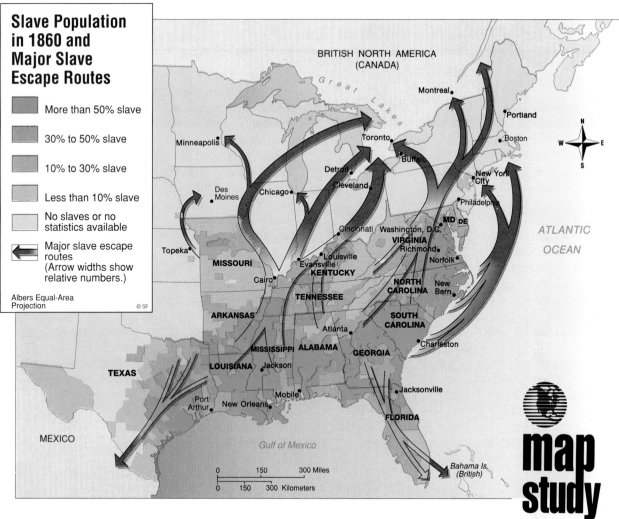

Slave Population in 1860 and Major Slave Escape Routes

- More than 50% slave
- 30% to 50% slave
- 10% to 30% slave
- Less than 10% slave
- No slaves or no statistics available
- Major slave escape routes (Arrow widths show relative numbers.)

Albers Equal-Area Projection
© SF

BRITISH NORTH AMERICA (CANADA)

Great Lakes

Montreal
Portland
Toronto
Buffalo
Boston
Minneapolis
Detroit
Cleveland
New York City
Des Moines
Chicago
Philadelphia
Cincinnati
Washington, D.C.
MD DE
ATLANTIC OCEAN
Topeka
MISSOURI
Louisville
Evansville
VIRGINIA
Richmond
Cairo
KENTUCKY
Norfolk
TENNESSEE
NORTH CAROLINA
New Bern
ARKANSAS
SOUTH CAROLINA
Atlanta
MISSISSIPPI
ALABAMA
GEORGIA
Charleston
TEXAS
LOUISIANA
Jackson
Jacksonville
Port Arthur
Mobile
New Orleans
FLORIDA
MEXICO
Gulf of Mexico
Bahama Is. (British)

0   150   300 Miles
0   150   300 Kilometers

Dred Scott remained a slave although his protest reached the Supreme Court. The Court ruled in 1857 that slaves were "beings of an inferior order [with] no rights which white men were bound to respect."

ing that rocked the nation. Its decision involved **Dred Scott**, a Missouri slave whose owner had taken him to the free territory of Wisconsin. Scott's owner then returned him to Missouri. In 1846 Scott sued his owner for freedom, contending that his residence in free territory entitled him to his freedom. In March 1857 the case reached the Supreme Court, which had a southern majority.

Under the leadership of Chief Justice Roger Taney, the Court ruled that Dred Scott was not a citizen and consequently had no legal right

(text continues on page 192)

map study

Regions
Runaway slaves usually worked their way on their own to border or free states. There, a network of way stations called the Underground Railroad helped them move north. Which slave states bordered free states? Did all slaves escape north?

Critical Thinking
Why might the percentages of slaves vary within the South and even within one state?

MARTIN VAN BUREN

Martin Van Buren was the first president born an American citizen rather than a British subject; ironically, his first language was Dutch. He also mastered the language of politics, which he learned in his father's tavern in Kinderhook, New York. Van Buren's famous cunning earned him spiteful nicknames ("Little Magician") and high office (senator, governor, vice president, and president).

Though Van Buren took office as the grateful heir of Andrew Jackson's policies and popularity, he saw both quickly drain away in one of the first

Born: December 5, 1782
Died: July 24, 1862
In office: 1837–1841

great national depressions, the Panic of 1837. He lost his bid for reelection in 1840, then tried twice more for the White House. In 1848, as the Free Soil candidate, Van Buren finished third.

The first vice president to succeed a president who died in office, John Tyler set a vital precedent by refusing to be "acting president" and insisting on the full powers of the presidency.

An ex-Democrat from Virginia, Tyler shared few goals with the Whigs. As president, he vetoed important Whig bills, provoking a riot outside the White House, a mass resignation of his cabinet, and the first-ever attempt to impeach a president.

A widower by 1844, Tyler became the first president to wed while in office when he married

JOHN TYLER

Born: March 29, 1790
Died: January 18, 1862
In office: 1841–1845

Julia Gardiner, 30 years younger than himself. Tyler fathered 15 children in his two happy marriages. This domestic record, at least, has not been equalled by any other president.

William Henry Harrison caught a cold at his inauguration and died of pneumonia a month later. He was the nation's briefest president, the first to die in office.

Born into a prominent Virginia family—his father had signed the Declaration of Independence—Harrison embarked on a military and political career in the Northwest Territory that made him a general, a territorial governor, and a U.S. senator.

In the 1840 campaign, the Whigs deliberately avoided issues and concentrated on shaping Harrison's image as a "man of the people."

WILLIAM HENRY HARRISON

Born: February 9, 1773
Died: April 4, 1841
In office: 1841

The campaign became a circus of symbols and slogans ("Tippecanoe and Tyler too"). In short, 1840 produced the first modern, image-based campaign.

Few presidents of any era have equalled the achievements of James Polk's single ambitious term of office. He set four major goals and accomplished them all: reduction of the tariff; reestablishment of an independent treasury; settlement of the Oregon dispute; and the acquisition of California.

A lawyer befriended by Andrew Jackson, Polk moved from the Tennessee legislature to Congress, where he was elected speaker of the house. Though he later served as governor of Tennessee, he was not known nationally. His nomination for president

JAMES POLK

Born: November 2, 1795
Died: June 15, 1849
In office: 1845–1849

was a colossal political surprise.

Only 49 when elected, Polk aged rapidly in office. He was the first president not to seek a second term.

ZACHARY TAYLOR

Born: November 24, 1784
Died: July 9, 1850
In office: 1849–1850

The nickname "Old Rough and Ready" serves equally well as a description of Zachary Taylor's casual dress, his approach to war, and his political aptitude. Taylor was a lifetime soldier who had held no political office—who had never even voted—before running for president in 1848.

Though southern-born and an owner of more than 100 slaves, Taylor firmly opposed the extension of slavery and strongly supported the admission of California and New Mexico as free states. These rough and ready positions pushed the country to a perilous choice between compromise and civil war. Taylor was no compromiser. His unexpected death in July was a critical ingredient of the Compromise of 1850.

FRANKLIN PIERCE

Born: November 23, 1804
Died: October 8, 1869
In office: 1853–1857

Born to politics, Franklin Pierce never lost an election in his life. Nomination was more difficult: it took 49 ballots to make him the Democratic presidential candidate. His wife fainted at the news.

Pierce made a smooth transition from college to law to politics, becoming by age 33 the youngest member of the Senate. He was equally quick to become a general in the Mexican War.

As president, Pierce had some success in his aims for prosperity and expansion, but his term was dominated by the issue of sectional strife. Tensions were only made worse by Pierce's obvious tilt toward "southern principles." His signature on the Kansas-Nebraska Act (1854) would eventually cost him his party's renomination for president.

MILLARD FILLMORE

Born: January 7, 1800
Died: March 8, 1874
In office: 1850–1853

Millard Fillmore's life followed a classic American path from log cabin to schoolhouse to law office to legislature to the White House. One of nine children of a poor farm family on the New York frontier, Fillmore rose through the study of law to a political career that included terms in the state legislature and in Congress.

Added to the Whig ticket in 1848 to provide regional balance, Fillmore became, on the death of Zachary Taylor, the second U.S. vice president to take office on the death of a president. He inherited as well the dangerous national crisis over the extension of slavery.

By signing the compromise measures that ended the crisis—especially the Fugitive Slave Act—Fillmore enraged the North and effectively ended his political career. He was the last Whig president.

JAMES BUCHANAN

Born: April 23, 1791
Died: June 1, 1868
In office: 1857–1861

James Buchanan entered the White House with 43 years of experience in politics and diplomacy. It was not enough. Buchanan endured his term as an irritable witness to events he could not control: the Dred Scott decision, the Panic of 1857, Harpers Ferry, secession.

The second of 11 children, Buchanan was born in a one-room log cabin. He picked up part of his education while clerking in his father's store.

Buchanan was the last of three northern presidents who sought national unity by favoring southern interests. He felt powerless to intervene when Lincoln's election caused seven states to secede. Though much criticized, Buchanan's inaction held eight slave states in the Union and left to the South the honor and error of firing the first shot of the Civil War.

ABRAHAM LINCOLN

Born: February 12, 1809
Died: April 15, 1865
In office: 1861–1865

No American life is more familiar; yet no life retains more mystery. How did Abraham Lincoln, the failed storekeeper and 90-day militia private, become the great war leader? How did the undereducated country politician become the master statesman? How did the man who struggled all his life for emotional balance become the unbreakable rock of the Union during the most tormented years in national history? More books have been written about Lincoln than any other American; the questions remain.

Lincoln's name is forever linked with union, emancipation, and government of the people. He once disclaimed any power to control events, but he did—and does. Lincoln's will and his vision endure through his words. They continue to shape America's understanding of its worst war and its best purposes.

Northern Democrat Stephen A. Douglas and Republican Abraham Lincoln are shown as rivals for the presidency in 1860. The Constitutional Union candidate, John Bell, looks on from the ring while the South's Democratic candidate, John C. Breckinridge, a few steps from the White House, thumbs his nose at the other contenders.

to sue. Secondly, the Court said that since slaves were property, and no one could be deprived of property without due process of law, slaveholders could take them into a territory without restrictions. In other words, the Missouri Compromise was unconstitutional.

White southerners hailed the Dred Scott decision as sound doctrine. In the North and the West, however, it was angrily denounced as a prosouthern political maneuver. Learning of the decision, Henry Highland Garnet arranged a large African American antislavery meeting at his church. He declared:

❙Our people, will not always consent to be trodden under foot; they will arm themselves some day, if need be, to secure their rights . . . armed with a box of lucifer matches [friction matches], the black man will have the power in his hands.

AN AMERICAN ★ SPEAKS

The emergence of Lincoln brought on a final crisis.

In 1858 attention shifted to a political contest in Illinois. Stephen A. Douglas was running for reelection to the Senate. His Republican opponent was **Abraham Lincoln**, a popular and successful Illinois lawyer. (In accordance with the Constitution, senators were elected by state legislatures until the 17th Amendment, ratified in 1913, allowed for the direct vote by the people of a state. Lincoln and Douglas, therefore, were really campaigning to be their parties' candidates to the state legislature.)

Lincoln and Douglas agreed to a series of seven debates that began to attract national attention. Large crowds assembled to hear the candidates, and the press printed full accounts of each debate. At Freeport, Illinois, scene of the second debate, Lincoln, with the Kansas-Nebraska Act in mind, asked Douglas how a territory could forbid slavery if Congress could not. Douglas said, in what became known as the **Freeport Doctrine**, that it did not matter what the Supreme Court ruled because, as a practical matter, slavery could not exist in a territory unless it was supported by local police regulations. Without such protection, no slaveholder would risk bringing valuable slave property into the territory. Although Lincoln's Republican candidates won more popular votes in the election, the Democrats main-

THE UNDECIDED POLITICAL PRIZE FIGHT

tained control of the Illinois legislature, which elected Douglas to another term.

As the presidential election of 1860 approached, divisions over slavery dimmed the hope of maintaining unity within the Democratic party. Stephen A. Douglas, a presidential hopeful, was no longer acceptable to the South because of his Freeport Doctrine. The national convention disintegrated into angry name-calling and finally adjourned without naming a candidate.

The Republicans were jubilant over the Democratic squabble. By this time they had adopted a number of important positions in addition to their opposition to the spread of slavery. They called for free homesteads for western settlers, protective tariffs for northern industries, internal improvements, and a railroad to the Pacific—all opposed by powerful southern interests. The convention chose Abraham Lincoln as its presidential candidate.

When the Democrats met again, matters had gone from bad to worse. Many southerners talked of secession and then walked out of the convention. Those remaining chose Douglas, who became, in effect, the candidate of the northern wing of the party. The southern wing met separately and nominated John C. Breckenbridge of Kentucky.

Meanwhile, a group of former Whigs, alarmed over the prospect of disunion, met in a hastily-called convention. Calling themselves the Constitutional Union party, they refused to say anything specific about the slavery question. They stressed their loyalty to the Union and their determination to uphold the Constitution. For their candidate they chose John Bell of Tennessee.

In the election, Lincoln received 40 percent of the popular vote and carried all the states of the North and West, winning a majority of the electoral vote and the presidency. In ten southern states he was not on the ballot and failed to receive a single vote. The nation had elected a sectional president.

Repeatedly during the campaign, the South had vowed to secede from the Union if Lincoln should win. They began now to carry out their threat. On December 20, 1860, South Carolina withdrew from the Union. Within six weeks Mississippi, Florida, Alabama, Georgia, Louisiana, and Texas followed. Delegates from the seceding states met in February 1861 at Montgomery, Alabama, and set up the Confederate States of America. The delegates then chose **Jefferson Davis** of Mississippi as provisional president. The Deep South had left a Union that no further compromise could hold together. Years of bitter civil war would be required to restore that Union.

SECTION **5** REVIEW

Identifying Key People and Terms
Write a sentence to identify: Wilmot Proviso, Free Soil party, Henry Clay, Millard Fillmore, Compromise of 1850, Fugitive Slave Law, Stephen A. Douglas, popular sovereignty, James Buchanan, Dred Scott, Abraham Lincoln, Freeport Doctrine, Jefferson Davis

Locate Key Places
Where was the slave trade abolished as a result of the Compromise of 1850?

Master the Main Ideas
1. **Comparing economies:** How did the economies of the North and the South differ?
2. **Recognizing the value of compromise: (a)** How did the Compromise of 1850 attempt to satisfy both the North and the South? **(b)** Why did the compromise fail to settle the conflict over slavery?
3. **Analyzing major political and constitutional issues:** How did the Kansas-Nebraska Act and the Dred Scott decision deepen sectional strife?
4. **Analyzing the results of major elections:** Why did seven states decide to secede from the Union?

Applying Critical Thinking Skills: Making Generalizations
How valid is the generalization that compromise is essential in a democratic society? Use evidence from your own experience as well as historical knowledge to support your conclusion.

Tecumseh Fights the Sale of Indian Lands

4A

TIME FRAME
1810

GEOGRAPHIC SETTING
Indiana

In 1810 the Shawnee chief Tecumseh [tə kum′ sə] complained to William Henry Harrison, first governor of the Indiana Territory, that Indian land was being stolen by white people. At that time Tecumseh (1768?–1813) and his twin brother, Tenskwatawa, who was known as "the Prophet," had formed an Indian confederacy along the western border of the Indiana Territory. Tecumseh spoke outside the governor's mansion at Vincennes, which he refused to enter. Excerpts from his speech follow.

A curious contemporary portrait of the Shawnee chief Tecumseh shows him in European dress, posed as though he were a successful member of America's merchant class.

Houses are built for you to hold councils in; Indians hold theirs in the open air. I am a Shawnee. My forefathers were warriors. Their son is a warrior. From them I take my only existence. From my tribe I take nothing. I have made myself what I am. And I would that I could make the red people as great as the conceptions of my own mind, when I think of the Great Spirit that rules over us all. . . . I would not then come to Governor Harrison to ask him to tear up the treaty [the 1795 Treaty of Greenville, which gave the United States parts of the Northwest Territory. Tecumseh had refused to attend the Greenville peace council]. But I would say to him, "Brother, you have the liberty to return to your own country."

You wish to prevent the Indians from doing as we wish them, to unite and let them consider their lands as the common property of the whole. You take the tribes aside and advise them not to come into this measure. . . . You want by your distinctions of Indian tribes, in allotting to each a particular, to make them war with each other. You never see an Indian endeavor to make the white people do this. You are continually driving the red people, when at last you will drive them onto the great lake [Lake Michigan], where they can neither stand nor work.

Since my residence at Tippecanoe, we have endeavored to level all distinctions, to destroy village chiefs, by whom all mischiefs are done. It is they who sell the land to the Americans. Brother, this land that was sold, and the goods that was given for it, was only done by a few. . . . In the future we are prepared to punish those who propose to sell land to the Americans. If you continue to purchase them, it will make war among the different tribes, and, at last I do not know what will be the consequences among the white people. . . .

The way, the only way to stop this evil, is for the red men to unite in claiming a common and equal right in the land, as it was at first, and should be now—for it was never divided, but belongs to all. No tribe has the right to sell, even to each other, much less to strangers. . . .

Sell a country! Why not sell the air, the great sea, as well as the earth? Did not the Great Spirit make them all for the use of his children?

How can we have confidence in the white people? When Jesus Christ came upon the earth you killed Him and nailed him to the cross. You thought he was dead, and you were mistaken. You have Shakers among you, and you laugh and make light of their worship.

Everything I have told you is the truth. The Great Spirit has inspired me.

Discussing the Reading

1. Is the way in which Tecumseh received his religious insights similar to the way in which Anne Hutchinson (Source Reading 2A) received hers? Explain.

2. The sect of the Shakers, whom Tecumseh mentioned in lines 61–63, came to America from England in 1774. The Shaker communities owned property in common and employed dancing in their religious services. What seems to have been Tecumseh's attitude toward the Shakers? Why might he have felt this way?

CRITICAL THINKING
Recognizing Values

How did Tecumseh want the Indian people to view land ownership? How did this view differ from that of the whites toward land ownership?

Lucy Stone and Henry Blackwell Get Married

TIME FRAME
1855

GEOGRAPHIC SETTING
Massachusetts

In 1853 the reformer Henry Blackwell (1825–1909) heard Lucy Stone (1818–1893) address a Massachusetts legislative hearing on the subject of women's rights. He spent two years persuading her to abandon her intention never to marry. They married in 1855 after Blackwell agreed to devote his life to the cause of women's rights. Insisting that they become equal partners in marriage, the couple wrote their own wedding vows and the following protest against the marriage laws of the time that forced a woman to give up her legal identity and property rights. (Stone never took her husband's name, only substituting *Mrs.* for *Miss* Lucy Stone.)

While acknowledging our mutual affection by publicly assuming the relationship of husband and wife, yet in justice to ourselves and a great principle, we
5 deem it a duty to declare that this act on our part implies no sanction [approval] of, nor promise of voluntary obedience to such of the present laws of marriage, as refuse to recognize the wife as an inde-
10 pendent, rational being, while they confer upon the husband an injurious and unnatural superiority, investing him with legal powers which no honorable man would exercise, and which no man should

possess. We protest especially against the laws which give to the husband:

1. The custody of the wife's person.
2. The exclusive control and guardianship of their children.
3. The sole ownership of her personal property, and the use of her real estate, unless previously settled upon her or placed in the hands of trustees, as in the case of minors, lunatics, and idiots.
4. The absolute right to the product of her industry.
5. Also against laws which give to the widower so much larger and more permanent an interest in the property of his deceased wife, than they give to the widow in that of the deceased husband.
6. Finally, against the whole system by which "the legal existence of the wife is suspended during marriage," so that in most States, she neither has a legal part in the choice of her residence, nor can she make a will, nor sue or be sued in her own name, nor inherit property.

We believe that personal independence and equal human rights can never be forfeited, except for crime; that marriage should be an equal and permanent partnership, and so recognized by law; that until it is so recognized, married partners should provide against the radical injustice of present laws by every means in their power.

We believe that where domestic difficulties arise, no appeal should be made to legal tribunes [officials] under existing laws, but that all difficulties should be submitted to the equitable adjustment or arbitrators [persons with full power to judge and decide] mutually chosen.

Thus reverencing law, we enter our protest against rules and customs which are unworthy of the name, since they violate justice, the essence of law.

(Signed) Henry B. Blackwell
Lucy Stone

Stitched in 1820 by Ruth Titus, this embroidered sampler typifies traditional beliefs about women's roles. Probably sewn with linen or silk thread on a linen backing, this sampler's design was created by counting individual threads in the linen backing to determine the precise placement of each stitch. On the opposite page, a marriage certificate published in 1848 by Nathaniel Currier, New York City, lists the duties of the husband and of the wife as excerpted from the Old and New Testaments.

WOMAN

As some fair violet loveliest of the glade
Sheds its mild fragrance on the lonely shade
So Woman born to dignify retreat
Unknown to flourish and unseen be great
To give domestic life its sweetest charm
With softness polish and with virtue warm
With angel kindness should behold distress
And meekly pity where she cant redress

Ruth . Titus
1820

Discussing the Reading

1. Stone and Blackwell claimed that the American marriage laws refused to recognize not only a woman's independence but even her status as a "rational being" (lines 9–10). What did they mean by this? What attitude toward women were they attributing to American society?

2. What proposal did Stone and Blackwell make in lines 49–55? Does this seem to you like a workable solution to domestic disputes? Why or why not?

CRITICAL THINKING
Recognizing Values

If Lucy Stone and Henry Blackwell were alive today, do you think that they would agree with contemporary attitudes toward marriage? Explain.

Santa Anna Besieges the Alamo

In *The Battle of the Alamo,* by F. C. Yohn, Davy Crockett wields his rifle, having fired his last shot, against Mexican soldiers. The painting reflects the superiority of the Mexican forces, both in number and arms, against the last defenders of the Alamo.

Between February 23 and March 6, 1836, the 188 defenders of the Alamo, an abandoned mission in San Antonio, Texas, held off an army of several thousand Mexicans commanded by General Antonio López de Santa Anna [san'tə an'ə]. Santa Anna (1795?–1876) had come to suppress rebellious Texans, most of them originally from the United States, who wanted independence from Mexico. The defenders of the Alamo were commanded by William Barrett Travis (1809–1836) and James Bowie (1796–1836), and included Davy Crockett (1786–1836), the most famous American frontiersman of his day. Many of the Hispanic residents of Texas, the *Tejanos* [tä-hän'ōz], also opposed Santa Anna, and eight of them were among the defenders of the Alamo. During the siege Travis issued several appeals for help; the last, dated

March 3, 1836, is the first of the two passages below. (The spelling of the original has been retained.) On March 6, Santa Anna's troops captured the Alamo, killing the few surviving defenders. Francisco Ruiz, the mayor of San Antonio, entered the mission about 30 minutes after the battle ended. The second of the following passages is an excerpt from his report.

I beg leave to communicate to you the situation of this garrison. . . .

From the 25th to the present date, the enemy have kept up a bombardment. . . .
5 During this period the enemy have been busily employed in encircling us with entrenched encampments on all sides. . . .

I have so fortified this place, that the walls are generally proof against cannon balls; and I still continue to intrench on the inside, and strengthen the walls by throwing up the dirt. . . . The spirits of my men are still high, although they have had much to depress them. We have contended [struggled] for ten days against an enemy whose numbers are variously estimated at from 1,500 to 6,000 men. . . .

I sent an express [message] to Col. Fannin, which arrived at Goliad on the next day, urging him to send us reinforcements—*none have yet arrived.* I look to the *colonies alone* [Texas] for aid; unless it arrives soon, I shall have to fight the enemy on his own terms. I will, however, do the best I can under the circumstances; and I feel confident that the determined valor, and desparate courage, heretofore evinced [shown] by my men, will not fail them in the last struggle: and although they may be sacrificed to the vengeance of a gothic [uncivilized] enemy, the victory will cost the enemy so dear, that it will be worse for him than a defeat. . . .

A blood red banner waves from the church of Bejar, and in the camp above us, in token that the war is one of vengeance against rebels: they have declared us as such, and demanded that we should surrender at discretion, or that this garrison should be put to the sword. Their threats have had no influence on me, or my men, but to make all fight with desperation, and that high souled courage which characterizes the patriot, who is willing to die in defence of his country's liberty and his own honor. . . .

The bearer of this will give your honorable body, a statement more in detail, should he escape through the enemies lines—*God and Texas—Victory or Death!*
Your obedient servant,
W. BARRETT TRAVIS,
Lieutenant Colonel Commanding
P.S. The enemies troops are still arriving, and the reinforcement will probably amount to two or three thousand.

On the 6th of March 1836, at 3 A.M., General Santa Anna at the head of 4,000 men advanced against the Alamo. The infantry, artillery and cavalry had formed about 1,000 varas [1,000 yards] from the walls of the same fortress. The Mexican army charged and were twice repulsed by the deadly fire of Travis' artillery, which resembled a constant thunder. At the third charge the Toluca battalion commenced to scale the walls and suffered severely. Out of 830 men only 130 of the battalion were left alive. . . .

The gallantry of the few Texans who defended the Alamo was really wondered at by the Mexican army. Even the generals were astonished at their vigorous resistance, and how dearly victory was bought.

Discussing the Reading

1. What was the meaning of the "blood red" flags that waved from the church at Bejar and the camp of the Mexican troops besieging the Alamo? What effect might the sight of these banners have had on the defenders of the mission?

2. According to Francisco Ruiz, what was the Mexican army's view of the defenders after the battle?

CRITICAL THINKING
Determining Relevant Information

William Barrett Travis could only guess at the number of Mexican troops besieging the Alamo, estimating them at between 1,500 and 6,000 men. Ruiz reported that there were 4,000 Mexicans; modern estimates are closer to 3,000. Estimates of the size of large groups of people, such as a crowd at a rally or an invading army, often vary a great deal depending on who is doing the counting. What different factors might affect the reliability of such estimates?

Lalu Nathoy Arrives in San Francisco

TIME FRAME
1872

GEOGRAPHIC SETTING
California

Lalu Nathoy (1853–1933) was raised in a poor and drought-stricken peasant village in North China. Seized from her family by bandits, she was shipped as a slave to America, where she was auctioned off to a Chinese saloon-keeper in an Idaho mining camp. Gaining her freedom, she married, ran a boarding-house, and eventually homesteaded a twenty-acre farm in Idaho. The following passage, an excerpt from *Thousand Pieces of Gold,* a novel by Ruthanne Lum McCunn based on the life of Lalu Nathoy, describes Lalu's arrival in San Francisco. The "Madam" to whom the narrator refers was the woman in China who had arranged Lalu's passage to America. The "demons" are Americans.

L ike the hold of the ship, the San Francisco customs shed was dimly lit, but at least the lanterns did not pitch and sway; and the air, though stale and stinking from
5 the press of unwashed bodies, did not reek of vomit or human waste. If anything, the din from hundreds of voices, mostly male, had grown louder. But there was life and excitement in the shouting, joyful ex-
10 pectation in the rush for luggage, relatives, and friends.

Lalu, waiting for her turn to come before the customs officer, caught the contagion of nervous excitement, and she felt
15 the same thrill, bright and sharp as lightning, that had shot through her when the Madam had told her she was going to America, the Gold Mountains at the other end of the Great Ocean of Peace.
20 "I have never been there, but Li Ma, the woman for whom I bought you, says there is gold everywhere. On the streets, in the hills, mountains, rivers, and valleys. Gold just waiting to be picked up. . . . "
25 Hugging herself inwardly, she had pictured her parents' and brothers' faces when she gave her father the gold that

would make him the richest man in the village. The pride they would have in her,
30 their qianjin [kē ān jin, "thousand pieces of gold," Lalu's family nickname]. And she had held fast to this picture, as to a talisman [good-luck charm]. First, when the Madam had turned her over to Li Ma,
35 the crotchety, foulmouthed woman who would take her to the Gold Mountains. Then, during the long voyage, when only the men's talk of gold had kept alive her dream of going home. And now, as she
40 folded and refolded the forged papers Li Ma had given her. For the demons who ruled the Gold Mountains wished to keep their gold for themselves, and in order to

gain the right to land, Lalu must successfully pretend to be the wife of a San Francisco merchant.

Over and over, during the long weeks crammed in the hold of the ship, Li Ma had forced Lalu and the other five women and girls in her charge to rehearse the stories that matched their papers, sternly warning, "Pass the examination by customs, and you will soon return to China a rich woman, the envy of all in your village. Fail, and you will find yourself in a demon jail, tortured as only the demons know how."

Could the torture be worse than the journey she had just endured? Lalu thought of the sweltering, airless heat and thirst that had strangled the words in her throat, making her stumble when she recited for Li Ma, earning her cruel pinchings and monotonous harangues. The aching loneliness that came from homesickness and Li Ma's refusal to permit the girls to talk among themselves. The bruising falls and the tearing at her innards each time the ship rocked, tossing her off the narrow shelf that served as bed, knocking her against the hard wood sides of the hull. The long, black periods of waiting for the hatch to bang open as it did twice each day, bringing a shaft of sunlight, gusts of life-giving salt air, the smell of the sea. . . .

Lalu tossed her head, straightened her jacket, and smoothed her hair. That was all over. Behind her. No more than a bad dream. She was in America, the Gold Mountains. And soon, just as soon as she gathered enough gold, she would go home.

"Next."

Lalu felt herself shoved in front of the customs officer. She had never been close to a white man before and she stared amazed at the one that towered above her. His skin was chalk white, like the face of an actor painted to play a villain, only it was not smooth but covered with wiry

golden hair, and when his mouth opened and closed, there were no words to make an audience shake with anger or fear, only a senseless roaring. Beside him, a Chinese man spoke.

"Your papers. Give him your papers," Li Ma hissed.

"My papers?" Lalu said in her native Northern dialect. "I've . . . "

Li Ma snatched the papers from Lalu. "Don't mind the girl's foolish rambling. You'll see everything's in order. Here's the certificate of departure and the slip with her husband's address here in the Great City."

Gold flashed as she passed the papers up to the Chinese man beside the demon officer. "A respected tradesman he is. Could have his pick of beauties. Why he wants this simpleton back is anyone's guess. . . ."

The Chinese man laughed. He passed the papers to the customs officer. Again gold flashed. They talked between them in the foreign tongue, their eyes stripping Lalu, making her feel unclean. Finally, the demon officer stamped the papers. Smirking, he thrust them down at Lalu. Her face burning with embarrassment, she hugged the precious papers against her chest and followed Li Ma past the wooden barricade. She was safe.

Lalu Nathoy shown on her wedding day, August 13, 1894, when she was married to miner Charlie Bemis.

Discussing the Reading

1. What does Lalu Nathoy believe about America? What does she believe about Americans?

2. How is her entry into America arranged?

CRITICAL THINKING
Identifying Assumptions

When Lalu gets her close view of a white American, of what is she reminded? How does this impression reinforce her preconceptions about Americans?

A Slave Recalls Her Mother's Courage

TIME FRAME
1840s

GEOGRAPHIC SETTING
Tennessee

In the 1850s white Southerners referred defensively to slavery as "the peculiar domestic institution of the South." The human situation disguised in that abstract phrase is revealed by the following two selections. The first is an account from an 85-year-old former slave of her mother's efforts to maintain her independence. The second is the spiritual "Go Down, Moses." The spirituals were the religious folk songs of African American slaves. Many spirituals, such as "Go Down, Moses," expressed the slaves' misery and their desire for freedom in terms borrowed from the Old Testament story of the bondage of Israel in Egypt, a captivity seen by the slaves to be similar to their own.

I began to exist in the year 1844, in a small town in Tennessee. Eden, Tennessee, was between Nashville and Memphis. . . .

I was the personal property of Mr. Jen-
5 nings. . . . Mr. Jennings was a good man. There was no disputing that. He seemed to always be in debt, and I reasoned that he was too easy, that people took advantage of his good nature. He had married a
10 woman of the same mold, and they had three children. . . .

My mother was the smartest black woman in Eden. She was as quick as a flash of lightning, and whatever she did
15 could not be done better. She could do anything. She cooked, washed, ironed, spun, nursed and labored in the field. She made as good a field hand as she did a cook. I have heard Master Jennings say to
20 his wife, "Fannie has her faults, but she can outwork any [slave] in the country. I'd bet my life on that."

My mother certainly had her faults as a slave. . . . Ma fussed, fought, and kicked all
25 the time. I tell you, she was a demon. She said that she wouldn't be whipped, and

when she fussed, all Eden must have known it. . . . With all her ability for work, she did not make a good slave. She was
30 too highspirited and independent. . . .

The one doctrine of my mother's teaching which was branded upon my senses was that I should never let anyone abuse me. "I'll kill you, gal, if you don't stand up
35 for yourself," she would say. "Fight, and if you can't fight, kick; if you can't kick, then bite." Ma was generally willing to work, but if she didn't feel like doing something, none could make her do it. At least, the
40 Jennings couldn't make, or didn't make her. . . .

I was the oldest child. My mother had three other children by the time I was about six years old. It was at this age that I
45 remember the almost daily talks of my mother on the cruelty of slavery. I would say nothing to her, but I was thinking all the time that slavery did not seem so cruel. Master and Mistress Jennings were
50 not mean to my mother. It was she who was mean to them. . . .

One day my mother's temper ran wild. For some reason Mistress Jennings struck her with a stick. Ma struck back and a fight
55 followed. . . .

About a week later, [my mother] called me and told me that she and pa were going to leave me the next day, that they were going to Memphis. She didn't know
60 for how long. [They were hired out for a year.]

"But don't be abused, Puss." She always called me Puss. My right name was Cornelia. I cannot tell in words the feelings I
65 had at that time. My sorrow knew no bound. My very soul seemed to cry out, "Gone, gone, gone forever." I cried until my eyes looked like balls of fire. I felt for the first time in my life that I had been
70 abused. How cruel it was to take my

A small-town minister is shown taking dinner with one of the families in his parish in *A Pastoral Visit* (1881), a painting by Richard Norris Brooke (1847–1920). The scene was painted from life in Brooke's home town of Warrenton, Virginia.

mother and father from me, I thought. My mother had been right. Slavery was cruel, so very cruel.

Go Down, Moses

When Israel was in Egypt's land,
    Let my people go!
Oppress'd so hard dey could not stand,
    Let my people go!

5 *Chorus*
Go down, Moses,
    Way down in Egypt's land.
Tell ole Pha-raoh,
    Let my people go!

10 Thus say de Lord, bold Moses said,
    Let my people go!
If not I'll smite your first-born dead,
    Let my people go!

No more shall dey in bondage toil,
15   Let my people go!
Let dem come out wid Egypt's spoil,
    Let my people go!

Discussing the Reading

1. Why did the speaker in the first selection think her mother was such an outstanding woman? How did her mother's character make her unfit for slavery?

2. What was the speaker's first reaction to her mother's lectures on the cruelty of slavery? What episode changed her mind?

3. Would the speaker's mother have approved of the feeling expressed by "Go Down, Moses"? Why or why not?

CRITICAL THINKING
Predicting Consequences

Imagine that the speaker and her family were owned by less easygoing people than Mr. and Mrs. Jennings. Would her mother have been likely to be more independent or less so under a harsher discipline than that of the Jennings?

Chapter Summary

Write supporting details under each of the following main ideas as you review the chapter.

Section 1
1. New economic forces shaped American life.
2. A new system of party politics developed.
3. Andrew Jackson dominated his Administration.
4. The Whig party emerged to challenge the Democrats.

Section 2
1. Religious movements inspired widespread reform.
2. Social crusaders tried to reform American life.
3. The abolition movement dominated the era.

Section 3
1. Texans fought a revolution to achieve independence from Mexico.
2. The United States acquired the Oregon Country by treaty.
3. Pioneers sought gold in California and religious freedom in Utah.

Section 4
1. The annexation of Texas triggered a war with Mexico.
2. Not all Americans and Mexicans supported the war.
3. Geography helped delay the American victory in Mexico.

Section 5
1. Economic factors contributed to sectional conflict.
2. The slavery issue intensified after the Mexican War.
3. The Kansas-Nebraska Act heightened sectional conflict.
4. The emergence of Lincoln brought on a final crisis.

Chapter Themes

1. **Religious and ethical framework:** The overwhelming majority of social reforms and many cultural achievements of the Age of Reform were inspired by religious movements, especially that of the Second Great Awakening.
2. **National destiny:** America's belief that it was uniquely destined to possess the continent from coast to coast led it into violent confrontation with Mexico over Texas and into peaceful negotiation with Britain over Oregon.
3. **Constitutional and representative government:** From the 1820s to the 1860s, Americans resolved their sectional differences through the federal legislative process and compromise. These compromises, however, were upset by territorial expansion, the decisions of the Supreme Court, and the reform movement of the abolitionists.

Chapter Study Guide

Identifying Key People and Terms

Name the key person or key term that describes the:
1. group of people who wanted to do away with slavery
2. idea of U.S. westward expansion
3. treaty that ended the Mexican War
4. law that allowed California to enter the Union
5. Illinoisan who debated Lincoln

Locating Key Places

1. Where was the first women's rights convention held?
2. Which former mission served as a refuge for Texans in 1836?
3. In which location was the slave trade abolished in 1850?

Mastering the Main Ideas

1. What was the role of religion in the Age of Reform?
2. How did the Mountain Men open the West?
3. How were the economies of the North and South different?
4. What was the significance of the Dred Scott decision?

Applying Critical Thinking Skills

1. **Recognizing values:** What values did the abolitionists hold? How did they demonstrate these values?
2. **Drawing conclusions:** Do you think the United States was justified in declaring war against Mexico? Why or why not?
3. **Identifying alternatives:** How successful were the compromises made to hold the Union together? What other alternatives might there have been in trying to prevent war?
4. **Testing conclusions:** What conclusions did the Supreme Court reach in the Dred Scott case? Why do you think the Court ruled the way it did on the Dred Scott case?

1825 Erie Canal opens | **1828** Andrew Jackson elected president

1832–1833 Nullification crisis occurs

1848 Gold is found at Sutter's Mill | **1857** Supreme Court decides against Dred Scott

1860 Lincoln elected president

1821 Mexico achieves independence

1830 Indian Removal Act passed

1846 United States and Mexico go to war

1851 *Moby Dick* (Melville)

Chapter Activities

Learning Geography Through History

1. How did the Erie Canal help further westward expansion?
2. What sections of the country were pitted against each other in the battle between reformers and slaveholders?
3. What region of Texas did Mexico object most strongly to losing and why?
4. Why was the Kansas-Nebraska Act so important to southern slaveholders?

Relating the United States to the World

1. What country's interest in Texas prompted the United States to annex it?
2. What countries had abandoned their claims to the Pacific Northwest by 1825?
3. How did northern states benefit from unsettling political and economic conditions in Europe?

Linking Past and Present

1. What are some reform movements today and how are they alike and different from reform movements in the 1800s?
2. What is the relationship between the United States and Mexico today? Consult magazines, newspapers, and other resources to identify areas of cooperation and conflict between the two nations.
3. Douglas wanted to build a railroad through Kansas. The Republicans wanted to build one west through Iowa and Nebraska. Davis wanted to build one west through Texas. Using a modern transportation map of the United States, find the railroads that made these dreams come true.

Using the Time Line

1. How long had Mexico been independent when it went to war with the United States?
2. Which time line events relect the westward movement of population across the continent?
3. Which events reflect growing sectionalism and a possible civil war?

Practicing Critical Thinking Strategies

Analyzing Cause and Effect

Many Mexicans supported the Mexican War. Use your text and other sources to determine how Mexicans viewed the causes for this war. Write a paragraph describing the Mexican view of the war.

Learning More About Expansion, Reform, and Constitutional Conflicts

1. **Using Source Readings:** Read the Source Readings for this chapter and answer the questions.
2. **Writing a newspaper article:** Write a newspaper article from the perspective of a conservative male reporter who has just witnessed an abolitionist meeting. Describe the speeches you might have heard and give your own thoughts about the content of these speeches.
3. **Using primary sources:** Read a pioneer account like that of Jesse Applegate quoted on pages 163 and 178 (*Westward Journeys,* edited by Martin Ridge; Chicago: Lakeside Press, 1989). For a Native American perspective, read *The Education of Little Tree,* by Forrest Carter (Albuquerque: University of New Mexico Press, 1986), a true story of a North Carolina Cherokee youth in the 1930s whose ancestors refused to comply with the Indian Removal Act.

Linking Past to Present

The painting of three runaway slaves riding to freedom before the Civil War, inset, and the contemporary photograph of a young college graduate and her proud parents, convey a significant effect of the Civil War and Reconstruction— the long, hard journey of African Americans to participation in the American Dream.

Civil War and Reconstruction

1 8 6 0 – 1 8 7 7

5

S outh Carolina seceded from the Union on December 20, 1860. By March 2, 1861, six additional states—Mississippi, Florida, Alabama, Georgia, Louisiana, and Texas—had also seceded. Although many people in those states had opposed leaving the Union, secession was accomplished quickly and with much public rejoicing.

In the North there was an air of uncertainty. President-elect Lincoln was still in Springfield and would not take the reins of government until March 4. President Buchanan was serving his last months in office, presiding over a government that, like the Union, was falling apart. An air of uncertainty hung over Washington, D.C., as Southerners resigned from federal service in droves. Colleagues and friends parted company, wondering if they might meet next as enemies on some battlefield.

The eight slave states still in the Union were teetering on the edge. Any provocation might cause them to secede. Most Northerners were apprehensive, not knowing how the government in Washington should respond to the worst crisis in the nation's history. Could the seven states that had formed the Confederacy be brought back into the Union peaceably? Would the remaining slave states remain loyal to the Union? What would—what *could*—the new president do?

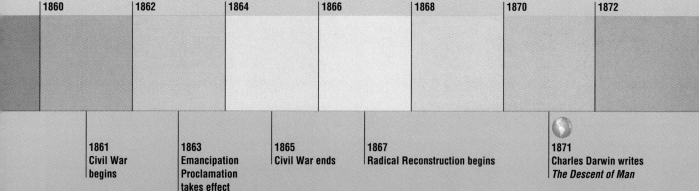

1860	1862	1864	1866	1868	1870	1872

1861 Civil War begins

1863 Emancipation Proclamation takes effect

1865 Civil War ends

1867 Radical Reconstruction begins

1871 Charles Darwin writes *The Descent of Man*

The Civil War
A PICTORIAL HISTORY

The Confederates attacked Fort Sumter.

The Civil War began on April 12, 1861, as a Confederate battery opened fire on Union forces at Fort Sumter in South Carolina's Charleston Bay. Forty hours later the Confederate flag waved victoriously over the battered fort. President Lincoln responded by ordering state militias in the loyal states to put down the insurrection. When Union forces drove Confederate troops out of western Virginia in May, recruitment broadsides such as the one at left called for volunteers to defend "our homes and firesides, the honor of our wives and daughters, and the sacred graves of our ancestors."

Stonewall Jackson prevailed at Bull Run.

The war's first major battle ended disastrously for Union forces. On July 21, 1861, General Thomas J. Jackson, right, earned the nickname "Stonewall" for his courageous stand against a Northern assault at Bull Run Creek at Manassas Junction, Virginia. Jackson, who then counterattacked and routed the invading Union forces led by General Irvin McDowell, later wrote his wife: "Whilst great credit [for the victory at Bull Run] is due to other parts of our gallant army, God made my brigade more instrumental than any other." The soldiers under Jackson also believed an element of divine intervention had been present at Bull Run. They fittingly named four of the cannons used at the battle, below, Mathew, Mark, Luke, and John because "they spoke a powerful language."

The Confederacy claimed important victories in 1862.

Above, weary Federal soldiers pursue Stonewall Jackson in the Shenandoah Valley. Jackson emerged triumphant in four battles in the valley in May and June. At the end of June, federal gunners, right, fire upon advancing Confederate troops near Richmond during the last of the Seven Days' battles. General Robert E. Lee's troops forced the Union to retreat from the capital.

Grant won the first significant victory for the North at Fort Donelson.

Although the North experienced heavy losses on the eastern front in 1862, it made significant strides in the west. On February 6, federal forces under General Henry W. Halleck captured Fort Henry in western Tennessee. Ten days later, General Ulysses S. Grant forced 13,000 Confederate troops at nearby Fort Donelson to surrender unconditionally. The painting at center shows Grant, on horseback, observing his troops advance on Fort Donelson. The portrait of Grant, right, shows him sporting a recently cultivated square-cut beard.

Grant narrowly prevailed at Shiloh.

Overconfident, General Grant had his guard down when 40,000 Confederate troops overran his lines at Shiloh in southern Tennessee on April 6, 1862. Although the casualties were high, the Union claimed a victory. Among Confederate forces at Shiloh were the Rutledge Rifles, right, a Tennessee light artillery battery. Their commander, Captain A.M. Rutledge, leans on one of the six-pound cannons that were responsible for many of the deaths at Shiloh.

"Keep still and don't blink."

Many soldiers commissioned portraits of themselves to send to their loved ones.

Bugle sounded the call to battle.

Private Frederick Barnhart of Company B of the 15th Indiana militia had this bugle shot from his hands as he sounded the call to battle at Shiloh. Barnhart saved the bugle as a memento of the bloody battle.

The Northern blockade suffocated the South.

A confident-looking young "powder monkey" poses by a huge gun aboard a Northern ship. His job was to make sure that each of the ship's guns was filled with gun powder. The ship was part of a huge fleet of boats and ships that formed a blockade along Southern ports during the war. The blockade helped prevent essential supplies from reaching the South.

Federal gunboats helped secure the Mississippi.

Union troops on the western front were greatly aided by ironclads such as the ones above, which are shown firing at Fort Henry on the Tennessee River. The *Cincinnati*, left, was hit 31 times by cannon balls but suffered only superficial damage.

Lee and McClellan battled at Antietam.

Federal signal corpsmen viewing Antietam on September 16, 1862, above left, had no way of knowing that the war's bloodiest one-day battle would be fought the next day. When the smoke had cleared, above, a total of 5,000 soldiers had been killed and more than 18,000 wounded. Although the battle was a draw, the Union claimed victory because General George McClellan had forced General Robert E. Lee to retreat.

The Confederate victory at Fredericksburg was a blow to the North.

Less than two weeks before Christmas, the Union's General Ambrose E. Burnside attacked Robert E. Lee and his depleted forces at Fredericksburg, Virginia. Burnside's troops suffered a devastating defeat, one which punctuated a year of bitter failure for the North on the eastern front.

Musicians led the troops into battle.

Boys as young as twelve led both sides to battle. The federal musicians at left were in their teens. Drums such as those below were often decorated with colorful insignia.

Artists and photographers brought news of the war to the homefront.

Photographers such as Mathew Brady and Alexander Gardner and artists such as Alfred R. Waud enabled Americans on the homefront to keep up with the war. Waud, an artist for *Harper's Weekly*, is shown above sketching a scene from the Battle of Gettysburg.

Victory at Gettysburg turned the tide for the Union.

Left, federal defenders repel a valiant yet foolhardy charge led by General George E. Pickett during the Battle of Gettysburg. General Robert E. Lee, shown below offering encouragement to his battered troops, blamed himself for the defeat. After Gettysburg, the Confederacy never again would be able to mount a major offensive against Northern armies.

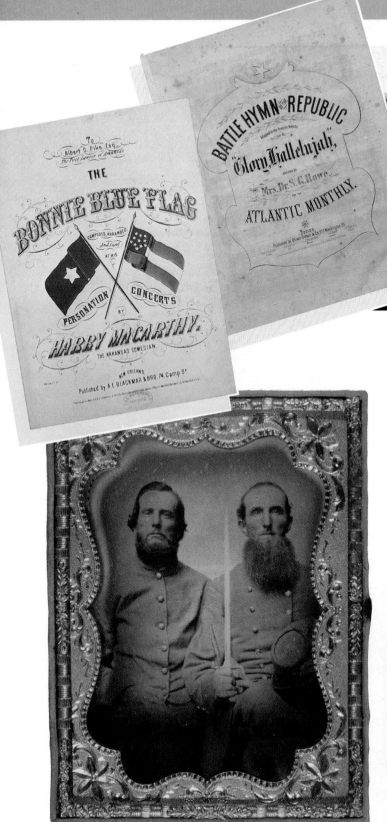

Patriotism soared on both sides of the conflict.

The war stirred passions in the North and the South. A Virginian wrote, "all of us are . . . ripe and ready. . . . I go for taking Boston and Cincinnati. I go for wiping them out." According to a New Yorker: "It seems as if we were never alive until now; never had a country until now." The populace clearly wanted to fight. Fathers and sons, such as those shown at left from the 13th Virginia Infantry, volunteered together to fight the North. Songs such as "The Bonnie Blue Flag" and "The Battle Hymn of the Republic" fueled the patriotic fires and promoted the "glory of war."

The glorious aspects of the war, in the end, were overwhelmed by its tremendous inhumanity and horror. To the many Southern civilians who were forced to leave their homes by invading troops, below, the war was anything but glorious.

African Americans helped the North.

Almost 200,000 African Americans, most of them newly freed slaves, eventually served in the Union armed forces and made a vital contribution to the North's victory. Left, members of Battery "A" of the 2nd U.S. Colored Artillery prepare a cannon for firing.

Women filled many important roles during the war.

During the long conflict, many women replaced skilled male workers in the labor force. They made uniforms, such as the Northern women shown above, rolled bandages, stuffed cartridges, and ran businesses and farms. Members of the U.S. Sanitary Commission, above left, distributed food, clothing, and medicine to the Union army and instructed its members in matters of sanitation, water supplies, and cooking. Women volunteers also cared for the sick and wounded at hospital wards such as the one shown at left.

Troops valued their battle flags.

The flags carried into battle by Union and Confederate armies provided practical as well as emotional value: They served as guides for infantry moving into battle and as rallying points for units forced to scatter under fire. The Confederate sharpshooters, above right, carried the above flag in their victory at the Battle of Chickamauga Creek in northern Georgia in September 1863. According to a Union officer in the battle, the heavily wooded area along the Creek made for a "mad, irregular battle, very much resembling guerrilla warfare on a vast scale, in which one army was bushwhacking the other."

Grant delivered a crushing blow to the South.

Two months after the Union defeat at Chickamauga Creek, General Grant quickly restored federal fortunes in the campaign for Chattanooga, Tennessee. Generals Granger, Grant, and Thomas, on the ledge on the left side of the painting at right, watch as their troops swarm Missionary Ridge, background. The Union victory at Chattanooga split the South and allowed entrance into Georgia and the heart of the Confederacy.

Lee's army disintegrated.

Grant's army pounded Lee's men mercilessly during the Wilderness Campaign at such places as Spotsylvania Court House and Cold Harbor, Virginia. By mid-June 1864 Lee's army had been reduced by one-third. Left, General Grant, beneath the tree sitting cross-legged and smoking a cigar, plots strategies with senior officers in a country churchyard near Petersburg, Virginia, toward the end of the Wilderness Campaign.

"Dictator" pounded Petersburg.

The 17,000-pound mortar, aptly called "Dictator," helped the Union capture Petersburg in early April 1865. The Confederate soldier at left was among the many casualties at the Virginia battlefield.

217

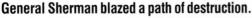

Savannah Ga Dec 22.186*
Via Ft. Monroe Va Dec 25.

His Excellency
Prest. Lincoln.
        I beg to present you as a
Christmas gift the city of Savannah
with 150 heavy guns & plenty
of ammunition & also about
25.000 bales of cotton.
                W.T. Sherman
                major Genl

General Sherman blazed a path of destruction.

Intending to "demonstrate the vulnerability of the South and make its inhabitants feel that war and individual ruin are synonymous terms," General William Tecumseh Sherman waged total war, systematically cutting a path of unprecedented destruction through Georgia and the Carolinas in late 1864 and early 1865. Charleston, South Carolina, below, was one of the cities leveled by Sherman's relentless troops.

Lee surrendered to Grant at Appomattox Court House.

As word of Sherman's devastating march reached Lee's battered troops at Petersburg, they began deserting in droves, wanting to return home to their families. The watercolor below by W.L. Sheppard depicts the homecoming of a Confederate soldier. The situation was now all but hopeless. Left, on the evening of April 2, 1865, Confederate officials fled Richmond across the James river. "The waters sparkled and rushed on by the burning city," recalled a Confederate guard at the bridge. On April 6, above, 2,000 retreating Confederate troops surrendered outside Richmond. Three days later Lee met with Grant and surrendered at Appomattox Court House. The Thomas Lovell depiction of the surrender, below center, is considered one of the most accurate. Lovell painted the work during the centennial of the Civil War.

219

Secession led to war.

Key Terms: border states, Battle of Bull Run, *Merrimac, Monitor,* Battle of Antietam, Emancipation Proclamation

Reading Preview

As you read this section, you will learn:

1. where the Civil War began.
2. which side appeared to have the advantage in the war.
3. what period of the war was discouraging for the Union.
4. how President Lincoln dealt with the issue of slavery.

Confederate soldiers survey the damage inside Fort Sumter on April 15, 1861, the day after Major Robert Anderson surrendered the fort to Confederate officers. According to a British journalist who was touring the South at the time, Southerners were elated with the news that Sumter had been taken. He recalled that the region was filled with "flushed faces, wild eyes, screaming mouths hurrahing for 'Jeff Davis' and 'the Southern Confederacy,' so that yells overpowered the discordant bands which were busy with 'Dixie's Land.' "

In his inaugural address on March 4, 1861, Abraham Lincoln was firm but conciliatory. He promised not to attack the seceding states but said he would do what was necessary to preserve the Union, stating:

I hold, that in contemplation of universal law, and of the Constitution, the Union of these states is perpetual. . . . no State, upon its own mere motion, can lawfully get out of the Union.

AN AMERICAN ★ SPEAKS

President Lincoln concluded by addressing the people of the South:

In *your* hands, my dissatisfied fellow countrymen, and not in *mine* is the momentous issue of civil war. The government will not assail *you*. You can have no conflict, without being yourselves the aggressor. *You* can have no oath registered in heaven to destroy the government, while *I* shall have the most solemn one to "preserve, protect, and defend" it.

The war began at Fort Sumter.

One of the few Southern military installations still in federal hands was **Fort Sumter**, located on an island at the entrance to Charleston harbor, an important Southern port. The surrender of Fort Sumter was inevitable unless provisions were sent to the troops holding it. On April 6 Lincoln informed the governor of South Carolina that he was going to send a supply ship, taking care to add that "no effort to throw in men, arms, or ammunition will be made." The Confederate government responded to Lincoln's message by demanding the surrender of Fort Sumter. When the Union commander at Sumter rejected the demand, Confederate forces in Charleston began shelling the fort. On April 13, after 33 hours of bombardment, Fort Sumter surrendered.

The months of waiting were over. War had begun. Lincoln immediately called for 75,000 volunteers to crush the rebellion. Within the next five weeks, Virginia, Arkansas, North Carolina, and Tennessee voted to join the Confederacy, which shifted its capital to **Richmond**, Virginia. The **border states**—the slave states of Delaware, Maryland, Kentucky, and Missouri—remained with the Union, although each of them contained many Confederate sympathizers. Several western counties of Virginia also stayed loyal to the Union. In 1863 western Virginia would be admitted into the Union as the new state of West Virginia.

The North appeared to have the advantage.

People of both regions enthusiastically supported their governments as the war began.

Union and Confederacy, 1861

Union (free) states

Border (slave) states loyal to the Union

Confederate (slave) states seceding before Ft. Sumter, April 1861

Confederate (slave) states seceding after Ft. Sumter, April 1861

Free territories

⊛ Capitals

Albers Equal-Area Projection

© SF

map study

Regions In early 1861 several states were uncommitted to either the Union or the Confederacy. Many people in these border states had mixed feelings about the war. Which border states stayed in the Union? Which border states seceded after April 1861?

Critical Thinking Part of Virginia became a separate new state during the war. Why might this have happened?

Recruiting broadsides such as this one asked for volunteers to "vindicate the honor of the Flag so ruthlessly torn by traitor hands from the walls of Sumter."

The North and the South were each confident of victory, and both sides expected that the war would soon be over. On the surface the North appeared to have all the advantages necessary to win a swift victory. Its population in 1860 was 22 million to the South's 9 million, one third of whom were slaves. The Union had more than three times as many service-age men. Although the South was able to use its slaves as workers, it did not dare arm them to fight. The North, on the other hand, eventually included 200,000 African Americans in its armed forces.

The North had a stronger and more varied economy. Almost all of the nation's manufacturing and more than two-thirds of its railroads were in the North. In addition, the North contained greater agricultural and mineral resources and owned most of the nation's merchant shipping. The Union also had an or-

ganized government and bureaucracy in place and a wealthy treasury to support its war effort.

The South, however, had a number of factors in its favor. The Confederate States needed to fight only a defensive war. Southerners merely had to beat back Northern armies to win their independence, whereas the North would have to invade and conquer the South. In a short war this advantage would offset the North's superiority in numbers and resources.

Because the South was mainly rural and agricultural, most white, male Southerners were skillful horseback riders and knew how to use firearms. Furthermore, the South had a strong military tradition. Seven

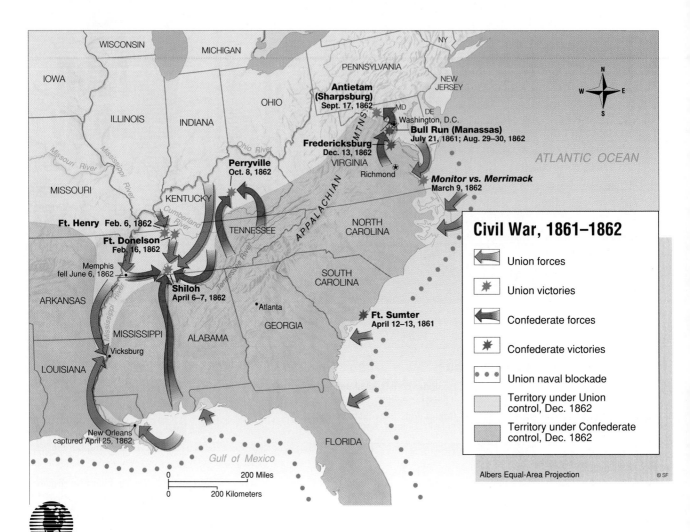

Civil War, 1861–1862

←	Union forces
✳	Union victories
←	Confederate forces
✳	Confederate victories
• • •	Union naval blockade
	Territory under Union control, Dec. 1862
	Territory under Confederate control, Dec. 1862

Albers Equal-Area Projection   © SF

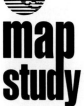

map study

Movement What border state saw particularly heavy action as Union forces moved down the Mississippi Valley?

Critical Thinking Why was it important for the Union to control the Mississippi?

of the nation's military colleges were in the South, and many of the U.S. Army's best officers were Southerners who resigned their commissions to fight for the Confederacy. Lincoln, in fact, had offered the command of the Union army to **Robert E. Lee**, who decided to fight on the side of his native Virginia. The loss of such talented officers was a severe blow to the North, and Lincoln would spend much of the war seeking able generals.

The early years of war were discouraging for the Union.

With the impatient Northern public clamoring for action, General Irvin McDowell was ordered to move against Confederate forces gathering at Manassas, only 25 miles from

Washington, D.C. In the battle, fought on July 21 near a stream called Bull Run, Confederate forces under General P. T. Beauregard routed the larger but mostly untrained Union force, which panicked and retreated in wild disarray.

The Northern strategy. The hope of both sides for a short war quickly vanished after the **Battle of Bull Run**. The North developed a three-point strategy to win what it now realized would be a long war. First, it would mount a blockade to halt Southern cotton shipments and prevent supplies from reaching Confederate ports. Second, the Union would gain control of the Mississippi River. This would divide the Confederacy—isolating Texas, Arkansas, and Louisiana from the rest of the South—and would clear the way for an attack on Georgia and the Carolinas from the west. Third, the North would build a well-trained army—the Army of the Potomac—to defend Washington, D.C., and undertake an offensive against Confederate forces in Richmond.

The naval war. The blockade was not totally successful at first. The North had only 90 ships, of which fewer than half were steam driven. The remainder were antiquated sailing vessels. Such a force was not adequate to patrol 3,500 miles of Confederate coastline. Gradually, the North captured or blockaded the major Southern ports, but not until near the end of the war did the Union have a force sufficient to totally seal off the South. Until then, the South's fleet of small, fast blockade runners were able to slip through the Union blockade and pick up ammunition and other supplies from British ships docked in Caribbean ports.

In addition to the blockade runners, the South developed another naval weapon in the **Merrimac**. The Confederacy revamped this steam-powered wooden ship by covering its sides with four-inch armorplate. On its first day of action, March 8, 1862, it easily sank two Union ships and ran three more aground. Although pounded with heavy shells from Union warships, the *Merrimac* remained undamaged. Hope inspired in the South by these easy victories vanished the next day when the *Merrimac* was confronted by an equally impressive Northern ironclad, the **Monitor**.

The two ships met at the mouth of the James River near Hampton Roads, Virginia, and pounded each other with shells for more than three hours. Neither ship was seriously damaged, but the *Merrimac* finally returned to harbor. Both sides built additional ironclads, but only the North had the resources to keep its ships running smoothly.

Lincoln's search for a general. Following the Union loss at Bull Run, Lincoln put General **George McClellan** in command of the Army of the Potomac. McClellan's task in the summer of 1862 was to defeat the forces protecting Richmond and capture the Confederate capital. After lengthy delays in which McClellan continued to put off an attack, the two sides engaged in a series of bitter battles on the peninsula southeast of Richmond. Locate that peninsula on the map on page 222. When McClellan met defeat, Lincoln replaced him with other generals who proved equally unable to match the daring and brilliant strategy of Confederate generals such as Robert E. Lee and Thomas J. "Stonewall" Jackson. After General John Pope met defeat at a second battle at Bull Run, Lincoln turned again to McClellan.

The *Merrimac*, left, and the *Monitor* pound each other with heavy shells on March 9, 1862. Both ironclads were soon lost. The *Merrimac* was disabled in Norfolk Harbor one month later. The *Monitor* went down in a gale in December.

Wearing his familiar stovepipe hat, President Lincoln urges General George McClellan to go on the offensive after the draw at Antietam. While McClellan struggled in the East, General Ulysses S. Grant, right, won an important string of victories in the West.

Emboldened by Union ineffectiveness, Lee led a force across the Potomac River and into Maryland. He reasoned that a victory on Union soil could convince France and England to extend diplomatic recognition to the Confederacy. On September 17, 1862, Lee met McClellan's forces at Sharpsburg, on the Antietam Creek. The **Battle of Antietam** was a draw, with heavy casualties on both sides. Lee retreated to Virginia, but the cautious McClellan, to Lincoln's dismay, failed to follow in pursuit.

The Union had somewhat greater success in the West—the theater of the war west of the Appalachian Mountains. Union forces managed to hold on to Missouri in spite of serious opposition by pro-South forces there. Confederate hopes of winning Kentucky were dashed in late 1861 when Union troops occupied strategic points at the mouths of the Kentucky and Cumberland rivers. In February 1862 Confederate-held Fort Henry and Fort Donelson in Tennessee fell to Union forces led by General **Ulysses S. Grant**.

With another Grant victory at the bloody Battle of Shiloh in southwestern Tennessee the following April, the Union was on the way to gaining control of the Mississippi Valley. However, a strongly fortified Vicksburg, Mississippi, continued to keep the Union from gaining complete control of the Mississippi River. Meanwhile, in the East, Lincoln had yet to find a leader who could take Richmond or outsmart Robert E. Lee.

Lincoln issued the Emancipation Proclamation.

Although slavery was clearly the root cause of the Civil War, abolition was not a Northern war aim. Lincoln had tried to assure the South that their domestic institutions were safe. His main aim was to save the Union. Personally he disliked slavery, but he recognized the legal basis given the institution by the United States Constitution. There were slave states fighting on both sides of the North-South struggle. Had President Lincoln called for abolition, the border states probably would have deserted the Union banner.

As the war progressed, Republicans in Congress urged Lincoln to free the slaves. England and France would be less likely to side with the Confederacy if abolition were to become a Union war aim. African American Southerners, wherever they could, were supporting the Union cause. Moved by these factors, the president prepared a proclamation of emancipation. However, he did not issue it immediately. To do so when the South was winning battle after battle, he reasoned, would make it look like an act of desperation by the North. Lincoln decided to wait for a Northern victory.

The Battle of Antietam was not quite the victory Lincoln had hoped for, but it had forced

The 54th Massachusetts Colored Regiment charges Fort Wagner, South Carolina, in July 1863. The 54th was the first African American unit recruited by the Union during the war. Charles and Lewis Douglass, the sons of Frederick Douglass, the abolitionist writer and lecturer, served with this regiment.

225

Top, African American slaves, some clad in Union uniforms, plant sweet potatoes on a South Carolina plantation shortly before Lincoln issued his Emancipation Proclamation. Above, Christian Fleetwood, who was one of many African Americans to win the Medal of Honor during the war, poses for a Union photographer.

Lee to retreat from Union soil. On September 22, 1862, five days after the battle, he issued the **Emancipation Proclamation**, which would take effect on January 1, 1863:

I, Abraham Lincoln, President of the United States, . . . order and declare that all persons held as slaves within . . . [the states in rebellion against the United States] are and henceforward shall be free, and . . . the executive government of the United States, including the military and naval authorities thereof, will recognize and maintain the freedom of said persons.

AN AMERICAN
★ SPEAKS

President Lincoln, of course, had no way of enforcing the Emancipation Proclamation. It applied only to the states in rebellion, not to the slave states that had remained loyal to the Union. Nevertheless, this historic document put the nation on a course toward freedom that would not be reversed.

By early 1863 African Americans began serving in the Union armed forces. African American recruits were generally formed into all-black units commanded by white officers. Until 1864, black soldiers were paid less than white soldiers. Nevertheless, 200,000 African Americans fought for the Union. Their enthusiasm and fighting spirit contributed significantly to the Northern victory.

SECTION 1 REVIEW

Identify Key People and Terms
Write a sentence to identify: border states, Robert E. Lee, Battle of Bull Run, *Merrimac, Monitor,* George McClellan, Battle of Antietam, Ulysses S. Grant, Emancipation Proclamation

Locate Key Places
1. Why was Fort Sumter's location a strategic one?
2. What was the capital of the Confederacy?

Master the Main Ideas
1. **Supporting the Constitution:** Why did President Lincoln take a firm stand against secession?
2. **Analyzing information:** What were the major advantages of each side in the Civil War?
3. **Evaluating information:** Explain the purpose of each part of the North's three-point strategy for winning the war.
4. **Examining the social impact of the Civil War:** Why did Lincoln refuse to call for the end of slavery at the beginning of the war?

Apply Critical Thinking Skills: Drawing Conclusions
Was it inevitable that the North would win the Civil War? Support your answer with facts presented in the chapter.

The war brought a Northern victory.

Key Terms: Battle of Gettysburg, greenbacks, Copperheads

Reading Preview
As you read this section, you will learn:

1. what victories turned the tide for the North.
2. which general led the North to victory.
3. what provided the North the winning edge.

After Antietam Lincoln renewed his search for a general who could defeat Lee decisively and end the war. He replaced McClellan with General Ambrose E. Burnside, who was defeated in December 1862 at Fredericksburg, Virginia. Next Lincoln tried General Joseph Hooker, who continued the Union's misfortune the following spring by losing to Lee at the Battle of Chancellorsville in May 1863. The victory was costly for the South, however, for among the dead was "Stonewall" Jackson, accidently shot by his own men. Said Lee, who had called Jackson his right arm, "I know not how to replace him."

The North turned the tide at Gettysburg and Vicksburg.

The stunning victories at Fredericksburg and Chancellorsville proved to be the high water mark for the Confederacy. Realizing the demoralized state of public opinion in the North, Lee planned an all-out invasion of Union territory. He hoped that a decisive win on Northern soil would force the Union to make peace. Lee and his invading army moved north into Pennsylvania, where they prepared to confront a large Union army near Gettysburg.

Gettysburg. The **Battle of Gettysburg** lasted three days: July 1–3, 1863. The first day belonged to Lee. The Confederate forces drove the Union troops out of Gettysburg to a defensive position on Cemetery Hill south of the town. The bulk of the Union army, under General **George Meade**, did not arrive until later that evening. On the second day, the Confederates tried but failed to break through the Union's entrenched positions. At one o'clock on the third day, the Confederate forces began the heaviest artillery barrage of the war.

Two hours of shelling had little effect on weakening the Union position. Through the smoke, Meade's men could see Southern forces massing for a frontal assault. Major General George Pickett led 13,000 Confederate troops, marching in perfect order, in an attempt to smash through the main Union position at Cemetery Ridge. Pickett's Charge, as the valiant but doomed assault became known, failed to break the Union hold. The attackers were cut down by Union fire. Nearly half of them failed to return to their own lines. "It's my fault," a distraught Lee muttered to the battered survivors. "The blame is mine." Having lost a third of his army in the three-day battle, Lee fell back to the safety of Confederate soil. When Meade made only a halfhearted attempt to pursue the retreating army, President Lincoln became enraged. Although he contem-

Before leading his valiant but disastrous charge against Union forces at Gettysburg, Major General George Pickett told his regiment: "Up men and to your posts! Don't forget today that you are from old Virginia." Although Pickett's men "advanced magnificently, unshaken by shot and shell," more than half of them were killed within 20 minutes.

VOICES FROM THE PAST

The Gettysburg Address

On November 19, 1863, Lincoln gave this brief speech at the dedication of the national cemetery at Gettysburg. How does this speech define what is at stake in the Civil War?

Four score and seven years ago our fathers brought forth on this continent, a new nation, conceived in Liberty, and dedicated to the proposition that all men are created equal.

Now we are engaged in a great civil war, testing whether that nation or any nation so conceived and so dedicated, can long endure. We are met on a great battle-field of that war. We have come to dedicate a portion of that field, as a final resting place for those who here gave their lives that that nation might live. It is altogether fitting and proper that we should do this.

But, in a larger sense, we can not dedicate—we can not consecrate—we can not hallow—this ground. The brave men, living and dead, who struggled here, have consecrated it, far above our poor power to add or detract. The world will little note, nor long remember what we say here, but it can never forget what they did here. It is for us the living, rather, to be dedicated here to the unfinished work which they who fought here have thus far so nobly advanced. It is rather for us to be here dedicated to the great task remaining before us—that from these honored dead we take increased devotion to that cause for which they gave the last full measure of devotion— that we here highly resolve that these dead shall not have died in vain—that this nation, under God, shall have a new birth of freedom—and that government of the people, by the people, for the people, shall not perish from the earth.

General William Tecumseh Sherman's men rip up railroad track in Atlanta in September, 1864. The tracks were destroyed so that supplies could no longer be shipped to rebel armies.

plated reprimanding the general for his failure to capture Lee, he decided not to because the tremendous importance of the victory overshadowed the military blunder. After Gettysburg, the Confederacy would never again be able to mount a major invasion of Union territory.

Victories in the West. On July 4, 1863, the day after General Robert E. Lee was forced to retreat at Gettysburg, Pennsylvania, General Grant's six-week siege of **Vicksburg**, Missis-

sippi, ended with the town's surrender. Vicksburg was the last obstacle standing in the way of gaining full control of the Mississippi River. Confederate control of the steep river bluffs near Vicksburg had let herds of cattle and other supplies reach the Confederate forces from Arkansas, Louisiana, and Texas. The city's fall cut off those states from the rest of the Confederacy. Josiah Gorgas, a Confederate officer, wrote in his diary a few weeks later:

One brief month ago we were apparently at the point of success. . . . Now the picture is just as sombre as it was bright then. . . . Yesterday we rode on the pinnacle of success—today absolute ruin seems to be our position. The Confederacy totters to its destruction.

AN AMERICAN ★ SPEAKS

The Union's next goal in the west was the capture of Chattanooga, on the Tennessee River near the Georgia border. Union armies won battles at Lookout Mountain and Missionary Ridge in November 1863. When Chattanooga fell soon thereafter, the way was opened for an invasion of Georgia and the lower South.

Grant led the North to victory.

Lincoln now sought to hasten the end of the conflict by placing Grant in overall command of the Union armies. Grant was a commander with a no-nonsense view of war:

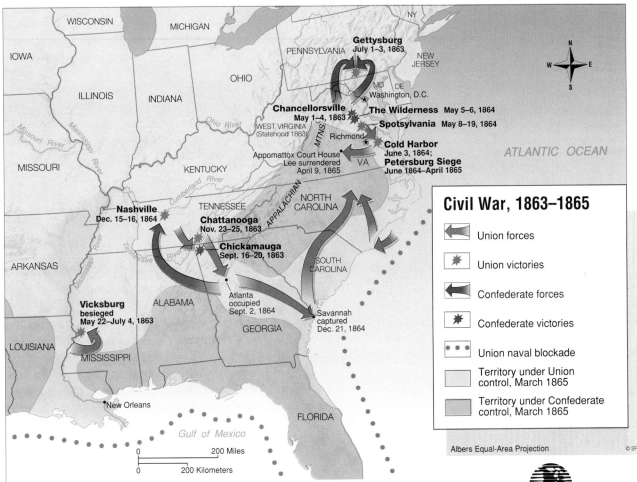

Civil War, 1863–1865

◄	Union forces
✸	Union victories
◄	Confederate forces
✸	Confederate victories
• • •	Union naval blockade
	Territory under Union control, March 1865
	Territory under Confederate control, March 1865

Albers Equal-Area Projection   © SF

AN AMERICAN
★ SPEAKS

The art of war is simple enough. Find out where your enemy is. Get at him as soon as you can. Strike him as hard as you can and as often as you can, and keep moving on.

The new commander set about at once designing a strategy to end the war. The strategy called for General **William Sherman** to lead the western armies in an attack on **Atlanta**, Georgia, one of the South's most important sources of munitions and other supplies and a major rail center. Grant himself would lead the Army of the Potomac toward Richmond.

Sherman took Atlanta in September 1864. Then he began his daring and destructive 285-mile march to the sea at Savannah, Georgia. Sherman believed in practicing total war. His object was to do everything possible to destroy the enemy's will and make it difficult for them to fight. Sherman observed that:

AN AMERICAN
★ SPEAKS

We cannot change the hearts of those people of the South, but we can make war so terrible, . . . make them so sick of war that generations would pass away before they would again appeal to it.

His troops cut a path of devastation 60 miles wide through Georgia, seizing or destroying anything that might be of use to the enemy. From Savannah, Sherman turned northward through the Carolinas, cutting an even more destructive path through South Carolina, the first secessionist state.

Meanwhile, Grant's army suffered enormous losses but moved relentlessly on toward Rich-

map study

Movement In 1864 and 1865 Union armies gradually closed in on Lee's Confederate forces in Virginia. Where did the war end?

Critical Thinking

Why was the Battle of Gettysburg a turning point in the Civil War?

After agreeing to General Grant's terms at Appomattox Court House, General Lee returned to his men to give them the news. "Are we surrendered?" several men called out. Tears streaming down his cheeks, Lee told them: "Men, we have fought through the war together. I have done the best I could do for you. My heart is too full to say more."

mond. Lee was gradually worn down by the Union's superior numbers. On April 3, 1865, the first Union troops marched into the Confederate capital. It remained only for Grant to trap Lee's exhausted army and force a surrender. On April 9, 1865, the war's most brilliant commanders, Robert E. Lee and Ulysses S. Grant, met at a private house in **Appomattox Court House**, Virginia, to arrange the surrender terms. General Joseph E. Johnson surrendered his Confederate army to General Sherman in North Carolina a few days later. The war that had cost more American lives than all others from the Revolution to Vietnam combined—more than 620,000 on both sides—was over.

Northern resources provided the winning edge.

It was clear from the beginning that the side that excelled in mobilizing its human, industrial, financial, and agricultural resources would have the advantage, particularly in a long war. Aware of this, the South had hoped for a quick resolution of the conflict.

As the war dragged on, the North became stronger and the South weaker. The North was able to finance the war by a variety of means. These included low-interest loans to private war contractors, the sale of bonds through banks operating under the direction of the

Women played a variety of crucial roles on both sides during the war. Some women, such as Union soldier Frances Clalin, right, disguised themselves as men and joined the front lines. Others, such as Clara Barton, opposite page, performed important medical tasks.

National Banking Act of 1863, and the issuing of **greenbacks**—paper currency not backed by gold. The South lacked good banks and was soon unable to borrow money from Europe. The only solution was to issue paper money that gradually lost its face value.

Women in the war. In both North and South, women served in many wartime roles. They replaced men on farms and in factories. They collected money to support the war effort, rolled bandages, and served as nurses in military hospitals. They also worked in distributing food, clothing, and medicines. Some on both sides worked as spies, and a few even engaged in combat.

Under the leadership of women such as **Elizabeth Blackwell** and **Clara Barton**, sanitary conditions and nursing were improved in military hospitals. Blackwell, the first American woman to earn a medical degree, helped recruit and train nurses. Barton, who would later found the American Red Cross, nursed in many battlefield hospitals, including those at Antietam and Fredericksburg.

Southern women of the planter class became plantation managers and overseers. Many of them kept the fields producing in spite of obstacles—runaway slaves, lack of supplies, broken-down machinery, and invading and occupying armies. Many women worked the fields by hand because horses and mules often were taken by the army. Frontier women in the West had the added burden of fending off Indian attacks once protective garrisons were called to serve in the war.

THE CIVIL WAR: A WATERSHED IN AMERICAN HISTORY

Human tragedy is synonymous with war—any war. Yet no other conflict in United States history produced calamity on such a large scale as the Civil War. The war also produced many revolutionary innovations and long-term effects. Below is a list of some of these changes and effects.

The Civil War:

- resulted in 618,000 military deaths—360,000 Union soldiers and 258,000 Confederate soldiers.

- produced a large number of widows, many of whom began engaging in careers or other activities outside the home to support themselves and their children.

- brought about the emancipation of four million slaves.

- paved the way for the passage of the 13th, 14th, and 15th amendments.

- was the first modern war. It was the first war in which submarines, ironclads, mines, and repeating rifles were used.

- demolished the antebellum way of life in the South, causing economic ruin and social chaos, but also providing new opportunities and liberties for many Southerners.

- produced a bitterness between Northerners and Southerners that lasted for decades.

- contributed to increased ethnic tolerance in the North. Immigrant groups such as the Irish and Germans, which had suffered from discrimination, were more readily accepted in society because of their heroism during the war.

- established that states do not have the right to secede from the Union, therefore crushing the idea of state sovereignty.

- strengthened the central government, enabling the U.S. to grow into a more unified nation and a global power.

The leaders. Both the Union and the Confederacy had reasonably able leadership at the top. Confederate President Jefferson Davis was competent and thoroughly devoted to the Confederacy. However, he had difficulty in delegating authority and had a tendency to interfere in military matters best left to the generals. His preoccupation with military affairs often left him with too little time to devote to other pressing concerns.

Lincoln, on the other hand, proved to be an ideal man for a crisis. He quickly showed that

chart study

According to the chart, how many military deaths occurred during the Civil War?
Critical Thinking How did the Civil War affect the values of Americans?

Jefferson Davis, top, and Abraham Lincoln both were capable leaders who nonetheless received a fair share of criticism during their tenures. Lincoln was criticized for arresting 10,000 suspected Confederate sympathizers. Davis was criticized for implementing conscription and other policies that violated the tradition of states' rights.

he was a superb leader with clear purpose, steadfast resolve, and infinite patience. He had the wisdom to choose strong men for cabinet positions and as commanders in the field, but he always remained their master.

Both presidents were criticized for dictatorial acts. Lincoln made far-reaching decisions without consulting Congress and spent money before it was appropriated by Congress. He ignored constitutional rights of citizens by suspending habeas corpus and ordering civilians suspected of disloyalty held without trial. President Davis acted in much the same way, claiming, as Lincoln did, that the war emergency justified his actions.

The election of 1864. In a supreme test of constitutional democracy, the Union went through a presidential election in the midst of the war—the first such election in the nation's history. With an enemy army not far from the national capital, the election was held on schedule and the results quietly accepted.

Lincoln was renominated by the Republicans. In a bid for national unity, they chose Andrew Johnson of Tennessee, a Democrat who supported the Union cause, for vice president. To make the ticket even more attractive to the voters, the name Republican was dropped from the ballot in favor of the name National Union party. The Democrats nominated General George McClellan, the popular commander who could claim that he had never lost a major battle—although he had never decisively won one either.

The campaign came at a time when morale in the North was low. The war had dragged on for more than three years, and the end was still not in sight. Many Northerners favored some sort of negotiated peace with the South, even if it meant failing to restore the Union. Most of these **Copperheads**, as their enemies named them (after the poisonous snake), supported General McClellan.

In the early stages of the campaign, Lincoln was sure he would lose, but his prospects brightened with Sherman's capture of Atlanta in September. The vote on election day gave Lincoln a victory with 55 percent of the popular vote and 212 electoral votes to his opponent's

21. The following March 4, less than a month before Lee's surrender, Lincoln began his second term with a brief, moving inaugural address. He concluded:

With malice toward none; with charity for all; with firmness in the right, as God gives us to see the right, let us strive on to finish the work we are in; to bind up the nation's wounds; to care for him who shall have borne the battle, and for his widow, and his orphan—to do all which may achieve and cherish a just, and a lasting peace, among ourselves, and with all nations.

AN AMERICAN ★ SPEAKS

SECTION **2** REVIEW

Identify Key People and Terms
Write a sentence to identify: Battle of Gettysburg, George Meade, William Sherman, greenbacks, Elizabeth Blackwell, Clara Barton, Copperheads

Locate Key Places
1. What Confederate stronghold, until its surrender, had kept the Union from gaining complete control of the Mississippi River?
2. From what Southern city that he had captured did General Sherman begin his march to the sea?
3. Where did Lee surrender to Grant?

Master the Main Ideas
1. **Analyzing information:** Why did the Battle of Gettysburg and the fall of Vicksburg turn the tide for the Union?
2. **Analyzing information:** What was the purpose of Sherman's march through Georgia and the Carolinas?
3. **Examining the economic impact of war:** Why were Northern efforts at financing the war more successful than Southern efforts?

Apply Critical Thinking Skills: Identifying Alternatives
General Sherman's troops destroyed cities, towns, farms, factories, and railroads. Southerners criticized his "total war" tactics because they affected civilians as well as soldiers. Do you agree or disagree with Sherman's way of making war? What other alternatives did Sherman have?

Plans for restoring the Union created conflict.

Key Terms: Radical Republicans, Wade-Davis bill, equality before the law, Freedmen's Bureau, 13th Amendment, Black Codes, Civil Rights Act of 1866, 14th Amendment, Tenure of Office Act

Reading Preview

As you read this section, you will learn:

1. about President Lincoln's and Congress' views about Reconstruction.
2. which issue caused a dispute between Congress and President Johnson.
3. how presidential Reconstruction fared.

One of the great issues of Reconstruction was a constitutional question: Who had the authority to take charge of reconstructing the Union—the president or Congress? Lincoln insisted that the Constitution did not allow for secession. Therefore, secession—and the Confederacy—had no legal basis. The South had never really left the Union, and the war had been simply an insurrection against the United States. The chief executive, therefore, had the authority to end the insurrection and restore the Union.

Many Republicans in Congress maintained that secession *had* taken place. The Confederate states had left the Union and would need to be readmitted into it, just as new states were admitted. The admission of states was clearly a responsibility of Congress, as Article IV, Section 3 of the U.S. Constitution states, not of the president.

The framers of the Constitution had not anticipated the secession of one or more states from the Union. The document, therefore, says nothing about it. Contrary opinions about this constitutional question, along with the desire of some Republicans to restructure Southern society, dominated the debate between Congress and the president over Reconstruction.

Lincoln and Congress differed over Reconstruction.

In December 1863, with the outcome of the Civil War still uncertain, Lincoln announced his plan for Reconstruction. He offered a pardon to nearly all supporters of the Confederacy who took an oath of loyalty and pledged to accept the end to slavery. Only certain high-ranking officials of the Confederacy would not be pardoned. When ten percent of a state's prewar voters took the oath, they could establish a state government and apply for readmission to the Union. Lincoln decreed that new state constitutions must prohibit slavery, but otherwise he promised the Southern states a free hand dealing with their own affairs.

Lincoln's plan—a wartime ploy intended to lure Confederates back into the Union—was based on leniency and forgiveness. The plan offered the former slaves no role in shaping the South's political future. This did not mean abandoning concern for their rights. The president publicly endorsed the idea of limited black suffrage. He singled out former soldiers and those with some education as being particularly qualified. This was the first time any president had suggested granting African Americans the right to vote.

As the war progressed, many Republicans in Congress came to believe that the federal government had a responsibility to protect the basic rights of the former slaves. The radical wing of the party, the **Radical Republicans**, insisted that Reconstruction could not be secure without black suffrage. Although never a majority, the Radical Republicans did much to shape the politics of the next few years. Foremost among this group were Congressman **Thaddeus Stevens** of Pennsylvania and Senator **Charles Sumner** of Massachusetts. They both believed that the Civil War had created the opportunity to make America "a perfect republic," free at last of the burden of racism.

These men were also practical politicians. They could see that without black votes, the Republicans would continue to be a minority party. If the Southern Democrats who had led the secession movement regained power, Northern sacrifices would have been in vain.

Radical Republicans Charles Sumner, bottom, and Thaddeus Stevens, top, championed the cause of racial equality. Sumner's legal brief for desegregated schools, which he wrote in 1849, was a forerunner of the 1954 Supreme Court ruling that integrated the nation's schools.

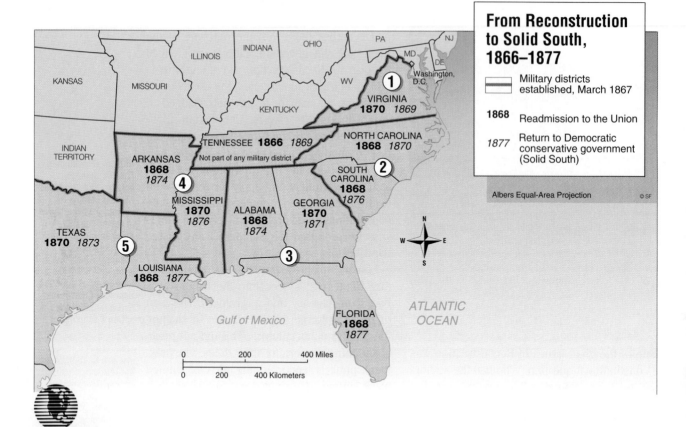

From Reconstruction to Solid South, 1866–1877

Military districts established, March 1867

1868 Readmission to the Union

1877 Return to Democratic conservative government (Solid South)

Albers Equal-Area Projection

© SF

KANSAS

MISSOURI

ILLINOIS

INDIANA

OHIO

PA

NJ

MD

DE

Washington, D.C.

WV

KENTUCKY

VIRGINIA **1870** *1869*

INDIAN TERRITORY

ARKANSAS **1868** *1874*

TENNESSEE **1866** *1869*

Not part of any military district

NORTH CAROLINA **1868** *1870*

SOUTH CAROLINA **1868** *1876*

MISSISSIPPI **1870** *1876*

ALABAMA **1868** *1874*

GEORGIA **1870** *1871*

TEXAS **1870** *1873*

LOUISIANA **1868** *1877*

FLORIDA **1868** *1877*

Gulf of Mexico

ATLANTIC OCEAN

0   200   400 Miles

0   200   400 Kilometers

map study

Regions In 1867 Congress divided the South into five districts headed by military governors. Congress also set up steps by which states could be readmitted to the Union. How many states were readmitted in 1868?

Critical Thinking Why did the first stages of Reconstruction include military supervision?

Thus, the Radicals looked to the establishment of new Southern governments based on an alliance of former slaves and whites who had never supported the Confederacy.

Convinced that Lincoln's plan of Reconstruction was too lenient, Congress in 1864 passed the **Wade-Davis bill**. This measure called for delaying Reconstruction until a majority of white males—not just the ten percent Lincoln had proposed—had taken a loyalty oath. Moreover, anyone who had aided the Confederacy would be excluded from voting in elections. The new state governments were to not only prohibit slavery but to guarantee black Southerners **equality before the law**—that is, equal legal rights, such as the right to a fair trial, for all citizens.

Lincoln sidestepped the issues raised by the Wade-Davis bill with a pocket veto. He did, however, sign a bill creating the **Freedmen's Bureau**, an agency empowered to protect the legal rights of former slaves, provide them with

an education and medical care, and give them the opportunity to lease land.

Lincoln also worked with Congress in securing approval of the **13th Amendment**, which abolished slavery. Unlike the Emancipation Proclamation, which had excluded the border states, the 13th Amendment barred slavery throughout the nation. Its ratification in 1865 made the prohibition of slavery part of the Constitution, thus assuring that no future Congress could restore it.

Congress and the president clashed over the rights of the former slaves.

It is likely that Lincoln, master politician that he was, could have come up with a workable compromise between his plan for Reconstruction and that of the Radicals, but he did not get an opportunity to do so. On April 14, 1865—five days after Lee's surrender at Appomattox Court House—Lincoln was shot by John Wilkes Booth, a pro-Confederate actor.

LINCOLN'S ASSASSINATION: On Good Friday, April 14, 1865, the president and Mrs. Lincoln attended the play *Our American Cousin* at Ford's Theatre in Washington, D.C. During the performance, as shown in the illustration below, John Wilkes Booth, a pro-Confederate actor, crept into the Lincolns' private box. Heavily intoxicated after a day of drinking at the adjoining Taltavul's Star Saloon, Booth staggered out of the shadows behind the presidential box and fired his .44-caliber single-shot derringer, above, at the president, hitting him just below the left ear. The chair Lincoln sat upon and the hat he wore that fateful night are also pictured above.

The president died the following day and Vice President **Andrew Johnson** assumed the presidency according to law.

Johnson was a Jacksonian Democrat from **Tennessee** who despised the old Southern, plantation-class leadership. When another Tennessean had commented during the war that the conflict was becoming a crusade against slavery, Johnson replied "Damn the negroes! I am fighting these traitorous aristocrats, their masters." He shared few of the concerns of the Republican party and had little sympathy for the former slaves.

Because Congress was not in session when he took office, Johnson had the opportunity to shape Reconstruction in his own way. He is-

Schools for the Emancipated

A Northern teacher, below, helps students in Beaufort, South Carolina, in 1866. "The children were eager for knowledge," an official reported. Right, a teacher assembles her students outside a Freedmen's Bureau school in North Carolina in 1866. By this time the Bureau was operating 965 schools.

[They are] all hopeful . . . every one pleading to be taught, willing to do anything for learning. They are never out of our rooms and their cry is for "Books! Books!" and "When will school begin?"

This hunger for education was reported by a teaching missionary in Louisiana in 1863. The eager pupils were newly free African Americans.

Beginning in the 1860s, thousands of abolitionists, many of them missionaries from New England, traveled to the war-torn South to open up schools for slaves who had just been freed. Free African Americans who had already gained an education also served as teachers in the new schools. Co-sponsored by the Freedmen's Bureau and missionary societies, these schools drew African Americans of all ages, from young children to grandparents. All were eager to make new lives for themselves aided by the advantages of education.

Because teaching slaves to read and write was a crime in the antebellum South, most students who came to the freedmen's schools had to begin with the basics. Elementary reading, writing, and arithmetic were taught in all schools. A sample lesson might discuss freed African Americans, such as Phillis Wheatley or Frederick Douglass, who had made important contributions to society. Advanced students interested in continuing their studies might attend one of the colleges or universities, such as Howard University in Washington, D.C., or Fisk University in Tennessee.

During Reconstruction, hundreds of thousands of students enrolled in the Freedmen's Bureau schools every year. As a result, the literacy rate for African Americans rose dramatically throughout the South.

Highlights of American Life

sued a proclamation of general amnesty, pardoning all Southerners except for certain categories that made up the old leadership class. He appointed governors for the seceded states and ordered state conventions held. These conventions, which would include only white men who had taken the oath of allegiance, were to ratify the 13th Amendment and repudiate secession and the Confederate debt. The states could then elect governors, legislatures, and representatives to Congress.

Johnson believed that the emancipated slaves should agree to work for their former owners and take no interest in politics. His Reconstruction for whites only had little appeal for African Americans, who sought to give real meaning to their new freedom. Throughout the South in 1865 former slaves left the plantations in search of family members, better jobs, or simply for a taste of personal freedom. African Americans withdrew from churches dominated by whites and established independent congregations that laid the foundation for modern black churches. Former slaves pooled their resources to establish schools that would provide the education denied them as slaves.

Throughout 1865 African Americans organized mass meetings and parades and petitioned for equality before the law and the right to vote. Their complaints against their lack of civil and political rights under Andrew Johnson's Reconstruction policy helped to turn many Northern Republicans against the president. It quickly became clear that the Republican majority and the president were on a collision course.

Presidential Reconstruction failed.

Southern actions further undermined Northern support for President Johnson's plan for Reconstruction. The new state governments passed **Black Codes,** laws designed to regulate the lives of former slaves much as the slave statutes had done before the war. They granted African Americans certain limited civil rights, but barred them from serving on juries, testifying against white people, and voting. The Black Codes regulated the labor of the former slaves by requiring them to show written

M E E T   T H E   P R E S I D E N T

ANDREW JOHNSON

Born: December 29, 1808
Died: July 31, 1875
In office: 1865–1869

Andrew Johnson was the only senator from the South to remain loyal to the Union in 1861. That solitary distinction was sufficient to make him vice president in 1865; Booth's bullet did the rest.

Apprenticed to a tailor at 12, Johnson had never attended school; he later learned writing and arithmetic from his wife. Elected mayor of Greeneville, Tennessee, at 21, Johnson soon tailored a political career in the state legislature and in Congress.

Johnson's stubborn and reckless presidency was not the ideal antidote to the raw tempers of the Reconstruction period. However, his defiant stand against the excesses of the Radical Republicans was an essential service to the nation—and its Constitution.

Johnson had the satisfaction in 1874 of being elected to the Senate, returning to the chamber where he was once so nearly convicted. He died a few months later.

evidence of employment. Those who failed to sign a labor contract could be arrested and forced to work for a white employer.

When Congress reconvened in December 1865, Johnson announced that because governments had been established in all Southern states, Reconstruction had been accomplished. Radicals responded that these governments were under the control of rebels. Moderate Republicans joined with the Radicals in refusing to seat the Southerners recently elected to Congress.

Early in 1866 Congress passed two bills aimed at assisting the former slaves. One of the bills extended the life of the Freedmen's Bureau. The second was the **Civil Rights Act of 1866**, which defined all persons born in the United States (except Indians) as American

Impeachment of Andrew Johnson

Point

Johnson should be impeached

- Johnson was in violation of the Tenure of Office Act.
- Johnson vetoed laws that provided for basic civil rights for African Americans.
- Johnson denounced the 14th Amendment.

Counterpoint

Johnson should not be impeached

- The Tenure of Office Act was an unconstitutional law intended to limit presidential power.
- The Constitution provides the president the right to veto bills he considers unwise.
- The First Amendment right to free speech is accorded to the president even when what he says is unpopular.

Despite pressure from Radical Republicans, the Senate acquitted President Johnson by one vote during his 1868 impeachment trial.

citizens, guaranteeing them the same legal rights (except for the right to vote). President Johnson vetoed both bills, claiming that they threatened to centralize power in the national government and deprive the states of their authority to regulate their own affairs. Because Southern congressmen had been denied their seats in Congress, both measures were easily passed over the president's veto.

Fearing that a later Democratically controlled Congress might repeal the Civil Rights Act of 1866, and thereby weaken the federal government's power to protect the rights of African Americans, Congress next approved and sent to the states the **14th Amendment** to the Constitution. One of the most important changes ever made to the Constitution, the 14th Amendment stated that all native-born or naturalized persons were citizens of the United States and of their state. Basically, this provision extended citizenship to the former slaves. In addition, the amendment:

1. prohibited the states from denying any citizen the equal protection of the law or taking anyone's life, liberty, or property without due process of law;
2. provided that any state denying any male citizens the right to vote could lose some of its seats in Congress;
3. barred former Confederate officeholders from state and national office.

The 14th Amendment became a key element in the congressional plan of Reconstruction that was emerging to take the place of Johnson's. Congress also demanded that the Southern states must ratify the 14th Amendment in order to regain their seats in the House of Representatives and Senate.

The breach between Congress and the president widened when Johnson denounced the proposal. On a speaking tour of the North in the fall of 1866 he made wild accusations against the Radicals that cost him support in the mid-term elections. The Republicans returned with increased majorities, sufficient to pass Reconstruction legislation over a presidential veto.

When ten of the eleven Southern states rejected the 14th Amendment, Congress moved to implement a new plan of Reconstruction. Over Johnson's veto, Congress divided the South into five military districts, each com-

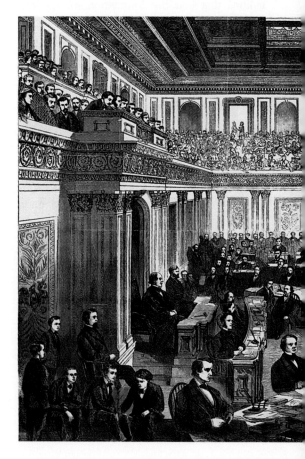

manded by a major general of the U.S. Army and occupied by federal troops. Congress then set forth procedures by which new state governments could be created in the South. States had to call constitutional conventions with members elected by both black and white Southerners. Former Confederate officials could neither vote nor serve as delegates. New state constitutions could not restrict the right to vote because of race, and new legislatures had to ratify the 14th Amendment. Once these steps had been taken, the states could be readmitted into the Union.

In order to limit Johnson's ability to interfere with its Reconstruction plans, Congress passed the **Tenure of Office Act**. This measure barred the president from removing officeholders, including cabinet members, without the consent of the Senate. Believing the law unconstitutional, Johnson dismissed Secretary of War Edwin M. Stanton, an ally of the Radi-

cals. To congressional Republicans, Johnson's action was the last straw. The House voted to impeach him—that is, order him tried before the Senate for high crimes and misdemeanors. If found guilty, he would be removed from office. Seven Republicans joined the Democrats in voting to acquit Johnson, some because they feared that a conviction would damage the separation of powers. The attempt to remove the president failed by one vote. Johnson remained in office, but his power had been broken.

This ticket facsimile admitted bearers to the impeachment trial of Andrew Johnson in 1868.

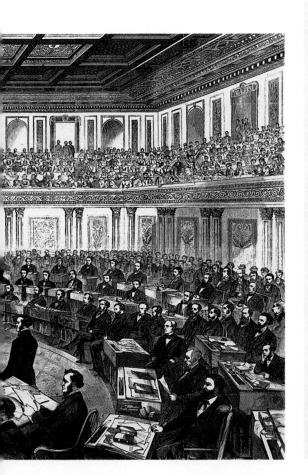

SECTION **3** REVIEW

Identify Key People and Terms
Write a sentence to identify: Radical Republicans, Thaddeus Stevens, Charles Sumner, Wade-Davis bill, equality before the law, Freedmen's Bureau, 13th Amendment, Andrew Johnson, Black Codes, Civil Rights Act of 1866, 14th Amendment, Tenure of Office Act

Locate Key Places
President Andrew Johnson was a native of which state?

Master the Main Ideas

1. **Examining major political issues:** Why did the Radical Republicans object to Lincoln's plan for Reconstruction?
2. **Examining the political effects of Reconstruction:** What were the major pieces of legislation that led to a clash between President Johnson and Congress?
3. **Examining the political effects of Reconstruction:** How did Congress undermine Johnson's efforts to control Reconstruction?

Apply Critical Thinking Skills: Making Comparisons
What qualities do you think made Lincoln an effective leader? Which of these qualities did Andrew Johnson lack?

SECTION 4

Reconstruction ended and white supremacy was restored.

Key Terms: 15th Amendment, carpetbaggers, scalawags, sharecropping, crop-lien system, Ku Klux Klan, enforcement acts, Compromise of 1877

Reading Preview
As you read this lesson, you will learn:

1. what political changes occurred during Radical Reconstruction.
2. how Radical Reconstruction affected the South's economy.
3. how some Southern whites intimidated African Americans.
4. what occurred in the South after Reconstruction.

Southern voters during Reconstruction, below, gave power to many whites who were new to Southern politics as well as African Americans such as Blanche K. Bruce, above left, and Hiram R. Revels, above right. Bruce and Revels were elected U.S. senators from Mississippi.

For the presidential election of 1868, the Republicans turned to the North's greatest war hero, General Ulysses S. Grant. The Democrats nominated Horatio Seymour, a former governor of New York. Grant won the election with strong support in the South, where newly enfranchised black voters supported him overwhelmingly. Soon afterwards Congress approved the **15th Amendment** to the Constitution, prohibiting any state from limiting the vote because of race. Bitterly opposed by the Democrats, the amendment was ratified in 1870. Congressional Reconstruction was now nearly complete. Said William Lloyd Garrison:

Nothing in all history [equalled] this wonderful, quiet, sudden transformation of four millions of human beings from . . . the auction-block to the ballot-box.

AN AMERICAN ★ SPEAKS

New groups achieved political power during Radical Reconstruction.

The period of Radical Reconstruction lasted for ten years, from 1867 to 1877, when Democrats regained control of the South. By 1870 all the Southern states had met the congressional requirements and had been readmitted to the Union. Their new democratic constitutions guaranteed civil and political rights to all citizens, black and white, although in some states those who had supported the Confederacy could not vote for a few years.

Throughout the South, new groups achieved political power. Anxious to exercise their new rights as citizens, former slaves by the thousands joined the Union League, which became their political voice. At black churches, societies, leagues, clubs, picnics, and other gatherings, these new citizens listened to and participated in political discussions. For the first time in American history, African Americans were elected to major offices at the state and national level. Fourteen African Americans sat in the House of Representatives and two, **Hiram Revels** and **Blanche K. Bruce**, represented **Mississippi** in the Senate. About 600

served in Southern legislatures, and others held national office and such state positions as lieutenant governor, secretary of state, and superintendent of education. Hundreds more served at the state and local levels as justices of the peace, sheriffs, and school-board officials. Throughout Reconstruction, black voters provided the bulk of the Republican party support in the South.

The new Republican party in the South also brought to power whites who were new to Southern politics. Many were Northerners who came South during and after the war. Their opponents dubbed them **carpetbaggers**, implying that they had gone South to reap the spoils of office, carrying their belongings in a piece of luggage known as a carpetbag. Most were former soldiers who had remained in the South without any thought of going into politics. Others were investors who saw economic advantages in the postwar South. Still others had volunteered to come south to help the freedmen.

Former Confederates reserved their greatest scorn for the so-called **scalawags**, native-born Southerners who joined the Republican party. Most scalawags were white farmers who hoped the Reconstruction governments would help them recover from wartime economic losses.

The South's traditional leaders opposed the new state governments, charging that black supremacy had been forced on them. They also complained that the new governments were corrupt and incompetent, a charge with little merit considering the widespread corruption elsewhere in the nation at the time. Given their inexperience, the Reconstruction governments left a remarkable record of achievement. They established the South's first state-supported public school system, free to both black and white children. They enacted civil rights laws that made it illegal for railroads, hotels, and other public facilities to discriminate on the basis of race. They repealed the Black Codes and made the tax system more equitable. They fostered economic development by financing railroad construction and attracting industry to the South.

MEET THE PRESIDENTS

ULYSSES S. GRANT

Born: April 27, 1822
Died: July 23, 1885
In office: 1869–1877

Few American lives have tossed so dramatically between mediocrity and greatness. A graduate of West Point, Ulysses Grant resigned from the army in near disgrace in 1854 and failed in a series of efforts to support his family. In 1861 Grant, at 39, was clerking in his brother's harness shop.

Three years later, Grant was supreme commander of all Union armies; five years after that, he entered the White House. There Grant's two terms of political innocence and bad judgment deepened the pain of Reconstruction and contributed to an epidemic of corruption and scandal. Returning to private life, Grant slid into familiar grooves of failure. By 1884 he was bankrupt and dying of throat cancer.

Grant then wrote his way back to greatness. His *Personal Memoirs*, completed only days before his death, are among the finest war commentaries in all literature.

RUTHERFORD B. HAYES

Born: October 4, 1822
Died: January 17, 1893
In office: 1877–1881

A sleazy secret deal in 1876 gave the country one of its most honest and high-minded presidents. Rutherford B. Hayes is the only man ever to become president despite the inconvenience of losing the election.

Hayes' reckless bravery in the Civil War cost him four horses and five wounds; he emerged with the rank of general. He served three terms as governor of Ohio.

At his subdued inauguration Hayes announced, "he serves his party best who serves the country best"—a statement exactly contrary to the sentiments of the age. Hayes spent his term swimming against the tides of patronage and corruption. His idealism was not contagious, and his reform efforts had little effect beyond earning him the dubious nickname "Old Granny."

The South failed to develop a prosperous economy.

Because few of the former slaves could afford to acquire land, most had to seek employment from white landowners. After attempts to restore the old plantation system failed, a new economic system called **sharecropping** emerged. Under this system each participating family rented a piece of land and worked it relatively free from outside supervision. Because few freed blacks had any money, the rent they paid was a share of the year's crops, which were divided between the sharecropper and the landowner at harvest time.

Sharecropping gave former slaves a degree of personal freedom, but many were exploited by the system. They quickly fell into debt, unable to pay merchants who advanced them credit at ruinous rates. Often, the merchants were also the landowners, who thereby kept their tenants tied to their land by debt.

Many white farmers in the South, and the few blacks who owned their land, also suffered economic hardships during Reconstruction.

Federal officers model Ku Klux Klan masks and robes confiscated from Klan members in Alabama in 1868.

Plunged into poverty by wartime destruction, they were forced to borrow, pledging their future crops against the loans. Often merchants would exchange money only for a lien, or pledge, on a future cotton crop. Thus, farmers who had grown food crops before the war were forced into the cotton economy. Like sharecropping, the **crop-lien system** made it hard for most farmers to escape poverty.

Thus, the South failed to develop a prosperous, diversified economy. Reconstruction brought both a political revolution and a social revolution to the South, but not an economic revolution to accompany them.

Some Southern whites used violence to intimidate African Americans.

A significant number of former Southern leaders, embittered by their defeat in the Civil War, were determined to overthrow the Reconstruction governments. They complained of corruption and the increase in taxes needed to pay for schools and other public facilities. Many poor whites withdrew their support of the new Southern governments when their economic situation did not improve. Most of all, few white Southerners were ready to accept the idea of black former slaves holding office and enjoying equality before the law. They viewed African Americans as an inferior race whose proper place was as dependent laborers.

In an effort to restore white supremacy, Reconstruction opponents resorted to violence and terror. Many supported organizations such as the **Ku Klux Klan**, whose purpose was to terrorize African Americans who attempted to vote and stand up for their rights. The Klan was responsible for a wave of beatings and lynchings—illegal hangings without trial. There were cases of wholesale assault on black communities resulting in mass murder. Scalawags and Northerners also became victims of Klan violence.

When the new Southern governments proved unable to restore order, the federal government stepped in. In 1870 and 1871 Congress passed **enforcement acts** outlawing terrorist societies and authorizing the use of the army against them. After the arrest and trial

THE BLACK CODES
Skill: Identifying Assumptions

Introducing the Skill. When the Emancipation Proclamation freed slaves in the states in rebellion, many of their former owners reacted with bitterness. Some sought retaliation by persuading Southern legislatures to pass laws designed to force African Americans into situations similar to those they had known in slavery. These laws became known as the Black Codes. Upon what principles and values were these codes based? Were these principles valid?

Learning the Skill. To evaluate the Black Codes, you might begin by **identifying assumptions** underlying their creation. An assumption is an idea, generally unstated, that someone takes for granted as being true and valid. Some assumptions may be accurate and based on fact, though others are questionable and even false. To identify an assumption,

carefully examine the given statement or information. Are there any claims or phrases expressed that lack clear support or evidence? What principles or values might lie behind the person's words or actions?

Applying the Skill. Study the following examples of Black Codes from the state of South Carolina. Then answer the questions.

a. Persons of color may not be part of the militia of this state.

b. No person of color shall migrate and reside in this state unless, within 20 days after his arrival, he shall post a bond swearing to his good behavior.

c. Upon seeing a crime committed by a person of color, any person may arrest the offender and take him before a magistrate.

d. Marriage between a white person and a person of color shall be illegal and void.

e. All persons of color who make contracts for service or labor shall be known as servants and those with whom they contract shall be known as masters.

1. What did the authors of these Black Codes assume or take for granted?
2. Were these underlying assumptions based on fact or opinion? Explain.
3. How would you describe the difference between life under the Black Codes and life under slavery? Explain your reasoning.

of hundreds of Klansmen, most Klan activity ceased. By 1872, for the first time since the beginning of the Civil War, peace reigned in the former Confederacy.

Despite the Grant Administration's effective response to Klan terrorism, many Northerners were losing interest in Southern affairs. Many of the Radical leaders who had championed black rights were passing from the scene. The idealism of Thaddeus Stevens, who died in 1868, was fading in the Republican party. Many felt that the South should be allowed to solve its own problems without interference from

Washington. Rising taxes because of the expenses of public schools and other state programs and reports of corruption placed the new Southern governments in an unfavorable light.

Although President Grant was overwhelmingly reelected in 1872, Northerners became increasingly concerned with other matters. In 1873 the country plunged into a severe economic depression. Distracted by economic problems and by scandals in the Grant Administration involving bribery and favors for certain business interests, Republicans were in no mood to devote further attention to the South. In spite of the changing political climate, Congress did enact one final piece of Reconstruction legislation, the Civil Rights Act of 1875, which outlawed discrimination in places of public accommodation and entertainment. However, the Supreme Court would declare the act unconstitutional in 1883.

In the mid-1870s, violence again erupted throughout the South. This time the Grant Administration showed little interest in taking action as Republicans were openly threatened and some were murdered. On election day armed Democrats destroyed ballot boxes and drove former slaves from the polls. In Louisiana a white supremacist organization announced that black workers who supported Reconstruction would be dismissed from their jobs. The result was a Democratic landslide in the South.

White supremacy was restored in the South.

The fate of Reconstruction was sealed with the presidential election of 1876. In the popular vote, **Rutherford B. Hayes**, the Republican candidate from Ohio, lost to **Samuel J. Tilden**, the Democratic candidate from New York. However, a dispute erupted over the electoral vote in several states where Reconstruction governments survived. Whoever won these states in the electoral vote would become president. The dispute was settled by the **Compromise of 1877**. In this agreement the Republicans gained the election of Hayes as president. The Democrats gained a promise of the withdrawal of all remaining federal troops from the South and federal support for internal improvements such as the expansion of the Southern railway system.

The bitter period of Reconstruction was over. It had been a time of both success and failure. The Union had been restored, and the rebuilding of the South had begun. The South's new public school systems and the independent community and religious life created by the former slaves were lasting accomplishments. Reconstruction had, however, failed to solve the South's serious economic problems.

Few African Americans managed to acquire land or to achieve economic independence in other ways.

In the next decades, whites in the South gradually nullified the civil and political rights of the former slaves and ignored the 14th and 15th amendments. By the early 20th century, virtually no African Americans could vote anywhere in the South. The Republican party faded from the scene, leaving the South solidly Democratic. Not until the 1950s and 1960s—a period sometimes called the Second Reconstruction—was the nation again ready to accord African Americans the rights they had held only briefly during Reconstruction.

SECTION **4** REVIEW

Identify Key People and Terms
Write a sentence to identify: 15th Amendment, Hiram Revels, Blanche K. Bruce, carpetbaggers, scalawags, sharecropping, crop-lien system, Ku Klux Klan, enforcement acts, Rutherford B. Hayes, Samuel J. Tilden, Compromise of 1877

Locate Key Places
What state sent two African Americans to the Senate during Reconstruction?

Master the Main Ideas
1. **Understanding the social effects of Reconstruction:** How did Radical Reconstruction affect the lives of the former slaves?
2. **Understanding economic developments:** How did the labor system change in the South, and what effect did this have on the Southern economy?
3. **Analyzing the social impact of Reconstruction:** How did some white Southerners attempt to undermine Reconstruction?
4. **Examining political issues:** What were the terms of the compromise that ended Reconstruction in 1877?

Apply Critical Thinking Skills: Demonstrating Reasoned Judgment
On the whole, would you judge Reconstruction as a success or a failure? Give reasons for your opinion.

Reconstruction tested national ideals.

Key Terms: body politic, free inquiry

Reading Preview
As you read this section, you will learn:

1. what dream of African Americans was dashed after Reconstruction ended in the South.
2. what Radical Reconstruction contributed toward the goal of racial equality.

Although the Civil War has long been over, the sounds and clashes of that struggle are still echoing. The failure of Reconstruction postponed for a century efforts to find for African Americans a place in American society consistent with the national heritage of freedom and equality. Reconstruction was not a total failure, however. Although the Radicals were only influential for a brief time, they managed to push through the passage of the 14th and 15th amendments. Twentieth-century America has reason to applaud their achievements. In many respects the Radicals helped lay the groundwork for the civil rights movement of the 1950s and 1960s. Without Radical Reconstruction the principle of African American equality might never have been realized.

African Americans saw the dream of equality temporarily dissolve.

Efforts to achieve true racial equality illustrate better than anything else the difficulties Americans have experienced in living up to the high ideals of the Declaration of Independence and putting into practice the positive side of the themes that define our history. As noted earlier in our study of the American past, racial, ethnic, and religious diversity define our society. We have gained strength from a great blending of religious ideas that produced acceptance of a common core of moral and ethical precepts. Our record in racial and ethnic matters, however, has been blemished. From colonial times to the present, every sizeable ethnic immigrant group has had to face varying degrees of discrimination, legal or not. Particularly with African Americans, this discrimination has spilled over into every aspect of our life and culture, sometimes making a cruel mockery of our professed ideals.

The commitment to free enterprise and private property—a key theme of our national development—meant nothing to African Americans held in bondage. Tragically, it meant very little even after passage of the Reconstruction amendments. Only in the late 20th century has there been anything even approximating economic equality for blacks. Free enterprise was a powerful economic principle for white America. For African Americans, it was an irrelevance.

Frederick Douglass believed that "Our reconstruction measures were radically defective" because they failed to give the ex-slaves any land. He said that the measures had:

AN AMERICAN ★ SPEAKS

Left the former slave completely in the power of the old master, the loyal citizen in the hands of the disloyal rebel against the government. . . . When the serfs of Russia were emancipated, they were given three acres of ground upon which they could live and make a living. But not so when our slaves were emancipated. They were sent away empty-handed, without money, without friends, and without a foot of land to stand upon. Old and young, sick and well, were turned loose to the open sky, naked to their enemies.

The same principle of exclusion applied in the political arena. The inclusion of African Americans in the political system was not a goal of either the North or the South prior to Radical Reconstruction. Moreover, when advanced by the Radical Republicans, the principle won out only temporarily. Inclusion of African Americans in the nation's political life was, as one historian has said, "a dawn without noon." After the last Northern troops were withdrawn from the South, African Americans

African Americans created many useful inventions during the postwar years. Charles Thomas Christmas' cotton-baling press, above, greatly improved cotton production methods. Elijah McCoy, below, invented the device shown below him, a drip cup used to lubricate locomotive engines.

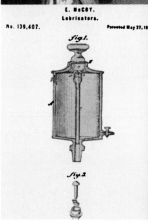

E. McCOY.
Lubricators.
No. 139,407.   Patented May 27, 18

fig.1

fig.2

Radical Reconstruction brought new educational opportunities for African Americans such as these 1875 graduates of Virginia's Hampton University.

were virtually excluded from the **body politic** —the people who make up a unit under a single government.

Radical Reconstruction planted the seeds of racial equality.

Americans in the 1840s, 1850s, and 1860s continued, as they had in earlier decades, to define public and private morality by religious and ethical principles. Racist attitudes, however, prevented most of them from applying these principles to African Americans. How could it have been otherwise, considering the fact that the basic instrument of government, the Constitution, referred to enslaved African Americans as "other persons"—that is, persons other than citizens? Those "other persons," the slave population of the South, had to await the day

when the aroused conscience of a determined minority prevailed in its efforts to apply ethical and moral principles in amending constitutional doctrine. For this, the nation owes the Radicals an enduring debt.

Fortunately, the American political system devised by the Founding Fathers allows for the kind of peaceful change engineered by the Radicals. Our Constitution can be amended, our national legislature can pass new laws, and our courts can adjust their rulings to discard outdated or unjust decisions.

Throughout the years from 1840 to 1870, Americans continued to believe in a unique national destiny—another theme that defines the American character. The expansionist spirit was particularly strong in the 1840s, before the sectional crisis derailed it. The "mission complex" that in 1630 inspired John Winthrop and the Puritans to build in **Massachusetts** "a city on a hill," as an example to the world, found its equivalent in the westward-bound pioneers of the mid-19th century. Again, however, it was not until the period of Radical Reconstruction that the former slaves could dream the same dreams in the same terms. African Americans went to Texas in the 1840s not as a people on a mission of destiny, but as the lackeys of their white masters.

Although African Americans were excluded from participating in missions of white America, they developed their own dreams and vigorously set about to achieve them. The ex-slaves, through community, church, and political organizations, funded schools and self-help groups that sought to overcome all the limits set by 250 years of bondage. This mission had the potential of transforming the South and promoting a climate of equality and racial harmony. The liberal state constitutions set up during Reconstruction were an example of what could be done. When the North lost interest in Reconstruction, however, and allowed the return of white supremacy, the flames of equality burned out. They would not be rekindled until leaders such as the Rev. Dr. Martin Luther King, Jr., appeared in the 1950s.

The vitality of American civilization rested in the mid-19th century, as it does today, on the interrelationship of ideas from the fields of religion, politics, economics, and science. Constitutional government and the rule of law created the climate in which free enterprise and individual initiative could flourish. The restraining principles of ethics and morality gave to both the quality of fairness that promoted a vigorous and mainly harmonious society. In such an atmosphere, **free inquiry**—the act of freely seeking solutions, an essential ingredient of scientific investigation and technological advance—can flourish. The exclusion of any element in society from full participation in the interplay of politics, economics, and free inquiry deprives society of the full benefit of the inventive genius of all its people. The contributions of African Americans to science and technology since the end of slavery can only

suggest the extent of the national loss during the years of their bondage.

The tragedy of Reconstruction was that except for the idealistically driven Radicals, neither North nor South was ready to accept the principle of racial equality. The Reconstruction amendments struck at two ingrained Southern principles—black inferiority and states' rights. At the same time, these additions to the Constitution did advance, if only haltingly, the North's sense of mission and reform.

Finally, then, the Civil War, the Emancipation Proclamation, and Radical Reconstruction were three acts in a wrenching drama that tested the ability of the American people to resolve fundamental issues of freedom and equality. The men and women of that period, both black and white, undertook the difficult task of repairing imperfections in the national fabric so that it might one day truly reflect the Jeffersonian idea of equality.

SECTION 5 REVIEW

Identify Key People and Terms
Write a sentence to identify: body politic, free inquiry

Locate Key Places
Where did the Puritans attempt to build "a city on a hill"?

Master the Main Ideas

1. **Studying the social impact of Reconstruction:** What factors were responsible for the dream of African Americans of the Reconstruction period remaining unrealized?
2. **Supporting democratic processes:** What is there about the American political system that gives hope to an oppressed minority?

Apply Critical Thinking Skills: Analyzing Cause and Effect
Do you think Radical Reconstruction might have succeeded in the long term if the North had been more supportive, or was the ultimate victory of white supremacy in the South inevitable? Give reasons for your opinion.

TOURING THE PAST

Gettysburg National Military Park

The peaceful landscape of Gettysburg belies its history as the site of one of the Civil War's most fateful battles.

The best way to see Gettysburg National Military Park is to march its fields and woods as tens of thousands of soldiers did during the first three days of July 1863. Although nature and encroaching civilization have changed the landscape somewhat, much of the terrain looks as it did when the Union and Confederate armies clashed in some of the most lethal action of the Civil War. The soldiers are all gone now, but the rolling fields and hills, the stone walls and boulders, and even trees dating from the war—some still containing in their heartwood the embedded stray metal of combat—remain.

Some 2,000 handcrafted memorials—statues, tablets, cannons—are placed on the battlefield in tribute to soldiers and deeds. Dwarfing these gestures of remembrance are the monuments of the land itself, the contested places that stand out in American legend.

Cemetery Hill. Here at the end of the first day, beaten Union troops frantically dug in against a final Confederate assault. The attack never came, and the hill became the fortress of the Union line.

Culp's Hill. Just to the east of Cemetery Hill, Culp's became the anchorpoint of the Union line. Fighting swept up and down the hill all during the second day; the Confederate attacks fell just short of success.

Seminary Ridge. This became the base line of the Southern army. Here a magnificent statue of Robert E. Lee still stares across the shallow valley to the Union positions he never quite captured.

Emmitsburg Road. On the high ground near here, General Sickles foolishly placed his Union troops. As his corps was smashed in by charging Confederates, ordinary farm sites were lifted in capital letters into the pages of history: *The Peach Orchard, The Wheat Field.* A jumble of boulders became a fatal *Devil's Den.*

Little Round Top. As the Sickles disaster unfolded on the second day, General Warren discovered this strategic high ground was undefended. He rushed Union troops up the hill; they arrived ten minutes before the Confederates, fought to the last bullet, and held. A statue of Warren still gazes through binoculars from Little Round Top.

The most ordinary, but perhaps the most fateful monuments at Gettysburg are a clump of trees and a low stone wall on Cemetery Hill. It was at those trees that 13,000 Confederates aimed their final attack on the third day; it was at that stone wall that Pickett's charge crested and ebbed away.

The Gettysburg battleground became a National Military Park in 1895. It is presently operated by the National Park Service. The Gettysburg National Cemetery lies next to the park, sheltering the graves of some 4,500 Union soldiers. (The Confederate dead were eventually relocated to cemeteries in the South.) It was at the dedication of this cemetery in November 1863 that Lincoln spoke the few words that would forever after make Gettysburg hallowed ground for all Americans.

GETTYSBURG
The National Military Park is located in southern Pennsylvania, about 35 miles southwest of Harrisburg near the Maryland border.

NY
PA
Harrisburg
Gettysburg
NJ
MD
WV
Washington
Manassas
VA
Chancellorsville
Richmond

A Union officer describes his experiences at Gettysburg:

One of the most vivid accounts of the Battle of Gettysburg was written two weeks afterward by Frank Haskell, a young Union officer. Here Haskell describes the aftermath of Pickett's charge. What sharp contrasts do you find in his description?

Just as the fight was over, and the first outburst of victory had a little subsided, when all in front of the crest was noise and confusion—prisoners being collected, small parties in pursuit of them far down into the fields, flags waving, officers giving quick, sharp commands to their men—I stood apart for a few moments upon the crest. . . Near me, saddest sight of the many of such a field and not in keeping with all this noise, were mingled alone the thick dead . . . who, not yet cold, with the blood still oozing from their death-wounds, had given their lives to the country upon that stormy field.

Mary Chesnut Watches the Attack on Fort Sumter

5A

TIME FRAME
1861

GEOGRAPHIC SETTING
Charleston

Mary Boykin Chesnut (1823–1886) of South Carolina was a daughter of a former governor of her home state and was married to one of its senators in November 1860 when South Carolina voted to secede. Her husband was the first Southern senator to resign and return home. Mary Chesnut recorded her experiences during the Civil War period in her diary. She was, observed American critic Edmund Wilson, "a woman of exceptional intelligence" and her diary is "an extraordinary document—in its informal department, a masterpiece." In the following excerpts from her diary, Mary Chesnut described the bombardment of Fort Sumter, in Charleston Harbor, on April 12–13, 1861. The "Anderson" she mentioned was Major Robert Anderson (1805–1871), commander of the Federal troops at Fort Sumter. He had been ordered on April 11 to immediately surrender the fort.

12th.—Anderson will not capitulate [surrender]. Yesterday's was the merriest, maddest dinner we have had yet. Men were audaciously [boldly] wise and witty. We had an unspoken foreboding that it was to be our last pleasant meeting. . . .

I do not pretend to go to sleep. How can I? If Anderson does not accept terms at four, the orders are he shall be fired upon. I count four, St. Michael's bells chime out, and I begin to hope. At half past four the heavy booming of a cannon. I sprang out of bed, and on my knees prostrate [humble] I prayed as I never prayed before.

There was a sound of stir all over the house, pattering of feet in the corridors. All seemed hurrying one way. I put on my double gown and a shawl and went too. It was to the housetop. The shells were bursting. In the dark I heard a man say, "Waste of ammunition." I knew my husband was rowing a boat somewhere in that dark bay. If Anderson was obstinate [stubborn], Colonel Chesnut [her husband had joined the Confederate army] was to order the fort on one side to open fire. Certainly fire had begun. The regular roar of the cannon, there it was. And who could tell what each volley accomplished of death and destruction?

The women were wild there on the housetop. Prayers came from the women and imprecations [curses] from the men. And then a shell would light up the scene. Tonight they say the forces are to attempt to land. We watched up there, and everybody wondered that Fort Sumter did not fire a shot. . . .

We hear nothing, can listen to nothing; boom, boom, goes the cannon all the time. The nervous strain is awful, alone in this darkened room. "Richmond and Washington ablaze," say the papers—blazing with excitement. Why not? To us these last days' events seem frightfully great. We were all women on that iron balcony. Men are only seen at a distance now. . . .

13th.—Nobody has been hurt after all. How gay we were last night! Reaction after the dread of all the slaughter we thought those dreadful cannon were making. Not even a battery the worse for wear. Fort Sumter has been on fire. Anderson has not yet silenced any of our guns. So the aides, still with swords and red sashes by way of uniform, tell us. But the sound of those guns makes regular meals impossible. None of us goes to table. Tea trays pervade the corridors, going everywhere. Some of the anxious hearts lie on their beds and moan in solitary misery. Mrs. Wigfall and I solace ourselves with tea in my room. These women have all a satisfying faith. "God is on our side," they say.

During the 34-hour bombardment of Fort Sumter, Confederate gunners fired 4,000 artillery rounds at the fort, destroying large portions of it. Despite the intensity of the shelling—indicated by this contemporary Currier and Ives lithograph—no one was killed on either side in the engagement. (One soldier—the first man to die in the Civil War—was killed later in an explosion that took place when a 50-gun salute to the American flag was fired during the surrender ceremonies.)

When we are shut in Mrs. Wigfall and I ask, "Why?" "Of course, He hates the Yankees," we are told, "You'll think that well of Him."

Not by one word or look can we detect any change in the demeanor [manner] of these Negro servants. Lawrence sits at our door, sleepy and respectful, and profoundly indifferent. So are they all, but they carry it too far. You could not tell that they even heard the awful roar going on in the bay, though it has been dinning in their ears night and day. People talk before them as if they were chairs and tables. They make no sign. Are they stolidly stupid? or wiser than we are; silent and strong, biding their time?

Discussing the Reading

1. What reaction does anxiety about the possibility of war seem to have had on Mary Chesnut?

2. How did Mary Chesnut's women friends defend their belief that God was on the Confederacy's side?

CRITICAL THINKING
Recognizing Bias

How did Mary Chesnut present the behavior and manner of the "Negro servants" (lines 71–83)? Can anything about her attitudes toward slavery and toward African Americans be inferred from this passage? Explain your answer.

"Sarah My Love for You Is Deathless"

TIME FRAME
1861

GEOGRAPHIC SETTING
Washington, D.C.

The first major battle of the Civil War was fought on Sunday, July 21, 1861, at a stream called Bull Run, which was about 25 miles southwest of Washington, D.C. Citizens of the capital, confident of a Union victory, packed picnic lunches and went to see the action. However, after a promising start, by mid-afternoon the First Battle of Bull Run had turned into a Northern rout, with the federal forces falling back to Washington in panic. With 2,700 Union and 2,000 Confederate casualties, Bull Run was a grim warning that the nation was in for a long and bloody struggle. Among the Union dead was Major Sullivan Ballou of the 2nd Rhode Island Volunteers. A 32-year-old lawyer and former Speaker of the Rhode Island House of Representatives, Ballou had left a promising political career to enlist in the Union army. Stationed at Camp Clark near Washington, on July 14 Ballou wrote the following letter—his last—to his wife Sarah. (The spelling of the original has been retained.)

My very dear Sarah:

The indications are very strong that we shall move in a few days—perhaps tomor-
5 row. Lest I should not be able to write again, I feel impelled to write a few lines that may fall under your eye when I shall be no more. Our movements may be of a few days duration and full of pleasure—
10 and it may be one of some conflict and death to me. "Not my will, but thine, O God be done." If it is necessary that I should fall on the battle field for my Country, I am ready.
15 I have no misgivings about, or lack of confidence in the cause in which I am engaged, and my courage does not halt or falter. I know how strongly American Civilization now leans on the triumph of the
20 Government, and how great a debt we owe to those who went before us through the blood and sufferings of the Revolution. And I am willing—perfectly willing—to lay down all my joys in this life, to
25 help maintain this Government, and to pay that debt.

But my dear wife, when I know that with my own joys, I lay down nearly all of your's, and replace them in this life with
30 cares and sorrows, when after having eaten for long years the bitter fruits of orphanage myself, I must offer it as the only sustenance to my dear little children, is it weak or dishonorable, that while the ban-
35 ner of my forefathers floats calmly and fondly in the breeze, underneath my unbounded love for you, my darling wife and children should struggle in fierce, though useless contests with my love of Country?
40 I cannot describe to you my feelings on this calm Summer Sabbath night, when two-thousand men are sleeping around me, many of them enjoying perhaps the last sleep before that of death, while I am
45 suspicious that death is creeping around me with his fatal dart, as I sit communing with God, my Country and thee. I have sought most closely and diligently and often in my heart for a wrong motive in thus
50 hazarding the happiness of those I love, and I could find none. A pure love of my Country and of the principles I have so often advocated before the people—another name of Honor that I love more than
55 I fear death, has called upon me and I have obeyed.

Sarah my love for you is deathless, it seems to bind me with mighty cables that nothing but Omnipotence could break;
60 and yet my love of Country comes over me like a strong wind and bears me unresistably on with all these chains to the battle field.

The memories of the blissful moments
65 I have spent with you come creeping over

A departing Confederate soldier says goodbye to his wife in *Off to the Front,* a painting done by an unknown artist sometime during the 1860s. The theme of the soldier's farewell to his family was a common one in late 19th-century American art.

children from harm. But I cannot. I must watch you from the Spirit-land and hover
90 near you, while you buffit the storm, with your precious little freight, and wait with sad patience, till we meet to part no more.

But, O Sarah! if the dead can come back to this earth and flit unseen around those
95 they loved, I shall always be near you; in the gladest days and in the darkest nights, advised to your happiest scenes and gloomiest hours, *always, always,* and if there be a soft breeze upon your cheek, it
100 shall be my breath, as the cool air fans your throbbing temple, it shall be my spirit passing by. Sarah do not mourn me dead; think I am gone and wait for thee, for we shall meet again.

105 As for my little boys—they will grow up as I have done, and never know a father's love and care. Little Willie is too young to remember me long—and my blue eyed Edgar will keep my frolics with him
110 among the dim memories of childhood. Sarah I have unlimited confidence in your maternal care and your development of their characters, and feel that God will bless you in your holy work.

115 Tell my two Mothers I call God's blessing upon them. O! Sarah I wait for you there; come to me and lead thither my children.

Sullivan

me, and I feel most gratified to God and to you that I have enjoyed them so long. And hard it is for me to give them up and burn to ashes the hopes of future years, when,
70 God willing, we might still have lived and loved together, and seen our sons grown up to honorable manhood, around us. I have, I know, but few and small claims upon Divine Providence, but something
75 whispers to me—perhaps it is the wafted prayer of my little Edgar, that I shall return to my loved ones unharmed. If I do not my dear Sarah, never forget how much I love you, and when my last breath escapes me
80 on the battle field, it will whisper your name. Forgive my many faults, and the many pains I have caused you. How thoughtless and foolish I have often times been! How gladly would I wash out with
85 my tears every little spot upon your happiness, and struggle with all the misfortunes of this world to shield you, and your

Discussing the Reading

1. What reasons did Sullivan Ballou offer for his willingness to give his life—if necessary—for the Union cause?

2. What consolation did he offer his wife if he were killed?

CRITICAL THINKING
Recognizing Values

Based on this letter, what things did Sullivan Ballou value? Did these values conflict with or strengthen one another? Explain.

253

Augustus Saint-Gaudens Honors an African American Regiment

TIME FRAME
1896

GEOGRAPHIC SETTING
Boston

Colonel Robert Gould Shaw (1837–1863), member of a family of abolitionists, was the commander of the 54th Massachusetts Regiment, the first African American troops from a free state mustered into the United States Army. Shaw and many of his men were killed on July 18, 1863, in the assault on Fort Wagner in South Carolina. On October 10, 1896, the American sculptor Augustus Saint-Gaudens [sānt gôd′nz] completed a monument to Shaw that shows Colonel Shaw on horseback leading his soldiers. The project had taken Saint-Gaudens (1848–1907) over 12 years to finish. What both the sculptor and Shaw's family wanted was a memorial honoring the entire regiment as much as the colonel. One of Saint-Gaudens' major problems was that most of the 54th Massachusetts had been killed in action, and the few that had survived were now old men, so the sculptor had to find other models. He depicted the figures on the monument, which are slightly over life-size, with photographic precision. At the dedication in Boston in 1897, Harvard philosopher William James felt he could almost hear the soldiers breathe. One art historian observed that the monument's "meticulous realism of detail strengthens, rather than distracts from, the rhythmic forward movement of these solemn and determined men."

Omnia Reliquit Servare Rem Publicam ("He sacrificed all to serve the state") reads the Latin inscription on St. Gaudens' sculpture of Colonel Shaw and his African American troops.

An inscription on the back of the monument, commemorating the joint achievement of the men of the 54th Massachusetts and their white officers, observes, "Together they gave to the nation and the world undying proof that Americans of African descent possess the pride, courage, and devotion of the patriot soldier."

Discussing the Sculpture

1. The robed figure floating over Shaw and his men personifies both fame and death (symbolized by the laurel leaves and poppies she carries). Does this imaginary being seem out of place associated with the realism of the figures of the soldiers. Why or why not?

2. Describing the figure of Shaw on the monument, poet Robert Lowell wrote, "He has an angry wrenlike vigilance,/ a greyhound's gentle tautness." Do Lowell's comparisons seem apt? Explain.

CRITICAL THINKING
Recognizing Values

According to Lowell, Shaw's father wanted no monument for his son, except the common grave in which he had been buried along with those of his men who were killed at Fort Wagner. Given his abolitionist principles, why might he have felt this way?

Frank Haskell Observes the Artillery at Gettysburg

TIME FRAME
1863

GEOGRAPHIC SETTING
Pennsylvania

Around 11:00 A.M. on the morning of July 3, 1863, the third and final day of the battle of Gettysburg, there was a lull in the combat. "Not a sound of a gun or musket can be heard in all the field," observed Frank Haskell (1828–1864), colonel of a Wisconsin regiment. Precisely at 1:00 P.M. the Confederate artillery began a massive barrage against the center of the Union lines. The sudden roar of the guns, one soldier remembered, "burst in on the silence, almost as suddenly as the full notes of an organ would fill a church." Soon answered by the Union artillery, this Confederate cannonade was in preparation for what became the climax of the battle—the heroic, doomed frontal assault by Southern troops led by General George Pickett (1825–1875). "Pickett's Charge," as it is known, failed to break the Union lines, and the next day the Confederate forces began to withdraw southward. In the following excerpt from his account of the battle, written for his brother shortly after the event, Frank Haskell described the fierce artillery duel between Confederate and Union gunners on the afternoon of July 3. The "Whitworth bolts" he mentioned were the shells fired by a new rifled cannon developed by an English engineer, Joseph Whitworth (1803–1887).

Imported from England, the breechloading Whitworth Cannon was largely used by Confederate artillerymen, one of whom observed that its "projectiles never failed to fly in the most beautiful trajectory."

W̲ho can describe such a conflict as is raging around us? To say that it was like a summer storm, with the crash of thunder, the glare of lightning, the shriek-
⁵ ing of the wind, and the clatter of hail-

stones, would be weak. The thunder and lightning of these two hundred and fifty guns and their shells, whose smoke darkens the sky, are incessant [unceasing], all
¹⁰ pervading, in the air above our heads, on the ground at our feet, remote, near, deafening, ear-piercing, astounding; and these hailstones are massy [heavy] iron, charged with exploding fire. And there is
¹⁵ little of human interest in a storm; it is an absorbing element of this. . . . We thought that at the second Bull Run, at the Antietam and at Fredericksburg on the 11th of December, we had heard heavy cannon-
²⁰ ading; they were but holiday salutes compared with this. Besides the great ceaseless roar of the guns, which was but the background of the others, a million various minor sounds engaged the ear. The
²⁵ projectiles shriek long and sharp. They hiss, they scream, they growl, they sputter; all sounds of life and rage; and each has its different note, and all are discordant [harsh]. Was ever such a chorus of sound
³⁰ before? We note the effect of the enemies' fire among the batteries and along the crest. We see the solid shot strike axle, or pole, or wheel, and the tough iron and heart of oak snap and fly like straws. The
³⁵ great oaks there by Woodruff's guns heave down their massy branches with a crash, as if the lightning smote them. The shells swoop down among the battery horses standing there apart. A half a
⁴⁰ dozen horses start, they tumble, their legs stiffen, their vitals and blood smear the ground. And these shot and shells have no respect for men either. We see the poor fellows hobbling back from the crest, or
⁴⁵ unable to do so, pale and weak, lying on the ground with the mangled stump of an arm or leg, dripping their life-blood away; or with a cheek torn open, or a shoulder

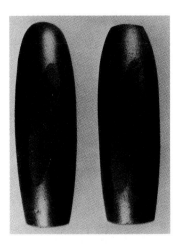

These shells for the Whitworth cannon show the hexagonal shape that fit the unique bore design of the weapon produced by the English engineer.

mashed. And many, alas! hear not the roar as they stretch upon the ground with up-turned faces and open eyes, though a shell should burst at their very ears. . . .

Strange freaks [tricks] these round shot play! We saw a man coming up from the rear with his full knapsack on, and some canteens of water held by the straps in his hands. He was walking slowly and with apparent unconcern, though the iron hailed around him. A shot struck the knapsack, and it and its contents flew thirty yards in every direction, the knap-sack disappearing like an egg, thrown spitefully against a rock. The soldier stopped and turned about in puzzled sur-prise, put up one hand to his back to as-sure himself that the knapsack was not there, and then walked slowly on again unharmed, with not even his coat torn. . . .

All the projectiles that came near us were not so harmless. Not ten yards away from us a shell burst among some bushes, where sat three or four orderlies holding horses. Two of the men and one horse were killed. Only a few yards off a shell exploded over an open limber box [am-munition box] in Cushing's battery, and at the same instant, another shell over a neighboring box. In both the boxes the ammunition blew up with an explosion that shook the ground, throwing fire and splinters and shells far into the air and all around, and destroying several men. We watched the shells bursting in the air, as they came hissing in all directions. Their flash was a bright gleam of lightning radi-ating from a point, giving place in the thousandth part of a second to a small, white, puffy cloud, like a fleece of the lightest, whitest wool. These clouds were very numerous. We could not often see the shell before it burst; but sometimes, as we faced towards the enemy, and looked above our heads, the approach would be heralded [signaled] by a prolonged hiss, which always seemed to me to be a line of something tangible [touchable], terminat-ing [ending] in a black globe, distinct to the eye, as the sound had been to the ear. The shell would seem to stop, and hang suspended in the air an instant, and then vanish in fire and smoke and noise. We saw the missiles tear and plow the ground. All in rear of the crest for a thousand yards, as well as among the batteries, was the field of their blind fury. Ambulances, passing down the Taneytown road with wounded men, were struck. The hospitals near this road were riddled. The house which was General Meade's headquarters was shot through several times, and a great many horses of officers and order-lies were lying dead around it. . . . The per-cussion shells would strike, and thunder, and scatter the earth and their whistling fragments; the Whitworth bolts would pound and ricochet, and bowl far away sputtering, with the sound of a mass of hot iron plunged in water; and the great solid shot would smite the unresisting ground with a sounding "thud," as the strong boxer crashes his iron fist into the jaws of his unguarded adversary. Such were some of the sights and sounds of this great iron battle of missiles. . . .

Discussing the Reading

1. What did Frank Haskell's account of Gettysburg suggest about his emotions under fire? Was he re-laxed? Elated? Frightened? Dis-gusted? Angry? Explain.

2. Do you think Haskell was probably a good officer? Why or why not?

CRITICAL THINKING
Testing Conclusions

Did Haskell's observations about the damage done by the Confeder-ate barrage suggest that the Southerners were aiming their guns too high? Explain.

Elizabeth Keckley Mourns the Death of Lincoln

TIME FRAME
1865

GEOGRAPHIC SETTING
Washington, D.C.

Within hours after Lincoln's death, Mary Todd Lincoln sent for Elizabeth Keckley (1818–1907), an African American who was her dressmaker and also her close friend. Born a slave in Virginia, Keckley later gained her freedom and became a prominent dressmaker in Washington, D.C. As seamstress for Lincoln's wife, she had called almost daily at the White House and had come to know and revere the President. In the following reading, Keckley describes her meeting with the President's widow on the morning of April 15 and expresses her own grief in the presence of Lincoln's body.

M orning came at last, and a sad morning was it. The flags that floated so gayly yesterday now were draped in black, and hung in silent folds at halfmast. The
5 President was dead, and a nation was mourning for him. Every house was

Phillippi. Photo

draped in black, and every face wore a solemn look. People spoke in subdued tones, and glided whisperingly, wonderingly, silently about the streets.

About 11 o'clock on Saturday morning a carriage drove up to the door, and a messenger asked for "Elizabeth Keckley,"

"Who wants her?" I asked.

"I come from Mrs. Lincoln. If you are Mrs. Keckley, come with me immediately to the White House." . . .

[Mrs. Lincoln] was nearly exhausted with grief, and when she became a little quiet, I asked and received permission to go into the Guests' Room, where the body of the President lay in state. When I crossed the threshold of the room, I could not help recalling the day on which I had seen little Willie lying in his coffin where the body of his father now lay. I remembered how the President had wept over the pale beautiful face of his gifted boy, and now the President himself was dead. The last time I saw him he spoke kindly to me, but alas! the lips would never move again. The light had faded from his eyes, and when the light went out the soul went with it!

What a noble soul was his—noble in all the noble attributes of God. Never did I enter the solemn chamber of death with such palpitating [violently beating] heart and trembling footsteps as I entered it that day. No common mortal had died. The Moses of my people had fallen in the hour of his triumph. Fame had woven her choicest chaplet [wreath] for his brow. Though the brow was cold and pale in death, the chaplet should not fade, for God had studded it with the glory of the eternal stars.

When I entered the room, the members of the Cabinet and many distinguished officers of the army were grouped around the body of their fallen chief. They made room for me, and, approaching the body, I lifted the white cloth from the white face of the man that I had worshipped as an idol—looked upon as a demi-god. Notwithstanding the violence of the death of the president, there was something beautiful as well as grandly solemn in the expression of the placid [peaceful] face. There lurked the sweetness and gentleness of childhood, and the stately grandeur of godlike intellect. I gazed long at the face, and turned away with tears in my eyes and a choking sensation in my throat. Ah! never was a man so widely mourned before. The whole world bowed their heads in grief when Abraham Lincoln died.

The nine black-draped cars of Abraham Lincoln's funeral train pull into a depot in the photograph on the facing page. The train carrying his body home for burial traveled from Washington to Springfield, Illinois, stopping at Philadelphia, New York, Cleveland, Indianapolis, and other cities. On the right is the portrait of Elizabeth Keckley that appeared as the frontispiece of her memoir, *Behind the Scenes, or Thirty Years a Slave, and Four Years in the White House* (1868).

Discussing the Reading

1. How did Elizabeth Keckley characterize the manner of the people in the streets of Washington on the morning of Lincoln's death?

2. Why did she compare Lincoln to Moses?

CRITICAL THINKING
Identifying Assumptions

What attitude did Elizabeth Keckley have toward Abraham Lincoln? Might this attitude have made her grief over his death easier to bear? Why or why not?

Chapter Summary

Write supporting details under each of the following main ideas as you read the chapter.

Section 1

1. The war began at Fort Sumter.
2. The North appeared to have the advantage.
3. The early years of war were discouraging for the Union.
4. Lincoln issued the Emancipation Proclamation.

Section 2

1. The North turned the tide at Gettysburg and Vicksburg.
2. Grant led the North to victory.
3. Northern resources provided the winning edge.

Section 3

1. Lincoln and Congress differed over Reconstruction.
2. Congress and the president clashed over the rights of former slaves.
3. Presidential Reconstruction failed.

Section 4

1. New groups achieved political power during Radical Reconstruction.
2. The South failed to develop a prosperous economy.
3. Some Southern whites used violence to intimidate African Americans.
4. White supremacy was restored in the South.

Section 5

1. African Americans saw the dream of equality temporarily dissolve.
2. Radical Reconstruction planted the seeds of racial equality.

Chapter Themes

1. **Conflict and cooperation:** After the war, the South's Reconstruction governments brought about landmark social and political changes such as state-supported public schools and sweeping civil rights legislation. Meanwhile, resistance to Radical Reconstruction was evident in the formation of violent societies such as the Ku Klux Klan.
2. **Constitutional and representative government:** For the most part throughout the Civil War, both Union and Confederacy remained faithful to their constitutions.

Chapter Study Guide

Identifying Key People and Terms

Name the key person or key term that describes the:
1. two ironclads that battled to a draw in 1862
2. document that released some slaves from bondage
3. concept whereby all citizens have certain legal rights
4. three amendments passed during Reconstruction
5. violent white supremacist organization

Locating Key Places

1. Where was the final capital of the Confederacy located?
2. What city was the main source of munitions and a major rail center for the South?
3. From which southern state did senators Hiram Revels and Blanche K. Bruce come?

Mastering the Main Ideas

1. What were some of the Northern advantages and Southern advantages in the Civil War?
2. What was the "total war" strategy of the North?
3. How did African Americans and women contribute to the war effort?
4. How did Radical Reconstruction plant the seeds of racial equality in the United States?

Applying Critical Thinking Skills

1. **Predicting consequences:** Lincoln issued the Emancipation Proclamation after a battle that could be interpreted as a Union victory. What might have been the consequences of his edict if he had issued it after a battlefield loss?
2. **Making comparisons:** Compare the war strategies of the North and the South.
3. **Expressing problems:** What was the basic quarrel between the Radicals and President Johnson regarding African Americans?
4. **Identifying assumptions:** What basic beliefs formed the foundation of President Lincoln's Reconstuction plan? Johnson's plan? The Radicals' plan?
5. **Recognizing values:** What American values are evident in the 13th, 14th, and 15th amendments?

1861
Civil War
begins

1863
Battle of
Gettysburg;
Lincoln issues
Emancipation
Proclamation

1865
Lee surrenders
to Grant at
Appomattox
Court House;
Lincoln is assassinated;
Mark Twain publishes
The Celebrated Jumping Frog of Calaveras County

1867
Radical Reconstruction begins

1871
Charles Darwin writes
The Descent of Man

1870
Last of Southern states
rejoins the Union

Chapter Activities

Learning Geography Through History

1. Use a map to explain the Union's three-part strategy to win the war.
2. What effect do climate and geography have on the Southern economy?
3. Between which two rivers lies the peninsula southeast of Richmond, Virginia, where McClellan lost an early chance to take the city?

Relating the United States to the World

1. How might the issuing of the Emancipation Proclamation have helped keep Britain and France from formally recognizing and supporting the Confederacy?
2. How might the Union blockade of the Confederacy have brought it into conflict with foreign powers?
3. According to Frederick Douglass, how did the serfs freed in Russia compare with the slaves freed in America?

Linking Past to Present

1. Watch a videotape of the 1989 film *Glory*, about the 54th Massachusetts Volunteer Infantry Regiment and the unit's white colonel, Robert Gould Shaw. Then answer these questions: **(a)** What were some obstacles the black soldiers had to overcome? **(b)** How did the black soldiers show their determination to participate in the war against slavery?
2. In 1954 the Supreme Court ruled that "separate but equal schools" were unconstitutional. On what Reconstruction amendment could this decision have been based? Why?

Using the Time Line

1. Approximately how many more years of war were there after the Battle of Gettysburg?
2. When did Radical Reconstruction begin?
3. Who wrote *The Descent of Man*?

Practicing Critical Thinking Strategies

Identifying Assumptions
President Johnson vetoed the Civil Rights bill and the bill to extend the life of the Freedmen's Bureau in 1866. What underlying assumptions probably contributed to Johnson's decision to veto these two bills?

Learning More About the Civil War and Reconstruction

1. **Using Source Readings:** Read the Source Readings for this chapter and answer the questions.
2. **Using Literature:** Read the excerpt from Stephen Crane's *The Red Badge of Courage* on pages 330–331. This classic Civil War novel describes the experiences of a young man who desperately tries to be a hero, only to find that he's human.
3. **Recreating a battle:** Research one of the famous battles of the Civil War. Recreate this battle using the necessary props to show how geography, human ingenuity and error, and other factors contributed to the victory for one side and the defeat for the other.

Linking Past to Present

Americans' means of travel have undergone many transformations since the late 1800s. Thomas Otter's painting *On the Road*, inset, portrays an age in which the railroad was first making its way into the West—a land of horses and wagons. Today the airplane, such as this one landing in Phoenix, Arizona, and the automobile serve the transportation needs of most Americans. (Painting from Nelson-Atkins Museum of Art, Kansas City, Missouri)

America's Economic Transformation

1 8 6 0 – 1 9 0 0

6

In 1860 America was still a nation of small communities, largely isolated from one another. These communities formed little economic islands to which individual farmers and their families, independent businesspeople, and skilled craft workers contributed their talents and energies. Travel and communication between communities was often slow and difficult, especially when it involved the still-uncharted western reaches of the country.

Tremendous changes swept across America in the late 1800s. A Pacific railroad opened up the western frontier to increasing numbers of settlers, primarily white Americans whose actions threatened the way of life of the western Indians. The railroad also changed the economic life of the United States. From a nation of isolated communities, America was transformed into an industrial society with a complex national economy. A new wave of immigrants arrived to help power the factories that fueled America's industrial transformation.

Questions developed in the minds of many Americans about this rapid technological transformation. Had economic growth developed in accord with America's commitment to free enterprise and private property, or at its expense? Furthermore, how did this economic development affect America's diverse racial and ethnic groups?

CHAPTER PREVIEW

In this chapter you will learn how America experienced a surge of growth and change.

SECTIONS IN THIS CHAPTER:
1. **The railroads altered the character of the West.**
2. **The close of the frontier threatened the Indians.**
3. **Industrial growth affected the American way of life.**
4. **America experienced massive economic growth.**
5. **Immigrants challenged American society.**

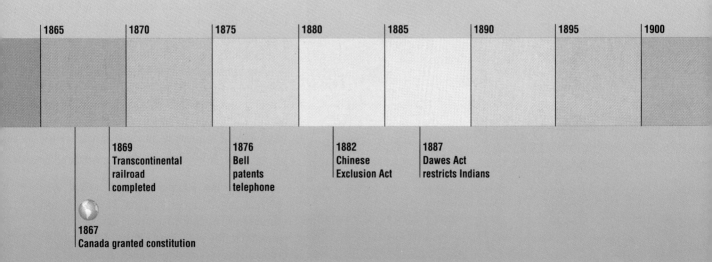

1865	1870	1875	1880	1885	1890	1895	1900

1869
Transcontinental railroad completed

1876
Bell patents telephone

1882
Chinese Exclusion Act

1887
Dawes Act restricts Indians

1867
Canada granted constitution

The railroads altered the character of the West.

Key Term: Chisholm Trail

Reading Preview
As you read this section, you will learn:

1. where the government encouraged the growth of railroads.
2. which two groups helped to open up the West.
3. about the relationship between the growth of ranching and the American cowboy.

Chinese immigrants, shown here building a railroad bridge in the Sierra Nevada, also made important contributions to western farming, mining, and wine industries.

In 1860 the options available to someone traveling to the American West were both limited and dangerous. People and products leaving the eastern states endured months of difficult travel by land or by sea. Since the 1830s many Americans had clamored for a Pacific railroad as a way to make the route to the West faster and safer. Little did they imagine the immense changes such a railroad would bring.

The government encouraged the westward expansion of railroads.

Although many government leaders professed that a Pacific railroad should or could never be built, most Americans did not listen to their doubts. The promise of the West was a powerful attraction, and the building of a Pacific railroad inevitable.

Planning the Pacific railroad. The railroad's starting point and route were not nearly as clear as its purpose. Much of the West had yet to be carefully mapped and surveyed, and nobody knew if a safe route existed that would allow for the engineering demands of a railroad. In addition, politicians of all sorts, eager for the economic benefits that would surely go along with the railroad, argued that their territory offered the only perfect location. As the Civil War drew closer, the debate focused on two routes—a southern trail, supported by Jefferson Davis, and the Emigrant Trail, a route that followed the basic path of westward-bound settlers through America's midsection.

After a series of surveys and debates that spanned three decades, President Lincoln ended the argument in 1862. The Civil War emphasized to the federal government the need for a railroad that would provide the quickest way to move troops, ammunition, and medical supplies. In the midst of the war, Congress took advantage of the South's absence, and that of Davis, and passed the Pacific Railway Act, which Lincoln signed. The act set up charters for two railroad lines, which, when they met, would span the country. The first, the Union Pacific, would build a rail system extending westward from Omaha, in the Nebraska Territory. The second, the Central Pacific, would build eastward from Sacramento, California. In addition, the U.S. government agreed to provide financial assistance for the railroad companies, giving them loans and land grants.

Building the Pacific railroad. Civil War veterans, freed slaves, Indians, Mormons, and immigrants, mainly Irish and Chinese—all responded to the recruiting efforts of the railroad companies. To provide shelter, food, and en-

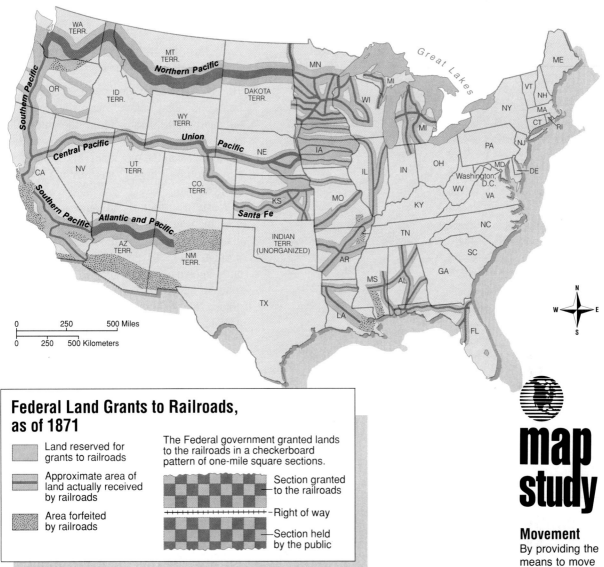

Federal Land Grants to Railroads, as of 1871

- Land reserved for grants to railroads
- Approximate area of land actually received by railroads
- Area forfeited by railroads

The Federal government granted lands to the railroads in a checkerboard pattern of one-mile square sections.

- Section granted to the railroads
- Right of way
- Section held by the public

Albers Equal-Area Projection

© SF

map study

Movement

By providing the means to move people and goods, the railroads increased the value of western lands. To encourage railroad building, the federal government granted land as shown. In what region was the most land forfeited by the railroads?

Critical Thinking

Why did the federal government support railroad building in the West?

tertainment for these rail crews, semipermanent camps or villages sprouted up at intervals along the route.

Among the workers, the Chinese men proved to be particularly valuable to the railroad. Championed by Charles Crocker, the bull-headed boss contractor of the Central Pacific, some 6,000 Chinese men worked for the railroad company by 1866. They were recruited both from California Chinatowns and from rural districts in China. The Chinese workers endured much discrimination on the job. They were scorned for being different and ridiculed for their unfamiliar diet, long pigtails, straw hats, and floppy blue pajamalike clothing. Still, they were respected for their strength, endurance, and courage.

The work of the railroad crews was strenuous, dangerous, and slow. At the peak of their labors, the work crews laid two to five miles of track a day. Most of the work was heavy physical labor, made more challenging by the extreme weather conditions of both the open prairie and mountains. Slowly, determined crews armed with hammers, sledges, iron hand drills, and kegs of black powder forged tunnels through thick walls of solid rock and spanned wide rivers and valleys with wooden bridges.

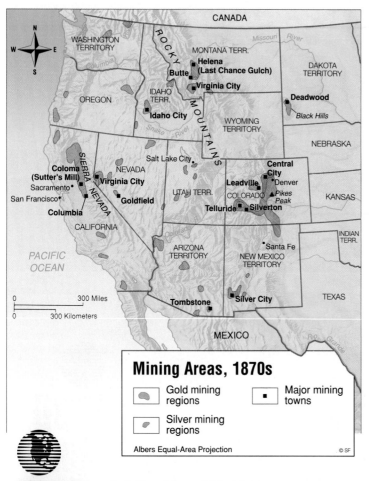

Mining Areas, 1870s

Gold mining regions

Silver mining regions

Major mining towns

Albers Equal-Area Projection

© SF

map study

Relationships within Places Mining towns spread throughout the West. Were there more states or territories in the West in the 1870s?

Critical Thinking How might the map help predict the loss of Indian lands in the late 1800s?

On May 10, 1869, six years after construction had begun, the tracks of the two rail lines met at **Promontory Point, Utah**. At the celebration, four specially forged spikes—two gold, one silver, and a fourth a composite of metals—were hammered into place. A final spike was wired into the nationwide telegraph system so that a blow to it would signal to the outside world that the task of linking the country's oceans was complete. Although the two men given the honor of striking the final blow missed the spike on the first try, the telegraph operator sent the signal anyway. Joyous celebrations erupted around the country.

Miners and ranchers opened up the West.

The American West, despite the success of the transcontinental railroad, was still believed to be nearly worthless land in the mid-1800s. However, as first miners and then ranchers found riches in the mountains and prairies, the perception of America's western half gradually changed.

Western mining. Miners sparked the movement eastward from California and populated many parts of the West. From 1859 through the 1870s, news of big gold and silver finds, known as strikes, kept hundreds of thousands of hopeful miners traveling through Colorado, Nevada, Washington, Idaho, Montana, Arizona, and the Dakota territories. The lure of gold drew large numbers of foreign-born miners—Irish, Chinese, Chilean, Peruvian, Mexican, French, German, and English.

An extremely mobile group, the miners flocked from strike to strike, and new camps and mining towns sprang up overnight. These mining camps quickly provided refinements not available on other frontiers—newspapers, theaters, schools, lending libraries, and the latest fashions. The camps were run by democratic governments, laying the foundation for the political organization of the West.

Western ranching. The railroads played an important role in creating new ways to exploit the land. In addition to mineral wealth, the region had two other plentiful resources: grass and cattle. Railroads provided the means to get the cattle to eastern cities, where urban residents wanted good beef to eat. At first, ranching did not require much investment. Both the grass and the cattle, some five million wild Texas longhorns, were free. In Chicago, Illinois, steers sold for $30 to $50 a head. All that was needed was a way to get them from Texas to Chicago.

Joseph G. McCoy, a livestock shipper from Illinois, came up with a solution. He realized that if he could get the cattle to a railroad, he could ship them the rest of the way to Chicago. He established the first cow town in the 1860s at Abilene, Kansas, where he built stock pens

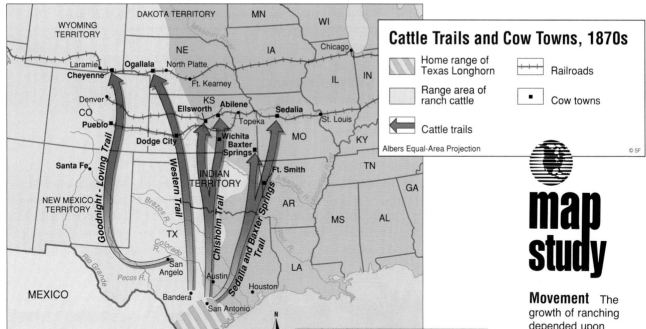

Cattle Trails and Cow Towns, 1870s

Legend	
Home range of Texas Longhorn	Railroads
Range area of ranch cattle	Cow towns
Cattle trails	

Albers Equal-Area Projection

© SF

map study

Movement The growth of ranching depended upon railroads moving cattle to midwestern cities such as Chicago for processing. Where did the Western Trail begin and end? How many miles long was it?

Critical Thinking Why was the era of long cattle drives short lived?

and loading chutes. One of the most famous trails to lead into Abilene was the **Chisholm Trail**. Follow it on the map above as it stretches northward from San Antonio, Texas. It took two to three months to travel.

The growth of ranching gave birth to the American cowboy.

To move the cattle from southern Texas to Kansas, a new type of worker—the American cowboy—was born. Since longhorns could not be easily captured or herded on foot, the Americans borrowed the methods of the Mexican *vaqueros*, horse-mounted herders who were expert at branding, roping, and roundups. The American cowboys also borrowed much of their equipment, all suited for the rough life of the range, from their southern neighbors—the Mexican saddle, the lariat, chaps, boots, spurs, and hat. The word "chaps," for example, comes from the Spanish *chaparreras*, meaning the thick leather trousers worn to protect one's legs.

267

The lanky, gray-eyed cowboy of Hollywood fame rarely existed on the range. At least a quarter of the cowboys were African Americans and possibly another quarter were Mexicans. Although cowboys celebrated heartily at the end of a long drive, the booming cow towns experienced little violence. The cowboys established their own laws and enforced them fairly.

Nat Love, an ex-slave from Tennessee, was a black cowboy who became a proud, rugged, self-made frontier hero. As a teenager after the Civil War, Love found his opportunities limited in the South and headed west. In 1869 he arrived in Dodge City, Kansas, and embarked on a 20-year stint on the cattle trails. Seven years later, he entered a rodeo at Deadwood City in the Dakota Territory and left with his most treasured prize, as he later recalled:

I never had a horse pitch with me so much as that mustang, but I never stopped sticking my spurs in him . . . until I proved his master. Right there the assembled crowd named me Deadwood Dick and proclaimed me champion roper of the western cattle country.

AN AMERICAN ★ SPEAKS

By 1880 the era of the big cattle drive was ending. As the rail network expanded into Texas, many ranchers switched from rounding up stray cattle to raising and breeding the longhorns. Eventually, a surplus supply of cattle resulted, and the price of beef plummeted to $10

Barbed Wire

This is the finest fence in the world. Light as air. Stronger than whiskey. Cheaper than dirt. All steel, and miles long. The cattle ain't born that can get through it.

With these words, John W. Gates, one of Texas' first barbed wire vendors, began a demonstration of his product. He had spent several days stringing up a barbed-wire corral in the middle of San Antonio. Curious onlookers had not been able to get a word out of Gates about the purpose of the project until the corral was complete.

On that day in the mid-1870s, a crowd gathered at the barbed-wire enclosure. Several dozen Texas longhorn steers were milling around in the background. Gates calmly told the crowd that he was going to drive the cattle into the corral. Some spectators laughed, some jeered, some made bets, and some moved back for safety.

On Gates' command, the cattle were driven into the corral. The cattle bolted for space, but the prickly wire

Highlights of American Life

a head, pushing poor producers out of the industry entirely.

After some bloody battles among the remaining competitors, the "Wild West" was largely tamed by the 1890s. Farmers who had received land through federal grant programs began to grow wheat on the lands where cattle once roamed freely. Barbed wire, developed in 1873, cut across the cattle trails and divided up the big ranches. Finally, the ranchers themselves turned to scientific and technological innovations to make their work easier. To the dismay of the cowboys, mowing machines and hay rakes became as important as chuck wagons and branding irons. "I tell you times have changed," one cowboy said sadly.

held them back. Furious, they charged against it again and again, then slowly gave up. Gates made a windfall that day, selling miles and miles of barbed wire.

Before the invention of barbed wire, good fencing material was difficult to come by on the western plains. Natural fencing, such as stones and lumber, was scarce and impractical for the large areas to be enclosed. With barbed wire, farmers could keep cattle from trampling their fields. Ranchers could bar their animals from dangerous obstacles. Large herds of cattle no longer roamed freely across the plains but were fenced in by barbed wire. Thus, the devil's wire, as some called it, helped tame the West.

SECTION 1 REVIEW

Identify Key People and Terms
Write a sentence to identify: Chisholm Trail, Nat Love

Locate Key Places
What was significant about Promontory Point, Utah?

Master the Main Ideas

1. **Supporting the role of profit:** How did the U.S. government encourage the westward expansion of the railroad system?
2. **Examining natural resources and population patterns: (a)** How did mining influence the settlement of the West? **(b)** How did ranching utilize the railroad to open up the West?
3. **Perceiving cause-effect relationships:** How did western ranching lead to the rise of the American cowboy?

Apply Critical Thinking Skills: Recognizing Bias
In the 1840s Daniel Webster, a senator from Massachusetts, presented the following argument against building a Pacific railroad: "What do we want with this region of savages and wild beasts, of deserts, of shifting sands and whirlwinds of dust, of cactus and prairie dogs?" In what ways does Webster use language to express his opinion about the need for a western railroad? Point out how specific words or phrases indicate his bias against the West. What effect might Webster's speech have on his audience?

Ads for barbed wire, at left, stressed the invention's value to farmers and ranchers around the country. Nat Love, at right, won his rodeo championship when he "roped, threw, tied, bridled, saddled, and mounted [his] mustang in exactly nine minutes from the crack of the gun."

SECTION 2

The close of the frontier threatened the Indians.

Key Terms: reservations, Battle of the Little Bighorn, Dawes Act

Reading Preview
As you read this section, you will learn:

1. how the Indians' way of life was threatened.
2. about the final result of Native American resistance.
3. what happened to the frontier in 1890.

As the American West changed, the cowboys were not alone in finding their way of life threatened. The American Indians, who had flourished on the Plains for hundreds of years, were nearly destroyed by the western railroads and the settlers who followed their trails. So-called progress on the western frontier threatened some 250,000 Native Americans, including Sioux, Cheyenne, and Arapaho, who followed the buffalo on the Great Plains.

Westward movement of white Americans threatened the Indians.

White Americans held little respect for the old and established Indian cultures. Racism, which is the belief that a particular race, especially one's own, is superior to other races, prevailed among white American society. To many Americans, the Indians were an inferior race of people, seen merely as barriers to white western expansion.

Echoing the feelings of many white Americans, the U.S. government led a campaign of racism and aggression against the western Indians. In general, U.S. Indian policy focused on getting more territory for white settlement. The government signed treaties that divided land between Indians and settlers and restricted the movement of each on the lands of the other.

Frequently, however, the government did not obtain Indian consent fairly, and the Indians were denied fair compensation for their lands.

In addition, most Plains Indians relied upon the buffalo for practically all of their needs—from food and clothing to shelter and fuel. As nomads following the herds of buffalo, many Indians had no concept of private property. **Chief Joseph** of the Nez Percé [nez′ pèrs′] eloquently expressed the perspective of many Native Americans:

The earth was created by the assistance of the sun, and it should be left as it was. . . . The country was made without lines of demarcation, and it is no man's business to divide it.

AN AMERICAN ★ SPEAKS

Furthermore, white respect for Indian ownership of land depended on how desirable the land was for settlement. Many settlers ignored both the treaties and Indian land rights. The U.S. government would not, or could not, honor its commitments.

Hostility between the Indians and the U.S. government intensified after the Sand Creek Massacre of 1864. Tired of years of fighting with gold miners who had entered their lands, the Cheyenne and Arapaho Indians accepted an offer of protection from the territorial governor of Colorado. They traveled in peace to Fort Lyon on Sand Creek, which is located in the southeastern corner of the Colorado territory. Instead of peace, however, the Indians met with disaster. Colonel J. M. Chivington's militia attacked their camp. Chief Black Kettle tried to stop the ambush, raising first an American flag and then a white flag for surrender. Neither worked. Chivington's troops killed 450 Indian men, women, and children—under his order of "Kill and scalp all, big and little." The scalps were brought back for public display.

Before long the powerful Sioux fought back. In 1865 an invasion of gold miners touched off a war, which flared even more intensely when the U.S. government announced plans for a wagon road to aid miners and travelers. The Bozeman Trail ran between Colorado and Virginia City, Montana, directly through the heart of the Sioux hunting grounds. Red Cloud, the

Relationships within Places Indians and settlers clashed as settlers moved onto Indian lands. In which states did Chief Joseph's route begin and end?

Critical Thinking
How do these maps show the hostile relationship between Indians and settlers?

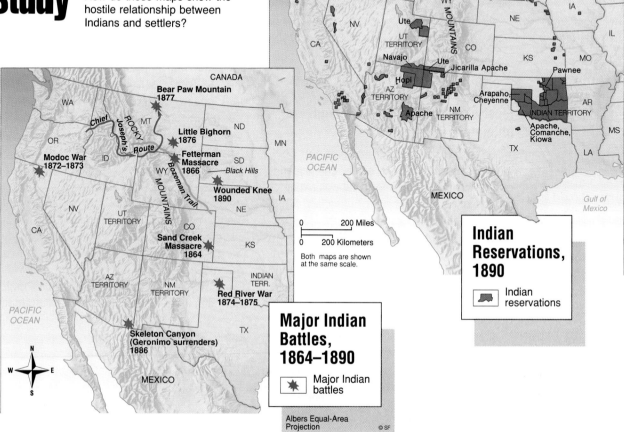

Indian Reservations, 1890

⬛ Indian reservations

Major Indian Battles, 1864–1890

✸ Major Indian battles

Albers Equal-Area Projection   © SF

Both maps are shown at the same scale.

Sioux chief, was determined to stop the trail. In 1866, while being pursued by army troops led by Captain William J. Fetterman, Red Cloud lured the careless Fetterman deep into the wilderness. Red Cloud then struck from ambush and wiped out all 82 of the soldiers.

The Fetterman fight, coming so soon after the Sand Creek Massacre, sparked a public debate over the nation's Indian policy. In the eastern United States, some reform and church groups wanted a humane peace policy, aimed at educating and "civilizing" the Native Americans. Others, East and West, questioned this approach, convinced that Indians were savages unfit for civilization. White westerners in gen-

eral favored a policy of firm control over the Native Americans.

In 1867 the advocates for peace won the debate. Construction on the Bozeman Trail was halted, and Congress created a Peace Commission to correct the causes of the Indian wars. The commission's actions, however, did little to change the Indians' situation. In 1867 and 1868, Indian chiefs were asked to restrict their groups to undesirable lands in two areas: one in the Black Hills of the Dakotas and the other in what would become Oklahoma.

These **reservations**, tracts of land under the jurisdiction of the federal government, became the primary element of U.S. Indian policy: to

Point

Pro-reform

- supported a humane policy
- advocated education

Counterpoint

Anti-reform

- viewed Indians as "savages"
- supported firm control

isolate the Indians, teach them to farm, and gradually "civilize" them. The land chosen for these reservations was usually so poor that white settlers did not want it.

Final challenges by the Indians ultimately failed.

Many western Indians resisted both the white invasion and the offer of safety and dependency on a reservation. The result was a quarter century of conflict between Indian and white culture. Many Americans recognized the justice of the Indian cause, even as they fought to destroy it. Even with this knowledge, the federal government continued the war against the western Indians, eventually killing or subduing them all.

The Sioux led one of several Indian attempts to defend their lands. In 1874 gold was found in the Black Hills territory of the Sioux, and greedy white miners poured in. Led by chiefs **Sitting Bull** and **Crazy Horse**, the Sioux resisted the white invasion. Their most stunning victory came at the **Battle of the Little Bighorn**, on the river of the same name in Montana. Here, on June 25, 1876, the overconfident young Lieutenant Colonel George A. Custer led his 264 U.S. troops into battle against 2,500 Sioux and Cheyenne. He and all of his men were overcome by the superior numbers of the Sioux in what came to be known as "Custer's Last Stand." Despite this victory, the Sioux eventually lost their war, surrendering to the United States in 1877.

As the Sioux war ended, another began. In 1877 the once-peaceful Nez Percé of Oregon and Idaho chose to fight rather than accept resettlement. Sensing that his cause was hopeless, their brilliant leader, Chief Joseph, made a desperate attempt to save his people from a reservation. He took his remaining followers on a harrowing 1,600-mile trek to Canada, regularly defeating larger U.S. army forces along

In this 1898 watercolor, Amos Badheart Buffalo, a Sioux participant in the Battle of Little Bighorn, depicts its aftermath. As Sitting Bull and others stand watching, Sioux and Cheyenne warriors ride horseback over the corpses of Custer (left center) and his men.

the way. Only 30 miles from the border, the Nez Percé were captured and sent south to Oklahoma. An exhausted and defeated Chief Joseph declared:

It is cold and we have no blankets. The little children are freezing to death. My people, some of them, have run away to the hills and have no blankets, no food; no one knows where they are—perhaps freezing to death. I want to have time to look for my children and see how many of them I can find. Maybe I shall find them among the dead. Hear me, my chiefs. I am tired; my heart is sick and sad. From where the sun now stands, I will fight no more forever.

The final act of the Indian tragedy came in December 1890 in South Dakota. First, Sitting Bull was killed by an Indian police officer in a dispute over a controversial Indian religion. Two weeks later, a band of Sioux men, women, and children were arrested by white soldiers as they left their reservation. Fierce fighting broke out at **Wounded Knee**, killing 170 Sioux and 29 soldiers. Many more, including Indian women and children, were wounded.

In the end, the railroad, not the army, defeated the western Indians. The railroad carried the troops and the settlers. Even worse, it split the herds of buffalo and brought the hunters who systematically destroyed the animals for sport and business. The decline of the buffalo, from some 15 million at the close of the Civil War to only about 1,000 in 1889, made the Plains Indian way of life impossible.

The U.S. government then acted to officially destroy the Indians' way of life. In 1887 Congress passed the **Dawes Act**, which was designed to force the Indians to accept the values of white American culture. Tribal groups were dissolved, and group ownership of lands ended. Whatever its intentions, the Dawes Act doomed the Plains Indians to poverty. The land granted to them was infertile and difficult to farm. Too often the best land of the reservations went to greedy white settlers.

By 1900 the Native American population in the United States, which may have numbered

millions in the time of Columbus, had declined to 237,000. Although the Indians were seen as vanishing Americans, they never vanished altogether. Many Native Americans have kept their cultures alive to this day, and their populations have grown, reaching 1.5 million by the year 1990.

The frontier closed in 1890.

The story of the West between 1860 and 1900 is one of dramatic change. That change was not always perceived by the people who lived through it as progress. Some felt it as loss. The taming of the frontier, celebrated by white American society, was mourned as a tragedy by western Indians. The culture they had developed over centuries was almost completely destroyed. The buffalo that had roamed the Plains providing food, clothing, and shelter were virtually exterminated.

For white society, the frontier stood as a challenge to American self-sufficiency, inge-

This portrait of Chief Joseph, taken in 1903, illuminates his rocklike dignity and calm. An unswerving proponent of peace, the Nez Percé leader once proclaimed, "The earth and myself are of one mind."

THE LAST BUFFALO

What did this mean? Among other things, it meant that it was no longer possible to leave the mistakes of the past behind and move on to the "edge of the unused," to new lands and new hopes. Soon there would be no escaping the consequences of centuries of expansion. Of course, there was still unsettled land and many people continued to move west. Progress and change continued. In important ways, however, the closing of the frontier, like the ongoing eclipse of the small town, changed the way America defined itself. Two sets of American values, the self-confidence and individualism of the frontier family and the stability and morality of the small community, no longer seemed to belong as the 20th century began.

SECTION **2** REVIEW

Identify Key People and Terms
Write a sentence to identify: Chief Joseph, reservations, Sitting Bull, Crazy Horse, Battle of the Little Bighorn, Dawes Act

Locate Key Places
In which state is Wounded Knee located?

Master the Main Ideas

1. **Identifying the effect of European colonization on Native Americans:** How did western movement threaten the Indians' existence?
2. **Respecting the beliefs of other cultures:** What factors led to the end of the Indians' way of life?
3. **Examining patterns of settlement:** What did the closing of the western frontier mean to different groups of Americans?

Apply Critical Thinking Skills: Recognizing Values
In setting out westward, many white Americans saw the promise of hope and progress. By taming the western frontier, however, these same Americans trampled the lives of the Indians and changed the face of the western landscape. In what ways did the ethical values of Americans shape their progress westward? Support your answer with evidence.

Thomas Nast's *The Last Buffalo* appeared in *Harper's Weekly* in 1874, heralding the demise of this majestic beast. The cartoon caption read, "Don't shoot, my good fellow! Here, take my 'robe,' save your ammunition, and let me go in peace."

nuity, and as a symbol of opportunity. Transforming the frontier into farmland, creating towns and cities where none had been—these acts confirmed the American belief in progress. Because these changes on the frontier were seen as accomplishments and achievements, any sensitivity to the losses involved was generally dulled.

It is hard to imagine now, given our intense and urgent environmental concerns, that few 19th-century Americans ever gave thought to the consequences of their conquest of nature. No one seemed to even consider that the frontier itself would disappear. Yet it did. In 1890 the U.S. government declared the frontier officially "closed." There were farms, mines, and settlements in every corner of what was to become the continental United States. The westward movement, begun in 1607 on the shores of Virginia, was over.

Industrial growth affected the American way of life.

Key Terms: trunk lines, mass production

Reading Preview

As you read this section, you will learn:

1. how competition affected the railroad industry.
2. about technological advances that changed the American way of life.
3. how mass production affected the workplace.

The building of a transcontinental railroad network acted as a spur to the American free-enterprise economy. More than anything else, railroads transformed a continent of isolated communities into a unified nation with an interdependent economy. This American economy underwent expansive industrial growth, affecting the way people lived and worked.

Competition pushed the railroads to grow rapidly.

Growth on the railroads came rapidly. By 1870 railroad workers had laid almost 52,000 miles of track across America. Just five years later, the nation boasted some 74,000 miles. Within the next 15 years, the figure had doubled.

Despite the great length of track laid, the early railroads were strictly local. Many railroads extended fewer than 50 miles and their locations often followed no rule or reason. To avoid cooperating with other lines, they adopted conflicting schedules, built separate depots, and above all, used different gauges. Gauges, the distance between the rails, ranged from 4 feet 8 1/2 inches to 6 feet. Without special equipment, trains of one gauge could not run on tracks of another. Around 1865 passengers and cargo traveling between New York and Chicago had to be unloaded and reloaded as many as six times.

Gradually, however, four major rail lines, known as **trunk lines**, took shape, all intended to link eastern seaports with the rich traffic of the Great Lakes and western rivers. These trunk lines drew traffic from dozens of smaller feeder lines and carried it to major markets. The four were the Baltimore and Ohio (B & O), the Erie Railroad, the New York Central Railroad, and the Pennsylvania Railroad. Other major lines eventually tied the South into a national transportation network.

Over the country's united rail system, passengers and freight moved in relative speed, comfort, and safety. Accidents were still commonplace, but such advances as air brakes, refrigerator cars, heated cars, and stronger locomotives transformed railroad service. Passenger comfort improved further when George Pullman created luxury cars to be attached to passenger trains—sleeping cars, dining cars, and parlor cars. Slowly, other changes took place that simplified rail travel. The railroads adopted standard schedules, signals, equipment, and finally in 1886, a standard gauge.

In November 1883 the railroads even changed time. You can read about the change in *Voices from the Past* on page 277. Before the 1880s each location determined its time by the position of the sun. Even in cities fairly close together, clocks were set differently. New York City and Boston, for example, were 12 minutes apart, and Illinois alone had 27 different local times. To make rapid rail travel simpler, the railroad companies established four standard time zones, which are still in use today.

In their flurry of growth and improvement, the railroad companies often failed to see that they did not have enough passengers or freight to go around. Competition among rail lines was fierce, and managers fought desperately for business. They offered special rates and favors: free passes for large shippers, low rates on bulk freight, and above all, rebates—secret, privately negotiated reductions below published rates. Rate wars broke out frequently, and many railroad companies went out of business.

The survivors, also feeling the pinch of competition, turned to bankers, who imposed order on the industry. The head of a New York

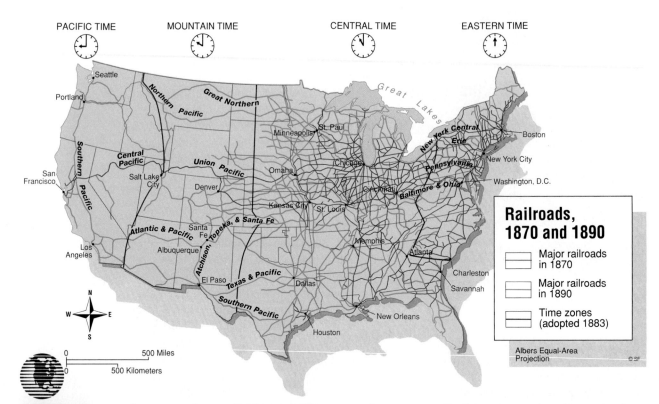

PACIFIC TIME   MOUNTAIN TIME   CENTRAL TIME   EASTERN TIME

Railroads, 1870 and 1890

Major railroads in 1870

Major railroads in 1890

Time zones (adopted 1883)

Albers Equal-Area Projection

0   500 Miles

0   500 Kilometers

map study

Movement The growth of railroads broke down the frontier. Railroads expanded into Texas, the far Southwest, and the Northwest—moving settlers, businesses, and government to these areas. How many time zones were set in 1883?

Critical Thinking Why were the time zones set up from east to west?

investment house, **J. Pierpont Morgan**, took the lead. Massively built, with eyes so piercing they seemed like the headlights of an onrushing train, Morgan was the most powerful figure in American finance. He liked efficiency, combination, and order and disliked "wasteful" competition. Morgan arranged traffic-sharing agreements, reorganized several railroad companies, and took over a half dozen other important railroads. By 1890 he dominated the American rail industry. For good or ill, a national transportation network, centralized and relatively efficient, was now in place.

Technological advances transformed American life.

In the late 19th century, technology dramatically changed the way in which most Americans lived. Bewildering as the changes sometimes were, the public generally welcomed new inventions with wide-eyed awe. Some of the most important public events of the time were devoted to new technology. For example, at the Philadelphia Centennial Exposition of 1876, visitors encountered for the first time a wild array of inventions: the gar-

gantuan Corliss steam engine, Alexander Graham Bell's telephone, the bicycle, the typewriter, the elevator, Charles Hires' root beer, and the "floor covering of the future"—easy-to-clean linoleum. You can see some of the same sights on page 278. By the time of the World's Columbian Exposition at Chicago in 1893, the Corliss engine was obsolete, and many of the miracles of 1876 were already commonplace necessities.

The impact of new inventions was enormous. Technological change affected the lives of people far more than any political developments of the time. For example, the invention of the typewriter in 1867 and the development of a practical adding machine in 1888 mechanized offices. Women moved increasingly into the field of clerical work, though they received lower pay and less prestige than men had enjoyed in the same field.

Innovations in communication also changed the nation, bringing people around the country in closer contact with one another. Links to the rest of the world also increased when a permanent transatlantic telegraph cable was completed in 1866. Inventions in the field of printing made popular newspapers with wide circulations a reality, along with mass advertising. Few innovations, though, rivaled Bell's invention of the telephone in 1876. By 1900 the telephone was seen as a necessity, and more than 1.5 million were installed.

Many of the new inventions relied upon cheap and efficient sources of electricity. Here **Thomas A. Edison** took the lead. Establishing a research lab at **Menlo Park, New Jersey**, in 1876, Edison promised to produce "a minor invention every ten days and a big thing every six months or so." He very nearly kept his promise, inventing the phonograph in 1877 and the incandescent light bulb in 1879, as well as hundreds of other devices. In the process, he obtained more than 1,000 patents.

Mass production techniques altered how and where people worked.

Changes in technology also affected how people worked. Inventors developed machines that displaced many skilled workers and farmers. In their place came workers whose pay came increasingly from a large company. In 1880, instead of going to a small shop each morning, most workers entered a newly built factory filled with the noise and activity of hundreds of employees. Instead of spending the day creating a product from start to finish, making a shoe or crafting a tool, most workers passed their hours performing one task in the production process, over and over again. Often, they were aided and directed by a machine. The new process, known as **mass production**, was efficient, for more goods than ever were produced and at a cheaper rate. Mass production, though, was at the very least a boring work pattern. Because each function was planned and routinized, the workers lost any opportunity to use their own judgment about production. Factory supervisors made the decisions that individual artisans or craftspeople had once made for themselves about productivity and work routines, hours, and pace. In turn, these supervisors were dependent upon the factory owners who set quotas and determined workplace policies.

VOICES FROM THE PAST

The Sun is Demoted

Railroads officially "synchronized their watches" at noon on November 18, 1883, when Standard Time went into effect. One writer joked that the changeover made everyone in Boston 16 minutes younger. To many Americans, however, this was no laughing matter. The editorial writer of the Indianapolis Sentinel *was not alone in contending that the railroads had at last gone too far. What is the basis of the writer's objections?*

The sun is no longer boss of the job. People—55,000,000 of them—must eat, sleep, and work as well as travel by railroad time. It is a revolt, a rebellion. The sun will be requested to rise and set by railroad time. . . . People will have to marry by railroad time, and die by railroad time. Ministers will be required to preach by railroad time.

Work in a factory was tiring and the hours were long. Before 1900 men, women, and even children spent 10 to 15 hours a day, six and sometimes seven days a week, in the factory or mill. If skilled, they earned about 20 cents an hour, but without skills, just half that. On average they earned between $400 and $500 a year, at a time when it took about $600 to live decently. Few could count on a steady income, for jobs could be lost without warning.

Young people accounted for much of the factory labor. By 1900 about 1.8 million children worked for wages. For example, in Paterson, New Jersey, an important industrial city, about half of all boys and girls aged 11 to 14 had jobs.

Work was not only grueling, but also highly dangerous. Safety standards were low, and accidents were common. Thousands of workers suffered from chronic illness, a result of their unknowing contact with dust, chemicals, and pollutants. The workers' pain, sweat, and misery, however, powered much of America's push for a strong industrial economy.

The Philadelphia Centennial Exposition attracted a wide range of exhibits. The Corliss engine, far right, awed visitors with its massive size. The world's first modern typewriter, the Remington No. 1, below right, also inspired curiosity—but no buyers. The most memorable foreign exhibit was from Japan. As Japanese workers built a teahouse and bazaar, above, many Americans mocked them. However, upon seeing the completed exhibit, this disparaging attitude changed to open admiration. The year 1876 thus marked the beginning of a lasting Japanese influence on American architecture and design.

SECTION 3 REVIEW

Identify Key People and Terms
Write a sentence to identify: trunk lines, J. Pierpont Morgan, Thomas A. Edison, mass production

Locate Key Places
Where did Thomas Edison establish his research lab?

Master the Main Ideas

1. **Supporting economic competition:** How did America's railroads grow into a national transportation network in the late 1800s?
2. **Assessing the impact of technological innovations:** In what ways did the sweeping technological advances transform American life in the late 1800s?
3. **Assessing the impact of technological innovations:** How did mass production techniques change American work patterns?

Apply Critical Thinking Skills: Drawing Conclusions
The technological changes that swept the late 1800s meant new ways of living and working to most Americans. In what ways do the scientific and technological advances of our times affect the way you live today? Think of ways in which technology has changed your life in the past five years. Draw a conclusion about how Americans respond to such changes.

SECTION **4**

America experienced massive economic growth.

Key Terms: Social Darwinism, capital, corporation, dividends, limited liability, pool, trust, monopoly

Reading Preview
As you read this section, you will learn:
1. how religious and social principles affected the growth of industrial America.
2. why the corporation developed.
3. why trusts were formed.
4. what pattern the economy developed.

The American free-enterprise economy quickly moved into high gear. Factory production soared, until, by the turn of the century, the United States was producing almost as much as England, France, and Germany combined. This extraordinary industrial growth changed the face of America.

Religious and social principles created an environment for growth.

The industrial growth of the late 1800s, though bountiful, did not come easily. New figures dominated this period—"captains of industry," to some, "robber barons" to others—who controlled the major industries of the nation and much of American society as well. The wealth of such leaders as Andrew Carnegie and John D. Rockefeller was legendary and their power absolute. Their actions, however, brought ruin to their competitors and poverty to many Americans. Ruthlessness not only became increasingly necessary for financial success, it was also transformed into a virtue by two social principles of the era—Social Darwinism and the Gospel of Wealth. These two theories, along with the principle of laissez-faire economics, combined to provide an environment rich in support for growth, whatever the cost to the American people.

Social Darwinism. The new doctrine of **Social Darwinism** was drawn from the biological concepts of Charles Darwin. The British philosopher Herbert Spencer wrote that a process was at work in society that was similar to Darwin's concept of natural selection in the animal world. The "survival of the fittest"—a phrase invented by Spencer, not Darwin—preserved the strong in society and weeded out the weak. Within this framework, survival of the fittest was thought to enrich not only the winners but society as a whole.

For such wealthy industrial giants as Andrew Carnegie of **Pittsburgh**, the work of the Social Darwinists helped to relieve any unwelcome guilt they may have felt about poverty in society. It allowed them to overlook the profound misery to be found in urban slums, and even to argue against any governmental or charitable aid to improve the conditions of the poor.

Gospel of Wealth. Some business leaders who found the ruthlessness of Social Darwinism too distasteful turned instead to the Gospel of Wealth. This religious rationale for wealth rested on the Protestant work ethic that viewed success as evidence of being among God's chosen people.

Carnegie became a strong supporter of this principle. He wrote,

Not evil, but good, has come to the race from the accumulation of wealth by those who have the ability and energy that produces it.

AN AMERICAN ★ SPEAKS

Carnegie took the concept one step further by saying that society's fittest had both the talent and responsibility for deciding what was best for society. He put his beliefs into action with charitable works.

Laissez-faire economics. In 1776 Adam Smith's *The Wealth of Nations* presented arguments that would long be used to explain the workings of a free economy and government's role in that economy. Smith believed that the market was directed and controlled by an "invisible hand" made up of a multitude of individual choices. In effect, if everyone were left free to act in their own self-interest, the result should be an economy best suited to

279

meet the needs of the general society, with supply and demand in balance.

Acceptance of the invisible hand theory led to a policy called "laissez-faire," from the French "to let one do." This policy held that government's proper role was to leave the economy alone. Supporters of laissez-faire economics believed that any government interference would disrupt the natural forces at work in the economy. Business leaders naturally agreed with the notion that government should not regulate their industries. At the same time, however, they saw no contradiction in asking for government aid to foster industrial development. In the end the business leaders got what they wanted—a laissez-faire policy that left them alone, except when they wanted financial help.

The corporation developed to meet changing economic demands.

As American industries grew, new demands were placed on businesses. To establish and run all of America's new industries, huge amounts of capital were needed. **Capital** is the amount of money, property, or other resources a company or person uses to carry on a business. Factories had to be built, expensive machinery had to be installed and maintained, and thousands of workers had to be paid. No single individual had the resources to begin such a business. The solution lay in the adaptation of a form of group ownership and investment, the corporation.

A **corporation** is a type of business organization that is created when three or more people apply for a charter or license from a state government. Under this charter of incorporation, they are allowed to sell shares in the company in order to raise capital. In return for investing their money, the shareholders receive **dividends**, which are a portion of the company's yearly profits.

The corporation had other advantages as well. The courts defined the corporation as separate from the people who owned it. This meant that the corporation could make its own contracts, buy and sell property, or take legal action in court. This definition also granted stockholders **limited liability**, which meant that if the corporation failed, a stockholder was responsible only for the amount of money he or she had originally invested. Limited liability encouraged investment and also allowed the corporation to take risks. Today the corporation remains the most important form of business organization.

Trusts were formed to limit competition in the business world.

Most American entrepreneurs had been raised to believe that competition was the key to American prosperity. Yet, competition made their businesses unpredictable and risky. Thus, in the 1870s and 1880s, they began a steady trend away from competition and toward a form of cooperation. The results sometimes troubled both reformers and consumers and challenged the free-enterprise basis of the American economy.

The first signs of the shift came early, as corporations within the same industry began to consolidate, that is, to merge or combine, so that they could create larger, more powerful, and more stable businesses. These mergers occurred in most of America's major industries, including steel, oil, sugar refining, tobacco, leather, meat packing, and manufacturing. The results were the same in each case: competition was limited or eliminated.

Consolidation took several forms. The railroads introduced one of the earliest forms of cooperation, the **pool**. Companies in a pool remained independent, but they divided up the market and agreed on rates and charges. The railroad owners argued that the pool was a rational step, but other Americans saw it as a conspiracy to raise prices and profits. In 1887 the U.S. government outlawed pools, declaring them to be against the public interest.

After the pool was banned, businesses made use of the trust. In a **trust**, the major stockholders of several companies turned over their shares to "trustees" in return for certificates promising them dividend payments. The trustees, who now held a majority of the shares in the companies, were able to control the policies of each company. In other words, the trus-

19TH-CENTURY TRUSTS
Skill: Formulating Appropriate Questions

Introducing the Skill. In the late 1800s, trusts gained in power and influence. The individuals who headed them came to control both a staggering percentage of the nation's wealth and a wide range of industries. As a result, many Americans became increasingly concerned about the potential for abuse that such power and wealth carry. How might you determine whether or not abuses occurred?

Learning the Skill. To test for such abuses, you must **formulate appropriate questions** by which to seek the information you need. To be effective, your questions need two features.

First, they must be appropriate, that is, fitting, to your task or purpose. Different questions serve different purposes and will elicit different responses. For instance, if your purpose is to find out if a trust is harmful to the American public, then questions about the trustees' leisure activities would not be appropriate.

Second, your questions must fit your source and type of information. If you are interviewing John D. Rockefeller, the head of the Standard Oil trust, effective questions would focus on areas of concern in which Rockefeller had information available. Different questions would need to be posed if you were interviewing consumers, studying corporate records, or reviewing stock market prices.

Applying the Skill.

1. Study the political cartoon on this page. What view does the cartoonist hold of the relationship between trusts and the U.S. Senate?

2. Imagine that you are a political reporter in the late 1800s, investigating reports that the trusts unfairly influenced the actions of senators. Who or what might you target for your research?

3. Formulate a list of ten questions with which to make your investigation. Consider a number of interview subjects and research sources. Make sure that the questions are appropriate both to your purpose—verifying the influence of trusts—and to your chosen source of information.

The industrial trusts of the late 1800s made their size and power well known in the U.S. Senate.

matic way, these depressions brought home to Americans the changes in their economic environment. The economic islands of the early 19th century, with their local markets and local production centers, were gone. In their place was a national market, with large corporations controlling entire industries. Decisions made in distant parts of the country affected everyone. What J. P. Morgan did in New York, or Carnegie in Pittsburgh, truly had an impact on the lives of farmers in Kansas and school-teachers in California.

A hungry Standard Oil Company extends its tentacles of influence. As the head of Standard Oil, John D. Rockefeller created a trust with far-flung holdings and immense power.

tees could run several large firms as if they were one giant company. The major stockholders profited because a trust could make deals more easily with suppliers of raw materials, with railroads, and with banks.

What was to the advantage of the trusts, however, was not necessarily in the best interests of the ordinary American consumer. Through consolidation, a trust could destroy smaller companies within the same industry. The final result was a **monopoly**, which meant that a trust had complete control over an industry—production, supply, quality, price, and workers' wages.

The economy developed a pattern of boom and bust.

With the aid of investment bankers such as J. P. Morgan, American business and industry grew, but it did not grow steadily or smoothly. On occasion, production of a certain good was greater than the consumer demand. The over-supply that resulted led to declining profits and frequently to corporate bankruptcy. The post–Civil War economy began to resemble a roller coaster ride, and its alternating periods of expansion and contraction became known as "booms" and "busts."

When the busts hit, millions suffered. The depressions of 1873, 1884, and 1893 were each worse than the one that preceded it. In a dra-

SECTION **4** REVIEW

Identify Key People and Terms
Write a sentence to identify: Social Darwinism, capital, corporation, dividends, limited liability, pool, trust, monopoly

Locate Key Places
Where was Andrew Carnegie's empire based?

Master the Main Ideas

1. **Examining religious motivations:** How did wealthy industrial leaders use religious and social principles to foster economic growth?
2. **Understanding economic development:** In what ways was the corporation a response to the industrial development of the late 19th century?
3. **Analyzing information: (a)** Why did corporations of the late 1800s create trusts? **(b)** What were some of their techniques?
4. **Analyzing information:** Describe the pattern that emerged in the economy during the late 19th century.

Apply Critical Thinking Skills: Drawing Conclusions
In what ways did the rampant consolidation of businesses in the late 19th century run counter to the principles on which the American economy was based? Give examples to support your answer.

Immigrants challenged American society.

Key Terms: nativism, xenophobia, Chinese Exclusion Act

Reading Preview
As you read this section, you will learn:

1. how the new immigrants compared to those who came before them.
2. how the new immigrants were received.
3. how the immigrants created new lives for themselves.

The growth experienced by America's industries was fueled largely by new arrivals to the United States. Between 1877 and 1890, some six million immigrants poured into the nation, many finding work in factories, steel mills, and packing plants. Their reasons for coming to the United States were many. Some came to escape intolerable conditions at home, others came to work and earn some money for their families. Still others came seeking the promise of America, the hope for a better future for them and for their children. The words of Emma Lazarus, which were placed on a plaque at the base of the Statue of Liberty in 1903, spoke to many a weary traveler as they made their way to **Ellis Island**, the reception center for immigrants entering the United States at New York City:

Give me your tired, your poor,
Your huddled masses yearning to breathe free,
The wretched refuse of your teeming shore.
Send these, the homeless, tempest-tossed to me,

I lift my lamp beside the golden door.

Immigrants of the late 1800s were different from previous newcomers.

Despite the statue's words of welcome and promise, the immigrants who entered the United States at the end of the 19th century were not always greeted with open arms. The country that was built upon the ideals and labor of immigrants was now having second thoughts about extending the invitation of citizenship to others.

An important difference was the immigrants themselves. During the 1880s a shift occurred in the origins of America's immigrants. Before this time, immigrants to this country had come primarily from northern and western Europe—England, Ireland, France, Germany, and Scandinavia. They were always white, mostly literate, and except for the Irish and some Germans who were Roman Catholic, mostly Protestant. They were also accustomed to living under a constitutional government. Assimilation into American society was relatively easy for them.

By contrast, the new immigrants came mainly from eastern and southern Europe and from Asia—Greeks, Poles, Russians, Italians, Slavs, Turks. They found blending into the existing culture much more difficult. The new immigrants were different both from earlier immigrants and from native-born Americans in several significant ways. They brought a new set of political, religious, and cultural values. In addition, their reasons for leaving Europe or Asia and their visions of America led them to seek out new variations of the American promise.

Essentially two types of immigrants came to America at this time—migrant workers and permanent settlers. The migrant workers, often called birds of passage, never intended to make the United States their home. Unable to earn a living in their home country, they came to America, worked and saved, and then returned home. Most were young men in their teens and twenties, principally Italian, Chinese, Greek, or Mexican. The permanent settlers, several million of them, came with no intention of ever returning to the land of their birth. They came with their families, looking for political and religious freedom and economic opportunity. The Jews who fled nearly unbearable hardships in Poland and Russia were typical of this group of immigrants.

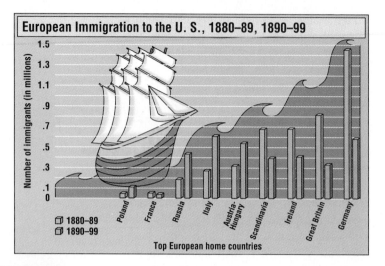

European Immigration to the U. S., 1880–89, 1890–99

Number of immigrants (in millions)

1.5
1.3
1.1
.9
.7
.5
.3
.1
0

Poland, France, Russia, Italy, Austria-Hungary, Scandinavia, Ireland, Great Britain, Germany

☐ 1880–89
☐ 1890–99

Top European home countries

chart study

Ethnic sheet music was one of the signs of America's growing immigrant population. How did the source of immigration from Europe change from one decade to the next?
Critical Thinking
Why might this change have occurred?

Mary Antin, a Jewish girl from Russia, was one of the new permanent immigrants. In 1894, when she was 13 years old, Mary left her home in Polotzk, Russia, to be reunited with her father, who had emigrated three years earlier to Boston. To reach the freedom that they yearned for in America, Mary, her mother, and her three sisters endured a long and grueling voyage. At one point in a train ride across Germany, Mary recalled a scene of:

Bewildering confusion, parents losing their children, and   **AN AMERICAN ★ SPEAKS** little ones crying; baggage being thrown together in one corner of the yard, heedless of contents . . . the confused passengers obeying all orders like meek children, only questioning now and then what was going to be done with them.

Eventually, Mary arrived in Boston, only to be frustrated by the slow efforts of the customs officials. They asked "a hundred or so stupid questions," examined all of their baggage, and checked their health—but finally they let the Antins pass into Boston. At long last, Mary had reached America, which, to her mind, was "like a nest to homeless birds."

The new immigrants were met with hostility.

At this point in American history, when economic hard times came frequently, the new immigrants were not warmly welcomed. Na-tive-born Americans were both suspicious and resentful of immigrants, especially those from southern and eastern Europe. If American business leaders saw in the immigrants a bottomless pool of cheap labor, other Americans saw something different.

Anti-immigrant attitudes, called **nativism**, took many forms. Workers saw competition, in particular competition that was willing to work for lower wages. Protestants saw Catholics and Jews. Educators saw illiterate hordes. Politicians saw peasants, unfamiliar with the workings of democracy and a constitutional government. Still others saw dark-skinned, thick-browed peoples whom they considered inferior and possibly dangerous.

In short, many Americans developed a sense of **xenophobia**, a hatred or fear of foreigners or strangers. They acted accordingly. They posted signs that read, "No Jews or Dogs Allowed." They called the Chinese "coolies" and the Italians "wops" and "dagos," all derogatory names. The ethnic jokes that still surface today have their roots in this period of ethnic hostility and violence.

The fears of Americans led the U.S. government to enact several laws in the late 1800s that restricted immigration. The Chinese were the first to feel the golden door closing on them. In 1882 the **Chinese Exclusion Act** suspended Chinese immigration for ten years and dramatically restricted the rights of the Chinese already in the United States. The act, which was later extended, demonstrated the lengths to which nativism and racism could go and set a precedent for the future exclusion of other immigrants.

The new immigrants forged new lives with religion and education.

Once firmly in the United States, the new immigrants faced a world vastly different from the one they left. An unfamiliar language, new freedoms, and a different set of customs all forced these new Americans to adjust and adapt. They did so in remarkable ways.

Most new immigrants settled in America's growing cities, where unskilled factory labor was much in demand. As a walk through the ethnically diverse cities of New York, Chicago, Miami, or Los Angeles would show you even today, the immigrants began to shape the cities around them. Most new arrivals tried to balance the old and the new—retaining their traditional culture for their families while also adapting to life in their new country. To do this, they spoke their native language, practiced their religion, and read their own newspapers. Tightly knit ethnic communities developed in many of America's large cities.

Immigrant associations sprang up to help the newcomers. Groups such as the Polish National Alliance provided assistance in finding housing and work, offered insurance plans, and sponsored such community activities as baseball teams and youth programs.

Religion and education were two important means of support for the immigrants. For many Polish and Irish immigrants, the Roman Catholic Church offered spiritual guidance, education, and a sense of community. Another group of immigrants, Eastern European Jews, established synagogues and religious schools wherever they settled, teaching the Hebrew language and raising their children with a Jewish heritage.

For Mary Antin, the young Jewish immigrant, education was her father's "chief hope for [his] children, the essence of American opportunity." In America, this too was possible, and free to all. For Mary, her introduction to American education was a special treat, a step on her way to becoming the author of the book *Promised Land.*

Father himself conducted us to school. He would not have delegated that mission to the President of the United States. He had awaited the day with impatience equal to mine. . . . At last the four of us stood around the teacher's desk; and my father, in his impossible English, gave us over in her charge, with some broken word of his hopes for us that his swelling heart could no longer contain. . . . I think Miss Nixon guessed what my father's best English could not convey. I think she divined that by the simple act of delivering our school certificates to her he took possession of America.

SECTION **5** REVIEW

Identify Key People and Terms
Write a sentence to identify: nativism, xenophobia, Chinese Exclusion Act

Locate Key Places
What purpose did Ellis Island serve?

Master the Main Ideas

1. **Analyzing reasons for immigration:** How did the new immigrants differ from the old?
2. **Analyzing reactions to immigration:** What was the prevailing attitude of native-born Americans toward the new immigrants?
3. **Synthesizing information:** In what ways did the immigrants create their new lives in America's cities?

Apply Critical Thinking Skills: Distinguishing False from Accurate Images
For many years people thought of the United States as a melting pot, in which immigrants of various backgrounds blended together into a common American culture. Recently, however, people have been referring to the country as a salad, in which the different ingredients come together in a bowl while still retaining their individual qualities. In this image, immigrants to the United States create together an interesting mix of cultures. Which image do you find to be the more accurate in the United States today? Use evidence to support your answer.

Immigrant children learn to salute the American flag in a New York City school around 1889. As this photograph by the Danish American journalist and reformer Jacob Riis (1849–1914) suggests, urban schools were important centers for sharing both old and new culture and knowledge.

Joseph McCoy Describes a Stampede

TIME FRAME
Late 1860s–early 1870s

GEOGRAPHIC SETTING
Great Plains

In 1867 Joseph G. McCoy (1837–1915), who was in the cattle business in Illinois, went to Texas with the hope of getting beef from the southwest for the northern and eastern markets, where there was a great scarcity and consequently high prices. In Texas he found vast herds of longhorn steers. Cut off from markets by the Civil War, they had little value and had been allowed to run wild. His idea was to drive these cattle hundreds of miles north to Abilene, Kansas, to be loaded on railroad cars and shipped east. The first cattle drive along this route, which became known as the "Chisholm Trail," took place in September 1867, and by 1872 1.5 million steers had reached Abilene. In the following excerpt from McCoy's book, *Historic Sketches of the Cattle Trade of the West and Southwest* (1874), he described one of the worst hazards of the cattle drive, a stampede.

W e left the herd fairly started upon the trail for the northern market. Of these trails there are several, one leading to Baxter Springs and Chetopa, another called the "old Shawnee trail" leaving Red River and running eastward, crossing the

Racing through a thunderstorm on the Great Plains, cowboys attempt to regain control of a runaway herd of cattle in *Stampeded by Lightning* (1908), a painting by Frederic Remington (1861–1909), an American artist famous for his depictions of life in the Old West.

Courtesy of the Thomas Gilcrease Institute of American History and Art, Tulsa, Oklahoma.

Arkansas not far above Fort Gibson, thence bending westward up the Arkansas River; but the principal trail now traveled is more direct and is known as "Chisholm trail," so named from a semi-civilized Indian who is said to have traveled it first. It is more direct, has more prairie, less timber, more small streams and less large ones, and altogether better grass and fewer flies—no civilized Indian tax or wild Indian disturbances—than any other route yet driven over, and is also much shorter in distance because direct from Red River to Kansas. Twenty-five to thirty-five days is the usual time required to bring a drove from Red River to the southern line of Kansas, a distance of between 250 and 300 miles, and an excellent country to drive over. So many cattle have been driven over the trail in the last few years that a broad highway is tread out looking much like a national highway; so plain, a fool could not fail to keep in it.

Few occupations are more cheerful, lively and pleasant than that of the cowboy on a fine day or night; but when the storm comes, then is his manhood and often his skill and bravery put to test. When the night is inky dark and the lurid lightning flashes its zig-zag course athwart the heavens, and the coarse thunder jars the earth, the winds moan fresh and lively over the prairie, the electric balls dance from tip to tip of the cattle's horns—then the position of the cowboy on duty is trying far more than romantic.

When the storm breaks over his head, the least occurrence unusual, such as the breaking of a dry weed or stick, or a sudden and near flash of lightning, will start the herd, as if by magic, all at an instant, upon a wild rush, and woe to the horse, or man, or camp that may be in their path. The only possible show for safety is to mount and ride with them until you can get outside the stampeding column. It is customary to train cattle to listen to the noise of the herder, who sings in a voice more sonorous than musical a lullaby consisting of a few short monosyllables. A stranger to the business of stock-driving will scarce credit the statement that the wildest herd will not run so long as they can hear distinctly the voice of the herder above the din of the storm. But if by any mishap the herd gets off on a real stampede, it is by bold, dashing, reckless riding in the darkest of nights, and by adroit, skillful management that it is checked and brought under control. The moment the herd is off, the cowboy turns his horse at full speed down the retreating column, and seeks to get up beside the leaders, which he does not attempt to stop suddenly, for such an effort would be futile, but turns them to the left or right hand, and gradually curves them into a circle, the circumference of which is narrowed down as fast as possible, until the whole herd is rushing wildly round and round on as small a piece of ground as possible for them to occupy. Then the cowboy begins his lullaby note in a loud voice, which has a great effect in quieting the herd. When all is still, and the herd well over its scare, they are returned to their bed-ground, or held where stopped until daylight.

Discussing the Reading

1. According to Joseph McCoy, why is it critical that the cowboys train the herd to listen to their voices? What might happen if the cattle could no longer hear the voices of the cowboys?

2. What strategy did McCoy say was used by cowboys to control a stampede?

CRITICAL THINKING
Recognizing Bias

What attitude does Joseph McCoy appear to have had toward Native Americans? Cite lines from the reading to support your answer.

The Buffalo Go

TIME FRAME
1860s–1880s

GEOGRAPHIC SETTING
Great Plains

The traditional way of life of the Plains Indians had centered on hunting the buffalo, which provided most of their food, as well as raw material for clothing, shelter, and other needs. Beginning in the 1860s, this way of life was destroyed by the coming of the railroads to the Great Plains. The railroads transported the troops that fought the Plains tribes, as well as the farmers, ranchers, and other settlers who entered tribal lands. More importantly, the railroads brought the professional hunters and sportsmen who systematically destroyed the buffalo. By 1885 the once vast herds had been reduced to around 1,000 surviving animals. In the following folktale, Old Lady Horse, a woman of the Kiowa [kī′ə wə] people of the southern Great Plains, described the departure of the last of the buffalo.

E verything the Kiowas had came from the buffalo. Their tipis were made of buffalo hides, so were their clothes and moccasins. They ate buffalo meat. Their

5 containers were made of hide, or of bladders or stomachs. The buffalo were the life of the Kiowas.

Most of all, the buffalo were part of the Kiowa religion. A white buffalo calf must 10 be sacrificed in the Sun Dance. The priests used parts of the buffalo to make their prayers when they healed people or when they sang to the powers above.

So, when the white men wanted to 15 build railroads, or when they wanted to farm or raise cattle, the buffalo still protected the Kiowas. They tore up the

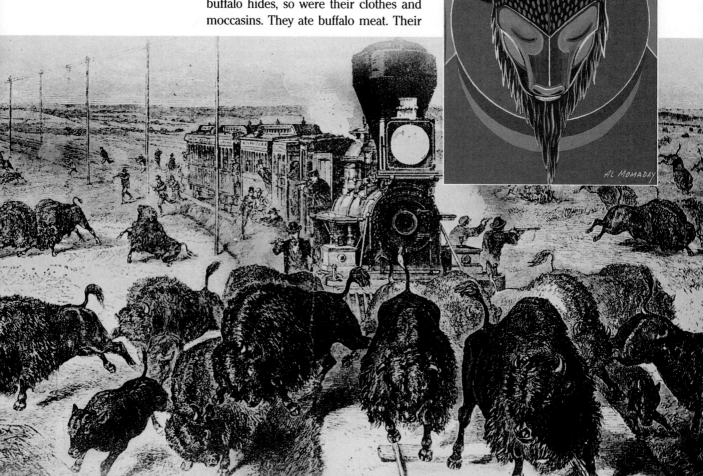

railroad tracks and the gardens. They chased the cattle off the ranges. The buffalo loved their people as much as the Kiowas loved them.

There was war between the buffalo and the white men. The white men built forts in the Kiowa country, and the woolly-headed buffalo soldiers [African American cavalrymen] shot the buffalo as fast as they could, but the buffalo kept coming on, coming on, even into the post cemetery at Fort Sill [Oklahoma]. Soldiers were not enough to hold them back.

Then the white men hired hunters to do nothing but kill the buffalo. Up and down the plains those men ranged, shooting sometimes as many as a hundred buffalo a day. Behind them came the skinners with their wagons. They piled the hides and bones into the wagons until they were full, and then took their loads to the new railroad stations that were being built, to be shipped east to the market. Sometimes there would be a pile of bones as high as a man, stretching a mile along the railroad track.

The buffalo saw that their day was over. They could protect their people no longer. Sadly, the last remnant of the great herd gathered in council, and decided what they would do.

The Kiowas were camped on the north side of Mount Scott, those of them who were still free to camp. One young woman got up very early in the morning. The dawn mist was still rising from Medicine Creek, and as she looked across the water, peering through the haze, she saw the last buffalo herd appear like a spirit dream.

Straight to Mount Scott the leader of the herd walked. Behind him came the cows and their calves, and the few young males who had survived. As the woman watched, the face of the mountain opened.

Inside Mount Scott the world was green and fresh, as it had been when she was a small girl. The rivers ran clear, not red. The wild plums were in blossom, chasing the red buds up the inside slopes. Into this world of beauty the buffalo walked, never to be seen again.

Buffalo are slaughtered by hunters riding a train, in the picture from *Frank Leslie's Illustrated Newspaper* (June 3, 1871) shown below on the facing page. Above is a painting of a buffalo by the Kiowa artist Al Momaday. The photograph below shows an immense pile of buffalo hides stacked up at Dodge City, Kansas, in 1874.

Discussing the Reading

1. According to Old Lady Horse, was the buffalo more than simply a source of the necessities of life for the Kiowa? Explain.

2. In the young woman's vision of the "world of beauty," (lines 63–69), how was the appearance of the rivers different from those of the Great Plains? Explain the reason for this difference.

CRITICAL THINKING
Distinguishing Fact from Opinion

Like many folk tales, Old Lady Horse's story is a mixture of myth and fact. Decide whether each of the following details from the story was mythical or factual.
a. The buffalo destroyed the settlers' gardens.
b. The buffalo loved the Kiowa.
c. Mile-long piles of buffalo bones lined the railroad tracks.
d. The buffalo disappeared into Mount Scott.

"Don't Come Back Till You Sell Them All"

TIME FRAME
Around 1900

GEOGRAPHIC SETTING
New York City

A Polish immigrant girl recalled her first experience as a street peddler in the following anonymous account. Growing up in New York's Lower East Side at the turn of the century, her previous contact with peddlers had been only as a customer. Her father, a tailor who was "experiencing one of his idle periods," tried to earn some money sewing petticoats, which she was directed to sell.

M other was having a Baby in an East Broadway Maternity Hospital. So I became the cook. Also, standing on a box, I scrubbed the children's overalls and
5 stockings. My dad was experiencing one of his idle periods.

He sat at his sewing machine, thinking of his father in the Old Country; he, too, had sat at just such a sewing-machine;
10 and what did he make? Petticoats! So be it! If it was good enough for his father, it would be good enough for him! He took his last few dollars that he had saved to get mother out of the hospital, and bought
15 some white calico and yards of white lace and began to make some petticoats. Perhaps he could sell them quickly before mother came home from the hospital; but who could sell them on a push-cart for
20 him? He swallowed a dry tear in his throat and called me with downcast eyes.

"Here, take these down across the street and put them on a paper on the sidewalk. Whatever they will offer you for
25 them, take it; maybe 25¢ or 35¢ or even

15¢ but don't come back without money; don't come back till you sell them all."

I was dumbfounded. Me... did he mean me? I should sell them like a street
30 peddler? What would my poor mother think, in the hospital there, if she knew? Mama! I screamed and ran down the steps, as though possessed. Hugging the bundle close to my heart, I flopped down
35 on the last step in the dark hall—and thought to myself—Lillian, next door— she has no father, her mother has a push- cart, just downstairs—they eat every day—I saw them myself through the fire-
40 escape window, yesterday.—They seemed happy, and unashamed, even proud! Lillian helps her mother some- times at the pushcart, when her mother goes to buy chicken. How will my mother
45 feel? She won't know. I whispered to my- self; we must eat too . . . the kids are hun- gry and yesterday we made hamburgers; today I don't see any meat in the store.

Stoically I arose, put out my chest, and
50 crossed the street, walked a few feet, lest someone who knew me should see me, and determined, set my wares on the ground. In a few minutes women began

Lined with stalls and pushcarts, bustling Hester Street (shown in the photograph on the facing page) was the heart of the Jewish neighborhood in New York's Lower East Side. The photograph of a bread vendor's stall on this page was taken by the Danish American journalist and reformer Jacob Riis [rēs] (1849–1914), famous for his crusade against slum conditions in New York.

picking at them. "Such fine work! How
much? Poor child, don't you know? I'll
give you 20¢, but really you can get from
someone else maybe 35¢; maybe even
50¢." I sold her two of them. A little more
courageous, then, I sold some at 35¢ and
eventually some with a little soil, at 15¢.
Late into the night, I stood there, afraid to
go home without a complete sell out; until
it commenced to rain . . . Then I sold out
at any price, and hurriedly pushed my way
through the crowds, back across to my father. What his thoughts were while I was
away, I cannot say. He said not a word,
pocketed the money and the next day, he
sent me for my mother. He was too proud
to be annoyed by charity and could not
bear the questions they asked. He just
would not go and lower himself; that is all
there was to it.

Discussing the Reading

1. What seems to have been the father's attitude toward sewing petticoats? Toward having his daughter
peddle them on the street?

2. What appears to have been the principal reason for the girl's reluctance
to peddle the clothing her father had
made?

CRITICAL THINKING
Recognizing Values

In this young Polish immigrant's account of her first experience as a
street peddler, there are several indications of what values her family regarded as important. What are these
values? Cite lines from the reading to
support your answer.

Japanese "Picture-Brides" Adjust to America

6D

TIME FRAME
1890s–1920s

GEOGRAPHIC SETTING
Far West and Midwest

The great majority of the first Japanese immigrants that came to the United States were males; in the years immediately after 1900, for example, they outnumbered female immigrants 6 to 1. When these men wanted to marry, those who could afford to returned to Japan to find wives. Some of the others employed the "picture-bride" system, in which friends or relatives back in Japan arranged a marriage after the immigrant and his prospective wife had exchanged photographs. According to Bill Hosokawa's history of the Japanese in the United States, *Nisei: The Quiet Americans,* "Such marriages were usually solemnized by proxy. Under Japanese law a woman was considered married when her name was entered on her husband's family record, strictly a bookkeeping process." The following excerpt from Hosokawa's book describes the picture-bride system. (The Japanese refer to immigrants as *Issei* [ē′sā′], "first generation"; the children of the Issei are the *Nisei* [nē′sā′], "second generation.")

The picture-bride system provides intensely interesting human studies. Both parties to a proxy marriage were anxious, of course, to put on the best face possible both before and at the time of meeting. Men and girls from the same village who were matched were likely to know at least something about each other. But often brides and grooms, seeing each other for the first time at dockside, discovered that the marriage partner looked nothing like the photograph submitted for examination. A bald or gray-haired man was likely to be photographed with his hat on. Men who did not have a decent suit to their names were photographed in borrowed or rented outfits. A butler or a janitor might be photographed in front of the mansion or factory building where he worked, and if he neglected to provide the details, it was easy for the bride to assume that in the wonderful land of America where everyone was wealthy, her husband owned the building. It was not unusual for brides to learn the husband was a virtually penniless laborer, an itinerant farmhand or a coarse, uncultured misfit. On the other hand, many was the man who dreamed of a tender, gentle mate and found he had drawn a shrew. One *Issei* woman recalls that her husband met her in San Francisco and took her home to a sod house on the Nebraska prairie. She could not understand that many Caucasian farmers in the Midwest of that time were living in soddies because of the shortage of lumber, and that the soddies were comfortably cool in summer and warm in winter. "You made me come all the way across the Pacific to live in a hole in the ground like a wild animal?" she raged. Some of the women never got over their disappointments—"I wept for ten years, and then I gave up," said one—but a surprising number quickly made adjustments as pioneer women from other lands had done before them. The development of genuine love matches was not at all unusual.

Yoshito Fujii, [a] Seattle hotel operator . . . , recalls that the innkeepers had a busy time of it during the picture-bride period. Days before a ship was due, the bridegrooms would come into the city from farms and sawmill camps and engage a room. They would be waiting anxiously at dockside when the ship approached, some duded up with derbies and walking sticks, searching the girls lined along the rail for a face they could recognize. Usually it took several days for the brides to clear immigration, and each day the men would congregate outside the immigration station hoping for a glimpse of their brides.

Chojiro Fujii [an earlier immigrant], who was an old hand and well-known to the immigration authorities, would be showered with questions each time he emerged from the building with a bride who had been cleared. She and her husband, shy and awkward in each other's presence, would be whisked to the Fujii Hotel. There she was quickly taken to an outfitter in the same building and provided with a complete set of American clothing and her feet, broadened by a lifetime of freedom in sandals, were jammed into the narrow, high-laced shoes that were the fashion of the day. Stripped of the familiar kimono, trussed into a corset, the bride's severance from all that she had known was quick and complete.

Looking somewhat uncertain as she perhaps contemplates her future in an unknown land, a Japanese picture-bride is shown just before leaving Japan for American in 1910 in the photograph on the facing page. The photograph below shows picture-brides arriving in San Francisco in 1919.

Discussing the Reading

1. According to Bill Hosokawa, how did the familiar illusion of an America where wealth was universal operate within the picture-bride system?

2. What was the first process of "Americanization" that the Japanese picture-brides underwent on arriving in the United States? Do you think that this generally had a positive or negative effect on their attitudes toward their new lives in America? Explain.

CRITICAL THINKING
Identifying Alternatives

At the time the picture-bride system was in operation, arranged marriages were common in many parts of the world. What are the advantages and disadvantages of arranged marriages?

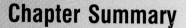

Chapter Summary

Write supporting details under each of the following main ideas as you review the chapter.

Section 1
1. The U.S. government encouraged the westward expansion of the railroads.
2. Miners and ranchers opened up the West.
3. The growth of ranching gave birth to the American cowboy.

Section 2
1. Westward movement of white Americans threatened the Indians.
2. Final challenges by the Indians ultimately failed.
3. The frontier closed in 1890.

Section 3
1. The railroads grew rapidly in the late 1800s.
2. Technological advances transformed American life.
3. Mass production techniques altered how and where people worked.

Section 4
1. New religious and social principles fostered economic growth.
2. The corporation developed to meet changing economic demands.
3. Trusts were formed to limit competition in the business world.
4. The economy developed a pattern of boom and bust.

Section 5
1. Immigrants of the late 1800s were different from previous newcomers.
2. The new immigrants were met with hostility.
3. The new immigrants forged new lives with religion and education.

Chapter Themes

1. **Racial, ethnic, religious diversity:** During the second half of the 19th century, Americans' reputation for ethnic and religious toleration was tarnished—first with Indians then with immigrants.
2. **Free enterprise:** The westward expansion of the railroads extended the industrial economy of the East across the continent and created a national economy that was characterized by mass-produced goods and new forms of business organization.

Chapter Study Guide

Identifying Key People and Terms

Name the key person or key term that describes the:
1. tracts of land on which the movement and activity of Native Americans was restricted
2. inventor of the electric light bulb
3. means of producing many goods cheaply
4. complete control over an industry
5. hatred and fear of foreigners or strangers

Locating Key Places

1. In which state did the Chisholm Trail originate?
2. Name two present-day states where land was set aside for huge Indian reservations.

Mastering the Main Ideas

1. How did the government encourage the westward expansion of the railroads?
2. How did the reservation system and the Dawes Act threaten the Plains Indians' traditional way of life?
3. In what way did technological advances transform American society?
4. Why did some big businesses seek to discourage economic competition?
5. How did some Americans show their hostility to the immigrants of the 1800s?

Applying Critical Thinking Skills

1. **Recognizing bias:** In the 1870s a government official said of the buffaloes of the Great Plains, "There is no law which human hands can write . . . that will stay the disappearance of these wild animals before civilization. They eat grass. They trample the plains. They are as uncivilized as the Indian." How does the language of this quotation demonstrate the bias of the speaker? What motives might the speaker have had in wanting the buffalo and the Indians off the Great Plains?
2. **Analyzing cause and effect:** List three causes for the defeat of the Plains Indians between 1865 and 1890, and describe three effects the defeat had on Indian lifestyles in the years to come.
3. **Making comparisons:** Compare the way early immigrants to the United States were treated by the American people and how the newcomers from 1880 to 1900 were treated.

1860	1865	1870	1875	1880	1885	1890	1895	1900

1864 Sand Creek massacre

1869 Transcontinental railroad completed

1876 Battle of the Little Bighorn

1877 U.S. Army defeats Sioux

1887 Dawes Act

1890 Frontier closed

1884 *The Adventures of Huckleberry Finn* (Twain)

1867 Canada granted constitution

1882 Chinese Exclusion Act

Chapter Activities

Learning Geography Through History

1. The first transcontinental railroad passed between Omaha, Nebraska, and Sacramento, California. Using the physical map on page 1004, name some of the geographical regions passed.
2. On the map on page 1001, locate some of the nations in eastern and southern Europe and in Asia from which the new immigrants came. Then write in these nations on an outline map of the world.

Relating the United States to the World

1. What ideas originating in Britain did many American industrialists incorporate into their philosophies of life and business? Describe those ideas.
2. Why did the new immigrants of the late 1800s leave their European and Asian homes to come to America?

Linking Past to Present

1. The railroads devised the standard time zones for more efficient scheduling of trains. How many time zones are in effect today in the United States? What is daylight-saving time?
2. What are some modern-day immigrant groups to the United States and from where do they come?

Practicing Critical Thinking Strategies

Formulating Appropriate Questions

As the transcontinental railroad was being planned, several possible routes were debated. Imagine that you were one of the people making the final selection. Formulate at least three appropriate questions with which to determine the advantages and disadvantages of each route.

Using the Time Line

1. How many years have passed since the official closing of the American frontier?
2. When did the United States government first act to restrict the immigration of Chinese people?

Learning More About America's Economic Transformation

1. **Using Source Readings:** Read the Source Readings for this chapter and answer the questions.
2. **Collecting information:** Collect information about the following "cow towns" of Kansas: Abilene, Ellsworth, Hays City, and Dodge City. Use the following questions as a guide for your search for information: (a) Where were these towns located? (b) When did they come into existence? (c) Who were some key western figures who lived in each town and what role did they play in the town's history? (d) How many head of cattle passed through each town yearly on their way to market? (e) What interesting events occurred in each town? (f) What role did the U.S. Army play in establishing or protecting these towns? (g) What are these towns like today? Use the following sources of information as guides: libraries, chambers of commerce, state bureaus of information and tourism. After you have collected the information you need, report your findings to the rest of the class.

Linking Past to Present

Conspicuous displays of wealth continue to provoke controversy in American life. Society hostess Alva Vanderbilt, shown in the inset in her costume as a Venetian princess, lavishly entertained 1,200 on the Monday after Easter in 1883. Publisher Malcolm Forbes, shown at the center with actress Elizabeth Taylor, ostentatiously celebrated his 70th birthday in Morocco in August 1989 with 600 friends.

Politics and Daily Life in the Gilded Age

1 8 7 0 – 1 9 0 0

7

In New York City, on March 26, 1883, the most costly private party ever given in the United States was about to begin at the mansion of Alva and William Kissam Vanderbilt. A police cordon held back shivering onlookers as some 1,200 invited guests in rich and fanciful costumes arrived in carriages and hurried inside. There, they ate, drank, and danced until dawn at an estimated cost of $250,000—a figure that would equal at least $3 million today.

The newspapers that devoted many columns to the Vanderbilts' fancy-dress ball also reported tersely that the wages of iron workers in Trenton, New Jersey, were being forced down by 10 percent when such workers averaged less than $9 for a 66-hour week. No one seemed to mind however, so powerful was the myth that even the poor, by their own effort, could rise from rags to riches, much like the Vanderbilts.

Conspicuous consumption and corruption marked much of American society from 1870 to 1900. This period in U.S. history takes its name from a novel written in 1873 by Mark Twain, *The Gilded Age*. The name suggests both the golden gleam of a gilded surface and the cheapness of the base metal underneath.

Does the opportunity to gain wealth and power give the incentive needed to encourage the investment and risk-taking that make our economy thrive? Does the concentration of wealth and power in the hands of a few pose risks to our society and our democratic system?

CHAPTER PREVIEW

In this chapter you will encounter some aspects of life in the Gilded Age, with both its glitter and its corruption.

SECTIONS IN THIS CHAPTER:
1. Gilded Age politicians avoided controversy.
2. City life transformed American culture.
3. Workers struggled to adapt to the industrial age.
4. Discontented farmers revolted.
5. Theme Essay: School reformers broadened the three R's.

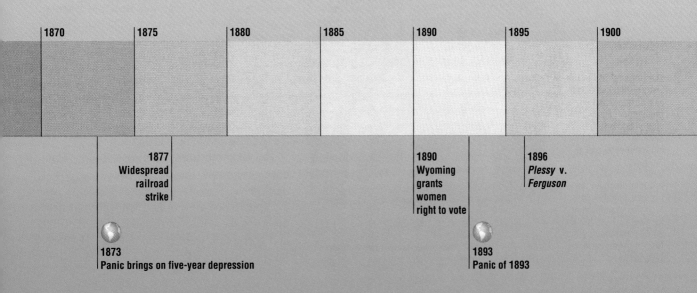

1870	1875	1880	1885	1890	1895	1900

1877 Widespread railroad strike

1890 Wyoming grants women right to vote

1896 *Plessy* v. *Ferguson*

1873 Panic brings on five-year depression

1893 Panic of 1893

Gilded Age politicians avoided controversy.

Key Terms: Crédit Mobilier, Pendleton Act, disfranchisement, Interstate Commerce Commission (ICC), Sherman Antitrust Act

Reading Preview
As you read this section, you will learn:

1. what marred national politics in the Gilded Age.
2. what supporters of women's suffrage hoped to achieve.
3. when African Americans lost ground to segregation.
4. whose policies promoted economic growth.
5. what effect popular pressure had on government regulation.

Politics in the Gilded Age was a popular source of entertainment. Although only men could vote, political parties roused the whole community with torchlight parades and massive barbeques. Patriotic oratory flourished. Most

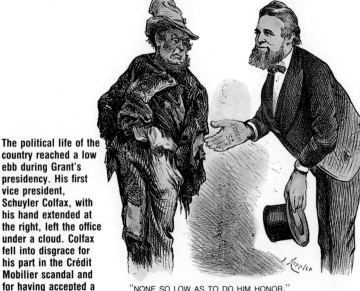

The political life of the country reached a low ebb during Grant's presidency. His first vice president, Schuyler Colfax, with his hand extended at the right, left the office under a cloud. Colfax fell into disgrace for his part in the Crédit Mobilier scandal and for having accepted a $4,000 campaign gift from a government supplier.

"NONE SO LOW AS TO DO HIM HONOR."
S.C.—"Why, my old friend, how do you do?"
OLD F.—"I can't take your hand. I have some reputation to lose."

politicians, however, avoided the serious issues of the day—the tariff, monetary policy, women's suffrage, and the prohibition of alcoholic beverages. Congress responded slowly, if at all, to problems brought by economic and social changes. Recurring episodes of political corruption also deeply troubled Americans.

Graft, corruption, and scandal marred national politics.

During the Gilded Age, Republicans drew their voters primarily from groups that supported the Union during the Civil War. Among them were African Americans loyal to the party of Emancipation, business leaders who wanted the government to encourage economic growth, and most rural, Protestant northerners. Democrats' support came from southern white voters, northern city machines, Irish and German immigrants, and business leaders who did not want government to interfere in the economy.

Close party competition. The two parties were evenly balanced in voter support. In 1876 Samuel Tilden, the Democrat, received more popular votes than Rutherford B. Hayes but lost the election when neither candidate secured a majority in the electoral college. A committee dominated by Republicans had to decide the outcome. Many felt that Republican party bosses had stolen the election. The Democratic presidential candidate **Grover Cleveland** was elected twice by a narrow margin, in 1884 and again in 1892. In the intervening presidential election of 1888, Cleveland won the popular vote but lost in the electoral college to Benjamin Harrison, the Republican.

Given the close balance, neither party seemed willing to risk taking on reform issues. Candidates for president tended to be bland party loyalists. Furthermore, the Senate included so many wealthy businessmen that critics called it the Millionaires' Club.

The troubled Grant Administration. State and local party bosses continued in power through successive terms of the presidents during the Gilded Age. Allied with big business interests, the bosses ran national politics. Graft and corruption were commonplace, especially during the presidency of Ulysses S. Grant

(1869–1877). Three scandals involving large sums of public money marred the Grant Administration. In the **Crédit Mobilier** [kred'it mō bēl yā' or mō bēl'yer] scandal of 1872 a newspaper revealed that Vice President Schuyler Colfax and other prominent Republicans had defrauded the government of millions of dollars granted for railroad construction in the West. In 1875 several highly placed officials, including Grant's private secretary, along with hundreds of whiskey-distilling companies, were charged with evading the federal tax on whiskey and keeping the tax money for themselves. A year after the Whiskey Ring scandal, the House of Representatives impeached William Belknap, Grant's secretary of war, for selling trading-post concessions in the Indian territories. The trading posts made enormous profits, often by cheating their Native American customers.

Although Grant himself was honest, he was a poor judge of character and put too much trust in his subordinates. The Grant Administration set the tone for the Gilded Age, an age the historian Henry Adams described as "poor in purpose and barren in results."

Civil service reform. Patronage, or the spoils system, had long permitted winning candidates to reward their supporters by appointing them to government jobs. President James A. Garfield, who succeeded Hayes, was assassinated in 1881 by Charles Guiteau, thought to be a disappointed office seeker. Guiteau's crime added to public indignation over the spoils system and finally brought reform of the civil service—civilian government workers who are appointed rather than elected.

Sponsored by Senator George Pendleton, the **Pendleton Act** (1883) created the Civil Service Commission which classified about 15,000 federal jobs. This meant that these jobs would be filled through competitive examinations rather than patronage. The law also made it illegal for political parties to require federal jobholders to make campaign contributions, a practice that had yielded most party campaign funds. Ironically, one result of civil service reform was to make political parties more dependent on business contributions.

HARPER'S WEEKLY. JOURNAL OF CIVILIZATION.
Vol. XXI.—No. 1096. NEW YORK, SATURDAY, OCTOBER 20, 1877.

HALT!
SENTINEL HAYES. "You can't come in here, Gentlemen, with that Flag!"

A steadfast President Rutherford B. Hayes stands firm against the spoils system in this 1877 engraving. Hayes had called for a "thorough, radical, and complete" reform of the civil service, but Congress blocked any effective legislation to end the spoils system until 1883. Then Congress passed the Pendleton Act.

Women hoped to achieve social and political rights.

While some reformers worked to end the spoils system, others fought for women's suffrage. A number of bold and determined women also asserted their rights to higher education and entrance into male-dominated professions—medicine, law, and the ministry.

After the Seneca Falls Convention launched the movement for women's rights in 1848, little progress took place until after the Civil War ended in 1865. Then in 1869 two rival groups formed to work for women's suffrage: the National Woman Suffrage Association (NWSA) and the American Woman Suffrage Association (AWSA). **Elizabeth Cady Stanton** and **Susan B. Anthony** led NWSA, which began a national campaign for a constitutional amendment giving the vote to women. **Lucy Stone** with her husband

Of their tireless effort to improve the position of women, Elizabeth Cady Stanton, below right, wrote her friend Susan B. Anthony in 1865, "our work is one, we are one in aim and sympathy."

JAMES GARFIELD

Born: November 19, 1831
Died: September 19, 1881
In office: 1881

Garfield was winning his struggle against the spoils system when he was shot by a disappointed office seeker. Garfield was president for only 200 days, 80 of them spent on his deathbed.

James Garfield's life included the brightest and darkest motifs of White House history. He made a stunning rise from log-cabin origins, only to become the second president cut down by an assassin's bullet.

Garfield's rise included diverse employment: he was a tow boy on the Ohio Canal, a teacher, a preacher (for the Disciples of Christ), and a college president. He became the youngest Union general in the Civil War before taking a seat in Congress at Lincoln's personal request. In 1880 he became a dark horse victor of the deadlocked Republican convention.

CHESTER A. ARTHUR

Born: October 5, 1829
Died: November 18, 1886
In office: 1881–1885

disappointment to his former Republican cronies, who denied him the presidential nomination in 1884.

Chester Arthur's presidency came as a pleasant surprise to a nation that had been dreading the worst. An undistinguished party hack, Arthur proved to be an honest and responsible president.

Son of a Baptist minister, Arthur practiced law before immersing himself in the boss-ridden swamps of New York Republican politics. Arthur's knack for playing machine politics while keeping his own hands clean won him the title "the Gentleman Boss." Aside from his me-too win as Garfield's vice president, Arthur had never been elected to public office.

Arthur's unexpectedly respectable term was a grave

Henry Blackwell helped found AWSA, which favored a state-by-state approach to winning suffrage.

Eight states voted on suffrage between 1867 and 1890. All rejected it. Some groups feared the power of the women's vote. Liquor interests, for example, believed that reform-minded women would vote for prohibition. Whatever their reasons, these enemies of women's political rights were many and powerful.

The first victory for suffrage came in the Wyoming Territory in 1869. Men outnumbered women there by six to one, and Wyoming officials hoped that the right to vote would attract more women. **Wyoming** became a state in 1890, the first with women's suffrage. Colorado approved women's suffrage in 1893, as did Idaho and Utah in 1896.

Susan B. Anthony had said in 1875 that winning the vote must be the "first and most urgent demand," but that women also needed equality in the "making, shaping, and controlling of the circumstance of life." Improved educational opportunities were important in helping women reach these larger goals.

Mary Lyon founded Mount Holyoke College in Massachusetts in 1837, promising its students an education as rigorous as that given in the men's colleges. In the next decades, other women's colleges opened—Mills in California, Vassar in New York, Wellesley and Smith in Massachusetts. The new state universities west of the Mississippi River admitted women without question, and many midwestern universities began to do so. In fact, by 1900 women equaled men at most universities in the Midwest and West, causing some to limit female enrollment. Still, few women ever attended college, and most women who did took teacher training or home economics programs.

A handful of women eventually gained admission to such professions as law, the ministry, and medicine. For example, Myra Bradwell studied law, but only after repeated appeals over more than 20 years did she finally gain admission to the Illinois bar.

At a time when few women could even gain admission to the ministry, **Mary Baker Eddy** founded a new religious denomination known as Christian Science. In 1876, as the leader of a small group of Christian healers in Lynn, Massachusetts, she published *Science and Health,* a statement of the Christian Science beliefs. In 1879 Eddy and others organized the First Church of Christ, Scientist, in Boston, which was followed by a number of branch churches. The *Christian Science Monitor,* the newspaper she founded in 1908 during her 88th year, has become one of the leading daily newspapers in the United States. Today the church has more than 3,000 congregations in 57 countries.

African Americans lost ground to segregation in the 1880s.

During the Gilded Age, the federal government moved backward in its treatment of African Americans. The desire to win the political support of southern white voters and a growing wave of racism led to the sharp restriction of African Americans' civil rights. In 1883 the Supreme Court denied the ideal of equal rights in the Civil Rights Cases. The Court held that the Civil Rights Act of 1875, which guaranteed equal accommodations in public places, protected African Americans' rights only against infringements by state governments, not those by individuals or private organizations. Not until the 1960s did the federal government make further efforts to protect African Americans against racial discrimination by private citizens.

After the end of Reconstruction, white voters again dominated southern state governments. Still, southern African Americans continued to vote and sometimes to hold office. Mississippi changed its constitution in 1890 to prevent African Americans from voting or holding office, a practice called **disfranchisement**. The same year, Congress defeated a bill that would have required the federal government to protect African Americans' voting rights. By the early 1900s, the other southern states had all enacted similar measures.

During the 1890s and after, all southern states and some northern states passed laws requiring segregation—separation of the races. More segregation laws began to appear after the Supreme Court, in the case of *Plessy* v. *Ferguson*, decided in 1896 that states could permit separate facilities for African Americans as long as they were equal to their facilities for others. That case made complete segregation of the races legal for more than half a century. Southerners rushed to provide separate facilities, but those for African Americans were rarely equal to those for others.

Booker T. Washington became the most prominent African American in the country after a speech he made in Atlanta, Georgia, in

Students in an American history class at Tuskegee Normal and Industrial Institute in Alabama, below left, mastered academic subjects as well as practical skills. Born a slave, Booker T. Washington, below, opened Tuskegee in 1881 as principal and the only teacher for 30 students. At his death in 1915, the school had many fine buildings and 185 teachers for 1,500 students.

GROVER CLEVELAND

Born: March 18, 1837
Died: June 24, 1908
In office: 1885–1889;1893–1897

He was the only president to serve two separated terms of office. Grover Cleveland was also the first and second Democratic president since the Civil War.

Son of a minister, Cleveland worked his way into the legal profession. He then fashioned a reform-minded public career, first as sheriff, then as mayor of Buffalo, finally as governor of New York. In 1884 he narrowly survived the most unpleasant presidential campaign in American history.

Against the corruption of his time, Cleveland offered the sturdy virtues of honesty, hard work, and good intentions. These were not enough to offset the blasts of a severe depression and a hostile Congress.

Cleveland retired to Princeton, New Jersey. His own last words are perhaps his best epitaph: "I have tried so hard to do right."

BENJAMIN HARRISON

Born: August 20, 1833
Died: March 13, 1901
In office: 1889–1893

He had the usual presidential qualifications of his time: he had been born in Ohio, had been a Union officer, and was Republican. Benjamin Harrison offered as well an historic bloodline: his great-grandfather had signed the Declaration of Independence and his grandfather had been president.

Harrison had been raised on an Ohio farm and prospered as an attorney. In the Civil War his soldiers dubbed him "Little Ben," but his stern leadership won him the rank of general.

Harrison lost the popular vote in 1888 but won the electoral count convincingly. High tariffs, costly pension programs, and economic problems during his Administration soon returned Grover Cleveland to the White House and Benjamin Harrison to private life.

1895. Washington headed Tuskegee Normal and Industrial Institute in Alabama, an industrial and agricultural school for African Americans. In the speech known as the Atlanta Compromise, Washington told African Americans in a racially mixed audience they should strive for self-improvement and forget about social equality for the time being. Stressing the need for all races to work together, he declared, "In all things social we can be as separate as the fingers, yet one as the hand in all things essential to mutual progress."

Many Americans, North and South alike, welcomed this acceptance of segregation. Washington's ideas mirrored the prevailing racism in white society, a society that seemed obsessed with industrialization, commerce, and the worship of power.

Two government policies promoted economic growth.

Despite setbacks and depressions, the Gilded Age was a period of progress. For one reason, the federal government became a full partner in U.S. economic growth. The government actively aided economic development through two main policies. First, a high tariff protected young industries. Second, the opening of the public domain in the West encouraged the development of natural resources. The public domain is land belonging to the federal government that has never been privately owned.

The tariff was a key issue in Gilded Age political campaigns. The issue was important to voters because tariff duties raised the price of imported goods, dividing the interest of consumers from that of producers. Republicans claimed that a protective tariff helped infant industries by making foreign-produced goods costlier and thus less attractive than goods produced in the United States. The Republicans defended the tariff as a necessary protection of American business and workers against competition from foreign goods. Democrats denounced the tariff and said it was only a tax passed on to consumers.

As for the management of the public domain, the government sold some public lands outright and set aside other lands for public purposes. It also sold rights to use the land in certain ways—grazing animals or cutting timber, for example. Between 1862 and 1871, Congress gave railroad companies almost 102 million acres—an area roughly the size of the state of Colorado. These subsidies helped build a huge railroad network, spurring the growth of the iron and steel industry and agriculture.

Popular pressure brought two weak attempts at government regulation.

Republicans used the federal government to further economic development. Most Democratic party leaders, however, remained committed to laissez faire, permitting trade, business, and industry to work with the least possible government interference. Since the Age of Jackson, leading Democrats argued that government intervention helped a favored few at the expense of the many. Those who held this view reasoned that the fairest policy was to allow unlimited free enterprise, with neither subsidy nor restriction. In keeping with this principle, President Grover Cleveland—the only Democrat to win the White House between 1861 and 1913—urged Congress to lower the tariff. Although Democrats and Republicans disagreed about the role of government in encouraging economic growth, few political leaders in either major party challenged laissez faire by calling for government regulation of economic matters or restriction of business.

Farmers and other railroad shippers, however, sought federal laws regulating the railroads. Congress finally responded in 1887 with the Interstate Commerce Act, which set up the **Interstate Commerce Commission (ICC)**. The law outlawed a number of questionable practices: special low rates or rebates (partial refunds or discounts) to large shippers, pooling (a practice that allowed several companies to divide up a market among themselves), and charging higher rates for a short haul than for a long haul. The ICC did not set rates but required them to be reasonable and just. Most importantly for farmers, the law required that shipping charges be the same in the South and West as they were back East.

Role of the federal government in the economy

Point	Counterpoint
Laissez faire	**Government intervention**
■ Government must provide only basic government services. ■ Government must not interfere by regulation or subsidy with the development of the economy. ■ The laws of supply and demand and natural selection will result in the strongest economy.	■ Government must support and even subsidize certain economic activities. ■ Government must regulate monopolies and other practices that restrain trade or limit markets. ■ Government must mediate between competing economic interests, such as management and labor, farmers and the railroads.

The Dingley Tariff, passed in 1897, rekindled farmers' resentments against the moneyed East with its tariff-protected industries. This tariff raised rates to a new high—57 percent—and imposed heavy duties on wool. President McKinley smiles slyly from his porch at left.

Public concern about the growth of huge corporations also brought demands for federal action in the 1880s. Congress in 1890 passed the **Sherman Antitrust Act**, a vaguely worded law that made combinations, trusts, and conspiracies "in restraint of trade" illegal. The law was largely symbolic. Few cases were brought to trial. Like the ICC, the Sherman Antitrust Act awaited a president determined to use the power of the federal government to regulate and control big business.

SECTION 1 REVIEW

Identify Key People and Terms
Write a sentence to identify: Grover Cleveland, Crédit Mobilier, Pendleton Act, Susan B. Anthony, Lucy Stone, Henry Blackwell, Mary Baker Eddy, disfranchisement, Booker T. Washington, Interstate Commerce Commission (ICC), Sherman Antitrust Act

Locate Key Places
Which was the first state to grant women's suffrage?

Master the Main Ideas
1. **Understanding political developments:** How did graft, corruption, and scandal during the Gilded Age affect civil service reform?
2. **Analyzing reform movements:** Why did women progress slowly in their fight for political rights?
3. **Analyzing the long-term social impact of Reconstruction:** Why did African Americans lose ground to segregation in the 1880s?
4. **Understanding economic growth:** How did the federal government promote economic growth during the Gilded Age?
5. **Understanding economic growth:** Why were the first two attempts at federal regulation weak and ineffective?

Apply Critical Thinking Skills: Making Comparisons
Do you think civil service workers should be barred from making campaign contributions? What do you think is the best way of financing political campaigns?

City life transformed American culture.

Key Terms: dumbbell tenement, political machines, Tammany Hall, Tweed Ring, settlement houses

Reading Preview
As you read this section, you will learn:

1. how new technologies affected the cities.
2. what kind of techniques changed city living spaces.
3. how the growth of cities affected politics.
4. who began the settlement movement.

The Gilded Age was an age of cities on the rise. For rural folk, the city seemed a cesspool of crime and immorality. Yet the city also promised opportunity along with anonymity, adventure, and excitement.

New technologies helped cities spread out geographically.

Before the Civil War, most American cities were geographically compact. Warehouses,

factories, and residences clustered near a downtown business center. Ordinary city dwellers worked and shopped within walking distance of their homes.

Between 1870 and 1900, immigration almost doubled U.S. population from about 39 million to 76 million. Most of these new Americans and many native-born Americans from rural areas flocked to the cities.

As urban areas grew more crowded, new technologies allowed cities to spread outward. The German American engineer John Augustus Roebling designed a series of impressive suspension bridges that allowed cities hemmed in by rivers to expand. The most celebrated of his works was the Brooklyn Bridge, which spanned the East River in 1883. As a result, New York City reached beyond Manhattan Island to take in nearby Brooklyn.

New forms of mass transportation also helped cities expand geographically, as the history of Boston, Massachusetts, in the late 19th century shows. Horses pulled the first streetcars in the 1850s, at which time Boston reached out about two miles from City Hall. By 1887 this distance had been doubled, and half a dozen streetcar suburbs ringed the city proper. The streetcar suburbs were residential districts, often quite rural, linked by streetcar

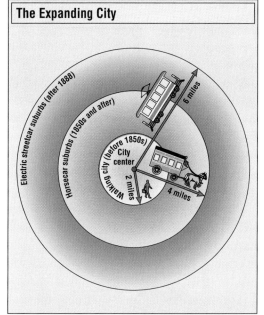

The Expanding City

Electric streetcar suburbs (after 1888)

Horsecar suburbs (1850s and after)

Walking city (before 1850s) City center

2 miles

4 miles

6 miles

chart study

How did improvements in transportation make one community out of many?
Critical Thinking
How does public transportation affect city life today?

to a nearby city. Suburbanites could commute by streetcar to work or to shop. Eleanor Hallowell Abbott described the two-hour trip by horsecar into Boston from one of its suburbs—Cambridge, Massachusetts—in the 1880s:

In winter for warmth and comfort, straw was heaped in the center of the car, and we children were only too glad to cuddle down into its sumptuous depths. Even so I remember perfectly well the cold and discomfort of the long winter ride into Boston and back.

AN AMERICAN ★ SPEAKS

The Brooklyn Bridge, left, at its opening in 1883, curved high above the East River so ships could pass beneath. In 1875 horsecars served New York City's Grand Central Station, below.

New construction techniques created new kinds of city living spaces.

Before the Civil War, most buildings were less than four stories tall. Height was limited because the walls carried the full weight of the building to the foundation. Taller buildings required excessively thick walls at the base. Americans began to use iron skeleton frames for five- and six-story buildings in the 1850s. With the addition of an American invention—Elisha Otis' safety elevator also developed in the 1850s—taller buildings became possible.

The postwar building boom brought the construction of the first skyscrapers, often regarded as America's greatest architectural achievement. **Chicago** became the center of architectural innovation after a terrible fire on October 8–10, 1871, destroyed nearly 2,000 acres in the heart of the city. Architects such as Daniel H. Burnham and Louis Sullivan designed ten-story buildings of brick and stone over iron and steel skeletons in the 1870s and 1880s. Soon even taller buildings transformed city skylines everywhere.

As people who could afford to do so moved to the city's outskirts, new owners subdivided the vacated residences into separate dwellings or boarding houses. There a family might live in a single, tiny room.

People also crowded into tenements, houses built exclusively for many tenant families. The dumbbell tenement, designed in New York City in 1879 by James E. Ware, tapered in at the middle to let light and air enter. Ware won a competition for plans that met minimum standards of a new tenement house law. However, little light ever entered the dank, murky interior of a dumbbell tenement, where a dozen families might share one cold-water tap and a toilet.

Displays of commercially canned foods tower over bargain hunters in the crowded interior of New York City's Siegel Cooper department store in 1897, above.

In 1888, one year after the nation's first electric streetcar appeared in Richmond, Virginia, Boston's horsedrawn streetcars gave way to electrified trolleys. Once again, Boston spread outward, this time reaching six miles from City Hall.

Andrew Hallidie, a Scottish immigrant, used a moving underground cable to pull streetcars in San Francisco in 1873. Twenty cities built cable-car systems over the next 20 years.

With improved urban transport, specialized central business districts grew up in large cities. Banks, insurance companies, and headquarters of large corporations grouped together in a financial district. Retail shopping districts, anchored by department stores, emerged nearby. Department stores began to appear in the mid-1800s. They became a popular feature of most big cities, making available ready-made clothes and greatly easing the work of women. Crowded Chinatowns and poor working-class sections occupied by African Americans and other ethnic groups squeezed in between business and industrial districts. More prosperous neighborhoods skirted the ring of suburbs.

This 1879 dumbbell floor plan, right, was meant to provide four apartments to a floor. However, a whole family might live in each room. Crowded, unsanitary conditions contributed to the spread of tuberculosis, the chief cause of death in the United States until 1909. Note the two flush toilets (marked W.C., for water closet), not widely available until the 1880s.

YARD

PARLOR | LIVING ROOM
11'4"x13'0"

LIVING ROOM 9'0"x10'0" | BED ROOM

BED RM 7'8"x8'4" | BED RM 7'8"x10'6"

HALL | W.C. | W.C.

BED RM 7'8"x8'4" | BED RM 7'8"x10'6"

BED RM 7'8"x8'4" | BED RM 7'8"x8'4"

BED RM 9'0"x10'0" | LIVING ROOM

LIVING ROOM 11'4"x13'0" | PARLOR

Jacob Riis [rēs], a Danish immigrant, became a crusading police reporter in New York City in 1877. His vivid articles and photographs confronted viewers with tenement life:

Be a little careful, please. The hall is dark and you might stumble over the children pitching pennies back there. Not that it would hurt them; kicks and cuffs are their daily diet. They have little else. Here where the hall turns and dives into utter darkness is a step, and another, another. A flight of stairs. You can feel your way, if you cannot see it. . . . That was a woman filling her pail by the hydrant you just bumped against. The sinks are in the hallway, that all the tenants may have access. . . . This gap between dingy brick walls is the yard. That strip of smoke-colored sky up there is the heaven of these people.

Two-thirds of New York City's population was packed into 32,000 tenements in 1890 when Riis wrote *How the Other Half Lives*. Although Riis' books helped win reforms, the problem of finding adequate housing for the poor still plagues large cities today.

The growth of cities gave rise to powerful urban political machines.

Growing populations placed many other demands on cities besides the need for better housing and transportation. City dwellers also needed a safe water supply, waste disposal systems, protection from fire and crime, and more hospitals, schools, and parks. To meet the demand for services, political organizations appeared drawing their support from the poor, many of whom were new immigrants. The organizations were called **political machines** because, people said, they were efficient like a machine. A leader called a boss ran the typical city machine. The boss gained power for the machine by supplying services to the voters.

The machine might give a food basket to a poor family, provide a carriage for a funeral, help an immigrant find a job or deal with legal problems. By giving a little help to those most in need, machine politicians built a loyal base of support among poor voters who had nowhere else to turn for social services.

George Washington Plunkitt explained how the power of the machine rested on poor voters. Plunkitt was a leader of **Tammany Hall**—the Democratic machine in New York City, popularly named for its headquarters building on Madison Avenue.

W hat tells in holdin' your grip on your district is to go right

AN AMERICAN ★ SPEAKS

down among the poor families and help them in the different ways they need help. . . . the poor look up to George W. Plunkitt as a father, come to him in trouble—and don't forget him on election day.

Besides ordinary voters, machines also gained support from banks and private companies, by aiding their dealings with city government—for a bribe or kickback. A company wishing to build a new streetcar line, for example, could get a franchise (the exclusive right) to do so by bribing machine leaders.

Some machine leaders amassed large fortunes. Christopher Buckley owned a modest

Children stand in a typical narrow, dark alley in a New York City tenement district. Jacob Riis photographed them in 1888 or 1889. As many as 30,000 children less fortunate than these were homeless and adrift in New York City, according to newspapers at the time. Dressed in rags, they picked through garbage and slept in cellarways or packing crates.

VOICES FROM THE PAST

Honest Graft

George Washington Plunkitt, a veteran Tammany politician, despised reformers who didn't know the difference between honest and dishonest graft. What new motto for political corruption is found in his remarks?

Yes, many of our men have grown rich in politics. I have myself. I've made a big fortune out of the game, and I'm getting richer every day, but I've not gone in for dishonest graft—blackmailin' gamblers, saloonkeepers, disorderly people, etc.—and neither has any of the men who have made big fortunes in politics.

There's an honest graft, and I'm an example of how it works. I might sum up the whole thing by saying: "I seen my opportunities and I took 'em."

Thomas Nast's sharp pen makes Boss Tweed a cruel Roman as the Tammany Tiger mauls honest government.

saloon before becoming boss of San Francisco Democrats in the 1880s. Known as the "blind boss" because of his impaired vision, he soon acquired a lavish home and a fortune in bonds from companies dealing with the city.

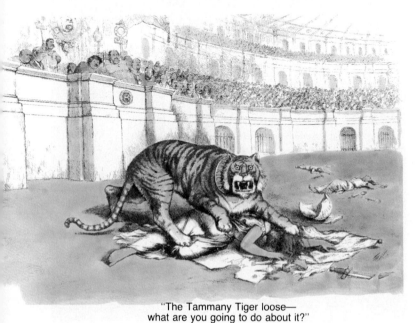

"The Tammany Tiger loose— what are you going to do about it?"

The most notorious case of graft and corruption was New York City's **Tweed Ring**, formed by William Marcy Tweed and powerful accomplices in Tammany Hall. The Tweed Ring plundered the city treasury of anywhere from $75 to $200 million before Tweed's arrest in 1871.

Well-intentioned reformers in New York and other cities tried periodically to defeat the machines, but the poverty that gave the machine its base of support always remained. As a result, reformers were rarely able to eliminate machine politics.

Social reformers began the settlement movement to assist the urban poor.

Other groups did try to relieve poverty. One approach they took was the settlement movement. Settlement leaders wanted to go beyond merely helping the needy to remedying social and economic problems that made people poor. Located in crowded immigrant neighborhoods, **settlement houses** offered such social services as English language and American citizenship classes and child care. Protestant and Roman Catholic churches, Jewish synagogues, and other religious groups took up the settlement idea.

The best-known settlement houses in the United States were Chicago's Hull House, established by **Jane Addams** in 1889; Boston's South End, founded by **Robert A. Woods** in 1892; and New York City's Henry Street Settlement, founded by **Lillian Wald** in 1893. Addams had started to become a doctor to "help the poor," but her health failed. When she recovered, Addams observed a settlement house in England and committed herself to helping end poverty. Addams and a college classmate, Ellen Gates Starr, began their pioneering work in a decaying mansion on Halsted Street in Chicago. Addams later wrote,

From the first it seemed understood that we were ready to perform the humblest neighborhood services. We were asked to wash the new-born babies, and to prepare the dead for burial, to nurse the sick, and to "mind the children."

AN AMERICAN ★ SPEAKS

The Hull House staff made some of the first studies of slums and took an active interest in strikes, labor legislation, and immigration problems. Hull House lobbied for more schools when its staff found 3,000 more children in the ward than there were seats in the schoolrooms. Addams and her staff also worked for and won public parks, municipal baths, and better garbage collection.

The settlement house movement also gave a new purpose to educated, politically conscious women who found it hard to pursue conventional lives. Nurturing the children of the poor opened a new profession, social work, started by Jane Addams, Edith Abbott, and others through Hull House and the University of Chicago. Following their example, many other college-educated women and men would find a way to make their social convictions count during the Gilded Age.

SECTION **2** REVIEW

Identify Key People and Terms
Write a sentence to identify: dumbbell tenement, political machines, Tammany Hall, Tweed Ring, settlement houses, Jane Addams, Robert A. Woods, Lillian Wald

Locate Key Places
Which city became a center for architectural innovation after a terrible fire in 1871?

Master the Main Ideas

1. **Understanding geographic influences:** How did new technologies make urban growth possible?
2. **Analyzing the impact of technology:** How did new construction techniques change city living spaces?
3. **Understanding political developments:** Why did urban growth enable political machines to acquire and use power?
4. **Recognizing societal values:** Why did the settlement houses have a special meaning for college-educated women?

Apply Critical Thinking Skills: Drawing Conclusions
What are some positive and negative qualities of political machines?

SECTION **3**

Workers struggled to adapt to the industrial age.

Key Terms: Knights of Labor, American Federation of Labor (AFL), United Mine Workers (UMW), blacklist, Great Railroad Strike of 1877, Haymarket riot, Homestead strike, Pullman strike

Reading Preview
As you read this section, you will learn:

1. what the goal of labor organizations was.
2. what groups remained outside the craft unions.
3. what effect labor disputes had on the nation during the Gilded Age.

During the Gilded Age, large-scale farming, new means of production, and mass marketing brought an abundance of products for those who could afford them. Women's lives changed dramatically as canned foods and ready-made clothes and home furnishings became commonplace. Yet ordinary working people were often too poor to enjoy the benefits their own labor produced.

Women on the H. J. Heinz Company production line pack tins of baked beans for shipment throughout the world around 1900. The rush to the gold fields of California in 1849 triggered an increasing demand for canned foods because they could be easily carried and quickly prepared.

Labor Strikes, 1870–1900

▨ Counties reporting strikes between 1870 and 1900

✷ Major strikes

1. Great Railroad Strike of 1877 (railroad workers)

2. Haymarket riot (farm equipment workers) 1886

3. Homestead strike (steelworkers) 1892

4. Pullman strike (railroad workers) 1894; Chicago and nationwide

Albers Equal–Area Projection ©SF

map study

Location
More than 14,000 strikes occurred in the 1880s and early 1890s, involving millions of workers. Where were the major strikes?

Critical Thinking
The map shows that few strikes occurred in the Great Plains states though more took place in the West. How can you explain that pattern? What other area shows the fewest strikes?

Labor organizations sought to improve the lot of American workers.

For the first time in history, the United States began to have an overall surplus of unskilled or semiskilled workers competing for jobs. A depression in the 1870s, a bad recession in the 1880s, and another depression in the 1890s all brought widespread unemployment. During depressions and at other times of low demand, manufacturers reacted by cutting production or closing down, reducing wages, and putting people out of work. When factories shut down, workers were left on their own without unemployment payments or other benefits available today.

Craft unions had existed for many years to protect the interests of skilled tradespeople—printers, carpenters, bootmakers, and others. The idea behind the union was that one worker alone was weak but many together could stand up against an employer who threatened to lower wages or increase working hours.

The **Knights of Labor**, founded in 1869, was the first important national labor organization. Unlike craft unions, this organization welcomed all workers—skilled and unskilled, male and female, black and white, immigrant and native-born. The Knights wanted to unite all those who by "honorable toil" produced something of value. Shopkeepers and farmers could join as well as laborers. Excluded were bankers, lawyers, gamblers, and liquor dealers. In Chicago the Knights were led by Elizabeth Flynn Rodgers, who was the mother of ten and later founded a large insurance company. In the South, one-third to one-half of the Knights were African Americans.

One of the Knights' genuine assets was their grand master workman, **Terence V. Powderly**, the son of Irish Catholic immigrants, a machinist by trade, and a flamboyant speaker with an elegant mustache. Under Powderly's leadership, the Knights promoted a broad platform of political reforms. They demanded an eight-hour workday, an end to child labor, equal pay for equal work regardless of sex, safety codes in the workplace, and the graduated income tax.

The Knights grew rapidly to a high point of more than 700,000 members in 1886 but soon entered a decline. Unsuccessful strikes in 1886 and 1887 together with competition from a new labor group, the American Federation of Labor, ended the Knights' effectiveness.

In contrast to the Knights, the **American Federation of Labor (AFL)**, formed in December 1886, was a loose federation of craft unions. The founders of the AFL hoped to preserve and extend the craft union movement with a separate union for every skill, rather than one union for all workers. English-born **Samuel Gompers**, the short, crusty head of the cigarmakers' union, was elected the first president. Under Gompers' direction, the AFL ignored politics and concentrated on building strong organizations among skilled workers. When depression struck in the 1890s, the AFL and most of the national craft unions survived. Previously, unions had grown in times of prosperity and collapsed in times of depression.

Women and unskilled workers remained outside the craft unions.

Despite steps toward labor reform, most workers did not belong to the AFL or any other union. Unskilled and easily replaceable workers found it hard to organize. Their ranks included a rising number of women, both married and single.

Like most women, African Americans and Asian immigrants were also excluded from the AFL craft unions. Both groups awakened white fears of a lower class that would depress wages. In the 1890s, as segregation was becoming the law of the land in the South, most AFL craft unions ignored the AFL policy that prohibited discrimination against African Americans. Only the interracial **United Mine Workers (UMW)**, formed in 1890, had a significant number of African American members. Unions on the West Coast had grown in the 1880s by blaming Chinese immigrants for driving down wage levels. Exclusion of Chinese immigrants became a political demand of unions, and no union admitted Chinese workers as members.

Some African Americans and women did join the unions. Richard L. Davis, twice elected to the national board of the UMW, worked as a coal miner and union organizer in West Virginia and Ohio until he was blacklisted in 1898. The **blacklist**, a list of workers who were considered troublemakers, became a powerful weapon when circulated among employers.

Workers whose names were on the list usually found it impossible to get another job. Davis expressed the cruelty of the blacklist:

> **AN AMERICAN ★ SPEAKS**
>
> I have been threatened; I have been sandbagged; I have been stoned, and last of all deprived of the right to earn a livelihood for myself and family. I do not care so much for myself, but it is my innocent children that I care for most, and heaven knows that it makes me almost crazy to think of it.

While still in his forties, Davis died of black lung disease, caused by breathing coal dust.

Mary Harris Jones devoted herself to the labor movement after losing her husband and four young children to yellow fever in the 1860s. An outspoken Irish immigrant, she was known as Mother Jones and the "miners' angel." Jones led marches and fought child labor. Criticized once for not being ladylike, she warned that powerful industrialists such as John D. Rockefeller wanted women to be timid. She told them, "Don't be ladylike. God almighty made women and the Rockefeller gang of thieves made ladies."

Women delegates to the 1886 national meeting of the Knights of Labor gather around one of their leaders, Elizabeth Flynn Rodgers, holding her two-week-old son, above. Rodgers headed the Chicago chapter in 1886 and 1887.

Mother Jones is shown below toward the end of her career.

Labor violence before 1900 brought a public clamor against the unions. The locomotive repair facilities of the Pennsylvania Railroad at Pittsburgh lie in ruins, top right, burned by striking workers in 1877. When an anarchist handbill, top left, called a meeting that ended in the Haymarket riot of 1886, foreign-born people became feared as mad bomb throwers.

Savage labor disputes racked the nation during the Gilded Age.

The growth of national labor unions brought a series of explosive clashes between workers and employers during the years from 1870 to 1900. Although tens of thousands of labor strikes took place during the Gilded Age, four violent strikes in particular seriously weakened the labor movement—the Great Railroad Strike of 1877, the Haymarket riot of 1886, the Homestead strike of 1892, and the Pullman strike of 1894.

The Great Railroad Strike. In 1877 a depression led railroad companies to cut wages. Workers in West Virginia went on strike. The **Great Railroad Strike of 1877** spread rapidly, paralyzing railways in the East and Midwest. In Pittsburgh, strikers rioted, and the state militia, trying to restore order, killed at least ten people. The strikers fought back by setting fire to freight cars and buildings and tearing up tracks. Finally, President Rutherford B. Hayes sent in the army to put down the strike. Union membership plummeted from 300,000 to 50,000.

The Haymarket riot. In Chicago in May 1886, bitter labor battles for an eight-hour workday at the McCormick Reaper Works led to a mass meeting at Haymarket Square. An unidentified person threw a bomb, killing seven police officers, and many people were wounded when the police opened fire. Eight anarchist leaders were convicted of conspiracy and sentenced to death in the **Haymarket riot**, even though their connection with the unknown bomb thrower was unproven and only four of them had been at the meeting. (Anarchists are people who favor the overthrow of all government.) One of the eight committed suicide. August Spies, the editor of an anarchist newspaper, and three others were hanged. Illinois governor John Peter Altgeld braved a public outcry and pardoned the remaining three in 1893, ending his own political career in the process.

The Homestead strike. In 1892 the Carnegie Steel Company refused to bargain with strikers at Homestead, in southwestern Pennsylvania, the site of a large steelworks. After months of hostility, the company decided to end the **Homestead strike** by bringing in new, non-union workers, under protection of armed guards from the Pinkerton Detective Agency. The guards fought a pitched battle with the striking workers, who had taken over the plant. After ten strikers were killed, the governor sent in 8,000 state troops to restore order. The union was all but destroyed.

The Pullman strike. The nation, while in the throes of a depression, faced another major strike in 1894, the **Pullman strike**. A new union, the American Railway Union (ARU), had formed in 1893 to unite all white railway workers regardless of skill. In 1894 the ARU told its members not to handle any Pullman cars, luxury sleeping or parlor cars built for the railroads at the company-owned town of **Pullman, Illinois**, now part of Chicago.

The leader of the ARU, **Eugene V. Debs**, acted in support of striking workers at Pullman, who had had their wages cut because of the depression. The boycott soon turned into a nationwide rail strike centered in Chicago.

The U.S. government entered the dispute on the employers' side, arguing that the strikers were obstructing the mails. A federal judge issued an injunction (court order) requiring the ARU to end the strike. Debs refused, and President Grover Cleveland sent in the army. The judge then jailed Debs and other leaders of the ARU, effectively destroying the union.

After the Pullman strike, labor relations became calmer because the effect of the labor injunction was to make strikes illegal. The issues that divided workers and employers, however, remained unresolved.

S E C T I O N **3** R E V I E W

Identify Key People and Terms
Write a sentence to identify: Knights of Labor, Terence V. Powderly, American Federation of Labor (AFL), Samuel Gompers, United Mine Workers (UMW), blacklist, Mary Harris Jones, Great Railroad Strike of 1877, Haymarket riot, Homestead strike, Pullman strike, Eugene V. Debs

Locate Key Places
What town built by a sleeping-car company was a center of strike activity in 1894?

Master the Main Ideas

1. **Understanding the development of labor unions:** How did the first labor organizations seek to improve the lot of American workers?
2. **Understanding the development of labor unions:** How did the groups that remained outside the craft unions try to improve working conditions?
3. **Understanding economic growth:** What does the violent nature of labor relations tell you about this period?

Apply Critical Thinking Skills:
Checking Consistency
Imagine you are a Gilded Age employer. Why would you oppose employees organizing a union? Then imagine you are a worker. Why would you want a union?

S E C T I O N **4**

Discontented farmers revolted.

Key Terms: Grange, Farmers' Alliances, Populists, Depression of 1893, Coxey's army

Reading Preview
As you read this section, you will learn:

1. what the farmers' chief problem was.
2. what solution the Populists proposed.
3. what event brought about demands for federal action.
4. what effect the 1896 election had on the Republican party.

In the 1890s hard times among farmers gave birth to new pressure groups and political parties that challenged prevailing notions of laissez faire. A depression beginning in 1893—the worst in history to that time—brought hardship to many Americans. As times grew steadily worse, farmers pressed for reforms that would put agriculture on an equal footing with business and industry.

Farmers struggled to adapt to the new market economy.

A major trend of the Gilded Age was the spread of agriculture west of the Mississippi River and in the South following the breakup of the plan-

Members of the Patrons of Husbandry, popularly called the Grangers, meet in the woods at Winchester, in west central Illinois, in 1873. The 13,000 local Granges worked to advance the interests of farmers much as the Knights of Labor did for other workers.

tation system. New machinery, fertilizers, and better kinds of seeds increased productivity. In 1880, for example, it took about 152 hours of work to produce 100 bushels of wheat. By 1900 it took only 108 hours. However, to pay for the machinery and other things that would increase their productivity, farmers had to raise more crops for sale.

Farmers became more and more committed to a few staple crops, especially wheat, corn, and cotton. You can see from the table on the opposite page how production increased between 1870 and 1900. Supply so outstripped demand that prices for farm products fell drastically. Wheat that sold for $2 a bushel around 1870 fell to 50 cents by the early 1890s. Corn and cotton prices dropped sharply as well.

Many farmers were in debt, both in the South and in newly developed areas west of the Mississippi. In this part of the West, farmers had borrowed money to start new farms and buy machinery. As prices fell, farmers had to raise more and more crops to earn the same cash income, which they owed as payment on their debts. The more they raised, the lower prices fell. Farmers were also discontented

Ordering By Mail

It was considered one of the best-read books of its time. Many people not only read it, they dreamed about it. This "wish book" of the late 1800s was the Montgomery Ward catalog. Families pored over its pages, astounded at the goods they could get simply by sending away for them.

Before Aaron Montgomery Ward started his mail-order business in 1872, farmers depended on the country store in small towns for practically all their supplies. Selection was small and prices were high, as wholesalers, distributors, and retailers each made their profit. Farmers generally had little choice but to buy from the country store; in sparsely settled areas it was not practical to shop around.

Ward had the idea of eliminating the middle men and selling to the farmers directly, through the mail. Ward bought large amounts of goods at favorable prices. He advertised his merchandise in a free catalog that he sent to prospective customers. The customers sent in orders and paid when the goods arrived. If the goods were not satisfactory, Ward refunded the customer's money, shipping price and all.

People were skeptical at first, but Ward's high quality merchandise and reassuring guarantee soon convinced them that mail-order was no hoax. Within 20 years, Ward's catalog had grown from a 4-page pamphlet to a 500-page tome. Competition had sprung up, including a mail-order company started by a man named Richard Sears. With their mail-order businesses, Ward and Sears spread the comforts of middle-class living across the continent in the late 1800s.

Ward's 1875–1876 catalog listed thousands of items, all at savings of 40 percent. Later, detailed illustrations enticed buyers.

Highlights of American Life

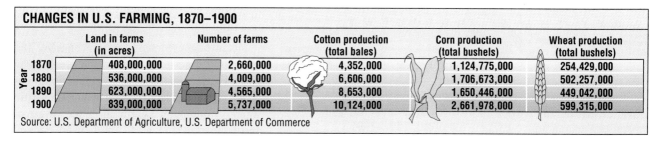

CHANGES IN U.S. FARMING, 1870–1900

Year	Land in farms (in acres)	Number of farms	Cotton production (total bales)	Corn production (total bushels)	Wheat production (total bushels)
1870	408,000,000	2,660,000	4,352,000	1,124,775,000	254,429,000
1880	536,000,000	4,009,000	6,606,000	1,706,673,000	502,257,000
1890	623,000,000	4,565,000	8,653,000	1,650,446,000	449,042,000
1900	839,000,000	5,737,000	10,124,000	2,661,978,000	599,315,000

Source: U.S. Department of Agriculture, U.S. Department of Commerce

about high interest rates on their loans and about the high rates railroads charged to carry their crops to market.

Increasingly, farmers joined the **Grange**, a farm organization founded in 1867, and through it voiced their concerns. Offshoots of the Grange, political parties called Granger parties, pushed through laws in several states regulating railroads. In addition to the Granger laws, they also set up local cooperative stores, sometimes called consumers' co-ops, in order to lower the prices they had to pay merchants. (To meet this kind of competition, Montgomery Ward introduced the mail-order method of selling merchandise.)

In the late 1870s and 1880s, some farmers turned to the Greenback party, and the Granger movement began to decline. The Greenbackers advocated many popular reforms, but their primary goal was to maintain or increase the amount of paper money in circulation. The federal government at that time was slowly withdrawing the paper money, called greenbacks, issued during the Civil War. In addition, Congress decided in 1873 to base all money on the gold standard rather than using both gold and silver. Problems had arisen in using two metals because the value of each fluctuated, and speculators tried to profit from these differences. Although Congress restored the silver dollar on a limited basis in 1878, farm prices soon fell again.

The Populists advocated government intervention to protect free enterprise.

In the late 1880s, farmers of the Middle West and South formed new groups to address their problems: the **Farmers' Alliances**. Three Alliance organizations formed, one in the North and two segregated groups in the South. All three Alliances held similar views on farmers' problems, favoring cooperative buying and marketing and political action.

In Kansas and the Dakotas, the Alliances took the lead in forming new political parties in 1890. In 1892 Alliance leaders organized a new national party, the People's party, whose members became known as **Populists**, from the Latin word *populus*, meaning "people."

The Populists opposed the large corporations that had appeared in the previous 15 years, arguing that such concentrations of power and wealth threatened individual opportunity. The Populists wanted to greatly expand the powers of the federal government. For example, they thought the government should own and operate the nation's railroads and the telephone and telegraph systems, and they hoped to restore to the public domain lands that were now owned by the railroads. The Populists also proposed a subtreasury plan to solve the farmers' problem of inadequate credit. The plan would create warehouses to hold farmers' nonperishable crops off the market while prices were low. Farmers could borrow money against the crop until it was sold after prices rose.

The Populists elected representatives, senators, and governors in the Midwest and in the South. They favored silver money, which brought support in Rocky Mountain mining regions. In the 1892 presidential election, the Populist candidate won 8.5 percent of the vote and carried several western states.

The depression of 1893 brought demands for federal action.

When Democrat Grover Cleveland became president for the second time in early 1893, the **Depression of 1893** was about to begin.

chart study

Corn, wheat, and cotton harvests more than doubled between 1870 and 1900, and millions of acres of new land were brought into production. By the turn of the century, the United States had developed one of the most efficient and competitive agricultural sectors in the world. Why could farmers produce more crops in 1900 than in 1870?

Critical Thinking How can farmers prosper in a market economy if prices always tend to fall as agricultural production increases?

WILLIAM McKINLEY

Born: January 29, 1843
Died: September 14, 1901
In office: 1897–1901

"I have never been in doubt since I was old enough to think intelligently that I would someday be made president." William McKinley's youthful confidence was justified by his 1896 election.

After one term in college McKinley became the first in his town to enlist in the Civil War; by its end he was a 22-year-old major. He practiced law, served seven terms in Congress, and was twice elected governor of Ohio. That public career never distracted McKinley from devoted care for his invalid wife, Ida.

During McKinley's presidency the United States was victorious in a "splendid little war" and prosperous in peace. The American flag flew in new outposts around the world. McKinley was resoundingly re-elected in 1900 and received in full measure the public esteem that he so desired. His popularity was no shield against the madness of a lone assassin, however. McKinley was fatally wounded in 1901.

Fifteen thousand businesses collapsed in that year, and four of the five transcontinental railroads declared bankruptcy. Unemployment increased from 3 percent in 1892 to 12 percent in 1893 to 18 percent in 1894, and higher in urban and industrial areas.

President Cleveland's response to the Depression of 1893 came straight from laissez faire thinking. He asked Congress to stop all silver coinage in order to reassure European creditors of the soundness of the dollar. Then he negotiated with J. P. Morgan to buy a new issue of government bonds in order to replenish the gold in the treasury.

As the depression deepened in 1894, **Coxey's army**—some 500 unemployed workers led by Ohio Populist Jacob S. Coxey—marched on **Washington, D.C.** Congress refused to hear Coxey's request for public works jobs, and the police jailed him.

Meanwhile, Cleveland's actions on silver and other issues severely divided the Democratic party. Democrats from the West and South opposed repeal of silver coinage, which Cleveland wanted. Moreover, shortly after the arrest of Jacob Coxey, Cleveland had used federal troops against the Pullman strikers, which alienated many workers. As a result, in the congressional elections in 1894 Democrats lost strength outside the South, ending the long period during which the major parties were equally balanced.

The 1896 election revitalized the Republican party.

The Republicans in 1896 nominated as their presidential candidate **William McKinley**, a former congressman who was then governor of Ohio. In Congress as chairman of the committee that set tariffs, he took the lead in creating the McKinley Tariff of 1890, which set the highest rates in 60 years. In 1896 McKinley thought that the solution to the depression lay in again raising tariff rates, and promised voters a "full dinner pail." He also was against silver coinage as a means of increasing the money supply. "Good money," he said, "never made hard times."

When the Democrats met to nominate a candidate in 1896, they were deeply divided. Some supported Cleveland's laissez faire approach. Others favored an activist approach including free and unlimited coinage of silver. During the debate on the silver issue, **William Jennings Bryan**, a young former congressman from Nebraska, electrified the convention with a stirring speech that ended with the words:

Having behind us the producing masses of this nation and the world, supported by the commercial interests, the laboring interests, and the toilers everywhere, we will answer their demand for a gold standard by saying to them: You shall not press down upon the brow of labor this crown of thorns, you shall not crucify mankind upon a cross of gold.

AN AMERICAN ★ SPEAKS

Inspired by Bryan's impassioned eloquence, the convention nominated him for president. The Populists soon nominated Bryan as their candidate too.

Where McKinley claimed that higher tariffs would end the depression, Bryan believed that prosperity would return with the free coinage of silver. His free silver policy was based on the idea that there was not enough gold in the United States to provide an adequate money supply for the expanding American economy. Bryan's followers also thought that free silver would help farmers pay their debts.

The campaign aroused much interest and excitement. McKinley stayed at home, as was traditional for presidential candidates, and greeted crowds of well-wishers from his front porch. Marcus Hanna, his campaign manager, raised in the neighborhood of $10 to $16 million dollars, mostly from big business, and used it to flood the country with flyers, pamphlets, and buttons, praising McKinley and the tariff and painting dismal pictures of the consequences of a Bryan victory. Bryan raised only $300,000 to run his campaign and decided to take his case directly to the people. He traveled 18,000 miles, visited 27 states, and spoke to 5 million people, arguing the need for silver coinage and criticizing McKinley and the tariff.

Bryan won nearly 6.5 million votes, more than any previous presidential candidate, but McKinley received even more—7.1 million. Bryan carried 22 states, McKinley took 23.

The Republican victory in 1896 marked the end of the period of close competition between the two parties and the beginning of a generation of Republican ascendancy. From 1896 to 1932, Republican presidential candidates won seven times, Democrats only twice. Republicans also usually won sizeable majorities in Congress. Although the Democrats emerged as the minority party, the Bryan campaign had begun to transform Democratic views from Cleveland's laissez faire philosophy toward a commitment to government intervention in the economy on behalf of the farmer and worker. This transformation laid the basis for the activist presidencies of Woodrow Wilson (1913–1921) and Franklin D. Roosevelt (1933–1945).

Although defeated for the presidency three times, silver-voiced William Jennings Bryan influenced Americans as few others have. At left, he stumps the country for the first time in 1896. Below, voters could choose Bryan's cocked hat or McKinley's goldbug pin.

SECTION **4** REVIEW

Identify Key People and Terms
Write a sentence to identify: Grange, Farmers' Alliances, Populists, Depression of 1893, Coxey's army, William McKinley, William Jennings Bryan

Locate Key Places
Where did Coxey's army march?

Master the Main Ideas

1. **Examining U.S. economic development:** Why did farmers face problems in adapting to the new commercial marketplace?
2. **Examining economic and cultural influences:** Why did the Populist party advocate government intervention?
3. **Examining U.S. economic development:** How did President Cleveland respond to the Depression of 1893?
4. **Understanding major elections:** How did the presidential election of 1896 revitalize the Republican party?

Apply Critical Thinking Skills: Drawing Conclusions
Why would a debt-ridden farmer favor inflation? How would an urban wage-earner feel about it? A business person? A money-lender?

317

Theme Essay: School reformers broadened the three R's.

Key Terms: progressive education

Reading Preview
As you read this section, you will learn:

1. what Americans expected their schools to create.
2. what forces shaped education in city schools.
3. how rural schools were organized.

One of the best-selling novels of the Gilded Age, Edward Bellamy's *Looking Backward*, published in 1888, depicted Boston 100 years in the future. In that utopian city to come, all children went to the finest schools from the age of 6 to 21, and higher education was open by right to every citizen. Men and women had to be well educated because they usually retired at age 45 to pursue their own interests. Like Edward Bellamy, most Gilded Age Americans were deeply committed to the idea of popular education.

The belief in the importance of universal education to a democratic society relates to several of the key themes in American history that you have read about, particularly the belief in a unique national destiny for the American people. Thomas Jefferson expressed his faith in the power of education to shape that destiny when he said:

By far the most important bill in our whole code, is that for **AN AMERICAN ★ SPEAKS** the diffusion of knowledge among the people. For no other sure foundation can be devised for the preservation of freedom and happiness.

Jefferson's fellow Virginians had been unwilling to accept his comprehensive educational system in its entirety. By the Gilded Age, however, most Americans had become deeply committed to education at all levels, not only as the basis for sound government but also as the principal means of achieving long-term reforms.

Americans expected their schools to create a unified society.

A society where one person in seven was foreign born placed heavy demands on its schools. Education, reformers stressed, would instill good work habits and give rise to a common culture. One goal of reformers was to require elementary education for all, extending throughout the United States the improvements in public schooling that Horace Mann had begun in Massachusetts in the 1830s. Reformers also wanted a longer school year, more public high schools, and kindergartens.

The curriculum for all ages in a one-room country school was "readin' and 'ritin' and 'rithmetic, taught to the tune of a hick'ry stick." *The New England Country School*, painted in 1871, was among many scenes of country life captured by Winslow Homer (1836–1910).

19TH-CENTURY EDUCATION
Skill: Recognizing Values

Introducing the Skill. In 1884 Roman Catholic church officials set the goal of having every Catholic child attending a Catholic school. A good many parents belonging to other religious groups, particularly Lutherans, had also chosen to educate their children with a curriculum infused with religious values and principles. By establishing their own schools, such parents hoped to instill their religious values in their children. What were those values, and how did they compare with the values promoted in the public schools of the time?

Learning the Skill. Values, that is, one's established ideals of life, may differ significantly among groups. **Recognizing values** of a particular group thus helps to understand the group's goals and actions.

To recognize the values of a person or group, be alert to both words and actions. What ideals does a person support? By what values does a person live and work?

Applying the Skill. Read the following words from a speech given in 1890 by the Roman Catholic Archbishop John Ireland about public education in America.

It (the public school) treats of land and sea, but not of Heaven; it speaks of statesmen and warriors, but not of God and Christ; it tells how to attain success in this world, but says nothing about the world beyond the grave. The pupil sees and listens, and sensibly forms the conclusion that religion is of minor im-

portance. Religious indifference becomes his creed; his manhood will be, as was his childhood in school, estranged from God and the positive influences of religion.

1. According to Archbishop Ireland, what values were taught in public schools? What values did he believe were neglected?
2. The archbishop's speech was controversial with both Catholics and Protestants because in it he went on to say that the public schools should provide religious instruction. Why do you think the plan was controversial? How would such a plan mesh with the principle of the separation of church and state written into the U.S. Constitution?

The broad goals of compulsory education were widely accepted, but not without controversy about the content of this education and who would provide it. Conflicts flared up repeatedly between Protestants and Roman Catholics, who by 1880 constituted the largest single U.S. denomination. Since the early 1800s, some Catholics had established separate parochial schools, sensing that American education had a Protestant orientation. Responding to a concern about the direction of public school education, the Catholic bishops met in 1884 in a council at **Baltimore, Maryland**. The Council of Baltimore charged every American Catholic community with building an elementary school. Faced with this burden and

the realization that Catholic schools would reduce the demand on the public schools, some Catholics sought tax money to aid parochial education. Their demands brought strong antiforeign and anti-Catholic outbursts.

Catholics and Protestants also fought over other issues, including the issue of language, in California. When statehood came in 1850, English became the language of instruction almost everywhere public schools were started. Only in Santa Barbara, where two-thirds of the townspeople spoke only Spanish, did influential residents force Spanish instruction. As a result, Spanish-speaking southern Californians established a Catholic school system in reaction to Yankee opposition to Spanish culture.

Compulsory Education Since 1852

Enactment of compulsory education laws

- 1852–1866
- 1867–1881
- 1882–1896
- 1897–1911
- 1912–1929

Albers Equal-Area Projection © SF

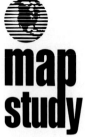

map study

Region
The states enacted compulsory education laws at different times. In which region were such laws first enacted? State laws also varied as to who should attend for how long and what should be taught.

Critical Thinking
Why might compulsory education have been introduced?

New reform movements shaped education in city schools.

What was life like for a student in the Gilded Age? In many cities of the North and West, schools probably had "no frills and little nonsense," like the one Henry Seidel Canby attended in the 1890s. He wrote,

> We went to school for facts and got them. Facts about Latin, facts about history, facts about algebra. . . . But of education there was very little.

AN AMERICAN ★ SPEAKS

Looking back on his lost school days in Wilmington, Delaware, Canby, publisher of the *Saturday Review of Literature,* saw "the same confusion of values" in 1934 as in the 1890s. He wrote, "Isolation from the major problems of society, memorizing of facts instead of training in thought, seem to be as confidently believed in as before."

By the 1890s critics began to find serious flaws in the system of public education. Like Canby, the critics saw too many schools as memorization factories where teachers used corporal punishment to instill rote learning. For example, Edward Bok, the influential editor of the *Ladies' Home Journal,* recalled that striking the palms of pupils' hands with a stick was the prevailing punishment when he started school in New York City at age seven. A recent immigrant from the Netherlands, Bok then knew scarcely a word of English, yet he stubbornly refused to practice the ornate Spencerian handwriting that was being taught. The principal struck his right hand until it was swollen, thus making all writing impossible.

One of the foremost school critics was **Joseph Mayer Rice,** a New York pediatrician who started a national school reform movement in the 1890s. Rice undertook a firsthand study of the public schools in 36 American cities. His book, *The Public-School System of the United States,* published in 1893, charged that mindless memorization and poor teaching were widespread. Rice also found a handful of fine schools—in Minneapolis, Minnesota; Indianapolis and LaPorte, Indiana; and Cook County, Illinois—where teachers encouraged students' interests. Rice's book led to a new movement called **progressive education.** The movement had three broad goals: first, the application of new research in psychology to school programs; second, the broadening of school programs to include health education and vocational training; and third, the tailoring of instruction to individual needs.

Many rural students attended one-room schools.

School days in a country environment were likely to be short and attendance irregular. Ungraded schools were still common in many rural areas during the Gilded Age. There, children from three to eighteen or older all studied in the same room. Millard Fillmore Kennedy began teaching in such a school near Franklin, in central Indiana, in September 1883. He had had only a few months of college and was not yet 20 years old.

The building was only eight-een by twenty-four feet in  AN AMERICAN ★ SPEAKS size, and there were thirty-five pupils, the majority of them former schoolmates of mine and ranging in age from six to twenty-three, packing in it on that opening day. When you allowed space for wraps and a stove and wood box and a teacher's desk, it will be evident that sardines in their can were positively isolated and lonely by comparison with us. . . . The six little beginners, who sat on a front bench almost under my feet and couldn't see anything but my legs without leaning backward, had to lay their primers on the seat beside them.

Though most teachers relied on endless recitations, the ungraded classrooms had their advantages. Anne Gertrude Sneller started in an ungraded school in Cicero, New York, in 1889. She found her front seat there a "listening post" as the older students recited aloud lessons that were mysterious and fascinating. She wrote:

I could not bear to have the physiology lesson come to an AN AMERICAN ★ SPEAKS end just as it was in the middle of talking about the hammer, anvil, and stirrup inside our ears—of all places!—and the twenty-four vertebrae and thirty-two teeth.

Around 1900 the isolated district schools gave way to consolidated schools, graded from the primary to the high-school level. In Eldorado, Kansas, where editor William Allen White went to school in the 1870s, the public schools were "the best money could buy."

Country or city, the schools of the Gilded Age made unprecedented advances. These schools brought literacy among native-born white Americans to a level with the advanced countries of western Europe and narrowed the gap between the educated and the uneducated.

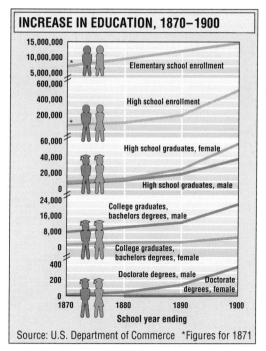

INCREASE IN EDUCATION, 1870–1900

Source: U.S. Department of Commerce *Figures for 1871

chart study

Education advanced steadily at all levels between 1870 and 1900. Why do you think this was so? **Critical Thinking** How could you account for the fact that women high-school graduates outnumbered men yet only one college graduate in five was a woman?

SECTION **5** REVIEW

Identify Key People and Terms
Write a sentence to identify: Joseph Mayer Rice, progressive education

Locate Key Places
Where did American Catholic bishops meet in 1884 when they made parochial schools mandatory?

Master the Main Ideas
1. **Recognizing societal values:** How did American schools attempt to create a unified society?
2. **Understanding reform movements:** Why did some Gilded Age Americans think education in city schools needed reform?
3. **Understanding U.S. cultural development:** How would you describe education in a country school?

Apply Critical Thinking Skills: Recognizing Values
What arguments can be made for and against public support of private schools? What do you say to the argument that private schools that meet state standards reduce the tax burden on the whole community and should therefore be entitled to some public funding?

Thomas Nast Attacks Boss Tweed

TIME FRAME
1871

GEOGRAPHIC SETTING
New York City

The art of political cartooning familiar in today's newspapers and magazines developed in England and France during the 18th and 19th centuries. In the United States, during the years following the Civil War, Thomas Nast (1840–1902) became America's most influential political cartoonist. Nast created or popularized images that have remained part of the American political cartoonist's stock in trade ever since. These images include the elephant as the symbol of the Republican party and the donkey as the symbol of the Democrats.

Nast's most famous cartoons are a series he drew in 1871 attacking the group of corrupt politicians who controlled the government of New York City in the 1860s and early 1870s. Headed by "Boss" William Marcy Tweed (1828–1878), the "Tweed Ring" benefited from bribes, kickbacks, and payoffs to the extent of perhaps $200 million, possibly more. One example of Tweed Ring corruption concerned the remodeling of the New York City courthouse in 1871. Original estimates placed the cost at $250,000; but with expenditures such as the $50,000 a day paid to a single plasterer (he alone received $2.8 million before the job was done), the final figure was considerably higher. Outraged by the Tweed Ring's flagrant corruption, Thomas Nast, then a young artist on the staff of *Harper's Weekly,* created the cartoons on these pages, along with many others attacking Tweed and his cronies. (Tweed is the fat figure with the huge nose and diamond stickpin.)

Nast's series helped overthrow the Tweed Ring. Tweed himself admitted the effectiveness of Nast's cartoons, telling an editor, "I don't care a straw for your newspapers articles. My constituents don't know how to read, but they can't help seeing them . . . pictures." While most members of the ring avoided punishment, Tweed himself finally went to jail. He escaped, but was arrested in Spain after someone identified him with the aid of a Nast cartoon.

One of Nast's most famous cartoons, *A Group of Vultures Waiting for the Storm To "Blow Over"—"Let Us Prey,"* is shown on the facing page. The title of the cartoon was an allusion to a remark by a member of the Tweed Ring that the scandal surrounding them "will soon blow over." In the double cartoon below, the upper panel shows Tweed and his cronies saluted by the police as they emerge with bulging pockets from the City Treasury; the lower panel shows the same police beating up a poor man for stealing a loaf of bread.

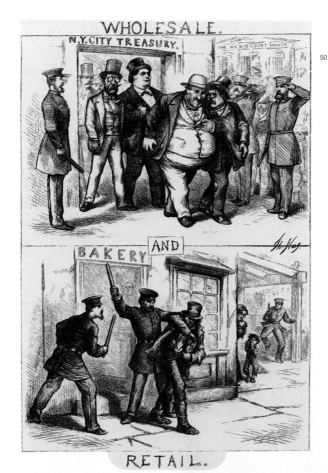

WHOLESALE.

N.Y. CITY TREASURY.

BAKERY AND

RETAIL.

Discussing the Cartoons

1. A caricature is a drawing of a person in which one or more features are exaggerated. In cartoons, people whose faces are familiar to the public are often caricatured rather than labeled. Did Thomas Nast label or caricature William Marcy Tweed?

2. What point about the punishment of theft is Nast making in *Wholesale and Retail*?

CRITICAL THINKING
Distinguishing False from Accurate Images

Does Nast's portrayal of the Tweed Ring as a group of vultures seem appropriate? Why or why not?

TIME FRAME
1886

GEOGRAPHIC SETTING
Chicago

Moments after the explosion of a dynamite bomb, Chicago police are shown exchanging fire with demonstrators in this drawing of the Haymarket Riot.

On May 3, 1886, six men were killed during a fight between police and striking workers at the McCormick Harvester Works in Chicago. On the following night, a crowd gathered at Chicago's Haymarket Square to protest police violence. As the rally broke up, someone threw a bomb into a group of policemen who had been watching the demonstration. The explosion killed one policeman, and in the riot that followed, six more officers and four demonstrators died. Although the person who threw the bomb was never discovered, eight men—most of them German immigrants—were quickly arrested and charged with inciting the Haymarket riot. Most of the eight men were also anarchists, political radicals who opposed all forms of government. In the ex-

cited atmosphere surrounding the trial, their radical views were felt sufficient to convict them of murder. Four were hanged, and one committed suicide in jail. The following passages are excerpted from the speech made on October 7 by the radical journalist August Spies [spēz], one of the four defendants who were hanged. The "Grinnell" mentioned by Spies was one of the State's Attorneys in the Haymarket trial.

Grinnell's main argument against the defendants was—"They were foreigners; they were not citizens." I cannot speak for the others. I will only speak for
5 myself. I have been a resident of this state fully as long as Grinnell, and probably have been as good a citizen—at least, I should not wish to be compared with him. Grinnell has incessantly appealed to the
10 patriotism of the jury. To that I reply in the language of [Samuel] Johnson, the English litterateur [literary man], "an appeal to patriotism is the last resort of a scoundrel." . . .
15 Grinnell has intimated to us that anarchism was on trial. The theory of anarchism belongs to the realm of speculative philosophy. There was not a syllable said about anarchism at the Haymarket meet-
20 ing. At that meeting the very popular theme of reducing the hours of toil was discussed. But, "Anarchism is on trial!" foams Mr. Grinnell. If that is the case, your honor, very well; you may sentence me,
25 for I am an anarchist. I believe that the state of castes and classes—the state where one class dominates over and lives upon the labor of another class, and calls this order—yes, I believe that this bar-
30 baric form of social organization, with its legalized plunder and murder, is doomed to die and make room for a free society, voluntary association, or universal broth-

erhood, if you like. You may pronounce the sentence upon me, honorable judge, but let the world know that in A.D. 1886, in the state of Illinois, eight men were sentenced to death because they believed in a better future; because they had not lost their faith in the ultimate victory of liberty and justice! . . .

You, gentlemen, are the revolutionists! You rebel against the effects of social conditions which have tossed you, by the fair hand of fortune, into a magnificent paradise. Without inquiring, you imagine that no one else has a right in that place. You insist that you are the chosen ones, the sole proprietors. The forces that tossed you into the paradise, the industrial forces, are still at work. They are growing more active and intense from day to day. Their tendency is to elevate all mankind to the same level, to have all humanity share in the paradise you now monopolize. You, in your blindness, think you can stop the tidal wave of civilization and human emancipation by placing a few policemen, a few Gatling guns [early machine guns], and some regiments of militia on the shore; you think you can frighten the rising waves back into the unfathomable depths whence they have arisen by erecting a few gallows in the perspective. You who oppose the natural course of things, you are the real revolutionists. You and you alone are the conspirators and destructionists! . . .

Look upon the economic battlefields! Behold the carnage and plunder of the Christian patricians [upper class]! Accompany me to the quarters of the wealth creators in this city. Go with me to the half-starved miners of the Hocking Valley. Look at the pariahs [outcasts] in the Monongahela Valley, and many other mining districts in this country, or pass along the railroads of that great and most orderly and law-abiding citizen Jay Gould. And then tell me whether this order has in it any moral principle for which it should be preserved. I say that the preservation of such an order is criminal—is murderous.

It means the preservation of the systematic destruction of children and women in factories. It means the preservation of enforced idleness of large armies of men, and their degradation. It means the preservation of intemperance, and sexual as well as intellectual prostitution. It means the preservation of misery, want, and servility on the one hand, and the dangerous accumulation of spoils, idleness, voluptuousness, and tyranny on the other. It means the preservation of vice in every form. And last, but not least, it means the preservation of the class struggle, of strikes, riots, and bloodshed. That is your "order," gentlemen. Yes, and it is worthy of you to be the champions of such an order. You are eminently fitted for that role. You have my compliments!

The Haymarket bomb marked the first time that dynamite was used as a weapon in the United States.

Discussing the Reading

1. August Spies quoted State's Attorney Grinnell as having said "Anarchism is on trial." Why might Grinnell have wanted to stress this point?

2. Spies argued (lines 50–54) that "the industrial forces" were historically tending "to elevate all mankind to the same level." Do you think that this estimate was true at the time when Spies made it? Is it true today?

CRITICAL THINKING
Demonstrating Reasoned Judgment

Many argued at the time of the Haymarket trial that Spies' ideas about anarchism were dangerous and threatening to the stability of society. To what extent should "dangerous" or unpopular ideas be protected by the First Amendment? What risks does the government take when it tries to curb free speech?

Elizabeth Cady Stanton Urges Higher Education for Women

TIME FRAME
1869

GEOGRAPHIC SETTING
Michigan

A leader in the movement for women's rights in the 19th century, Elizabeth Cady Stanton (1815–1902) helped organize the Seneca Falls Convention in 1848. After the Civil War, she and Susan B. Anthony (1820–1906) founded and edited *Revolution,* a newspaper that called for equal rights for women in all areas of life. In 1869 she helped organize the National Woman Suffrage Association. Between 1869 and 1881, Stanton lectured widely on a variety of topics, including education, family life, women's suffrage, and childrearing. In the following excerpt from her autobiography, *Eighty Years and More: Reminiscences, 1815–1897,* Stanton recalled a lecture she delivered at the University of Michigan at Ann Arbor in November 1869, where she discussed higher education for women.

The students, in large numbers, were there, and strengthened the threads of my discourse with frequent and generous applause; especially when I urged on the
5 Regents [governing board] of the University the duty of opening its doors to the daughters of the State. There were several splendid girls in Michigan, at that time, preparing themselves for admission to the
10 law department. As Judge [Thomas M.] Cooley, one of the professors, was a very liberal man, as well as a sound lawyer, and strongly in favor of opening the college to girls, I had no doubt the women of Michi-
15 gan would soon distinguish themselves at the bar. Some said the chief difficulty in the way of the girls of that day being admitted to the University was the want of room. That could have been easily obvi-
20 ated by telling the young men from abroad to betake themselves to the colleges in their respective States, that Michigan might educate her daughters. As the women owned a good share of the

25 property of the State, and had been heavily taxed to build and endow that institution, it was but fair that they should share in its advantages.

The Michigan University, with its

Hooting and jeering from the galleries, men attempt to disrupt a women's rights convention in 1857. A woman in the lower left corner of the picture is shown wearing bloomers, the loose-fitting trousers for women popularized by reformer Amelia Bloomer (1818–1894). This wood engraving appeared in *Harper's Weekly* in 1859.

extensive grounds, commodious buildings, medical and law schools, professors'
residences, and the finest laboratory in the
country, was an institution of which the
State was justly proud, and, as the tuition
35 was free, it was worth the trouble of a long,
hard siege by the girls of Michigan to gain
admittance there. I advised them to organize their forces at once, get their minute guns, battering rams, monitors,

40 projectiles, bombshells, cannon, torpe-
does, and crackers ready, and keep up a
brisk cannonading until the grave and
reverend seigniors [feudal lords; the Re-
gents] opened the door, and shouted,
45 "Hold, enough!" . . .

My visit ended with a pleasant reception, at which I was introduced to the
chaplain, several professors, and many ladies and gentlemen ready to accept the
50 situation. Judge Cooley gave me a glowing
account of the laws of Michigan—how
easy it was for wives to get possession of
all the property, and then sunder the marriage tie and leave the poor husband to
55 the charity of the cold world, with their
helpless children about him. I heard of a
rich lady, there, who made a will, giving
her husband a handsome annuity as long
as he remained her widower. It was evi-
60 dent that the poor "white male," sooner or
later, was doomed to try for himself the
virtue of the laws he had made for women.
I hope, for the sake of the race, he will not
bear oppression with the stupid fortitude
65 we have for 6,000 years.

Discussing the Reading

1. What arguments did Elizabeth
Cady Stanton make in favor of admitting women to universities?

2. Explain the meaning of the last two
sentences of this excerpt.

CRITICAL THINKING
Making Comparisons

Abigail Adams, in the excerpt from
one of her letters to her husband
John that is part of Source Reading
3D, urged that in the new American government then being
formed, women be given more independence. How does the tone of
her remarks about women's rights
differ from that of Stanton's? What
similarities are there between the
tones employed by the two
women?

Chapter Summary

Write supporting details under each of the following main ideas as you review the chapter.

Section 1

1. Graft, corruption, and scandal marred national politics.
2. Women hoped to achieve social and political rights.
3. African Americans lost ground to segregation in the 1880s.
4. Two government policies promoted economic growth.
5. Popular pressure brought two weak attempts at government regulation.

Section 2

1. New technologies helped cities spread out geographically.
2. New construction techniques created new kinds of city living spaces.
3. The growth of cities gave rise to powerful urban political machines.
4. Social reformers began the settlement movement to assist the urban poor.

Section 3

1. Labor organizations sought to improve the lot of American workers.
2. Women and unskilled workers remained outside the craft unions.
3. Savage labor disputes racked the nation during the Gilded Age.

Section 4

1. Farmers struggled to adapt to the new market economy.
2. The Populists advocated government intervention to protect free enterprise.
3. The depression of 1893 brought demands for federal action.
4. The 1896 election revitalized the Republican party.

Section 5

1. Americans expected their schools to create a unified society.
2. New reform movements shaped education in city schools.
3. Many rural students attended one-room schools.

Chapter Themes

1. **Conflict and cooperation:** Throughout the Gilded Age, labor, minorities, and women struggled to gain their rightful share of economic and political power. These groups gradually won basic rights.
2. **Free enterprise:** Economic power was clearly in the hands of big business during the Gilded Age. Powerful forces in business and government favored a laissez-faire approach—protection without regulation. Challenges to that power from unions and splinter parties such as the Populists were unsuccessful.

Chapter Study Guide

Identifying Key People and Terms

Name the key person or key term that describes the:
1. act designed to create a Civil Service and abolish the spoils system
2. name of a particularly corrupt political group in New York's Tammany Hall
3. list of workers, considered troublemakers, circulated among employers to prevent certain people from obtaining jobs
4. worst economic downturn in the nation's history before 1900

Locating Key Places

1. Which state first gave women the vote?
2. What city was destroyed by fire in 1871 and later became a center of architectural innovation?
3. Into what city did Jacob Coxey lead his army of unemployed workers?

Mastering the Main Ideas

1. Why were Gilded Age politicians more concerned with encouraging economic growth than with taking on reform issues?
2. How did political machines gain and maintain power?
3. In a chart, compare the Knights of Labor, the AFL, the UMW, and the ARU. Use the following as a model.

Comparison of Unions, 1869–1900

Name	Membership requirements	Goals	Method of achieving goal	Success

4. **(a)** What programs did the Populists propose? **(b)** To whom did the Populists' programs appeal and why?
5. **(a)** What did Americans expect of their schools in the late 1800s? **(b)** Explain how the schools helped reach those goals.

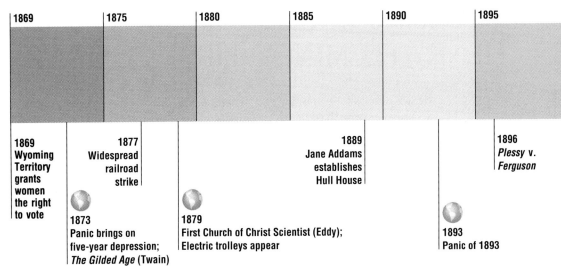

1869	1875	1880	1885	1890	1895	1900

1869
Wyoming Territory grants women the right to vote

1877
Widespread railroad strike

1873
Panic brings on five-year depression; *The Gilded Age* (Twain)

1879
First Church of Christ Scientist (Eddy); Electric trolleys appear

1889
Jane Addams establishes Hull House

1893
Panic of 1893

1896
Plessy v. *Ferguson*

Applying Critical Thinking Skills

1. **Expressing problems: (a)** Why were high tariffs a problem for consumers? **(b)** Why were low—or no—tariffs a problem for American businesses?
2. **Recognizing values:** What values are evident in the work of Jane Addams, Robert A. Woods, and Lillian Wald?
3. **Identifying central issues:** What are some of the social, political, and economic problems that became evident during the Gilded Age that the United States would have to deal with in the 1900s?
4. **Making comparisons:** Explain in what ways McKinley can be said to have represented the old ways of politics and Bryan the politics of the future.
5. **Formulating appropriate questions: (a)** If you were to interview students of the 1890s, what would you ask city students? **(b)** What would you ask rural students?

Chapter Activities

Learning Geography Through History

1. How did technology promote the outward spread of cities in the late 1800s?
2. How did improvements such as elevators and steel frames for buildings affect the physical geography of the city?

Relating the United States to the World

1. The cartoon on page 218 pictures an "alien anarchist" trampling on American law and order. Why might foreign-born anarchists appeal for violence more strongly than native-born Americans?
2. Foreign investors provided much of the capital that built U.S. industries and railroads. What benefits and drawbacks does such investment offer?

Using the Time Line

1. What key events indicate that the Gilded Age was a period of social upheaval?
2. What events show that women were actively seeking to influence social change?

Linking Past to Present

1. The Civil Rights Act of 1964 prohibited all discrimination because of race, color, religion, and national origin. How did it differ from the 1883 Supreme Court decision regarding the Civil Rights Act of 1875?
2. How many of the Knights of Labor goals have become realities?

Practicing Critical Thinking Strategies

Recognizing Values
Commodore Vanderbilt's oldest son, William, said in 1877: "Our men feel that although I . . . may have my millions and they the rewards of their daily toil, still we are about equal in the end." In what respects were Vanderbilt and the employees of his railroads equals? In what ways are workers and employers more nearly equal today?

Learning More About Politics and Daily Life in the Gilded Age

1. **Using Source Readings:** Read the Source Readings for this chapter and answer the questions.
2. **Creating Original Material:** As a Gilded Age teenager, prepare a short talk or create a poster advocating or opposing giving the vote to women.

HENRY FLEMING'S FIRST COMBAT

Stephen Crane (1871–1900) interviewed veterans, studied photographs, and read first-hand accounts of battles in order to master the historical details needed for his Civil War novel, *The Red Badge of Courage* (1895). Although he does not mention actual places or dates, the combat that Crane described resembles the battle of Chancellorsville, fought in northern Virginia in May 1863. In the following excerpt from Crane's novel, his hero, a young recruit named Henry Fleming, gets his first taste of combat.

He was at a task. He was like a carpenter who has made many boxes, making still another box, only there was furious haste in his movements. He, in his thought, was careering off in other places, even as the carpenter who as he works, whistles and thinks of his friend or his enemy, his home or a saloon. And these jolted dreams were never perfect to him afterward, but remained a mass of blurred shapes.

Presently, he began to feel the effects of the war atmosphere—a blistering sweat, a sensation that his eyeballs were about to crack like hot stones. A burning roar filled his ears.

Following this came a red rage. He developed the acute exasperation of a pestered animal, a well-meaning cow worried by dogs. He had a mad feeling against his rifle, which could only be used against one life at a time. He wished to rush forward and strangle with his fingers. He craved a power that would enable him to make a world-sweeping gesture and brush all back. His impotency appeared to him, and made his rage into that of a driven beast.

Buried in the smoke of many rifles his anger was directed not so much against men whom he knew were rushing toward him as against the swirling battle phantoms which were choking him, stuffing their smoke robes down his parched throat. He fought frantically for respite for his senses, for air, as a babe being smothered attacks the deadly blankets.

> **He wished to rush forward and strangle with his fingers.**

There was a blare of heated rage mingled with a certain expression of intentness on all faces. Many of the men were making low-toned noises with their mouths, and these subdued cheers, snarls, imprecations, prayers, made a wild, barbaric song that went as an undercurrent of sound, strange and chantlike with the resounding chords of the war march. The man at the youth's elbow was babbling. In it there was something soft and tender like the monologue of a babe. The tall soldier was swearing in a loud voice. From his lips came a black procession of curious oaths. Of a sudden another broke out in a querulous way like a man who has mislaid his hat. "Well, why don't they support us? Why don't they send supports? Do they think ———"

The youth in his battle sleep heard this as one who dozes hears.

There was a singular absence of heroic poses. The men bending and surging in their haste and rage were in every impossible attitude. The steel ramrods clanked and clanged with incessant din as the men pounded them furiously into the hot rifle barrels. The flaps of the cartridge boxes were all unfastened, and bobbed idiotically with each movement. The rifles, once loaded, were jerked to the shoulder and fired without apparent aim into the smoke or at one of the blurred and shifting forms which upon the field before the regiment had been growing larger and larger like puppets under a magician's hand.

The officers, at their intervals, rearward, neglected to stand in picturesque attitudes. They were bobbing to and fro roaring directions and encouragements. The dimensions of their howls were extraordinary. They expended their lungs with prodigal wills. And often they nearly

An excerpt from
THE RED BADGE OF COURAGE
by Stephen Crane

stood upon their heads in their anxiety to observe the enemy on the other side of the tumbling smoke.

The lieutenant of the youth's company had encountered a soldier who had fled screaming at the first volley of his comrades. Behind the lines these two were acting a little isolated scene. The man was blubbering and staring with sheeplike eyes at the lieutenant, who had seized him by the collar and was pommeling him. He drove him back into the ranks with many blows. The soldier went mechanically, dully, with his animal-like eyes upon the officer. Perhaps there was to him a divinity expressed in the voice of the other—stern, hard, with no reflection of fear in it. He tried to reload his gun, but his shaking hands prevented. The lieutenant was obliged to assist him.

The men dropped here and there like bundles. The captain of the youth's company had been killed in an early part of the action. His body lay stretched out in the position of a tired man resting, but upon his face there was an astonished and sorrowful look, as if he thought some friend had done him an ill turn. The babbling man was grazed by a shot that made the blood stream widely down his face. He clapped both hands to his head. "Oh!" he said, and ran. Another grunted suddenly as if he had been struck by a club in the stomach. He sat down and gazed ruefully. In his eyes there was mute, indefinite reproach. Farther up the line a man standing behind a tree, had had his knee joint splintered by a ball. Immediately he had dropped his rifle and gripped the tree with both arms. And there he remained, clinging desperately and crying for assistance that he might withdraw his hold upon the tree.

> The enemy were scattered into reluctant groups.

At last an exultant yell went along the quivering line. The firing dwindled from an uproar to a last vindictive popping. As the smoke slowly eddied away, the youth saw that the charge has been repulsed. The enemy were scattered into reluctant groups. He saw a man climb to the top of the fence, straddle the rail, and fire a parting shot. The waves had receded, leaving bits of dark *débris* [rubbish; here, bodies] upon the ground.

Some in the regiment began to whoop frenziedly. Many were silent. Apparently they were trying to contemplate themselves.

After the fever had left his veins, the youth thought that at last he was going to suffocate. He became aware of the foul atmosphere in which he had been struggling. He was grimy and dripping like a laborer in a foundry [metalworks]. He grasped his canteen and took a long swallow of the warmed water.

A sentence with variations went up and down the line. "Well, we've helt 'em back. We've helt 'em back; derned if we haven't." The men said it blissfully, leering at each other with dirty smiles.

The youth turned to look behind him and off to the right and off to the left. He experienced the joy of a man who at last finds leisure in which to look about him.

Under foot there were a few ghastly forms motionless. They lay twisted in fantastic contortions. Arms were bent and heads were turned in incredible ways. It seemed that the dead men must have fallen from some great height to get into such positions. They looked to be dumped out upon the ground from the sky.

CRITICAL THINKING
Identifying Central Issues
Indicate different ways in which Stephen Crane suggested the dream-like nature of Henry Fleming's first experience of combat.

331

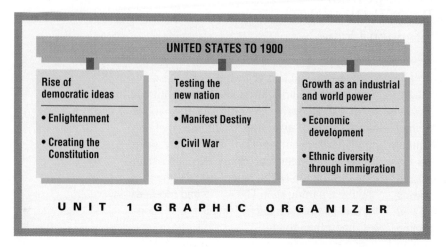

UNITED STATES TO 1900

Rise of democratic ideas	Testing the new nation	Growth as an industrial and world power
• Enlightenment	• Manifest Destiny	• Economic development
• Creating the Constitution	• Civil War	• Ethnic diversity through immigration

U N I T 1 G R A P H I C O R G A N I Z E R

CHAPTER SURVEY

The Meeting of Three Cultures
Pre-Columbian Era–1624

New World voyages began a rich cultural exchange. The explorations of Columbus led the way. Native Americans soon shared North America with thousands of Europeans and Africans. Conquest, disease, and slavery were some of the bitter results of the meeting of these cultures. However, both the New World and the Old were enriched by discoveries of new crops, animals, religions, and ways of life. Together, Native Americans, Europeans, and Africans would create a new and lasting culture in North America.

The first Americans spread throughout both continents. Different conditions across the country created different ways of life for each group of Native Americans. However, they shared many social customs and religious beliefs.

African cultures had also been shaped by various conditions of their continent. West Africans, the first to come to America, were farmers, hunters, and traders.

Europeans in the 1400s had taken new interest in trade, art, learning, and invention. One result of this awakening — called the Renaissance — was that European sailors began long ocean voyages of trade and exploration.

Spain led the way in exploring the New World. First came conquerors, who killed, destroyed, and discovered as they searched for glory and treasure. Colonists came next, bringing the Christian faith to the New World and sending great riches back to Spain. During the 1500s, Spain built a large colonial empire in North and South America. Indians were forced to do the hardest work in the colonies, and many died. To replace them, thousands of Africans were brought to America as slaves.

France and England began colonies in North America. France used the discoveries of Verrazano and Cartier to claim its share of the New World. French traders roamed deep into North America in search of furs. New France grew large in territory, but it held only a few colonists and permanent settlements.

After defeating Spain in a great sea battle, England also turned to America. The first successful English colony began at Jamestown. John Smith helped the colony to survive. Tobacco crops gave the colony financial success. In 1619, the colony elected members to the House of Burgesses, starting the first representative form of government in colonial America.

2

The Enlightenment and the Revolutionary Era
1600–1788

Different goals brought colonists to America.
Some colonists came to find religious freedom. Some looked for the profits of farming and trade. Others were forced to come, leaving British jails.

Gradually colonists developed a unique, American character. In the 1700s the ideas of the European Enlightenment spread through the colonies, bringing new ways to think about freedom and government.

The French and Indian War tested colonial partnership.
Colonists had fought side by side with British soldiers in the conflict. Their victory, however, began their separation. The British demanded new taxes to pay for the war. Colonists bitterly resisted. In the 1770s, rising anger stirred acts of violence, including the Boston Massacre and the Boston Tea Party. The British sent soldiers to control the city of Boston, a center of colonial unrest. In 1744 the colonists formed the First Continental Congress to plan united action. Other colonists gathered weapons and trained for war.

The fighting began at Lexington and Concord in April 1775.
The Continental Congress sent George Washington to command American forces. Washington's task was to create a national army and to keep that tattered force together to the end. Despite mistakes, defeats, and great hardship, Washington succeeded.

In spite of many victories, British generals did not succeed. Problems of geography — the wide Atlantic Ocean, the deep American wilderness — became fatal to the British. At two key points in the war, British armies were trapped beyond supply lines. In 1777 General Burgoyne's army surrendered at Saratoga, New York. This American victory brought France into the war on the American side. In 1781 a combined French and American force trapped a British army at Yorktown. After General Cornwallis surrendered his army, the war came to an end.

Americans won the Revolution and tried a new government.
Under the Articles of Confederation, the national government had no main leader and depended on the voluntary cooperation of the states. In 1787 the states sent delegates to Philadelphia to fix the many problems of the Confederation. Instead, the delegates wrote a new Constitution.

The framers wanted to give the national government enough power to solve problems. However, they also wanted to guard against abuse of power. The framers divided power among the three branches of government — the executive, the legislative, and the judiciary. Each branch had some control over the others. The Constitution also divided powers carefully between the national government and state governments. After almost a year of debate, the states accepted the new Constitution.

C H A P T E R
S U R V E Y

Examining the Constitution
1787–1824

George Washington led the new federal government.

Congress created a federal court system and proposed the Bill of Rights. Washington selected a cabinet of advisers. Alexander Hamilton won acceptance for his economic plans, including payment of the national debt and the creation of a national bank.

As Americans built new democratic traditions, they were challenged by France and Great Britain. They were also torn by disagreements among themselves. Territorial growth, the rise of political parties, and war would soon test the strength and flexibility of the new Constitution.

The Constitution created a complex but effective system.

The framers carefully balanced the powers of the national and the state governments in a system known as federalism. The work of the national government was assigned to three branches. The legislative branch, Congress, makes laws. The executive branch, the president, puts laws into action. The judicial branch, or court system, interprets the laws. A system of checks and balances gives each branch some control over the others to limit government power and to prevent tyranny.

The Constitution is flexible, allowing for change through interpretation and an amendment process. Other changes have come about through tradition, creating an "unwritten constitution."

The Constitution safeguarded many valued civil liberties, though it did not at first include a bill of rights. Those safeguards included the right of *habeas corpus* and protections against *ex post facto* laws and bills of attainder.

The many compromises in the Constitution included the continued existence of slavery. The rights and hopes of African Americans, women, Indians, and others were not advanced in 1789.

Early struggles helped form two political parties.

The Federalists and the Republicans each had quite different ideas about the purpose and working of government. Led by Alexander Hamilton, the Federalists wanted a powerful commercial nation. The Republicans, led by Thomas Jefferson, favored a quiet agricultural country.

The second president, Federalist John Adams, avoided a war with France after that nation began seizing American ships. However, Adams had difficulty finding political peace at home. The harsh Alien and Sedition Acts passed by the Federalists only increased political conflict within the country. The election of 1800 brought the Republicans to power.

President Jefferson let the Alien and Sedition Acts expire and ended Federalist control of the court system. During this time the Supreme Court established its power of judicial review.

In 1803 Jefferson bought the Louisiana Territory from France, doubling the nation's size. He tried to avoid conflict with Great Britain with the Embargo Act in 1807. The act stopped Americans from doing business with other countries, and the result was economic disaster.

A dispute with Great Britain exploded into war in 1812.
President James Madison led a divided and unprepared United States into the conflict. Opposition to the war was especially strong in New England.

The U.S. Navy stung the British with unexpected defeats. However, the Americans experienced shocks of their own. An attempt to conquer Canada ended in disaster. Later, a British army succeeded in burning Washington, D.C. The war ended in 1814 without solving the original disputes. However, their tardy victory at New Orleans gave Americans a sense of triumph.

Peace produced an era of good feelings. The two terms of James Monroe were marked by a new national unity, prosperity, and growth. The addition of new states sparked tension between North and South over the issue of slavery. However, Congress won a temporary solution to the problem with the Compromise of 1820.

In 1823 the president published the Monroe Doctrine, setting the Western Hemisphere off limits to European colonization. With this firm statement, the young nation began to take its place in world affairs.

Expansion, Reform, and Constitutional Conflicts
1824–1860

Andrew Jackson takes charge.   As the United States grew in size, population, and wealth, it also grew more democratic. Almost all white men gained the right to vote. Their enthusiasm elected Andrew Jackson in 1828 and transformed American politics. New campaign styles were developed. New parties formed: Democrats to support Jackson, Whigs to oppose him. Jackson introduced the spoils system to reward his supporters with federal jobs.

Jackson met many challenges with boldness. In 1832, South Carolina tried to nullify, or ignore, federal tariffs. This action brought an early threat of civil war. When Jackson threatened to use troops to enforce the tariff, the crisis passed. Jackson opposed the Bank of the United States and succeeded in closing it in 1832. During Jackson's Administration, thousands of eastern Indians were driven from their homelands and forced to relocate in the West. Wise or not, fair or not, Jackson dominated his time.

A revival of religious faith began a time of social reform
Some reformers fought the abuse of alcohol. Dorothea Dix drew attention to conditions of the mentally ill; others brought aid to people with physical disabilities. Horace Mann began a transformation of American public education. A women's rights movement began with the Seneca Falls Convention in 1848.

No reform movement was more powerful or passionate than the anti-slavery cause. African American and white abolitionists published, preached, and paraded in the cause of human freedom.

It was a costly struggle. By April 1865 620,000 soldiers were dead. Abraham Lincoln was dead. Slavery, too, was dead — and three million African Americans lived in freedom.

The United States extended its boundaries.
Belief in a so-called Manifest Destiny produced a period of settlement and territorial growth. Americans crossed into the Mexican territory of Texas, fought for their independence in 1836, and joined the United States in 1845. The next year, the huge Oregon Territory was added through a treaty with Great Britain.

The American push for more territory led to war with Mexico. American forces invaded Mexico and won by capturing Mexico City. The United States gained the territories of California and New Mexico in the treaty that ended the war.

Growing sectional differences divided North and South.
Should a new state be slave or free? In answering that question, the North and South saw their long, uneasy truce over slavery fall apart. One by one, political compromises failed in the 1850s. The presidential election in 1860 brought the country to a breaking point. When Northern votes elected a Republican president — Abraham Lincoln — seven states seceded from the Union. These states formed their own government, the Confederacy.

5

Civil War and Reconstruction
1860–1877

The attack on Fort Sumter plunged the nation into war.
Citizens in the North and South greeted the long-awaited conflict with enthusiasm. Both sides expected easy victory. However, it would take four cruel years to end the war. Northern soldiers marched in order to save the Union. Southern troops defended states' rights. Gradually many Americans, including Abraham Lincoln, came to realize that slavery was the true issue of the war. By issuing the Emancipation Proclamation in 1863, Lincoln committed the Union to the cause of human freedom.

The South won many battles in the early years of the war.
The South began the war with smaller armies but better generals. These leaders had the advantage of fighting a defensive war on familiar lands.

In the east, the Union goal was to capture the Confederate capital of Richmond. The first Union drive ended in Southern victory at Bull Run in July 1861. Again and again Union armies would be stopped by Southern victories. Lincoln searched for a commander able to defeat Robert E. Lee and Thomas J. Jackson.

Confederate success shocked the North, but did not bring an end to the war. After brilliant victories in the spring of 1863, Lee invaded the North to force a decisive battle. In a three-day battle at Gettysburg, Lee was defeated. This was a major turning point of the war.

Northern advantages finally led to victory in the Civil War.

The North began the war with huge advantages in population and economic power. During the war, these advantages only increased. Thousands of freed African Americans joined the Union forces. Gradually, the navy blockade of Southern ports began to damage the South's economy

Northern failures against Lee's army had been balanced by better success in the west. In July 1863 Ulysses S. Grant captured Vicksburg, giving the North complete control of the Mississippi River.

Grant was placed in overall command of Union forces. He planned a campaign that used the superior force of the North against a weakening Confederacy. Grant attacked Lee's army in Virginia in the spring of 1864. Despite defeats and huge losses, Grant kept moving forward, keeping Lee on the defensive. Meanwhile, Union armies won victories in the west. William Sherman captured Atlanta in September 1864. The march of Sherman's army through the heart of Georgia was the beginning of the end for the South. Lee surrendered his worn-out army in April 1865. America's deadliest war was over.

Peace brings the challenges of Reconstruction.

Lincoln had hoped to restore Southern states to the Union on simple and generous terms. Radical Republicans in Congress had harsher plans. After Lincoln's assassination in April 1865, President Andrew Johnson tried to carry on Lincoln's policies. Radical Republicans struck back with their own proposals. After a bitter political struggle, Radicals finally passed their programs and tried to remove Johnson from office. Johnson became the first president to be impeached. He survived his Senate trial by one vote, but his political power was broken. Ulysses S. Grant was elected president in 1868. Radical Republicans gained full control of Reconstruction in the South. They would maintain that control for the next nine years.

A key to Radical Reconstruction was the 14th Amendment, which gave full citizenship to ex-slaves and banned Confederate officials from public office. To rejoin the Union, Southern states had to write new constitutions and ratify the 14th Amendment. Later Radicals proposed the 15th Amendment to make sure African American men had the right to vote.

Radical Reconstruction gave temporary political gains.

The new constitutions brought new groups to power in the South. Northerners who came to the South during Reconstruction were called carpetbaggers by their opponents. Southerners who joined in Reconstruction were called scalawags.

African Americans exercised their new political rights. Many former slaves were elected to major offices. Several served in Congress.

The new governments established public schools and passed civil rights laws. However, they failed to solve the deep poverty of the postwar South or to heal the bitterness of former Confederates.

Most Southern whites rejected the new social and political system. Some resorted to violence; some joined organizations such as the Ku Klux Klan. Reconstruction governments needed help from the federal government to restore order. Over the years, however, Northerners lost interest in Reconstruction. A political deal in 1877 put Rutherford B. Hayes in the White House and put an official end to Reconstruction. White Southerners were gradually able to erase the political and civil rights gains of former slaves.

At times the government outlawed business practices that harmed the public interest. Usually, however, the government let business alone. This hands-off attitude allowed a few wealthy individuals to control large industries. J.P. Morgan, Andrew Carnegie, and John D. Rockefeller were among those who achieved great power, fame, and influence in American business.

C H A P T E R
S U R V E Y

America's Economic Transformation
1860-1900

Changes swept across the United States after 1860.

The nation was transformed from a collection of small communities into a single powerful economy. Travel and communication increased in speed. Some traditional ways of life were lost forever. New groups of immigrants contributed to American society. New inventions and fresh ideas changed business and industry. Americans lived and worked in new ways. The great symbol and main cause of this time of change was the American railroad.

The transcontinental railroad ushered in a new age.

The completion of the Pacific railroad in 1869 brought rapid settlement of the West. People poured into the region between the Mississippi River and California. The American frontier came to an end. Buffalo herds were wiped out. Soldiers and Indians fought their last tragic battles. The Sioux won a stunning victory at Little Big Horn in 1876. They also endured a terrible loss at Wounded Knee in 1890. Indians were forced onto reservations, their way of life all but destroyed.

The railroad opened new markets for American business. Industries expanded and developed new methods of mass production. Inventions such as the telephone created a revolution in communication. These changes combined to create a national economy.

New ways of organizing businesses were discovered.

The corporation was developed to raise the great sums of money to build new factories. Some businesses learned ways to combine the power of several companies. Schemes such as trusts and monopolies allowed certain businesses to eliminate their competition, fix prices, and increase their profits.

A new wave of immigrants arrived from Europe and Asia.

Millions of these newcomers crowded into American cities and took low-paying factory jobs. They were not always welcomed by Americans. Some disliked the religion, culture, or race of the new immigrants. Others resented the additional competition for jobs during hard times. In 1882 the Chinese Exclusion Act became the first of several laws that restricted immigration.

Despite these unfriendly attitudes, immigrants made new lives for themselves. They enriched American society with their unique customs and beliefs.

CHAPTER SURVEY 7

Politics and Daily Life in the Gilded Age
1870–1900

The Gilded Age was a time of sharp social differences. A few Americans enjoyed wealth and ease, but many others suffered terrible hardship. Cities were dirty and over-crowded. Workers were mistreated and underpaid. Farmers struggled with debts.

Politicians of the Gilded Age ignored these serious problems. Instead, many used government power to enrich themselves. Given little help from corrupt politicians, Americans began to act for them-selves. Individuals and groups worked to improve education, and living and working conditions. A time of political corruption would lead to an age of reform in the United States.

Politicians enriched both themselves and big business. Graft and bribery became a way of life in many city governments. Scandals in President Ulysses S. Grant's Administration cheated the public out of millions of dollars. Disputes over patronage — control of government jobs — led to the assassination of President James Garfield in 1881. Garfield's death shocked both political parties into changes in the patronage system.

Government policies favored busi-ness in the Gilded Age. Other groups lost out. Women won little progress toward voting and other rights. African Americans saw their voting rights disappear and discrimination increase.

American cities grew rapidly during the Gilded Age. Millions of people moved to cities to work in shops and factories. New building techniques created tall office and apartment structures. New methods of building bridges and new forms of public transportation helped cities expand. However, rapid growth produced many problems, including lack of clean water supplies and proper sewage treatment. Poor people — many of them immigrants — were forced to live in crowded, unclean conditions. Reformers such as Jane Addams in Chicago used settlement houses to help with the everyday problems of city residents.

Working people and farmers fought for improvements. Workers formed labor unions to try to change their low wages and working conditions. Large corporations resisted changes that would lessen their profits. A series of violent strikes occurred during the Gilded Age. Government soldiers were used against the strikers, and the labor movement weakened.

New equipment and methods helped farmers produce more food than Americans needed. As a result, crop prices fell as the farmer's costs increased. Faced with growing debt, farmers joined organizations such as the Farmer's Alliance and the Grange. They also supported the Populists, a national political party that pushed for stronger powers for the federal government.

Liberty

"Give me your tired, your poor, your huddled masses yearning to breathe free," invites the famous inscription on the pedestal of the Statue of Liberty. Having welcomed generations of immigrants to the United States, Lady Liberty is probably—after the American flag—the most deeply beloved symbol of our country. Although Americans treasure the ideal of liberty she represents, they have not always agreed on what the proper limits of our freedoms ought to be. The following quotations reflect both Americans' love of liberty and their disagreements about its limits.

1774

The God who gave us life, gave us liberty at the same time.
▲ **Thomas Jefferson, "Summary View of the Rights of British America"**

1792

It requires some experience of liberty to know how to use it.
▲ **Hugh Henry Brackenridge, Modern Chivalry**

1865

Everybody has asked the question, and they learned to ask it of the Abolitionists, "What shall we do with the Negro?" I have had but one answer from the beginning. Do nothing with us! Your doing with us has already played the mischief with [injured] us. Do nothing with us! If the apples will not remain on the tree of their own strength, . . . let them fall. And if the Negro can not stand on his own legs, let him fall also. All I ask is, give him a chance to stand on his own legs! If you see him on his way to school, let him alone,—don't disturb him. If you see him going to the dinner table at a hotel, let him go! If you see him going to the ballot-box, let him alone,—don't disturb him! If you see him going into a work-shop, just let him alone,—your interference is doing him a positive [real] injury. . . . Let him fall if he can not stand alone!
▲ **Frederick Douglass, "What the Black Man Wants"**

1919

The most stringent protection of free speech would not protect a man in falsely shouting fire in a theater and causing a panic. . . . the question in every case is whether the words used in such circumstances are of such a nature as to create a clear and present danger that they will bring out the substantive [real] evils that Congress has a right to prevent.
▲ **Oliver Wendell Holmes, Jr., opinion in Schenk v. United States**

1920

No woman shall call herself free who does not own or control her body. No woman can call herself free until she can choose conciously whether she will or will not be a mother.
▲ **Margaret Sanger, Woman and the New Race**

1968

His headstone said
FREE AT LAST, FREE AT LAST
But death is a slave's freedom
We seek the freedom of free men
And the construction of a world
Where Martin Luther King could
    have lived and preached
    nonviolence.
▲ **Nikki Giovanni, "The Funeral of Martin Luther King, Jr."**

1987

. . . As I stood with the Statue of Liberty towering over me, I realized again what many have felt before—that America is another name for freedom.

Yet many Americans take their freedom for granted. I cannot. For 6½ years I was in solitary confinement in a Communist Chinese prison, falsely accused of being a spy for the West. My ordeal began on a very different August day 22 years ago, when 30 or 40 Red Guards [gangs of teenagers used by the government to attack the "enemies" of communist leader Mao Zedong] came to destroy my house. I had been alone in my study reading, and though I knew it was a futile [useless] gesture, I picked up a copy of the Chinese constitution. "It's against the constitution of the People's Republic of China to enter a private house without a search warrant," I challenged.

The young Red Guards grabbed the constitution from my hands and tore it up. "The constitution is abolished," they said. "We recognize only the teaching of our Great Leader Chairman Mao." . . .

A constitution is only as strong as the beliefs of its people.

▲ **Nien Chang,** *Life and Death in Shanghai*

Paraphrase and Discuss

"Men, their rights and nothing more; women, their rights and nothing less," declared Susan B. Anthony at the conclusion of a speech she gave in 1873 urging that American women be free to vote. What did she mean? One method that might help you understand what Anthony said would be to paraphrase her conclusion; that is, restate it in your own words. Which of the following would be the best paraphrase of Anthony's conclusion: (a) men and women are fundamentally the same; (b) men deserve only their rights and women shouldn't settle for less than their rights; (c) women deserve the right to vote. The best paraphrase is (b), because it most closely restates Anthony's words.

Assignment: In a paragraph, paraphrase the excerpt from Frederick Douglass' speech "What the Black Man Wants" that appears on the facing page. Then, in a second paragraph, discuss the central point that Douglass was making. Use the following process.

Paraphrase the excerpt. Read the passage carefully. What attitude would the Abolitionists have had toward African Americans? Examine the language that Douglass used. What did he mean by such terms as *mischief, disturb, interference,* and *positive injury*? Rewrite the excerpt sentence by sentence, using simple, everyday English.

Think about what Douglass was saying. What was Douglass' central point? What examples did he provide to expand on it? How does his central point fit in with the American ideal of liberty? How does his position apply to the lives of African Americans and other minority groups today? How do you feel about Douglass' point?

Discuss Douglass' statement in a paragraph. Present his central point as your topic sentence. In the remaining sentences of your paragraph, explore one or more of the questions in the preceding step. Provide specific examples to support your points. Be sure to use appropriate transitional words and phrases to link up your sentences. Write an effective concluding sentence in which you sum up the points you have made about Douglass' statement.

Edit both paragraphs. Look over your paraphrase of the excerpt and your discussion of Douglass' central point. Does your paraphrase restate Douglass' points in the order in which he made them? Is the topic sentence of your discussion paragraph clear? Is your concluding sentence an effective summary of the points you have made?

Proofread and rewrite your paragraphs. Go over both paragraphs, correcting any errors in grammar, spelling, and punctuation. Rewrite both paragraphs.

341

Unit 2

Your Song - My Song - Our Boys' Song

OVER THERE

WORDS AND MUSIC BY
GEORGE M. COHAN

You Are There

Johnnie get your gun, get your
  gun, get your gun,
Take it on the run, on the run,
  on the run;
Hear them calling you and me;
Every son of liberty.
Hurry right away, no delay, go
  today,
Make your daddy glad, to have
  had such a lad,
Tell your sweetheart not to
  pine,
To be proud her boy's in line.
Over there, over there,
Send the word, send the word
  over there,
That the Yanks are coming, the
  Yanks are coming,
The drums rum-tumming
  everywhere.
So prepare, say a prayer,
Send the word, send the word
  to beware,
We'll be over, we're coming
  over,
And we won't come back till it's
  over over there.
—*Composer George M.
Cohan's (1878–1942) song,
Over There.*

**Norman Rockwell's painting of
World War I soldiers adorned
Over There's original
sheet-music cover.**

342

America at Peace and at War

Unit Themes

In this unit you will analyze the following themes of U.S. history:

► The American political system is built upon constitutional and representative government.

► Americans express social and political concerns within a religious and ethical framework.

► The American belief in a unique national destiny influences its relations with other nations.

► Americans have made choices based on geography as they interacted with the environment.

1890	1895	1900	1905	1910	1915	1920

1893
Americans in Hawaii overthrow Queen Liliuokalani

1898
Spanish-American War begins

1900
Decade of peak immigration begins, mainly from Europe and Asia

1906
Upton Sinclair's *The Jungle* spurs reform

1917
United States declares war on Germany

1914
World War I begins; Panama Canal opens

1918
Armistice declared

Linking Past to Present

Homelessness haunts the American conscience today as it did for Robert La Follette in the 1880s. The children in the inset, photographed around 1900 by Jacob Riis in New York City, sought shelter in a doorway. For the family shown in the background photograph in San Jose, California, in 1987, the family car provided the only roof over their heads.

The Progressive Era

1 9 0 0 – 1 9 1 7

8

When Robert M. La Follette and his wife, Belle, took up the study of law in the 1880s, they were only a few steps from poverty. Yet the idea of making money from their law practice, then and later in life, meant little to these idealistic, young University of Wisconsin graduates. In one of his first cases, Bob La Follette successfully defended a homeless person in the Madison, Wisconsin, municipal court. He shrugged off the praise of his friends, saying they did not seem to realize that

AN AMERICAN ★ SPEAKS I did it . . . because I thought he was innocent—that I was simply fighting a fight for the truth—that his vindication [being cleared of guilt] was a *truth.* That is the way I like to think of it and the way I did think of it else I should not have tried so earnestly to win.''

The La Follettes were typical of the serious, thoughtful Americans who would soon usher in a new era of reform. The rapid pace of technological change had opened up the vision of an abundant future, when poverty and other social ills would become obsolete. Because of a widespread belief in human progress and determination to seek reform, historians later called the years from 1900 to 1917 the Progressive Era.

How and why did so many Americans work so hard then for reform? Answering these questions will help us understand American politics and government today.

CHAPTER PREVIEW

In this chapter you will learn about reforms that changed America in the early 1900s.

SECTIONS IN THIS CHAPTER:
1. **The American people clamored for reform.**
2. **Progressive ideas transformed politics.**
3. **Progressive reforms reached the national level.**
4. **The West gained political power.**
5. **Woodrow Wilson won sweeping reforms.**

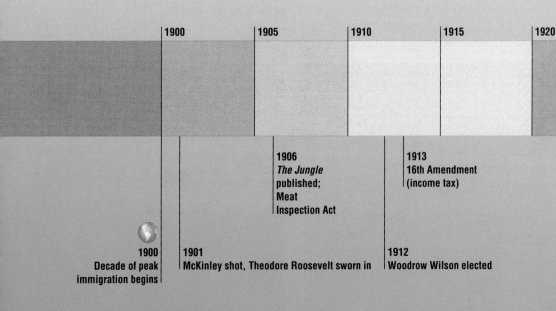

1900	1905	1910	1915	1920

1906
The Jungle published;
Meat Inspection Act

1913
16th Amendment (income tax)

1900
Decade of peak immigration begins

1901
McKinley shot, Theodore Roosevelt sworn in

1912
Woodrow Wilson elected

The American people clamored for reform.

Key Terms: progressivism, muckrakers, *The Jungle*, Socialist Party of America, *Muller* v. *Oregon*, National Association for the Advancement of Colored People (NAACP)

Reading Preview
As you read this section, you will learn:

1. who powered the reform impulse in the early 1900s.
2. what a new brand of journalism revealed about society and politics.
3. what kinds of changes the socialist movement hoped to bring about.
4. what reform women worked to achieve.
5. what social and political restrictions African Americans fought.

Night-shift workers at a Bridgetown, New Jersey, glass factory pose for the photographer, sociologist Lewis Hine, in November 1909, below left. Another Hine photograph, below right, shows a young girl tending a spinning machine in a North Carolina cotton mill. Hine (1874–1940) often had to smuggle his bulky camera into factories to capture his vivid photo stories, which played an important part in bringing about labor reforms.

As the new century began, Americans could look back on the last 30 years of their history with a sense of pride. The size, wealth, and power of the country had grown. The states in the Union now numbered 45, and the census counted 76 million Americans—20 percent more than in 1890. Having overcome the severe depression of 1893, the United States was now enjoying general prosperity. Yet prosperity brought its own problems. Private interests were wasting natural resources. Young children labored in factories and mines. Giant corporations manipulated markets and exploited workers without restraint. The festering slums of America's cities bred crime and disease. Many turn-of-the-century Americans also fretted about the flood of immigrants, now arriving at the rate of more than a million a year. Anti-immigrant, anti-Catholic, and anti-Semitic bigotry flourished.

Many special interests powered the reform impulse.

In the early 1900s people like Bob and Belle La Follette, along with other men and women from every region and class, mobilized to expose the ills of society and write new laws to correct social problems. Their movement, called **progressivism**, drew upon the heritage of Populism and the labor movement and had wide support from farmers and labor. The progressive movement also included industrialists and merchants fighting mismanagement and high taxes or looking to the government for protection against monopolies and price-fixing in a chaotic marketplace. However, many leading progressives were middle-class college graduates like the La Follettes, living in towns and cities.

Progressivism was like a large umbrella under which many different reformers could huddle. Some who called themselves progressives worked against poverty. Others wanted the regulation of corporations. Still others fought to

end corruption and waste in government. Although progressives often disagreed on specific points, some basic beliefs united the movement. First, progressives placed their faith in progress, technology, and science. They believed that society could be studied scientifically and that impartial experts could help politicians make good laws. Second, progressives rejected the laissez-faire attitudes of the Gilded Age. They called for an active government and pressed for laws that would improve American life.

Protestant moral values shaped progressivism, and many ministers and the sons and daughters of ministers became leaders in the progressive movement. However, Roman Catholics, Jews, and people belonging to no religious group also worked to achieve progressive goals.

What defined progressivism more than anything else was not a specific platform but a new view of the purpose of government. The progressives wanted more than governmental and legislative reforms. They sought to use government as an instrument of social change, to reform social institutions and to check the misuse of power wherever it took place.

One way to understand progressivism is to examine what some reform groups did. Close to the mainstream of progressivism were two diverse groups—writers, who began a new form of popular journalism; and women, who worked to improve people's lives and open the political process. On the fringes of progressivism were two other reform movements—socialism, which sought public ownership of the means of production, and the racial justice movement, which wanted equal rights for African Americans.

A new brand of journalism exposed flaws in society and politics.

In our time, crusading reporters who write about corruption are commonplace. Writers of the Progressive Era pioneered this investigative journalism. These men and women were called **muckrakers** after President Theodore Roosevelt said that they were so busy raking the muck at their feet that they ignored the glories of the heavens above. Roosevelt had become the nation's youngest president in 1901 when an assassin shot President William McKinley. Roosevelt meant to insult the muckraking journalists, but they accepted the name proudly.

The progressives found a strong voice for reform in such popular magazines as *McClure's, Cosmopolitan,* and *Collier's.* New printing press technologies beginning in the 1870s made these lively publications possible. The enormous change brought about by the new mass-circulation newspapers and magazines then was much like the impact of television in the 1940s and 1950s.

McClure's Magazine led the way in muckraking journalism. In January 1903 *McClure's* carried a report by Lincoln Steffens on the ties between business and the corrupt Minneapolis political machine, an exposé of John D. Rockefeller's Standard Oil Trust by Ida Tarbell, and a report by Ray Stannard Baker about labor union violence. The issue sold out. Clearly, muckraking was profitable.

Ida Tarbell's exposé of the Standard Oil trust began in *McClure's* magazine in 1902. S. S. McClure, the publisher, said, "Miss Tarbell has our capitalists conspiring among themselves, deliberately, shrewdly, upon legal advice, to break the law . . . and to misuse it to restrain others who were in their way."

Muckraking articles became muckraking books. The article on corruption in Minneapolis was part of a brilliant series by Lincoln Steffens, a young California journalist, that later became *Shame of the Cities* (1904). Steffens' careful research revealed that corrupt bankers and corporations bought their own laws in St. Louis, Pittsburgh, Philadelphia, Chicago, New York, and Minneapolis.

Even novels took a muckraking turn, helping to dramatize reform issues. The novelist Frank Norris told about the stranglehold of the Southern Pacific railroad on California's sheep ranchers in *The Octopus* (1901). The most famous of the muckraking novels was Upton Sinclair's **The Jungle** (1906), which described

Chicago's meat-packing industry. In one passage, a stockyards worker explained how sausages were made:

> There was never the least attention paid to what was cut up for sausage; there would come all the way back from Europe old sausage that had been rejected, and that was mouldy and white—it would be dosed with borax and glycerine, and dumped into the hoppers, and made over again for home consumption.... There would be meat stored in great piles in rooms; and the water from the leaky roofs would drip over it, and thousands of rats would race about on it.... These rats were a nuisance, and the packers would put poisoned bread out for them; they would die, and then rats, bread, and meat would go into the hoppers together.

Sinclair shocked the nation. President Roosevelt could barely eat his breakfast sausages.

Workers make sausage at a meatpacking plant in Chicago, 1902. After reading *The Jungle*, "Mr. Dooley" (Finley Peter Dunne), one of America's shrewdest humorists, observed that he had been unable "to ate annything more nourishin' thin a cucumber in a week."

A vigorous socialist movement sought economic and political change.

Upton Sinclair, a socialist, filled *The Jungle* with socialist propaganda. He hoped to raise an outcry over working conditions under capitalism and win people over to socialism. Instead, the book drew attention to unsanitary conditions in the meat-packing industry. Sinclair said, "I aimed at the public's heart and by accident I hit it in the stomach."

Sinclair was part of a growing worldwide socialist movement. The socialists thought it was "the historic mission of the working class to do away with capitalism" and institute a classless society. People who called themselves socialists proposed a number of reforms, but most wanted a society in which workers controlled both the government and the means of production—factories and farmland. Before the Russian Revolution in 1917, socialist ideas did not arouse the suspicion and fear they later would receive.

Socialist parties in the United States drew their members chiefly from the foreign born. American socialists also counted in their ranks farmers, labor organizers, and Christian Socialists—urban Protestant groups that favored socialism. The **Socialist Party of America**, formed in 1901, was led for many years by Eugene V. Debs, a charismatic labor leader from Indiana.

Under the leadership of Debs, the socialist vote rose steadily, and 18 cities elected socialist mayors in 1911. Debs received 900,000 votes, or six percent of the total, in the 1912 presidential election. Despite Debs' tireless work, however, most Americans feared socialism because of its association with radical socialism in Europe where its leaders preached class war and the destruction of capitalism. U.S. workers, with their better pay and long tradition of political rights, generally remained committed to the values of private property and the free-enterprise system.

Women worked to achieve equality.

As more women worked for wages before and during the Progressive Era, the idea that a woman's place was in the home came into question. Charlotte Perkins Gilman, who wrote *Women and Economics* (1898), called for child-care centers and common dining facilities so that women could work more efficiently. Women's rights advocates in the 1960s voiced the same ideas.

Feeling threatened by the large number of immigrants, some progressive reformers advocated birth control as a means of limiting population growth. Although families began to have fewer children, women found it hard to get reliable birth-control material. The laws defined such information as pornography and prohibited its publication.

Mary Ware Dennett and Margaret Sanger worked for repeal of these laws. Sanger, a nurse, was sent to jail in 1916 for running a birth-control clinic. She formed a lobbying group that in 1942 became the Planned Parenthood Federation.

Other groups tried to limit or abolish child labor and improve working conditions for women. Both women and children often labored ten or twelve hours a day, six or seven days a week in hazardous factories or sweatshops—places that employ workers at low pay for long hours under bad conditions.

Rose Cohen started her first job in a sweatshop at age 12, sewing sleeve linings in coats 12 hours a day for a gruff, miserly boss.

He paid me three dollars [a week] and for this he hurried **AN AMERICAN ★ SPEAKS** me from early until late. He gave me only two coats at a time to do. When I took them over and as he handed me the new work he would say quickly and sharply, "Hurry!" . . . Late at night when the people would stand up and begin to fold their work away and I too would rise, feeling stiff in every limb and thinking with dread of our cold empty little room and the uncooked rice, he would come over with still another coat.

The death of 146 workers in the Triangle Shirtwaist Company fire in 1911 brought the grim reality of sweatshop labor before the public. Many of the victims were young Jewish immigrants like Cohen.

Florence Kelley, a Pennsylvania-born social worker at Chicago's Hull House, saw children as young as four working long hours in tenement sweatshops.

An energetic, dynamic person, Kelley helped write a factory inspection law in Illinois and became the state's first factory inspector. Later, as head of the National Consumers' League, she lobbied for state laws restricting women's work hours. However, a conservative Supreme Court had repeatedly ruled that such laws violated the due process clause of the Fourteenth Amendment. Kelley persuaded lawyer Louis Brandeis to present historical and economic data in court to support an Oregon law (then considered enlightened) that said women could work no more than ten hours a day. On the basis of this Brandeis brief, the Supreme Court upheld the ten-hour law in ***Muller*** v. ***Oregon*** in 1908.

As women fought for progressive causes, support for women's suffrage grew. Between 1910 and 1914 seven western states and the Territory of Alaska voted for women's suffrage.

In 1900 **Carrie Chapman Catt**, a former Iowa superintendent of schools, became head of the National American Woman Suffrage Association (NAWSA). Catt, who had impressive organizational skills, mapped out a long-term campaign to convince Congress to support an amendment to the U.S. Constitution that would give women the right to vote in every state. Alice Paul and the Congressional Union (later

Young girls add their support to the suffrage movement in this photograph of a 1913 parade on Long Island, New York. Many women were arrested and some went on hunger strikes and endured force feeding before Congress passed the 19th Amendment granting women's suffrage in 1919.

the National Woman's party) aroused public opinion through demonstrations. However, suffrage for all women in the United States through the 19th Amendment did not come until 1920 after women had promoted their cause by selling war bonds and working in factories during World War I.

African Americans fought segregation and restriction of their civil rights.

Like reformers in many eras, the progressives were captives of many prejudices of the world they hoped to reform. Accordingly, despite their desire for social justice, progressives often remained blind to the problems of African Americans and other minorities. The progressive movement did not press for racial equality. In fact, southern white progressives often took the lead in pushing disfranchisement and segregation in the South where nine of every ten African Americans still lived in 1900.

Many African American leaders cautioned patience in the face of such harsh measures. For example, Booker T. Washington, probably the best known African American in the early 1900s, argued that African Americans should focus on economic advancement and be willing temporarily to accept a lower status. He said, "it is at the bottom of life we must begin, and not at the top."

However, not all black leaders agreed with Washington. **W. E. B. Du Bois** [dù bois'], the first African American to receive a Ph.D. from Harvard and the author of some of the first black histories, charged that Washington's strategy was "leading the way backward" for African Americans.

Leaders of the Niagara Movement pose in 1905 before the falls that gave their movement its name. W. E. B. Du Bois, middle row, second from the right, urged his followers to see "Beauty is Black."

His doctrine has tended to make the whites, North and South, shift the burden of the Negro problem to the Negro's shoulders . . . when in fact, the burden belongs to the nation, and the hands of none of us are clean if we bend not our energies to righting these great wrongs.

AN AMERICAN ★ SPEAKS

In 1905 Du Bois and others met in Canada at **Niagara Falls** and drew up demands for full civil rights and an end to segregation. In 1909 Jane Addams and other white progressives joined leaders of this Niagara Movement to establish the **National Association for the Advancement of Colored People (NAACP)**. For years to come, Du Bois and the NAACP would lead the fight against racism.

SECTION 1 REVIEW

Identify Key People and Terms
Write a sentence to identify: progressivism, muckrakers, *The Jungle,* Socialist Party of America, Florence Kelley, *Muller* v. *Oregon,* Carrie Chapman Catt, W. E. B. Du Bois, National Association for the Advancement of Colored People (NAACP)

Locate Key Places
Where did W. E. B. Du Bois and others draft demands for racial equality in 1905?

Master the Main Ideas

1. **Understanding reform movements:** Why did so many special interests want reforms during the Progressive Era?
2. **Examining cultural contributions:** How did a new brand of journalism expose flaws in U.S. society and politics?
3. **Understanding reform movements:** How did the socialists' goals differ from those of the progressives?
4. **Understanding reform movements:** How did women work to achieve equality during the Progressive Era?
5. **Identifying ethnic, racial, and cultural contributions:** How did African Americans fight segregation and the limitation of their civil rights during the early 1900s?

Apply Critical Thinking Skills: Analyzing Cause and Effect
The progressives enjoyed the support of many diverse groups. In what ways would this be an advantage? A disadvantage?

SECTION 2

Progressive ideas transformed politics.

Key Terms: commission system, city-manager plan, direct primary, initiative, referendum, recall, Pure Food and Drug Act, Meat Inspection Act

Reading Preview

As you read this section, you will learn:

1. where demands for reform usually started.
2. how reformers tried to deal with corruption at the state level.
3. in what ways reformers changed state and federal governments.

Well-dressed citizens of Toledo, Ohio, seek a cool breeze at a lakefront park in July 1898. A few children even venture near the water. Samuel M. Jones, Toledo's colorful reform mayor, opened public playgrounds and golf links during his "Golden Rule" administration.

In the early 1900s, American cities grew rapidly, concentrating populations that had once been spread out in small towns and on farms. At the same time, large corporations gained economic power with the growth of huge trusts in such fields as steel, railroads, and banks. Yet the institutions of government from the local to the national level stayed the same as in the 1700s when most Americans lived in rural areas and businesses and banks were small. The progressives saw the need to modernize government and to expand its powers in order to stop corruption.

This new view of government changed policies, programs, and even the structure first of state and local government and finally the federal government. In these changes in the years from 1900 to 1917 may be seen the origins of modern American politics.

Demands for reform usually started at the local level.

Most progressives pointed to urban corruption and poor city government as major problems of the day. Advocates of municipal reform won elections in many cities even before Lincoln Steffens' exposés stirred cries for change. Hazen S. Pingree of Detroit, elected in 1889, was

the first of the reform mayors. Pingree was soon followed by others—Edwin U. Curtis of Boston, Tom L. Johnson of Cleveland, and Seth Low of New York. All ousted notorious political bosses.

The most colorful of the reform mayors was Samuel "Golden Rule" Jones, an Ohio manufacturer. Jones, who took office as the mayor of Toledo in 1897, began applying the golden rule to his administration of that city as he had in his factory. Jones pushed for lower utility rates and set a minimum wage for city employees. Toledo soon boasted better courts, new parks, free concerts, free public baths, and even a form of welfare.

The election of a progressive mayor did not, of course, always end corruption. What was needed, decided some progressives, was to separate politics from government. To achieve this, the progressives invented two new forms of city government: the commission system and the city-manager plan. Both plans copied corporate forms of organization.

Under the **commission system**, voters often elected five commissioners comparable to the directors of a corporation. The commissioners were elected without party affiliations but with expertise needed to head such city departments as police, fire, or public works. Galveston, Texas, in 1901 became the first city to test commission government to meet the crisis

351

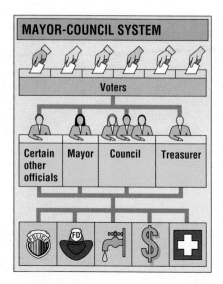

MAYOR-COUNCIL SYSTEM

Voters

Certain other officials | Mayor | Council | Treasurer

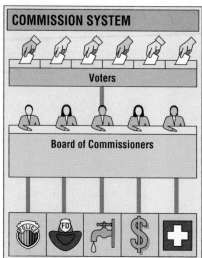

COMMISSION SYSTEM

Voters

Board of Commissioners

COUNCIL-MANAGER SYSTEM

Voters

Council

Manager

What services do all cities provide?
Critical Thinking
Which plans focus on efficiency?

A hurricane in 1900 led Galveston, Texas, to try the commission system.

caused by a terrible hurricane that killed 6,000 people and caused extensive property damage. The idea spread, and 160 cities had commission governments by 1911. Its popularity has since waned, in part because of the leaderless nature of commission government. The mayor of Wichita, Kansas, where the new plan failed, said it was like "a ship with five captains."

The **city-manager plan** also tried to take city government out of politics by electing a city council to make laws and set policy. The council in turn appointed a manager trained in city government. Staunton, Virginia, first tried this system in 1908. Today half of the U.S. cities with 25,000 people or more use the city-man-

ager form of government. More than a third, including most of the largest cities, use the mayor-council plan. Only about 50 cities of 25,000 or more use the commission system.

Both the commission system and the city-manager plan insulated city government from the popular will. This showed the progressives' faith in the use of experts and their fear of the power of immigrant voters. This undemocratic aspect of progressivism at the local level stands at odds with the progressives' declared support for popular rule.

Reformers also tackled corruption at the state level.

Reform movements also swept the states during the Progressive Era. The most famous reform governors were Wisconsin's Robert La Follette and California's Hiram Johnson. Both of these progressive governors won a reputation for reform by battling powerful railroad interests in their states.

Robert M. La Follette served in Congress before running for governor of Wisconsin in 1900. Voters supported the fiery, energetic governor against the regular party politicians. In order to bypass corrupt party machinery, La Follette established a direct primary system for nominating candidates, a system now used in every state. In a **direct primary**, a party's candidates are chosen by the voters instead of by party members at a convention.

Experts at the University of Wisconsin advised La Follette and set up a legislative reference bureau to help in writing laws. The bureau took the drafting of bills out of the hands of lobbyists, a key part of the movement for good government. **Wisconsin** became known as the "laboratory of democracy."

In addition to the direct primary, reformers developed the initiative and referendum to give voters more power in city and state elections. The **initiative** allows voters to introduce laws through petitions and to enact laws directly by a popular vote. Under a **referendum** citizens may approve or reject a proposed law or put

Frank Lloyd Wright and the Prairie Style

As American cities grew in the 1900s, so did American architecture, breaking with European traditions and embracing new ideas and technologies. In this period Frank Lloyd Wright, America's greatest architect, launched his career.

Wright began in Chicago as a draftsman for the firm of Dankmar Adler and Louis Sullivan. There he was strongly influenced by Sullivan's belief that "form follows function," that a design should reflect the purpose of the building. Wright developed Sullivan's idea into his own concept of "organic simplicity": that a design should blend purpose and materials in harmony with a building's surroundings. At a time when many architects were focusing on commercial buildings and

vertical, skyscraping designs, Wright applied his ideas to a variety of buildings and emphasized horizontal designs.

Working independently, Wright in the early 1900s produced a series of houses in the now-famous "prairie style." In contrast to the houses of the time, consisting of boxes-within-boxes, Wright's prairie houses had open interiors, low ceilings, and extensive windows. Wright combined a strong horizontal design with earth-toned building materials to blend the houses into their surroundings. Wright built about 50 prairie homes between 1900 and 1910. The Robie House in Chicago is regarded as the classic statement of Wright's prairie

style. Another Wright masterpiece of the decade is the Unity Temple in Oak Park, Illinois. In this church Wright combined a revolutionary design with an innovative use of reinforced concrete.

Wright's career would span 70 years and produce more than 700 houses, schools, office buildings, churches, and museums—each of them "organic," each of them indelibly stamped with Wright's originality. His last project, the Guggenheim Museum in New York, is as bold and distinctive as anything he ever produced.

Wright was once asked what he considered his most satisfying achievement. He answered, "The next one, of course."

Frank Lloyd Wright designed fabrics, furniture, and stained glass, including the skylight photographed below, to complement the low, horizontal lines of his prairie houses. The February 1901 *Ladies' Home Journal* featured his plans for a model suburban home shown in the drawing.

Highlights of American Life

Good city goverment: two views

Point	Counterpoint
Government by experts	**Government under a boss**
■ Experts make decisions scientifically ■ Government is honest, efficient, economical ■ Nonpartisan citywide elections center power in business-dominated hands	■ Decisions of boss reflect will of most voters ■ Government reaches out to problems of the community that experts ignore ■ Elections by ward give power to minorities and working class

an existing law to a vote. South Dakota became the first state to approve the initiative and referendum in 1898. Many states later adopted these measures even though the processes are cumbersome. Some cities and states also have **recall** laws, allowing voters to remove an official from office.

A reform in politics and government swept California after Hiram Johnson's election as governor in 1910. The square-jawed governor had campaigned on one theme: "Kick the Southern Pacific out of politics." The railroad was the largest landowner and the largest employer in California and had dominated state politics for 40 years. Under Johnson's leadership, California adopted a number of laws and constitutional amendments that regulated the railroad and public utilities and limited their political power. The legislature also instituted the direct primary, initiative, referendum, recall, the non-partisan ballot, and cross-filing, which allowed candidates, without stating their party affiliation, to place their names on the primary ballots of all parties. In contrast to these liberal measures, Johnson had the legislature pass a law in 1913 aimed at Japanese immigrants that prohibited aliens from owning land in California. The courts finally held the law unconstitutional in 1952.

Reformers broadened activities of state and federal governments.

Upton Sinclair's novel *The Jungle* caused a national sensation. President Theodore Roosevelt appointed a commission to investigate, and it confirmed Sinclair's charges. Congress responded by passing two reform measures in 1906. The **Pure Food and Drug Act** banned impure or mislabeled foods and drugs. The **Meat Inspection Act** provided for federal meat inspection. Both were milestones on the road to today's consumer-conscious government.

The Interstate Commerce Commission, set up in 1887 to control railroad rates, was the first federal regulatory agency. Calls for reform had led states to establish similar independent regulatory commissions. These governmental bodies usually could investigate and apply government regulations to ensure competition or protect consumers or employees. Many such commissions exist today, at both state and federal levels. In most states, for example, regulatory commissions control the rates charged by utilities serving the public, such as telephone, electric, or natural gas companies. Regulatory commissions show a key element in reform: a desire to settle conflicts between special interests scientifically through investigation and mediation by experts.

SECTION 2 REVIEW

Identify Key People and Terms
Write a sentence to identify: commission system, city-manager plan, Robert M. La Follette, direct primary, initiative, referendum, recall, Pure Food and Drug Act, Meat Inspection Act

Locate Key Places
What state was called the "laboratory of democracy"?

Master the Main Ideas

1. **Understanding reform movements:** Describe two new reforms progressives demanded at the local level.
2. **Understanding democratic beliefs:** What measures did reformers introduce to end corruption at the state level?
3. **Understanding economic development:** How did reformers expand the activities of state and federal governments?

Apply Critical Thinking Skills: Identifying Central Issues
What contradictions might exist between the progressives' goal of extending the role of the voter in politics and the progressives' tendency to rely on experts?

SECTION **3**

Progressive reforms reached the national level.

Key Terms: trustbusting, Hepburn Act, arbitration

Reading Preview
As you read this section, you will learn:

1. how Theodore Roosevelt changed the presidency.
2. how Roosevelt dealt with the trusts.
3. whose action ended the coal strike.

Progressivism came to the White House when **Theodore Roosevelt** became the 26th president of the United States in 1901. A young person with enormous energy, Roosevelt became an active, progressive leader, in many ways the forerunner of our modern presidents.

Theodore Roosevelt expanded the power of the presidency.

President McKinley had set the stage for a stronger presidency by enlarging his staff and putting a telephone and a telegraph in the White House. Roosevelt continued to strengthen the office. He became the first president to deliberately cultivate personal popularity. As a result, watching the president became a national habit. Cartoonists delighted in his bristling mustache, pince-nez glasses, and large front teeth. Roosevelt later wrote, "I cannot say that I entered the Presidency with any deliberately planned and far-reaching scheme of social betterment." Nonetheless, he set his mark on the office and on the nation more strongly than any president since Lincoln.

Born into a wealthy New York family, Teddy Roosevelt had every advantage. He went to Harvard University, where a generation of gentlemen were taught to avoid the messy world of politics. Roosevelt, however, seemed to have politics in his blood. Straight out of school, he threw himself into New York politics and eventually was elected governor in 1898. In 1900,

when McKinley needed a running mate, Roosevelt's political enemies in New York pushed the governor for the vice presidency in order to get him out of the state.

Unlike many politicians, who thought in terms of favors and deals, Roosevelt saw politics as a noble duty. Calling himself a "radical conservative," he viewed political power as a means to a moral, ordered society. As president, he took bold initiatives in foreign affairs and attacked powerful corporations. He looked on the presidency as a "bully pulpit" from which to preach a message of character and duty to the nation. Saddled with a conservative Congress, Roosevelt nonetheless became an active and strong chief executive. He used the powers of his office and his own popularity to get around congressional opposition.

Roosevelt challenged the trusts.

The formation of large and notorious trusts alarmed Roosevelt. He said later,

When I became President, the question as to the method **AN AMERICAN** ★ **SPEAKS** by which the United States Government was to control the corporations was not yet important. The absolutely vital question was whether the Government had power to control them at all.

The Sherman Antitrust Act of 1890 had outlawed monopolies, but the courts had drastically limited its use. Roosevelt set out to establish the power of the federal government over big business. He ordered his attorney general in 1902 to use the Sherman Act against the newly formed Northern Securities Company, which consolidated railroads north and west of Chicago.

Roosevelt's action was popular, for the power of large corporations, trusts, and monopolies alarmed Americans. Roosevelt won his fight in 1904, when the Supreme Court ordered the Northern Securities Company dissolved. The Court's decision breathed new life into the Sherman Act, allowing Roosevelt to continue **trustbusting**, that is, trying to break up monopolies through antitrust suits. Roosevelt's Administration brought 44 antitrust suits, though not all were successful.

He was, in no particular order, a cowboy, a cop, a conservationist, a boxer, a war hero, a naturalist, a hunter, a historian, an explorer, a trustbuster, a mountain climber, a ditchdigger. Theodore Roosevelt pursued "the strenuous life," yet he found sufficient time to write more than 30 books, to earn the Nobel Peace Prize, and to be president of the United States.

Roosevelt famously believed in the West African proverb, "Speak softly and carry a big stick" (he sometimes forgot the first part). Under his leadership, the United States took its place as a world power, its role in part defined by the enormous energy and confidence of its youngest president. He left the Panama Canal and millions of acres of protected wilderness as his legacy.

THEODORE ROOSEVELT

Born: October 27, 1858
Died: January 6, 1919
In office: 1901–1909

Roosevelt did all that he did with a robust style and a wide toothy grin that wordlessly proclaimed what he also declared: "No president has ever enjoyed himself as much as I have."

Despite his highly publicized trustbusting, Roosevelt came to believe that large corporations were inevitable and that it made more sense to regulate them than to break them up. There were "good" trusts and "bad" trusts, Roosevelt decided. Good trusts were those that met Roosevelt's standards and accepted the role of the White House in the economy. For them, Roosevelt promised a "Square Deal" in which every person—worker and industrialist alike—was treated fairly. Trusts that misbehaved could expect the big stick—trustbusting.

Dissatisfied with the trustbusting approach, Roosevelt set about to shape an alternative in the form of regulation. He started by asking Congress to bar railroads from giving rebates.

Public opinion strongly opposed rebates, which gave large corporations lower rates than small shippers. Congress passed the Elkins Act forbidding rebates in 1903, but Roosevelt wanted more. Working closely with reformers in Congress, he won passage of the **Hepburn Act** in 1906, which gave the Interstate Commerce Commission power to set maximum railroad rates.

Roosevelt took bold action to end a crippling coal strike.

Like his trustbusting activities, Roosevelt's role in the 1902 coal strike increased the power of the presidency. The United Mine Workers of America (UMW), a young industrial union, had called a strike in May 1902. The UMW wanted higher wages, an eight-hour workday, and recognition of the union. The miners, many of them foreign born, worked underground ten to twelve hours a day in the anthracite (hard) coal region of northeastern **Pennsylvania**. Death and injury were common.

More than 99 percent of the hard coal mined in the United States at that time—and three-quarters of the world production—came from Pennsylvania's anthracite fields. The mines were largely owned by the railroads and under the control of a powerful trust headed by J. P. Morgan. The mine owners hindered attempts to organize the miners, and played on racial and ethnic differences to defeat the union. John Mitchell, an idealistic young labor leader who had gone into the mines at age 12, became UMW president in 1899. Mitchell, who spoke more than a dozen languages, began to preach brotherhood to the Pennsylvania miners. "The coal you dig isn't Slavish or Polish or Irish coal. It's just coal," he told them.

The strike dragged on through the summer and early fall. As winter approached, public concern grew because coal was essential for heating homes, schools, and hospitals as well as providing the principal source of energy for operating steamships, railroads, and factories.

In early October Roosevelt called both sides to the White House and urged them to arbitrate their differences. **Arbitration** is a method of settling disagreements between employers and workers through a legally binding decision by an impartial person or group. The mine owners refused arbitration. Their spokesman, George F. Baer, called Mitchell an anarchist (one who advocates the destruction of government and law). "The unions," Baer said, "are corrupting the children of America by letting them join their illegal organizations."

Roosevelt forced the mine owners into arbitration by threatening to send in troops to take over the mines. Then an arbitration commission named by Roosevelt agreed to higher wages and a nine-hour workday but denied the union recognition. The mine owners were allowed to raise coal prices ten percent.

Roosevelt's actions set new precedents. Instead of using the army to break up the strike—in order to protect property or to assure a government service—the president had intervened on behalf of the strikers. Conservatives attacked Roosevelt, but he argued that he had acted to protect private property by righting wrongs that bred discontent. It was the "extreme reactionary," Roosevelt felt, who was most likely to "incite revolution" and was therefore the greatest danger to free enterprise.

Roosevelt's trustbusting and his actions in the coal strike brought him great popularity. When he ran for election in 1904, on a platform based on the Square Deal, he won a sweeping victory with more than 56 percent of the popular vote against Alton B. Parker, a little-known Democrat.

SECTION **3** REVIEW

Identify Key People and Terms
Write a sentence to identify: Theodore Roosevelt, trustbusting, Hepburn Act, arbitration

Locate Key Places
In which state did coal miners strike in 1902?

Master the Main Ideas

1. **Recognizing major political leaders:** How did Theodore Roosevelt expand the power of the presidency?
2. **Understanding the American economic system:** How did Roosevelt establish the power of the federal government over the trusts?
3. **Comparing the treatment of public and private property:** How did Roosevelt end the coal strike in 1902?

Apply Critical Thinking Skills: Demonstrating Reasoned Judgment
Roosevelt referred to himself as a "radical conservative." What do you think he meant, and how do Roosevelt's actions as president reflect this philosophy?

Anthracite miners parade through Shenandoah, Pennsylvania, during a strike in 1902. "The laborer who asks for shorter hours asks for a breath of life," said John Mitchell, the UMW president. Theodore Roosevelt's stand against the mine owners created broad support for his action against the bloated trusts shown in the cartoon below.

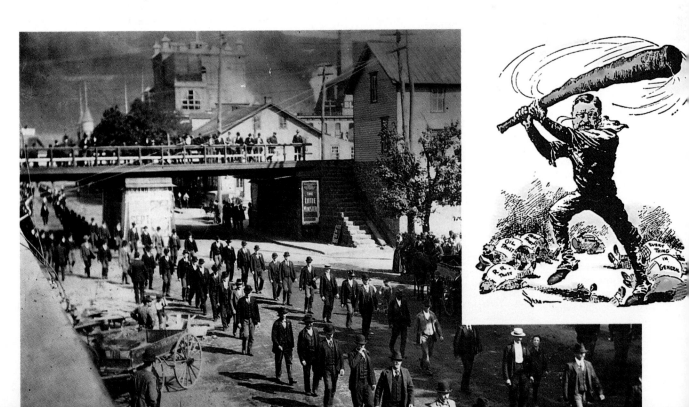

Western United States: Climate and Precipitation

Very dry

Dry

Precipitation less than 20 inches per year

Precipitation between 20 and 100 inches per year

Precipitation more than 100 inches per year

Albers Equal-Area Projection

© SF

map study

Regions
This map clearly shows why the western region is concerned with water rights. Note the large dry areas that receive little precipitation. To make this region productive, state and federal governments have regulated the water supply. Which states have "very dry" areas?

Critical Thinking
According to the map, which areas might not be concerned with water rights? Why?

Spring moisture brightens a desert landscape in southwestern Arizona.

The West gained political power.

Key Terms: water rights, conservation, reclamation, 16th Amendment, 17th Amendment, Progressive party

Reading Preview
As you read this section, you will learn:
1. where the geographic distribution of water was vitally important.
2. what broader effects western economic growth had.
3. how Theodore Roosevelt responded to the threat of dwindling natural resources.
4. what group William Howard Taft alienated.
5. how a split in the Republican party affected the presidential election of 1912.

Three western states—Idaho, Wyoming, and Utah—had joined the Union as the 20th century opened, and Arizona and New Mexico won statehood soon after. These and the other western states—California, Oregon, Washington, Nevada, Colorado, and Montana—became a powerful political force during the Progressive Era. Struggles over the development of this last frontier brought one of the bitterest conflicts in American history. The conflict racked the presidency of William Howard Taft, Roosevelt's hand-picked successor, and caused a major split in the Republican party.

The geographic distribution of water shaped the West.

Except for the coast and some mountainous areas, water is scarce throughout the West. For this reason, population centered mainly along the coast and near rivers. The arid regions, which you can see on the map on this page, were untouched by development. Unlike the East, which has plenty of rain, **water rights** were of primary importance. In much of the West, these rights were subject to complex state laws and local customs even on federal lands.

Both progressive reformers and middle-class Americans came to fear the growing poverty in the crowded eastern cities and saw the western lands as a safety valve against social unrest. A young California lawyer, George H. Maxwell, spearheaded the drive for federally financed irrigation projects. Maxwell and others were certain that the country faced ruin unless more city dwellers moved back to the land. Western political leaders favored these projects as a way to aid the economic development of the region.

Economic growth gave rise to the conservation movement.

Congress had surveyed water resources in the West in the 1880s and 1890s under Major John Wesley Powell, a geologist. Powell gained a place in history as the first person to survey the Colorado River and traverse its 900-mile course through the Grand Canyon and other dangerous gorges.

A young engineer named Frederick Haynes Newell, who worked under Powell, became one of the chief leaders of the conservation movement. In fact, the term **conservation** came into use as Newell and others planned huge reservoirs to conserve and store the runoff from winter snows and spring rains for use during the almost rainless growing season.

Thousands of acres of irrigated land were already under cultivation in the West, but confusing water-rights laws limited irrigation before 1900. Progress in irrigation, refrigeration, and marketing opened new farmlands and brought economic and political power to regions that had been lightly populated.

Roosevelt promoted the conservation of resources.

One of Theodore Roosevelt's first acts as president was to endorse irrigation and conservation measures. Early in his presidency, in 1902, Congress passed the National Reclamation Act, sponsored by Representative Francis Newlands of Nevada. The Newlands act began a federal program of **reclamation**—the restoration to productivity—of dry lands through irrigation. Intended to help family farmers, the law also played a role in the development of large-scale

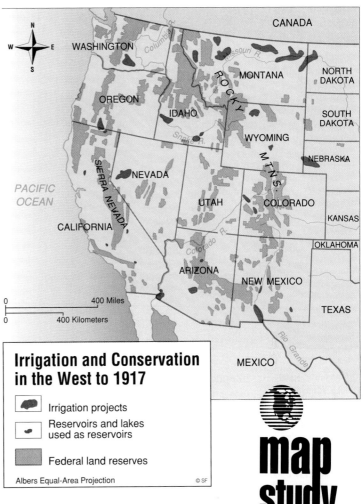

Irrigation and Conservation in the West to 1917

- Irrigation projects
- Reservoirs and lakes used as reservoirs
- Federal land reserves

Albers Equal-Area Projection   © SF

corporate farms, "factories in the fields," in the words of one California historian. Roosevelt promoted conservation by adding five national parks and more than 50 wildlife refuges during his presidency. As the map above shows, all the western states had federal irrigation or conservation projects by 1917.

Preservationists such as **John Muir** [myūr], who founded the Sierra Club to protect scenic places, applauded the creation of parks and reserves. Muir wanted wilderness areas to be kept forever safe from developers. Conservationists such as **Gifford Pinchot**, Roosevelt's chief adviser on natural resources, thought differently. Like preservationists, the conservationists favored parks and wildlife refuges. However, the conservationists believed that federally owned resources should be used productively. With Roosevelt's approval, Pinchot

map study

Regions
Compare this map with the one opposite. Note how irrigation projects affected some dry areas. In addition to irrigation, the federal government also created land reserves in the early 1900s. Does any western state not have federal land reserves?

Critical Thinking
Why might resource planning require federal as well as state control?

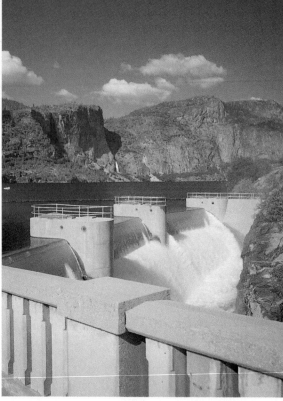

The beautiful Hetch Hetchy Valley, on the Tuolumne [tü ol′ə mē] River, is shown at the left above before it was dammed. The view at the right shows a portion of the O'Shaughnessy Dam, which transformed the verdant valley into a reservoir.

intended to withdraw some federal lands from sale and then manage them scientifically. Pinchot planned to permit mining, logging, and grazing under federal control. That way, he hoped, the lands would "produce the largest amount of whatever crop or service will be most useful, and keep on producing it for generation after generation." During his Administration, Roosevelt withdrew nearly 200 million acres from sale.

Of course, not all westerners favored irrigation projects or federal reserves. Timber, mining, and grazing interests often united to fight proposed federal programs. Disagreements over the best use of public resources continue to this day.

The bitterest controversy between the preservationists and conservationists took place over the beautiful **Hetch Hetchy Valley** of California, in the northwestern part of Yosemite National Park. San Franciscans wanted to flood the floor of the valley and use it as a city water supply. John Muir insisted that other sources of water could be found. The city applied to the federal government, and Pinchot approved the project. In doing so, he said that supplying water for a city was a higher use than

recreation or the preservation of scenic places. Speaking for the preservationists, Muir cried,

These temple-destroyers . . . instead of lifting their eyes to the God of the mountains, lift them to the Almighty Dollar. Dam Hetch Hetchy! As well dam for water tanks the people's cathedrals and churches, for no holier temple has ever been consecrated by the heart of man.

AN AMERICAN ★ SPEAKS

After years of controversy, San Francisco won the right to flood the Hetch Hetchy in 1913, a year before Muir died.

The struggle over conservation continued as Roosevelt yielded the presidency to Taft in 1909. Unfortunately, Taft proved unable to maintain harmony on the issue, either in the country at large or within the Republican party.

William Howard Taft alienated the conservationists.

When Roosevelt won the election of 1904, he rashly vowed that he would not run again for the presidency. Following his wishes, the Republican party in 1908 nominated as his successor **William Howard Taft**. Both Taft and the Democratic nominee, William Jennings

U.S. LAND POLICY: DEVELOPMENT VERSUS CONSERVATION
Skill: Identifying Central Issues

Introducing the Skill. A century after Thomas Jefferson purchased the Louisiana Territory for the United States, most Americans still acted as though the country's soil and its forests were unlimited resources. Conservationists insisted that the country reexamine its wasteful ways. President Theodore Roosevelt sided with the conservationists. When he took steps to control and manage the country's natural resources, he met with controversy. What were the issues central to this continuing debate over land use?

Learning the Skill. The first step in understanding any debate is to **identify central issues**, that is, to list the important points of the problem. Start by defining clearly the problem or situation at hand. In this instance the problem involves deciding how best to use the country's natural resources. Then think about the different aspects of the problem, narrowing them down to the most important, or central, issues. In this case consider questions such as: Who is responsible for making decisions about land use in the United States? Who do such decisions affect? How can natural resources be protected?

Applying the Skill.
1. Consider the list at the right of events that have affected the use of public lands in the United States from 1849 to 1916. What purposes did the various government agencies and actions concerning the environment serve? What values was the government promoting?
2. After analyzing the events of this period here and in this section, how do you believe that public lands should be used today? Upon what issues did you base your decision?

1849 Department of the Interior founded to manage and protect natural resources
1872 Yellowstone, the first national park, created
1892 Sierra Club established by John Muir to promote preservation and conservation
1902 National Reclamation Act passed to allow irrigation of arid lands
1906 National Antiquities Act gave the president power to preserve national monuments
1914 Hetch Hetchy Valley flooded to supply water for San Francisco
1916 National Park Service established to promote and regulate the use of national parks and other preserves

Bryan, ran as progressives. Roosevelt's support made all the difference, however. Taft won with almost 52 percent of the vote, and Republicans continued their control of Congress. Soon after Taft took office, a smiling Roosevelt went off to hunt big game in Africa.

William Howard Taft of Ohio boasted a distinguished record of public service as a federal judge, governor of the Philippines, and Roosevelt's secretary of war. Cautious, with a lawyer's respect for procedure, Taft rejected Roosevelt's broad use of presidential power. However, Taft seemingly planned to continue the programs and policies begun by Roosevelt.

Taft's cautious approach to change often led him to side with Republican conservatives. To please conservatives in Congress, Taft signed the Payne-Aldrich Tariff, which actually raised tariff rates, despite his campaign promise to lower tariffs. Republican progressives were outraged when Taft defended the new tariff as "the best bill that the Republican party ever passed." Taft also sided with the conservatives when Republican progressives tried to weaken the power of House Speaker Joseph G. Cannon of Illinois, a leading conservative. Democrats and insurgent Republicans finally broke Cannon's power in March 1910.

Hand-picked as the successor to Theodore Roosevelt, William Howard Taft was a reluctant candidate and an unhappy president. He found the White House "the lonesomest place in the world."

Born to wealth and well educated, Taft eventually became a judge. In 1901 he was appointed governor of the Philippines and later became Roosevelt's most trusted cabinet officer.

Taft's smoothly paved career had not prepared him for party bosses or patronage. He was clearly no Teddy Roosevelt—a fact that galled Roosevelt more than anyone else. The old Rough Rider charged out of retirement in 1912 to kill Taft's chances of re-election.

Woodrow Wilson was impelled through his public life by the conviction that he was right. The tragedy of Wilson's presidency was that being right was not enough.

Wilson briefly practiced law, then chose an academic career. He had been president of Princeton University for eight years when, in 1910, his first political race made him governor of New Jersey. His second race, two years later, made him president of the United States.

Though Wilson had planned to focus on his ambitious, progressive domestic program, his presidency was soon dominated by world war. Wilson fought to transfuse democratic ideals into the European bloodbath, to

WILLIAM HOWARD TAFT

Born: September 15, 1857
Died: March 8, 1930
In office: 1909–1913

Taft gladly returned to the field of law. He taught at Yale until President Warren G. Harding gave him the happiest years of his life by appointing him Chief Justice of the Supreme Court in 1921.

WOODROW WILSON

Born: December 28, 1856
Died: February 3, 1924
In office: 1913–1921

win an honorable peace, and to create a League of Nations. His failed effort to share this vision with his own fellow citizens shattered his health in 1919.

However, a battle over conservation became the key issue bringing all of Taft's policies under attack. At issue was a dispute between Gifford Pinchot, head of the Forest Service under Roosevelt and Taft, and Taft's secretary of the interior, Richard A. Ballinger, over Taft's conservation policies. Both Ballinger and Pinchot favored development of the western lands. However, Ballinger preferred private or state control rather than federal control. Pinchot charged Ballinger with abandoning Roosevelt's policies and favoring the water and power companies. He also said that Ballinger had cooperated with private coal companies to plunder Alaskan reserves. Taft investigated the matter with his usual thoroughness and decided that Ballinger had done nothing wrong. When Pinchot objected vigorously, Taft fired him. Once again, congressional progressives were infuriated. This long and bitter controversy hurt the Republican party badly. In the 1910 election, the Democrats won control of the house for the first time in 16 years.

Two constitutional amendments passed during Taft's years in the White House, both initiated by progressives. The **16th Amendment**, proposed in 1909 and ratified in early 1913 with Taft's support, permitted the federal government to collect income taxes. The Supreme Court had declared earlier income-tax laws unconstitutional. Reformers considered tariff duties, long the main source of federal revenues, as a kind of taxation that favored business at the expense of the common people. They believed an income tax a fairer means of financing the government. The **17th Amendment**, proposed in 1912 and adopted in May 1913, changed the method of electing U.S. senators. Instead of state legislatures electing senators, the voters of the state now elected them directly. Taft took no position on this proposal, another longtime goal of reformers.

When Theodore Roosevelt returned from Africa in 1910, bringing back nearly 300 hunting trophies, he discovered his party badly split. Taft stood with one wing against the progressives. Early in 1911 some Republican progressives organized to defeat Taft and chose La Follette as their candidate. Roosevelt disliked

La Follette but at first was unwilling to challenge Taft. Finally, disturbed by Taft's poor party leadership and by his antitrust policies, which ignored Roosevelt's distinctions between good and bad trusts, Roosevelt declared himself a candidate. He quickly won the support of most progressive Republicans.

A split in the Republican party ensured Democratic victory in 1912.

In June 1912 the Republican National Convention met in Chicago. Progressives battled conservatives to determine which group would be seated. Taft delegates controlled the credentials committee, and most contested seats went to Taft's supporters. Roosevelt's supporters stomped out of the hall, shouting that Taft had stolen the nomination. The remaining delegates chose Taft on the first ballot.

In August Roosevelt's supporters formed a third party: the **Progressive party**. The new party was nicknamed the "Bull Moose" party from Roosevelt's boast that he felt "as fit as a bull moose." Roosevelt called his platform the New Nationalism. He asked for the regulation of corporations and such progressive reforms as women's suffrage, an end to child labor, and a minimum wage.

Meanwhile, the Democrats met in Baltimore, certain that the Republican split offered them their greatest opportunity in 20 years. After 46 ballots, they nominated **Woodrow Wilson**, the governor of New Jersey. The Democratic platform also called for a wide range of reforms, under the title of the New Freedom.

Roosevelt's New Nationalism differed sharply from Wilson's New Freedom on the issue of big business. Roosevelt favored regulation but did not oppose big business. Roosevelt said, "We are in favor of honest business, big or little. We propose to penalize conduct and not size."

Wilson and the Democrats saw monopoly itself as a serious problem. Competition, they believed, benefited consumers through better products and lower prices. Regulated monopolies, they feared, would seek to control the federal government, which alone could restrict their power. Wilson argued in his book *The*

New Freedom (1913) that by opposing big business "I am fighting for the liberty of every man in America." Thus, both Roosevelt and Wilson called for government action against big corporations, but presented very different plans.

Taft had a stronger record as a trustbuster than Roosevelt, but he nonetheless ran as the undisputed conservative. In the end, Roosevelt and Taft split the Republican vote, 27 percent for Roosevelt and 23 percent for Taft, and Wilson won the election with 42 percent of the vote. Democrats also won majorities in both houses of Congress.

SECTION **4** REVIEW

Identify Key People and Terms
Write a sentence to identify: water rights, conservation, reclamation, John Muir, Gifford Pinchot, William Howard Taft, 16th Amendment, 17th Amendment, Progressive party, Woodrow Wilson

Locate Key Places
What controversy surrounded the flooding of the Hetch Hetchy Valley?

Master the Main Ideas

1. **Understanding geographic influences:** Explain how the geographic distribution of water shaped western development.
2. **Understanding geographic influences:** How did the western economic growth give rise to conservation as a national movement?
3. **Comparing the control of public and private property:** How did Theodore Roosevelt act to promote the conservation of natural resources?
4. **Understanding major political issues:** How did William Howard Taft alienate the conservationists?
5. **Understanding major political campaigns:** Explain how a split in the Republican party cost the Republicans the presidential election of 1912.

Apply Critical Thinking Skills: Drawing Conclusions
Historians have maintained that the 16th Amendment "probably did more to transform the relationship of the government to the people than all other progressive measures combined." Support or refute this statement.

GEOGRAPHY IN AMERICAN HISTORY

Yosemite National Park

Miwok Indians once inhabited the parklike floor of California's Yosemite Valley in the Sierra Nevada. Both men and women adorned themselves with tattoo marks as shown in this 1822 lithograph. Miwok women played a ball game with woven rackets like the one at right above. ▶

Relationships Within Places On the map of Yosemite National Park below, find the rock formations named Half Dome and El Capitan at either end of Yosemite Valley. Is it possible to tour the valley by bus?

Critical Thinking How does the nature of Yosemite's terrain affect the fragile relationship between visitors and the environment?

Sawtooth Ridge

TUOLUMNE MEADOWS

Benson Lake

Tenaya Lake

Half Dome

Nevada Fall

Grand Canyon of the Tuolumne River

Vernal Fall

Illilouette Fall

Yosemite Falls

Glacier Point

YOSEMITE VALLEY

El Capitan

Merced River

HETCH HETCHY RESERVOIR

Bridalveil Fall

LAKE ELEANOR

CHERRY LAKE

Panorama of Yosemite National Park

Location The map below shows that America's first national parks were all located in the West, which had available land with dramatic features. After 1917, parks were established in other parts of the country. Which was the first national park?

Critical Thinking
What physical, natural, or cultural features are represented among the park names on the chart at left below?

The eloquent naturalist John Muir first hiked into Yosemite Valley in 1868. He was then 30 years old. He wrote:
The walls are made up of rocks, mountains in size, partly separated from each other by side canyons, and they are so sheer in front, and so compactly and harmoniously arranged on a level floor, that the Valley . . . looks like an immense hall or temple lighted from above.
President Theodore Roosevelt, below right, came to Yosemite in 1903 to seek John Muir's advice on conservation. The massive bulk of Half Dome looms behind them.

National Parks, to 1917

Dates of Founding

1.	Yellowstone	1872
2.	Sequoia	1890
3.	Yosemite	1890
4.	Mount Rainier	1899
5.	Crater Lake	1902
6.	Wind Cave	1903
7.	Mesa Verde	1906
8.	Glacier	1910
9.	Rocky Mountain	1915
10.	Hawaii (changed to Hawaii Volcanoes, 1961)	1916
11.	Lassen Volcanic	1916
12.	Mount McKinley (changed to Denali, 1980)	1917

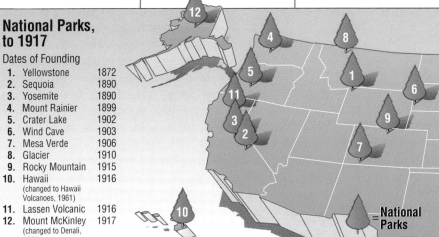

= National Parks

The majestic sequoias are the world's largest plants. Outraged by the lumbering of these giants, Muir urged government protection. His articles helped establish Yosemite and Sequoia national parks in California in 1890. Yosemite's Wawona Tree finally fell in a snowstorm in 1969.

SECTION **5**

Woodrow Wilson won sweeping reforms.

Key Terms: workmen's compensation, Underwood Tariff, Federal Reserve Act, Federal Trade Commission Act, Clayton Antitrust Act

Reading Preview
As you read this section, you will learn:

1. what program of reform Woodrow Wilson launched.
2. how Wilson dealt with banking and the trusts.
3. how Wilson's record of reform fared.

As his presidency began in April 1913, Woodrow Wilson broke the precedent established by Thomas Jefferson of submitting messages to Congress in writing rather than speaking "from the throne." In his speech Wilson boldly denounced the tariff as "not a system of protection, but a system of favoritism, of privilege, too often granted secretly and by subterfuge."

Until the Bull Moose campaign hopelessly divided the Republican party in 1912, Theodore Roosevelt, Robert La Follette, and other charismatic Republican figures dominated the Progressive Era. After 1912 Woodrow Wilson led the Democratic party and the progressive movement throughout the country.

Wilson launched his New Freedom.

Woodrow Wilson was born in Staunton, Virginia, five years before the Civil War, and his earliest memories were of this bitter conflict. As the son of a Presbyterian minister, he was raised in an atmosphere of stern morality and commitment to public service. These values would later color his understanding of presidential responsibility. A professor of political science at Princeton University and later its president, Wilson was elected reform governor of New Jersey in 1910. In just two years as governor, Wilson pushed through a direct primary system and state control of railroads and public utilities. He also secured the passage of **workmen's compensation**—laws making an employer pay a worker who is injured or contracts a disease because of his or her job. **New Jersey** gained nationwide attention for its progressive legislation. Wilson's success in New Jersey won him the support of many Democratic progressives when he sought the 1912 presidential nomination.

Once in the White House, Wilson determined to be an active, progressive president. Unlike Roosevelt, Wilson was in a position to

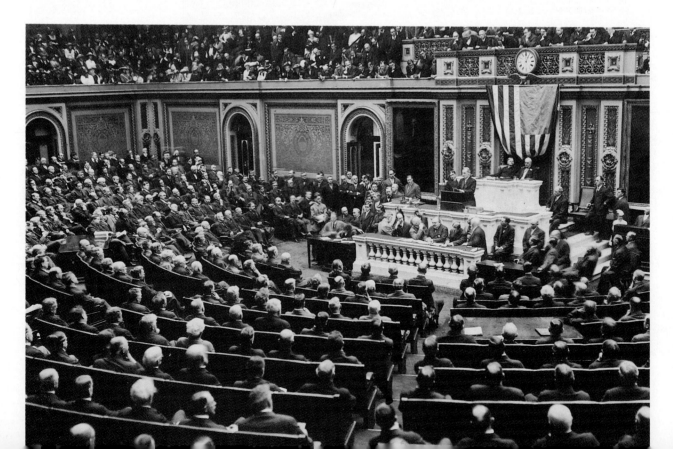

do so for he had the support of a Congress controlled by Democrats and progressives.

Wilson greatly admired the British parliamentary system. In Britain leading members of Parliament control the government in both its executive and legislative branches. He believed that all important decisions of the president should be shared with Congress. "The whole purpose of democracy," Wilson said, "is that we may hold counsel with one another, so as not to depend upon the understanding of one man, but to depend upon the counsel of all." As president, he hoped to use the Democratic party to bridge the gap between president and Congress.

When Wilson's presidency began, he called Congress into special session in April 1913. He wanted to explain his New Freedom policies and deal with tariff reform. An eloquent speaker, he addressed Congress in person, the first president since John Adams to do so.

Wilson believed that high tariffs helped create monopolies by reducing competition. Despite the opposition of industry, Congress passed the **Underwood Tariff** bill in October 1913. This law significantly reduced the tariffs for the first time since the Civil War. To make up for the lost revenue, the law provided for a small income tax, the first since the passage of the 16th Amendment.

Wilson established powerful controls over banking and the trusts.

Wilson and the Democrats next tackled banking and financial reforms. The national banking system had been created in 1863 to supply a safe and uniform currency. However, the system provided neither flexibility in the money supply nor central direction in times of financial crisis. Conservatives, led by Carter Glass of Virginia, joined with the powerful eastern banking interests in opposing bank regulation.

Wilson finally won a compromise in December 1913. The **Federal Reserve Act** divided the country into 12 districts, each with a Federal Reserve bank. The Federal Reserve Board, a central board in Washington, D.C., directed U.S. monetary policy and supervised the Federal Reserve Banks and the commercial banks

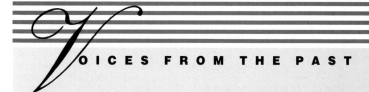

OICES FROM THE PAST

A Work of Restoration

Woodrow Wilson's gift of public eloquence has often been compared to that of Lincoln. In his Inaugural Address on March 4, 1913, Wilson powerfully expressed the progressive intentions of his administration. What standards did Wilson intend to use to measure national progress?

We have been proud of our industrial achievements, but we have not hitherto stopped thoughtfully enough to count the human cost, the cost of lives snuffed out, of energies overtaxed and broken, the fearful physical and spiritual cost to the men and women and children upon whom the dead weight and burden of it all has fallen pitilessly the years through. . . .

At last a vision has been vouchsafed us of our life as a whole. We see the bad with the good, the debased and decadent with the sound and vital. With this vision we approach new affairs. . . .

We have made up our minds to square every process of our national life again with the standards we so proudly set up at the beginning and have always carried at our hearts. Our work is a work of restoration.

"WELL!—*MY* HUSBAND WILL HAVE TO PAY AN INCOME TAX!"

Only the upper income groups had to pay any income tax at all in 1913 when C. R. Weed made this drawing for *The Independent.* Therefore most Americans favored the tax. The woman on the right even regards it as a status symbol.

How the Federal Reserve System Regulates the Money Supply

BOARD OF GOVERNORS

- appointed by the president and confirmed by the Senate
- administers the Federal Reserve System (FRS)
- sets reserve requirements (percentage of deposits that must be set aside as currency or as Federal Reserve deposits) and with the Federal Reserve Banks, sets discount rates (the interest rate at which banks can borrow money from the Federal Reserve Banks)
- lowers discount rate or reserve requirements to enable banks to make more loans, which increases money supply; takes the opposite actions to shrink money supply

FEDERAL OPEN MARKET COMMITTEE

- members of the Board of Governors and five Federal Reserve Bank presidents
- regulates purchase and sale of government securities, such as treasury bills, bonds, and notes
- buys government securities to increase the money supply or sells to shrink the supply

When the FRS buys government securities, checks paid to dealers are deposited in member banks. The increase in deposits gives the banks more money to loan and increases the amount of money and credit in the economy. Opposite actions shrink the money supply.

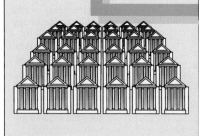

12 FEDERAL RESERVE BANKS

- carry out day-to-day operations to serve 25 branch banks and 5,100 member banks
- help set discount rates
- provide funds to member banks through discounting (lending) operations, which also regulate the money supply

5,100 MEMBER BANKS

- includes all national commercial banks and state banks that accept membership and certain regulations of the Federal Reserve System
- money supply expands when lower discount rate, open-market purchases, or lower reserve requirements enable banks to make more loans

chart study Before the Federal Reserve System, each bank attempted to maintain enough reserves to meet any possible demand by its depositors. Furthermore, the supply of money was not flexible enough to meet the normal ebb and flow of private enterprise. The Fed, as it is called, meets these needs by pooling member banks' resources. What actions taken by the Fed will affect the money supply?

Critical Thinking Why is a flexible money supply desirable?

that were members. All national banks were required to become members of this Federal Reserve System, and state banks were invited to join. A key instrument of economic policy-making today, the Federal Reserve System stands as Wilson's greatest domestic achievement. This reform transferred the control of U.S. monetary policy from powerful private bankers to the federal government. It also provided for an elastic money supply and resolved conflicts that had led to earlier struggles such as President Jackson's war on the Second Bank of the United States.

Wilson's reform programs continued. In 1914 he gained passage of the **Federal Trade Commission Act**, designed to end unfair business practices in interstate commerce. Congress also clarified the Sherman Antitrust Act by passing the **Clayton Antitrust Act**. This act freed unions from antitrust actions and barred interlocking directorates, an arrangement in which the same person sits on the board of directors of more than one company. Despite this burst of progressive legislation, Wilson never reached his goal of breaking up big business and ended by accepting something close to Roosevelt's New Nationalism.

Wilson's record of reform proved uneven.

Throughout his presidency, Woodrow Wilson worked to unify the Democratic party and keep it in power. During his 1912 campaign, he had appealed to African Americans for support. As president, however, Wilson gave way to pressure from southern Democrats and allowed southerners in his Cabinet to segregate African American and white workers in their departments. When prominent African Americans asked the president to reverse his policy, he declared, "I sincerely believe it to be in their interest." After a visit to the nation's capital in 1913, Booker T. Washington wrote to a leader of the NAACP, "I have never seen the colored people so discouraged and so bitter as they are at the present time." However, no new departments were segregated after 1914, and the Treasury Department quietly ended segregation there.

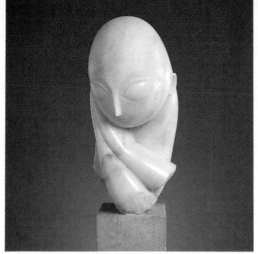

awakening of concern for the environment, the Federal Reserve Act and the income tax, and progress toward votes for women, among other changes. In winning these reforms, the progressives demonstrated that the American people through hard work could peacefully change their society and their economy.

Wilson's racial policies disturbed some progressives. He later resisted anti-Catholic and anti-Semitic bigotry, however, and named Louis Brandeis, a Jew, to the Supreme Court.

At the end of 1914, Wilson announced that he would not seek further reforms. Early in 1916, however, Wilson changed his mind. He had received less than half the popular vote in 1912. Now, with many Roosevelt followers back in the Republican fold, Wilson feared that the Democrats might lose the election.

Wilson pushed through several measures intended to lure more progressives into the Democratic camp. The new laws gave workmen's compensation to federal employees and ended child labor (later overturned by the courts). Armed with these reforms, Wilson won a close election with 49 percent of the popular vote to 46 percent for Charles Evans Hughes, a progressive Republican.

Progressivism declined after the nation entered World War I in 1917. The war drew public attention from reform, and the end of the war brought different political concerns. Yet historians continue to examine the Progressive Era and respect its legacy of reforms. These years brought control over big business, the

SECTION 5 REVIEW

Identify Key People and Terms
Write a sentence to identify: workmen's compensation, Underwood Tariff, Federal Reserve Act, Federal Trade Commission Act, Clayton Antitrust Act

Locate Key Places
In which state did Woodrow Wilson establish an impressive reform government?

Master the Main Ideas

1. **Understanding U.S. economic development:** What reform did Congress enact to launch Woodrow Wilson's New Freedom?
2. **Understanding development of the U.S. banking system:** Describe the controls over banking and the trusts that Woodrow Wilson established.
3. **Recognizing major reform movements:** In what ways was Woodrow Wilson's record of reform uneven?

Apply Critical Thinking Skills: Recognizing Values
To what extent do you think Woodrow Wilson showed a willingness to compromise principles in order to consolidate Democratic power?

America's Most Influential Art Show

While the business world was in an uproar over tariffs and trusts, the 1913 Armory Show shook the art world and shocked the American public. The controversial exhibit of some 1,100 paintings, drawings, and sculptures by American and European artists exposed ordinary Americans for the first time to modern European art. The most sensational painting without a doubt was *Nude Descending a Staircase, No. 2*, far left, by the French artist Marcel Duchamp [mär sel' dY shäN'] (1887–1968). One critic identified it as "an explosion in a shingle factory." Critics also savagely attacked *Mlle. Pogany*, the work of the Romanian sculptor Constantin Brancusi [kon'stən tēn' brän kü'zē] (1876–1957). The plaster version that appeared in the show is now lost, but Brancusi also sculpted a similar marble version, above left, in 1912. In four weeks 56,000 visitors saw the exhibit at the 69th Regiment Armory in New York City, and some 240,000 others later flocked to see many of the works in Chicago and Boston.

Ellis Island

Once a three-acre dot in New York Harbor, Ellis Island has had many names, owners, and uses. It was purchased from Indians by Dutch colonists in 1630. Fisherman dried their nets there, and families came to picnic. The island was privately owned for many years, most notably by namesake Samuel Ellis, a New Jersey farmer. The federal government acquired the island in 1808 and used it as a fort and an ammunition depot.

Ellis Island found new purpose in 1890 when the federal government assumed direct control of immigration in New York City. The island was doubled in size, old buildings were remodeled, and new ones constructed. Completed in 1892, the wooden immigration facility was destroyed by fire in 1897. Construction began immediately on a fireproof complex of brick and limestone structures. These were crowned by the French Renaissance splendor of the main building.

The new facilities opened in 1900, just in time to catch the crest of the great "third wave" of immigration in the years 1900 to 1914. Immigrants arrived in numbers far beyond the dreams of

Gateway to 12 million newcomers, Ellis Island embodies the heritage of a nation of immigrants.

government planners—more than a million in the peak year of 1907. Construction raced to keep pace, and Ellis Island expanded to more than 27 acres.

New arrivals were transferred from their ships to Ellis Island by barges. As they entered the main building, they checked their baggage, then headed for the Great Hall on the second floor. The stair climb itself was their first test; inspectors watched for those who had difficulty. After passing a brief medical exam, immigrants proceeded to the registry room—the Great Hall—for an examination of their documents, their finances, and, in later years, their learning. Generally, adult immigrants had to show that they were capable of work, had the price of a rail ticket (about $25), and could read and write. Immigrants who passed were given a landing card and were free to enter the United States.

The outbreak of World War I quickly pinched the flow of immigrants to a few hundred thousand per year; restrictive laws of the 1920s would maintain the squeeze. For several decades Ellis Island was as much a detention and deportation center as a gateway for newcomers.

Virtually unused after World War II, Ellis Island closed in 1954. Vacant buildings were abandoned to the ravages of rust and rot as the government occasionally debated the island's fate. Not until the 1970s did the government commit itself to restoring Ellis Island, and not until the 1980s did a public fund-raising drive generate the hundreds of millions of dollars necessary for the task.

In 1990 the Ellis Island Immigration Museum opened in the restored magnificence of the main building. The Great Hall now echoes to the footsteps of new visitors, many of them remembering grandparents and great-grandparents who walked there long before, crossing an extraordinary threshold and winning for themselves and their descendants a new destiny as Americans.

A Russian immigrant describes her experiences:

The examination process at Ellis Island was stressful to most immigrants. Nina Goodenov, who arrived in 1911, explains why. What factors contributed to her ordeal?

As far as Ellis Island was concerned, it was a nightmare. After all, none of us spoke English. We had no idea where we were going and no idea what was to be done to us. We had no idea what they wanted of us. There were hundreds and hundreds of people and they were treated exactly like sheep. "Go here. Go sit here. Wait here. Wait there." It took a day and a night. You had no place to sleep. You had to sleep on the benches, just sitting up.

A medical inspector folds back the upper eyelid over a special instrument, 1913.

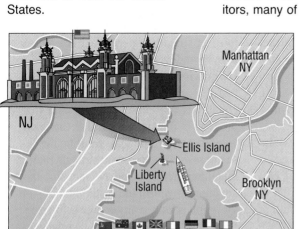

ELLIS ISLAND
The Ellis Island Immigration Museum is located in New York Harbor, approximately one mile southwest of Manhattan.

371

Booker T. Washington and W. E. B. Du Bois Disagree

8A

TIME FRAME
1895–1903

GEOGRAPHIC SETTING
Atlanta

The two great spokesmen for African Americans at the turn of the century were Booker T. Washington and W. E. B. Du Bois. Born into slavery, Washington (1856–1915) helped found Tuskegee Institute, a vocational and teacher's college for African Americans, in Alabama in 1881. He felt that African Americans should wait to press for civil rights until they had grown stronger economically. He outlined this position, known as the "Atlanta Compromise," in a speech before the Atlanta Exposition on September 18, 1895. An excerpt from this speech is the first of the following two selections. Du Bois (1868–1963) was a sociologist and historian who in 1909 helped organize the National Association for the Advancement of Colored People. In the second of the following selections, which is an excerpt from Du Bois' most famous book, *The Souls of Black Folk,* he explained how his view of the struggle of African Americans for equality differed from that of Washington.

A ship lost at sea for many days suddenly sighted a friendly vessel. From the mast of the unfortunate vessel was seen a signal, "Water, water; we die of thirst!" The

5 answer from the friendly vessel at once came back, "Cast down your bucket where you are." A second time the signal, "Water, water; send us water!" ran up from the distressed vessel, and was answered,

10 "Cast down your bucket where you are." And a third and fourth signal for water was answered, "Cast down your bucket where you are." The captain of the distressed vessel, at last heeding the injunction, cast

15 down his bucket, and it came up full of fresh, sparkling water from the mouth of the Amazon River. To those of my race who depend on bettering their condition in a foreign land or who underestimate

20 the importance of cultivating friendly relations with the Southern white man, who

is their next-door neighbor, I would say: "Cast down your bucket where you are"— cast it down in making friends in every

25 manly way of the people of all races by whom we are surrounded.

Cast it down in agriculture, mechanics, in commerce, in domestic service, and in the professions. And in this connection it

30 is well to bear in mind that whatever other sins the South may be called to bear, when it comes to business, pure and simple, it is in the South that the Negro is given a man's chance in the commercial world,

35 and in nothing is this Exposition more eloquent than in emphasizing this chance.

Our greatest danger is that in the great leap from slavery to freedom we may overlook the fact that the masses of us are

40 to live by the productions of our hands, and fail to keep in mind that we shall prosper in proportion as we learn to dignify and glorify common labor and put brains and skill into the common occupations of

45 life.... No race can prosper till it learns that there is as much dignity in tilling a field as in writing a poem. It is at the bottom of life we must begin, and not at the top. Nor should we permit our grievances

50 to overshadow our opportunities....

The wisest among my race understand that the agitation of questions of social equality is the extremest folly, and that progress in the enjoyment of all the privi-

55 leges that will come to us must be the result of severe and constant struggle rather than of artificial forcing. No race that has anything to contribute to the markets of the world is long in any degree ostracized.

60 It is important and right that all privileges of the law be ours, but it is vastly more important that we be prepared for the exercise of these privileges. The opportunity to earn a dollar in a factory just now is worth

Challenge, a collage created in 1969 by the African American artist Lois Mailou Jones (1905–   ), displays a gallery of people who have played significant roles in African American history and culture. Booker T. Washington is shown full face between the large red letters *A* and *M* in the upper left corner. W. E. B. Du Bois appears in profile directly above him.

65 infinitely more than the opportunity to spend a dollar in an opera-house.

———————————————

Mr. Washington represents in Negro thought the old attitude of adjust-ment and submission; but adjustment at such a peculiar time as to make his pro-
5 gram unique. This is an age of unusual ec-onomic development, and Mr. Washing-ton's program naturally takes an eco-nomic cast, becoming a gospel of Work

and Money to such an extent as apparently almost completely to overshadow the higher aims of life.

Moreover, this is an age when the more advanced races are coming in closer contact with the less developed races, and the race-feeling is therefore intensified; and Mr. Washington's program practically accepts the alleged inferiority of the Negro race. . . .

In other periods of intensified prejudice all the Negro's tendency to self-assertion has been called forth; at this period a policy of submission is advocated. In the history of nearly all other races and peoples the doctrine preached at such crises has been that manly self-respect is worth more than lands and houses, and that a people who voluntarily surrender such respect, or cease striving for it, are not worth civilizing.

In answer to this, it has been claimed that the Negro can survive only through submission. Mr. Washington distinctly asks that black people give up, at least for the present, three things,—

First, political power; Second, insistence on civil rights; Third, higher education of Negro youth,—and concentrate all their energies on industrial education, the accumulation of wealth, and the conciliation of the South. This policy has been courageously and insistently advocated for over 15 years, and has been triumphant for perhaps 10 years. . . .

[On] the whole the distinct impression left by Mr. Washington's propaganda is, first, that the South is justified in its present attitude toward the Negro because of the Negro's degradation; secondly, that the prime cause of the Negro's failure to rise more quickly is his wrong education in the past; and, thirdly, that his future rise depends primarily on his own efforts.

Each of these propositions is a dangerous halftruth. The supplementary truths must never be lost sight of: first, slavery and race-prejudice are potent if not sufficient causes of the Negro's position; second, industrial and common-school training were necessarily slow in planting because they had to await the black teachers trained by higher institutions . . . and, third, while it is a great truth to say that the Negro must strive and strive mightily to help himself, it is equally true that unless his striving be not simply seconded, but rather aroused and encouraged, by the initiative of the richer and wiser environing group, he cannot hope for great success.

In his failure to realize and impress this last point, Mr. Washington is especially to be criticized. His doctrine has tended to make the whites, North and South, shift the burden of the Negro problem to the Negro's shoulders and stand aside as critical and rather pessimistic spectators; when in fact the burden belongs to the nation, and the hands of none of us are clean if we bend not our energies to righting these great wrongs.

Discussing the Readings

1. Booker T. Washington implied that political and social power cannot exist without economic power. Do you agree or disagree with that?

2. According to W. E. B. Du Bois, for what failure was Booker T. Washington especially to be criticized? What did Du Bois think was the consequence of that failure?

3. In the context of their time, do you think that Washington or Du Bois had a better strategy for improving the social and economic conditions of African Americans? Why?

CRITICAL THINKING
Testing Conclusions

In your opinion, has history favored the viewpoint of Booker T. Washington or W. E. B. Du Bois? Explain.

Ida Wells Calls for Action Against Lynching

8B

TIME FRAME
1901

GEOGRAPHIC SETTING
Chicago

Lynching is a form of mob violence in which a person accused of a crime is executed—usually by hanging—without a trial. Lynchings have occurred in many places in unsettled times. They were particularly common in the post-Reconstruction South, when thousands of people, most of them African Americans, were killed by mobs. In 1892, the peak year for such crimes, 230 people were lynched in the United States. In that year, the African American journalist Ida B. Wells (1862–1931) began a lifelong campaign against lynching when three of her friends were killed by a mob. After the office of the Memphis newspaper in which she had published her attacks on lynching was destroyed by a mob, Wells moved to Chicago, where she continued to work as a journalist, lecturer, and organizer of anti-lynching societies. In the following article, she attacked the belief, widely held at the time, that lynch mobs were formed primarily to punish African American males for crimes against white women.

condemn lynching, the condemnation is tempered with a plea for the lyncher—that human nature gives way under such awful provocation and that the mob, insane for the moment, must be pitied as well as condemned. It is strange that an intelligent, law-abiding, and fair-minded people should so persistently shut their eyes to the facts in the discussion of what the civilized world now concedes to be America's national crime.

This almost universal tendency to accept as true the slander which the lynchers offer to civilization as an excuse for their crime might be explained if the true facts were difficult to obtain; but not the slightest difficulty intervenes. The Associated Press dispatches, the press clipping bureau, frequent book publications, and the annual summary of a number of influential journals give the lynching record every year. This record [contradicts the view] that Negroes are lynched only because of their assaults upon womanhood. . . .

It would be supposed that the record would show that all, or nearly all, lynchings were caused by outrageous assaults upon women; certainly that this particular offense would outnumber all other causes for putting human beings to death without a trial by jury and the other safeguards of our Constitution and laws.

But the record makes no such disclosure. Instead, it shows that five women have been lynched, put to death with unspeakable savagery, during the past five years. . . . It shows that men, not a few but hundreds, have been lynched for misdemeanors, while others have suffered death for no offense known to the law, the causes assigned being "mistaken identity," "insult," "bad reputation,"

Issued February 1, 1990, this postage stamp honors Ida Wells for her work as a reformer on behalf of African Americans and women.

Among many thousand editorial clippings I have received in the past five years, 99 percent discuss the question upon the presumption that lynchings are the desperate effort of the Southern people to protect their women from black monsters, and, while the large majority

Ida B. Wells

25

Black Heritage USA

375

Clipped from Texas, Arkansas, Mississippi, and Georgia newspapers during the early months of 1919, these accounts give testimony to a continuing pattern of mob violence against African Americans decades after Ida Wells began her anti-lynching campaign in 1892.

ACCUSED WAS SENTENCED TO HANG FEBRUARY 21

The Dallas Express

TAKEN IN HAND BY AN "ORDERLY MOB" AND EXECUTED WITH LITTLE EXCITEMENT. OFFICERS OFFER NO RESISTANCE. SEVERAL HUNDRED TOOK PART IN THE DEMONSTRATION.

It must be true for we take the following despatch from the front page of the Dallas News of Tuesday, Jan. 21, 1919. Comment unnecessary. The despatch says:

Hilsboro, Texas, Jan. 20.—Bragg Williams, Negro, who confessed to the murder of Mrs. George Wells and her little son at their home near Itasca, Dec. 2, was taken from jail here at 1 o'clock this afternoon and burned to death on the public square. Earlier in the day he had been sentenced to be hanged on Feb. 21. He was convicted last week.

Williams, who had been in jail in Dallas for safe keeping, was brought to Hillsboro this morning to receive sentence, which was passed by Judge Horton Porter of the District Court. Williams was then taken to the county jail.

Attorneys Walter Collins and A. M. Frazier, who were appointed to defend Williams served under protest. The defense moved for a new trial an, on this being refused, gave notice of appeal.

Shortly afternoon a crowd went to the jail and demanded that Williams be turned over to them. The demand was refused. The outer door of the jail was broken with a sledgehammer and preparations were made to batter down the cell door, but some one in the crowd secured possession of the cell keys by overpowering a guard. The Negro was brought out and led to the public square. Williams was chained to the concrete "safety first" post on the square. Hay, wood and coal were piled about him and over the mass was poured several gallons of coal oil. Then a match was applied. Williams lived but a few minutes in the flames, probably not more than five. He is said to have made no outcry at his fate further than to say "Help me, Cap," three times.

At the jail Williams is said to have denied outraging his victim.

While a great many persons gathered around the burning Negro, business was not suspended and there was very little excitement.

MAN'S ATTEMPT TO LEAVE FARM ENDS FATALLY

Special to The Freeman.

DUBLIN, Ga., June 4.—James Waters, was accused of assaulting a white girl in Johnson county two weeks ago, was turned over by Sheriff O. L. Smith to a mob while on his way to the county jail. It appeared that the real reason for the lynching of Waters was that he had served notice on the farmer for whom he had worked for a number of years that he was going to leave. This appears to have angered his employer who, it is claimed, had his daughter to declare that Waters had attempted to assault her. And when he was about to leave his employer the sheriff placed him under arrest, at the same time telling him that he was charged with attempted assault upon the farmer's daughter. Waters denied the allegation and offered in his own defense the fact that he had been employed for a number of years and was one of the most trusted men on the farm. His protestations, however, were of no avail, and while on his way to the county jail the mob, which had previously formed, was turned over to them without any attempt at protection by the sheriff and lynched. A coroner's jury was called the following day and reported on their finding that Waters had come to his death at the hands of "parties unknown." It was said on good authority that the members of the coroner's jury were drawn from an aggregation of men who comprised the mob. As a result of this horrible murder hundreds of our people are preparing to leave.

Arkansas Negro Is Hanged By Mob.

Forest City, Aak., April 24.—Sam McIntyre, negro, was taken from the county jail by an armed mob and hanged to a telegraph pole near the city. McIntyre was charged with having murdered John Johnson, negro farmer, Feb. 4. The jailer said he was lured to the door by two men pretending to be an officer and a prisoner and that he was quickly overpowered.

Another Lyn... Mississipp...

Secretary Shillady Information ...

New York, March 10, 191...

National Association for the A... ment of Colored People, thro... Secretary, John R. Shillady... York, makes public the follow... egram to Governor Theodore ... of Mssissippi and Sheriff O. ... ner of Belzoni, Miss., asking i... tion regarding Eugene Gr... ung Negro, who was take... il at Belzoni, Miss., at two ... st Sunday morning by a m... as not been seen since, and ... s believed, has been lynched. ... telegrams follow:

March 8, 1919.

Hon. Theodore G. Bilbo, G... Jackson, Mississippi.

Ntional Association for A... ment of Colored People, with ... embers and 180 branche... tates, and furnishing inform... press of country regarding ... requests information concer... fate of Eugene Greene, a Ne... was taken from Belzoni, M... early Sunday morning, Mar... mob. Memphis papers of We... report inability of Sheriff O. ... ner to ascertain Greene's fa... he been lynched, and if so, wh... have been and are being ta... Missisippi authorities to deal ... uation. Information reques... our press service.

National Association for Advan...

of Colored People.

JOHN R. SHILLADY, Sec...

March 8, 191...

376

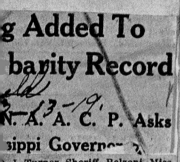

g Added To
baRity Record

N. A. A. C. P. Asks
sippi Govern--

), J. Turner, Sheriff, Belzoni, Miss.
National Association for Advance-
nt of Colored People with forty-
ht thousand members and 180
nces in 38 states, and furnishing
ormation to press of country re-
ding lynching, requests informa-
a as to whether Eugene Greene, a
--o, taken from Belzoni jail Sun-
-, March 2, has been lynched and
to steps being taken by your office
l other authorities to deal with the
ation.

ional Association for Advancement
of Colored People,
OHN R. SHILLADY, Secretary.

GRO ATTEMPTS
0 PULL YOUNG
OMAN FROM HORSE

pular Girl of Parks'
Mill Neighborhood
Escapes from Villian
and He Is Put to
Death

For the past few days there has
n a good deal of suppressed ex-
ement in the Parks' Mill neigh-
rhood, three miles beyond Ralph.
e story has been kept quite, as
people of the neighborhood were
ing to get their hands on a negro
uth by the name of Cicero Cage,
of Sam Cage, who attempted an
sault on one of the most prominent
d popular young ladies of that
ghborhood.

She was riding along a road, some
tance from any residence, when
cero ran out from a clump of
shes and placed his hands on her
fore she could whip up her horse

headed the horse on and made another attempt to pull her from the
animal, when she succeeded in whip-
ping up the animal and made good
her escape.

She knew the negro and reported
the matter and a watch has been
kept for Cicero, the outraged men
of the neighborhood swearing ven-
feance if they could lay their hands
on him.

A pretty well authenticated rumor
reach the city Saturday that on account of the matter being kept so
quiet Cicero thought there was no
danger and came back to his old
haunts, with the result that his dead
body was found Friday morning,
with his throat cut and many stabs
in different parts of his body.

The matter has been kept so still
that very few people at Ralph, only
three miles from the scene, knew
anything about the attempted assault
or the death of the negro boy at the
hands of parties unknown.

Late Saturday afternoon Sam Cage,
the father of Cicero, was in the city
and confirmed the above rumor that
his son had been killed. He says
he was literally cut to pieces. He
related the killing to Hon. Walter
D. Seed, who knew Sam and so the
story of the death of the negro is
a fact, instead of being a rumor.

FIVE NEGROES DEAD
IN JENKINS FEUD

MACON GA NEWS
APRIL 14, 1919

Church, Lodge Rooms and Auto-
mobiles Belonging to Negroes
Destroyed by Fire Last Night.
No More Trouble Expected.

MILLEN.—As results of the shooting
at Carswell Grove church Sunday, five
negroes have been killed. The principal, Joe Ruffin, is in jail in Augusta
slightly wounded. Lewis Ruffin, who
is accused of beating Night Marshal
Stephen's head into a pulp is still at
large with prospects of being captured
within the next few hours.

Last night the Carswell Grove church
was burned and three automobiles belonging to the negroes were destroyed
by fire and two negro lodge rooms in
this city were also burned to the
ground. Things are quiet at this time
and no more trouble is expected.

A plan is being put on foot to raise
funds for the two widows and to assist them in providing a home. W. C.
Brown's remains will be buried at
Summertown this afternoon, and the
remains of T. P. Stepens will be buried at Sardis about the same hour.

The officers were the victims of a
plot laid by the negroes to kill W. C.
Brown, and Deputy Sheriff F. A. Mar-
bach on account of their activities in
running down the illicit distillers in
this county. They were phoned to
come to the church to quell a disturbance and when they reached there and
arrested Edmund Scott the shooting

"unpopularity," "violating contract," "running quarantine," "giving evidence,"
"frightening child by shooting at rabbits,"
etc. Then, strangest of all, the record
55 shows that the sum total of lynchings for
these offenses—not crimes—and for the
alleged offenses which are only misdemeanors greatly exceeds the lynchings
for the very crime universally declared to
60 be the cause of lynching. . . . Negroes are
lynched for "violating contracts," "unpopularity," "testifying in court," and "shooting rabbits," As only Negroes are lynched
for "no offense," "unknown offenses," of-
65 fenses not criminal, misdemeanors, and
crimes not capital, it must be admitted
that the real cause of lynching in all such
cases is race prejudice, and should be so
classified.

70   The Christian and moral forces of the
nation should insist that misrepresenta-
tion should have no place in the discussion of this all important question, that
the figures of the lynching record should
75 be allowed to plead, trumpet-tongued, in
defense of the slandered dead, that the
silence of concession be broken, and that
truth, swiftwinged and courageous, sum-
mon this nation to do its duty to exalt jus-
80 tice and preserve inviolate the sacred-
ness of human life.

Discussing the Reading

1. According to Ida Wells, what justification was typically offered for the
actions of lynch mobs?

2. What did Wells claim was the basic
cause of lynching?

CRITICAL THINKING
Formulating Appropriate
Questions

Ida Wells rejected one justification for
lynching and offered what she felt
was the real reason. Suggest at least
two questions that would need to be
answered to determine whether her
theory was more valid than the one
she rejected.

Chapter Summary

Write the supporting details under each of the following main ideas as you review the chapter.

Section 1

1. Many special interests powered the reform impulse.
2. A new brand of journalism exposed flaws in American society and politics.
3. A vigorous socialist movement sought economic and political change.
4. Women worked to achieve equality.
5. African Americans fought segregation and restriction of their civil rights.

Section 2

1. Demands for reform usually started at the local level.
2. Reformers also tackled corruption at the state level.
3. Reformers broadened activities of state and federal governments.

Section 3

1. Theodore Roosevelt expanded the power of the presidency.
2. Roosevelt challenged the trusts.
3. Roosevelt took bold action to end a crippling coal strike.

Section 4

1. The geographic distribution of water shaped the West.
2. Economic growth gave rise to the conservation movement.
3. Roosevelt promoted the conservation of resources.
4. William Howard Taft alienated the conservationists.
5. A split in the Republican party ensured Democatic victory in 1912.

Section 5

1. Wilson launched his New Freedom.
2. Wilson established powerful controls over banking and the trusts.
3. Wilson's record of reform proved uneven.

Chapter Themes

1. **Constitutional and representative government:** Progressives expanded government after 1900 in order to protect and extend the rights of the people. Reforms included controls over big business, the Pure Food and Drug Act, the 16th and 17th Amendments, and the Federal Reserve Act.

2. **Geography and environmental interaction:** Theodore Roosevelt treasured the American wilderness and helped save it for future generations. He urged conservation and created 51 wildlife refuges and five national parks.

Chapter Study Guide

Identifying Key People and Terms

Name the key person or key term that describes the:

1. movement that placed its faith in progress, expanding government to help people
2. kind of writer who tried to expose corruption
3. political tool that allows citizens to vote on a new law or do away with an existing law
4. president noted for his trustbusting
5. reform president, author of the New Freedom

Locating Key Places

1. Which state, home to Robert La Follette, was called a laboratory of democracy?
2. Where was most anthracite coal mined in the early 1900s?

Mastering the Main Ideas

1. Complete a chart about the reform groups in Section 1. Use the following as a model:

	Major issues or activities	Achievements
(a) writers		
(b) socialists		
(c) women		
(d) African Americans		

2. What progressive ideas changed politics in Wisconsin, California, Texas, and Virginia?
3. How did the Supreme Court ruling on the Northern Security Company affect Theodore Roosevelt's later antitrust activities?
4. How did the use of presidential power change during Taft's term in office?
5. Why was Wilson more successful than Roosevelt in getting reform legislation?

Applying Critical Thinking Skills

1. **Expressing problems:** Which groups were not sharing in America's prosperity at the turn of the century?
2. **Analyzing cause and effect:** How did the commission system and city-manager plan propose to reform city government?

1900	1905	1910	1915	1920

1904
Trustbusting begins

1906
The Jungle published; Meat Inspection Act

1909
NAACP formed

1913
16th Amendment (income tax)
17th Amendment (direct election of senators)

1900
Decade of peak immigration begins; Hurricane ravages Galveston, Texas

1901
McKinley shot; Theodore Roosevelt sworn in; Socialist Party of America formed

1912
Woodrow Wilson elected

3. **Making comparisons:** How did Theodore Roosevelt's ideas change between 1900 and 1904 concerning the president's role in protecting the nation from monopolies?

4. **Analyzing cause and effect:** How did federal irrigation projects affect the growth of power in the West?

5. **Recognizing values:** In what way was the Federal Reserve Act a clear example of progressive principles?

Chapter Activities

Learning Geography Through History

1. Was the progressive movement limited to one geographical area? Explain.
2. How did the Hetch Hetchy Valley become an issue between conservationists and preservationists?

Relating the United States to the World

1. In 1903 Emmeline Pankhurst founded the Women's Social and Political Union to work for women's suffrage in England. What similar activities were occurring in the United States?
2. Explain the similarities and differences of the American progressive movement and the socialist movement that brought revolution to Russia in 1917.

Linking Past to Present

1. About three million 14- to 17-year-olds work part-time today. What are the costs and benefits of students working?
2. How does the government continue today to regulate the food industry?

Using the Time Line

1. In what year was the NAACP established?
2. Which time line events reflect the movement toward reform in American life?

Practicing Critical Thinking Strategies

Identifying Central Issues
What main point is the artist trying to make in the cartoon below?

Learning More About the Progressive Era

1. **Using Source Readings:** Read the Source Readings for this chapter and answer the questions.
2. **Analyzing Journalism:** Read an article by Lincoln Steffens, S. S. McClure, Ida M. Tarbell, Ray Stannard Baker, Edward Bok, or Upton Sinclair. Summarize the article and analyze the author's main arguments.

Linking Past to Present

Nine years after the Spanish-American War President Theodore Roosevelt flaunted American naval power by sending a force of warships around the world. Painter Henry Reuterdahl (1871–1925) pictured the Great White Fleet, inset, as it entered San Francisco Bay in 1908 on its way to Japan. A U.S. nuclear submarine cruises at left. The most modern U.S. submarine today can carry eight times the destructive force of all explosives fired in World War II.

America's Rise to World Power

1 8 9 0 — 1 9 1 4

9

Americans in the late 1890s found themselves in a heated debate over foreign policy. The American victory in the war with Spain in 1898 placed the key issues squarely before the American public: Should the United States acquire island outposts to promote commerce and aid defense? Would the residents of those areas become American citizens or subjects of an American colonial empire? Did the idea of empire contradict the principles of the Declaration of Independence?

Perhaps no Americans had more conflicting emotions than the men of the four African American regiments—veterans of campaigns against the Indians in the West—sent to Cuba and the Philippines to fight that war. These men at times had to fight people of their own color who wanted neither Spanish nor American rule.

John W. Galloway, a sergeant major in the 24th Infantry, wrote from the Philippines in 1899:

AN AMERICAN ★ SPEAKS We black men here are so much between the Devil and the Deep Blue. . . . The future of the Filipino, I fear, is that of the Negro in the South. . . . He is kicked and cuffed at will and he dare not remonstrate [protest].

The United States went on to become a world power by 1900 and a superpower by 1945. However, as Galloway feared, wielding colonial power proved difficult. Americans today ask, as they did in 1890, can the United States ever really be both an imperialist power and a force for good beyond its borders?

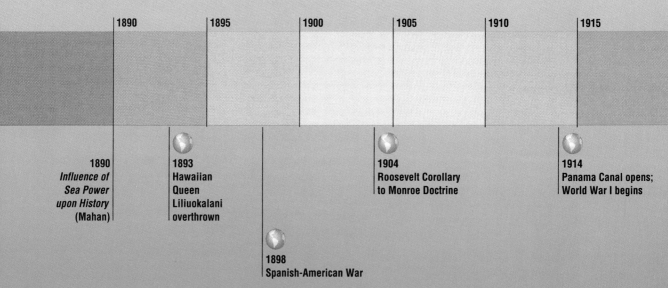

1890	1895	1900	1905	1910	1915

1890
Influence of Sea Power upon History (Mahan)

1893
Hawaiian Queen Liliuokalani overthrown

1898
Spanish-American War

1904
Roosevelt Corollary to Monroe Doctrine

1914
Panama Canal opens; World War I begins

SECTION 1

U.S. expansion laid the foundation for world power.

Key Terms: expansionists, imperialism, Open Door policy

Reading Preview
As you read this section, you will learn:

1. how U.S. continental expansion was completed.
2. what guided U.S. relations with Latin America.
3. what groups focused American attention on the Pacific.
4. what goal led Americans to compete with European powers in Africa.
5. when the United States rose to world power.

The wonders of electricity dazzled visitors to the World's Columbian Exposition at Chicago in 1893. President Grover Cleveland pushed a button in the White House, and crowds at the Fair witnessed the first public demonstration of the new alternating current system of distributing energy. The American Impressionist painter Childe Hassam (1859–1935) captures the shimmering light of the Palace of Electricity.

Visitors from all over the world thronged to Chicago in 1893 to visit a spectacular World's Fair, the Columbian Exposition, which opened a year late to celebrate the 400th anniversary of the discovery of the Americas. While crowds attended the fair, American historians also gathered in Chicago at a special meeting. Some

heard a young historian from the University of Wisconsin deliver a brief lecture, possibly the most influential lecture ever given on American history. Noting that, according to the 1890 census, a frontier line no longer existed in the country, Frederick Jackson Turner traced the influence of the frontier in shaping American character. He observed,

And now, four centuries from the discovery of America, at the end of a hundred years of life under the Constitution, the frontier has gone, and with its going has closed the first period of American history.

AN AMERICAN ★ SPEAKS

With the frontier gone, **expansionists** wanted Americans to seek new frontiers overseas, to extend "American influence to outlying islands and adjoining countries."

The purchase of Alaska completed U.S. continental expansion.

From its earliest days as a nation, the United States pressed westward across the whole continent. Under the rallying cry of Manifest Destiny, the United States in the 1840s had annexed Texas, divided the Pacific Northwest with Great Britain, and fought an expansionist war with Mexico, gaining California and the

Southwest. As you can see from the map on page 1006, these huge acquisitions gave the United States its familiar, present-day contours. Yet some expansionists hoped to go further.

William H. Seward, secretary of state under Lincoln and Johnson, was an ardent expansionist and at various times proposed the acquisition of Cuba, Central America, Mexico, and Canada. He also foresaw the need for a canal through Central America so that ocean-going vessels could avoid the long trip around South America.

In 1867 Seward succeeded in negotiating the purchase of **Alaska** from Russia for $7.2 million. The Senate promptly ratified the treaty, but the House balked at buying the frozen wasteland they called "Seward's Folly." He finally convinced them that Alaska's rich mineral and animal resources and its position as a bridge to Asia justified the expense.

The treaties by which the United States had acquired earlier territories made their residents U.S. citizens and specified that the territories could eventually become states. The Alaskan purchase treaty also extended citizenship to the residents of Alaska but made no promise of statehood. Few expected Alaska's population ever would grow enough to justify statehood.

Some Americans saw the purchase of Alaska as a prelude to the annexation of Canada. Talk of annexing Canada arose when the United States accused Great Britain of a breach of neutrality during the Civil War. Congress demanded payment for damages caused by Confederate naval vessels built in England, notably the *Alabama*, and hoped Britain would simply sign over Canada as restitution. The *Alabama* claims, however, were settled by arbitration, and the cession of Canada or any other territory never entered the negotiations.

The Monroe Doctrine guided U.S. policy in Latin America.

The United States maintained a leading role in Latin America, basing its policies there on the Monroe Doctrine, proclaimed by President James Monroe in 1823. The Monroe Doctrine asserted that the Americas were not to be considered as subjects for future colonization by

any European powers, and that the United States would not interfere in Europe's internal affairs. However, for many years European nations refused to recognize the Monroe Doctrine.

Consequently, Seward decided not to rest his case on the Monroe Doctrine when he maneuvered the United States through a confrontation with Mexico in the 1860s over France's designs on that country. After the Mexican War with the United States in 1846–1848, struggling factions within Mexico and the interference of foreign business interests left the country weak and unstable. France's emperor Napoleon III, taking advantage of the U.S. preoccupation with the Civil War, established a puppet emperor, Archduke Maximilian of Austria, on a Mexican throne in 1864. Seward protested, and after the Civil War he posted 50,000 American troops at the Mexican border. Napoleon withdrew his army in 1867, and the Mexican people, led by their president, **Benito Juárez** [bā nē′tō hwä′res], were able to depose and execute the hapless Maximilian.

Secretary of State William H. Seward, bowing deeply, and President Andrew Johnson, greet the new Alaskan representative. In 1867 few Americans viewed Alaska as a bargain though they gained an area more than twice the size of Texas for two cents an acre.

President of Mexico from 1861 to 1872, Benito Juárez carried out major reforms to promote social equality.

Congregational Christian missionaries erected the first Mission House in Honolulu in 1820, using lumber carried with them when they sailed from Boston around Cape Horn at South America's southernmost tip. Christianity spread quickly among the Hawaiians.

The United States did, however, cite the Monroe Doctrine in 1895 when it supported Venezuela in a boundary dispute with British Guiana after gold was discovered in that part of South America. Secretary of State Richard Olney demanded that Great Britain submit to arbitration and boldly declared "the United States is practically sovereign on this continent." In 1896 Britain finally agreed in order to avoid conflict with the United States during a time of mounting difficulties with Germany in South Africa. Britain's recognition of U.S. dominance in Latin America marked the beginning of a special relationship between Great Britain and the United States.

Traders and missionaries focused American attention on the Pacific.

From the earliest years of the Republic, Americans had traded with East Asia. The first New England merchant ship reached China in 1784 and reaped a return of 30 percent on its $120,000 investment. In 1854 Japanese ports, long closed to foreigners, were finally opened to American commerce through negotiations between the Japanese rulers and Commodore Matthew C. Perry, backed by an intimidating U.S. naval squadron.

American missionaries also had a keen interest in Asia and the Pacific islands. In 1885

a Congregational minister, **Josiah Strong**, wrote a small but influential book called *Our Country*, in which he urged the spread of Protestant Christianity "down upon Mexico, down upon Central and South America, out upon the islands of the sea, over upon Africa and beyond." Missionaries of many different Christian denominations took up the challenge.

Both Protestant and Roman Catholic missionaries were particularly successful on the beautiful islands of Hawaii. Located 2,000 miles southwest of San Francisco, the islands also provided an important base for ships crossing the Pacific.

Many of the missionaries' descendants became wealthy planters of sugar cane and eventually dominated Hawaii's economy, which became closely tied to that of the United States. In 1875 the sugar growers obtained a reciprocity treaty that exempted Hawaiian sugar from American tariff duties. Hawaii's economy boomed. The McKinley Tariff of 1890 gave an advantage to sugar grown in the United States. This triggered an economic crisis in Hawaii.

An energetic, new queen, **Liliuokalani** [li lē′ ə wō kə lä′nē], came to the Hawaiian throne in 1891. Liliuokalani resolved to restore Hawaii to the Hawaiians. When she proposed to disfranchise American settlers who were not married to native women, the planters overthrew her monarchy in 1893. An American diplomat in Honolulu had ordered a U.S. naval unit there to support the planters. The rebellious planters set up their own government and asked the United States to annex the islands. However, President Grover Cleveland opposed expansionism and rejected annexation although he did recognize the new government. Hawaii was finally annexed by a joint resolution of Congress in 1898 during the administration of President McKinley.

Americans competed with European powers for markets in Africa.

Americans first looked to Latin America and Asia for markets, but by the 1870s they turned to Africa as well. Hundreds of missionary societies from the United States, Great Britain, and Europe were also active there.

By this time the race for new colonies had begun. Weak countries in Africa and Asia became prey for European nations with superior weapons. In their search for colonies, the European powers were practicing **imperialism**, which is the policy of extending the rule of one country over other countries or colonies, usually in order to protect trading interests or investments but sometimes to protect national security. Although similar to the U.S. policy of Manifest Destiny, imperialism usually implied seizing distant regions and holding them in a dependent, unequal status.

Meeting at Berlin, Germany, in 1884 and 1885, Great Britain, France, Germany, Russia, and ten other nations proceeded to lay claim to almost the entire African continent. U.S. delegates urged an **Open Door policy** that would allow all countries to trade in western Africa on equal terms. To win this concession, the United States wound up supporting a cruel Belgian regime in the Congo. George Washington Williams went to Africa and reported on conditions in the Congo in 1890. Williams was a Baptist minister, Ohio's first black state legislator, and an important African American historian. From the headwaters of the Congo, he wrote in an *Open Letter* to the Belgian king:

Your majesty's government has [seized the Congolese] **AN AMERICAN ★ SPEAKS** land, burned their towns, stolen their property, enslaved their women and children, and committed other crimes too numerous to mention in detail.

Published in the United States in 1890, the letter turned U.S. opinion against Belgium.

The United States rose to world power in the 1890s.

"Some nations achieve greatness; the United States had greatness thrust upon it," wrote historian Ernest R. May in describing America's emergence as a world power during the last years of the 19th century. Other historians have argued that major credit must be given to the individuals who shaped U.S. expansionist policies—especially President William McKinley, who made the crucial decision of war against

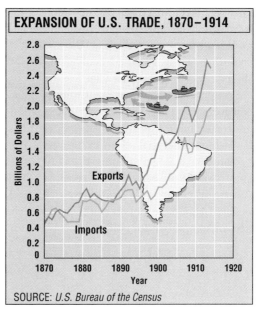

EXPANSION OF U.S. TRADE, 1870–1914

Billions of Dollars (vertical axis: 0, 0.2, 0.4, 0.6, 0.8, 1.0, 1.2, 1.4, 1.6, 1.8, 2.0, 2.2, 2.4, 2.6, 2.8)

Exports

Imports

Year (horizontal axis: 1870, 1880, 1890, 1900, 1910, 1920)

SOURCE: *U.S. Bureau of the Census*

chart study

When the United States exports more goods and services to other countries than it imports, it has a trade surplus. When it imports more than it exports, it has a trade deficit. During which years did the U.S. balance of trade show a surplus? **Critical Thinking** How has the U.S. trade picture changed?

Spain in 1898. A book by a U.S. naval officer, **Alfred Thayer Mahan** [mə han′], *The Influence of Sea Power Upon History*, also had a profound effect on U.S. policy.

In his book, published in 1890, Mahan wrote that to support American diplomacy and commerce, the United States needed a modern

Africans carry raw rubber out of German Cameroon, below. Gathering wild rubber became the principal industry in the Congo River Basin after the Belgian king Leopold II seized it as virtually his own private property in the 1880s.

navy with steel-hulled warships powered solely by steam. Because a steam navy could operate no farther from its shores than the amount of coal it carried in its holds, coaling stations at strategic locations became vital.

Secretary of the Navy Benjamin F. Tracy convinced Congress in 1889 and 1890, to modernize the navy. Construction began on three battleships equal to the best in the world.

Mahan's strategic arguments and Tracy's construction of battleships came as some Americans began, in Mahan's phrase, to "look outward." Soon the United States would use its new military might for conquest.

SECTION 1 REVIEW

Identify Key People and Terms
Write a sentence to identify: expansionists, William H. Seward, Benito Juárez, Josiah Strong, Liliuokalani, imperialism, Open Door policy, Alfred Thayer Mahan

Locate Key Places
Next to which country is Alaska located?

Master the Main Ideas

1. **Understanding U.S. land policies:** How did the Alaska purchase treaty differ from previous treaties by which the United States had acquired large territories?
2. **Understanding historic documents:** Give an example showing how the Monroe Doctrine guided U.S. policy in Latin America in 1890.
3. **Examining economic and cultural influences:** How did American missionaries and traders focus U.S. attention on the Hawaiian Islands?
4. **Analyzing information:** Why did American opinion change regarding the partitioning of Africa among European powers in the 1880s and 1890s?
5. **Recognizing notable men and women:** What individuals or ideas contributed to the U.S. rise to world power in the 1890s?

Apply Critical Thinking Skills: Recognizing Values
How did the U.S. acquisition of Mexican lands before the Civil War differ from the race for empire among European nations at the end of the 19th century?

SECTION 2

War with Spain opened the path to empire.

Key Terms: *reconcentración*, De Lôme letter, *Maine*, Teller Amendment, Rough Riders

Reading Preview
As you read this section, you will learn:

1. what effect the Cuban revolt had on the American public.
2. about the outcome of negotiations with Spain.
3. how Spain lost the Philippines and Cuba.

"It has been a splendid little war," **John Hay** wrote shortly after Spain acknowledged its defeat in 1898. Hay was the American ambassador to Great Britain and would serve as secretary of state under Presidents McKinley and Roosevelt. The term "splendid little war" soon became the best-known description for the Spanish-American War, which brought America to world power.

A Cuban revolt aroused the American public.

By 1890 Cuba, Puerto Rico, the Philippines, and the Pacific island of Guam were all that remained of the once vast Spanish empire. Cuba had repeatedly tried to throw off the Spanish yoke, notably between 1868 and 1878. After the ten-year insurrection came to an end, some of the insurgents (revolutionaries) fled to the United States. Led by the poet and journalist **José Martí**, the exiles gained American support for Cuban independence.

Cuba's economy, like that of Hawaii, flourished or faltered according to the tariff advantage given its sugar by the United States. By 1894 the United States received nearly 90 percent of Cuba's exports, primarily sugar. That year a new tariff put a sizable duty on Cuban sugar, causing a depression in Cuba.

Discontent erupted into a new insurrection, and Martí returned to Cuba to lead the fight for independence. He was soon killed in battle. The Spanish government sent General Valeriano Weyler [bä′le ryä′nō wā′ler] to Cuba in 1896 to combat the guerrilla warfare waged by the insurgents. Weyler instituted a policy of *reconcentración* (concentration), herding the civilian population into fortified towns. Anyone outside the towns was assumed to be an insurgent and was subject to military action. Disease and starvation swept through the camps. Within two years, by one estimate, these conditions killed one of every four Cubans.

American newspapers vied with each other in portraying Spanish atrocities and referred to the Spanish governor general as "Butcher" Weyler. Two New York newspapers were engaged in intense competition to gain readers—the *World*, published by **Joseph Pulitzer**, and the *Journal*, published by **William Randolph Hearst**. To attract readers, Pulitzer and Hearst used large headlines, unscrupulously sensational stories, and comics. The papers sent their best reporters to Cuba and exaggerated the reports to attract readers, a practice called yellow journalism. (The name came from a *World* cartoon, "The Yellow Kid," featuring a child in a yellow dress.)

Novelist Stephen Crane and such noted journalists as Richard Harding Davis rushed to Cuba to cover the war together with photographers and famous artists—Frederic Remington, Howard Chandler Christy, William J. Glackens, and John T. McCutcheon, among others. After several weeks of inactivity, Remington wired Hearst from Cuba that there would be no war. Hearst is said to have wired back, "You furnish the pictures and I'll furnish the war."

Negotiations with Spain failed to prevent war.

Fed a steady diet of stories from the yellow press, many Americans began clamoring for war to free Cuba from Spain. President McKinley redoubled U.S. diplomatic efforts to prevent a clash of arms. In February 1898 two events made a negotiated solution less likely.

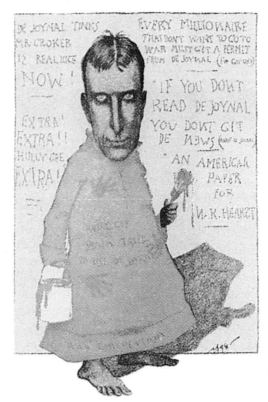

William Randolph Hearst promoted— some say created—the Spanish-American War in order to build the circulation of his newspapers. Mr. Croker, at top left, refers to Tammany boss Richard Croker. Hearst's *Journal* first opposed Croker then sought his favor when Hearst ran for Congress in 1902.

That month Cuban rebels stole and made public a letter critical of President McKinley that had been written by Enrique Dupuy de Lôme [en rē′kä dY pwē′ də lōm], the Spanish minister to the United States. A few days after publication of the **De Lôme letter**, a mysterious explosion destroyed the American battleship *Maine* in the harbor of Havana, Cuba. More than 260 Americans died. The yellow press blamed Spain, and an official inquiry reported that an underwater mine had caused the explosion. Despite this report, the cause has never been exactly determined although in 1976 U.S. Admiral Hyman G. Rickover demonstrated that the explosion probably resulted from internal causes.

President McKinley quietly began preparing for war. He issued a new set of demands for Spain including negotiations, with McKinley as mediator, leading to Cuban independence. The Spanish government promised reform but made no commitment regarding independence. McKinley responded in April by telling

THE SPANISH-AMERICAN WAR
Skill: Making Comparisons

Introducing the Skill. You have read how the Spanish-American War became known as the "Splendid Little War." Some historians also have named it the "Newspapers' War," primarily because of the influence of two New York newspapers—the *World* and the *New York Journal*. How did these newspapers, both proponents of yellow journalism at its peak, compare with one another?

Learning the Skill. By looking for similarities and differences between the two newspapers, you are practicing the skill of **making comparisons**. As you learned earlier, the skill really involves two steps—comparing, that is, determining how two or more things are alike, and contrasting, determining

how two or more things are different.

Follow these five steps:
1. Identify the main features of each item.
2. Select a feature in one item and determine whether it can be found in all the other items.
3. Classify as a similarity any feature found in all the given items.
4. Classify as a difference any feature not found in all the given items.
5. Repeat this process for each main feature.

Applying the Skill.
1. Study the front-page headlines that appeared in the *World* and in the *Journal* on February 17,

1898—directly following the explosion of the *Maine*. Below the headlines both newspapers featured stories that were filled with drama and conjecture.

The *Journal* announced a $50,000 reward for the "detection of the perpetrator of the Maine outrage" five different times on its front page.

The front-page focus of the *World* was an illustration based on eyewitness accounts of the ship's fiery explosion. An article also announced that the newspaper had sent a special tug to Havana to investigate the explosion.

2. Compare and contrast the coverage and actions of the two newspapers. Were the journalists acting responsibly?

Congress that "the war in Cuba must stop." Congress authorized him to use force and added a statement by Senator Henry M. Teller of Colorado. The **Teller Amendment** pledged that the United States would not annex Cuba once the island was free and peace restored. Spain declared war on April 24, 1898.

Spain lost the Philippines and Cuba after humiliating naval defeats.

The first action in the Spanish-American War occurred not in Cuba but on the other side of the world in the Philippine Islands, a Spanish colony for more than 300 years. Like Cuba, the Philippines had rebelled repeatedly against

Spanish rule. Assistant Secretary of the Navy Theodore Roosevelt understood the islands' strategic location. You can see from the map at right how these islands could aid American trade or travel in East Asia. In late February, anticipating war with Spain, Roosevelt cabled the American naval commander in the Pacific, **George Dewey**, and ordered him, in the event war was declared, to proceed immediately to the Philippines and destroy the Spanish fleet at **Manila Bay**. Use the map at right to trace the path of Dewey's fleet.

The fleet fought the enemy in Manila Bay on May 1, five days after President McKinley had signed the war resolution. The Spanish ships anchored there moved to shallower waters as Commodore Dewey gave a soon-to-be-famous order to the commander of his flagship, "You may fire when ready, Gridley." The obsolete Spanish ships proved no match for the modern American navy. Dewey sent the ten enemy vessels to the bottom of Manila Bay. The Spanish lost 381 men. The Americans lost none. Dewey instantly became a national hero.

Attention now shifted to Cuba. When war was declared, the U.S. Army numbered only 30,000, but a call for volunteers soon brought a quarter of a million men to the colors. In training camps in the South, chaos and confusion reigned. Food and supplies arrived at one location while the men for whom they were intended arrived at another. Disease ran rampant through some camps, killing many soldiers. Others died from tainted food. The first transports did not sail for Cuba until June, almost two months after war was declared.

Among the volunteers was Theodore Roosevelt, who as Assistant Secretary of the Navy resigned to become lieutenant colonel of a cavalry regiment soon known as the **Rough Riders**. The energetic Roosevelt had recruited a collection of western cowboys and rangers (he specified "young, good shots, and good riders") as well as upper-class easterners, whose riding experience came from playing polo.

The Rough Riders—on foot except for Roosevelt because their horses had not yet reached Cuba—participated in the successful assault on the fortifications surrounding the port city of

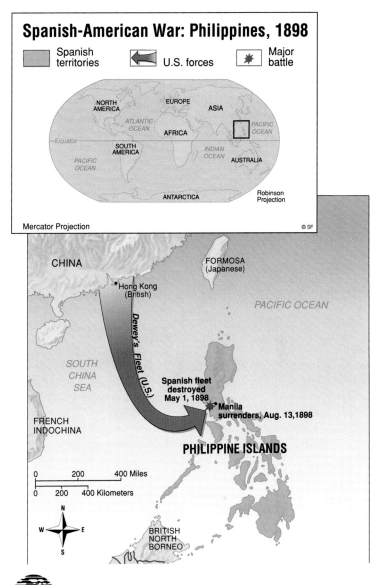

map study

Relationships Within Places   The first action of the Spanish-American War took place in Spain's colony in the Philippines. Dewey's victory there eventually led to the United States gaining control of this territory. How far are the Philippine Islands from the Asian mainland?

Critical Thinking   Why did U.S. business and military leaders want a controlling relationship with the Philippines?

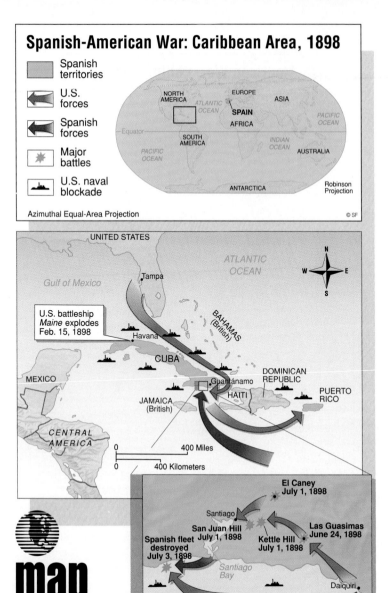

Spanish-American War: Caribbean Area, 1898

- Spanish territories
- U.S. forces
- Spanish forces
- Major battles
- U.S. naval blockade

Azimuthal Equal-Area Projection

© SF

NORTH AMERICA • EUROPE • ASIA • SPAIN • AFRICA • PACIFIC OCEAN • ATLANTIC OCEAN • Equator • SOUTH AMERICA • PACIFIC OCEAN • INDIAN OCEAN • AUSTRALIA • ANTARCTICA

Robinson Projection

UNITED STATES
ATLANTIC OCEAN
Gulf of Mexico
Tampa

U.S. battleship *Maine* explodes Feb. 15, 1898

Havana
CUBA
BAHAMAS (British)
MEXICO
Guantánamo
JAMAICA (British)
HAITI
DOMINICAN REPUBLIC
PUERTO RICO
CENTRAL AMERICA

0 _____ 400 Miles
0 _____ 400 Kilometers

El Caney July 1, 1898
Santiago
San Juan Hill July 1, 1898
Spanish fleet destroyed July 3, 1898
Kettle Hill July 1, 1898
Las Guasimas June 24, 1898
Santiago Bay
Daiquiri
CARIBBEAN SEA

0 _____ 4 Miles
0 _____ 4 Kilometers

map study

Relationships Within Places

American actions in the Caribbean began with a naval blockade. Where did the major sea and land battles take place?

Critical Thinking

What geographic factors help explain U.S. interest in Cuba and Puerto Rico?

---

peated Dewey's feat at Manila, destroying every vessel with the loss of only one U.S. life.

With the Spanish fleet destroyed, Santiago surrendered. A week later American forces took Puerto Rico. Spanish land forces in the Philippines surrendered in mid-August. The "splendid little war" lasted only 16 weeks.

By the Treaty of Paris, signed in December 1898, Spain surrendered all claim to Cuba, ceded Puerto Rico and the island of Guam to the United States, and sold the Philippines for $20 million. The treaty did not specify that the residents would immediately become American citizens, nor did it mention statehood. In these critical respects, these acquisitions differed significantly from earlier ones. America had become an imperial power.

Santiago. You can see from the map above where U.S. troops moved into Santiago by land. Roosevelt led a charge of Rough Riders and of the 9th and 10th cavalry, elite units of African Americans popularly known as Buffalo Soldiers. The yellow press made Roosevelt the hero of the Battle of San Juan Hill.

The Spanish Atlantic fleet was anchored in Santiago Bay. As the Spanish squadron attempted to escape, the American navy re-

---

SECTION 2 REVIEW

Identify Key People and Terms
Write a sentence to identify: John Hay, José Martí, *reconcentración*, Joseph Pulitzer, William Randolph Hearst, De Lôme letter, *Maine*, Teller Amendment, George Dewey, Rough Riders

Locate Key Places
1. Where did Admiral Dewey defeat the Spanish fleet?
2. What Cuban port was the center of military activity in the Spanish-American War?

Master the Main Ideas
1. **Perceiving cause/effect relationships:** Describe three elements that contributed to the concern of the American public over the Cuban revolt.
2. **Perceiving cause/effect relationships:** How did the yellow press influence negotiations to prevent war with Spain?
3. **Understanding international conflicts:** Why were Spain's naval defeats in the Philippines and Cuba so one-sided?

Apply Critical Thinking Skills: Making Comparisons
Compare and contrast the yellow press of the 1890s with media today in terms of their characteristics and influence.

The nation debated the status of its new territories.

Key Terms: Platt Amendment, Foraker Act, Insular Cases

Reading Preview
As you read this section, you will learn:

1. how Americans felt about annexation of the Philippines.
2. in which presidential election imperialism became a key issue.
3. about what happened to Cuba and Puerto Rico.

When Admiral Dewey destroyed the Spanish fleet at Manila Bay, some Americans began to change their view of the Spanish-American War as simply a humanitarian effort. Imperialists argued that the United States should retain the Philippines to help spread American influence around the world. Other Americans disagreed. Retaining control over a distant land, said these anti-imperialists, violated the principle of self-determination expressed in the Declaration of Independence.

Americans were sharply divided over annexation of the Philippines.

The debate over annexation of the Philippines divided the U.S. Congress and the American public. Although Theodore Roosevelt and such congressional leaders as **Henry Cabot Lodge** of Massachusetts supported the idea of an American empire from the beginning, they were clearly a minority at the time the nation went to war against Spain. The spirit of the Teller Amendment—rejecting in advance any idea of territorial acquisition and fighting simply "to free Cuba"—was much closer to the views of the majority. As the war progressed, Americans began to accept the idea of acquiring distant colonies.

Arguments for annexation. The imperialists argued for annexation of the Philippines

on two main grounds: first, that U.S. trade would be enhanced; and second, that the United States should keep the Philippines in order to fulfill its special mission in the world. Each argument made several points.

According to the first argument, the location of the Philippines' principal port, Manila, 600 miles from the Asian mainland, could make it the base for a prosperous China trade. The severe economic depression of 1893 had convinced many Americans that the United States, as a major industrial nation, needed more foreign markets to ward off future depressions. Senator **Albert Beveridge** of Indiana argued for economic expansion when he said, "Today, we are raising more than we can consume, making more than we can use. Therefore, we must find new markets for our produce." In keeping with this position, imperialists said that if the United States did not take over the Philippines, one of its trading rivals would.

The second argument basically expressed Americans' sense of their special responsibility toward the Philippines, "not to exploit but to develop, to civilize, to educate, to train in the science of self-government," to use President

Draped in a Roman toga befitting an eloquent orator, the youthful Albert Beveridge prepared for his first term in the Senate by making an exhaustive tour of the Philippines, still in the throes of war. He became a national figure within a month. An uncompromising imperialist, Beveridge later defended the U.S. Army in the Philippines against Senate charges of misconduct and cruelty. Democratic Senator Edward Carmack and Populist Ben Tillman take an opposite view in this 1902 cartoon.

Midnight Thoughts of American Imperialism

American imperialism in the early 1900s mixed economic rivalry, racism, and greed with national pride and good intentions. In justifying his decision to annex the Philippines, President McKinley tossed in most of the ingredients of the imperialist recipe. Would a president today explain his decisions in such a way? Why or why not?

I walked the floor of the White House night after night until midnight. . . . And one night it came to me in this way . . . (1) that we could not give them back to Spain—that would be cowardly and dishonorable; (2) that we could not turn them over to France or Germany—our commercial rivals in the Orient—that would be bad business and discreditable; (3) that we could not leave them to themselves—they were unfit for self-government . . . and (4) that there was nothing left for us to do but to take them all, and to educate the Filipinos, and uplift and civilize and Christianize them.

McKinley's words. Senator Beveridge expressed this idea most forcefully. He said,

God has made us the master organizers of the world to es- **AN AMERICAN ★ SPEAKS** tablish a system where chaos reigns. He has marked the American people as His chosen Nation to finally lead in the regeneration of the world.

The English poet Rudyard Kipling expressed a similar feeling in a poem dedicated to the United States and the Philippines in 1899 in which he urged the United States to "take up the White Man's burden." That phrase came to describe a self-imposed obligation to go into distant lands, to bring the benefits of civilization to other peoples, and to Christianize them. Kipling was applying the concepts of Social Darwinism to nations. According to this belief, the peoples of the world were climbing a ladder of civilization, with Europe and the United States in the lead. With nations as with individuals, the fittest would survive.

Imperialists usually believed in the superiority of Anglo-Saxons, that is, people of English descent. Their attitudes expressed a racist point of view. In this respect, imperialists appealed to Americans' prejudices as well as to their desire for prosperity and pride in their country's special mission.

Arguments against annexation. On the other side, a strong anti-imperialist movement formed and flourished between 1898 and 1900. Leaders included William Jennings Bryan—the popular Democratic presidential candidate in 1896 and 1900—business leader Andrew Carnegie, and writer Mark Twain. The movement attracted Democrats and Republicans, labor organizers and business leaders, progressives and conservatives. They argued that any denial of self-government ran contrary to the principles upon which America was founded.

The brutality of the war in the Philippines also troubled Americans. **George F. Hoar**, a Massachusetts senator and founder of the Republican party, fought his party's policies on moral grounds. He said:

We changed the Monroe Doctrine from a doctrine of **AN AMERICAN ★ SPEAKS** eternal righteousness and justice, resting on the consent of the governed, to a doctrine of brutal selfishness looking only to our own advantage. . . . We put children to death. We devastated provinces. We baffled the aspirations of a people for liberty.

Despite their opposition to imperialism, the anti-imperialists had one major attribute in common with the imperialists. They were both often racist. For example, Samuel Gompers, the American Federation of Labor president, fought expansion because the "half-breeds and semi-barbaric people" of the new colonies would work too cheaply and undercut American labor.

Imperialism became a key issue in the 1900 presidential election.

The terms of the Treaty of Paris dismayed Democrats, Populists, and conservative Republicans. Bryan urged his followers in the Senate to approve the treaty. In that way he hoped the

United States would grant the Philippines their independence. By a slim margin, the Senate did approve the treaty but rejected the proposal for Philippine independence.

The Republicans renominated McKinley in 1900 and chose Theodore Roosevelt, the hero of San Juan Hill, for vice president. The Democrats nominated Bryan and condemned imperialism. McKinley and Roosevelt defended expansion, and Republicans questioned the patriotism of anyone who proposed to pull down the flag where it had once been raised. President McKinley won a second term with nearly 52 percent of the vote. He carried most of the western states where Populism had once flourished, and Republicans won secure majorities in both houses of Congress.

Cuba and Puerto Rico came under the American flag.

The Teller Amendment had proclaimed that the United States would not keep Cuba. The McKinley Administration, however, refused to recognize the revolutionaries as constituting a legitimate government. Instead, the U.S. Army ran Cuba, modernizing transportation, expanding the public school system, and improving sanitation. After two years of army rule, Cuban voters were permitted to elect delegates to a constitutional convention.

U.S. officials drafted provisions outlining Cuba's future relationship with the United States for inclusion in the new Cuban constitution. Those conditions became known as the **Platt Amendment** because they were presented by U.S. Senator Orville Platt as an amendment to the army appropriations bill of 1901.

The most important provisions of the Platt Amendment were (1) Cuba could not make a treaty with a foreign power that might impair its independence, (2) the Cuban government gave the United States the right to intervene in Cuban affairs in order to preserve independence and maintain order, and (3) the Cuban government agreed to lease facilities for U.S. naval and coaling stations. These restrictions effectively made Cuba a protectorate of the United States.

The Cubans reluctantly accepted these conditions as part of their new constitution. In this way, the United States gained the naval base at **Guantánamo** [gwän tä′nä mō] **Bay** in Cuba, a base it still holds. The other provisions of the Platt Amendment continued in force until 1934. The United States intervened in Cuba several times between 1902 and 1934.

The Teller Amendment did not apply to Puerto Rico. The U.S. Army ruled Puerto Rico for a year and a half before Congress in 1900 gave that island a civil government by passing the **Foraker Act**. Under this act, Puerto Ricans were citizens of Puerto Rico but not citizens of the United States. They were permitted to elect a legislature, but final authority lay with a governor and a council appointed by the president of the United States.

Imperialism

Point

Imperialists: Keep the Philippines

- U.S. mission to develop, educate, and uplift the Filipinos
- Philippines' location an ideal base for U.S. trade with East Asia

Counterpoint

Anti-imperialists: Grant Philippines independence

- denying self-government to others contrary to the Declaration of Independence
- people in new colonies would undercut U.S. labor

'LET ME IN.'

Threatened by a ravenous wolf, Puerto Rico begs for admission to the United States in this 1898 woodcut by W. A. Rogers. Actually, Puerto Rico was about to gain parliamentary government under Spain but submitted to U.S. domination without a struggle.

The status of citizens of Puerto Rico was further clarified by the U.S. Supreme Court in 1901. In a series of historic decisions known as the **Insular Cases**, the Court ruled, in effect, that Puerto Rico and the other new possessions were not fully part of the United States and that their people were not automatically entitled to the guarantees of the U.S. Constitution. In other words, these decisions said, the Constitution does not follow the flag.

Congress passed the Jones Act in 1917, conferring U.S. citizenship on the Puerto Ricans and making the upper house of their legislature elective. The governor and supreme court continued to be appointed by the president, and its laws subject to presidential veto until 1952 when Puerto Rico became a self-governing commonwealth. A referendum was planned for the 1990s offering Puerto Ricans a range of options from statehood to independence.

SECTION 3 REVIEW

Identify Key People and Terms
Write a sentence to identify: Henry Cabot Lodge, Albert Beveridge, George F. Hoar, Platt Amendment, Foraker Act, Insular Cases

Locate Key Places
Where is the U.S. naval base in Cuba located?

Master the Main Ideas
1. **Analyzing U.S. foreign policy:** **(a)** How did the imperialists justify annexation of the Philippines? **(b)** Why did the anti-imperialists oppose annexation?
2. **Analyzing political campaigns:** How did the issue of imperialism affect the 1900 presidential election?
3. **Analyzing U.S. foreign policy:** **(a)** How did the Platt Amendment define the status of Cuba? **(b)** How did the Jones Act in 1917 change the status of Puerto Rico?

Apply Critical Thinking Skills: Recognizing Values
Was American imperialism a betrayal or a fulfillment of the nation's ideals, or both? Explain.

The United States became a Pacific power.

Key Terms: Philippine insurrection, spheres of influence, Boxer Rebellion, indemnity, Russo-Japanese War

Reading Preview
As you read this section, you will learn:

1. what action Americans took regarding the independence movement in the Philippines.
2. what policy Americans defended in China.
3. what country the United States refused to challenge in Asia.

The acquisition of the Philippines and Guam gave the United States two potentially important sites for naval bases near China and Japan. During the Spanish-American War, Congress annexed Hawaii. Late in 1899 Great Britain, Germany, and the United States agreed that Germany and the United States would divide Samoa. These possessions made the United States a major power in the Pacific.

Americans suppressed independence in the Philippines.

McKinley's re-election in 1900 ended any prospect for immediate Philippine independence. When Dewey's victory came in early May 1898, the Philippine independence movement, led by **Emilio Aguinaldo** [ä mē′lyō ä gē näl′dō], established a provisional government and took control throughout the islands except for Manila. The revolutionaries were divided among themselves, however, and the American military forces, which began to arrive in August, carefully avoided any actions that might imply recognition of the rebel government. The revolutionary assembly declared independence from U.S. rule early in 1899, and the Filipinos attacked U.S. forces in Manila. American authorities termed the Filipinos' struggle for independence the **Philippine insurrection**.

Quelling the independence movement in the Philippines required three years, the lives of 4,000 American soldiers and at least 20,000 guerrillas, and more than $170 million. In crushing the uprising, American troops resorted to the same policy of *reconcentración* that had been so widely condemned when used by the Spanish in Cuba. Resistance continued into mid-1902 even though American troops captured Aguinaldo in 1901.

In 1900, before the army had suppressed the Philippine insurrection, President McKinley appointed William Howard Taft to head a commission governing the Philippines. Under his leadership, public schools, hospitals, and modern sanitation came to the islands along with much-needed reform in land ownership.

In 1902 Congress set up a government for the Philippines similar to that in Puerto Rico. Under the act, Filipinos became citizens of the Philippine Islands but not citizens of the United States. The Philippine Islands were to have a legislative body, one house of which was to be popularly elected and the other appointed by the governor. The president of the United States appointed the governor.

When the first Philippine legislature met in 1907, half of its members favored independence from the United States. Congress made both houses of the Philippine legislature elective in 1916 and promised independence. However, independence was delayed until 1946.

Americans defended the Open Door in China.

From its new Asian bases, the United States began to expand its trade and investment in East Asia, especially in China. Weakened by corruption, natural disasters, and civil wars, the Chinese government could not resist attempts by European powers to gain control over large parts of its territory. By the turn of the century, several nations had carved out trading areas in China, called **spheres of influence**, where

After the United States acquired the Philippines by conquest and purchase from Spain, Filipino insurgents at outposts like this fought hundreds of engagements against American soldiers. Many Americans, including the African American soldiers who fought against them, sympathized with the Filipinos' desire for independence. Emilio Aguinaldo, inset, led the rebellion.

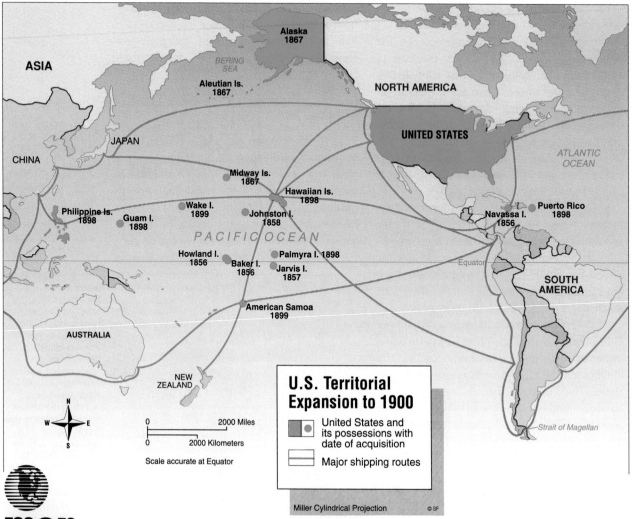

U.S. Territorial Expansion to 1900

Alaska 1867

BERING SEA

ASIA

Aleutian Is. 1867

NORTH AMERICA

JAPAN

UNITED STATES

ATLANTIC OCEAN

CHINA

Midway Is. 1867

Hawaiian Is. 1898

Wake I. 1899

Johnston I. 1858

Philippine Is. 1898

Guam I. 1898

PACIFIC OCEAN

Puerto Rico 1898

Navassa I. 1856

Howland I. 1856

Palmyra I. 1898

Equator

Baker I. 1856

Jarvis I. 1857

SOUTH AMERICA

American Samoa 1899

AUSTRALIA

NEW ZEALAND

Strait of Magellan

N W E S

0   2000 Miles

0   2000 Kilometers

Scale accurate at Equator

U.S. Territorial Expansion to 1900

☐ ● United States and its possessions with date of acquisition

☐ Major shipping routes

Miller Cylindrical Projection   © SF

map study

Location Note that most new U.S. territories were islands. Which future state was a "crossroads of the Pacific" by 1900?

Critical Thinking How did the location of the new territories support U.S. trade interests?

they enjoyed special rights. Because the United States claimed no special privileges, American merchants feared they would be excluded from the China market.

Secretary of State John Hay realized that the new American military presence in the Philippines, 600 miles from the Chinese mainland, strengthened the U.S. position in China. He tried to guarantee continued access to China's market by establishing an Open Door policy there under which all nations would enjoy equal trading privileges. By the time Hay announced his Open Door policy in 1899, however, it was too late to have much effect. He asked Great Britain, Germany, Russia, France, Italy, and Japan to agree to keep the ports of

China open to ships of all nations. Their response was discouraging. Nevertheless, even though the United States lacked the authority to enforce its position, Hay announced that the Open Door policy was in effect.

Americans promoted trade and free enterprise indirectly through a wide variety of cultural contacts. China became a major target of missionary efforts. By 1890 more than 1,000 U.S. missionaries were working in China, many of them women or college students who were part of the Student Volunteer Movement of the Young Men's Christian Association. The mission schools responded eagerly to the Chinese demand for instruction in the "new learning"— science and Western languages.

The year after the United States declared its Open Door policy, in 1900, a Chinese secret society called the Boxers rose up to expel foreigners from China, and 242 missionaries were murdered. The Boxers were so-called by Westerners because their name translated to "righteous harmony fists." Among the Americans forced to flee during the **Boxer Rebellion** were Absalom and Caroline Sydenstricker, Presbyterian missionaries who came to China from Hillsboro, West Virginia, as newlyweds in 1879. Their seven children learned to speak Chinese before they learned English, and four of them died in China, victims of tropical diseases. Their daughter, Pearl Comfort, was eight years old at the time the Boxers rebelled and later described how bewildered she felt when their Chinese friends began to avoid her and her family. Her mother tried to explain:

The Sydenstricker family with Pearl, left, her younger sister, Grace, and Wang Amah, their Chinese nurse, are shown on their return to China after the Boxer Rebellion. An older brother, Edwin, was then a college student in the United States.

It had nothing to do with Americans, she said, for

AN AMERICAN ★ SPEAKS

surely we had never been cruel to the Chinese nor had we taken their land or their river ports. Other white people had done the evil, and our friends, she promised me, understood this and did not hate us. . . . I could not understand why we, who were still ourselves and unchanged, should be lumped with unknown white men from unknown countries who had been what we were not, robbers and plunderers. It was now that I felt the first and primary injustice of life. I was innocent, but because I had the fair skin, the blue eyes, the blond hair of my race I was hated, and because of fear of me and my kind I walked in danger.

Later, the Sydenstrickers returned to China where the mission movement again prospered. Pearl married an American agricultural expert there. As the popular novelist Pearl Buck, she became the first woman to win a Nobel Prize in literature for her books about China.

The United States took part in an armed intervention by Great Britain, France, Germany, Russia, and Japan that crushed the Boxer Rebellion. However, Secretary of State Hay took a firm stand against those who wanted to punish China by dividing up more of its territory. Instead, China was required to pay a huge **indemnity** (repayment for damage or loss) to these nations. After paying its citizens for losses suffered during the rebellion, the U.S. government returned its share of the indemnity to China. The Chinese government used the money to send students to the United States.

In spite of this sign of mutual friendship, Chinese students and merchants often experienced discrimination in the United States. Furthermore, the 85,000 to 90,000 Chinese already living in the United States were frequently the victims of anti-Chinese prejudice. The Chinese Exclusion Act was renewed indefinitely in 1902, barring Chinese nationals from immigration into the United States—a step favored by American labor leaders. The exclusion policies were extended to Hawaii, the Philippines, and Cuba to make certain no Chinese laborers entered the United States indirectly.

The United States refused to challenge Japan in Asia.

Americans kept a close watch on East Asian developments, especially the rise of Japan as a major power. Before 1904, both Russia and Japan had coveted **Manchuria**, a northern region of China rich in coal and other resources and with the potential for industrialization. President Roosevelt hoped that neither Russia nor Japan would gain dominance.

Japan went to war with Russia in 1904 and 1905 over Manchuria and nearby Korea, winning a stunning victory. For the first time, an

Chinatowns

Just as American forces were establishing outposts and influence near China, Chinese immigrants in the United States were creating small outposts of their own within American cities. These Asian communities came to be known as Chinatowns.

Though American diplomats spoke of an "open door policy" for China, in America itself Chinese people were finding only closed doors during difficult economic times. In the late 1800s many Chinese miners, farmers, and workers left the small western towns where they had settled and gathered together in the larger urban centers. By the early 1900s, Chinatowns had sprung up in San Francisco, Los Angeles, Seattle, Chicago, New York, and Boston.

The streets of Chinatowns were lined with Chinese restaurants and grocery stores. Chinese lanterns hung outside of ornately decorated temples. Merchants painted their wrought-iron balconies bright yellow and green and planted flower boxes of cheerful flowers. Chinese notices hung on wooden walls, and men with long, braided hair would stand before the wall, reading the community news. Peddlers hawked traditional Chinese sweets and tempted children with colorful, hand-painted toys.

Chinatowns, with their exotic sights and sounds, drew tourists from near and far. However, tourism was of secondary importance to the people who lived in these communities. One resident of Chinatown remarked:

It is only in Chinatown that a Chinese immigrant has society, friends and relatives who share his dreams and hopes, his hardships, and adventures. Here he can tell a joke and make everybody laugh with him; here he may hear folktales told which create the illusion that Chinatown is really China.

Today many Chinatowns continue their historic role as haven communities and as bright beacons of Asian contributions to American history.

恭
喜
發
財

The characters above translate "Goun She Fa Szi" and wish someone good fortune and much wealth in the new year.

Firecrackers pop as masked dragon dancers wind through the narrow, crowded streets of New York City's Chinatown to celebrate the Chinese New Year.

Highlights of American Life

Asian nation decisively vanquished a European power. Japan gained recognition as an advanced country, better qualified than Russia to instruct backward China.

Roosevelt acted as mediator to bring this **Russo-Japanese War** to an end. The peace conference held in Portsmouth, New Hampshire, in the summer of 1905 gave Japan control over Korea and the principal Russian holdings in Manchuria—Port Arthur and the region's railroads—but preserved Manchuria as part of China. For his role in mediating the Treaty of Portsmouth, President Roosevelt received the Nobel Peace Prize in 1906. In later agreements, the United States and Japan pledged to respect each other's new acquisitions: the Philippines for the United States, and Korea and southern Manchuria for Japan.

SECTION 5

Americans expanded their influence in Latin America.

Key Terms: Hay-Pauncefote Treaty, Hay-Bunau-Varilla Treaty, Roosevelt Corollary, dollar diplomacy

Reading Preview
As you read this section, you will learn:

1. about the part of the Americas through which geography dictated the building of a canal.
2. what Theodore Roosevelt did to the Monroe Doctrine.
3. what action President Wilson took with regard to Mexico.

SECTION 4 REVIEW

Identify Key People and Terms
Write a sentence to identify: Emilio Aguinaldo, Philippine insurrection, spheres of influence, Boxer Rebellion, indemnity, Russo-Japanese War

Locate Key Places
Why did both Russia and Japan want Manchuria?

Master the Main Ideas

1. **Understanding U.S. foreign affairs:** Why was it so hard for the United States to suppress the independence movement in the Philippines?
2. **Analyzing U.S. foreign policy:** How did Secretary of State John Hay hope the United States would benefit by proposing the Open Door policy in China?
3. **Analyzing U.S. foreign policy:** After the Boxer Rebellion, why did the United States refuse to challenge Japan in Asia?

Apply Critical Thinking Skills: Predicting Consequences
What beneficial or harmful consequences might result when a powerful nation announces a foreign policy but lacks the authority to enforce it? Use the U.S. Open Door policy in China to support your answer.

After the victory over Spain, American policy makers acted to exclude foreign rivals from the Caribbean in order to protect U.S. interests there. Part of their efforts centered on the construction of a canal through Central America.

 ## Geography dictated the building of a Central American canal.

Many people had dreamed of a waterway between the Atlantic and Pacific oceans at the **Isthmus of Panama**. The isthmus is the narrow, mountainous land link between North and South America. You can see from the map on the next page that a Panamanian route would save thousands of miles of sea travel on voyages between the East and West coasts.

No one attempted the project until 1879 when a French company began work on a canal through Panama, which was then part of Colombia. Leading the project was the French diplomat Ferdinand de Lesseps, who had directed construction of the Suez Canal joining the Mediterranean and the Red seas in 1869. The Panama project proved too costly for his company and had to be abandoned.

During the Spanish-American War, interest in a canal revived after the frantic dash of a U.S. warship, the *Oregon*, from the Pacific

Coast around the tip of South America to the waters off Cuba. Its 12,000-mile voyage took 68 days. A canal through the isthmus might have cut the voyage to 20 days.

American leaders began by removing an obstacle to a U.S. canal. Under the Clayton-Bulwer Treaty signed in 1850, Great Britain and the United States had each agreed not to build a canal without the other. John Hay negotiated a new agreement in 1901, the **Hay-Pauncefote** [hā pôns′fút] **Treaty**, permitting the United States to build and control a canal on condition that it would remain open to the ships of all nations, even in wartime.

With British opposition removed, the next task was selection of a site. One possible route lay through Nicaragua, the other through Panama. Those who favored the Panama route argued that it was shorter, that Colombia seemed willing to grant a right-of-way, and that some work had been completed by the French company. That company wanted to sell its interest to the United States and hired a special agent, Philippe Bunau-Varilla [fē lēp bü′nō-va′rē′yä], to promote the Panamanian route. Opponents pointed to the rugged terrain and fever-ridden swamps. They also argued that Lake Nicaragua formed part of the Nicaraguan canal route, so there would be less excavation. Just then a volcano overlooking Lake Nicaragua erupted. The Senate chose the Panamanian route.

Negotiations with Colombia bogged down when its representatives asked for more money than the United States was willing to pay. Bunau-Varilla quickly organized an independence movement, which was able to gain control of Panama with the aid of an American warship that prevented Colombian troops from landing. The Panamanians declared their independence, and the United States promptly extended diplomatic recognition. Now, as Panama's foreign minister, Bunau-Varilla negotiated the **Hay-Bunau-Varilla Treaty** (1903). The treaty gave the United States complete control over the **Canal Zone**—a strip of Panamanian territory ten miles wide—for a price of $10 mil-

Philippe Bunau-Varilla proved a master of public relations. He gave each U.S. senator one of these postage stamps to impress upon them the perils of a canal route through Nicaragua. The volcano promptly erupted.

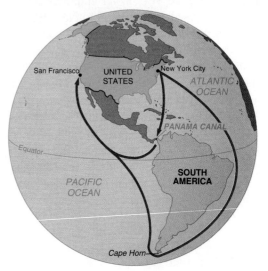

Panama Canal: East/West Shortcut

← Water routes to California

Orthographic Projection   © SF

lion and annual rent of $250,000. The treaty effectively made Panama an American protectorate. The United States began construction of the canal in 1904.

Colombia was furious and became more so when Theodore Roosevelt, the president who had so quickly recognized Panamanian independence, boasted in 1911, "I took the canal zone and let Congress debate." He always denied, however, that he had been involved in the revolution. The United States paid Colombia $25 million in 1921 in an attempt to restore relations but made no apology.

Building the canal proved difficult. A U.S. Army surgeon, **William C. Gorgas**, led a vigorous campaign to rid the swamps and jungles of the *Anopheles* [ə nof′ə lēz′] mosquito, which transmits malaria, and the *Aedes* [ā ē′dēz] mosquito, which transmits yellow fever. These diseases had taken 7,000 lives a year during the French construction. Within two years, yellow fever had been eradicated and malaria brought under control.

The canal took ten years to build and cost nearly $400 million. Completed in 1914, just as World War I was beginning, it was consid-

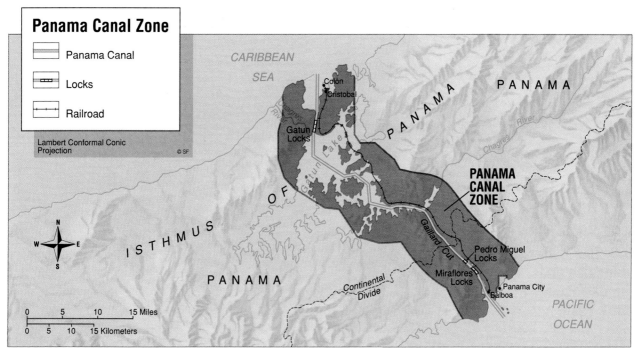

Panama Canal Zone

- ▭ Panama Canal
- ▭ Locks
- ┼ Railroad

Lambert Conformal Conic
Projection © SF

CARIBBEAN SEA

Colón
Cristobal
Gatun Locks
Gatun Lake

PANAMA

PANAMA

Chagres River

PANAMA CANAL ZONE

Gaillard Cut

Pedro Miguel Locks

Miraflores Locks

Continental Divide

Panama City
Balboa

PACIFIC OCEAN

ISTHMUS OF PANAMA

PANAMA

N
W E
S

0   5   10   15 Miles
0   5   10   15 Kilometers

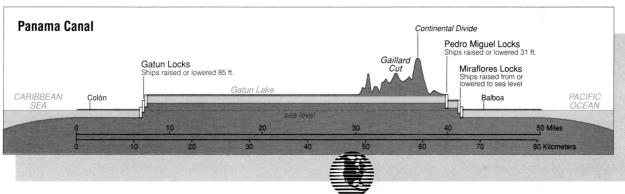

Panama Canal

Continental Divide

Gaillard Cut

Pedro Miguel Locks
Ships raised or lowered 31 ft.

Gatun Locks
Ships raised or lowered 85 ft.

Miraflores Locks
Ships raised from or lowered to sea level

CARIBBEAN SEA
Colón
Gatun Lake
sea level
Balboa
PACIFIC OCEAN

0   10   20   30   40   50 Miles
0   10   20   30   40   50   60   70   80 Kilometers

ered one of the world's engineering wonders.

Even before the canal was finished, protecting the waterway became a primary concern of U.S. foreign policy. The United States fortified the Canal Zone, and the U.S. naval base at Guantánamo Bay protected one of the major sea approaches to the canal. To complete the protective shield, the United States purchased the Virgin Islands from Denmark in 1916.

President Roosevelt extended the Monroe Doctrine.

Strengthening its position in the Caribbean drew the United States into the affairs of other Latin American countries. Several of the smaller countries had borrowed large amounts of money from foreign banks. In 1902 Great

The *Anopheles* mosquito transmits malaria.

map study

Movement The Panama Canal greatly shortened the distance between the East and West coasts of the United States. This shortcut saved time and expense in travel, freight shipment, and military operations. Compare the two routes on the map at left above. Although the Panama Canal is only 51 miles long, it took ten years to complete, partly because of geography. Near which ocean did the canal cross through mountains? What were two advantages of the Isthmus of Panama as a site for the canal?

Critical Thinking How did the Panama Canal help make the United States a world power?

401

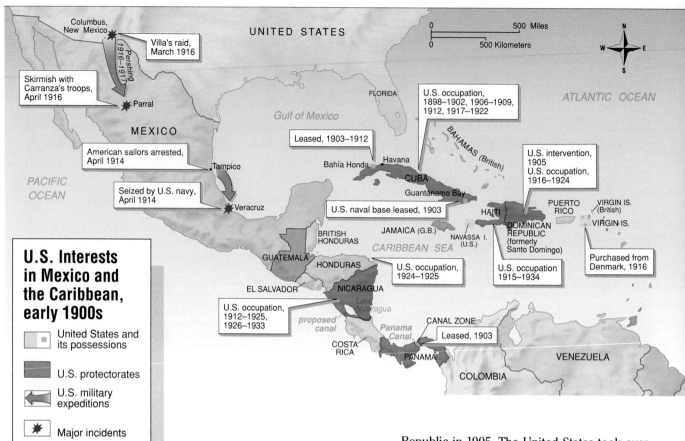

Columbus, New Mexico

Villa's raid, March 1916

Pershing 1916–1917

Skirmish with Carranza's troops, April 1916

Parral

UNITED STATES

0   500 Miles

0   500 Kilometers

N W E S

FLORIDA

ATLANTIC OCEAN

U.S. occupation, 1898–1902, 1906–1909, 1912, 1917–1922

MEXICO

Gulf of Mexico

Leased, 1903–1912

Havana

BAHAMAS (British)

U.S. intervention, 1905 U.S. occupation, 1916–1924

American sailors arrested, April 1914

Tampico

Bahía Honda

CUBA

PACIFIC OCEAN

Guantánamo Bay

PUERTO RICO

VIRGIN IS. (British)

Seized by U.S. navy, April 1914

Veracruz

U.S. naval base leased, 1903

HAITI

DOMINICAN REPUBLIC (formerly Santo Domingo)

VIRGIN IS.

JAMAICA (G.B.)

NAVASSA I. (U.S.)

CARIBBEAN SEA

Purchased from Denmark, 1916

BRITISH HONDURAS

GUATEMALA

HONDURAS

U.S. occupation, 1924–1925

U.S. occupation, 1915–1934

EL SALVADOR

NICARAGUA

U.S. occupation, 1912–1925, 1926–1933

Lake Nicaragua

proposed canal

Panama Canal

CANAL ZONE

Leased, 1903

COSTA RICA

PANAMA

VENEZUELA

COLOMBIA

U.S. Interests in Mexico and the Caribbean, early 1900s

☐ United States and its possessions

■ U.S. protectorates

◄ U.S. military expeditions

✹ Major incidents

Azimuthal Equal-Area Projection

© SF

map study

Relationships Within Places

The Roosevelt Corollary led to U.S. intervention in the Caribbean. Note the major American actions. Which U.S. territories shield the Panama Canal?

Critical Thinking

Why was the Caribbean sometimes called an "American lake"?

Britain and Germany declared a blockade of Venezuela to force that country to pay its debts. In a similar situation in 1904, President Theodore Roosevelt decided to assert American power—his "big stick"—when the Dominican Republic refused to pay its foreign debts. In his annual message to Congress, he presented what became known as the **Roosevelt Corollary** (extension) to the Monroe Doctrine. He said:

Chronic wrongdoing, or an impotence which results in a general loosening of the ties of civilized society, may in America, as elsewhere, ultimately require intervention by some civilized nation.

AN AMERICAN ★ SPEAKS

If intervention were necessary in the Western Hemisphere, Roosevelt announced, the Monroe Doctrine required that the United States undertake the intervention.

The most typical form of intervention was patterned after U.S. actions in the Dominican Republic in 1905. The United States took over collection of customs (usually the major form of government revenue) and supervision of government expenditures. This was often accompanied by an American military force in the nation's capital to discourage the overthrow of the government.

The United States continued to intervene in the Caribbean under President Taft, who succeeded Roosevelt in 1909, and President Wilson, who took office in 1913. You can see from the map above where and when U.S. presidents found it necessary to enforce order in Latin America.

American investment in Latin America swelled to more than $1 billion by 1908. Roosevelt and his successors worked actively to promote U.S. business interests and to exercise the nation's growing economic power, instead of military force, to protect American security interests. To encourage private investment, the United States made loans to Nicaragua, Honduras, and other countries. Soon U.S. interests owned plantations, markets, railroads, and banks in Central America. Taft's critics branded this policy **dollar diplomacy**, but Taft insisted that he was "substituting dollars for bullets."

President Wilson intervened in Mexico.

Woodrow Wilson had criticized the way Roosevelt and Taft intervened in Latin America, but when he came into the White House, revolutions had begun to shake the world. By the time he left office in 1921, Wilson had ordered U.S. troops into Mexico, Haiti, Santo Domingo, and Cuba. The expedition into Mexico nearly ended in war.

Since 1877 **Porfirio Díaz**, a dictator, had ruled Mexico. Díaz gave foreign companies free rein in developing Mexico's resources. Although this policy helped modernize Mexico's economy, ordinary Mexican people gained little from it.

More than $1 billion had been invested in Mexico by American companies, which owned more than 75 percent of Mexico's mines, 60 percent of the oil, 70 percent of the rubber plantations, and most of the railroads. Because of this investment, and because some 50,000 U.S. citizens lived in Mexico, Americans were deeply concerned about what took place there.

Díaz was ousted in a revolution in 1911. His successor, Francisco Madero, who had been educated in the United States, called for democratic reforms. However, Madero was murdered in 1913 by one of his subordinates, **Victoriano Huerta** [bēk tō ryä′nō wer′tä]. Huerta declared himself president. Wilson refused to recognize the blood-splattered Huerta regime, believing that without American recognition, Huerta's government would not last. In April 1914 a minor incident gave Wilson an excuse to seize the seaport of Veracruz. By occupying this major Mexican port, Wilson deprived Huerta of income and arms.

Huerta's regime collapsed. His successor, **Venustiano Carranza** [bä nüs tyä′nō kä rän′sä], soon faced revolts throughout the country. In northern Mexico, Francisco Villa, known as **Pancho Villa** [pän′chō bē′yä], hoped to topple Carranza by involving the United States. He raided Columbus, New Mexico, killing 17 Americans.

With reluctant assent from Carranza, Wilson sent a 6,000-man army led by General **John Pershing** into Mexican territory. His force was called a punitive expedition because its purpose was to punish Villa. Villa hoped to draw Pershing's troops deep into Mexico and precipitate a conflict with Carranza's forces. He nearly succeeded. On the verge of war, both Carranza and Wilson drew back. A commission set up to study the situation urged Wilson to withdraw and recognize the Carranza government. Increasingly preoccupied with events in Europe, where war had been raging since 1914, Wilson agreed, and soon the American people were swept into European affairs. However, Wilson's attempt to control events in Mexico added to the legacy of distrust many Latin Americans felt toward their neighbor to the north.

SECTION 5 REVIEW

Identify Key People and Terms
Write a sentence to identify: Hay-Pauncefote Treaty, Hay-Bunau-Varilla Treaty, William C. Gorgas, Roosevelt Corollary, dollar diplomacy, Porfirio Díaz, Victoriano Huerta, Venustiano Carranza, Pancho Villa, John Pershing

Locate Key Places
1. Why is the Isthmus of Panama of such strategic importance?
2. Where is the Canal Zone in relation to the Panama Canal?

Master the Main Ideas
1. **Understanding geographic influences:** Why did geography dictate the building of the Panama Canal?
2. **Understanding historic documents:** How did Theodore Roosevelt extend the Monroe Doctrine?
3. **Analyzing U.S. foreign policy:** How did Wilson's intervention in Mexico affect U.S. relationships with Latin America?

Apply Critical Thinking Skills: Demonstrating Reasoned Judgment
Decide whether or not Congress should give its consent before a president deploys American forces around the world. Support your position.

Commodore Perry Visits Japan

9A

TIME FRAME
1853–1854

GEOGRAPHIC SETTING
Japan and the United States

Fearing foreign influences—including Christianity—on Japanese culture, the rulers of Japan had closed their country to European traders and missionaries in the 1630s. Japan remained isolated from contact with Western nations until an American diplomatic mission headed by Commodore Matthew Perry (1794–1858) arrived in July 1853. During his brief first stay, Perry received permission to return the following year; which he did, arriving in February 1854, this time in command of nine heavily armed warships. In addition to this display of American sea power, Perry also brought an array of gifts to help convince Japanese officials to open their country to foreign trade. In return, the Japanese sent gifts to the Americans. The following lists indicate some of the gifts exchanged during Perry's second visit.

Some of the American Presents for the Japanese

For the Emperor

Miniature steam engine, 1/4 size, with track, tender, and car.
2 telegraph sets, with batteries, three miles of wire, gutta percha [rubber-like
5   substance] wire, and insulators.
1 Francis' copper lifeboat.
1 surfboat of copper.
Collection of agricultural implements.
Audubon's Birds, in nine vols.
10 *Natural History of the State of New York,* 16 vols.
Annals of Congress, 4 vols.
Laws and Documents of the State of New York.
15 *Journal of the Senate and Assembly of New York.*
Lighthouse Reports, 2 vols.
Bancroft's History of the United States, 4 vols.
20 Morris, *Engineering.*
Farmers' Guide, 2 vols.

1 series of United States Coast Survey Charts.
Silver-topped dressing case.
25 8 yards scarlet broadcloth, and scarlet velvet.
Series of United States standard yard, gallon, bushel, balances and weights.
Quarter cask of Madeira [wine].
30 Barrel of whiskey.
Box of champagne and cherry cordial and maraschino.
3 boxes of fine tea.
Maps of several states and four large
35   lithographs.
Telescope and stand, in box.
Sheet-iron stove.
An assortment of fine perfumery.
5 Hall rifles.
40 3 Maynard muskets.
12 cavalry swords.
6 artillery swords.
1 carbine.
20 Army pistols in a box.
45 *Catalogue of New York State Library and of Postoffices.*

For the Empress

Flowered silk embroidered dress
Toilet dressing-box gilded.
6 dozen assorted perfumery.

Some of the Japanese Presents for the Americans

1st. For the Government of the United States of America, from the Emperor

1 gold lacquered writing apparatus.
1 gold lacquered paper box.
1 gold lacquered book case.
1 lacquered writing table.
5 1 censer [incense-burner] of bronze, (cow-shape,) supporting silver flower and stand.

The Japanese called the fleet of warships with which Commodore Perry returned to Japan in early 1854 the ''Black Ships.'' A picture of one of these vessels by a Japanese artist conveys the alien quality—both strange and menacing—that Perry's warships had for the people of Japan.

1 flower holder and stand.
2 braziers [charcoal-burners].
10 10 pieces fine red pongee [pon jē', silk].
10 pieces white pongee.
5 pieces flowered crape [silk].

2nd. From Hayashi, 1st commissioner

1 lacquered writing apparatus.
1 lacquered paper box.
15 1 box of paper.
1 box flowered note paper.
5 boxes stamped note and letter paper.
4 boxes assorted sea shells, 100 in each.
1 box of branch coral and feather in silver.
20 1 lacquered chow-chow [preserved fruit] box.
1 box, set of three, lacquered goblets.
7 boxes cups and spoons and goblet cut from conch shells.

Discussing the Reading

1. Do the gifts from the Americans seem more concerned with the public aspects of life, such as government and commerce, or the private aspects, such as leisure-time activities and the arts? Do the Japanese gifts seem more concerned with public or private life? Explain.

2. What aspects of 19th-century American culture are reflected by the gifts that Perry brought the Japanese?

CRITICAL THINKING
Drawing Conclusions

Assuming that the gifts from the Japanese reflected their public life, what conclusions could you draw about its character?

Queen Liliuokalani Objects to American Annexation and Manners

6B

TIME FRAME
1891–1898

GEOGRAPHIC SETTING
Hawaii

Taken in 1887 while Queen Liliuokalani was in London attending the celebration of the Golden Jubilee of England's Queen Victoria, this portrait of Hawaii's queen displays her regal appearance and suggests her determined personality.

In 1820 a shipload of New England missionaries reached Hawaii. By the 1890s, descendants of these missionaries, the so-called "missionary party," dominated the native Hawaiian ruler, King Kalakaua [kä-lä kou'ə]. When he died in 1891, his sister Liliuokalani [li lē'ə wō kə lä'nē] came to the throne. Queen Liliuokalani (1838–1917) attempted to restore the power of the Hawaiian monarchy, but in 1893 the missionary party deposed her and organized a provisional government, which asked for annexation by the United States. The American minister to Hawaii, John L. Stevens, recognized the new government and landed U.S. troops to keep order. Although President Grover Cleveland disapproved of the overthrow of Queen Liliuokalani, the United States formally recognized the new government in 1894, and annexed Hawaii in 1898. In the following excerpt from her memoirs, written in 1898, Queen Liliuokalani commented on these events.

K alakaua's reign was, in a material sense, the golden age of Hawaiian history. The wealth and importance of the Islands enormously increased, and always
5 as a direct consequence of the king's acts. It has been currently supposed that the policy and foresight of the "missionary party" is to be credited with all that he accomplished, since they succeded in abro-
10 gating [ending] so many of his prerogatives [privileges], and absorbing the lion's share of the benefits derived from it. It should, however, be only necessary to remember that the measures which brought
15 about our accession of wealth were not at all in line with a policy of annexation to

the United States, which was the very essence of the dominant "missionary" idea. In fact, his progressive foreign policy was
20 well calculated to discourage it.

And for this reason, probably, they could not be satisfied even with the splendid results which our continued nationality offered them. They were not grateful
25 for a prosperity which must sooner or later, while enriching them, also elevate the masses of the Hawaiian people into a self-governing class, and depose them from that primacy in our political affairs
30 which they chiefly valued. They became fiercely jealous of every measure which promised to benefit the native people, or to stimulate their national pride. Every possible embarrassment and humiliation
35 were heaped upon my brother. And because I was suspected of having the welfare of the whole people also at heart (and what sovereign with a grain of wisdom could be otherwise minded?), I must be
40 made to feel yet more severely that my kingdom was but the assured prey of these "conquistadores." . . .

After the so-called Provisional Government had been recognized by Minister
45 Stevens, and I had referred in writing my case to the United States, there was no more for me to do but retire in peace to my private residence, there to await the decision of the United States government.
50 This I did, and cautioned the leaders of my people to avoid riot or resistance, and to await tranquilly, as I was doing, the result of my appeal to the power to whom alone I had yielded my authority. . . .
55 It has been my endeavor, in these recollections, to avoid speaking evil of any person, unless absolutely demanded by the exigencies [needs] of my case before the public. I simply state facts, and let oth-
60 ers form their own judgment of the individuals. But of Minister John L. Stevens it must be said that he was either mentally incapable of recognizing what is to be expected of a gentleman, to say nothing of a
65 diplomatist, or he was decidedly in league with those persons who had conspired against the peace of Hawaii [since] 1887. Several times in my presence, to which he had access by virtue of his official position,
70 he conducted himself with such a disregard of good manners as to excite the comment of my friends.

His official despatches to his own government, from the very first days of his
75 landing, abound in statements to prove (according to his view) the great advantage of an overthrow of the monarchy, and a cession of my domains to the rule of the United States. His own daughter went as a
80 messenger to the largest one of the islands of my kingdom to secure names for a petition for the annexation of the Hawaiian Islands to the American Union, and by an accident lost her life, with the roll contain-
85 ing the few names she had secured. All this took place while he was presumed to be a friendly minister to a friendly power, and when my minister was under the same relation to his government. Of his
90 remarks regarding myself personally I will take no notice, further than to say that, by his invitation, I attended a very delightful lunch party at his house a few months before the United States troops were landed.

Discussing the Reading

1. What did Queen Liliuokalani claim was the motive behind the missionary party's desire for annexation of Hawaii by the United States?

2. Apart from opposing him politically, what appear to have been Queen Liliuokalani's feelings about John Stevens personally?

CRITICAL THINKING
Recognizing Bias

How would Liliuokalani's political views affect her judgment of Kalakaua's success in governing Hawaii?

407

"I Have Two Countries: Cuba and the Night"

TIME FRAME
1887–1888

GEOGRAPHIC SETTING
Exile from Cuba

The Cuban poet José Martí [hō sā′ mär tē′] was a leader in the revolution that broke out against Spanish rule in 1895. Exiled from Cuba in 1871 and again in 1879 for his political activities, Martí lived from 1881 to 1895 in New York City, where he wrote poetry, essays, and journalism that made him famous throughout Latin America. His death in a skirmish with Spanish forces little more than a month after returning to Cuba in 1895 made Martí a national hero. Although he died three years before Cuban independence, he is credited with doing more than any other individual to win his nation's freedom. The following poem, "Dos Patrias," was written by Martí while in exile from Cuba in the late 1880s.

Conveying an impression of formality, sensitivity, and scholarship, this painting of José Martí by New York artist Herman Norman was the only portrait of the poet done from life.

Dos patrias

Dos patrias tengo yo: Cuba y la noche.
¿O son una las dos? No bien retira
su majestad el Sol, con largos velos
y un clavel en la mano, silenciosa
5 Cuba cual viuda triste me aparece.
¡Yo sé cuál es ese clavel sangriento
que en la mano le tiembla! Está vacío
mi pecho, destrozado está y vacío
en donde estaba el corazón. Ya es hora
10 de empezar a morir. La noche es buena
para decir adiós. La luz estorba
y la palabra humana. El universo
habla mejor que el hombre.
                                Cual bandera
15 que invita a batallar, la llama roja
de la vela flamea. Las ventanas
abro, ya estrecho en mí. Muda,
        rompiendo
las hojas del clavel, como una nube
20 que enturbia el cielo, Cuba, viuda,
        pasa. . . .

Two countries

I have two countries: Cuba and the night.
Or are both one? No sooner does
        the sun
Withdraw its majesty, than Cuba,
5 With long veils and holding a carnation,
Appears as a sad and silent widow.
I know about that bloodstained
        carnation
That trembles in her hand! My breast
10 Is empty, destroyed and empty
Where the heart lay. Now is the time
To commence dying. Night is a good
        time
To say farewell. Light is a hindrance
15 As is the human word. The universe
Talks better than man.
                        Like a flag
That calls to battle, the candle's
Red flame flutters. I feel a closeness
20 And open windows. Crushing the
        carnation's
Petals silently, widowed Cuba passes by
Like a cloud that dims the heavens. . . .

A group of Cuban rebels in New York is shown meeting in this illustration from *Harper's Weekly.* Such gatherings, inspired by the words of José Martí, occurred frequently in many large American cities.

Discussing the Reading

1. Why might José Martí have seen Cuba as "a sad and silent widow"? What was Cuba mourning?

2. What does the association of the "bloodstained carnation" with the poet's absent heart suggest about what Martí felt Cuban independence required of him?

CRITICAL THINKING
Drawing Conclusions

In "Dos Patrias," was José Martí more concerned with expressing the sorrow he felt as an exile or with issuing a call for action? Cite lines from the poem in your answer.

"Villa Is Coming!"

9D

TIME FRAME
1914

GEOGRAPHIC SETTING
Northern Mexico

In November 1910, a revolution began in Mexico against the dictatorial government of President Porfirio Díaz [dē′äz]. Led by an idealistic reformer named Francisco Madero [mä dā′rō], the Mexican Revolution was initially successful. However, the assassination of Madero by one of his generals, Victoriano Huerta [wer′tä], plunged Mexico into years of brutal civil war in which the former rebel leaders first battled Huerta (1854–1916), and after his overthrow, each other. The most famous fictional account of this period is *Los de Abajo* [lōs′dā ä bä′hō, usually translated as "the underdogs"], a novel by Mariano Azuela [ä zwā′lä]. Azuela (1873–1952) was a doctor who served with the forces of the most famous of the rebel leaders, Francisco "Pancho" Villa [bē′yä]. Villa (1877–1923) created an international incident in 1916 with his raids into the United States. The following two excerpts from Azuela's novel are set about two years earlier. In the first, Solís [sō lēs′] and Luis Cervantes [lü ēs′ ser vän′tās], two intellectuals who have each joined small rebel bands in northern Mexico, discuss their disillusionment with the revolution. In the second, the "high hats," their peasant comrades-in-arms, react to the possibility of joining the already legendary Pancho Villa.

H m," Solís went on, offering Cervantes a chair, "since when have you turned rebel?" 30

"I've been a rebel the last two months!"

5 "Oh, I see! That's why you speak with such faith and enthusiasm about things we all felt when we joined the revolution...."

"What about you? Are you tired of the 10 revolution?" asked Cervantes sharply.

"Tired? My dear fellow, I'm twenty-five years old and I'm fit as a fiddle! But am I disappointed? Perhaps!"

"You must have sound reasons for feel-15 ing that way."

"I hoped to find a meadow at the end of the road, I found a swamp. Facts are bitter; so are men. That bitterness eats your heart out; it is poison, dry-rot. Enthusiasm, 20 hope, ideals, happiness—vain dreams, vain dreams.... When that's over, you have a choice. Either you turn bandit, like the rest, or the time-servers will swamp you...."

25 Cervantes writhed at his friend's words; his argument was quite out of place... painful.... To avoid being forced to take issue, he invited Solís to cite the circumstances that had destroyed his illusions.

30 "Circumstances? No—it's far less important than that. It's a host of silly, insignificant things that no one notices except yourself... a change of expression, eyes shining—lips curled in a sneer—the deep 35 import of a phrase that is lost! Yet take these things together and they compose the mask of our race... terrible... grotesque... a race that awaits redemption!"

He drained another glass. After a long 40 pause, he continued:

"You ask me why I am still a rebel? Well, the revolution is like a hurricane: if you're in it, you're not a man... you're a leaf, a dead leaf, blown by the wind."

V illa is coming!"

The news spread like lightning. Villa—the magic word! The Great Man, the salient profile, the unconquerable 5 warrior who, even at a distance, exerts the fascination of a reptile, a boa constrictor.

"Our Mexican Napoleon!" exclaimed Luis Cervantes.

"Yes! The Aztec Eagle! He buried his 10 beak of steel in the head of Huerta the

A group of peasant soldiers of the Mexican Revolution, some holding weapons and others musical instruments, is shown in a relaxed moment in the photograph above. Bandoliers of ammunition crisscrossing his chest, the young fighter below shows a fiercer, more military, appearance.

serpent!" Solís, Natera's Chief of Staff, remarked somewhat ironically, adding: "At least, that's how I expressed it in a speech I made at Ciudad Juárez!"

15 The two sat at the bar of the saloon, drinking beer. The "high hats," wearing mufflers around their necks and thick rough leather shoes on their feet, ate and drank endlessly. Their gnarled hands

20 loomed across table, across bar. All their talk was of Villa and his men. The tales Natera's followers related won gasps of astonishment from Demetrio's men. Villa! Villa's battles! Ciudad Juárez . . . Tierra

25 Blanco . . . Chihuahua . . . Torreón. . . .

The bare facts, the mere citing of observation and experience meant nothing. But the real story, with its extraordinary contrasts of high exploits and abysmal cruel-

30 ties was quite different. Villa, indomitable Lord of the Sierra, the eternal victim of all Governments. . . . Villa tracked, hunted down like a wild beast . . . Villa the reincarnation of the old legend; Villa as Prov-

35 idence, the bandit, that passes through the world armed with the blazing torch of an ideal: to rob the rich and give to the poor. It was the poor who built up and imposed a legend about him which Time itself was

40 to increase and embellish as a shining example from generation to generation.

"Look here, friend," one of Natera's men told Anastasio, "if General Villa takes a fancy to you, he'll give you a ranch on

45 the spot. But if he doesn't, he'll shoot you down like a dog! God! You ought to see Villa's troops! They're all northerners and dressed like lords! You ought to see their wide-brimmed Texas hats and their

50 brand-new outfits and their four dollar shoes, imported from the U.S.A."

As they retailed the wonders of Villa and his men, Natera's men gazed at one another ruefully, aware that their own

55 hats were rotten from sunlight and moisture, that their own shirts and trousers were tattered and barely fit to cover their grimy, lousy bodies.

"There's no such a thing as hunger up

60 there. They carry box cars full of oxen, sheep, cows! They've got cars full of clothing, trains full of guns, ammunition, food enough to make a man burst!" . . .

Anastasio Montáñez questioned the

65 speaker more particularly. It was not long before he realized that all this high praise was hearsay and that not a single man in Natera's army had ever laid eyes on Villa.

Discussing the Reading

1. In the first excerpt from Mariano Azuela's novel, how do Solís and Cervantes differ in their attitudes to the revolution?

2. Why is Solís still a rebel?

3. In the second excerpt, the peasant rebels react to and further embellish the already larger-than-life figure of Pancho Villa. What characteristics do they attribute to him? Are some of these characteristics contradictory? Explain.

CRITICAL THINKING
Identifying Assumptions

Solís and Luis Cervantes are both educated men. In the second excerpt, how are their reactions to Villa (lines 7–14) different from those of their peasant comrades?

Chapter Summary

Write supporting details under each of the following main ideas as you review the chapter.

Section 1
1. The purchase of Alaska completed U.S. continental expansion.
2. The Monroe Doctrine guided U.S. policy in Latin America.
3. Traders and missionaries focused American attention on the Pacific.
4. Americans competed with European powers for markets in Africa.
5. The United States rose to world power in the 1890s.

Section 2
1. A Cuban revolt aroused the American public.
2. Negotiations with Spain failed to prevent war.
3. Spain lost the Philippines and Cuba after humiliating naval defeats.

Section 3
1. Americans were sharply divided over annexation of the Philippines.
2. Imperialism became a key issue in the 1900 presidential election.
3. Cuba and Puerto Rico came under the American flag.

Section 4
1. Americans suppressed independence in the Philippines.
2. Americans defended the Open Door in China.
3. The United States refused to challenge Japan in Asia.

Section 5
1. Geography dictated the building of a Central American canal.
2. President Roosevelt extended the Monroe Doctrine.
3. President Wilson intervened in Mexico.

Chapter Themes

1. **Free enterprise:** America rose to world power by pursuing a policy widely practiced by other nations: imperialism. Naval theorists, traders, and missionaries helped extend American culture and find markets and resources in other, less-developed countries.

2. **Geography and environmental interaction:** Geography played an important role in America's expansionist period. The building of the Panama Canal, the enforcement of the Monroe Doctrine (strengthened by the Roosevelt Corollary), and the extension of American interests into the Caribbean and the Pacific Rim were all actions based on geographic factors including the location of the United States.

Chapter Study Guide

Identifying Key People and Terms

Name the key person or key term that describes the:
1. ruler who wanted to restore Hawaii to the Hawaiians
2. policy of extending the rule of one country over other countries or colonies
3. U.S. battleship that was destroyed in the harbor at Havana, Cuba
4. leader of the Philippine independence movement

Locating Key Places

1. What was Seward's Folly?
2. In what Philippine harbor did George Dewey's American fleet destroy a Spanish fleet?
3. What was the coal-rich country fought over in the Russo-Japanese War?

Mastering the Main Ideas

1. List at least three reasons 19th-century Americans gave for favoring expansionism.
2. Why did many feel that the Spanish-American War was a "splendid little war"?
3. Given the terms of the Foraker Act and the Platt Amendment, who won—the imperialists or the anti-imperialists? Explain.
4. On a chart similar to the one below, list at least three methods the United States used to influence affairs in the Pacific between 1890 and 1914. Then tell when and where each method was used.

Method	When used	Where used

5. How did the building of the Panama Canal, the Roosevelt Corollary, and dollar diplomacy affect relations between the United States and Latin America?

1890	1895	1900	1905	1910	1915

1893
Hawaiian Queen Liliuokalani overthrown

1900
Boxer Rebellion in China

1904
Russo-Japanese War begins; Roosevelt Corollary to Monroe Doctrine

1914
Panama Canal opens; World War I begins

1890
Influence of Sea Power upon History (Mahan)

1898
Spanish-American War; U.S. acquires Puerto Rico, Guam, Philippines; U.S. annexes Hawaii

Applying Critical Thinking Skills

1. **Analyzing cause and effect:** How might the Columbian Exposition have fostered acceptance of expansionism?
2. **Making comparisons: (a)** Compare the following U.S. territorial acquisitions: California, Alaska, and the Philippines. **(b)** Which proved the most valuable?
3. **Identifying central issues:** Compare the central idea of the "White Man's burden" with the economic reasons for advocating imperialism.
4. **Recognizing bias:** What influenced Congress to renew the Chinese Exclusion Act in 1902?
5. **Analyzing cause and effect:** How did the building of the Panama Canal help make the United States a world power?

Chapter Activities

Learning Geography Through History

1. What area of the world is covered by the Monroe Doctrine and the Roosevelt Corollary?
2. How did the acquisition of Hawaii, Guam, and the Philippines affect U.S. actions toward China and Japan before 1914?

Relating the United States to the World

1. What position did the United States take when European colonial powers divided up Africa?
2. How did the Chinese react in 1900 after European powers tried to divide up their country?

Using the Time Line

1. Which countries on the time line were victims of American imperialism?
2. How many years after Mahan's book on sea power did the Panama Canal open?

Linking Past to Present

1. Explain how Chinese policy today might be related to the Boxer Rebellion.
2. In 1978 the U.S. Senate agreed to turn over control of the Panama Canal to Panama by December 31, 1999. At that time, how long will the United States have controlled the Canal Zone?

Practicing Critical Thinking Strategies

Making Comparisons
Compare U.S. policies toward Cuba and the countries bordering the Caribbean with U.S. policies toward the Philippines, Japan, and China in the early 1900s.

Learning More About America's Rise to World Power

1. **Using Source Readings:** Read the Source Readings for this chapter and answer the questions.
2. **Role-playing:** With several other students, assume the role of key imperialists and anti-imperialists and debate the annexation of the Philippines.
3. **Preparing a speech:** Research and prepare a short speech on the current status of Hawaii, the Philippines, Puerto Rico, Guam, or Cuba. Include information on how the status of the area has changed since the Spanish-American War.

Linking Past
to Present

Freshly fallen snow
casts a somber mood
over Arlington National
Cemetery in Arlington,
Virginia, where
thousands of the
nation's war dead are
buried. American
wounded and German
prisoners stagger back
from the brutal,
grinding horror of
Meuse-Argonne in a
painting by Harvey
Dunn (1884–1952),
inset. Dunn was one of
eight official artists
with the American
Expeditionary Force.

The Great War

1 9 1 4 — 1 9 1 8

10

"I loved and trusted old Uncle Sam and I have always believed he did the right thing," said Alvin Cullum York, who grew up in the remote mountains of Tennessee. Deeply religious and equally patriotic, York was drafted in 1917, at the age of 29, to serve in the U.S. Army. The nation was at war, and many of those drafted would be sent to fight against Germany. York found his religious values at conflict with his nation's call.

> **AN AMERICAN ★ SPEAKS** I was worried clean through. I didn't want to go and kill. I believed in my Bible. And it distinctly said, 'THOU SHALT NOT KILL.' And yet old Uncle Sam . . . said he wanted me most awful bad.

World War I posed a serious moral choice for Alvin York and for many other young men in the United States in 1917 and 1918. The war also created deep conflicts in American society. Ethnic loyalties to old homelands clashed with America's historic opposition to entanglements in European quarrels. Would these conflicts and confusion of purpose affect the outcome of the war? How would U.S. involvement in that war challenge Americans' traditional attitudes and assumptions?

CHAPTER PREVIEW

In this chapter you will learn how events in Europe and elsewhere drew the United States into the First World War and what impact that war had upon the United States.

SECTIONS IN THIS CHAPTER:
1. **Peace movements failed to stop world war.**
2. **The United States went to war in 1917.**
3. **U.S. economic power won the war.**
4. **World leaders debated the peace.**
5. **Theme essay: Americans drew back from world leadership.**

1914	1915	1916	1917	1918	1919

1914
World War I begins

1916
Verdun: French lose 315,000; Germans 280,000

1917
Submarine warfare resumes; U.S. declares war; Russian Revolution begins

1918
Armistice declared November 11

Peace movements failed to stop world war.

Key Terms: pacifists, Triple Alliance, Triple Entente, Central Powers, Allies, nationalism, Armenian massacre

Reading Preview
As you read this section, you will learn:

1. when worldwide peace movements gained popularity.
2. for what purpose opposing alliances emerged in Europe.
3. what incident ignited war in Europe in 1914.
4. what stand Americans took during the early years of the war.
5. what role geography played in the timing of the war.

chart study

The fateful events of August 1914 set the course of World War I and shaped the world today. How much time elapsed between the assassination at Sarajevo and the first declaration of war?

Critical Thinking
How does the time line show that alliances and the arms buildup contributed to the outbreak of war?

By the turn of the century, many Americans believed that a conflict among industrialized nations would be so brutal that war must be made obsolete. Some became **pacifists**—people who believed that all wars should be outlawed. At the same time, however, the leading nations of Europe were developing efficient new weapons, stockpiling munitions, and entering into elaborate alliances in preparation for war.

COUNTDOWN TO WAR, 1914		
JUNE	28	Austrian archduke assassinated at Sarajevo, Bosnia
JULY	28	Austria-Hungary declares war on Serbia
	30	Russia mobilizes in support of Serbia
AUGUST	1	Germany declares war on Russia
	3	Germany declares war on France
	4	Germany invades Belgium Great Britain declares war on Germany
	12	Great Britain declares war on Austria-Hungary

Worldwide peace movements gained popularity in the early 1900s.

The world's first peace societies formed in the United States back in 1815, and by the 1890s several hundred organizations on both sides of the Atlantic worked for the peaceful settlement of disputes between nations. Women, especially a rising women's suffrage movement, played a major role in the American peace movement.

Interest in peace increased in 1897 when **Alfred Nobel**, the Swedish discoverer of dynamite, set aside some of his millions to establish an international peace prize. The next year, in 1898, the young Tsar Nicholas II, leader of the large and expanding Russian nation, electrified the world by calling for world disarmament. U.S. delegates attended the international peace conferences in 1899 and 1907 called by the tsar and held at The Hague, a city in the Netherlands.

The Hague Peace Conferences made no progress toward world disarmament but did create the Permanent Court of Arbitration, known as The Hague Court, to provide nations with neutral arbitrators for their disputes. Andrew Carnegie donated the money for a gleaming marble Peace Palace at The Hague in which The Hague Court has its seat. Beginning in 1902 the Hague Court arbitrated 25 disputes in which all parties agreed to accept the court's decision as binding.

Two opposing alliances emerged in Europe to create a balance of power.

Despite many activities in the cause of peace, a new era of violence seemed to be threatening. The five major powers of Europe—Great Britain, France, Germany, Austria-Hungary, and Russia—had maintained an uneasy peace since the Franco-Prussian War of 1870–1871. In that war, Germany had taken the frontier region of **Alsace-Lorraine** from France. Fearing retaliation from France, Germany had formed the **Triple Alliance** with Austria-Hungary and Italy. Opposing the Triple Alliance was a second major alliance system, the **Triple Entente**, which included Great Britain,

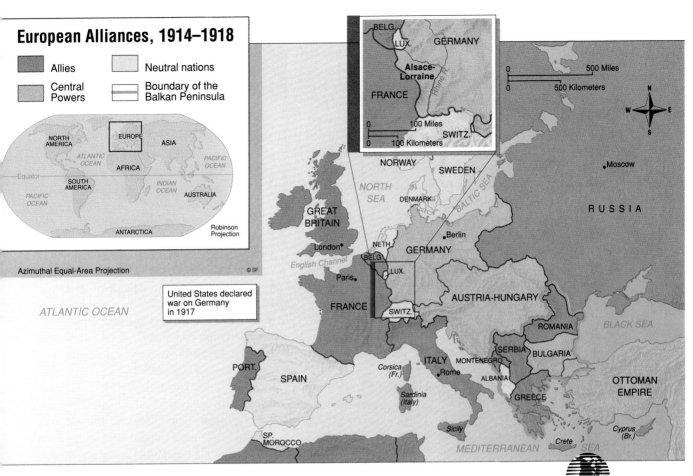

European Alliances, 1914–1918

Legend:
- Allies
- Central Powers
- Neutral nations
- Boundary of the Balkan Peninsula

Azimuthal Equal-Area Projection © SF

Robinson Projection

United States declared war on Germany in 1917

France, and Russia. Britain was also allied with Japan after 1902. You can see on the inset map above why Alsace-Lorraine might interest both France and Germany. The main map shows the countries of the Triple Alliance, later known as the **Central Powers**, and the Triple Entente, later known as the **Allies**.

As European governments formed their alliances, they often found themselves in conflict over colonies and world markets. At the same time, forces of nationalism were stirring, especially in the huge, ethnically diverse Russian, Austro-Hungarian, and Ottoman empires. **Nationalism** means an intense feeling of patriotism or the desire and plans for national independence. Nationalist movements grew especially strong among the Slavs (a language grouping that includes the Russians, Poles, and other peoples of southeastern Europe).

On the **Balkan Peninsula** in southeastern Europe, the weakness of the Ottoman Empire

encouraged Greece, Serbia, Montenegro, Romania and Bulgaria to revolt between 1829 and 1908. Austria-Hungary also took part of the Balkans from the Turks. The political instability of these new countries gave the Balkans the nickname "the powder keg of Europe." As you can see on the map above, the Balkans might well form a convenient corridor to the Mediterranean for the Russian, Austro-Hungarian, or Ottoman empires as they existed in 1914.

The forces of imperialism and nationalism encouraged a massive arms build-up in Europe. Germany's huge Krupp Works and other arms makers in Britain, France, and Austria-Hungary sold weapons to all sides. Each year, technological advances made their products more deadly. By 1900 most of the major European powers required all young men to serve for a time in the army. Some nations—especially Germany—glorified the military.

map study

Region Two regions in Europe, Alsace-Lorraine and the Balkan Peninsula, played key roles in the buildup of World War I. Describe the locations of these regions.

Critical Thinking Why might Slavic nationalism cause conflict in the Balkans?

At right the Austrian archduke Franz Ferdinand and his wife, Sophie, seated at the rear of the motorcar, leave the Sarajevo senate building on their fateful ride June 28, 1914. Minutes later both were shot and killed. The resulting crisis flamed into world war.

The shooting of an Austrian prince ignited war in 1914.

Despite the arms race, Europe managed to avoid war, partly because the contending alliance systems were so evenly matched that neither side felt it could score a decisive victory. On June 28, 1914, however, a young Slavic nationalist linked to Serbia, Gavrilo Princip [gä vrē′lō prēn′tsēp], assassinated the heir to the Austrian throne, Archduke Franz Ferdinand, and his wife, Sophie.

Austria-Hungary first made sure that it had the backing of its ally Germany and then moved to punish Serbia. Hoping to prevent further Austrian penetration into the Balkans, Russia mobilized its army in support of Serbia on July 30. Germany responded by declaring war on Russia on August 1 and on Russia's ally France on August 3. Belgium refused to let Germany cross its territory to attack France, so

Germany declared war on Belgium. Because Germany violated Belgian neutrality, Great Britain entered the conflict against Germany on August 4. By the end of August 1914, the Central Powers—Austria-Hungary and Germany—were at war with the Allies—Serbia, Russia, France, Belgium, Great Britain, Montenegro, and Japan.

The Ottoman Empire joined the Central Powers on October 19, and other nations, including the United States, later joined each side, as you can see on the list of combatants at left. The alliance system dragged nation after nation into a deadly conflict first known as the Great War and now as World War I.

Americans struggled to remain neutral in the early years of the war.

European nations on both sides went to war with a naive confidence that they would win a quick, decisive victory. Most Americans saw no reason for the United States to become involved at all.

Wilson hoped America could remain above the conflict and hoped too that he might serve as peacemaker. He argued that the only real solution was a "peace without victory," in which neither side would gain territory or compensation at the expense of the other. Such gains, he believed, would plant the seeds for future wars.

On August 4, 1914, President Wilson issued a Neutrality Proclamation, announcing that the

chart study

Use the map on page 417 and a dictionary, if necessary to determine where the Allies and the Central Powers were located. During which year did the largest number of nations enter the war?

Critical Thinking
Do you think "World War" is a fitting title to describe the conflict of 1914–1918? Why or why not?

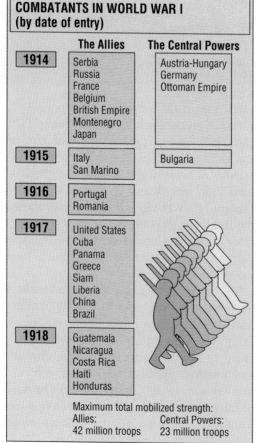

COMBATANTS IN WORLD WAR I (by date of entry)		
	The Allies	**The Central Powers**
1914	Serbia Russia France Belgium British Empire Montenegro Japan	Austria-Hungary Germany Ottoman Empire
1915	Italy San Marino	Bulgaria
1916	Portugal Romania	
1917	United States Cuba Panama Greece Siam Liberia China Brazil	
1918	Guatemala Nicaragua Costa Rica Haiti Honduras	

Maximum total mobilized strength:
Allies: Central Powers:
42 million troops   23 million troops

United States was not committed to either side and was to be treated as a neutral. On August 19 he urged Americans to be "neutral in fact as well as in name . . . impartial in thought as well as in action." Many Americans disregarded Wilson's suggestion, however. Of the 97 million people in the United States, more than 34 million had at least one foreign-born parent.

Geography ruled out a swift victory on land and at sea.

Despite the hopes for an early end to the war, certain geographical factors made a swift victory on land unlikely. The geographical contours of the North Sea and the Mediterranean also ruled out a swift victory at sea, as historian Paul Kennedy has pointed out.

The Central Powers held a strong advantage in a land war because Germany and Austria-Hungary formed a single connected territory, as you can see from the map on page 417. Efficient railroads permitted the rapid movement of troops and supplies. As for the Allies, Britain was separated from the others by the English Channel. The two largest Allies, France and Russia, were also widely separated, and coordination of their operations proved almost impossible. Russia was also handicapped with poor roads and inefficient railroads.

The long European coastlines worked to the advantage of the Allies. Great Britain's control of the seas meant that it could blockade the Central Powers and assured the Allies of access to vital supplies. Furthermore, Italy's extensive coastline made it especially vulnerable to British sea power. As a consequence, Italy remained neutral for a time and then finally joined the Allies in 1915.

Fighting on the western front. Since 1905 the German army's general staff had developed a plan to launch a quick strike against France in the event war broke out. According to this Schlieffen [shlē′fən] Plan, German forces would first defeat France, then launch a full-scale assault on Russia. In order to avoid the heavily fortified Franco-German border, Germany attacked Belgium on August 4, 1914.

The small Belgian army resisted the German advance long enough for Great Britain and France to move troops into northern France where they stopped the German invasion near the Marne River. The First Battle of the Marne marked the first turning point in the war, when Germany lost its chance for a quick victory.

The western front quickly became stalemated, with neither side able to move, as their armies settled into defensive positions covering 600 miles of French and Belgian countryside. Both sides dug elaborate networks of trenches, separated from each other by coils of barbed wire and a no-man's land where any movement brought a burst of machine-gun fire. During the next three years, millions of men achieved little.

Members of a French machine-gun crew become robots in a world of machine forms in this 1915 painting by British painter C. R. W. Nevinson (1889–1946). The machine gun could fire 600 bullets a minute, making trench warfare a necessity.

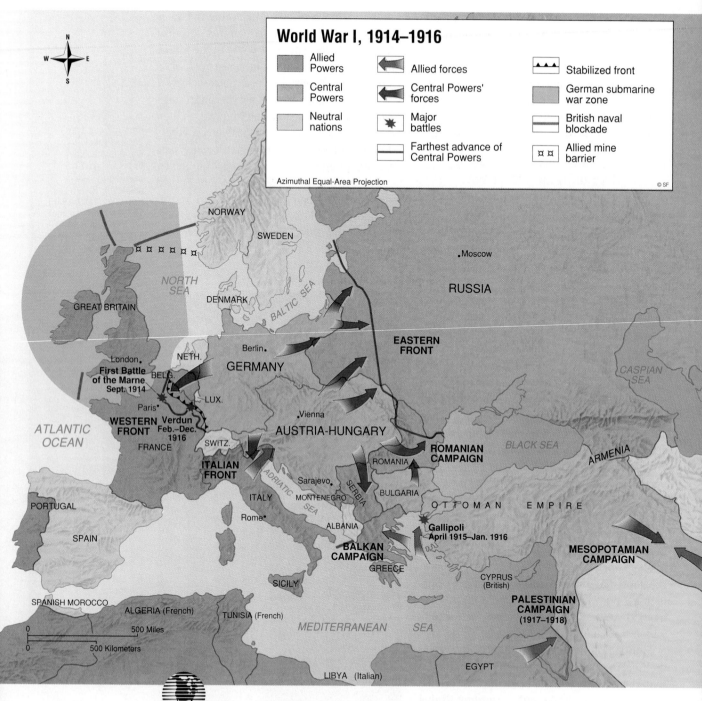

World War I, 1914–1916

■	Allied Powers	◄	Allied forces	▲▲▲	Stabilized front
■	Central Powers	◄	Central Powers' forces		German submarine war zone
■	Neutral nations	✦	Major battles		British naval blockade
			Farthest advance of Central Powers	¤ ¤	Allied mine barrier

Azimuthal Equal-Area Projection   © SF

Movement Much of World War I was a land war in which the Central Powers had a geographical advantage. Arrows on the map clearly illustrate the Central Powers plan to move west, east, and south into all of Europe. What were the results of this plan on the western and eastern fronts? What naval strategies were used by the Allies and Central Powers?

Critical Thinking The western front changed little from 1914 to 1916. At Gallipoli one battle lasted 11 months. Why would such prolonged battles be less likely today?

At the Battle of Verdun, which started in February 1916 and lasted the rest of that year, French casualties totaled more than 315,000 men, and the Germans lost more than 280,000. In the end, the French won back Verdun. Despite unbelievable carnage, the western front changed little between 1914 and 1916.

The Germans used a new weapon in 1915— chlorine gas, which attacked soldiers' eyes and throats. Before the war ended, both sides had tried many other chemicals. To protect against gas, the troops carried gas masks, invented by an African American, Garrett A. Morgan. Tanks—developed by the British—and aerial bombings failed to break the deadlock.

The Central Powers were more successful on the eastern front, driving deep into Russia. Again, however, with millions of troops spread over hundreds of miles of battle lines, neither side could hope to deal a single decisive blow. Fighting also took place along the Italian-Austrian frontier from the Swiss border to the Adriatic Sea. Other battlefronts included Egypt; German colonies in Asia, Africa, and the Pacific Ocean; and parts of the crumbling Ottoman Empire—the southern Balkans, Mesopotamia (now Iraq), and Palestine.

In the mountainous region of Armenia, now divided by Turkey, the Soviet Union, and Iran, the growth of a nationalist movement among Christian Armenians provoked cruel repression. In 1915–1916, after Armenians formed volunteer battalions to help Russia fight the Turks, the Turkish government deported 1,750,000 Armenians to the deserts of Mesopotamia. At least 600,000 men, women, and children were killed outright or died of starvation in this **Armenian massacre**. Those who escaped death were forced into exile.

Fighting for control of the seas. With their armies at an impasse, the Central Powers and the Allies turned to their navies. Actions by both sides immediately threatened neutral nations' freedom of the seas. The British stopped and searched all ships approaching the continent and confiscated contraband (prohibited war supplies). As the war progressed, they defined contraband more broadly to include food, medical supplies, and most other items.

To break the British blockade, the German navy turned to underwater warfare. The German submarines, known as U-boats from the German *Unterseeboot* (undersea boat), attacked surface shipping to keep war supplies from reaching the Allies. The U-boats were small, cramped vessels with no room to carry survivors of the ships they torpedoed.

The Germans proclaimed a war zone around the British Isles within which Allied merchant ships would be sunk upon sight. When British ships took to flying the flags of neutral nations, Germany served warning that a neutral flag did not guarantee protection.

SECTION 1 REVIEW

Identify Key People and Terms
Write a sentence to identify: pacifists, Alfred Nobel, Triple Alliance, Triple Entente, Central Powers, Allies, nationalism, Armenian massacre

Locate Key Places

1. Which frontier region did France lose to Germany in 1871?
2. What countries were located in the Balkan Peninsula in 1914?

Master the Main Ideas

1. **Understanding U.S. foreign affairs:** Why did Americans seek peace during the early 1900s?
2. **Understanding international conflicts:** Why did the nations of Europe split into two opposing alliances before 1914?
3. **Understanding international conflicts:** How did the shooting of an Austrian prince ignite war in 1914?
4. **Understanding U.S. foreign policy:** Why did the United States choose neutrality in the early years of the war?
5. **Understanding geographic influences:** Why did geography rule out a swift victory?

Apply Critical Thinking Skills: Recognizing Values
Why would Americans in World War I accept the machine gun and the tank more readily than they accepted the U-boat and poison gas?

The United States went to war in 1917.

Key Terms: *Lusitania, Sussex* pledge, Zimmermann note, convoy, Bolsheviks

Reading Preview
As you read this section, you will learn:

1. what effect Germany's U-boat campaign had on the United States.
2. what Americans did in regard to the war effort.
3. what the United States needed to do to prepare an army for war.
4. what role the U.S. Navy played in the war.
5. what part U.S. troops took in the war in France.

As the war in Europe continued into 1915, President Wilson struggled to maintain U.S. neutrality. He sent his most trusted adviser, Colonel Edward M. House, to Europe to propose American mediation. The British, French, and German leaders, however, refused the president's offer.

The sinking of the British ocean liner *Lusitania* off the coast of Ireland May 7, 1915, by a German U-boat hardened U.S. opinion against Germany. The headline at right underestimated the death toll by almost 300. President Wilson, struggling to remain neutral, said there was such a thing as being "too proud to fight."

Germany's U-boat campaign pushed America into war.

On May 7, 1915, a German torpedo sliced through the waters off the coast of Ireland, sinking the British ocean liner *Lusitania*. Nearly 1,200 passengers died, including 128 Americans. Half of the *Lusitania*'s cargo was war supplies, although the public would not know that until years later. After Wilson protested repeatedly, Germany announced that it would sink no more unarmed passenger ships without warning.

Despite these promises, less than a year later, in March 1916, a U-boat torpedoed the French cross-channel steamer *Sussex*, injuring two Americans. Again, Wilson protested. In what became known as the **Sussex pledge**, Germany promised not to sink passenger or merchant ships "without warning and without saving human lives."

In the summer of 1916, Congress passed laws increasing the size of the army and authorizing many new ships for the navy. Americans also turned their attention to the 1916 presidential election. Wilson and the Democrats ran on the slogan "He kept us out of war." The Republicans nominated Charles Evans Hughes, a Supreme Court justice and former governor of New York.

The election proved so close that the final outcome hung in the balance for three days while the California vote was counted. Wilson won with 49 percent of the popular vote. The Democrats retained control of Congress.

Shortly after the election, on February 1, 1917, Germany renewed its program of unrestricted submarine warfare. Germany had by then built a large submarine fleet and hoped to defeat Great Britain and France before American troops could arrive in force. The United States broke off diplomatic relations with Germany and began arming American merchant ships.

In early March 1917, the president released to the press an intercepted, coded message from German foreign minister Arthur Zimmermann to the German minister in Mexico. Zimmermann proposed that if the United

States entered the war, Mexico should attack the United States. As its reward, Mexico would recover its lost territory of Texas, New Mexico, and Arizona. The **Zimmermann note** outraged most Americans. That same month U-boats sank three American merchant ships.

On April 2, 1917, Wilson faced a special session of Congress and asked for a declaration of war against Germany. In the most memorable words from the address, he pleaded that "the world must be made safe for democracy." He also asked Americans to fight to "end all wars" and to bring "peace and safety to all nations."

I WANT YOU
for the U.S. ARMY
UNITED STATES ARMY RECRUITING SERVICE

World War I Posters

On April 17, 1917, a group of well-known artists met in New York City to determine how they could contribute to America's war effort. Less than two weeks had passed since the United States had declared war against Germany. The government faced the massive job of mobilizing millions of troops, amassing tons of food and supplies, and raising hundreds of millions of dollars to pay for the war. What could a group of artists do that would be of service to the war effort?

A telegram from George Creel, director of the government's Committee on Public Information, offered an answer. Creel advised Charles Dana Gibson, a leading member of the artist group, to organize a committee of volunteer artists to produce whatever artwork the government might need in connection with the war effort. Gibson took the floor and presented Creel's proposal. The group was enthusiastic. Within a few weeks, hundreds of artists were mobilized to work on government posters.

Over the next two years, these war posters became a common sight throughout American cities. During this time, more than 2,000 different posters were issued and about 20 million copies of these posters were printed. The posters relied on strong, forceful images and simple slogans to get their messages across in a flash. As Creel pointed out, "The printed word might not be read, people might not choose to attend meetings or to watch motion pictures, but the billboard [poster] was something that caught even the most indifferent eye."

Figures from World War I posters lived on in popular culture long after the war was over. Uncle Sam, from a poster by James Montgomery Flagg, has come to represent patriotic duty, pride, and courage shared by many Americans. The image is so strong, it continues to be used in government posters and pamphlets even today.

The pointing Uncle Sam by U.S. illustrator James Montgomery Flagg (1877–1960) was a self-portrait. The image was inspired by an extremely successful 1914 British recruiting poster by Alfred Leete (1882–1933) featuring Field Marshal and Secretary of State for War Lord Horatio Kitchener.

Highlights of American Life

Joan of Arc Saved France

W.S.S. WOMEN OF AMERICA SAVE YOUR COUNTRY *Buy* WAR SAVINGS STAMPS

UNITED STATES TREASURY DEPARTMENT

Not all members of Congress agreed. Senator **George W. Norris**, a Progressive Republican from Nebraska, Senator Robert La Follette of Wisconsin, and four other senators voted against the war resolution. Opponents in the House included **Jeannette Rankin** of Montana, who had just become the first woman representative. Rankin declared, "I want to stand by my country, but I cannot vote for war. I vote no." After four days of debate, Congress declared war.

Posters like that above made the selling of Liberty bonds into a crusade. For those with limited means, bonds could be purchased on an installment plan or war savings stamps could be pasted in a book and redeemed for bonds. Although this poster addresses women, most savings stamps—more than a billion dollars' worth—were bought by schoolchildren.

American propaganda sometimes incited anger and hatred. The cartoon at right appeared the day before a German American immigrant, Robert Paul Prager, was seized by a mob, wrapped in an American flag, and killed as a suspected spy near Collinsville, Illinois.

Americans united to support the war effort.

The American decision to enter the war came at a crucial point. The Allied armies were exhausted, and U-boats were making quick work of Allied merchant ships.

Financing the war. When the war began, British control of the seas put the Allies in a strong position to buy supplies from the United States. By early 1917 American companies had loaned $1.5 billion to Great Britain and half that amount to the other Allies to pay for war materials and foodstuffs. At this point, the U.S. economy was heavily dependent on selling war supplies.

The secretary of the treasury, William Gibbs McAdoo, who was Wilson's son-in-law, convinced the president that he could find money to fight the war and also fight inflation by borrowing from the public. Posters and bond rallies with such film stars as Douglas Fairbanks and Mary Pickford encouraged Americans to purchase Liberty bonds or Victory bonds, as the loans were called. The government raised $21 billion in five well-publicized bond drives and an additional $11 billion through taxation.

Silencing opposition to the war. Not all Americans fully supported the war. For ex-

ample, a pro-German weekly editorialized that German American draftees should not be forced to fight their kin. Some Irish Americans also refused to rally to the British cause, especially after the British government brutally suppressed an Irish independence movement in 1916. The Socialist party condemned the war as an evil that was part of the capitalist system. Many people came to regard all socialists and pacifists as pro-German traitors.

In order to encourage support for the war, President Wilson established the Committee on Public Information. George Creel, a young newspaper editor and muckraker, was chosen to head the committee. Artists, writers, and speakers helped whip up enthusiasm for the American cause in what Creel called "the world's greatest adventure in advertising."

Unfortunately the fervor whipped up by Creel had its ugly side. Patriotism became an excuse for persecuting people with German names and for banning the music of Bach, Beethoven, and Wagner. Even eating German

Life, 4 April 1918

WE WOULD HAVE LESS OF THIS

IF WE HAD MORE OF THIS

foods was considered disloyal, so sauerkraut was renamed liberty cabbage. Many schools stopped teaching the German language, and German-language books were burned.

As early as 1894 Theodore Roosevelt had condemned "hyphenated Americans"—persons whose loyalties were divided between the United States and the old country. Woodrow Wilson took up the theme. He further added to wartime hysteria by telling Americans that the "military masters of Germany" had "filled our unsuspecting communities with vicious spies and conspirators."

Congress passed the Espionage Act in 1917, aimed at checking espionage (spying) and treason and prohibiting use of the mails to send treasonable materials. The act, used to ban socialist publications from the mails, seriously crippled the socialist movement. The Sedition Act, passed in 1918, barred "disloyal utterances," which included criticism of the government or the Constitution and disrespect for the American flag.

Some 1,500 people were arrested for violating these laws. John Schrag was a Mennonite farmer in Burrton, Kansas, whose religious beliefs forbade support of the war. Schrag was attacked by a mob. When a flag thrust at him fell to the ground, they covered him with yellow paint and had him jailed for flag desecration (treating the flag with disrespect). Many others went to prison, including Eugene V. Debs, the socialist leader. When opponents of the war challenged the laws as unconstitutional, the Supreme Court ruled that freedom of speech was never absolute. No one has the right to shout "fire" in a crowded theater, said Justice Oliver Wendell Holmes, Jr., nor to say things that might endanger the security of the nation.

The United States needed to raise, train, and equip an army.

The army was far from ready for action in April 1917. Congress passed the Selective Service Act in May, requiring all men between the ages of 21 and 31 (later 18 through 45) to register for the draft. Local draft boards then determined who would be called to duty. Of the 29

divisions that saw combat in the war, 11 were formed of draftees.

When Alvin York registered for the draft, he asked for an exemption on religious grounds. His draft board denied the request because, they said, the Church of Christ in Christian Union to which he belonged was not a "well-recognized" sect. York was inducted in November 1917.

Private York excelled on the rifle range, but his mind was troubled. He told his company commander, "Sir, I am doing wrong. Practicing to kill people is against my religion." After a furlough, and hours spent in prayer, York resolved his crisis of conscience and returned to the army. Eventually, along with about two million other American soldiers, he served in France.

Nearly 400,000 African Americans also served during World War I in segregated army and navy units. The war proved a bitter exper-

America's most celebrated war hero, Sergeant Alvin C. York, is photographed at the end of the war wearing, left to right, the Congressional Medal of Honor, for gallantry in action, and the French Croix de Guerre [krwä də ger'], meaning war cross, for bravery. York's draft registration card, claiming exemption as a conscientious objector, is also shown.

A War Prophecy

World war would create world change, W. E. B. Du Bois knew. As African American regiments prepared to fight overseas, Du Bois, an activist and a scholar, addressed them with visionary words. Have his prophecies come true?

You are not fighting simply for Europe; you are fighting for the world, and you and your people are a part of the world.

This war is an End and, also, a Beginning. Never again will darker people of the world occupy just the place they had before. Out of this war will rise, soon or late, an independent China; a self-governing India; an Egypt with representative institutions; an Africa for Africans . . . . Out of this war will rise, too, an American Negro, with the right to vote and the right to work and the right to live without insult. These things may not and will not come at once; but they are written in the stars. . . .

ience for many black soldiers and sailors, revealing the deep vein of prejudice in American society at that time. Under a discriminatory plan that was kept confidential, about 70 percent of the soldiers served as stevedores, loading and unloading ships, or in labor companies.

Despite these injustices, almost 200,000 African Americans served overseas, including the 92nd and 93rd infantry divisions that fought in France. More than 600 African Americans earned commissions as officers. Four African American infantry regiments joined French divisions where they served bravely and well. The 369th infantry regiment, from New York City's Harlem district, served 191 days in combat, longer than any other American regiment. France decorated the entire unit.

Athough women were not allowed to join the army, almost 11,000 women enlisted in the navy and about 300 in the marines. Most of them served as clerk-typists, telephone operators, or nurses. Many women who joined the Red Cross and the Army Corps of Nurses served in France.

Members of the 369th Regiment won high praise for their fighting in the Meuse-Argonne. They are shown here on the return voyage to the United States in 1919 after receiving the French Croix de Guerre for bravery.

The U.S. Navy ferried a huge army across dangerous waters.

As the army began training recruits, the U.S. Navy took action against the U-boats. Rear Admiral William S. Sims convinced the British to plant mines across the North Sea between Scotland and Norway to contain the German navy. Sims also urged the use of a **convoy** system, with several merchant ships sailing together under the protection of destroyers. By spring 1918 the U-boat danger had passed.

In addition to escorting cargo vessels, destroyers protected troopships carrying soldiers across the Atlantic. During the course of the war, the navy ferried two million men without the loss of a single troopship.

U.S. troops turned the tide in France.

In June 1917 the first troops from the American army, officially called the American Expeditionary Force (AEF), arrived in France. Commanding the force was Major General John J. Pershing, who had recently returned from the punitive expedition to Mexico and was highly regarded as a tough and competent officer.

The Central Powers seemed on the verge of a stunning victory. In Russia riots had broken out in March 1917 (February under the old Russian calendar), and workers and soldiers overthrew the tsar. The Russian soldiers refused to continue the war, and the Bolsheviks seized power in November 1917. The **Bolsheviks** were a minority socialist party led by Vladimir Ilyich Lenin [vlə dē′myir il yēch′ len′ən]. They were also called communists.

With the collapse of Russia as an ally, huge numbers of seasoned German troops were shifted to the western front. At a terrible cost, the German armies broke through the British lines for a gain of 14 miles, the largest advance in three and a half years. Mutiny swept through the French troops. The French soldiers reportedly baaed like sheep going to slaughter as they marched to the front.

However, improved Allied organization and the fresh American troops finally halted the German advance. From May to November 1918, the AEF fought bravely and effectively, especially at Château-Thierry [sha tō′ tye rē′], Belleau [be lō′] Wood, Saint-Mihiel [san mē-yel′], and Meuse-Argonne [myüz är gän′], which was the last major French and American

The failure of poorly planned missions cast a pall of gloom over British and French troops. British artist John Nash (1893–1977) painted an eyewitness record in *Over the Top* at left. Nash—one of 12 survivors out of a company of 80—recalled, "It was bitterly cold and we were easy targets against the snow and in daylight."

U.S. forces took a leading part in the final offensives of the war. American doughboys, or infantrymen, below, move into action in France carrying sacks of grenades.

427

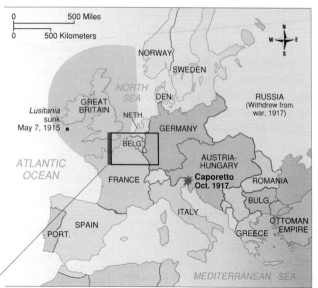

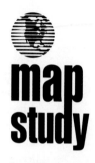

map study

Location Cantigny was the first battle fought by the American Expeditionary Force. There the Germans retreated and were continually driven back toward Germany from June to November of 1918. Trace this final campaign of World War I on the map. Where was it fought?

Critical Thinking Why was it imperative to stop the German advance in this location?

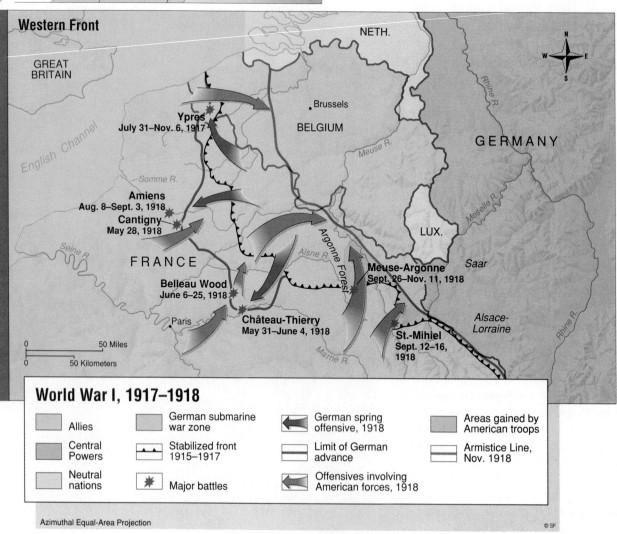

Western Front

Ypres
July 31–Nov. 6, 1917

Amiens
Aug. 8–Sept. 3, 1918

Cantigny
May 28, 1918

Belleau Wood
June 6–25, 1918

Château-Thierry
May 31–June 4, 1918

St.-Mihiel
Sept. 12–16, 1918

Meuse-Argonne
Sept. 26–Nov. 11, 1918

World War I, 1917–1918

- Allies
- Central Powers
- Neutral nations
- German submarine war zone
- Stabilized front 1915–1917
- Major battles
- German spring offensive, 1918
- Limit of German advance
- Offensives involving American forces, 1918
- Areas gained by American troops
- Armistice Line, Nov. 1918

Azimuthal Equal-Area Projection

© SF

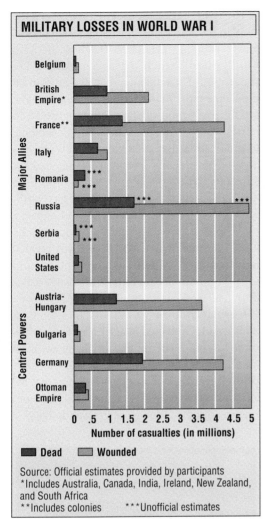

MILITARY LOSSES IN WORLD WAR I

Major Allies
- Belgium
- British Empire*
- France**
- Italy
- Romania ***/***
- Russia ***/***
- Serbia ***/***
- United States

Central Powers
- Austria-Hungary
- Bulgaria
- Germany
- Ottoman Empire

Number of casualties (in millions): 0 .5 1 1.5 2 2.5 3 3.5 4 4.5 5

■ Dead   ▨ Wounded

Source: Official estimates provided by participants
*Includes Australia, Canada, India, Ireland, New Zealand, and South Africa
**Includes colonies   ***Unofficial estimates

offensive of the war. The **Meuse-Argonne** sector occupied the upper valley of the Meuse River in northeastern France, as you can see on the map on the opposite page. The Meuse is crossed there by a rugged and thickly wooded ridge, the Argonne Forest.

About 900,000 Americans participated in the Meuse-Argonne offensive, among them Alvin York. On October 8, 1918, York silenced 35 German machine guns that protected a railroad carrying German supplies to the front. In doing so, he killed 17 German soldiers with just 17 shots, and, with only seven men under his command, captured 132 more. Promoted to the rank of sergeant, he became America's most celebrated war hero.

The German General Staff knew they had lost the war by late July. On the 11th hour of

the 11th day of the 11th month in 1918, an armistice was signed.

A whole generation was swept away in the war. Use the chart at the left to see the major participants' battle losses. Altogether, the war killed more than nine million troops and five million civilians. Millions more lost their lives through starvation or in a deadly epidemic of Spanish influenza that swept across the world in 1918 and 1919, infecting a billion people and killing tens of millions. Four empires collapsed during the war, a dozen new nations emerged, and the maps of Europe, Asia, and Africa were all redrawn.

S E C T I O N **2** R E V I E W

Identify Key People and Terms
Write a sentence to identify: *Lusitania*, *Sussex* pledge, Zimmermann note, George W. Norris, Jeannette Rankin, convoy, Bolsheviks

Locate Key Places
Describe the geographical location of the last major offensive of the war.

Master the Main Ideas
1. **Understanding international conflicts:** How did Germany's U-boat compaign push America into war?
2. **Analyzing economic impact of wars: (a)** How did American efforts to finance the war affect inflation? **(b)** How did attempts to silence opposition to the war affect civil liberties?
3. **Analyzing economic impact of wars:** How did racial discrimination enter into plans to raise and train the American army?
4. **Understanding international conflicts:** How did the U.S. Navy deal with the submarine menace as it ferried troops across the Atlantic?
5. **Understanding international conflicts:** How did U.S. troops contribute to the final victory in France in 1918?

Apply Critical Thinking Skills: Demonstrating Reasoned Judgment
How do you think African American soldiers felt fighting a war to preserve democracy?

chart study

More than 9 million troops were killed in World War I and almost 22 million wounded. Losses of Greece, Japan, Montenegro, and Portugal are not shown. Which nation suffered the largest number of deaths among military personnel?
Critical Thinking How might feelings of the various participants about their war losses have influenced postwar events?

U.S. economic power won the war.

Key Terms: assembly line, Great Migration, Urban League

Reading Preview
As you read this section, you will learn:

1. what role new government agencies played in the war effort.
2. what attracted African Americans to the cities of the North and West during the war.
3. to what region of the United States Mexicans migrated.
4. what benefits the war brought women.

The war affected every aspect of American life. Manufacturers who had once worried about finding markets for their goods now had but one aim: to turn out war materials as rapidly as possible. Wartime also multiplied the activities of the federal government and brought a degree of federal intervention in the economy that has never been matched. At the same time, the war opened new opportunities for many Americans, especially African Americans and Mexican immigrants. The war also drew into the labor force many more women of all racial and ethnic backgrounds.

New government agencies marshaled U.S. economic resources for war.

The responsibility for overseeing America's economic mobilization fell to a cabinet committee created in 1916, the Council for National Defense. Aiding the Council was a seven-member Civilian Advisory Board—officials from business, industry, railroads, and labor unions. The council soon created several other bodies to allocate scarce resources, untangle railway transportation snarls, and coordinate specific economic sectors such as manufacturing, agriculture, fuel production, and transportation.

The War Industries Board (WIB), created early in the war, came to wield near-dictatorial power over the economy. Heading the WIB was **Bernard Baruch**, a financier who had become a self-made millionaire at age 30. Baruch drew up a blueprint for industrial mobilization, setting production quotas, allocating raw materials, standardizing products, and developing new industries. For example, the WIB set up a division to procure special wood needed for airplanes. Private Alvin York served in it for a time, felling spruce trees in the Pacific Northwest, before his unit shipped out to France.

To win the support of labor unions for the war effort, the War Labor Board was created in 1918. The board protected the right of workers to form unions, and it also mediated labor disputes.

Herbert Hoover was the nation's food administrator. Orphaned at age eight, Hoover became a successful mining engineer with an international reputation and a large fortune. Hoover also headed the relief program that fed ten million people in Belgium and northern France after the outbreak of the war. In his post

Posters like the one at right exhorted Americans to plant war gardens and preserve the fruits and vegetables they raised for home use. Such posters were only part of a campaign that included house-to-house calls and articles in women's magazines featuring meatless recipes. The Kaiser was Kaiser Wilhelm II, the German ruler.

as U.S. food administrator, Hoover guaranteed a high price for wheat so that farmers would increase production. With the slogan "Food will win the war!" the Food Administration also sent people door to door with pledge cards, urging housewives to observe meatless Mondays and wheatless Wednesdays. Food shipments to the Allies tripled.

To conserve energy, the Fuel Administration ordered that electric advertising signs remain dark on Thursdays and Sundays. Congress also enacted the first use of daylight-saving time.

The war gave the world its first real idea of what American assembly-line methods could accomplish. Cyrus McCormick used the principle of the **assembly line** in the manufacture of reapers as far back as the 1850s. Henry Ford applied the principle to the manufacture of cars in 1913. An assembly line employs a power-driven conveyor that carries each element of a product past workers. As it passes, each worker adds or fixes some part in place. During the first year of the war, the production of machine guns increased from 20,000 a year to 225,000. By war's end, Philadelphia shipyards were turning out a 7,500-ton vessel every 72 hours.

As manufacturing rose in volume, goods clogged terminals and railroads, and railway workers threatened to strike. The federal government took over the railroads for the duration. The government also ran the telegraph and telephone systems for a year.

The promise of jobs attracted African Americans to the North and West.

The war curtailed European immigration, adding to the labor shortages created by wartime demands. The promise of jobs drew approximately 500,000 African Americans to the cities of the North and West during and immediately after the war.

African Americans had always moved about the country in search of opportunity. Before the war, however, about 90 percent of all African Americans lived in the South. Beginning in 1916, in what historians have termed the **Great Migration**, the first mass movement of black southerners to northern and western cities began.

If You are a Stranger in the City

If you want a job   If you want a place to live
If you are having trouble with your employer
If you want information or advice of any kind
CALL UPON
The CHICAGO LEAGUE ON URBAN CONDITIONS AMONG NEGROES
3719 South State Street

Telefone Douglas 9098   T. ARNOLD HILL, Executive Secretary

No charges—no fees. We want to help YOU

Stimulating the drive, northern labor agents offered free transportation to Chicago, Milwaukee, Philadelphia, Pittsburgh, and other northern cities. Many agents represented railroads, mines, and meat-packing plants, seeking new workers.

An emotion-packed weekly newspaper, the Chicago *Defender*, also contributed to migration. The *Defender* was founded by Robert S. Abbott in 1905, published from his home with a starting capital of only 25 cents. It had become the largest-selling black newspaper in the United States by World War I with a national circulation of 230,000.

Abbott, born and raised in Georgia and the son of former slaves, used the *Defender* to give African Americans an effective means of self-improvement. The *Defender* spread news of racial injustices in the South and opportunities in the North. More convincingly, it pictured a ramshackle one-room black school in the South side by side with Chicago's integrated Robert Lindblom High School, an imposing, modern brick structure.

Northbound migrants crowded onto railroad cars, chalking on the side such slogans as "Farewell—We're Good and Gone" or "Bound for the Promised Land." In Chicago, a mecca for many migrants, the newcomers found help from established black churches, the Bethlehem Baptist Association, and the Chicago branch of the **Urban League**, a national group formed in 1910 to aid the adjustment of African Americans to cities.

The Chicago Urban League passed out cards like the one above to help African Americans from the rural South adjust to city life. Through "Strangers Meetings," door-to-door visits, and other programs, members of the Urban League encouraged newcomers to leave country ways behind and become respected members of the urban community.

Women took pride in learning new job skills in mills and factories. The shipyard workers above posed in front of their handiwork. The women carried hot rivets in cone-shaped holders and used tongs to insert the rivets into holes that had been drilled in two metal plates. Another worker hammered the open end of the rivets to meld the plates together. Note that the women wore slacks, which did not become popular generally until World War II.

The Hispanic woman at right posed for the photographer at Beeville, in southern Texas, in the early 1900s. Many Mexicans came to Texas then as the cattle industry began to give way to cotton farming.

Helene Abbott Sayre was one of the Chicago Urban League's first social workers from 1917 to 1932. Sayre, a Canadian by birth, was in her forties and married with four children when she started and had already pioneered the kindergarten program for African American students in the St. Louis, Missouri, schools. Her first League post was as a League liaison charged with the well-being of 600 African American women employed at Montgomery Ward's mail-order business. She helped black women succeed in their jobs and smoothed racial tensions among workers.

Seeking better jobs and higher pay, African Americans also found discrimination and prejudice. Racial tensions in some places led to lynchings. In the factory city of **East St. Louis**, Illinois, at least 39 African Americans were killed and as many as 6,000 left homeless after the burning of their neighborhood in a 1917 race riot.

Mexicans migrated to the Southwest.

A large wave of Mexican immigrants entered the United States between 1910 and 1921 for three main reasons. First, the completion of rail lines in northern Mexico in 1910 drew Mexican workers to the Southwest. Mexican labor played a key role in this region's emergence as an agricultural empire. Second, the Mexican Revolution in 1911 and the confusion and disorders before, during, and after the revolution drove many Mexicans to the United States in search of some means of earning a livelihood. Third, the U.S. wartime labor shortage brought an easing of immigration restrictions.

One of many thousands of new immigrants, Ernesto Galarza, came to Sacramento, California, with his mother and two uncles in 1911 when Ernesto was just six. Sacramento in 1911 was a melting pot of nationalities—Mexicans, Japanese, Koreans, Yugoslavs, Poles, and Irish, as well as many "home-grown Americans." "The Americanization of Mexican me was no smooth matter," Galarza later wrote. He described his first school there as "not so much a melting pot as a griddle where Miss Hopley [the principal] and her helpers warmed knowledge into us and roasted racial hatreds out of us." An Italian schoolmate helped Galarza get a job selling newspapers.

AN AMERICAN ★ SPEAKS

It was Matti also who pointed out that I could keep a copy of the *Union* to take home, the first regular newspaper we had in the house. At night I picked out words from the headlines and read them to whoever would listen. It was I who brought the headlines home that said an Austrian duke had been assassinated and that there was a war.

The Spanish influenza struck Sacramento in 1919, killing Galarza's mother and uncle. After working his way through high school and college, Galarza became a noted author and teacher. He also became a leading crusader in efforts to organize Mexicans and other farm workers.

The war brought new jobs and political power to women.

As war called men to the front, the labor potential of women became an important part of each nation's war effort. Much of the work fell within the area of volunteer labor—making bandages, knitting sweaters, planting victory gardens, or canning fruits and vegetables. However, demands for increased production also opened opportunities for women in industry. For example, women learned to rivet battleships, stitch wings for airplanes, and mix chemicals for explosives. They drove delivery trucks, loaded and unloaded ships, carried the mail, and served as streetcar conductors. As white women took advantage of new opportunities, African American women moved into jobs in department stores, meat-packing plants, and textile mills that had once been reserved for white workers.

Friction sometimes developed between men and women workers. In Bethlehem, Pennsylvania, where steelworkers had to put in a 13-hour day, machinists deliberately slowed down production to improve their bargaining position. The men were hostile toward women machinists who worked quickly.

Some wartime gains were later lost. However, the war did prove the potential strength of women as a skilled and semiskilled workforce.

Leaders of the women's suffrage movement had high hopes that the war would help women at last win political as well as economic equality. President Wilson had refused to support women's suffrage in 1913, but in 1918 he told Congress the women's suffrage amendment was "vital to the winning of the war." You will read about the success of the suffrage movement in the next chapter.

SECTION 3 REVIEW

Identify Key People and Terms
Write a sentence to identify: Bernard Baruch, Herbert Hoover, assembly line, Great Migration, Urban League

Locate Key Places
What city was the site of a violent race riot in 1917?

Master the Main Ideas

1. **Analyzing the economic impact of wars:** How did the new government agencies marshal U.S. economic resources for total war?
2. **Understanding contributions of racial and ethnic groups:** Why did African Americans migrate to the cities of the North and West during World War I?
3. **Understanding causes for immigration:** Why did Mexican Americans migrate to the U.S. Southwest between 1910 and 1921?
4. **Analyzing the economic impact of wars: (a)** How did the war affect women's job opportunities? **(b)** Their political power?

Apply Critical Thinking Skills: Analyzing Cause and Effect
Given Americans' longstanding fear of powerful governments and their tradition of laissez faire, how do you explain their willingness to accept wartime controls over the economy in 1917 and 1918?

World leaders debated the peace.

Key Terms: Fourteen Points, self-determination, reparations, League of Nations, mandate

Reading Preview

As you read this section, you will learn:

1. what kind of vision of the postwar world President Wilson offered.
2. where the Allies intervened to stop the spread of bolshevism.
3. what position Wilson finally took in regard to his Fourteen Points.
4. what kind of peace treaty was created at Versailles.
5. what action the U.S. Senate took regarding the peace treaty.

Allied war leaders met at Versailles in 1919 to write a treaty that would reconcile their opposing views. The Big Four, from left to right, are Britain's David Lloyd George, Italy's Vittorio Orlando, France's Georges Clemenceau, and the U.S. president, Woodrow Wilson.

When the war ended, President Wilson was the most popular and powerful leader in the world. Despite immense popularity, however, Wilson faced strong opposition at home, partly as a result of political blunders in the 1918 congressional elections. In October, while the

war was still being fought, the president had challenged the loyalty of the Republican opposition by appealing for the election of a Democratic majority. When the ballots were counted November 5, the Republicans had won control of both houses. Congress also deeply resented the president's war-magnified powers.

Though Wilson's party no longer commanded a majority of American voters, the Allies unanimously accepted him as their spokesperson in the armistice negotiations. Some of the Allies, however, seemed more interested in territorial gains than in creating a just and lasting peace.

President Wilson offered a new vision of the postwar world.

In his 1917 war message and after, Wilson held the United States somewhat apart from the Allies. This stemmed, to an extent, from his distrust of the Allies' war aims.

When the Bolsheviks seized power in Russia, they found and published secret treaties made in 1915 in which the Allies agreed to divide among themselves extensive territory and colonies of the Central Powers. In disclosing the selfish motives of the Allies, the Bolsheviks challenged war-weary Europeans to end the fighting and join together in a worldwide communist revolution.

The Bolshevik appeal prompted Wilson to issue his own war objectives on January 8, 1918. Wilson's **Fourteen Points**, the list of war aims he presented to Congress, were designed to seize the initiative from the Bolsheviks. Wilson stressed that U.S. policies were based on "the principle of justice to all peoples and nationalities, and their right to live on equal terms of liberty and safety with one another, whether they be strong or weak."

Points one through five provided a general context for lasting peace: no secret treaties, freedom of the seas, removal of trade barriers, reduction of armaments, and the adjustment of colonial claims based partly on the interests of the people of the colonies. Points six through thirteen addressed particular situations in Europe: return of Alsace-Lorraine to France and self-determination in central Europe, the Balkans, and the remnants of the Ottoman Empire. By **self-determination**, Wilson meant the right of an ethnic group to determine what form of government it should have, without reference to the wishes of any other nation. The Fourteenth Point called for a league of nations that would afford "mutual guarantees of political independence and territorial integrity to great and small states alike."

The Allies intervened in Russia to stop the spread of bolshevism.

Article six of Wilson's Fourteen Points called for the evacuation of and nonintervention in Russia. Soon after Wilson's speech, the new Russian government signed a peace treaty with Germany at the Russian city of Brest-Litovsk in March 1918. Under the terms of the treaty, Russia lost about one-third of its population and one-fourth of its territory.

As the final stages of the war disrupted governments in Europe and Asia, however, the Allies feared the spread of bolshevism, especially into western Europe. Accordingly, the British and French governments decided to intervene in Russia against the Bolshevik regime. After much anguish, Wilson cooperated with the Allies. American troops originally went in to aid 20,000 Czech and Slovak soldiers trapped in the Russian region of Siberia. Wilson also wanted to keep an eye on the Japanese, who had moved into eastern Siberia, and protect Allied military supplies at the Russian ports of Archangel and Vladivostok. Wilson's intervention did little to improve the U.S.–Russian relationship, a relationship that would come to dominate the 20th century.

President Wilson compromised on many of his Fourteen Points.

While Allied forces waited out their first long winter in northern Russia, their representatives gathered in Paris to discuss the peace. Wilson sailed for France in December 1918, the first time that an American president had gone to Europe while in office. No senators and no leading Republicans were among the American delegates.

WILSON'S FOURTEEN POINTS

1. An end to all secret diplomacy

2. Freedom of the seas in peace and war

3. The removal of trade barriers among nations

4. The general reduction of armaments

5. The adjustment of colonial claims in the interest of the inhabitants as well as of the colonial power

6. The evacuation of Russian territory and the independent determination by Russia of its own national policies

7. The restoration of Belgium

8. The evacuation of all French territory and return of Alsace-Lorraine

9. The readjustment of Italian boundaries along clearly recognizable lines of nationality

10. Independence for various national groups in Austria-Hungary

11. The restoration of the Balkan nations and free access to the sea for Serbia

12. Protection for minorities in Turkey and the free passage of the ships of all nations through the Dardanelles

13. Independence for Poland, including access to the sea

14. A general association of nations to protect "mutual guarantees of political independence and territorial integrity to great and small states alike"

When the peace conference opened in January 1919, Austria-Hungary had crumbled as Poland, Czechoslovakia, Yugoslavia, and Hungary declared their independence. Amid the ruins of the Russian Empire, Finland and the Baltic States—Estonia, Latvia, and Lithuania—also asserted their independence. Finally Arabs revolted from Ottoman rule as well with the help of Great Britain and France.

Although 32 nations were represented at the peace conference, the major decisions were made by the leaders of the four strongest nations. Called the Big Four, they were Wilson, David Lloyd George of Great Britain, Georges Clemenceau of France, and Vittorio Orlando of

chart study

Wilson's Fourteen Points were idealistic and offended some Allied leaders. Which point was most important to Wilson, and why? **Critical Thinking** Which points do you think might offend some of the Allies? Which would appeal to separate ethnic groups seeking identity as a nation?

Regions
Compare boundaries on this map with those on page 417. What are the new or reorganized nations?

Critical Thinking
Why might German losses shown on the map lead to future conflicts?

Italy. The peace conference met at the Palace of Versailles [ver sī'], outside Paris.

Clemenceau carried strong memories of the humiliating defeat of France by Germany in 1871. Nicknamed "the Tiger," he was determined to prevent Germany from ever again invading his nation. Lloyd George, fresh from his victory in the first British parliamentary elections in eight years, came to Paris determined to exact heavy reparations from Germany. **Reparations** are payments made by a defeated country to compensate for war damages. Italy joined the Allies in 1915 because of the promise of territorial gains. Orlando came to Paris to secure the gains his country had been promised.

Wilson quickly learned that the European leaders wanted to pursue their own national interests rather than a peace based on the Fourteen Points. Their main concerns were territorial gains and reparations. Wilson's goals, as expressed in the Fourteen Points, were the self-determination of peoples, free trade, and, above all, the creation of a **League of Nations**. Wilson was confident that the League would correct any injustices of the peace treaty. Every compromise he made on other issues intensified his commitment. He demanded that the Covenant, or constitution, of the League be written into the peace treaty with Germany and threatened to make a separate peace with Germany unless the Allies agreed.

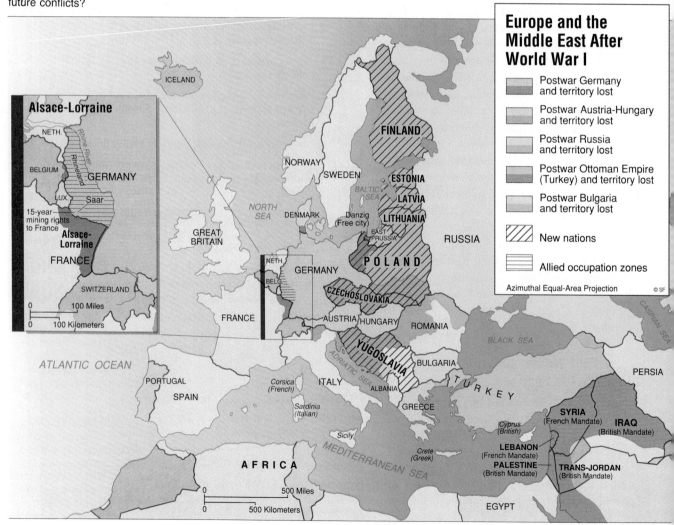

Europe and the Middle East After World War I

- Postwar Germany and territory lost
- Postwar Austria-Hungary and territory lost
- Postwar Russia and territory lost
- Postwar Ottoman Empire (Turkey) and territory lost
- Postwar Bulgaria and territory lost
- New nations
- Allied occupation zones

Azimuthal Equal-Area Projection

THE VERSAILLES TREATY
Skill: Formulating Appropriate Questions

Introducing the Skill. In an effort to overcome U.S. Senate opposition to the Versailles Treaty, President Wilson invited all members of the Senate Foreign Relations Committee to meet at the White House. At the conference the senators had an opportunity to ask questions and present any concerns they had about the treaty. If you were one of the senators, what questions might you have asked?

Learning the Skill. As you learned earlier, **formulating appropriate questions** means asking questions that fit both your task or purpose and your source of information. To come up with questions that serve these needs, you might follow these five steps:
1. Identify and define clearly the topic or subject of interest.
2. Identify and define clearly your purpose or task.
3. Determine what the given information might reveal to you.
4. Brainstorm to identify specific questions that will provide answers directly related both to your purpose and to your given information.
5. Select those questions most likely to help you achieve your purpose and for which the given information appears best suited.

Applying the Skill. Imagine that you are one of the senators meeting with President Wilson at the White House in 1919. Your purpose is to determine what U.S. membership in the League of Nations would mean for the country and for your constituents, many of whom are tired of foreign involvements. Your specific concerns relate to Article ten of the League covenant, which pledges member nations to defend any League member whose territory or independence is threatened. Formulate a list of at least five questions to ask of President Wilson.

The Versailles Treaty contained serious flaws.

Wilson won inclusion of the Covenant in the Versailles Treaty. However, the treaty was written hurriedly and contained grave weaknesses.

Despite Wilson's efforts, the Allies insisted on the harsh punishment of Germany. The treaty exacted massive reparations, returned Alsace-Lorraine to France, and gave France mining rights in the **Saar Valley**, a mineral-rich border region. However, Wilson held firm that Germany's colonies should not go to the Allies. Instead, these lands as well as parts of the Ottoman Empire would be administered as separate mandates by one of the Allies on behalf of the League. A **mandate** is a territory or colony taken from defeated nations and placed under the control of the victors. Open Door policies were to apply in all of the mandated territories.

The peacemakers also wanted the treaty to guard against the spread of bolshevism into Germany, which was Lenin's immediate goal. As a result, the peacemakers distorted Wilson's principle of self-determination to create a "quarantine zone" between Russian bolshevism and the nations of western Europe. New nations formed much of Russia's western border, as you can see on the map opposite. Boundaries of the new nations were hastily drawn on the basis of ethnic groupings and historic claims. No one thought about their future economic stability or the defensibility of their borders. The consequences of the war placed especially heavy burdens on these small, new nations.

The Senate rejected the peace treaty.

While Wilson was in Paris, opposition mounted at home. The Republican-controlled Senate needed to approve any treaty, but Wilson did

437

League of Nations

Point	Counterpoint
Proponents of the League of Nations	**Opponents of the League of Nations**
■ League will resolve world problems without war ■ League will guarantee self-determination of peoples	■ League will involve the United States in others' wars ■ Only Congress can authorize U.S. wars

little to involve the Senate Republicans.

The Senate split into three groups. **Henry Cabot Lodge**, head of the Senate committee on foreign relations, led the largest group, the reservationists as they were usually called. Lodge, like Wilson an able historian, had developed reservations (meaning "amendments") to the treaty. His chief objection was that Article ten of the Covenant, guaranteeing the "territorial integrity and existing political independence" of members of the League, might commit American troops to war. Another group, mostly Republicans, earned the name Irreconcilables because they saw no reason for the United States to be involved in European affairs, in the defense of colonial empires. A third group, mostly Democrats, supported the treaty.

Wilson decided to appeal directly to the people. In early September 1919, he boarded a special train to begin an ambitious speaking tour—9,500 miles with speeches in 29 cities. He brought out huge crowds to hear his arguments on the League. The effort proved too much for his health. On September 25th he collapsed in Pueblo, Colorado, and returned to Washington. There he soon suffered a serious stroke. Half-paralyzed, Wilson lay so ill that he could carry on few of his duties. Edith Galt Wilson, the president's strong-willed second wife, controlled access to the sick room.

Lodge proposed that the Senate accept the treaty with reservations about defending other League members and requiring congressional approval of a president's commitments to the League. Wilson rigidly refused any changes. Raising himself from his sick bed, he whispered "Let Lodge compromise!"

Wilson's supporters opposed the treaty with the Lodge reservations. Lodge's supporters opposed the treaty without the reservations. The Irreconcilables opposed the treaty either way. On November 19, 1919, the Senate defeated the treaty with the Lodge reservations by votes of 39 to 55 and 41 to 50 and then defeated the unamended version of the treaty by 38 to 53. The treaty with reservations came up for a vote again in March 1920. This time the treaty did win a majority, 49 to 35, but approval required a two-thirds vote. The United States would not join the League. Congress terminated the war by joint resolution. The League began to operate in 1920 without U.S. membership.

SECTION 4 REVIEW

Identify Key People and Terms
Write a sentence to identify: Fourteen Points, self-determination, reparations, League of Nations, mandate, Henry Cabot Lodge

Locate Key Places
In which region of Germany did France gain mining rights?

Master the Main Ideas

1. **Understanding historic documents:** How did Wilson's new vision of the postwar world differ from that of the Allies?
2. **Understanding U.S. foreign policy:** Why did the Allies fear the spread of bolshevism?
3. **Understanding historic documents:** How did the peace aims of European leaders differ from Wilson's Fourteen Points?
4. **Understanding international conflicts:** Why was the Versailles Treaty seriously flawed?
5. **Understanding international conflicts:** Why did the U.S. Senate fail to ratify the Versailles Treaty?

Apply Critical Thinking Skills: Analyzing Cause and Effect
To what extent were the seeds of future wars contained in the Versailles Treaty?

Theme Essay:
Americans drew back from world leadership.

Key Terms: isolationism

Reading Preview
   As you read this section, you will learn:

1. what factors encouraged U.S. optimism.
2. on what principles Wilson hoped to rebuild the world.
3. what position Americans took concerning a binding commitment to world peace.

The 50 years from the end of the Civil War in 1865 to World War I have been called "the confident years." During that half century, the nation became a powerful industrial giant with a leading role in world affairs.

Economic growth and political reform encouraged U.S. optimism.

The editor and author **Herbert Croly** wrote an influential book in 1909, *The Promise of American Life*. Although the book was not a popular success, it apparently inspired both Theodore Roosevelt's New Nationalism and Woodrow Wilson's New Freedom. The keynote of Croly's book was, for Americans, "that the future will have something better in store for them individually and collectively than has the past or the present."

During those 50 years, Americans' experience often justified confidence, and that period strengthened many of the positive themes you have read about in your study of American history. The pace of growth was remarkable, whether measured by population increase, miles of railroad track, or bushels of wheat. Technology produced the skyscraper, streetcar, electric light, and telephone, transforming the way Americans worked and lived. Opportunities seemed without parallel.

For Croly, economic opportunity was only half of the picture. The United States was also for him the Land of Democracy. Yet politics after the Civil War often seemed to call into question the health of democracy in America. Corruption in government, the degeneration of the Senate into a rich man's club, and the rise of political bosses, together with underlying social and economic changes, led to cries for reform. Reform came, in the years after 1900. Charismatic political figures—William Jennings Bryan, Theodore Roosevelt, Robert M. La Follette, Woodrow Wilson—led the way. They pushed through laws intended to regulate big business, curb corruption, protect workers and consumers, and increase the people's control over political processes. The idea of progress—that people, through rational effort, could improve themselves and their world—became so central to Americans' thinking that people today describe those hopeful years as the Progressive Era.

Childe Hassam's painting of a wet, flag-filled city street on Flag Day, 1917, seems to herald the beginning of the end to the confident years. Americans did feel patriotic pride and confidence during the country's first year as a participant in the war, but also a sense of loss for the fallen. Hassam studied in Paris and used the Impressionist technique of conveying light with strokes of pure, bright color.

Woodrow Wilson hoped to rebuild the world on American principles.

Roosevelt, La Follette, Wilson, and others all appealed to Americans' ideals in their campaigns for progressive reform, and Wilson invoked the same ideals in calling for war. Wilson knew that the nation was unlikely to go to war just to protect American commerce with the Allies. He sought to justify it in noble terms. Accordingly, he presented the war as one to make the world "safe for democracy," as a righteous crusade for justice, liberty, and peace. Americans accepted Wilson's view that the United States had a unique destiny to fulfill among the nations of the world community and responded to his appeal based on moral issues.

For those who believed that rational, civilized people had outgrown war, the war itself was a disillusioning experience. For others, the wartime suppression of civil liberties called into question their belief in democratic principles. For many Americans, however, disillusionment stemmed from the contrast between the lofty idealism expounded by Wilson and the selfishness and greed of the Allies at Versailles. The war to make the world safe for democracy really turned out to be a war for the victorious Allies to take territory from their defeated enemies and to force a change of colonial masters in Africa and Asia.

Americans rejected a binding commitment to world peace.

Historians have frequently attacked Wilson's lofty idealism. If he had been willing to compromise, they argue, he could have won U.S. membership in the League of Nations, thereby forestalling future wars. Yet the president was a realist as well as an idealist, in the opinion of Walter LaFeber, a noted historian of American foreign policy. "Indeed," LaFeber wrote,

> *Wilson has become the most influential architect of twentieth-century U.S. foreign policy in part because he so eloquently clothed the bleak skeleton of U.S. self-interest in the attractive garb of idealism.*

Moreover, LaFeber believes, U.S. membership in the League would not have removed the threat of future wars. Enormous problems were inherent in the boundaries, mandates, and reparations agreed to at Versailles.

The first public criticisms of the Versailles Treaty had come from a newly formed peace organization led by Jane Addams, the Women's International League for Peace and Freedom

The first woman member of the U.S. House of Representatives, Jeannette Rankin, continued to oppose U.S. involvement in wars after her historic vote against Wilson's war resolution in 1917. Rankin, who was then a progressive Republican, lost her House seat in 1919 and was defeated in a bid for the Senate as a member of the newly organized National party. However, she continued her pacifist campaigning as an official of the Women's International League for Peace and Freedom. She is shown here in 1932 several years before being re-elected to Congress from Montana as a Republican pacifist.

(WILPF). While Wilson and the Allies hammered out the peace treaty, women from all over the world established the WILPF at the city of Zurich in **Switzerland**. That small, mountainous country was a fitting home for an organization committed to ending war. The Swiss had pledged their country in the early 1500s to permanent neutrality in the European wars that raged around it.

Although highly critical of the Versailles Treaty, Addams and Emily Greene Balch, another prominent member of WILPF, strongly favored the League of Nations and hoped to shape its development. Balch, an economist, had been fired from her post at Wellesley College for her outspoken pacifist views. Addams in 1931 and Balch in 1946 became the first American women to win the Nobel Peace Prize.

American voters had an opportunity to endorse or reject membership in the League in the presidential election of 1920, about which you will read in the next chapter. Wilson himself had suggested that the election should be a "great and solemn referendum" on the League, and that Americans should show their support by voting for his party, the Democrats.

As that election approached, members of WILPF campaigned vigorously for the League. They looked forward to voting for the first time for the office of president and hoped the women's vote would make a difference in the outcome. It did not. Even more emphatically than the U.S. Senate, American voters rejected the League of Nations. The Republicans walked away with 16 million votes to a mere 9 million for the Democrats. Tired of war, Americans drew back from any binding commitment to maintain the peace.

Though Americans rejected membership in the League, they did not retreat into total isolationism. Under a policy of **isolationism**, a nation avoids both political alliances and economic relationships with other nations. The United States did retreat from center stage in its diplomatic relations, yet it continued to promote both political and economic expansion. In the years ahead, as in decades past, American business and political leaders were quick to apply the principles of the Monroe Doctrine in the Western Hemisphere and the policy of the Open Door in Africa and Asia.

"Our isolation was ended 20 years ago," President Wilson, far left, declared as he presented the Treaty of Versailles to the Senate. "The only question is whether we can refuse the moral leadership that is offered, whether we shall accept or reject the confidence of the world." Wilson was photographed in Los Angeles, California, as he carried his fight to promote the League of Nations to the people in 1919. The president attracted cheering crowds wherever he went, but after 34 major speeches, he collapsed in Pueblo, Colorado, and was forced to give up his tour.

SECTION **5** REVIEW

Identify Key People and Terms
Write a sentence to identify: Herbert Croly, isolationism

Locate Key Places
What geographic factors might have influenced Switzerland's policy of permanent neutrality?

Master the Main Ideas

1. **Examining economic and cultural influences:** How did economic growth and political reform encourage American optimism before World War I?
2. **Understanding U.S. foreign affairs:** To what extent did Wilson succeed in his attempt to rebuild the world on American principles?
3. **Analyzing U.S. foreign policy:** Why did the women's vote make little difference in winning U.S. acceptance of a binding commitment to world peace?

Apply Critical Thinking Skills: Recognizing Values
In view of President Wilson's willingness to consult with Congress at the very beginning of his presidency, how do you account for his inability to compromise concerning the Versailles Treaty?

Arshile Gorky Is Haunted by Armenia's Sufferings

10A

TIME FRAME
Late 1920s

GEOGRAPHIC SETTING
New York City

Before World War I, the Christian Armenians who lived within the boundaries of the Ottoman Empire had been subject to periodic persecutions by their Muslim rulers. Widespread massacres in the mid-1890s prompted the first large-scale emigration to the United States. When World War I broke out, this emigration was virtually halted; and in 1915 the Ottoman government—which had joined the Central Powers and claimed that its Armenian subjects supported the Allies—began to massacre and deport the Armenians. Exactly how many died is difficult to estimate; but according to Armenian American writer Michael Arlen, in his book *Passage to Ararat,* "it is possible to say, not precisely but with a general respect for accuracy and plausibility, that in the course of the 1915–1916 massacres and deportations close to a million Armenians—more than half the Armenian population of Turkey—disappeared;

which is to say were killed, outright by police or soldiers, or by roadside massacres, or by forced marches, or by starvation, or by sickness, or by conditions in the concentration camps." On August 31, 1915, the Turkish Minister of the Interior reported to his German allies, "The Armenian problem no longer exists."

Among the Armenians who survived the Turkish massacres was Vosdanig Adoian (1904–1948), who emigrated to the United States in 1920. He eventually settled in New York City and became a painter, using the name Arshile Gorky [är'shĭl gôr'kē] (The Russian word *gorky* means "bitter.") As a recent study of Armenian Americans observed, "Gorky's art was always haunted by memories of his experiences in Armenia." Painted in the late 1920s, *The Artist and His Mother* reflects these experiences. Basing his painting on an old photograph, Gorky portrayed himself as a young boy standing beside his mother, her face a mask drained of feeling. (She had died of starvation in March 1918 after the family had fled from Turkey.) Gorky himself committed suicide when he was only 43 years old.

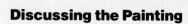

Discussing the Painting

1. In Arshile Gorky's *The Artist and His Mother,* what feeling is conveyed by the expression on the boy's face? on his mother's face?

2. Does the background of the two figures give any suggestion of place? Explain.

CRITICAL THINKING
Identifying Central Issues

The two figures in Arshile Gorky's painting, while positioned close together, still seem starkly separate. How does this separateness contribute to the dominant mood of the painting?

George M. Cohan Contributes to the War Effort

TIME FRAME
1917

GEOGRAPHIC SETTING
New York City

After the United States entered World War I in 1917, many artists, writers, and actors were pressed into service to publicize the American cause. The main contribution to America's war effort by actor, playwright, and composer George M. Cohan (1878–1942) was the song "Over There." Performed by famous singers at Liberty Bond rallies and used as a marching song by the troops of the American Expeditionary force, the popularity of "Over There," observes one literary historian, "showed that [Cohan] possessed an uncanny instinct for catching the exact vibrations of mass feeling." The word *Hun* (line 18) was a term of abuse for the enemy that was widely used during the war in the English-speaking Allied countries. *Tanks* (line 22) is short for *tank-towns,* very small towns, composed of little more than a railroad water tank.

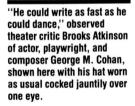

"He could write as fast as he could dance," observed theater critic Brooks Atkinson of actor, playwright, and composer George M. Cohan, shown here with his hat worn as usual cocked jauntily over one eye.

Over There

Johnnie get your gun, get your gun, get
    your gun,
Take it on the run, on the run, on
    the run;
Hear them calling you and me;
Every son of liberty.
5 Hurry right away, no delay, go today,
Make your daddy glad, to have had
    such a lad,
Tell your sweetheart not to pine,
To be proud her boy's in line.

Chorus:
Over there, over there,
10 Send the word, send the word over
    there,
That the Yanks are coming, the Yanks
    are coming,
The drums rum-tumming everywhere.
So prepare, say a prayer,
Send the word, send the word to
    beware,
15 We'll be over, we're coming over,
And we won't come back till it's over
    over there.

Johnnie get your gun, get your gun, get
    your gun,
Johnnie show the Hun, you're a
    son-of-a-gun,
Hoist the flag and let her fly,
20 Like true heroes do or die.

Pack your little kit, show your grit, do
    your bit,
Soldiers to the ranks from the towns
    and the tanks,
Make your mother proud of you,
And to liberty be true.

Discussing the Reading

1. What different kinds of emotional appeals did George M. Cohan use in "Over There"?

2. What kinds of sound devices did he employ to create the song's overall mood? What is this mood?

CRITICAL THINKING
Making Comparisons

As an expression of patriotic sentiment, how did "Over There" differ from "The Ballad of Jane McCrea" (Source Reading 2F)? Upon what did each song base its appeal to patriotism?

Saying farewell to wives and sweethearts, the soldiers of New York's famous "Fighting 69th" Regiment, formed primarily of Irish Americans, are shown in October 1917 boarding the train that will take them to their transport ship.

Shirley Millard Serves Behind the Lines

TIME FRAME
1918

GEOGRAPHIC SETTING
France

Throughout most of 1918, Shirley Millard served as a nurse at a French army hospital near the front lines. Because she spoke French, she also acted as an interpreter for the English-speaking wounded. The hospital was a makeshift affair in a beautiful old chateau. It held 3,500 cots, which at times were completely filled with wounded men. Sometimes after heavy fighting, men might wait outside on stretchers for as long as three days before attendants could make room for them inside. While most of the patients were French or British, there were Arabs, Zouaves (members of some regiments in the French army usually stationed in North Africa), Senegalese, a number of Americans, and many Germans. The first diary entry was written shortly after Shirley Millard joined the hospital staff. The last entries were written just before the war ended.

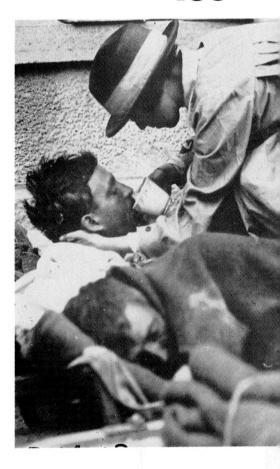

Tenderly cradling the head of a badly wounded British soldier, an American Red Cross volunteer gives him water on the platform of a railroad station in France.

April 1st
The big drive is over and the terrific rush has stopped, at least temporarily, but the hospital is still filled.

5 Most of the men are too badly wounded to be moved, although we need the space, for we are swamped with influenza cases. I thought influenza was a bad cold, something like the grippe, but this is much 10 worse than that. These men run a high temperature, so high that we can't believe it's true, and often take it again to be sure. It is accompanied by vomiting and dysentery. When they die, as about half of them 15 do, they turn a ghastly dark gray and are taken out at once and cremated.

November 8th
More and more Americans in the death 20 ward [a ward where dying cases are quartered]. Gas cases are terrible. They cannot breathe lying down or sitting up. They just struggle for breath, but nothing can be done . . . their lungs are gone. . . . [Some 25 are] covered with first degree burns. We try to relieve them by pouring oil on them. They cannot be bandaged or even touched. We cover them with a tent of propped-up sheets. Gas burns must be ag- 30 onizing because usually the other cases do not complain even with the worst of wounds. But gas cases invariably are beyond endurance and they cannot help crying out. . . .

35 November 10th
Charley [an American sergeant who was almost completely paralyzed] died this morning. I held his hand as he went and could not keep back the tears. Near the

This shattered church in the ruins of the French town of Neuvilly furnished temporary shelter for the Americans wounded on the first day of the offensive in the Meuse-Argonne in September 1918. Lasting six weeks, the battle eventually cost 117,000 American casualties.

end he saw me crying and patted my hand with his two living fingers to comfort me. I cannot describe that boy's sweetness. He took part of my heart with him. Everybody around the place was in tears.

Just after he went someone came into the ward and said: "Armistice! The staff cars have just passed by the gate on their way to Senlis to sign an Armistice!"

What a time and place to come in shouting about an Armistice! I said: "Sh! Sh!"

There is no armistice for Charley or for any of the others in that ward. One of the boys began to sob. I went and talked soothingly to him, but what could I say, knowing he would die before night?

Well, it's over. I have to keep telling myself, it's over, it's over, it's over.

But there is still that letter to write to Charley's mother. I can hear commotion and shouting through the hospital as I write this. The chapel bell is ringing wildly.

I am glad it is over, but my heart is heavy as lead. Must write that letter.

One of the girls came looking for me. They have opened champagne for the staff in the dining hall. I told her to get out.

Can't seem to pull myself together.

Discussing the Reading

1. What epidemic added to the hospital's case load? From Shirley Millard's reaction to these cases, what can you infer about the character of this epidemic?

2. What was Millard's reaction to news of the Armistice?

CRITICAL THINKING
Expressing Problems

Why were the gas cases so terrible? Do you think the use of poison gas in war is any worse than using conventional weapons? Why or why not?

Chapter Summary

Write supporting details under each of the following main ideas as you review the chapter.

Section 1
1. Worldwide peace movements gained popularity in the early 1900s.
2. Two opposing alliances emerged in Europe to create a balance of power.
3. The shooting of an Austrian prince ignited war in 1914.
4. Americans struggled to remain neutral in the early years of the war.
5. Geography ruled out a swift victory on land and at sea.

Section 2
1. Germany's U-boat campaign pushed America into war.
2. Americans united to support the war effort.
3. The United States needed to raise, train, and equip an army.
4. The U.S. Navy ferried a huge army across dangerous waters.
5. U.S. troops turned the tide in France.

Section 3
1. New government agencies marshaled U.S. economic resources for war.
2. The promise of jobs attracted African Americans to the North and West.
3. Mexicans migrated to the Southwest.
4. The war brought new jobs and political power to women.

Section 4
1. President Wilson offered a new vision of the postwar world.
2. The Allies intervened in Russia to stop the spread of bolshevism.
3. President Wilson compromised on many of his Fourteen Points.
4. The Versailles Treaty contained serious flaws.
5. The Senate rejected the peace treaty.

Section 5
1. Economic growth and political reform encouraged U.S. optimism.
2. Woodrow Wilson hoped to rebuild the world on American principles.
3. Americans rejected a binding commitment to world peace.

Chapter Themes

1. **Religious and ethical framework:** Many Americans hoped the United States would not become involved in World War I for a variety of religious and ethical reasons. Their reasons ranged from personal religious convictions to a general belief that people of the Western Hemisphere ought to hold themselves aloof from European quarrels.
2. **Relations with other nations:** Woodrow Wilson expressed a growing American belief that the United States should participate in World War I in order to preserve democratic ideals for Americans and for all other peoples of the world.

Chapter Study Guide

Identifying Key People and Terms

Name the key person or key term that describes the:
1. intense feeling of patriotism or the desire and plans for national independence
2. members of a minority socialist party led by Lenin; also called communists
3. World War I head of industrial mobilization
4. first mass movement of African Americans to northern and western cities
5. list of war aims outlined by Woodrow Wilson

Locating Key Places

1. Where was the last major offensive of World War I?
2. Where did France gain mining rights after the war?

Mastering the Main Ideas

1. **(a)** What two alliance systems emerged in Europe before 1914? **(b)** What issues created conflict between the major powers?
2. **(a)** Why was it important for the British and Americans to insist on freedom to use Atlantic shipping lanes? **(b)** Why was it just as important for the German navy to deny free use of the seas?
3. How did the war affect the economic fortunes of African Americans, Hispanic Americans, and women?
4. Why did the U.S. Senate defeat the Treaty of Versailles?
5. How widely accepted were Woodrow Wilson's plans for preserving world peace?

1914	1915	1916	1917	1918	1919

1914
World War I begins

1916
Verdun: French lose 540,000, Germans 430,000

1917
Submarine warfare resumes; U.S. declares war; Russian Revolution begins; AEF wins last offensive at Meuse-Argonne

1918
Worldwide flu epidemic strikes; Armistice declared November 11

1919
Senate defeats Versailles treaty

Applying Critical Thinking Skills

1. **Identifying assumptions:** What false assumptions did Woodrow Wilson have about the American people when he went to Versailles to participate in treaty talks?
2. **Recognizing values:** Briefly describe the values of two groups concerning World War I. One group opposes war because it will benefit only the ruling classes, another opposes war on religious grounds. Explain how their values conflict or agree.
3. **Determining relevant information:** Which of these statements *does not* describe a cause of World War I? Explain your answer:
   (a) The countries of Europe suffered from an excess of nationalistic spirit.
   (b) Several European political leaders believed that the balance of military power had tipped their way.
   (c) The communists seized power in Russia.

Chapter Activities

Learning Geography Through History

1. What nations were collectively known as the "powder keg of Europe"?
2. Which northern cities in the United States acquired significant numbers of African Americans because of the Great Migration?

Relating the United States to the World

1. What role did most Americans want the United States to have in the international community after World War I?
2. How did the United States show its attitude toward the Bolshevik regime in Russia at the end of World War I?

Using the Time Line

1. Which events on the time line had causes other than the war in Europe?
2. How many years did the United States participate in the war?

Linking Past to Present

1. What present-day international organization parallels the League of Nations?
2. What present-day eastern European nations emerged from the Austro-Hungarian Empire, Serbia, and Montenegro?

Practicing Critical Thinking Strategies

Formulating a Question
Formulate a question that would lead to a deeper understanding of the competing arguments about U.S. entry into World War I.

Learning More About the Great War

1. **Using Source Readings:** Read the Source Readings for this chapter and answer the questions.
2. **Writing a letter:** Imagine that you are Alvin York writing a letter home from Europe to your sweetheart. Express your feelings about your religious convictions, your patriotism, your fear of chemical weapons, your feelings about being far from home and facing death each day.
3. **Holding a debate:** Divide the class into two groups. One group should argue on behalf of Woodrow Wilson's concept of a postwar world, including the Versailles Treaty and the League of Nations. Another group should argue on behalf of Henry Cabot Lodge and his concept of America's role in the postwar period.

A FARM GIRL DOES A MAN'S WORK

Like Jim Burden, the narrator of her novel *My Ántonia* (1918), Willa Cather moved as a child to the vast, empty prairies of frontier Nebraska. There she witnessed first-hand the brutalizing effects of pioneer life on many recent immigrants. In the following excerpt from *My Ántonia,* Jim describes the change in the heroine of the novel, a 15-year-old immigrant girl named Ántonia Shimerda [än′tōn ē′ä shi mėr′dä], when she is forced to do a man's work on the family farm after the suicide of her father.

When spring came, after that hard winter, one could not get enough of the nimble air. Every morning I wakened with a fresh consciousness that winter was over. There were none of the signs of spring for which I used to watch in Virginia, no budding woods or blooming gardens. There was only—spring itself; the throb of it, the light restlessness, the vital essence of it everywhere; in the sky, in the swift clouds, in the pale sunshine, and in the warm, high wind—rising suddenly, sinking suddenly, impulsive and playful like a big puppy that pawed you and then lay down to be petted. If I had been tossed down blindfold on that red prairie, I should have known that it was spring.

> I wakened with a fresh consciousness that winter was over.

Everywhere now there was the smell of burning grass. Our neighbors burned off their pasture before the new grass made a start, so that the fresh growth would not be mixed with the dead stand of last year. Those light, swift fires, running about the country, seemed a part of the same kindling that was in the air.

The Shimerdas were in their new log house by then. The neighbors had helped them to build it in March. It stood directly in front of their old cave, which they used as a cellar. The family were now fairly equipped to begin their struggle with the soil. They had four comfortable rooms to live in, a new windmill,—bought on credit,—a chicken-house and poultry. Mrs. Shimerda had paid grandfather ten dollars for a milk cow, and was to give him fifteen more as soon as they harvested their first crop.

When I rode up to the Shimerdas' one bright windy afternoon in April, Yulka [Ántonia's sister] ran out to meet me. It was to her, now, that I gave reading lessons; Ántonia was busy with other things. I tied my pony and went into the kitchen where Mrs. Shimerda was baking bread, chewing poppy seeds as she worked. By this time she could speak enough English to ask me a great many questions about what our men were doing in the fields. She seemed to think that my elders withheld helpful information, and that from me she might get valuable secrets. On this occasion she asked very craftily when grandfather expected to begin planting corn. I told her, adding that he thought we should have a dry spring and that the corn would not be held back by too much rain, as it had been last year.

She gave me a shrewd glance. "He not Jesus," she blustered; "he not know about the wet and the dry."

I did not answer her; what was the use? As I sat waiting for the hour when Ambrosch [Ántonia's brother] and Ántonia would return from the fields, I watched Mrs. Shimerda at her work. She took from the oven a coffee-cake which she wanted to keep warm for supper, and wrapped it in a quilt stuffed with feathers. I have seen her put even a roast goose in this quilt to keep it hot. When the neighbors were there building the new house they saw her do this, and the story got abroad that the Shimerdas kept their food in their feather beds.

When the sun was dropping low, Ántonia came up the big south draw with her team. How much older she had grown in eight months! She had come to us a child, and now she was a tall, strong young girl, although her fifteenth birthday had just slipped by. I ran out

An excerpt from
MY ÁNTONIA
by Willa Cather

and met her as she brought her horses up to the windmill to water them. She wore the boots her father had so thoughtfully taken off before he shot himself, and his old fur cap. Her outgrown cotton dress switched about her calves, over the boot-tops. She kept her sleeves rolled up all day and her arms and throat were burned as brown as a sailor's. Her neck came up strongly out of her shoulders, like the bole of a tree out of the turf. One sees that drafthorse neck among the peasant women in all old countries.

She greeted me gayly, and began at once to tell me how much ploughing she had done that day. Ambrosch, she said, was on the north quarter, breaking sod with the oxen.

"Jim, you ask Jake [a farmhand who works for Burden's grandfather] how much he ploughed to-day. I don't want that Jake get more done in one day than me. I want we have very much corn this fall."

While the horses drew in the water, and nosed each other, and then drank again, Ántonia sat down on the windmill step and rested her head on her hand.

"You see the big prairie fire from your place last night? I hope your grandpa ain't lose no stacks?"

"No, we didn't. I came to ask you something, Tony. Grandmother wants to know if you can't go to the term of school that begins next week over at the sod schoolhouse. She says there's a good teacher, and you'd learn a lot."

Ántonia stood up, lifting and dropping her shoulders as if they were stiff. "I ain't got time to learn. I can work like mans now. My mother can't say no more how Ambrosch do all and nobody to help him. I can work as much as him. School is all right for little boys. I help make this land one good farm."

> I ain't got time to learn. I can work like mans now.

She clucked to her team and started for the barn. I walked beside her, feeling vexed. Was she going to grow up boastful like her mother, I wondered? Before we reached the stable, I felt something tense in her silence, and glancing up I saw that she was crying. She turned her face from me and looked off at the red streak of dying light, over the dark prairie.

I climbed up into the loft and threw down the hay for her, while she unharnessed her team. We walked slowly back toward the house. Ambrosch had come in from the north quarter, and was watering his oxen at the tank.

Ántonia took my hand. "Sometime you will tell me all those nice things you learn at the school, won't you, Jimmy?" she asked with a sudden rush of feeling in her voice. "My father, he went much to school. He know a great deal; how to make the fine cloth like what you not got here. He play horn and violin, and he read so many books that the priests in Bohemie [Bohemia; today part of Czechoslovakia] come to talk to him. You won't forget my father, Jim?"

"No," I said, "I will never forget him."

Mrs. Shimerda asked me to stay for supper. After Ambrosch and Ántonia had washed the field dust from their hands and faces at the wash-basin by the kitchen door, we sat down at the oilcloth-covered table. Mrs. Shimerda ladled meal mush out of an iron pot and poured milk on it. After the mush we had fresh bread and sorghum molasses, and coffee with the cake that had been kept warm in the feathers. Ántonia and Ambrosch were talking in Bohemian; disputing about which of them had done more ploughing that day. Mrs. Shimerda egged them on, chuckling while she gobbled her food.

Presently Ambrosch said sullenly in English:

"You take them ox to-morrow and try the sod plough. Then you not be so smart."

His sister laughed. "Don't be mad. I know it's awful hard work for break sod. I milk the cow for you to-morrow, if you want."

Mrs. Shimerda turned quickly to me. "That cow not give so much milk like what your grandpa say. If he make talk about fifteen dollars, I send him back the cow."

"He doesn't talk about the fifteen dollars," I exclaimed indignantly. "He doesn't find fault with people."

"He say I break his saw when we build, and I never," grumbled Ambrosch.

I knew he had broken the saw, and then hid it and lied about it. I began to wish I had not stayed for supper. Everything was disagreeable to me. Ántonia ate so noisily now, like a man, and she yawned often at the table and kept stretching her arms over her head, as if they ached. Grandmother had said, "Heavy field work'll spoil that girl. She'll lose all her nice ways and get rough ones." She had lost them already.

After supper I rode home through the sad, soft spring twilight. Since winter I had seen very little of Ántonia. She was out in the fields from sun-up until sun-down. If I rode over to see her where she was plough-ing, she stopped at the end of the row to chat for a moment, then gripped her plough-handles, clucked to her team, and waded on down the furrow, making me feel that she was now grown up and had no time for me. On Sun-days she helped her mother make garden or sewed all day.

> Heavy field work'll spoil that girl.

Grandfather was pleased with Ántonia. When we complained of her, he only smiled and said, "She will help some fellow get ahead in the world."

Nowadays Tony could talk of nothing but the prices of things, or how much she could lift and endure. She was too proud of her strength. I knew, too, that Ambrosch put upon her some chores a girl ought not to do, and that the farm-hands around the country joked in a nasty way about it. Whenever I saw her come up the fur-row, shouting to her beasts, sunburned, sweaty, her dress open at the neck, and her throat and chest dust-plastered, I used to think of the tone in which poor Mr. Shimerda, who could say so little, yet managed to say so much when he exclaimed, "My Ántonia!"

After I began to go to the country school, I saw less of the Bohemians. We were sixteen pupils at the sod school-house, and we all came on horseback and brought our dinner. My school-mates were none of them very in-teresting, but I somehow felt that, by making comrades of them, I was getting even with Ántonia for her indifference. Since the father's death, Am-brosch was more than ever the head of the house, and he seemed to direct the feelings as well as the fortunes of his women-folk. Ántonia often quoted his opinions to me, and she let me see that she admired him, while she thought of me only as a little boy. Before the spring was over, there was a distinct coldness between us and the Shimerdas. . . .

CRITICAL THINKING
Identifying Assumptions
What seems to be Jim Bur-den's attitude toward the change he notes in Ántonia? What assumptions about the different types of work appropriate to men and women does this attitude reflect?

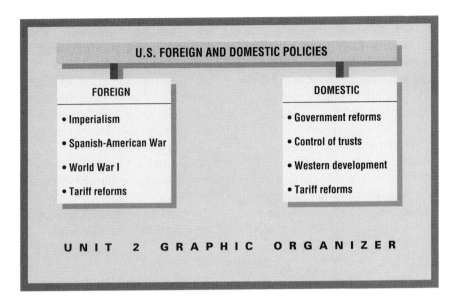

U.S. FOREIGN AND DOMESTIC POLICIES

FOREIGN	DOMESTIC
• Imperialism	• Government reforms
• Spanish-American War	• Control of trusts
• World War I	• Western development
• Tariff reforms	• Tariff reforms

UNIT 2 GRAPHIC ORGANIZER

Reform also came to state and national governments. For example, at the state level, Wisconsin reformers developed the direct primary in an effort to make the political process more democratic. At the national level, Theodore Roosevelt pushed through new laws banning impure foods and providing for government meat inspection.

The West became a significant political force. Hunger for land brought Americans west, and irrigation and conservation became key issues in the development of these dry lands. A battle over conservation racked the presidency of William Howard Taft, who succeeded Roosevelt in 1909. Finally, a split in the Republican party opened the door to a Democratic victory for Woodrow Wilson in 1912.

C H A P T E R
S U R V E Y

The Progressive Era
1900–1917

In 1900 Americans began to make much-needed changes in society. Many Americans called themselves reformers or progressives in the period from 1900 to 1917, known as the Progressive Era. Crusading journalists — the muckrakers — wrote story after story challenging corrupt city bosses as well as the rich and powerful in the land. The progressives proposed that experts collect facts, study society, and provide solutions to its problems. Although most Americans remained blind to the plight of African Americans, the Niagara Movement in 1905 stirred some progressives to fight for racial equality.

Reformers changed city, state, and national governments. Even before the Progressive Era began, reformers applied pressure to clean up city governments and root out the causes of urban ills. To make city government both honest and efficient, progressives introduced two new forms of city government — the commission system, and the city-manager plan.

Woodrow Wilson fulfilled the progressives' aims. A scholar and an idealist, President Woodrow Wilson translated progressive goals into federal law. Wilson reformed the tariff, redirected monetary policies, and further restricted the trusts. The entry of the United States into the European war in 1917, however, brought the Progressive Era to a close.

America's Rise to World Power
1890–1914

Americans turned from continental expansion to look overseas. "The frontier has gone," said American historian Frederick Jackson Turner in 1893, "and with its going has closed the first period of American history." With these words, the noted historian looked back on a century of U.S. continental expansion. Others looked ahead toward an empire overseas. William H. Seward, secretary of state under Lincoln, had dreamed of such an empire and purchased Alaska in 1867 as a steppingstone to Asia. Seward also handled French interference in Mexico forcefully. He told the French puppet emperor, Maximilian, to get out of Mexico and sent American troops to the Mexican border to enforce his demand. Troops under Benito Juárez, president of the Republic of Mexico, deposed Maximilian and executed him.

Traders and missionaries had spread U.S. influence in Latin America, Asia, and Africa. Now, with a modern, well-equipped navy, Americans began to look overseas with greater ambitions.

The Spanish-American War brought America to world power. Sensational accounts in the U.S. press had fanned flames of revolt against Spanish colonial rule in Cuba. The resulting conflict, the Spanish-American War, brought the United States new holdings in the Caribbean and the western Pacific, most notably, the Philippines.

American opinion was sharply divided on the question of annexing the Philippines. In the end, the U.S. Senate approved annexation. The American voters confirmed the decision by re-electing President McKinley in 1900, with Theodore Roosevelt, the hero of San Juan Hill, as vice president.

The United States became an important Pacific power. America's base in the Philippines spurred interest in China, where foreign nations had carved out huge spheres of influence. Secretary of State John Hay's Open Door note asked that all countries have equal trade opportunities there.

Elsewhere in Asia, Japan inflicted a stunning defeat on Russia in 1904 and 1905. As a result, Japan was allowed to keep Korea but pledged to respect U.S. control over the Philippines.

A canal through Panama spread U.S. influence in the Caribbean. During the Spanish-American War, Americans realized that a Central American canal was vital to U.S. defense and trade. When Colombia refused to cooperate, the United States quietly supported a revolution in Panama, the Colombian province in which the canal was later built.

President Roosevelt extended the Monroe Doctrine, stating that the United States had the right to intervene to keep peace in the hemisphere. Again and again, Roosevelt and his successors, William Howard Taft and Woodrow Wilson, took steps to control events in Latin America.

The Great War
1914–1918

America tried to remain neutral as war broke out in Europe.
World War I began in August 1914 with a conflict in the Balkans between Serbia and Austria-Hungary. Archduke Franz Ferdinand, heir to the throne of Austria-Hungary, was killed by a terrorist, and Austria blamed Serbia for the assassination. Austria made a list of demands and then declared war on Serbia. Soon Europe divided into a bloody conflict between two alliances—the Central Powers (Germany, Austria-Hungary, and the Ottoman Empire) and the Allies (Serbia, Russia, France, Belgium, and Great Britain). The United States struggled to remain neutral.

The United States entered the war in 1917. Germany launched all-out submarine warfare in January 1917, and in March sank three U.S. merchant ships without warning. With this, Congress approved U.S. entry into the war on the side of the Allies. The U.S. government quickly harnessed its economy for total war. The government also acted firmly to suppress dissent. Soon fresh American troops helped beat back German advances, and on November 11, 1918, the war came to an end.

President Wilson envisioned a peace based on Fourteen Points. Allied leaders met in Paris to debate the peace treaty. A Bolshevik revolution had ended Russia's part in the war in 1917, and fear of the spread of bolshevism infected the peacemakers. Wilson was forced to surrender some of his Fourteen Points—his goals for peace—as the Allies demanded harsh reparations from Germany.

At home the Versailles Treaty faced stiff opposition. Many Americans feared the treaty might lead to future entanglement in Europe's quarrels. Finally, after much debate, the U.S. Senate rejected the treaty and with it membership in the League of Nations.

With Wilson's defeat, America drew back from world affairs. Economic growth and political reform had inspired an age of confidence in the United States following the Civil War. Confidence turned to disillusion for many Americans with the advent of World War I.

At the war's end, American members of peace organizations campaigned vigorously for U.S. membership in the League of Nations. Their hopes were dashed when the Democratic party, the party of Wilson, was soundly defeated in the presidential election of 1920. However, Americans did not retreat into isolationism. Instead, the United States continued to apply the policies of the Monroe Doctrine and the Open Door as it pursued economic and political goals throughout the world.

Reform

"For we must consider that we shall be as a city upon a hill," John Winthrop admonished a group of Puritans arriving in Massachusetts Bay Colony in 1630. From the first, many Americans felt that our nation had a special destiny to serve as a moral example to the rest of the world. Perhaps as a result of this sense of mission, the United States has always possessed a large class of people intent on reforming the lives of their fellow citizens. Of course, not every American was equally sure about the wisdom of these reformers.

1838

It will scarcely be denied, I presume, that as a general rule, men do not desire the improvement of women. . . . As *they* have determined that Jehovah has placed woman on a lower platform than men, they of course wish to keep her there; and hence the noble faculties of our minds are crushed, and our reasoning powers are almost wholly uncultivated. . . .

▲ **Sarah Grimké, letter to her sister Angelina**

1841

What is man born for but to be a reformer, a remaker of what he has made; a renouncer of lies; a restorer of truth and good, imitating the great Nature which embosoms us all, and which sleeps no moment on an old past, but every hour repairs herself, yielding us every morning a new day, and with every pulsation a new life?

▲ **Ralph Waldo Emerson, lecture**

1850

There is a higher law than the Constitution.

▲ **William H. Seward, speech**

1851

They talk about this thing in the head; what's this they call it? [Intellect, someone whispers.] That's it, honey. What's that got to do with women's rights or Negro's rights? If my cup won't hold a pint, and yours holds a quart, wouldn't you be mean not to let me have my little half-measure full?

▲ **Sojurner Truth, speech to a women's rights convention**

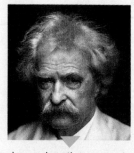

1867

Soap and an education are not as sudden as a massacre, but they are more deadly in the long run.

▲ **Mark Twain, "The Facts Concerning My Recent Resignation"**

1900

A man that'd expict to thrain lobsters to fly in a year is called a looneytic; but a man that thinks men can be tu-rrned into angels be an illiction is called a rayformer an' remains at large.

▲ **Finley Peter Dunne, *Mister Dooley's Philosophy***

1928

A reformer is a guy who rides through a sewer in a glass-bottomed boat.

▲ **James J. "Jimmy" Walker, speech**

1978

BLEEDING HEARTS, an ultraconservative view of ultraliberals, as those whose "hearts bleed" for the poor, who are "suckers" for every "sob story," and who place tax burdens on all, in a mistaken effort to cure social ills.

▲ **William Safire,** *Safire's Political Dictionary*

1984

Ten days ago, President Reagan admitted that although some people in this country seemed to be doing well nowadays, others were unhappy, even worried, about themselves, their families, and their futures. The President said that he didn't understand that fear. He said, "Why, this country is a shining city on a hill." And the president is right. In many ways we are "a shining city on a hill." But the hard truth is that not everyone is sharing in this city's splendor and glory.

▲ **Mario Cuomo, speech to the Democratic National Convention**

1990

The American people do not want judges, acting without any warrant in the Constitution, settling their social issues for them.

▲ **Robert H. Bork, editorial in** *The New York Times*

Define and Explain

"Whenever A annoys or injures B on the pretense of improving X," grumbled critic H. L. Mencken (1880–1956) about reformers, "A is a scoundrel." How would you define *reform*? Do you think reformers, in the long run, improve or injure American society?

Assignment: Write a clear, well-organized paragraph of 150–200 words defining *reform* and discussing whether reformers, on the whole, help or hurt their fellow citizens.

Explore the idea of reform. Begin by reading through the quotations on these two pages. To define *reform*, identify one or more characteristics associated with reform or reformers by many of the people quoted. (For example, some of the quotations associate an attempt to improve society with reform; some of them also associate with reformers a belief in a higher moral standard.) Divide the quotations into two groups— those that support reform and those that attack it. Select the two items from each group that seem to you to make the most effective case for or against reform.

Write a draft of your paragraph. Using the characteristic or characteristics associated with reform that you have identified, write a definition of *reform*. (For example, using the characteristics in the preceding paragraph a definition might read, "Reform is the attempt to improve society in accord with the reformer's belief in a higher moral standard.")

In the body of your paragraph discuss the four quotations you have selected, considering the pro-reform statements first, and then the anti-reform statements. Use your concluding sentence to indicate your opinion as to whether those who attempt to reform American society are useful or not.

Revise the draft. Examine the organization and writing of your paragraph, asking yourself the following questions: (1) Is the definition clearly stated? (2) Are the quotations correctly classified as pro- or anti-reform groups? (3) Does the conclusion effectively present your feelings about reform? (4) Are the parts of the paragraph connected using appropriate transitional words and phrases?

Proofread the essay and make a final copy. Read the paragraph again. Correct any errors in grammar, punctuation, and spelling. Write a final copy of the paragraph.

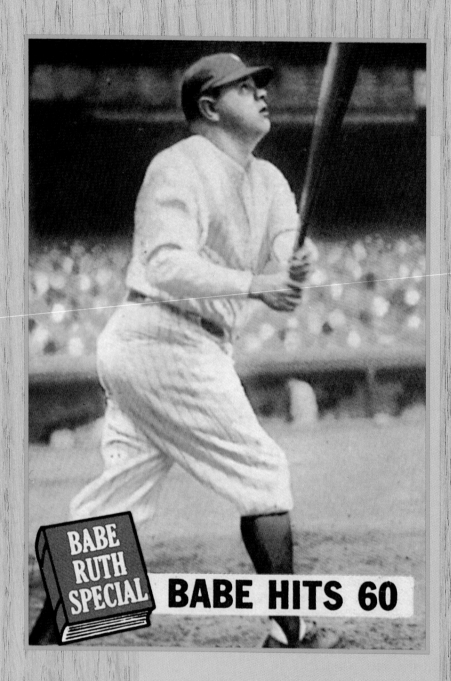

BABE RUTH SPECIAL

BABE HITS 60

Unit 3

You Are There

Babe Ruth scaled the hitherto unattained heights yesterday. Home run 60 . . .

While the crowd cheered and the Yankee players roared their greetings the Babe made his triumphant, almost regal tour of the paths. He jogged around slowly, touched each bag firmly and carefully and when he imbedded his spikes in the rubber disk to record officially Homer 60, hats were tossed into the air, papers were torn up and thrown liberally and the spirit of celebration permeated the place.
—*journalist James Carolan*

This special baseball card commemorates Babe Ruth's record 60th home run.

Prosperity and Depression

Unit Outline

CHAPTER 11	**Society and Politics in the 1920s**	**1919–1929**
CHAPTER 12	**Technology and Culture in the 1920s**	**1919–1929**
CHAPTER 13	**The Great Depression**	**1929–1935**
CHAPTER 14	**The New Deal**	**1933–1940**

Unit Themes

In this unit you will analyze the following themes of U.S. history:

- ▶ Our society reflects racial, ethnic, and religious diversity.
- ▶ Our economic system is organized around free enterprise and the protection of private property.
- ▶ Encouraging technological and scientific innovation has helped American society.

1915 | 1920 | 1925 | 1930 | 1935 | 1940 | 1945

- **1919** Red Scare; 18th Amendment (Prohibition) ratified
- **1920** Women gain the vote
- **1922** Soviet Union established
- **1925** *The Great Gatsby* (Fitzgerald); Louis Armstrong begins recording jazz
- **1927** Babe Ruth hits record 60 home runs
- **1929** Stock market crash sparks the Great Depression
- **1933** President Roosevelt initiates the New Deal
- **1935** Dust Bowl conditions worsen
- **1939** World War II begins in Europe

Linking Past to Present

Racial tensions of the post–World War I decade come to life in this inset photograph of a white mob chasing an African American man during the Chicago race riots of 1919. More than 70 years later, an interracial group comes together to protest the racist activities of the Ku Klux Klan.

Society and Politics in the 1920s

1 9 1 9 – 1 9 2 9

11

In 1920 a young African American veteran of World War I was leaving a factory job just outside of Chicago. As he was about to board the streetcar that would take him home to Chicago's south side, he was attacked by 20 white men. He jumped into the car, and they followed. The man jumped off at 51st Street, still chased by the angry gang, and ran for blocks before finding a safe place to hide. As he lay down among some weeds, he thought about the injustice of his situation.

AN AMERICAN ★ SPEAKS — Had the ten months I spent in France been all in vain? Were those little white crosses over the dead bodies of those dark-skinned boys lying in Flanders fields for naught? Was democracy merely a hollow sentiment? What had I done to deserve such treatment? . . . Must a Negro always suffer merely because of the color of his skin?

This African American, having risked his life to fight the country's enemies, found himself facing new enemies at home. He was not alone. The 1920s, often seen as a time of laughter and frivolity, was also a time of intense hatred and intolerance.

How do the personal and public attacks bred by this intolerance speak for the protections promised to citizens under the U.S. Constitution? Must the conditions of a diverse society necessarily lead to conflict?

CHAPTER PREVIEW

In this chapter you will learn how the United States adopted a social and political agenda aimed at "normalcy."

SECTIONS IN THIS CHAPTER:
1. Intolerance and conflict marked postwar society.
2. Social change threatened traditionalists.
3. Republicans dominated 1920s politics.
4. Women and farmers pushed for change.

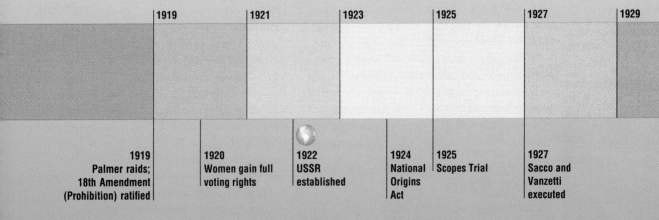

1919	1921	1923	1925	1927	1929

1919
Palmer raids;
18th Amendment
(Prohibition) ratified

1920
Women gain full
voting rights

1922
USSR
established

1924
National
Origins
Act

1925
Scopes Trial

1927
Sacco and
Vanzetti
executed

SECTION 1

Intolerance and conflict marked postwar society.

Key Terms: welfare capitalism, red scare, American Civil Liberties Union, *barrio*, Sacco-Vanzetti case, ghetto

Reading Preview
As you read this section, you will learn:

1. how workers reacted to the unfavorable postwar economy.
2. how the federal government responded to communist threats.
3. about the significance of the Sacco-Vanzetti case.
4. what expectations African Americans had after World War I.
5. why Marcus Garvey was important.

John L. Lewis, elected president of the United Mine Workers in 1920, held that post until he retired in 1960.

As the U.S. soldiers returned home, they were greeted by a country ready for a celebration. Parades flowed, with flags waving and people cheering, down main streets all across the United States. The soldiers, however, were more interested in life's basics—finding a job and a place to live. Both were scarce. As war contracts were canceled and few orders for consumer goods took their place, factories shut down and people were left without work. As for housing, a low level of residential construction during the war had left the growing country short about one million dwellings by 1918.

At the same time, inflation soared. Prices skyrocketed, and Americans complained bitterly about the high cost of living. The result was widespread fear and restlessness, both of which contributed to a time in which intolerance for ethnic and racial differences reigned.

Four million workers went on strike in 1919.

As inflation soared, so did union membership. The American Federation of Labor had enrolled two million members in 1916, and by 1920 that membership had doubled. Organized or not, American workers demanded higher wages. If they could not get them, they were willing and ready to strike.

American coal miners organized the largest of the 1919 strikes. During the war they had made an agreement with the U.S. Fuel Administration. In return for inflation-related wage increases, the miners agreed not to strike. When the wage agreements came to an end in 1919, the miners insisted upon their freedom to bargain freely with the mine owners. The government rejected their plea, maintaining that there had not yet been an official end to the country's state of war. The angry miners, meeting in September, called for nationalization of the mines.

Under the leadership of **John L. Lewis**, the acting president of the United Mine Workers (UMW), the miners entered negotiations for better hours and a 60 percent increase in base pay. When the talks broke down, Lewis called for a strike. Meanwhile, U.S. Attorney General **A. Mitchell Palmer** secured a court order declaring the strike illegal. In his arguments Palmer claimed that the strike was a communist plot to bring down the government. Despite the injunction, some 450,000 members of the UMW stayed home on November 1. In secret negotiations with the federal government, Lewis secured a 31 percent pay hike but failed to win improvements in hours or safety. After ten days, Lewis ordered his men back to work. Although some 50,000 miners stubbornly refused, the mines reopened. For his efforts Lewis became the president of the UMW, the second most powerful figure in union politics.

By the end of 1919, the most strikebound year in U.S. history, some four million workers had participated in more than 3,000 strikes. Although nearly all the major walkouts failed, they created for organized labor a legacy of public fear and anger. Union membership declined throughout the 1920s, largely because corporations began to provide benefits designed to keep workers both happy and productive. Through **welfare capitalism**, companies introduced pensions, cafeterias, paid vacations, profit-sharing plans, and other company-sponsored programs.

Attorney General Palmer launched an attack against the "red menace."

American anxiety over a communist threat did not fade with the weakening of the unions. Ever since World War I had ended, the public had been obsessed with the idea of a communist takeover of the government. The **red scare**, as this obsession was known, got its name from the color of the communist party's flag—with red symbolizing Marxist revolution. Newspapers were splashed with sensational reports of strikes and anti-communist riots. Many people were thus quick to take action against anything or anyone that seemed at all anti-American. For example, in February 1919 a jury in Indiana took only two minutes to acquit a man charged with shooting and killing an immigrant who had said, "To hell with the United States."

A disturbing series of bombings, however, sent even rational Americans into a panic. In the spring of 1919, 36 crude homemade bombs were mailed to leading government officials and capitalists—such people as A. Mitchell Palmer and J.P. Morgan. Only a couple reached their destination, but the bombings created widespread terror. One month later, bomb explosions damaged the homes of officials in New York, Pittsburgh, and Boston. Another bomb shattered the front of Palmer's home in Washington. Found outside the house were copies of a pamphlet titled *Plain Words*, which called on the working masses to rise up and overthrow the government.

Shortly thereafter, Palmer began his campaign against radicalism. From a Quaker family in a small Pennsylvania town, Palmer had served as a three-term member of Congress and wartime alien property custodian before becoming U.S. attorney general. In August 1919 he created the General Intelligence Division within the Justice Department and appointed 24-year-old **J. Edgar Hoover** as its chief. Hoover, who had entered government service as a file clerk at the Library of Congress, later would become the director of the Federal Bureau of Investigation. At first, Hoover's division was charged only with the task of collecting information about politically dangerous people and activities. His determined assistants rapidly built up a store of information, undeterred by a frequent lack of clear, hard evidence.

The division's intelligence work gave way to more active measures when the secretary of labor ruled that membership in a radical organization, such as the communist party, was grounds for deportation. Palmer and his aides used the ruling to go into the deportation business. Beginning in November 1919, the Justice Department, with the assistance of local police, raided the meeting places of alleged radical groups across the country. The raiders ripped buildings apart and seized tons of "anarchist" literature. They ignored the need for search warrants and the right of *habeas corpus*. Palmer's agents arrested thousands of "aliens," many of whom were loyal American citizens. Most were treated roughly and thrown into crowded jail cells. Some were beaten until they made confessions, even if they were innocent. Only a few hundred were actually deported.

Palmer was hailed as a popular hero, and the support fueled his political ambitions. His dream of winning the Democratic presidential

Palmer raids

Point	Counterpoint
Pro-raids	**Anti-raids**
■ fought supposed communist threat to U.S. government ■ responded to public fears	■ neglected constitutional protections and civil liberties ■ targeted few real radicals or criminals

"UNGRATEFUL SCUM!"

THE LAND OF OPPORTUNITY

VICIOUS ALIENS

DEPORTATION

In "The Only Thing They Fear," cartoonist John T. McCutcheon comments on the U.S. government's anti-immigrant policies of the 1920s. (1929, Chicago Historical Society)

463

nomination in 1920 led him to keep up the intensity of his antiradical campaign. The red scare kept Palmer's name in the press and on the minds of voters.

The facts of the Palmer raids did not support the need for the widespread suppression of civil liberties. Few of the men and women arrested were aliens or revolutionary agitators. The Palmer raids had netted some revolutionary pamphlets, but only three guns.

Palmer's concern that foreign revolutionaries were invading the United States, however, was shared by many. Almost one-third of the states passed strict laws designed to punish radicals.

These laws applied to men and women who advocated violence as well as to those who actually took violent political action.

Other Americans came to believe that the red scare and the Palmer raids were a greater threat to civil liberties than were the communists. In 1920 some of these people formed the **American Civil Liberties Union** (ACLU) to challenge the constitutionality of laws that violated the Bill of Rights.

Many also questioned Palmer's personal motives for the raids, and his credibility began to suffer. The attorney general's downfall came in the spring of 1920. First, a new secretary of

In Their Own Voice

Immigrants in the United States may have been distressed by the social turbulence of the 1920s, but at least they had the advantage of reading about events in their own language. Virtually every big city in the nation had newspapers published for the needs of its ethnic citizens.

At their peak early in the 20th century, about 1,000 foreign language newspapers were published in nearly 40 languages, including German, Lithuanian, Italian, Polish, Spanish, Chinese, Japanese, and Yiddish. About 140 of these papers were published daily.

African Americans had their own journalistic tradi-

tion, first forged in the cause of antislavery. *Freedom's Journal* (1827) and Frederick Douglass' *North Star* (1847) were two that led the way. Eventually,

more than 3,000 African American newspapers appeared. Today prominent African American newspapers include the *Chicago Daily Defender,* New York's *Amsterdam News,* the *Pittsburgh News Courier,* and the *Los Angeles Sentinel.*

Highlights of American Life

labor was appointed. Louis F. Post, who was outraged by the lack of order and justice in Palmer's actions, canceled thousands of his warrants and released hundreds of people from custody. Palmer then announced that a massive communist demonstration would take place in New York City on May 1, a day of celebration in honor of working people. The holiday, known as Labor Day, was associated with socialism and communism. Palmer ordered a great show of force, with police and federal agents flooding the city. May 1 came and went, with no sign of radical activity. Popular confidence in Palmer quickly faded, and the Palmer raids came to an end.

Workers prepare *La Prensa*, a Spanish-language newspaper in San Antonio, Texas, in 1928. The masthead below is from a Lithuanian paper.

The *Cherokee Phoenix* (1828) was the first Native American newspaper. More than 300 Native American newspapers are now published in 34 states.

Over the years the foreign language press has declined in circulation and in number of papers. Today about 40 dailies and 200 weeklies are publishing. The robust exceptions to the decline are Spanish-language newspapers. About 100 of them are currently being published. Though most are in the Southwest, the two largest are *El Diario-La Prensa* in New York City and *Diario de las Americas* in Miami. These papers help sustain the journalistic tradition of keeping people informed in their own voice.

The Sacco-Vanzetti case focused anti-immigrant sentiment.

Although Americans lost confidence in Palmer, hostility toward immigrants persisted. Books with titles such as *The Passing of the Great Race* warned that Anglo-Saxon citizens were losing their nation to hordes of "twisted . . . filthy" southern Europeans and Jews, who were, and would remain, un-American. Nativism, with its anti-immigrant attitudes, was clearly on the rise. Two laws were passed in the early 1920s to slow immigration—the Emergency Quota Act in 1921 and the National Origins Act in 1924. The second law set an immigration quota of two percent of each national group counted in the 1890 census. Since southern and eastern Europeans had not arrived in large numbers until 1900, the law gave western and northern Europeans an advantage. For example, Great Britain and Ireland could send 62,574 people a year, Italy only 3,845. Japan, China, India, and other Asian nations were each limited to 100 immigrants a year.

The newest immigrants to the United States came from Mexico and Puerto Rico. As in the 1800s, many Mexicans moved north to work as agricultural laborers in the Southwest. Large numbers of Mexicans also flowed into growing cities such as Denver, San Antonio, Los Angeles, and Tucson. They often lived in low-rent, inner-city districts in which services and conditions were poor. These urban Hispanic communities, known as **barrios**, were often rich in Mexican culture and tradition. Puerto Rican immigrants likewise headed to American cities in the 1920s. Most moved to New York City where they formed *barrios* in parts of Brooklyn and Manhattan. These Puerto Ricans usually found work in manufacturing, hotels, restaurants, and domestic service. As with the Mexicans, however, Puerto Rican communities also contained well-educated professionals such as doctors, lawyers, and business owners, many of whom served as leaders of their ethnic communities.

In 1920 hostile attitudes toward immigrants came to the forefront with the **Sacco-Vanzetti case**, involving two Italian immigrants. Nicola

THE SACCO-VANZETTI CASE
Skill: Distinguishing False from Accurate Images

Introducing the Skill. At midnight on August 22, 1927, a group of Italian immigrants waited for word of the Sacco and Vanzetti executions. When the news of their deaths arrived, the people wept—for the two men whom they believed to be innocent and for the American dream that had failed them. Americans wondered about the red scare and the national hysteria about immigrants that threatened the American ideal of "liberty and justice for all." Why were Nicola Sacco and Bartolomeo Vanzetti convicted of a crime for which the prosecution had not proven guilt beyond a reasonable doubt? How might the public's image of immigrants in the 1920s have influenced the court's final decision?

Learning the Skill. Sorting out the events and emotions of the trial of Sacco and Vanzetti calls for the

skill of **distinguishing false from accurate images**. Much of the popular opinion at the time of the trial portrayed recent immigrants as undesirable troublemakers and agitators. Was this an accurate image of the immigrants in the 1920s? Or were the members of the Sacco-Vanzetti jury showing signs of prejudice, that is, a bias that has become a firm and unreasonable judgment about someone or something?

In the robbery and murder trial of these two men, many observers and historians believed that prejudice, and a false image of immigrants, played a role in the conviction. To support this claim, people point to the fact that Bartolomeo Vanzetti had 14 witnesses to confirm his alibi that he was not at the crime scene. Still, the jury decided that these witnesses, all Italian Americans, were unreliable and found Vanzetti guilty as charged.

To identify images as false or accurate requires you to compare the given image to evidence presented in a source that is considered credible on the subject. Check also to see if actions or statements can be supported by fact or evidence—or only by opinion.

Applying the Skill. Consider the image presented in the following story: While gathering information for a novel based on the Sacco-Vanzetti case, writer Upton Sinclair visited the Sacco family. Frustrated with the family's lack of cooperation, Sinclair concluded that there was "some dark secret there." He evidently believed that the family was hiding some knowledge of Sacco's guilt. What other conclusions might Sinclair have drawn from the situation? How might false images of immigrants have affected his judgment?

Sacco and Bartolomeo Vanzetti stood accused of robbing a shoe factory in South Braintree, Massachusetts, and killing its paymaster and a guard. Both men had given false statements during the initial interrogation, but neither had a criminal record. None of the stolen money was found in their possession. Despite a weak case against the men, a jury found them guilty of murder in July 1921. Sacco and Vanzetti were sentenced to death.

Were the two men guilty? No one can be sure. Their defenders, among whom were a large group of Italian Americans, claimed that they had been convicted because of their political views and ethnicity instead of the evidence. Both men were anarchists who believed that any form of government was an unnecessary evil and should be abolished. It was their political radicalism, supporters insisted, and the fact that they were immigrants, that produced a verdict of guilty. Read Building Critical Thinking Strategies at left to learn more.

Sacco and Vanzetti were executed in 1927. In death they became heroes to some who were critical of the apparent bias against the foreign born, the poor, and the politically radical. On the 50th anniversary of their deaths in 1977, Massachusetts Governor Michael Dukakis pardoned Sacco and Vanzetti.

African Americans sought new opportunities after World War I.

African Americans were eager to share in the prosperity of the 1920s. Black veterans were particularly optimistic. More than 350,000 black men had served in the armed forces during World War I, primarily in Europe. In the service they had experienced more freedom and less discrimination than they had ever known at home. Because they had helped to fight for a democratic world, these veterans believed their nation would treat them with honor when they returned.

The hope that racial discrimination would decline at home quickly faded. The short but intense postwar economic depression and the fierce competition for peacetime employment intensified racial tensions. A severe housing shortage in northern cities further aggravated the situation. In 1919 black frustration and white anger and fear prompted a new wave of racial incidents across the country.

The worst of these race riots occurred in Chicago. A young African American boy, playing in Lake Michigan, floated across an imaginary line dividing Chicago's white and black beaches. The boy was hit by a rock, believed to be thrown by a white man, and knocked unconscious. He then drowned. Fighting on the beach followed, and streets filled with angry and protesting crowds that night. After five days of violence, 6,000 national guard troops were called in to restore order. In all, 38 people were dead and 537 injured. About 1,000 African Americans were left homeless, their houses destroyed by white mobs.

Despite the intolerance they encountered, African Americans continued to flood northern cities. By 1930 some 2.5 million African Ameri-

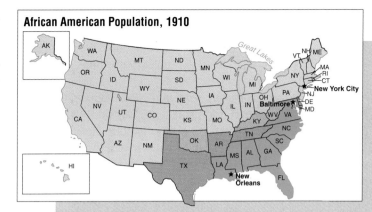

African American Population, 1910

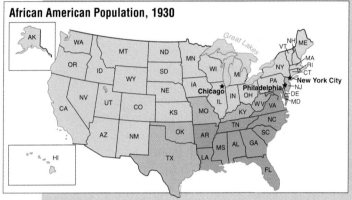

African American Population, 1930

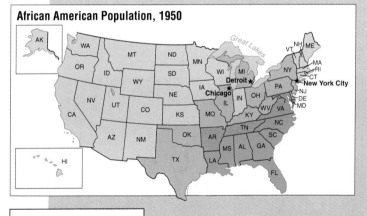

African American Population, 1950

African American Population Shift: 1910, 1930, 1950

- More than 30% black
- 15% to 30% black
- 5% to 15% black
- Less than 5% black
- ★ Top three black urban centers

Albers Equal-Area Projection
© SF

map study

Regions
Which southern states lost the most African Americans by 1950?

Critical Thinking
Why did Illinois and New York show gains in black population from 1910 to 1950?

467

cans had fled the repressive poverty of the rural South in search of a better life. In many northern cities, white people abandoned neighborhoods as they filled with these black migrants. Racial segregation in housing became established in many cities, including Chicago, Detroit, Cleveland, and New York City.

Harlem, a neighborhood in New York City, attracted many of the southern migrants. In 1900 Harlem was home to a primarily white, well-to-do population. By 1930 many of the white residents had left the neighborhood, replaced by some 165,000 African Americans. In Harlem, as in other urban ghettos, the result was overcrowding, housing shortages, and rising rents. A **ghetto** is a segregated slum, some of which began to appear in America's cities around World War I.

The one-room kitchenette was home for many African Americans during and after World War I. A typical building owner might take a seven-room apartment, which rented to white tenants for $50 a month, divide it into seven separate apartments, each with a small gas stove and one small sink. These tiny kitchenettes would then rent to African Americans for $42 a month, thus bringing in nearly six times as much rent for the owner. Sometimes five or six people lived together in these single-room apartments, so that one toilet might have to function for thirty or more tenants.

The high rents, however, gave rise to a staple of ghetto entertainment—the rent party. The cost of admission varied, from a nickel to a quarter, and went to pay the host's rent. More profitable, though, was the sale of illegal liquor and homemade soul food. In Harlem, in particular, rent parties were wild, exuberant affairs.

Young black girls gather for a children's fashion show in Harlem, 1928. African Americans of all economic classes lived in the segregated community.

Fall in line, and watch your step, For there'll be Lots of Browns with plenty of Pep At

A Social Whist Party

Given by

Lucille & Minnie

149 West 117th Street, N. Y. Gr. floor, W,

Saturday Evening, Nov. 2nd 1929

Refreshments Just It   Music Won't Quit

Colorful cards such as the one above, stuck in the grille of apartment house elevators, gave notice of Harlem rent parties.

Marcus Garvey led a new movement of black militancy in the North.

The hardships of life in the urban ghetto were met with a new spirit of militancy in the 1920s. A central figure in urban black activism was **Marcus Garvey**. A Jamaican immigrant, he founded the Universal Negro Improvement As-

Marcus Garvey

sociation in Jamaica in 1914. Garvey argued that the white majority in the United States would never treat African Americans as equals within their society. He urged African Americans to look within their own culture for dignity and pride and to abandon efforts at winning white society's approval.

Thousands of ghetto residents responded to the call for black pride and black solidarity. In August 1920 some 50,000 Garvey support-

ers paraded through Harlem behind their leader, who was dressed "in a dazzling uniform of purple, green, and black, with gold braid, and a thrilling hat with white plumes." African Americans responded as well to Garvey's self-help philosophy, which led to the creation of black-run businesses, including restaurants, grocery stores, and a company that manufactured black dolls for children.

In 1919, with more than four million people paying dues to his organization, Garvey set up the Black Star Line Steamship Company. The company was to provide transportation for the return of African Americans to Africa. Such a triumphant return to Africa was never realized. In 1923 Garvey's steamship company went bankrupt. Soon after, Garvey was tried and convicted of defrauding his followers. He was sent to prison and later deported.

The voices of other leaders, calling for equality in America rather than a withdrawal to Af-

rica, grew stronger after Garvey's movement collapsed. The National Association for the Advancement of Colored People (NAACP), which had been founded in 1909, led this struggle for civil rights. Its most eloquent spokesperson, W. E. B. Du Bois, became a familiar and respected figure in both black and white communities. As Du Bois and others would learn, the fight for civil rights and racial equality in the United States would prove to be both long and difficult.

SECTION **1** REVIEW

Identify Key People and Terms
Write a sentence to identify: John L. Lewis, A. Mitchell Palmer, welfare capitalism, red scare, J. Edgar Hoover, American Civil Liberties Union, *barrio*, Sacco-Vanzetti case, ghetto, Marcus Garvey

Locate Key Places
What New York City neighborhood was a center for African American life in the 1920s?

Master the Main Ideas

1. **Understanding labor unions:** How did the labor strikes of 1919 affect most workers' lives?
2. **Valuing tolerance of different opinions:** What tactics did A. Mitchell Palmer use to fight communists and radicals?
3. **Recognizing the impact of immigration:** How did anti-immigrant attitudes affect the Sacco-Vanzetti case?
4. **Understanding racial discrimination:** How did the expectations of African Americans after the war compare with their experiences?
5. **Recognizing social leaders:** How did Marcus Garvey reflect the new spirit of militancy and activism among African Americans in the 1920s?

Apply Critical Thinking Skills: Expressing Problems
In situations such as the red scare, the United States has struggled with the problem of finding a balance between the right of Americans to dissent and the need for national security. What issues are important to both sides of this balance?

Social change threatened traditionalists.

Key Terms: 18th Amendment, Prohibition, Volstead Act, speakeasies, fundamentalism, Scopes trial

Reading Preview
As you read this section, you will learn:
1. what happened to the Ku Klux Klan during the 1920s.
2. what Prohibition involved.
3. why the Scopes trial was significant.

The rise of cities and their ghettos, the mass influx of Catholic and Jewish immigrants, and the African American migration north—these social changes all posed a threat to traditional white Protestants living in rural areas. In response, many of these traditionalists participated in fierce campaigns against immigrants, alcohol, and evolution in the 1920s.

The Ku Klux Klan was revived in the 1920s.

In the atmosphere of fear and intolerance that followed World War I, organizations such as the Ku Klux Klan returned. The Klan was brought back to life in 1915 by William J. Simmons, a 35-year-old one-time Methodist minister and soldier. Aiding him were two advertising specialists, Elizabeth Tyler and Edward Young Clark. They hired an army of people to travel the countryside selling memberships in the Klan at $10 each. The salespeople molded each pitch to their clientele and were hugely successful at what a southern newspaper editor called "selling people their own prejudices."

The new Klan may have seemed the same as the earlier, post–Civil War Klan since it revived the old secret rituals, white robes, and burning crosses. Yet important differences arose. Instead of being limited to the South, the new Klan gained its strength in the small towns of the Midwest, Southeast, and the Far West. It was also successful in the rapidly urbanizing cities of the South and Midwest. Furthermore, the Klan broadened its violent attacks to include not only African Americans but also Jews, Roman Catholics, foreigners, and anyone who did not conform to the Klan's moralistic standards. This last group included alcoholics, adulterers, and criminals. To restore "100 percent pure Americanism," that is, a white, Protestant ideal, Klan groups embraced a program of terrorism, often beating, mutilating, and sometimes murdering their victims.

By 1925 Klan membership had soared to five million men, including five U.S. senators and four state governors. Indeed, by August 1925, some 50,000 Klan members felt respectable enough to parade down the streets of the nation's capital past the White House.

As quickly as it rose, the Ku Klux Klan fell. Its destruction did not come about because people rejected its prejudice or its violent tactics. Instead, the Klan members themselves abandoned the organization when they became aware of their leaders' hypocrisy and greed. Members learned that Klan leaders had pocketed millions of dollars in dues and that a prominent Indiana Klan member was convicted of sexually assaulting and killing a young woman. By 1930 the Klan's membership had dwindled to 9,000 men.

Prohibition outlawed the manufacture, transport, and sale of liquor.

Another popular target of the traditionalists was alcohol. Their campaign ultimately inspired a constitutional amendment and had widespread effects on American society during the 1920s.

Reasons for Prohibition. Many crusaders pointed to the physical and emotional dangers of even moderate drinking. In addition, many people openly linked alcohol with corrupt politicians and immigrants, both of whom tended to gather in working-class saloons. The Anti-Saloon League led the attack against alcohol. The ASL, headed by Wayne B. Wheeler, was an organization founded in 1895 by evangelical Protestant churches. Wheeler, an effective lobbyist, recruited many to his cause. By 1914

23 states had voted to ban alcoholic liquor, known as going dry. Two years later, the prohibition of liquor was the primary issue in state elections across the country.

When the United States entered World War I, though, prohibition took on new urgency and a patriotic tone. People tended to link alcohol with the enemy since most breweries had German names. The use of grain in domestic alcohol production also came under attack when distilleries were closed in order to conserve food and fuel supplies. Much of the public was clearly in support of banning intoxicating alcohol, and Congress obliged them by passing the **18th Amendment** to the Constitution in December 1917. The amendment banned the sale, manufacture, and transportation of "intoxicating liquor," but did nothing to forbid buying or drinking it. By January 1919 the necessary 36 states had ratified the amendment, and it went into effect the following January. **Prohibition**, the era in which restrictions on alcohol were in effect, had begun.

Enforcement of Prohibition. To enforce the amendment, Congress passed the **Volstead Act**. The legislation provided a lengthy list of exceptions to the 18th Amendment. These exceptions included allowances for religious and medicinal uses of alcohol. The Treasury Department was assigned to enforce the law, but financial support was minimal.

As soon as the Volstead Act took effect, Americans by the thousands became voluntary lawbreakers. Neighborhood saloons and fancy cabarets shut down, but secret clubs known as **speakeasies** sprang up to take their place. A knock on the door, and a softly spoken password gave the person "speaking easy" a place to drink or socialize. The police usually knew about the local speakeasies but tended to ignore them, often in return for payoffs or free drinks (or both). Prohibition agents who were willing to turn their eyes became wealthy, the more notorious of whom rode in chauffeured limousines and sported diamond rings.

Americans were determined to find ways to drink, and the understaffed federal agencies could do little to stop them. Some parts of the country completely ignored the amendment.

Two federal agents, Izzy Einstein and Moe Smith, endeared themselves to the nation during Prohibition. They donned clever disguises to con speakeasy owners into selling them alcohol. To try to get around the feds, speakeasies provided numbered membership cards.

Diners in San Francisco or Boston could order wine with their meals and go undisturbed.

Smuggling and producing illegal liquor became big business. People built stills and concocted bathtub gin, actually made in gallon jugs. The lawbreaking reached every level of society. President Warren Harding even served liquor confiscated by federal authorities to his fellow poker players who met at a little green house on K Street. The liquor was reportedly delivered in a Wells Fargo armored truck.

471

Effects of Prohibition.

Although many Americans found that speakeasies and bootlegged liquor added a little adventure to their lives, the leaders of organized crime took Prohibition seriously. They saw enormous profits to be made from the popular rebellion against the Volstead Act. Gangsters seized control of the production and distribution of illegal alcohol and built extensive money-making organizations. Violence was often used as the answer to competition from rival gangs. Trucks carrying liquor were highjacked, and competitors were gunned down in broad daylight on crowded city streets.

Murder became common in Chicago, where **Al Capone** headed one of the country's most infamous crime syndicates. Capone flaunted his wealth before frustrated police, at least those who weren't already on his payroll. He wore lime-green suits and dazzling silk ties, drove in a custom-made, armor-plated Cadillac, and used the press to cultivate an image of wealth and power. The Bureau of Internal Revenue estimated that Capone took in $105 million in 1927 from operations involving alcohol, gambling, and prostitution.

The crime syndicates stopped fighting each other only when they were busy fighting against federal law enforcement agents. Between 1920 and 1928, 135 gangsters and 55 agents lost their lives in the fight over Prohibition. The federal effort to arrest Al Capone was one of the most involved and dangerous of investigations. Elliot Ness led a team of Justice Department agents known as "The Untouchables" for their unwillingness to take bribes. Eventually, Ness won the battle in 1931, when Capone was convicted on charges of tax evasion and sent to prison.

Overall, besides increasing crime, the 18th Amendment failed to have a clear impact on American drinking habits. Thus, in 1929 President Herbert Hoover appointed Attorney General George W. Wickersham to head a commission investigating its effectiveness. The Wickersham Commission presented a report that was inconclusive and contradictory. It admitted that Prohibition was a failure since the public was indifferent or downright hostile to

Al Capone, though he was a ruthless mobster, liked to think of himself as a businessman, saying, "All I do is supply a public demand."

it. Still, it argued that the ban on alcohol should continue. An amused New York newspaper parodied the report:

> Prohibition is an awful flop.
> We like it.
> It can't stop what it's meant to stop.
> We like it.
> It's left a trail of graft and slime.
> It's filled our land with vice and crime.
> It don't prohibit worth a dime.
> Nevertheless we're for it.

The pressure for repeal grew steadily. In 1932 President Hoover reluctantly abandoned his support for Prohibition. By December of the next year, the 21st Amendment, repealing the 18th, was ratified.

Prohibition had lasted for more than 10 years. During this time alcohol consumption did indeed decline, and so did the number of deaths caused by alcoholism. Yet, the benefits that may have been gained failed to convince all Americans that the government had the right to violate their personal liberties.

The Scopes trial challenged a state's right to ban the teaching of evolution.

Many of the opponents of alcohol also attacked the teaching of evolution in public schools. Religion played an important role in the daily life of the 1920s, with fundamentalism gaining strength. **Fundamentalism**, a term originating about 1910, referred to the belief in a literal interpretation of the Bible. Most fundamentalists, who lived mainly in the South, came from Baptist, Methodist, or Presbyterian backgrounds.

The fundamentalists got their day in court in 1925, when the **Tennessee** legislature passed a law that made it unlawful for any public school or university to "teach any theory that denies the story of the Divine Creation of man as taught in the Bible, and to teach instead that man has descended from a lower order of animals." No one at the time paid much attention to the law, believing that it would not actively be enforced. However, the law caught the attention of the ACLU, which set out to find a test case with which to challenge the law.

John Scopes, a biology teacher in the small town of Dayton, became the ACLU test case. He was brought to trial in the summer of 1925 for deliberately breaking the Tennessee law banning the teaching of evolution. Scopes' defense team was led by **Clarence Darrow**, a famous trial lawyer and self-proclaimed agnostic (someone who believes that nothing is known or can be known about the existence of God). The prosecutor was William Jennings Bryan, a prominent fundamentalist known as rural America's defender of the faith and three-time presidential candidate.

The trial was played out like a circus. Stands selling hot dogs and lemonade filled the sidewalks, and little cotton apes appeared in windows. When the trial opened, it became the first ever carried on the radio. In addition, loudspeakers relayed the courtroom action to the thousands of people camped out on the courthouse lawn. Journalists then sent the news out to an excited American public.

Scopes' guilt was never much of an issue in the trial. Darrow instead raised the constitutional question of whether the state had the right to forbid him to teach evolution. He first attempted to bring scientists to the stand as expert witnesses arguing that evolution was true. The judge refused to allow this, saying that their testimony could only be hearsay since they were not present when lower life forms evolved into human beings. Darrow's case seemed to be lost, but the lawyer, in a flash of brilliance, tried another path. He called to the stand William Jennings Bryan himself.

Confronted with Darrow's sarcastic questions about God and religion, Bryan revealed an unshakable faith in the literal truth of the

OICES FROM THE PAST

Testifying at the Scopes Trial

As a sophomore, Bud Shelton had been a student in John Scopes' biology class. Shelton was one of ten students called to testify at the trial in the summer of 1925. What is his opinion about the famous trial?

It was a rigged affair. I think it was all done for the publicity. But I didn't know that at the time. I was just a kid; I would rather have been playing baseball, or swimming. The trial was held during summer vacation. They asked if I believed in the Bible, and I said yes. They didn't ask if I objected to being instructed in evolution, but I would have said no. I don't think the trial ever settled anything. It was all hoopla. . . .

The important question [Darrow] asked was whether Scopes' teaching of evolution had affected my religion in any way. He asked if I still attended church and Sunday School and believed in the Bible. I said I was still religious.

Clarence Darrow, representing John Scopes, argues his case before the jury.

Bible. Darrow tried to ridicule Bryan's testimony as "fool ideas that no intelligent Christian on earth believes." Bryan, however, held his own, insisting that "it is better to trust in the Rock of Ages than to know the ages of rocks."

As for Scopes, he was convicted and fined $100, though Tennessee's Supreme Court set aside the conviction on a technicality. The **Scopes trial** exposed the intolerance common in the United States of the 1920s. However, as with the red scare, Ku Klux Klan, and Prohibition, the reactionary forces of fundamentalism eventually declined. The people calling for a return to an America of white, native-born Protestants simply could not compete with the realities of a rapidly urbanizing society.

SECTION **3**

Republicans dominated 1920s politics.

Key Term: Teapot Dome scandal

Reading Preview
As you read this section, you will learn:

1. why Warren G. Harding's election was important.
2. what brought about the downfall of President Harding's administration.
3. who succeeded Harding as president.
4. what the election of 1928 demonstrated about American society.

SECTION **2** REVIEW

Identify Key People and Terms
Write a sentence to identify: 18th Amendment, Prohibition, Volstead Act, speakeasies, Al Capone, fundamentalism, Clarence Darrow, Scopes trial

Locate Key Places
Which state passed the law that led to the Scopes trial?

Master the Main Ideas

1. **Valuing tolerance of different opinions:** In what ways was the Ku Klux Klan of the 1920s different from the Klan of post–Civil War times?
2. **Understanding reform movements:** **(a)** What arguments were used to support the need for Prohibition? **(b)** How did Prohibition contribute to the rise of organized crime?
3. **Identifying religious issues:** Why did the Scopes trial attract widespread attention?

Apply Critical Thinking Skills: Identifying Central Issues
Do you think that the government has the right to ban a substance such as tobacco, demonstrated to cause harm to smokers and nonsmokers alike? How might restrictions affect an American's personal liberties?

During the presidential election of 1920, the United States arrived at a crossroads. The nation was spiritually tired, done in by the raw excitement of the war and the nervous tension of the red scare. Sick of Woodrow Wilson and his talk of America's duty to humanity, Americans simply wanted a chance to pursue their private affairs without government interference and to forget about public matters. They found their man in **Warren G. Harding**, a senator from **Ohio** and Republican candidate for president who promised a return to "normalcy." To Harding, the term, his own twist on "normality," meant "not heroism but healing, not agitation but adjustment, not surgery but serenity." With his election, he would lead the way for his party's domination of politics in the 1920s.

Harding's election signaled a new direction for government.

Warren G. Harding looked as Americans believed the president of the United States should look. He was as handsome as a movie star and exceedingly friendly. Perhaps it did not matter therefore that he was not particularly bright. He had difficulty answering questions of policy, and he constantly twisted the English language with inappropriate or nonexistent words. A leading journalist of the time called him "almost unbelievably ill-informed." Neither was Harding very ambitious. In fact, he had no real desire to be president but ran because party leaders insisted that he was their best hope for the office. Still, he was immensely popular and won by a landslide. The Republicans captured a 309–132 advantage in the House and one of 59–37 in the Senate.

As Harding settled into the White House, a new mood fell upon Washington, D.C. A feeling of good will returned to the city, so long banished by the depressing illness and seclusion of President Wilson. Harding opened up the White House to visitors and warmed their hearts with his dog named Laddie Boy. The fighting reform spirit of the Wilson administration faded, the laissez-faire principles of the Gilded Age returned, and the nation turned back to isolationism.

Harding himself had little to do with his administration's new direction. He was content to leave policy to his high-level appointees. This willingness to let others run the government for him might have been harmless had Harding chosen his aides wisely. Some of his Cabinet choices served the president well—men such as Charles Evans Hughes as secretary of state, Herbert Hoover as secretary of commerce, and Andrew Mellon as secretary of the treasury. Others brought only trouble. Harding appointed to office many of his old friends and political cronies from Ohio, most of whom were not qualified to hold their positions. Instead, members of the so-called Ohio Gang spent much of their time playing golf, drinking whiskey, and playing poker.

The government took a conservative turn under Harding, with big business as the winner. Mellon dismantled Progressive era restraints on business and convinced Congress to lower taxes for the wealthy. He also instituted the Bureau for the Budget, allowing the government to set priorities and limits for federal spending for the first time. Secretary of State Hughes in turn championed American business interests abroad.

Herbert Hoover, more of a progressive than his peers in the Cabinet, was nonetheless one of Harding's most popular appointments. Every

MEET THE PRESIDENT

Warren G. Harding's presidential career was born in a "smoke-filled room" in Chicago; it ended three years later in a fog of scandal in San Francisco. He once said, "I knew this job would be too much for me." History agrees.

An easygoing small-town newspaper publisher, Harding was nudged into politics by the ambitions of others. His Senate career was distinguished mainly by his tireless job-hunting for friends.

In place of the strenuous idealism of Woodrow Wilson, Harding offered a return to "normalcy." He won the 1920 election in an historic landslide.

Harding was superbly equipped for ordinariness, but in addition to "normalcy" he brought in a gang of Ohio pals who proceeded to loot the country with both hands.

WARREN G. HARDING

Born: November 2, 1865
Died: August 2, 1923
In office: 1921–1923

Just before the worst of the scandals became public in 1923, he took a long train journey that ended with his death.

one knew his name but no one knew much about him. He did not have a striking appearance and did not say clever things, but he had boundless energy. Hoover was driven largely by two ideas, both based on progressivism—greater democracy and greater efficiency. With these goals he turned the commerce department into one of the most powerful and well-organized in the federal government.

Scandal harmed the Harding administration.

Harding's inability to say "no" to his inept friends soon brought him public embarrassment. The first in a long line of political scandals involved Attorney General Harry M. Daugherty [dô′ər tē], who had sold pardons to criminals and received payoffs from people who violated prohibition laws. Daugherty was forced to resign and was then prosecuted for fraud. He refused to testify, hinting that Harding himself could be implicated in the corruption. The troubled jury could not agree on a verdict, so Daugherty went free.

Rumors of other scandals circulated around Washington. Harding soon began to realize the depth of his poor judgment. He exclaimed,

This is a terrible job. I have no trouble with my enemies. . . . But my friends . . . they're the ones who keep me walking the floors nights!

AN AMERICAN ★ SPEAKS

By the summer of 1923, Harding's health began to fail. He had become overweight, and suffered from hypertension and nervous disorders. When doctors recommended a rest, Harding left on a long train ride, intent on combining cam-paign stops with long games of poker. When the train reached San Francisco at the end of July, Harding collapsed. He was dead by August 2, presumably from a cerebral hemorrhage or a coronary thrombosis. Rumors of poisoning, however, have never been disproved. Millions of Americans, still full of love and affection for their leader, watched as the train carried his coffin back across the country to Washington.

After Harding's death, reports of more scandals came to light. In 1924 the largest of them became big news. Several senators, suspicious of the luxurious life led by Secretary of the Interior Albert B. Fall, began the investigation that unearthed the **Teapot Dome scandal**. Fall had convinced the secretary of the navy to transfer the administration of oil-rich properties in Teapot Dome, Wyoming, and Elk Hills, California, to the Department of the Interior. Although these lands were specifically reserved for the navy, Fall secretly leased them to private business interests. This secret arrangement netted Fall $200,000 in government bonds and $185,000 in cash. Fall and his partners were brought to trial but acquitted. Later, Fall was convicted of bribery, fined $100,000, and sentenced to a year in prison.

Attorney General Harry M. Daugherty, an Ohio friend of President Harding, is shown struggling to keep hidden the many skeletons of his scandalous administration.

President Harding was known to relax with some of the country's most successful business leaders. On this particular camping trip, Harding (third from left) joined friends Henry Ford, Thomas Edison, and Harvey Firestone.

Scandals continued to unfold, and as they did, two government officials committed suicide to avoid punishment. Harding's name remained relatively clean. Most Americans understood that the president was guilty only of poor judgment and lack of control. The Republicans, however, continued to carry the burden left by Harding's friends.

Calvin Coolidge took over Harding's presidency.

Harding's sudden death put Vice-President **Calvin Coolidge** into the White House and into the national spotlight. The new president clearly understood that his first task was to restore the reputation of his office and of his political party.

Coolidge began a major house cleaning. By the time the Republican convention met for the 1924 election, the honest and conservative Coolidge had rid Washington of all the Harding-era scoundrels. He was rewarded for his efforts with his party's nomination and the public's respect. The Republicans cheerfully urged the nation to "Keep Cool with Coolidge" for the next four years.

The Democratic party, meanwhile, was having trouble keeping cool. After 103 ballots, their convention delegates had still not agreed on any candidate. The Ku Klux Klan, which was opposed by nearly half the population, had managed to place delegates at the convention. By doing so the nominating process was thrown into confusion. An uproar went up, but

At a time of booming prosperity, Thomas Hart Benton's *Boom Town* captured the spirit of Borger, Texas, "as it was in 1926 in the middle of its rise from road crossing to an oil city." (1927–1928, Memorial Art Gallery of the University of Rochester, New York)

"Keep Cool with Coolidge" was an unlikely slogan for the hot, jazzy era of the Roaring Twenties. Despite the paradox, quiet and colorless Calvin Coolidge became one of America's most popular presidents.

Raised on a Vermont farm, Coolidge trained as a lawyer and, in 20 years, held 19 different public offices. His firm response to a police strike in Boston while governor of Massachusetts gave him a national reputation and the second spot on the 1920 Republican ticket.

Coolidge's flinty integrity restored public confidence after Harding's scandal-ridden administration. Coolidge developed a reputation for wisdom by keeping his mouth closed and a reputation for leadership by letting things be. "Coolidge luck" produced "Coolidge prosperity"—a sizzling but endangered econ-

CALVIN COOLIDGE

Born: July 4, 1872
Died: January 5, 1933
In office: 1923–1929

omy. Coolidge was luckiest of all in his decision, announced with typical terseness, not to run in 1928, the year before the Great Depression.

The vote reflected the general satisfaction with conservative leadership. Prosperity had returned, business was booming, and Coolidge won by a landslide. He was an excellent spokesperson for the new mood of the nation. He had earned a reputation for law and order as governor of Massachusetts and for honesty after the Harding scandals. In addition, his personal style fit his conservative principles perfectly. He was known as "Silent Cal" and became famous for his commitment to inactivity and hours of sleep. "Four-fifths of all our troubles in this life would disappear," Coolidge declared, "if we would sit down and keep still."

The Coolidge administration continued the policies begun under Harding. "Silent Cal" was an open admirer of American business people and believed that they should be left alone to accomplish what they wished. "The man who builds a factory," Coolidge observed, "builds a temple. The man who works there, worships there." The president used his influence to transform regulatory agencies into support systems for private business policies. Both the Interstate Commerce Commission and the Federal Reserve Board thus became allies of private enterprise rather than its watchdogs. Coolidge's philosophy was summed up in his most famous comment: "The business of America is business."

The 1928 election revealed deepseated intolerance.

Calvin Coolidge chose not to run for reelection in 1928. The Republicans turned instead to Secretary of Commerce Herbert Hoover, who campaigned on a platform promising continued prosperity. Hoover, a native of Iowa, portrayed himself as a simple farmboy who had worked his way to being both rich and famous. He told folksy tales of growing up in rural America, a childhood filled with swimming holes, fishing trips, and moonlit romps in fresh snow. In truth, Hoover's childhood was more complicated than that. Orphaned as a child, he was raised by a variety of relatives before heading off to Stanford University, where he graduated with a degree in mining. After a year of working in the mines, he got a job as an en-

a resolution to condemn the Klan by name failed by less than a single vote. As a result, the Democratic party was hopelessly split between William Gibbs McAdoo, former secretary of the treasury, and Al Smith, governor of New York. A compromise candidate was eventually found—John W. Davis, a largely unknown Wall Street attorney.

Faced with two conservative candidates, the remaining Progressive factions decided to run a third party candidate. The aging but still energetic reformer "Battling Bob" LaFollette was the natural choice.

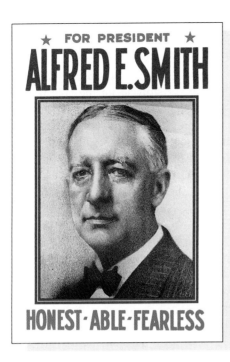

★ FOR PRESIDENT ★
ALFRED E. SMITH

HONEST·ABLE·FEARLESS

The difference in style between Hoover and Smith was made instantly and dramatically evident to voters during the campaign. For theirs was the first political contest to be broadcast on the radio. Smith's casual, slang-laden speech contrasted sharply with Hoover's well-bred tones.

To no one's real surprise, Hoover scored an overwhelming victory at the polls. The Republicans broke into the South for the first time since the Civil War, winning Kentucky, Virginia, Tennessee, North Carolina, Florida, and Texas. However, Smith carried the vote in the 12 largest U.S. cities, demonstrating the shift in Democratic strength from rural to urban areas. Still, contentment with Republican prosperity coupled with intolerance of immigrant culture swept Hoover's party into the White House once again.

Alfred E. Smith, known as the "Happy Warrior," used this campaign poster in his unsuccessful 1928 presidential race against Herbert Hoover.

gineer with an international firm and became a millionaire within 12 years.

When the Democratic Party nominated New York governor **Alfred E. Smith**, the contest was set between the two opposite faces of America—one rural, the other urban. Smith was strikingly different from Hoover. In fact, Smith was not a typical national candidate at all. He was Catholic, the son of Irish immigrants, rather than a native-born Protestant. He had been raised in the Lower East Side slums of New York City, not a log cabin or a white house with a front porch and a picket fence. He was an urban politician who had risen to power as the faithful son of Tammany Hall. A foe of Prohibition, he spoke for urban, ethnic Americans.

From the beginning, Al Smith himself was the biggest issue in the campaign. Smith represented all the elements of city life that many rural Americans thought were destroying their country. His religion and his urban upbringing acted like magnets for intolerance and fear. As the Ku Klux Klan roused itself to oppose Smith, conservative Democrats abandoned their party in droves, seeking refuge with the Republicans as "Hoovercrats."

SECTION 3 REVIEW

Identify Key People and Terms
Write a sentence to identify: Warren G. Harding, Teapot Dome scandal, Calvin Coolidge, Alfred E. Smith

Locate Key Places
From what state did President Harding come?

Master the Main Ideas

1. **Understanding relationships of government and economy:** What policies under Harding signaled the new conservative orientation of government?
2. **Perceiving cause/effect relationships:** How did Harding's management style lead to widespread scandal?
3. **Identifying political leaders:** How did Calvin Coolidge restore the reputation of the Republican presidency?
4. **Analyzing political campaigns:** What were the primary campaign issues of the 1928 election?

Apply Critical Thinking Skills: Identifying Central Ideas
The 1928 election revealed the increasing tensions between rural and urban America. In what organizations, events, or attitudes of the 1920s were the tensions evident?

SECTION 4

Women and farmers pushed for change.

Key Terms: 19th Amendment, McNary-Haugen bill

Reading Preview
As you read this section, you will learn:

1. what was granted under the 19th Amendment.
2. what sort of job-related progress women made in the 1920s.
3. how successful American farmers were in improving their economic situation.

As the 1920s progressed, various groups tried to use legislation to improve their situations. Two groups in particular, women and farmers, had different experiences with the strategy.

The 19th Amendment gave American women the right to vote.

As described in Chapter 8, the 20th-century phase of the struggle for the vote was led by Carrie Chapman Catt and Alice Paul. By 1916 their push for women's suffrage had begun to falter. Too many factions battled for control of the women's movement, disrupting its work and dissipating its energies and resources.

Catt realized that something had to be done, and done quickly, if the suffrage movement were to survive. She called her solution the "Winning Plan," the first step of which was to gain the cooperation of local suffrage groups. At the 1916 NAWSA convention, Catt persuaded the officers of more than 36 state suffrage associations to sign a secret agreement. The officers agreed to support Catt in a new campaign for a national suffrage amendment. Thus, the Winning Plan meant abandoning the movement's earlier state-by-state tactic and risking everything on a Congressional cam-

In November 1919 a group of California women celebrate upon hearing the news that their state just ratified the 19th Amendment. A year later, a voting woman graced the cover of a popular women's magazine.

paign. Each state suffrage organization was given a specific role to play.

Catt's approach worked. By January 10, 1918, support for the national amendment on suffrage had mushroomed. On that cold winter day, a large crowd of suffragists gathered outside the House of Representatives waiting to hear its decision. Three years earlier, the House had voted down the measure. Now, however, by a vote of 274 to 136, the House declared its support for an amendment ensuring that "the right of citizens of the United States to vote shall not be denied or abridged by the United States or any state on account of sex." Two more years passed while the state legislatures approved the amendment. Finally, on August 26, 1920, the **19th Amendment** became part of the Constitution, guaranteeing women the right to vote. The dream of 19th-century reformers such as Elizabeth Cady Stanton and Lucretia Mott had at last been realized.

Sadly, the right to vote did not guarantee equality for women in the United States. Discrimination in hiring practices, in salaries and wages, in access to education and training, and in many legal matters were not directly affected by the suffrage amendment. To compensate, some women called for the passage of an Equal Rights Amendment to legislate an end to discrimination based on gender. In 1923 Alice Paul led the National Woman's Party in taking up a new reform campaign to complete the quest for equality for women. In truth, however, most American women of the 1920s paid little attention to the struggles of suffrage or equal rights. Even once they had the right to vote, few women bothered to use it. Their energies were focused instead on private concerns.

Women made little progress in the work force in the 1920s.

Limited reform for women in the political arena was matched by slow progress in the work force. Although large numbers of women worked—more than eight million in 1920, more than ten million in 1930—most remained in low-paying, female-dominated occupations. Women were most likely to work as domestic workers, secretaries, typists, and clerks. Union organization provided little help. With the exception of the garment industry, women's efforts to unionize failed. In addition, the AFL was openly hostile to women since it did not want them competing with men for jobs.

Professional women encountered a similar lack of progress. Although the proportion of

map study

Regions

Between 1869 and 1919, women gained full voting rights in many states. In 1920 the 19th Amendment granted full rights to women in the remaining states. Did your state grant these rights before 1920?

Critical Thinking

Which regions of the country were most affected by the 19th Amendment?

AK 1913
(Statehood 1959)

HI
(Statehood 1959)

WA 1910
OR 1912
ID 1896
MT 1914
ND
MN
NV 1914
UT 1870
WY 1869
SD 1918
WI
IA
NE
CA 1911
CO 1893
KS 1912
MO
IL
IN
OH
MI 1918
PA
NY 1917
VT
NH
ME
MA
RI
CT
NJ
DE
MD
WV
VA
KY
TN
NC
AZ 1912
NM
OK 1918
AR
MS
AL
GA
SC
TX
LA
FL

Great Lakes

Women's Voting Rights Before 1920

- Full voting rights for women with date granted
- Partial voting rights for women (limited to local or presidential elections)
- No voting rights for women

Albers Equal-Area Projection   © SF

African American women both worked in and patronized fancy tearooms such as this one in Harlem. These establishments generally catered exclusively to black clients.

Although poor women worked throughout their lives out of economic necessity, most middle-class women quit as soon as they got married. They were expected to make homemaking and childraising their career, and few tried to combine career with marriage. For many women, the decade of the 1920s represented a flight from feminism and a resurgence of domesticity.

For working-class women, work usually began by the age of 14 or 15. Girls, in particular those whose parents were unskilled laborers, often left school to find jobs in factories or shops. Women also found work as textile or garment workers, lumber workers, woodchoppers, blacksmith apprentices, stone cutters, and boardinghouse keepers. What little money a girl earned went to support her family, with much of her income going directly to her mother. Edythe Greth, a young Pennsylvania woman, described the frustrations she felt upon learning from her mother that she would have to leave school at the age of 15. Her father had been injured and could no longer support their family of six.

female workers in the professions rose between 1920 and 1930, more than 75 percent of these women worked in so-called "female" occupations—teaching and nursing. Women who entered other fields, such as law, medicine, architecture, or accounting, were not common and usually made less money than their male counterparts. For example, there were only 60 female certified accountants and 151 female dentists in the entire country in the late 1920s.

Other educated women entered new and expanding fields. Some women began careers in publishing and advertising, others in real estate or tearoom management. Many women opened their own shops, selling antiques or clothing. Others, including college-educated women, went to work for large department stores such as Macy's in New York City or Marshall Field's in Chicago in the hopes of becoming buyers. With these jobs came a sense of economic independence, and many young unmarried women left their family's home to set themselves up in apartments of their own.

Although I was but fifteen years old, I suddenly realized

AN AMERICAN ★ SPEAKS

it was my duty as the oldest child to go to work. I tried to fight off the idea, by telling myself I probably wouldn't after all.

I slept little that night and as I rolled and tossed my conscience seemed to be shouting at me, "Would you see your mother go to the factory for the sake of your school? Would this be fair?"

The next morning I awoke with my mind resolved to take the step which I would do anything to avoid. Instead of telling the principal at once when I got to school, I went to all the classes that day, and after my last class at three-ten, I told her with much reluctance.

I shall never forget how, as I walked home that hot day, my heart seemed to sink lower with each step. I walked along seeing nothing, for the thought that I had left school forever was driving me mad. Thus, the next day I entered the factory with the door to education slammed in my face.

African American women went to work in larger numbers than white women. In 1922 Elizabeth Ross Haynes, Domestic Service Secretary of the U.S. Employment Service and an African American herself, issued a report on working black women. She noted that in that year two million African American women worked in three types of jobs—domestic and personal service, agriculture, and manufacturing and mechanical industries. These jobs generally offered low wages, long hours, and poor working conditions in such places as private homes, hotels, laundries, and factories.

Farmers failed to solve their economic problems.

The world's return to peace after World War I brought hardship to the American farm community. During the war American farm produce had been in great demand. **Europe**'s farms were often battlefields, so American farmers responded by expanding their own production, often going heavily into debt. When peace returned and farming revived in Europe, the American farmer was left with an unwanted surplus and high debt payments. As prices plummeted, a serious agricultural depression spread across the nation.

Just as prices began to tumble, costs began to soar. To remain competitive, farmers were forced to purchase new equipment, which most could not afford. Even worse for farmers, the powerful new machines produced larger crops, which created still greater surpluses. Prices fell again. Technology, once the farmer's ally, had become the enemy.

In the 1920s midwestern and southern farmers organized to pressure the government for aid to agriculture. From 1924 to 1928, the farm bloc, a group of legislators that favored laws to help farmers, fought in Congress for passage of the **McNary-Haugen bill**. This legislation proposed to raise farm prices by having the government purchase farm surplus to sell in foreign markets. President Coolidge vetoed the bill twice. He felt that price fixing, which is what the plan established, would encourage overproduction and at the same time force consumers to pay higher prices.

During the decade, farm families suffered setbacks from which they never recovered. A half-million farmers lost their farms, and others stood at risk of losing theirs as well. The decline in farm income affected nonfarmers as well. As farmers stopped buying tractors, cars, furniture, and other goods, the effects of farm troubles spread throughout the American economy. In addition, the country's banks were hard hit as millions of farmers defaulted on their debts. Between 1920 and 1929, more than 5,000 of the country's 30,000 banks went out of business. Afraid to put their money into a troubled banking system, people began to hoard cash, taking more than $1 billion out of circulation. Hard times on the farm soon gave way to the economic doom of the Great Depression.

S E C T I O N **4** R E V I E W

Identify Key People and Terms
Write a sentence to identify: 19th Amendment, McNary-Haugen bill

Locate Key Places
Fighting on which continent contributed to America's farm troubles?

Master the Main Ideas

1. **Understanding the struggle for equal rights:** How did Carrie Chapman Catt's new strategy help her secure women's right to vote?
2. **Recognizing the contributions of women: (a)** What changes did professional women experience in the 1920s? **(b)** In what fields were working-class and African American women mainly employed?
3. **Recognizing the impact of depressions: (a)** What situation was the McNary-Haugen bill intended to improve? **(b)** How did farm hardships affect the rest of the U.S. economy?

Apply Critical Thinking Skills: Making Comparisons
During the 1920s both women and farmers tried to use legislation to further their causes. Compare their experiences. What factors affected their success?

George F. Babbitt Describes the Ideal American

11A

TIME FRAME
Early 1920s

GEOGRAPHIC SETTING
Zenith (a fictional
Midwestern city)

Among the most important American literary works to appear during the 1920s were the novels of Sinclair Lewis (1888–1951). In books such as *Main Street* (1920) and *Babbitt* (1922), Lewis memorably depicted Midwestern life as marked by smug mediocrity and petty social cruelties. *Babbitt,* a satirical portrait of a middle-aged businessman, gave the name to a type of vulgar, self-satisfied, conformist American (and added a word to the language). In the following passage from *Babbitt,* the title character, George F. Babbitt, is giving a speech to a group of businessmen in which he sketches his ideal American.

Our Ideal Citizen—I picture him first and foremost as being busier than a bird-dog, not wasting a lot of good time in day-dreaming or going to sassiety [soci-
5 ety] teas or kicking about things that are none of his business, but putting the zip into some store or profession or art. At night he lights up a good cigar, and climbs into the little old 'bus, and maybe cusses
10 the carburetor, and shoots out home. He mows the lawn, or sneaks in some practice putting, and then he's ready for dinner. After dinner he tells the kiddies a story, or takes the family to the movies, or
15 plays a few fists of bridge, or reads the evening paper, and a chapter or two of some good lively Western novel if he has a taste for literature, and maybe the folks nextdoor drop in and they sit and visit
20 about their friends and the topics of the day. Then he goes happily to bed, his conscience clear, having contributed his mite to the prosperity of the city and to his own bank-account.
25 In politics and religion this Sane Citizen is the canniest man on earth; and in the arts he invariably has a natural taste which makes him pick out the best, every time.

In no country in the world will you find so
30 many reproductions of the Old Masters and of well-known paintings on parlor walls as in these United States. No country has anything like our number of phonographs, with not only dance records and
35 comic but also the best operas, such as Verdi, rendered by the world's highest-paid singers.

In other countries, art and literature are left to a lot of shabby bums living in attics
40 and feeding on booze and spaghetti, but in America the successful writer or picture-painter is indistinguishable from any other decent business man; and I, for one, am only too glad that the man who has the
45 rare skill to season his message with interesting reading matter and who shows both purpose and pep in handling his literary wares has a chance to drag down his fifty thousand bucks a year, to mingle with
50 the biggest executives on terms of perfect equality, and to show as big a house and as swell a car as any Captain of Industry! But, mind you, it's the appreciation of the Regular Guy who I have been depicting
55 which has made this possible, and you got to hand as much credit to him as to the authors themselves.

Finally, but most important, our Standardized Citizen, even if he is a bachelor,
60 is a lover of the Little Ones, a supporter of the hearthstone which is the basic foundation of our civilization, first, last, and all the time, and the thing that most distinguishes us from the decayed nations of
65 Europe.

I have never yet toured Europe—and as a matter of fact, I don't know that I care to such an awful lot, as long as there's our own mighty cities and mountains to be
70 seen—but, the way I figure it out, there must be a good many of our own sort of

Looking the embodiment of smug respectability that the word "Babbitt" has come to mean, the actor Willard Louis is shown as George F. Babbitt in a 1924 silent film version of Sinclair Lewis' novel.

folks abroad. Indeed, one of the most enthusiastic Rotarians I ever met boosted the tenets of one-hundred-per-cent pep in a burr that smacked o' bonny Scutland and all ye bonny braes o' Bobby Burns. But same time, one thing that distinguishes us from our good brothers, the hustlers over there, is that they're willing to take a lot off the snobs and journalists and politicians, while the modern American business man knows how to talk right up for himself, knows how to make it good and plenty clear that he intends to run the works. He doesn't have to call in some highbrow hired-man when it's necessary for him to answer the crooked critics of the sane and efficient life. He's not dumb, like the old-fashioned merchant. He's got a vocabulary and a punch.

With all modesty, I want to stand up here as a representative business man and gently whisper, "Here's our kind of folks! Here's the specifications of the Standardized American Citizen! Here's the new generation of Americans: fellows with hair on their chests and smiles in their eyes and adding-machines in their offices. We're not doing any boasting, but we like ourselves first-rate, and if you don't like us, look out—better get under cover before the cyclone hits town!"

So! In my clumsy way I have tried to sketch the Real He-man, the fellow with Zip and Bang. And it's because Zenith has so large a proportion of such men that it's the most stable, the greatest of our cities. New York also has its thousands of Real Folks, but New York is cursed with unnumbered foreigners. So are Chicago and San Francisco. . . .

But it's here in Zenith, the home for manly men and womanly women and bright kids, that you find the largest proportion of these Regular Guys, and that's what sets it in a class by itself; that's why Zenith will be remembered in history as having set the pace for a civilization that shall endure when the old time-killing ways are gone forever and the day of earnest efficient endeavor shall have dawned all round the world!

Some time I hope folks will quit handing all the credit to a lot of moth-eaten, mildewed, out-of-date, old, European dumps, and give proper credit to the famous Zenith spirit, that clean fighting determination to win Success that has made the little old Zip City celebrated in every land and clime, wherever condensed milk and pasteboard cartons are known! Believe me, the world has fallen too long for these worn-out countries that aren't producing anything but bootblacks and scenery and booze, that haven't got one bathroom per hundred people, and that don't know a looseleaf ledger from a slip-cover; and it's just about time for some Zenithite to get his back up and holler for a showdown!

I tell you, Zenith and her sister-cities are producing a new type of civilization. There are many resemblances between Zenith and these other burgs, and I'm darn glad of it! The extraordinary, growing, and sane standardization of stores, offices, streets, hotels, clothes, and newspapers throughout the United States shows how strong and enduring a type is ours. . . .

Discussing the Reading

1. George F. Babbitt makes a number of references to the arts in this excerpt from his speech. What quality is common to most of these references?

2. What attitudes toward foreigners does Babbitt express?

CRITICAL THINKING
Identifying Assumptions

Babbitt takes certain things for granted about his audience. What assumptions does he make? What makes you think so?

"Depressions Are Farm Led and Farm Fed"

11B

TIME FRAME
Late 1920s–early 1930s

GEOGRAPHIC SETTING
South Dakota

While European agriculture was disrupted during World War I, American farm produce was in great demand. American farmers responded to this wartime demand by expanding their production. When peace came and agriculture resumed in Europe, American farmers, especially in the Midwest, were left with an unwanted surplus. Farm prices plummeted and a serious agricultural depression set in. In the following excerpt from Studs Terkel's oral history of the Great Depression, *Hard Times,* Emil Loriks, a South Dakota farmer who had served as a state senator from 1927 to 1934, recalled how farmers were radicalized by their economic problems.

In 1924, our grain elevator went broke. Farm prices collapsed. I remember signing a personal note, guaranteeing the commission company against loss. I didn't
5 sleep very good those nights. The banks were failing all over the state. The squeeze was beginning to be felt. The stock market panic didn't come as any surprise to us. Our government had systematically done
10 everything wrong. . . . We were going to take the profits out of war. The only thing we did was put a ceiling on wheat. We passed high protective tariffs, other countries retaliated. . . .
15 There's a saying: "Depressions are farm led and farm fed." That was true in the Thirties. As farmers lost their purchasing power, the big tractors piled up at the Minneapolis-Moline plant in the Twin Cities.
20 One day they closed their doors and turned their employees out to beg or starve. My cousin was one of them. I took my truck to Minneapolis and brought him and his family out to my farm for the du-
25 ration. They stayed with us until the company opened up again, two or three years later.

During my first session in the state senate, in 1927, five hundred farmers came
30 marching up Capitol Hill. It thrilled me. I didn't know farmers were intelligent enough to organize. (Laughs.) They stayed there for two days. It was a strength I didn't realize we had.
35 The day after they left, a Senator got up and attacked them as anarchists and bolsheviks. (Laughs.) They had a banner, he said, redder than anything in Moscow, Russia. What was this banner? It was a
40 piece of muslin, hung up in the auditorium. It said: "We Buy Together, We Sell Together, We Vote Together." This was the radical danger. (Laughs.) They'd been building cooperatives, which the farmers
45 badly needed.

I was the first man to answer him from the senate floor. Eleven others took turns. He never got re-elected. In the lower house, we had about thirty or forty mem-
50 bers of the Farmer's Union. It was quite an education for me. . . .

Oh, the militancy then! At Milbank, during a farm sale, they had a sheriff and sixteen deputies. One of them got a little trig-
55 ger-happy. It was a mistake. The boys disarmed him so fast, he didn't know what happened. They just yanked the belts off 'em, didn't even unbuckle 'em. They took their guns away from 'em. After that, we
60 didn't have much trouble stopping sales.

Thirteen highways to Sioux Falls were blocked. They emptied the stockyards there in a day or two. There was some violence, most of it accidental.
65 I'll never forget a speech by a Catholic priest at a Salem meeting, straight south of here about forty miles. It was the most fiery I ever heard. He said, "If you men haven't got the guts to picket the roads
70 and stop this stuff from going to market,

Farmers in Hastings, Nebraska are shown gathered for the auction of a neighbor's land in this 1938 photograph by Arthur Rothstein.

put on skirts and get in the kitchen and let your wives go out and do the job." (Laughs.) The boys used the police stations as their headquarters. (Laughs.) The
75 police couldn't do much. The sheriffs and deputies just had to go along.

That judge situation in Iowa was a warning. In Brown County, farmers would crowd into the courtroom, five or six hun-
80 dred, and make it impossible for the officers to carry out the sales. (Laughs.)

Deputies would come along with whole fleets of trucks and guns. One lone farmer had planks across the road. They ordered
85 him to remove them. They came out with guns. He said, "Go ahead and shoot, but there isn't one of you ... getting out of here alive." There were about fifteen hundred farmers there in the woods. The
90 trucks didn't get through. It was close in spirit to the American Revolution.

Discussing the Reading

1.In the context of the 1920s and '30s, what did the saying, "Depressions are farm led and farm fed" mean?

2.Do you agree with Emil Loriks' feeling that the farmers' radicalism "was close in spirit to the American Revolution"? Why or why not?

CRITICAL THINKING
Expressing Problems

During economic hard times, when farmers cannot keep up with the mortgage payments on their land, the banks who own the property will often sell the farms in order to recover their money. Do farmers have a right to stop such sales, as Loriks reported was done in the 1920s and '30s? Why or why not?

Chapter Summary

Write supporting details under each of the following main ideas as you review the chapter.

Section 1

1. Four million workers went on strike in 1919.
2. Attorney General Palmer launched an attack against the "red menace."
3. The Sacco-Vanzetti case focused anti-immigrant sentiment.
4. African Americans sought new opportunities after World War I.
5. Marcus Garvey led a new movement of black militancy in the North.

Section 2

1. The Ku Klux Klan was revived in the 1920s.
2. Prohibition outlawed the manufacture, transport, and sale of liquor.
3. The Scopes trial challenged a state's right to ban the teaching of evolution.

Section 3

1. Harding's election signaled a new direction for government.
2. Scandal harmed the Harding administration.
3. Calvin Coolidge took over Harding's presidency.
4. The 1928 election revealed deepseated intolerance.

Section 4

1. The 19th Amendment gave American women the right to vote.
2. Women made little progress in the work force in the 1920s.
3. Farmers failed to solve their economic problems.

Chapter Themes

1. **Racial, ethnic, religious diversity:** Until the 1920s the United States had been basically rural in its values and culture. The 1920s brought a shift to urban culture. Not everyone believed this trend to be in the best interests of the nation. Fear and mistrust were reflected in the resurgence of the Ku Klux Klan, Prohibition laws, the interest in the Scopes trial, the passage of stricter immigration laws, and in the election results of 1924 and 1928.
2. **Representative and constitutional government:** In 1919 and 1920, the Constitution was modified by two new amendments, both of which demonstrated the ability of interest groups to be heard. The 18th Amendment, which brought about Prohibition, reflected the interest of traditionalists, especially fundamentalists and others who linked alcohol with crooked politicians and radical foreigners. The 19th Amendment, which finally brought the vote to American women, came, as Carrie Chapman Catt said, after "52 years of pauseless campaign."

Chapter Study Guide

Identifying Key People and Terms

Name the key term that describes the:
1. segregated slum area of a city
2. belief in the literal interpretation of the Bible
3. group, founded in 1920, that is dedicated to challenging the constitutionality of laws that violate the Bill of Rights

Locating Key Places

1. To what section of New York City did many black southerners migrate during and after World War I?
2. In what state did Clarence Darrow and William Jennings Bryan argue the Scopes case?

Mastering the Main Ideas

1. Fear became an overriding theme for some people in the 1920s. Complete a chart that shows at least five different groups, what each feared, and how they coped with the fear. Use the model below.

Group	Fear	Action

2. In what ways did some traditionalists violate the personal liberties of other Americans in the 1920s?
3. Both Harding and Coolidge were said to take inactive roles as president. Why, then, did Harding's management style lead to scandals, whereas Coolidge's led to national prosperity?
4. Why was the passage of the 19th Amendment a victory for perseverance and cooperation?

Applying Critical Thinking Skills

1. **Analyzing cause and effect:** What caused the jubilation of the World War I victory to degenerate into a decade of unrest in the 1920s?

1918	1920	1922	1924	1926	1928

1919 Palmer raids; 18th Amendment (Prohibition) ratified

1920 Women gain the vote

1922 USSR founded

1923 Coolidge replaces Harding

1924 National Origins Act; Teapot Dome

1925 Scopes trial

1927 Sacco and Vanzetti executed

1928 Hoover defeats Smith

2. **Recognizing values:** For what values did each of the following groups stand? **(a)** fundamentalists **(b)** Ku Klux Klan members **(c)** prohibitionists?
3. **Expressing problems:** How was the switch from Wilson's progressive reform program to Harding's and Coolidge's laissez-faire conservatism a problem for the nation's poor and disadvantaged?
4. **Making comparisons:** What similarities can be found in the problems of black and white working-class women and farmers in the 1920s?

Chapter Activities

Learning Geography Through History

1. Why did many African American veterans and farmers move to cities in the 1920s?
2. Immigrants from which part of the world were favored in the National Origins Act of 1924? Which were largely excluded?

Relating the United States to the World

1. From what Spanish-speaking nations did America's newest immigrants come?
2. What event in the Soviet Union fueled the hysteria that gave rise to Palmer's raids?

Linking Past to Present

1. Compare the welfare capitalism practiced by today's companies with that of companies in the 1920s.
2. **(a)** Who led the National Women's Party to propose the Equal Rights Amendment in 1923? **(b)** What happened to the idea when it resurfaced in Congress in 1972? **(c)** What happened to the amendment in 1982?

Using the Time Line

1. List three events from the time line that reflect intolerance of foreigners.
2. What event on the time line was meant to control alcohol consumption and sales by Americans?

Practicing Critical Thinking Strategies

Distinguishing False from Accurate Images

Like the Sacco-Vanzetti jury, the Palmer raids relied heavily on false images of immigrants. How did the agency's failure to distinguish false from accurate images lead to widespread violations of civil liberties? Use the guidelines you learned on page 466 to answer the question. Provide evidence to support your response.

Learning More About Society and Politics in the 1920s

1. **Using the Source Readings:** Read the Source Readings for this chapter and answer the questions.
2. **Writing an editorial:** Research the Sacco and Vanzetti trial using books from your library. Then write an editorial supporting the innocence or guilt of the two based on your research. Do you agree or disagree with Governor Dukakis' action in this case? Why or why not?
3. **Giving a speech:** Research one of the following topics and give a three-minute speech on your finding to the class.
   (a) Ku Klux Klan: the 1920s and today
   (b) Alfred E. Smith: Urban Candidate
   (c) St. Valentine's Day Massacre
   (d) John L. Lewis: "No Contract, No Work"

Linking Past to Present

Teenagers—in both the 1920s and 1990s—often found an identity rebelling against societal traditions in clothing and appearance. Both the John Held, Jr., drawing of a flapper and her date, inset, and the contemporary photograph of a punk-inspired couple offer a spirited look at youth culture in America.

Technology and Culture in the 1920s

1 9 1 9 — 1 9 2 9

12

*N*one of the Victorian mothers—and most of the mothers were Victorian—had any idea how casually their daughters were accustomed to be kissed. . . . Amory saw girls doing things that even in his memory would have been impossible: eating three-o'clock, after-dance suppers in impossible cafés, talking of every side of life with an air half of earnestness, half of mockery, yet with a furtive excitement that Amory considered stood for a real moral let-down. But he never realized how wide-spread it was until he saw the cities between New York and Chicago as one vast juvenile intrigue.

The observations of Amory Blaine, a handsome, young aristocrat, appeared in the 1920 novel, *This Side of Paradise*, an instant success for its author F. Scott Fitzgerald. In this and other literary classics of the decade, Fitzgerald explored the light-hearted side of the 1920s—the era that earned such nicknames as the Roaring Twenties and the Jazz Age. At a time when race riots, labor strikes, and the red scare were consuming their parents' energies, the young people of the 1920s played with wild abandon. They rode around in new automobiles, danced to jazz in nightclubs, cheered for baseball and movie stars, and went crazy over every passing fad and fashion.

This young generation of dreamers lived in a world of constant change. In what ways did innovations in science and technology shape and guide their lives? Moreover, how did their culture—the music, art, and literature—respond to these changes?

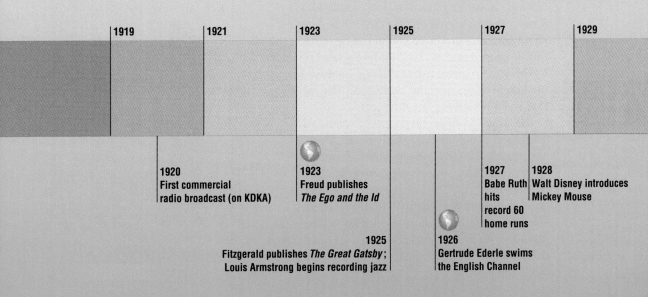

1919	1921	1923	1925	1927	1929

1920
First commercial radio broadcast (on KDKA)

1923
Freud publishes *The Ego and the Id*

1927
Babe Ruth hits record 60 home runs

1928
Walt Disney introduces Mickey Mouse

1925
Fitzgerald publishes *The Great Gatsby*; Louis Armstrong begins recording jazz

1926
Gertrude Ederle swims the English Channel

SECTION 1

Technology transformed American society.

Key Term: scientific management

Reading Preview
As you read this section, you will learn:

1. the effect electricity had on Americans' lives in the 1920s.
2. who dominated the U.S. auto industry.
3. how the automobile changed the United States.

Two energy sources, electricity and oil, fueled the production and the prosperity of the 1920s. Neither source of energy was new, of course. Ben Franklin experimented with electricity in the 18th century, and Edwin L. Drake, a retired railroad conductor, drilled the first oil well in the United States in Titusville, Pennsylvania, in 1859. Yet, new technologies developed in the 1920s that gave both energy sources a more powerful role in American life.

Electricity changed how people lived and worked in the 1920s.

By 1882, when Thomas Edison built the first electrical power plant, Americans had learned to harness electricity for manufacturing and lighting. However, Edison's plant, located in New York City, served only 85 customers. The direct current it produced could only be transmitted short distances, limiting its usefulness. In the 1890s George Westinghouse improved on Edison's idea with an alternating current that could be sent farther distances.

The switch to alternating current broadened the uses of electricity and revolutionized American society. Electricity now could be used to power everything from small gadgets to large machinery. By 1930 the tiny electrical industry grew to include ten huge corporations. These companies produced more electricity for the American home and workplace than all other nations of the world combined.

The availability of electricity changed the American home. Before World War I, only one-fifth of America's households had electricity. By 1929 two-thirds of them did. Families soon became accustomed to electric refrigerators, vacuum cleaners, and toasters. Electricity also transformed American industry. By the 1920s electrically powered machines dominated the country's manufacturing. Industrial productivity rose even as the work force remained constant. More efficient methods of mass production bolstered productivity still further. The champion of mass production, engineer **Frederick W. Taylor**, had long advocated **scientific management**, a business approach that focused on efficiency and speed. By the 1920s Taylor's ideas had found a ready audience. He conducted time and motion studies, charting every movement in a worker's routine. Using the principles of scientific management, he then combined steps that were complementary and eliminated any that were unnecessary. As a result, workers could produce goods more quickly and efficiently.

chart study

How did the percentage of dwelling units with electric service change from 1920 to 1929?
Critical Thinking
How did this shift affect American life?

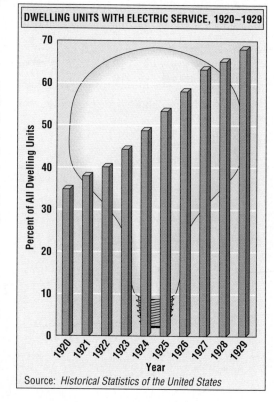

DWELLING UNITS WITH ELECTRIC SERVICE, 1920–1929

Percent of All Dwelling Units / Year

Source: *Historical Statistics of the United States*

492

The moving assembly line, used effectively during World War I, came to symbolize efficient production. As manufacturers increased the speed of their lines, production costs decreased and productivity increased. Workers, however, resented the speeding-up of the lines and objected to the dehumanizing effects of their work. Because workers had to keep pace with the machinery, opportunities for individual judgment and decision-making disappeared. Skill was sacrificed to efficiency, and work was boring and exhausting.

Henry Ford dominated the early automobile industry.

The assembly-line production used by **Henry Ford** best symbolized the new methods and benefits of mass production in the 1920s. Ford was a self-taught Michigan mechanic who had a lifetime love affair with cars. For a while, he worked for the Edison Illuminating Company in Detroit as its chief engineer, but in 1903 he quit to organize his own Ford Motor Company.

In 1908 Ford introduced the Model T Ford, a strong but very stark automobile. Compared to the comfortable and sleek cars of today, the Model T was a utilitarian torture chamber, available only in the color black. Still, the public, in need of a cheap, durable car, adored the car, giving it the endearing nickname, "Tin Lizzie." The Model T quickly became such a huge success that Ford could not keep up with the demand. Henry Ford turned to Walter E. Flanders, a disciple of Frederick Taylor, for a solution. Flanders introduced line production, an idea adapted from the meat-cutting plants of Chicago. He thus increased production to more than 10,000 cars a year. When Ford built a moving belt assembly line a few years later, costs fell still further and production skyrocketed. The time required to produce a Model T dropped from 12½ hours to 90 minutes, and production rose to 10,000 cars a week.

Ford's achievements brought the automobile within financial reach of the average American for the first time in history. In 1920 more than

Salespeople display their new electric appliances in front of their store in Louisville, Kentucky. Such electric appliances as vacuum cleaners and washing machines dramatically changed the way women spent their time at home.

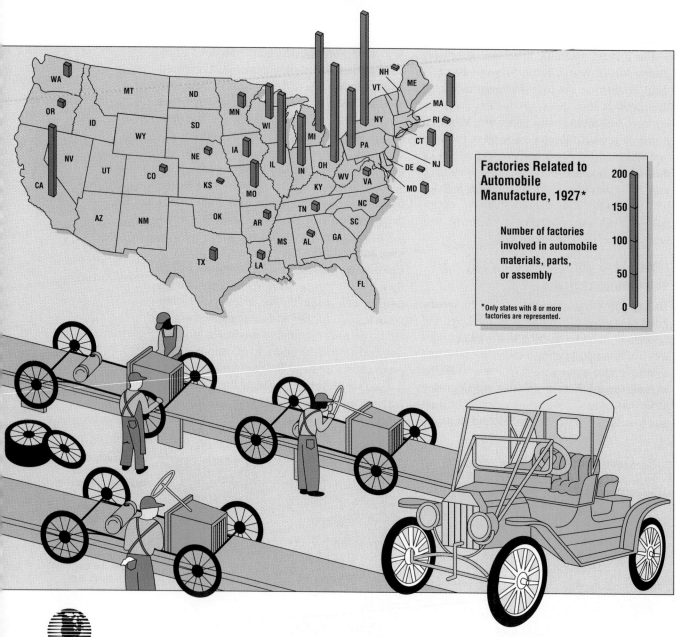

Factories Related to Automobile Manufacture, 1927*

Number of factories involved in automobile materials, parts, or assembly

	200
	150
	100
	50
	0

*Only states with 8 or more factories are represented.

map study

Location In which two regions of the country were most automobile-related factories located in 1927?

Critical Thinking What economic consequences might you predict for these regions if car sales slumped?

nine million cars traveled the nation's roadways, and by 1930 there were 26.5 million, one vehicle for every five Americans. These cars were no longer the stark, black Model Ts that forced the driver out of the car, in any sort of weather, to crank the engine. The Fords, though still common, were surpassed by General Motors' Chevrolets and Ford's own Model A's. The Chevrolet impressed car buyers with a self-starter and a palette of many colors.

The automobile industry, dominated by Ford and General Motors and centered in **Detroit, Michigan**, was the largest in the country. Not surprisingly, it had a major impact on the national economy. The success of the auto industry and its many dependent industries did much to create the business boom of the 1920s. Car makers needed massive quantities

494

of steel, rubber, glass, paint, lead, nickel, and petroleum. By 1929 the automotive industry was using 15 percent of the nation's steel, 75 percent of its plate glass, and 80 percent of the rubber produced. The oil industry quickly adjusted to this new market, switching from kerosene to gasoline production. Almost four million Americans worked in industries related to the construction, maintenance, or powering of the automobile.

The automobile changed both culture and geography.

Only a generation before Henry Ford came along, song writers had seen romance in a ride "on a bicycle built for two." By the 1920s a ride offering romance, excitement, or adventure required an automobile. The car changed America's culture, and in doing so, transformed America's landscape as well.

Effects on culture. If the car transformed the economy, it revolutionized American culture. The automobile changed people's sense of distance and space, affecting where they lived and worked. Cars made it possible for people to reach the suburbs, those towns or villages ringing the traditional central city, easily and relatively inexpensively. Because employees were more mobile, businesses began to move outside the city to less expensive or more convenient locations. Small neighbor-

hood shops gave way to the large department stores, within reach of shoppers in their Fords or Oldsmobiles.

The car's effect on families was widely debated. Some enthusiasts claimed that the automobile promoted family togetherness through evening rides, picnics, and weekend trips. Critics, however, complained about family arguments that developed, much as they do today, between parents and teenagers about the use of the car. They worried too that an apparent decline in church attendance resulted from all-day Sunday outings. Critics also claimed that the automobile gave young people too much freedom and privacy. Before the arrival of the automobile, teen courtship was most commonly practiced in the family parlor, where teenagers could be within earshot of parents or other relatives. Now, with a car, young people had a private room they could take anywhere—much to the dismay of their conservative parents.

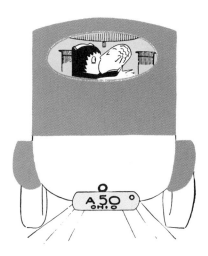

This 1926 *Vanity Fair* cartoon gently satirized young people and their use of cars.

With the huge increase in car sales, filling stations became a hub of activity during the 1920s. Stations such as this one in New York City often sold groceries and sandwiches as well as gasoline.

Cars and Family Life

Point

Promoted family life

- brought families together through car trips
- allowed parents to work closer to home
- promoted family gatherings

Counterpoint

Weakened family life

- provoked family arguments over car use
- contributed to apparent decline in church attendance
- allowed too much freedom for teenagers

As roads and highways multiplied around the country, few people paid much attention to developing road signs. By mid-decade America's motorists found themselves looking with puzzlement and dismay at such displays as this one showing (among other things) a detour between Manitowoc and Sheboygan, Wisconsin, by way of Highway 17. Drivers seemed to need a compass and talents of celestial navigation to get where they wanted to go. Some people tried a more creative means of route-marking—painting distinctive bands of color on telephone poles, trees, and fences along the way. In the East, however, there were more intersecting highways than there were colors to go around, and in the West—not enough trees and fences.

Effects on geography. The popularity of the car affected the geographic face of America as well. The federal government took a major role in building new roads and highways. Road construction became the largest item in the federal budget, providing jobs to more men and women than any other project. Virtually thousands of roads and highways were constructed during the 1920s, crisscrossing the countryside with ribbons of pavement.

Villages that had once prospered because of their placement on a rail line suffered as travelers took to the new roads and highways in their cars. Gas stations, hot dog stands, restaurants, and camping sites sprang up along the country's highways to serve cars and their passengers. In the countryside, billboards took their place beside grazing cows. In cities, streets were widened, parking spaces created, and traffic rerouted in complex one-way patterns. By the end of the decade, green and red stoplights made their entrance.

SECTION 1 REVIEW

Identify Key People and Terms
Write a sentence to identify: Frederick W. Taylor, scientific management, Henry Ford

Locate Key Places
Where was the auto industry centered in the 1920s?

Master the Main Ideas

1. **Recognizing the impact of science and technology:** In what ways did electricity change the American home and workplace?
2. **Identifying notable business leaders:** What was Henry Ford's contribution to the auto industry?
3. **Recognizing the impact of science and technology:** In what ways did the automobile change American culture and geography?

Apply Critical Thinking Skills: Drawing Conclusions
Technological changes often have mixed effects upon society. Analyze the long-term effects, both positive and negative, of the automobile on American society.

A new consumer society arose.

Key Terms: installment plan, tabloid, *The Jazz Singer*

Reading Preview
As you read this section, you will learn:

1. what new marketing techniques achieved in the 1920s.
2. what place sports had in 1920s society.
3. through what forms a national media developed.
4. what Hollywood and Broadway offered to Americans.

As Chrysler, Dodge, and others joined Ford and General Motors in the big business of selling cars, competition for the customer's eye and loyalty became quite fierce. As automobile manufacturers began to rely heavily on consumer advertising to win and keep customers, other industries joined in. An American public culture soon developed, growing to include sports, the media, and entertainment.

New marketing techniques created more eager consumers in the 1920s.

Throughout the decade manufacturers mass-produced a wide variety of new appliances and gadgets. Out of this vast grab bag of consumer products, Americans could choose not only vacuum cleaners or refrigerators, but also electric irons and electric fans. They could also purchase inexpensive wristwatches, cigarette lighters, or cameras. And purchase they did. In an era of prosperity, the question was not would people buy, but what products would they select. This willingness to spend money promoted the appearance of ever more consumer goods. Optimistic inventors filed for more than 80,000 patents for new or improved gadgets each year of the 1920s. To sustain this buying spree, manufacturers turned to two developing fields—advertising and financing.

Advertising. Manufacturers needed to convince Americans who had been raised to value thrift that spending for the present was preferable to saving for the future. Advertising thus took on the task of persuading people to buy what they wanted, whether they needed it or not. Jingles spilled from the radio, itself a newcomer to the 1920s, and print ads filled the pages of newspapers and magazines. The success of this new advertising strategy was so tremendous that economists today search for ways to persuade Americans to return to habits of thrift and saving.

Advertising prospered by appealing to people's deepest needs and anxieties. For example, deodorant manufacturers warned of terrible social consequences if their products were not used faithfully. The makers of Listerine actually dug the term "halitosis" out of medical dictionaries to excite fears of bad breath and sell their mouthwash. Car manufacturers appealed to Americans' desire for novelty by changing the design of their cars each year. Other ad campaigns urged Americans to keep pace with their neighbors, who might own more and live better than they. As one General Motors Company executive put it, advertising was essential because it made people "healthily dissatisfied with what they have."

Advertising also created big new markets for existing products, sometimes with lasting effects. For example, Albert Lasker, the most influential advertising executive of the 1920s, introduced Americans to the habit of drinking a daily glass of orange juice. For years people had been eating oranges, but they weren't consuming enough to keep up with the supply pouring forth from the new orange groves of California. So Lasker launched a campaign

In 1929 the Lambert Company presented the saga of lonely Marvin as a way to sell their Listerine mouthwash. Between 1920 and 1927, clever advertising helped raise the company's profits from roughly $100,000 a year to more than $4 million.

1920S ADVERTISING
Skill: Determining Relevant Information

Introducing the Skill. The advertising industry came into its own during the 1920s. Ad agencies combined powerful words and attractive images to entice consumers to buy such products as new automobiles and household appliances. To make smart purchases, consumers needed to be able to evaluate the information in these ads. How might consumers, then and now, make such evaluations?

Learning the Skill. Making evaluations involves **determining relevant information**, that is, recognizing whether or not data or evidence relates or applies to your purpose or problem. For example, if you were figuring out your grade for history class, your test scores would be relevant, but your performance in the school play or on the soccer team would not. To distinguish relevant information from irrelevant information, follow the steps at right:

1. Define your problem, topic, or issue.

2. Identify the general kinds of information that might be related to it. Consider definitions, details, examples, or explanations.

3. Evaluate each piece of information to determine whether it is relevant.

Applying the Skill. Study the advertisement on this page for Johnston & Murphy shoes. Determine which pieces of information presented are relevant to a decision on whether or not to buy these particular shoes. Which pieces of information are irrelevant?

This Johnston & Murphy shoe ad appeared in *Vanity Fair* magazine in August of 1929.

to convince people that it was healthy to drink orange juice, daily if possible.

Financing. The new emphasis on buying rather than saving was helped along by the availability of easy credit. Cars, refrigerators, sewing machines, and radios—along with scores of other products—were sold on the **installment plan.** Under the plan, a customer made an initial down payment and then spread the balance out over several months or years. People with modest incomes thus could purchase goods that would otherwise be outside their reach. As one popular song put it, Americans could buy anything with "a dollar down and a dollar a week." In a few short years, the American national motto went from the Puritan ethic of "waste not, want not" to "wait not, want not."

Sports became an American obsession.

In the 1920s many Americans enjoyed a new luxury—a combination of more leisure time, more money, easy credit, and the freedom of the road. They soon learned to fill their leisure hours with new forms of entertainment, with sports occupying a huge role.

Spectator sports such as baseball, football, and boxing enjoyed tremendous popularity, and sports heroes such as George "Babe" Ruth, Harold "Red" Grange, and Jack Dempsey became national stars. Across the country, tens of thousands of Americans gathered in enormous stadiums, cheering on their favorite baseball or football teams. Still more listened to the games over their radios.

Babe Ruth, the New York Yankee home run king, brought power hitting to baseball and millions of screaming fans to their feet. In 1927 Ruth hit a record-breaking 60 home runs in one season (154 games) and made the 1927 Yankees one of the best baseball teams ever. Babe Ruth, an orphan from Baltimore, Maryland, became a national hero, though his blazing temper and weakness for alcohol and women often landed him in trouble.

From the growing sport of college football emerged one of the decade's most famous sports heroes, "Red" Grange of Wheaton, Illinois. Grange played extraordinary football for the University of Illinois. In the first 12 minutes of a 1924 game against a strong Michigan team, Grange carried the ball four times and scored four touchdowns, running 263 yards. This feat escalated him to the heights of football legend and drew hundreds of thousands of fans to college football. When he

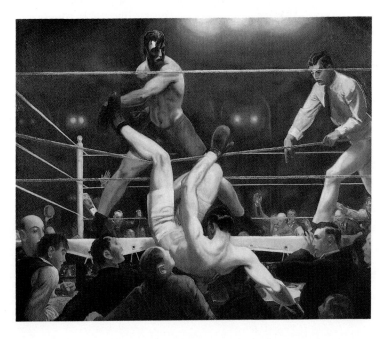

Red Grange

turned professional the next year, Grange worked his magic before huge crowds in Chicago and New York. He also graced a 1925 cover of *Time* magazine, the first athlete to do so, and won a lucrative movie contract.

Like Babe Ruth and Red Grange, Jack Dempsey electrified his chosen sport. Boxing fans went wild in 1921 when he successfully defended his world heavyweight title by knocking out the European champ, France's Georges Carpentier. Fans paid $1.8 million to watch the fight in the new 60,000-seat stadium built near Jersey City, New Jersey, specifically for the fight. The match was the first important sporting event ever broadcast on radio, heard in thousands of speakeasies, poolrooms, lodge halls, and living rooms up and down the East Coast. It paved the way for the sports extravaganzas of modern day.

Heroes emerged in other sports as well. In 1926, 19-year-old **Gertrude Ederle** thrilled women and men alike by swimming 31 miles across the English Channel in the fastest time yet recorded—14 hours and 31 minutes. Ederle, a gold-medal winner at the 1924 Olympics, was the first woman to accomplish this feat. Another stellar athlete, Bobby Jones, played game after game of technically flawless golf to raise the American game to the stan-

Artist George Bellows captures the drama and intensity of a Jack Dempsey fight in *Dempsey and Firpo* (The Whitney Museum of American Art, New York City).

dards of world golf competition. As Jones won tournament after tournament, amateur golfers flocked to American courses and the game grew tremendously. Still another athlete, William Tilden, transformed American tennis. Before Tilden became the first American to win the men's singles title at Wimbledon in 1920, few Americans took the game seriously. Another American tennis champion was Helen Wills, who was known for both her poise and her ability to hit the ball harder than any woman she faced. Between 1923 and 1938, California-born Wills won the U.S. women's title seven times and Wimbledon eight times. After Tilden and Wills infused energy into the sport, tennis attracted millions of weekend athletes and fans.

A national media developed through newspapers and radio.

A national popular culture depended in large part on the rise of a national communications system. By the 1920s men and women learned about world events, domestic politics, entertainment news, social happenings, and their favorite pitcher's statistics through two main sources, large newspaper chains and radio.

During the 1920s Americans began to read standardized news, that is, news written by national press associations such as the Associated Press and United Press and distributed to newspapers around the country. Many people were tempted to read a newspaper every day because of the appearance of a new type of paper: the **tabloid**. Tabloids caught the eye with banner headlines, revealing photos, and plenty of stories about sex and violence.

Americans also began to turn to the radio for information and entertainment. The first commercial radio broadcast occurred on November 2, 1920, over station KDKA in Pittsburgh. By 1927 nearly 700 radio stations were beaming their signals across the country.

Like the newspapers, the radio helped create mass culture by blurring regional differences. Listeners heard the same news and serial shows, spoken in the same dialect. They also

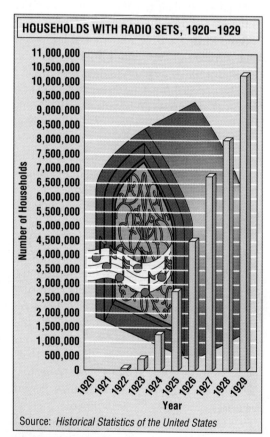

HOUSEHOLDS WITH RADIO SETS, 1920–1929

Number of Households (y-axis): 0 to 11,000,000

Year (x-axis): 1920, 1921, 1922, 1923, 1924, 1925, 1926, 1927, 1928, 1929

Source: *Historical Statistics of the United States*

chart study How many more households owned radios in 1929 than in 1920?

Critical Thinking What effect did widespread radio usage have on American society?

Helen Wills and William Tilden captured the hearts of American tennis fans with their exceptional talent and grace.

heard the same advertisements telling them what to buy. With its national audience, the radio had the power to create folk heroes overnight. When **Charles Lindbergh** became the first person to fly nonstop across the Atlantic Ocean from New York to Paris in 1927, the radio brought his amazing feat into American homes and made him an instant celebrity.

Radio programming, though, also reinforced national prejudices. One of the most popular radio shows, "Amos 'n' Andy," spread demeaning stereotypes about African Americans into homes whose occupants knew little about black life. Other minorities received similar treatment. Radio shows relied on such stock characters as the Italian gangster, the bloodthirsty Indian, the Mexican with the sing-song voice, and the tight-fisted Jew.

Hollywood and Broadway brought entertainment to millions.

Movies formed the center of the new national popular culture. During the 1920s some 60 million Americans on average flocked to the movies each week, almost half the entire population of the United States. In the darkness of lavishly decorated movie palaces, people enjoyed adventure, glitter, and fantasy.

Moviemaking was the fourth largest industry in the country, and **Hollywood** was at its heart. Located in the southern part of California, Hollywood nurtured one of the most influential film directors of all time—Cecil B. De Mille. His style, always spectacular, set the standard both on and off the screen. Americans took their cues on fashion and manners from such De Mille classics as *The Ten Commandments* (1923) and *Forbidden Fruit* (1921). His shows were filled with romance and glamour, por-

When pilot Charles Lindbergh took off alone from Long Island on a misty day and landed near Paris 33½ hours later, he became an overnight hero. American children could soon play with the toy version of Lucky Lindy's airplane, the *Spirit of St. Louis.*

A still from Charlie Chaplin's classic film *The Gold Rush* serves as a backdrop for some of the most memorable actors and films of the 1920s. Mickey Mouse, top left, debuted in *Steamboat Willie* (1928), the first cartoon to use sound. Rudolph Valentino, top right, performed the role of the handsome Arab seducer with Agnes Ayres in *The Sheik* (1921). Paul Robeson, lower right, achieved worldwide fame with his 1930 London appearance as the lead actor in Shakespeare's *Othello*. He was the most respected African American actor of his time. Al Jolson, lower left, introduced Americans to their first movie with sound, *The Jazz Singer*. Jolson performed the role in blackface, wearing makeup to look like an African American. A Jewish immigrant from Lithuania, Jolson brought an electric energy to the screen.

traying a world of luxury and leisure, of moral freedom and hard-won success.

Charlie Chaplin was the most popular film star of the 1920s. Chaplin's tramp-clown, in baggy pants and derby hat, became the universal symbol of American cinema. His films were quite different from the showy spectacles of De Mille. Through such classics as *A Woman of Paris* (1923) and *The Gold Rush* (1925), Chaplin criticized the social order of the 1920s. The filmmaker offered sympathetic portraits of the poor while spoofing the pretensions of the wealthy. Other film stars included Mary Pickford and Douglas Fairbanks—America's favorite couple—and Rudolph Valentino, an Italian-born heartthrob.

In 1927 Warner Brothers added to the movie mania by introducing the first "talkie," ***The Jazz Singer***. With the addition of sound, the popularity of films increased still more. The animated cartoon, a product of the genius of Max Fleischer and Walt Disney, drew younger Americans into the theaters as well. Disney's famous creation Mickey Mouse debuted in the first cartoon to use sound, *Steamboat Willie*, in 1928. Walt Disney himself provided Mickey Mouse's voice.

Like the radio, the movies did little to promote positive attitudes toward different ethnic groups. Mexicans generally appeared as sleepy-eyed peasants. Likewise, roles for African American actors were limited to those portraying humiliating stereotypes.

African American actors fared somewhat better in the realm of live theater, where shows with all-black casts or black stars played on Broadway in New York City every year of the 1920s. In New York's Greenwich Village, Charles Gilpin played an important role in Eugene O'Neill's classic *Emperor Jones* (1920), a successful play performed in Harlem. On Broadway the hit of the 1921 season was *Shuffle Along*, a musical with an all-black cast whose star was a talented young woman named Florence Mills. Black actors continued to win featured roles in Broadway hits in the 1920s and 1930s with such shows as *Runnin' Wild*, *Porgy and Bess*, and *Green Pastures* (1929 Pulitzer Prize winner for drama). One

African American actor in particular, **Paul Robeson**, became a huge success. A former All-American football star, Robeson first triumphed in O'Neill's *All God's Chillun Got Wings*. He later starred in the Broadway hit musical *Showboat* and in a London production of William Shakespeare's *Othello*, gaining worldwide fame. However, Robeson's support of radical causes ultimately hurt his popularity.

Together—advertising, sports, tabloids, radio, and movies—all created an American popular culture, with common speech, dress, behavior, and heroes. In most cases information and entertainment drew people together in the 1920s, molding and mirroring a society infatuated with novelty and obsessed with spectacle.

SECTION **2** REVIEW

Identify Key People and Terms
Write a sentence to identify: installment plan, Babe Ruth, Gertrude Ederle, tabloid, Charles Lindbergh, Charlie Chaplin, *The Jazz Singer*, Paul Robeson

Locate Key Places
What city was the center of the moviemaking business?

Master the Main Ideas

1. **Perceiving cause/effect relationships:** How did new marketing techniques create more customers for products in the 1920s?
2. **Understanding cultural development:** Why did sports heroes become popular in the 1920s?
3. **Understanding cultural development:** How did newpapers and radio contribute to the creation of a national media culture?
4. **Understanding cultural development: (a)** What forms of entertainment did Hollywood and Broadway provide? **(b)** Who were some of the leading stars?

Apply Critical Thinking Skills: Making Comparisons
What do you think are the major elements in today's popular culture? Which, if any, were not present in the 1920s?

Young women took the lead in the 1920s.

Key Terms: flapper, Grand Ole Opry

Reading Preview
As you read this section, you will learn:

1. what the flapper symbolized.
2. how women's lives changed during the 1920s.
3. how urban and rural culture both developed in the 1920s.

Often historians speak of a national mood during a decade or an era, which though not shared by everyone, is strong enough among middle-class Americans to dominate national life. The nicknames given to the 1920s—the Jazz Age, the Roaring Twenties—support the notion that the mood of that decade was more self-indulgent than the pre-war Progressive mood of self-sacrifice. As the contemporary writer F. Scott Fitzgerald put it, the postwar generation was disillusioned with reform and idealism for they had "grown up to find all Gods dead, all wars fought, all faiths in man shaken." The goal of many young men and women of the Jazz Age was to live for the here and now.

The flapper was the symbol of a new youth culture.

The essential elements of the new culture were freedom and spontaneity. Young white Americans seemed, to their elders at least, determined to ignore all traditional rules of behavior. The older generation was shocked as their sons and daughters abandoned the waltz for the rhythms of jazz, drank bootlegged liquor out of hip-pocket flasks, and raced their cars at breakneck speeds.

The symbol of this revolution in morals and manners was the **flapper**. She was a young woman who had abandoned all older views of femininity and women's roles. The flapper preferred to be sexy and daring rather than shy and innocent. She smoked in public, drank liquor, swore, and flirted openly with men.

Her appearance advertised her new mood. Hemlines rose above the knees, waistlines dropped below the hips, and body-restricting corsets were thrown away entirely. Long hair, which in previous decades was a woman's crowning glory, was left on the barber shop floor. "Bobbed" hair, the shorter the better, replaced it. Cosmetics, once the mark of a woman of loose morals, became a standard part of the new look. Entrepreneurs were quick to see the potential. Beauty parlors opened up in cities across the country, and the cosmetics industry grew quickly.

The flappers were by no means only white women. Young African American women in New York City and other urban areas chose to abandon their long skirts as did Chinese American teenagers in San Francisco. A worker at

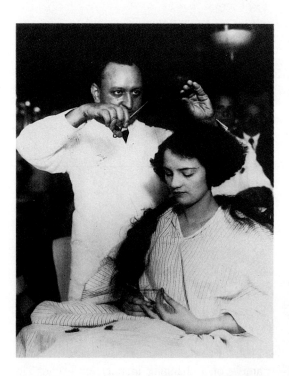

Actress Muriel Redd of Chicago has her hair bobbed at the Hotel McAlpin barber shop in New York City in 1920.

the Congregational Mission in San Francisco's Chinatown described the young women of 1924: "The Chinese girls bob their hair, wear sleeveless dresses, and look just like American flappers." The Chinese teenagers created a unique cultural blend for themselves. One girl commented, "On weekends we'd go eat *won-ton* and drink orange freeze at the soda fountain." Their parents, though, often had difficulty understanding their children, especially when they changed their given names to American ones. "My parents wanted me to grow up a good Chinese girl, but I am an American and I can't accept all the old Chinese ways and ideas," explained Flora Belle Jan of Fresno, California.

To a modern American teenager, the flapper is hardly shocking. In the 1920s, however, this new female ideal disturbed adults who had been raised with Victorian images of the sexes. The new woman seemed to them to signal the collapse of the nation's moral standards.

The flappers and other Jazz Age young people borrowed, and largely misinterpreted, **Sigmund Freud**'s theories of psychoanalysis in order to justify their behavior. The Austrian-born scientist and doctor had developed a new method for treating troubled patients, a method based upon the theory that abnormal behavior was often the result of unconscious and suppressed fears or desires. By examining a person's thoughts and feelings through a process called psychoanalysis, Freud hoped to cure certain mental disorders. Without reading Freud's complex theory carefully, or at all, American followers of this new psychology claimed that mental health depended on satisfying all one's desires. Repression, that is, control over human drives or desires, thus led to emotional problems. They concluded that freedom and lack of inhibition were necessary to one's mental health.

Women's lives were changed by new technologies.

The flapper was only the most sensational example of a changing identity for women. In fact, changes in hair style or hemline, in appearance or courtship rituals, may not have

These young Chinese American women show the influence of two cultures. Their clothing is Chinese, but their hair is bobbed in the latest American fashion. They are playing mahjong, a Chinese game that became an American fad in the 1920s.

been particularly important to millions of married or older women. For them, the new scientific technologies and the consumer orientation of the era had a more revolutionary impact on their lives.

One developing technology had a dramatic impact on many women's lives. Because of the availability of inexpensive and safe birth control, the national birth rate fell for the first time during the 1920s. As discussed in Chapter 8, Margaret Sanger led the battle for women's access to birth control. Throughout the decade she encountered fierce and well-organized opposition from the Roman Catholic Church and others who believed that sexual abstinence was the only moral means to prevent conception.

Other new technologies had unexpected effects. Although electric appliances were promoted as labor-saving devices, they did not lighten the average homemaker's workload. Instead, advice columnists and product advertisements encouraged women to use the new appliances to meet higher standards of cleanliness. They equated cleanliness with motherly love and tried to make women who did not keep spotless homes feel like failures. In addition, the availability of household appliances stopped a trend toward such jobs as taking in laundry and baking outside of the home. As a result, the household chores expected of women increased in the 1920s.

Ruhe López, a young Mexican American woman, was born in Mazatlán, Mexico, but moved to Los Angeles, California, with her American husband, a mechanic. López, though she considered herself to be Mexican by heart and by "race," adapted herself quite easily to the life of a young American woman. She took on a number of different jobs—landlord, real estate agent, chauffeur, and movie studio extra—so that she and her husband would be able to dress and live well. Ruhe López described their good life to an interviewer:

I get up in the morning at seven and make breakfast for

AN AMERICAN
★ SPEAKS

my husband and myself. This consists of mush, eggs, milk, and coffee. I also prepare his lunch and take him to his work in the automobile which we have bought and then I go to mine. At noon when I come home I make ham and eggs or anything for lunch or take my lunch in a restaurant. I come early in the afternoon if I don't have anything to do, and after I have fixed and swept the house, I get supper ready. That is our big meal, as it is with the Americans. I make Mexican stews, vegetables, and American side dishes, chocolate, milk, and coffee, *frijoles*, etc. I buy pies and sweets and we have a good supper. Then we go out to a movie or some dance hall or riding in the automobile.

Urban and rural culture developed separately in the 1920s.

The 1920 census showed that for the first time in the nation's history more people lived in towns and cities than in the countryside. About 54 million Americans lived in urban areas, compared to 52 million in rural areas. These figures did not mean that the average American lived in a major urban center. Only one in four resided in a city of more than 100,000 people. Nevertheless, the population shift was significant.

Despite the trend to an urban society, rural culture in this country remained strong. Many people resisted the spread of urban culture and

values fostered by the radio, syndicated newspapers, and movies. In particular, rural-based churches fought to preserve their traditions from this invasion of new manners, morals, and ideas. Prohibition, strongly supported by rural Protestant Americans, was one example of the resistance to urban culture.

Some advocates of rural culture realized that the media could be used to spread their values and traditions as well. Singing groups such as the Carter Family acquired a national following through their appearances on a weekly broadcast from the **Grand Ole Opry**, a musical hall in **Nashville, Tennessee**. With these Saturday night performances at the Opry, the Carters and similar groups introduced Americans to a form of country music that kept alive the ballad tradition of the English, Scottish, and Irish settlers of the mountain regions of the American continent.

SECTION **3** REVIEW

Identify Key People and Terms
Write a sentence to identify: flapper, Sigmund Freud, Grand Ole Opry

Locate Key Places
In what city was the Grand Ole Opry located?

Master the Main Ideas
1. **Understanding cultural development:** What was the significance of the flapper as a new image for women?
2. **Recognizing the impact of science and technology:** In what ways did technological innovations affect women's lives during the 1920s?
3. **Understanding cultural development: (a)** What evidence is available that America was becoming an urban culture in the 1920s? **(b)** How did rural America respond?

Apply Critical Thinking Skills: Demonstrating Reasoned Judgment
Historians and writers have said that the national mood of the 1920s was one of disillusionment and self-indulgence. How might you characterize your decade of the 1990s?

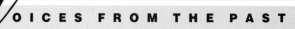

Art and music shaped the Jazz Age.

Key Term: Harlem Renaissance

Reading Preview

As you read this section, you will learn:

1. who made up the Lost Generation of artists.
2. what artistic movement developed in the African American community during the 1920s.
3. what role music and dance played in the culture of the 1920s.

Not all young Americans embraced the politics and cultural changes of their generation. The most articulate critics of the Jazz Age could be found within the country's artistic and intellectual community.

Writers and artists made up the Lost Generation.

The 1920s spawned a group of discontented artists known as the Lost Generation, alienated from a society whose values they rejected. Critical of their nation, yet too pessimistic to be reformers, these artists were unlike those of the Progressive era. They believed that all ideals, all causes, all dreams of a better society were pointless. The only possible salvation came from art.

As these talented men and women took refuge in the world of art, they produced a major flowering of American creativity—an outpouring of literature and painting. Many Lost Generation artists gathered together in New York's Greenwich Village, an urban neighborhood of tenements and brownstones. Others left the country for the artist communities of Paris and Rome. Although these exile artists loudly renounced their native land, they continued to carry the United States with them in their hearts and minds.

VOICES FROM THE PAST

A Leaky Inheritance

The behavior of "flaming youth" in the 1920s produced a predictable friction between generations. John F. Carter, Jr., responded to the older generation with an aggressive defense. Do his words have a familiar ring? Explain.

In the first place, I would like to observe that the older generation had certainly pretty well ruined this world before passing it on to us. They gave us this Thing, knocked to pieces, leaky, red-hot threatening to blow up; and then they are surprised that we don't accept it with the same attitude of pretty, decorous enthusiasm with which they received it . . . . Now, with loving pride, they turn over their wreck to us; and, since we are not properly overwhelmed with loving gratitude, shake their heads and sigh, "Dear! dear! We were so much better-mannered than these wild young people."

American literature. Two young novelists became the major chroniclers—and eventually, symbols—of the Lost Generation: F. Scott Fitzgerald and Ernest Hemingway. **F. Scott Fitzgerald** was handsome and gifted, rising to sudden fame with his first novel, *This Side of Paradise* (1920). The book described the life of

F. Scott and Zelda Fitzgerald set off on a motoring adventure in their car, a Marmon. The couple was famous in their youth for enjoying a fun-filled, indulgent life.

507

Ernest Hemingway

his generation, a life of frenzied activity and gaiety that the author felt hid the fear and bewilderment of those living for "the here and now." Fitzgerald, who for much of his life lived the same lavish, excessive, self-destructive life as his fictional characters, also wrote *The Great Gatsby* (1925) and *Tender is the Night* (1934). In each novel, he painted the tragedy and disillusionment that underlay the lavish wealth and glitter of the Jazz Age.

Ernest Hemingway served during World War I as an ambulance driver in Europe. By his 19th birthday, he found himself badly wounded in Italy and profoundly disillusioned by what he saw occurring on the battlefields. When the war ended, Hemingway settled into self-imposed exile in Europe. He soon attracted attention for his spare, unadorned writing style and for the appeal of his courageous heroes. In *The Sun Also Rises* (1926), Hemingway captured the world of the American refugees who spent their days in Parisian cafes, living lives of aimlessness and quiet desperation.

Many writers who remained in the United States focused on the confining, narrow, often

The Paintings of Georgia O'Keeffe

In December 1916 Georgia O'Keeffe sent a set of drawings she had done to her friend Anita Pollitzer. O'Keeffe had been working on these drawings throughout the autumn. To her the drawings were personal and private and she asked that Pollitzer show them to no one else. On viewing them however, Pollitzer was struck by their beauty and vitality. She took them to photographer and art patron Alfred Stieglitz, who also was awed by their strength, sensitivity, and candor. Without O'Keeffe's permission, Steiglitz exhibited them. The drawings were widely acclaimed, and

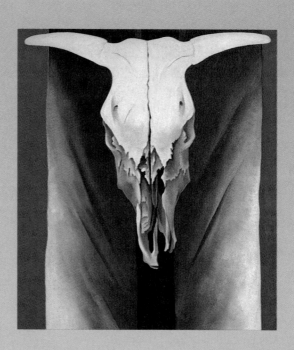

Georgia O'Keeffe soon became a prominent figure in the New York art world.

O'Keeffe painted *Cow's Skull, Red, White, and Blue* in 1931. (Metropolitan Museum of Art, New York City)

O'Keeffe did some of her most well-known paintings in the 1920s. She painted delicate flower blossoms, enlarged to fill entire canvases. She painted bold scenes of New York that highlighted the sharp lines and contrasting colors of the city. She did a series of

Highlights of American Life

hypocritical world of small-town life. In his first novel, *Main Street* (1920), **Sinclair Lewis** drew a scathing picture of middle America. The book made him an instant success. Lewis went on to attack American businesspeople, doctors, and religious charlatans in novels such as *Babbit* (1922), *Arrowsmith* (1925), and *Elmer Gantry* (1927). In 1930 Lewis, one of the most successful novelists of the Jazz Age, became the first American to receive the Nobel Prize for literature.

The South produced a group of novelists who presented an unromantic and complex portrait of the life and culture of their region. The most renowned, **William Faulkner**, began his writing career with *The Sound and the Fury* (1929) just as the Jazz Age was ending. Faulkner created a remarkable universe in the fictional Yoknapatawpha [yok′nə pə tô′fə] County, modeled after the area around his hometown in Mississippi.

Another voice, that of H. L. Mencken, editor of *Mercury* magazine, consistently provided one of the most cynical commentaries on the 1920s. He wrote hundreds of essays mocking almost every aspect of American life, saving his worst barbs for the middle class (the "booboisie," a turn on "bourgeoisie") and social reformers.

American poetry. American poetry and drama also blossomed in the soil of disillusionment. T. S. Eliot, Edna St. Vincent Millay, e.e. cummings, Ezra Pound, Amy Lowell, Robert Frost, and Carl Sandburg all experimented with new forms of expression during the 1920s. In several major poems, **T. S. Eliot** captured the loneliness and alienation he found in modern life. The very titles of many of Eliot's poems express his cold criticism: *The Waste Land* (1922) and *The Hollow Men* (1925). Eliot became a major voice in modern literature.

Robert Frost chiseled his deceptively simple poetry from different materials: from nature, from farm life, from plain New England speech. Using images of falling snow and empty woods in "Stopping by Woods on a Snowy Evening" (1923), Frost subtly suggested the complexities of human fate.

American art. Painters too were breaking new ground in the 1920s. **Georgia O'Keeffe** and **Edward Hopper** expanded the subject matter and the techniques of art. O'Keeffe painted the natural environment using a powerful simplicity of form and dramatic colors. She gained particular fame for her treatment of the American Southwest. You can learn more about O'Keeffe's work in the *Highlights of American Life* at left. Hopper painted starkly lighted scenes of lonely roads, vacant rooms, and women seated alone, lost in thought. His most famous work is *Nighthawks* (1942), a late-night scene of a sparsely populated diner, showing the loneliness and feeling of isolation the artist saw in American big-city life.

still-life paintings that developed from the concrete to the abstract. About her work, one 1920s art critic wrote:

Miss O'Keeffe is perhaps the most original painter in America. . . . She has discovered a beautiful language, with unsuspected melodies and rhythms, and has created in this language a new set of symbols; by these means she has opened up a whole area of human consciousness.

Georgia O'Keeffe continued to paint for another 60 years. Her work hangs in all of America's leading art museums. The power and grace of her paintings has made Georgia O'Keeffe one of America's most popular and respected artists.

A cultural renaissance occurred within the African American community.

Ironically, the decade in which one of the fiercest waves of racial hatred and violence against African Americans occurred also included one of the major explosions of their creativity. As a result, the 1920s became famous throughout the world as the age of jazz.

New York City's Harlem, the world's largest urban African American community, was the black cultural capital—drawing theatrical companies, poets, writers, painters, and musicians. The excitement of the place and the time, known as the **Harlem Renaissance**, was captured by poet **Langston Hughes**, who described his arrival in Harlem:

I can never put on paper the thrill of the underground ride

AN AMERICAN ★ SPEAKS

to Harlem. I had never been in a subway before and it fascinated me—the noise, the speed, the green lights ahead. At every station I kept watching for the sign: 135TH STREET. When I saw it, I held my breath. I came out on the platform with two heavy bags and looked around. It was still early morning and people were going to work. Hundreds of colored people! I wanted to shake hands with them, speak to them. I hadn't seen any colored people for so long—that is, any Negro colored people.

I went up the steps and out into the bright September sunlight. Harlem! I stood there, dropped my bags, took a deep breath and felt happy again.

The African American artists and writers of the Harlem Renaissance were often harsh critics of American race relations. They used their skills to dramatize the injustices of segregation and the horrors of lynching and to capture the tragedy of black poverty. Yet Hughes, James Weldon Johnson, Claude McKay, Countee Cullen, Zora Neale Hurston, and Jessie Redmond Fauset also expressed the pride of African Americans in their own history and culture. Hurston, born in Eatonville, Florida, joined the Harlem community to pursue her writing and her education. She celebrated African American culture in a series of novels and collections of folklore.

Together the men and women of the Harlem Renaissance gave other Americans a better un-

Langston Hughes, born in 1902 in Joplin, Missouri, went on to become one of America's leading writers. He grew up in Lawrence, Kansas, raised by his grandmother until he was 12. After her death, Hughes moved first to Illinois, then to Ohio with his mother.

Artist Archibald Motley, Jr., captured the energy of the African American community in *Black Belt*. (1934, Hampton University Museum, Hampton, Virginia)

derstanding of the daily lives of black citizens and the immorality of racism. Jean Toomer's *Cane* (1923) and Claude McKay's *Home to Harlem* (1928) both captured the rich life of the 1920s African American community.

By the end of the 1920s, the spirit of the Harlem Renaissance had spread to other cities with large African American populations such as Detroit, Chicago, Houston, and Los Angeles. The literary and musical contributions of its many artists helped project the image of the "new Negro," proud of one's race and heritage.

Music and dance shaped the culture of the 1920s.

In Harlem and across the country, music was everywhere—and the most influential sounds of the 1920s came from the African American community. Decades before the 1920s, black musicians in **New Orleans** developed the sounds of jazz. Jazz had its roots in various musical traditions from the African slave spirituals to the blues. It was a music that was both black and American, born from the music of protest against injustice, of a spirit that celebrated its joy in the face of scorn and oppression. Jazz could not have originated with white musicians, nor could it have arisen in Africa. It was a unique African American contribution. Since its beginnings, jazz has influenced many forms of modern music ranging from rock and roll to rap.

In the 1920s, when jazz reached the North and the tens of thousands of transplanted black southerners, the musical form finally came into its golden age. In Chicago jazz was adopted by the gangsters, who filled their speakeasies and nightclubs with its brassy sounds to keep the customers coming. In New York, as well, jazz made a spectacular entrance. Upon their return from World War I, the 369th U.S. Infantry, known by their nickname of the Harlem Hell Fighters, paraded in full glory up Fifth Avenue. With them marched the African American musician Lt. James Reese Europe and his big jazz band. A New York City high school student watching the parade rejoiced in the sounds of the day. Years later he remembered his excitement upon viewing Jim Europe's band:

AN AMERICAN ★ SPEAKS

Then we heard the music! Somewhere in the line of march was Jim Europe and his band that the French had heard before we ever did. Major Little claims they played no jazz until they got to Harlem later that day—but if what we along the curbs heard was not jazz, it was the best substitute for it I've ever heard in my life.

Louis Armstrong, a master of the jazz trumpet, sends his melodic sounds out to a large radio audience.

Many of the originators of jazz were unacknowledged in their society and remain unrecognized today. Not until the white community embraced jazz did African American jazz musicians receive national attention and find financial security. **Louis Armstrong**, a master of improvisation on the trumpet, and **Duke Ellington**, a leading jazz composer, bandleader, and pianist, were the first to win fame and glory. Sadly, Ferdinand "Jelly

Bessie Smith, an African American star of the blues scene of the 1920s, defied many odds to become a celebrity.

Jim Europe's Army band, at left, brought American jazz music to France and back to New York City. The band traveled with the 369th U.S. Infantry, a troop of African American soldiers who fought during World War I. Upon the regiment's triumphant return to Harlem in 1919, black families such as the ones at right watched with excitement and pride.

Roll" Morton, the first jazz composer and one of the most innovative jazz pianists of all time, missed out on his deserved acclaim at the time. Born in New Orleans, Morton was on the West Coast during the 1920s, spending much of the decade suing record companies who copied his ideas without paying him a dime. His experience was typical of African American jazz and blues musicians, many of whom never received credit for their accomplishments.

As these African American men were perfecting their jazz playing, African American women were concentrating on the blues. At the height of the Jazz Age, **Bessie Smith** and **Ma Rainey** were among the young black blues queens who could be seen driving through town in their smart automobiles and wearing fur coats that matched the leopard skin interior of their cars. They wore fancy feathered hats and richly beaded gowns, and their parties and appearances were routinely reported in the papers. Talented and hypnotic performers, these young women sold millions of records, many through mail-order ads in the *Chicago Defender*, an African American newspaper. Chicago was, and continues to be, the home of the classic blues, which like jazz, traveled northward with migrating black southerners.

As white musicians adapted the sounds and rhythms of jazz, the music was transformed into a style perfect for ballroom dancing. The Paul Whiteman orchestra, led by the plaintive cornet sounds of Leon "Bix" Beiderbecke, was the most successful of the white jazz bands. His orchestra's one lasting masterpiece was *Rhapsody in Blue*, written by George Gershwin especially for the group.

Parties for young people invariably included dancing, usually involving close contact between partners. Some parents objected, but churches held dances to attract the young, and schools taught dancing to their students. Flappers had special enthusiasm for the art of dancing, learning every variation of the fox-trot and mastering such steps as the camel-walk, tango, and toddle. The most popular dance of the 1920s, though, was the Charleston. Appearing first in a black musical called *Runnin' Wild*, this dance swept the country within six months. Teenagers spent hours learning its difficult steps and rhythms, becoming expert at such moves as crossing hands and knocking knees.

walking in off the street. And where awful bootleg whiskey and good fried fish or steaming chitterlings were sold at very low prices. And the dancing and singing and impromptu entertaining went on until dawn came in at the windows.

These parties, often termed whist parties or dances, were usually announced by brightly colored cards stuck in the grille of apartment house elevators. Some of the cards were highly entertaining in themselves.

Almost every Saturday night when I was in Harlem I went to a house-rent party. I wrote lots of poems about house-rent parties, and ate thereat many a fried fish and pig's foot—with liquid refreshments on the side. I met ladies' maids and truck drivers, laundry workers and shoe shine boys, seamstresses and porters. I can still hear their laughter in my ears, hear the soft slow music, and feel the floor shaking as the dancers danced.

The look, complete with the flapper's short dresses and long beads, became forever the symbol of the Roaring Twenties.

The Harlem Renaissance and the birth of jazz, for all of the positive attention they brought to African Americans, did little to promote permanent change in the black community. Economic hardship and racial prejudice remained, and the white Americans who rode the subway to visit Harlem's exciting nightclubs soon lost interest and went elsewhere. The black residents of Harlem went on with their lives. Langston Hughes described the experience in his autobiography:

The Saturday night rent parties that I attended were often **AN AMERICAN ★ SPEAKS** more amusing than any night club, in small apartments where God knows who lived—because the guests seldom did—but where the piano would often be augmented by a guitar, or an old cornet, or somebody with a pair of drums

SECTION **4** REVIEW

Identify Key People and Terms
Write a sentence to identify: F. Scott, Fitzgerald, Ernest Hemingway, Sinclair Lewis, William Faulkner, T. S. Eliot, Georgia O'Keeffe, Edward Hopper, Harlem Renaissance, Langston Hughes, Louis Armstrong, Duke Ellington, Bessie Smith, Ma Rainey

Locate Key Places
In which city did jazz originate?

Master the Main Ideas

1. **Understanding developments in art and literature:** Who were the Lost Generation artists and what did they represent?
2. **Understanding developments in music and literature:** What were the central themes of the works produced by the Harlem Renaissance?
3. **Understanding developments in music:** What forms of music and dancing shaped the culture of the 1920s?

Apply Critical Thinking Skills: Identifying Central Ideas
Imagine that you are an artist living during the 1920s. Explain to fellow Americans why you have chosen to move away from the United States and live in exile in Paris.

Mann's Chinese Theatre retains the splendor of Hollywood's star-struck, glamorous past.

TOURING THE PAST

ann's Chinese Theatre

On April 23, 1886 the motion picture had its world premiere in Koster and Bial's Music Hall in Manhattan. The audience, sitting on wooden chairs in a small dark room, watched in captivated amazement as Thomas Alva Edison's latest invention, the Vitascope, threw moving images in black and white across a blank wall. The silent show lasted only a few minutes, but the public was hooked. Not ten years later, thousands of movie halls, called nickelodeons (because of the five-cent admission charge), had sprung up.

By 1913 Hollywood, California, was the center of a new entertainment industry. On its temporary stages Mary Pickford, Charlie Chaplin, Rudolph Valentino, and other performers rose to stardom, groomed and promoted by the fledgling studios of Twentieth Century Fox, Paramount, and Warner Brothers. Rising with this new form of show business, and far removed from the darkness of the nickelodeon, was a new type of movie hall, one that richly deserved its name—the movie palace.

By 1920 nearly every large city in the country had a movie palace. On the outside, these great halls of film masqueraded as Greek temples, ancient shrines, and

Maya palaces, but their true identities were revealed by the glittering marquees that stretched across their fronts. Inside, patrons entered a world of pure Hollywood luxury. Lobbies and lounges were outfitted with marble staircases, crystal chandeliers, and ornate furniture. Designed to accommodate a thousand people or more in plush velvet seats (including box seats), the auditoriums were decorated with gilded plaster work, rich carpeting, and silk wallpaper. Enhancing the luxury was a complete orchestra that performed music for the live stage shows that were featured with the films.

One of the most fanciful movie palaces ever built was Grauman's (now Mann's) Chinese Theatre in Hollywood. From the outside it resembles an elaborate Chinese pagoda, complete with large stone lions guarding the main entrance. Inside, the theater is an exotic blend of carved red and gold doors, ornate murals, and dragon-

shaped chandeliers. The 2,258-seat pagoda palace opened in 1927, and for a few years patrons were treated to a movie and a stage show that featured dancers, musicians, and even animals. When the show was about to begin, two large Oriental gongs were sounded.

The Chinese Theatre was the creation of Sidney Grauman, who got his taste for show business while traveling with his father in minstrel shows. In 1906 young Sid persuaded his father to open a nickelodeon in San Francisco. After a shaky start—they lost their first building to the San Francisco earthquake—the Graumans soon owned two thriving movie houses. In 1917 Sid took his profits and headed for Hollywood. Over the next ten years he built four lavish movie palaces, of which the Chinese Theatre is his masterpiece.

Mann's Chinese Theatre has survived the years with virtually all of its original architecture and decorations intact. Here visitors can relive the gold-and-velvet fantasy of a glamorous past while inhaling the aroma of fresh popcorn and watching a new movie—all for the price of admission.

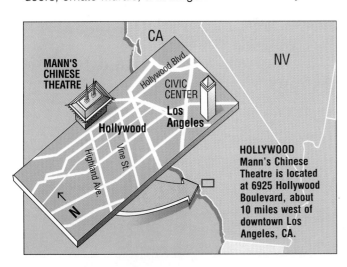

HOLLYWOOD
Mann's Chinese Theatre is located at 6925 Hollywood Boulevard, about 10 miles west of downtown Los Angeles, CA.

A Hollywood director, 1939:

The Chinese Theatre became—and remains—famous for the imprints in its concrete courtyard. William de Mille, an old Hollywood hand, offers an ironic description of this movieland ritual in his memoir. Why do you think this "imprint tradition" was so popular?

In the pavement of its impressive entrance-yard were set concrete blocks containing footprints and handprints of famous stars, from Mary Pickford down to Rin Tin Tin. This gave a fine effect of deathless age . . . with the added improvement that should one of these celebrities be so unfortunate as to become an unwelcome memory . . . the stone record of his personality could be removed overnight and that of the latest favorite substituted in a simple but touching ceremony which made every tourist feel that he had been present while history was being made.

The Age of Advertising Arrives

12A

TIME FRAME
1920s

GEOGRAPHIC SETTING
United States

As the advertising business became a specialized industry, advertising agencies hired the best writers, illustrators, and graphic designers to create messages that would persuade traditionally thrifty Americans to purchase the wares of American manufacturers.

The most distinctive feature of the new consumer-oriented economy of the United States after World War I was its emphasis on advertising. American business discovered marketing. "No longer was it considered enough to recommend one's goods in modest and explicit terms," observed Frederick Lewis Allen in *Only Yesterday,* his social history of the 1920s. "The advertiser must plan elaborate national campaigns, consult with psychologists, and employ all the eloquence of poets to cajole, exhort, or intimidate the consumer into buying." Below are two examples of advertisements from the 1920s.

Discussing the Ads

1. Does the General Electric ad make rational appeals? Emotional appeals? Both? Explain. To what kind of buyer was General Electric trying to appeal?

2. Was the appeal made by the Ford car ad basically the same as that of the refrigerator ad? Why or why not?

CRITICAL THINKING
Identifying Assumptions

How do each of these ads emphasize social status?

Her habit of measuring time in terms of dollars gives the woman in business a keen insight into the true value of a Ford closed car for her personal use.

This car enables her to conserve minutes, to expedite her affairs, to widen the scope of her activities. Its low first cost, long life and inexpensive operation and upkeep convince her that it is a sound investment value.

And it is such a pleasant car to drive that it transforms the business call which might be an interruption into an enjoyable episode of her busy day.

TUDOR SEDAN, $590   FORDOR SEDAN, $685   COUPE, $525   (All prices f. o. b. Detroit)

Ford
CLOSED CARS

THE SATURDAY EVENING POST   December 14, 1929

Happy to own it ... proud to show it

Really, you can't blame her. Who wouldn't drag her friends out into the kitchen to show off her new General Electric? There it stands, gleaming white, strong as a safe, incredibly quiet ... the envy of all who see it.

For a gift that gives all-year usefulness, that makes every-day tasks lighter, that safeguards health, the General Electric is really ideal. It makes a generous supply of ice cubes and, of course, freezes those luscious desserts which every hostess enjoys serving.

When you buy a General Electric you are choosing the one and only electric refrigerator which has an *all-steel* cabinet. It is rust-proof, warp-proof. Its doors are finished with trim black Textolite edges, an attractive contrast to the whiteness of the cabinet. The inside corners are rounded so that they are

most easy to clean. And the graceful legs leave plenty of broom-room under the cabinet. In fact, this refrigerator has every detail that makes for greatest sanitation and cleanliness.

And the General Electric is the only refrigerator which has all its mechanism mounted on top in an hermetically sealed

Prices on the new all-steel models now start as low as $215 at the factory.

steel casing . . . . out of the way, dust-proof. It never needs oiling and leaves the greatest cabinet area for food storage. It allows the heat to rise *above* the cabinet—not up through it. It has an accessible freezing regulator and it creates absolutely no radio interference.

When you are deciding on the gift that will best serve the whole family, consider the sound value which the General Electric offers. The operating cost is but a few cents a day and not a single owner has thus far paid a dollar for repairs or service. No other refrigerator approaches this record. Conveniently spaced payments can be arranged.

For complete information about all the models, write to Electric Refrigeration Department of General Electric Company, Hanna Building, Cleveland, Ohio. Ask for an illustrated Booklet—S-12.

GENERAL ℰ ELECTRIC
STEEL REFRIGERATOR

The Babe Slams Number Sixty

12B

TIME FRAME
1927

GEOGRAPHIC SETTING
New York City

Many of the characteristic features of modern American culture began to assume their present form and influence during the 1920s. Like advertising (see Reading 12A), spectator sports were a typical product of the new national popular culture emerging during this period. Sports figures such as boxer Jack Dempsey, golfer Bobby Jones, and football player Red Grange became national heroes. The preeminent sports hero of the 1920s was George Herman "Babe" Ruth (1895–1948) of the New York Yankees, who became the first great home-run hitter in baseball. Born into poverty, Ruth typified the American "rags-to-riches" success story, and his flamboyant style of living reflected the Roaring '20s. Ruth's greatest year was 1927, when he hit 60 home runs, a major-league record that assumed an almost magical quality in baseball tradition. The first of the following readings is the account of Ruth's sixtieth home run from the *New York Times* of October 1, 1927. The second is a column, entitled "The Babe," by journalist Heywood Broun [brün] (1888–1939).

Babe Ruth scaled the hitherto unattained heights yesterday. Home run 60, a terrific smash off the southpaw pitching of Tom Zachary, nestled in the Babe's
5 favorite spot in the right-field bleachers, and before the roar had ceased it was found that this drive not only had made home-run record history but also was the winning margin in a 4–2 victory over the
10 Senators. The Yanks' last league game of the year will be played today. . . .

The first Zachary offering was a fast one for a called strike. The next was high. The Babe took a vicious swing at the third
15 pitched ball and the bat connected with a crash that was audible in all parts of the stand. It was not necessary to follow the course of the ball. The boys in the bleachers indicated the route of the record

20 homer. It dropped about half way to the top. Boys, No. 60 was some homer, a fitting wallop to top the Babe's record of 59 in 1921.

While the crowd cheered and the Yan-
25 kee players roared their greetings, the Babe made his triumphant, almost regal tour of the paths. He jogged around slowly, touched each bag firmly and carefully and when he imbedded his spikes in
30 the rubber disk to record officially Homer 60, hats were tossed into the air, papers were torn up and thrown liberally and the spirit of celebration permeated the place. . . .

35 The only unhappy individual within the stadium was Zachary. He realized he was going down in the records as the historical home-run victim, in other words the goat. Zachary was one of the most interested
40 spectators of the home-run flight. He tossed his glove to the ground, muttered to himself, turned to his mates for consolation and got everything but that. There is no denying that Zachary was putting
45 everything he had on the ball.

The ball that the Babe drove was a pitch that was fast, low and on the inside. The Babe pulled away from the plate, then stepped into the ball, and wham! Accord-
50 ing to Umpire Bill Dinneen at the plate and Catcher Muddy Ruel the ball traveled

on a line and landed a foot inside fair territory about half way to the top of the
bleachers. . . .

55   The ball which became Homer 60 was
caught by Joe Forner of 1937 First Avenue, Manhattan. He is about 40 years old

and has been following baseball for thirty-
five, according to his own admission. He
60 was far from modest and as soon as the
game was over rushed to the dressing
room to let the Babe know who had the
ball. . . .

George Herman "Babe" Ruth steps up to bat, perhaps to hit a record-breaking home run. Here he is playing for the New York Yankees. He began his career with the Baltimore Orioles in 1914 and also played with the Boston Red Sox and the Boston Braves. Baseball cards were as popular in his day as they are today. Shown here are three Babe Ruth baseball cards that have become valuable collector's items.

The distinction between the amateur and the professional cannot be reduced to a simple formula. In any field of endeavor your true and authentic amateur is a man who plays a game gleefully. I have never seen any college player who seemed to get half so much fun out of football as Babe Ruth derives from baseball. Ruth is able to contribute this gusto to his game spontaneously. Nobody makes him a set speech in the dressing room before he embarks to meet his test. The fans will not spell out "N-E-W Y-O-R-K" with colored handkerchiefs to inspirit him. There will be no songs about hitting the line. Indeed, Ruth will not even be asked to die for the cause he represents.

Instead of running out at top speed, Babe Ruth may be observed ambling quite slowly in the general direction of the diamond. He approaches a day's work. This thing before him is a job and it would not be fitting for him to run. But a little later you may chance to see a strange thing happen. The professional ball players take up their daily tasks. Soon, in the cause of duty, Ruth is called upon to move from right center all the way to the edge of the foul line. And now he is running. To the best of my knowledge and belief there is no current gridiron hero who runs with the entire earnestness of Ruth. Once I saw him charge full tilt against the wall of the Yankee Stadium. It was a low wall and Ruth's big body was so inextricably committed to forward motion that a wall was insufficient to quell the purpose inhering in the moving mass. And so his head and shoulders went over the barrier and, after a time, his feet followed. The resulting tumble must have been at least as vicious as any tackle ever visited upon a charging halfback. But for Ruth there was no possibility of time out. He could not ask so much as the indulgence of a sponge or a paper drinking cup. Shaking the disorders out of his spinning head, he tumbled himself back over the wall again and threw a runner out at the plate.

It is my impression that in the savage charge up to the wall and over, Ruth was wholly in the grip of the amateur spirit. If he had stopped short of the terrific tumble his pay would have still continued. To me there is nothing very startling in the fact that young men manage to commit themselves whole-heartedly to sport without hope of financial return. That is a commonplace. Recruiting volunteer workers for any cause is no trouble at all. I grow more sentimental over a quality much rarer in human experience. I give my admiration utterly to that man who can put the full sweep of effort into a job even though he is paid for it.

Discussing the Readings

1. Both the *New York Times* story and Heywood Broun's column emphasized the careful, deliberate quality of Babe Ruth's performance as a baseball player. How was this quality exhibited in the news story? in Broun's column?

2. When Broun wrote that the outfield wall "was insufficient to quell the purpose inhering in the moving mass," he meant that it couldn't stop Ruth running at full speed. What effect does Broun's use of such formal language have in this context? Considering the overall impression of Ruth created by this column, do you think that Broun intended that his description of the Yankee outfielder chasing a fly ball would make him seem less heroic?

CRITICAL THINKING
Recognizing Values

What quality displayed by Babe Ruth did Heywood Broun praise? Why did Broun admire this quality? Do you agree with his high estimate of the value of this quality?

"Homesick Blues Is a Terrible Thing to Have"

TIME FRAME
1920s

GEOGRAPHIC SETTING
New York City

During the 1920s, New York City's Harlem district, which had become the largest African American community in the United States, also became a cultural capital, housing theatrical companies, libraries, writers, painters, musicians, and other artists. This outburst of creativity was called the Harlem Renaissance. One of the major figures of this African American cultural movement was the poet Langston Hughes (1902–1967), who became famous with the publication of his first book of verse, *The Weary Blues,* in 1926. Hughes made a notable use of the motifs and verse patterns of the blues in this book. The following readings are excerpts from *The Weary Blues.* The first is an explanatory "Note on Blues" that Hughes prefaced to a group of poems written in the blues form. This is followed by two of these poems, "Homesick Blues" and "Bound No'th Blues."

A Note on Blues

The following poems are written in the manner of the Negro folk songs known as Blues. The Blues, unlike the Spirituals, have a strict poetic pattern: one long line,
5 repeated, and a third line to rhyme with the first two. Sometimes the second line in repetition is slightly changed and sometimes, but very seldom, it is omitted. Unlike the Spirituals, the Blues are not group
10 songs. When sung under natural circumstances, they are usually sung by one man or one woman alone. Whereas the Spirituals are often songs about escaping from trouble, going to heaven and living hap-
15 pily ever after, the Blues are songs about being in the midst of trouble, friendless, hungry, disappointed in love, right here on earth. The mood of the Blues is almost always despondency, but when they are
20 sung people laugh.

Langston Hughes reads his account of the Spanish Civil War battle of Teruel. Hughes was an eyewitness to the fighting, and he is shown here describing his experiences to an audience in Paris in January 1938. Throughout his career, Hughes toured the lecture circuit, speaking or reading from his works.

Homesick Blues

D e railroad bridge's
A sad song in de air.
De railroad bridge's
A sad song in de air.
5 Ever time de trains pass
I wants to go somewhere.

I went down to de station.
Ma heart was in ma mouth.
Went down to de station.
10 Heart was in ma mouth.
Lookin' for a box car
To roll me to de South.

Homesick blues, Lawd,
'S a terrible thing to have.
15 Homesick blues is
A terrible thing to have.
To keep from cryin'
I opens ma mouth an' laughs.

Bound No'th Blues

G oin' down de road, Lawd,
Goin' down de road.
Down de road, Lawd,
Way, way down de road.
5 Got to find somebody
To help me carry dis load.

Road's in front o' me,
Nothin' to do but walk.
Road's in front o' me,
10 Walk . . . and walk . . . and walk.
I'd like to meet a good friend
To come along an' talk.

Hates to be lonely,
Lawd, I hates to be sad.
15 Says I hates to be lonely,
Hates to be lonely an' sad,
But ever friend you finds seems
Like they try to do you bad.

Road, road, road, O!
20 Road, road . . . road . . . road, road!
Road, road, road, O!
Oh de No'thern road.
These Mississippi towns ain't
Fit fer a hoppin' toad.

Discussing the Readings

1. What paradox, or apparent contradiction, did Langston Hughes note about people's reaction to the blues? How is this paradox expressed in the last lines of "The Homesick Blues"?

2. What historical process is reflected in "Bound No'th Blues"?

CRITICAL THINKING
Making Comparisons

Using the distinctions between the blues and spirituals that Langston Hughes made in his "Note on Blues," compare "Homesick Blues" and "Bound No'th Blues" to the spiritual "Go Down, Moses" (page 203).

Chapter Summary

Write supporting details under each of the following main ideas as you review the chapter.

Section 1

1. Electricity changed how people lived and worked in the 1920s.
2. Henry Ford dominated the early automobile industry.
3. The automobile changed the culture and geography of the United States.

Section 2

1. New marketing techniques created more eager consumers in the 1920s.
2. Sports became an American obsession.
3. A national media developed through newspapers and radio.
4. Hollywood and Broadway brought entertainment to millions of Americans.

Section 3

1. The flapper was the symbol of a new youth culture in the 1920s.
2. Women's lives were changed by new technology.
3. Urban and rural culture developed separately in the 1920s.

Section 4

1. Writers and artists made up the Lost Generation.
2. A cultural renaissance occurred within the African American community in the 1920s.
3. Music and dance shaped the culture of the 1920s.

Chapter Themes

1. **Technological and scientific innovation:** In the 1920s various technological innovations, such as electricity and the automobile, produced profound effects on American life and geography. Technological advances in communications helped form a mass society that shared common interests in consumer goods, sports, and entertainment.
2. **Geography and environmental interaction:** Widespread use of the automobile changed the landscape of the United States in the 1920s. Changes included the construction of new roads and highways, shifts in population away from villages located on rail lines, and the appearance of new types of businesses such as gas stations.

Chapter Study Guide

Identifying Key People and Terms

Name the key person or key term that describes the:

1. person who dominated the early automobile industry
2. period of vitality in African American art and entertainment
3. person who wrote *The Great Gatsby*
4. young women who abandoned traditional views of femininity and women's roles

Locating Key Places

1. What city was the center of the moviemaking business?
2. In which city was the Grand Ole Opry located?

Mastering the Main Ideas

1. How did Henry Ford's industrial innovations alter the way people in factories produced goods?
2. How did easy credit help create a new consumer society in the United States during the 1920s?
3. How did national media help create a sports- and entertainment-oriented American society?
4. What was the Lost Generation of American artists and writers? How did the horrors of World War I contribute to the creation of this group of people?
5. Who were some of the foremost authors of the 1920s and what were some of the themes of their writing?

Applying Critical Thinking Skills

1. **Predicting consequences:** The principles of scientific management and assembly-line production dramatically increased industrial output, an advantage for factory owners and consumers. Predict some consequences of scientific management that might prove to be disadvantages for the workers on the assembly lines.
2. **Recognizing values:** What values were associated with rural society in the United States during the 1920s? With American urban society?
3. **Testing conclusions:** Because of developments in the 1920s, many Americans concluded that New York City was the cultural capital of the United States. Test this conclusion by listing events,

1920	1922	1924	1926	1928	1930

1920
First commercial radio broadcast on KDKA

1922
The Waste Land (Eliot); *Babbit* (Lewis)

1923
The Ego and the Id (Freud); Chaplin stars in *A Woman of Paris*

1925
The Great Gatsby (Fitzgerald); First Louis Armstrong jazz records

1926
Gertrude Ederle swims the English Channel

1927
Babe Ruth hits record 60 home runs

1928
Walt Disney introduces Mickey Mouse

movements, and personalities described in this chapter that had New York City as their scene. Draw your own conclusion that either confirms or disputes the idea that in the 1920s, New York City was the cultural capital of the United States.

Chapter Activities

Learning Geography Through History

1. How did a national media, the automobile, and the American entertainment and sports fields blur regional differences during the 1920s?
2. During the 1920s why might the Harlem Renaissance have been more likely to take place in a northern rather than a southern environment?

Relating the United States to the World

1. Why was Charles Lindbergh an international popular hero as much as an American popular hero?
2. In what way did European ideas about the personality affect American culture?

Linking Past to Present

1. Compare the popular attitudes of the young people of the 1920s with those of today's American youth. How are they alike and different?
2. How has the automobile, a development of the 1920s, affected life today? Include both advantages and disadvantages.

Using the Time Line

1. In what year did the radio industry produce its first local commercial broadcast?
2. When did Gertrude Ederle swim the English Channel?

Practicing Critical Thinking Strategies

Determining Relevant Information
Read the copy on the Listerine ad on page 497. What information is relevant to the mouthwash producer's sales pitch?

Learning More About the 1920s

1. **Using Source Readings:** Read the Source Readings for this chapter and answer the questions.
2. **Analyzing popular films:** Secure a copy of Walt Disney's *Steamboat Willie* from a film library along with a cartoon featuring Mickey Mouse, such as *The Sorcerer's Apprentice*. Watch the films and compare the character of Steamboat Willie with that of Mickey Mouse. Compare also the production values of the two cartoons. Make lists of likenesses and differences between Disney's early and later efforts.
3. **Defining the term "popular hero":** The following personalities were among the popular heroes of the 1920s: Henry Ford, George "Babe" Ruth, Harold "Red" Grange, Jack Dempsey, Gertrude Ederle, Helen Wills, Charles Lindbergh, Charlie Chaplin, Paul Robeson. Use a biographical dictionary or encyclopedia to gather information about the exploits and achievements of each. Then make a few generalizations about the characteristics of these popular heroes.

523

Linking Past to Present

Nearly 58 years to the day after the Stock Market Crash of 1929, the New York Stock Exchange was dealt the blow of Black Monday. On October 19, 1987, stock prices plunged 508.32 points—a drop of 22.6 percent, far more severe than the worst day of 1929. A sense of panic characterized both days at the Stock Exchange—1929, shown inset, and 1987.

The Great Depression

1 9 2 9 – 1 9 3 5

13

Winston Churchill, a member of the British parliament who happened to be visiting New York City, stood in the visitors' gallery of the New York Stock Exchange, looking down at a scene of unfolding panic. The date was Thursday, October 24, 1929, and stock prices—which for more than a year had enjoyed steady, spectacular, some believed almost miraculous increases—were plummeting more rapidly than anyone could count. Later in the afternoon, the visitors' gallery was closed, as if preventing outsiders from witnessing the scene would limit the damage. Churchill, who would later become Britain's prime minister, never forgot the moment. It was the beginning of a series of momentous crises that would ultimately change the United States, Britain, and the rest of the world forever.

How would the Great Depression, an economic disaster of immense proportion, affect life in the United States and throughout the world in the 1930s? How would different groups of Americans—men and women, adults and children—respond to the challenges of this era? In effect, how would the Depression shape their lives and their futures?

1929	1930	1931	1932	1933	1934	1935
1929 Stock market crashes on October 29	**1930** Revolutions occur in six South American countries	**1931** Scottsboro case begins	**1932** Franklin Roosevelt defeats Hoover for the presidency			**1935** Dust bowl conditions worsen

The Depression brought economic hardship.

Key Term: Great Depression

Reading Preview
As you read this section, you will learn:

1. how the stock market crash affected the American economy.
2. what worsened America's economic crisis after 1929.
3. what groups of people were affected by unemployment.
4. how the Dust Bowl added to the economic hardship of the 1930s.

The same afternoon that Winston Churchill witnessed panic on the floor of the New York Stock Exchange, five of the nation's most powerful bankers gathered across the street. In the office of Thomas W. Lamont of J. P. Morgan and Company, the men discussed how they might help save the stock market. Each pledged to spend millions of dollars buying up stocks, a gesture they believed would restore confidence and return stock prices to their upward climb.

The stock market collapse led to the Great Depression.

chart study

In which year did stock prices reach their highest level? In which year did prices hit their lowest point?
Critical Thinking
How might the steady rise in stock prices in the 1920s have contributed to the severe drop in 1929?

The bankers' gesture had a striking impact, and the market quickly revived. However, despite reassuring statements from bankers, economists, even President Hoover, fears slowly revived. The following Monday, stock prices began falling again. Then, the next day, Tuesday, October 29, the stock market crashed, experiencing the worst day in its history. So many investors were trying to sell their stocks, and so few investors were buying them, that prices fell to almost unimaginable lows. Some traders could not find buyers for the stocks they were trying to sell at any price.

For the next few weeks, the market continued to deteriorate. By the middle of November,

stocks had lost more than 40 percent of their value. Hundreds, perhaps thousands, of investors—large and small, institutions and individuals—were wiped out. The economic boom of the 1920s had come to an end. Not until the 1940s, with an economic boom created by World War II, would prosperity finally return to the nation. The **Great Depression** was not only the longest, but also the worst, economic crisis in the nation's history. It reached nearly every area of society and affected millions of Americans.

INDEX OF COMMON STOCK PRICES, 1920–1935

Standard and Poor's Index of Common Stocks

Source: *Historical Statistics of the United States*

Crowds gathered in front of the New York Stock Exchange as the market crashed on October 29, 1929.

Debate over the causes of the Great Depression has never stopped. Economists, historians, and others generally agree that several factors, many of them interrelated, contributed to the collapse. These experts disagree, however, about which causes were the most important.

For one thing, the American economy had weakened significantly during the 1920s. Had the economy of 1929 been stronger, it might have had a better chance of weathering the crash on Wall Street. The economic difficulties felt by farmers increasingly were shared by such distressed industries as coal, railroads, and textiles. As a result, by 1929, unsold inventories were stacking up, investments were shrinking, workers were being laid off, and consumers were buying fewer products.

Second, the American business system was unbalanced, with a few industries carrying the weight of the economy. Automobiles and housing construction, in particular, fueled the economic boom of the 1920s. Newer industries, such as chemicals, were still not fully developed. Thus when the market for houses and cars began to weaken, as it did in 1928, other industries were not able to take up the slack.

Third, poor distribution of purchasing power weakened the economy. Although the wages of most Americans increased in the 1920s, they grew at a much slower rate than the economy as a whole. Farmers and other workers were not, therefore, earning enough money to buy the products they were making.

Fourth, an enormous amount of debt threatened the country's economic health. Farmers carried large mortgages on their land and were unable to keep up payments as their crop prices fell. Small banks, particularly the ones that had loaned money to farmers, were having serious problems as borrowers defaulted on their loans. Some large banks also were taking on dangerous amounts of debt, part of it to allow them to speculate in the stock market. The market itself was largely unregulated, and investors created for themselves an elaborate, and shaky, house of cards.

Finally, debt problems with the international community deepened the domestic credit crisis. All the nations of Europe owed large debts to the United States in the 1920s, some of them left over from World War I. In order to pay those debts, Europe needed dollars. To raise the necessary dollars, they needed to sell goods in the United States. In 1922, however, Congress had passed the Fordney McCumber Tariff, the highest in American history. International trade declined, particularly once European governments had raised their own tariff rates in retaliation.

A poster urged Americans to help the economy by buying a car. Still, a tinsmith wondered, "How'd they expect us to buy autos when we can't buy food?"

When You BUY an AUTOMOBILE You GIVE 3 Months' Work to Someone Which Allows Him to BUY OTHER PRODUCTS

BUY A CAR NOW—HELP BRING BACK PROSPERITY

A banking crisis hastened the economic collapse after 1929.

Partly as a result of the stock market crash, investment declined rapidly after 1929. What really hastened the economic collapse, though, was the crisis of the American banking system. Between 1930 and 1933, more than 9,000 banks were forced to close. Since bank deposits were not insured, millions of bank depositors lost their money—more than $2.5 billion altogether. Americans who had saved faithfully for a rainy day found themselves without a cent, just as they were losing their jobs and homes. The decline of the banking system also reduced the amount of money available for loans and investments.

The Federal Reserve system, which controlled the flow of money into American banks, responded slowly to the Depression. In 1931 the agency finally acted by raising interest rates—precisely the wrong thing to do, most economists now argue, because in doing so it shrank an already inadequate money supply still further. Some believe that the Federal Reserve's misguided policies were the main reason the Great Depression grew so severe and lasted so long.

The economy reached bottom late in 1932. By then the dimensions of the crisis were evident to everyone. The gross national product had declined by 25 percent since 1929. Investment was only about three percent of what it had been before the stock market crash. Prices had fallen by between a quarter and a third, and farm income had been cut by almost two-thirds. Unemployment, according to the crude estimates of the day, had reached 25 percent. That is, one of every four Americans of working age was out of work.

Unemployment hit all segments of the population.

No area of the country was unaffected by the Depression, but the impact was most immediately visible in the industrial cities of the Northeast and Midwest. Fully half the workers in Cleveland, Ohio, were unemployed in 1932. In Toledo, Ohio, the number hit 80 percent.

The mass unemployment of the 1930s was traumatic. It came at a moment when those who lost their jobs had little chance of finding another and when relief and welfare mechanisms were almost nonexistent. Most small- and medium-sized cities offered no assistance, and relief programs in many large cities went bankrupt by the fall of 1931. It affected not just industrial workers, to whom layoffs were always a danger, but middle-class people, who were accustomed to thinking of their jobs as being secure.

GLOSSARY OF ECONOMIC TERMS

CREDIT money extended in return for a promise to pay later

DEBT obligation to pay something to another

DEFAULT to fail to pay a loan or mortgage when due

DEFLATION a general decline in prices

DEPRESSION a sharp and sustained decline in economic activity

GROSS NATIONAL PRODUCT (GNP) the total value of final goods and services produced in a country during a year

INFLATION a general rise in prices

INVESTMENT outlay of money for income or profit

MARKET ECONOMY economy in which the individuals in the marketplace make decisions about production and distribution of goods and services

MORTGAGE loan contract used to finance home purchases

PURCHASING POWER the amount of goods and services money will buy

RECESSION modern name for a depression, when GNP declines for two consecutive quarters

STOCK share of ownership in a company

TARIFF tax on imported goods

---

chart study

The chart above lists key economic terms common to the Depression. Using the chart at the right, determine in which year the highest number of Americans were unemployed.
Critical Thinking How might mass unemployment affect a local economy?

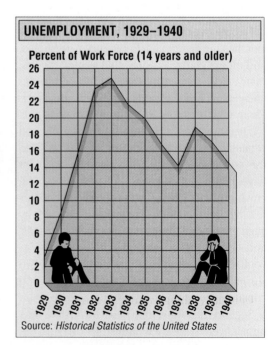

UNEMPLOYMENT, 1929–1940

Percent of Work Force (14 years and older)

Source: *Historical Statistics of the United States*

Ward James, for example, had seldom thought about unemployment. As the Depression began, he was working for a publishing house in New York City. "It was a good job," he recalled years later for Studs Terkel's well-known oral history of the Great Depression, *Hard Times*. "It looked like a permanent situation. I was feeling rather secure."

The Depression destroyed James' sense of security and his self-esteem. In 1935, without explanation, he was fired from his job. For the next six months, he went from one publishing house to another looking for work, but without success. "I never got past the telephone operator," James recalled. Unable to support his family, he sent his wife and child to live with his wife's parents in Ohio.

Ward James struggled with feelings of boredom and humiliation. As he told Terkel:

One of the worst things was occupying your time, sensibly. You'd go to the library. You took a magazine to the room and sat and read. I didn't have a radio. I tried to do some writing and found I couldn't concentrate. The day was long. There was nothing to do evenings. I was going around in circles, it was terrifying. So I just vegetated.

With some people I knew, there was a coldness, shunning: I'd rather not see you just now. Maybe *I'll* lose my job next week. On the other hand, I made some very close friends, who were merely acquaintances before. If I needed $5 for room rent or something, it was available.

Eventually, James exhausted all his friends' resources and turned to the state for relief. He described the humiliation:

It's an experience I don't want anybody to go through. . . . You sit in an auditorium and are given a number. The interview was utterly ridiculous and mortifying.

In the end, the relief office gave him $9 a month. "I came away feeling I didn't have any business living any more. I was imposing on somebody."

Ultimately, things turned around for Ward James. He found a job, reunited his family, and rebuilt his life. The experience of unemploy-

AN AMERICAN ★ SPEAKS

During the later years of the Depression, Alice Conniffe, an unemployed schoolteacher, earned an average of $3 a day blacking shoes. At the time, she was Philadelphia's only female bootblack.

ment left permanent scars however. "Everyone was emotionally affected," he said decades later. "We developed a fear of the future which was very difficult to overcome."

Many people like Ward James had no choice but to turn to public relief systems in order to eat. Through the first years of the Depression, however, the overwhelmed relief system could not come close to meeting their demands. The federal government provided almost no funding for relief, and state and local governments—whose tax revenues were declining—could not find the resources to keep the system going. In some cities relief agencies simply closed down for lack of funds. In others they offered such minimal benefits that many recipients were still forced to beg in order to feed their families.

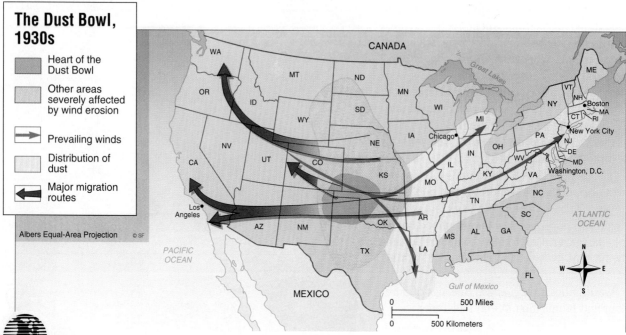

The Dust Bowl, 1930s

- **Heart of the Dust Bowl**
- **Other areas severely affected by wind erosion**
- **Prevailing winds**
- **Distribution of dust**
- **Major migration routes**

Albers Equal-Area Projection © SF

---

map study

Relationships within Places

The Dust Bowl was part of the Great Plains region of the United States. Note on the map that though the worst drought area was relatively small, its effects were far-reaching. What northern Plains states suffered severe wind erosion?

Critical Thinking

Why did conditions in the Dust Bowl region affect other parts of the country?

◆ The Dust Bowl added geographic crisis to economic hardship.

Although unemployment was most visible in the cities, people were equally distressed in the countryside. Crop prices were so low that even a good harvest would not pay for itself.

Still worse, good harvests were impossible in much of the farm belt because of the **Dust Bowl**—a natural disaster that struck the country's midsection. In the mid-1930s lower than average rainfall plagued the Plains from the Dakotas to Texas. The area worst hit centered in the panhandles of Texas and Oklahoma and parts of Kansas, Colorado, and New Mexico. Lakes and rivers dried up, plants withered, and animals died. In addition, heavy winds ripped the weakened crops out of the ground. No longer anchored by plants, the precious topsoil was picked up and blown eastward. At times huge dust storms carried Plains-area dirt as far as Chicago and Boston.

In his classic novel, *The Grapes of Wrath*, **John Steinbeck** described the scene after a dust storm swept through Oklahoma:

The dawn came, but no day. In the gray sky a red sun appeared, a dim red circle that gave

a little light, like dusk; and as that day advanced, the dusk slipped back toward darkness, and the wind cried and whimpered over the fallen corn.

Men and women huddled in their houses, and they tied handkerchiefs over their noses when they went out, and wore goggles to protect their eyes. . . .

In the morning the dust hung like fog, and the sun was as red as ripe new blood. All day the dust sifted down from the sky, and the next day it sifted down. An even blanket covered the earth. . . .

The people came out of their houses and smelled the hot stinging air and covered their

A gigantic dust cloud moves to engulf this modest ranch in Boise City, Oklahoma. The dust storms, which tore top soil from farming areas and buried range and pastures in sand and silt, caused many farm families to leave the land. One of the agencies set up to help ease their suffering used artist Ben Shahn to publicize its services.

YEARS OF DUST

RESETTLEMENT ADMINISTRATION
Rescues Victims
Restores Land to Proper Use

cause many came from Oklahoma), they experienced more hardship and poverty working as low-paid agricultural migrants. In addition, nearly half a million migrants from the northern Plains traveled to the Pacific Northwest.

Despite the declining productivity of the Dust Bowl, American agriculture continued to produce many more crops than consumers could buy. Thus, prices of farm products declined at least as rapidly as those of manufactured goods.

Many migrant families left their ruined farms with their meager possessions packed into cars or pickup trucks. This family was photographed by Dorothea Lange, one of the decade's leading recorders.

noses from it. And the children came out of the houses, but they did not run or shout as they would have done after a rain. Men stood by their fences and looked at the ruined corn, drying fast now, only a little green showing through the film of dust. The men were silent and they did not move often. And the women came out of the houses to stand beside their men—and to feel whether this time the men would break. The women studied the men's faces secretly, for the corn could go, as long as something else remained.

Hundreds of thousands of families in the Dust Bowl either lost their land or ceased to be able to make a living off it. Many of them packed their possessions into cars or pickup trucks and traveled west. Others walked or hitched rides. More than a million people headed along Route 66 to California, where they heard crops were good and jobs were plentiful. Once the travelers arrived in California (where they were known as "Okies," be-

SECTION **1** REVIEW

Identify Key People and Terms
Write a sentence to identify: Great Depression, John Steinbeck

Locate Key Places
Which five states were the worst hit by the Dust Bowl?

Master the Main Ideas

1. **Understanding the impact of depressions:** In what way did the stock market crash of 1929 signal the coming of the Great Depression?
2. **Understanding the development of the U.S. banking system: (a)** What crisis hit the U.S. banking system after 1929? **(b)** How did the crisis worsen the country's existing economic problems?
3. **Recognizing the impact of depressions:** How were unemployed Americans able to survive?
4. **Recognizing the influence of physical features:** How did the geographic crisis of the Dust Bowl intensify agricultural hardships throughout the United States?

Apply Critical Thinking Skills: Identifying Alternatives
Consider the causes leading up to the Great Depression. If you were an economic adviser to President Hoover in 1929, what might you recommend as possible solutions? Be sure to support your response with evidence.

The Depression challenged people's culture and values.

Key Term: individualism

Reading Preview
As you read this section, you will learn:

1. what values guided many Americans during the Great Depression.
2. against what systems some Americans protested in the 1930s.
3. how Americans felt about big business in the 1930s.

The culture of a nation and the values of its people do not change quickly or easily, nor are they entirely constant. For the American people, the shock of the Great Depression—coming as it did after a decade of unprecedented prosperity—both confirmed and changed the way they viewed their world.

Americans retained their faith in the value of the individual.

Robert and Helen Merrell Lynd were noted sociologists. In the 1920s they spent a year in **Muncie, Indiana**—which they considered a representative, medium-sized American city. They then wrote a book entitled *Middletown* (the fictional name they gave Muncie), describing the nature of the community's life and culture. Ten years later, they went back to see how Muncie had changed as a result of the Depression. They found it poorer, of course, with more unemployed people and more anxiety about the present and the future. On the whole, however, they reported, "the texture of Middletown's culture has not changed. . . . Middletown is overwhelmingly living by the values by which it lived in 1925."

The most important of those values, perhaps, was the belief in the importance of the individual–a value known as **individualism**. Cer-

tainly the Depression severely tested the idea that individuals were in control of their own futures. The old Horatio Alger myth—that anyone who worked hard enough could become a success—was difficult to believe in a time when hardworking, successful people were losing jobs, businesses, and homes through no fault of their own.

In some ways, however, the Depression strengthened the American faith in self-reliance and individual initiative. Unemployed people tended to blame themselves for their problems, to hide themselves at home to avoid the shame of appearing in public without work. Books such as Dale Carnegie's *How to Win Friends and Influence People* (1936), the best-selling book of the decade, told Americans that with a winning personality they could advance over any obstacle.

Some Americans protested against social and political systems.

The Depression also encouraged many Americans to look more critically at the nation's social and political systems. Although many

Boys from Muncie, Indiana, take a few minutes away from rollerskating to pose on the front steps of their city's YMCA. The photograph, taken in 1930, is part of the *Middletown* collection.

Dorothea Lange became famous for her moving portraits of people touched by economic hardship. This migrant family was photographed on the road in Tule Lake, California, in 1939.

for *Life* magazine, writer Erskine Caldwell, and artist Ben Shahn. Shahn became famous in the 1930s for his series of paintings of the Sacco-Vanzetti trial.

Woody Guthrie, a musician, developed into an authentic folk hero by celebrating the strength and dignity of common Americans. Throughout the Depression, Guthrie rode the rails, playing his guitar and harmonica for struggling people from Oklahoma to California. As the "voice of the people," Guthrie put into words the most important themes of the 1930s—the common person's defiant pride and will to survive in the face of adversity. As he saw the hardships people endured, Guthrie came to blame politicians for not doing more to relieve the people's suffering. Woody Guthrie also reflected the genuine love that Americans felt for their country. His most famous song was "This Land Is Your Land," sung by generations of Americans.

Political protest. The failure of capitalism to keep people fed and sheltered led a small group of Americans toward radical politics. Some of these people—whose ranks included intellectuals, artists, and African Americans disappointed by racial divisions in the United States—joined the Communist party. In American history the communists had not enjoyed much success, however, and the 1930s did not prove to be an exception. The party remained relatively small, peaking at about 100,000 members. Most workers shunned the party,

people looked to radical solutions, ultimately most returned to familiar government institutions for relief.

Social protest. Writers, artists, and photographers took special note of poverty in the United States in the 1930s—not just the new poverty of unemployed people in cities, but the longstanding poverty in parts of the countryside. Some toured the deep South and produced searing pictures and descriptions of the plight of sharecroppers and tenant farmers. James Agee, a writer, and Walker Evans, a photographer, produced one of the most compelling documents of rural poverty, *Let Us Now Praise Famous Men* (1941).

Dorothea Lange is perhaps the best known of the Depression-era photographers. She offered honest and sympathetic portrayals of migrant farm workers, usually victims of drought and poverty. Her photographs appeared in several newspapers and magazines of the 1930s, spurring interest in government relief programs for migrant workers.

Other well-known recorders of the time were Margaret Bourke-White, a photographer

Lange left the security of a portrait studio to cover the world of people too poor to pay for a sitting. (Courtesy of the Dorothea Lange Collection. © The City of Oakland, The Oakland Museum, 1934.)

most African Americans ignored its recruiting drives, and most farmers rejected its call that they abandon individual ownership of property. Many of those initially attracted to Marxism as a means of social change and economic planning later rejected the party's rigid discipline and attachment to the Soviet Union.

One person who felt first attraction then disillusionment with the Communist party was the African American writer **Richard Wright**. As a young man in the 1930s, Wright believed that communism could overcome racial oppression. Through some of his early writings—including the acclaimed novel, *Native Son* (1940)—Wright struggled with the role communism could play in American society. He ultimately rejected its discipline and use of thought control.

Other groups on the left were also active in the 1930s. The Socialist party, led by **Norman Thomas**, emphasized reform rather than the radical revolution supported by the communists. Still, the party had attracted only 17,000 members by 1932. Thomas, commenting on his party's lack of attraction to Americans, found it "amazing that the workers were so comparatively quiet." Indeed, few Americans looked to left-wing parties, protest marches, or violence for relief from their misery. They turned instead to more familiar and stable institutions—their local, state, and federal governments.

Americans became hostile toward big business.

Even many Americans who spurned the radical positions of the communists and socialists were dismayed by the performance of American capitalism. In the 1920s the "captains" of industry and finance had been among the most revered people in America. In the 1930s Americans experienced a massive loss of faith in business and its leaders.

The portrayal of business leaders in popular literature in the 1930s showed how quickly their reputation had declined. Once respected titans began to be portrayed as greedy, bloated "plutocrats" who lived off the suffering of the people. J. P. Morgan, the financial leader be-

fore whom even presidents usually stood in awe, was treated with open contempt when he appeared before a congressional committee. Richard Whitney, the aristocratic head of the New York Stock Exchange, was sentenced to prison for fraud. Samuel Insull, head of a giant utilities empire, was denounced as a fraud and a crook as his businesses unraveled and evidence of corruption became public.

Eventually American business would regain much of the luster the Depression took from it. Never again, though, would the "captains of industry" enjoy the unchallenged prestige and power they held in the 1920s.

This air pump in Kern County, California, spells out the hostile feelings that many Americans held for big business during the Depression. (Courtesy of the Dorothea Lange Collection. © The City of Oakland, The Oakland Museum, 1938.)

S E C T I O N **2** R E V I E W

Identify Key People and Terms
Write a sentence to identify: individualism, Dorothea Lange, Woody Guthrie, Richard Wright, Norman Thomas

Locate Key Places
Upon which city did the Lynds base their sociological study, *Middletown*?

Master the Main Ideas

1. **Recognizing societal values:** In what ways was Americans' faith in individualism apparent?
2. **Understanding reform movements:** What forms did American protest take in the 1930s?
3. **Supporting economic competition:** Why were many Americans hostile toward big business?

Apply Critical Thinking Skills: Recognizing Values
In what ways is individualism reflected in modern American society? How has American culture changed since the 1930s in respect to individualism?

SECTION **3**

A diverse society dealt with the Depression.

Key Term: Scottsboro case

Reading Preview
As you read this section, you will learn:

1. how families survived the Depression.
2. what special problems women faced during the Depression.
3. how the Depression affected African Americans.
4. how the Depression-era experience of Mexican Americans was unique.
5. how Asian Americans fared during the Depression.

Some middle-class families, such as the Lees of San Francisco, were able to afford car travel during the Depression. Both May and Leo Lee, shown with their son Stanford in 1935, were accomplished photographers operating their own studio.

The Depression affected nearly all Americans, but not always in the same ways or to the same degrees. People who had been successful and powerful before the crash generally suffered less than those who had already been weak or poor or both.

Families made do with less during the Depression.

Economic hardship forced many American families—including many middle-class families—to give up things they had come to take for granted in the 1920s. Many women re-

turned to sewing clothes for their families rather than buying them. Some families grew their own food in gardens and stored preserves to feed the family through the winter. Others started home businesses—taking in laundry, selling baked goods, accepting boarders. The sizes of many households expanded (even if the size of houses did not) as relatives crowded together to share the hardship.

The Depression experience affected families differently. Some families crumbled under the strain of financial stress, conflict, and role changes. Others pulled together to share the struggle and adversity as a unit. As one observer noted, "Many a family has lost its automobile and found its soul."

The Jones family of Bauxite, Arkansas, a small mining town, was one of the more fortunate. Each family member contributed whatever he or she could to the group's survival. They never went hungry, but they learned to live with few luxuries. The father worked in the mines, and the mother scrubbed floors at the company hospital. The couple's two sons earned a few extra dollars as caddies at a local golf course. The three daughters helped tend the family garden, can fruits and vegetables, and slaughter chickens and an occasional calf.

The Jones family purchased one pair of shoes for each child when school started in the fall. When the soles wore out, the children had to continue to wear the tops even as their bare feet touched the ground. Years later, one of the daughters recalled that her worn-out shoes almost prevented her from walking to school in a terrible snowstorm. After she had shed many tears over breaking her perfect attendance record, her older brother offered to help:

He carried me the whole way [about three miles roundtrip] on his back. You see, he was a football star in high school, and the company [sponsoring the team] had bought him football shoes. So he could walk on the snow.

AN AMERICAN ★ SPEAKS

Despite the financial hardships, many families found ways to entertain themselves with new technologies and leisure activities. Car travel continued to occupy middle-class Americans, since the family car was nearly the last thing Americans were willing to give up in times of trouble. Other leisure activities included listening to records on jukeboxes, playing pinball machines, and competing at the new game of Monopoly.

As in the 1920s, radio programs and movies also were popular. Families gathered around the radio at night to listen to Jack Benny, laugh at Edgar Bergen and Charlie McCarthy, or try to solve a murder mystery with Mr. and Mrs. North. Another popular show, "The Lone Ranger," had 20 million listeners by 1939. Movies too attracted huge audiences, with 60 to 90 million Americans going to the movies every week of the 1930s. Shirley Temple, a young girl with adorable blond curls, was the leading box-office attraction between 1935 and 1938.

Going to the Movies

The following advertisement from March 1932, tells it all: "NO MONEY—Yet New York [residents] dug up $89,931 to see *King Kong* at Radio City." The Depression had been raging for two-and-a-half years. Millions of people were out of work. Nevertheless, they still managed to scrimp and save 25 cents each week to escape to the movies. Movie attendance averaged 80 million viewers a week throughout the 1930s. In other words, half the U.S. population indulged in this compelling form of entertainment every week.

Two technological achievements helped keep the movie industry booming: sound and color. In the early 1930s, "talkies" suddenly became the rage in films. Before that time, movies had been silent with printed placards interspersed with action sequences to supply information about the plot. Color movies were also slowly perfected in the 1930s. At first, the color was crude, and few movie theaters had the equipment to project color film. However, by the late 1930s, color film and the developing process had greatly improved. Some people who went to see the movie *Gone With the Wind* (1939) shielded their eyes during scenes of the burning of Atlanta, so realistic was the color. In *The Wizard of Oz* (1939), the film bursts gloriously into color as Dorothy discovers she's "not in Kansas anymore."

These new developments and the more natural acting styles that evolved with them made the 1930s and early 1940s the "Classic Age of Movies." People still enjoy watching some of the era's brilliant stars: Humphrey Bogart, Fred Astaire, Ginger Rogers, James Cagney, Ingrid Bergman, and Greta Garbo. The movies that helped take ache out of the hard times continue to transport us from our troubles today.

Shirley Temple, in *The Little Colonel* (1935), and Vivien Leigh, in *Gone With the Wind* (1939) were two of the decade's most popular actresses. Leigh won the Academy Award for her portrayal of Scarlett O'Hara.

Highlights of American Life

Women faced wage and job discrimination during the Depression.

Most men, and many women as well, believed that in a time of high unemployment, what jobs there were should be reserved for men—that female workers were taking jobs away from male breadwinners. Women whose husbands were employed were especially strongly discouraged or legally forbidden from taking jobs. For example, for several years in the 1930s, it was illegal for more than one member of a family to hold a federal civil service job.

Nevertheless, the number of women with paid jobs rose 25 percent during the 1930s, at a time when overall employment was shrinking. The largest number of women workers in these years were those who took jobs to supplement their dwindling family incomes. These new women workers generally took modest, non-professional jobs.

Other women were pushed out of professional occupations that had traditionally been open to them. Teaching and social work, for example, had once been heavily female activities. In the 1930s men who could not find jobs elsewhere began moving into these areas as women began to be eased out.

Women were also much more likely to be laid off or fired than male workers. Still, women had certain advantages, since the service jobs they traditionally dominated—salesclerks, secretaries, and the like—were less likely to be cut back than industrial jobs.

African American women had no such advantages. They suffered massive unemployment in the South and elsewhere, in part because so many worked as domestic servants. White families cut back on servants more quickly than on anything else once the hard times hit.

African Americans experienced deep poverty and intense racism.

Throughout the Depression years, African Americans withstood fierce racial and economic discrimination. As a result, black Americans generally were harder hit by the Depression than were white Americans.

Economic hardship. In 1930 about three-quarters of all African Americans lived in the South. Most worked as sharecroppers or tenant farmers on someone else's land and struggled with poverty, disease, and illiteracy. With few resources, they had nothing to protect them from the collapse of prices and credit that hit the country in the late 1920s and early 1930s.

Southern African Americans tried to cope in different ways. Some tried to scrape together a living by selling their crops, though they generally received little from their efforts. Many survived mainly through hunting, fishing, and foraging—dropping out of the market economy almost entirely. Other African Americans migrated to southern cities and looked for work. Their search often proved fruitless. Unemployed white workers now took any job they could find, including the low-paying jobs usually held by African Americans. At times white Americans went so far as to demand that no black workers be hired for any position as long as white people were unemployed. Nor could the unemployed African Americans depend on much help from southern relief agencies. What little help they could offer they usually reserved for white Americans.

Women continued to work throughout the Depression, both to support themselves and their families, as Raphael Soyer depicted in *Office Girls*. (1936, The Whitney Museum of American Art, New York City)

At right a black man's sandwich board pleads for an end to the lynching of African Americans.

In the course of the 1930s, therefore, as many as 400,000 African Americans moved out of the South altogether and into northern cities, following the course set during World War I. Conditions in the North, however, were not much better than those in the South. Unemployment rates for African Americans were much higher than those for white Americans. As in the South, African Americans tended to be the last people hired and the first fired.

Racial discrimination. In both the North and the South, the position of African Americans was growing increasingly desperate. In addition to economic hardship, black Americans found themselves excluded from social and political justice. Most could not vote or serve on a jury, nor enroll at a university. In addition, many could not be treated at the local hospital, play at the public park, or swim at the public pool.

More serious was the increasing intensity of racial violence. Because President Hoover rejected appeals for a federal anti-lynching law, African Americans continued to be denied basic American justice. In 1933, for example, the worst year of the Depression, 24 African Americans were killed by the noose.

The **Scottsboro case** quickly came to symbolize the ugliness of race relations in the Depression era. One afternoon in March 1931, nine African American teenagers were arrested in the small town of **Scottsboro, Alabama**. The young men, who had been traveling in a freight train's boxcars, were charged with roughing up some white hobos and throwing them off the train earlier in the day. When two white women were pulled off the same freight train, they claimed that the young men had raped them. No real evidence surfaced that could prove that the rapes had occurred or that the "Scottsboro boys," as they were forever known, had committed any crime. Only the accusations of the two women existed, and some speculation remains that they may have invented the charges to avoid being arrested themselves on charges of prostitution. Regardless, an accusation by a white woman against a black man was seldom dismissed in the South of the 1930s.

The Scottsboro defendants stood trial before a jury (composed, as virtually all southern juries were, solely of white people) and were convicted of rape. Eight of the nine were sentenced to death. White southerners generally believed justice had been done.

However, over the next several years, the case attracted intense interest among those who protested its injustice. In 1932 the Supreme Court overturned the original convictions on the grounds that the accused had not been granted adequate legal counsel. New trials began in 1933, again with all-white juries. In these, the Scottsboro defendants were represented by Samuel Leibowitz, a talented lawyer from the International Labor Defense, an organization closely tied to the Communist party. Leibowitz helped bring widespread publicity to the case, but also cost the defendants some potential support by connecting their cause with the unpopularity of communists.

The Scottsboro defendants meet with their lawyer, Samuel Leibowitz, in an Alabama jail. The case attracted attention to the explosive issue of race relations in the United States.

Herbert Hoover lost his battle with the economy.

Key Terms: Agricultural Marketing Act, Reconstruction Finance Corporation, Bonus Army

Reading Preview
As you read this section, you will learn:

1. how Herbert Hoover approached the nation's economic problems.
2. what happened to Hoover's popularity as the Depression worsened.
3. what event made Hoover finally take direct action in the economy.
4. how veterans protested in the 1930s.
5. who emerged as a political leader after Hoover.

The crisis in the American economy forced many people to seek assistance. This man was waiting in the White Angel Breadline in San Francisco, California. (Courtesy of the Dorothea Lange Collection. © The City of Oakland, The Oakland Museum, 1933.)

Herbert Hoover owed his election to the presidency in 1928 to the confidence of the American people in the health of their economy. Perhaps more than any other figure of the 1920s, he was a symbol of the belief that rational, scientific intelligence could produce prosperity and growth. Eight months after he entered office, the economic success that had propelled him to the White House began to evaporate. Hoover spent the rest of his troubled presidency trying, and failing, to bring it back.

Hoover tried to restore confidence in the American economy.

Herbert Hoover tried first to stop the panic that he and many others believed was the principal cause of the Depression. He summoned business and financial leaders to Washington for meetings and assured them, and the public, that "the fundamental business of this country . . . is on a sound and prosperous basis." He tried to get business owners to keep production up and preserve jobs for their workers. He also persuaded labor leaders to drop demands for higher wages. Under other circumstances, these voluntary efforts might have had some

effect, but the economic crisis was now too severe for them to be successful. By mid-1931 the voluntary agreements Hoover had so carefully constructed were collapsing everywhere as the economy plunged into a new and more desperate phase.

Hoover rejected the demands of many conservatives that he cut government spending in order to balance the budget in a time of falling tax revenues. Instead, he proposed an increase in federal spending for public works and urged state and local governments to do the same. These projects, he argued, would create jobs and spur economic activity. Once in place, however, the public works projects helped few people. Hoover's commitment to public spending was limited.

American agriculture was in trouble long before the Depression began in other sectors of the economy. In April 1929, six months before the stock market crash, Hoover asked Congress to approve what became the **Agricultural Marketing Act**, establishing the first government agency with responsibility for stabilizing farm prices. Under the act, the government could spend up to $500 million to help farmers create cooperative marketing associations and achieve more efficient production. An amendment allowed the Farm Board to attempt to keep the market for agricultural products stable by establishing minimum prices. As the economy declined, however, the Farm Board's efforts proved inadequate.

Hoover also supported a new tariff on agricultural products—the Hawley-Smoot Tariff of 1930—which added protections against foreign competition to about three-fourths of all American farm products. It raised tariff rates to the highest level in the nation's history.

Despite the unprecedented nature of these efforts, farmers remained in trouble. The Marketing Act was unable to do what the farm economy needed most: force or encourage farmers to limit production to prevent surpluses. In addition, the Hawley-Smoot Tariff proved to be a costly mistake. Like most tariffs, it provoked retaliation abroad, which meant that American farmers could not sell as many goods overseas.

Hoover's popularity declined as the Depression worsened.

In the 1930 congressional elections, Democrats won control of the House of Representatives for the first time in more than a decade. They also made major gains in the Senate. Clearly, the Republican party was in danger.

Much of the public had begun to hold Hoover personally responsible for the Depression. The shantytowns on the edges of cities, where unemployed people took shelter, came to be known as "Hoovervilles." An empty pocket turned inside out was called a "Hoover flag," and newspapers were "Hoover blankets."

Compounding the problem was Hoover's chilly public personality. An aloof and formal man, he never developed a capacity to demonstrate compassion for those who were suffering. As he became a target of popular abuse, he publicly denied the existence of problems that were painfully obvious to millions of Americans. "No one is actually starving," he once said, infuriating a public struggling with survival. On another occasion, he took note of the thousands of men selling apples on street corners, widely cited as a sign of hard times, and insisted that many of them had left other jobs for this "more profitable" task.

Hoover believed that "rugged individualism" was the foundation of the American way of life. He held that direct aid for the needy should come from private charities or local communities, not the federal government. In a speech, he said:

Victory over this depression and over other difficulties will

AN AMERICAN ★ SPEAKS

be won by the resolution of our people to fight their own battles in their own communities, by stimulating their ingenuity to solve their own problems, by taking new courage to be masters of their own destiny in the struggle for life. This is not the easy way, but it is the American way.

A 1931 financial crisis in Europe sparked action by Hoover.

In May 1931 a major bank failed in Austria, sparking a financial panic that spread across

M E E T   T H E   P R E S I D E N T

HERBERT HOOVER

Born: August 10, 1874
Died: October 20, 1964
In office: 1929–1933

Herbert Hoover's lifetime of personal success and public achievement was marred only by the great misfortune of winning the 1928 presidential election. Hoover had neither the politics nor the personality to deal effectively with the traumas of the Great Depression.

An orphan at eight, Hoover worked his way to an engineering degree. He began his mining career pushing a cart for two dollars a day. Within a decade Hoover was an internationally famous engineer and a millionaire. World War I brought Hoover into public service, and his management of food relief in Europe during and after the war saved millions of people from starvation.

Hoover could not, however, save Americans from their ravaged economy as president. Scornfully dismissed after one ill-fated term, Hoover continued to devote his organizational genius to public service. He lived long enough to recover the esteem of his country, dying at age 90.

Europe over the next several months. The Depression was quickly becoming an international crisis, and American economic conditions grew worse as a result. Because so many European banks owed large sums of money to American ones, their troubles affected the United States both directly and indirectly.

To Hoover the problems in Europe demonstrated that domestic reforms in the United States would not suffice to end the Depression. Only an international solution would effectively restore prosperity, he claimed. He proposed a moratorium on the repayment of international debts to allow financial institutions to stabilize themselves—a sound proposal, but one that came too late to halt the panic.

Point

pro-Hoover

- relied on individual initiative
- suggested aid from local communities or charities
- supported voluntary agreements

Counterpoint

anti-Hoover

- insufficient to meet severe economic crisis
- unresponsive to Americans unable to help themselves
- contributed to unequal relief distribution

By the end of 1931, with conditions continuing to deteriorate in America, Hoover began supporting several new policy initiatives. Among them were increased support for American lending institutions to prevent bank failures and foreclosures on properties; a banking reform bill; and the creation of the **Reconstruction Finance Corporation**, or RFC. The RFC was, in effect, a government bank set up to loan funds to struggling banks, savings and loan associations, railroads, and life insurance companies. It also supported public works programs and, to a limited degree, assisted local relief agencies. Its budget in 1932 was $1.5 billion, which made it one of the largest spending programs in American history. However, the RFC never had enough money, and never spent it aggressively enough, to have more than a modest impact on the Depression. Under its chairman, the conservative Texas banker Jesse Jones, the RFC was so cautious in making loans that it only released a relatively small proportion of its funds.

Veterans protested by marching the Bonus Army into Washington.

In the meantime, distressed Americans were beginning to mobilize behind a variety of protest movements. One that attracted much attention was that of American veterans. In 1924 Congress had approved

bonus payments to all World War I veterans, to be distributed in 1945. In 1932, however, many veterans began to demand that the bonus be paid early. Hoover refused.

In June 1932 some 20,000 veterans marched into **Washington, D.C.**, calling themselves the Bonus Expeditionary Force (BEF). More popularly known as the **Bonus Army**, the veterans tried to persuade Congress to pay the bonus over Hoover's objections. They camped out in vacant public lots and in empty government buildings.

Although the House supported the early payments, the Senate voted down the proposal. Upon hearing the news, one disgusted veteran shouted, "We were heroes in 1917, but we're bums today." After their defeat, many members of the Bonus Army stayed in the city anyway, likely for lack of anywhere else to go. In mid-July Hoover asked the Washington, D.C., police to clear the few thousand remaining veterans out of federal buildings. A clash broke out between police officers and Bonus Marchers, and two veterans died. Hoover, who was embarrassed by the presence of the marchers and eager for an excuse to expel them, saw this as evidence of dangerous radicalism and violence. He ordered the army to drive the veterans out.

General Douglas MacArthur, the imperious chief of staff of the army, took command and exceeded the president's orders. He sent a large military force—armed with tanks, tear gas, rifle fire, sabers, and torches—against the

World War I veterans took over the steps of the U.S. Capitol in Washington, D.C. on July 5, 1932. They carried waving flags and banners announcing their home states.

THE GREAT DEPRESSION
Skill: Distinguishing Fact from Opinion

Introducing the Skill. As the economy worsened, apple vendors became one of the best-known symbols of the Depression. Because of an oversupply of apples, the fruit was offered on credit to unemployed people for them to sell. In New York City alone, some 6,000 apple vendors took to the streets. Many were well-dressed men—a sign that professionals were suffering as much as laborers. President Hoover, however, noted that these apple vendors had left other jobs because apple selling was more profitable. How might you determine whether Hoover's statement was true or simply his own opinion?

Learning the Skill. One of the most important skills in history is **distinguishing fact from opinion**. A fact is an accurate piece of information for which objective evidence exists. An opinion is a personal viewpoint that cannot be objectively tested. However, not all pieces of information are clearly fact or opinion. For example, a historian's interpretation of a historical event, which is an opinion, may become a fact if objective evidence is revealed in the future to prove it. Still, you can generally distinguish fact from opinion by testing a given piece of information against the definitions for both.

Applying the Skill. Study the cartoon on this page and answer the following questions.
1. What images or ideas has the cartoonist presented in this work?
2. Determine whether the images or ideas presented are facts or opinions.

Drawing by Peter Arno; © 1931, 1959
The New Yorker Magazine, Inc.

"WELL, SO LONG. I'LL SEE YOU AT LUNCH AT THE BANKERS CLUB."

unarmed veterans. Dozens were injured as the Bonus Marchers fled in terror and confusion.

Vivid photographs of the rout appeared in newspapers around the country the next day, inflaming the public. Conservative newspapers largely applauded the government action. By contrast, most of the public took it as evidence of the government's—and Hoover's—insensitivity. The veterans after all had worn the same uniforms as their attackers 15 years earlier. They were not radicals or revolutionaries, but simply unemployed, desperate men looking to their government for help. "What a pitiful spectacle is that of the great American Government,

Electoral Shift, 1928–1932

1932 Election

	Popular Vote	Electoral Vote
Roosevelt (Democratic party)	22,809,638 (57%)	472 (89%)
Hoover (Republican party)	15,756,901 (40%)	59 (11%)

Switched from Republican in 1928 to Democratic in 1932

Remained Republican, 1928 and 1932

Remained Democratic, 1928 and 1932

Albers Equal-Area Projection   © SF

map study

Regions As the map and chart show, the Democratic party gained huge numbers of followers at the expense of the Republicans. Which regions voted Democratic? Which regions remained Republican?

Critical Thinking Why might the country's severe economic problems contribute to the shift in party preference shown on the map?

mightiest in the world, chasing unarmed men, women and children in Army tanks," commented one Washington newspaper.

The counterattack on the president was to some degree unfair, since Hoover had never ordered an attack like the one that actually occurred. Still, the public was unable to make such distinctions. As a result, the bonus march hastened Hoover's political demise.

Roosevelt emerged as a political leader.

As the 1932 presidential election approached, Hoover had no opposition within the Republican party, in part because he was the incumbent and in part because few Republicans expected their party to win. The Democrats, after a spirited preconvention battle, settled on the governor of New York, **Franklin Delano Roosevelt**, to oppose the president.

Roosevelt had been a well-known politician for many years before 1932. He was the son of a wealthy railroad executive from the Hudson Valley and had grown up in aristocratic surroundings. As a child he spent summers in Europe and studied at home with a private tutor. As a young man, he attended such prestigious Massachusetts institutions as Groton School and Harvard University. A distant cousin of

Theodore Roosevelt, he strengthened the connection by marrying TR's niece, Eleanor. Largely because of his magic political name, but also because he was handsome, charming, and energetic, he rose quickly in the Democratic party.

In 1921 Roosevelt suffered a severe attack of polio and lost the use of his lower body. After years of rehabilitation, he learned how to stand with the use of braces and even to walk short distances with crutches. However, his legs remained paralyzed for the rest of his life.

Roosevelt remained active in politics and in 1928, when Governor Al Smith of New York was nominated for the presidency, Roosevelt was nominated to succeed him as governor. He won the election that fall (as Smith was losing to Hoover) and won again in 1930. Governors of New York, then the nation's largest state, were almost always considered potential presidents. Roosevelt's modestly progressive record in dealing with the Depression in his state increased his attractiveness.

In Roosevelt's acceptance speech to the 1932 Democratic convention, he promised "a new deal for the American people." The phrase stuck. His programs would always be known as the "New Deal," though his campaigning against Herbert Hoover gave only a few hints

of the kinds of programs Roosevelt had in mind. The Democratic candidate believed—correctly, it turned out—that Hoover and the Republicans were now so unpopular that it was not necessary to be specific in order to beat the president.

In November 1932 Roosevelt won by a landslide. He received 57 percent of the popular vote to Hoover's 40 and carried every state but Pennsylvania, Connecticut, Vermont, New Hampshire, and Maine. Democrats won large majorities in both houses of Congress as well.

The months between the election in November 1932 and the inauguration of the new president in March 1933 were among the most desperate of the entire Depression. President Hoover tried to pressure Roosevelt to join him in devising a recovery program even before taking office. Roosevelt resisted, aware that Hoover was trying to trap him into endorsing Hoover's own prescriptions for recovery.

In February, only weeks before the inauguration, the nation began to experience a severe banking crisis. One of Detroit's largest banks collapsed, and many smaller banks fell in its wake. Panic began to spread. Frightened depositors stood in line outside banks all over the country waiting to withdraw their money, fearful that the banks would collapse before they could get it. Since banks kept only a fraction of their deposits in cash, lending the rest out, these bank runs were disastrous for many of them. They simply did not have enough money on hand to cover the withdrawals.

In the middle of February, the governor of Michigan (where the banking crisis had begun) ordered all banks to close temporarily. Other states followed. By the beginning of March, as Roosevelt prepared to take office, banking activity was suspended or limited in 47 of the 48 states. The country's financial system was in crisis.

On March 4, 1933, Roosevelt rode up to Capitol Hill to take the oath of office in an open car, a glum Herbert Hoover seated beside him. Waiting to hear him were millions of Americans in near despair, wondering what the new president would do to solve the worst economic crisis in the nation's history.

On March 4, 1933, Roosevelt rode with a glum-looking Hoover to his inauguration. In the car Roosevelt tried very hard to be pleasant to his companion, who remained quite downcast. "I made some perfectly inane remarks to the president," he told his wife that afternoon. "When we passed that big building under construction I said to him, 'What beautiful steel!' "

SECTION 4 REVIEW

Identify Key People and Terms
Write a sentence to identify: Agricultural Marketing Act, Reconstruction Finance Corporation, Bonus Army, Franklin Delano Roosevelt

Locate Key Places
In what city did the Bonus Army march?

Master the Main Ideas
1. **Recognizing the changing relationship of government and economy:** What steps did Hoover take to try to restore confidence in the economy?
2. **Perceiving cause/effect relationships:** Why did Hoover's popularity decline as the Depression deepened?
3. **Understanding the impact of depressions:** How did a financial crisis in Europe affect Hoover's response to the Depression in the United States?
4. **Valuing civic participation:** Why did veterans march on Washington, D.C.?
5. **Identifying major political leaders:** What strengths did Franklin Delano Roosevelt bring to the Democratic presidential ticket?

Apply Critical Thinking Skills: Testing Conclusions
Consider these words from Herbert Hoover's speech as quoted on page 543: "This is not the easy way, but it is the American way." Do you agree that rugged individualism is the American way? Why or why not? Should it be?

Muriel Rukeyser Expresses the Despair of the Unemployed

13A

TIME FRAME
Late 1930s

GEOGRAPHIC SETTING
New York City

In her second book of verse, *U.S. 1* (1938), poet Muriel Rukeyser [rü′kī zər] explored the impact of the Depression on people living along the highway of the title (one of the earliest interstates, running along the east coast of the United States from Maine to Florida). In her early work Rukeyser dis-

played both her left-wing political convictions and a poetic imagery derived from the urban, industrial world around her. As one critic observed, "Mack trucks, not meadowlarks, are city-bred Muriel Rukeyser's symbols of dawn." In the following poem from *U.S. 1,* "Boy with His Hair Cut Short," Rukeyser pictured an unemployed young man and his sister attempting to encourage each other about his prospects of getting a job.

Boy with His Hair Cut Short

Sunday shuts down on this twentieth-
century evening.
The L passes. Twilight and bulb define
the brown room, the overstuffed plum
5   sofa,
the boy, and the girl's thin hands above
his head.
A neighbor radio sings stocks, news,
serenade.

10 He sits at the table, head down, the young
clear neck exposed,
watching the drugstore sign from the
tail of his eye;
tattoo, neon, until the eye blears, while
15   his
solicitous tall sister, simple in blue,
bending

Looking tired yet hopeful, unemployed men and one woman wait their turns in Isaac Soyer's 1937 painting, *Employment Agency.* Soyer (1902–1981) depicted the Depression as he saw and lived it in the 1930s and 1940s. On the opposite page a young African American straightens his tie, perhaps preparing to look for work, in this photograph by Arthur Rothstein. Employed for many years by the Farm Security Administration, Rothstein (1915–1985) joined other photographers, such as Dorothea Lange and Walker Evans, in recording the lives and times of the Great Depression.

behind him, cuts his hair with her
   cheap shears.

20 The arrow's electric red always reaches its
   mark,
successful neon! He coughs, impressed
   by that precision.
His child's forehead, forever protected
25   by his cap,
is bleached against the lamplight as he
   turns his head
and steadies to let the snippets drop.

Erasing the failure of weeks with level
30   fingers,
she sleeks the fine hair, combing:
   "You'll look fine tomorrow!
You'll surely find something, they can't

keep turning you down;
35 the finest gentleman's not so trim as
   you!" Smiling, he raises
the adolescent forehead wrinkling
   ironic now.

He sees his decent suit laid out, new-
40   pressed,
his carfare on the shelf. He lets his head
   fall, meeting
her earnest hopeless look, seeing the
   sharp blades splitting,
45 the darkened room, the impersonal
   sign, her motion,
the blue vein, bright on her temple,
   pitifully beating.

Discussing the Reading

1. What images did Muriel Rukeyser use to suggest the poverty of the boy and his sister?

2. What did Rukeyser convey about the boy's feelings by describing his "adolescent forehead wrinkling ironic now"? Is he really encouraged by his sister's words?

CRITICAL THINKING
Identifying Assumptions

According to the widely accepted belief in America as a land of unlimited opportunity, any decent, energetic young person could succeed here. How did Muriel Rukeyser attack this assumption in "Boy with His Hair Cut Short"?

Dorothea Lange Documents the Depression

TIME FRAME
Mid-1930s

GEOGRAPHIC SETTING
California and Texas

In the mid-1930s, the state of California hired photographer Dorothea Lange [lang] (1895–1965) to document the problems of the migrant farm workers
5 flooding the state as the Depression wors- ened and the Dustbowl drove small farmers out of the Great Plains. Among the photographs that resulted was the portrait of the migrant mother surrounded by her
10 children that appears on this page. The

In her photograph of five tenant farmers from Hardeman County, Texas, who have lost their farms, Dorothea Lange captures the boredom and frustration of the unemployed. On the opposite page, a mother and her three small children reflect the economic and personal devastation of the Depression.

example of Lange's work for California led to the establishment of the brilliant group of photographers, including Lange, who provided an extraordinary record of rural
15 poverty for the New Deal's Farm Security

Administration (FSA). Among Lange's photographs for the FSA was the picture above of a group of unemployed tenant farmers in Texas.

Discussing the Photographs

1. What is the dominant emotion expressed by the face of the migrant mother in Dorothea Lange's portrait? What other feelings does this photograph convey?

2. What is the atmosphere created by Lange's photograph of the tenant

farmers? Do the men seem frightened? angry? resigned?

CRITICAL THINKING
Making Comparisons

Compare Lange's interpretation of the rural poor with Muriel Rukeyser's assessment of the urban unemployed. How are the two similar? Explain.

Chapter Summary

Write supporting details under each of the following main ideas as you review the chapter.

Section 1

1. The stock market collapse led to the Great Depression.
2. A banking crisis hastened the American economic collapse after 1929.
3. Unemployment hit all segments of the population.
4. The Dust Bowl added geographic crisis to economic hardship.

Section 2

1. Americans retained their faith in individualism.
2. Some Americans protested against social and political systems.
3. Americans became hostile toward big business.

Section 3

1. Families made do with less.
2. Women faced wage and job discrimination during the Depression.
3. African Americans experienced deep poverty and intense racism.
4. Many Mexican Americans were forced to leave the country during the Depression.
5. Asian Americans were forced out of the general labor market during the Depression.

Section 4

1. Hoover tried to restore confidence in the American economy.
2. Hoover's popularity declined as the Depression worsened.
3. A 1931 financial crisis in Europe sparked action by Hoover.
4. Veterans protested by marching the Bonus Army into Washington.
5. Roosevelt emerged as a political leader.

Chapter Themes

1. **Racial, ethnic, religious diversity:** The economic hardships of the Great Depression helped emphasize the divided nature of American society. Unemployment and discrimination were rampant.
2. **Free enterprise:** The Great Depression severely challenged the American economic system. Most people, however, kept their faith in the essential strength of a free economy.

Chapter Study Guide

Identifying Key People and Terms

Name the key person or key term that describes the:
1. economic hardship of the 1930s
2. court case that illustrates how unjustly African Americans were treated in the 1930s
3. organization set up by Hoover to help failing banks, savings and loans, railroads, and insurance companies
4. group of unemployed veterans who went to Washington to demand early payment of promised money

Locating Key Places

1. What is the name of the five-state area hardest hit by the drought in the 1930s?
2. In what southern state did the Scottsboro case take place?
3. From what city did General Douglas MacArthur drive the Bonus Army?

Mastering the Main Ideas

1. Make a cause-effect chart for the Great Depression. A cause may produce several effects; and an effect might have several causes. Also an effect might become a cause. Show these relationships with arrows. Use the model below.

The Great Depression		
Cause(s)	$\longrightarrow$	Effect(s)

2. **(a)** How did the Depression affect America's belief in the Horatio Alger myth? **(b)** How was this change reflected in the changed attitude of many Americans toward business?
3. What methods did minorities use to cope with the hardships of the Depression?
4. What factors contributed to Roosevelt's election?

Applying Critical Thinking Skills

1. **Making comparisons:** Compare the situation of a Wall Street stock broker with that of a Dust Bowl farmer during the Depression years.
2. **Identifying central issues:** How might Americans' belief in individualism have affected the social and political protests of the Great Depression?

1929	1930	1931	1932	1933	1934	1935

1929	1930	1931	1932	1933		1935
Stock market crash; Depression begins	Six revolutions occur in South America	Scottsboro case begins	Depression hits low point; Bonus Army marches	FDR takes office; Hitler comes to power		Dust bowl conditions worsen

3. **Expressing problems:** What social, political, and judicial problems became evident during the Depression?
4. **Analyzing cause and effect:** Why did Hoover's attempts to improve the economy fail?

Chapter Activities

Learning Geography Through History

1. Many Dust Bowl farmers traveled, in search of work, to California by way of Route 66. Using photographs, books, music, magazines and so forth from this time, find out what it would have been like to travel this road—the states it passes through, the geography of the regions it crosses, the culture of the people who lived along the road, and so on.
2. In what country did a bank fail in 1931 and start the European depression?

Relating the United States to the World

1. How did foreign nations react to the Hawley-Smoot Tariff?
2. How did the relationship between the Philippines and the United States affect Filipinos in America?

Linking Past to Present

1. What progress has been made in recent years to find solutions to the social, political, and judicial problems that first became evident during the Depression?
2. In every period of history, entertainers such as singer Woody Guthrie have described people's feelings and problems while providing escape and hope for those in difficulty. Name and discuss entertainers who are doing that today.

Using the Time Line

1. How many years elapsed between the beginning of the Great Depression in the United States and its low point?
2. Which two world leaders took office in the same year—1933?

Practicing Critical Thinking Strategies

Distinguishing Fact from Opinion

When President Hoover ordered General Douglas MacArthur to use military force against the Bonus Army, the president believed that these marchers were dangerous to the public interest. What facts can you find out that would support or contradict the president's opinion?

Learning More About The Great Depression

1. **Using Source Readings:** Read the Source Readings for this chapter and answer the questions.
2. **Using Literature:** Read the excerpt from John Steinbeck's novel *The Grapes of Wrath* on pages 588–589. The selection deals with the migration of Dust Bowl farmers to California during the Great Depression.
3. **Examining films:** Obtain a video of the original *King Kong*, *Gone with the Wind*, or any Shirley Temple film. After your viewing, try to describe how you think that the particular movie might have helped people deal with their lives during the Great Depression.

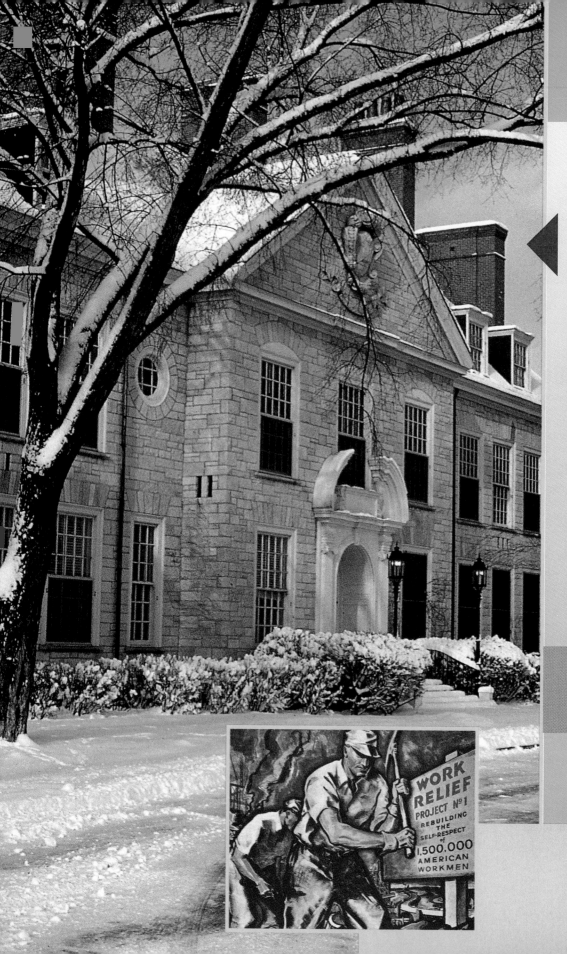

Linking Past to Present

The legacy of New Deal workers, such as those shown in the inset WPA poster, remains today in such institutions as schools, hospitals, museums, and government buildings. An example is Lake Forest High School, Lake Forest, Illinois, which was built in 1935 with WPA funds and workers.

WORK RELIEF PROJECT Nº 1
REBUILDING THE SELF-RESPECT of 1,500,000 AMERICAN WORKMEN

The New Deal

1 9 3 3 – 1 9 4 0

14

CHAPTER PREVIEW

As you read this chapter you will learn about New Deal programs set up to overcome the Depression.

SECTIONS IN THIS CHAPTER:
1. Franklin D. Roosevelt launched the New Deal.
2. New federal programs helped many Americans.
3. Organized labor grew more powerful during the 1930s.
4. Theme Essay: The New Deal changed the role of government.

Alfred Landon, governor of Kansas, was the Republican candidate for president in 1936, fighting to prevent the re-election of Franklin D. Roosevelt. Many of Landon's advisers—citing unscientific polls and their own wishful thinking—told him again and again that he was ahead. At times Landon half believed it. However, one day midway through the fall campaign, he rode a train into Chicago. Looking out the window as he passed shabby apartment buildings in working-class neighborhoods, he saw Roosevelt campaign posters in almost every window. He knew then that his candidacy was hopeless.

The image of Roosevelt was everywhere in the 1930s—not just in working-class homes in Chicago, but in modest farmhouses in the Midwest and in the cabins of black and white sharecroppers in the South, where pictures of the president were often tacked to bare wooden walls. He inspired a hatred as intense as the adoration. Wealthy conservatives so despised Roosevelt—and the policies he represented, which were known as the New Deal—that they would not say his name. They referred to him as "that man."

What made Roosevelt such an important and controversial figure? How did the programs and reforms he helped create affect traditional notions of free enterprise and private property? How did the New Deal meet the challenge of social diversity? How did it change the role of government in American life?

1933	1934	1935	1936	1937	1938	1939	1940
1933 Roosevelt launches New Deal	1934 Indian Reorganization Act	1935 Social Security Act	1936 AAA declared unconstitutional		1938 Orson Welles broadcasts *War of the Worlds*	1939 World War II begins in Europe	

SECTION 1

Franklin D. Roosevelt launched the New Deal.

Key Terms: Agricultural Adjustment Administration, Tennessee Valley Authority, National Industrial Recovery Act, National Recovery Administration, Public Works Administration, pump priming, Securities and Exchange Commission, Civilian Conservation Corps

Reading Preview
As you read this section, you will learn:

1. about Roosevelt's first task as president.
2. what impact early New Deal programs had on rural poverty.
3. how industry fared under the New Deal.
4. what effect the New Deal had on banks and financial markets.
5. how the New Deal helped the unemployed.

Entering office in the midst of a severe banking crisis, Roosevelt recognized that his first task was to stop the panic. He began doing so with his calming Inaugural Address, in which he assured the American people that "the only thing we have to fear is fear itself." From then on, he tried to present an image of confidence and optimism.

Roosevelt set out to reassure a troubled nation.

In contrast to his dour predecessor, Herbert Hoover, Roosevelt was an ebullient, cheerful public presence, whose charm and enthusiasm were infectious. He reached out to the public in many ways. Perhaps most effective was his use of radio. He was the first president to grasp the impact of broadcasting, and he inaugurated a series of informal addresses. Through these "fireside chats," he explained his programs to the American people and asked for their support. Roosevelt also took care to cultivate good relations with the press. The new president held informal news conferences as often as two

or three times a week and made friends with individual reporters.

In Roosevelt's first "Hundred Days" in office, he and Congress produced an amazing amount of legislation. The key to recovery, according to the president, was action. "Take a method and try it," he once told his staff members. "If it fails, try another. But above all, try something!"

Two days after his inauguration, Roosevelt issued a proclamation suspending the operation of all American banks. This "bank holiday," which lasted four days, threw investors into a panic but provided a welcome breathing spell in which new legislation could be devised. In the meantime Congress overwhelmingly passed the Emergency Banking Act. The act established new procedures by which the Treasury Department would inspect all banks, allowing only sound institutions to resume normal business.

Early New Deal programs had a limited impact on rural poverty.

Within weeks the Roosevelt Administration began introducing legislation to deal with larger problems in more enduring ways. Among the first was an effort to stabilize the troubled farm economy.

Agricultural reform. In May 1933 Congress passed legislation dealing with the most

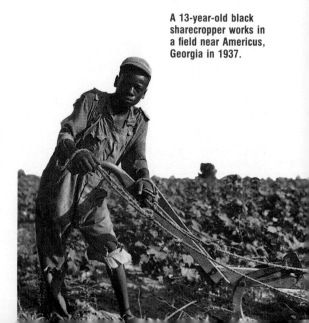

A 13-year-old black sharecropper works in a field near Americus, Georgia in 1937.

pressing farm problems: production surpluses and low prices. The new law created the **Agricultural Adjustment Administration** (AAA), which paid farmers to make idle one-fourth to one-half of their tillable land. Farmers eventually removed millions of acres from cultivation. The agency financed its farm subsidies through a tax levied on farm processing (for example, flour milling).

The AAA had only a mixed record of success. Farm prices rose after 1933, and the farm economy grew healthier. However, the AAA generally favored large landowners over tenant farmers and sharecroppers, who were often those most in need. Some New Deal farm programs unintentionally encouraged landowners to dispossess tenants and sharecroppers or fire field hands by making it cheaper to leave the land idle.

In 1936, amid widespread criticism of the AAA, the Supreme Court declared the agency unconstitutional. The Court ruled that the government had no authority to compel farmers to limit production. Instead of disappearing, however, many of the core AAA programs, including the farm subsidies, reappeared in other, slightly different forms.

Tennessee Valley Authority. One of the most celebrated accomplishments of the New Deal was the creation of the **Tennessee Valley Authority** (TVA), a bold experiment in government economic planning. For many years progressives in Congress had advocated federal development of water resources to produce cheap electrical power. They hoped to reduce the ability of utility monopolies to charge high rates, thereby making electricity more widely available.

One project in particular attracted the attention of progressives. During World War I, the government had begun building, but had never finished, a dam at a spot known as Muscle Shoals, on the Tennessee River in Alabama. Progressives wanted the dam completed and operated by the government. For many years the private power companies successfully opposed them.

All that changed in 1933 with the beginning of the New Deal and, perhaps equally signifi-

MEET THE PRESIDENT

For a rich kid and a mama's boy, Franklin D. Roosevelt had a remarkably combative spirit: "There's nothing I love as much as a good fight." He proved it three times, first in a personal battle against disabling illness, then as president during both the Great Depression and World War II.

Roosevelt entered the White House with a gust of try-anything energy, creating an alphabet soup of new programs and agencies. He attracted many great talents into government service. Perhaps the most essential talent was Roosevelt's own gift for awakening hope and renewing confidence in demoralized Americans.

Not since Lincoln has a president risen so dramatically to such grave challenge—or been so hated and so loved. In an unprece-

FRANKLIN D. ROOSEVELT

Born: January 30, 1882
Died: April 12, 1945
In office: 1933–1945

dented 12 White House years, Roosevelt's policies and his personality thumped America like a drum. The reverberations linger to the present day.

cantly, the spectacular collapse of the huge utility company of Samuel Insull. In May of that year, Congress approved the creation of the TVA as a government-owned corporation. Although one of its purposes was to complete the dam at Muscle Shoals, the TVA had a much larger agenda. It was designed to redevelop the entire **Tennessee Valley**, a region of 40,000 square miles that stretched into seven states—Tennessee, Kentucky, Virginia, North Carolina, Georgia, Alabama, and Mississippi. The TVA built a series of 20 dams and took control of five others in the region. The TVA then sold

(text continues on page 560)

557

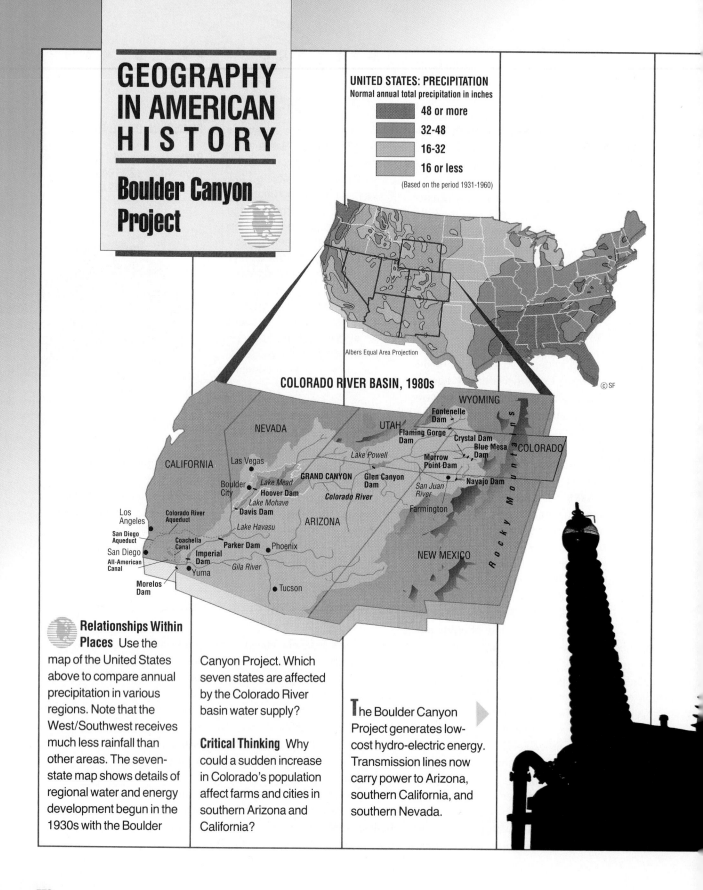

GEOGRAPHY IN AMERICAN HISTORY

Boulder Canyon Project

UNITED STATES: PRECIPITATION
Normal annual total precipitation in inches

- 48 or more
- 32-48
- 16-32
- 16 or less

(Based on the period 1931-1960)

Albers Equal Area Projection

© SF

COLORADO RIVER BASIN, 1980s

WYOMING

Fontenelle Dam

Flaming Gorge Dam

Crystal Dam
Blue Mesa Dam

UTAH

Morrow Point Dam

COLORADO

NEVADA

Lake Powell

Rocky Mountains

Las Vegas

GRAND CANYON

Glen Canyon Dam

Navajo Dam

CALIFORNIA

Boulder City

Lake Mead

Colorado River

San Juan River

Hoover Dam

Lake Mohave

Davis Dam

Farmington

Los Angeles

Colorado River Aqueduct

ARIZONA

Lake Havasu

San Diego Aqueduct

Coachella Canal

San Diego

Imperial Dam

Parker Dam

Phoenix

NEW MEXICO

All-American Canal

Yuma

Gila River

Morelos Dam

Tucson

Relationships Within Places Use the map of the United States above to compare annual precipitation in various regions. Note that the West/Southwest receives much less rainfall than other areas. The seven-state map shows details of regional water and energy development begun in the 1930s with the Boulder Canyon Project. Which seven states are affected by the Colorado River basin water supply?

Critical Thinking Why could a sudden increase in Colorado's population affect farms and cities in southern Arizona and California?

The Boulder Canyon Project generates low-cost hydro-electric energy. Transmission lines now carry power to Arizona, southern California, and southern Nevada.

At the peak of the project, in June 1934, the federal government and the six contracting firms involved together employed 5,218 men.

At right is a river level view of Hoover Dam. Seven-story buildings at the base of the dam house powerplant control rooms and administrative offices.

President Roosevelt noted at the dam's dedication: "This is an engineering victory of the first order — another great achievement of American resourcefulness, skill, and determination."

Arizona Spillway

Drum Gates

Intake Towers 395' in height

Maximum depth, 589'

Canyon Wall Outlet Works

Arizona Spillway Tunnel 50' Diameter 2200' in length

Stoney Gate 50' x 35'

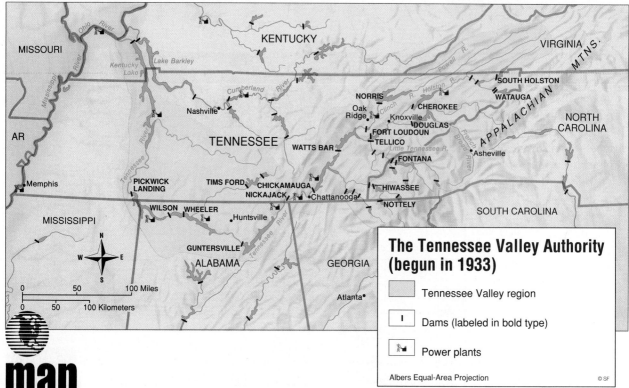

The Tennessee Valley Authority
(begun in 1933)

Tennessee Valley region

Dams (labeled in bold type)

Power plants

Albers Equal-Area Projection   © SF

map study

Relationships within Places

As the map above shows, the Tennessee Valley Authority (TVA) served a seven-state region in the Southeast. Developing such a vast project required federal funding and management, both of which were provided through a federally owned corporation. What two rivers are part of the TVA?

Critical Thinking

How have people in the TVA region tried to control their environment? What advantages and disadvantages has this effort brought to the region?

the electricity produced by the dams at reasonable prices, establishing a standard for electricity prices elsewhere.

The founders of the TVA also envisioned an ambitious effort at social reform throughout the region. They wanted it to help create local industries, to teach farmers new and more efficient techniques, to plant new forests, to stop flooding, and to improve education and social services. Many of the most expansive reform ideas were soon abandoned, but the TVA did make some important contributions to the region. Its system of dams and waterways virtually ended flooding and made water transportation more efficient. It also brought electricity to more than 400,000 residents, many using it for the first time. In addition, the TVA produced cheap new fertilizers, helped reduce soil erosion, and increased the productivity of the region.

The New Deal attempted to reform and revive American industry.

Although the federal government had been involved in assisting industry since the early 1800s, not until the Great Depression had it tried to intervene directly in the private economy as a means of restoring prosperity. The Hoover Administration had begun such efforts, but with little success. The Roosevelt Administration now began searching for its own approach to the economic crisis.

In June 1933 the Roosevelt Administration proposed and Congress passed the **National Industrial Recovery Act** (NIRA), which the president called "the most important and far-reaching legislation ever enacted by the American Congress." Whether or not that was true, it was certainly one of the most ambitious government programs in history.

At the heart of the NIRA was a series of "codes of fair competition," regulations that limited work production, established minimum wages, and set limits on work hours. Many of these codes had been drawn up by trade associations in the 1920s, but under the NIRA, they became enforceable by law. Old antitrust laws were set aside as industries were urged to cooperate.

To write, coordinate, and implement the new codes, Roosevelt established the **National Recovery Administration** (NRA). As its head, the president appointed General Hugh Johnson, a red-faced, aggressive ex-cavalry officer who tried to turn the agency into a popular, patriotic movement. Johnson staged large parades and demonstrations and devised both a vivid symbol, the Blue Eagle, and a slogan, "We Do Our Part." He also encouraged homemakers and shopowners to post NRA posters and stickers in their windows.

The NIRA brought a measure of strength to organized labor. To ensure that wages would rise along with prices, section 7(a) of the law guaranteed workers the right to form unions and bargain collectively with their employers. This was the first time in American history the federal government had recognized unions by law. The measure helped inspire the formation of many new unions, but the absence of effective enforcement mechanisms limited the ability of the unions to gain recognition from employers.

The NIRA also tried to help consumers by creating the **Public Works Administration** (PWA). This agency oversaw an ambitious program of publicly funded construction projects (dams, bridges, roads, and public buildings). It was designed to provide jobs for the unemployed and pump purchasing power into the economy. The use of public spending to stimulate private industry became known as **pump priming**. Under the cautious administration of Secretary of the Interior Harold Ickes, however, the PWA spent its money too slowly and carefully to have much impact.

Despite initial popular enthusiasm, the NIRA failed to have any significant effect on industrial recovery. In fact, industrial activity declined in the first months after its creation. By early 1934 many groups began to attack the agency. Business leaders complained that the government was interfering too directly in their affairs. Workers argued that the provisions of the law's section 7(a) were inadequate to pro-

A woman from San Antonio, Texas, prepares a quilt decorated with the NRA logo (shown above) to be sent to President Roosevelt. The NRA symbol came to represent patriotism and loyalty in a time of duress.

As the painting at left shows, the Public Works Administration (PWA) hired workers to build a multitude of schools, irrigation canals, sewage treatment plants, and bridges across the United States.

tect them. In addition, consumers complained that businesses were conspiring to raise prices to artificially high levels.

Finally, in the spring of 1935, the Supreme Court—in *Schechter* v. *United States*—ruled the NRA unconstitutional. In the suit the Schechter brothers who owned a poultry company claimed that since their business was not involved in interstate commerce, operating as it did only in New York, it should not be subject to the NRA codes. The government argued that interstate commerce should be more broadly defined. For example, the Schechters used products and equipment manufactured outside New York, even if they sold their own products only in that state. The Court agreed with the Schechters, ruling further that Congress had unconstitutionally delegated powers to the executive branch of government by permitting the NRA to draft industrial codes.

By closing down the NRA, the Supreme Court eliminated a failed agency that had become a political embarrassment. Nevertheless, Roosevelt was angry and alarmed by the decision. He realized that by taking a narrow view of the interstate commerce clause of the Constitution, the Supreme Court was signaling its intention to strike down other New Deal measures as well.

New Deal legislation regulated the banks and financial markets.

After the first, hurried response to the banking crisis in March 1933, Roosevelt's administration began to consider more lasting reforms in the nation's unstable financial system. Its first act was to change the country's monetary system. Until 1933 the economy had been based on the gold standard, which meant that all currency had to be backed up by gold. In April of that year, Roosevelt took the nation off the gold standard by making the price of gold—which had long been fixed—variable. In 1934, for example, the United States proclaimed that gold was worth only about half what it had been worth the year before. In that way, the government allowed itself to raise and lower the amount of currency in circulation simply by revaluing gold.

Many conservatives believed that the gold standard was essential to national economic stability, and even some people who otherwise supported the New Deal were hostile to the president's efforts to tamper with the currency. However, the gradual improvement of the economy after Roosevelt's actions suggests that, even if the currency reforms may not have caused the gains, they at least did not work against them.

Roosevelt turned next to the banking industry. In June 1933 Congress passed the Glass-Steagall Banking Act, which prohibited commercial banks from selling stock or financing corporations. The new law also created the Federal Deposit Insurance Corporation (FDIC), which insured individual bank deposits up to $2,500. That money was thus protected by the government. Today deposits are insured up to $100,000. The bill was designed to eliminate irresponsible banking practices and increase public confidence in the banks.

The Administration was also concerned about irresponsible trading practices in the nation's stock exchanges—the kind of practices that had helped create the 1929 crash. In 1934 Roosevelt persuaded Congress to establish the **Securities and Exchange Commission** (SEC), a new regulatory agency that would supervise the financial markets. Its first chairman was Joseph P. Kennedy, a wealthy financier and supporter of Roosevelt (and father of future president John F. Kennedy). The SEC became one of the most successful of all American regulatory commissions and oversaw a much needed reform of the way the stock markets did business. It also intensified resentment of the president among conservative business leaders, who saw the SEC as a "socialistic" intervention in private economic activity.

The New Deal helped the unemployed through work relief programs.

Like Hoover before him, Roosevelt entered office believing that aid to the poor and unemployed was the responsibility of local governments and private philanthropies. Unlike his predecessor, however, Roosevelt also recognized that the severity of the Depression made it impossible for traditional agencies to perform their tasks. "I see millions of families trying to live on incomes so meager that the pall of family disaster hangs over them day by day," Roosevelt once said. "I see one-third of a nation ill-housed, ill-clad, ill-nourished."

In his first months as president, therefore, Roosevelt established the first of many New Deal relief agencies. The Federal Emergency Relief Administration (FERA), created in May, funneled federal money to state and local governments to assist their own struggling relief efforts. It had a budget of $500 million, which its dedicated director, **Harry L. Hopkins**, spent as quickly and efficiently as he could.

By the end of the summer, however, Hopkins and Roosevelt both realized that the FERA budget would not be enough to get unemployed and otherwise dependent Americans through the cold winter months ahead. In November they won congressional approval of a new relief agency, the Civil Works Administration (CWA). The agency provided federal jobs for the unemployed—a significant departure from the FERA, which subsidized existing state and local agencies. CWA workers labored on road and school repairs, airport expansion, and other relatively small public works projects.

Harry Hopkins, in his capacity as the head of FERA, had the wisdom to hire a talented journalist, Lorena Hickok, to report to him on how Americans were dealing with the Depression. During three years of traveling, Hickok

V OICES FROM THE PAST

This I Remember

Mexican American leader Cesar Chavez was only a child during the Depression, but he will never forget the losses and dislocations that the Chavez family shared with millions of others. Why is Chavez determined to remember these events?

Oh, I remember having to move out of our house. My father had brought in a team of horses and a wagon. We had always lived in that house, and we couldn't understand why we were moving out. . . .

And then we were in California, and migratory workers. There were five kids—a small family by those standards. It must have been around '36. I was about eight. Well, it was a strange life. We had been poor, but we knew every night there was a bed *there,* and that *this* was our room. . . . But that all of a sudden changed. When you're small, you can't figure these things out. You know something's not right and you don't like it, but you don't question it and you don't let that get you down. You sort of just continue to move. . . .

This I remember. Some people put this out of their minds and forget it. I don't. I don't want to forget it. I don't want it to take the best of me, but I want to be there because this is what happened. This is the truth, you know. History.

CWA workers in Florence County, Wisconsin, make repairs and improvements in one of the county's public buildings.

observed scores of Americans and listened to their stories, recording her experiences in letters to Hopkins and **Eleanor Roosevelt**, the wife of the president and a close friend. As Hickok assembled her letters for a book that was published after her death, she recalled:

AN AMERICAN ★ SPEAKS

One by one, sometimes bold, sometimes hesitant, sometimes demanding, sometimes faltering, they emerged—individuals. People, with voices, faces, eyes. People with hope. People without hope. People still fighting. People with all courage squeezed out of them. People with stories.

There was a Negro woman in Philadelphia who used to walk eight miles every day over the scorching pavements just on the chance of getting, perhaps, a little cleaning to do, at 10 cents an hour. . . .

There was the little Mexican girl, aged 6, in Colorado, who said, sure, she'd worked "in the beets" two Summers already and, yes, sometimes she did get pretty tired. . . .

There were those little boys who refused to go to school in Houston, Texas, wearing the trousers of terribly conspicuous black-and-white-striped ticking that had been given to them, because everybody would know they were on relief.

There were those two small boys, a year or so later, in Salt Lake City, who were overheard boasting about whose father had been on relief longer.

There was the small town woman in Iowa who spent part of her husband's first CWA check for oranges, because she hadn't tasted any for three years.

There was the architect who said he didn't mind working on a road as a day laborer because "at least my children can tell the teacher their father is working."

To help some of the people Hickok met on her travels, Roosevelt himself proposed one of the New Deal's most popular relief programs. The **Civilian Conservation Corps** (CCC) was established in March 1933 to employ young, unemployed men between the ages of 18 and 25, most of them city residents. The young men were assigned to camps in the countryside, paid $30 a month (a portion of which they were required to send home to their families), and put to work. CCC projects included replanting forests, restoring historic battlefields, stocking lakes and streams with fish, building parks, and fighting forest fires.

To Roosevelt, it also served another purpose: It gave young, urban men a chance to work in what he considered a "healthy and wholesome atmosphere." The semimilitary organization of the camps, Roosevelt liked to believe, also instilled a sense of discipline in those who served in them. By 1940 more than two million young men (no women) had served in the CCC. Most workers were white, but a few segregated camps were established for African American youths.

Most of the relief efforts of the early New Deal were intended to be temporary, and only a few of them survived for very long. However, they were a first step in what would be more enduring efforts to create a system of social protection for Americans.

SECTION 1 REVIEW

Identify Key People and Terms
Write a sentence to identify: Agricultural Adjustment Administration, Tennessee Valley Authority, National Industrial Recovery Act, National Recovery Administration, Public Works Administration, pump priming, Securities and Exchange Commission, Harry L. Hopkins, Eleanor Roosevelt, Civilian Conservation Corps

Locate Key Places
In which seven states does the Tennessee Valley lie?

Master the Main Ideas

1. **Identifying major political leaders:** How did Roosevelt work to calm public fear?
2. **Understanding the development of the federal government:** Why did early New Deal programs such as the AAA and the TVA have only limited success?
3. **Acknowledging the role of government in regulating competition:** How did New Deal programs plan to reform and stimulate American industry?
4. **Understanding the development of the U.S. banking system:** How were banks and financial markets regulated during the New Deal?
5. **Respecting beliefs of other individuals:** Why did many unemployed Americans favor work relief programs over other relief programs?

Apply Critical Thinking Skills: Making Comparisons
Compare Roosevelt's early actions in regard to the economy with Hoover's responses while in office. How were the approaches of the two presidents different?

SECTION 2

New federal programs helped many Americans.

Key Terms: American Liberty League, Social Security Act of 1935, Works Progress Administration

Reading Preview
As you read this section, you will learn:

1. why conservatives attacked the New Deal.
2. about the general goal of the most popular dissident movements of the 1930s.
3. how Roosevelt responded to dissident challenges.
4. what the Social Security Act accomplished.
5. whom new programs of work relief helped.

Although Franklin Roosevelt enjoyed extraordinary popularity during his first two years in office, by the end of 1934, he began to encounter serious challenges. These challenges led the president into a new period of reform known as the Second New Deal.

Conservatives attacked the New Deal as a step toward socialism.

During the first years of Roosevelt's administration, the president had tried to win over the business community. He invited corporate leaders to help shape some of his early programs, most notably the NRA.

To many conservative business leaders, however, any government interference with private enterprise seemed a dangerous step on the road to socialism. They were also outraged at what they saw as the New Deal's "reckless" spending policies and tampering with currency. Many were particularly embittered by the Administration's support for organized labor.

As a result, in August 1934, a group of powerful industrialists formed a well-funded political organization to oppose the New Deal. Led by the Du Pont family and executives of the

General Motors Corporation, which the Du Ponts partially controlled, the members of this group, mostly northern Republicans, called themselves the **American Liberty League**.

The Liberty League claimed to have two objectives: the personal and property rights of individuals and the right of private enterprise to function without government interference. The leading Liberty Leaguers did not, however, oppose all connections between business and government. They strongly favored active government policies to assist and encourage business enterprise, and they saw an important role for business leaders in taking positions in the federal government.

The Liberty League attracted widespread publicity, but it never won very much popular support. The Liberty League was important in that it convinced Roosevelt that there was no point in trying to make friends with big business. By 1936 the president was ready to make attacks on "organized money" a major element of his campaign for re-election.

Several popular dissident movements supported a redistribution of wealth.

More successful than the Liberty League in attracting popular support were several dissident movements that attacked the New Deal for not doing enough to help those in need. Among the most prominent were those led by Francis Townsend, Father Charles Coughlin [käg′lən], and Senator Huey Long.

In California an elderly physician named Dr. **Francis E. Townsend** proposed a plan by which the government would pay $200 each month to every American over the age of 60. Each recipient would have to spend the money within a few weeks. The Townsend Plan, as it became known, was designed both to assist the elderly and to pump money into circulation to promote economic growth. Townsend was virtually unknown when he first presented his plan in a letter to the editor of a local newspaper. Within a few years, he had developed a national following estimated at five million.

Father **Charles E. Coughlin**, a Catholic priest from the Detroit suburb of Royal Oak, Michigan, attracted a still larger following through a weekly series of sermons broadcast over national radio. Some 30 million Americans listened each week to Coughlin's rich, warm voice as he mixed religious commentary with attacks on capitalists and bankers, whom he blamed for the Depression. Coughlin targeted Jewish bankers in particular since many

Senator Huey Long

Father Charles Coughlin

Dr. Francis Townsend

of the most successful banking families were Jewish. His anti-Semitic message was immensely appealing to his audience, largely from the urban, lower-middle class. Coughlin came to popularity during a decade in which anti-Semitism peaked in the United States, when Jews, rather than Catholics, bore the brunt of nativist fury.

A fervent supporter of Franklin Roosevelt in 1932, by 1934 Coughlin was beginning to turn against the president. He claimed that Roosevelt had not done enough to curb the "money power." Late in 1934, Coughlin went a step further and established the National Union for Social Justice, an organization that would mobilize popular support behind his demands. He was demonstrating considerable influence in Congress and was emerging as a major political figure. Some believed his National Union was the nucleus of a new political party, which Coughlin would use to mount a challenge to Roosevelt in 1936.

Most frightening to Roosevelt himself was Senator **Huey P. Long** of **Louisiana**, whom the president once called "one of the two most dangerous men in America." (The other was General Douglas MacArthur.) Long had risen to power in his home state by attacking the oil companies, the utilities, and the conservative political establishment. Elected governor in 1928, he dominated the politics and the government of Lousiana so completely that he was widely known as a dictator. Even his supporters called him the "Kingfish." In 1930 he won a seat in the U.S. Senate and prepared to make himself a national political figure as well.

Long had a colorful and often engaging public personality. He wore brightly colored shirts and loud ties. He made fun of everyone he considered stuffy or old-fashioned. He led marching bands across football fields and belted out songs in night clubs. Long, though, was not the clown he sometimes pretended to be. Once in Washington, he quickly set out to develop a national political following. He supported Roosevelt in 1932 but broke with him only a few months after the inauguration.

Long then attacked the Administration for not doing more to redistribute the nation's wealth. In 1934 he created the Share Our Wealth Society to promote his own implausible solution to the Great Depression: a redistribution of the nation's wealth. The federal government would confiscate the "excess" wealth and income of the rich and give it to the poor. Senator Long's Share-Our-Wealth Plan would guarantee every American a minimum annual income of $2,500. Share Our Wealth clubs began forming all over the country, with membership estimated at four million or more. Many people believed Long was planning to run for president in 1936, and some members of the Roosevelt Administration feared that the Democrat could tip a close election to the Republicans.

Roosevelt reacted aggressively with the Second New Deal.

The rise of Townsend, Coughlin, Long, and other dissident challenges to the New Deal created concern in the Administration. Roosevelt sensed that he had to move aggressively in 1935 to deal with the continuing problems of the Depression and to consolidate his own political position as a reform leader. He knew that to act would take much of the punch away from the popular protests. The result was a new flurry of legislative activity that often has been labeled the Second New Deal.

One of the most conspicuous elements of this new phase of the New Deal was the changed attitude of the Administration toward big business. In his speeches and public statements, Roosevelt now openly attacked the influence of the corporate world. He also introduced legislation to limit its power. One of the most controversial proposals was aimed at the utility companies.

In 1935 Roosevelt proposed reforms in the tax code to shift burdens to the wealthy, a proposal conservatives labeled a "soak-the-rich" tax. Although the bill called for the highest income tax rates in peacetime history, Congress readily passed it. It was not, however, the radical wealth redistribution measure conservatives feared and Huey Long advocated. The bill had important symbolic value for the president, but it did relatively little to redistribute wealth.

Organized labor grew more powerful during the 1930s.

Key Terms: Congress of Industrial Organizations, Wagner Act, National Labor Relations Board

Reading Preview
As you read this section, you will learn:

1. what issue divided the labor movement in the 1930s.
2. how labor unions won the right of recognition from employers.
3. which group of Americans strongly supported Roosevelt in his 1936 bid for re-election.

The Supreme Court's Schechter decision in 1935 declaring the National Recovery Administration unconstitutional destroyed not only the NRA itself, but NIRA's section 7(a), which guaranteed workers the right to organize and bargain collectively. However, the decision could not stop the growth of a powerful labor movement, which continued to put pressure on both employers and the government to respond to its demands.

The labor movement divided over the issue of unskilled workers.

The new militancy of American workers began to become evident in 1934, when labor staged a wave of strikes to win recognition of their unions. Some of these strikes displayed a strength and radicalism not seen among workers in many years. Relatively few of them, however, produced major victories for the strikers.

During the 1930s the principal labor organization in the country was the American Federation of Labor (AFL), which increased its efforts at unionization in response to the Depression. The AFL was committed to the idea of craft unions, which were organizations that represented a particular craft or skill, such as carpentry, plumbing, or bricklaying. Many labor leaders argued that in an age of giant corporations the craft union model was obsolete. Craft unionism divided the work force into too many groups, each too small to bargain effectively on its own. It also excluded altogether the fastest growing element of the working class: unskilled factory workers, who fit into no craft category at all. Instead, these leaders argued, workers should organize themselves into industrial unions—unions that represented all the employees of such industries as steel, automobiles, or mining.

Leading the drive to create industrial unions was John L. Lewis, the president of the United Mine Workers, the oldest industrial union in the country. Lewis, who had achieved national stature during the 1919 mine workers' strike, was a flamboyant and charismatic figure who inspired enormous loyalty from his followers and deep loathing from his enemies. At first he tried to work within the AFL, but he found it impossible to avoid conflict between the new organizations he was promoting and the older craft unions he was often threatening. He decided that a new and different type of labor organization was needed.

In 1935 Lewis created the Committee for Industrial Organization within the AFL. However, a year later, the AFL suspended the group and

This 1937 cartoon showed the concern of AFL leadership about the growing dominance of John L. Lewis in the CIO. The caption read, "Boys, we'd better go out and stop it!"

then finally expelled it altogether. (The two groups did not reunite until 1955.) Lewis renamed his union the **Congress of Industrial Organizations** (CIO) and made it into a direct rival of the AFL.

Although the split weakened the labor movement of the 1930s, it also provided a home for the new industrial unions. The CIO attempted to organize unions in industries where there were virtually no skilled workers at all—industries the AFL had traditionally ignored: laundries, textiles, tobacco factories, and others. Much of this new, unskilled work force consisted of African Americans and women, two groups the AFL had largely excluded from membership.

Labor unions won the right of recognition in the Wagner Act.

Even before the Supreme Court's Schechter decision, progressives in Congress (led by Senator Robert Wagner of New York) were pressing for new legislation to assist labor unions in winning recognition from employers. With the death of NIRA's section 7(a), they stepped up their efforts. Roosevelt was reluctant to support the new legislation at first, but when it became clear that it was going to pass anyway, he changed his mind. In May 1935 the president signed the National Labor Relations Act, better known as the **Wagner Act**.

The Wagner Act reinstated the provisions of section 7(a), guaranteeing workers the right to bargain collectively with employers through unions. It also went further by specifically outlawing a group of "unfair labor practices" commonly practiced by employers to keep unions out of their plants. Most importantly, the act created the **National Labor Relations Board** (NLRB) to enforce the provisions of the law—something section 7(a) had conspicuously lacked. The NLRB had the power to compel employers to recognize and bargain with unions that had the support of a majority of the employees.

The empowering of unions, reflected in the Wagner Act, influenced industrial workers throughout the nation. In 1932 only three million workers were members of unions officially recognized by employers. By the end of 1937, that number had risen to eight million.

Evelyn Macon was one worker who used the union to win both a major improvement in her working life and a new measure of self-respect. Macon was an African American who lived in New York City during the Depression. She was working in a commercial laundry, whose labor force was largely female and black.

Laundry workers strike in front of their Brooklyn, New York, workplace. In a 1937 organizing drive, the United Laundry Workers enrolled nearly 14,000 new members.

Slavery is the only word that could describe the conditions **AN AMERICAN ★ SPEAKS** under which we worked. At least 54 hours a week, it was speed up, speed up, eating lunch on the fly, perspiration dropping from every pore for almost ten hours per day.

Fearful of losing her job in a time of high unemployment, she kept her complaints to herself. One day, however, a new man arrived at the plant and disrupted the normal working routine. When the boss told him to work faster, he laughed and continued to work at his own pace. When the boss told the workers to eat lunch "on the fly"—without stopping work—the new man picked up his lunch and walked out. He came back exactly one hour later. He was promptly fired.

That night Macon met the man on the street and learned that he was a CIO organizer, sent to the laundry to investigate working conditions. He handed her a leaflet advertising a union organizing meeting that night. "As disgusted as I was with my lot," Macon recalled, "I was the first one to reach the meeting." Almost everyone from the plant was there. Within six months everyone had joined the CIO's new United Laundry Workers Union except for one woman, who informed the boss about the organizing.

"The boss was frantic," Macon remembered. He tried to intimidate the workers, then tried to start a company union unaffiliated with the CIO. The employees stood their ground. Finally, after the entire work force walked out, the boss relented and recognized the United Laundry Workers. The workers won higher wages and better hours. "Conditions in the laundry are a hundred times better than they were two years ago," Macon said in 1939, two years after the strike.

The working class resoundingly returned Roosevelt to office in 1936.

The mobilization of the working class, and the New Deal's support of their efforts, had a major effect on the 1936 election. Millions of American workers mobilized to help return Franklin Roosevelt to office. Roosevelt launched his campaign with a stinging attack on the forces of "organized greed" and a ringing endorsement of the rights of American workers.

The Republicans nominated the moderate Alfred Landon, whose record as governor of **Kansas**, like the man himself, was solid but unexciting. Supporters of Father Coughlin, Dr. Townsend, and Huey Long (who had been assassinated in 1935 by a political enemy) gathered under the banner of the new Union Party and nominated Representative William Lemke of North Dakota for president.

Neither the Republican nor the Union party was able to mount an effective challenge to the magnetic and popular Roosevelt. Not long before the election, the president's chief political adviser, Postmaster General James Farley, predicted that Roosevelt would win every state except Maine and Vermont. He was right. Roosevelt polled a record 60.8 percent of the popular vote and 523 electoral votes to Landon's 8. The Democrats also increased their already large majorities in both houses of Congress. In the election the country seemed to validate Roosevelt's New Deal. The president would soon learn otherwise.

S E C T I O N **3** R E V I E W

Identify Key People and Terms
Write a sentence to identify: Congress of Industrial Organizations, Wagner Act, National Labor Relations Board

Locate Key Places
Of which state was Alfred Landon governor?

Master the Main Ideas

1. **Understanding the development of labor unions:** How did the issue of unskilled workers divide the AFL into two separate organizations?
2. **Understanding the development of labor unions:** How did the Wagner Act guarantee the right of recognition for labor unions?
3. **Understanding major political elections:** Why did the working class support Roosevelt in 1936?

Apply Critical Thinking Skills: Drawing Conclusions
How did the development of the CIO reflect changes in the country's work force in the 1930s?

Throughout the 1930s industrial workers pushed for the right to unionize their workplaces. This group from Detroit's Ford Motor Company protested Ford's refusal to allow unions to represent auto workers.

Theme Essay:
The New Deal changed the role of government.

Key Terms: court-packing plan, Fair Labor Standards Act of 1938

Reading Preview

As you read this section, you will learn:

1. which institution presented problems for Roosevelt's New Deal.
2. when New Deal activity began to slow down.
3. how the New Deal affected minorities and women.
4. about the significance of the New Deal.

The magnitude of Roosevelt's victory in 1936 seemed to promise an expansion of the New Deal in the president's second term. However, more quickly than anyone could have imagined that November, Roosevelt's political and legislative fortunes declined. His legacy, though, remained. The New Deal changed both the way the U.S. government operated and the way it was viewed by the American public. Throughout the 1930s Roosevelt crafted a government that played an increasingly active role in the economic and social health of the country. Through federal agencies and legislation, the president sought to meet the needs of a highly diverse population. In doing so, he consistently tested the U.S. Constitution and challenged the powers and relationships of the three branches of government.

The Supreme Court presented problems for the New Deal.

Roosevelt's most serious problem, he believed at the end of 1936, was the conservatism of the Supreme Court. The Court had already struck down several important pieces of New Deal legislation, including the NIRA and the AAA, as unconstitutional. New Dealers feared that it would also use its power of judicial review to

invalidate the Wagner Act, the Social Security Act, and perhaps more. Some hoped that Roosevelt would be able to shape the Court more to his liking with new appointments. However, no justices retired during his first term as president, and there were few signs that any intended to leave soon as he began his second.

Roosevelt toyed with a number of ideas for meeting the challenge of the Court. He finally decided that the best solution would be to win the authority to appoint more justices even if the present ones did not retire. Early in 1937, therefore, he proposed a Judiciary Reorganization bill to Congress. The bill proposed, among other things, to give the president authority to appoint one new justice to the Supreme Court for every sitting justice who had reached the age of 70 and failed to retire. The Constitution did not specify the number of justices, but the Court had consisted of nine members since the mid-1800s. Roosevelt's plan would allow it to expand to as many as 15 justices.

Roosevelt's real motives for proposing the plan were clear. He wanted to name more liberal justices and protect his programs from judicial review. The **court-packing plan**, as it soon became known, was intensely controversial from the beginning. Conservatives saw it as confirmation of what they had long claimed: that Roosevelt aspired to be a dictator. Roosevelt's supporters defended it as the only way to preserve the New Deal. At first it seemed that the bill might pass. Then, late in March, the Court voted to uphold a state minimum-wage law, reversing its position of a year before. Two justices—Chief Justice Charles Evans Hughes and Associate Justice Owen Roberts, both of whom had generally opposed the New Deal in the past—had switched and sided with the supporters of the New Deal.

The Court, it seemed clear, had deliberately moderated its course to protect itself from attack. Support for Roosevelt's judicial reform plan quickly faded, and months later it was defeated in Congress. Over the next several years, a number of justices retired and Roosevelt appointees ensured that the Court would not again be an obstacle to the president. The in-

THE COURT-PACKING PLAN
Skill: Identifying Assumptions

Introducing the Skill. By the end of 1936, President Roosevelt had become frustrated with the Supreme Court. The nine justices had struck down several major New Deal measures, and Roosevelt was anxious to stop the assault on his programs by expanding the Court to 15 justices. How did the president's plan to secure a supportive Court reflect his assumptions about people and government?

Learning the Skill. Understanding Roosevelt's plan requires **identifying assumptions** made by the president. As you learned on page 243, an assumption is an idea, generally unstated, that someone takes for granted as being true. Some assumptions may be accurate and based on fact. Others, however, are questionable or even false. To recognize an assumption, examine the given information to see if there are any claims or statements being expressed that lack obvious support or evidence. Assumptions based on fact are more likely to be valid than those based on opinion.

Applying the Skill. Study the cartoon on this page and answer the following questions.
1. What assumption does the cartoonist suggest President Roosevelt made about his relationship with the Supreme Court? Give evidence for your response.
2. Was Roosevelt's assumption valid?

cident brought lasting political damage to Roosevelt, emboldening conservatives to oppose him openly. Never again would he have the same influence in Congress he had enjoyed in his first term.

New Deal activity slowed down after 1937.

More damaging to the Administration was a severe recession that began in the fall of 1937. Although the recession had many causes, one of them was the Administration's own confidence in the success of its economic policies. Believing that the Depression was now finally over, the president agreed in the spring of 1937 to reduce federal expenditures on relief and other programs in an effort to balance the budget.

By early fall, however, the fragile economic boom had collapsed, and economic conditions quickly grew worse than at any time since the worst days of 1932. This time, however, the Administration seemed to recognize the problem. Early in 1938 Roosevelt asked Congress for a large new spending program for relief and public works, which would, he promised, pump needed purchasing power back into the economy. A few months later, a modest recovery had begun. It seemed to vindicate the idea that government deficit spending in a recession could help the economy recover, an idea central to the teachings of the British economist **John Maynard Keynes** and others.

The Supreme Court fight, the recession, the resurgence of conservative opposition in Congress, and the apparent lack of new ideas from the Administration itself all combined to make the late 1930s a period in which the New Deal accomplished relatively little. The principal legislative victory of Roosevelt's second term was the **Fair Labor Standards Act of 1938**, which for the first time established a national minimum wage and placed limits on the number of hours people could be required to work. The bill made only a slight immediate impact because it excluded many workers and established low standards.

Perhaps the biggest reason for the decline of the president's reform energies in the late

1930s, however, was his growing preoccupation with the outside world. In particular, Roosevelt faced the rise of dictator Adolf Hitler in **Germany**. International crises would soon draw the United States into war.

The New Deal had a limited effect on minorities and women.

As you read previously, the Depression hit minority groups especially hard. The last-hired, first-fired syndrome hurt them from the very beginning, bringing high unemployment and widespread poverty.

The New Deal and African Americans. In many ways the Roosevelt Administration was more sympathetic to the cause of racial equality than any of its predecessors. The president appointed a number of African Americans to positions in the federal government. For example, Roosevelt appointed **Mary McLeod Bethune**, a black educator, to the advisory committee of the National Youth Administration, an agency set up to provide jobs for needy young people. Because of her efforts, African Americans received a fair share of NYA funds. In addition, Harold Ickes, a strong sup-

The Blues

I been down so long,
It seems like up to me.

This line, common to many blues songs, could have been sung with feeling by millions of people during the Depression of the 1930s. The blues, a type of music developed by African Americans in the South in the late 1800s, first gained recognition with white audiences in the 1920s. Such artists as Gertrude (Ma) Rainey, Bessie Smith, and later, Billie Holiday, belted out their gutsy lyrics as band members imitated the rhythm of their singing with the saxophone, piano, or trumpet. These and other blues artists used their music to combine humor with despair. The release many people felt from listening to the blues helped them keep their sanity through the Depression.

Although the blues can take many forms, most blues songs have 12-bar verses with three lines each. The second line is usually a repeat of the first, and the third line completes the thought. Blues lyrics are highly personal, dealing with sorrows, rejection, and anger, often in a witty or amusing manner.

Blues musicians use many elements of African music. These include simple instrumentation that mimics or echoes the singer's voice in a call-response pattern, a musical shout that changes pitch suddenly and dramatically, complex patterns of rhythm, and improvisation. Admired and imitated around the world, the blues is a unique African American product.

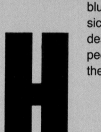

Ma Rainey, Bessie Smith, and Billie Holiday adorned many record labels in their time, also appearing live at such clubs as New York City's Savoy, center. Ma Rainey led the band shown below during the 1920s.

Highlights of American Life

Black southerners, educated separately from their white neighbors, generally did not receive equal schooling.

Mary McLeod Bethune, the most influential member of the black cabinet, became the first African American woman to head a federal agency.

The New Deal and Mexican Americans.

Fewer in number and scattered throughout the Southwest, Mexican Americans had less political clout than African Americans. Like black Americans, though, they were deeply affected by such New Deal programs as the AAA. Migrant farm workers were often laid off when acreage was reduced.

Still, the New Deal did help in some ways. For example, the Farm Security Administration set up camps for migrant farm workers in California. In addition, FERA, CCC, and WPA programs hired unemployed Mexican Americans for relief jobs.

However, many people of Mexican descent had difficulty qualifying for relief assistance. As non-citizens, Mexican aliens could not get assistance. Mexican American migrant workers also had trouble because they did not live long enough in the same place to meet residency requirements. Also, legal statutes excluded farm workers from the benefits of such programs as Social Security and the National Labor Relations Act.

The New Deal and Native Americans.

A brighter side of the New Deal's treatment of minorities was the so-called Indian New Deal. In 1933 President Roosevelt appointed **John Collier** as commissioner of Indian affairs. In this role Collier had Congress create the Indian Emergency Conservation Program, a CCC-type project for the reservations. Through this program, tens of thousands of Native Americans built dams and reservoirs, installed fences and lookout towers, and conducted extensive pest and weed control projects. Collier also worked to make sure that the PWA, WPA, CCC, and NYA actively hired Native Americans.

Collier also pursued another pressing issue in Congress—the breaking up of Indian tribal lands. As a result, Congress passed the Indian Reorganization Act in 1934. The act ended the government's 47-year-old program of allotting tribal lands to individual Native Americans and white settlers and provided funds for Indian groups to purchase new lands. It also recognized tribal constitutions and lifted bans on the use of Native American languages, ceremonies, and traditional dress on the reservations.

porter of civil rights, hosted the much publicized black cabinet in the Department of the Interior. This group—which included Clark Foreman, as Ickes' personal assistant, and Robert C. Weaver and William H. Hastie as lawyers—worked together to push the Administration to end segregation.

In addition, many New Deal relief programs provided African Americans with fair assistance. Programs poured federal funds into black schools and hospitals in the South, and provided work relief to unemployed African Americans in the North.

There were strict limits, however, to how far Roosevelt would go to assist African Americans. He feared that to do more would so antagonize powerful southerners in Congress that he would be unable to win approval of any of his programs. So he opposed the demand of the NAACP and others for legislation to make lynching a federal crime. Roosevelt also did little to challenge hiring and wage discrimination in the local administration of New Deal relief projects.

The New Deal and women.

The New Deal provided an important moment for American women to gain a foothold in national politics. Roosevelt appointed the first female member of the cabinet in American history: **Frances Perkins**, his secretary of labor. He named more than 100 other women to positions throughout the Administration. Eleanor Roosevelt, by becoming an active and outspoken champion of reform causes, served as an example to thousands of women.

Again, there were limits. Few of the women in the New Deal could be called feminists by any modern definition of the term. They were less interested in winning equality for women than in winning special protections for them—such as barring women from especially arduous and dangerous work. Perkins, for example, opposed the Equal Rights Amendment, fearing it would eliminate the female protective legislation for which she had fought throughout her career.

Mexican American teenagers receive training in food catering.

John Collier meets with Blackfoot chiefs in 1934.

Navajo women in New Mexico practice the traditional craft of weaving blankets.

KEY NEW DEAL LEGISLATION, 1933–1938

Year	Act or Agency	Provisions
1933	Agricultural Adjustment Administration (AAA)	Granted farmers direct payments for reducing crop production; funds for payment provided by a processing tax, later declared unconstitutional
1933	Tennessee Valley Authority (TVA)	Constructed dams and power projects and developed the economy of a seven-state area in the Tennessee River Valley
1933	National Industrial Recovery Act (NIRA)	Sought to revive business through a series of fair–competition codes; created National Recovery Administration (NRA) to write, coordinate, and implement these codes; NIRA's Section 7a guaranteed labor's right to organize (act later declared unconstitutional)
1933	Public Works Administration (PWA)	Sought to increase employment and business activity through construction of roads, buildings, and other projects
1933	Banking Act of 1933 (Glass– Steagall Act)	Prohibited commercial banks from selling stock or financing corporations; created FDIC
1933	Federal Deposit Insurance Corporation (FDIC)	Insured individual bank deposits
1933	Federal Emergency Relief Act (FERA)	Provided federal funds for state and local relief efforts
1933	Civil Works Administration (CWA)	Provided federal jobs for the unemployed
1933	Civilian Conservation Corps (CCC)	Employed young men in reforestation, road construction, and flood control projects
1934	Federal Housing Administration (FHA)	Insured loans provided by banks for the building and repair of houses
1935	Social Security Act	Created a system of social insurance that included unemployment compensation and old age survivors' insurance; paid for by a joint tax on employers and employees
1935	Works Progress Administration (WPA)	Employed more than eight million people to repair roads, build bridges, and work on other projects; also hired artists and writers
1935	National Labor Relations Act (Wagner Act)	Recognized the right of employees to join labor unions and to bargain collectively (reinstating the provisions of NIRA's Section 7a); created the National Labor Relations Board (NLRB) to enforce laws against unfair labor practices
1935	National Youth Administration (NYA)	Provided job training for unemployed youths and part–time jobs for students in need
1938	Fair Labor Standards Act	Established a minimum wage of 25 cents an hour and a standard workweek of 44 hours for businesses engaged in interstate commerce

Roosevelt's New Deal

Point

In support of the New Deal

- responded to social injustices
- created a more humane and responsible government
- changed the role of the federal government

Counterpoint

Against the New Deal

- defied the U.S. Constitution
- ignored individual freedoms and the rights of private enterprise
- made modest alterations when radical changes were necessary

lation established the trade union movement as an important and powerful part of the industrial economy. Its farm subsidies became the basis of a permanent federal involvement in agriculture pricing and production. The Social Security program formed the foundation of the modern welfare state and remains the single most important program of government social provision. Above all, perhaps, the New Deal helped break down traditional ideas about what government should and should not do and inspired future generations to think of even larger roles for the state in regulating and reforming American life.

The New Deal also endorsed the belief that in hard times, women should leave the work force to open up jobs for unemployed men. New Deal relief agencies generally excluded women. The Social Security program made no provision for such overwhelmingly female occupations as domestic and restaurant service.

The New Deal had a lasting effect on American institutions.

The New Deal was intensely controversial in the 1930s, and it has remained so to some degree ever since. To its defenders, it was a long overdue response to social injustices—a transforming moment that created a more humane and responsible government. To its critics on the right, it was a dangerous radical experiment that defied the Constitution and trampled on individual freedoms and the sanctity of private enterprise. To its critics on the left, it was a timid defense of capitalism, making modest alterations in the existing structure to fight off demands for more basic changes. As with so many issues in history, how one evaluates the New Deal depends in large part on one's own values and assumptions.

Despite these and many other limits, the New Deal was a vital moment in shaping the kind of society we know today. Its labor legis-

SECTION **4** REVIEW

Identify Key People and Terms
Write a sentence to identify: court-packing plan, John Maynard Keynes, Fair Labor Standards Act of 1938, Mary McLeod Bethune, John Collier, Frances Perkins

Locate Key Places
In which country did Adolf Hitler rise to power?

Master the Main Ideas

1. **Recognizing constitutional developments: (a)** How did various decisions by the Supreme Court disturb Roosevelt? **(b)** How did the president try to outmaneuver the Court?
2. **Understanding the development of the federal government:** What caused New Deal activity to slow down after 1937?
3. **Perceiving cause/effect relationships:** Why did the New Deal have a limited impact on minorities and women?
4. **Understanding the development of the federal government:** What lasting contributions did the New Deal make to American life?

Apply Critical Thinking Skills: Identifying Assumptions
With the New Deal, Roosevelt created a flood of federal relief and regulatory agencies. What assumptions might the president have been making about the role of the federal government in the economy and in American life?

chart study

What New Deal agencies listed on page 578 dealt with geographic issues?
Critical Thinking
In what ways does today's society reflect the New Deal programs of the 1930s?

Diego Rivera Paints Murals in the United States

14A

TIME FRAME
1931–1933

GEOGRAPHIC SETTING
San Francisco and Detroit

The painter Diego Rivera (1886–1957) was one of an extraordinary group of Mexican artists who employed murals, or wall paintings, to express the ideals of the Mexican Revolution. It was the example of these Mexican muralists that prompted the creation of the New Deal's Federal Arts Projects. Part of the Works Progress Administration (WPA), the public-works agency of the New Deal, the Federal Arts Projects employed out-of-work artists, many of whom painted murals on the walls of post offices and other public buildings. The style of Mexican muralists such as Rivera strongly influenced the style of this WPA art. Rivera himself executed a number of murals in the United States, including the two shown here.

This section of Diego Rivera's mural *Detroit Industry* is part of a sequence picturing the manufacture of automobiles. Rivera's *Allegory of California*, which appears on the facing page, was painted on one of the walls of the Pacific Stock Exchange in San Francisco.

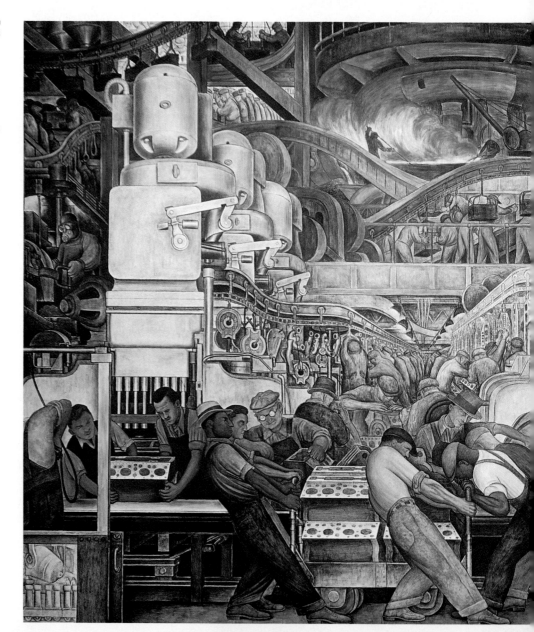

Painted in San Francisco in 1931, the work
20 shown above, *Allegory of California,* was
the first mural that Rivera did in the
United States. He personified California as
a gigantic serenely beautiful woman
(whose features were based on those of
25 Californian Helen Wills, a tennis champion of the 1920s and 1930s). The figure
bending over a plant in the center right is
California horticulturist Luther Burbank.

The figure immediately below him is
30 James Marshall, discoverer of gold in California. The mural on the left is a portion
of a series, *Detroit Industry,* which Rivera
painted on the walls of the Detroit Institute of Arts between May 1932 and March
35 1933. Rivera based these images on research he had done at the Ford Motor
Company's huge Rouge River Plant in
April 1932.

Discussing the Paintings

1. What kind of expression did Diego Rivera give James Marshall in *Allegory
of California*? Did he make Marshall
look exultant or anxious about his discovery of gold at Sutter's Mill?

2. What attitude toward its subject does
Detroit Industry express? Did Rivera
make the process involved in producing automobiles seem heroic or dehumanizing? Did he emphasize

the workers or the machines in the
composition of this painting?

CRITICAL THINKING
**Distinguishing False From Accurate
Images**

An *allegory* is a picture or story in which
abstract ideas are personified, as in Diego Rivera's *Allegory of California*.
What images would you employ to create an allegorical picture of the state in
which you live?

"Which Side Are You On?"

TIME FRAME
1931

GEOGRAPHIC SETTING
Kentucky

Kentucky's Harlan County was the scene of bitter and frequently violent labor disputes between coal-mine operators and miners. In 1931, with the Depression reducing the demand for coal, miners struck to force mineowners to maintain wage rates. Both sides resorted to violence, and several miners were killed. It was against the background of these events that Florence Reece, the wife of a union leader, wrote the famous song "Which Side Are You On?" Folksinger Pete Seeger, who met Reece in the 1940s, gave the following account of the song's composition: "Mrs. Florence Reece, wife of a rank-and-file organizer for the old National Miners' Union in Harlan County, Kentucky, was at home one day in 1931 when High Sheriff J. H. Blair and his 'deputies' ('they were really company gun thugs,' she said) came to her house. One of her little girls began to cry. 'What you crying for?' said a deputy. 'We ain't after you, we're after your old man.' They poked their rifles into closets, under beds, even into piles of dirty clothes, and finally left. Mrs. Reece tore an old calendar off the wall and wrote these now famous verses. She fitted them to an old hymn tune, and her little girls used to sing it at the union hall." In the early 1960s "Which Side Are You On?" was rewritten by civil-rights leader James Farmer for use by the Freedom Riders.

Which Side Are You On?

C ome all of you good workers,
Good news to you I'll tell
Of how the good old union
Has come in here to dwell.

A miner's wife stands amid the evidence of her family's poverty in this Bureau of Mines photograph of the kind of housing provided by mineowners for their workers.

Chorus:

5 Which side are you on?
Which side are you on?
Which side are you on?
Which side are you on?

My daddy was a miner
10 And I'm a miner's son,
And I'll stick with the union
Till every battle's won.

They say in Harlan County
There are no neutrals there;
15 You'll either be a union man
Or a thug for J. H. Blair.

Oh, workers, can you stand it?
Oh, tell me how you can.
Will you be a lousy scab
20 Or will you be a man?

Don't scab for the bosses,
Don't listen to their lies.
Us poor folks haven't got a chance
Unless we organize.

Discussing the Reading

1. How did Florence Reece describe the political situation in Harlan County in 1931?

2. Reece used the word *scab* (line 19) to refer to a nonunion miner. What attitude did she express toward these workers?

CRITICAL THINKING
Testing Conclusions

Some people argue that unions have served their purpose and are no longer needed in the American workplace. These people would point out that many of the reforms in working conditions sought by unions have been implemented. Others feel that only the permanent presence of unions in the workplace protects the gains made by American workers over the years. With which position do you agree? Explain.

The Depression Lingers in Spanish Harlem

TIME FRAME
1941

GEOGRAPHIC SETTING
New York City

Despite New Deal recovery programs, the Depression lingered on throughout the 1930s. Real economic recovery and full employment did not return to the United States until World War II rearmament stimulated American industry, and military manpower needs reduced the workforce. Piri Thomas (1928–) is a Puerto-Rican American who grew up in New York City's Spanish Harlem. In the following excerpt from his autobiographical novel, *Down These Mean Streets,* he recalled the waning of the Depression in 1941. His father had recently lost his job and was working for the WPA, or Works Progress Administration, the New Deal agency that provided jobs for the unemployed in public works projects.

It was 1941, and the Great Hunger called Depression was still down on Harlem. But there was still the good old WPA. If a man was poor enough, he could dig a
5 ditch for the government. Now Poppa was poor enough again.

The weather turned cold one more time, and so did our apartment. In the summer the cooped-up apartments in
10 Harlem seem to catch all the heat and improve on it. It's the same in the winter. The cold, plastered walls embrace that cold from outside and make it a part of the apartment, till you don't know whether it's
15 better to freeze out in the snow or by the stove, where four jets, wide open, spout futile, blue-yellow flames. It's hard on the rats, too.

Snow was falling. "My *Cristo,*" Momma
20 said, "*qué frío* [kā frē′ō, how cold!]. Doesn't that landlord have any *corazón* [kô rä sôn′, heart]? Why don't he give more heat?" I wondered how Pops was making out working a pick and shovel in
25 that falling snow.

Momma picked up a hammer and be-gan to beat the beat-up radiator that's copped a plea from so many beatings. Poor steam radiator, how could it give out
30 heat when it was freezing itself? The hollow sounds Momma beat out of it brought echoes from other freezing people in the building. Everybody picked up the beat and it seemed a crazy, good idea. If eve-
35 rybody took turns beating on the radiators, everybody could keep warm from the exercise. . . .

584

The door opened and put an end to the kitchen yak. It was Poppa coming home from work. He came into the kitchen and brought all the cold with him. Poor Poppa, he looked so lost in the clothes he had on. A jacket and coat, sweaters on top of sweaters, two pairs of long johns, two pairs of pants, two pairs of socks, and a woolen cap. And under all that he was cold. His eyes were cold; his ears were red with pain. He took off his gloves and his fingers were stiff with cold.

"*Cómo está* [kō′mō es tä′, how are you]?" said Momma. "I will make you coffee."

Poppa said nothing. His eyes were running hot frozen tears. He worked his fingers and rubbed his ears, and the pain made him make faces. "Get me some snow, Piri," he said finally.

I ran to the window, opened it, and scraped all the snow on the sill into one big snowball and brought it to him. We all watched in frozen wonder as Poppa took that snow and rubbed it on his ears and hands.

"Gee, Pops, don't it hurt?" I asked.

"*Sí*, but it's good for it. It hurts a little first, but it's good for the frozen parts."

I wondered why.

"How was it today?" Momma asked.

"Cold. My God, ice cold."

Gee, I thought, *I'm sorry for you, Pops. You gotta suffer like this.*

"It was not always like this," my father said to the cold walls. "It's all the fault of the damn depression."

"Don't say 'damn,' " Momma said.

"Lola, I say 'damn' because that's what it is—*damn*."

And Momma kept quiet. She knew it was "damn."

My father kept talking to the walls. Some of the words came out loud, others stayed inside. I caught the inside ones—the damn WPA, the damn depression, the damn home relief, the damn poorness, the damn cold, the damn crummy apart-ments, the damn look on his damn kids, living so damn damned and his not being able to do a damn thing about it. . . .

The next day the Japanese bombed Pearl Harbor.

"My God," said Poppa. "We're at war."

"*Dios mío,*" said Momma.

I turned to James. "Can you beat that," I said.

"Yeah," he nodded. "What's it mean?"

"What's it mean?" I said. "You gotta ask, dopey? It means a rumble is on, and a big one, too."

I wondered if the war was gonna make things worse than they were for us. But it didn't. A few weeks later Poppa got a job in an airplane factory. "How about that?" he said happily. "Things are looking up for us."

Things *were* looking up for us, but it had taken a damn war to do it. A lousy rumble had to get called so we could start to live better. . . .

I couldn't figure it out, and after a while I stopped thinking about it. Life in the streets didn't change much. . . . War or peace—what difference did it really make?

Slum children are shown playing on a tenement fire escape in one of the images from *One Third of a Nation*, a series shot in New York City's East Side and Chelsea districts in 1937 by WPA photographers Arnold Eagle and David Robbins.

Discussing the Reading

1. What aspects of life caused the narrator's father to repeatedly curse the family's situation?

2. What event improved the economic situation of the narrator's family? What was his attitude toward this event?

CRITICAL THINKING
Making Comparisons

Compare the narrator's family to the Polish immigrant family of Source Reading 6C. What seems to be the position of the mother within each of these families? How do the children interact with their parents?

Chapter Summary

Write supporting details under each of the following main ideas as you review the chapter.

Section 1

1. Roosevelt set out to reassure a troubled nation.
2. Early New Deal programs had a limited impact on rural poverty.
3. The New Deal attempted to reform and revive American industry.
4. New Deal legislation regulated the banks and financial markets.
5. The New Deal helped the unemployed through work relief programs.

Section 2

1. Conservatives attacked the New Deal as a step toward socialism.
2. Several popular dissident movements supported a redistribution of wealth.
3. Roosevelt reacted aggressively with the Second New Deal.
4. The Social Security Act created a system of social insurance.
5. New programs of work relief aided writers, artists, and other unemployed workers.

Section 3

1. The labor movement divided over the issue of unskilled workers.
2. Labor unions won the right of recognition in the Wagner Act.
3. The working class resoundingly returned Roosevelt to office in 1936.

Section 4

1. The Supreme Court presented problems for the New Deal.
2. New Deal activity slowed down after 1937.
3. The New Deal had a limited effect on minorities and women.
4. The New Deal had a lasting effect on American institutions.

Chapter Themes

1. **Constitutional and representative government:** During the New Deal, Congress worked hard to produce legislation that would meet the critical needs of the times. At the same time, the courts zealously examined the legislation to ensure that it did not exceed the limits of the Constitution. Within this balance of power, Roosevelt believed that the Supreme Court was being too conservative so he proposed an ill-fated Judiciary Reorganization bill.

2. **Free enterprise:** Many critics of the New Deal believed that Roosevelt's legislation infringed on people's economic rights. During the Progressive Era, government's role had been that of an economic regulator of big business. During the New Deal, however, with such legislation as the Wagner Act, the Fair Labor Standards Act, and Social Security, the federal government became more active in the economy.

Chapter Study Guide

Identifying Key People and Terms

Name the key person or key term that describes the:
1. federal project to develop water and electrical resources
2. key New Deal legislation that established codes and regulations for fair competition and working conditions
3. Roman Catholic priest who advocated sweeping social changes in America
4. John L. Lewis' union that sought to organize all industrial workers, regardless of craft specialty
5. Roosevelt's effort to protect his New Deal programs from judicial condemnation

Locating Key Places

1. What river did the United States government plan to develop in an effort to bring electricity to much of the South?
2. From what state did Huey Long come?

Mastering the Main Ideas

1. Create a chart summarizing the purpose and success of five New Deal programs established in 1933. Use the following categories to organize your chart: "New Deal Program," "Purpose," and "Result."
2. What were the principal accomplishments of the Second New Deal?
3. What was the issue dividing the AFL and the CIO in the 1930s? How did each group reflect the times in which it was founded?
4. How was the conflict between Roosevelt and the Supreme Court resolved?

Applying Critical Thinking Skills

1. **Distinguishing fact from opinion:** Roosevelt said that "the only thing we have to fear is fear itself." Was his statement a fact, an opinion, or both? Support your response with evidence.

1933	1934	1935	1936	1937	1938	1939	1940

1933	1934	1935	1936	1937	1938	1939	
Roosevelt launches New Deal	Indian Reorganization Act	Social Security Act; NRA declared unconstitutional	AAA declared unconstitutional	Court-packing plan fails	Second New Deal; CIO formed	World War II begins	

2. Testing conclusions: Some historians have concluded that Townsend, Coughlin, and Long actually did Roosevelt a favor by proposing programs that were even more liberal than those of the president's New Deal. Why would they draw this conclusion? Do you think that there is any political evidence to support it? Explain.

3. Identifying assumptions: What different assumptions about the extent and responsibility of the federal government did New Deal critics on the right and left make?

4. Predicting consequences: The fortunes of many women and minorities were advanced because of New Deal legislation. What political consequences might you predict for Roosevelt and the Democratic party as a result?

Chapter Activities

Learning Geography Through History

1. How did the Tennessee Valley Authority project affect the geographic conditions of the southern United States?

2. In what city did Harold Ickes host the black cabinet during Roosevelt's administration?

Relating the United States to the World

1. From what nation did many immigrants to the southwestern United States come?

2. In what country did many of Roosevelt's ideas about government monetary and fiscal policies originate?

Linking Past to Present

1. What are some government programs that have been added to further the original goals of the Social Security Act?

2. Roosevelt tried to use a court-packing plan to influence the Court to preserve laws that he considered essential. How have recent presidents influenced the Court?

Using the Time Line

1. What events on the time line might have led President Roosevelt to create his court-packing plan?

2. In what years did Roosevelt initiate his two phases of the New Deal?

Practicing Critical Thinking Strategies

Identifying Assumptions

Many New Deal programs relied on the concept of pump priming. Upon what assumptions was this concept based? Use evidence from your reading of the chapter or other sources.

Learning More About the New Deal

1. Using Source Readings: Read the Source Readings for this chapter and answer the questions.

2. Gathering and analyzing data: From the library, get a copy of the *Historical Statistical Abstract of the United States*. Locate statistics about the nation's Gross National Product from the years 1925 to 1940. Also locate America's unemployment records for the same years. Finally, locate statistics for the United States government's annual expenditures from 1925 to 1940. Construct tables and graphs that illustrate the statistical ups and downs related to the Great Depression. Use the figures to describe the events of the Great Depression.

3. Analyzing popular films: From a film library, get a copy of the film *The Grapes of Wrath*. This film version of John Steinbeck's novel shows some of the consequences of the Great Depression for common people living in Dust Bowl America, many of whom traveled to California in search of work. (a) After viewing the film, write a short report describing the purposes of the film or (b) memorize one particular scene from the movie and deliver it to the class.

DUST BOWL MIGRANTS MOVE WESTWARD

In the 1930s a combination of drought, the Depression, and the increasing mechanization of American agriculture forced many small farmers in the Great Plains off their land. Large numbers of displaced farm families headed west to California, where they hoped to find work in the fields and orchards. Eventually more than a million of these migrants reached California, though their economic plight rarely improved when they arrived there. This vast migration was the subject of John Steinbeck's novel *The Grapes of Wrath* (1939). In the following excerpt he described the temporary communities established by the migrants at each night's rest stop as they traveled westward.

The cars of the migrant people crawled out of the side roads onto the great cross-country highway, and they took the migrant way to the West. In the daylight they scuttled like bugs to the westward; and as the dark caught them, they clustered like bugs near to shelter and to water. And because they were lonely and perplexed, because they had all come from a place of sadness and worry and defeat, and because they were all going to a new mysterious place, they huddled together; they talked together; they shared their lives, their food, and the things they hoped for in the new country. Thus it might be that one family camped near a spring, and another camped for the spring and for company, and a third because two families had pioneered the place and found it good. And when the sun went down, perhaps twenty families and twenty cars were there.

In the evening a strange thing happened: the twenty families became one family, the children were the children of all. The loss of home became one loss, and the golden time in the West was one dream. And it might be that a sick child threw despair into the hearts of twenty families, of a hundred people; that a birth there in a tent kept a hundred people quiet and awestruck through the night and filled a hundred people with the birth-joy in the morning. A family which the night before has been lost and fearful might search its goods to find a present for a new baby. In the evening, sitting about the fires, the twenty were one. They grew to be units of the camps, units of the evenings and the nights. A guitar unwrapped from a blanket and tuned—and the songs, which were all of the people, were sung in the nights. Men sang the words, and women hummed the tunes.

Every night a world created, complete with furniture—friends made and enemies established; a world complete with braggarts and with cowards, with quiet men, with humble men, with kindly men. Every night relationships that made a world, established; and every morning the world torn down like a circus.

At first the families were timid in the building and tumbling worlds, but gradually the technique of building worlds became their technique. Then leaders emerged, then laws were made, then codes came into being. And as the worlds moved westward they were more complete and better furnished, for their builders were more experienced in building them.

The families learned what rights must be observed—the right of privacy in the tent; the right to keep the past black hidden in the heart; the right to talk and to listen; the right to refuse help or to accept, to offer help or to decline it; the right of son to court and daughter to be courted; the right of the hungry to be fed; the rights of the pregnant and the sick to transcend all other rights.

> In the evening a strange thing happened: the twenty families became one family.

An excerpt from
THE GRAPES OF WRATH
by John Steinbeck

And the families learned, although no one told them, what rights are monstrous and must be destroyed: the right to intrude upon privacy, the right to be noisy while the camp slept, the right of seduction or rape, the right of adultery and theft and murder. These rights were crushed, because the little worlds could not exist for even a night with such rights alive.

And as the worlds moved westward, rules became laws, although no one told the families. It is unlawful to foul near the camp; it is unlawful in any way to foul the drinking water; it is unlawful to eat good rich food near one who is hungry, unless he is asked to share.

And with the laws, the punishments—and there were only two—a quick and murderous fight or ostracism; and ostracism was the worst. For if one broke the laws his name and face went with him, and he had no place in any world, no matter where created.

In the worlds, social conduct became fixed and rigid, so that a man must say "Good morning" when asked for it, so that a man might have a willing girl if he stayed with her, if he fathered her children and protected them. But a man might not have one girl one night and another the next, for this would endanger the worlds.

The families moved westward, and the technique of building the worlds improved so that the people could be safe in their worlds; and the form was so fixed that a family acting in the rules knew it was safe in the rules.

There grew up government in the worlds, with leaders, with elders. A man who was wise found that his wisdom was needed in every camp; a man who was a fool could not change his folly with his world. And a kind of insurance developed in these nights. A man with food fed a hungry man, and thus insured himself against hunger. And when a baby died a pile of silver coins grew at the door flap, for a baby must be well buried, since it has had nothing else of life. An old man may be left in a potter's field, but not a baby.

A certain physical pattern is needed for the building of a world—water, a river bank, a stream, a spring, or even a faucet unguarded. And there is needed enough flat land to pitch the tents, a little brush or wood to build the fires. If there is a garbage dump not too far off, all the better; for there can be found equipment—stove tops, a curved fender to shelter the fire, and cans to cook in and to eat from.

> **A man with food fed a hungry man, and thus insured himself against hunger.**

And the worlds were built in the evening. The people, moving in from the highways, made them with their tents and their hearts and their brains.

In the morning the tents came down, the canvas was folded, the tent poles tied along the running board, the beds put in place on the cars, the pots in their places. And as the families moved westward, the technique of building up a home in the evening and tearing it down with the morning light became fixed; so that the folded tent was packed in one place, the cooking pots counted in their box. And as the cars moved westward, each member of the family grew into his proper place, grew into his duties. . . .

CRITICAL THINKING
Recognizing Values
Are individual or group rights more important in the migrant communities described by John Steinbeck? Support your answer by citing evidence from the passage.

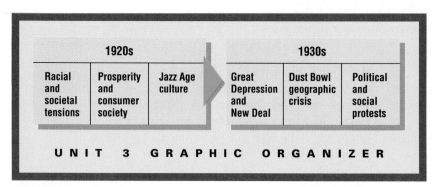

1920s			1930s		
Racial and societal tensions	Prosperity and consumer society	Jazz Age culture	Great Depression and New Deal	Dust Bowl geographic crisis	Political and social protests

U N I T   3   G R A P H I C   O R G A N I Z E R

11

C H A P T E R
S U R V E Y

Society and Politics in the 1920s

1919–1929

Postwar America was a restless and divided country.
The 1920s are famous as a time of prosperity and pleasures. However, they were also years of fear and social conflict. Major labor strikes in 1919 combined with a series of terrorist bombings to create panic about a communist takeover. Attorney General A. Mitchell Palmer responded to this "red scare" by ignoring constitutional rights and rounding up thousands of suspected radicals.

Racial injustice led to several riots across the country. Millions of African Americans left the South to crowd segregated sections of northern cities. Their old enemy, the Ku Klux Klan, celebrated renewed strength and influence by holding a huge parade in the nation's capital in August 1923.

Traditionalists tried to shape American conduct and thought.
During the 1920s, some political and religious conservatives promoted their beliefs by passing laws. The Prohibition Amendment was an attempt to improve American morals by changing the Constitution. The making and selling of alcoholic beverages were forbidden. Many Americans ignored Prohibition, however, and large criminal empires developed to satisfy the public's illegal thirst.

Another traditionalist effort succeeded in banning the teaching of evolution in some public schools. In Tennessee, this law was tested in the Scopes trial of 1925. In this contest between science and religion, traditionalists won a brief victory.

One legal measure signaled social progress. American women won the right to vote with the 19th Amendment, which became law in 1920. Along with millions of American men, most women promptly voted Republican.

Republicans controlled the White House in the 1920s.
Warren G. Harding won the 1920 presidential election with a promise of "normalcy." He fulfilled that promise, but his careless leadership led to major scandals. Harding died before he was disgraced. His successor, Calvin Coolidge, said and did little except to use his powers of office to help American business. A third Republican, Herbert Hoover, won the presidency in 1928, expecting to continue the same system of

prosperity. There were troubling signs, however, that Republican prosperity was reaching a limit. American farmers struggled with serious problems during the 1920s. Hundreds of thousands of farm failures caused thousands of banks to go out of business. The ripples of these problems would spread through the American economy.

C H A P T E R
S U R V E Y

Technology and Culture in the 1920s
1920–1929

Energy and technology created prosperity.   In the 1920s American industries found new ways of using the energies of oil and electricity. Workers could produce goods more quickly and cheaply. The results

would be revolutionary. Henry Ford's use of the assembly line in his factories produced a car that average families could afford. Americans bought cars by the millions, creating millions of jobs — not only in factories, but in road construction, gas stations, oil fields, and many other businesses.

The automobile did more than create prosperity. Cars changed the American landscape and influenced where Americans worked, where they lived, and what they did for fun.

Americans learned new ways to spend money and time.
Powerful new methods of mass production poured out thousands of new products, from cars to mouthwash. New techniques of advertising made Americans eager to buy. Pay-later financing plans made buying easy, and Americans went on a spending spree.

Prosperity gave most Americans more free time. As a result, interest in sports, movies, and other forms of entertainment increased greatly in the 1920s. New developments in communication, including newspaper chains and radio, helped Americans share the same experiences. Americans across the country might listen to the same game, see the same movie, and read the same comic strip.

New generations chose their own styles and values.   In the 1920s many young Americans ignored the traditions and values of earlier generations. Enjoying the new freedom created by cash and cars, many young people shocked their parents by following their own ideas. Daring young women known as flappers became symbols of this rebellion. In dress and behavior, flappers signaled a revolution in fashion and morals. Though not all young women became flappers, many were affected by the changes of the 1920s. The national birth rate fell due to effective, inexpensive methods of birth control. American households were transformed by modern electric appliances.

The 1920s were rich in literature, art, and music.   A "lost generation" of writers and artists rejected the carefree values of American popular culture. They transformed their critical feelings into an outpouring of novels, poems, and paintings. In the Harlem Renaissance, African American writers and artists expressed the pride and pain of their unique experience. African American musicians gave the 1920s a sound, a rhythm, and a name: The Jazz Age.

CHAPTER SURVEY 13

The Great Depression
1929–1932

A stock-market collapse began the Great Depression.   The uncontrolled fall of stock prices in October 1929 jolted the American economy. By the time the economic crisis reached its worst point late in 1932, almost every area of American life had been affected. Many businesses were wiped out. More than 9,000 banks were closed. Millions of Americans lost their jobs, homes, lands, and life savings. One out of four Americans was out of work; in some cities eight out of ten were jobless. Natural disaster deepened the crisis as dry weather created a Dust Bowl on the American plains. Worried Americans faced the deepest economic crisis in the nation's history.

The Depression tested the American way of life.   Stunned by their losses, Americans reacted with anger, despair, protest, and determination. Some families collapsed; others were drawn closer together by the struggle to survive. The Depression caused many citizens to ask angry questions about the American way of life and of business. However, relatively few citizens looked for answers in socialism, communism, or radical action. Throughout the 1930s most Americans still struggled to believe in self-reliance, hard work, and free enterprise.

Economic stress produced intolerance.   Women and minority Americans were the first to be squeezed out of a shrinking job market. Already hit hard by poverty, African Americans felt the additional pains of injustice and racism. The Scottsboro trials of nine African American teenagers in 1931 and 1933 showed to many angry citizens that even the legal system was against them. Other minorities also experienced injustice. Large numbers of Mexican Americans were forced to leave the United States for Mexico. Chinese Americans and Filipinos were paid unequal wages when they could find work at all. In these ways, the Depression increased the level of unfairness in American life.

Americans turned to new leadership in 1932.   A strong believer in "rugged individualism," President Herbert Hoover at first tried to talk Americans out of the Depression. He was slow to use the powers of federal government to aid businesses and citizens during the crisis. He was quick, however, to use force against a "Bonus Army" of unemployed veterans who had come to Washington, D.C., for help in 1932.

In contrast to Hoover's reluctant efforts, his Democratic opponent in the 1932 election boldly promised "a new deal for the American people." Franklin Delano Roosevelt won the presidency in a landslide.

14

The New Deal
1933–1940

Roosevelt confronted the problems of the Depression.

The new president was eager to use the powers of the federal government. Roosevelt's Administration quickly produced new laws to reform and restore key areas of the nation's economy, including banks, financial markets, farming, and industry. Relief agencies and job programs were created to help people with problems of poverty and unemployment. Taken together, Roosevelt's economic and social programs are known as the New Deal. Early New Deal programs included the Tennessee Valley Authority (TVA) and the Public Works Administration (PWA).

If one program failed, Roosevelt soon tried another. His energy and optimism encouraged Americans.

The New Deal is challenged.

The first phase of the New Deal was criticized by some people for being too reckless and radical. Other critics felt that the New Deal did not go far enough in sharing the wealth of America among all its citizens. Roosevelt responded with a second phase of New Deal laws that increased taxes for the rich, started new job programs such as the Works Progress Administration (WPA), and produced the historic Social Security Act of 1935. This law gave the United States its first system of social insurance.

Organized labor gained power and political influence.   During the Depression American workers became more assertive about improving their conditions. John L.

Lewis and other labor leaders urged a change from small, craft-based organizations to giant unions that included all workers within an industry. The creation of the National Labor Relations Board in 1936 made it easier for workers to join unions and to bargain with employers.

Roosevelt was quick to see the political power of organized workers. He began to campaign against the interests of wealth and big business, and he supported the rights of American workers. In the 1936 presidential election, Roosevelt won easily over Alfred Landon.

The New Deal changed ideas about American government.

Despite Roosevelt's triumphant re-election, New Deal programs faded in his second term. A plan to pack the Supreme Court with justices who favored the New Deal caused Roosevelt to lose much of his political support. The recession of 1937 slowed economic recovery.

Americans disagreed about the New Deal in the 1930s. Differences of opinion about the benefits and costs of the New Deal still exist today. However, no one questions the fact that the New Deal reshaped American ideas about the role of government in American life.

Equality

Human equality was the first of the "self-evident" truths recognized by the Declaration of Independence. Of course, the society that produced this document was still a very unequal one, with few civil rights for women and none for slaves or Native Americans. Our subsequent history has been a struggle to expand our notions of equality to include all Americans.

1782

What, then, is the American, this new man? He is either an European or the descendant of an European; hence that strange mixture of blood, which you will find in no other country. I could point out to you a family whose grandfather was an Englishman, whose wife was Dutch, whose son married a French woman, and whose present four sons have now four wives of different nations. . . . Here individuals of all nations are melted into a new race of men, whose labors and posterity will one day cause great changes in the world.

▲ **Hector St. John de Crèvecoeur,** *Letters from an American Farmer*

1835

No novelty in the United States struck me more vividly during my stay here than the equality of conditions. It is easy to see the immense influence of this basic fact on the whole course of society. It gives a particular turn to public opinion and a particular twist to the laws, new maxims to those who govern and particular habits to the governed.

▲ **Alexis de Tocqueville,** *Democracy in America*

1848

We hold these truths to be self-evident: that all men and women are created equal . . .

▲ **Elizabeth Cady Stanton, Seneca Falls Declaration of Sentiments**

1919

Years ago, I recognized my kinship with all living things, and I made up my mind that I was not one bit better than the meanest [lowest] of the earth. I said then, I say now, that while there is a lower class, I am in it; while there is a criminal element, I am of it; while there is a soul in prison, I am not free.

▲ **Eugene Debs, speech at his trial for sedition**

1939

Be the inferior of no man, nor of any man be the superior. Remember that every man is a variation of yourself. No man's guilt is not yours, nor is any man's innocence a thing apart.

▲ **William Saroyan,** *The Time of Your Life*

1961

The year was 2081, and everybody was finally equal. They weren't just equal before God and the law. They were equal every which way. Nobody was smarter than anyone else. Nobody was better looking than anyone else. Nobody was quicker or stronger than anyone else. All this equality was due to the 211th, 212th, and 213th Amendments to the Constitution, and to the unceasing vigilance of agents of the United States Handicapper General.

Some things about living still weren't quite right though. April, for instance, still drove people crazy by not being springtime. And it was in that clammy month that the H-G men took George and Hazel Bergeron's 14-year-old son, Harrison, away.

It was tragic, all right, but George and Hazel couldn't think about it very hard. Hazel had a perfectly average intelligence, which meant that she couldn't think about anything except in short bursts. And George, while his intelligence was way above normal, had a little mental handicap radio in his ear. He was required by law to wear it at all times. It was tuned to a government transmitter.

Every twenty seconds or so, the transmitter would send out some sharp noise to keep people like George from taking unfair advantage of their brains.

▲ **Kurt Vonnegut, "Harrison Bergeron"**

1963

Democracy does not necessarily result from majority rule, but rather from the forged compromise of the majority with the minority . . . The philosophy of the Constitution . . . is not simply to grant the majority the power to rule but is also to set out limitation after limitation upon that power. . . .

▲ **Senator Daniel Inouye, Senate debate**

1974

"We, the people." It is a very eloquent beginning. But when the document was completed on the seventeenth of September in 1787 I was not included in that "We, the people." I felt that somehow for many years that George Washington and Alexander Hamilton just left me out by mistake. But through the process of interpretation and court decision I have finally been included in "We, the people."

▲ **Barbara Jordan, speech**

Analyze

Ralph Waldo Emerson (1803–1882) once observed that the schoolyard boast, "I'm as good as you be," contained the "essence" of the Declaration of Independence. Whether or not Emerson was right, it is true that the American tradition of equality is a complex mixture of political, social, and economic elements.

Assignment: To *analyze* is to separate or distinguish the elements of something that is complex. Write a paragraph of 150–200 words in which you analyze the American tradition of equality, isolating the elements that seem the most important to you. Use the following process.

Explore the idea of equality. Begin by examining the quotations on these two pages. Write down a phrase or two for each quotation, indicating what aspect of equality it reflects. (Crèvecoeur, for example, stressed the leveling effect of America's ethnic "melting pot"; Elizabeth Cady Stanton asserted the fundamental equality between men and women; Eugene Debs affirmed his solidarity with the lower class; and so on.) Look over your list and pick out those aspects of equality that seem the most important to you. Write a clear topic sentence that states these central points. (For example, your topic sentence might be the following: "The American tradition of equality has a lofty intellectual side to it that aims at a political ideal; and it has a more folksy, cultural side that reflects the everyday social equality of American neighborhoods and towns."

Plan the paragraph. Write an outline that presents your topic sentence and the evidence you are offering in its support (which can combine ideas drawn from these quotations, your knowledge of American history and current events, and your own experience.)

Write a draft of the paragraph. Using your outline as a plan, write a complete draft of the paragraph. Begin with your topic sentence and then the sentences containing your supporting evidence. End with a summary sentence that refocuses the reader's attention on your central points. (For example, you might conclude by saying, "So while intellectuals might only be satisfied with an ideal equality that is probably unobtainable, the majority of Americans are content to cherish the feeling, like Emerson's schoolboy, that 'I'm as good as you be.' "

Revise the draft. Examine the organization of the paragraph. Ask yourself the following questions: (1) Is the topic sentence stated clearly? (2) Is the evidence presented effectively? (3) Have appropriate transitional words and phrases been used? (4) Does the summary refocus the reader's attention on the central points?

Proofread the paragraph and make a final copy. Correct any errors in grammar, punctuation, and spelling.

Unit 4

You Are There

This is London, ten minutes before five in the morning. . . . A German bomber came boring down the river. We could see his exhaust trail like a pale ribbon stretched straight across the sky. Half a mile downstream there were two eruptions and then a third, close together. The first two looked like some giant had thrown a huge basket of flaming golden oranges high in the air. The third was just a balloon of fire enclosed in black smoke above the housetops.
—*Edward R. Murrow broadcasting during the Battle of Britain, 1940*

A solitary figure makes his way through a London street, choked with debris from air raids.

War and Cold War

Unit Outline

Unit Themes

In this unit you will analyze the following themes of U.S. history:

▶ The American belief in a unique national destiny influences its relations with other nations.

▶ Encouraging technological and scientific innovation has helped American society.

▶ Conflict and cooperation have been essential elements in the development of the United States.

1930	1935	1940	1945	1950	1955	1960	1965

1940
British turn back Nazi air force at Battle of Britain

1941
Japanese attack Pearl Harbor; the United States enters the war

1942
Japanese Americans sent to relocation camps

1945
United States drops atomic bombs on Hiroshima and Nagasaki; World War II ends

1948
Berlin airlift marks beginning of Cold War

1950
Korean War begins

1957
Soviet Union launches *Sputnik*, beginning space age

Linking Past to Present

Hoping that Hitler and his Nazi party would return their nation to greatness, Germans enthusiastically showed support for their *führer* at a Nazi rally in Berlin in the 1930s, inset. Hitler's actions would only lead to war, the division of the two Germanies in 1945, and the erection of the Berlin Wall in 1961. Background, the wall finally crumbled in 1989, setting off joyous celebrations all along the concrete and barbed-wire edifice. One year later the two Germanies were reunified.

The World At War

1 9 3 9 – 1 9 4 1

15

The Great Depression hit most Americans as hard as a death in the family. Financially and emotionally drained, they turned inward, preoccupied with their own problems—putting food on the table, finding a job, making the house payment. The government also looked inward. It promised no entangling alliances abroad.

In the meantime the Depression took an even greater toll on the rest of the world. Germany was particularly hard hit. The nation, which already had been financially drained because of World War I reparations, neared collapse. Frustrated and with seemingly no recourse, Germans turned to a charismatic dictator for guidance. He promised to solve all their problems. They listened and they followed, and before they realized the mistake they had made, their leader had taken the nation on a new road of military conquest in Europe. Other dictators also began conquests, and by the mid-1930s a second world war was inevitable.

Although most Americans were not indifferent to the aggression that was taking place across the sea, they did not want to be drawn into another world war. By supporting neutrality in the face of the conquest abroad, however, Americans were walking on a frayed tightrope. Could the United States remain uninvolved? Could the nation sit back idly and watch one country after another be swallowed up?

CHAPTER PREVIEW

In this chapter you will learn how world events caused the United States to abandon isolationism and gradually become more involved in World War II.

SECTIONS IN THIS CHAPTER:
1. **World depression led to the rise of dictators.**
2. **Britain and France answered aggression with appeasement.**
3. **Germany attacked with new methods of warfare.**
4. **America aided Britain and the Soviet Union.**

1930	1932	1934	1936	1938	1940	1942

1931
Japan invades Manchuria

1938
Germany annexes Austria; Britain and France appease Hitler at Munich

1939
Germany invades Czechoslovakia; Britain and France declare war against Germany; Soviet Union invades Poland and Finland

1940
Germany begins *blitzkrieg* against France; Battle of Britain occurs

1941
Lend-Lease Act passes; Germany invades the Soviet Union

599

SECTION 1

World depression led to the rise of dictators.

Key Terms: *Lebensraum*, Stimson Doctrine, Nazi party, genocide, anti-Semitism, Third Reich, *führer*, *Kristallnacht*

Reading Preview
As you read this section, you will learn:

1. the means Germany, Italy, and Japan chose to improve their economic conditions and gain new resources.
2. what caused many people to support dictators.
3. the result of Japan's first act of aggression.
4. how Hitler achieved total power in Germany.

Although two vast oceans insulated the Americans and fostered their isolationism, the people of Germany, Italy, and Japan had no such protection. Nor did they have the territory and resources to dig themselves out of the Great Depression that the Americans, the British, the French, and the Soviets had. Consequently, the dictatorial leaders in these nations sought to expand their borders as a way to gain new resources and solve economic problems.

 Germany, Italy, and Japan sought geographical expansion.

Germany, Italy, and Japan had several things in common. All were experiencing economic problems, all were relatively small in size, and all were heavily dependent on foreign trade for food and raw materials.

By contrast, the world's leading powers had access to plentiful sources of wealth. The United States, for example, controlled a continent rich in resources. In addition, it controlled much of Latin America's natural resources. For more than a century, the British

Empire had ruled nearly a quarter of the surface of the earth and commanded its strategic waterways. France had vast holdings as well, especially in Africa. The Soviet Union stretched for 6,000 miles across northern Europe and Asia. Even small nations such as the Netherlands and Belgium had large colonial territories in Asia and Africa.

If Germany, Italy, and Japan were going to compete with these nations, their leaders argued that they would have to build empires that extended far beyond their homelands. It was against this backdrop that German nationalists proposed that Germany's eastern neighbors would provide *Lebensraum* (lā′ bəns-room′), or living space for the nation. This was also the setting in which **Benito Mussolini**, the Italian dictator, dreamed of turning the "Mediterranean into an Italian lake." In other words, he dreamed of building a new Roman Empire that would control the entire Mediterranean basin. Military leaders in Japan shared this imperialistic dream and clearly intended to dominate China.

The new leaders in Germany, Italy, and Japan were very convincing when they told their people that expansion was the only solution to their problems. Many people firmly believed that expansion was necessary. The new leaders also garnered support from the masses because of a basic fear that they shared: the fear of being subjugated by communism.

Fear of communism caused many people to support dictators.

The fear of being trampled by the evils of communism was a worldwide phenomenon after World War I. **Joseph Stalin** had taken control of the Soviet Union in 1926. Driven by the principles of communism, he envisioned an atheistic, classless society based on the equal distribution of goods. He announced a plan that called for government ownership of all property and businesses.

By 1930 the Soviets had uprooted half of the peasants from their farms and resettled them on collective farms controlled by the central government. In the years that followed, millions of Soviet citizens were killed or sent to prisonlike work camps run by the secret police. By eliminating people and enforcing slave labor, Stalin was able to rebuild the Soviet economy. However, he did so at an enormous cost to the Soviet people.

Communists the world over looked to the Soviet Union for leadership in achieving their goal of an eventual global revolution. Fear and paranoia spread as communist agents tried to infiltrate the press, labor unions, and government agencies around the world. In this atmosphere, the strongly nationalistic and totalitarian governments in Germany, Italy, and Japan were able to convince their people that communism was their number one enemy. By posing as the only alternative to this evil system, they were able to frighten their people into believing that aggression was the only way to stop communism. Thus, under the guise of stopping communism in its tracks and gaining new territory in order to bring about economic recovery, the totalitarian states began their campaigns of expansion and aggression in the early 1930s. Japan was the first expansion-minded nation to make its move.

Japanese military leaders captured Manchuria.

As a result of Japan's victory in the Russo-Japanese War in 1905, Japan already controlled a small portion of the northern Chinese province of **Manchuria**. Japanese military leaders and business people had long wanted to gain control of the entire province, however. Manchuria was rich in natural resources and fertile farmland. When the Depression hit, Japan's desire for Manchuria increased considerably. It desperately needed Manchuria to supply the growing needs of its expanding population of 70 million. Besides, Japanese military leaders wanted the land to serve as a buffer state between Korea, which it controlled, and the Soviet Union. The threat of Soviet communism was a chief concern in Japan.

In 1931 conditions for a successful Japanese invasion of Manchuria could not have been better. China was in the midst of a civil war between nationalist and communist groups and was thus in no position to defend itself. In

September, acting without the knowledge of the Japanese civilian government, Japanese military leaders swiftly captured Manchuria. Within months the military leaders proclaimed Manchuria an independent state under the protection of Japan. They renamed the new state Manchukuo, which means "the land of the Manchu." Although Japan's civilian government protested the actions of its military, it had little power to do anything. The military leaders had established a firm base of power.

To the surprise of the world community, it was the isolationists in the United States that first protested Japan's invasion of Manchuria. The so-called **Stimson Doctrine**, named for the American secretary of state, denied diplomatic recognition to any territory taken over by force. Although this was hardly a deadly threat to Japan, the rest of the world did little else but react with harmless words. France did not even react at all. When the League of Nations passed a resolution calling for Japanese withdrawal from Manchuria, the Japanese instead scornfully withdrew from the League. They then defiantly continued their invasion of China, pushing toward the central provinces. This episode showed the world that naked aggression could succeed. The lesson was not lost on Germany and Italy.

Italy's Benito Mussolini adopted the German goose step as a parade march, renaming it the "Roman step." Here he leads a parade of high-stepping militiamen in 1938.

Japanese soldiers rejoice in their capture of a railroad station and train at Hankow, China, in 1938.

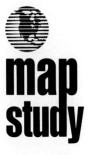

map study

Movement

In 1905 Japan gained Korea and Port Arthur in Manchuria. These territories gave Japan a foothold on the Asian mainland. Use the map to describe the extent of Japanese mainland territories by 1941. Note that because of Japanese expansion the Chinese were forced to move their national capital. What was the Chinese capital after 1938?

Critical Thinking

As the map shows, Japan is a small island nation. In the early 1900s its population grew rapidly to 70 million. How do these facts help explain Japanese expansion into Asia and the Pacific area?

Hitler gained power by promising to make Germany strong again.

Born in 1889 in an Austrian town near the German border, **Adolf Hitler** was an unlikely candidate for leadership. When Hitler was 18 years old he moved to Vienna, where he failed the entrance exam for the Academy of Fine Arts, one of the world's most prestigious schools of art. Until World War I broke out, the failed artist spent his time drifting, reading newspapers, and talking politics. Hitler often seemed enthralled by the power of his own voice. He used gestures and facial expressions as though he were in a theatrical production. In later years Hitler would have his personal photographer take pictures of him making an assortment of these gestures and expressions. (See the photographs on page 603.) He then would study the photos to see which ones were the most effective and those that he should delete from his repertoire. Afterward, he would practice his favorite poses in front of a mirror.

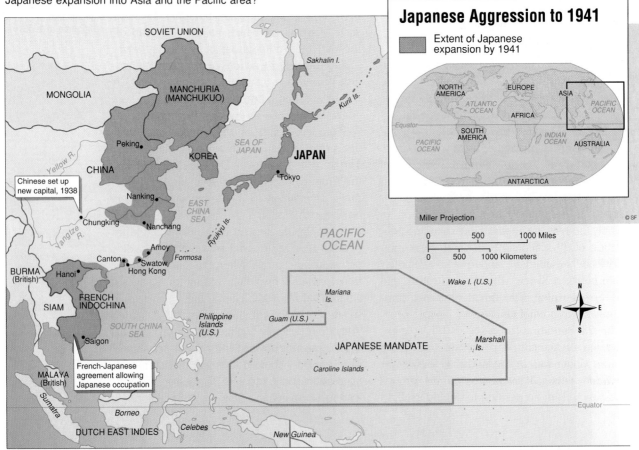

Japanese Aggression to 1941

Extent of Japanese expansion by 1941

Miller Projection   © SF

0   500   1000 Miles
0   500   1000 Kilometers

Bigotry was widespread in Vienna in the early 1900s. Consequently, Hitler had no problem adopting this sickness wholeheartedly:

Disgusting to me was the conglomerate of races which characterized Vienna, disgusting the whole mixture of peoples, Czechs, Poles, Hungarians, Ruthenians, Serbs, and Croats.

When Hitler left for Munich in 1913, he was convinced that a worldwide conspiracy of Jews and other "inferior" peoples was at work to destroy Germany. By volunteering for service in World War I, he found a purpose in life. When the war was over, he joined a small nationalistic party that was against capitalism and communism and violently hostile to Jews.

The Nazi party. By 1930 the small party had become known as the Nationalist Socialist German Workers' party, shortened to **Nazi party**, and Hitler had become its leader. Hitler offered hope and promised recovery to the millions of unemployed Germans who were suffering from the Great Depression. By 1932 five million people were without work. To make matters worse, the government proposed cutting unemployment benefits. Extreme measures were needed and Hitler took advantage of the times to offer solutions.

Albert Speer, a teacher of architecture who would become one of Hitler's top advisers and who would write *Inside the Third Reich* after the war, described his first personal exposure to Hitler:

I was carried away on the wave of enthusiasm which, one could almost feel this physically, bore the speaker along from sentence to sentence. It swept away any skepticism, any reservation. Opponents were given no chance to speak. This furthered the illusion, at least momentarily, of unanimity. Finally, Hitler no longer seemed to be speaking to convince; rather he seemed to feel that he was expressing what the audience, by now transformed into a single mass, expected of him. It was as if it were the most natural thing in the world to lead the students and part of the faculty of two of the greatest academies in Germany by a leash.

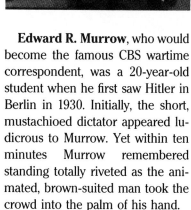

Edward R. Murrow, who would become the famous CBS wartime correspondent, was a 20-year-old student when he first saw Hitler in Berlin in 1930. Initially, the short, mustachioed dictator appeared ludicrous to Murrow. Yet within ten minutes Murrow remembered standing totally riveted as the animated, brown-suited man took the crowd into the palm of his hand.

To those Germans who wanted to confront the communists at home and make their country respected once again, Hitler offered a plan. He would make Germany strong again by uniting the blond, blue-eyed members of the Aryan race, as he called it, in a "pure" state free of "undesirables." He would avenge the shame of the Versailles Treaty, regain lost territories, and conquer more territory to ensure that the master race would rule a glorious, longstanding empire. His plan called for **genocide**, or the killing of a whole national or ethnic group. Specifically he planned to kill all Jews. Others, such as Gypsies and homosexuals, would also be killed.

Among the poisonous ingredients of Hitler's plan was **anti-Semitism**, the hatred of Jewish people. When faced with Germany's defeat in World War I and humiliation at Versailles, Hitler refused to blame the German military. He

Hitler stirred audiences with his extraordinarily powerful speeches. Fascinated early on by his own ability, Hitler hired a photographer in 1925 to take a series of photographs of him as he mimed the fanatical actions and dramatic gestures for which he would later be famous.

Young Germans were encouraged to join the Nazi effort. Recruiting posters such as the one at right urged students to participate in the Nazi youth movement. Girls and boys alike trained in athletics as a way of promoting strength and purity.

DER DEUTSCHE STUDENT

KÄMPFT FÜR FÜHRER UND VOLK IN DER MANNSCHAFT DES NSD-STUDENTENBUNDES

Radio enabled Hitler to reach a huge audience. His Nazi party, which had begun as little more than a racist street gang, was poised to rule Germany. The speed with which Hitler brought down the German government, known as the Weimar Republic, and dominated the country surprised the whole world. The Weimar Republic was based on a democratic constitution and had been in existence since 1919. The German people had had no previous experience with democracy and after years of political division and economic chaos the voters welcomed a return to the martial glory and discipline the Nazi party offered.

The Third Reich. After being appointed chancellor of Germany in 1933 by President Paul von Hindenburg—the same year Franklin Roosevelt became president of the United States—Hitler rapidly consolidated his power. The **Third Reich**, or the third German empire, had begun.

In the spring of 1933, the Reichstag, Germany's parliament, gave Hitler dictatorial powers. Soon after he stripped the Reichstag of all its power, dissolved all opposition parties, ended freedom of the press, and discarded all laws not in line with Nazi goals. Then in August 1934, just hours before the death of President von Hindenburg, Hitler abolished the office of president. That same day he declared himself *führer* (the leader) of Germany and immediately demanded that each member of the armed forces take an oath of loyalty to him.

Soon Hitler's Storm Troopers, a group of physically imposing veteran soldiers whom Hitler used as bodyguards and thugs, began building concentration camps for political prisoners. Many of these prisoners were Jews who had lost their civil rights as a result of the Nuremberg Laws of 1935. These laws forbade Jews to practice medicine. They called for segregation on public transportation and restricted Jews from shopping except during specified hours. They set an 8:00 P.M. curfew for Jews and required them to wear a Jewish star on their clothing for identification. These laws were the forerunners of Hitler's future plans.

Hitler could not achieve his goals without coming into conflict with other world powers

proposed instead that Jewish traitors within Germany had betrayed the country. In a propaganda master stroke, Hitler also blamed communism and the Depression on Jewish plots. Although these accusations were false, the German people believed them because they desperately needed to find a scapegoat for their economic troubles. Through his deep personal hatred for Jews, Hitler brought anti-Semitism to the surface in Germany.

sooner or later. His greed for territory was so great and his plans for domination of other peoples were so monstrous that eventually he was bound to provoke resistance. Furthermore, the notion of racial impurity, so central to Hitler's thinking, deeply offended many people throughout the world.

Jesse Owens' triumph. The 1936 Summer Olympic Games in Berlin, Germany, which were hosted by Hitler, provided the dictator with a prime opportunity to demonstrate the "superiority" of the Aryan race to the world. As it turned out, however, the games provided Hitler only embarrassment and humiliation.

Jesse Owens, a determined 23-year-old African American athlete, caused much of Hitler's embarrassment by capturing four gold medals during the games. Owens' feat, which earned him the title "the fastest man in the world," was accomplished under incredibly adverse conditions. He recalled his feelings prior to an important jump during the qualifying round of the broad jump competition (now called long jump):

> I looked around nervously, panic creeping into every cell **AN AMERICAN ★ SPEAKS** of my body. On my right was Hitler's box. Empty. His way of saying I was a member of an inferior race who would give an inferior performance. In back of that box was a stadium containing more than a hundred thousand people, almost all Germans, all wanting to see me fail.

Despite the pressure, Owens went on to capture the gold medal in the long jump. Surprisingly, his performance won over just about everyone in the stands except Hitler. Owens recalled:

> After he [Owens' German competitor, Luz Long] failed in his last attempt to beat me, ★ he leaped out of the pit and raced to my side. To congratulate me. Then he walked toward the stands pulling me with him while Hitler was glaring, held up my hand and shouted to the gigantic crowd, "Jesse Owens! Jesse Owens!" The stadium picked it up. . . . I'd heard people cheering me before, but never like this. Many of those men would end up killing my countrymen, and

mine theirs, but the truth was they didn't want to, and would only do it because they "had" to. Thanks to Luz [who became a good friend of Owens and who would die fighting for Germany in northern Africa], I learned that the false leaders and sick movements of this earth must be stopped in the beginning, for they turn humanity against itself.

Kristallnacht. The world received a taste of Hitler's bigotry during the 1936 Olympics, but few people fully realized the depths of Hitler's hatred. Many Jews did not have to wait long, however. In November 1938 Hitler accelerated his violent campaign against the Jews by organizing a night of terror. During this horror-filled evening, which became known as ***Kristallnacht***, or the Night of Broken Glass, Nazi gangs broke into Jewish homes, beat up the occupants, burned synagogues, and looted Jewish businesses. According to Nazi records, 35 Jews were killed during the night. In addition, more than 7,500 Jewish businesses and synagogues were destroyed. Not even Jewish hospitals or schools were spared.

Three days later the Nazis heavily fined German Jews. The Ministry of Education barred Jewish children from German schools. In addition, the Nazis forbade the Jews to purchase or sell real estate, to drive cars, or to use public transportation. Their aim was to eliminate Jews from all aspects of German society.

Jesse Owens stunned and thrilled Germans with his stellar performance at the 1936 Olympics in Berlin.

A Jewish storekeeper cleans up broken glass the morning after *Kristallnacht*.

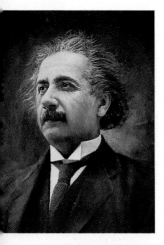

In 1939 Hitler announced his intentions regarding the Jews to his national legislature:

Today I will be a prophet again. If international finance Jewry within Europe and abroad should succeed once more in plunging the people into a world war, then the consequences will be . . . the destruction of the Jewish race in Europe.

Between 1933 and 1938, thousands of Jewish refugees came to America. In 1939, however, isolationist and anti-immigrant feelings were so strong that Americans rejected a bill to relax the immigration laws and admit 20,000 German children—most of whom would have been Jewish. It was this reluctance to become involved on the part of the world's democracies that contributed to Hitler's success.

Mathematician and physicist Albert Einstein was the most famous of Germany's Jewish refugees. Among his many accomplishments was the development of the special theory of relativity in 1905 and the law of photoelectric effect, for which he won the Nobel Prize in physics in 1921. Persecuted by Hitler as a Jew, Einstein moved to the United States in 1933.

SECTION 1 REVIEW

Identify Key People and Terms
Write a sentence to identify: *Lebensraum*, Benito Mussolini, Joseph Stalin, Stimson Doctrine, Adolf Hitler, Nazi party, Edward R. Murrow, genocide, anti-Semitism, Third Reich, *führer*, Jesse Owens, *Kristallnacht*

Locate Key Places
Why did the Japanese invade Manchuria?

Master the Main Ideas

1. **Perceiving cause/effect relationships:** Why were Germany, Italy, and Japan at a disadvantage in the race for world power?
2. **Analyzing information**: Why did so many people fear communism?
3. **Analyzing information:** Why were the Japanese successful in their invasion of Manchuria?
4. **Analyzing information:** How did Adolf Hitler persuade the German people to follow him?

Apply Critical Thinking Skills: Making Comparisons
Consider how the United States, Britain, and France obtained territory before the 1900s. How did their methods compare with the efforts of Japan? What similarities and differences do you note?

SECTION 2

Britain and France answered aggression with appeasement.

Key Terms: appeasement, Nazi-Soviet Nonaggression Pact, panzer divisions, *Luftwaffe*, Maginot Line, fifth columnists

Reading Preview
As you read this section, you will learn:

1. how appeasement affected German and Italian acts of aggression.
2. how the Munich Pact affected Czechoslovakia.
3. the result of Stalin's deal with Hitler.
4. where Hitler shifted his attention after defeating Poland.

During the 1920s France and Britain resolved to maintain the freedom of the newly independent countries of eastern Europe. However, the Great Depression seriously compromised the willingness and ability of these powers to use military force to uphold the provisions of the Versailles Treaty.

Germany and Italy took the offensive virtually unimpeded.

Eastern Europe was an unstable, dangerous power vacuum. In place of the Austro-Hungarian Empire, a number of smaller states —Poland, Czechoslovakia, Austria, Hungary, and Yugoslavia—came into existence with the signing of the Versailles Treaty. These countries, which are shown on the map on page 610, were too militarily and economically weak to protect themselves without assistance. In the long run, most would fall into the geographical sphere of either Germany or the Soviet Union.

Although Germany did suffer greatly after World War I, its long-term strategic situation looked promising because of the weaknesses of its rivals. By 1930 Germany was once again the strongest economic state in Europe. France and Britain both had smaller populations than

Germany. The Soviet Union, although possessing a larger population, needed two decades to recover from World War I, a civil war, and the bloody consolidation of communism.

Surrounded by countries weaker than his own, Hitler saw an opportunity to take the offensive. According to the Versailles Treaty, the **Rhineland**, the region along the Rhine River, was to be a buffer zone between Germany and France. To accomplish this, the Rhineland was to be permanently free of military units or fortifications. In 1936, however, Hitler began a remarkable campaign of bluff and diplomacy by moving military forces into the Rhineland. Hitler made this bold move despite the real weakness of the German army and air force at that time. His generals worried that the more powerful French would easily sweep the German forces out of the Rhineland. Nevertheless, Hitler was confident that France would not act. He was right. Thus, a major early opportunity to stop Hitler in his tracks had been missed.

With this success, Hitler began rebuilding the German war machine in earnest and resumed the military draft. In 1938 Hitler's army invaded Austria and quickly proclaimed *Anschluss*, the "union" of Germany and Austria. Although the Nazis refused American media requests to cover the invasion, Edward R. Murrow convinced authorities to allow him to broadcast the news of their victory from Vienna. The broadcast was done under duress—a censor stood by ready to break off Murrow's report should he say the wrong thing. However, he gave Americans a good idea of what it was like to be in a city under siege. As a crowd waited for Hitler to arrive, Murrow reported:

On March 7, 1936, at Hitler's order, the first German troops marched across the Hohenzollern Bridge into the Rhineland. By entering this demilitarized zone, the Germans violated the terms of the Versailles Treaty.

AN AMERICAN ★ SPEAKS

Young storm troopers are riding about the streets, riding about in trucks and vehicles of all sorts, singing and tossing oranges out to the crowd. . . . Nearly every principal building has its armed guard, including the one from which I am speaking. There are still huge crowds. . . . There's a certain air of expectancy about the city, everyone waiting and wondering where and [when] Herr Hitler will arrive.

Several days later, back in the United States, Murrow once again broadcast the news of Austria's fall. This time he had no storm trooper standing over his shoulder. He reported:

I would like to . . . forget the haunted look on the faces of . . . people trying to get away . . . the thud of hobnail boots and the crash of light tanks in the early hours of the morning. . . . I'd like to forget the sound of the smashing glass as the Jewish shop streets were raided; the hoots and jeers at those [Jews] forced to scrub the sidewalk.

Hitler's actions were blatant violations of the Versailles Treaty. Yet neither France nor Britain took any action against the Nazi aggression. Both nations had a variety of reasons for not acting. First, many people believed that Germany had indeed been wronged by the strict terms of the Versailles Treaty. The terms made it virtually impossible for the nation to solve its economic problems. Second, British and French officials were more worried about the spread of communism than they were about Hitler. They reasoned that a stronger Germany might be needed to combat future threats from the Soviet Union. Third, the French and British underestimated Hitler's abilities and misinterpreted his intentions. They believed that letting Hitler win several small victories would satisfy, or appease, him and quench his thirst for conquest. This policy, known as **appeasement**, would be employed increasingly by France and Britain as well as other nations as totalitarian regimes aggressively began to swallow up nations in other parts of the world. One of these aggressors was Italy.

As Germany was expanding its power, Italy was also on the move. Benito Mussolini, intent on establishing a base for his Mediterranean empire, invaded **Ethiopia**, an independent country in northeast Africa on the Red Sea. Using aircraft, flame throwers, poison gas, and machine guns, the Italians attacked the poorly armed Ethiopians. The emperor of Ethiopia, Haile Selassie, appealed to the League of Nations. Although the League voiced disapproval of the Italian invasion and imposed some economic sanctions, it failed to take actions that might have forced the Italians to abandon their mission. As a result, Selassie fled into exile and Italy conquered Ethiopia in 1936. Once again, aggression won an easy prize.

Soon after the invasion of Ethiopia, Germany and Italy formed an alliance. They combined to support a right-wing Spanish general, Francisco Franco, in his revolt against the republican government in Spain. Both the Germans and the Italians used the savage civil war in Spain (1936–1939) as a testing ground for their new weapons and tactics. With their assistance, Franco won the war.

The American writer, Ernest Hemingway, was a war correspondent in Spain from 1936–1937. He was one of thousands of Americans who supported the republican cause against Franco. He wrote:

The Spanish Civil War offered something which you could **AN AMERICAN ★ SPEAKS** believe in wholly and completely, and in which you felt an absolute brotherhood with the others who were engaged in it.

Although the governments of Britain, France, and the United States were opposed to Franco, they did not intervene. The Soviet Union was the only government to come to the aid of the Spanish loyalist republicans.

Time and again democracies voiced their opposition to the totalitarian regimes, but in the end they decided not to risk war over their aggressive actions. Time and again the democracies hoped that "this is the last time." This path of appeasement ultimately led Britain and France to the shame of Munich.

The bombing of the Spanish town of Guernica inspired artist Pablo Picasso to paint his masterpiece of the same name. *Guernica* (1937) now hangs in the Prado Museum in Madrid, Spain.

The Munich Pact betrayed Czechoslovakia.

A land-locked democracy with only 15 million people, Czechoslovakia had been created after World War I from parts of the old Austro-Hungarian Empire. Determined to safeguard their independence, the Czechs had built a string of strong fortifications in the hills ringing the heart of their country. They had a well-trained, well-equipped army of 34 divisions.

A significant German minority lived among the predominantly Slavic people of Czechoslovakia. Hitler intended to destroy Czechoslovakia as part of his grand plan to make all of eastern Europe a German colony. Under the pretense of protecting the German minority, Hitler demanded in 1938 that the Czechs cede the **Sudetenland** to Germany. This mountainous region contained most of the fortresses protecting Czechoslovakia. Czechoslovakia's leaders knew that their nation would be defenseless without the Sudetenland.

Resolved to resist Hitler, the Czechs recognized their need for help; they called upon the French and the British. War seemed imminent. As tensions rose Edward R. Murrow logged the events from the CBS newsroom in London. Murrow's personal friend, Jan Masaryk, was the Czech ambassador to London. Masaryk spoke to late-night radio listeners assuring them that the Czechs would somehow resist, "in full confidence that this time England and France will not forsake us." On Saturday, September 24, Hitler issued an ultimatum: unconditional and immediate surrender of the Sudetenland by October 1—one week away.

Day by day, Murrow reported the events that followed. Trenches were dug in London parks and gas masks were distributed to civilians. Fear stalked Europe as people recalled the horror of World War I—only 20 years earlier.

Hoping to peacefully solve the crisis, the leaders of Britain, France, Germany, and Italy met in Munich. **Neville Chamberlain**, the peace-loving British prime minister, managed to extract an agreement from Hitler. The British and the French would agree to the surrender of the Sudetenland to Germany in exchange for Germany's promise to seek no

further territorial expansion. Czech officials were not invited to participate in the decision to dismantle their country, nor was the Soviet Union.

Despite previous pacts, Britain and France had betrayed the last surviving democracy in eastern Europe. The result of the Munich Conference was that Czechoslovakia surrendered 10,000 square miles of territory and 3.5 million of its people to Germany. Czechoslovakia also lost additional land and people to Poland and Hungary because Hitler supported these nations' claims to eastern Czech territory. The Munich Conference constituted a coup for Hitler. It enabled him to gain a large tract of land. In addition, it allowed him to seize large stockpiles of Czechoslovakian arms.

Chamberlain returned home from the Munich Conference to proclaim to joyous crowds that he had achieved "peace in our time." Although a wave of relief swept over millions of apprehensive Europeans, it was not, as future British prime minister **Winston Churchill** pointed out, the end of fear. It was, he declared, "only the first sip, the first foretaste of a bitter cup. . . . " The bitterness would soon be tasted as Hitler used his diplomatic skills to set the stage for an invasion of Poland.

Sudetenland, largely populated by Germans, reacted with mixed emotions to Hitler's advance into Czechoslovakia. Many residents welcomed the Nazi forces by flying huge Nazi flags and throwing flowers. Others worried that Hitler's actions foreboded an ominous future for their country.

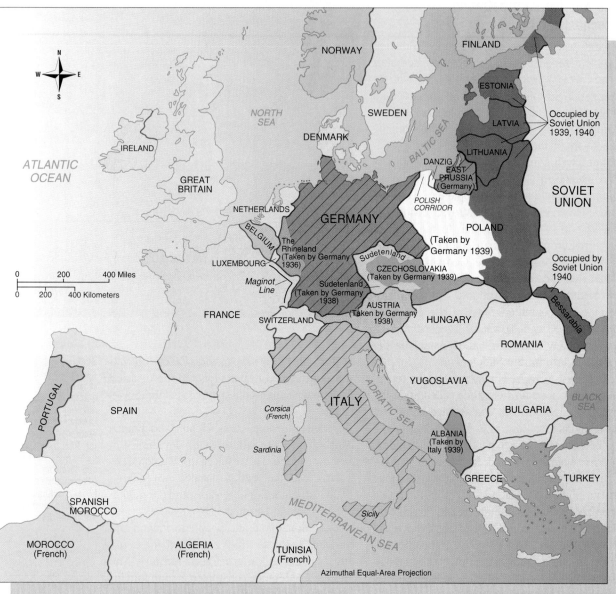

NORWAY

SWEDEN

FINLAND

NORTH
SEA

BALTIC SEA

ESTONIA

LATVIA

Occupied by
Soviet Union
1939, 1940

IRELAND

ATLANTIC
OCEAN

GREAT
BRITAIN

DENMARK

LITHUANIA

DANZIG

EAST
PRUSSIA
(Germany)

SOVIET
UNION

NETHERLANDS

GERMANY

POLISH
CORRIDOR

POLAND
(Taken by
Germany 1939)

BELGIUM

The
Rhineland
(Taken by Germany
1936)

Sudetenland

Occupied by
Soviet Union
1940

LUXEMBOURG

CZECHOSLOVAKIA
(Taken by Germany 1939)

Bessarabia

Maginot
Line

Sudetenland
(Taken by Germany
1938)

AUSTRIA
(Taken by
Germany
1938)

FRANCE

SWITZERLAND

HUNGARY

ROMANIA

YUGOSLAVIA

BULGARIA

BLACK
SEA

PORTUGAL

SPAIN

Corsica
(French)

ITALY

ADRIATIC SEA

Sardinia

ALBANIA
(Taken by
Italy 1939)

GREECE

TURKEY

SPANISH
MOROCCO

MEDITERRANEAN SEA

Sicily

0   200   400 Miles

0   200   400 Kilometers

MOROCCO
(French)

ALGERIA
(French)

TUNISIA
(French)

Azimuthal Equal-Area Projection

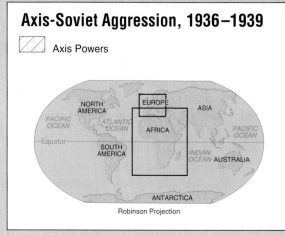

Axis-Soviet Aggression, 1936–1939

/// Axis Powers

NORTH
AMERICA

EUROPE

ASIA

PACIFIC
OCEAN

ATLANTIC
OCEAN

AFRICA

PACIFIC
OCEAN

Equator

SOUTH
AMERICA

INDIAN
OCEAN

AUSTRALIA

ANTARCTICA

Robinson Projection

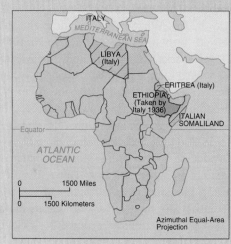

ITALY

MEDITERRANEAN SEA

LIBYA
(Italy)

ERITREA (Italy)

ETHIOPIA
(Taken by
Italy 1936)

ITALIAN
SOMALILAND

Equator

ATLANTIC
OCEAN

0   1500 Miles

0   1500 Kilometers

Azimuthal Equal-Area
Projection

© SF

Stalin's deal with Hitler doomed Poland and triggered World War II.

The Treaty of Versailles had given Poland a corridor through Prussia to provide it with an outlet to the Baltic Sea. Danzig, the port city of the corridor, was declared a free city under the protection of the League of Nations. Although 90 percent of the corridor's population was Polish, Germans predominated in Danzig.

On March 23, 1939, Hitler demanded that Danzig be ceded to Germany and that the Nazis be allowed to occupy a narrow strip of the corridor connecting Germany with East Prussia. Poland was suspicious of these demands and appealed to Britain for support. Hitler's demands on Poland convinced Chamberlain that his effort to appease Hitler at Munich had been futile. Therefore, Britain abandoned the policy of appeasement and began to take steps toward war preparedness. A military draft was introduced and in a short time British military expenditures topped $5 million a day. Similar preparations occurred in France. Both nations warned Hitler that, in the event of action threatening Polish independence, they would come to the aid of Poland.

The position of the Soviet Union was critical. In the months following their declaration about Poland, Britain and France competed with Germany for an alliance with the Soviet Union. Britain suggested that a united front, including the Soviet Union, be formed against Nazi aggression. Joseph Stalin, who had been ignored at the Munich Conference, was not eager to join the democracies that had long been antagonistic toward his communistic regime. He also distrusted Hitler, who had persecuted German communists. However, he came to feel that Hitler as a friendly enemy would be far better than Hitler as a fighting enemy. When

the German leader suggested a military pact with the Soviet Union, Stalin was receptive. As a result, Germany and the Soviet Union signed the **Nazi-Soviet Nonaggression Pact** on August 23, 1939. The pact was mutually beneficial to both parties. Hitler was able to secure his eastern flank from Soviet attack and Stalin was given extra time to build up his military.

Early on the morning of September 1, 1939, the German army invaded Poland without a declaration of war. On September 3 Britain demanded that the invasion be halted immediately. Hitler did not bother to answer the ultimatum. That same day Britain and France declared war on Germany.

The Nazi army wasted no time in Poland. Massed tank formations—**panzer divisions**—sliced through the Polish frontier defenses and plunged deep into the country, cutting communications and isolating pockets of brave

Hitler receives the salutes of Nazi faithful as he announces that German troops and tanks had invaded Poland in September, 1939.

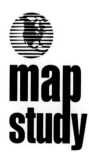

map study

Movement
The Axis nations, Germany and Italy, began their territorial takeovers in 1935 and 1936 with Ethiopia and the Rhineland. As the map shows, Axis conquests followed throughout Europe. Note the sequence of German invasions, first to the east then west and north. What nations were occupied by the Soviets in 1939–1940?

Critical Thinking
Though Germany and the Soviet Union were not allies, they signed the Nonaggression Pact in 1939. What effect did this pact have on Poland?

WONDER HOW LONG THE HONEYMOON WILL LAST?

Cartoonist James Berryman questioned the future of the Nazi-Soviet alliance, forged by Hitler and Stalin in 1939.

but poorly armed Poles. The German air force, or *Luftwaffe*, quickly eliminated Polish air cover and then bombed cities and machine-gunned roads crowded with refugees. The Poles, who met the enemy with an outmoded horse cavalry, were overwhelmed by the Germans.

Meanwhile, Soviet forces advanced into Poland from the east. Realizing that Poland's fate was sealed, France and Britain failed to aid the Poles. Forced to fend for themselves against two superior enemies, Poland's defenders were conquered by the end of September. Then, without any hesitation, Germany and the Soviet Union divided Poland between them.

Along the French-German border the British and French failed to take the offensive. They believed that Nazi Germany could be defeated by a naval blockade and by firm defensive action along the **Maginot Line**, the entrenched fortifications built by the French along their nation's eastern border. As you can see on the map on page 616, this system of concrete bunkers and underground artillery positions ran along the French-German border, from the Rhine River to Luxembourg.

For almost seven months, from September 1939 until the end of March 1940, almost no fighting took place along the western front. This period became known as the "phony war," or *Sitzkrieg*.

Hitler seized Denmark and Norway.

When the conquest of Poland had been completed, Hitler and his generals took advantage of inaction in the west to plan an invasion of the Scandinavian countries. On April 9, 1940, Hitler's paratroopers, disguised in the uniforms of other nations, prepared the way for ground forces which invaded Denmark and Norway. Denmark surrendered without much resistance. Norway proved to be more stubborn, but

its resistance had been softened in advance by **fifth columnists**. The fifth columnists were undercover agents who created fear and dissension in towns prior to an invasion. Foremost among the fifth columnists was the Norwegian fascist Vidkun Quisling, whose name became synonymous with a traitor. After months of secret collaboration with the Nazis, his followers opened the way for a German victory in Norway.

Hitler's Scandinavian conquests enabled him to gain new air bases, additional food supplies, and valuable natural resources. With Germany's economy bolstered, Hitler was ready to begin setting his sights on France and the Low Countries—Belgium, Luxembourg, and the Netherlands.

SECTION 2 REVIEW

Identify Key People and Terms
Write a sentence to identify: appeasement, Neville Chamberlain, Winston Churchill, Nazi-Soviet Nonaggression Pact, panzer divisions, *Luftwaffe*, Maginot Line, fifth columnists

Locate Key Places
1. The Rhineland was supposed to serve as a buffer zone between which two countries?
2. Ethiopia is located in which part of Africa?
3. Why was the Sudetenland important to Czechoslovakia?

Master the Main Ideas
1. **Evaluating information:** Why did Britain and France fail to stop the aggressions of Hitler and Mussolini?
2. **Perceiving cause/effect relationships:** What German demand led to the Munich pact?
3. **Analyzing information:** What did Stalin gain by making the Nonaggression Pact with Hitler?
4. **Perceiving cause/effect relationships:** Why did the Germans attack Norway and Denmark?

Apply Critical Thinking Skills: Predicting Consequences
What might have been the consequences if Neville Chamberlain had refused to sign the Munich Pact in 1938?

SECTION 3

Germany attacked with new methods of warfare.

Key Terms: *blitzkrieg*, Royal Air Force

Reading Preview

As you read this section, you will learn:

1. why the German war machine was so successful.
2. what the Germans accomplished in May 1940.
3. what happened when Germany invaded France in June 1940.

Ju 87B Stuka dive bombers were a destructive force in the Nazi *blitzkrieg* in Poland. The planes ranged over Poland's undefended skies, hammering at railways and breaking up divisions of soldiers.

Many of the armies in Europe in 1939 were equipped and trained to fight the wrong war. Polish generals took pride in 12 brigades of horse-mounted cavalry that were the best in the world. French engineers constructed massive fortifications that would certainly win World War I all over again. By contrast, German generals had used the 1930s to create new strategies. The result was a new kind of warfare and an early flood of German victories.

Tanks and aircraft spearheaded German attacks.

Although tanks and aircraft had been utilized toward the end of World War I, the full potential of these weapons remained untapped. It was the Germans who developed methods of combining the speed and firepower of massed tanks with the precision-bombing of fighter planes. The resulting attack became known as **blitzkrieg**, or "lightning war."

The Germans would concentrate tanks and planes for an attack on a very narrow part of an enemy's line. Dive bombers would blast enemy strong points, tanks would punch a hole in the line, and masses of motorized guns and troops would then flood through the gap. Using speed and surprise tactics, they would paralyze communications and overrun supply dumps. The German panzer divisions spearheaded the *blitzkriegs* throughout the war.

The Polish campaign was a classic example of the effectiveness of the *blitzkrieg*. However, the lesson was lost on the British and French. They attributed Poland's rapid defeat to faulty Polish efforts rather than to superior German tactics. They made no changes in their own military organizations and battle plans, which tended to use tanks only as infantry support weapons. As a result, the British and French had no concentrated force to match the staggering punch of a panzer attack.

The German army would conquer France not by sheer numerical superiority or by better equipment, but by superior planning and organization. The French and British had more men and more tanks on the western front than did the Germans in the spring of 1940. The Germans, however, were far better prepared.

The Germans forced Britain and France to retreat to Dunkirk.

The French doubted that the Nazis would be able to penetrate their fortifications along the Maginot Line. They were never so wrong.

In a brilliantly executed attack starting on May 10, 1940, the Germans invaded Belgium

613

WORLD WAR II
Skill: Drawing Conclusions

Introducing the Skill. When the German army penetrated Belgium's Ardennes Forest on its way into France in 1940, the French confidence in the Maginot Line was misplaced. The French leadership had assumed that this formidable line of defensive works would hold back the Nazis. Why had they been so mistaken?

Learning the Skill. The ability to **draw conclusions** from available information is important in many areas but particularly crucial in matters of war. A conclusion is a claim that someone has formed, based on supporting evidence or reasons. To draw a conclusion, follow these three steps:

1. Collect and study all available information on a given subject, for instance, why the Maginot Line could not defend France effectively. Form a preliminary claim based on this research.
2. Identify specific facts or principles that support the same claim. Specific facts should be accurate pieces of information—dates, statistics, quotations, or details. Principles are accepted rules or guidelines.
3. Form a final statement that summarizes your findings.

Applying the Skill. Read the following excerpt from historian William L. Shirer's book, *The Collapse of the Third Republic* (1969):

The trouble with the Maginot Line was that it was in the wrong place. The classical invasion route to France which the Germans had taken since the earliest tribal days—for nearly two millennia—lay through Belgium. This was the shortest and the easiest, for it lay through level land with few rivers of any consequence to cross. It was the route the Germans had taken again in 1914.

1. What conclusion has Shirer drawn about France and the Maginot Line?
2. What evidence does he use to support his conclusion?

Britain's massive evacuation at Dunkirk in 1940 strengthened the country's resolve to turn back the Nazis. As bombs burst on the sands of the narrow beach, British and French soldiers scrambled aboard the makeshift rescue fleet.

and the Netherlands, drawing major French and British units north. Then the Germans attacked through the **Ardennes Forest**, a hilly region in southern Belgium too far north to be protected by the Maginot Line, but well south of the French and British forces in Belgium.

In a major military blunder, the French failed to place significant reserve troops behind the Ardennes Forest. The French had wrongly calculated that German panzer units would be unable to penetrate the dense Ardennes Forest. When the German tanks broke through the French lines at the Meuse River behind the Ardennes, they had open country before them.

This German force swept through northwestern France and pushed on toward the English Channel. Suddenly, hundreds of thousands of British and French soldiers realized that they were trapped between the German armies in the Low Countries and the second

German force and the English Channel. While the French and British became cornered, both the Netherlands and Belgium surrendered to the Germans.

Trapped by the German forces, the French and British troops had no choice but to retreat to the coast of France at **Dunkirk**, where their capture and destruction seemed inevitable. However, in one of the most amazing events of the war, Britain called into service more than 800 civilian yachts, tugs, barges, and other assorted motorboats. These civilian craft crossed the Channel to Dunkirk under cover of darkness to rendezvous with 200 British naval vessels. With the aid of the **Royal Air Force** (RAF), which provided air protection, this hastily assembled fleet, "in a miracle of deliverance," evacuated more than 335,000 soldiers to Britain by June 4. For the British, so badly defeated in France, the dramatic rescue at Dunkirk restored morale.

Hitler's armies seized France and divided it into zones.

After Dunkirk, Hitler's armies turned south to conquer the rest of France. The French, having placed too much confidence in the Maginot Line, were otherwise militarily unprepared to defend their country.

Early in June 1940, following a relentless, all-out Nazi attack, the French army collapsed. French government officials and thousands of terrified French civilians and military personnel fled to the south of France. Deserted and lifeless, Paris was easily captured on June 14. Ironically, Marshal Henri Pétain signed an armistice with the Germans in the same railroad car in which Germany had signed the agreement ending World War I.

The terms of the armistice split France into two zones. One zone, known as Occupied France, included northern France and the Atlantic coastline. This zone was governed by Germany. The second zone became known as Unoccupied France and was administered by Marshal Pétain at Vichy. The Nazis, however, actually controlled Pétain's Vichy government. For this reason it was opposed by many patriots who refused to give up hope for French liberty. These patriots were represented in London by an exile government known as the Free French government, headed by **Charles de Gaulle** (də gōl′). The Free French government sponsored an underground group in France, the Maquis (mä kē′), which proved to be an effective guerrilla force against the Nazis during the rest of the war.

When the German defeat of France became certain, Italy's dictator, Benito Mussolini, believed that the war would soon be over. On June 10, 1940, he declared war on France and Britain in hopes of gaining benefits for Italy at a future peace settlement. Mussolini was wrong, however. The war was far from being over.

The hour of Hitler's greatest triumph had come. His armies had conquered Poland, Denmark, Norway, the Netherlands, Belgium, and France at little cost, especially when compared to the First World War. The Soviet Union, neutral in the war so far, delivered large amounts of war supplies to Germany. The United States, though sympathetic to Britain, continued to heartily embrace isolationism. No major army remained in the field against Germany anywhere in the world. The American journalist **Walter Lippmann** wrote a stinging commentary summarizing his reaction to Germany's *blitzkrieg* of Europe. He told Americans that it was their duty:

To begin acting at once on the basic assumption that . . . before the snow flies again we may stand alone and isolated, the last great Democracy on earth.

AN AMERICAN ★ SPEAKS

Parisian children cling to one another after the Nazi invasion of France turned them into refugees.

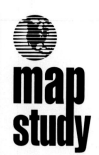

map study

World War II: German Advances, 1940–1941

 Axis Powers, early 1940

 Occupied by Germany, early 1940

 German offensives

Limit of German advances

British and French retreat

Azimuthal Equal-Area Projection © SF

Movement

A glance at the arrows reaching out from Germany in all directions on this map gives the clear impression of German movements in 1940–1941. World War II began in earnest in 1940 with the German takeover of France and the British defeat at Dunkirk. In 1941, searching for total victory in Europe, Germany moved east against the Soviet Union. Follow these developments on the map. What region of the Soviet Union was taken by the Germans in 1941?

Critical Thinking

Why did Hitler avoid attacking the Soviet Union until 1941? Why was it important for Germany to have Italy as an ally?

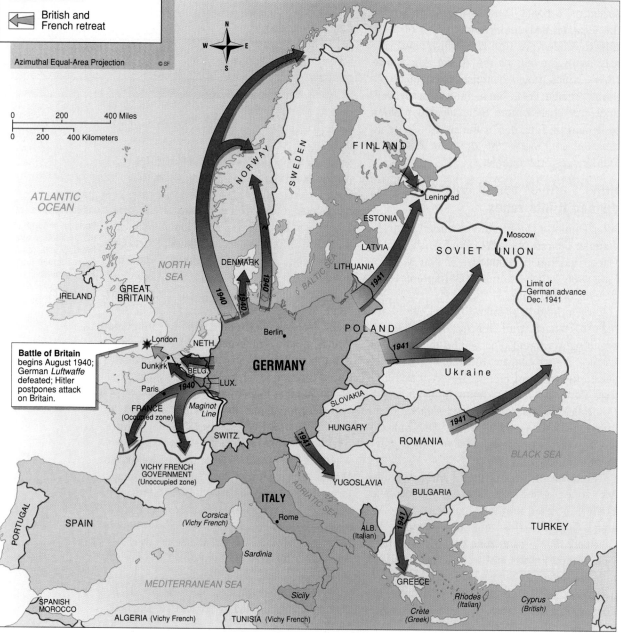

0   200   400 Miles
0   200   400 Kilometers

ATLANTIC OCEAN

NORWAY

SWEDEN

FINLAND

Leningrad

ESTONIA

LATVIA

LITHUANIA

SOVIET UNION

Moscow

NORTH SEA

DENMARK

BALTIC SEA

IRELAND

GREAT BRITAIN

Berlin

POLAND

Limit of German advance Dec. 1941

Battle of Britain begins August 1940; German *Luftwaffe* defeated; Hitler postpones attack on Britain.

London

NETH.

Dunkirk

BELG.

GERMANY

Ukraine

Paris

LUX.

1940

FRANCE (Occupied zone)

Maginot Line

SLOVAKIA

SWITZ.

HUNGARY

ROMANIA

BLACK SEA

VICHY FRENCH GOVERNMENT (Unoccupied zone)

YUGOSLAVIA

BULGARIA

ITALY

PORTUGAL

SPAIN

Corsica (Vichy French)

Rome

ADRIATIC SEA

ALB. (Italian)

TURKEY

Sardinia

MEDITERRANEAN SEA

GREECE

Sicily

Rhodes (Italian)

Cyprus (British)

SPANISH MOROCCO

ALGERIA (Vichy French)

TUNISIA (Vichy French)

Crete (Greek)

Only Britain continued to resist. Its ability to hurt the Germans, however, was limited. The small, defeated British army had left thousands of guns and all transport and armored vehicles on the beaches at Dunkirk. Despite help from Canada, Australia, New Zealand, India, and other parts of the Empire, the British were no match for the German might. At best, the army was able to conduct relatively small-scale operations in Africa or the Middle East, but not in Europe. The navy busied itself chasing German and Italian raiders and submarines, and protecting convoys. The Royal Air Force (RAF) prepared itself for the inevitable attacks from occupied Europe. Determined to continue resistance but facing a hostile continent just 21 miles away, the British knew that they would need massive help from the United States in order to survive.

SECTION **3** REVIEW

Identify Key People and Terms
Write a sentence to identify: *blitzkrieg*, Royal Air Force, Charles de Gaulle, Walter Lippmann

Locate Key Places
1. What is the name of the hilly region in southern Belgium?
2. In which country is Dunkirk located?

Master the Main Ideas
1. **Analyzing information**: What was new about *blitzkrieg* warfare?
2. **Perceiving cause/effect relationships:** What factor enabled the Germans to break through French lines at the Meuse River?
3. **Analyzing information:** How did Hitler divide France?

Apply Critical Thinking Skills: Identifying Assumptions
The Maginot Line was built to be far superior to the defensive fortifications that dominated World War I. What assumptions were the French making about a possible future war? What was wrong with those assumptions?

SECTION **4**

America aided Britain and the Soviet Union.

Key Terms: Battle of Britain, *Spitfire*, Neutrality Acts, Lend-Lease Act, Atlantic Charter

Reading Preview
As you read this section, you will learn:

1. how Britain resisted Germany.
2. how the United States responded to Britain's resistance.
3. why Germany failed to conquer the Soviet Union.
4. how the United States helped the Allies.

The conquest of France made Hitler the master of the western European continent. Only the British Isles remained unvanquished. Britain had not been successfully invaded since 1066, when William the Conqueror had done so. The English Channel, only 21 miles wide at its narrowest point between France and Britain, had long helped protect the island nation from enemies to the east. In light of Hitler's successes on the continent of Europe, Britain realized the extent of its own unpreparedness. This feeling produced great alarm because Adolf Hitler seemed poised to order a massive invasion of the island.

Britain resisted Germany with air power and radar.

The British prepared to fight, and Prime Minister Chamberlain, a broken man because of the failure of his policy of appeasement, resigned. On May 10, 1940, King George VI asked Winston Churchill to form a new government.

In the face of almost hopeless odds, Churchill announced a policy of defiance against Hitler and his armies, telling them that Britain would never consider a negotiated surrender. Following the defeat and evacuation of the British army at Dunkirk, Churchill rallied the British people, declaring:

We shall defend our Island, whatever the cost may be. We shall fight on the beaches, we shall fight on the landing grounds, we shall fight in the fields, and in the streets, we shall fight on the hills; we shall never surrender. . . .

Although Hitler began to strengthen his navy, the invasion by sea never materialized. Hermann Goering, commander of the *Luftwaffe*, had convinced Hitler that the battle against Britain could be won by aerial warfare, thus making an invasion by sea unnecessary.

On August 8, 1940, the first of Germany's nightly bombing missions droned over Britain. The Blitz, or the **Battle of Britain**, had begun. The *Luftwaffe* concentrated its bombs on British cities in hopes of quickly breaking Britain's will to resist. By the end of October, thousands of civilians had lost their lives and large areas of Britain had been destroyed. However, British morale was far from broken.

The battle in the air was by no means one-sided. With the help of a new device called radar and an elusive fighter plane named the ***Spitfire***, the RAF gradually gained superiority over the *Luftwaffe*.

Preparing for a Nazi invasion of Britain, Londoners removed road signs to confuse the would-be invaders. The attack never occurred. The signs, shown here awaiting storage, ended up tormenting only British drivers.

Radar, first used to locate aircraft by Robert Watson-Watt in 1935, enabled the British to detect German planes at a great distance and to make accurate estimates of the size of the attacking force, its probable target, and its time of arrival. RAF pilots could wait on the ground until just before the attack, rather than maintaining an exhausting air patrol.

Despite the British advantage with radar, the *Luftwaffe* came close to pounding Britain into submission during the early stages of the battle. Edward R. Murrow, reporting from London, told his American radio listeners:

Much of it you can't see. . . . Even when the Germans come down to dive-bomb. . . . You just see a bomber slanting downward toward its target; three or four things that look like marbles fall out, and it seems to take a long time for those bombs to hit the ground.

AN AMERICAN ★ SPEAKS

Eighteen-year-old Londoner Len Jones had a different perspective of the incessant bombing. He was standing in a crowded section of London's working class East End when the German bombers attacked:

RAF pilots run to their Hurricanes in an effort to repel enemy aircraft during the Battle of Britain. American volunteers, such as the one in the inset, kept track of their Nazi hits on the side of their planes.

That afternoon, around five o'clock, I went outside the house. I'd heard the aircraft, and it was exciting, because the first formations were coming over without any bombs dropping, but very majestic; terrific. And I had no thought that they were actually bombers. Then from that point on I was well aware, because bombs began to fall, and shrapnel was going along King Street, dancing off the cobbles [cobblestones]. Then the real impetus came. . . . After an explosion of a nearby bomb, you could actually feel your eyeballs being sucked out. I was holding my eyes to try to stop them going. And the suction was so vast, it ripped my shirt away, and ripped my trousers. Then I couldn't get my breath, the smoke was like acid and everything around me was black and yellow.

On September 15, British *Spitfires* inflicted heavy losses on the *Luftwaffe*. When Churchill praised the RAF with the words "never in the field of human conflict was so much owed by so many to so few," most people probably thought he was referring only to British fighter pilots. Although it was against U.S. law to join

the war, the RAF included at least seven American volunteer pilots who fought in Britain. Within three months, the British and the small group of American volunteers had destroyed 1,880 aircraft, almost twice the number that they themselves had lost. On September 17 Hitler postponed his invasion of Britain. Hitler had suffered his first major setback.

The "keep going" courage of the British people did more than foil a German invasion. Besides Edward R. Murrow in London, other American journalists such as Eric Sevareid in Paris and William Shirer in Berlin, transmitted the drama of the events in Europe to Americans. In addition to delivering on-the-spot radio broadcasts over the thunder of bombs, they sent film footage and wrote powerful descriptions of what they saw. Americans were also deeply moved by Churchill's defiant eloquence. Though they did not yet see the world war as their fight, most Americans could no longer pretend to be neutral. That represented a significant change from their former attitude.

The United States moved from isolation to concern.

Isolationism has sturdy roots in American history. George Washington's parting advice to the nation had been to avoid the "rivalries" of Europe. For much of its history, the United States preferred to mind its own business behind the twin moats of the Atlantic and the Pacific. During the 1930s the domestic troubles of the Great Depression gave Americans good reason to ignore events in Europe.

The sour memory of America's last attempt to make the world "safe for democracy" increased their resistance to involvement. Of all its allies in World War I, only Finland had repaid the massive war loans that had been extended by the United States. For the average citizen, this was disturbing—not only was America put to the trouble of saving the world—and look how that turned out—but it was also stuck with the bill.

In a curiously delayed reaction, the disillusionment and cynicism about World War I became more intense in the 1930s than it had been immediately after the war. The "lost generation" that fought the war finally found its voice, and powerful books proclaimed the horror, waste, and stupidity of the so-called Great War. In a popular opinion by no means confined to the United States, the war was seen as a monstrous conspiracy of crooked politicians, bankers, and arms merchants.

Politicians caught the antiwar mood. No "merchants of death" would ever again lure American boys into the "slaughter pens of Europe." Slogans such as those won elections in America and produced a Congress that was decidedly isolationist. The U.S. Army withered to a mere 110,000 underequipped soldiers by 1936. Congress passed neutrality laws in 1935, 1936, and 1937 to make sure the United States would not trip again over the mistakes of the recent past. The **Neutrality Acts** included the following provisions: (1) The transportation of weapons and other items of war to warring nations was banned. (2) Other materials that could also be used for war, such as oil, rubber, and steel were to be sold on a "cash and carry" basis. Warring clients were extended no credit and had to carry the materials in their own ships. (3) No warring nations could borrow money from the United States. (4) American citizens were prohibited from traveling on vessels belonging to warring nations.

By 1937 President Franklin D. Roosevelt was beginning to realize that the Nazi threat in Europe was not just another European power struggle. He saw that Hitler planned aggression on a scale that would eventually involve the United States, no matter how much Americans might desire peace. The racism and terrorism of the Nazi state began to get worldwide attention. In finding ways to aid those who stood

Broadcasting the Blitz

"This is London." Despite trans-Atlantic static, Americans instantly recognized the radio voice of correspondent Edward R. Murrow. That deep, steady voice spilled neither fear nor excitement as it narrated another harrowing night of war. In the background listeners could hear the scream of sirens, the rumble of distant explosions, the shouts of nearby gun crews. It sounded desperately real. It was real. Murrow was broadcasting from a London rooftop as the Battle of Britain raged around him.

British officials had at first rejected the requests of Murrow and CBS for permission to try outdoor broadcasts during bombing raids. Reportedly, Winston Churchill himself cleared the way, instantly grasping the value of giving Americans a more vivid sense of Britain's solitary struggle against Nazism.

Murrow and his crew used as many as a dozen microphones to pick up the sounds of the Blitz. He supplemented his on-air reporting with tireless background coverage of the embattled city—assessing damage, interviewing citizens, and gathering the eyewitness detail he found so essential to his work. "I have a peasant's mind," he once said. "I can't write about anything I haven't seen." Murrow preferred to drive a convertible, the better to follow the sound of falling bombs. He and his wife never took to underground shelter during raids, though they occasionally sat under their kitchen table.

More than 120 American journalists were on assignment in London during the Blitz, but none could match the daily you-are-there immediacy of Murrow's innovative reports. He brought the London Blitz to American living rooms, a feat of no small importance as Americans slowly chose their side in World War II.

Highlights of American Life

against Hitler, Roosevelt had to deal with the legal obstacles of the neutrality laws.

In September 1939 Congress lifted the ban on arms shipments. The following summer Congress voted funds to begin rebuilding the army and navy. In September 1940 it authorized the first peacetime military draft in the nation's history. That same month Roosevelt negotiated a deal that sent 50 old American destroyers to the British in return for 99-year leases on bases in the Caribbean. The United States in 1940 had clearly chosen sides, but the depth of its commitment was far short of what it would take to stop Hitler.

The Soviet Union's geography stopped the German invasion.

Despite his Nonaggression Pact with Stalin, Hitler regarded the Soviets as his true enemies. He yearned to conquer the Soviet Union both to gain its vast territory and to destroy the communist system he loathed. His moment came in the spring of 1941. The invasion, originally planned for mid-May, did not get underway until late in June. The delay would have chilling consequences for Germany.

Stalin, the Soviet dictator, received many warnings of the impending attack, but he refused to believe them. His instincts told him that his anticommunist enemies were trying to promote a conflict between the Soviet Union and Germany. Meanwhile, three million German soldiers, plus many Romanian, Hungarian, and Finnish divisions, lined up on the Soviet border. German panzer divisions with more than 3,000 tanks provided the spearhead for the *blitzkrieg*, with more than 500,000 trucks supporting this effort.

Amazingly, given the size of the attack forces, the Germans caught the Soviets by surprise on June 22, 1941. Stalin was so sure that the Germans would not attack that he neglected to take even the most basic precautions. The Soviet Air Force lost 1,200 planes by noon of the first day.

After the initial attack, the German armies sliced through the opposing forces and raced deep into the interior of the Soviet Union. In the north the German armies overran Soviet-controlled Estonia, Latvia, and Lithuania—taken over by the Soviets after the Nazi-Soviet Nonaggression Pact—and proceeded to surround Leningrad. In the south the Germans captured most of the Ukraine, the populous southern region with half of all the Soviet grain-producing lands. In the center the

Murrow strides past London's All Souls Church, at right, and the BBC building from whose roof he often broadcasted during bombings. Murrow avoided bomb shelters except in pursuit of news. "Once you start going into shelters," he said, "you lose your nerve."

Isolationism

Point

In favor of isolationism

■ War is a monstrous conspiracy of crooked politicians, bankers, and arms merchants.
■ World War I failed "to make the world safe for democracy."
■ Americans still are suffering from the effects of the Great Depression.
■ The polls show that most American people are against going to war.

Counterpoint

Against isolationism

■ If Germany conquers Britain, the United States will be in grave danger.
■ From a moral standpoint, Americans cannot claim freedom for themselves and remain secure while freedom is being denied to others around the world.

America First!

The most prominent figure in the American isolationist movement was Charles Lindbergh, the "Lone Eagle" whose nonstop solo flight from New York to Paris had been the most celebrated accomplishment of its time. In a speech on April 23, 1941, how does Lindbergh spotlight a crucial difficulty in involving a democracy in war?

War is not inevitable for this country. Such a claim is defeatism in the true sense. No one can make us fight abroad unless we ourselves are willing to do so. No one will attempt to fight us here if we arm ourselves as a great nation should be armed. Over a hundred million people in this nation are opposed to entering the war. If the principles of democracy mean anything at all, that is reason enough for us to stay out. If we are forced into a war against the wishes of an overwhelming majority of our people, we will have proved democracy such a failure at home that there will be little use fighting for it abroad.

Germans pushed toward the prize of **Moscow**, the Soviet capital. In the process, hundreds of thousands of Soviet soldiers became prisoners of the Germans. The Soviets, although fighting desperately, appeared to be the next hapless victims of the German war machine.

This time, however, the German *blitzkrieg* failed. The Soviet Union was simply too big. The Soviet road system was primitive compared to that of France, and the deeper the Germans drove into the Soviet Union, the longer their supply lines stretched. No matter how many Soviets the Germans killed, Stalin never ran out of soldiers. The Soviet armies, aided by unfavorable weather, held up the German advance. October rains reduced the roads to impassable rivers of mud.

At first the Germans welcomed the winter. As the ground hardened and tanks could maneuver, they made their final push for Moscow. Then the cold deepened to 20 degrees below

zero. Tank engines froze and German soldiers, unprepared for winter weather, suffered from frostbite. The German attack on the Soviet Union shuddered to a halt just 30 miles from Moscow on December 5, 1941.

The United States supported the Allies with weapons and supplies.

In the United States, President Roosevelt's big problem was how to use American power to prevent a Nazi victory. He clearly understood the dangerous world situation but also knew that the American electorate was not ready to commit itself to war. Britain and the Soviet Union might suffer defeat or exhaustion before the United States became involved.

The prospect of securing a declaration of war still seemed remote. In the 1940 election Roosevelt, who was seeking an unprecedented third term in office, pledged aid to the Allies. However, so did his Republican opponent, Wendell Willkie. Both candidates promised to avoid war. Responding to pressure from the isolationists, Roosevelt vowed, "Your boys are not going to be sent into any foreign wars." Roosevelt won the election with 53 percent of the popular vote and 449 electoral votes.

Although isolationist spirit remained strong, the United States did make several decisive moves against the Germans in 1941. Roosevelt argued that if a neighbor's house were on fire it would only be common sense to lend the person a hose. Accordingly, he signed the **Lend-Lease Act** on March 11, which allowed Britain to place orders for American weapons and supplies without payment. Roosevelt described the United States as "the arsenal of democracy," a far cry from the intent of the Neutrality Acts.

In April American troops landed on the island of Greenland, a Danish colony, to help protect American-European shipping routes. Two months later President Roosevelt ordered all German and Italian assets frozen. Then he directed the U.S. Marines to occupy Iceland, another Danish colony.

In August the Americans extended Lend-Lease to the Soviet Union. Even though the Soviets themselves had a repressive totalitarian

government, both the British and the Americans funneled supplies to them in order to fight the common German enemy.

That same month Roosevelt and Churchill met on an American warship off the coast of Newfoundland to decide their next step. The two leaders negotiated the **Atlantic Charter**, a statement of war aims that Roosevelt saw as his equivalent of President Wilson's Fourteen Points. The Atlantic Charter affirmed the right of people to choose their own governments and to be free of foreign aggression. Given these aims, the participation of the Soviet Union in the anti-Nazi effort proved an embarrassment, especially since the Soviet Union announced its intention to keep Polish territory after the war.

Although these measures significantly helped the Allies, the commitment of the United States fell far short of the effort needed to defeat Hitler. Even with so much at stake, many Americans remained firmly opposed to war. As late as May 1941 an opinion poll indicated that 79 percent of Americans opposed war. Although Roosevelt announced that the Battle of the Atlantic was "coming very close to home," America's military remained

woefully unprepared for war. In August 1941 the House of Representatives passed a bill to extend the draft by only one vote.

In September American ships began to escort merchant vessels carrying war material to Britain and the Soviet Union. American escort ships and German submarines started to shoot at one another. In October a German submarine sank an American naval vessel, the destroyer *Reuben James*, killing 115 sailors. Americans were provoked to outrage, but no further. What would it take to bring the United States into the war?

Members of the "Mother's Crusade" took up vigil near the Capitol in Washington, D.C. They wanted to convince Congress not to pass the Lend-Lease Act.

SECTION **4** REVIEW

Identify Key People and Terms
Write a sentence to identify: Battle of Britain, *Spitfire*, Neutrality Acts, Lend-Lease Act, Atlantic Charter

Locate Key Places
Where was the German attack on the Soviet Union halted in December 1941?

Master the Main Ideas

1. **Analyzing information:** Why was radar so important to Britain?
2. **Analyzing U.S. foreign policy:** What actions taken by Congress in 1939 and 1940 showed that the United States was moving away from isolationism?
3. **Perceiving cause/effect relationships:** Why did the *blitzkrieg* fail against the Soviet Union?
4. **Studying the causes and effects of U.S. involvement in international conflicts:** What steps brought the United States near open war with Germany?

Apply Critical Thinking Skills: Identifying Alternatives
The Soviet Union under Stalin was a totalitarian regime similar in many ways to Hitler's Germany. The communist party maintained complete control over the Soviet people and the economy. In your judgment, should the United States and Britain have allied themselves with such a regime in order to defeat Hitler? What other alternative might they have had?

"This is London . . ."

15A

TIME FRAME
1940

GEOGRAPHIC SETTING
London, England

After the Fall of France in June 1940, Germany prepared to invade England. In an attempt to destroy British defenses, the Germans began an intensive air assault against England in August 1940. Early in September the focus of the German air raids shifted to the British capital, London. A 32-year-old American newsman, Edward R. Murrow (1908–1965), became famous for his radio broadcasts from London during the Battle of Britain. The following is an excerpt from his broadcast for October 10, 1940.

This is London, ten minutes before five in the morning. Tonight's raid has been widespread. London is again the main target. Bombs have been reported from more than fifty districts. Raiders have been over Wales in the west, the Midlands, Liverpool, the southwest, and northeast. So far as London is concerned, the outskirts appear to have suffered the heaviest pounding. The attack has decreased in intensity since the moon faded from the sky.

All the fires were quickly brought under control. That's a common phrase in the morning communiqués. I've seen how it's done; spent a night with the London fire brigade. For three hours after the night attack got going, I shivered in a sandbag crow's-nest atop a tall building near the Thames. It was one of the many fire-observation posts. There was an old gun barrel mounted above a round table marked off like a compass. A stick of incendiaries bounced off rooftops about three miles away. The observer took a sight on a point where the first one fell, swung his gun sight along the line of bombs, and took another reading at the end of the line of fire. Then he picked up his telephone and shouted above the half gale that was blowing up there, "Stick of incendiaries—between 190 and 220—about three miles away." Five minutes later a German bomber came boring down the river. We could see his exhaust trail like a pale ribbon stretched straight across the sky. Half a mile downstream there were two eruptions and then a third, close together. The first two looked like some giant had thrown a huge basket of flaming golden oranges high in the air. The third was just a balloon of fire enclosed in black smoke above the housetops. The observer didn't bother with his gun sight and indicator for that one. Just reached for his night glasses, took one quick look, picked up his telephone, and said, "Two high explosives and one oil bomb," and named the street where they had fallen. . . .

There was peace and quiet inside for twenty minutes. Then a shower of incendiaries came down far in the distance. They didn't fall in a line. It looked like flashes from an electric train on a wet night, only the engineer was drunk and driving his train in circles through the streets. One sight at the middle of the flashes and our observer reported laconically, "Breadbasket at 90—covers a couple of miles." Half an hour later a string of fire bombs fell right beside the Thames. Their white glare was reflected in the black, lazy water near the banks and faded out in midstream where the moon cut a golden swath broken only by the arches of famous bridges.

We could see little men shoveling those fire bombs into the river. One burned for a few minutes like a beacon right in the middle of a bridge. Finally those white flames all went out. No one bothers about the white light, it's only when it turns yellow that a real fire has started.

St. Paul's Cathedral in London is illuminated by the light of nearby burning buildings after a bombing raid on the night of December 29th, 1940. A team of scientists led by Sir Henry Tizard had developed the radar system that signaled approaching *Luftwaffe* planes and helped assure the RAF victory in the Battle of Britain.

I must have seen well over a hundred fire bombs come down and only three small fires were started. The incendiaries aren't so bad if there is someone there to deal with them, but those oil bombs present more difficulties.

As I watched those white fires flame up and die down, watched the yellow blazes grow dull and disappear, I thought, what a puny effort is this to burn a great city. Finally, we went below to a big room underground. It was quiet. Women spoke softly into telephones. There was a big map of London on the wall. Little colored pins were being moved from one point to another and every time a pin was moved it meant that fire pumps were on their way through the black streets of London to a fire. One district had asked for reinforcements from another, just as an army reinforces its front lines in the sector bearing the brunt of the attack. On another map all the observation posts, like the one I just left, were marked. . . .

We picked a fire from the map and drove to it. And the map was right. It was a small fire in a warehouse near the river.

Not much of a fire; only ten pumps working on it, but still big enough to be seen from the air. The searchlights were bunched overhead and as we approached we could hear the drone of a German plane and see the burst of antiaircraft fire directly overhead. Two pieces of shrapnel slapped down in the water and then everything was drowned in the hum of the pumps and the sound of hissing water. Those firemen in their oilskins and tin hats appeared oblivious to everything but the fire. We went to another blaze—just a small two-story house down on the East End. An incendiary had gone through the roof and the place was being gutted. A woman stood on a corner, clutching a rather dirty pillow. A policeman was trying to comfort her. And a fireman said, "You'd be surprised what strange things people pick up when they run out of a burning house."

And back at headquarters I saw a man laboriously and carefully copying names in a big ledger—the list of firemen killed in action during the last month. There were about a hundred names. . . .

Discussing the Reading

1. What impression did Edward R. Murrow give of the British under attack?

2. What quality of Murrow's report reflected the fact that his broadcast medium was radio?

CRITICAL THINKING
Drawing Conclusions

The principal German objective in shifting the focus of their bombing raids to London was to terrorize the British people into surrendering. Based on Murrow's broadcast from near the end of the Battle of Britain (when London had been being bombed nightly for over a month), was the German strategy succeeding?

An Isolationist Speaks Out

TIME FRAME
1941

GEOGRAPHIC SETTING
New York City

The America First Committee, formed in 1940, strongly opposed United States intervention in World War II. Charles Lindbergh (1902–1974), a national hero since his solo transatlantic flight in 1927, was a prominent America Firster during 1940 and 1941, traveling across the country presenting the case for isolationism. The following passages are excerpted from a speech Lindbergh gave in New York City in April 1941. At about this time, in response to criticism of his isolationist views from President Roosevelt, Lindbergh resigned his commission in the Army Air Corps. After the United States entered the war, Lindbergh became a consultant for an aircraft manufacturer, accompanying 50 combat missions in the Pacific.

It is not only our right, but it is our obligation as American citizens to look at this war objectively and to weigh our chances for success if we should enter it. I
5 have attempted to do this, especially from the standpoint of aviation; and I have been forced to the conclusion that we cannot win this war for England, regardless of how much assistance we extend.
10 I ask you to look at the map of Europe today and see if you can suggest any way in which we could win this war if we entered it. Suppose we had a large army in America, trained and equipped. Where
15 would we send it to fight? The campaigns of the war show only too clearly how difficult it is to force a landing, or to maintain an army, on a hostile coast.
Suppose we took our Navy from the Pa-
20 cific, and used it to convoy [escort] British shipping. That would not win the war for England. It would, at best, permit her to exist under the constant bombing of the German air fleet. Suppose we had an air
25 force that we could send to Europe. Where could it operate? Some of our

squadrons might be based in the British Isles; but it is physically impossible to base enough aircraft in the British Isles alone
30 to equal in strength the aircraft that can be based on the Continent of Europe.
I have asked these questions on the supposition that we had in existence an Army and an air force large enough and
35 well enough equipped to send to Europe; and that we would dare to remove our Navy from the Pacific. Even on this basis, I do not see how we could invade the Continent of Europe successfully as long as all
40 of that Continent and most of Asia is under Axis domination. But the fact is that none of these suppositions are correct. We have only a one-ocean Navy. Our Army is still untrained and inadequately
45 equipped for foreign war. Our air force is deplorably lacking in modern fighting planes because most of them have already been sent to Europe. . . .
There are many . . . interventionists in
50 America, but there are more people among us of a different type. That is why you and I are assembled here tonight. There is a policy open to this nation that will lead to success—a policy that leaves
55 us free to follow our own way of life, and to develop our own civilization. It is not a new and untried idea. It was advocated by Washington. It was incorporated in the Monroe Doctrine. Under its guidance, the
60 United States has become the greatest nation in all the world.
It is based upon the belief that the security of a nation lies in the strength and character of its own people. It recom-
65 mends the maintenance of armed forces sufficient to defend this hemisphere from attack by any combination of foreign powers. It demands faith in an independent American destiny. This is the policy of the
70 America First Committee today. It is a

Represented as a skunk, Hitler and "Hitlerism" are sanitized in this 1941 political cartoon attacking the American First Committee, to which Charles Lindbergh and Montana Senator Burton Wheeler (1882–1975) belonged. After the Japanese attack on Pearl Harbor in December 1941, even isolationists like Lindbergh and Wheeler supported the American war effort.

policy not of isolation, but of independence; not of defeat, but of courage. It is a policy that led this nation to success during the most trying years of our history, 75 and it is a policy that will lead us to success again. . . .

The United States is better situated from a military standpoint than any other nation in the world. Even in our present 80 condition of unpreparedness no foreign power is in a position to invade us today. If we concentrate on our own defenses and build the strength that this nation should maintain, no foreign army will ever 85 attempt to land on American shores.

War is not inevitable for this country. Such a claim is defeatism in the true sense. No one can make us fight abroad unless we ourselves are willing to do so. 90 No one will attempt to fight us here if we arm ourselves as a great nation should be armed. Over a hundred million people in this nation are opposed to entering the war. If the principles of democracy mean 95 anything at all, that is reason enough for us to stay out. If we are forced into a war against the wishes of an overwhelming majority of our people, we will have proved democracy such a failure at home 100 that there will be little use fighting for it abroad.

Discussing the Reading

1. What was Charles Lindbergh's main argument for opposing American entry into World War II? Do you find it convincing?

2. How did Lindbergh link this argument to what he presented as the traditional foreign policy of the United States? Was he justified?

CRITICAL THINKING
Identifying Assumptions

Did Charles Lindbergh make any relative moral judgments of the English and German causes?

Chapter Summary

Write supporting details under each of the following main ideas as you review the chapter.

Section 1
1. Germany, Italy, and Japan sought geographical expansion.
2. Fear of communism caused many people to support dictators.
3. Japanese military leaders captured Manchuria.
4. Hitler gained power by promising to make Germany strong again.

Section 2
1. Germany and Italy took the offensive virtually unimpeded.
2. The Munich Pact betrayed Czechoslovakia.
3. Stalin's deal with Hitler doomed Poland and triggered World War II.
4. Hitler seized Denmark and Norway.

Section 3
1. Tanks and aircraft spearheaded German attacks.
2. The Germans forced Britain and France to retreat to Dunkirk.
3. Hitler's armies seized France and divided it into zones.

Section 4
1. Britain resisted Germany with air power and radar.
2. The United States moved from isolation to concern.
3. The Soviet Union's geography stopped the German invasion.
4. The United States supported the Allies with weapons and supplies.

Chapter Themes

1. **Representative government:** Unlike in Germany, where one dictator made all of the important decisions, the United States made its decision to stay out of war by electing representatives who campaigned on isolationist platforms. Even Roosevelt, who by 1940 was conceding to aid the Allies, pledged not to send American troops "into any foreign wars."
2. **Conflict and cooperation:** During the opening years of World War II, Roosevelt found ways to cooperate with Europe and with the Soviet Union. However, it was the will of the American people to avoid joining the conflict. Compromise was reflected in such actions as sending war material on a cash-and-carry basis and later on the more liberal Lend-Lease program. Yet another approach for cooperation was through the Atlantic Charter, a statement of principle and support for democracy and against all aggression.

Chapter Study Guide

Identifying Key People and Terms

Name the key person or key term that describes the:
1. systematic killing of a whole national or ethnic group
2. title Hitler took in 1934
3. policy used by Britain and France because they hoped to satisfy Hitler's thirst for conquest without going to war with him
4. three laws passed by Congress to guarantee that the United States would not go to war

Locating Key Places

1. What country did Japan invade in 1931?
2. What was the first area that Hitler took, correctly assuming that Britain and France would not respond?
3. What African country did Italy invade to begin its conquest of the Mediterranean basin?
4. The invasion of what country caused Britain and France to declare war on Germany?

Mastering the Main Ideas

1. What problems experienced by Germany, Japan, and Italy was "empire building" expected to solve?
2. How did Germany and Italy's aggression test the resolve of other nations in the 1930s?
3. **(a)** By 1940 what had Germany accomplished with its *blitzkrieg* attacks? **(b)** How had this tactic of war affected Britain?
4. **(a)** What two major setbacks did Hitler face in 1940 and 1941? **(b)** Why did each setback occur?

Applying Critical Thinking Skills

1. **Predicting consequences:** What future treatment could the Jews expect from Hitler given their experience with the Nuremberg Laws and with *Kristallnacht*?
2. **Identifying alternatives:** In each of the following situations, list the action that the League of Nations or Britain, France, or other nations took, and next list alternative

1931
Japan invades Manchuria; Stimson Doctrine

1934
Hitler assumes absolute power

1935
Nuremberg Laws; Neutrality Acts

1936
Olympic Games; Hitler takes the Rhineland

1938
Kristallnacht; Hitler annexes Austria; Munich Conference

1939
Nazi-Soviet Nonaggression Pact; World War II begins

1940
Hitler takes Denmark, Norway, Belgium, the Netherlands, and France; Battle of Britain

1941
Lend-Lease Act; Atlantic Charter

actions that they might have taken that would have created a stronger stance against aggression. **(a)** Japan invades Manchuria. **(b)** Germany takes the Rhineland. **(c)** Germany invades Austria. **(d)** Italy invades Ethiopia. **(e)** Germany takes Sudetenland.

3. Analyzing cause and effect: Explain how both the German preparedness and the lack of French and British preparedness led to the fall of France.

4. Recognizing values: (a) What were the values espoused by Britain and America in the Atlantic Charter? **(b)** How would Hitler have responded to such values? Why? **(c)** How would Manchuria, Poland, and France have responded?

Chapter Activities

Learning Geography Through History

1. (a) Where was the Maginot Line located and what kind of troop movements was it designed to stop? **(b)** Did the Maginot Line work? Explain.

2. What body of water separated British and German soldiers by just 21 miles during the Battle of Britain? How did this body of water protect Britain?

Relating the United States to the World

1. How was Hitler embarrassed by the United States in the 1936 Summer Olympics?

2. Fear of war motivated the foreign policy of the American government during the 1930s. How did fear of communism and Jews play a part in Hitler's foreign policy during the same period?

Using the Time Line

1. How many years elapsed between Hitler's becoming dictator of Germany and his victory in France?

2. In what year did Japan begin its aggression in China?

Linking Past to Present

1. Compare how Hitler used radio to gain power with how politicians today use TV.

2. How are the principles set forth in the Atlantic Charter used today as a United Nations' rationale for condemning aggression, for instance the aggression by Iraq on Kuwait in 1990?

Practicing Critical Thinking Strategies

Drawing Conclusions
The Iraqi attack on Kuwait in 1990 and the Nazi attack of the Rhineland in 1936 were both unprovoked attacks by nations that were weak militarily. What belief do you think the leaders of both Iraq and Germany held that gave them the confidence to initiate these aggressive acts?

Learning More About the World At War

1. Using Source Readings: Read the Source Readings in this chapter and answer the questions.

2. Using Primary Sources: Two types of firsthand accounts of history are the diary and the transcribed oral history. Choose one or the other type by reading books such as *The Diary of a Young Girl* by Anne Frank or *The Good War* by Studs Terkel. Report to the class about the content of the book, as well as the reliability and usefulness of source material in such forms.

Linking Past to Present

The memory of the Japanese surprise attack of the American naval base at Pearl Harbor on December 7, 1941, inset, lives on today at the Battleship *Arizona* Memorial, background. The memorial is positioned directly above the sunken remains of the *Arizona*. A glass floor provides visitors a clear view of the battleship.

The Allied Victory

1 9 4 1 – 1 9 4 5

16

Although events in Europe had dominated the headlines in the 1930s, it was the Japanese, not the Nazis, who finally plunged the United States into World War II. America's neutrality came to an abrupt end on the fateful morning of December 7, 1941, when Japanese bombers attacked Pearl Harbor, an American naval base in Hawaii. Isolationism, which Americans had clung to tenaciously as Hitler marched through Europe, now quickly dissolved.

For the United States, the war really consisted of two almost entirely separate conflicts, one in the Pacific against Japan, and one in Europe and Africa against Germany and Italy. This meant that the American perspective of the war differed from that of the British, for whom the war in the Pacific was never as important as the war at home.

Fighting a global war on two fronts would create a challenge for American leaders not only during the war but afterward. They would be forced to answer some very important questions: Who would the United States fight first, Hitler or the Japanese militarists? What strategies at home as well as on the battlefield would they employ? What role would the United States assume in building a new global and political economic order after the dust of war had settled?

CHAPTER PREVIEW

In this chapter you will learn how the United States and its Allies defeated Germany, Italy, and Japan.

SECTIONS IN THIS CHAPTER:
1. Japan began its march toward empire.
2. The Allies concentrated on defeating Germany and Italy.
3. The United States led the offensive against Japan.
4. The war changed America's role in the world.

1940	1941	1942	1943	1944	1945	1946

1941
Japanese attack Pearl Harbor; United States enters World War II

1942
Battles of Coral Sea and Midway; U.S. Marines invade Guadalcanal

1943
Casablanca Conference; Allies invade Italy

1944
Allies invade France (D–Day); Battle of the Bulge

1945
President Roosevelt dies; Germany surrenders; U.S. drops atomic bombs on Japan; Japanese surrender

Japan began its march toward empire.

Key Terms: Tripartite Pact, Axis, Allies, Bataan Death March

Reading Preview
As you read this section, you will learn:

1. what was the main objective of the Japanese militarists.
2. how Congress reacted to the Japanese bombing of Pearl Harbor.
3. who won the early victories following Pearl Harbor.

Hitler's conquests in eastern Europe and Mussolini's victories in the Mediterranean encouraged the Japanese to begin their own march toward world dominance. China, with its tremendous natural resources and economic potential, became Japan's primary target. Japan's strategy was to nibble away at the edges of China and then plunge into the interior.

Japan's thirst for Chinese land already had been partially quenched. In 1895 Japan took the island of Formosa (Taiwan) from China. Ten years later, in the Russo-Japanese War (1904–1905), Japan demonstrated its military strength by defeating the Russians in the Chinese province of Manchuria. In the Battle of Tsushima, the Japanese navy destroyed the entire Russian fleet. Japan emerged from this battle a recognized world power, the first Asian nation in modern times to defeat a western power.

Spurred on by their new status, the Japanese annexed Korea in 1910. Then, in 1914, they took advantage of World War I to seize strategically located islands in the Pacific from Germany. World War I also gave the Japanese the opportunity to increase their influence in China at the expense of American and European trade rivals who were preoccupied with defeating Germany.

For a short time in the 1920s, the Japanese seemed to move toward democracy. When the Great Depression ruined their much-needed markets for exports, however, military leaders insisted on invading China to make Japan more economically self-sufficient.

Japanese militarists sought the complete conquest of China.

As you read previously, the Japanese seized resource-rich Manchuria in 1931. Despite objections from the League of Nations and the United States, Japan incorporated Manchuria—renamed Manchukuo—into its expanding empire. The Japanese militarists, who had begun consolidating their power before the invasion, now had their first major prize in their quest for China.

In 1937 the Japanese invaded the rest of China, capturing Shanghai, Nanking, and other large cities. When the Japanese captured the Chinese capital of Nanking, their soldiers subjected the civilians to days of atrocities. The Chinese refused to surrender, however. Instead, 50 million of them fled to the western part of the nation, taking machinery, farm implements, and whatever else they could carry or put into a cart. As the map on page 602 shows, they then set up a new capital for China at Chungking in 1938.

The League of Nations and the United States once again condemned Japanese aggression.

Chinese peasants in Shanghai angrily demonstrate against Japanese invaders in October 1939 after being refused rations of rice, a Chinese staple.

However, still preoccupied with the Depression, neither the United States nor the members of the League were willing to use military force against Japan. They feared that their domestic economic problems would be increased if they antagonized Japan. This failure to act against Japan dealt a heavy blow to the prestige of the League.

With no one trying to stop them, the Japanese militarists continued on their course of aggression. After Germany defeated France and the Netherlands in 1940, these nations' possessions in Indochina and the East Indies were particularly vulnerable. Japan, in great need of oil and other natural resources, immediately took steps to acquire these resource-rich European colonies.

As the League sat by passively, the Roosevelt Administration finally decided to take action. In July 1940 it enacted a series of economic sanctions against Japan in an attempt to make it back off from Indochina and the East Indies. The sanctions included a reduction in the amount of oil Japan could import from the United States (Japan's largest supplier) and the cutoff of all gasoline.

The U.S. economic sanctions failed to stop Japanese aggression. In September 1940 Japanese troops landed in northern French Indochina. Shortly afterward, Japan signed a defensive pact with Germany and Italy—the **Tripartite Pact**. This pact established these nations as the **Axis** powers and confirmed what many people had already known for some time—Japan had become a major threat to world peace.

During the following months, Japan and the United States held talks to try to solve their differences. The talks were unsuccessful, however, because Japan refused to consider the American demand that it withdraw from China.

Shortly after the talks, U.S. naval intelligence experts broke the Japanese diplomatic code used to send messages between Tokyo and the Japanese embassy in Washington, D.C. One message indicated that Japan had once again gone on the offensive, this time in southern French Indochina. Immediately, the Roosevelt Administration responded by freezing all

Japanese assets in the United States and stopping all oil shipments to Japan. The Dutch government-in-exile, another major supplier of oil to Japan through the Dutch East Indies, also shut off Japan's oil supply. Japan's choices were now extremely clear: either it could end its aggression and regain its oil supply or it could attack the Dutch East Indies and take the oil it needed. The Japanese knew that attacking the Dutch East Indies would mean war.

In the meantime General **Hideki Tojo** became Japan's new premier. Tojo, like other militarists in Japan, draped himself with illusions of military grandeur and national destiny. He reasoned that foreigners had never defeated Japan in a war and that there was no reason to believe that they ever could. After all, Japan's emperor was a direct descendant of a powerful divinity. With divine power on its side, Tojo reasoned, no nation could ever stop Japan's quest for empire. Indeed, the question of whether the nation should go to war to achieve its expansionist goals never entered Tojo's mind. The only question that remained was when Japan should make its move.

Laden with military medals, Japan's war minister, Hideki Tojo, salutes his troops on August 1, 1941. Six weeks later Tojo became premier of Japan, staffing his cabinet with high-ranking military men. At the end of the war, Tojo was convicted of war crimes and then hanged for his offenses.

FINAL MORNING EXTRA

San Francisco Chronicle

U.S. AT WAR!
PARATROOPS LAND IN PHILIPPINES!

Japs Bomb Hawaii, Invade Thailand

350 Slain—Then Tokyo Declares War on U.S., Britain

President Roosevelt Will Go Before Congress Today

While banner
headlines flashed news
of the bombing of
Pearl Harbor to
shocked Americans, a
rescue crew in a small
boat attempts to locate
survivors. The
battleship *West
Virginia*, seen in the
foreground, was
heavily damaged
during the surprise
attack.

On December 7, 1941, that question was answered with crystal clarity. A message from Tokyo to Washington revealed that Japan had totally rejected all American demands. An attack of U.S. naval bases in the Pacific was imminent. Immediately, American officials sent urgent warnings to its bases in the Pacific. By the time the warnings arrived, however, the Japanese had already struck.

Congress declared war on Japan.

Just before 8:00 A.M. on a peaceful Sunday morning, December 7, 1941, Japanese warplanes attacked the undefended American fleet at **Pearl Harbor**, Hawaii. An American radar operator picked up the incoming Japanese planes but failed to inform the defenses. Despite many recent alerts, the U.S. fleet was unprepared for an aerial attack.

By 10:00 A.M. the bombing was over. The Japanese had sunk or severely damaged all 8 American battleships and destroyed about 149 airplanes before they even got off the ground. Altogether, 2,403 American soldiers, sailors, marines, and civilians were killed. Another 1,178 were wounded. The American navy alone suffered more casualties than it had in all of World War I.

John Garcia, a 16-year-old pipe fitter apprentice employed at the Pearl Harbor Navy Yard in December 1941, recalled the aftermath of December 7:

> I was asked by some other officer to go into the water and get sailors out that had been blown off the ships. Some were unconscious, some were dead. So I spent the rest of the day swimming inside the harbor, along with some other Hawaiians. I brought out I don't know how many bodies. . . .

AN AMERICAN ★ SPEAKS

Despite the enormous losses at Pearl Harbor, the consequences could have been worse. The Japanese missed the aircraft carriers,

634

which were at sea during the attack. They also missed the repair yards and the fuel storage tanks, the loss of which would have crippled the American navy for months.

Speaking to Congress the day after the Pearl Harbor bombing, an emotional yet determined President Roosevelt described December 7 as "a date which will live in infamy." Knowing that the United States had to act and act quickly, he asked Congress to declare war on Japan. Later that day it honored his request. Only one dissenting vote was cast. Britain, knowing that it would need American help in Europe, also declared war against Japan on December 8. Three days later Germany and Italy declared war against the United States. Nearly four years would pass before the American people would know peace again.

The Japanese claimed victory after victory during the first six months.

In January 1942 in Washington, D.C., 26 nations, headed by the United States, Britain, and the Soviet Union, pledged themselves to fight together until the Axis powers were defeated. These countries referred to themselves formally as the United Nations, but were popularly known as the **Allies**, or Allied nations.

The Allies were startled by the relentlessness exhibited by the Japanese during the first six months of the war. The Japanese war machine, reminiscent of the German *blitzkrieg*, quickly seized Guam, Wake Island, Hong Kong, Thailand, Malaya, Burma, Singapore, the Philippines, and the Dutch East Indies. These victories, accomplished without the loss of a single warship, provided ample proof that the Japanese would be a most formidable opponent.

For the United States, the defeat in the Philippines was an even worse disaster than Pearl Harbor. Despite more than eight hours advance warning, the Americans once again had their air force destroyed on the ground. General **Douglas MacArthur**, the American commander in the Philippines, originally planned to fight the Japanese on the beaches. When this plan failed, however, he retreated to the **Bataan Peninsula** across the bay from the Philippine capital of Manila. There he hoped to hold out until reinforcements could arrive from the United States.

Although the American and Filipino troops on Bataan fought bravely, they had no air cover and little hope of reinforcement because the United States had lost much of its naval fleet and many of its planes at Pearl Harbor. In addition, the Japanese had overrun the rice stockpiles in the Philippines. Consequently, many of the troops and refugee civilians on Bataan died from starvation. Diseases such as malaria also took a toll.

Informed of the bleak situation, President Roosevelt ordered MacArthur to flee the island. He did not want to lose one of his best military strategists for a cause that appeared hopeless. MacArthur escaped by PT boat and airplane through Japanese-controlled territory to Australia. However, he was not a man to give up easily. He promised, "I shall return."

The 78,000 isolated, disease-ridden American and Filipino troops left on Bataan finally surrendered to the Japanese in April 1942. This was the largest surrender of American troops in the nation's military history. The Japanese soldiers then forced their prisoners to walk 65 miles with little food or water on the infamous **Bataan Death March**. Thousands of the

Shouldering litters bearing injured comrades, half-starved American and Filipino prisoners of war near the end of the long and arduous Bataan Death March. Many prisoners were bayonetted or beaten for getting out of step or for trying to help a fallen marcher. According to one survivor: "I know we've heard of Hitler starving and killing people by the thousands. . . . And we've heard of the [Japanese] using living Chinese for bayonet practice. But we're Americans. . . . Those things don't happen to Americans!"

American and Filipino troops captured at Bataan died during or shortly after this march.

By early May 1942, the Japanese had accomplished all of their original objectives. Several reasons accounted for their astounding success. The United States was not prepared for war. Britain was fighting for its life in Europe and could not spare enough troops for Asia. France and the Netherlands, occupied by the Germans, could not reinforce their colonies. Only in the Philippines did the colonial subjects fight vigorously against the Japanese. Elsewhere, especially in the Dutch East Indies and Burma, many people greeted the Japanese as liberators because they resented the racism of their colonial rulers.

SECTION **1** REVIEW

Identify Key People and Terms
Write a sentence to identify: Tripartite Pact, Axis, Hideki Tojo, Allies, Douglas MacArthur, Bataan Death March

Locate Key Places
1. Why did the Japanese attack Pearl Harbor?
2. Why did the American and Filipino troops retreat to the Bataan Peninsula?

Master the Main Ideas
1. **Studying American foreign policy:** What actions did President Roosevelt take in an attempt to stop Japanese aggression in China and elsewhere?
2. **Analyzing the effects of U.S. involvement in international conflicts:** What damage did the Japanese inflict on the United States at Pearl Harbor?
3. **Perceiving cause/effect relationships:** Why were the Japanese so successful in southeast Asia and in the western Pacific in the first six months of the war?

Apply Critical Thinking Skills: Identifying Assumptions
What assumptions made by Japanese militarists supported Japanese aggression throughout the early 1900s?

SECTION **2**

The Allies concentrated on defeating Germany and Italy.

Key Terms: Operation Torch, Casablanca Conference, Operation Overlord, D-Day, Battle of the Bulge, Yalta Conference, Final Solution, Holocaust

Reading Preview
As you read this section, you will learn:

1. why the Allies believed the Germans were more dangerous than the Japanese.
2. where American and British troops decided to confront the Germans in 1942.
3. what happened to the German army on the eastern front.
4. where the Allies decided to attack Germany in June 1944.
5. the result of the Allied invasion of Germany.

When Germany and Italy declared war on the United States on December 11, 1941, President Roosevelt was relieved. He had worried that the American peoples' eagerness to take revenge on Japan would overshadow the greater danger from Nazi Germany.

Once the United States joined the war, President Roosevelt and his allies had to agree on a joint strategy for winning. Unlike the Japanese, who refused German requests to declare war on the Soviet Union, the Americans knew from the start that they would have to fight on two fronts. Which front was to be given top priority? This was a question that needed to be addressed at the outset.

German technology was superior to that of the Japanese.

Roosevelt favored the "Europe first" strategy as did Churchill, Stalin, and General **George Marshall**, the army chief of staff. In their view, Germany was more dangerous because of its technological lead in such fields as jet aircraft and rocketry and because Germany posed an immediate threat to the Soviet Union. In essence, they believed that Germany could win the war without Japan. Japan, however, could not win the war without Germany.

The decision to give top priority to the war in Europe met with some resistance. General MacArthur wanted the Pacific theater's needs to come first. He was supported by the navy and by those Americans who wanted quick revenge for Pearl Harbor. Chiang Kai-shek (chyäng′ kī′shek′), the Chinese leader, pleaded for aid against the Japanese who occupied most of his country. In the end, however, Roosevelt and the others who favored concentrating on Europe first prevailed.

American and British troops attacked the Germans in North Africa in 1942.

Roosevelt was determined to attack the Germans somewhere in 1942. The military planners, however, disagreed about where to stage the attack. The Americans argued that the best way to defeat Germany was to drive across northern France and occupy the German industrial heartland along the Rhine River Valley. The British, especially Prime Minister Churchill, fiercely opposed this plan. Recalling the tragic losses suffered in the trench-style warfare of World War I, they feared that war in France would result in another bloodbath.

Victory in North Africa. Despite Soviet protests, the British finally persuaded President Roosevelt to agree to attack the Germans in North Africa. In **Operation Torch** British and American troops invaded North Africa in November 1942. The plan was to have British forces, under the command of Field Marshal Bernard Montgomery, attack Field Marshal Erwin Rommel's Afrika Korps at El Alamein in Egypt. Montgomery would then push Germany's Afrika Korps toward General **Dwight D. Eisenhower**'s American forces that would be moving eastward from Morocco. The British succeeded in pushing Rommel, who had gained the nickname the "Desert Fox" because of his uncanny ability to outmanuever his opponents in desert combat, westward across Libya to Tunisia. The Americans, however, were delayed by bad weather and were unable to trap Rommel as planned. Instead, the Desert Fox characteristically turned adversity into victory. He attacked General Eisenhower at Kasserine Pass, shown on the map on page 638, and soundly defeated the inexperienced American troops.

President Roosevelt went to Casablanca, Morocco, in January 1943. There, in the middle of the North African campaign, he met with Churchill and other Allied leaders at the **Casablanca Conference**. The Allies, partially

Field Marshal Erwin Rommel, the Desert Fox, shown below sporting a pair of captured British sun glasses, was finally routed from Africa by British and American forces in May 1943. Rommel would later be implicated in a plot to kill Hitler and be forced to ingest a fatal dose of poison. Below left, a member of Rommel's Afrika Korps surrenders to charging British troops at El Alamein.

map study

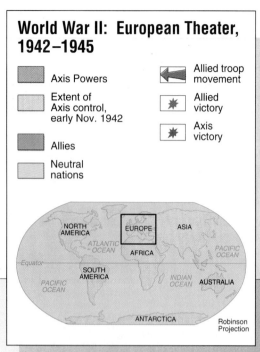

World War II: European Theater, 1942–1945

- Axis Powers
- Extent of Axis control, early Nov. 1942
- Allies
- Neutral nations
- Allied troop movement
- Allied victory
- Axis victory

NORTH AMERICA
ATLANTIC OCEAN
EUROPE
ASIA
AFRICA
PACIFIC OCEAN
Equator
SOUTH AMERICA
INDIAN OCEAN
AUSTRALIA
PACIFIC OCEAN
ANTARCTICA

Robinson Projection

Albers Equal-Area Projection   © SF

Movement   Compare this map with the one on page 616 showing German advances in 1940–1941. Note the change in direction of the arrows. In the winter of 1942–43, the tide of battle shifted in the Allies' favor. The German advance on the eastern front was turned back at Stalingrad and Soviet troops moved toward Germany through eastern Europe. The Allies recaptured North Africa and fought their way north through Italy. In 1944 the massive Allied invasion at Normandy began the final assault on Germany. Follow these events on the map. What is the last major battle shown?

Critical Thinking   Why did Soviet participation in World War II lead to Soviet domination of eastern Europe after the war?

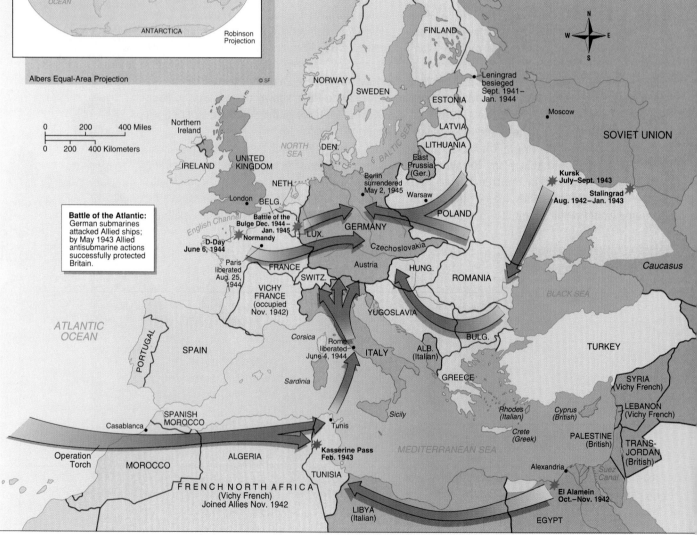

0   200   400 Miles
0   200   400 Kilometers

Battle of the Atlantic: German submarines attacked Allied ships; by May 1943 Allied antisubmarine actions successfully protected Britain.

FINLAND

Leningrad besieged Sept. 1941– Jan. 1944

Moscow

NORWAY
SWEDEN
ESTONIA
LATVIA
LITHUANIA
SOVIET UNION

Northern Ireland
NORTH SEA
DEN.
East Prussia (Ger.)

IRELAND
UNITED KINGDOM
NETH.
Berlin surrendered May 2, 1945
Warsaw
Kursk July–Sept. 1943
Stalingrad Aug. 1942–Jan. 1943

London
BELG.
BALTIC SEA
POLAND

English Channel
Battle of the Bulge Dec. 1944– Jan. 1945
LUX.
GERMANY
D-Day June 6, 1944
Normandy
Czechoslovakia

Paris liberated Aug. 25, 1944
FRANCE
SWITZ.
Austria
HUNG.
ROMANIA
Caucasus

VICHY FRANCE (occupied Nov. 1942)
YUGOSLAVIA
BLACK SEA

ATLANTIC OCEAN
Corsica
Rome liberated June 4, 1944
ITALY
BULG.
TURKEY

PORTUGAL
SPAIN
Sardinia
ALB. (Italian)
GREECE
SYRIA (Vichy French)
LEBANON (Vichy French)

Sicily
Rhodes (Italian)
Cyprus (British)
PALESTINE (British)
TRANS-JORDAN (British)

SPANISH MOROCCO
Tunis
Crete (Greek)
MEDITERRANEAN SEA
Alexandria
Suez Canal

Casablanca
Kasserine Pass Feb. 1943

Operation Torch
MOROCCO
ALGERIA
TUNISIA
El Alamein Oct.–Nov. 1942

FRENCH NORTH AFRICA (Vichy French) Joined Allies Nov. 1942
LIBYA (Italian)
EGYPT

as a result of pressure applied by Stalin, agreed to insist on the unconditional surrender of Germany, Italy, and Japan. They did this to reassure Stalin that Soviet lands would not end up in the hands of Germany at the end of the war. In addition, both Churchill and Roosevelt believed that calling for unconditional surrender would discourage Stalin from making a separate peace with Hitler, as Lenin had done with Germany during World War I.

In the meantime, General **George Patton** visited the American troops that had suffered defeat at the hands of the Desert Fox and gave them an inspiring talk that helped restore morale. Eventually, in May 1943, the American and British armies accomplished their goal of driving the Germans from Africa.

The battle for Italy. After achieving victory in North Africa, the Americans wanted to plan for the invasion of northern France. However, Winston Churchill and the British once again prevailed. They successfully argued for the invasion of the strategic Italian island of **Sicily** and then mainland Italy. Sicily was important, the British maintained, because it commanded supply routes through the Mediterranean region.

In July 1943 the Allies invaded Sicily. Within two weeks Mussolini was forced out of office and imprisoned. A new government, formed by Marshal Pietro Badoglio, signed an armistice on September 8, surrendering unconditionally to the Allies one day before the Allied invasion of Italy was scheduled to begin.

Shortly afterward, Nazi forces rescued Mussolini from prison and took him to northern Italy where he was installed by Hitler as head of a makeshift government. On October 13, however, Badoglio's government declared war on Germany.

Stiff German resistance hindered the Allies, but finally, on June 4, 1944, the Allies entered Rome. The Germans would continue to hold northern Italy until the spring of 1945, however, fighting a brutal rear-guard action.

The Battle of the Atlantic. While some Americans were battling Italy's rugged terrain, others were turning the tide in the Atlantic. The struggle for the control of the seas had begun with the British naval blockade of Germany at the outset of the war. Britain planted mines from Scotland to Norway and across the English Channel. Because the British navy was considerably superior to the German navy, Hitler realized the futility of challenging Allied supremacy at sea by the use of surface craft.

Although the Germans planted magnetic mines near the approaches to British harbors, British naval experts learned how to neutralize the magnetic fields of their ships and render them safe. The Germans then resorted to a familiar alternative: U-boat, or submarine, warfare. As in World War I, Germany hoped that Britain's lifeline could be cut by persistent,

African American pilots and support staff, above left, plot targets and formulate strategies during the campaign to liberate Italy from the Nazis. Above, Americans victoriously enter Palermo, Sicily, on July 22, 1943.

unrelenting attack. During the early months of the war, more than 650 Allied ships were destroyed by German submarines. The British countered by organizing a convoy system with covering aircraft that protected vessels near shore. The Nazi U-boats inflicted severe damage to Allied shipping, but by May 1943 the antisubmarine campaign, which was greatly aided by the United States, had succeeded in stemming German efforts to cripple Britain.

The German army suffered defeat on Europe's eastern front.

While the Americans and the British were fighting the Germans in Italy and on the Atlantic, the Soviet Union was making gigantic strides toward the defeat of the Nazis on Europe's eastern front. Hitler's armies suffered their greatest defeat in **Stalingrad**, the city named in honor of the Soviet dictator, in the bitter cold Russian winter of 1942–1943. At Stalingrad, located on the map on page 638, the Red Army stopped Hitler's drive eastward by surrounding and either killing or capturing more than 300,000 German soldiers.

The Germans launched one last grand attack in the Soviet Union in the summer of 1943 at Kursk, which developed into the biggest tank battle of the war. Despite some initial success for the Germans, the Battle of Kursk turned into an overwhelming victory for the Soviets. After Kursk, the German army could never again launch a major offensive against the Soviet Union. The Germans fought desperately against the Soviets for the rest of the war, but the Red Army drove relentlessly across the Soviet Union, through eastern Europe, and into Germany itself. Nazi propaganda terrified Germans with stories of Soviet atrocities.

A winter-camouflaged Soviet ski patrol, below, prepares to engage Nazi forces in the Soviet Union's Murmansk wilderness. Soviet troops were far better prepared for fighting in the harsh winters of the north than were the Germans. Below right, General Eisenhower briefs paratroopers for the D-Day invasion.

Hordes of German refugees fled westward from the Soviets. Hitler had intended to turn all of eastern Europe into a German-controlled slave empire. Ironically, his war virtually emptied eastern Europe of Germans who had lived there for centuries.

The British and the Americans attacked Germany at Normandy.

Plans for the invasion of France had been one of the major considerations of the Allies since 1942. Preparations for the assault neared the final stages in early 1944. Nearly three million trained Allied troops massed in Britain; ships and landing craft collected at British ports. Utmost secrecy was maintained. Diversionary raids along the English Channel put the Germans off guard. They did not expect the Allies to invade the **Normandy Peninsula**, because this part of the French coast lacked natural ports and had extreme tidal variations that presented navigational hazards. Furthermore, it was defended by Hitler's "Atlantic Wall," which included many miles of underwater obstacles.

Operation Overlord, the name given to the Normandy invasion plan, was under the supreme command of General Eisenhower. On June 6, 1944, the day known as **D-Day**, Eisenhower's troops moved across the English Channel. The Germans were subjected to a *blitzkrieg*, Allied style. Five thousand ships approached German beach emplacements while paratroopers were dropped behind the German coastal defenses. Allied fighterplanes out-

numbered the *Luftwaffe* 50 to 1. After a week of fighting, the invasion army held a 60-mile strip of the Normandy beach. In July the Allied armored divisions broke through the German lines, opening the door to the rest of France. By August Paris was liberated.

The Allied invasion of Germany forced the Nazis to surrender.

In October the advancing Allied columns entered Germany near Aachen. Two months later, however, Hitler surprised them by staging his last major offensive of the war in the West. This bloody offensive became known as the **Battle of the Bulge** because German tanks formed a bulge 80 miles long and 50 miles wide into Allied territory. Although the Nazis made impressive gains initially, American and British airpower eventually overwhelmed them. In addition, the advance of Soviet troops toward Berlin forced Hitler to dispatch most of his troops to the eastern front.

The Yalta Conference. As the Allied air offensive destroyed or seriously damaged every major German city and the Soviets moved closer to Berlin, the Allies sensed victory. In February 1945 Roosevelt, Churchill, and Stalin met at Yalta, a Soviet seaport and resort on the Black Sea. During the historic **Yalta Conference**, Roosevelt wanted Stalin to promise to fight Japan when the war in Europe ended. Stalin wanted to keep Poland and much of eastern Europe in a Soviet zone of influence. Although Churchill was against Stalin's proposal, the Soviet Union was in a strong negotiating position. Its armies already occupied most of eastern Europe. Roosevelt, although he also did not want to give Stalin too many concessions, was in a weak position because he faced a savage war against Japan.

In the end, Stalin promised to enter the Pacific War three months after Germany's surrender. In return, Roosevelt offered extensive concessions in eastern Europe and Asia. Stalin was allowed to claim lands in eastern Europe under the condition that free elections be held after the war. No method of supervision or enforcement was provided, however. In addition, Stalin was allowed to control Manchuria.

OICES FROM THE PAST

Showing What We Could Do

World War II brought significant changes to Winona Espinosa. She moved from Colorado to California to become a riveter, a wife, a mother, and a bus driver. How does she describe the war's impact on American women?

I just saw a sign on a bus downtown one day that said, "I need you," and I went and applied. I hadn't even been driving very long. I only learned to drive a car after I got to San Diego, and I didn't know anything about driving a big vehicle like that. But the war really created opportunities for women. It was the first time we got a chance to show that we could do a lot of things that only men had done before. . . .

I drove buses and streetcars for about two and a half years. In fact, I was driving a bus the day the war ended. I let everybody ride my bus free that day.

Although some historians have charged that Roosevelt "sold out" at Yalta, others believe that the president had done as well as he could have considering the circumstances. Regardless, Yalta represented a major diplomatic victory for Stalin, one that reflected the Soviet Union's tremendous contribution to the Allied victory in Europe.

The D-Day invasion of the Normandy Peninsula by the Allies on June 6, 1944, was a massive undertaking. In one day alone, more than 150,000 Allied forces stormed the heavily mined beaches. By day's end, the Allies suffered 10,000 casualties.

The Holocaust.

This painting depicts the suffering of the people of Warsaw, Poland, where as many as a half million Jews were executed or left to die from disease or starvation. The artist, Zygmunt Menkes, lost his entire family to the Nazis.

Hitler's hold on the German people lasted almost until the end of the war. Nazi propaganda kept the people's hope alive with talk of secret weapons and terrified them with the prospect of occupation by the Soviet Union. Hitler's strong-arm tactics had made him many enemies, however.

After an unsuccessful bid to assassinate him in July 1944, Hitler and his fanatical Nazi leaders took the opportunity to eliminate their enemies, including top-ranking generals. Hitler spent the last months of his life in an underground bunker in Berlin, drifting further and further from reality. He sent orders to units that had long ceased to exist. He dismissed officers who protested that they no longer had soldiers. He remained obsessed with the murder of the Jews.

Following Hitler's orders, his death squads worked feverishly into the last months of the war. This they did in spite of the fact that almost all hope for a German victory had evaporated. Hitler had directed persecution policies against the Jews since the mid-1930s, but the **Final Solution**, which was the plan to murder all Jews and other "racially inferior" peoples, only began in earnest in 1942. During that year Hitler's henchmen had begun building extermination and concentration camps throughout Germany and other eastern European nations.

As the Allies moved farther into Germany, they uncovered these camps and their horrifying truths. They discovered the gas chambers and the incinerators in which six million Jews were mercilessly put to death. Perhaps as many as five million people considered "undesirable" to the Nazis—Poles, Czechs, Russians, Gypsies, homosexuals, and the mentally and physically handicapped—were also slaughtered. The **Holocaust**, as the mass murders became known, shocked the world as its gruesome details came to light. General Omar Bradley, who toured Germany's Ohrdruf concentration camp on April 12, 1945, would never forget what he saw that day:

The smell of death over- **AN AMERICAN ★ SPEAKS** whelmed us even before we passed through the stockade. More than 3,200 naked, emaciated bodies had been flung into shallow graves. Others lay in the street where they had fallen.

Petr Fischl, a Polish Jew, died in a Nazi extermination camp in Auschwitz, Poland, in 1944 at the age of 15. One of 15,000 children who passed through the Terezin Concentration Camp before being sent to Auschwitz, he left this descripton of his final days:

We got used to undeserved slaps, blows and executions. We got accustomed to seeing people die in their own excrement, to seeing piled-up coffins full of corpses, to seeing the sick amidst dirt and filth and to seeing the helpless doctors. We got used to it that from time to time, one thousand unhappy souls would come here and that, from time to time, another thousand souls would go away. . . .

Germany's surrender. On March 17 Allied forces under the command of General Eisenhower began advancing on Berlin in a wide front. Soviet forces began moving in from the east. In the last week of April, both forces descended upon the capital.

On April 30, with the Soviets only miles away from Hitler's bunker in central Berlin, the deranged dictator finally realized that his grand plans had failed. In despair, he passed a cyanide capsule to Eva Braun, his longtime mistress. She positioned herself comfortably on a couch in the corner of the bunker and then bit the capsule. Within seconds she was dead. After shooting Blondi, his German shepherd, Hitler then bit a cyanide capsule himself. Before the pill did its work, he positioned himself next to his mistress on the couch and then raised a pistol to his head and fired. Hitler's guards, loyal to the last minute, hurriedly burned their führer's remains and buried him in a shallow grave. The Soviets arrived moments later.

With or without Hitler, the Nazis were doomed. On May 8, 1945, General Eisenhower accepted their unconditional surrender. The Allies were victorious in Europe and the United States could now turn its firepower on Japan.

SECTION 2 REVIEW

Identify Key People and Terms
Write a sentence to identify: George Marshall, Operation Torch, Dwight D. Eisenhower, Casablanca Conference, George Patton, Operation Overlord, D-Day, Battle of the Bulge, Yalta Conference, Final Solution, Holocaust

Locate Key Places
1. Why did the British want to capture Sicily before invading France?
2. Why was Stalingrad a watershed on Europe's eastern front?
3. Why was the Normandy Peninsula chosen as the site for the D-Day invasion?

Master the Main Ideas
1. **Studying international cooperative efforts:** Why did the Americans agree to make the defeat of Nazi Germany their top priority?
2. **Analyzing information: (a)** Where did the Americans commit most of their troops in 1942 and 1943? **(b)** Why were they sent there?
3. **Evaluating information:** Why did the Nazis have such a difficult time fighting the Soviets on the eastern front?
4. **Perceiving cause/effect relationships:** Why did Operation Overlord work so well?
5. **Analyzing international cooperative efforts:** Explain why Hitler's defeat was a cooperative effort.

Apply Critical Thinking Skills: Identifying Assumptions
What assumptions did the Germans make about the Normandy Peninsula before June 1944?

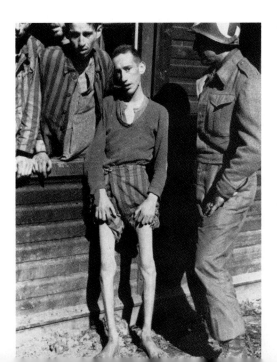

Margaret Bourke-White's haunting photograph of prisoners at the Buchenwald concentration camp, opposite page, right, and other photos of Holocaust survivors taken by Allied troops as they liberated the camps, told the world the true nature of the Holocaust. The Jewish women, opposite page, left, were liberated near Bergen-Belsen a week before the end of the war. The boxcar behind them is loaded with Jewish victims. Left, a Jewish man liberated from the Langenstein concentration camp lifts his trousers to show his emaciated condition. He once weighed 190 pounds.

SECTION 3

The United States led the offensive against Japan.

Key Terms: Battle of the Coral Sea, Battle of Midway, Manhattan Project

Reading Preview
As you read this section, you will learn:

1. why Japan began suffering setbacks in mid-1942.
2. how the Battle of Midway affected the Japanese.
3. how geography helped dictate war strategy in the Pacific.

A carrier-launched American dive-bomber buzzes a Japanese warship during the Battle of Midway in June 1942. The American victory at Midway severely crippled Japan's ability to carry on an offensive war.

Several months before the Japanese bombed Pearl Harbor on December 7, 1941, Prime Minister Tojo of Japan asked Admiral Isoroku Yamamoto if Japan could defeat the United States in a war. Yamamoto replied: "In the event of such a war, the Navy could give the enemy great trouble for six months or a year. After that I do not know." His prediction proved uncannily accurate.

Complacency and greed led to Japanese setbacks.

The Japanese enjoyed an almost unbroken series of victories for six months after Pearl Harbor. These easy victories led to complacency and conquests beyond the original plan. The Japanese militarists decided to seize a series of lightly defended islands in the southwest Pacific. They also intended to take **Midway Island**, which the map on page 648 shows is strategically located between Hawaii and Japan. While the Japanese planned these attacks, they received a shock from the Americans.

In April 1942 a special team of American airmen, led by the famous racing pilot Jimmy Doolittle, took off on a daring mission. They flew long-distance, land-based bombers from the aircraft carrier *Hornet* to launch a surprise attack on Japan itself. Although Doolittle's 16 raiders did little physical damage, they severely embarrassed Japanese leaders. In retaliation, the Japanese massacred more than 250,000 Chinese peasants in the districts where the American aircraft landed after the raid. They also decided to lessen the chance of another attack by extending their zone of control.

For the Japanese the time was now ripe to go ahead with their plan to isolate Australia, an Allied nation, by seizing a chain of islands anchored to New Guinea, the second largest island in the world. When the American code breakers uncovered this plan, the United States Navy marshalled its scarce resources to prevent it from being carried out.

What followed was the **Battle of the Coral Sea**, which took place in May 1942. This battle proved conclusively that the aircraft carrier had replaced the battleship as the most formidable naval weapon. The Japanese and American fleets never sighted one another during the course of the battle. All of the combat took place among the opposing aircraft.

Although both sides suffered many losses, the Battle of the Coral Sea was a strategic victory for the Americans because it halted the advance on Australia. Coral Sea was a significant setback for the Japanese, but the next major sea battle would prove to be a disaster.

The Japanese never recovered from their defeat at the Battle of Midway.

In June 1942 the Japanese assembled more than 150 warships for a major attack on Midway Island. They intended not only to capture the island but also to destroy the last remnants of the American fleet.

Such arrogance cost the Japanese. They grossly underestimated American strength and will to fight. The Japanese also failed in their effort to pull off a surprise attack because, once again, the Americans had broken the Japanese code and knew the attack was coming.

Although the Americans suffered high casualties initially, carrier-launched American dive bombers caught three Japanese carriers by surprise. Mitsuo Fuchida, who had led the aerial attack on Pearl Harbor, was on the flagship aircraft carrier *Akagi* when the Americans hit. He later recalled:

> *We had been caught flatfooted in the most vulnerable position possible—decks loaded with planes armed and fueled for attack. Looking about, I was horrified by the destruction that had been wrought in a matter of seconds. There was a huge hole in the flight deck just behind the amidship elevator. The elevator itself, twisted like molten glass, was drooping into a hangar. Deck plates reeled upward in grotesque configurations. Planes stood tail up, belching livid flame and jet-black smoke. Reluctant tears streamed down my cheeks as I watched the fires spread, and I was terrified at the prospect of induced explosions which would surely doom the ship.*

Within minutes, explosions tore apart the three carriers. The Japanese fleet retreated, thus marking the first defeat ever suffered by the modern Japanese navy.

The **Battle of Midway** was a significant victory for the Americans. Not only did it allow them to gain a foothold in the central Pacific, it severely crippled Japan's ability to carry on an offensive war. A long, difficult war still lay ahead, but the Japanese would soon become reactors instead of actors in the Pacific theater of war.

Geography dictated an island-hopping strategy in the Pacific.

Strategically, the war against Japan in the Pacific was very different from the war against Germany in Europe. Japan's empire, which included many Pacific islands south and east of Japan, could not be conquered in the same fashion that the Soviets and Americans swept over Germany. The vast expanses of the Pacific dictated that victories would be secured through amphibious, island-hopping campaigns. The navy, the army and navy air forces, and the marines would be the key players.

American military strategists believed that two separate American operations would be needed to defeat Japan. The first operation called for the American forces based in Australia to rout Japanese forces from New Guinea, pushing northward. From New Guinea these forces would then liberate the Philippines, a U.S. territory that had fallen to the Japanese early in the war. General Douglas MacArthur, who had promised to return after the disastrous American defeat at Bataan, would spearhead this operation. The second operation, headed by Admiral **Chester Nimitz**, would involve capturing Japanese-held islands

Japan's suicide air corps, known as the kamikazes, wreaked havoc on American ships toward the end of the war. In the Philippines alone, 424 kamikaze pilots met their deaths as they attempted to crash-dive their Zero fighterplanes into Allied ships. U.S. Vice Admiral Charles R. Brown, who witnessed many kamikaze attacks, recalled that: "There was a hypnotic fascination to a sight so alien to our Western philosophy. We watched each plunging kamikaze with the detached horror of one witnessing a terrible spectacle rather than as the intended victim. . . . And dominating it all was a strange mixture of respect and pity."

in the central Pacific. Once far enough west, both operations would be able to build air bases from which to conduct bombing missions on Japan.

Nimitz's forces made the first move in the Pacific by orchestrating the invasion of the Solomon Islands. Their main target was the key island of **Guadalcanal**. Guadalcanal was important to the Americans because intelligence reports indicated that the Japanese were beginning to build an air base there. As the map on page 648 shows, a Japanese air base on Guadalcanal would mean that Japanese planes could reach other Pacific islands that were still controlled by the Allies. If these islands were taken, Japan would be able to wreak havoc on U.S.–Australian shipping lanes.

Determined to prevent such a disaster, members of the 1st Marine Division fought a savage six-month battle with the Japanese. Not only did the marines have to fight the enemy,

they had to contend with a most inhospitable environment. According to one marine:

Guadalcanal was a mass of slops and stinks and pestilence; of scum-crusted lagoons and swamps inhabited by giant crocodiles; a place of spiders as big as your fist and wasps as long as your finger. . . . And Guadalcanal stank. She was sour with the odor of her own decay, her breath so hot and humid, so sullen and so still, that the Marines cursed and swore to feel the vitality oozing from them in a steady stream of enervating sweat.

AN AMERICAN ★ SPEAKS

Despite the hardships on Guadalcanal, the marines persevered and emerged victorious. For the Japanese, who had lost 23,000 of the 36,000 men they sent to fight, the defeat was wrenching. In the future they would aptly refer to Guadalcanal as the "Island of Death."

Guadalcanal inspired the Americans. In late 1943 and early 1944, American forces under the command of Admiral Nimitz swept northward through the central Pacific with blinding speed, scoring victories in the Gilbert, Marshall, and Caroline islands.

The victories in these island chains—at such places as Tarawa in the Gilbert Islands—were not easy ones. The tenacious, disciplined Japanese soldiers proved to be formidable adversaries time and time again. They believed that surrender was so shameful that they often fought to the last man. Rather than give in, many preferred suicide. On many occasions a soon-to-be-captured Japanese soldier would pull the pin of a grenade just in time to take a few marines along with him to the afterlife. At other times, Japanese soldiers would commit *seppuku*, an honorable form of suicide practiced for many years by members of the Japanese warrior class. *Seppuku* involved ripping one's abdomen apart with a knife.

Victory in the Marianas. In June and July of 1944 Americans penetrated the inner defense of the **Mariana Islands**. One of these islands, **Saipan**, was the scene of one of America's most important World War II victories. In terms of American casualties, it was also one of the costliest.

Henry Bake, at left, and George Kirk, Navajos in the U.S. Marine Corps, operate a radio in 1943 on Bougainville Island in the Pacific. More than 400 Navajo marine "code talkers" helped maintain security by transmitting orders in a Navajo code.

On June 15 an armada of 535 American ships carrying about 130,000 marines and army troops began their assault of the 70-square-mile island. Their goal was to dislodge 30,000 Japanese troops that had burrowed into the tropical island's hilly terrain. The marines who stormed Saipan's beaches on the first day were hit hard by Japanese artillery. The 2nd Marine Division alone lost 2,000 men that day.

Over the next three weeks, the Americans slowly pushed the Japanese soldiers toward the cliffs that guarded the island's north shore. Accompanying the soldiers were more than 20,000 Japanese civilians—men, women, and children—who were permanent residents of the island. During the drive northward 12,000 more American soldiers lost their lives. The Japanese casualties, both soldiers and citizens, were even higher.

As the retreating Japanese reached the cliffs, with no hope of reinforcement and no place else to go, defeat was a certainty. The Japanese commander refused to give up, however. He organized one last counterattack during which up to 5,000 charging soldiers were killed. Finally recognizing the hopelessness of the situation, he committed *seppuku* rather than surrender. Although American commanders assured the Japanese over their loudspeakers that they would be treated honorably, many were convinced that the Americans would brutalize them. Rather than subject themselves to such treatment, they decided to take what they considered to be a more honorable way out of their predicament. As the Americans looked on in disbelief and horror, as many as 20,000 Japanese soldiers and civilians leaped from the cliffs to their deaths. In the end, only 11,000 of the more than 50,000 Japanese on Saipan survived to surrender.

The victory at Saipan and on other islands in the Marianas enabled the Americans to begin building airfields from which they could base air attacks on Japan itself. Only 1,300 miles separated Japan from the Marianas, an easy journey for the nation's new super plane, the B-29 bomber. By October 1944 the first of these airfields, Saipan's Isley Field, was completed. From Isley scores of B-29s began the first of many successful bombing missions of Japan. Within the next ten months, they would severely damage 66 Japanese cities. Their success proved to the U.S. military establishment that air power had come into its own. Two years after the war this accomplishment was recognized with the establishment of the U.S. Air Force, a separate branch of the military on equal footing with the army and navy.

Victory in the Philippines. While Nimitz's forces fought for the Marianas, General MacArthur was busy completing his campaign in New Guinea. By September 1944 New

Three years after fleeing the Philippines, General Douglas MacArthur fulfills his promise to return to the islands. The American victory in the Philippines effectively destroyed all that remained of the Japanese imperial fleet.

THE ATOMIC BOMB
Skill: Testing Conclusions

Introducing the Skill. In June of 1945, an advisory committee on nuclear energy sent a report to President Truman. The report recommended that the atomic bomb be used against Japan as soon as possible and without prior warning about the nature of the weapon. From the report, Truman concluded that dropping the atomic bomb on Japan was a justifiable way to end the war quickly. Was the president's decision valid?

Learning the Skill. To answer this question requires **testing conclusions** made by Truman. Were his reasons for deciding to drop the bomb accurate? Were they the right reasons? To test a conclusion, use these guidelines:
1. State the conclusion clearly.
2. Identify any stated or unstated reasons given to support the

conclusion, including specific facts, rules, or generalizations.
3. Distinguish relevant reasons from irrelevant reasons, omitting the irrelevant ones.
4. Evaluate the reasons, based on accuracy and consistency. In effect, do all the reasons logically support the conclusion?

Applying the Skill. Consider the following list of information, given as reasons for Truman's decision to use the atomic bomb against Japan.

a. Plans for defeating Japan without the atomic bomb called for the direct involvement of some five million men and for fighting until at least late 1946.

b. Continuing the air and sea bombardment and blockade would mean heavy losses for both the Allies and Japanese. Japanese suicide planes had already sunk 34

American ships and damaged 285 others. Likewise, an Allied bombing mission on Tokyo had left an estimated 97,000 Japanese dead, 125,000 wounded, and 1.2 million homeless.

c. The Japanese government had rejected terms for an unconditional surrender and had given indications that its intention was to fight to the death.

d. Test results from New Mexico indicated that the atomic bomb could be deployed successfully, with a power so destructive that Japan would be forced to surrender.

1. Review the above information and your text. Do you believe the information Truman considered warranted the use of the bomb?
2. What other information might you consider relevant to testing the president's conclusion?

prepared to fight to the last man rather than unconditionally surrender.

Truman, meanwhile, did not want to sacrifice American lives in what would certainly be a bloody confrontation on Japan. He also did not want to soften the conditions for surrender. Truman believed he had no choice but to authorize the use of the bomb.

Truman's authorization was carried out swiftly. During the early morning of August 6, 1945, an American B-29 named the *Enola Gay* quietly passed over the city of **Hiroshima** and dropped a single bomb from its cargo bay. The hundreds of thousands of citizens below—

scurrying to their jobs, eating breakfast, dressing their children—never knew what hit them. The solitary explosion produced a fireball so powerful that 60,000 people were instantly incinerated. Four square miles of city were literally leveled within the blink of an eye. The effects of the bomb were not all experienced instantaneously, however. The radiation that emanated from the explosion caused numerous slow and agonizing deaths. In all, the casualties from the single bomb would exceed 200,000 in the years ahead.

Despite the unprecedented destruction, President Truman believed he was fully justified in authorizing the dropping of the bomb. He said:

AN AMERICAN ★ SPEAKS

We have used [the bomb] against those who attacked us without warning at Pearl Harbor, against those who have starved and beaten and executed American prisoners, against those who have abandoned all pretense of obeying international laws of warfare. We have used it to shorten the agony of war.

Yasuo Takeyama, a 22-year-old naval officer, had just boarded a train when the bomb hit:

I clawed my way out of the station precincts and ran to seek the designated shelter at the Imperial Army's east drill ground, only to step right into an inferno of piles and piles of dead bodies, with their thin summer clothes ripped off and their faces, heads, and torsos scorched, some of them half-immersed in muddy pools of water, and faint and dying groans of "water, water" rising on all sides. . . . The next thing I knew I found myself in one of the shelters the Army had managed to set up all across the city, in the company of a young girl cradling herself in tattered shreds of what must have been a white summer blouse, and miserably sobbing at the reflection of her terribly burned face in her hand mirror.

On August 9 another atomic bomb destroyed **Nagasaki**. Then, as promised at Yalta, the Soviet Union entered the war and quickly overran the Japanese forces in Manchuria, where the war had started 14 years before. Japan's Emperor Hirohito finally insisted upon surrender, saying to his government: "That it is unbearable for me to see my loyal troops disarmed goes without saying, but the time has come to bear the unbearable."

The emperor's radio broadcast on August 15 came as a severe shock to the Japanese people, many of whom were prepared to continue to fight for their nation's honor. General MacArthur accepted the formal surrender on the battleship *Missouri* in Tokyo Bay on September 2, 1945, and the American occupation of Japan proceeded without resistance.

Top, a mushroom cloud rises from the atomic explosion at Nagasaki. Above, a wounded youngster grasps a ball of rice given to him by a relief agency shortly after the bomb hit Hiroshima. Left, modern Hiroshima has retained some of the ruins of the blast as a memorial to those who lost their lives.

The dropping of the atomic bombs produced widespread feelings of relief in America at the time. These powerful weapons had brought an end to the war. The bombs seemed to be a quick method of producing the same effects that the B-29 raids had been producing for months. In time, however, as the full horror of radiation poisoning became known, Americans realized the enormous destructiveness of these weapons and some people began to question the morality of nuclear warfare.

SECTION 3 REVIEW

Identify Key People and Terms
Write a sentence to identify: Battle of the Coral Sea, Battle of Midway, Chester Nimitz, Harry S. Truman, Manhattan Project

Locate Key Places
1. The following places were the sites of major World War II battles: Guadalcanal, Leyte Gulf, Midway Island, Mariana Islands. Using the map on page 648, describe the location of each of these places in relation to either Japan or Hawaii.
2. Why was Saipan important to the United States?
3. What memories will probably always be associated with the cities of Hiroshima and Nagasaki?

Master the Main Ideas
1. **Studying the effect of U.S. involvement in international conflicts:** Why did the Japanese begin to suffer setbacks after their early victories?
2. **Perceiving cause/effect relationships:** Why was the Battle of Midway a significant American victory?
3. **Sequencing historical data:** Arrange the following Pacific battles in chronological order: Guadalcanal, Philippines, Saipan, Iwo Jima

Applying Critical Thinking Skills: Identifying Alternatives
What alternatives did President Truman have before making his decision to use the atomic bomb?

The war changed America's role in the world.

Key Terms: rationing, internment camps

Reading Preview
As you read this section, you will learn:
1. how the war helped America.
2. why Japanese Americans were forced into internment camps during the war.
3. how American perceptions of their role in the world were changed by the war.

Although their losses were enormous, the American people were spared the devastation commonplace in Europe and east Asia after the war. By contrast, the war had stimulated the American economy, brought new job opportunities to women and minorities, and changed America's role in world affairs.

World War II stimulated the American economy.

As orders for war supplies flooded American factories, ten years of economic depression came to an end. Federal spending rose from $9.6 billion in 1940 to $95 billion in 1945. Of this amount, $85 billion went to the armed forces. This high level of government spending stimulated the American economy and brought back full employment.

The demand for workers was so great that it produced massive internal shifts in the population. As 12 million Americans entered military service, another 20 million left their homes to seek work in the booming war industries. California's population grew by almost two million as Midwesterners and Mexican Americans from the Southwest relocated there.

African Americans. Although America needed workers, discriminatory policies prevented African Americans from landing high paying jobs in defense-related industries during the early years of the war. In addition, African Americans suffered from discriminatory practices in the armed forces. Although they wanted to do as much as they could to defeat Germany and Japan, very few African Americans were allowed to join the marines. They were allowed to join the army, which 700,000 blacks did, but they were forced to serve in segregated units that were usually led by white officers. These soldiers even had segregated entertainment facilities.

In 1941 **A. Philip Randolph**, head of the Brotherhood of Sleeping Car Porters, organized a March on Washington to bring an end to discrimination in defense jobs and to segregation in the armed forces. In return for a promise not to conduct the march, President Roosevelt issued an executive order prohibiting discrimination in the war industries. However, nothing was done to improve the situations of the African American military personnel. President Roosevelt's actions left a bittersweet taste in Randolph's mouth. He expressed the views of other African Americans when he said:

Though I have found no Negroes who want to see the **AN AMERICAN ★ SPEAKS** United Nations [Allies] lose this war, I have found many who, before the war ends, want to see the stuffing knocked out of white supremacy and of empire over subject peoples. American Negroes, involved as we are in the general issues of the conflict, are confronted not with a choice but with the challenge both to win democracy for ourselves at home and to help win the war for democracy the world over.

As a result of Randolph's efforts to gain job opportunities for African Americans, more than one million African Americans left the South and moved to northern cities such as **Detroit** during the war. Detroit, with its huge Chrysler Tank Arsenal and a new Ford factory, was the wartime defense production capital.

Although many blacks landed good paying jobs in Detroit and other cities, they suffered from discriminatory housing practices and other forms of discrimination. By 1943 disgruntled African Americans began to speak out against these unfair policies. During the summer riots broke out in Detroit between blacks

and whites. Twenty-five blacks and nine whites were killed. Another 700 people were injured.

Detroit was not the only scene of racial violence that summer. However, as more job opportunities opened up because of labor shortages, wages and housing conditions for those in the cities improved.

Despite the improved conditions, African Americans learned a valuable lesson during the war. Positive changes were not going to just happen. If blacks were going to achieve racial equality and full civil rights, they were going to have to take the initiative. To Jesse Hall, an African American who moved his family from Arkansas to Detroit in 1942, the war symbolized the beginning of an era of improvement. He said:

We aren't going to go back to where we were before the **AN AMERICAN ★ SPEAKS** war. We've shed our blood and proved our loyalty, and we're going to fight for all that is rightfully due us. We won't turn back.

Women. The war brought new opportunities for women as well as for African Americans. More than 250,000 women joined the military forces in noncombat postings and millions of women entered the work force.

Most of the women who joined the military entered the Women's Army Corps (WAC). Texas newspaper publisher, **Oveta Culp Hobby**, directed the WAC throughout the

American women aided the war effort on the homefront as well as in every theater of the war. Below left, women rivet sections of an aircraft engine compartment. Below, posters such as this one helped recruit women for a variety of positions in the armed forces.

war. Other women enlisted in the navy (WAVES), the Coast Guard (SPARS), and the Women's Auxiliary Ferrying Squadron (WAFS). Some women also entered the Women's Reserve of the Marine Corps.

Before the war, married women were encouraged to stay at home with their families. By 1942, however, songs such as "We're the Janes Who Make the Planes" urged women to put on pants, tie up their hair in bandannas, and contribute to the war effort. More than six million previously unemployed women joined the work force. " Rosie the Riveter" in her overalls and cap soon became the symbol of the woman wage earner "making history working for victory."

As more and more women were trained for skilled jobs, union membership climbed. Eight hundred thousand women belonged to unions in 1940. By 1944 the number had risen to more than three million.

Despite the number of American women who were drawn into the work force, mobilization levels did not reach those of Britain, where women were drafted into war work. Nor did they match those of the Soviet Union, where women served in combat units. After the war, three-quarters of the female wartime

Go for Broke!

The 442nd Regimental Combat Team was called the "Christmas Tree regiment" for its many decoratons for bravery. No American army unit in history ever earned more awards and few endured more casualties. The 442nd had one further distinction: its soldiers were Nisei (nē sā'), second-generation Japanese Americans.

The unit began with the 100th Battalion of the Hawaiian National Guard, which was largely composed of Nisei. Called up after Pearl Harbor, these soldiers helped man Hawaii's defenses for months, but then they were abruptly recalled, shipped to Wisconsin, and issued wooden rifles for training. The men clamored for a chance to

fight, and in 1943 the War Department formed a Nisei unit, the 442nd, with the 100th Battalion as its nucleus. Most of the all-volunteer unit came from Hawaii; about a third enlisted from the mainland.

Some of the Nisei soldiers had been living in the internment camps where many Japanese Americans had been placed during the war. Ironically, many of the volunteers who would be

fighting to free Europe had friends and families living behind barbed wire in the United States.

Sent to Europe, the 442nd fought against the Germans house by house, hill by hill up the length of Italy. In seven costly campaigns, the 442nd attacked with a headlong intensity reflected in its motto, "Go for broke!" The Nisei soldiers suffered more than 9,000 casualties and accumulated more than

Members of the 442nd Regimental Combat Team, right, head for the Italian front in 1943. Nisei soldiers, far right, visit their families and friends while on furlough at a USO club in Heart Mountain, Wyoming.

Highlights of American Life

workers remained employed, but the majority saw their wages fall.

As labor unions increased their membership, their bargaining power also increased. Ordinary working people prospered because plentiful overtime increased their wages.

Once people had more money to spend, the demand for goods increased. By using price controls and increased taxation, the government kept inflation under control. Through **rationing**, or issuing coupons to limit how much a person can buy, the government reduced demand, but assured people of a minimum supply of scarce goods.

18,000 individual citations for valor, including one Medal of Honor, 52 Distinguished Service Crosses, and 560 Silver Stars.
By war's end the 442nd had received seven Presidential Distinguished Unit Citations. In saluting the Nisei soldiers, President Truman said, "You fought not only the enemy, but you fought prejudice—and you won."

Mexican Americans. Besides bringing new job opportunities to women and to African Americans, the wartime labor shortage also stimulated an influx of Mexican workers. Almost 400,000 Mexican Americans served in the military. Although prejudice resulted in some wartime riots and discrimination against Hispanics—even those in uniform—the economic conditions of most improved significantly. The most blatant incidents of discrimination took place on the West Coast against the Japanese Americans.

Racism forced Japanese Americans into internment camps.

Racial prejudice against Japanese Americans was deeply rooted in the United States long before the Japanese attack of Pearl Harbor. Some West Coast farmers resented Japanese American success in truck farming. This was evident in an article published in the *Saturday Evening Post* in May 1942 in which the Grower-Shipper Vegetable Association expressed their racist views: "We're charged with wanting to get rid of the [Japanese] for selfish reasons. We might as well be honest. We do. . . . They came into this valley to work, and they stayed to take over. . . ."

After Pearl Harbor prejudice against the Japanese Americans intensified as anti-Asian groups spread fears that they would commit acts of sabotage. Although some officials genuinely believed that a danger of sabotage or espionage existed, no evidence of such conspiracies ever surfaced.

In February 1942, however, President Roosevelt responded to pressure from paranoid military officers and self-seeking farmers and politicians by ordering the establishment of the War Relocation Authority. This agency had the job of evacuating more than 110,000 Japanese Americans from the West Coast and shipping them off to **internment camps** located in isolated parts of California, Arizona, Utah, Colorado, Wyoming, Arkansas, and Idaho. The barbed-wire-enclosed internment camps were like prisons. The men, women, and children who were forced to stay in them lived in wooden shacks furnished only with the barest

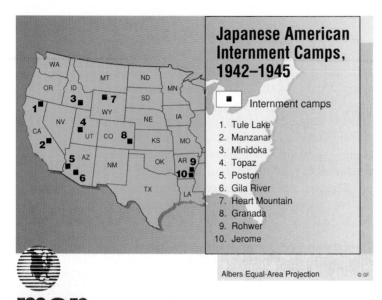

Japanese American Internment Camps, 1942–1945

■ Internment camps

1. Tule Lake
2. Manzanar
3. Minidoka
4. Topaz
5. Poston
6. Gila River
7. Heart Mountain
8. Granada
9. Rohwer
10. Jerome

Albers Equal-Area Projection   © SF

map study

Location
The map shows locations of camps set up to intern Japanese Americans during World War II. The move for internment gained momentum after the Japanese attack on Pearl Harbor in December, 1941. More than 110,000 people were sent to these camps under the authority of the federal government. In which states were internment camps located?

Critical Thinking
Why were internment camps located in isolated areas away from the West Coast?

of necessities—cots, light bulbs, and not much else. Food, medical care, and schools were inadequate at best.

Sumio Nichi was in the food business in California in the 1930s. A second-generation Japanese American, he was ordered in 1942 to leave for an internment camp. Years later, he was asked how this order affected his activities. He explained:

We had a big farm near Salinas, California. Lettuce, celery, cauliflower. . . . We had our own packinghouse. . . . We had an inventory of $80,000 worth of equipment. The people around, the whites, knew we had to leave. They were just standing around, waiting. I was thinking of storing it, but they told us we couldn't do it. It would be hampering the war effort. So they set up appraisers. I got $6,000 for it. After the war . . . I took a trip back to Salinas. I couldn't lease one acre of land. Nothing available. The people who took over our place, they're doing quite well.

AN AMERICAN ★ SPEAKS

Despite their treatment, Japanese Americans were eager to prove their loyalty to the United States in whatever way they could. As soon as the government permitted them to do so, 18,000 signed up for military duty and went to Europe to fight in the 442nd Regimental Combat Team. In the hills of Italy and in eastern France, the 442nd saw some of the heaviest

fighting of the war. At the war's end, it had won fame as one of the most decorated units in United States military history.

In December 1944 the Supreme Court heard the case of *Korematsu* v. *United States*. The Court upheld the constitutionality of the evacuation order. However, Justice Frank Murphy voiced a dissenting opinion when he said that the internment of the Japanese Americans reminded him of the Nazi treatment of the Jews.

In 1976 President Gerald Ford proclaimed:

We now know what we should have known then— not only was the evacuation wrong but Japanese Americans were and are loyal Americans. On the battlefield and at home the names of Japanese Americans have been and continue to be written in American history for the sacrifices and the contributions they have made to the well-being and the security of this, our common Nation.

AN AMERICAN ★ SPEAKS

In 1988 Japanese Americans received a formal apology from the United States government for the harm it had caused in violating their civil rights during World War II. Congress also voted to compensate the survivors in the amount of $20,000 each. Arthur Morimitsu expressed the views of many survivors:

Frankly, a lot of us [internees] were not looking for monetary [payments]. We wanted recognition that we were loyal, that interning loyal American citizens was wrong.

AN AMERICAN ★ SPEAKS

Americans perceived new global responsibilities.

Germany, Italy, and Japan emerged from World War II completely at the mercy of their conquerors, with their governments overthrown and their economies shattered. Countless numbers of refugees swarmed through central Europe destitute and with little hope.

Throughout Europe and east Asia the scene was equally bleak. The British had fought constantly since September 1939. By August 1945 their country was in severe economic distress. Their merchant navy had suffered from

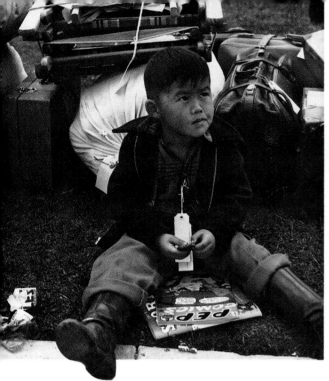

German submarines, and many of their overseas investments had been sold to pay for arms. The French army was also ruined. France had been a major battleground of the war. At the war's end, the country was left with a bombed-out transportation system and deep internal political divisions. The war had left the Soviet Union with a staggering 20 million dead, including many civilians. A million people had died of starvation in Leningrad alone. Millions of Chinese were also on the verge of starvation. After 14 years of fighting with the Japanese, China still faced a savage civil war. Around the world, colonial empires had begun to crack. Taking advantage of Europe's weakened position, colonial subjects began organizing independence movements.

By contrast, the United States emerged from the war stronger and more powerful than it had ever been. Although nearly 400,000 American lives had been lost, very few of these were civilians. Confronted with such a broken world, the nation discarded its isolationist foreign policy and started to assume responsibility for building a new global political and economic order. Part of this dramatic shift in policy came in an effort to avoid the mistakes of appeasement, which had done so much to bring about the most destructive war in history.

SECTION 4 REVIEW

Identify Key People and Terms
Write a sentence to identify: A. Philip Randolph, Oveta Culp Hobby, rationing, internment camps

Locate Key Places
What U.S. city was the nation's wartime defense production capital?

Master the Main Ideas
1. **Analyzing the economic impact of war:** In what ways did World War II affect the American economy, particularly the labor force?
2. **Analyzing information:** How did Japanese Americans show their loyalty to the United States during the war?
3. **Studying the effects of U.S. involvement in foreign affairs:** How did the nation regard the policy of isolationism after the war?

Apply Critical Thinking Skills: Recognizing Bias
With enemies such as Hitler and the Japanese militarists, it was easy for Americans to think of themselves as fighting a war against racism. However, the United States itself was not free of racism in the 1940s. Where could one find evidence of racism and discrimination in the United States during World War II?

Above, a Japanese American family from Los Angeles loads their belongings onto a truck that will take them to an internment camp in 1942. Above left, a Japanese American youth, with identification tags dangling from his shirt, patiently waits for his parents to be processed.

TOURING THE PAST

Oak Ridge, Tennessee

Thousands of Americans lived and worked in Oak Ridge without realizing they were keeping one of the deepest secrets of World War II.

In 1939, one month before Germany plunged the world into war, Albert Einstein and other scientists urged President Franklin D. Roosevelt to establish an American nuclear research program. At the time it was known that German physicists were experimenting with a new energy source capable of creating the most destructive weapon ever known—the atomic bomb.

In 1942, a year after the United States entered World War II, President Roosevelt approved plans for a top-secret, full-scale bomb development program. Its code name was the Manhattan Project. Its mission: to produce an atomic bomb within three years.

Three locations were selected by the U.S. government for the secret design and production of the bomb. Site X, later named Oak Ridge, would house the largest variety of operations. The 92-square-mile area lay in protected valleys with level land for the construction of three huge plants, and could draw on power generated by the Tennessee Valley Authority. In addition, Knoxville was near enough to provide a large work force, and the southern climate permitted year-round outdoor work.

Construction of Oak Ridge began in late 1942. By 1945 it was a military boom town, home to 75,000 residents and the employer of 100,000 workers. Oak Ridge did not appear on any maps, however, and few who lived or worked there were aware of the true purpose of the military installation. Most knew the place as the Clinton Engineer Works. Only a select group of people knew that K-25, Y-12, and X-10, the three plants at Oak Ridge, were facilities for the secret production of the uranium isotope U-235, which was needed to fuel the atomic bomb.

In part to keep the secret from being discovered, the U.S. government tried to create at Oak Ridge a typical American town. Oak Ridge had houses and front yards, schools, churches, stores, gas stations, and even a town orchestra. Unlike the typical American town, however, Oak Ridge was surrounded by a barbed-wire fence, and was patrolled by armed guards. All residents and workers at Oak Ridge, including children, were required to wear identification badges, which were routinely checked. No one could enter or leave the town without passing through security gates.

Residents and workers at Oak Ridge weren't told of the town's top-secret purpose until August 6, 1945, when the first atomic bomb was dropped, destroying Hiroshima, Japan. The Uranium 235 for the bomb had been produced at Oak Ridge. Oak Ridgers reacted to this news with surprise, shock, and wonderment. They poured into the streets on August 6 to celebrate the victory in Japan and the important role they had played in bringing it about. Nine days later the war was over.

In 1949 the fence surrounding Oak Ridge was taken down, and the town was opened to the public. Today about 30,000 people live in Oak Ridge. The town's three plants no longer produce uranium for atomic bombs, but they are in use as energy-related research and production facilities for the U.S. Department of Energy. Preserved at the X-10 plant is the graphite reactor, which dates from 1943 and is now a National Historic Landmark.

Horace Sherrod describes his experiences at Oak Ridge:

Since Oak Ridge did not appear on any maps, merchants sometimes had trouble getting suppliers to deliver goods to the secret city. Horace Sherrod, a grocery store manager in Oak Ridge, recalled some of the difficulties of doing business with the outside world. Could the United States create a "secret city" today? Why or why not?

I started filling my shelves in 1943 and didn't manage to get them completely filled until 1946. When I asked big shippers to send me food, they'd say "We never heard of Oak Ridge. It can't be a priority city." A carload of merchandise I ordered hadn't arrived in four weeks and I inquired about it. The shipper wrote back and said nobody could tell him where Oak Ridge was; he said he didn't believe there was such a place.

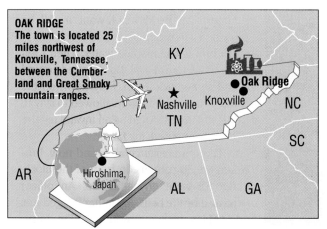

OAK RIDGE
The town is located 25 miles northwest of Knoxville, Tennessee, between the Cumberland and Great Smoky mountain ranges.

KY
Oak Ridge
Nashville Knoxville
TN
NC
SC
AR
Hiroshima, Japan
AL GA

DUPLICATE
Serial No. CV- 166425
COMMERCIAL VISITOR PASS
OAK RIDGE, TENN.
CEW Form 166 (Sept. 1, 1947) GPO
DATE ISSUED
3-19-49
NAME OF VISITOR
Horner, Clay C.
EXPIRES: MAR 19 1949
NAME OF APPLICANT Deakr Sgt.
ORGANIZATION AFC
I HEREBY CERTIFY that the above-named visitor is not a newspaper or magazine writer or photographer, motion picture photographer, radio commentator, alien, inspector or investigator (State or Federal).
(Signature of applicant or visitor)

Eugene Sledge Fights on Okinawa

16B

TIME FRAME
1945

GEOGRAPHIC SETTING
Southwestern Pacific

By early 1945, Allied forces in the Pacific had forced the Japanese back to the vicinity of their home islands. At this point the United States struck at two islands that were almost in Japan's backyard—Iwo Jima [ē′wō jē′mä] and Okinawa [ō kē nä′wä]. These two islands had been held by Japan for centuries, and they were among the most strongly defended in the entire Pacific. Bloody battles were fought for both of them. 5,000 marines were killed on Iwo Jima, and 11,000 more died on Okinawa. Among the American marines who fought on Okinawa was Eugene Sledge. Of his account of his wartime experiences, *With the Old Breed at Peleleiu and Okinawa,* critic Paul Fussell commented that it "is one of the finest memoirs to emerge from any war." In the following excerpt from his book, Sledge described the horrors of the Okinawa battlefield at night.

By day the battlefield was a horrible scene, but by night it became the most terrible of nightmares. Star shells and flares illuminated the area throughout the nights but were interspersed with moments of chilling, frightening blackness.

Sleep was almost impossible in the mud and cold rain, but sometimes I wrapped my wet poncho around me and dozed off for brief periods while my foxhole mate was on watch and bailing out the hole. One usually had to attempt sleep while sitting or crouching in the foxhole. . . .

When a flare or star shell lighted the area, everyone froze just as he was, then moved during the brief periods of darkness. When the area lighted up with that eerie greenish light, the big rain drops sparkled like silver shafts as they slanted downward. During a strong wind they looked as though they were being driven along almost horizontal to the deck. The light reflected off the dirty water in the craters and off the helmets and weapons of the living and the dead.

I catalogued in my mind the position of every feature on the surrounding terrain. There was no vegetation, so my list consisted of mounds and dips in the terrain, foxholes of my comrades, craters, corpses, and knocked-out tanks and amtracs [armored vehicles]. We had to know where everyone, living and dead, was located. If one of us fired at an enemy infiltrating or on a raid, he needed to know where his comrades were so as not to hit them. The position and posture of every corpse was important, because infiltrating Japanese also would freeze when illuminating shells lit up. . . . I reached the state where I would awake abruptly from my semi-sleep, and if the area was lit up, note with confidence my buddy scanning the terrain for any hostile sign. I would glance about, particularly behind us, for trouble. Finally, before we left the area, I frequently jerked myself up into a state in which I was semiawake during periods between star shells.

I imagined Marine dead had risen up and were moving silently about the area. I suppose these were nightmares, and I must have been more asleep than awake, or just dumbfounded by fatigue. . . . The pattern was always the same. The dead got up slowly out of their waterlogged craters or off the mud and, with stooped shoulders and dragging feet, wandered around aimlessly, their lips moving as though trying to tell me something. I struggled to hear what they were saying. They seemed agonized by pain and despair. I felt they were asking me for help. The most horrible thing was that I felt unable to aid them.

At that point I invariably became wide awake and felt sick and half-crazed by the horror of my dream. I would gaze out intently to see if the silent figures were still there, but saw nothing. When a flare lit up, all was stillness and desolation, each corpse in its usual place.

Among the craters off the ridge to the west was a scattering of Marine corpses. . . . Next to the base of the ridge, almost directly below me, was a partially flooded crater about three feet in diameter and probably three feet deep. In this crater was the body of a Marine whose grisly visage has remained disturbingly clear in my memory. If I close my eyes, he is as vivid as though I had seen him only yesterday.

The pathetic figure sat with his back toward the enemy and leaned against the south edge of the crater. His head was cocked, and his helmet rested against the side of the crater so that his face, or what remained of it, looked straight up at me. His knees were flexed and spread apart. Across his thighs, still clutched in his skeletal hands, was his rusting BAR [automatic rifle]. Canvas leggings were laced neatly along the sides of his calves and over his boondockers [boots]. His ankles were covered with muddy water, but the toes of his boondockers were visible above the surface. His dungarees, helmet, cover, and 782 gear appeared new. They were neither mud-spattered nor faded.

I was confident that he had been a new replacement. Every aspect of that big man looked much like a Marine "taking ten" on maneuvers before the order to move out again. He apparently had been killed early in the attacks against the Half Moon, before the rains began. Beneath his helmet brim I could see the visor of a green cotton fatigue cap. Under that cap were the most ghastly skeletal remains I had ever seen— and I had already seen too many.

Every time I looked over the edge of that foxhole down into that crater, that half-gone face leered up at me with a sardonic [bitter, mocking] grin. It was as though he was mocking our pitiful efforts to hang on to life in the face of the constant violent death that had cut him down. Or maybe he was mocking the folly of the war itself: "I am the harvest of man's stupidity. I am the fruit of the holocaust. I prayed like you to survive, but look at me now. It is over for us who are dead, but you must struggle, and will carry the memories all your life. People back home will wonder why you can't forget."

Battle-fatigued and begrimed Marines drink coffee on an assault transport after taking Eniwetok Atoll, the westernmost Japanese base in the Marshall Islands.

Discussing the Reading

1. What different interpretations did Eugene Sledge make of the expression on the face of the dead marine?

2. Compare Frank Haskell's description of the battle of Gettysburg (Source Reading 5D) with Sledge's account of Okinawa. Which of the two men seems the more horrified by what confronts him? Which of the two accounts deals primarily with the sounds of battle and which primarily with its sights?

CRITICAL THINKING
Checking Consistency

What attitude toward warfare did Eugene Sledge express in this excerpt? Was the view he expressed inconsistent with patriotism? Explain.

Harry Truman Defends Dropping the Atomic Bomb

16C

TIME FRAME
1945

GEOGRAPHIC SETTING
United States

When President Franklin Roosevelt died suddenly in April 1945, he was succeeded by Vice-President Harry S. Truman (1884–1972). One of the most daunting of the new president's responsibilities involved the secret weapon that U.S. scientists had developed—the atomic bomb. Truman later claimed that the research on the bomb had been so secret that even as Vice-President he had known nothing of its existence. Yet within a few months of taking office he had to make the momentous decision whether or not to use the atomic bomb against Japan. In the following excerpts from his memoirs he gave his reasons for his decision to drop the bomb, thus opening the world to a future of possible nuclear war.

The historic message of the first [test] explosion of an atomic bomb was flashed to me in a message from Secretary of War Stimson on the morning of July 16. The most secret and the most daring enterprise of the war had succeeded. We were now in possession of a weapon that would not only revolutionize war but could alter the course of history and civilization. . . .

We knew that the bomb would receive its first test in mid-July. If the test of the bomb was successful I wanted to afford Japan a clear chance to end the fighting before we made use of this newly gained

The remains of a wristwatch found in the rubble at Hiroshima (above) record the beginning of the nuclear age. Survivors of the blast (below) wait to receive first aid. Although the explosion devastated Hiroshima, and over 75,000 people were killed, the Japanese rebuilt the city and in 1949 erected an international shrine to peace.

power. If the test should fail, then it would be even more important to us to bring about a surrender before we had to make a physical conquest of Japan. General Marshal told me that it might cost half a million American lives to force the enemy's surrender on his home grounds. But the test was now successful. . . .

. . . I had then set up a committee of top men and had asked them to study with great care the implications the new weapon might have for us. It was their recommendation that the bomb be used against the enemy as soon as it could be done. They recommended further that it should be used without specific warning and against a target that would clearly show its devastating strength. I had realized, of course, that an atomic bomb explosion would inflict damage and casualties beyond imagination. On the other hand, the scientific advisers of the committee reported, "We can propose no technical demonstration likely to bring an end to the war; we see no acceptable alternative to direct military use." It was their conclusion that no technical demonstration they might propose, such as over a deserted island, would be likely to bring the war to an end. It had to be used against an enemy target.

The final decision of where and when to use the atomic bomb was up to me. Let there be no mistake about it. I regarded the bomb as a military weapon and never had any doubt that it should be used. . . .

In deciding to use this bomb I wanted to make sure that it would be used as a weapon of war in the manner prescribed by the laws of war. That meant that I wanted it dropped on a military target. I had told Stimson that the bomb should be dropped as nearly as possibly upon a war production center of prime military importance.

Stimson's staff had prepared a list of cities in Japan that might serve as targets. Kyoto, though favored by General Arnold as a center of military activity, was eliminated when Secretary Stimson pointed out that it was a cultural and religious shrine of the Japanese. Four cities were finally recommended as targets: Hiroshima, Kokura, Kiigata, and Nagasaki. . . .

On August 6, the fourth day of the journey home from Potsdam, came the historic news that shook the world. I was eating lunch with members of the *Augusta's* crew when Captain Frank Graham, White House Map Room watch officer, handed me the . . . message: Following message regarding Manhattan received. "Hiroshima bombed visually with only one tenth cover at 052315A. There was no fighter opposition and no flak. Parsons reports 15 minutes after drop as follows: 'Results clear cut successful in all respects. Visible effects greater than in any test. Conditions normal in airplane following delivery.' "

I was greatly moved. I telephoned Byrnes aboard ship to give him the news and then said to the group of sailors around me, "This is the greatest thing in history. It's time for us to get home."

Discussing the Reading

1. What did President Truman mean when he said, "This is the greatest thing in history"? On what assumption did he base his remark? Do you agree with him?

2. What result did Truman expect from his decision to use the atomic bomb? Did he have adequate information to make his decision? What consequences did he not foresee?

CRITICAL THINKING
Demonstrating Reasoned Judgment

What circumstances, if any, would warrant the use of modern nuclear weapons?

Sybil Lewis Does Defense Work

16D

TIME FRAME
1942–1945

GEOGRAPHIC SETTING
California

As the World War II draft swept up male workers, and as American industry expanded to meet defense needs, millions of women joined the workforce, providing a key source of labor. By 1944, the peak year of female wartime employment, women comprised 36 percent of the American workforce. Many of these women took jobs that before the war had been done by males, such as riveting, welding, and operating heavy equipment. Although female defense workers often performed these jobs very ably, they frequently encountered prejudice in their new roles. "Women who remained at home criticized them for wearing slacks, for 'neglecting' their children, and for working alongside, and therefore presumably tempting, married men," observed one recent social history of the period. "Black women suffered the added burden of racism. . . ." One of these African American defense workers was Sybil Lewis.

When I first arrived in Los Angeles, I began to look for a job. I decided I didn't want to do maid work anymore, so I got a job as a waitress in a small black restaurant. I was making pretty good money, more than I had in Sapulpa [city in Oklahoma], but I didn't have the knack for getting good tips. Then I saw an ad in the newspaper offering to train women for defense work. I went to Lockheed Aircraft and applied. They said they'd call me, but I never got a response, so I went back and applied again. You had to be pretty persistent. Finally they accepted me. They gave me a short training program and taught me how to rivet. Then they put me to work in the plant riveting small airplane parts, mainly gasoline tanks.

The women worked in pairs. I was the riveter, and this big strong white girl from a cotton farm in Arkansas worked as the bucker. . . . Bucking was harder than shooting rivets; it required more muscle. Riveting required more skill.

I worked for a while as a riveter with this white girl, when the boss came around one day and said, "We've decided to make some changes." At this point he assigned her to do the riveting and me to do the bucking. I wanted to know why. He said, "Well, we just interchange once in a while." but I was never given the riveting job back. That was the first encounter I had with segregation in California, and it didn't sit too well with me. It brought back some of my experiences in Sapulpa—you're a Negro, so you do the hard work. . . .

So I applied to Douglas Aircraft in Santa Monica and was hired as a riveter there. On that job I did not encounter the same prejudice. . . . the foreman was more congenial. But Maywood, where Lockheed was located, was a very segregated city. Going into that city, you were really going to forbidden territory. Santa Monica was not as segregated a community.

I worked in aircraft for a few years, then in '43 I saw an ad in the paper for women trainees to learn arc welding. The salary sounded good, from a dollar to a dollar-twenty-five an hour. . . . I answered the ad and they sent me to a short course at welding school. After I passed the trainee course, they employed me at the shipyards. That was a little different than working in aircraft, because in the shipyard you found mostly men. There I ran into another kind of discrimination: because I was a woman I was paid less than a man for doing the same job.

I was an arc welder, I'd passed both the army and navy tests, and I knew I could do the job, but I found from talking with . . . the men that they made more money. You'd ask about this, but they'd say, "Well,

Two women work together at riveting what is probably a portion of an aircraft. "Rosie the Riveter," a song written in 1942, popularized women's new place in the war-time labor force.

you don't have the experience," or "The men have to lift some heavy pieces of steel and you don't have to," but I knew that I had to help lift steel, too.

They started everyone off at a dollar-twenty an hour. There were higher-paying jobs, though, like chippers and crane operators, that were for men only. Once, the foreman told me I had to go on the skids—the long docks alongside the hull. I said, "That sounds pretty dangerous. Will I make more than one-twenty an hour?" And he said, "No, one-twenty is the top pay you'll get." But the men got more.

It was interesting that although they didn't pay women as much as men, the men treated you differently if you wore slacks. I noticed, for example, that when you'd get on the bus or the streetcar, you stood all the way, more than the lady who would get on with a dress. I never could understand why men wouldn't give women in slacks a seat. And at the shipyards the language wasn't the best. Nobody respected you enough to clean up the way they spoke. It didn't seem to bother the men that you were a woman. During the war years men began to say, "You have a man's job and you're getting paid almost the same, so we don't have to give you a seat anymore, or show the common courtesies that men show women." All those little niceties were lost.

I enjoyed working at the shipyard; it was a unique job for a woman, and I liked the challenge. But it was a dangerous job. The safety measures were very poor. Many people were injured by falling steel. Finally I was assigned to a very hazardous area and I asked to be transferred into a safer area. They said, "You have to work where they assign you at all times." I thought it was getting too dangerous, so I quit.

The war years had a tremendous impact on women. I know for myself it was the first time I had a chance to get out of the kitchen and work in industry and make a few bucks. This was something I had never dreamed would happen. In Sapulpa all that women had to look forward to was keeping house and raising families. The war years offered new possibilities. ... This was the beginning of women's feeling that they could do something more. We were trained to do this kind of work because of the war, but there was no question that this was just an interim period. We were all told that then the war was over we would not be needed anymore.

Discussing the Reading

1. What example of racial discrimination did Sybil Lewis recall from her time as a riveter?

2. According to Lewis, how did the increased presence of women in the workforce affect "all those little niceties" of male courtesy (lines 81-99)? How much did she seem to regret this?

CRITICAL THINKING
Predicting Consequences

What would be the probable long-term effects on women of experiences such as those of Sybil Lewis? Explain.

Daniel Inouye Defends the War-Time Record of Japanese Americans

16E

TIME FRAME
1941–1945

GEOGRAPHIC SETTING
Hawaii

Daniel Inouye [ē nō'wā] was 17 years old when Japanese warplanes attacked Pearl Harbor on December 7, 1941. After graduation from high school in 1942, Inouye enlisted in an army combat team composed entirely of *Nisei* [nē' sā'] volunteers. (Nisei—"second generation"—are children of Japanese immigrants.) Inouye's unit fought in Italy, where he was badly wounded, losing his right arm. After the war, Inouye became a lawyer and entered politics in Hawaii. In 1963 he became the first Japanese American elected to the Senate. In the following excerpt from his autobiography, *Journey to Washington* (1967), Inouye described the "grief and shame and anger" he experienced on the morning of the attack on Pearl Harbor by Japan. After the first wave of Japanese planes attacked, Inouye reported to a Red Cross aid station to help with the wounded.

It was past 8:30—the war was little more than half an hour old—when I reported in at the aid station, two classrooms in the Lunalilo Elementary School. I had gained the first six years of my education in this building and before the day was out it would be half-destroyed by our own anti-aircraft shells which had failed to explode in the air. Even now confusion was in command, shouting people pushing by each other as they rushed for litters and medical supplies.... I grabbed a litter and rounded up a couple of fellows I knew.

"Where're we going?" one yelled at me.

"Where the trouble is! Follow me!"

In a small house on the corner of Hauoli and Algaroba Streets, we found our first casualties. The shell had sliced through the house. It had blown the front out and the tokens of a lifetime—dishes, clothing, a child's bed—were strewn pathetically into the street.

I was propelled by sheerest instinct. Some small corner of my mind worried about how I'd react to what lay in that carnage—there would be no textbook cuts and bruises, and the blood would be real blood—and then I plunged in, stumbling over the debris, kicking up clouds of dust and calling, frantically calling to anyone who might be alive in there. There was no answer. The survivors had already fled and the one who remained would never speak again. I found her half-buried in the rubble, one of America's first civilian dead of the Second World War....

Remembering those traumatic days, the great turning point of my life, I can see how my need to become totally involved in the war effort sprang from that invidious [unjust] sense of guilt, the invisible cross lashed to the back of every *Nisei* at the instant when the first plane bearing that rising sun appeared in the sky over Pearl Harbor. In actual fact, of course, we had nothing to feel guilty about, and all rational men understood this. And still I knew of no American of Japanese descent who didn't carry this special burden, and who didn't work doubly hard because of it.

The provocations were sometimes severe. We began to hear disturbing stories of what was happening to the Japanese on the mainland. Along the West Coast, thousands of families were summarily uprooted, taken from their homes, often on twelve hours notice, and moved to "relocation" camps on the incredible grounds that this whole class of Americans, rich and poor, alien and citizen, men, women, and children, was a security risk....

I think that most Americans now agree that this was a dreary chapter in our history. But I believe it to be equally impor-

Recently inducted Asian American recruits (above) arrive at Basic Training, Camp Shelby, Mississippi, in 1943. Daniel Inouye (above right) delivers a speech before Congress. Inouye's political career began in what was then the territorial Hawaiian House of Representatives, followed by two terms in the territorial Senate. He served two terms in the United States House of Representatives before being elected to the U.S. Senate.

tant that they understand that greed, as much as war hysteria, made possible this momentary triumph of the vigilante mentality. In every city and town where Japa-
70 nese-Americans settled, there were those who envied their neat little farms, those who coveted their homes and gardens and jobs. And when their hour came, these human vultures struck with cunning
75 and cruelty, offering two hundred dollars for land that was worth two thousand, five dollars for a nearly new refrigerator. And stunned by this upheaval in their lives, unable to make a better arrangement in the
80 few hours given them to settle their affairs, the *Nisei* were forced to surrender the fruits of a lifetime's labor, for a pittance.

Had it not been for a few courageous
85 and outspoken men, the same bitter situation might have prevailed in Hawaii. . . . [But] despite widely published concern that the *Nisei* were a sort of built-in fifth column [group of traitors] in Hawaii, not a
90 single act of sabotage or subversion was ever charged to an American of Japanese ancestry from the day the war began until the day it ended. The *Nisei* bought more war bonds than any other group in the Is-
95 lands. And when the Army finally permitted them to volunteer for the service, more than ten thousand men showed up

at their draft boards, approximately eighty percent of all qualified males of military
100 age.

And still we could not escape humiliation, discrimination, even internment. . . . And even those of us whose personal liberty was never threatened felt the sting of
105 suspicion. We felt it in the streets where white men would sneer at us as they passed. We felt it in school when we heard our friends called Jap-lovers. We felt it in our homes when military police and F.B.I.
110 men came looking for shortwave sets, letters in code and only the good Lord knows what else. Everywhere there were signs that admonished us to "Be American! Speak American!"

Discussing the Reading

1. Why did Daniel Inouye feel the need "to become totally involved in the war effort" (lines 39–40)?

2. How do you imagine he reacted to the slogans "Be American! Speak American!"? Are the two synonymous? Explain.

CRITICAL THINKING
Distinguishing False from Accurate Images

What image did Daniel Inouye use to describe those who bought up Japanese American property when the owners were sent to internment camps? Was he justified in using this image? Why or why not?

Chapter Summary

Write supporting details under each of the following main ideas as you review the chapter.

Section 1
1. Japanese militarists sought the complete conquest of China.
2. Congress declared war on Japan.
3. The Japanese claimed victory after victory during the first six months of the war.

Section 2
1. German technology was superior to that of the Japanese.
2. American and British troops attacked the Germans in North Africa in 1942.
3. The German army suffered defeat on Europe's eastern front.
4. The British and the Americans attacked Germany at Normandy.
5. The Allied invasion of Germany forced the Nazis to surrender.

Section 3
1. Complacency and greed led to Japanese setbacks.
2. The Japanese never recovered from their defeat at the Battle of Midway.
3. Geography dictated an island-hopping strategy in the Pacific.

Section 4
1. World War II stimulated the American economy.
2. Racism forced Japanese Americans into internment camps.
3. Americans perceived new global responsibilities.

Chapter Themes

1. **Free enterprise:** Ironically, World War II was a boon to the American economy, dramatically propelling it out of the Depression. In the process of responding to the demands for guns, tanks, and airplanes, thousands of women and African Americans rushed to fill job openings.
2. **Relations with other nations:** After being forced out of its isolationist stance by the attack on Pearl Harbor, the United States began a new era in world affairs. Conferences of Allied leaders in Casablanca, Yalta, and Potsdam established American leaders in positions of power and also helped to decide the course of the war. American leaders also helped shape the political direction of postwar Europe, Asia,

and Africa for decades to come. Finally, with the development of the atomic bomb, the United States became the undisputed leader on the world scene.

Chapter Study Guide

Identifying Key People and Terms

Name the key person or key term that describes the:
1. agreement between Japan, Germany, and Italy that established the Axis powers
2. systematic mass murder by the Nazis of more than six million Jews and millions of Poles, Czechs, Russians, Gypsies, and others between 1942 and 1945
3. name given to the program that created the atomic bomb
4. issuing of coupons to limit the number of items a person can buy, especially during periods of limited supply

Locating Key Places

1. From what base did MacArthur try to fight the Japanese in the Philippines but ultimately had to surrender?
2. After routing the Germans from North Africa, which Italian island did the Allies target?
3. Where did D-Day take place?

Mastering the Main Ideas

1. America's isolationism and preoccupation with the Depression led to a lack of preparedness both psychologically and militarily. How did this fact influence the results of Japanese attacks on Pearl Harbor, the economic sanctions against Japan, and the attacks on the Philippines?
2. Why did the Allies decide to first concentrate on defeating Germany rather than Japan?
3. Explain the strategy of island-hopping. What were the costs of such a strategy?
4. How were the internment camps and the riots in Detroit symbols of one of America's most persistent problems—racism?

Applying Critical Thinking Skills

1. **Identifying central issues: (a)** What were the economic reasons for Japanese aggression? **(b)** What were the psychological reasons Japanese militarists used to support their policy of aggression?

1940	1941	1942	1943	1944	1945	1946

1941
Japanese attack Pearl Harbor; United States enters World War II

1942
Battles of Coral Sea and Midway; U.S. Marines invade Guadalcanal

1943
Casablanca Conference; Allies invade Italy

1944
Allies invade France (D–Day); Battle of the Bulge

1945
President Roosevelt dies; Germany surrenders; U.S. drops atomic bombs on Japan; Japanese surrender

2. Identifying assumptions: What assumptions did Hitler seem to make about himself and others when he ordered the start of the Holocaust?

3. Analyzing cause and effect: List some of the reasons Truman decided to order atomic bombs dropped on Hiroshima and Nagasaki despite the fact that the effect of the bombs would be devastating. State what you consider to be the most important reason first.

4. Making comparisons: Compare the effects of the war in Europe and Asia with its effects in the United States.

Chapter Activities

Learning Geography Through History

1. What nations made up the eastern and western fronts in Europe during World War II?

2. What large island had to be won from Japan to protect Australia during World War II?

Relating the United States to the World

1. Penicillin was first used in medicine in 1941. How might this development have helped the war effort internationally?

2. In what way were Soviet-American relations a matter of compromise during the war?

Linking Past to Present

1. To what extent did the dropping of the bombs on Hiroshima and Nagasaki permanently change the world?

2. How was the reunion of the two Germanies in 1990 the logical conclusion of agreements made during World War II?

Using the Time Line

(a) When did the war in North Africa end?
(b) Europe? **(c)** Pacific?

Practicing Critical Thinking Strategies

Testing Conclusions
Based on information in the text, do you think there is enough evidence to support the conclusion that the United States would not have entered the war had Japan decided not to bomb Pearl Harbor? Why or why not?

Learning More About the Allied Victory

1. Using Source Readings: Read the Source Readings for this chapter and answer the questions.

2. Holding a discussion: Research the internment of the Japanese Americans during the war. You might wish to read chapters 16–20 in *Nisei: The Quiet Americans* by Bill Hosokawa. Learn of the dilemma that faced these loyal Americans as they were wrongly accused of possible war crimes, lost most of their worldly possessions, and were herded like cattle into fenced and guarded camps with minimal supplies. After research, participate in a discussion regarding the civil rights of American citizens during war time.

3. Enjoying firsthand accounts: Read chapters 16 and 20 of *Plain Speaking: An Oral Biography of Harry S. Truman* by Merle Miller. This anecdotal book will give you a sense of how Truman felt on the day Roosevelt died and he took office and how he felt about dropping the bomb. It is a warm book, complete with the folksy, firm flavor of President Truman.

Linking Past to Present

The Cold War began with fundamental disagreements about who could control postwar Europe. Such disagreements among the victorious Allies surfaced at the Potsdam Conference in 1945, inset. Shown seated from left to right: Clement Attlee of Britain, Harry Truman of the United States, Joseph Stalin of the Soviet Union. Forty-five years later, the Cold War ended as Eastern European nations denounced communism. In the background, jubilant Czechs celebrate in Prague in 1989 after the collapse of the communist regime that had ruled since 1948.

Truman and the Cold War

1 9 4 5 — 1 9 5 2

17

CHAPTER PREVIEW

In this chapter you will learn how an intense rivalry between the United States and the Soviet Union developed after World War II.

SECTIONS IN THIS CHAPTER:
1. **The Cold War began.**
2. **The United States vowed to contain communism.**
3. **The Cold War spread to Asia.**
4. **The Cold War affected life at home.**

Harry Truman was stunned by Roosevelt's death on April 12, 1945. He had never expected to be a senator, let alone president, and he felt unprepared for the task ahead. As vice president, he had little to do but ask about FDR's deteriorating health. He was kept in the dark about the complex questions of foreign policy that he was soon to face. The day after he took the presidential oath he told reporters:

AN AMERICAN ★ SPEAKS Boys, if you ever pray, pray for me now. I don't know whether you fellows ever had a load of hay fall on you, but when they told me yesterday what had happened, I felt like the moon, the stars and all the planets had fallen on me.

Indeed, President Truman needed the prayers of his fellow Americans. The months preceding and immediately after the end of the war would call for him to exhibit the highest of diplomatic skills. Would the president be up to the task? Would he be able to guide the nation into an era of worldwide peace and prosperity inspired by American ideals of freedom and democracy? Would he be able to work effectively with an increasingly hostile Soviet Union to develop a solution regarding the control of postwar Europe? How would the new president respond to the spread of communism abroad as well as at home?

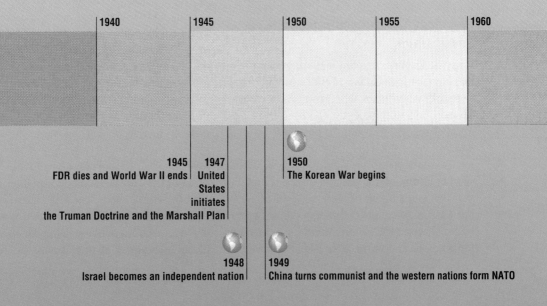

| 1940 | 1945 | 1950 | 1955 | 1960 |

1945
FDR dies and World War II ends

1947
United States initiates the Truman Doctrine and the Marshall Plan

1950
The Korean War begins

1948
Israel becomes an independent nation

1949
China turns communist and the western nations form NATO

The Cold War began.

Key Terms: Cold War, self-determination, satellite

Reading Preview

As you read this section, you will learn:

1. how President Truman reacted to Soviet aggression in Europe.
2. how successful the United Nations was.
3. how the Cold War affected Europe.

Instead of the peace that everyone hoped for, the end of World War II brought about a new rivalry between the United States and the Soviet Union. The **Cold War**, as it soon became known, marked a power struggle between the United States and the Soviet Union. In the devastated world of 1945, these two countries were the only ones possessing enough military strength to threaten each other. With different cultures, ideologies, and past experiences, they soon became locked in a rivalry that began in Europe, spread to Asia, and would last for more than four decades.

President Truman confronted the Soviet Union.

Harry S. Truman was the first American president to face the burdens of the Cold War. Sixty years old when he reached the White House, Truman had only recently emerged from political obscurity after years of adversity. Born of hardy pioneer stock in Missouri, he had farmed for ten years, fought in World War I, and then went bankrupt in the clothing business in Kansas City. Undaunted, he entered politics, serving as county judge in Independence, a city east of Kansas City. Truman won a reputation for integrity and fairness that helped him win

election to the Senate in 1934. A decided underdog when he ran for reelection in 1940, he amazed everyone by winning a second term.

It was easy to underestimate Harry Truman. Modest and unassuming in manner, he was in fact a shrewd politician. Widely read in American history, he had a clear sense of the power and prestige of the presidency. He was determined not to do anything to dishonor the office and to try his best to serve the nation. He knew Washington well but had little experience with world affairs. For guidance in foreign policy he relied on such experienced advisers as Secretary of State James F. Byrnes and Secretary of War Henry Stimson. Candid and outspoken, Truman had the ability to learn quickly and to make decisions boldly without agonizing over them. The plaque on his desk read, "The buck stops here."

The gravest challenge facing Truman was the growing hostility toward the Soviet Union. A deal for a coalition government in Poland reached at Yalta was beginning to unravel as the Soviets installed a communist regime. At Potsdam the new president had resisted Soviet demands for large reparations from Germany that would have forced the United States to support the German population for the indefinite future. When Soviet Foreign Minister Molotov visited Washington in late April 1945, Truman spoke bluntly, telling the Soviet Union to honor its agreements, or else! The president later recalled that he had given Molotov a "straight one-two to the jaw." Molotov responded by saying that he had never been talked to like that before. Truman then countered by saying, "Carry out your agreements and you won't get talked to like that." Molotov left Washington furious.

Truman's tough talk, however, could not hide the fact that the Soviet Union was in a strong position in Europe. Having borne the brunt of the war against Germany, Soviet armies had overrun all of Eastern Europe and much of the heart of the continent was under their military control. The United States had exclusive possession of the atomic bomb as well as superior financial resources, but with the American people demanding that their troops be returned

Europe After World War II

- Western bloc
- American zone
- British zone
- French zone
- Communist bloc or Soviet zone
- Nonaligned nations
- "Iron Curtain"
- Berlin airlift 1948–1949

Azimuthal Equal-Area Projections

Germany

Berlin

map study

Regions
The heavy black line on the map shows the division of Europe into western and communist blocs. Note that Germany was divided between the two blocs. How many occupation zones were there in West Germany?

Critical Thinking
In 1948 the Soviets set up a land blockade between West Germany and Berlin. Why was the Berlin airlift necessary?

home, Truman lacked the military strength to force a showdown with the Soviet Union for dominance in Europe.

The United Nations proved to be generally ineffective.

During World War II, most Americans had put their faith in the future United Nations (UN) to keep the postwar peace. After FDR's death, Truman went ahead with arrangements for a conference in San Francisco in April 1945 to complete plans for the new world organization.

Despite tensions between the American and Soviet delegations, the San Francisco Conference was successful. The delegates adopted the United Nations Charter, which provided for a General Assembly composed of all member states and a Security Council on which the United States, the Soviet Union, China, France, and Britain had the power to veto any action.

In contrast to the fate of the League of Nations after World War I, this time the U.S. Senate voted overwhelmingly for American membership in the new world body. Unfortunately, the UN would prove to be as ineffective

CULTURAL DIVERSITY AND THE UNITED NATIONS
Skill: Expressing Problems

Introducing the Skill. In 1945 President Harry Truman spoke to the delegates of the newly formed United Nations, urging them, "Let us not fail to grasp this supreme chance to establish a worldwide rule of reason—to create an enduring peace under the guidance of God." For much of its history, however, the role and power of the United Nations has been limited by issues of international conflict and domestic politics. What problems have prevented the organization from creating the enduring peace Truman envisioned?

Learning the Skill. In order to evaluate why the United Nations

has not been as effective as planned, you need first to **express the problems** plaguing the organization. Expressing problems involves stating clearly any difficulties present in the given situation. For example, your text states that one of the main problems that has faced the United Nations is that the five permanent members of the Security Council have the power of veto over any proposal before this body. Consider other questions as well: Who makes up the membership of the United Nations? How is the body funded? What arrangements exist for enforcing UN declarations or investigations?

Applying the Skill.
1. Express the problems facing the United Nations of the Cold War era. What prevented the world body from consistently taking effective actions around the globe?
2. How does the effectiveness of the United Nations during the Middle East crisis that began in August 1990 compare with that of the Cold War era? Why might there be more potential for global cooperation in the modern world? You could use newspapers and magazines from August 1990 to March 1991 to help you answer these questions.

U.S. Secretary of State Edward Stettinius signs the UN Charter on June 25, 1945.

as the earlier League. The Security Council could rarely act effectively to keep the peace because any one of the five major nations could block any action by the veto. In addition, the General Assembly became little more than a debating society. Thus, the United Nations soon became the first casualty of the Cold War.

The Cold War led to the division of Europe.

The conflict between the United States and the Soviet Union developed gradually. Although Soviet and American diplomats met regularly from 1945 to 1947 to discuss plans for a European settlement, they never were able to construct one.

The greatest obstacle to a negotiated peace was Soviet insecurity. Invaded repeatedly from the west throughout their history, the Soviets wanted to control the countries on their borders. The United States insisted on the principle of national **self-determination**—the right of the people of a country to choose their leaders in free elections. Aware that such elections might lead to anti-Soviet regimes in Poland and other parts of Eastern Europe, Stalin repeatedly refused to allow them.

Germany was the key to a European settlement. Instead of reaching agreement on a new German state, the United States and the Soviet Union gradually allowed the zones of occupation, designed to be only temporary, to become permanent dividing lines. By 1947 the United States, Britain, and France were merging their zones, preparing the way for an independent West Germany. The Soviet Union, meanwhile, established a communist regime in East Germany, which included the jointly occupied city of Berlin.

Throughout 1946 and 1947, Stalin created **satellites**, or nations loyal to Moscow, throughout Eastern Europe. One by one, Poland, Hungary, Romania, and Bulgaria emerged as communist nations. The climax to this thrust toward Soviet domination of Eastern Europe came in March 1948 when a coup in **Czechoslovakia** overthrew a democratic government and gave the Soviet Union a

MEET THE PRESIDENT

HARRY S. TRUMAN

Born: May 8, 1884
Died: December 26, 1972
In office: 1945–1953

When Harry Truman was first addressed as "Mr. President" he sighed, "I wish you hadn't called me that." His anxiety was shared by many Americans concerned that the untried Missouri politician would not measure up to the office filled so grandly and for so long by Franklin Roosevelt.

The shoe fit after all. Truman presided over the conclusion of World War II and responded with vigor to the first chilling moves of the Cold War. He could make bold decisions without apology: to drop an atomic bomb; to drop an ambitious general. He knew his own mind and seldom refrained from speaking it. When that outspokenness brought him near political extinction in 1948, Truman engineered the most stunning election upset in presidential history.

Truman said of himself, "I wasn't one of the great presidents, but I had a good time trying to be one."

strategic foothold in the heart of Europe. Note on the map on page 675 that Czechoslovakia is directly south of Soviet-controlled Poland and Germany.

In a speech in Fulton, Missouri, in 1946, Winston Churchill gave a graphic warning of the way the Soviets were dividing Europe. "From Stettin in the Baltic to Trieste in the Adriatic," the British statesman declared, "an iron curtain has descended across the Continent. . . . I do not believe that Soviet Russia desires war. What they desire is the fruits of war and the indefinite expansion of their power and doctrines." Fearful of free elections, Joseph Stalin had imposed this iron curtain that would divide Europe into rival camps until 1989, when democracy would finally begin its triumphant return to the countries of Eastern Europe.

The British statesman Winston Churchill warned Americans of the Soviet plan to dominate Eastern Europe in his famous speech in Fulton, Missouri, in 1946.

The United States vowed to contain communism.

Key Terms: covert, containment, Truman Doctrine, Marshall Plan, North Atlantic Treaty Organizaton (NATO)

Reading Preview
As you read this section, you will learn:

1. how President Truman dealt with foreign policy.
2. what new foreign policy was announced.
3. how the Marshall Plan affected Europe.
4. what the principal effect of NATO was.
5. how Stalin tried to intimidate the United States.

SECTION 1 REVIEW

Identify Key People and Terms
Write a sentence to identify: Cold War, self-determination, satellite

Locate Key Places
In relation to Poland, where is Czechoslovakia located?

Master the Main Ideas

1. **Studying major political leaders:** Why couldn't Truman force the Soviets to honor their agreements?
2. **Examining international cooperative efforts:** Why was the UN Security Council unable to make important international decisions?
3. **Understanding foreign conflicts:** What specific events led to the division of Europe in the early postwar years?

Apply Critical Thinking Skills: Drawing Conclusions
Do you think the rivalry between the United States and the Soviet Union was bound to develop after World War II? Why or why not? Support your answer with evidence from the text.

In 1947 the United States changed its foreign policy to meet the challenges of the Cold War. New structures, new leaders, and above all, a new strategy designed to stop Soviet expansion, would shape America's role in the world for the next two decades.

President Truman chose a new foreign policy team.

Pearl Harbor had shown Americans the need for closer cooperation between the armed forces and greater effort at coordinating military and diplomatic activities. Accordingly, in 1947, Congress established the Department of Defense. The secretary of defense, a civilian with cabinet rank, heads the department. He or she presides over the three military services—the Army, Navy, and Air Force. Congress also established the Joint Chiefs of Staff, which is composed of top military and naval officers. They advise both the secretary of defense and the president on strategic issues.

Two other bodies were designed to meet the nation's new global responsibilities. The first is the National Security Council (NSC). The NSC is composed of the secretaries of the three military branches, as well as the secretaries of defense and state. They advise the president on all issues affecting the nation's security. The second body is the Central Intelligence Agency (CIA). The CIA coordinates all the government's foreign intelligence-gathering bodies in an effort to warn of possible external dangers. The CIA is also authorized to conduct **covert**, or secret, operations to help ensure friendly regimes abroad.

An equally important change in foreign policy personnel took place in 1947 with the appointment of George Marshall as secretary of state. The army chief of staff in World War II, Marshall had shown the ability to think in broad, global terms in guiding the nation to victory. Calm, mature, and orderly of mind, Marshall was a very good judge of character. He quickly chose two men of exceptional talent to help him develop an effective approach to the problems of the Cold War.

The first man chosen by Marshall was **Dean Acheson**, the new undersecretary of state. A Washington lawyer and experienced diplomat, Acheson combined a shrewd intelligence with supreme self-confidence. Marshall's other deputy was **George Kennan**, a career foreign service officer who had become an expert on the Soviet Union. In his post as director of the newly created Policy Planning Staff, Kennan used his years of experience in Moscow and his knowledge of Russian history and culture to devise a new strategy for the Cold War. Kennan's strategy became known as **containment**.

Containment was based on Kennan's belief, borne out by postwar experience, that the Soviet Union was bent on an expansionist policy. Kennan compared the Soviet Union's actions to those of a toy car:

Once a given party line has been laid down on a given issue of current policy, the whole Soviet governmental machine . . . moves inexorably along the prescribed path, like a persistent toy automobile wound up and headed in a given direction, stopping only when it meets with some unanswerable force.

AN AMERICAN ★ SPEAKS

STEP ON IT, DOC!

The Truman Administration had good reason to be wary of Soviet intentions in Europe after World War II. This cartoon reflects this concern.

The United States announced the Truman Doctrine.

The containment policy, which developed in three phases, was soon put to the test. On February 21, 1947, Britain, the traditional guardian of western interests in the Mediterranean, informed the United States that it could no longer support the governments of Greece and Turkey. Soviet leaders demanded that Turkey give up control of the **Dardanelles**, a strategic waterway leading from the Black Sea to the Mediterranean Sea. The Soviet Union needed this waterway so that it could gain access to warm-water ports in the Mediterranean. At the same time in Greece, communist rebels tried to overthrow a conservative regime supported by Britain.

In the belief that the Soviets were responsible for organizing the communist rebels in Greece, which in fact they were not, Marshall, Acheson, and Kennan quickly decided that the United States would have to take Britain's place in the eastern Mediterranean. In late February they met with congressional leaders to stress the need for American action.

President Truman, in a reference to Nazi Germany, agreed with his advisers and told the American public that "We must not go through the thirties again." Then, before a joint session of Congress on March 12, 1947, Truman asked for $400 million in military and economic aid for Greece and Turkey. He then made it clear that more was involved than just the fate of these two countries:

The free peoples of the world look to us for support in maintaining their freedoms. If we falter in our leadership, we may endanger the peace of the world—and we shall surely endanger the welfare of our own nation. Great responsibilities have been placed upon us by the swift movement of events. I am confident that the Congress will face these responsibilities squarely.

AN AMERICAN ★ SPEAKS

After only a short debate, Congress approved the president's request for aid by a heavy margin. The **Truman Doctrine**, as the president's policy became known, marked an informal declaration of war against the Soviet Union. In less than two years, American military advisers helped defeat the communist insurgents in Greece and helped Turkey withstand Soviet pressure. More importantly, America had served notice on the Soviet Union that it would resist communist encroachment anywhere.

The Marshall Plan aided European recovery.

Western Europe was far more vital to the United States than Greece and Turkey. By 1947 it had also become vulnerable to communist takeover. Despite American financial loans Britain, France, and Italy had been unable to recover from the economic devastation that World War II had wrought.

Secretary of State George Marshall returned from a futile diplomatic meeting in Moscow filled with despair. "The patient is sinking while the doctors deliberate," he warned. Then, with help from Acheson, Kennan, and economic experts, Marshall drew up a plan for massive American aid to put Europe back on its feet. This ambitious endeavor, the **Marshall Plan**, became the second phase of containment.

The Marshall Plan turned out to be a great success. During the years of the Marshall Plan, from 1948 through 1952, the United States loaned or gave $13 billion to the countries taking part in the plan. As a result, by 1952 Western Europe was economically healthy. The Marshall Plan also provided a large market for American goods, and it held back the spread of Soviet influence.

NATO put Europe under the American nuclear shield.

The third major phase of containment came in 1949 with the establishment of the **North Atlantic Treaty Organization (NATO)**. As the people of Western Europe recovered from World War II, they began to worry about the danger of Soviet military aggression. As one American diplomat explained, "People could not go ahead and make investments for the future without some sense of security."

Dean Acheson, who succeeded George Marshall as secretary of state in 1949, was the primary architect of NATO. He presided over the

Recipients of Marshall Plan aid felt this plan was ''the most straightforwardly generous thing any country had ever done for others, the fullest expression so far of that American idealism on which all the hopes of the West depend.''

★ ★ ★ ★

STRENGTH FOR THE FREE WORLD

FROM THE
UNITED STATES OF AMERICA

negotiations that led to the signing of the North Atlantic Treaty in Washington on April 4, 1949. Breaking with its historic tradition of having no entangling alliances, the United States joined with Canada and ten European nations in a broad mutual defense pact.

The principal effect of NATO was to put Europe under the American nuclear shield. The key clause in the treaty stated that "an armed attack against one or more" members of NATO "shall be considered an attack on all." President Truman, who had said that he was "tired of babying the Russians," appointed General Dwight D. Eisenhower as supreme commander of NATO. Truman believed that the appointment of Eisenhower, who was greatly respected in Europe, would help reassure worried Europeans that the United States

would come to their defense in case of such an attack. The president also authorized the stationing of four American divisions in Europe (180,000 soldiers including supporting units) as the nucleus of the NATO forces.

Some historians believe that the United States may have paid too high a price to guarantee European security. Despite many warning signs, no concrete evidence existed that showed that the Soviets ever intended to invade Western Europe. They did not even respond with the Warsaw Pact, the communist counterpart of NATO, until 1955. The attempt by Acheson to apply the lesson of Munich—that the Soviet Union could pick off the European countries one by one as Hitler had done—ignored the fact that there were many differences between Hitler's Germany and Stalin's Soviet Union. All NATO did was intensify the Cold War by reinforcing a Soviet fear of being encircled by the West.

Stalin imposed a land blockade of Berlin in 1948.

The main Soviet response to containment came at the West's most vulnerable point. American, British, French, and Soviet troops each occupied a section of Berlin, but the city was located more than 100 miles within the Soviet zone of Germany. Stalin decided to see

Soviet guards check German citizens before allowing them to enter the western sector of Berlin during the blockade. U.S. pilots hauled in almost 2 million tons of food, fuel, and medicine by the time the airlift ended on September 30, 1949.

whether the Americans were prepared to stand by their European commitments by imposing a land blockade of Berlin on June 24, 1948. Soviet troops stopped all highway, railroad, and barge traffic between the western zones of Germany and Berlin.

The United States was caught unprepared by the Berlin blockade. The policy choices were not very appealing. President Truman could withdraw American forces and lose not just a city, but the confidence of all of Europe; he could try to send reinforcements by land to Berlin and risk a military defeat by much larger Soviet forces; or he could just sit tight and try to find a diplomatic solution. The president made the basic decision in characteristic fashion, telling the military that there would be no thought of pulling out of the city. "We're going to stay, period," he reportedly said.

The Berlin Airlift

The children of West Berlin called American soldiers who staffed the airlift the "chocolate pilots." Flying low over the streets of Berlin, the pilots dropped thousands of chocolate bars, each with its own tiny parachute. The candy floated down to the children, who waited with outstretched hands. For many, this was the only treat they got during the dreary year of the Soviet blockade.

Between June 24, 1948, and September 30, 1949, British and American soldiers made about 400,000 flights into West Berlin,

hauling almost two million tons of food, coal, clothes, and other necessities. During the busiest days, a plane landed every 45 seconds at one of the three airports in West Berlin. Pilots even used the rivers as runways to bring in their essential cargo. Berlin's Havel River was the landing site for amphibious aircraft participating in the airlift.

However, even with the supplies donated by western nations, blockaded Berliners did not have an easy year. Fuel was in such short supply that power plants could supply electricity for only a few hours each day. Food rations consisted

mainly of dehydrated potatoes, and fresh foods were not available at all. In the winter, the sun set before four o'clock. The people of West Berlin huddled in their cold, dark homes, without heat, light, or a warm meal to cheer them.

Nevertheless, West Berliners were determined not to give in to Soviet pressure. They refused to accept food from the communist government of East Berlin.

The Berlin airlift, known as "Operation Vittles," provided fuel and food for West Berliners in 1948 and 1949. Here, children wait for the candy that American pilots dropped in handkerchief parachutes.

Highlights of American Life

Over the next few weeks, Truman and his military advisers worked out a two-fold response. The first part was a massive airlift of food, fuel, and supplies for both the 10,000 U.S. troops and the two million Germans who lived in the western sectors of Berlin. Fleets of C-47 and C-54 cargo planes began making two daily round-trip flights to Templehof airfield, bringing in 2,500 tons of supplies every 24 hours. Then, to guard against Soviet interference with the airlift, Truman announced the second part of his response—the transfer of 60 American B-29s, planes that supposedly carried atomic bombs, to bases in Britain. The president was bluffing, however. The planes never really had atomic cargoes.

Although the world tottered on the edge of war during the last months of 1948, the Soviets finally gave in in early 1949. They ended the blockade in return for a diplomatic meeting about Germany—a conference that proved as unproductive as all the earlier meetings between East and West.

The Berlin airlift was a striking political victory, showing the world the triumph of American ingenuity over Soviet stubbornness. Yet it could not hide the fact that behind the iron curtain the Soviets had consolidated their control over areas won by their troops in World War II. The Truman Doctrine, the Marshall Plan, and NATO had saved Western Europe, but a divided continent was a far cry from the wartime hopes for a peaceful world.

Americans who flew planes into West Berlin were inspired by the courage and spirit of the citizens of that city. Many of them volunteered to make six flights a day through the narrow corridor that connects West Germany to West Berlin.

SECTION **2** REVIEW

Identify Key People and Terms
Write a sentence to identify: covert, Dean Acheson, George Kennan, containment, Truman Doctrine, Marshall Plan, North Atlantic Treaty Organization (NATO)

Locate Key Places
Which two bodies of water are connected by the Dardanelles?

Master the Main Ideas

1. **Supporting basic civic values:** What civic responsibilities did President Truman hope to fulfill with the appointment of his new foreign policy team?
2. **Understanding U.S. foreign policy:** What global foreign policy goals did the United States establish with the Truman Doctrine?
3. **Analyzing the economic impact of war:** How did the Marshall Plan provide for postwar European recovery?
4. **Perceiving cause-effect relationships:** How did the establishment of NATO affect the Cold War?
5. **Applying decision-making skills:** What options did President Truman have when the Soviet Union blockaded Berlin?

Apply Critical Thinking Skills: Making Comparisons
How does American policy toward Europe after World War I compare with the policy established after World War II? Why did the United States abandon isolation in favor of containment? What difference did it make?

GEOGRAPHY IN AMERICAN HISTORY

Cold War

Defense Systems in the Cold War, 1950s-1960s

| | NATO countries | | Warsaw Pact countries | | Trouble spots |

Warsaw Pact

Bulgaria	Hungary
Czechoslovakia	Poland
East Germany	Romania
	Soviet Union

Map labels:
ARCTIC OCEAN
SOVIET UNION
H-bomb test, 1953
U-2 shot down, 1960
Sputnik launched, 1957
Berlin, 1958-1959
Korean War, 1950-1953
UNITED STATES
PACIFIC OCEAN
ATLANTIC OCEAN
Equator
INDIAN OCEAN
PACIFIC OCEAN

0   4,000 Miles
0   4,000 Kilometers
Robinson Projection
Scale accurate for the Equator

North Atlantic Treaty Organization (NATO)

Britain	France	Luxembourg	Turkey
Belgium	Greece	Netherlands	United States
Canada	Iceland	Norway	West Germany
Denmark	Italy	Portugal	*Spain joined NATO in 1982

Middle East

TURKEY
LEBANON, 1958
Beirut
SYRIA
IRAN, 1953
MEDITERRANEAN SEA
ISRAEL
IRAQ
JORDAN
Suez Canal, 1956
KUWAIT
SAUDI ARABIA
PERSIAN GULF
EGYPT
RED SEA

0   500 Miles
0   500 Kilometers
©SF

Regions Regional conflicts escalated the Cold War in the 1950s. In 1949 the western nations organized NATO; the Soviet Union and Eastern Europe created the Warsaw Pact in 1955.

Which two nations were dominant in the Cold War? Where was *Sputnik* launched?

Critical Thinking Once NATO was formed, why was it probable that the Warsaw Pact would be created?

On April 4, 1949, Italy's foreign minister, Count Carlo Sforza, signed the historic pact that created the North Atlantic Treaty Organization (NATO).

In 1960 this Pittsburgh family participated in a government-sponsored study conducted to gauge how well people would adapt to living in a cramped bomb shelter for an extended time, below. During the Cold War, NATO stockpiled thousands of nuclear missiles, bottom.

North American Defense System (NORAD), 1950s-1960s

Ballistic Missile Early Warning System		Strategic Air Command bases (SAC)	●
Other Warning Lines		Nuclear submarine shipyards	○

Polar Projection

SOVIET UNION

ARCTIC OCEAN

EUROPE

GREENLAND
Thule Radar Station

Clear Radar Station

Distant Early Warning Line (DEW)   Alaska

Mid-Canada Warning Line   CANADA

ATLANTIC OCEAN

Pinetree Warning Line

UNITED STATES

PACIFIC OCEAN

U.S. Naval Space Surveillance System

MEXICO

© SF

Location The main parts of NORAD are located in North America; other components are in Europe and Asia. What defenses are shown north of the lower 48 states? What defenses are located within the lower 48 states?

Critical Thinking Why were the major lines of defense established in Canada?

The Cold War spread to Asia.

Key Terms: H-bomb, 38th parallel

Reading Preview
As you read this section, you will learn:

1. which nation ended the American nuclear monopoly.
2. what new political system China adopted.
3. why the United States became involved in the Korean War.
4. why Truman dismissed MacArthur.

The rivalry between the United States and the Soviet Union intensified in the late 1940s. Both sides began to rebuild their military forces and develop new weapons. In the United States, where American military strength had fallen from 12 million men and women in uniform in 1945 to only 1.5 million by 1947, Truman began increasing the armed forces. Congress approved a peacetime draft in 1948 and began approving larger defense budgets. Truman would soon need his beefed-up army to combat the spread of communism in Asia.

The fearsome power of the H-bomb was demonstrated to the world when a U.S. test bomb destroyed an entire uninhabited island in the Pacific on November 1, 1952. In the next ten years both the Soviet Union and the United States developed bombs 15 times more powerful than the one shown here.

The Soviet Union developed the atomic bomb.

In September 1949 the American people were shocked to learn that the Soviet Union had tested its first atomic bomb, thus ending the American nuclear monopoly. When some advisers urged the president to conduct nuclear arms control negotiations with the Soviets, Truman decided instead to outstrip the Soviet Union by building the **H-bomb**, or hydrogen bomb. After two years of intense effort, the United States tested the first H-bomb in late 1952. This weapon used an atomic device to trigger a powerful fusion explosion. The test bomb was a thousand times more destructive than the bomb that leveled Hiroshima at the end of World War II.

At the same time, Secretary of State Acheson ordered the Policy Planning Staff of the National Security Council to draw up a new statement of national defense to meet the Soviet challenge. NSC-68, as the document eventually became known, began with the charge that the Soviet Union sought "to impose its absolute authority over the rest of the world" and thus "mortally challenged" the United States. It then called for a massive expansion of American military power.

China turned communist.

The promise of the Truman Doctrine to support anticommunist governments around the world was soon put to the test in China. **Chiang Kai-shek**, the Nationalist Chinese leader, had been at war off and on since the 1930s with the Chinese Communists led by **Mao Zedong** [mou′ dzu′dùng]. Chiang's cause had strong support from many Americans.

The United States provided Chiang with extensive economic and military support. Corruption was widespread among the Nationalist leaders, however, and a raging inflation that reached 100 percent devastated the Chinese middle classes and thus eroded Chiang's base of power. The Soviets backed Mao, giving him control over Manchuria in 1946. More important than Soviet support, however, Mao was able to garner the support of the masses in the countryside. He appealed to the desire of the

Chinese people for industrial modernization and agricultural reform. He promised land to the peasants and an end to inflation.

With the masses behind them, the Chinese Communists soon gained the upper hand, despite having a smaller army. In late 1949 Chiang was forced to leave the mainland for Taiwan. Taiwan is about 130 miles east of mainland China. On Taiwan, Chiang set up the Nationalist Chinese government in exile. Meanwhile, Mao became the ruler of the newly proclaimed People's Republic of China. In February 1950 Mao and Stalin signed a treaty of mutual assistance that clearly marked China as a Soviet ally.

The United States responded to Mao's triumph in China in two ways. First, the State Department refused to recognize the People's Republic. Instead, the government claimed that the Nationalists on Taiwan were still the legal rulers of China. Second, the nation began relying on a restored Japan to contain the spread of communism in Asia.

In 1952 the United States ended its occupation of Japan and signed a peace treaty. Under its terms, Japan granted the United States the rights to military bases designed to guard against further communist advances in Asia.

The United States acted to halt communist aggression in Korea.

A major American effort to halt the spread of communism came in Korea. In 1945 American and Soviet forces had arbitrarily divided the nation of Korea at the **38th parallel**, shown on the map on page 688. In the industrial area north of this line, the Soviets installed a communist government under Kim Il-Sung. In the agrarian south, Syngman Rhee, a conservative nationalist, emerged as the American-sponsored ruler. Each seeking total control, neither leader heeded a call from the UN to hold elections to unify the country.

By 1949 the United States and the Soviet Union had pulled out most of their occupation forces. The Soviet Union, however, had helped train a powerful Korean army in the north. For reasons of their own, the Soviets encouraged Kim. Although the Soviet Union and China

were both communist countries, there was a deep animosity between Stalin and Mao. The Soviets knew that a unified Korea under Soviet control would be a blow to Chinese prestige and create a potential enemy on China's flank. It would also pose a threat to Japan.

On June 25, 1950, the North Korean army suddenly crossed the 38th parallel in great numbers. Kim Il-Sung, with the reluctant approval of Stalin, hoped to win control of all of Korea. President Truman, however, did not view the fighting as a civil war, but rather as a clear-cut case of Soviet-inspired aggression. In his memoirs he recalled thinking that: "Communism was acting in Korea just as Hitler, Mussolini, and the Japanese had acted ten, fifteen, and twenty years earlier."

The president put the Korean invasion before the UN Security Council for action. With a Soviet walkout preventing a Soviet veto, the Security Council branded North Korea the aggressor and called on the member states to engage in a collective security action. Within a few days, American troops stationed in Japan were in combat in South Korea. The conflict, which would last more than three years, technically was not a "war." Truman called it a "police action" because the Constitution states that

Red troops march through Beijing spreading propaganda just before the communist takeover of China in 1949. The truck in the center carries a red star with Mao Zedong's picture in it.

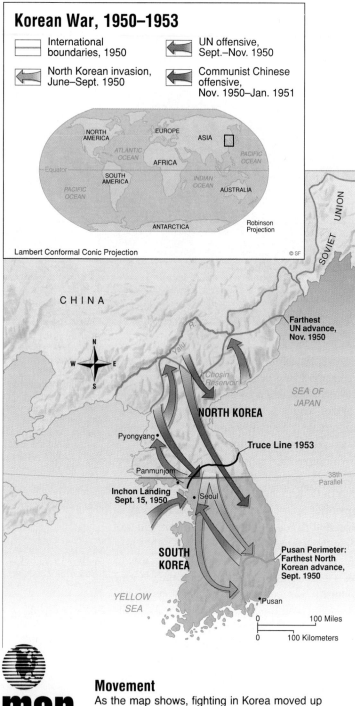

Korean War, 1950–1953

International boundaries, 1950

North Korean invasion, June–Sept. 1950

UN offensive, Sept.–Nov. 1950

Communist Chinese offensive, Nov. 1950–Jan. 1951

NORTH AMERICA
EUROPE
ASIA
ATLANTIC OCEAN
AFRICA
PACIFIC OCEAN
Equator
SOUTH AMERICA
INDIAN OCEAN
PACIFIC OCEAN
AUSTRALIA
ANTARCTICA
Robinson Projection

Lambert Conformal Conic Projection
© SF

CHINA
SOVIET UNION
Yalu R.
Chosin Reservoir
SEA OF JAPAN
NORTH KOREA
Farthest UN advance, Nov. 1950
Pyongyang
Truce Line 1953
Panmunjom
38th Parallel
Inchon Landing Sept. 15, 1950
Seoul
SOUTH KOREA
Pusan Perimeter: Farthest North Korean advance, Sept. 1950
YELLOW SEA
Pusan

0   100 Miles
0   100 Kilometers

map study

Movement
As the map shows, fighting in Korea moved up and down the peninsula during the first year of war. When was the truce line dividing North and South Korea established?

Critical Thinking
China and the Soviet Union are both communist countries. Why did crossing the Yalu River become an important issue in the Korean War?

only Congress has the right to declare war. Truman justified his actions, which were implemented without congressional approval, on the grounds that in the atomic age the president must be able to make quick decisions without waiting for Congress to move through its lengthy debates. Technicalities aside, however, the United States had indeed become involved in a war—a war with a Soviet satellite.

In the beginning the fighting went badly as the North Koreans continued to drive down the peninsula. By August, however, American forces had halted the communist advance near the port of Pusan. As the map at left shows, Pusan is in southeastern Korea. In September General Douglas MacArthur, the American Far Eastern commander, reversed the tide of the war by carrying out a brilliant amphibious assault at Inchon, a coastal city directly west of Seoul, South Korea's capital. Within two weeks the North Korean army was driven back north of the 38th parallel. Encouraged by this unexpected victory, Truman began to shift from his orginal goal of restoring the 38th parallel to a new one—the unification of all Korea by military force.

The new American objective alarmed the Chinese. The Chinese openly warned that if Americans invaded North Korea they would respond with force.

The Truman Administration ignored the warnings from China. "I should think it would be sheer madness for the Chinese to intervene," Secretary of State Acheson told the president. MacArthur was even more confident. "The United States has nothing to fear from China," he told Truman.

Rarely had an American president received worse advice. With Truman's approval, the UN forces crossed the 38th parallel in October and advanced confidently toward the **Yalu River** in early November, preparing for what General MacArthur believed would be the final offensive of the war. (Note on the map at left that the Yalu River separates North Korea and China.) However, the Chinese did what no one thought they would do. They attacked the UN forces and drove them out of North Korea.

At left, American soldiers watch for enemy activity from a foxhole on a snow-covered hill near the 38th parallel. In the inset General MacArthur greets UN forces near Seoul shortly after his successful assault on Inchon.

The 1st Marine Division bore the brunt of the assault by 120,000 Chinese at Chosin Reservoir in bitter winter weather. The Americans fought their way 78 miles down a winding mountain road in a 30-degree-below-zero blizzard. One company lost four commanding officers in an hour. It was so cold that a medic dipped his fingers in blood to keep them warm.

Truman dismissed MacArthur for insubordination.

In early 1951 American forces finally halted the Chinese advance and gradually fought their way back close to the 38th parallel. Feeling he had momentum on his side, General MacArthur wanted to commit massive American forces to win a decisive victory in Korea. If necessary, he favored using the A-bomb against China. "There is no substitute for victory," he declared. Truman, however, insisted on a limited war for limited objectives. He

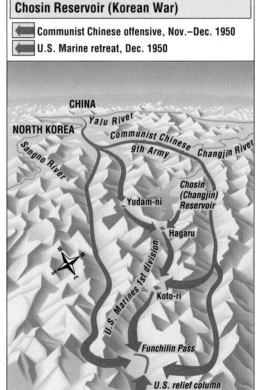

Marine Breakout from Chosin Reservoir (Korean War)

Communist Chinese offensive, Nov.–Dec. 1950

U.S. Marine retreat, Dec. 1950

CHINA
Yalu River
NORTH KOREA
Sangno River
Communist Chinese 9th Army
Changjin River
Chosin (Changjin) Reservoir
Yudam-ni
Hagaru
U.S. Marines 1st division
Koto-ri
Funchilin Pass
U.S. relief column

map study

Movement
A surprise attack of 120,000 communist Chinese forces trapped 20,000 American marines at Chosin Reservoir. How did the marines, an advance force cut off from the main army, manage to escape?

Critical Thinking
What physical factors made the marine retreat so difficult?

VOICES FROM THE PAST

A Soldier's Farewell

After his dismissal by President Truman, General Douglas MacArthur was hailed as a hero on his return to the United States. He closed 52 years of military service with these words to a joint session of Congress. Would it be possible for a person of his importance to simply "fade away"?

The world has turned over many times since I took the oath on the Plain at West Point, and the hopes and dreams have long since vanished. But I still remember the refrain of one of the most popular barrack ballads of that day . . . that old soldiers never die; they just fade away. And like the old soldier of that ballad, I now close my military career and just fade away, an old soldier who tried to do his duty as God gave him the light to see that duty. Good-by.

feared that a broader war in Asia could not be won. He was more worried by the prospect of the conflict turning into World War III.

Truman's policies were bitterly attacked by many conservative politicians. They idolized MacArthur and wanted to "unleash" Chiang Kai-shek and use the Korean conflict to defeat communism in China. MacArthur sided publicly with this viewpoint and insisted that he be allowed to pursue the war by bombing China if necessary. Truman considered this insubordination and relieved him of his command.

In *Plain Speaking*, an oral biography, Truman defended his actions:

If what MacArthur proposed had happened . . . had been allowed to take place, we would have wound up being at war not only with Red China, but with Russia, too, and . . . the consequences would have been . . . it might have meant the destruction of a good part of the world.

AN AMERICAN ★ SPEAKS

Backed by most of the other generals, Truman insisted that a commander, even one as popular as MacArthur, could not be allowed to override civilian authority.

The firing of General MacArthur in April 1951 was a courageous but highly unpopular act. Huge crowds greeted MacArthur to welcome him home from Korea and hear him call for victory over the communists in Asia. A Gallup poll indicated that only 29 percent of the American public had favored firing the popular general. In towns and cities all across the nation, enraged citizens burned President Truman in effigy.

In time, however, people came to accept the wisdom of MacArthur's recall. The Korean War settled into a stalemate near the 38th parallel. Truman could take heart from the fact that he had achieved his original goal, the defense of South Korea. Yet by taking the gamble to unify Korea by force, he had allowed America to be humiliated in the eyes of the world. The war proved more costly than anyone had thought— more than 33,000 American soldiers died in battle, and nearly 100,000 were wounded.

SECTION 3 REVIEW

Identify Key People and Terms
Write a sentence to identify: H-bomb, Chiang Kai-shek, Mao Zedong, 38th parallel

Locate Key Places

1. What two nations in eastern Asia were separated by the 38th parallel?
2. What two nations border the Yalu River?

Master the Main Ideas

1. Analyzing international conflicts: How did the United States respond to the Soviet development of the atomic bomb?
2. Assessing U.S. foreign policy: Why did the United States refuse to recognize China's communist government?
3. Analyzing international conflicts: (a) What was the primary American goal in the Korean War? **(b)** How did the American position shift during the war?
4. Studying political issues: Why was the dismissal of MacArthur originally so unpopular?

Apply Critical Thinking Skills: Identifying Assumptions
What risks did President Truman take when he decided to dismiss the tremendously popular General MacArthur?

The Cold War affected life at home.

Key Terms: Fair Deal, Taft-Hartley Act, Dixiecrats, McCarthyism

Reading Preview
As you read this section, you will learn:

1. how the American economy responded to a return to peace.
2. why Truman failed to get much support for his Fair Deal proposals.
3. who won the election of 1948.
4. how the Cold War affected domestic events.
5. which U.S. senator launched a new red scare.

For Americans generally, World War II restored the confidence shaken by the Great Depression. The United States emerged from the conflict clearly the strongest nation on earth. Most Americans expected that strength to show itself at home as well as abroad. As one nostalgic writer put it: "To have been an American then—the world must have seemed at one's feet."

The economy quickly adjusted to peacetime.

With the end of the war, Depression-era fears of unemployment returned to haunt the nation. Economists predicted that the nation would be unable to absorb returning veterans. Some experts believed that unemployment would affect between 8 and 20 million people.

Women in labor force. Thousands of women did lose their jobs to the returning GIs. For example, in 1943 women made up 25 percent of all automotive workers. By 1950 they were only 10 percent. Most of these women did not give up their jobs willingly. Company policies and social pressures forced them to make room for the veterans.

Frankie Cooper was one of the many women who lost a high-paying job when the war ended. During much of the war she had worked as a certified welder at a shipyard on the East Coast. She had liked the job and the independence it had given her so much that she had toyed with the idea of finding a job after the war. A new agenda for women, however, discouraged her from doing so:

After the war . . . you were supposed to become a feminine person. We laid aside our slacks, our checkered shirts, and we went in for ostrich feathers, ruffles, high-heeled shoes. All this was part of the propaganda in magazines and newspapers to put a woman back in her "rightful place" in the home. . . . Go home and make your bread, raise your children.

AN AMERICAN ★ SPEAKS

Like many other women, Cooper initially bowed to social pressure. She settled into her expected role as a dutiful wife and mother. The war had changed her outlook on life, however:

My husband would have been happy if I had gone back to the kind of girl I was when he married me—a little homebody there on the farm, in the kitchen, straining milk. But I wasn't that person anymore. I tried it for three years, but it just didn't work out. All at once I took a good look at myself, and I said no. No, you're not going to do it. You're not going back where you started from. From here on, you're your own person, you can do anything you want to do.

Frankie Cooper and thousands of other women lost high-paying jobs when the war ended. This classic Margaret Bourke-White photograph, titled "Women in Steel," first appeared in *Life* in 1943. The workers are beveling armored plates for use in the manufacture of tanks.

Doing what she wanted to do proved to be a difficult task. Her desire to find a job resulted in the breakup of her marriage and discrimination in the workplace. She moved to Cincinnati and applied through the mail for a job as a welder. When it came time for the interview, Cooper was rudely awakened:

When I met the personnel manager he said there had been a terrible mistake. They thought I was a man, because they had assumed my name was Frank. I said, "What about my qualifications?" And he agreed that I was highly qualified. . . . Finally he said, "I will go out in the plant and check with the men. . . . If you are acceptable to them . . . I'll hire you." When he came back he said, "I asked the men and the men said they would rather not work with a woman."

Although Cooper didn't get the job as a welder, she didn't give up hope:

It took a while, but eventually I got a job setting fuses for ninety-millimeter guns. Still it was a woman's job at a woman's pay. Then I found another job . . . assembling television tubes . . . and I ran for president of the union . . . and I won. I've been involved in labor work ever since.

Men in labor force. Although many women were thrown out of work, jobs for men in the postwar years were generally available. The credit for preventing a crisis in unemployment for men belongs in part to effective government planning. The economy returned to peacetime production more smoothly and efficiently than anyone had expected. By the end of 1945, more than 90 percent of the wartime industries were back to civilian production. This rapid revival plus GI unemployment benefits meant that the breadlines of the Depression never returned.

African Americans made important breakthroughs in the 1940s. In the field of sports Jackie Robinson became the first African American to play major league baseball when he joined the Brooklyn Dodgers in 1947. An exceptional hitter and fielder, he was elected to the National Baseball Hall of Fame in 1962.

Inflation, not unemployment, became the biggest postwar problem. During the war years, military production and strict rationing had limited the purchases people could make. With few consumer goods available, Americans saved some $140 billion. When the war ended, people wanted to spend those dollars on goods yet to be produced. As a result, prices of the limited goods available went sky-high.

The enormous growth of the economy, however, came to Truman's rescue. With more and more goods available, prices began to level off by 1950. Critics of the New Deal saw in this a vindication of their point of view. They argued that business, not government, had stifled inflation. To them the end of war and price controls signaled the end of the New Deal.

Americans were not interested in reform.

President Truman ignored his conservative critics and laid plans to extend the New Deal. He called his proposals the **Fair Deal**. Truman's Fair Deal called for an expansion of the Social Security system, an increase in the minimum wage from 40¢ to 75¢ an hour, and a full employment bill. His plan also called for an end to racial discrimination in housing, a stronger Fair Employment Practices Commission, and new public housing and slum clearance programs. In addition, Truman's Fair Deal proposed federal aid to education, national health insurance, and government support of scientific research.

In 1949 Congress raised the minimum wage and passed the Public Housing Act. In 1950 it extended Social Security coverage to ten million more Americans. Congress, however, refused to pass most of Truman's other proposals. The postwar mood of the nation was not conducive to a new outburst of reforms. Concerns such as the Cold War, inflation, and labor unrest were deemed more important.

Business and labor strife. After the war business and labor resumed the fierce fighting of the Depression years. As we have seen, the depression of the 1930s greatly weakened the public's view of American business. The success of industry in arming the Allies, however, revived public support of the business community. Their confidence renewed, members of the National Association of Manufacturers and other business owners began to take the offensive against organized labor and its allies.

Although organized labor had also gained in strength, it had some new problems. During the war, workers had not gone on strike because of patriotism and high wages. At the war's end, prices rose sharply and wages declined. Wages fell because of the end of overtime pay for war production, the end of well-paid defense work, and the growing surplus of labor as veterans flooded the labor market. Once more workers began to hit the bricks—to go out on strike. By January 1946, two million workers were on strike in the auto, oil refining, electrical, and steel industries.

The conflict between business and labor centered on how to divide growing profits. Between 1939 and 1945, productivity in American industry had doubled, but wages had not kept pace. Many companies grew prosperous on wartime contracts and then saw profits soar even higher after the war. Union leaders pointed to these enormous profits and argued that wages could be greatly raised without increasing prices. Management bitterly rejected these suggestions. They argued that such a path would lead to tyranny and socialism.

Taft-Hartley Act. The efforts of labor unions to win their goals led to growing resentment on the part of business. Even many unorganized workers objected to union demands. In 1947 antiunion sentiment led to the passage of the **Taft-Hartley Act** over Truman's veto. The main author of the measure was Senator Robert A. Taft of Ohio. Taft, the highly respected leader of the conservative forces in the Republican party, wanted to limit the power of unions. He claimed they had been made too strong by New Deal labor laws.

The Taft-Hartley Act outlawed such labor practices as the closed shop, which prevented employers from hiring nonunion members. Union shops, which required workers to join a union after they were hired, were still permitted. The Taft-Hartley Act also required unions to accept a 60-day "cooling-off period" before

Striking General Electric workers march to city hall in Philadelphia in February 1946. The workers were protesting the tactics used by police to break up picket lines at the GE plant. Across the country, workers in other industries also "hit the bricks" to protest declining wages.

striking. It also empowered the president to issue an injunction to prevent strikes that hurt the national safety.

Labor denounced the act as a slave-labor law designed to keep workers docile. The passage of the law over Truman's veto was only one sign of the growing conservative mood in the country. It also reflected the president's dwindling popularity.

Truman won an upset victory in 1948.

As the nation approached the presidential election of 1948, Truman-can't-win talk filled the air. Despite the popularity of Truman's militantly anti-Soviet foreign policy, the tide seemed to be moving with the Republicans. The Republicans thought the country was finally turning away from the active government spawned by the New Deal and back to business-oriented politics. They had captured Congress in 1946. In the past, when the party out of power won control of Congress during an off-year election, it had always gone on to win the next presidential election.

As their candidate in 1948, the Republicans nominated Governor Thomas E. Dewey of New York. Dewey, who had also been the Republican nominee in 1944, was confident about his chances. He expected to capitalize on the

Unions

Point

In favor of Taft-Hartley Act

- Socialism will result if unions are not regulated.
- Businesses in a free enterprise system should have the right to hire employees of their choice—union or nonunion.
- Businesses do not necessarily have to share their profits with workers.

Counterpoint

Against Taft-Hartley Act

- The closed shop is needed to prevent businesses from taking advantage of workers.
- Unions have the right to strike whenever they believe it is necessary.
- Profits are the direct results of productive labor; therefore, labor should benefit whenever businesses profit.

feeling that the Democrats had been in office for 16 years and "it was time to throw the rascals out."

Before Truman could face Dewey he had to fight off numerous challenges from within his own party. A number of moderate Democrats approached World War II hero General Dwight D. Eisenhower and asked him if he would be their standard-bearer, but he declined. On his political left, Truman faced Henry Wallace, who had left the Democratic party over what he felt was Truman's unnecessary belligerence toward the Soviet Union. Wallace's followers considered him the true heir to FDR. To his right, Truman faced the States' Rights Democrats, which the press called **Dixiecrats**, led by Senator Strom Thurmond of South Carolina. The Dixiecrats wanted to protect southern white interests and to limit the power of African Americans.

With many traditional Democratic votes lost to him because of the Fair Deal and his stand on civil rights, Truman seemed to have little chance of winning in 1948. Truman was stronger than he appeared, however. As a campaigner, his Republican opponent was "as dull as a dishrag." Riding around the country on his Victory Special train, Dewey was overconfident. Many people found him cold, smug, and overly slick. Truman, on the other hand, was an exciting campaigner. He crisscrossed the country by rail on a whistle-stop campaign, giving as many as a dozen speeches a day in his folksy, no-holds-barred style.

The campaign was nasty. The Republicans accused Truman of being soft on communism. Truman accused the Republicans of being tools of big business. Truman's masterstroke was to call the Republican Congress back into session midway through the campaign to enact measures that he said would relieve the average American of the burden of inflation. When Congress refused to approve his proposals, the president scored crucial points with the public. To a group of farmers in Iowa Truman shouted that: "Congress has stuck a pitchfork in the farmer's back."

The morning after the election, the headline in the *Chicago Tribune* read "Dewey Defeats Truman." The *Tribune* was wrong, however. To the surprise of almost everyone, Truman had won an upset victory. He had gained almost 50 percent of the popular vote, while Dewey received only 45 percent.

Elections are more than personal popularity contests. Looked at closely, they can be seen as X rays that reveal the inner anatomy of the country. When historians analyzed the 1948 election, they saw that Truman's victory was a testimony to the number of groups that had come to look to the federal government for assistance. The farmers, for instance, who were supposed to be mainly Republican, voted heavily for Truman. They had come to depend on New Deal price supports and were unwilling to risk a Republican administration. Blue-collar Americans feared that a Dewey presidency might bring more in the way of Taft-Hartley legislation. In addition, African Americans, voting in increasing numbers, abandoned the party of Lincoln for the party of civil rights.

High-level Americans were accused of being communists.

Although the Cold War helped Truman win re-election in 1948, it led to an intense outburst of anticommunist emotions that hurt the Democrats. Fear of radicalism had been a recurrent theme in American history, from the Alien and Sedition Acts of the 1790s to the red scare after World War I. The rivalry with the Soviet Union heightened the traditional belief that subversion from abroad endangered the Republic.

President Truman beams as he holds an early edition of the November 4, 1948, *Chicago Tribune* that had erroneously declared Dewey as the winner of the extremely close presidential election.

A series of revelations of communists penetrating American government agencies reinforced these fears. The most startling disclosure came in August 1948, when Whittaker Chambers, a repentant communist, accused **Alger Hiss**, a former high State Department official, of having been a Soviet spy in the 1930s. When Hiss denied the charges, Chambers led congressional investigators to a hollowed-out pumpkin on his Maryland farm. Inside the pumpkin were microfilms of secret government documents that Chambers claimed Hiss had passed to him in the 1930s. Although too much time had passed for Hiss to be tried for treason, he eventually was convicted of perjury and sentenced to five years in federal prison.

At first Truman dismissed the charges of disloyalty as a red herring, a ploy used to draw attention away from the real issue. He finally responded, however, by beginning a loyalty

map study

Regions
Truman did well in all regions of the country except which one?

Critical Thinking
How did regional voting in 1948 show the support of farmers and African Americans for Truman?

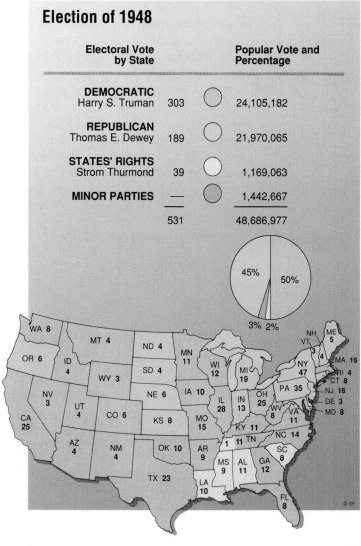

Election of 1948

Electoral Vote by State		Popular Vote and Percentage
DEMOCRATIC Harry S. Truman	303	24,105,182
REPUBLICAN Thomas E. Dewey	189	21,970,065
STATES' RIGHTS Strom Thurmond	39	1,169,063
MINOR PARTIES	—	1,442,667
	531	48,686,977

45% 50% 3% 2%

The execution of the Rosenbergs, shown here in a police van after their conspiracy conviction on April 5, 1951, remains a controversial topic even today as new evidence periodically surfaces supporting their guilt or innocence.

program designed to root out communists from the ranks of government workers. Often acting on rumors and not allowing the accused to face their accusers, Truman's Loyalty Review Board began to dismiss workers as security risks on the flimsy ground of reasonable doubt about their loyalty. Thousands of government employees lost their jobs. They were charged with guilt by association with radicals or with membership in left-wing organizations. In September 1949, when the Truman Administration revealed that the Soviets had detonated their first atomic bomb, many people jumped to the

conclusion that communist spies had helped end the nuclear monopoly.

A few months later, the United States government charged American communists **Ethel** and **Julius Rosenberg** with conspiracy to transmit atomic secrets to the Soviet Union. In 1951 a jury found the Rosenbergs guilty of treason. A judge then sentenced them to die for what he termed a "loathsome offense." Despite their insistent claims of innocence and worldwide appeals to spare their lives, the Rosenbergs were electrocuted on June 19, 1953.

Thus, by the early 1950s, nearly all the ingredients were at hand for a new outburst of hysteria. Fear of the Soviet Union, evidence of atomic espionage, and a belief in a vast unseen conspiracy would fuel this new red scare.

Joseph McCarthy launched a new red scare.

On February 9, 1950, **Joseph McCarthy**, a little-known U.S. senator from the midwestern state of **Wisconsin**, attracted national attention. Speaking in Wheeling, West Virginia, the Republican declared:

Senator Joseph McCarthy displays the infamous list of supposed communists in the U.S. State Department to the press.

I have here in my hand a list of 205—a list of names that   AN AMERICAN ★ SPEAKS
were made known to the Secretary of State as being members of the Communist party and who nevertheless are still working and shaping policy in the State Department.

McCarthy repeated the charge that there were communists in the State Department, although the number changed almost daily, from 205 to 57 to 81. Although McCarthy failed to prove that there was a single communist in the government, his strident accusations triggered a national crusade to hunt down subversives in the Truman Administration. This crusade soon became known as **McCarthyism**.

The senator's basic technique was the multiple untruth. Instead of offering evidence to prove his charges, he kept coming up with a steady stream of new ones. Relying on tips from disgruntled government workers, he accused Truman of hiring and protecting known communist agents. Everywhere he went, McCarthy carried a briefcase bulging with documents, but he did little actual research, relying instead on earlier congressional investigations. He was especially skillful in exploiting the press, calling news conferences just before newspaper deadlines to make startling accusations sure to win big headlines.

The secret of McCarthy's power was the fear he created among his Senate colleagues. In 1950 he succeeded in helping to defeat several senators who had spoken out against him. McCarthy delighted in taking on prominent public figures. He ridiculed Secretary of State Dean Acheson as the "Red Dean," and he even went after General George Marshall, calling this highly respected statesman an agent of the communist conspiracy. Although he concentrated on Democrats, not even Republicans were immune. One Republican senator was described as "a living miracle in that he is without question the only man who has lived so long with neither brains nor guts."

These attacks on the famous and privileged won McCarthy a devoted national following. He was especially popular among those groups who normally voted Democratic—working-class Catholics and ethnic voters of Irish, Polish, and Italian descent who held strongly anticommunist beliefs. Above all, he appealed to conservative Republicans in the Midwest who felt cheated by Truman's upset victory in 1948. Republican leaders such as Senator Robert Taft of Ohio found McCarthy's tactics personally distasteful, but they quietly encouraged him to continue attacking vulnerable Democrats.

By the early 1950s, Truman and the Democrats were in tremendously deep political trouble. McCarthyism had undermined the public's confidence in the Administration. The continued fighting in Korea, with no victory in sight, added to the public disillusionment. The Republicans had been overconfident in 1948, but now they had a second chance to capture the White House. All they needed was the right candidate to lead them to victory.

SECTION **4** REVIEW

Identify Key People and Terms
Write a sentence to identify: Fair Deal, Taft-Hartley Act, Dixiecrats, Alger Hiss, Ethel and Julius Rosenberg, Joseph McCarthy, McCarthyism

Locate Key Places
In which region of the United States is Wisconsin located?

Master the Main Ideas

1. **Analyzing the economic impact of war: (a)** How did the wartime economy affect the personal savings of Americans? **(b)** What effect did these savings have on the postwar economy?
2. **Assessing major political issues:** What economic issues distracted Americans from reform?
3. **Examining political elections:** Why was Truman's victory in the 1948 election so "miraculous"?
4. **Examining social issues:** How did the red scare reflect the American society's feelings about communism?
5. **Assessing political leaders:** What methods did Senator McCarthy use to fuel the new red scare?

Apply Critical Thinking Skills: Making Comparisons
Compare the campaign style of President Harry Truman to that of President George Bush. How would you characterize the style of each president? Which style do you prefer? Why?

Kuangchi Chang Flees Communism

17A

TIME FRAME
1949

GEOGRAPHIC SETTING
United States

In October 1949 the Chinese Communists, led by Mao Zedong [mou' tse'tŭng], proclaimed the birth of the People's Republic of China. In that same year, Kuangchi Chang [kwäng'chē jäng], an architect and art historian, came to the United States as a refugee from communism. Chang, who was born in Shanghai, reflected on his childhood and his experience as a refugee in the following poem. The Great Wall (line 3) is an ancient stone fortification 4,000 miles long that defended China's northern frontier from barbarian invaders. A juggernaut (line 13) is a force that destroys everything in its path. The Yangtse [yang'tsē] (line 14) is China's longest river.

Garden of My Childhood

"**R**un, run, run,"
Whispered the vine,
"A horde is on the march no Great Wall
  can halt."
5 But in the garden of my childhood
The old maple was painting a sunset
And the crickets were singing a carol;
No, I had no wish to run.

"Run, run, run,"
10 Gasped the wind,
"the horde has entered the Wall."
Down the scorched plain rode the
  juggernaut
And crossed the Yangtse as if it were a
15   ditch;
The proverbial rats had abandoned the
  ship
But I had no intention of abandoning
The garden of my childhood.

20 "Run, run, run,"
Roared the sea,
"Run before the bridge is drawn."
In the engulfed calm after the storm
The relentless tom-tom of the rice-sprout
25   song
Finally ripped my armor,
And so I ran.

I ran past the old maple by the terraced
  hall
30 And the singing crickets under the
  latticed wall,

And I kept on running down the walk
Paved with pebbles of memory big and
  small
35 Without turning to look until I was out of
  the gate
Through which there be no return at all.

Now, eons later and worlds away,
The running is all done
40 For I am at my destination: Another
  garden,
Where the unpebbled walk awaits
  tomorrow's footprints,
Where my old maple will come with the
45   sunset's glow
And my crickets will sing under the wake-
  ful pillow.

Discussing the Reading

1. Who did Kuangchi Chang mean by the "horde" in line 3?

2. What is the new "garden" (line 41) at which the narrator arrives? Why does its "unpebbled walk [await] tomorrow's footprints"?

CRITICAL THINKING
Recognizing Values

What attitude did Kuangchi Chang have toward the homeland he was leaving? Did his departure from China make him feel relieved or guilty?

A young marcher helps carry a huge red star in a parade held on August 1, 1949, to celebrate the conquest of the city of Shanghai by the Chinese Communists. The characters on the banner in the background identify the portrait of Communist leader Mao Zedong.

TIME FRAME
1950

GEOGRAPHIC SETTING
Wake Island in the Pacific
Ocean; Washington, D.C.

When President Truman fired General Mac-Arthur as commander in Korea in 1951, he set off a national uproar. In the following reading, Merle Miller, a Truman biographer, questioned the former President about the episode. Truman's physician, who was present at the Wake Island meeting of Truman and MacArthur in 1950, joined in the discussion, one of a series of interviews with Truman that took place in 1961 and 1962.

Mr. President, I know why you fired General MacArthur, but if you don't mind, I'd like to hear it in your own words.
Mr. Truman: "I fired him because he
5 wouldn't respect the authority of the President. That's the answer to that. I didn't fire him because he was . . . dumb . . ., although he was, but that's not against the law for generals. If it was, half to three-
10 quarters of them would be in jail. . .

[In the fall of 1950 Truman flew to Wake Island to meet MacArthur.]
Dr. Wallace Graham, Mr. Truman's personal physician:
15 "I was with the President when he was going to meet MacArthur on Wake Island. And MacArthur was always a showman type. He deliberately tried to hold up his

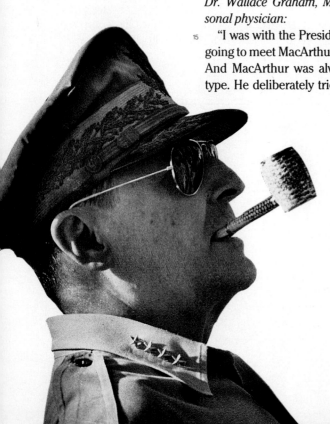

landing so that we would go in and land
20 ahead of them.
"Harry caught it right away, and he told MacArthur, 'You go ahead and land first. We've got plenty of gas. We'll wait for you.' And that's what happened. That's what we
25 did."
Mr. Truman: "MacArthur was always play acting, and he wasn't any . . . good at it. I knew what he was trying to pull with all that stuff about whose plane was going to
30 land first, and I wasn't going to let him get away with it.
"So I let . . . I made it quite clear that he was to go in first, and he did."
I understand that when you did get on
35 the ground, there was another delay.
Mr. Truman: "There was. After we landed, there was a welcoming party there on the ground, but I looked out the window, and MacArthur wasn't there . . .
40 "When he walked in, I took one look at him, and I said, 'Now you look here. I've come halfway across the world to meet you, but don't worry about that. I just want you to know I don't [care] what you do or
45 think about Harry Truman, but don't you ever again keep your Commander in Chief waiting. Is that clear?'
"His face got as red as a beet, but he said . . . he indicated that he understood
50 what I was talking about, and we went on from there. . . . "
Only a few days after President Truman's return to Washington from Wake Island and from MacArthur's assurance of
55 everlasting loyalty, the general directly countermanded the President's orders to use only South Korean troops near the northern borders. He personally ordered American forces into the vanguard of the
60 drive north to the Yalu. . . .
[After the Chinese pushed UN forces far south], MacArthur, still smarting, still

His trademark corncob pipe clenched between his teeth, General Douglas MacArthur surveys a World War II beachhead in the portrait on the facing page. The cartoon on the right, which appeared in April, 1951, reflects the dissatisfaction of the American public with Truman's firing of MacArthur, a national hero.

FIRING OF MACARTHUR

PUBLIC OPINION

issuing complaints about his treatment in Washington, regrouped his forces and started north again. By March they were once more back at the thirty-eighth parallel, and it was here that the final, bitter showdown between the general and the President began.

Truman and the Joint Chiefs wanted MacArthur to stop at the thirty-eighth parallel so that the President, with South Korea now cleared, could, it was hoped, begin to negotiate a ceasefire.

MacArthur was having none of that. He proposed not to stop the war, but to expand it; only in that way, he said publicly, would lasting peace be achieved. Otherwise, he would be fighting what he called "an accordion war," moving back and forth until first one side, then the other moved too far ahead of its supplies. As an alternative he proposed bombing China's industrial cities, blockading its coast, and, once again, using Chiang Kai-shek's army in Korea and to invade South China as well....

MacArthur paid no attention at all to the advice from Washington. Instead, four days later he issued a statement of his own. He said that he personally was ready to meet with the enemy [Red China] to discuss a settlement in Korea. Barring that, he threatened a general attack against China. And he suggested that if

North Korea were to be surrendered, it be surrendered to him personally....

Harry Truman waited two weeks. I didn't ask how he managed, but I did ask why.

Mr. Truman: "I wanted, if possible, an even ... better example of his insubordination, and I wanted it to be one that the ... that everybody would recognize for exactly what it was, and I knew that, MacArthur being the kind of man he was, I wouldn't have long to wait, and I didn't. He wrote that letter to [House minority leader] Joe Martin. And you've read it. He repeated that *he* wanted to use Chiang Kai-shek's troops and repeated that ... all that stuff about there being 'no substitute for victory.' ...

"We had a series ... several meetings with what they called the war cabinet; I never called it that, but that's what the papers called it. I called everybody together, and I said, 'I'm going to fire [him] *right now.'* And they all agreed.... And that's all there was to it. I went to bed, and Joe Short [press aide] called a press conference and read my statement, and it was all over but the shouting."

As I recall, there was plenty of shouting. *Mr. Truman:* "No more than I expected. I knew there'd be a big uproar, and I knew that MacArthur would take every advantage of it that he could, but I knew that ... in the end people would see through him, and it would all die down."

Discussing the Reading

1. Why did President Truman fire General MacArthur?

2. How did Truman's and MacArthur's ideas on the war conflict?

CRITICAL THINKING
Demonstrating Reasoned Judgment

Do you believe that President Truman was justified in firing General MacArthur? Why or why not?

Chapter Summary

Write supporting details under each of the following main ideas as you review the chapter.

Section 1

1. President Truman confronted the Soviet Union.
2. The United Nations proved to be generally ineffective.
3. The Cold War led to the division of Europe.

Section 2

1. President Truman chose a new foreign policy team.
2. The United States announced the Truman Doctrine.
3. The Marshall Plan aided European recovery.
4. NATO put Europe under the American nuclear shield.
5. Stalin imposed a land blockade of Berlin in 1948.

Section 3

1. The Soviet Union developed the atomic bomb.
2. China turned communist.
3. The United States acted to halt communist aggression in Korea.
4. Truman dismissed MacArthur for insubordination.

Section 4

1. The economy quickly adjusted to peacetime.
2. Americans were not interested in reform.
3. Truman won an upset victory in 1948.
4. High-level Americans were accused of being communists.
5. Joseph McCarthy launched a new red scare.

Chapter Themes

1. **Relations with other nations:** After World War II, the United States was the dominant power in the world. As such, Americans believed they should protect world freedom and democracy from a new threat, communist expansion.
2. **Conflict and cooperation:** The Cold War introduced Americans to new kinds of international conflict, such as the arms race, limited war, military alliances, and internal strife over communism.

Chapter Study Guide

Identifying Key People and Terms

Name the key person or key term that describes the:

1. post-World War II power struggle between the United States and the Soviet Union.
2. Truman's secretary of state, largely responsible for saving Western Europe from economic ruin.
3. broad mutual defense alliance formed by the United States, Canada, and ten European nations.
4. communist leader who ruled post-World War II China.
5. crusade to hunt down communist subversives in high places in American society.

Locating Key Places

1. Why is the 38th parallel significant?
2. What is the strategic waterway connecting the Black and Mediterranean seas?

Mastering the Main Ideas

1. Why did the United Nations prove to be ineffective during many post-World War II crises?
2. How did the Truman Administration carry out the containment strategy?
3. In what respect was the Korean conflict of the early 1950s a "limited" war?
4. How did the end of World War II affect many American women workers?

Applying Critical Thinking Skills

1. **Making comparisons:** How was Harry Truman like and unlike Franklin Roosevelt?
2. **Predicting consequences:** President Truman believed MacArthur's recommendation to use the atomic bomb against Chinese bases in Manchuria during the Korean War would have escalated the conflict into a third world war. Why did Truman predict this consequence, and do you think he was correct?
3. **Expressing problems:** What were the problems caused by the Soviets' blockade of West Berlin?
4. **Distinguishing false from accurate images:** Was Truman's description of the Korean conflict as a "police action" a false image or an accurate image? Explain.

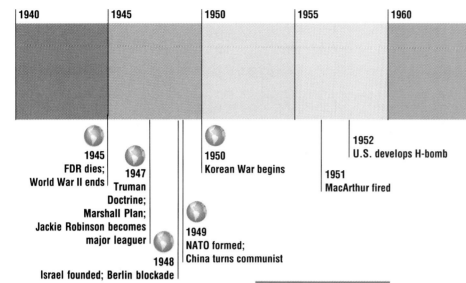

1940 | 1945 | 1950 | 1955 | 1960

1945
FDR dies;
World War II ends

1947
Truman
Doctrine;
Marshall Plan;
Jackie Robinson becomes
major leaguer

1948
Israel founded; Berlin blockade

1949
NATO formed;
China turns communist

1950
Korean War begins

1951
MacArthur fired

1952
U.S. develops H-bomb

Chapter Activities

Learning Geography Through History

1. On a map of Europe, trace a line from Stettin, Poland, (now called Szcezecin) to present-day Trieste, Italy. This line was Churchill's "iron curtain." In reality, this curtain's borders extended farther east. What were the actual western borders of the Soviet-ruled nations of Eastern Europe?
2. Which parallel divided North Korea and South Korea?

Relating the United States to the World

1. What international organizations did the United States join after World War II in an effort to defend peace and freedom?
2. How might the United States involvement in the Korean War have affected the communists' worldwide plans?

Linking Past to Present

1. The Cold War began immediately after the end of World War II. Why might the events of 1989–1990 in Eastern Europe be thought of as the end of the Cold War?
2. To his critics, certain aspects of Truman's Fair Deal of the 1940s seemed extreme. Do some research in the library. Investigate one of the following topics: minimum wage, full employment, racial discrimination in housing, fair employment practices, adequate public housing, federal aid to education, national health insurance, or government support of scientific research. Then rate the American people's success or failure to achieve Truman's goal regarding the topic you chose.

Using the Time Line

1. Why might 1949 be considered an important year of change for the world?
2. Who was the first African American major league baseball player?

Practicing Critical Thinking Strategies

Expressing Problems
MacArthur claimed that "there is no substitute for victory." Write an essay that expresses three problems that such a philosophy might create.

Learning More About the Cold War Era

Linking Past to Present

Suburbia was born in the late 1940s with the development of planned communities such as Levittown, New York, inset. The Levittown homes, which were built at the furious rate of 150 per week, had interiors that were identical in every detail right down to the venetian blinds. Today sprawling suburban communities such as Serramonte/ Westlake in San Francisco, background, fringe every city in the nation.

Eisenhower and Postwar Prosperity

1 9 5 3 – 1 9 6 0

18

On May 7, 1947, William Levitt announced plans to build 2,000 houses in a former potato field on Long Island, 30 miles from midtown Manhattan. Using mass production techniques he had mastered during the war, Levitt quickly built 4,000 homes. Young couples, crowded in city apartments or living with their parents, rushed out to buy Levitt's houses. They were inexpensive, comfortable, and efficient, and each came with a refrigerator, cooking range, and washing machine. By 1951 Levittown was a thriving suburban community with more than 17,000 homes. Just nine years later, one-third of the nation lived in suburbs such as Levittown. Suburban growth contributed significantly to an economic boom that brought unprecedented prosperity to most Americans.

At the same time Americans enjoyed affluence, the Cold War heated up, and America's chief rival, the Soviet Union, made stunning new achievements in science and technology. These developments as well as the flight to the suburbs raised a number of weighty questions. Were Americans becoming too concerned with material prosperity? Was affluence more important than the Cold War? Was the Soviet Union beginning to overtake the United States in science and technology?

CHAPTER PREVIEW

In this chapter you will learn how the American people lived during the 1950s.

SECTIONS IN THIS CHAPTER:
1. **The American economy boomed.**
2. **Eisenhower served as president.**
3. **The Cold War tested Eisenhower.**
4. **Americans questioned their values.**
5. **Theme Essay:** *Sputnik* shook the confidence of the American people.

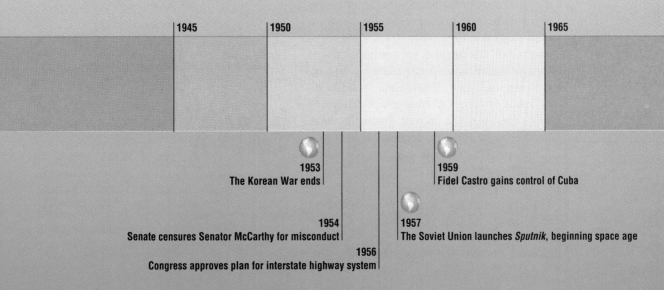

| 1945 | 1950 | 1955 | 1960 | 1965 |

1953
The Korean War ends

1959
Fidel Castro gains control of Cuba

1954
Senate censures Senator McCarthy for misconduct

1957
The Soviet Union launches *Sputnik*, beginning space age

1956
Congress approves plan for interstate highway system

SECTION 1

The American economy boomed.

Key Term: baby boom

Reading Preview
As you read this section, you will learn:

1. what two major factors sparked the economy in the postwar years.
2. how the nation's standard of living changed in the 1950s.
3. what impact television had on the American public in the 1950s.
4. how Americans changed when they moved to the suburbs.
5. how religion changed in the 1950s.

In the 15 years following World War II, the United States underwent an unprecedented period of economic growth. By the end of this period, most of the nation's population lived free of material want. With Europe and Japan still recovering from the war, America, with only six percent of the world's population, produced half of the world's manufactured goods.

Consumers and the Cold War sparked economic growth.

Two major factors were responsible for the nation's postwar prosperity. First, after years of depression and then wartime scarcities, there was a pent-up demand for consumer goods. Initially, American factories could not turn out cars and appliances fast enough to satisfy the appetites of hordes of savings-rich buyers. By 1950, however, the factory production lines finally caught up with demand. In that year Americans bought more than six million automobiles and the Gross National Product (GNP) was 50 percent higher than in 1940. The GNP represents the value of all goods and services produced in a nation during a specific period. Second, the Cold War provided the additional stimulus the economy needed when

postwar expansion slowed. The Marshall Plan and other foreign-aid programs led to a large increase in American exports. Then the Korean War and the continuing rivalry with the Soviet Union expanded defense spending fourfold in the early 1950s.

As a result of these economic factors, the nation achieved a level of affluence that erased any fears of another Great Depression. The growth of the suburbs continued as the nation underwent a **baby boom**, a period that has a substantially higher than normal number of births. Young married couples began to have three, four, or five children compared to only one or two children in the 1930s. This trend led to the largest rise in population in any decade since 1910.

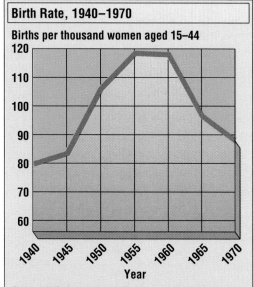

Birth Rate, 1940–1970

Births per thousand women aged 15–44

Source: U.S. Bureau of the Census, *Historical Statistics of the United States, Colonial Times to 1970,* Bicentennial Edition, Washington, D.C., 1975.

chart study

The nation experienced an unprecedented population explosion during the baby boom years. According to this graph, during which decade did the baby boom peak?
Critical Thinking Why do you suppose the late 1960s experienced such a plunge in the birth rate?

The nation enjoyed a high standard of living.

The national economy boomed as manufacturers turned out an ever-increasing number of refrigerators, ranges, and dishwashers to equip the kitchens of Levittown and other suburbs across the country. A multitude of new consumer products—ranging from frozen foods to high fidelity phonographs—appeared in stores. In the suburbs, the supermarket replaced the corner store.

The automobile industry thrived with suburban expansion as two-car families became commonplace. In 1955, in an era when gasoline sold for less than 30 cents a gallon, Detroit's auto industry sold a record 8 million cars. In addition, businesses snapped up office machines and the first generation of computers; industry installed electronic sensors and processors as it underwent extensive automation; and the military showed a growing hunger for electronic devices for its planes and ships.

Despite the economic abundance of the 1950s, not everyone shared in the prosperity. Long-established manufacturing areas such as

New England, which is located in the Northeast, experienced hard times, and farmers continued to suffer from low crop prices. Unemployment persisted, rising to more than seven percent in a year-long recession that hit the country in the fall of 1957.

The nation as a whole, however, was remarkably prosperous. The GNP grew to $440 billion by 1960, more than double the 1940

America's love affair with the automobile began with the flight to the suburbs in the 1950s. By the end of the decade, the nation had 40 million automobiles—about one car for every four-and-a-half people.

MUSIC OF THE 1950S: The record business boomed during the 1950s. From top to bottom, some of the period's most successful recording stars were: Chuck Berry, Buddy Holly, Ritchie Valens, Teresa Brewer, and Elvis Presley.

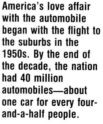

level. More importantly, workers now labored fewer than 40 hours a week. From 1945 to 1960, annual per-capita disposable income rose from $1,345 to $1,845. The American people, in one generation, had moved from poverty and depression to the highest standard of living the world had ever known.

Television changed American life.

The boom industry that had the greatest impact on American life in the 1950s was television. The new medium had a slow start, but it soon began to compete with radio and even undermined many leading mass circulation magazines such as *The Saturday Evening Post*. By 1957 the three networks—CBS, NBC, and ABC—controlled the airwaves. Their 500 stations reached 40 million TV sets.

In the early days of television, the insatiable demand for new programs led to a burst of creativity. Writers such as Reginald Rose, Rod Serling, and Paddy Chayefsky created a series of notable dramas in the 1950s. Broadcast live from cramped studios, these productions thrived on tight dramatic structures, movable scenery, and frequent closeups of the actors. *Marty*, Chayefsky's deceptively simple story of a butcher's decision to marry, epitomized the golden age of television.

Although the networks attempted to develop

The American Musical

Oh, what a beautiful mornin'. That lyric did more than open the musical *Oklahoma!*; it announced the dawn of a new era in the American musical theater. Following the lead of Jerome Kern's *Show Boat* (1927), composer Richard Rodgers and lyricist Oscar Hammerstein II introduced serious conflict to the musical comedy and combined words, melodies, dance, and drama in a new wholeness. Songs and dances (the rowdy ballets of Agnes de Mille) were not interruptions of the story, but became expressions of character and extensions of the action. The result was a new theatrical form known as the musical play, or musical.

Oklahoma! was a raging commercial success in the 1940s, running on Broadway for a record-breaking five years. Rodgers and Hammerstein contributed other works to a golden age of the American musical, including *Carousel* (1945), *South Pacific* (1949), *The King and I* (1951), and *The Sound of Music* (1959). Composer Frederick Loewe and lyricist Alan Jay Lerner

added *My Fair Lady* (1956) and *Camelot* (1960). Composer Leonard Bernstein, lyricist Stephen Sondheim, and choreographer Jerome Robbins brought new depths of contemporary realism and darkness of mood to their tragic *West Side Story* (1957).

In ensuing years the American musical continued to display a wide range of subject matter and musical styles. *Hair* (1967) jolted Broadway with protest and rock. Gospel, rhythm and

Highlights of American Life

informational shows in the 1950s, they soon discovered that viewers weren't interested in such programming. According to George Gallup, a pioneer public opinion pollster, people in the 1950s wanted to be entertained by TV, not informed:

AN AMERICAN ★ SPEAKS

I have known many a valiant attempt on the part of advertisers to put information shows on the air, only to be compelled by good business practice to withdraw them after it was clearly demonstrated that the public was not interested in this type of serious fare. . . .

The present lack of interest in the informative type of television show is shocking. The total number of hours devoted by the American public to just *two* shows, ''I Love Lucy'' and the ''Show of Shows,'' is greater than the total number of hours spent on all information or educational shows put together.

TELEVISION IN THE 1950S: Entertainment was the focus of TV programming in the 1950s. Two of the most popular shows were ''I Love Lucy,'' top, and ''The Mickey Mouse Club,'' above.

A scene from *West Side Story* is shown at left. The score for this successful musical was written by Leonard Bernstein. Bernstein was credited by many people as the savior of the American musical.

blues, and soul music pulsed in such productions as *Purlie* (1970), *The Wiz* (1975), and *Dreamgirls* (1982). In recent years, however, rising costs have reduced the number of musicals being produced.

The classic shows themselves have by no means disappeared. They live on in revivals and school productions, in recordings and film versions—and in the melodies that generations of Americans continue to warble in their showers.

Suburbanites developed new values.

The new suburban dwellers quickly discovered that the automobile was no longer a luxury but a necessity. Most workers needed an auto to commute from their suburban homes to their jobs in the city. The car was equally essential for people to reach the shopping centers that began to dot the countryside by the mid-1950s.

The charismatic Billy Graham, known for his exuberant, inspiring sermons, gained many followers as a result of his television ministry. Other preachers, realizing television's potential for gaining new followers, also took to the airwaves in the 1950s.

These large multi-store centers mushroomed in the 1950s almost as quickly as automobiles. In 1946 the entire nation had only eight shopping centers. Literally hundreds sprang up over the next 15 years.

In the 1950s the home became the focus for all activity. The young parents of the baby boom generation prized "more space" above everything else in the purchase of new houses. They wanted kitchens with built-in dishwashers, extra bedrooms for their growing families, large garages that could be converted into recreation rooms, and small, neat lawns that gave them areas for outdoor activities.

"Togetherness" became the code word of the 1950s. Families did things together. They gathered around the black-and-white TV sets that dominated living rooms. They attended community functions. In summer, they packed up their huge, gas-guzzling station wagons and headed off on vacation.

The new suburban lifestyle had no place for the extended family of the past, where several generations had lived in close proximity. The small, detached homes, as one historian noted, meant that "most children would grow up in intimate contact only with their parents and siblings." Grandparents, aunts and uncles, cousins, and more distant relatives would become remote figures, seen only on holidays.

Religion flourished in the 1950s.

Organized religion flourished in suburban America. Ministers, priests, and rabbis all commented on the rise in church and synagogue attendance in the new communities. For the first time in the 20th century, church membership climbed to more than 50 percent of the nation's population. Those who moved to the suburbs kept their religious identity, tending to associate mainly with people of the same faith.

Some observers condemned the bland nature of suburban churches, which seemed to be an integral part of the consumer society. "On weekdays one shops for food," wrote one critic, "on Saturdays one shops for recreation, and on Sundays one shops for the Holy Ghost." Other observers, however, disagreed. They believed that the new churches filled a genuine

human need. In their defense, they often pointed to the words of Norman Vincent Peale, a religious writer who drew many converts to his gospel that urged people to "start thinking faith, enthusiasm and joy."

Television provided a new way for members of the clergy to reach a broader public in the 1950s. **Billy Graham**, a popular Protestant revivalist, went from tent meetings to televised services to reach a wide audience. Roman Catholic Bishop **Fulton J. Sheen** built up a national following for his television ministry. At the height of the Cold War, these clergymen were successful in defending traditional American values while preaching against atheistic communism.

SECTION 1 REVIEW

Identify Key People and Terms
Write a sentence to identify: baby boom, Billy Graham, Fulton J. Sheen

Locate Key Places
In which part of the country is New England located?

Master the Main Ideas

1. **Analyzing the economic impact of war:** Why did the Cold War have a positive impact on the economy?
2. **Assessing our economy's contribution to the standard of living:** Why did the automobile industry grow so rapidly in the 1950s?
3. **Analyzing the impact of technology on culture:** According to George Gallup, what did the American public want from the television programmers of the 1950s?
4. **Analyzing cultural developments:** What impact did suburban life have on the American family?
5. **Studying religious issues:** What caused the growth in churches and synagogues in the 1950s?

Apply Critical Thinking Skills: Making Comparisons
Why do you think there was so much emphasis on material prosperity after World War II? How would you compare this trend with the 1980s and 1990s?

Eisenhower served as president.

Key Term: censure

Reading Preview
As you read this section, you will learn:

1. which candidate was victorious in the 1952 presidential election.
2. why Senator Joseph McCarthy disappeared from the public spotlight.
3. what type of domestic program Eisenhower developed.

The man who presided over the prosperity of the 1950s was Dwight D. Eisenhower. As a hero of World War II, General Eisenhower was the perfect candidate for the Republican party in 1952. Amiable in manner, with a winning smile and the ability to rise above partisan infighting, he was able to capitalize on the loss of confidence that had overtaken the nation during Truman's second term.

The stalemate in Korea and the turmoil created by McCarthy's reckless charges had produced a desire for political change. Disclosures of scandals by several of Truman's aides intensified the feeling that someone needed to clean up the "mess in Washington." Eisenhower was the man the Republicans needed to carry out their formula for success, K_1C_2—Korea, communism, and corruption.

Eisenhower won the election of 1952.

In the 1952 campaign, Eisenhower, popularly known simply as "Ike," displayed surprising skill as a politician in running against **Adlai Stevenson**, the eloquent Illinois governor whose appeal was limited to diehard Democrats and liberal intellectuals. Eisenhower allowed his young running mate, Richard M. Nixon of California, to hammer away at the Democrats on the communism and corruption issues, but Ike himself delivered the most telling blow of all on the Korean War. Speaking

MEET THE PRESIDENT

DWIGHT D. EISENHOWER

Born: October 14, 1890
Died: March 28, 1969
In office: 1953–1961

Eisenhower was twice swept into the White House by landslides created in part by his military glory, his engaging grin, and an irresistible slogan. America indeed liked "Ike."

One of six brothers raised in Abilene, Kansas, Ike followed a path first blazed by Ulysses S. Grant. He graduated from West Point in 1915. During World War II, he quickly rose from obscurity to the highest pinnacles of command. In 1952 he translated his war-won fame into a Republican presidency.

Ike promptly ended the Korean War and declined every chance to fight another. He disliked confrontation, steering for "the middle of the road" as a personal, domestic, and foreign policy.

Though he left office with problems of civil injustice and the Cold War still looming, Eisenhower retained the strong affection of most Americans. The slogan "I like Ike" never became obsolete.

in **Detroit**, Michigan, in late October, Ike promised that if elected he would "bring the Korean War to an early and honorable end."

"That does it—Ike is in," several reporters exclaimed after they heard this pledge. The World War II general had clinched his election by committing himself to end an unpopular war. Ten days later, he easily won the presidency, carrying 39 states, including four in the formerly solid Democratic South.

The Senate publicly condemned Joseph McCarthy.

The first problem facing the new president was Senator Joseph McCarthy's continuing anticommunist crusade. Instead of toning down his

LIFE

FIRST-PERSON REPORTS BY THE ASTRONAUTS

START OF CONTINUING EXCLUSIVE STORIES ON EPOCHAL MISSION

ONE OF SEVEN: FIRST AMERICAN IN SPACE

SEPTEMBER 14, 1959

Boys' Life
FOR ALL BOYS

SCIENTIST
1706
1790
STATESMAN
PHILOS
Poor Richard's Almanack
Benjamin Franklin

Seventeen

LIBRARY

Cheerleaders salute
Seventeen-by-the-yard
Sew for glory and for gain

Miss Young America in Girl Scouts

3 fiction stories   Dance! dance! dance!
Forecast of fall fashions

America's thirst for entertainment in the postwar years was quenched not only by television but by a wide variety of special interest magazines such as those shown.

however, saying, "I will not get into the gutter with that guy." The president preferred to play for time, hoping that the American people would eventually see McCarthy as the scoundrel he was.

The Wisconsin senator finally went too far. In early 1954 McCarthy accused the army of harboring suspected communists, telling one much-decorated general that he was "not fit to wear the uniform." The Senate then held the televised Army-McCarthy hearings in the spring of 1954. For six weeks, the senator revealed his crude, bullying behavior to a nationwide audience. TV viewers were repelled by his surly questions, frequent outbursts, and insistent cry, "Point of order, Mr. Chairman, point of order." McCarthy overreached himself when he attempted to smear a young lawyer assisting Army Counsel Joseph Welch. Welch immediately struck back, condemning McCarthy for "reckless cruelty" and asking rhetorically, as millions watched on television, "Have you no sense of decency, sir?"

Courageous Republicans joined with Democrats to bring about the Senate's **censure** of McCarthy in December 1954 by a vote of 67 to 22. Censure is the public condemnation of a member of Congress for misconduct. Once rebuked, McCarthy fell quickly from sight. He died three years later virtually unnoticed and unmourned.

Despite McCarthy's relatively short time in the national spotlight, his influence was profound. Not only did he paralyze national life with what a Senate subcommittee called "the most nefarious campaign of half-truth and untruth in the history of the Republic," but he left behind a legacy of political conformity. For years after his death, the nation tolerated loyalty oaths for teachers, the banning of books in public libraries, and the blacklisting of entertainers in radio, television, and Hollywood. Although President Eisenhower could claim that his policy of giving McCarthy enough rope to hang himself had worked, many historians and other observers believed that a bolder and more direct presidential attack would have spared the nation some of the excesses of McCarthyism.

red scare tactics after the Republican victory in 1952, McCarthy continued to search for communists on the federal payroll. He made a series of charges against State Department officials and demanded that certain books be banned from American information libraries overseas. Eisenhower's advisers urged the president to use his great prestige to stop McCarthy. Ike refused such a confrontation,

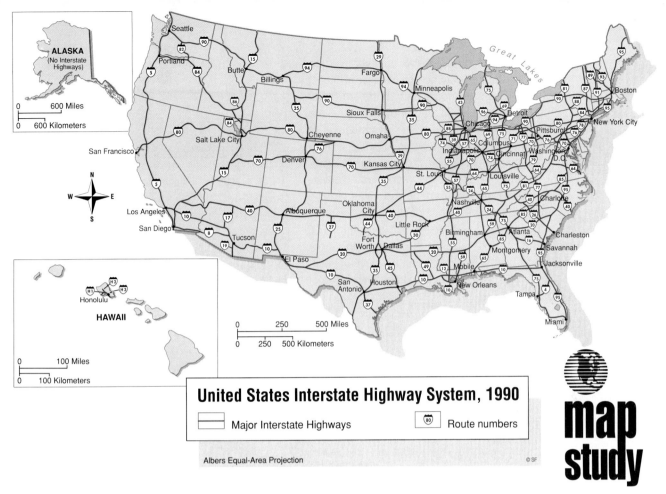

United States Interstate Highway System, 1990

▭ Major Interstate Highways ⑧⓪ Route numbers

Albers Equal-Area Projection © SF

map study

Movement The U.S. Interstate Highway System today covers about 45,000 miles, slightly more than originally planned in 1956. Does any state lack an interstate highway? If so, which one?

Critical Thinking Why does the United States need a federally controlled highway system?

Eisenhower developed a cautious domestic program.

Moderation was the keynote of the Eisenhower presidency. His major goal was to restore calm and tranquillity to a badly divided nation. Unlike FDR and Truman, he had no commitment to social change or economic reform. Ike was a fiscal conservative who was intent on balancing the budget, yet he had no intention of undoing the social reforms of the New Deal.

On domestic issues, Eisenhower preferred to delegate authority. The people he chose to run the nation reflected his high regard for successful corporate executives. Thus George Humphrey, an Ohio industrialist, carried out a policy of fiscal restraint as secretary of the treasury, and Charles E. Wilson, the former head of General Motors, sought to reduce military spending as secretary of defense.

Eisenhower was equally reluctant to play an active role in dealing with Congress. He left congressional relations to aides such as Sherman Adams, a former governor of New Hampshire who served as White House chief of staff. Adams' skill at resolving problems insulated Eisenhower from many of the nation's pressing domestic concerns.

Relations with Congress were weakened when the Democrats regained control of both houses in the midterm election of 1954. The result was that Ike achieved a very modest legislative record.

The one significant legislative achievement of the Eisenhower years came with the passage of the Highway Act of 1956. After a 12-year delay, Congress approved plans for a 41,000-mile interstate highway system consisting of multilane divided expressways that would connect all the nation's major cities. Built over the next 20 years, the interstate highway system had a profound influence on American life. It stimulated the economy and shortened travel time dramatically. In addition, the interstate system intensified the nation's dependence on the automobile and encouraged urban growth in long strips paralleling the new expressways.

Overall, the Eisenhower years marked an era of political moderation. The American people, enjoying the abundance of the 1950s, seemed quite content with legislative inaction. The president was sensitive to the nation's economic health. When recessions developed in 1953 and 1957, he quickly abandoned his goal of a balanced budget in favor of increased government spending to restore prosperity. As a result, Eisenhower achieved a balanced budget in only three of his eight years in office and the deficit of $12 billion in 1959 was larger than any ever before recorded in peacetime. Thus, Eisenhower maintained the New Deal legacy of federal responsibility for social welfare and the state of the economy while successfully resisting demands for more extensive government involvement in American life.

SECTION 2 REVIEW

Identify Key People and Terms
Write a sentence to identify: Adlai Stevenson, censure

Locate Key Places
In which state is Detroit located?

Master the Main Ideas
1. **Analyzing political elections:** Why did Eisenhower win so easily in 1952?
2. **Assessing major political issues:** How did Eisenhower deal with the issue of McCarthyism?
3. **Analyzing economic policies:** Describe President Eisenhower's view of the federal government's role in the economy.

Apply Critical Thinking Skills: Analyzing Cause and Effect
Moderation was the keynote of the Eisenhower Administration. Did this attitude help or hinder the nation during the McCarthy era? Why or why not?

SECTION 3

The Cold War tested Eisenhower.

Key Terms: massive retaliation, *Sputnik*

Reading Preview
As you read this section, you will learn:
1. who was primarily responsible for directing American foreign policy during the Eisenhower years.
2. how Eisenhower was able to bring about an end to the Korean War.
3. what method Eisenhower used to quell disturbances in the Middle East.
4. what types of activities Eisenhower permitted the CIA to engage in abroad.
5. what issue increased Cold War tensions.

Dwight D. Eisenhower was extremely well prepared to lead the nation at the height of the Cold War. His long years of military service had exposed him to a wide variety of international issues and to a broad array of world leaders, ranging from Winston Churchill to Joseph Stalin. His talents were primarily political and diplomatic rather than military. He was blessed with a sharp, practical mind and the organizational genius to plan and carry out large enterprises. Above all, he had an unshakable self-confidence. At the end of his first day in office, he confided in his diary: "Plenty of worries and difficult problems. But such has been my portion for a long time. . . ."

Eisenhower directed American foreign policy.

Eisenhower chose **John Foster Dulles**, a New York lawyer and foreign policy expert, as his secretary of state. Although many observers believed that Dulles was responsible for a majority of the major foreign policy decisions during the Eisenhower Administration, he in fact consulted with the president on a regular basis. Ike, who preferred to work behind the scenes, made all the major foreign policy decisions.

The Cost of Cold War

For a great general, Dwight Eisenhower became a remarkably unmilitary president. In one of his first major speeches as president, Eisenhower vividly describes the cost of the Cold War. What "currency" does he use to count the cost?

This world in arms is not spending money alone. It is spending the sweat of its laborers, the genius of its scientists, the hopes of its children. The cost of one modern heavy bomber is this: a modern brick school in more than 30 cities. . . . We pay for a single fighter plane with a half-million bushels of wheat. We pay for a single destroyer with new homes that could have housed more than eight thousand people.

This is not a way of life at all, in any true sense. Under the cloud of threatening war, it is humanity hanging from a cross of iron.

Above all else, Eisenhower was determined to bring the Cold War under control. In part, he was motivated by a deeply held fear of excessive federal spending for defense. Ike was convinced that the nation was in danger of going bankrupt unless military spending, which had increased from $13 billion to $50 billion a year under Truman, was reduced. Thus, Eisenhower began a "new look" for American defense, cutting back on expensive ground forces and relying more heavily on the air force and its nuclear striking power to keep the peace.

The new Administration's idea of relying on nuclear weapons in case of war was known as the policy of **massive retaliation**. Under this policy, the United States said it would no longer fight limited wars such as in Korea. Instead, it would consider using nuclear weapons to stop communist aggression. Dulles, who announced the new policy, explained that:

The way to deter aggression is for the free community to be willing and able to respond vigorously at places and with means of its own choosing.

AN AMERICAN ★ SPEAKS

Ike used nuclear threats to end the Korean War.

When Eisenhower entered office in January 1953, two years of back-and-forth fighting in Korea had left the two sides essentially where they had been when the North Korean invasion began the war. Although Secretary of State Dulles wanted the United States to win the war by engineering a new offensive, Eisenhower believed that such a move would be futile. He was convinced that "small attacks on small hills would not end the war." Instead, he turned to diplomacy, warning China that the United States would use nuclear weapons if it had to to end the war.

Before his election in 1952, General Eisenhower promised to go to Korea personally to work out an end to the war. A man of his word, Ike, above left, visits with U.S. troops in Seoul shortly before his inauguration. Within six months, the war would be over.

Eisenhower's threat of massive retaliation worked exceedingly well. Mao Zedong agreed to negotiate. On July 27, 1953, American and communist diplomats signed a truce that officially ended the Korean War.

Although the war had cost more than 54,000 American lives, and perhaps as many as two million Chinese and Korean casualties, little was achieved by either side. Korea remained divided, as it had been at the start of the war, close to the 38th parallel.

Ike used restrained force in the Middle East.

Eisenhower faced a grave crisis in the explosive Middle East in 1956. In July, Egyptian ruler Gamal Abdel Nasser [nä'sər] seized the **Suez Canal**. As you can see on the map on page 919, the Suez Canal is a 100-mile long canal that connects the Mediterranean and Red seas. America's allies, Britain and France, who were dependent on the canal for the flow of oil from the Persian Gulf, wanted to use force immediately against Egypt. President Eisenhower, however, strongly preferred a diplomatic solution. For three months, Dulles conducted futile negotiations with Nasser. Finally, Britain and France ran out of patience and took a desperate gamble—invading Egypt and capturing the canal while relying on the United States to prevent any Soviet interference.

Eisenhower was furious when Britain and France launched their attack against Egypt in early November. Ike, who was running for re-election against Adlai Stevenson on the slogan of "keeping the peace," was forced to stop campaigning to deal with the threat of war. "The White House crackled with barracks-room language," reported one observer. Angry as he was with Britain and France, however, the president took a firm stand against the Soviets when they threatened rocket attacks against America's allies. He said: "If those fellows start something, we may have to hit 'em—and, if necessary, with everything in the bucket."

Just after noon on election day, November 6, 1956, Britain and France informed the president that they were ending their invasion. American voters rallied behind Ike in a time of crisis, electing him to a second term in a near landslide. As a result of the Suez affair, the United States replaced Britain and France as the main western power in the Middle East. The Soviet Union, however, by backing Egypt, had gained significant influence with the Arab nations as the Cold War spread into a new battleground.

Two years later, Eisenhower found it necessary to intervene in the strategic Middle Eastern country of Lebanon. Fearful of Soviet or Egyptian military intervention in a possible civil war between contending Christian and Muslim groups, Eisenhower decided to send American forces into Lebanon in July 1958.

U.S. Marines quickly secured the Beirut airport, preparing the way for the arrival of some 14,000 U.S. troops airlifted from bases in Germany. The military wanted to occupy all of Le-

banon, but the president insisted on limiting American forces to the capital. Their mission, he argued, was "not primarily to fight," but simply to show the flag. When rival Lebanese political leaders finally reached agreement on a new government, the American soldiers left the country in October. This restrained use of force achieved Eisenhower's primary goal of quieting the explosive Middle East, whose oil was vital to American allies in Europe and Asia. It also served, as Secretary of State Dulles pointed out, "to reassure many small nations that they could call on us in a time of crisis."

The CIA engaged in secret activities abroad.

In addition to handling dangerous crises in Asia and the Middle East, President Eisenhower authorized the Central Intelligence

Agency (CIA) to use covert action to expand America's global influence. In 1953 a communist-backed political party seized control of **Iran**, located directly south of the Soviet Union, and attempted to assert control over the nation's rich oil fields. The shah of Iran, **Muhammed Reza Shah Pahlavi**, who had gained the Iranian throne in 1941, was deposed. Several days later, undercover American agents covertly helped overthrow the communist-dominated government and reinstated the shah as ruler. As a result of the CIA involvement in Iran, American oil companies gained lucrative concessions. In addition, the United States acquired an important, strategically located ally.

A far more dangerous situation developed in 1959, when Fidel Castro came to power in **Cuba**, an island only 90 miles south of the United States. After only a brief effort at good relations, the Eisenhower Administration took a negative stance against Castro that helped drive Cuba further under the Soviet sphere of influence. More regrettably, Ike ordered the CIA to begin planning a secret invasion of Cuba to overthrow Castro. You will read about the results of these plans later in the text.

The arms race increased Cold War tensions.

The most difficult challenge facing President Eisenhower in the 1950s was to manage the rivalry with the Soviet Union and, above all, the threat of nuclear war. In November 1952 the United States tested the hydrogen bomb successfully. Nine months later the Soviets also perfected the H-bomb. By 1955 both nations had added this dreaded new weapon to their nuclear arsenals and were capable of destroying each other completely. Peace, as Winston Churchill observed, now rested on a "balance of terror."

Throughout the 1950s Eisenhower sought ways to resolve the nuclear dilemma. First, shortly after the death of Joseph Stalin in March 1953, he called for the Soviets to join him in a new effort at disarmament. In a speech to the United Nations, the president pointed out that:

Fidel Castro, shown delivering a rousing speech in Havana, gained control of Cuba during a coup in 1959. Castro quickly showed his anti-American feelings by confiscating American-held properties and businesses in Cuba. Before the revolution, Fulgencio Batista, a right-wing dictator, had allowed American ownership of 90 percent of Cuba's mines, 80 percent of its utilities, and 40 percent of its sugar plantations. Castro's seizure of these properties and his close alignment with the Soviet Union, presented Eisenhower and future presidents with numerous foreign policy challenges.

717

Point

In favor of the policy of massive retaliation

- Limited wars are too costly in terms of lives and money.
- Communist aggressors cannot be stopped through conventional means.

Counterpoint

Against the policy of massive retaliation

- Nuclear threats will encourage the Soviet Union to use its own form of massive retaliation.
- Massive retaliation will result in nuclear proliferation.

Ten days after American pilot Francis Gary Powers was shot down by the Soviet Union, Soviet officials set up a display of three portraits of Powers and a group of assorted items confiscated from the pilot. The Soviet Union's foreign minister then warned U.S. officials that future spy missions over Soviet territory would be "smashed to smithereens."

E very warship launched, every rocket fired, signifies, **AN AMERICAN ★ SPEAKS** in the final sense, a theft from those who hunger and are not fed, those who are cold and are not clothed.

Despite this eloquent appeal, the United States and the Soviet Union were unable to reach agreement on disarmament plans at the Geneva summit conference in 1955. The only bit of progress came in 1958, when Eisenhower and the new Soviet leader, Nikita Khrushchev [krüsh chôv'] agreed to suspend nuclear tests in order to stop nuclear fallout, which threatened to poison the world's atmosphere.

Nonetheless, the Cold War became even more intense in the late 1950s. Khrushchev used the Soviet feat in launching *Sputnik*, the first artificial earth satellite, to boast that the Soviet Union had gained the upper hand in science and technology. He began to issue threats, proclaiming, "We will bury capitalism," and telling Americans, "Your grandchildren will live under communism."

A major confrontation developed in 1958 when Khrushchev tried to force the United States out of Berlin. Eisenhower stood as firmly as Truman had in this second Berlin crisis. He

refused to abandon the city, but he also tried to avoid a military showdown. The president met with Khrushchev in the United States in 1959. The two leaders agreed to hold a summit meeting in Paris in May 1960 designed to resolve the situation in Berlin and make progress toward nuclear arms limitation.

This meeting, however, was destined for failure. On May 1, only two weeks before the leaders were due to meet in Paris, the Soviet Union shot down an American U-2 plane piloted by **Francis Gary Powers**. Beginning in 1956 the United States had been sending the U-2, a high-altitude spy plane with cameras, to take pictures of Soviet military bases and missile sites. At first the United States claimed that the U-2 was just a weather plane that drifted off course. When Khrushchev produced the wreckage of the plane and then Gary Powers in person, however, Eisenhower was forced to

Iran was less admirable and effective only in the short run. His greatest failure lay in his inability to halt the nuclear arms race. Nevertheless, he did display an admirable quality of staying calm in moments of great tension. Above all, he could boast, as he did to the nation in 1962, of his ability to keep the peace:

AN AMERICAN ★ SPEAKS

In those eight years we lost no inch of ground to tyranny. . . . One war was ended and incipient wars were blocked.

SECTION **3** REVIEW

Identify Key People and Terms
Write a sentence to identify: John Foster Dulles, massive retaliation, Muhammed Reza Shah Pahlavi, *Sputnik*, Francis Gary Powers

Locate Key Places
1. Which two seas are joined by the Suez Canal?
2. Geographically, Iran is located where in relationship to the Soviet Union? Where is Cuba located in relationship to the United States?

Master the Main Ideas
1. Understanding U.S. foreign policy: What was the rationale behind Eisenhower's policy of massive retaliation?
2. Analyzing major political leaders: Instead of ordering "small attacks on small hills," what did Eisenhower do to convince Mao Zedong to negotiate?
3. Analyzing U.S. involvement in foreign affairs: What were the effects of U.S. involvement in the Suez Canal affair in 1956?
4. Applying decision-making skills: Was CIA involvement necessary in Iran? Why or why not?
5. Analyzing the impact of scientific developments: How did new developments in science and technology serve to increase Cold War tensions?

Apply Critical Thinking Skills: Identifying Assumptions
What assumptions could both the Soviet Union and the United States safely make after both sides developed the H-bomb?

admit that he had ordered this spy flight over Soviet territory. Khrushchev responded by denouncing the United States and leaving the conference.

The president deeply regretted the way the U-2 incident had broken up the summit and the chance for easing the Cold War. He told an aide that "the stupid U-2 mess" had ruined his efforts at peace and that "he saw nothing worthwhile left for him to do now until the end of his presidency."

Some historians believe that Eisenhower was too hard on himself. Although he had failed in his effort to ease Cold War tensions, he had scored a number of important foreign policy victories. He had ended the Korean War, kept the Suez crisis from developing into a major East-West confrontation, and had blocked Khrushchev's efforts to force the United States out of Berlin. His reliance on covert action in

Americans questioned their values.

Key Terms: white-collar workers, blue-collar workers, beats, abstract expressionism

Reading Preview
As you read this section, you will learn:

1. what critics found wrong with suburbia.
2. how some groups reacted to the trend toward conformity.
3. what the chief cause of the crisis in education in the 1950s was.

The continuing Cold War cast a long shadow over American life in the 1950s. Despite the growing affluence, Americans began to develop doubts about the consumer culture and the conformity of the suburban way of life. This lack of confidence would lead to a widespread questioning of traditional values.

Social critics lamented the sameness of suburbia.

A number of widely read books appeared in the 1950s that stressed the flaws in suburbia. One common theme was the loss of individual identity in the endless rows of tract houses in Levittown and other suburbs. Folk singer Malvina Reynolds, a Californian, wrote a song that clearly showed her views of life in suburbia:

Little boxes on the hillside,
Little boxes made of ticky tacky
Little boxes on the hillside,
Little boxes all the same.
There's a green one and a pink one
And a blue one and a yellow one
And they're all made out of ticky tacky
And they all look just the same.

Other writers stressed the changes in traditional American values brought about by the consumer culture. Harvard sociologist David Riesman, in his influential 1950 book *The Lonely Crowd*, bemoaned the decline of the "inner-directed" American of the past, who had relied on such traditional values as self-denial and frugality. Riesman stated this person

Women during the 1950s were expected by society to assume traditional roles as dutiful housewives and mothers. Career-oriented women who defied the norm often were looked down upon and suffered discrimination in the workplace.

had succumbed to the "other-directed" American of the consumer society, who always tried to conform to social pressures. The result was a decline in individualism, Riesman contended, which led to a bland society lacking in the creative and adventurous people every growth-oriented nation needs.

C. Wright Mills was even more critical of American society in the 1950s. Mills, a sociologist, pointed out the way a new class of **white-collar workers** (clerks, office workers, bank tellers) was taking the place of **blue-collar workers** (miners, factory workers, mechanics). According to Mills, the industrial assembly line of the 1940s had given way to an even more dehumanizing workplace in the 1950s, the modern office:

At rows of blank-looking counters sat rows of blank-looking girls with blank, white folders in their blank hands, all blankly folding blank papers.

AN AMERICAN ★ SPEAKS

Like the modern offices and the suburban tract houses, teenagers also succumbed to a bland sameness. Writer Frank Conroy, who went to high school and college during the 1950s, recalled that:

We became teen-agers when to be a teen-ager meant nothing, [we were] the lowest of the low. . . . Our clothing, manners and life-styles were unoriginal—scaled-down versions of what we saw in the adults. We had no sense of group identity, perhaps not so much less than the teen-age generations that had preceded us, but unquestionably less than the generation that was to follow ten years later.

AN AMERICAN ★ SPEAKS

In college we were named. The Silent Generation. The Apathetic Generation. There was no doubt about it. The sleepy Eisenhower years. America in a trance, drifting leisurely through a long golf game [Ike's favorite pastime] while the clouds gathered. Among the students it was hard to find a rebel, virtually impossible to find a Marxist, a mystic, a reformer, or indeed anyone who felt very strongly about anything.

We believed in civil rights but did nothing active about it. Picketing was unheard of, protest vaguely uncool. It was enough to send a few bucks to the N.A.A.C.P., an organization we believed to be utterly safe, no more and perhaps even less militant than the Parent Teachers Association. . . .

No one knew anything about drugs in those days. Marijuana, which was to sweep through all levels of American society during the next decade, was smoked, as far as I know, by only two students in my college of five hundred.

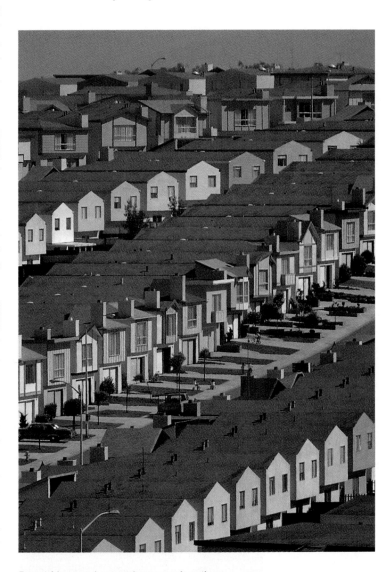

Rows of inexpensive tract houses such as these mushroomed outside of large cities all across the nation during the 1950s.

Beatniks such as those pictured above frequented urban coffeeshops during the 1950s to contemplate philosophies developed by the generation's anti-establishment gurus such as Jack Kerouac, right.

Some writers and artists rebelled against conformity.

The disenchantment with the consumer culture was most eloquently expressed by the **beats**, a literary group that rebelled against the materialistic society of the 1950s. The name came from the quest for beatitude, a state of inner grace that is sought in Zen Buddhism. The beats, or beatniks, as the middle-class Americans they were rebelling against called them, often gathered in small, dimly lit, urban coffeehouses to listen to folk music and poetry or to simply contemplate the deeper meanings of life. Many of the beats, including the poet Lawrence Ferlinghetti, exchanged ideas and

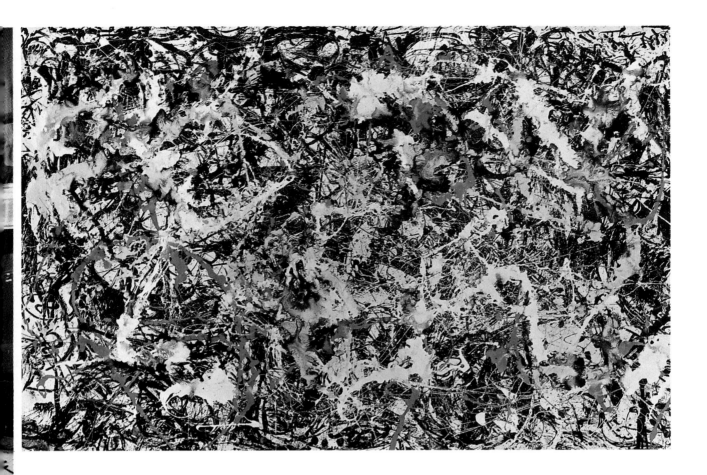

philosophies at the City Lights Bookstore in **San Francisco**. Dropping out of a society they found senseless and materialistic, the beats' cynical view of life was accurately summed up by Ferlinghetti: "I was a wind-up toy someone had dropped wound up into a world already running down."

Writer **Jack Kerouac** set the tone for the beats in his novel *On the Road*, published in 1957. The book, which Kerouac wrote during a three-week manic outburst, detailed the author's frantic search for "IT"—the ultimate moment when mind and experience supposedly come together. Despite the disapproval he and other beats evoked from mainstream Americans, Kerouac had only compassion for his detractors: "We love everything—Bill Graham, the Big Ten, Rock and Roll, Zen, apple pie, Eisenhower—we dig it all." As highly visible rebels in an age of conformity, the beat generation pioneered a style of social protest that

would flower into the counterculture of the turbulent 1960s.

The rebellion against traditional values reached its fullest expression in a style of painting—**abstract expressionism**. A new group of artists sought to break with the past by abandoning realism and filling their immense canvases with bold colors and lines. Instead of trying to depict a figure or a concept, they sought to express transcendental themes by capturing a moment in the artist's life. As one critic noted, their work "was not a picture but an event."

The two most successful abstract expressionists were Jackson Pollock and Mark Rothko, who stunned the art world with a striking exhibit at the Museum of Modern Art in New York City in 1951. Pollock physically involved himself in the artistic process by dripping random patterns of paint on floor-anchored canvases. Rothko's style, which

Abstract expressionist Jackson Pollock, above left, drips paint onto a canvas. His unorthodox technique became known as "action painting." An example of Pollock's work, "Convergence, 1952," is shown above.

featured bold masses of color, conveyed his somber view of reality. In rejecting the representational style of painting, Pollock and Rothko were committed to working "from within," as Pollock put it, rather than going to a "subject matter outside themselves."

Growing enrollments caused a crisis in education.

When the baby boom generation reached school age in the 1950s, school systems across the country scurried to find solutions to rapidly growing enrollments. The unprecedented increase in the number of school-age children overwhelmed the resources of many local districts. In California a new school was added every week throughout the decade. Nonetheless, the state could still not keep up with the demand for classrooms. Calls for federal assistance led Congress to grant limited help for areas where defense plants and military bases caused an influx of children. Eisenhower's commitment to a balanced budget, combined with the tradition of state control over public education, blocked efforts to use federal funds for new schools.

Besides dealing with overcrowding, school systems also debated educational goals. Critics of "progressive education," an educational philosophy that emphasized the teaching of practical skills that students would need to function in the workplace, called for a return to traditional curriculums that stressed basic academic skills such as reading, writing, and arithmetic. Many parents agreed that their children needed an extra dose of basic skills and were doubtful that professional educators could do the job. **Rudolph Flesch**, author of the best-selling 1955 book *Why Johnny Can't Read*, asserted, "Just as war is 'too serious a matter to be left to the generals,' so I think, the teaching of reading is too important to be left to the educators." Parents, in response to such thinking, began to demand educational reform. They called for kindergarten enrichment programs and foreign language instruction in grade schools. These programs were often costly, however, and many taxpayers resisted their implementation.

The one thing everyone in the 1950s seemed to agree on was the desirability of a college education. The number of young people attending colleges increased from 1.5 million in 1940 to 3.6 million by 1960.

The Soviet launching of *Sputnik* in 1957 persuaded President Eisenhower that it was time to begin spending federal funds to improve American education. Fearful of falling behind the Soviets in training scientists and engineers, Congress passed the National Defense Education Act in 1958. This legislation authorized federal financing of scientific and foreign language programs in the nation's schools and colleges. Soon American children were hard at work mastering the "new physics" and the "new math." The infusion of federal money and the effort at curriculum reform brought about a long-needed improvement in the quality of American education by the end of the decade.

SECTION **4** REVIEW

Identify Key People and Terms
white-collar workers, blue-collar workers, beats, Jack Kerouac, abstract expressionism, Rudolph Flesch

Locate Key Places
In which city did many of the beats exchange ideas?

Master the Main Ideas

1. **Analyzing social issues:** What was the chief fault that social critics found with life in the suburbs?
2. **Analyzing developments in art and literature:** Why did some writers and artists protest against the consumer culture?
3. **Analyzing developments in education:** What were the major problems facing American education in the 1950s?

Critical Thinking Skills: Recognizing Values
What values were probably held by the people who favored progressive education? What values were held by those who called for an end to progressive education?

SECTION 5

Theme Essay:
Sputnik shook the confidence of the American people.

Key Term: Commission on National Goals

Reading Preview
As you read this section, you will learn:

1. how the United States reacted to the launching of *Sputnik*.
2. what President Eisenhower did to help the nation regain a sense of national purpose.

The Soviet feat in putting *Sputnik* into orbit in October 1957 had an impact on the American people that went far beyond educational reform. Throughout their history, Americans had aspired to world leadership in science and technology. From Eli Whitney's cotton gin to Henry Ford's moving assembly line, they had taken pride in American inventive genius and the resulting economic progress. Now, suddenly, the Soviet Union had appeared to move ahead of the United States in technological progress. As a result, a sense of panic swept over the nation.

The United States intensified its missile and space efforts.

In the late 1950s, the president and Congress moved to restore national confidence. Eisenhower appointed James R. Killian, president of the Massachusetts Institute of Technology in **Cambridge**, Massachusetts, as his special assistant for science and technology to oversee a crash program in missile development. Despite Democratic cries of a missile gap, the president knew, thanks to the U-2 flights, that the nation was not behind the Soviets in developing intercontinental ballistic missiles (ICBMs). By 1960 the United States had not only deployed the Atlas, the nation's first operational ICBM, but had also perfected the Polaris submarine-

President Eisenhower, flanked by Vice President Richard Nixon and Soviet leader Nikita Khrushchev, holds a model of *Sputnik*. A closeup of the model is shown above.

THE U.S. SATELLITE PROGRAM
Skill: Recognizing Bias

Introducing the Skill. On October 4, 1957, the Soviet Union launched *Sputnik*, the world's first successful earth satellite. Americans reacted with dismay. They wondered how another country, an adversary at that, could have surpassed the United States in technological development. In fact, the United States remained a leader in space technology. However, because the Soviet astronauts were able to be the first in space, their country won a huge coup in terms of propaganda. As a result, Americans came to doubt their own technological capacity. On what was the American public's reaction to *Sputnik* based, and how accurate was it?

Learning the Skill. As you learned earlier, a bias is a slanted, one-sided view or inclination—either a preference for or a dislike of something. **Recognizing bias** in a political cartoon, such as the one on this page, involves adapting the procedures used for written material. Political cartoons by nature are biased, designed to call at-

tention to a particular point of view. Still, you can confirm that a bias exists by looking for the following clues:
1. the use of exaggeration in the art or written copy
2. the presentation of only one side of an issue
3. the use of emotionally charged language or symbols

Applying the Skill. Study the political cartoon on this page, printed in *The Detroit Free Press* in 1957.
1. What is the point of view of the cartoonist on the issue of the U.S. satellite program?
2. What clues did you recognize in the cartoon to alert you to the cartoonist's bias on this subject?

based missile, something the Soviets did not duplicate until a decade later.

The nation also moved quickly to overcome the apparent Soviet lead in space. At first, there was frustration and disappointment. In Decem-

ber 1957 the rocket bearing Vanguard, the first American satellite, rose only a few inches off the launch pad before it toppled over in full view of a nationwide television audience. It was a moment of national humiliation.

Many critics began to make jokes about the American "flopnik" and "dudnik." In January 1958, however, former German rocket scientist **Wernher von Braun** gave Americans something to cheer about when he sent an Explorer satellite into orbit around the earth.

Congress then created the National Aeronautics and Space Administration (NASA) and appropriated large sums to train astronauts for rocket ventures above the earth's atmosphere. By the time President Eisenhower left office in 1961, NASA was engaged in a comprehensive space program.

Ike beckoned the nation to pursue excellence.

Despite advances in missiles and space exploration, the American people continued to fear that the United States was losing its competitive edge in the world. They had long believed that their nation was unique—Americans were God's elect on earth and it was their destiny to lead the world. After *Sputnik*, however, the American people began to question their unique place in history. With a recession underway in 1957, economists pointed to a higher rate of Soviet economic growth, while social critics bemoaned a supermarket culture that stressed consumption over production.

President Eisenhower responded by appointing a **Commission on National Goals** to give the nation a new sense of purpose. After months of study, the Commission issued a report that called for increased military spending, broader educational opportunities, and more government support for scientific research and the advancement of the arts. The consensus was that all the United States really needed was a renewed commitment to the pursuit of excellence.

Despite his actions, Eisenhower never truly believed in his heart that the United States had ever fallen behind the Soviet Union. He did worry about the cumulative impact of the Cold War on the American economy, however. In January 1961, three days before he left the White House, he delivered a farewell address in which he gave a somber warning about the danger of massive military spending:

In the councils of government, we must guard against the acquisition of unwarranted influence, whether sought or unsought, by the military industrial complex. The potential for the disastrous rise of misplaced power exists and will persist.

AN AMERICAN ★ SPEAKS

Rarely has an American president been more prophetic. In the next few years, the level of defense spending would skyrocket as the Cold War escalated under his successors in the White House. The 1950s thus ended with a mixed legacy. On the one hand, the United States had achieved the highest standard of living the world had ever known. Yet the consumer culture left many Americans dissatisfied, worried about materialism, and wondering if the nation had lost the very qualities—a unique sense of national mission and a devotion to scientific innovation—that accounted for American greatness.

The "I Like Ike" campaign button worn by many of Eisenhower's supporters during the election campaigns of 1952 and 1956 summed up the nation's respect and warmth toward the popular president during his eight years in office.

SECTION 5 REVIEW

Identify Key People and Terms
Write a sentence to identify: Wernher von Braun, Commission on National Goals

Locate Key Places
In which city is the Massachusetts Institute of Technology located?

Master the Main Ideas

1. **Assessing the impact of science and technology:** What effect did *Sputnik* have on American life in the late 1950s?
2. **Examining social developments:** What did Eisenhower do in response to reports that suggested that the Soviet economy was growing more quickly than the American economy?

Apply Critical Thinking Skills: Demonstrating Reasoned Judgment
Do you think the American people overreacted to the Soviet feat in launching *Sputnik*? Why or why not?

Margaret Chase Smith Condemns McCarthyism

18A

TIME FRAME
1950

GEOGRAPHIC SETTING
Washington, D.C.

From early 1950 through 1954, American political life was dominated by the anti-communist crusade of Senator Joseph R. McCarthy (1908–1957). In 1949 the communist revolution in China and the successful detonation of an atomic bomb by the Soviet Union created a great deal of fear and frustration in the United States. A Republican from Wisconsin, McCarthy was a genius at publicizing his assertion that these setbacks for American foreign policy were evidence of a gigantic communist conspiracy at the heart of the United States government. McCarthy's charges of communist subversion in Washington created an atmosphere of bitter enmity and petty political strife in the Senate. Senator

Margaret Chase Smith (1897–   ), a Republican from Maine, was the first to speak out in the Senate against "McCarthyism" and the danger it represented to basic American principles. The following excerpt is taken from her speech to the Senate on June 1, 1950.

———————————————

The U.S. Senate has long enjoyed worldwide respect as the greatest deliberative body in the world. But recently that deliberative character has too often been debased to the level of a forum of hate and character assassination sheltered by the shield of congressional immunity.

Shielding a microphone with his hand, Roy Cohn (1927–1986), chief counsel to Senator Joseph McCarthy's Senate subcommittee, whispers to McCarthy at a hearing in 1954. During 1953–54, McCarthy, chairman of the Senate Permanent Investigating Subcommittee, conducted a long series of hearings intended to support his charges of communist subversion of the federal government and other sectors of American society.

It is ironical that we Senators can in debate in the Senate, directly or indirectly, by any form of words, impute to any American who is not a Senator any conduct or motive unworthy or unbecoming an American—and without that non-Senator American having any legal redress [remedy] against us—yet if we say the same thing in the Senate about our colleagues we can be stopped on the grounds of being out of order.

It is strange that we can verbally attack anyone else without restraint and with full protection, and yet we hold ourselves above the same type of criticism here on the Senate floor. Surely the U.S. Senate is big enough to take self-criticism and self-appraisal. Surely we should be able to take the same kind of character attacks that we "dish out" to outsiders. . . .

I think it is high time that we remembered that we have sworn to uphold and defend the Constitution. I think it is high time that we remembered that the Constitution, as amended, speaks not only of the freedom of speech but also of trial by jury instead of trial by accusation.

Whether it be a criminal prosecution in court or a character prosecution in the Senate, there is little practical distinction when the life of a person has been ruined.

Those of us who shout the loudest about Americanism in making character assassinations are all too frequently those who, by our own words and acts, ignore some of the basic principles of Americanism—

The right to criticize.

The right to hold unpopular beliefs.

The right to protest.

The right of independent thought.

The exercise of these rights should not cost one single American citizen his reputation or his right to a livelihood nor should he be in danger of losing his reputation or livelihood merely because he happens to know some one who holds unpopular beliefs. Who of us does not?

Otherwise none of us could call our souls our own. Otherwise thought control would have set in.

The American people are sick and tired of being afraid to speak their minds lest they be politically smeared as Communists or Fascists by their opponents. Freedom of speech is not what it used to be in America. It has been so abused by some that it is not exercised by others. . . .

As an American, I am shocked at the way the Republicans and Democrats alike are playing directly into the Communist design of "confuse, divide, and conquer." As an American, I do not want a Democratic administration to white wash or cover up any more than I want a Republican smear or witch hunt.

As an American, I condemn a Republican Fascist just as much as I condemn a Democrat Communist. I condemn a Democrat Fascist just as much as I condemn a Republican Communist. They are equally dangerous to you and to me and to our country. As an American, I want to see our Nation recapture the strength and unity it once had when we fought the enemy instead of ourselves.

Discussing the Reading

1. According to Senator Margaret Chase Smith, upon what basic freedom has McCarthyism encroached?

2. What does she mean by the statement that freedom of speech "has been so abused by some that it is not exercised by others" (lines 64–65)?

CRITICAL THINKING
Expressing Problems

Describe the policy of congressional immunity described by Margaret Chase Smith in this excerpt (lines 8–18). Do you think it is a wise policy? Why or why not?

Elvis Presley Reaches the Top of the Charts

TIME FRAME
1956

GEOGRAPHIC SETTING
United States

Americans in the 1950s used much of their new wealth and leisure time on recreational activities. Record sales, which had previously been counted in the thousands, were, in the mid-1950s, now tabulated in the millions. The records of the great jazz artists still sold, but they were overshadowed by a new music called rock 'n' roll, which started to become popular in 1954. The new music quickly became a craze among teenagers, who went wild over rock 'n' roll stars such as Chuck Berry and Elvis Presley. Presley (1935–1977), who before his early death would become perhaps the most famous entertainer in the world, made his first recording in Memphis in 1954. National recognition came in 1956 when his *Heartbreak Hotel* became the best-selling record in America. The following article on Presley appeared in *Time* magazine's May 14 issue that year.

Without preamble, the three-piece band cuts loose. In the spotlight, the lanky singer flails furious rhythms on his guitar, every now and then breaking a
5 string. In a pivoting stance, his hips swing sensuously from side to side and his entire body takes on a frantic quiver, as if he had swallowed a jackhammer. Full-cut hair tousles over his forehead, and sideburns
10 frame his petulant, full-lipped face. His style is partly hillbilly, partly socking rock 'n' roll. His loud baritone goes raw and whining in the high notes, but down low it is rich and round. As he throws himself
15 into one of his specialties—*Heartbreak Hotel, Blue Suede Shoes* or *Long Tall Sally*—his throat seems full of desperate aspirates ("Hi want you, hi need you, hi luh-huh-huh-huv yew-hew") or hiccup-
20 ing glottis strokes, and his diction is poor. But his movements suggest, in a word, sex.

He is Elvis Aaron Presley, a drape-suited, tight-trousered young man of 21,
25 and the sight and sound of him drive teen-age girls wild. All through the South and West, Elvis is packing theaters, fighting off shrieking admirers, disturbing parents, puckering the brows of psychologists, and
30 filling letters-to-the-editor columns with cries of alarm and, from adolescents, counter-cries of adulation. . . .

Heavy Beat. The perpetrator of all this hoopla was born in Tupelo, Miss. (pop.
35 11,527). His parents gave him a guitar before he was twelve. "I beat on it for a year

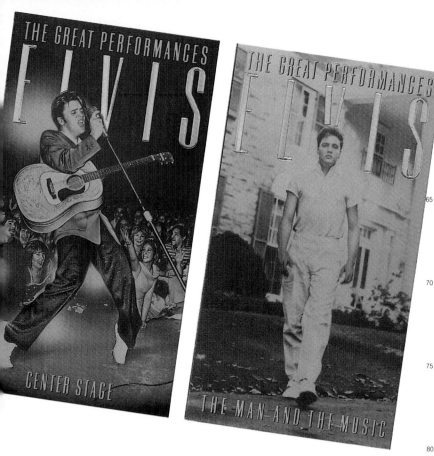

Presley's writhing, gyrating performances (above and opposite) prompted television's Ed Sullivan to describe him as "unfit for a family audience." But Elvis was turning rock'n'roll into a teenage obsession, and Sullivan later paid Presley $50,000 for three appearances on his show.

or two," he drawls. "Never did learn much about it." He learned to sing church hymns with a heavy beat, as Negro revival singers do, but gave no thought to a musical career. A couple of years ago, Presley, working as a truck driver, was seized with the urge to hear his own voice, took his guitar with him and made a recording in a public studio. "It sounded like somebody beatin' on a bucket lid." Presley recalls. "But the engineer at this studio had a recording company called Sun, and he told me I had an unusual voice, and he might call me up sometime."

When the call came, Presley was overcome by the stiffness that still bothers him when he sings without an audience. The session was about to fizzle when he started fooling around with a rock-'n'-roll beat, the same heavily accented style he uses today. Records started to sell, and Elvis set out to get himself a manager. The manager booked Presley with the words, "He may not sound like a hillbilly, but he gets the same response." It was not long before the response was even better, comparable to Johnnie Ray or Frankie Sinatra, with girls snatching Presley's shirt, belt, shoes, and RCA Victor buying out his recording contract for $35,000. Elvis now nets $7,500 a week for personal appearances, will net more than $100,000 this year; he owns three Cadillacs and a three-wheeled Messerschmitt [motorcycle] plus a dazzling wardrobe.

Dodgem, Too. Last week his *Heartbreak Hotel* was the nation's No. 1 best-selling record, and Elvis Presley himself was appearing at Las Vegas' New Frontier and getting a taste of more adult audiences. There was little screaming to be heard, but some fully grown female listeners matched the star squirm for squirm. As for Elvis, he spent some of his off-stage time amusing local showgirls, but most of it amusing himself in a small amusement park, where, for hours on end, he and his cronies rode the dodgem cars, having a wonderful time.

Discussing the Reading

1. What different musical influences did the *Time* articles note in Elvis Presley's music?

2. According to *Time,* what was the reaction of young people to Presley? Of older people?

CRITICAL THINKING
Making Comparisons

Babe Ruth (Source Reading 12B) and Elvis Presley were among the preeminent popular heroes of their respective eras. What do the differences between the two men suggest about how America had changed between the 1920s and the 1950s?

Chapter Summary

Write supporting details under each of the following main ideas as you review the chapter.

Section 1

1. Consumers and the Cold War sparked economic growth.
2. The nation enjoyed a high standard of living.
3. Television changed American life.
4. Suburbanites developed new values.
5. Religion flourished in the 1950s.

Section 2

1. Eisenhower won the election of 1952.
2. The Senate publicly condemned Joseph McCarthy.
3. Eisenhower developed a cautious domestic program.

Section 3

1. Eisenhower directed American foreign policy.
2. Ike used nuclear threats to end the Korean War.
3. Ike used restrained force in the Middle East.
4. The CIA engaged in secret activities abroad.
5. The arms race increased Cold War tensions.

Section 4

1. Social critics lamented the sameness of suburbia.
2. Writers and artists rebelled against conformity.
3. Growing enrollments caused a crisis in education.

Section 5

1. The United States intensified its missile and space efforts.
2. Ike beckoned the nation to pursue excellence.

Chapter Themes

1. **Free enterprise:** The American economy during the Eisenhower years grew because of consumer demand, technological advances, and increased military spending.
2. **Conflict and cooperation:** During the Eisenhower years, the Cold War continued to challenge Americans' concepts of their national destiny to lead the free world against communist aggression.

Chapter Study Guide

Identifying Key People and Terms

Name the key person or key term that describes the:
1. period that has a substantially higher than normal number of births.
2. Illinois governor who was the Democratic presidential candidate in 1952.
3. policy of threatening to use nuclear weapons to stop aggression.

Locating Key Places

1. The Suez Canal connects which large bodies of water?
2. Name the country in the eastern Mediterranean where Eisenhower sent troops in 1958.

Mastering the Main Ideas

1. How did the move to suburbia affect American society?
2. What is the Interstate Highway System and how did it influence American life?
3. What effects did the arms race have on international relationships?
4. How did artists and writers respond to the conformity of the 1950s?
5. What effects did the Soviet satellite *Sputnik* have on the American people?

Applying Critical Thinking Skills

1. **Identifying alternatives:** In the 1950s Americans first began to enjoy television as an entertainment medium. What are some alternative ways television is used today?
2. **Recognizing bias:** What bias does Malvina Reynolds' song "Little Boxes" display? What arguments might an admirer of suburban life put forth to counter Reynolds' opinions?
3. **Predicting consequences:** What challenges did Americans face as a result of the launching of *Sputnik*?
4. **Expressing problems:** What problems did Eisenhower cite in addressing the issue of the creation of a military-industrial complex? Have Eisenhower's predictions been realized? Explain.
5. **Making comparisons:** Compare the "containment" foreign policy with "massive retaliation."

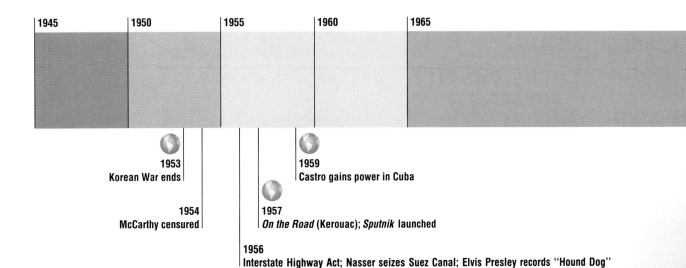

1945	1950	1955	1960	1965

1953
Korean War ends

1959
Castro gains power in Cuba

1954
McCarthy censured

1957
On the Road (Kerouac); *Sputnik* launched

1956
Interstate Highway Act; Nasser seizes Suez Canal; Elvis Presley records "Hound Dog"

Chapter Activities

Learning Geography Through History

1. How did the suburban way of life depend on the use of inexpensive natural resources?
2. Why might it have been in the interest of the United States to become involved in events in Lebanon and Egypt during the 1950s?

Relating the United States to the World

1. In the atomic age, with a military man as leader of the United States, how might other nations have viewed the doctrine of massive retaliation?
2. The launching of *Sputnik* spurred major reforms in education and promoted scientific research. What might have been the response of many of the other peoples of the world to the Soviets' achievement?

Linking Past to Present

1. In the 1950s Americans were concerned with events in Middle Eastern countries such as Lebanon, Egypt, and Iran. What events in the Middle East concern the American people today?
2. Suburbia was established in a time of inexpensive natural resources. Today natural resources have become expensive. What are some ways suburbia has had to change to respond to rising costs of housing and transportation and the conservation of natural resources?

Using the Time Line

What event or events signalled American artists' search for meaning in the 1950s?

Practicing Critical Thinking Strategies

Recognizing Bias
Many people in the 1950s did not think much of the work of abstract expressionists. People said that it wasn't really art at all. How could uncontrolled swirls of paint on a canvas mean anything? How did people's biases affect the way they looked at the work of the abstract expressionists?

Learning More About Eisenhower and Postwar Prosperity

1. **Using Source Readings:** Read the Source Readings for this chapter and answer the questions.
2. **Using Literature:** Read the excerpt from Lorraine Hansberry's play *A Raisin in the Sun*, which deals with African American life in the 1950s, on pages 736–737, and then answer the question.
3. **Analyzing literature:** The policy of massive retaliation caused much fear in the United States and the rest of the world about nuclear war. The writer Neville Shute wrote the novel *On the Beach* during the 1950s to alert the people of the world about the dangers of nuclear war. Read *On the Beach*. Report to the class about the fictional experiences of the people of Australia and the crew of an American nuclear submarine searching for a safe haven in a world whose atmosphere had been poisoned by nuclear fallout. How does the book end? What is its message to the people of the world?

733

AMERICAN LITERATURE

THE CASTILLO BROTHERS COME TO NEW YORK

The watershed event in the recent history of Cuba was the communist revolution, which produced a flood of refugees to the United States after Fidel Castro came to power in 1959. Even earlier, many Cubans had come to America seeking a better life. Some of these immigrants settled in New York City, where novelist Oscar Hijuelos [ē hwā′lōs] was born of Cuban parents in 1951. In his novel *The Mambo Kings Play Songs of Love* (1989), Hijuelos described the adventures of Nestor and Cesar Castillo, two young musicians who travel from Havana to New York in 1949.

The day the brothers arrived in New York, fresh from Havana, in January of 1949, the city was covered in two feet of snow. Flying out of Havana on a Pan Am Clipper to Miami for $39.18, they then took the Florida Special north. In Baltimore they began to encounter snow, and while passing through a station in northern Maryland, they came across a water tower that had burst and blossomed into an orchid-shaped, many-petaled cascade of ice. Pablo [their cousin] met them at Pennsylvania Station, and, *hombre* [ôm′brā, man! as an exclamation], the brothers in their thin-soled shoes and cheap Sears, Roebuck overcoats were chilled to the bone. On the streets, people and cars seemed to disappear in the snowy winds like shredding phantoms. (They dissolved in a snow that wasn't anything like the snow they'd seen in the movies in Havana, nothing like Bing Crosby's angelic "I'm Dreaming of a White Christmas" snow, or the snow they'd imagined in dreams, lukewarm like the fake frost on a movie house *Air-Conditioned* sign.) Their thin-soled Cuban shoes soaked through, and when they stomped their feet in Pablo's lobby, they could smell the fumes of gas and electric heaters in the halls.

Pablo and his family lived at 500 La Salle, west of 124th Street and Broadway, in uptown Manhattan. It was a six-story tenement, constructed around the turn of the century to house the servant class, and it had a simple stoop with black curlicue railings, a narrow doorway framed in a crenellated brick archway. Above this rose six floors of black wrought-iron fire escapes and lamplit Venetian-blinded windows. It was two minutes from the 125th Street El, an overnight train ride and forty-five-minute flight from Havana, and five minutes from Harlem, the heartland of syncopating rhythm, as they used to say in those days. From its roof you could see the Hudson River and the domed and pillared mausoleum that was Grant's Tomb toward the northern edge of Riverside Park at 122nd Street and all the way over to the docks, and the lines of commuters and cars waiting to board the ferryboats for New Jersey.

That same night, Pablo's wife cooked them a great feast, and because it had been snowing and their feet were cold, she washed their numb toes in a pan of hot water. She was a practical and kindhearted woman from Oriente [ō′rē en′tā, a province in Cuba], for whom marriage and childbearing were the great events in her life. She lived to take care of the men in that house, slaved washing their clothes, cleaning the house, cooking, and attending to the children. Those first cold days, the future Mambo King spent most of his time in the kitchen drinking beer and watching her prepare big pots of stew and rice and beans and fried *plátanos* [plä′tä nōs, plantains, a kind of banana]. Frying up steaks and pork chops and long strings of sausages that Pablito would bring home from his foreman's job at the meat plant. The smoke would escape out the windows, and neighbors, like their landlady, Mrs. Shannon, would shake their heads. Pablo's wife would cook breakfast, fried *chorizos* [chō rē′zōs, sausages] and eggs, and then iron their clothes. She sighed a lot, but

> A family and love make a man happy, not just playing the mambo.

An excerpt from
THE MAMBO KINGS PLAY SONGS OF LOVE
by Oscar Hijuelos

immediately after sighing, she smiled, a statement of fortitude; her plump, dimpled face highlighted by long, long eyelashes whose shadows were like the hands of a clock. That was what she was like, a clock, marking her day with her chores, her sighs punctuating the hours.

"A family and love," he heard again. "That's what makes a man happy, not just playing the mambo."

And in those days Pablo would drive them around in his Oldsmobile to see the sights, or the brothers would ride the subway all over the four boroughs, faces pressed against the windows, as if counting the pillars and flashing lights for fun. Cesar favored amusement parks, circuses, movie houses, burlesques, and baseball games, while Nestor, a more quiet, docile, and tormented man, enjoyed nature and liked going to the places that Pablo's children loved the most. He liked to take the children to the Museum of Natural History, where he would revel in walking among the remains of so many reptiles, mammals, birds, fish, insects which had once vibrated, shimmered, crawled, flown, swum through the world and which were now preserved in row after row of glass cases. On one of those days, he, Cesar, Pablo, and the kids posed proudly for a photograph before the looming skeleton of Tyrannosaurus Rex. Afterwards they walked over to Central Park, the brothers strolling together as they used to down in Havana. Back then it was tranquil and clean. Old ladies sunned themselves everywhere and young men snuggled in the grass with their girls. Picnicking on the green, they ate thick steak heroes and drank Coca-Colas, enjoying the sunshine as they watched boats float across the lake. Best was the Bronx Zoo in springtime, with its lions prowling in their dens, the buffalo with their great horns and downy fur foaming like whitewater beneath their chins, long-necked giraffes whose heads curiously peeked high into the skirts of trees. Beautiful days, beyond all pain, all suffering.

At this time in New York there was a bit of malevolent prejudice in the air, postwar xenophobia [zen′ə fõ′bē ə, a hatred or fear of foreigners], and budding juvenile delinquency on the streets. (And now? Years later? A few of the Irish old-timers stubbornly hanging on can't believe what happened on their street, the sidewalks jammed now with dominoes, shell games, card players, and radios and fruit-ice wagons, those old fellows wandering about furtively like ghosts.) Cesar would remember being shushed on the street for speaking to Nestor in Spanish, having eggs thrown at him from a rooftop as he marched up the hill to Pablito's in a flamingo-pink suit. They learned which streets to avoid, and not to go walking along the docks at night. And while they found this part of life in New York depressing at first, they took solace in the warmth of Pablo's household: the music of Pablo's record player, the aroma of cooking plantains, the affection and kisses from Pablo's wife and his three children made them happier.

That was the way it happened with most Cubans coming to the States then, when every Cuban knew every Cuban. Apartments filled with travelers or cousins or friends from Cuba. . . .

> There was a bit of malevolent prejudice in the air.

Critical Thinking
Drawing Conclusions
The narrator attributes some of the prejudice encountered by the Castillo brothers to "postwar xenophobia." Why might fear of foreigners be heightened after a war?

IN MY MOTHER'S HOUSE THERE IS STILL GOD

Set in Chicago's South Side in the 1950s, Lorraine Hansberry's play *A Raisin in the Sun* (1958), deals with the struggles of an African American family, the Youngers, to realize their different dreams. In the following excerpt from Act 1, the mother of the family discusses with her daughter, Beneatha, and her daughter-in-law, Ruth, the possibility of Beneatha marrying the wealthy young man she has been dating.

MAMA. (*To change the subject.*) Who you going out with tomorrow night?

BENEATHA. (*With displeasure.*) George Murchison again.

MAMA. (*Pleased.*) Oh—you getting a little sweet on him? . . .

BENEATHA. Oh—I like George all right, Mama. I mean I like him enough to go out with him and stuff, but—

RUTH. (*For devilment.*) What does *and stuff* mean?

BENEATHA. Mind your own business.

MAMA. Stop picking at her now, Ruth. (*A thoughtful pause, and then a suspicious sudden look at her daughter as she turns in her chair for emphasis.*) What *does* it mean?

BENEATHA. (*Wearily.*) Oh, I just mean I couldn't ever really be serious about George. He's—he's so shallow.

RUTH. Shallow—what do you mean he's shallow? He's *Rich!*

MAMA. Hush, Ruth.

BENEATHA. I know he's rich. He knows he's rich, too.

RUTH. Well—what other qualities a man got to have to satisfy you, little girl?

BENEATHA. You wouldn't even begin to understand. Anybody who married Walter could not possibly understand.

MAMA. (*Outraged.*) What kind of way is that to talk about your brother?

BENEATHA. Brother is a flip—let's face it.

MAMA. (*To* RUTH, *helplessly.*) What's a flip?

RUTH. (*Glad to add kindling.*) She's saying he's crazy.

> I couldn't ever really be serious about George.

BENEATHA. Not crazy. Brother isn't really crazy yet—he—he's an elaborate neurotic.

MAMA. Hush your mouth!

BENEATHA. As for George. Well, George looks good—he's got a beautiful car and he takes me to nice places and, as my sister-in-law says, he is probably the richest boy I will ever get to know and I even like him sometimes—but if the Youngers are sitting around waiting to see if their little Bennie is going to tie up the family with the Murchisons, they are wasting their time.

RUTH. You mean you wouldn't marry George Murchison if he asked you someday? That pretty, rich thing? Honey, I knew you was odd—

BENEATHA. No I would not marry him if all I felt for him was what I feel now. Besides, George's family wouldn't really like it.

MAMA. Why not?

BENEATHA. Oh, Mama—The Murchisons are honest-to-God-real-*live*-rich colored people, and the only people in the world who are more snobbish than rich white people are rich colored people. I thought everybody knew that. I've met Mrs. Murchison. She's a scene!

MAMA. You must not dislike people 'cause they well off, honey.

BENEATHA. Why not? It makes just as much sense as disliking people 'cause they are poor, and lots of people do that.

RUTH. (*A wisdom-of-the-ages manner. To* MAMA.) Well, she'll get over some of this—

BENEATHA. Get over it? What are you talking about, Ruth? Listen, I'm going to be a doctor. I'm not worried about who I'm going to marry yet—if I ever get married.

MAMA *and* RUTH. *If!*

MAMA. Now, Bennie—

An excerpt from
A RAISIN IN THE SUN
by Lorraine Hansberry

BENEATHA. Oh, I probably will . . . but first I'm going to be a doctor, and George, for one, still thinks that's pretty funny. I couldn't be bothered with that. I am going to be a doctor and everybody around here better understand that!

MAMA. (*Kindly.*) 'Course you going to be a doctor, honey, God willing.

BENEATHA. (*Drily.*) God hasn't got a thing to do with it.

MAMA. Beneatha—that just wasn't necessary.

BENEATHA. Well—neither is God. I get sick of hearing about God.

MAMA. Beneatha!

BENEATHA. I mean it! I'm just tired of hearing about God all the time. What has He got to do with anything? Does he pay tuition?

MAMA. You 'bout to get your fresh little jaw slapped!

RUTH. That's just what she needs, all right!

BENEATHA. Why? Why can't I say what I want to around here, like everybody else?

MAMA. It don't sound nice for a young girl to say things like that—you wasn't brought up that way. Me and your father went to trouble to get you and Brother to church every Sunday.

BENEATHA. Mama, you don't understand. It's all a matter of ideas, and God is just one idea I don't accept. It's not important. I am not going out and be immoral or commit crimes because I don't believe in God. I don't even think about it. It's just that I get tired of Him getting credit for all the things the human race achieves through its own stubborn effort. There simply is no blasted God—there is only man and it is he who makes miracles! (*MAMA absorbs this speech, studies her daughter and rises slowly and crosses to BENEATHA and slaps her powerfully across the face. After, there is only silence and the daughter drops her eyes from her mother's face, and MAMA is very tall before her.*)

MAMA. Now—you say after me, in my mother's house there is still God. (*There is a long pause and BENEATHA stares at the floor wordlessly. MAMA repeats the phrase with precision and cool emotion.*) In my mother's house there is still God.

BENEATHA. In my mother's house there is still God.

(*A long pause.*)

MAMA. (*Walking away from BENEATHA, too disturbed for triumphant posture. Stopping and turning back to her daughter.*) There are some ideas we ain't going to have in this house. Not long as I am at the head of this family.

BENEATHA. Yes ma'am.

(*MAMA walks out of the room.*)

RUTH. (*almost gently, with profound understanding*). You think you a woman, Bennie—but you still a little girl. What you did was childish—so you got treated like a child.

BENEATHA. I see. (*Quietly.*) I also see that everybody thinks it's all right for Mama to be a tyrant. But all the tyranny in the world will never put a God in the heavens! (*She picks up her books and goes out.*)

RUTH. (*goes to MAMA's door*). She said she was sorry.

MAMA. (*coming out, going to her plant*). They frightens me, Ruth. My children.

> Why can't I say what I want to around here?

CRITICAL THINKING
Recognizing Values
Beneatha appears to reject the material values represented by the Murchisons and the spiritual values represented by her mother. Does Beneatha give any indication of what values she feels are important? Explain.

THE PORTRAIT

"Up to the time I started teaching," wrote Tomás Rivera (1935–1984), "I was part of the migrant labor stream that went from Texas to . . . the Midwest. I lived and worked in Iowa, Minnesota, Wisconsin, Michigan, and North Dakota." This experience is reflected in his novel *And the Earth Did Not Devour Him* (1971), which deals with the lives of Mexican American migrant workers in the 1940s and '50s. The following reading, "The Portrait," comes from that novel.

As soon as the people returned from up north the portrait salesmen began arriving from San Antonio. They would come to rake in. They knew that the workers had money and that was why, as Dad used to say, they would flock in. They carried suitcases packed with samples and always wore white shirts and ties; that way they looked more important and the people believed everything they would tell them and invite them into their homes without giving it much thought. I think that down deep they even longed for their children to one day be like them. In any event, they would arrive and make their way down the dusty streets, going house to house carrying suitcases full of samples.

> Doesn't he look real, like he's alive?

I remember once I was at the house of one of my father's friends when one of these salesmen arrived. I also remember that that particular one seemed a little frightened and timid. Don Mateo asked him to come in because he wanted to do business.

"Good afternoon, traveler. I would like to tell you about something new that we're offering this year."

"Well, let's see, let's see . . ."

"Well, sir, see, you give us a picture, any picture you may have, and we will not only enlarge it for you but we'll also set it in a wooden frame like this one and we'll shape the image a little, like this—three dimensional, as they say."

"And what for?"

"So that it will look real. That way . . . look, let me show you . . . see? Doesn't he look real, like he's alive?"

"Man, he sure does. Look, vieja [vē ā′hä, old woman, an affectionate term for a man's wife]. This looks great. Well, you know, we wanted to send some pictures to be enlarged . . . but now, this must cost a lot, right?"

"No, I'll tell you, it costs about the same. Of course, it takes more time."

"Well, tell me, how much?"

"For as little as thirty dollars we'll deliver it to you done with inlays just like this, one this size."

"Boy, that's expensive! Didn't you say it didn't cost a lot more? Do you take installments?"

"Well, I'll tell you, we have a new manager and he wants everything in cash. It's very fine work. We'll make it look like real. Shaped like that, with inlays . . . take a look. What do you think? Some fine work, wouldn't you say? We can have it all finished for you in a month. You just tell us what color you want the clothes to be and we'll come by with it all finished one day when you least expect, framed and all. Yes, sir, a month at the longest. But like I say, this man, who's the new manager, he wants the full payment in cash. He's very demanding, even with us."

"Yes, but it's much too expensive."

"Well, yes. But the thing is, this is very fine work. You can't say you've ever seen portraits done like this, with wood inlays."

"No, well, that's true. What do you think, vieja?"

"Well, I like it a lot. Why don't we order one? And if it turns out good . . . My Chuy [Chwē] . . . may he rest in peace. It's the only picture

AND THE EARTH DID NOT DEVOUR HIM
by Tomás Rivera

we have of him. We took it right before he left for Korea. Poor m'ijo [mē hō′, *mi hijo,* my son], we never saw him again. See . . . this is his picture. Do you think you can make it like that, make it look like he's alive?"

"Sure, we can. You know, we've done a lot of them in soldier's uniforms and shaped it, like you see in this sample, with inlays. Why, it's more than just a portrait. Sure. You just tell me what size you want and whether you want a round or square frame. What do you say? How should I write it down?"

"What do you say, vieja, should we have it done like this one?"

"Well, I've already told you what I think. I would like to have m'ijo's picture fixed up like that and in color."

"All right, go ahead and write it down. But you take good care of that picture for us because it's the only one we have of our son grown up. He was going to send us one all dressed up in uniform with the American and Mexican flags crossed over his head, but he no sooner got there when a letter arrived telling us that he was lost in action. So you take good care of it."

"Don't you worry. We're responsible people. And we understand the sacrifices that you people make. Don't worry. And you just wait and see, when we bring it, you'll see how pretty it's gonna look. What do you say, should we make the uniform navy blue?"

"But he's not wearing a uniform in that picture."

"No, but that's just a matter of fixing it up with some wood fiber overlays. Look at these. This one, he didn't have a uniform on but we put one on him. So what do you say? Should we make it navy blue?"

"All right."
"Don't you worry about the picture."

And that was how they spent the entire day, going house to house, street by street, their suitcases stuffed with pictures. As it turned out, a whole lot of people had ordered enlargements of that kind.

"They should be delivering those portraits soon, don't you think?"

"I think so, it's delicate work and takes more time. That's some fine work those people do. Did you see how real those pictures looked?"

"Yeah, sure. They do some fine work. You can't deny that. But it's already been over a month since they passed by here."

"Yes, but from here they went on through all the towns picking up pictures . . . all the way to San Antonio for sure. So it'll probably take a little longer."

"That's true, that's true."

> Children found a sack full of pictures, all worm-eaten and soaking wet.

And two more weeks had passed by the time they made the discovery. Some very heavy rains had come and some children, who were playing in one of the tunnels leading to the dump, found a sack full of pictures, all worm-eaten and soaking wet. The only reason that they could tell that these were pictures was because there were a lot of them and most of them the same size and with faces that could just barely be made out. Everybody caught on right away. Don Mateo was so angry that he took off to San Antonio to find the so and so who had swindled them.

"Well, you know, I stayed at Esteban's house.

739

And every day I went with him to the market to sell produce. I helped him with everything. I had faith that I would run into that son of a gun some day soon. Then, after I'd been there for a few days, I started going out to the different barrios [bär'ē ōz, neighborhoods] and I found out a lot that way. It wasn't so much the money that upset me. It was my poor vieja, crying and all because we'd lost the only picture we had of Chuy. We found it in the sack with all the other pictures but it was already ruined, you know."

"I see, but tell me, how did you find him?"

"Well, you see, to make a long story short, he came by the stand at the market one day. He stood right in front of us and bought some vegetables. It was like he was trying to remember who I was. Of course, I recognized him right off. Because when you're angry enough, you don't forget a face. I just grabbed him right then and there. Poor guy couldn't even talk. He was all scared. And I told him that I wanted that portrait of my son and that I wanted it three dimensional and that he'd best get it for me or I'd let him have it. And I went with him to where he lived. And I put him to work right then and there. The poor guy didn't know where to begin. He had to do it all from memory."

"And how did he do it?"

"I don't know. I suppose if you're scared enough, you're capable of doing anything. Three days later he brought me the portrait all finished, just like you see it there on that table by the Virgin. Now tell me, how do you like the way my boy looks?"

"Well, to be honest, I don't remember too well how Chuy looked. But he was beginning to look more and more like you, isn't that so?"

"Yes, I would say so. That's what everybody tells me now. That Chuy's a chip off the old block and that he was already looking like me. There's the portrait. Like they say, one and the same.

> I don't remember too well how Chuy looked.

CRITICAL THINKING
Drawing Conclusions
One type of irony occurs when what happens in a literary work is contrary to what is expected. How is the conclusion of "The Portrait" ironic?

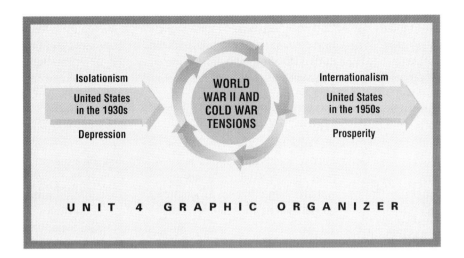

UNIT 4 GRAPHIC ORGANIZER

CHAPTER
SURVEY
15

The World at War
1939–1941

World economic depression helped bring the rise of Hitler.
Worldwide depression in the 1930s left five million Germans without jobs by 1932. In their distress, more and more Germans heeded the appeals of Adolf Hitler and the Nazi party. Hitler made the Jewish people the scapegoats for Germany's economic troubles. He began a brutal program

of genocide—the cold-blooded killing of a whole race.

Imperialistic leaders also came to power in Japan and Italy. Japan acted on its ambitions in 1931 by seizing Manchuria. The League of Nations called for Japanese withdrawal from Manchuria, but Japan instead withdrew from the League. Italy's dictator Benito Mussolini also hungered for glory and dreamed of reviving the once-magnificent Roman Empire.

Britain and France suffered Hitler's rise to power. Great Britain and France had agreed to protect the borders of the new countries created by the Versailles Treaty. Nevertheless, they hesitated to risk war as Germany seized first the Rhineland in 1936, then Austria and part of Czechoslovakia in 1938. At the same time, Italy moved into Ethiopia in 1936. Nazi Germany and Italy formed an alliance, the Axis powers, and together they supported a nationalistic, totalitarian dictator in Spain, General Francisco Franco.

Hitler and Russia's communist dictator, Joseph Stalin, sealed a nonaggression pact in August 1939. One month later, Hitler invaded Poland. Britain and France, who had guaranteed Poland's borders, declared war. World War II had begun.

German forces slashed across Europe. Hitler's army and airforce used new methods of warfare — massed tanks and precision bombing by air — to destroy Allied defenses. His divisions slashed across Belgium and the Netherlands to occupy much of Europe by June 1940. Only Britain continued to resist. German aircraft began to bomb London and other major cities, but Britain's Royal Air Force delivered punishing blows in return. As a result, Hitler turned from a planned invasion of Britain to attack the Soviet Union in June 1941.

America moved away from isolationism. Haunted by memories of World War I, Americans tried to avoid any direct involvement in the war. As the Nazi threat mounted, however, President Roosevelt began to move away from a policy of isolationism and neutrality. He

proposed a Lend-Lease Act to Congress. The United States would lend or lease munitions to Britain and its allies to be repaid when the war was over. Roosevelt and British prime minister Winston Churchill signed the Atlantic Charter in August 1941. The charter outlined war aims and affirmed the right of self-government by all people. To ensure that lend-lease goods reached Britain, American warships began to escort merchant vessels across the Atlantic.

The Allied Victory
1941–1945

Japan's secret attack drew America into war. Like Germany and Italy in Europe, Japan had

dreamed of conquest. After seizing Manchuria in 1931, Japanese forces opened a punishing drive into China in 1937. The United States and the League of Nations condemned Japan's aggressions but did little else. When Japan occupied French and Dutch colonial holdings in southeast Asia, relations with the United States grew less friendly. The United States sharply reduced its oil exports to Japan. The Japanese military retaliated with a devastating attack on the U.S. naval base at Pearl Harbor, Hawaii, on December 7, 1941. Congress declared war on Japan, and three days later Germany and Italy declared war on the United States. The United States was part of the global struggle.

Allied landings in Europe led to defeat of the Axis. Faced with war in both Europe and Asia, the Allies gave top priority to the war in Europe. Fearing a bloodbath would follow an invasion on the European mainland, the Allies agreed to attack the Germans in North Africa. After a seesaw campaign, the Allies finally forced the German army out of Africa in May 1943. The Allies then invaded Sicily and began a bloody drive through Italy.

Finally, on D-Day — June 6, 1944 — the Allies launched a full-scale invasion of France's Normandy coast. As Allied armies smashed through Germany, they discovered the horrors of the Holocaust — the mass murder of six million Jews. A shattered Germany surrendered on May 7, 1945.

Air bombardments, including the dropping of the first and second nuclear bombs on the Japanese cities of Hiroshima and Nagasaki, forced Japan's surrender on September 2, 1945. The war was over.

U.S. forces spearheaded the war against Japan in the Pacific. In the six months following Pearl Harbor, Japan spread its empire far into the Pacific. U.S. forces managed to stop the Japanese sweep in the Battle of the Coral Sea in May 1942. The turning point of the war in the Pacific came with the spectacular victory at Midway Island that June.

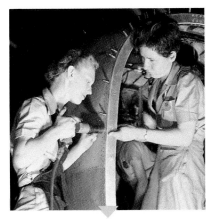

The war brought enormous changes in American life. With the attack on Pearl Harbor, the United States quickly converted to a wartime economy. The vast U.S. war production was the key to Allied victory. The surging economy brought opportunities for the nation's African Americans, women, and Mexican Americans in industry and in the armed forces. The war also fanned discrimination and prejudice, especially against thousands of loyal Japanese Americans who were moved to internment camps.

Germany, Italy, and Japan emerged from the war with their economies shattered. Britain and France faced economic distress at home and opposition in their former colonies. In contrast, the United States was more powerful than it had ever been. Americans also stood ready to discard their traditional isolationist role and take the lead in remaking a world shattered by years of destruction.

17

C H A P T E R
S U R V E Y

Truman and the Cold War
1945–1952

A cold war began in Europe.
Harry Truman became president after the sudden death of Franklin D. Roosevelt in April 1945. As World War II drew to a close, a cold war began between the world's two major powers, the United States and the Soviet Union. Having borne the brunt of the war against Germany, the Soviets insisted on setting up communist regimes in the countries they had overrun in Eastern Europe. The Soviets created satellites in Poland, Hungary, Romania, and Bulgaria. Then in 1948 the Soviets shocked the West by staging a coup in democratic Czechoslovakia.

Americans became locked in a struggle against communism.
The United States responded to Soviet pressure by forming a policy of containment. The centerpiece of that policy was the Marshall Plan, which revitalized Western Europe with financial aid. The most dramatic challenge to the Marshall Plan came in June 1948 when the Soviets set up a blockade of the Western-occupied section of Berlin. A giant airlift of food and provisions finally forced the Soviets to lift the Berlin blockade in early 1949.

U.S. forces tried to stop the spread of communism in Asia.
The promise of the Truman Doctrine to support anticommunist governments

around the world was soon put to a test in Asia. A communist takeover in China in 1949 stunned many Americans. The United States had sided with the Chinese Nationalists under Chiang Kai-shek, who were defeated after a 12-year war with Chinese Communists under their leader Mao Zedong.

Communism also threatened to consume all of Korea. That nation had been divided north and south in 1945. In 1950 communist North Koreans invaded South Korea. The United States, with the support of the United Nations, aided the South. When UN forces drove the North Korean army back across the 38th parallel that divided the two Koreas in late 1950, the Chinese intervened. The war ground brutally on for three more years without changing the military stalemate.

The transition to peace moved unevenly at home. With the end of the war, depression-era fears of unemployment returned to haunt the nation. Although many women and minorities were thrown out of work, returning veterans generally found jobs. Inflation, not unemployment, proved the biggest postwar problem. As prices continued to rise, wages fell

behind, partly because veterans were flooding the labor market. Hoping to quell bitter quarrels between business and labor, Congress passed the Taft-Hartley Act in 1947. The act, passed over Truman's veto, limited the power of labor unions. Despite the country's growing conservative mood, Truman won re-election in 1948, becoming president in his own right.

During Truman's years, public attention focused more and more on communism. Beginning in 1950 Republican Senator Joseph McCarthy of Wisconsin falsely accused hundreds of innocent Americans of being communists. The red scare inflamed the public, allying working-class Americans and conservative Republicans to sweep the Republicans into the White House in 1952.

C H A P T E R S U R V E Y
18

Eisenhower and Postwar Prosperity
1953–1960

Americans prospered during the Cold War years. The Suburban middle classes expanded dramatically following World War II. As the economy boomed, real income soared dramatically, and most white

Americans lived free of economic want. They purchased huge quantities of consumer goods, moved into suburban homes, and began large families. Americans used much of their new wealth and leisure time on recreational activities. Suburban life centered around the automobile and, increasingly, television. Only a few Americans worried about the impact of mass media on society.

Eisenhower followed middle-of-the-road policies at home.

World War II hero Dwight Eisenhower won the presidency in 1952 and soon built a thoroughly Republican presidency. Eisenhower took a low-key view of Senator McCarthy's vicious anticommunism. As the senator's charges grew more extreme, the Senate began to hold public hearings. Finally, the Senate's censure of McCarthy put an end to his assaults on the rights of many Americans.

An economic conservative, Eisenhower hoped to return as much of the economy as possible to private interests. Only in the 1956 Highway Act did the president launch an expensive new domestic program.

The nuclear threat shadowed U.S. policies abroad.

Experienced in dealing with international issues, Eisenhower was determined to bring the Cold War under control. He also believed firmly that the nation must not go bankrupt in its fight against communism. Both factors shaped his foreign policy of massive retaliation. The policy depended upon American willingness to use nuclear power to meet Soviet aggression. The threat of nuclear war helped end the Korean War in 1953, although the war cost many lives and the Korean nation remained divided. Nuclear threats also helped end a crisis in the Suez in 1956.

A nuclear arms race ensued between the United States and the Soviet Union. The resulting balance of power rested on fear of nuclear disaster. Plans for a Soviet-American summit to address arms control were ruined when the Soviets shot down an American spy plane over the Soviet Union in 1960.

Americans began to question the values of the 1950s.

Although many Americans enjoyed their growing affluence, thrusts against the consumer culture and conformity also appeared. Writers such as David Reisman and Jack Kerouac and artists such as Jackson Pollock questioned the effects of the supermarket culture and its numbing conformity. Disillusioned young adults, nicknamed the Beatniks, turned away from a life they saw as barren and stifling.

In spite of skyrocketing enrollments in American schools and colleges, critics challenged the effectiveness of these schools in teaching basic skills. The Soviet launching of *Sputnik* in 1957 abruptly ended popular complacency. In response, Congress approved long-debated federal financing of education in 1958. Expanded programs in science and foreign languages resulted. The president also appointed a Commission on National Goals that beckoned the nation to pursue excellence and renew its sense of national mission.

Optimism

"Every day, in every way, I'm getting better and better," chanted many health-conscious Americans in the 1920s, an exuberant decade when everything, from stock-market prices to major-league batting averages, seemed on the rise. Americans have tended throughout most eras of our history to be an optimistic people, confident in what the future would bring. "What will be will be well," wrote Walt Whitman, "for what is is well." What do you think Whitman meant? Try restating it in your own words.

The following are some American reflections on optimism.

1861

Hope is the thing with feathers
That perches in the soul,
And sings the tune without the
   words,
And never stops at all,

And the sweetest in the gale is
   heard,
And sore must be the storm
That could abash the little bird
That kept so many warm.

I've heard it in the chillest land,
And on the strangest sea;
Yet, never, in extremity.
It asked a crumb of me.
▲ **Emily Dickinson, "Hope Is the Thing with Feathers"**

1872

optimism, *n.* The doctrine or belief, that everything is beautiful, including what is ugly, everything good, especially the bad, and everything right that is wrong. . . . Being a blind faith, it is inaccessible to the light of disproof—an intellectual disorder, yielding to no treatment but death. . . .
▲ **Ambrose Bierce, *The Devil's Dictionary***

1926

The optimist proclaims that we live in the best of all possible worlds; and the pessimist fears that this is true.
▲ **James Branch Cabell, *The Silver Stallion***

1936

"I'll think of it all tomorrow, at Tara. I can stand it then. Tomorrow, I'll think of some way to get him back. After all, tomorrow is another day."
▲ **Scarlett O'Hara, in Margaret Mitchell's *Gone with the Wind***

1949

"Willy was a salesman. And for a salesman, there is no rock bottom to the life. He don't put a bolt to a nut, he don't tell you the law or give you medicine. He's a man way out there in the blue, riding on a smile and a shoeshine. And when they start not smiling back—that's an earthquake. And then you get a couple of spots on your hat, and you're finished. Nobody dast [dare] blame this man. A salesman is got to dream boy. It comes with the territory."
▲ **Charley, in Arthur Miller's *Death of a Salesman***

1951

I decline to accept the end of man. It is easy to say that man is immortal simply because he will endure: that when the last dingdong of doom has clanged and faded from the last worthless rock hanging tideless in the last red and dying evening, that even then there will be one more sound: that of his puny inexhaustible voice, still talking. I refuse to accept this. I believe that man will not merely endure, he will prevail. He is immortal, not merely because he alone among creatures has an inexhaustible voice, but because he has a soul, a spirit capable of compassion and sacrifice and endurance.
▲ **William Faulkner, Nobel Prize Acceptance Speech**

1953

Don't look back. Something may be gaining on you.

▲ **Satchell Paige, "How to Keep Young"**

1989

I want to . . . major in pharmacy. [My hero is] my second uncle. . . . [My uncle and aunt] came here to America and he didn't know how to speak a word of English. Now they've been here six years and he's a pharmacist. He makes a lot of money, they have a nice house, and when I went to where he works, he introduced me to his staff. I was shocked. They all understood his English! I said, "This is a miracle!" And he answered, "Sook, America is where miracles come true."

▲ **Sook, an 18-year-old Korean immigrant**

1990

I know that American films are often criticized for their happy endings, but I do not agree with this. I think that this is a remarkable quality, which gives the spectator hope and builds a healthy soul for the nation, so I like it.

In Russia there are no happy endings.

▲ **Russian actor Aleksandr Romantsov, in *New York Times* interview**

Paraphrase, Summarize, and Discuss

"You've got to AC-CENT-TCHU-ATE THE POSITIVE," urged an American popular song of the 1940s; "Eliminate the negative, Latch on to the affirmative, Don't mess with Mister In-between." How would you restate the song's message in your own words?

Assignment: Write a clear, well-organized paragraph summarizing and discussing the excerpt from William Faulkner's Nobel Prize Acceptance Speech on the facing page.

Paraphrase the speech. In order to ensure that you understand what Faulkner said, restate the excerpt from his speech in your own words. To do this, read the speech carefully. Determine the meanings of unfamiliar words from the context of the speech. Look up in the dictionary any words you still do not know. Rewrite the speech sentence by sentence. Use plain, straightforward English.

Summarize the speech. Reread the speech and your paraphrase of it. Ask yourself the following questions: What is Faulkner's central statement about mankind? Where in the speech does he present this main idea? Write Faulkner's central idea in a clear sentence. In a second sentence, summarize the assertions that he makes about this idea.

Discuss the speech. Think about Faulkner's central idea. Is Faulkner right, or is he being *too* optimistic? Does what you know of history support his assertions about human beings? What experiences in your own life cause you to believe in or doubt humanity's capacity for compassion, sacrifice, and endurance? Organize your thoughts on these questions and express them in several clearly written sentences. Be sure that your examples are specific.

Rewrite your draft. In a single paragraph of approximately 250 words, present your summary of Faulkner's central idea, your opinion of his view, and the supporting evidence you have gathered.

Edit and proofread your paragraph. Reread what you have written to improve the organization and to correct errors in grammar, punctuation, and spelling.

Unit 5

You Are There

I made four sorties into Saigon. . . . The night sorties were the worst. . . . To see a city burning gives one a strange sense of insecurity. . . .

It isn't very easy for me to even tell myself what the motivation was to come here. It was more the feeling than something concrete. I have been repaid. And that's possibly a funny way of saying it, but that's the way I feel. . . .
—*helicopter pilot Richard Van de Geer remembering the fall of Saigon, April 30, 1975; he was the last American to die in the Vietnam War.*

Vietnamese refugees run desperately for safety as Saigon falls to the communists.

Troubled Times

Unit Outline

Unit Themes

In this unit you will analyze the following themes of U.S. history:

▶ Our society reflects racial, ethnic, and religious diversity.

▶ The American political system is built upon constitutional and representative government.

▶ Americans express social and political concerns within a religious and ethical framework.

▶ Conflict and cooperation have been essential elements in the development of the United States.

| 1950 | 1955 | 1960 | 1965 | 1970 | 1975 | 1980 | 1985 |

1954
Brown v. *Board of Education of Topeka* establishes that separate educational facilities are unequal

1962
Cuban missile crisis threatens U.S.–Soviet peace

1963
President Kennedy assassinated

1964
Civil Rights Act of 1964; Gulf of Tonkin Resolution

1968
The Rev. Dr. Martin Luther King, Jr., and Robert F. Kennedy assassinated

1974
President Nixon resigns under threat of impeachment

1969
American astronauts make first moon landing

1975
South Vietnam falls to communist North Vietnam

1982
Vietnam Veterans Memorial dedicated

...UNTIL JUSTICE ROLLS DOWN LIKE WATERS AND RIGHTEOUSNESS LIKE A MIGHTY STREAM

MARTIN LUTHER KING JR

Linking Past to Present

Rosa Parks (inset) refused to give up her seat on a Montgomery, Alabama, bus in 1955. Her protest is one of the events inscribed on the Civil Rights Memorial in that city. The memorial, dedicated in 1989 to honor the 53 people who gave their lives during the civil rights struggle, was designed by Maya Lin. She wanted the tribute to possess the tranquility of a Japanese garden, a place in which to "appreciate how far the country has come in its quest for equality and to consider how far it has to go." The inscription above the disk is from the Rev. Dr. Martin Luther King, Jr.'s "I Have a Dream" speech, which is paraphrased from the Bible.

The Struggle for Civil Rights

1 9 5 4 — 1 9 6 8

19

CHAPTER PREVIEW

In this chapter you will learn about the African American quest for equal rights.

SECTIONS IN THIS CHAPTER:
1. **The struggle began with nonviolent protests.**
2. **Students strengthened the civil rights movement.**
3. **African Americans staged mass protests.**
4. **Many racial barriers remained in the South.**
5. **Militant black consciousness developed.**

When Rosa Parks boarded a Montgomery, Alabama, city bus on the afternoon of December 1, 1955, she anticipated rude treatment from the white bus driver. At the time, African Americans were allowed to ride Montgomery buses, but only if they sat at the very back. On several previous occasions a driver had taken Parks' fare at the front door of the bus and then forced her to reenter through the rear door. Before she could get in, however, the driver cruelly drove off, leaving Parks standing at the curb. After many years of such treatment, Parks finally reached a breaking point.

When white passengers came aboard the full bus on that December day in 1955, the bus driver told Parks to remove herself from her rear seat so that a white passenger could sit down. Defiantly, she refused to do so. The bus driver then warned, "I'm going to have you arrested." Parks still refused to move. Shortly afterward the police arrived and arrested Parks for violating one of Alabama's segregation laws.

Although Parks' solitary protest was a seemingly insignificant event at the time, it helped spark one of the nation's largest social movements in its history—the fight for African American civil rights. Why did Parks' protest cause such a furor? What other events and people played a part in this great movement? What elements in our history made such a movement inevitable?

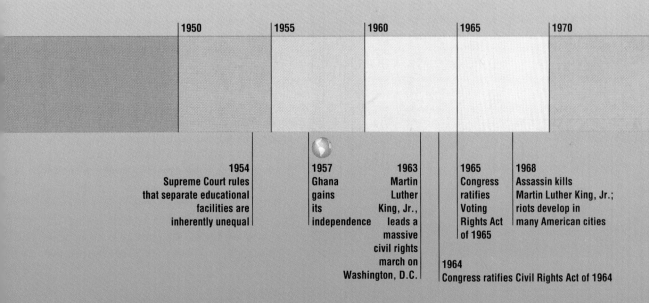

1950	1955	1960	1965	1970

1954
Supreme Court rules that separate educational facilities are inherently unequal

1957
Ghana gains its independence

1963
Martin Luther King, Jr., leads a massive civil rights march on Washington, D.C.

1965
Congress ratifies Voting Rights Act of 1965

1968
Assassin kills Martin Luther King, Jr.; riots develop in many American cities

1964
Congress ratifies Civil Rights Act of 1964

751

The struggle began with nonviolent protests.

Key Terms: Jim Crow laws, *Brown* v. *Board of Education of Topeka*, Southern Christian Leadership Conference (SCLC).

Reading Preview
As you read this section, you will learn:

1. what effect the Jim Crow laws had.
2. what method African Americans used to fight segregation in Montgomery.
3. when the new movement for black equality orginated.
4. what the effect of the Supreme Court's ruling in the Brown case was.
5. what the Rev. Dr. Martin Luther King, Jr., emphasized after the Brown decision.

This photograph of children in a Memphis schoolhouse in the early 1950s clearly showed Americans the unfairness of the "separate but equal" doctrine and helped begin the drive for integrated schools across the nation.

During the 1950s and 1960s, African Americans, especially those living in the southern states, became the first large group of Americans to launch a major protest movement for group advancement. Despite the passage of the 13th, 14th, and 15th amendments and other post-Civil War legislation aimed at providing African Americans various freedoms and rights, black southerners were still subjected to many forms of humiliating treatment, discrimination, and segregation. Why did these amendments fail to prevent such treatment?

Jim Crow laws made African Americans second-class citizens.

In the 1880s and 1890s, the Supreme Court dealt a serious blow to African American rights by handing down a series of decisions overturning Reconstruction legislation. These decisions limited federal protection for African Americans and encouraged segregation. In 1883, in the *Civil Rights Cases*, the Court said that Congress could not punish individuals for acts of racial discrimination. In the landmark case *Plessy* v. *Ferguson* in 1896 the Court held that separate public facilities for blacks and whites did not violate the 14th Amendment as long as these facilities were equal.

The "separate but equal" doctrine upheld by the Court in the Plessy case, and the general failure of society to counter the practice of segregation, led to the passage of many **Jim Crow laws** in the South. (Jim Crow was a term used by many whites to refer to African Americans.) More thorough than the black codes of 1865, the Jim Crow laws passed in the 1890s segregated blacks almost everywhere in the South. For example, in 1905 Georgia passed the first law requiring separate public parks for blacks and whites. In 1909 a city in Alabama passed a law requiring blacks to be off the streets by 10 P.M. South Carolina law prevented blacks and whites from working together in the same rooms in textile factories. Atlanta, Georgia, had separate Bibles for witnesses in the city courts. Hundreds of other southern communities also passed Jim Crow laws. Overall, the effects were devastating. African Americans were legally made second-class citizens.

Besides physically excluding African Americans from the mainstream, southern whites devised an elaborate "etiquette" of proper race relations. Blacks were expected to act in a subservient manner around whites, always addressing whites as Mr. and Mrs. even while whites addressed blacks of any age by their first names or as "boy" or "girl." Black men were taught to never challenge whites, either physically or verbally. "Uppity" blacks could be punished by severe beatings or worse. In 1955 a group of whites in Mississippi brutally murdered 14-year-old Emmett Till after he talked to a white woman on a dare from his friends.

The South's rigidly enforced system of racial domination instilled fear in the minds of many blacks. However, it also fed the desire to resist. The Rev. Dr. **Martin Luther King, Jr.**, for example, remembered going with his father to an Atlanta shoe store and being told to use only the rear seats. His father announced that he would not accept the discriminatory treatment. Taking his son by the hand, he walked out of the store in protest. King recalled:

This was the first time I had ever seen my father so angry. **AN AMERICAN ★ SPEAKS**
I still remember walking down the street beside him as he muttered, "I don't care how long I have to live with this system, I will never accept it."

African Americans used passive resistance to fight segregation.

In 1955 **Rosa Parks'** stunningly effective act of resistance began a new phase in the African American struggle against racial oppression. Black residents of **Montgomery**, the capital of Alabama, greatly respected Parks and quickly mobilized to support her. They arranged to have a sympathetic white attorney represent her and raised her bail. Members of the Women's Political Council proposed that blacks refuse to ride the buses for one day as a protest against discriminatory treatment. The boycott, which began on December 5, was an overwhelming success, with almost no blacks riding the buses. That afternoon, black residents decided to continue the boycott. They formed the Montgomery Improvement Association and selected the Rev. Dr. Martin Luther King, Jr., as president of the new group.

King was only 26 years old at the time. Before the boycott began, he had served less than two years as the pastor of Montgomery's Dexter Avenue Baptist Church. Despite his youth,

however, King's talents were evident to those who knew him. The son and grandson of ministers who were active in the Atlanta chapter of the National Association for the Advancement of Colored People (NAACP), King had spent much of his youth around Ebenezer Baptist Church, where his father had been pastor since the 1930s. As a young child he became aware of racial discrimination. When he resolved to hate whites after a young white friend was told not to play with him, King's parents told him that it was his Christian duty to love whites. However, King greatly admired his father's willingness to stand up to whites. On one occasion when a policeman stopped his father's car and addressed him as "Boy," the elder King pointed to his son. "He's a boy. I'm the Reverend King."

When Martin Luther King, Jr., grew older, and especially when he attended Morehouse College in Atlanta, he found other appealing role models, such as Benjamin E. Mays, the college's president. Mays combined strong religious convictions with a determination to fight against racial injustice.

By the time King graduated, he had decided to become a minister. Shortly before the Montgomery boycott started, he received his Ph.D. from Boston University. One of only a few black ministers to have a doctorate, King had an unusual ability to speak effectively to both white and black audiences.

When he spoke to the first mass meeting of the boycott movement on the evening of December 5, King demonstrated his ability to unify the black community to continue the protest. He knew that he could not sustain the boycott by himself. He later recalled:

I neither started the protest nor suggested it. I simply responded to the call of the people for a spokesman.

Rosa Parks, whose solitary act of defiance on a Montgomery bus in 1955 helped spark the civil rights movement, remained politically active in the 1980s. She is shown here, at the age of 75, campaigning for Jesse Jackson during the 1988 Democratic National Convention.

Point	Counterpoint
In favor of passive resistance	**Against passive resistance**
■ Violence only begets violence. ■ Change requires time and patience.	■ Passivity encourages oppression. ■ Action, not words, gets results.

With little time to prepare his remarks, he prayed for guidance and then drafted an outline that combined militancy with moderation. When he addressed the audience at crowded Holt Street Baptist Church, he pointed to the larger meaning of the boycott. He urged Montgomery blacks to remain nonviolent and true to the Christian values held by the nation:

> **AN AMERICAN ★ SPEAKS**
>
> And you know, my friends, there comes a time when people get tired of being trampled over by the iron feet of oppression. If we are wrong, the Supreme Court of this nation is wrong! If we are wrong, God Almighty is wrong!

After the meeting black residents were even more determined to continue their boycott. King was not the only boycott leader, but he played a crucial inspirational role. He was able to work well with other leaders, who respected him even when they disagreed with some of his positions. He also was a stimulating speaker who understood the larger significance of the boycott. He realized that the tactics used by the Indian leader **Mohandas K. Gandhi** in his country's independence movement could be used by southern blacks:

> I had come to see early that the Christian doctrine of love operating through the Gandhian method of nonviolence was one of the most potent weapons available to the Negro in his struggle for freedom.

King also proved that he was a courageous leader. As white resistance to the boycott became stronger and more violent, King and other black leaders were threatened with death. Despite these threats King maintained his nonviolent philosophy:

> Blood may flow in the streets of Montgomery before we receive our freedom, but it must be our blood and not that of the white man.

In January King's home was bombed. The following month, Montgomery officials indicted boycott leaders, including King and his close associate, the Reverend **Ralph Abernathy**, on charges of violating a state law against boycotts. Despite these efforts to intimidate the boycott leaders, however, the Montgomery movement continued.

On December 17, 1956, after the boycott had continued for more than a year, the Supreme Court rejected the arguments of Montgomery city officials and ruled against bus segregation. A few days later segregation on buses came to an end. Contrary to the warnings of segregationists, integrated bus seating did not result in major incidents of violence.

African Americans had won their first modern victory in the struggle for freedom. Montgomery blacks had demonstrated that individuals could successfully resist the humiliating Jim Crow system. They had also shown that nonviolent protests could succeed if blacks remained united and protest leaders refused to be intimidated. News reports of the victory in Montgomery soon encouraged blacks elsewhere to launch movements of their own.

Black activism originated during World War II.

Protest activity had long been a part of African American life, but the Montgomery movement signaled the beginning of a new era of massive African American advancement struggles. What caused this upsurge? Although spontaneous small-scale acts of resistance, such as Rosa Parks' refusal to give up her seat, sparked the struggles of the 1950s and 1960s, major underlying social changes were necessary to transform individual protests into social movements. These changes began to take place during World War II.

World War II had greatly affected the lives of many black Americans who served in the military and worked in war industries.

A. Philip Randolph's threatened march on Washington on the eve of America's entry into the war had demonstrated the effectiveness of militancy. Randolph pressured President Franklin Roosevelt into taking action against racial discrimination in war industries. As a result, African American employment in these industries rose tremendously during the war. Few gains were made in the private sector, however, because companies continued discriminatory practices.

Although many African Americans on the homefront benefited economically during the war, World War II served as a reminder that they were still considered second-class citizens. One black soldier who fought the Japanese in the Pacific remarked: "Just carve on my tombstone, here lies a black man killed fighting a yellow man [Japanese] for the protection of a white man."

In the postwar years, black veterans, especially those from the South, returned home with new determination to fight against racial oppression. On numerous occasions southern whites sought to remind black veterans that the Jim Crow system still remained. In 1946 a white mob in Monroe, Georgia, brutally murdered a black veteran, his wife, and another black couple. No one was punished for the crime, which was one of many directed against black veterans, often when they were wearing their uniforms. African Americans who had gained new employment because of wartime labor demands were determined to keep the new jobs they had obtained in defense plants and other industries.

Despite these limited opportunities, the Cold War crusade against communism that began after World War II sent a signal to African Americans that certain forms of leftist dissent would not be tolerated in postwar America. W. E. B. Du Bois, the author who helped form the NAACP in 1909, and Paul Robeson, an actor and singer, were among the black leaders who were charged with disloyalty in the new political climate. Eventually, however, the struggle against communism actually encouraged many Americans to eliminate racial practices that hurt the nation's democratic image.

The Reverend Ralph Abernathy, left, and the Rev. Dr. Martin Luther King, Jr., walk away from the Montgomery County Courthouse in February 1956 after being indicted for violating Alabama's law against boycotts. Eighty-seven other boycotters were also indicted. In spite of Alabama's attempt to thwart the protesters, the Montgomery bus boycott continued until the Supreme Court ruled against bus segregation in late 1956.

The Supreme Court reversed *Plessy* v. *Ferguson*.

Because African Americans generally saw education as a route to improvement, school desegregation became a major focus of racial advancement in the 1940s. African American lawyers, many of them graduates of Howard University's law school, spearheaded the NAACP's sustained effort to weaken the legal foundations of white racial domination in the South. Charles Houston, William Hastie, and **Thurgood Marshall**, who would become a Supreme Court justice during the Johnson Administration, filed lawsuits proving that southern black educational schools were not equal to those provided to whites. NAACP lawyers questioned why black children should be bused past white schools in order to attend inferior black ones. By the end of the 1940s, they had assembled evidence that black students were psychologically damaged when excluded from white schools.

On May 17, 1954, the NAACP won its most important victory. The Supreme Court ruled

Elizabeth Eckford, inset, and other African American students attempt to enter Little Rock's Central High but are turned away by a jeering mob. Federal troops, right, escort the students into school on September 26, 1957.

unanimously in the case of **Brown v. Board of Education of Topeka** that segregated schools were inherently inferior because they stigmatized blacks. According to Chief Justice Earl Warren, who wrote the landmark opinion in the Brown case:

Separate educational facilities are inherently unequal. [Separating children] solely because of their race generates a feeling of inferiority as to their status in the community that may affect their hearts and minds in a way unlikely to be undone.

AN AMERICAN ★ SPEAKS

Thus, this historic decision reversed the *Plessy v. Ferguson* decision that had legalized "separate but equal" facilities for blacks and whites.

Despite the Brown decision, African Americans had to overcome continued opposition to integration. When the Supreme Court announced in 1955 that the Brown decision would be enforced "with all deliberate speed," rather than immediately, southern white officials became more obstinate. They hoped to postpone integration in the public schools.

In 1957 Arkansas Governor Orval Faubus expressed this segregationist sentiment when he used National Guard troops to prevent nine black students from enrolling at Little Rock's Central High School. This open challenge to federal law encouraged white mobs to turn the students away from the school's doors.

Elizabeth Eckford, 15, was one of these students. She recalled being frightened as she and the other students tried to enter the school:

When I was able to steady my knees, I walked up to the guard who had let the white students [into the school]. . . . When I tried to squeeze past him, he raised his bayonet and then the other guards closed in and they raised their bayonets. . . . [The mob] came closer, shouting "No [black girl] is going to get in our school. . . . Someone hollered "Drag her over to this tree! Let's take care of [her]." Just then a white man sat down beside me, put his arm around me and patted my shoulder. He raised my chin and said, "Don't let them see you cry."

AN AMERICAN ★ SPEAKS

President Dwight D. Eisenhower questioned the wisdom of the Brown decision, but Faubus' public challenge to federal authority forced him to respond. The president placed the

Guard under federal control and sent soldiers to Little Rock. Backed by federal force, Elizabeth and the other black students were allowed to attend classes. In the years to come Elizabeth Eckford's resolve would prove to be an inspiration to others who would, with the backing of the Brown decision, eventually break the racial barriers that the Plessy decision had helped to build.

King emphasized the need for voting rights.

As the federal officials considered how rapidly to implement the Brown decision, the successful Montgomery movement demonstrated that blacks would seek to speed the pace of change in the South. In 1957 Martin Luther King, Jr., and other southern black ministers formed the **Southern Christian Leadership Conference (SCLC)**, with King as president. The following year King traveled to India to increase his understanding of the nonviolent tactics used by Gandhi. He returned with an even stronger commitment to use Gandhian tactics to overcome all aspects of southern racial oppression.

King was not sure about the future direction of the struggle, however. Although he had become the nation's best-known black spokesperson, he was reluctant to begin new mass protests. Instead, he emphasized the need for voting rights. In April 1957 he told 25,000 people gathered at the Washington Monument that voting rights were the key to black advancement: "Give us the ballot and we will no longer have to worry the federal government about our basic rights."

Many blacks agreed with King. They believed that the federal government would more than likely pass legislation protecting voting rights before it would act on more controversial issues such as the desegregation of schools. They were right.

In 1957 Congress passed the first civil rights act since Reconstruction. The act established a Civil Rights Commission to investigate civil rights violations and a Civil Rights Division of the Justice Department. It also authorized the attorney general to sue people who hindered voting for racial reasons.

By the end of the 1950s, black southerners knew that changes were underway. The Montgomery bus boycott strengthened their new sense of hope and increased their confidence that protest activity could be successful. King was widely admired as an example of an educated, successful black man who was willing to take risks in order to achieve advancement for the entire race. King could not predict nor control the events the Montgomery bus boycott had set in motion. Still a young man himself, he would soon share the stage with even younger leaders.

SECTION 1 REVIEW

Identify Key People and Terms
Write a sentence to identify: Jim Crow laws, Martin Luther King, Jr., Rosa Parks, Mohandas K. Gandhi, Ralph Abernathy, Thurgood Marshall, *Brown* v. *Board of Education of Topeka*, Southern Christian Leadership Conference (SCLC)

Locate Key Places
What southern capital was the site of a historic bus boycott in 1955?

Master the Main Ideas
1. **Studying the long-term political effects of the Civil War:** Provide two examples of Jim Crow laws.
2. **Recognizing the value of civic participation:** What was one result of the Montgomery bus boycott?
3. **Recognizing the value of civic participation:** How did A. Philip Randolph's actions provide more jobs for African Americans during World War II?
4. **Analyzing major court decisions:** Why do you think the Court overturned Plessy with the Brown decision?
5. **Studying reform movement leaders:** Why did King choose to concentrate on the issue of voting rights after the Brown decision?

Apply Critical Thinking Skills: Drawing Conclusions
Do you agree or disagree with Chief Justice Earl Warren's statement on the psychological effects of school segregation? Why or why not?

Students strengthened the civil rights movement.

Key Terms: sit-in, Student Nonviolent Coordinating Committee (SNCC), Freedom Riders, Albany Movement

Reading Preview
As you read this section, you will learn:

1. what method of protest black students used against segregation.
2. what student protesters did in order to maintain their independence from existing civil rights organizations.
3. what role African Americans played in the election of 1960.
4. what the Freedom Riders sought.
5. what the main strategy of the SNCC activists was.

Seventeen-year-old Diane Nash remembered feeling "stifled and boxed-in" after she left Chicago to attend Fisk University in **Nashville**, Tennessee. Fisk was one of the best black colleges in the South, but Nash realized that Nashville theaters and restaurants were segregated. She knew that the South was changing, however, and that young people, such as the

students in Little Rock, were helping to bring about change. Like many other students she knew, Nash was convinced that the pace of change was too slow. She believed the major civil rights organizations, even King's SCLC, were too cautious. As a result, Nash joined a workshop headed by **James Lawson**, a student at nearby Vanderbilt Divinity School. The purpose of the workshop was to teach students about Gandhian nonviolent protest tactics.

Black students organized sit-ins to protest segregation.

Before Nash and other Nashville students could take action, however, four black students—David Richmond, Franklin McCain, Ezell Blair, and Joseph McNeill—started a protest of their own in **Greensboro**, North Carolina. On February 1, 1960, these four freshmen at North Carolina Agricultural and Technical College, a predominately black school, began a wave of student demonstrations that would soon spread throughout the South. The four Greensboro students were disturbed that the store where they bought school supplies did not allow blacks to sit at the lunch counter to order food. After debating what they could do, the students finally decided to **sit-in**, that is, to remain seated at the lunch counter until they were served or arrested. Although the surprised store manager refused to serve them, he

David Richmond, one of the four students who participated in the 1960 Greensboro lunch-counter sit-in, reflects upon his role in the historic event in 1990. Richmond, who still lives in Greensboro, is shown in front of an exhibit built in remembrance of the sit-in. He is seated on one of the chairs that once lined the lunch counter of the Woolworth's store in which the sit-in took place. Behind Richmond is a poster of the students and other memorabilia.

also decided not to have the students arrested. Subsequently, the protesters returned to their campus to recruit more students. After several days of increasingly larger protests, both black and white students at nearby colleges decided to try the sit-in tactic.

During the following weeks, thousands of black and white college and high school students in many southern communities protested against segregation in eating places by launching their own sit-ins. Nash and the Nashville students quickly joined the new movement. Student protesters were not frightened when police came to arrest them. Many went to jail singing "freedom songs," adding their own words to church songs and popular rock and roll tunes. Although the SCLC and the NAACP attempted to provide guidance for student protesters after the initial sit-in in Greensboro, student activists had their own ideas and plans.

Student activists formed their own civil rights organization.

Although sit-in protesters admired and respected King, most wanted to maintain their independence from the existing civil rights organizations. James Lawson expressed the militant mood of the students when he questioned the cautious tactics of older leaders. He called upon Christians to overcome "social evil" and he warned against too much patience: "All of Africa will be free before the American Negro attains first-class citizenship."

Lawson had lived in India for several years, and he had learned that Gandhian nonviolence was more than a tactic; it was a philosophy of life. He expressed the idealism of many student protesters of the early 1960s:

Nonviolence as it grows from Judaic-Christian traditions **AN AMERICAN ★ SPEAKS** seeks a social order of justice permeated by love. [Love] matches the capacity of evil to inflict suffering with an even more enduring capacity to be evil, all the while persisting in love.

Ella Baker, director of SCLC's headquarters in Atlanta, was one of the few older civil rights leaders who gained the trust of militant students. Fifty-six years old when the sit-in move-

ment began, she had participated in social reform movements since the 1930s. Her experiences as an organizer in the NAACP and SCLC led her to sympathize with the students rather than with more cautious adult leaders. "She was much older in terms of age," Nashville student John Lewis explained, "but in terms of ideas and philosophy and commitment she was one of the youngest persons in the movement." Baker criticized King's charismatic form of leadership, believing that it made blacks feel dependent on him.

When Baker arranged for student leaders to meet during April 1960, she encouraged them to form their own independent organization. The result was the establishment of the **Student Nonviolent Coordinating Committee (SNCC)**. Baker urged the new organization to practice "group-centered" leadership rather than create a "leader-centered" group, such as King's SCLC. What the movement needed, she

PASSIVE RESISTANCE: Henry David Thoreau, above left, practiced passive resistance when he refused to pay his poll taxes in 1846. The gesture, which landed him in jail for a night, was the means Thoreau chose to protest the institution of slavery prior to the Mexican-American War. Mohandas K. Gandhi, top, the inspirational Indian leader who had such a great impact on Martin Luther King, Jr., above, studied Thoreau's ideas on passive resistance and utilized many of his techniques to help gain independence for India in 1947.

said, were "people who are interested not in being leaders as much as in developing leadership among other people."

African Americans helped Kennedy win the presidency in 1960.

In October 1960 Martin Luther King was jailed after he joined student protesters in Atlanta in a sit-in. King's arrest attracted much media coverage and forced the two candidates running for president to decide whether to take a stand on the case. Richard Nixon, the Republican candidate, had supported civil rights reforms in the past. However, John F. Kennedy, the Democratic candidate, gained the initiative by calling King's wife, Coretta Scott King. Kennedy expressed his concern for her husband's cause. He then helped gain King's release from jail. Kennedy's action and concern were appreciated in the black community. Kennedy won the election, with black voters helping to supply the narrow margin of victory.

After becoming president, Kennedy realized that African Americans were expecting him to support civil rights. He acted cautiously at first, however, because he did not want to lose southern white support. After he did not fulfill his promise to eliminate housing discrimination with "a stroke of the pen," many blacks sent pens to the White House to remind him of the need for action.

The Freedom Riders sought desegregation in the Deep South.

Black student protesters admired the new young president, but they soon began to push him toward more rapid action on civil rights. During the spring and summer of 1961, black and white protesters known as the **Freedom Riders** staged "freedom rides" to carry the civil rights struggle into the Deep South states of Alabama and Mississippi, where white resistance was strongest. A small group of white and black protesters recruited by the Congress of Racial Equality (CORE), a group of activists dedicated to stopping segregation nonviolently, traveled through the South and attempted to use segregated facilities at bus terminals. In **Birmingham**, a city in central Alabama, a mob

attacked the Freedom Riders as they came off the bus. After several of the riders were seriously injured, the initial CORE group decided to end their effort.

Diane Nash and other Fisk University students wanted the freedom ride to continue, however, and came to Alabama to replace the original group. The student Freedom Riders took buses into **Jackson**, the capital of Mississippi, where they were quickly arrested and charged with violating the states' segregation laws. Even after the first group of arriving students went to jail, however, other protesters, many affiliated with the SNCC, continued to come to the state. By the end of the summer, several hundred students had joined the freedom ride movement. Many of them spent their summer vacations in Mississippi prisons. Despite their arrests, the youthful protesters kept their spirits high, singing freedom songs and discussing how to continue their movement.

The freedom rides put the Kennedy administration on the defensive. Newspapers throughout the world carried reports of the attacks against the riders. When students continued the rides and asked the federal government for protection, Kennedy's commitment to

Freedom Riders helplessly watch their bus burn near Anniston, Alabama, in 1961. Moments before, hostile whites had tossed gas bombs into the vehicle.

focused on economic as well as civil rights issues. Influenced by Ella Baker, the SNCC activists favored a strategy based on local leadership and local issues. They urged blacks to challenge white officials whenever possible. Charles Sherrod, a young SNCC "field secretary" who came to Albany in 1961, explained what many young blacks wanted:

AN AMERICAN ★ SPEAKS

We want to go ahead in a new way—maybe not the way whites have shown. . . . We are not the puppets of the white man. We want a different world where we can speak, where we can communicate.

In contrast, King and SCLC officials saw the Albany protests as part of a national effort to achieve civil rights reform. They wanted to work with the SNCC but were concerned that undisciplined protests might decrease northern white support for black advancement.

During December 1961 a small group of young Freedom Riders were arrested protesting against segregated facilities at the Albany train station. Local blacks in an organization called the **Albany Movement** staged several mass marches and rallies during December. Despite the arrest of more than 500 demonstrators, however, white city officials refused to discuss desegregation and other issues.

Hoping to strengthen the movement and gain outside support, the Albany Movement leaders invited the Rev. Dr. Martin Luther King, Jr., to join the protests. On December 16 King led a prayer march to city hall where police arrested him and more than 250 demonstrators. The next summer he returned to Albany.

Despite King's efforts, however, young activists questioned his methods. They saw that King was unable to gain concessions in Albany. They also saw that the police were too easily able to stop the peaceful demonstrations.

During the early 1960s, black college students frustrated with the lack of progress brought a new militancy to the southern black

civil rights was put to a test. Because the president did not want to upset southern whites by openly backing the students, he tried to stop the rides through behind-the-scenes efforts. Kennedy and his brother, Attorney General Robert F. Kennedy, tried to convince the students to engage in voter registration efforts rather than freedom rides. They argued that white resistance to voting rights was not as great as resistance to desegregation. Although some student activists were interested in voter registration, they were disappointed by the Kennedys' unwillingness to take political risks to support civil rights. Student disillusionment with liberal leaders would increase as the southern movement expanded.

Student activists focused on local issues.

The clash between students' confrontation tactics and King's more cautious approach became more intense after the freedom rides. The differences became more apparent in 1961 and 1962 during a series of demonstrations in Albany, Georgia. These protests, unlike the relatively small-scale sit-ins of 1960, involved all segments of the black population. They also

struggle. Students felt they had less to risk than older blacks, who feared losing their jobs. The goal of the student protests was to end the exclusion of blacks from the mainstream of American society, but they also produced a new sense of pride among young blacks. Diane Nash remarked that in joining the student movement she became part of "a group of people suddenly proud to be called black." Nash and other students who participated in the sit-ins left school temporarily to become full-time activists. They realized that they were not simply part of a desegregation movement. Instead, they were part of a long-term freedom struggle seeking major social change.

SECTION 2 REVIEW

Identify Key People and Terms
Write a sentence to identify: James Lawson, sit-in, Ella Baker, Student Nonviolent Coordinating Committee (SNCC), Freedom Riders, Albany Movement

Locate Key Places
1. In which city is Fisk University located?
2. In which states are these cities located: Nashville, Greensboro, Birmingham, Jackson?

Master the Main Ideas
1. **Studying reform movements:** Why did college students protest not being allowed to sit at a lunch counter in Greensboro?
2. **Studying reform movements:** Why did students believe they had to form their own civil rights organization?
3. **Studying political elections:** Why did blacks support Kennedy in 1960?
4. **Analyzing political leaders:** How did President Kennedy react to the freedom rides?
5. **Studying reform movements:** How did the philosophy of the SNCC activists differ from that of King and the SCLC?

Apply Critical Thinking Skills: Making Comparisons
Martin Luther King, Jr., said that individuals have a moral obligation to disobey unjust laws. Give two arguments supporting the view that Americans have such an obligation and two arguments opposing this view.

African Americans staged mass protests.

Key Terms: Project C, the March on Washington for Jobs and Freedom, Civil Rights Act of 1964, National Woman's party

Reading Preview
As you read this section, you will learn:

1. where black leaders concentrated their protest efforts after the setback at Albany.
2. what the March on Washington demonstrated.
3. what the Civil Rights Act of 1964 eliminated.

The role of the church and of people's personal religious faith was central to the civil rights movement. For example, the Reverend **Fred Shuttlesworth** had been fighting for civil rights for many years before the Birmingham campaign of 1963. During the 1950s he had formed the Alabama Christian Movement for Human Rights, which held mass meetings every Monday. Shuttlesworth's church had been bombed, and he had been arrested while helping Freedom Riders. Yet he maintained his faith and conviction to this cause. By 1963 Shuttlesworth had decided that the Birmingham movement needed outside help. He invited King to come to Birmingham for a major campaign to overcome racial segregation.

Black leaders concentrated their efforts in Birmingham.

After the setback in Albany, King and the other SCLC leaders were determined to build a more effective movement in their new target city, Birmingham, Alabama. King also realized that the SNCC was not active in Birmingham, and therefore his organization would have a freer hand than in Albany in directing protests. SCLC leaders prepared a plan called **Project C**.

(The "C" represented confrontation.) King's strategy was to provoke confrontations with local white officials, especially the openly anti-black police commissioner, Eugene T. "Bull" Connor. King believed that such televised confrontations between nonviolent protesters and brutal police with clubs and police dogs would attract the sympathy of northern whites and would cause federal intervention on behalf of civil rights reforms.

During April SCLC officials and local black leaders organized a series of sit-ins, marches, and rallies in Birmingham. King warned that whites who refused to negotiate with nonviolent black leaders would soon have to deal with more militant leaders. Frustrated blacks, he argued, might turn to black nationalism, "a development that will lead inevitably to a frightening racial nightmare."

The Birmingham protests became increasingly large during the spring of 1963. By early May more than 3,000 blacks had been jailed. On May 7, after thousands of school children marched into Birmingham's business district, Governor George Wallace sent state patrolmen to reinforce Connor's police forces, who used water hoses to disperse the children. A few

days later, when bombs exploded at the home of King's brother and at a SCLC local office, angry demonstrators began to throw rocks at police. King and other SCLC representatives responded by appealing to black residents to refrain from violence. Finally, white officials indicated their readiness to make concessions, and the Birmingham protests subsided.

People of all religious faiths and creeds—people Martin Luther King, Jr., called "the true sons of faith"—were vital to the success of the civil rights movement and, in fact, were the guiding force behind this movement.

Montgomery school children recoil in terror as Alabama state patrolmen try to disperse them with powerful fire hoses in May 1963.

The March on Washington for Jobs and Freedom reflected the spirit and determination of the many people who believed in the African American cause. In his "I Have a Dream" speech, Martin Luther King, Jr., assured his 250,000 cheering listeners that: "This sweltering summer of the Negro's legitimate discontent will not pass until there is an invigorate autumn of freedom and equality."

By this time, however, the Birmingham protests had become only one of many such local protest movements. An estimated 930 public protest demonstrations in more than 100 cities would take place during the year. Unlike the lunch-counter protests, which were generally well-organized and peaceful, some of the larger protests during the spring and summer of 1963 involved poor blacks who had little sympathy for nonviolence. Each of the national civil rights organizations tried to offer guidance for the mass marches and demonstrations which culminated in the Birmingham protests of spring 1963. However, none of them could completely control these protests.

The March on Washington drew public support for civil rights laws.

During the steamy summer of 1963, veteran civil rights leader A. Philip Randolph proposed a march on Washington to give blacks an opportunity to express their discontent in a nonviolent way. When President John F. Kennedy initially objected to the idea of a march because of a fear that violence would erupt, Randolph told the president that "Negroes were already in the streets. It is very likely impossible to get them off."

The March on Washington for Jobs and Freedom, held August 28, 1963, was the largest single demonstration of the early 1960s. More than 250,000 people gathered at the **Lincoln Memorial** in Washington, D.C. Both black and white marchers demonstrated the increasing public support for legislation to outlaw racially segregated facilities. The march attracted support from a broad liberal coalition that included the major civil rights groups, labor unions, and religious leaders.

Martin Luther King, Jr., delivered a moving speech during the rally. Calling upon America to live up to its ideals, he recounted the

THE CIVIL RIGHTS ACT OF 1964
Skill: Analyzing Cause and Effect

Introducing the Skill. In 1948, seven years before Rosa Parks refused to give up her bus seat, Langston Hughes wrote:

> *What happens to a dream*
> *   deferred?*
> *Does it dry up*
> *like a raisin in the sun?*
> *Or fester like a sore—*
> *And then run?*
> *Does it stink like rotten meat?*
> *Or crust and sugar over—*
> *like a syrupy sweet?*
> *Maybe it just sags*
> *like a heavy load.*
> *Or does it explode?*

As Hughes' words suggest, the civil rights movement did not spring up overnight but rather was the result of many frustrating years of deferring dreams. What eventually led to the Civil Rights Act of 1964, and what changes did it bring?

Learning the Skill. Understanding the full story of the Civil Rights Act of 1964 calls for the skill of **analyzing cause and effect**. As you learned earlier, a cause leads to an effect, that is, an outcome or result. Usually an event, in particular one as sweeping as the civil rights movement, has several causes and produces several effects. Remember the following clues to identify cause-effect relationships:

1. Identify an event or idea as the focus point (such as the passage of the Civil Rights Act of 1964).
2. List related events that occurred before the focus point, then ask: "How did these events bring about the focus point?" These are your causes. Some will be long-term conditions, others will be single events.
3. List related events that occurred after the focus point, asking of each, "How might this have resulted from the focus point?" These are your effects.
4. Identify how each cause or effect is related to the focus point.

Applying the Skill. Consider the passage of the Civil Rights Act as your focus point. Following the steps given above, analyze possible causes and effects of this act. List several examples of each.

difficulties the black freedom struggle had faced. However, he remained very optimistic:

I still have a dream. I have a dream that one day this nation will rise up and live out the true meaning of its creed—we hold these truths to be self-evident, that all men are created equal.

AN AMERICAN ★ SPEAKS

King looked forward to the day when his four children would:

live in a nation where they will not be judged by the color of their skin but by the content of their character.

★

The March on Washington was a major event of a decade of struggle, but the black-white coalition that supported civil rights reform began to weaken in the following years. Civil rights leaders recognized that they were caught in the middle between increasingly angry blacks, frustrated by the slow pace of change, and political leaders resisting rapid social change. SNCC workers who faced violence from southern white officials wondered why the Kennedy Administration would not provide them with protection. Civil rights workers became even more concerned about the fate of Kennedy's proposed civil rights legislation when the president was assassinated on November 22, 1963. (You will read about the Kennedy assassination in Chapter 20.) The new president, Lyndon Baines Johnson, was not known as a strong advocate of civil rights. To the surprise of some activists, however, Johnson was able to push through Congress a major civil rights bill, the **Civil Rights Act of 1964**.

VOICES FROM THE PAST

I Have a Dream

He was the very last speaker on a very long program. The day was hot; some in the vast audience drowsed and others were starting to slip away when the Rev. Dr. Martin Luther King, Jr., came to the microphone to electrify his audience with his dream. Has the nation moved nearer to realizing King's dream since the 1963 March of Washington?

I have a dream that one day on the red hills of Georgia the sons of former slaves and the sons of former slaveowners will be able to sit down together at the table of brotherhood. . . .

This is our hope. This is the faith with which I return to the South. With this faith we will be able to hew out of the mountain of despair a stone of hope. With this faith we will be able to transform the jangling discords of our nation into a beautiful symphony of brotherhood. . . .

When we let freedom ring, when we let it ring from every village and every hamlet, from every state and every city, we will be able to speed up that day when all of God's children, black men and white men, Jews and Gentiles, Protestants and Catholics, will be able to join hands and sing in the words of the old Negro spiritual, "Free at last! Free at last! Thank God Almighty, we are free at last!"

The Civil Rights Act eliminated "whites only" public facilities.

Although the new legislation did not eliminate all barriers to racial equality, it was among the most important post–World War II reforms. The most dramatic result of the Civil Rights Act was the elimination of "whites only" public facilities. Blacks growing up after 1964 would never have to experience the humiliation of being denied service at a restaurant because of their race or having to use "colored" restrooms.

Although other provisions of the Civil Rights Act were less noticed, they also brought about major changes in American life, not only in the South but also in the North. Title VII of the Civil Rights Act was originally designed to deal with racial discrimination, but women and nonblack minorities were affected by provisions outlawing racial bias in hiring. A southern representative included protections for women in the legislation, believing that he would lessen support for the legislation by adding a clause that extended the bill's coverage to include sexual discrimination. Even many women's rights advocates at the time believed that female and male workers should not be treated equally. They believed women needed special protection at work.

Other women believed that it was wrong to pass legislation protecting the employment rights of blacks without doing the same for women. Among those supporting the expansion of the legislation to include women were members of the **National Woman's party**, a remnant of the women's suffrage movement of the early 1900s. To the surprise of many, the clause outlawing sexual discrimination was adopted. Thus, the Civil Rights Act had a result—the expansion of women's rights—that was not intended by its original supporters.

SECTION 3 REVIEW

Identify Key People and Terms
Write a sentence to identify: Fred Shuttlesworth, Project C, the March on Washington for Jobs and Freedom, Civil Rights Act of 1964, National Woman's party

Locate Key Places
In which city is the Lincoln Memorial?

Master the Main Ideas

1. **Studying social reform movements:** Why did Martin Luther King, Jr., choose Birmingham as the new target city for protests in 1963?
2. **Studying social reform movements:** What was the significance of the March on Washington?
3. **Analyzing major historic documents:** What were two provisions of the Civil Rights Act of 1964?

Apply Critical Thinking Skills: Demonstrating Reasoned Judgment
What responsibilities do people have when they engage in mass protests? What are the responsibilities of government officials in addressing such protests?

Many racial barriers remained in the South.

Key Terms: Mississippi Summer Project, freedom schools, Mississippi Freedom Democratic party (MFDP), Voting Rights Act of 1965, affirmative action programs

Reading Preview
As you read this section, you will learn:

1. what civil rights leaders did to try to end white political and economic domination in Mississippi.
2. what black civil rights organizers did to increase national awareness of the violence directed toward them.
3. how civil rights workers protested the exclusion of blacks from the Mississippi delegation to the 1964 Democratic National Convention.
4. what King's major goal in 1965 was.

Despite the passage of the Civil Rights Act of 1964, racial barriers remained in the South. This was particularly true in the rural areas of Mississippi and Alabama, where African Americans made up a large proportion of the population. In such areas widespread poverty among blacks made desegregation of public facilities less important to them as a goal than political and economic gains.

Civil rights leaders encouraged voter registration in Mississippi.

Because blacks made up such a large part of the population in Alabama and Mississippi, desegregation meant an end to white political and economic domination. Therefore, white resistance to civil rights reforms was particularly intense in these states.

The Deep South had become notorious because of its history of lynchings and other acts of racial violence. Mississippi, in particular, was known as the stronghold of southern segregation. In 1962 the United States Commission on Civil Rights reported that there was "danger of

a complete breakdown of law and order" in the state. "Citizens of the United States have been shot, set upon by vicious dogs, beaten and otherwise terrorized because they sought to vote," the Commission reported.

Although the major national civil rights organizations assisted the civil rights movement in Mississippi, students played a major role in the struggle there. The student activists who joined the Mississippi voter registration campaign realized that they faced strong opposition. During the fall of 1962, federal troops had to be sent to Oxford, Mississippi, when a large mob of whites rioted in a violent protest against the admission of **James Meredith**, a black student, to the University of Mississippi. During February 1963 white gunmen shot into a car, seriously wounding a SNCC worker. In June 1963 NAACP leader **Medgar Evers** was shot to death in Jackson, Mississippi.

These violent attacks discouraged many blacks from registering to vote, but civil rights workers were determined to continue the voter registration campaign. They tried to convince blacks that it was possible to resist the forces

James Meredith strides from the podium after receiving his bachelor of arts degree during commencement ceremonies at the University of Mississippi in 1963. Meredith was the university's first African American graduate.

The ominous clouds gathering above the black and white Americans who marched from Selma to Montgomery in the spring of 1965 provide a metaphor for the violence the peaceful marchers would encounter along the way.

residents create the all-black Lowndes County Freedom Organization. The SNCC field secretaries chose Lowndes County because it seemed a promising place to prove that blacks could build their own bases of power. Blacks were a majority of the population in the county, yet not a single black had been able to register to vote. The symbol chosen by the new political party—the black panther—reflected the new sense of militancy that took hold among African Americans in large cities all across the nation after 1964.

King concentrated on the voting rights issue in 1965.

While militants began to organize, Martin Luther King, Jr., and SCLC representatives began a new voting rights campaign in **Selma**, Alabama. As in other places, King hoped that by mobilizing marches and mass rallies he could attract national attention to the voting rights issue. Despite the passage of the 24th Amendment in 1964, which made it illegal for any state to make a poll tax a requirement for voting for federal officials, King believed more

needed to be done to ensure that African Americans could freely exercise their right to vote.

Early in March, SCLC leaders announced plans for a march from Selma to the state capitol in Montgomery. Because of a previous commitment, however, King was not present when several protesters left Selma on the afternoon of March 7. At Pettus Bridge on the outskirts of Selma, police on horseback using tear gas and clubs attacked the marchers when they refused to turn back. Television camera operators and newspaper photographers quickly communicated pictures to the national media of policemen attacking nonviolent protesters.

SNCC chairperson **John Lewis**, who suffered a fractured skull during the mêlée, afterwards expressed the anger that many marchers felt about the federal government's failure to protect blacks attempting to vote. Lewis complained: "I don't see how President Johnson can send troops to Vietnam . . . and can't send troops to Selma, Alabama."

News accounts of the attack at Pettus Bridge—activists referred to it as "Bloody

Sunday"—brought hundreds of civil rights sympathizers to Selma. White officials obtained a court order against further marchers, but many blacks were determined to mobilize another march. Young SNCC activists challenged King to defy the court order. However, King was reluctant to do anything that would lessen public support for the voting rights cause. Despite King's reluctance, the marchers conducted a second march to Pettus Bridge on March 10. That evening a group of Selma whites killed a northern white minister, James Reeb, who had joined the demonstrations. Reeb's murder led to national outrage and intensified efforts to bring an end to racial violence in Selma.

When the marchers arrived at the capitol in Montgomery, King delivered a poignant speech. He praised them for their bravery and commitment. Despite the racial violence encountered by the marchers who traveled to Montgomery, King told them that segregation was "on its deathbed." He reminded them to retain their faith in nonviolence.

The march to Montgomery produced important gains. Using the words of the most popular civil rights song, President Johnson told the nation "we *shall* overcome." Within a few months, Congress had passed the historic **Voting Rights Act of 1965**, which empowered the federal government to supervise voter registration practices in the South.

Yet King's and the black struggle's long-range objectives remained unachieved even after passage of the Voting Rights Act of 1965. Even as President Johnson urged Congress to pass the bill, he recognized the limitations of civil rights reforms. In June 1965 he spoke of the need for a new strategy in the campaign for racial equality. He said:

> Freedom is not enough. You do not wipe away the scars of centuries by saying "now you are free to go where you want, do as you desire . . . and still justly believe that you have been completely fair.

AN AMERICAN ★ SPEAKS

Johnson concluded by calling upon the nation to transform civil rights from theoretical equality to "equality as a fact and as a result."

Besides helping to push through major civil rights legislation, President Johnson took

Regions The Voting Rights Act of 1965 was a legislative milestone for civil rights. The act applied to the entire United States but its effects were felt most dramatically in the South. Which states had more than a 100 percent increase in registered voters in 1966?

Critical Thinking Why did some states have much greater increases than others in voter registration?

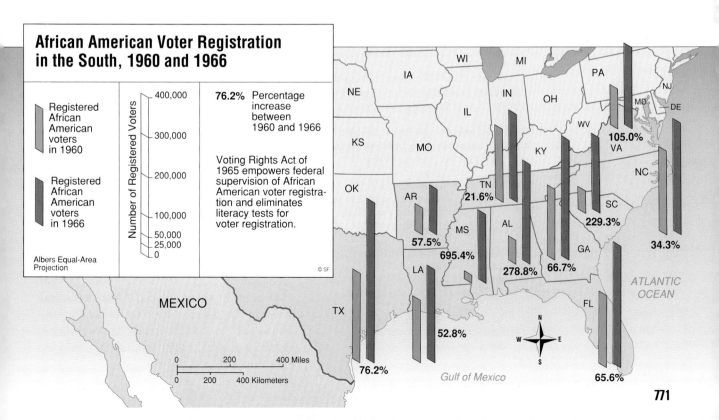

African American Voter Registration in the South, 1960 and 1966

Registered African American voters in 1960

Registered African American voters in 1966

Number of Registered Voters: 400,000 / 300,000 / 200,000 / 100,000 / 50,000 / 25,000 / 0

76.2% Percentage increase between 1960 and 1966

Voting Rights Act of 1965 empowers federal supervision of African American voter registration and eliminates literacy tests for voter registration.

Albers Equal-Area Projection

© SF

MEXICO

0   200   400 Miles
0   200   400 Kilometers

TX — 76.2%
LA — 52.8%
AR — 57.5%
MS — 695.4%
TN — 21.6%
AL — 278.8%
GA — 66.7%
VA — 105.0%
SC — 229.3%
NC — 34.3%
FL — 65.6%

Gulf of Mexico

ATLANTIC OCEAN

direct action by issuing executive orders for **affirmative action programs**. Affirmative action programs, which are still in effect today, set goals and timetables for the hiring of minority groups and women. To meet these goals, some employers are required to practice preferential hiring, choosing black and female applicants over equally qualified or even more qualified white males. Although this program had some setbacks, as you will read in Chapter 22, it did much to increase African American opportunities—as well as those for women—in areas such as employment and education.

S E C T I O N **4** R E V I E W

Identify Key People and Terms
Write a sentence to identify: James Meredith, Medgar Evers, Fannie Lou Hamer, Mississippi Summer Project, freedom schools, Mississippi Freedom Democratic party (MFDP), Stokely Carmichael, John Lewis, Voting Rights Act of 1965, affirmative action programs

Locate Key Places
Selma is located in which state?

Master the Main Ideas
1. **Understanding the importance of individual participation in civic affairs:** Why did civil rights leaders have a difficult time trying to convince African Americans in Mississippi to register to vote?
2. **Understanding the importance of individual participation in civic affairs:** Why did civil rights leaders recruit white volunteers in Mississippi?
3. **Studying minor political parties:** Why did civil rights workers think it was necessary to form the Mississippi Freedom Democratic party?
4. **Studying reform leaders:** What tactics did King believe he could use to attract national attention to the voting rights issue?

Apply Critical Thinking Skills: Drawing Conclusions
Martin Luther King, Jr., said "Our aim must never be to defeat or humiliate the white man but to win his friendship and understanding." Do you think King's goal has been realized? Why or why not?

Militant black consciousness developed.

Key Terms: Nation of Islam, Black Power, Black Panther party, Poor People's Campaign, de jure segregation, de facto segregation

Reading Preview
As you read this section, you will learn:
1. what Malcolm X's approach to the challenges faced by African Americans was.
2. what occurred after the death of Malcolm X.
3. what the civil rights movement accomplished.

Malcolm Little, better known as **Malcolm X,** was not invited to speak at the March on Washington, but he came to observe. He saw the event as a middle-class "picnic" that did not reflect the anger and frustrations of poor blacks. Malcolm did not believe that the black leaders gathered at the Lincoln Memorial represented most blacks. He listened to Martin Luther King, Jr.'s, speech. He insisted that no "American dream" existed for black Americans. He believed "the black masses in America were—and still are—having a nightmare."

Malcolm X emphasized black separatism and political power.

Militant blacks such as Malcolm X played an increasingly important role in redefining black objectives in the mid-1960s. He challenged the notion that blacks should allow themselves to be beaten in order to participate in a racist white society. Although not as well known as King, Malcolm served as a reminder in 1964 and 1965 that neither King nor other national civil rights leaders reflected the sentiments of all blacks.

Like many young African Americans who grew up in poverty, Malcolm gradually lost hope that he could succeed in the white-dominated world. Although he did well in school, teachers told him to forget about his dream to become a lawyer. Using racist language, one teacher told him: "We all here like you. . . . But you've got to be realistic about being a nigger. A lawyer—that's no realistic goal for a nigger. Why don't you plan on carpentry?"

His ego deflated and his dreams crushed, Malcolm dropped out of school and eventually became involved in criminal activities. He soon found himself behind bars. Although his time in jail was difficult, a letter he received from his brother changed his life forever. The letter explained the teachings of **Elijah Muhammad**, who was the head of a religiously inspired group called the **Nation of Islam**. Muhammad and his 100,000 Black Muslim followers believed in racial separation and black superiority. Muhammad demanded that whites give blacks their own territory or suffer the consequences. If whites refused to do so, Muhammad said the entire white race "will be destroyed and removed from this earth by Almighty God." In addition, Muhammad said that blacks who believed in integration would be "destroyed along with the whites."

Desperate to find meaning in his life, Malcolm joined the Black Muslims when he was released from prison in 1952. As the southern black protest movement expanded, Malcolm became the Nation of Islam's most well-known minister. His main message was that discrimination had led many African Americans to despise themselves. He said:

The worst crime the white man has committed has been to teach us to hate ourselves. Some of you hate your hair so much you put lye on it to get it straight.

AN AMERICAN ★ SPEAKS

This self-hatred, Malcolm said, caused African Americans to lose their identity. Consequently, he taught that blacks should do everything they could to get back in touch with their culture. This meant rejecting white cultural elements such as hair styles and names. Accordingly, Malcolm dropped the last name he had been born with, Little, and adopted the name Malcolm X. The letter X stood for the

Elijah Muhammad, left, and Malcolm X discuss philosophies shortly before Malcolm left the Nation of Islam in 1964.

name his ancestors had before they had been forced to accept "slave names."

Malcolm's beliefs were highly unpopular with whites as well as a vast majority of blacks. Whites called him a demagogue for statements such as "if ballots won't work, bullets will." Followers of Martin Luther King, Jr., about 85 percent of the black population according to a poll, were also critical of Malcolm.

In the early 1960s, Malcolm became disenchanted with the Nation of Islam. He questioned the racial doctrines of the Nation after discovering that many whites, particularly in the Middle East, also believed in Islam. He also became critical of the Nation's lack of involvement in the protest movement after hearing increasingly in the black community that the Muslims talk tough but never do anything.

Frustrated, Malcolm left the Nation of Islam in 1964 and formed his own organization, the Organization of Afro-American Unity. After softening his attacks on King, especially after the two men exchanged greetings during the spring of 1964, Malcolm gained increased influence in the black community. He recognized that despite their differences over tactics, he and King were part of the same struggle.

Malcolm's life came to a sudden end, however. In February 1965 he was assassinated

MANIFESTATIONS OF BLACK POWER: African Americans expressed their individuality in numerous ways beginning in the mid-1960s. Near right, athletes Tommie Smith and John Carlos, center and right respectively, display the Black Power salute during award ceremonies at the 1968 Summer Olympic games as the National Anthem was played. Top right, Muhammad Ali, a professional boxer, and Kareem Abdul-Jabbar, bottom right, a professional basketball player, both became part of the Black Power movement by becoming Muslims.

while giving a speech in New York. Members of the Nation of Islam were later convicted of the murder. Even after his death, however, Malcolm's ideas continued to influence the African American freedom struggle.

Urban black militancy increased in the mid-1960s.

Stokely Carmichael, the SNCC leader who coined the "Black Power" slogan in the late 1960s, speaks to a civil rights group in Washington, D.C., in 1970.

The racial divisions in American society became increasingly apparent during the period after Malcolm's death. The most visible indication of these divisions were the urban black rebellions or riots that spread throughout the country. The first major rebellion occurred in August 1965. The arrest of a black man in Los Angeles led to several days of violence in the black community of Watts. More than 30 blacks were killed by police. Many other large cities later experienced similar outbreaks of violence. During the summer of 1967, for example, 23 people were killed in Newark, New Jersey, and 43 in Detroit, Michigan.

Interracial civil rights organizations such as SNCC also became more racially divided during this period. SNCC staff members voted to replace John Lewis as chair when they decided he was not militant enough. To replace Lewis, they elected Stokely Carmichael, an organizer who had worked in Mississippi and Alabama. Carmichael soon provided a slogan for the new militant mood when he called for **Black Power**. Influenced by Malcolm X, Carmichael insisted that blacks should not be ashamed of being black. "We are black and beautiful," he told audiences. Carmichael and other Black Power advocates were also skeptical about continuing to work with white civil rights supporters. "They admonish blacks to be nonviolent," Carmichael said. "Let them preach nonviolence in the white community."

Although Black Power was a political slogan, it was only one aspect of broader cultural changes. African Americans began to express a new sense of pride through art and literature as well as political action. Playwright Leroi Jones, who changed his name to **Amiri Baraka**, became a leader of the Black Arts movement, which sought to create positive images for blacks. Popular black singers such as James Brown expressed the new spirit in their lyrics. Sports figures, such as boxing champion Muhammad Ali, also began to identify with Black Power sentiments. Black college students began to demand Black Studies programs that would teach courses emphasizing the contributions Africans and African Americans made to American culture.

In 1966 the SNCC, strongly associated with the Black Power movement, took steps toward black separatism. It dismissed all of its white members and then formed a new political party, the **Black Panther party**. The original goal of the Black Panthers was to gain political office for African Americans throughout the South. Their efforts were largely unsuccessful, however. In the late 1960s the party, which primarily attracted young, urban blacks, became increasingly militant in its demands for "land, bread, housing, education, clothing, justice, and peace." By the start of the new decade the party had all but dissipated.

Martin Luther King, Jr., was critical of many elements of the Black Power movement, believing that it would decrease white support for the black struggle. Nevertheless, he recognized that black people needed to build a positive sense of identity in order to advance. He pointed out that blacks could never be truly free unless they freed their minds. King urged blacks to say to themselves and the world:

I am somebody. I am a person. I am a man with dignity and honor. I have a rich and noble history.

AN AMERICAN ★ SPEAKS

As the civil rights movement progressed, King became increasingly aware of the need to instill a sense of hope among northern urban blacks whose lives had been virtually untouched by civil rights legislation. He launched a campaign in Chicago to address the problems of urban blacks—lack of jobs, poor housing, widespread crime, and drug use. King discovered, however, that the problems of northern blacks were even more difficult to solve than the problem of southern segregation. Eliminating segregation did not require the large expenditures that would be required to eliminate poverty. Northern liberals who supported the southern civil rights movement often were less willing to support black advancement efforts in their own cities.

By the end of 1967, King had decided that a **Poor People's Campaign** was needed to prod the nation into action. His plan was to bring to Washington thousands of poor people—blacks, poor whites, Native Americans, Mexican Americans, and other Hispanics. They would engage in protests designed to pressure President Johnson into increasing funding for his "War on Poverty." King criticized Johnson for diverting funds from antipoverty efforts to the war in Vietnam. Caught between Black Power advocates who thought he was too cautious and Johnson supporters who saw him as too militant, King lost much of his popularity as he focused on the issue of poverty.

In early April 1968, King came to **Memphis**, Tennessee, to offer his support for garbage workers who were striking for higher wages and better working conditions. He was depressed about the many difficulties he faced and disturbed that some young blacks in Memphis had turned to violence to express their

Along with Huey P. Newton, Bobby Seale, below, established the Black Panther party in Oakland, California, in 1966. Both men were greatly influenced by Malcolm X.

Rosa Parks Refuses to Move

19A

TIME FRAME
1955

GEOGRAPHIC SETTING
Montgomery, Alabama

If the American civil rights movement can be said to have begun with a single incident, it would certainly be Rosa Parks' famous act of passive resistance in Montgomery, Alabama, on December 1, 1955. At that time in Montgomery, as throughout the South, public facilities such as bus lines were racially segregated, with the front seats of the buses reserved for white passengers. On December 1, 1955, Parks (1913–   ), a seamstress and a respected member of the African American community in Montgomery, boarded a bus on the way home from work. The following reading is excerpted from her account of what happened next.

As I got up on the bus and walked to the seat, I saw there was only one vacancy that was just back of where it was considered the white section. So this was the seat that I took, next to the aisle, and a man was sitting next to me. Across the aisle there were two women, and there were a few seats at this point in the very front of the bus that was called the white section. I went on to one stop and I didn't particularly notice who was getting on the bus, didn't particularly notice the other people getting on. And on the third stop there were some people getting on, and at this

Rosa Parks contemplates the streets of Montgomery, Alabama, as she rides on one of the city's first integrated buses. Nearly a year had passed between the day Rosa Parks refused to give up her seat on a Montgomery bus and the day the United States Supreme Court ruled in favor of the city's African American bus riders, forcing Montgomery to integrate its buses.

point all of the front seats were taken. Now in the beginning, at the very first stop I had got on the bus, the back of the bus was filled up with people standing in the aisle and I don't know why this one vacancy that I took was left, because there were quite a few people already standing toward the back of the bus. The third stop is when all the front seats were taken, and this one man was standing and when the driver looked around and saw he was standing, he asked the four of us, the man in the seat with me and the two women across the aisle, to let him have those front seats.

At his first request, didn't any of us move. Then he spoke again and said, "You'd better make it light on yourselves and let me have those seats." At this point, of course, the passenger who would have taken the seat hadn't said anything. In fact, he never did speak to my knowledge. When the three people, the man who was in the seat with me and the two women, stood up and moved into the aisle, I remained where I was. When the driver saw that I was still sitting there, he asked if I was going to stand up. I told him, no, I wasn't. He said, "Well, if you don't stand up, I'm going to have you arrested." I told him to go on and have me arrested.

He got off the bus and came back shortly. A few minutes later, two policemen got on the bus, and they approached me and asked if the driver had asked me to stand up, and I said yes, and they wanted to know why I didn't. I told them I didn't think I should have to stand up. After I had paid my fare and occupied a seat, I didn't think I should have to give it up. They placed me under arrest then and had me to get in the police car, and I was taken to jail and booked on suspicion, I believe. The questions were asked, the usual questions they ask a prisoner or somebody that's under arrest. They had to determine whether or not the driver wanted to press charges or swear out a warrant, which he

did. Then they took me to jail and I was placed in a cell. In a little while I was taken from the cell, and my picture was made and fingerprints taken. I went back to the cell then, and a few minutes later I was called back again, and when this happened I found out that Mr. E. D. Nixon and Attorney and Mrs. Clifford Durr had come to make bond [money to guarantee that a person released from custody will return at an appointed time] for me.

In the meantime before this, of course . . . I was given permission to make a telephone call after my picture was taken and fingerprints taken. I called my home and spoke to my mother on the telephone and told her what had happened, that I was in jail. She was quite upset and asked me had the police beaten me. I told her, no, I hadn't been physically injured, but I was being held in jail, and I wanted my husband to come and get me out. . . . He didn't have a car at that time, so he had to get someone to bring him down. At the time when he got down, Mr. Nixon and the Durrs had just made bond for me, so we all met at the jail and we went home.

Discussing the Reading

1. Explain why Rosa Parks was arrested. Why did she refuse to move to the rear of the bus?

2. What is your opinion of Parks' action on the bus? If you had been faced with the same situation, what might you have done?

CRITICAL THINKING
Formulating Appropriate
Questions

Imagine that you are an oral historian interviewing Rosa Parks about the events of December 1, 1955. What sort of questions would you ask her to illuminate the atmosphere surrounding this episode and her feelings at the time?

"We Shall Overcome"

TIME FRAME
1950s–1960s

GEOGRAPHIC SETTING
United States

The Americans engaged in the struggle for civil rights in the 1950s and 1960s sang together to raise their spirits and express their common purpose. Some of these songs were traditional. For example, "We Shall Overcome" was first a hymn and then was adapted by union leaders and sung on picket lines. New words were added in 1960, and it quickly became the most popular song of the civil rights movement. Other songs, such as "Keep Your Eyes on the Prize," were probably more recent in origin.

We Shall Overcome

We shall overcome,
we shall overcome,
We shall overcome some day.
Oh, deep in my heart, I do believe,
5 We shall overcome some day.

We are not afraid,
    we are not afraid,
We are not afraid today.
Oh, deep in my heart, I do believe,
10 We shall overcome some day.

"We Shall Overcome" TRO—© Copyright 1960 (renewed) and 1963 Ludlow Music, Inc.

We are not alone,
 we are not alone,
We are not alone today.
Oh, deep in my heart, I do believe,
15 We shall overcome some day.

The truth will make us free,
 the truth will make us free,
The truth will make us free some day.
Oh, deep in my heart, I do believe,
20 We shall overcome some day.

We'll walk hand in hand,
 we'll walk hand in hand,
We'll walk hand in hand some day.
Oh, deep in my heart, I do believe,
25 We shall overcome some day.

The Lord will see us through,
 the Lord will see us through,
The Lord will see us through today.
Oh, deep in my heart, I do believe,
30 We shall overcome some day.

The only chain that a man can stand
Is that chain of hand in hand.

The only thing that we did wrong—
Stayed in the wilderness too long.

20 But the one thing we did right
Was the day we started to fight.

We're gonna board that big Greyhound,
Carryin' love from town to town.

We're gonna ride for civil rights,
25 We're gonna ride, both black and white.

We've met jail and violence too,
But God's love has seen us through.

Haven't been to heaven but I've been told
Streets up there are paved with gold.

Dr. Martin Luther King, Jr., is joined by his wife Coretta Scott King as they march through city streets, perhaps singing one of the songs reprinted here.

Keep Your Eyes on the Prize

Paul and Silas, bound in jail,
 Had no money for to go their bail.

Chorus:
Keep your eyes on the prize,
Hold on, hold on,
5 Hold on, hold on—
Keep your eyes on the prize,
 Hold on, hold on.

Paul and Silas begin to shout,
The jail door opened and they walked out.

10 Freedom's name is mighty sweet—
Soon one of these days we're going to
 meet.

Got my hand on the Gospel plow,
I wouldn't take nothing for my journey
15 now.

Discussing the Readings

1. Why would "We Shall Overcome" be particularly well suited to express the mood of the early stages of the civil rights movement? How does this song attempt to address fears? Does it envision an early victory? Explain.

2. In the New Testament, the Christian missionaries Paul and Silas are miraculously delivered from prison by God. Why might civil rights workers have chosen to sing about them?

CRITICAL THINKING
Recognizing Values

What do these songs suggest about the role of religion in the civil rights movement?

Malcolm X Talks to Young African Americans

TIME FRAME
1964

GEOGRAPHIC SETTING
New York City

Born Malcolm Little, Malcolm X (1925–1965) was a minister of the Nation of Islam, or Black Muslims, an African American separatist religious movement. (The letter *X* stood for the unknown name his African ancestors had before they were forced to accept "slave names" by American owners.) In 1964 he broke with the Black Muslim leadership, in part because the Muslims refused to participate in the civil rights movement. After forming the Organization of Afro-American Unity, Malcolm X continued to speak forcefully about the need for African American identity and pride. On December 31, 1964, he spoke to a group of African American teenagers from McComb, Mississippi, who were in New York City under the sponsorship of a civil rights group. The following passages are excerpted from this speech.

Malcolm X exhorts a crowd in Harlem on May 14, 1963. The two-hour rally, in support of African American protestors in Birmingham, Alabama, ended in a scuffle as some members of the crowd began to break nearby store windows.

I t is important for you to know that . . . you're not alone. As long as you think you're alone, then you take a stand as if you're a minority or as if you're outnumbered, and that kind of stand will never enable you to win a battle. You've got to know that you've got as much power on your side as that Ku Klux Klan has on its side. And when you know that you've got as much power on your side as the Klan has on its side, you'll talk the same kind of language with that Klan as the Klan is talking with you. . . .

I think in 1965, whether you like it, or I like it, or they like it, or not, you will see that there is a generation of black people becoming mature to the point where they feel that they have no more business being asked to take a peaceful approach than anybody else takes, unless everybody's going to take a peaceful approach. . . .

[We] do not go along with anybody telling us to help nonviolently. We think that

if the government says that Negroes have a right to vote, and then some Negroes come out to vote, and some kind of Ku Klux Klan is going to put them in the river, and the government doesn't do anything about it, it's time for us to organize and band together and equip ourselves and qualify ourselves to protect ourselves. And once you can protect yourself, you don't have to worry about being hurt. . . .

That doesn't mean we're against white people, but we sure are against the Ku Klux Klan and the White Citizens Councils; and anything that looks like it's against us, we're against it. Excuse me for raising my voice, but this thing, you know, gets me upset. Imagine that—a country that's supposed to be a democracy, supposed to be for freedom and all of that kind of stuff when they want to draft you and put you in the army and send you to Saigon to fight for them—and then you've got to turn around and all night long discuss how you're going to just get a right to register and vote without being murdered. Why, that's the most hypocritical government since the world began! . . .

I hope you don't think I'm trying to incite you. Just look here: Look at yourselves. Some of you are teen-agers, students. How do you think I feel—and I belong to a generation ahead of you—how do you think I feel to have to tell you, "We, my generation, sat around like a knot on a wall while the whole world was fighting for its human rights—and you've got to be born into a society where you still have that same fight." What did we do, who preceded you? I'll tell you what we did: Nothing. And don't you make the same mistake we made. . . .

You get freedom by letting your enemy know that you'll do anything to get your

freedom; then you'll get it. It's the only way you'll get it. When you get that kind of attitude, they'll label you as a "crazy Negro." . . . Or they'll call you an extremist or a subversive, or seditious, or a red or a radical. But when you stay radical long enough, and get enough people to be like you, you'll get your freedom. . . .

So don't you run around here trying to make friends with somebody who's depriving you of your rights. They're not your friends, no, they're your enemies. Treat them like that and fight them, and you'll get your freedom; and after you get your freedom, your enemy will respect you. And we'll respect you. And I say that with no hate. I don't have hate in me. I have no hate at all. I don't have any hate. I've got some sense. I'm not going to let somebody who hates me tell me to love him. . . . And you, young as you are, and because you start thinking, you're not going to do it either. The only time you're going to get in that bag is if somebody puts you there. Somebody else, who doesn't have your welfare at heart.

Discussing the Reading

1. Why did Malcolm X disagree with those who supported nonviolent actions to win civil rights?

2. What did he say about his attitude toward white people?

CRITICAL THINKING
Checking Consistency

Which of the following statements could be consistent with the views expressed by Malcolm X in this speech?

a. African Americans should regard all white people as their enemies.

b. Nonviolence is a worthless approach to gaining civil rights.

c. African Americans should only be expected to employ nonviolence if others do.

CHAPTER 19 REVIEW

Chapter Summary

Write supporting details under each of the following main ideas as you review the chapter.

Section 1
1. Jim Crow laws made African Americans second-class citizens.
2. African Americans used passive resistance to fight segregation.
3. Black activism originated during World War II.
4. The Supreme Court reversed *Plessy* v. *Ferguson*.
5. King emphasized the need for voting rights.

Section 2
1. Black students organized sit-ins to protest segregation.
2. Student activists formed their own civil rights organization.
3. African Americans helped Kennedy win the presidency in 1960.
4. The Freedom Riders sought desegregation in the Deep South.
5. Student activists focused on local issues.

Section 3
1. Black leaders concentrated their efforts in Birmingham.
2. The March on Washington drew public support for civil rights laws.
3. The Civil Rights Act of 1964 eliminated "whites only" public facilities.

Section 4
1. Civil rights leaders encouraged voter registration in Mississippi.
2. Civil rights leaders recruited white volunteers in Mississippi.
3. Civil rights workers formed their own political party.
4. King concentrated on the voting rights issue in 1965.

Section 5
1. Malcolm X emphasized black separatism and political power.
2. Urban black militancy increased in the mid-1960s.
3. The civil rights movement reaffirmed constitutional principles.

Chapter Themes

1. **Racial, ethnic, religious diversity:** Civil rights leaders and workers pressed for equality, using nonviolent techniques; they were motivated by religious and ethical principles as well as by political and economic necessity.
2. **Constitutional and representative government:** African American reformers wanted to enjoy political, social, and economic rights guaranteed by the Constitution but ignored for almost 100 years.

Chapter Study Guide

Identifying Key People and Terms

Name the key person or key term that describes the:
1. most prestigious civil rights leader.
2. Court case overturning segregation in the schools.
3. black and white protesters who traveled by bus into the Deep South to demonstrate against discrimination.
4. legislation eliminating whites-only public facilities.
5. segregation developed by custom rather than law.

Locating Key Places

1. In what southern city did Rosa Parks take actions that helped spark the civil rights movement?
2. What school district was sued because of its segregated schools?

Mastering the Main Ideas

1. What laws prompted civil rights protesters of the 1960s to act as they did?
2. Name some examples of the nonviolent protests supported by the Rev. Dr. Martin Luther King, Jr.
3. Describe Project C.
4. What was the significance of the March on Washington for Jobs and Freedom in 1963?
5. What was the Mississippi Summer Project and what was its impact on the civil rights movement?

1950	1955	1960	1965	1970

1954
*Brown v.
Board of
Education
of Topeka*

1955
Mont-
gomery
boycott

1960
Seventeen
African
nations
gain
indepen-
dence

1957
Ghana gains independence;
Central High School integrates

1963
March on
Washington;
Birmingham
protests

1965
Voting
Rights Act
of 1965;
Malcolm X
assassination

1968
Martin Luther King, Jr., assassination;
race riots

1964
Civil Rights Act of 1964

Applying Critical Thinking Skills

1. **Identifying central issues:** What were the central ideas of Martin Luther King, Jr.'s nonviolent philosophy?
2. **Analyzing cause and effect:** What steps did white officials of Birmingham take against African Americans? What were the effects of these steps? Why were these effects exactly the opposite of what the governor of Alabama and the police chief of Birmingham expected?
3. **Expressing problems:** In spite of the advances of the civil rights laws of 1964 and 1965, President Johnson identified a fundamental problem endured by African Americans. What was the problem?
4. **Making comparisons:** Compare de jure segregation with de facto segregation. Which do you believe is worse? Why?

Learning Geography Through History

What historical factors contributed to making the southern region of the United States the scene of most de jure segregation and the northern region the scene of much de facto segregation?

Relating the United States to the World

1. What events in Asia did King cite when he called on the U.S. government to respond to the needs of African Americans?
2. What religious principles guided African Americans during their push to secure civil rights?

Using the Time Line

1. What year may be called a turning point in the civil rights movement?
2. In what years were major figures of the civil rights era assassinated?

Linking Past to Present

1. Looking back on the 1960s from the 1990s, what do you think are the most important gains of the civil rights era?
2. In what ways did the African American civil rights movement spur the movement for equal rights for women?

Practicing Critical Thinking Strategies

Analyzing Cause and Effect
Reread President Johnson's account of the effects of centuries of racial segregation and discrimination on pages 771–772. What was one major effect of the president's call for "equality as a fact and as a result" rather than theoretical equality?

Learning More About the Struggle for Civil Rights

1. **Using Source Readings:** Read the Source Readings for this chapter and answer the questions.
2. **Role playing:** From a library, get the entire text of the Rev. Dr. Martin Luther King, Jr.'s "I Have a Dream" speech. Read the speech for understanding. Then read it dramatically before the class.
3. **Holding a debate:** Hold a debate in class. One side should argue the case for nonviolent civil rights protests. The other should argue on behalf of other forms of protests. Make sure both sides cite American traditions as they argue.

Linking Past to Present

The United States space program has come a long way since Alan B. Shepard, Jr., shown in the inset, became the nation's first space traveler in 1961. Today the backbone of the U.S. space program is a fleet of reusable transport vehicles called space shuttles. The *Discovery*, shown lifting off on a four-day mission from the Kennedy Space Center in October 1990, carried five astronauts.

The Turbulent Sixties

1 9 6 0 – 1 9 6 8

20

In this chapter you will learn why the 1960s began optimistically yet ended chaotically.

SECTIONS IN THIS CHAPTER:
1. **Liberal optimism swept the nation.**
2. **The Great Society emerged.**
3. **Liberalism influenced international affairs.**
4. **Discontent characterized the late 1960s.**

On the morning of May 5, 1961, ordinary activities ground to a halt in offices, schools, and homes in all parts of America. Millions of people sat down in front of their television sets to watch a tall, slender Mercury-Redstone rocket blast off from a launching pad at Cape Canaveral, Florida. On top of the rocket was a small capsule. Inside it was Alan B. Shepard, Jr., the first American to travel in space.

Less than a month earlier, Yuri Gagarin of the Soviet Union had orbited the earth in a similar space capsule. Shepard's flight was comforting to Americans because it suggested that the United States could compete with the Soviets in space exploration. However, the American manned space program—and the seven astronauts chosen as the nation's first space travellers—had already become a national preoccupation well before Gagarin's or Shepard's flight. The program had become a symbol of America's soaring optimism about the future—its faith in technological progress and its confidence in the nation's ability to lead the world.

The 1960s, which began with such hope, ended in chaos and division. What happened to produce such turbulence? Were the confidence and idealism that shaped the decade a cause of the later problems? To understand what went wrong in the late 1960s, it is necessary first to understand how the nation viewed itself in 1960.

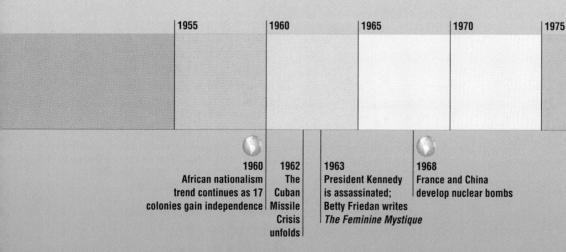

1955	1960	1965	1970	1975

1960
African nationalism trend continues as 17 colonies gain independence

1962
The Cuban Missile Crisis unfolds

1963
President Kennedy is assassinated; Betty Friedan writes *The Feminine Mystique*

1968
France and China develop nuclear bombs

Liberal optimism swept the nation.

Key Terms: New Frontier, Great Society

Reading Preview
As you read this section, you will learn:

1. who won the 1960 election.
2. what attribute of Kennedy made him so popular.
3. how Johnson continued the Kennedy legacy.

Election of 1960

Electoral Vote by State		Popular Vote and Percentage
DEMOCRATIC		
John F. Kennedy	303	34,227,096
Harry F. Byrd	15	—
REPUBLICAN		
Richard M. Nixon	219	34,108,546
MINOR PARTIES	—	502,363
	537	68,838,005

ALASKA 3
HAWAII 3

49.5% 49.7%

.8%

WA 9
OR 6
ID 4
MT 4
ND 4
MN 11
WI 12
NY 45
NH 4
VT 3
ME 5
MA 16
RI 4
CT 8
NJ 16
DE 3
MD 9
SD 4
MI 20
PA 32
WY 3
NE 6
IA 10
IL 27
IN 13
OH 25
WV 8
VA 12
NV 3
UT 4
CO 6
KS 8
MO 13
KY 10
NC 14
CA 32
AZ 4
NM 4
OK 1 7
AR 8
TN 11
SC 8
GA 12
MS 8
AL 6
TX 24
LA 10
FL 10
© SF

Relatively few Americans in 1960 would have predicted that the decade ahead was to be among the most turbulent of the century. Despite the growing restiveness of the nation's African American population, and despite undercurrents of protest and discontent from many other groups, most Americans faced the future with optimism.

Kennedy barely defeated Nixon.

The presidential campaign of 1960 was a reflection of the nation's optimism. It presented two young candidates, both of whom offered active leadership, both of whom emphasized the promise of the future. Vice President **Richard Nixon**, the Republican nominee, was already one of the most familiar figures in American politics, a man with both fervent admirers and passionate foes. He insisted that the United States would remain prosperous and strong by expanding upon the policies of the Eisenhower Administration.

Senator **John F. Kennedy** of Massachusetts, the Democratic candidate, was a relative newcomer to national politics, although he had narrowly missed becoming the party's vice-presidential nominee four years earlier. In 1960 he criticized the Republicans for allowing the nation to "drift" and promised what one columnist called "positive leadership and presidential power to the uttermost."

On only a few issues did the two candidates strongly disagree. Many believed the election would hinge not on questions of policy, but on religion and ethnicity. Kennedy was Roman Catholic and of Irish descent. No member of either group had ever been elected president. In 1928 religious intolerance had contributed to the defeat of Al Smith, the first Roman Cath-

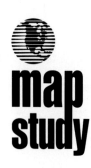

map study

Regions Note on the charts how close the popular vote was in this election in both numbers and percentages. In which region was Nixon strongest?

Critical Thinking How does the map help explain the winning electoral vote for Kennedy?

olic to run for president on a major party ticket. Kennedy did much to dispel whatever suspicions and prejudices survived that election, however. He was handsome, articulate, and poised—the Harvard-educated son of one of America's wealthiest men. He was a far cry from Smith, who was poorly educated and rather plain looking.

The election was one of the closest in American history. Kennedy received 49.7 percent of the popular vote to Nixon's 49.5. His electoral margin was similarly thin. The shift of a few thousand votes in Illinois and Texas (both states in which vote-counting irregularities were alleged) would have changed the result.

Kennedy's charisma captured American hearts.

Forty-three-year-old John F. Kennedy was inaugurated on a cold, sunny January day, made all the brighter by the fresh blanket of snow.

MEET THE PRESIDENT

JOHN F. KENNEDY

Born: May 29, 1917
Died: November 22, 1963
In office: 1961–1963

The first president born in the 20th century, John Kennedy proclaimed the rise of a new generation of American leadership, ready to meet the challenges of a New Frontier with intelligence, energy, and boldness.

Kennedy was the second son of a large, wealthy Massachusetts family that was a dynamic political force all by itself. He was a congressman by 29, a senator by 35.

In world affairs, Kennedy's new policies bore a striking resemblance to the old Cold War: he faced several tense confrontations with the Soviets. In domestic matters, Kennedy set goals for space exploration, started the Peace Corps, and encouraged the civil rights movement, but his ambitious legislative program was hampered by his razor-thin election margin. Kennedy needed more time to gather political strength in Congress. Time was one gift he never had, however. He was killed in Dallas at age 46.

The youngest man ever elected to the presidency (succeeding a man who was among the oldest), Kennedy spoke to the nation as a representative of a new generation filled with hopes and ideals. He challenged the nation to aspire to new greatness.

Once in office, however, Kennedy had great difficulty translating his lofty goals into practice. He called his domestic program the **New Frontier**, and in the course of his three years in office he proposed an ambitious series of social and economic programs. Lacking a resounding mandate from the electorate, however, and facing a conservative Congress, most of his proposals remained stalled.

Stymied in Congress, Kennedy looked elsewhere for opportunities to exert leadership. He launched a new round of trade negotiations

With characteristic charm and glamour, President Kennedy celebrates at his inaugural ball, January 1961. Jacqueline Kennedy, the new first lady, is seated behind the president.

designed to lower tariff rates and stimulate international trade. He used the authority of his office to browbeat the steel industry into rescinding a price increase that exceeded the informal guidelines his Administration had announced. Toward the end of his life, he lent the moral prestige of the presidency to the civil rights movement. Kennedy's greatest opportunities to provide leadership, however, would come in foreign policy, which he proposed to rescue from what he considered the rigidity and stagnation of the Eisenhower years.

Despite a relatively limited record of accomplishments, Kennedy attracted enormous popularity during his brief time in the White House, largely through the impact of his own

Shocked by the recent tragedy of her husband's assassination, Jacqueline Kennedy, right, looks on as Judge Sarah T. Hughes administers the presidential oath of office to Vice President Lyndon B. Johnson. They are aboard Air Force One on November 22, 1963, as it flies from Dallas to Washington, D.C. Lady Bird Johnson, the new first lady, is left of the president.

appealing personality. Charming, witty, energetic, he had what many admirers began to call charisma. His large and attractive family quickly became objects of national curiosity and fascination. Kennedy himself seemed to many to embody the boldness and energy of America at the peak of its power.

How important the image of Kennedy had become to the American imagination became clear on November 22, 1963. On that day the president and his wife Jacqueline, who were making a series of political appearances in Texas, rode slowly through downtown **Dallas** in an open car. Suddenly, shots rang out from a sixth-floor window of the Texas Book Depository. Kennedy was struck in the head. He died minutes later in a nearby hospital.

That same day police arrested Lee Harvey Oswald, a confused and embittered Marxist who had once asked for political asylum in the Soviet Union, and charged him with the murder of the president. Two days later, Jack Ruby, a Dallas nightclub owner, shot and killed Oswald as he was being moved to a new jail. The popular assumption at the time was that Oswald had acted alone, expressing through the assassination his personal anger and frustration, and that Ruby had killed Oswald in an effort to make himself a hero. Those assumptions were endorsed by a federal commission chaired by Chief Justice **Earl Warren**. It concluded its nine-month investigation with a report stating unequivocally that there had been no conspiracy. In subsequent years, however, questions arose about the assassination; and new investigations—including one commissioned by a committee of the House of Representatives in 1978—cast doubt on the Warren Commission's findings.

The death of President Kennedy traumatized the nation and left an indelible mark on virtually every American who lived through the event. For months after the assassination much of the public remained obsessed with the martyred president and his family. For years Americans continued to revere him in ways that the comparatively modest accomplishments of his brief presidency cannot explain. In later, more troubled times, when Americans looked back longingly to the stable, confident climate of the 1950s and early 1960s, many remembered November 22, 1963, as the moment when things began to unravel.

Johnson pushed Kennedy's programs.

Lyndon B. Johnson, the new president, was in many ways very different from the man he succeeded. A native of Stonewall, a small town in central Texas, Johnson had risen in politics

without the benefit of family money or personal glamor. His successes came primarily through sheer hard work. He had surrendered the powerful position of Senate majority leader to become Kennedy's running mate in 1960 and had chafed at the restrictions the vice presidency had placed on him. Now, because of a national tragedy, he had attained the position he had always wanted.

Johnson was a tall, gawky, inelegant man, a generally ineffective public speaker, often coarse, at times alarmingly cruel—a stark contrast to his smooth, urbane, unfailingly polite predecessor. However, he shared Kennedy's commitment to making active use of presidential power. He also brought to his office remarkable political skills, particularly in dealing with Congress, that Kennedy had not possessed. Although Kennedy had been unable to win passage of almost any of his major legislative proposals, Johnson succeeded in pushing both Kennedy's programs and his own through Congress with remarkable speed.

Indeed, in his first three years in office,

Johnson compiled the most impressive legislative record of any president since Franklin Roosevelt. He was assisted at first by the deep popular emotions the Kennedy assassination had stirred. He managed to win approval of many of the late president's measures as a tribute to Kennedy's memory. Later he benefited from the strength of the mandate he received in the 1964 presidential election. Running against Barry Goldwater, a Republican so conservative that even many members of his own party deserted him, Johnson triumphed by the largest popular margin of any presidential candidate to date and carried a strongly Democratic Congress into office with him.

Johnson used these advantages to construct a sweeping domestic program that went well beyond the proposals of the New Frontier. Searching for a name for it that would distinguish his record from that of Kennedy's (whose shadow he desperately sought to escape), he seized on the phrase **Great Society**.

Johnson displayed almost unbelievable energy in promoting his Great Society programs,

Courageous, yet too young to comprehend the tragedy, John F. Kennedy, Jr., salutes as the casket containing his father, the late President Kennedy, is taken from St. Matthew's Cathedral during the funeral. John Jr., stands next to his mother, Jacqueline, who is holding hands with her daughter, Caroline (partially concealed). The president's brother, Attorney General Robert F. Kennedy, is directly behind John, Jr.

LYNDON B. JOHNSON

Born: August 27, 1908
Died: January 22, 1973
In office: 1963–1969

If laws alone could create a "Great Society," Lyndon Johnson was the man for the job. No other president matched his mastery of law-making.

The son of schoolteachers, Johnson was himself briefly a teacher before he entered politics. He was one of the most powerful and effective leaders the Senate ever had.

As president, Johnson quickly achieved vital civil rights laws—his enduring legacy. Poverty and racism, however, could not be extinguished by Johnson's costly flood of programs—nor could the war in Vietnam be resolved by Johnson's ever more costly commitment of American power. Johnson's "Great Society" vanished in the haze of urban fires and turbulence of a divisive war.

Johnson always knew when he had the votes—and when he didn't. He abruptly withdrew from the 1968 campaign and afterwards retired to his Texas ranch.

using every tool in the presidential arsenal—flattery, patronage, promises, and threats—to push one bill after another through Congress. He was, for a time, one of the most effective legislative politicians ever to serve as president. At first he seemed to have a good chance to achieve his great ambition: to become the greatest reform president of the century.

Despite the differences between Kennedy and Johnson, their two presidencies can best be understood as a single, Democratic administration. Many of the same men and women who entered government to serve Kennedy stayed on to work with Johnson. Many of the broad policies of the Johnson Administration, both domestic and foreign, were continuations (and at times elaborations) of policies the Kennedy Administration had introduced. Many Kennedy admirers soon learned to dislike Lyndon Johnson, however. They insisted that if Kennedy had lived, the history of those years would have been very different. In fact, however, the Johnson presidency seldom departed in any significant way from the paths the Kennedy Administration had laid out.

Together, Kennedy and Johnson presided over the rise and fall of an extraordinary moment in modern American history: the climax of liberal confidence about America's role in the world and its potential at home. Seldom before, and never since, has the nation experienced such soaring confidence. Rarely has it embraced such soaring ambitions. Americans have always liked to believe that theirs is an exceptional land, graced with special moral virtues and endowed with a unique destiny. In the 1960s American liberals made those assumptions the basis of a dramatic experiment in active government.

SECTION 1 REVIEW

Identify Key People and Terms
Write a sentence to identify: Richard Nixon, John F. Kennedy, New Frontier, Earl Warren, Lyndon B. Johnson, Great Society

Locate Key Places
In which city was President Kennedy assassinated?

Master the Main Ideas

1. **Analyzing political elections:** By what margin did Kennedy defeat Nixon in the 1960 election?
2. **Studying political leaders:** Why was President Kennedy so popular with the American public?
3. **Studying political leaders:** What did President Johnson decide to do with many of the foreign and domestic programs and policies initiated or developed by Kennedy?

Apply Critical Thinking Skills: Making Comparisons
In what ways was President Johnson different from President Kennedy? How were they similar?

The Great Society emerged.

Key Terms: Medicare, socialized medicine, Medicaid, War on Poverty, redistribution of income

Reading Preview
As you read this section, you will learn:
1. how the federal government changed under Kennedy and Johnson.
2. how the federal government dealt with poverty.
3. what the results of the Great Society programs were.

The domestic programs of the Kennedy and Johnson administrations rested on two broad commitments. First, like their predecessors and like their successors, they agreed that the federal government should play an important role in maintaining the health of the nation's economy. Second, they sought to expand the government's role in protecting social welfare. In pursuing this second goal, they moved the government in new and unfamiliar directions.

The federal government expanded social welfare programs.

Not since the 1930s had there been a major expansion of the American welfare state. In the early and mid-1960s, however, the federal government moved rapidly to increase its role in American domestic life. Kennedy proposed many programs but won passage of few of them. Under Johnson, however, the Administration seemed able for a time to push almost anything it wanted through Congress, particularly after the 1964 election. In 1965 and 1966, the president managed to win passage of more than two-thirds of the measures he proposed.

Under Kennedy the federal government moved to expand the existing welfare state along lines liberals had been advocating for years. The Administration successfully pressed for an increase in the minimum wage and an expansion of social security benefits. Its most ambitious proposal, however, was for a system of federally subsidized health care for the elderly: **Medicare**.

Demands for national health insurance had been part of the liberal agenda since the 1940s. Liberals had never been able to overcome the strenuous opposition of the medical profession and conservatives in Congress, however. Federal involvement, critics argued, would threaten the freedom of doctors and patients and would violate the nation's commitment to private enterprise. It might ultimately produce what the medical profession called **socialized medicine**—a federally run health-care system.

The form Medicare assumed removed at least some of those objections, however. It became part of the existing, highly popular Social Security System. It offered benefits to all elderly Americans. Like Social Security, it immediately attracted a large middle-class constituency. In addition, physicians treating Medicare patients did not have to be employees of the government, a decision that defused fears of socialized medicine. Doctors would continue practicing privately and the government would simply reimburse them.

Even so, opponents managed to block Medicare for more than two years after Kennedy proposed it. In 1965, however, Congress finally approved the program. The following year Johnson moved to expand this new commitment to national health insurance by winning passage of the **Medicaid** program, which

Great Society

Point	Counterpoint
In favor of increasing social welfare programs	**Against increasing social welfare programs**
■ The federal government has a duty to provide for the social welfare of its citizens. ■ A person's ability to secure services such as medical care should not be dependent on his or her ability to pay for that care.	■ Increased social welfare undermines the free enterprise system. ■ Too much federal involvement in social programs will destroy or severly limit local decision-making ability.

subsidized the medical expenses of welfare recipients of all ages.

Responding to growing concerns about the problems of American cities, both Kennedy and Johnson won passage of measures offering federal aid to urban areas. New programs funded the construction of public housing, the expansion or creation of mass-transit systems, rent supplements for the urban poor, the preservation of open spaces, and—in 1966—the creation of a "Model Cities" program intended to explore comprehensive strategies for urban redevelopment. Johnson also won approval of the new Department of Housing and Urban Development (HUD), whose first secretary, **Robert Weaver**, became the first African American ever to serve in a president's cabinet.

In the 1960 campaign, Kennedy had attacked the Republican administrations of the 1950s for allowing American public education to "fall behind." As president, Kennedy pressed for legislation to provide federal aid to public schools. Substantial opposition remained from those who feared that such aid would lead to federal interference in local school districts. In 1965, however, Johnson finally steered the Elementary and Secondary Education Act through Congress, the first of several measures expanding Washington's role in funding education in the United States.

The Democratic governments of the 1960s broke precedent in other ways as well. They established agencies to provide federal assistance to the arts such as the National Endowments for the Arts and the Humanities. They funded public television through the Corporation for Public Broadcasting. They passed legislation to protect consumers from unsafe automobiles, largely in response to the efforts of **Ralph Nader**, a passionate consumer advocate. They created a new Department of Transportation. They established new rules governing air and water pollution. They reformed the immigration laws to eliminate discriminatory ethnic quotas. In addition, as you read previously, they produced the most important civil rights acts since Reconstruction.

The government waged a War on Poverty.

The most ambitious public effort of the Kennedy and Johnson administrations was the attempt to eliminate poverty from American life. The unprecedented effort was a response in part to a renewed popular interest in poverty in the early 1960s. Books, especially Michael Harrington's *The Other America*, television programs, and political demonstrations all drew attention to what became known as "the discovery of poverty." Many Americans could not understand why, in a society enjoying unprecedented prosperity, more than 20 percent of the population—35 million people—still lived below the poverty line.

Planning for what became known as the **War on Poverty** began in the Kennedy Administration. Johnson formally launched the "war" in 1964, with the creation of the Office of Economic Opportunity (OEO), which was to oversee a wide array of antipoverty efforts.

The War on Poverty ultimately became one of the most controversial domestic programs

President Johnson congratulates Robert Weaver upon his swearing in as Secretary of HUD.

Ralph Nader continues to be a vocal advocate of consumer rights. In 1988 he criticized the Food and Drug Administration for trying to repeal a rule requiring makers of fruit juice to reveal the percentage of real fruit juice in their products.

BUILDING
CRITICAL THINKING STRATEGIES

JOHNSON'S DOMESTIC POLICIES
Skill: Checking Consistency

Introducing the Skill. As president, Lyndon Johnson oversaw the creation of many social welfare programs. He believed, as had John F. Kennedy, that the federal government had a responsibility to provide directly for the welfare of its people. During the 1964 campaign, Johnson described his vision for America as a place:

where no child will go unfed and no youngster will go unschooled; where every child has a good teacher and every teacher has good pay, and both have good classrooms; where every human being has dignity and every worker has a job; where education is blind to color and unemployment is unaware of race.

Were Johnson's domestic policies as president aimed at achieving his vision of America, at winning the War on Poverty? Was he successful?

Learning the Skill. To know whether Johnson was successful in his domestic policies requires **checking consistency** in Johnson's statements and programs. Were the president's actions in agreement or in keeping with his stated goals and principles? Were they also consistent with one another?

To answer these questions, consider what you have learned about President Johnson's philosophies in the text or in other research. You might wish also to consult other sources, such as published speeches or biographies.

Applying the Skill. Read the newspaper headlines that follow. Which one do you think would be most consistent with the domestic policies of President Johnson? Give evidence to support your response.

a. President urges local volunteering efforts.
b. State legislatures forced by federal cuts to increase welfare spending.
c. President pushes new welfare legislation through Congress.
d. Business and industry leaders urged to donate personnel and profits to aid social programs.
e. President announces plan to cut federal spending in social services.

of the postwar era. At the time, however, it was carefully designed to avoid controversy. First, the Administration argued that the government could reduce or even eliminate poverty without raising taxes because economic growth was producing enough surplus revenue to fund the antipoverty programs. In addition, the government avoided such controversial approaches as **redistribution of income**, which involves the use of taxes and transfer payments to shift income from one group to provide financial help for another group. Instead, the government promised to fight poverty by helping the poor to help themselves—a self-help approach that Johnson once called "a hand up, not a handout." Finally, the War on Poverty adopted a

community-based approach. It committed itself to revitalizing poor communities rather than moving the poor into more affluent areas.

The antipoverty crusade produced a remarkable array of programs in pursuit of these goals. Its agencies sought to provide vocational training, remedial education, college work-study grants, and other subsidized training programs for the poor. It created the Job Corps, the Neighborhood Youth Corps, and other employment programs. It launched Project Head Start to prepare pre-school, low-income children for elementary school. It created Upward Bound to assist poor high school students in entering college. It established Volunteers in Service to America (VISTA), which sent

Named for their distinctive caps, the Green Berets are specially trained to infiltrate behind enemy lines to support guerrilla warfare operations.

Kennedy Administration sought to develop them through an approach to foreign policy that became known as **flexible response**.

Insurgent, or rebellious, groups in many developing areas such as Laos and South Vietnam had learned to employ unconventional methods, most notably guerrilla warfare, to spread communism. One of the most important initiatives of the flexible response strategy, therefore, was the search for ways to counter those methods. Kennedy supported the development of new "counterinsurgency" forces within the military and ordered the training of soldiers in the techniques of fighting a modern, limited war. These special forces, known as the **Green Berets** because of their distinctive headgear, were the vanguard of the liberal strategy.

Kennedy also promoted peaceful methods of expanding American influence in the Third World. His **Alliance for Progress** with Latin America, a series of cooperative projects and agreements, were designed to repair the badly deteriorating relationship between the United States and its southern neighbors. He also launched the Agency for International Development to coordinate foreign aid. In addition, he created the **Peace Corps**, which sent American volunteers to work in developing areas abroad. The Peace Corps, which is still active today, became one of Kennedy's most popular innovations.

The Bay of Pigs invasion ended disastrously.

A Peace Corps volunteer instructs students on how to do math problems in Honduras.

Kennedy's first major foreign policy initiative was a disaster. As you read previously, the Eisenhower Administration had been working through the Central Intelligence Agency (CIA) with a group of anti-Castro Cuban immigrants to prepare an invasion of Cuba. The invasion would, the planners hoped, trigger an anticommunist uprising in Cuba and restore a noncommunist government there. In the first weeks of his presidency, Kennedy decided to continue with the preparations. Then, on April 17, 1961, the invasion began.

Two thousand armed exiles landed in a swampy, isolated region of Cuba known as the *Bahia de Cochinas*, or **Bay of Pigs**. (The Bay of Pigs is on the southern coast of Cuba.) The invasion immediately became bogged down in the area's hostile terrain and soon encountered powerful resistance from Cuban forces. As things began to go badly, Kennedy attempted to limit American exposure and refused to authorize the Air Force to launch raids on Cuba. Within two days, the mission had collapsed.

Amid denunciations from around the world, Kennedy took public responsibility for the fiasco. Privately, he blamed the CIA and the military for providing him with unreliable information. Despite the humiliation, Kennedy refused to abandon his public commitment to overthrowing Castro.

The United States confronted the Soviet Union.

For all of Kennedy's concern about the Third World, the most critical foreign policy challenges of his presidency involved the Soviet Union. The city of Berlin, the former capital of Germany, was the source of special tension.

The communist government of East Germany controlled one sector of the city and the pro-western government of West Germany controlled the other. Because the city lay entirely within East Germany, the presence of western forces there had always been a particular irritant to the Soviet Union. Especially embarrassing was the steadily growing flow of refugees from East Germany to the West through the easily crossed border in the center of Berlin.

In June 1961 President Kennedy and Soviet Premier Nikita Khrushchev met briefly in Vienna to discuss, among other things, the German question. The chilly meeting produced no agreements, however. Two months later, on August 13, the East Germans (under the direction of the Soviet Union) began to construct the **Berlin Wall**, a concrete and barbed-wire barrier between East and West Berlin. Guards were then ordered to fire on anyone attempting to cross the now fortified border. The grim, gray barrier cutting through the heart of one of Europe's great cities remained for nearly three decades the most powerful symbol of the Cold War. The United States protested the Wall but made no effort to dismantle it. In the last chapter you will read about the dismantling of the Berlin Wall in 1990.

In 1962 a far more dangerous confrontation between the United States and the Soviet Union emerged. In October American U-2 reconnaissance planes discovered evidence through high-altitude photographs that the Soviet Union was installing missiles in Cuba, 90 miles from the coast of Florida. At first, the Administration assumed the missiles were, as the Soviets claimed, purely defensive. On October 14, however, Administration officials found conclusive evidence that they were, in fact, offensive nuclear weapons.

Why the Soviets decided to place nuclear weapons in Cuba remains the source of speculation. The best guess is that Khrushchev, aware of his nation's nuclear inferiority to the United States, was trying to compensate for the American advantage quickly and inexpensively. The United States had missiles in Turkey, near the Soviet border. He probably reasoned that placing Soviet missiles in Cuba would be little different. Khrushchev may also have believed that the weapons would deter the United States from launching another invasion of Cuba.

Whatever the reasons, the United States considered the presence of nuclear missiles in Cuba unacceptable. Kennedy faced the difficult decision of how to force Khrushchev to remove them. He rejected the advice of many of his advisers that he launch an air strike against the missile sites, fearing that an armed conflict

President Kennedy observes the Berlin Wall, which angry Berliners labeled *Schandmauer*, or wall of shame. The Brandenburg Gate, built in 1791, stands just inside what was the East German side of Berlin. The gate, one of Berlin's greatest landmarks, stands at the west end of *Unter den Linden*, Berlin's famous boulevard.

LAUNCH POSITION

MISSILE-READY TENTS

MISSILE ERECTORS

This is one of the many aerial reconnaissance photographs that alerted the Kennedy Administration to the construction of missile sites in Cuba. At the time, American officials never knew if nuclear warheads were actually in Cuba. In 1989, at a conference attended by American, Soviet, and Cuban officials involved in the crisis, the Soviets revealed that 20 warheads were in Cuba and could have been launched within two hours.

might escalate into a nuclear war. He chose instead what he considered a moderate response: imposing a naval blockade on Cuba to stop Soviet ships from carrying additional weapons to the island.

For several anxious days, Kennedy waited for a response from Khrushchev as Soviet ships continued to steam toward Cuba. At the last moment, the ships stopped and turned around, and Khrushchev sent a conciliatory message offering to remove the missiles if the United States would pledge not to invade Cuba. Kennedy agreed, and the most dangerous crisis of the Cold War, the **Cuban Missile Crisis**, came to a close.

Kennedy's handling of the Cuban Missile Crisis was widely considered the president's greatest triumph. It vastly increased his stature and popularity. In the immediate aftermath of the crisis, moreover, Cold War tensions appeared to ease. In June 1963 Kennedy made a conciliatory speech calling for a less confrontational relationship with the Soviet Union. That same summer the two superpowers concluded years of negotiation by agreeing to a treaty banning the testing of nuclear weapons in the atmosphere.

In the longer run, however, the Cuban Missile Crisis served to heighten Cold War tensions. Khrushchev emerged from the episode humiliated and badly weakened. Two years

later he was deposed and replaced by more militant leaders. Their first priority was to build up Soviet military might so that the nation would never again have to back down before an American threat. The United States, of course, soon felt obliged to match the Soviet Union. The long-range result of the crisis, therefore, was the largest peacetime military buildup in American history.

Johnson continued Kennedy's foreign policy.

Lyndon Johnson entered the presidency with almost no experience in international affairs. Even during his three years as vice president, he had remained on the periphery of most important decisions. Eager to prove that he was a strong world leader, Johnson quickly committed himself to continuing Kennedy's policies and almost immediately came to depend on the same foreign-policy advisers Kennedy had used.

Johnson soon absorbed the concern of the Kennedy Administration about communism in the Third World. The president expressed that concern when he acted to prevent what he said was a possible communist take-over of the **Dominican Republic**. (As you can see on the map on page 1000, the Dominican Republic shares an island in the Caribbean Sea with Haiti.) Various factions had been struggling to establish control over the Dominican Republic for four years, since the assassination in 1961 of its longtime dictator, Rafael Trujillo. In the spring of 1965, a popular insurgency led by the leftwing nationalist Juan Bosch threatened the conservative military regime. Johnson responded to the appeals of the existing government to intervene and dispatched more than 20,000 American troops to quell the rebellion. Only after a conservative candidate defeated Bosch in 1966 were the forces withdrawn.

Johnson also continued the general policies of his predecessors in dealing with the Soviet Union. He made occasional conciliatory gestures to the Kremlin, and at one point had a brief summit meeting with Soviet President Alexei Kosygin in Glassboro, New Jersey. After the 1964 overthrow of Khrushchev, however, and the elevation of **Leonid Brezhnev** to the chairmanship of the communist party, Soviet foreign (and domestic) policies hardened. That was one reason for Johnson's inability to advance the efforts Kennedy had begun in arms control and relaxation of tensions. The larger reason, however, was Johnson's (and the nation's) growing preoccupation with the war in Vietnam—a conflict that by the end of the 1960s had escalated to major proportions and had created a major political crisis in the United States.

SECTION 3 REVIEW

Identify Key People and Terms
Write a sentence to identify: Third World, flexible response, Green Berets, Alliance for Progress, Peace Corps, Berlin Wall, Cuban Missile Crisis, Leonid Brezhnev

Locate Key Places
1. In which country is the Bay of Pigs located?
2. What Caribbean country shares an island with the Dominican Republic?

Master the Main Ideas
1. **Analyzing U.S. foreign policy:** How was President Kennedy's foreign policy different from President Eisenhower's?
2. **Studying international conflicts:** Why was the Bay of Pigs invasion unsuccessful?
3. **Analyzing U.S. foreign policy:** **(a)** What actions did the United States take when the Soviet Union built the Berlin Wall? **(b)** What actions did the nation take when it discovered that the Soviet Union had missile sites in Cuba?
4. **Analyzing U.S. foreign policy:** In what ways was Johnson's foreign policy a continuation of Kennedy's foreign policy?

Apply Critical Thinking Skills: Predicting Consequences
President Kennedy decided not to send in the Air Force to Cuba during the Bay of Pigs invasion. Considering that Cuba still is a communist nation, and still a legitimate threat to the United States because of its geographical closeness, should the United States consider taking this action today? Why or why not?

SECTION 4

Discontent characterized the late 1960s.

Key Terms: SDS, Free Speech Movement, counterculture, hippies, National Organization for Women, American Indian Movement, United Farm Workers, bilingualism

Reading Preview
As you read this section, you will learn:
1. how the civil rights movement affected many northern white students.
2. how members of the counterculture defined themselves.
3. what movement affected women.
4. how the role of ethnic groups changed.

Even in the relatively tranquil Eisenhower years, signs of instability and discontent foreshadowed the difficult times ahead: the beginnings of a major revolt by African Americans against racial oppression; the stirrings of a new feminist movement; the origins of a rebellious youth culture; and a critique by intellectuals of the impersonal, alienating quality of modern life. These conflicts grew more pronounced in the 1960s, creating a major social crisis.

Some members of the counterculture, such as this family, showed their dissatisfaction with mainstream society by joining rural communes.

The civil rights movement spawned social activism.

Among the many effects of the civil rights movement as it gained momentum in the early 1960s was its impact on northern white students who were attracted to the cause. Beginning with the Greensboro sit-ins in 1960, accelerating with the 1961 Freedom Rides, and peaking in 1964 with the Mississippi Summer Project, white youths from the North found in the civil rights movement not only an outlet for their idealism, but an inspiration to pursue other causes as well. One result was the creation of a liberal reform movement that became known as the New Left.

Tom Hayden was one of the middle-class white youths who came to be associated with the New Left. Like others in this liberal movement, he began to question the nature of American society. Hayden grew up in Royal Oak, Michigan, a suburb of Detroit, and attended a conservative Roman Catholic school in the parish of the once-famous radio priest, Charles Coughlin. Later, he attended public high school in Royal Oak.

Hayden's family was reasonably secure, but far from wealthy. His parents divorced when he was a boy, and his family lived frugally on his mother's earnings as a school librarian. Tom did well in school, excelled as an athlete, and edited his high school newspaper. He also showed small signs of youthful rebellion. Part of Hayden's rebelliousness could be attributed to his attraction to J. D. Salinger's novel *The Catcher in the Rye*, whose alienated hero, Holden Caulfield, he came to admire.

In the fall of 1957, Hayden entered the University of Michigan at Ann Arbor. He hated what he considered the impersonality of the university. "I had to live in a dorm with thirteen hundred guys," he later wrote, "that was worse than a public housing project." He also rebelled against what seemed to him the university's petty and arbitrary rules and the absence of democratic procedures for students accused of breaking them. He began writing for the student newspaper and gravitated to "the fringe, bohemian culture of the campus."

In the spring of 1960, he read Jack Kerouac's novel *On the Road*, which was based on a wild cross-country trip Kerouac had taken with a friend. Hayden decided to take a similar trip, and that summer he hitchhiked to California and visited the campus of the University of California at Berkeley. At Berkeley Hayden became involved with student political activists. Later that summer, he joined pickets outside the Democratic National Convention in Los Angeles urging delegates to support a strong civil rights plank in the party platform. While he was there, he met the Rev. Dr. Martin Luther King, Jr. In the Michigan student newspaper he wrote:

Meeting King transformed me. There I was, trying to conduct an objective interview with Martin Luther King, whose whole implicit message was: 'stop writing, start acting.' That was a compelling moment.

AN AMERICAN ★ SPEAKS

Tom Hayden catches his breath as an assailant, angered by Hayden's coverage of a desegregation march, stands over him with clenched fists. The photos of the incident were reprinted in newspapers across the country and helped to focus national opinion against segregation.

When Hayden returned to Ann Arbor in the fall, he began writing editorials for the campus newspaper, of which he was now the editor. He called on students to begin protesting the condition of the university and the world. He also became involved with the growing community of political activists at Michigan and, with them, agitated against racial discrimination and "undemocratic" university policies.

In the fall of 1961 (after his graduation from Michigan), Hayden traveled south with a large group of white students from Michigan and elsewhere to participate in the Freedom Rides that civil rights activists were organizing to protest the segregation of interstate bus terminals. In October, in McComb, Mississippi, he and a friend were dragged from a car by a white racist and beaten. A photograph of the attack, which appears on page 802, appeared in newspapers around the country.

Participating in the civil rights movement excited him, not only because he believed in the cause he was fighting for, but because he was excited by the spirit of the movement:

We believed in wanting to make history and achieve civil **AN AMERICAN ★ SPEAKS** rights. But there was something else: the middle-class emptiness of alienation that people talk about, and then suddenly confronting commitment.

In 1962 Hayden joined a group of other disenchanted young people in Port Huron, Michigan. They wanted to form a group that would give voice to their beliefs. As a result, they created **Students for a Democratic Society (SDS)**, and they issued a proclamation explaining their concerns. Hayden wrote:

Many of us began maturing in complacency. As we grew, however, our comfort was penetrated by events too troubling to dismiss.

Those events included the exposure of racial injustice, the threat of nuclear war, and a general decline in the quality of human life.

SDS was not, as some charged, a communist organization. Most of its members deplored the oppressive nature of communist regimes

throughout the world. It was sympathetic to many Marxist ideas, however, including the idea that the working classes were the key to creating social change. For several years after 1962, Hayden and other SDS men and women pursued their goals by living in working-class communities and attempting to organize their neighbors for political struggle. Those efforts produced few results, however. SDS always had its greatest impact where it had begun, on college campuses, where a rising wave of discontent—both with society and with the universities themselves—was fueling a growing rebellion.

The first sign of student rebellion came in the fall of 1964 at the University of California at Berkeley. A small group of radical students resisted university efforts to deny them a place

In 1964 students at the University of California at Berkeley staged campus protests that commenced a nationwide student crusade against poverty, war, and racism that lasted into the 1970s.

This young woman prepares to enter her elaborately decorated van in the Haight-Ashbury neighborhood of San Francisco. Such vans were commonplace modes of transportation for members of the counterculture in the late 1960s and early 1970s. Inset, shoppers view wares in the window of a counterculture store in San Francisco.

to solicit volunteers and funds for off-campus causes. Forming the **Free Speech Movement**, they struck back by occupying administration buildings and blocking the arrest of a nonstudent protester. For the next two months, the campus was in turmoil. The administration overreacted, calling in the police; the faculty condemned the radicals' tactics but supported their goals; the rest of the student body, distraught at the size, complexity, and impersonality of the university, rallied behind the Free Speech Movement. In the end, the protesters won the rights of free speech and association that they championed, and youth everywhere had a new model for effective direct action.

As the decade continued, campus protests spread. In 1968 students seized an administration building at Columbia University to protest what the demonstrators claimed was the school's insensitivity to the poor black community surrounding it. A year later, the seizure of administrative offices at Harvard resulted in a bloody confrontation with local police, while

another rebellion convulsed the Berkeley campus. Over the next several years, hardly any major university escaped some level of disruption from radicals and activists among its student body.

The counterculture rejected traditional standards and styles.

The rise of political radicalism on college campuses occurred alongside an even larger change in the character of American youth: the emergence of what became known as the **counterculture**. Among the conspicuous features of the counterculture was a general contempt among young people for traditional standards. Youths displayed that contempt by wearing long hair, shabby or flamboyant clothing, using unconventional speech, and flaunting conventional standards of behavior. They also were attracted to drugs, particularly to marijuana and hallucinogens. In addition, they adopted a new and more permissive view of sexual behavior. Rock music (which was itself becoming more and more rebellious in style) also became an increasingly important part of the counterculture.

Lying behind these open challenges to traditional lifestyles were the outlines of a philosophy. Like members of the student left (with which it in many ways overlapped), the counterculture challenged the nature of modern American society for its hollowness and artificiality. It called for a more "natural" world in which men and women would live in closer harmony with nature and would have greater freedom to vent their instincts and emotions.

The counterculture was, in the end, a search for personal fulfillment. Popular phrases of the 1960s expressed something of its character: "Do your own thing" or "If it feels good, do it." So did the communities created by the so-called **hippies**: adherents of the counterculture who attempted to withdraw from the conventional world and live among people who shared their beliefs. Such communities emerged in the **Haight-Ashbury** neighborhood of San Francisco and then spread to other large cities. The hippies also established rural communes in Colorado, New England, and elsewhere.

The effects of the New Left and the counterculture spread well beyond the college campuses and the hippie communities. They reached out to the whole society and established a new set of social norms that many young people (and some adults) imitated. Long hair, flamboyant clothing, drug use, and sexual

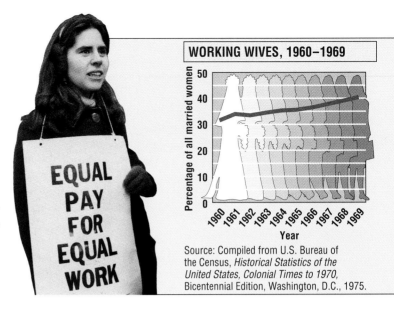

WORKING WIVES, 1960–1969

Source: Compiled from U.S. Bureau of the Census, *Historical Statistics of the United States, Colonial Times to 1970,* Bicentennial Edition, Washington, D.C., 1975.

freedom became badges not just of hippies and radicals, but of an entire generation.

Feminism experienced a rebirth.

American women also found inspiration in the civil rights movement. By the end of the 1960s women had launched a new feminist movement that soon profoundly changed the life of the nation.

Feminists in the 1960s did not draw just from the example of other groups, however. They drew from a long tradition, stretching back to the early 19th century, of women seeking to expand their rights. Gender discrimination was deeply embedded in American life, so deeply that most men—and many women—

chart study

The chart above depicts the percent of wives in the work force from 1960 to 1969. During which year did the percentage of working women drop? **Critical Thinking** Based on your understanding of the 1960s, what accounts for the trend illustrated in the chart?

Members of the National Women's Political Caucus hold a news conference in 1972 in which they state some of their objectives. From left to right are Gloria Steinem, Bella Abzug (who always wore outrageous hats), Shirley Chisholm, and Betty Friedan.

were not even aware of how fundamentally it shaped their lives. One of the most important results of the new feminism was to increase that awareness.

In the 40 years after the passage of the 19th Amendment, which gave women the right to vote in 1920, feminism had been a relatively weak force. Indeed, in the 1950s it had often seemed almost extinct. Its revival, however, was so rapid and so powerful that it seems clear that many women had never accepted the traditional roles society was prescribing for them.

One event that signalled the feminist revival was the publication in 1963 of *The Feminine Mystique* by **Betty Friedan**. Friedan had interviewed her classmates from the Smith College class of 1947, most of them affluent suburban housewives and mothers, and had discovered substantial discontent. Many of them found

Modern Art in America

Turmoil in Europe between the world wars brought many important artists to the United States. The creative interchange between European and American artists eventually produced a vigorous new style of painting called abstract expressionism. Abstract expressionist painters avoided representation (that is, painting objects or scenes as they appear to the eye). Instead, these artists used pure texture, color, and shape to express inner emotions. Abstract expressionism brought American artists, for the first time, to the forefront of international influence.

Jackson Pollock was among the earliest and most famous of abstract expressionists. His method was to dribble, smear, or fling paint at a piece of canvas laid on the floor.

When I am in the painting, I'm, not aware of what I'm doing . . . . I have no fears about making changes, destroying the image, etc., because the painting has a life of its own.

In the late 1950s, many American artists began to rebel against abstract expressionism and its emphasis on personal involvement. One result was pop art, a style of painting that freely borrowed images from popular culture. Robert

Andy Warhol's *4 Campbell's Soup Cans*, circa 1965, reflects his interest in banal images appropriated from popular culture. In *Map, 1961*, Jasper Johns combined the slashing brushstrokes of the abstract expressionists with an ordinary map of the United States, deliberately confusing the painterly with the precise.

Highlights of American Life

their home-centered lives unfulfilling. They wanted greater outlets for their intelligence, talent, and education. The "feminine mystique"—the illusion that women would find fulfillment in domestic roles—was responsible, Friedan claimed, for "burying millions of women alive."

By the time Friedan's book appeared, reform agitation had already begun among another, much larger group: the more than 20 million women in the paid workforce (including more than a third of all married women). Working women encountered widespread discrimination. In 1963 agitation by women's groups helped produce the Equal Pay Act, which banned the practice of paying women less than men for equal work. However, women remained effectively barred from advancement beyond a certain point in many professions and barred from some altogether.

In 1966 Friedan joined with other feminists to create the **National Organization for Women** (NOW), which announced its goal as confronting "the conditions which now prevent women from enjoying the equality of opportunity and freedom of choice which is their right as individual human beings." It drew inspiration, the founders claimed, from the civil rights movement.

At first, the focus of NOW and other feminist groups was primarily on jobs. Within a few years, however, the tone and direction of the women's movement had begun to change. Younger feminists produced more sweeping critiques of gender relations in the United States and challenged the traditional structure not just of the workplace, but of the family. Among other things, most feminists were committed to controlling their reproductive lives— through access to birth control and abortion. These and other female demands became a major feature of public debate, and the source of major social and cultural changes in American life in the 1970s and 1980s.

Ethnic groups gained more power.

Through much of American history, most of the nation's dominant institutions had been controlled by middle-class, Protestant, white males. Nonetheless, throughout those same years, American society was extraordinarily diverse. It included many groups whose political, economic, and social outlook was very different from those of the controlling white male population. African Americans, Native Americans, Hispanic Americans, and members of other ethnic groups were largely excluded from the mainstream of American life. Women lived within sharply defined boundaries. People

Rauschenberg used newspaper clippings and postcards in his collages. Jasper Johns painted images of the American flag. Roy Lichtenstein produced paintings that resembled giant cartoon strip panels. Andy Warhol, among the most famous of the pop artists, reproduced common commercial products, such as soft drink bottles and soup cans, frequently in multiple images. In taking up these ordinary and even banal subjects, artists were perplexing many Americans with the question, "What is art, after all?"

Most artists in the 1960s sought objectivity and avoided social commentary, but their works were often shaped by skepticism, irony, mockery, antitraditionalism, and a saving dash of humor. In a sense they were faithfully representing the skeptical and experimental spirit of their times.

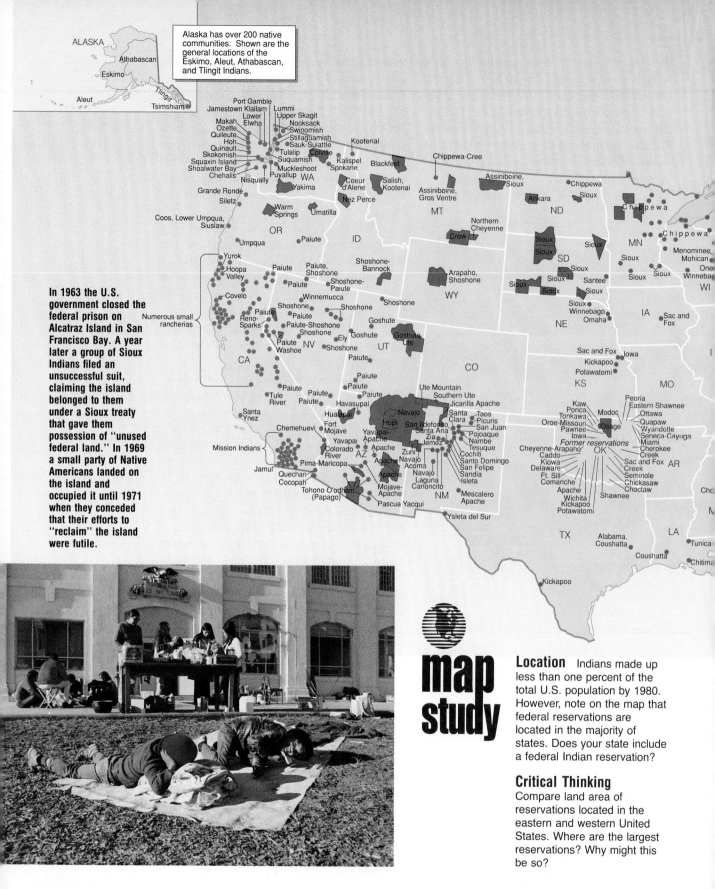

Alaska has over 200 native communities. Shown are the general locations of the Eskimo, Aleut, Athabascan, and Tlingit Indians.

In 1963 the U.S. government closed the federal prison on Alcatraz Island in San Francisco Bay. A year later a group of Sioux Indians filed an unsuccessful suit, claiming the island belonged to them under a Sioux treaty that gave them possession of "unused federal land." In 1969 a small party of Native Americans landed on the island and occupied it until 1971 when they conceded that their efforts to "reclaim" the island were futile.

map study

Location Indians made up less than one percent of the total U.S. population by 1980. However, note on the map that federal reservations are located in the majority of states. Does your state include a federal Indian reservation?

Critical Thinking
Compare land area of reservations located in the eastern and western United States. Where are the largest reservations? Why might this be so?

in the South and the West had different interests from those in the Northeast.

The existence of racial, ethnic, and religious diversity had been the source of many conflicts and adjustments for more than three centuries. In the 1960s, perhaps more than at any other moment in American history, that diversity erupted and helped redefine the nation's life. African Americans, students, and women all raised challenges to traditional practices and institutions. So did other groups who felt excluded from the centers of American life.

Native Americans.   No group had deeper or more justifiable grievances against the prevailing culture than American Indians—or Native Americans, as they began to call themselves in the 1960s. By the 1960s the rapidly growing Indian population was the least prosperous, least healthy, and least stable group in the nation. Indian unemployment rates were ten times as high as the national rate. They were particularly high on the reservations, where nearly half the Indians lived. Life expectancy among Indians was 20 years lower than the national average. Educational and employment opportunities were limited.

In 1961 representatives of 67 Indian tribes gathered in Chicago to begin the effort to attract attention to Native American grievances. They issued a Declaration of Indian Purpose declaring their "right to choose our own way of life." In 1968 a group of young Native Americans, inspired in part by the Black Power Movement, established the **American Indian Movement** (AIM). The movement received enough attention in Washington to help gain inclusion of Indians in the 1968 Civil Rights Act. Most Native Americans wanted a great deal more, however.

By 1968 AIM and other insurgent groups were becoming militant in demanding their rights. They fought with government officials over fishing rights in what they claimed were "tribal waters." They seized the abandoned federal prison on Alcatraz Island in San Francisco Bay and claimed it as Indian land. In 1972 militants occupied the offices of the Bureau of Indian Affairs in Washington, D.C. A year later, they seized the town of **Wounded Knee**, South

My Own Kind of American

The 1960s brought a new emphasis on the cultural diversity of the United States. Many Americans stepped forward to express pride in their racial and ethnic heritage. In 1964 one middle class Mexican American explained his sense of citizenship. How does John Salazar's very name express his dual heritage?

My first name is English and my second name is Spanish. My ancestry is Mexican, but if you ask me what I am, I'll tell you I'm an American and I'm a good American. I've worked for this country and fought for it. I would also die for it. But I want the right to be my own kind of American. I would no more renounce my Mexican heritage than the Anglos would renounce the English language. I am just as American as the Anglos, but my ancestors came from Mexico. I'm a Mexican American and I'm proud of it. We Mexican Americans can contribute to the greatness of our country. All we need to do is organize, state our wishes, and vote.

Dakota, holding it for two months while demanding changes in the reservation system.

Many Indian tribes also began filing law suits to regain lands and rights they claimed had been promised them in old treaties but then had been taken away by the government. By the early 1970s, some tribes were winning significant victories in these efforts.

Hispanic Americans. Many Hispanic Americans also responded to the turbulent climate of the late 1960s by developing a sense of ethnic identification and organizing for political and economic power. Far more numerous than Native Americans (more than nine million according to the 1970 census), Hispanics were also highly diverse in origin. Some were Puerto Rican immigrants, concentrated in New York City. Some were Cuban refugees, many of them living in southern Florida. Mexican Americans, who lived mostly in Texas, California, and other areas of the Southwest, made up the largest group of Hispanics. The

Mexican American group included descendants of families who had been living in Mexican territory when it was incorporated into the United States in the mid-19th century. It also included an uncounted (and growing) number of illegal immigrants who had come to America in search of employment.

Affluent, middle-class Hispanic Americans enjoyed impressive successes in the 1960s and 1970s in occupying major positions of political and economic power. They won seats in Congress, governorships, and mayoralties. They rose to the head of major businesses and professions. Most Hispanic Americans however, continued to encounter poverty and discrimination in much the same way that African Americans did.

Hispanics produced no civil rights movement equivalent to that of African Americans, women, or Native Americans. One group, however, attracted significant attention by organizing to protest oppression. In California,

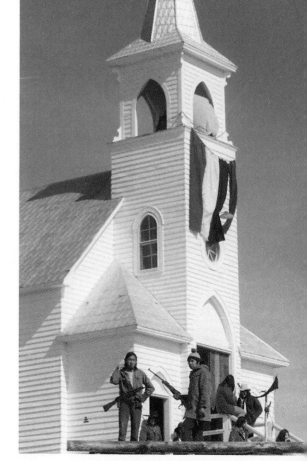

Native Americans from AIM stand guard in their two-month occupation of Wounded Knee, South Dakota, in 1973.

United Farm Workers leader Cesar Chavez speaks with Salinas, California, farm workers in 1981. Chavez's efforts with migrant farm workers helped spark an outburst of ethnic conciousness among Mexican Americans that swept through urban areas of the Southwest in the late 1960s and early 1970s.

describe a place where members of diverse immigrant groups blend together, or assimilate, by adopting the rules and values of a new society. Some older immigrant groups believed they had advanced in the New World by becoming a part of the melting pot. The more militant racial and ethnic movements of the 1960s, however, involved groups—blacks, Indians, Hispanics—who had long been barred from assimilating by legal and cultural discrimination. These groups seemed less willing to accept the standards of the mainstream society. They were demanding, instead, recognition of their own, distinctive identities. Their demand—a radical challenge to traditional notions of assimilation—was the recognition of ethnic and cultural diversity not as an obstacle to be overcome by the melting pot, but as a very positive force.

the Mexican American farm worker **Cesar Chavez** (who had been born in Arizona) created a union of migrant farm workers, most of whom were Hispanics. His **United Farm Workers** began a long strike against growers in 1965 to demand recognition of the union and increased wages and benefits. It also enlisted the support of liberals and students by organizing a nationwide boycott of table grapes and lettuce grown in the United States. In 1970 Chavez won a major victory when the growers of more than half of California's table grapes signed contracts with his union.

At the same time, some Hispanics were generating controversy by demanding that American public schools teach their children at least in part in Spanish. This call for **bilingualism**, teaching subjects in two languages, generated strong opposition from many non-Hispanics. They saw bilingualism as a threat to the nation's cultural unity.

The efforts of African Americans, Native Americans, Hispanic Americans, and others to emphasize their group identities, was a challenge to the traditional American idea of the "melting pot." Melting pot is a term used to

S E C T I O N 4 R E V I E W

Identify Key People and Terms
Write a sentence to identify: Tom Hayden, SDS, Free Speech Movement, counterculture, hippies, Betty Friedan, National Organization for Women, American Indian Movement, Cesar Chavez, United Farm Workers, bilingualism

Locate Key Places
1. Where is Haight-Ashbury located?
2. Where is Wounded Knee located?

Master the Main Ideas
1. **Analyzing reform movements:** Why did many northern white students turn to social activism?
2. **Studying cultural developments:** What were some of the ways in which the counterculture rejected traditional standards?
3. **Analyzing reform movements:** What caused the resurgence of feminism?
4. **Analyzing reform movements:** What were some of the gains made by ethnic groups during the 1960s?

Apply Critical Thinking Skills: Making Comparisons
In the 1960s some observers noted that the melting pot had changed to a tossed salad. What did they mean?

"What Keeps the Women Home?"

20A

TIME FRAME
1963

GEOGRAPHIC SETTING
United States

The 1960s were a time of change for women. This change resulted in part from a book, *The Feminine Mystique,* published by Betty Friedan (1921–   ) in 1963. In it, she accused advertising writers, educators, psychiatrists, and others of promoting what she labeled "the feminine mystique"—the idea that women could find fulfillment only in their roles as wives and mothers. Friedan argued that there was an overemphasis on becoming the "perfect" wife and mother to the exclusion of all other interests and occupations. She said that women should not feel compelled to conform to limited views of the ideal woman. In the following excerpts from this influential book, Friedan described how American business profited from the feminine mystique.

W hat keeps the women home? What force in our culture is strong enough to write "Occupation: housewife" so large that all the other possibilities for women
5 have been almost obscured?

Powerful forces in this nation must be served by those pretty domestic pictures that stare at us everywhere, forbidding a woman to use her own abilities in the
10 world. . . . When one begins to think about it, America depends rather heavily on women's passive dependence, their femininity. . . .

If, despite the nameless desperation of
15 so many American housewives, despite the opportunities open to all women now, so few have any purpose in life other than to be a wife and mother, somebody, something pretty powerful must be at
20 work. The energy behind the feminist movement [of the early 20th century] was too dynamic merely to have trickled dry; it must have been turned off, diverted, by something more powerful than that
25 underestimated power of women.

There are certain facts of life so obvious and mundane that one never talks about them. . . . Why is it never said that the really crucial function, the really impor-
30 tant role that women serve as housewives is *to buy more things for the house.* In all the talk of femininity and woman's role, one forgets that the real business of America is business. But the perpetuation of
35 housewifery, the growth of the feminine mystique, makes sense (and dollars) when one realizes that women are the chief customers of American business. Somehow, somewhere, someone must
40 have figured out that women will buy more things if they are kept in the underused, nameless-yearning, energy-to-get-rid-of-state of being housewives.

I have no idea how it happened. Deci-
45 sion-making in industry is not as simple, as rational, as those who believe the conspiratorial theories of history would have

Betty Friedan, pictured at right, poses with her influential book, *The Feminine Mystique*. A mother and daughter inspect a sheet of cookies in this vintage domestic scene shown below. Since the Second World War, advertising art directors and photograhers have excelled in helping to establish and perpetuate trends and tastes.

it. I am sure the heads of General Foods, and General Electric, and General Motors, and Macy's and Gimbel's and the assorted directors of all the companies that make detergents and electric mixers, and red stoves with rounded corners, and synthetic furs, and waxes, and hair coloring, and patterns for home sewing and home carpentry, and lotions for detergent hands, and bleaches to keep the towels pure white, never sat down around a mahogany conference table in a board room on Madison Avenue or Wall Street and voted on a motion: "Gentlemen, I move, in the interests of all, that we begin a concerted $50-billion campaign to stop this dangerous movement of American women out of the home. We've got to keep them housewives . . ."

A thinking vice-president says: "Too many women getting educated. Don't want to stay home. Unhealthy. If they all get to be scientists and such, they won't have time to shop. But how can we keep them home? They want careers now."

"We'll liberate them to have careers at home," the new executive with horn-rimmed glasses and the Ph.D. in psychology suggests. "We'll make home-making creative."

Of course, it didn't happen quite like that. It was not an economic conspiracy directed against women. It was a by-product of our general confusion lately of means with ends; just something that happened to women when the business of producing and selling and investing in business for profit—which is merely the way our economy is organized to serve man's needs efficiently—began to be confused with the purpose of our nation, the end of life itself. . . .

It is easy to see why it happened. I learned *how* it happened when I went to see a man who is paid approximately a million dollars a year for his professional services in manipulating the emotions of American women to serve the needs of business. . . . Properly manipulated ("if you are not afraid of that word," he said), American housewives can be given the sense of identity, purpose, creativity, the self-realization . . . they lack—by the buying of things. I suddenly realized the significance of the boast that women wield 75% of the purchasing power in America. I suddenly saw American women as *victims* of that ghastly gift, that power at the point of purchase.

Discussing the Reading

1. According to Betty Friedan, what is "the feminine mystique"? In her view, how did American business profit from it?

2. Did she think that companies directed an economic conspiracy against women? Explain.

CRITICAL THINKING
Distinguishing Fact from Opinion

In this excerpt, did Betty Friedan provide any facts to support her view of the involvement of American business in the promotion of "the feminine mystique"? If so, what were they?

Mary Crow Dog Describes the Occupation of Wounded Knee

TIME FRAME
1973

GEOGRAPHIC SETTING
South Dakota

On February 27, 1973 a group of Native Americans seized the tiny town of Wounded Knee, South Dakota, to dramatize Indian grievances. Wounded Knee was chosen because it was the site where in 1890 hundreds of Sioux had been massacred by the United States cavalry. Many of the occupiers were members of the radical American Indian Movement (AIM), which had been founded in 1968 by Chippewas in Minneapolis to protest alleged police brutality. Besieged by hundreds of law enforcement officers, the AIM militants held out for 71 days. One of the Native Americans at Wounded Knee was Mary Crow Dog (1953–   ). Pregnant at the time of the siege, she delivered her child during one of the firefights. In the following excerpt from her memoir *Lakota Woman,* she described the seizure of Wounded Knee.

When I heard the words "Wounded Knee" I became very, very serious. Wounded Knee—Cankpe Opi in our language—has a special meaning for our people. There is the long ditch into which the frozen bodies of almost three hundred of our people, mostly women and children, were thrown like so much cordwood. And the bodies are still there in their mass grave, unmarked except for a cement border. Next to the ditch, on a hill, stands the white-painted Catholic church, gleaming in the sunlight, the monument of an alien faith imposed upon the landscape. And below it flows Cankpe Opi Wakpala, the creek along which the women and children were hunted down like animals by Custer's old Seventh, out to avenge themselves for their defeat by butchering the helpless ones. That happened long ago, but no Sioux ever forgot it. . . .

Before we set out for Wounded Knee, Leonard [Crow Dog, AIM leader] and

Wallace Black Elk prayed for all of us with their pipe. I counted some fifty cars full of people. We went right through Pine Ridge. The half-bloods and goons, the marshals and the government snipers on their rooftop, were watching us, expecting us to stop and start a confrontation, but our caravan drove right by them, leaving them wondering. From Pine Ridge it was only eighteen miles more to our destination. Leonard was in the first car and I was way in the back.

Finally, on February 27, 1973, we stood on the hill where the fate of the old Sioux Nation, Sitting Bull's and Crazy Horse's nation, had been decided, and where we, ourselves, came face to face with our fate. We stood silently, some of us wrapped in our blankets, separated by our personal thoughts and feelings, and yet united, shivering a little with excitement and the chill of a fading winter. You could almost hear our heartbeats.

It was not cold on this next-to-last day of February—not for a South Dakota February anyway. Most of us had not even bothered to wear gloves. I could feel a light wind stirring my hair, blowing it gently about my face. There were a few snowflakes in the air. We all felt the presence of the spirits of those lying close by in the long ditch, wondering whether we were about to join them, wondering when the marshals would arrive. We knew that we would not have to wait long for them to make their appearance.

The young men tied eagle feathers to their braids, no longer unemployed kids, juvenile delinquents, or winos, but warriors. I thought of our old warrior societies—the Kit Foxes, the Strong Hearts, the Badgers, the Dog Soldiers. The Kit Foxes—the Tokalas—used to wear long sashes. In the midst of battle, a Tokala would sometimes dismount and pin the end of his sash to the earth. By this he signified his determination to stay and fight on his chosen spot until he was dead, or until a friend rode up and unpinned him, or until victory. Young or old, men or women, we had all become Kit Foxes, and Wounded Knee had become the spot upon which we had pinned ourselves. Soon we would be encircled and there could be no retreat. I could not think of anybody or anything that would "unpin" us. Somewhere, out on the prairie surrounding us, the forces of the government were gathering, the forces of the greatest power on earth. Then and there I decided that I would have my baby at Wounded Knee, no matter what.

Suddenly the spell was broken. Everybody got busy. The men were digging trenches and making bunkers, putting up low walls of cinder blocks, establishing a last-resort defense perimeter around the Sacred Heart Church. Those few who had weapons were checking them, mostly small-bore .22s and old hunting rifles. We had only one automatic weapon, an AK-47 that one Oklahoma boy had brought back from Vietnam as a souvenir. Altogether we had twenty-six firearms—not much compared to what the other side would bring up against us. None of us had any illusions that we could take over Wounded Knee unopposed. Our message to the government was: "Come and discuss our demands or kill us!" Somebody called someone on the outside from a telephone inside the trading post. I could hear him yelling proudly again and again, *"We hold the Knee!"*

Mary Ellen Crow Dog is shown below in a photograph by Richard Erdoes, who collaborated with her on her autobiography, *Lakota Woman,* which records her difficult and extraordinary life as a Native American in contemporary American culture.

Discussing the Reading

1. What was the attitude of Mary Crow Dog and the other Native Americans at Wounded Knee to the presence of a Catholic Church there?

2. What transformation did she see in the young Native American men present at the seizure of Wounded Knee?

CRITICAL THINKING
Recognizing Values

Judging from Mary Crow Dog's account, how did Native American tradition figure in the lives of the Indians at Wounded Knee?

"God Is Beside You on the Picketline"

20C

TIME FRAME
1966

GEOGRAPHIC SETTING
California

In March 1966, in the midst of a long and bitter strike by grape-workers, Mexican American labor organizer Cesar Chavez (1927–) led a 250-mile Easter march from Delano, California, to the state capital, Sacramento, to dramatize the plight of migrant farm laborers. As most of the farm workers were Catholics, the march took on the character of a religious pilgrimage. A sign on the union hall at Delano proclaimed, "God Is Beside You on the Picket Line"; and the marchers carried a banner with the image of the Virgin of Guadalupe, patroness of Mexico. In the following statement, Chavez expressed his view that the farm workers' cause was rooted in their religious faith.

In the "March from Delano to Sacramento" there is a meeting of cultures and traditions; the centuries-old religious tradition of Spanish culture conjoins with the very contemporary cultural syndrome of "demonstration" springing from the spontaneity of the poor, the downtrodden, the rejected, the discriminated against bearing visibly their need and demand for equality and freedom.

In every religion-oriented culture "the pilgrimage" has had a place: a trip made with sacrifice and hardship as an expression of penance and of commitment—and often involving a petition to the patron of the pilgrimage for some sincerely sought benefit of body or soul. Pilgrimage has not passed from Mexican culture. Daily at any of the major shrines of the country and in particular at the Basilica of the Lady of Guadalupe, there arrive pilgrims from all points—some of whom may have long since walked out the pieces of rubber tire that once served them as soles, and many of whom will walk on their knees the last mile or so of the pilgrimage. Many of the "pilgrims" of Delano will have walked such pilgrimages themselves in their lives—perhaps as very small children even—and cling to the memory of the day-long marches, the camps at night, streams forded, hills climbed, the sacral aura of the sanctuary, and the "fiesta" that followed.

But throughout the Spanish-speaking world there is another tradition that touches the present march, that of the Lenten penitential processions, where the *penitentes* would march through the streets, often in sack cloth and ashes, some even carrying crosses, as a sign of penance for their sins, and as a plea for the mercy of God. The penitential procession is also in the blood of the Mexican-American, and the Delano march will therefore be one of penance—public penance for the sins of the strikers, their own personal sins as well as their yielding perhaps to feelings of hatred and revenge in the strike itself. They hope by the march to set themselves at peace with the Lord, so that the justice of their cause will be purified of all lesser motivation.

These two great traditions of a great people meet in the Mexican-American with the belief that Delano is his "cause," his great demand for justice, freedom, and respect from a predominantly foreign cultural community in a land where he was first. The revolutions of Mexico were primarily uprisings of the poor, fighting for bread and for dignity. The Mexican-American is also a child of the revolution.

Pilgrimage, penance, and revolution. The pilgrimage from Delano to Sacramento has strong religio-cultural overtones. But it is also the pilgrimage of a cultural minority which has suffered from a hostile environment, and a minority which means business.

Cesar Chavez (center) joins a group of protestors at a farm workers' rally where symbols and emblems of the United States, Catholicism, and Mexican-American culture mingle. In the early 1960s Chavez was successful, where others had failed, in organizing the first agricultural workers' union, the United Farm Workers.

Discussing the Reading

1. What "meeting of cultures and traditions" did Cesar Chavez identify in the farm workers' march to Sacramento?

2. What function of "purification" did Chavez hope the march might serve?

CRITICAL THINKING
Making Comparisons

Compare the religious values underlying the songs of the civil rights movement (Source Reading 19B) with those identified by Cesar Chavez in his statement.

817

Chapter Summary

Write supporting details under each of the following main ideas as you review the chapter.

Section 1
1. Kennedy barely defeated Nixon.
2. Kennedy's charisma captured American hearts.
3. Johnson pushed Kennedy's programs.

Section 2
1. The federal government expanded social welfare programs.
2. The government waged a War on Poverty.
3. The Great Society programs had mixed results.

Section 3
1. Kennedy developed a more active foreign policy.
2. The Bay of Pigs invasion ended disastrously.
3. The United States confronted the Soviet Union in Germany and Cuba.
4. Johnson continued Kennedy's foreign policy.

Section 4
1. The civil rights movement spawned social activism.
2. The counterculture rejected traditional standards and styles.
3. Feminism experienced a rebirth.
4. Ethnic groups gained more power.

Chapter Themes

1. **Constitutional and representative government:** Congress and President Johnson cooperated to enact more than 200 pieces of landmark social legislation during the 1960s including key civil rights legislation for African Americans and women.
2. **Racial, ethnic, religious diversity:** During the 1960s ethnic groups such as African Americans, Native Americans, and Hispanic Americans demanded that the American dream be opened to them.

Chapter Study Guide

Identifying Key People and Terms

Name the key person or key term that describes the:
1. domestic program of John F. Kennedy
2. federally subsidized health care plan for the elderly
3. new foreign policy approach that replaced massive retaliation
4. organization created in 1966 to focus on feminist issues

Locating Key Places

1. In what country did the United States stage the abortive Bay of Pigs invasion and also force the Soviet Union to close its nuclear missile bases?
2. In which state did Cesar Chavez begin his successful grape boycott?

Mastering the Main Ideas

1. In what ways were the programs of the New Frontier and the Great Society similar?
2. Through which programs did the government attempt to improve the welfare of the young, the poor, and the elderly?
3. What was the two-pronged approach Kennedy used to exert American influence against communism in the Third World?
4. How was Tom Hayden typical of the New Left?

Applying Critical Thinking Skills

1. **Identifying assumptions:** What assumptions did both Kennedy and Johnson hold about the role of the federal government in improving the lives of the poor in America?
2. **Identifying central issues:** How does the name of Johnson's program—Great Society—reflect the outlook of many Americans in the 1960s?
3. **Recognizing values: (a)** How did the values of the Soviet leaders change in 1964? **(b)** How did this affect relations between the superpowers?
4. **Drawing conclusions:** How is the Peace Corps a living example of Kennedy's inaugural speech admonition: "Ask not what your country can do for you—ask what you can do for your country"?

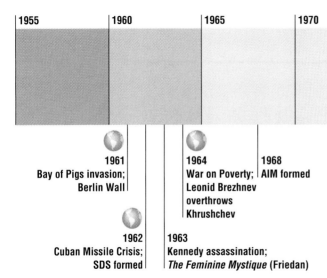

1955	1960	1965	1970	1975

1961
Bay of Pigs invasion;
Berlin Wall

1962
Cuban Missile Crisis;
SDS formed

1964
War on Poverty;
Leonid Brezhnev
overthrows
Khrushchev

1963
Kennedy assassination;
The Feminine Mystique (Friedan)

1968
AIM formed

Chapter Activities

Learning Geography Through History

1. Measure the distance between Florida and Cuba. Then use that information to explain why Kennedy so vehemently opposed the installation of Soviet missiles in Cuba in 1962.

2. What geographical reasons might be sighted for expanding American influence through the Alliance for Progress?

Relating the United States to the World

By 1965 most of the European colonial empires in Africa and Asia had been dismantled. Despite independence, most new African nations had severe social, political, and economic problems. Why did both the United States and the Soviet Union want to aid these countries?

Linking Past to Present

1. How have economic and political opportunity changed for women since the 1960s?

2. (a) Why was the Berlin Wall built in 1961? **(b)** Why was it torn down in 1989?

Practicing Critical Thinking Strategies

Checking Consistency

Which of the following statements would not be consistent with President Kennedy's foreign policy?

A. Eisenhower's policy of massive retaliation is appropriate for the 1960s.

B. The United States must stop the spread of communism in the world.

C. America needs to repair the badly deteriorating relationship between itself and Latin America.

D. The United States needs to develop "counterinsurgency" forces to stop communism.

Using the Time Line

1. What two events involved a Caribbean neighbor of the United States?

2. Which group on the time line was formed primarily to help achieve equal opportunity for its members?

Learning More About the Turbulent 1960s

1. Using Source Readings: Read the Source Readings for this chapter and answer the questions.

2. Using Literature: Read the excerpt from Scott Momaday's *The Way to Rainy Mountain*, which unites past and present in its account of the traditions of the Kiowa, on pages 900–901, and then answer the question.

3. Using the media: Watch the video "Woodstock." Analyze the dress and behavior of the participants, the lyrics of the music, and the reaction of the police and other authority figures. Using your analysis, write a two- or three-paragraph essay about the purpose and effectiveness of the counterculture of the 1960s.

4. Using sources: Read Chapter 19 of *Bury My Heart at Wounded Knee* by Dee Brown. Explain why militant Native American groups chose Wounded Knee, South Dakota, for their protest in 1973.

Linking Past
to Present

The 58,000 Americans
who died in the
Vietnam War live on in
memory at the starkly
beautiful Vietnam
Veterans Memorial in
Washington, D.C.
Marines, inset, defend
Khe Sanh, near the
border between North
and South Vietnam,
where some of the
most intense fighting
took place.
"Just waitin' and
diggin'," one marine
lamented about the 77
tense, bloody days of
battle. "That's all
we're doing. Just
waitin' and diggin'."

The Vietnam War and its Aftermath

1 9 5 4 — 1 9 8 2

21

On a July afternoon in 1965, President Lyndon Johnson walked into the East Room of the White House looking unusually grim. He was there to make a public announcement that would change the course of American history.

For some time, American military forces had been involved in a frustrating war against communist revolutionaries in South Vietnam. The GI's were there as "advisers," not combatants. Now, however, their mission had changed, Johnson reluctantly admitted. American troops would become actively involved in fighting the communist foe in Vietnam.

The president read a letter he had received from the mother of a U.S. soldier asking why it was necessary for Americans to fight in such a distant land. Johnson tried to explain that stopping communism in Vietnam was part of America's effort to stop communism everywhere. If Vietnam fell, so would other nations. Already, however, many Americans were beginning to question that explanation and to challenge the wisdom of the commitment to Vietnam. Within three years, those doubts would grow to become the basis of an enormous antiwar movement. How did the United States become involved in this strange and difficult war? Why was the American commitment so unpopular and so difficult to sustain?

CHAPTER PREVIEW

In this chapter you will learn about the Vietnam War and its long-term effects on the nation.

SECTIONS IN THIS CHAPTER:
1. **America gradually became involved in Vietnam.**
2. **President Johnson escalated the war.**
3. **Turbulence characterized 1968.**
4. **The war ended in 1975.**

1950	1955	1960	1965	1970	1975	1980	1985

1954
Geneva Accords partition Vietnam

1964
Congress approves Gulf of Tonkin Resolution

1975
Vietnam War ends

1982
Vietnam Veterans Memorial is dedicated in Washington D.C.

1970
National Guard kills student protesters at Kent State; police kill demonstrators at Jackson State

1972
Chinese-American relations improve after Nixon's historic visit to China

America gradually became involved in Vietnam.

Key Terms: Vietminh, domino theory, Geneva Accords, Viet Cong

Reading Preview
As you read this section, you will learn:

1. what Ho Chi Minh wished to achieve.
2. what type of government Ngo Dinh Diem established in South Vietnam.
3. how Diem responded to increased opposition from the Viet Cong.

French colonial rule in Vietnam could be summarized by this photograph of a 19th-century French woman and her Vietnamese rickshaw "driver." The French colonists, exploiting the availability of cheap labor, were able to live as well as the wealthiest Parisians. The Vietnamese, meanwhile, were forced to become little more than the servants of their French masters.

America's involvement in Vietnam began almost unnoticed in 1945. Vietnam had for many years been a colony of France. During World War II, the Japanese had seized control of the nation. After the defeat of Japan, the French wanted it back.

Ho Chi Minh sought Vietnamese independence.

Although France wanted Vietnam, a powerful nationalist movement had formed within that southeast Asian nation. The nationalist leader was **Ho Chi Minh**, a communist educated in Paris and Moscow, who was determined to win independence for his nation. To counter the French, Ho looked to the United States for help in 1945. He received no response, however, partly because his nation seemed so insignificant to American leaders and partly because his communist convictions were unacceptable to the architects of the Cold War.

Even so, Ho Chi Minh managed to launch a major challenge to the French attempt to reassert authority in Vietnam. His organization, the **Vietminh**, received substantial aid from the Soviet Union and, after 1949, communist China. The United States, in the meantime, was supporting the French. As war between France and the Vietminh grew fiercer in the early 1950s, America paid increasingly more of the French war costs.

In 1954, however, the French position grew desperate. Early in that year, 12,000 French troops became surrounded by Vietminh forces at the city of **Dien Bien Phu**. (As you can see on the map on page 823, Dien Bien Phu is in northern Vietnam.) The French government appealed to the United States for help. Some members of the Eisenhower Administration urged that American forces intervene in the conflict to rescue the French. A few of them even recommended using nuclear weapons against the Vietminh. Eisenhower himself spoke publicly about the importance of maintaining a "free" Vietnam and endorsed the so-called **domino theory**—the idea that if Vietnam fell to communism, the rest of Asia would soon follow.

In the end, Eisenhower refused to intervene to save the French. He was convinced that any such effort would be too costly and difficult. The defense of Dien Bien Phu collapsed on May 7, 1954, and the French agreed to negotiate a settlement of the conflict at an international conference scheduled for that summer in Geneva, Switzerland.

As you can see on the map at right, the **Geneva Accords**, the settlement agreed upon at the conference, established a supposedly temporary division of Vietnam along the 17th parallel. Ho Chi Minh and his followers would govern the northern part of the nation. An anticommunist regime tied to the West would govern the south. Democratic elections planned for 1956 would determine the terms for uniting the two parts of the country.

South Vietnam established a pro-American government.

As the French withdrew from Vietnam, the United States increased its own role there. The Eisenhower Administration was willing to accept a partition of Vietnam, but not willing to accept reunification under a communist regime. Realizing that the Vietminh would likely win any election in Vietnam, the United States did not sign the Geneva Accords. Instead, it helped establish a pro-American government in the south headed by **Ngo Dinh Diem**, a wealthy member of the country's Roman Catholic minority. With assurances of American military support, Diem refused to permit the promised elections. Instead, he set out to consolidate his power in the diverse and factionalized new nation of South Vietnam.

The North Vietnamese government of Ho Chi Minh, based in the city of **Hanoi**, never accepted the division of the country. For several years after the Geneva Accords, however, it made few active efforts to force reunification. Nonetheless, Ho had left many reunification supporters behind in the south when the nation was partitioned in 1954. They remained ready to revive the struggle.

Diem asked for American aid.

By 1958 forces loyal to Ho had launched a new civil war in the south, encouraged and supplied by Hanoi. In 1960 they organized the National Front for the Liberation of Vietnam (NLF), known to its opponents as the **Viet Cong**, or Vietnamese communists. When they gradually escalated their military challenge to the Diem regime, Diem appealed to the United States for more assistance. In response, the

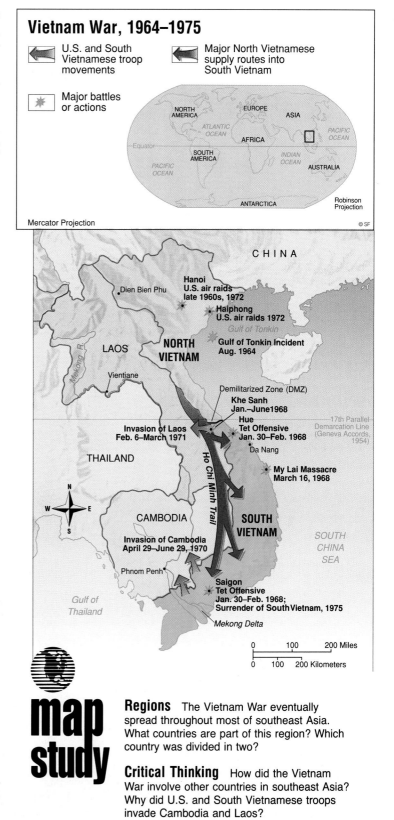

Vietnam War, 1964–1975

U.S. and South Vietnamese troop movements

Major North Vietnamese supply routes into South Vietnam

Major battles or actions

Mercator Projection

Robinson Projection

© SF

CHINA

Dien Bien Phu

Hanoi
U.S. air raids
late 1960s, 1972

Haiphong
U.S. air raids 1972

Gulf of Tonkin

Gulf of Tonkin Incident
Aug. 1964

LAOS

NORTH VIETNAM

Vientiane

Demilitarized Zone (DMZ)

Khe Sanh
Jan.–June1968

Hue
Tet Offensive
Jan. 30–Feb. 1968

Invasion of Laos
Feb. 6–March 1971

17th Parallel Demarcation Line (Geneva Accords, 1954)

Da Nang

THAILAND

My Lai Massacre
March 16, 1968

Ho Chi Minh Trail

CAMBODIA

Invasion of Cambodia
April 29–June 29, 1970

SOUTH VIETNAM

SOUTH CHINA SEA

Phnom Penh

Gulf of Thailand

Saigon
Tet Offensive
Jan. 30–Feb. 1968;
Surrender of SouthVietnam, 1975

Mekong Delta

0   100   200 Miles
0   100   200 Kilometers

map study

Regions The Vietnam War eventually spread throughout most of southeast Asia. What countries are part of this region? Which country was divided in two?

Critical Thinking How did the Vietnam War involve other countries in southeast Asia? Why did U.S. and South Vietnamese troops invade Cambodia and Laos?

Children, right, receive religious instruction at downtown Saigon's Market Temple. Although Saigon was called the "Paris of the Orient" and French culture was embraced by the wealthy, most Vietnamese remained Buddhist. Below, Thich Quang Duc, a Buddhist monk, protested Diem's harsh policies against Buddhists by setting himself on fire June 11, 1963. The immolation was witnessed by millions of television viewers around the world.

Eisenhower Administration sent additional weapons and about 650 military advisers. At the beginning of the Kennedy Administration, the American presence in South Vietnam remained small.

The plight of the South Vietnamese government grew steadily worse during the Kennedy years. The United States responded to each setback with more weapons and advisers. By 1963 American military personnel in South Vietnam numbered more than 15,000. They were of little help, however. The Diem regime continued to have little success in combatting the Viet Cong. At the same time, Diem created a major religious crisis by instituting harsh policies toward the country's Buddhists, who formed a majority of the nation's population. Brutal government raids of Buddhist temples particularly outraged members of the religion. Several Buddhist monks set themselves afire in the streets of **Saigon**—the capital of South Vietnam—to protest government policies. Americans who saw the events on television were horrified.

Members of the Kennedy Administration gradually realized that the war in Vietnam could not be won without removing Diem.

American officials gave quiet assurances to a number of South Vietnamese military leaders that they would not oppose an effort to topple the regime. Early in November 1963, these leaders staged a coup, seized control of the government, and executed Diem and his brother. Kennedy was shocked by the executions. In addition, he could not have taken much comfort from the character of the new government, an unstable military regime that seemed even less likely than that of Diem to bring order to South Vietnam. Before he could formulate a policy to deal with the new situation, however, Kennedy himself was killed in Dallas, Texas.

SECTION 1 REVIEW

Identify Key People and Terms
Write a sentence to identify: Ho Chi Minh, Vietminh, domino theory, Geneva Accords, Ngo Dinh Diem, Viet Cong

Locate Key Places

1. Where is the city of Dien Bien Phu located?
2. What were the capitals of North and South Vietnam?

Master the Main Ideas

1. **Respecting values in other cultures:** What values prompted Ho Chi Minh to seek Vietnamese independence?
2. **Perceiving cause/effect relationships:** Why do you think Diem established a pro-American government in South Vietnam?
3. **Analyzing information:** What was the result of American aid sent to Vietnam between 1960 and 1963?

Apply Critical Thinking Skills: Checking Consistency
How was the U.S. decision not to sign the Geneva Accords consistent with the Truman Doctrine? (The Truman Doctrine was a commitment to resist and contain communism anywhere in the world.)

SECTION 2

President Johnson escalated the war.

Key Terms: Gulf of Tonkin Resolution, napalm, pacification, My Lai massacre

Reading Preview
As you read this section, you will learn:

1. what happened when the North Vietnamese allegedly attacked an American destroyer in the Gulf of Tonkin.
2. what Johnson did about the Vietnam War after he won the 1964 presidential election.
3. what factor helped create a stalemate in the war.
4. how most U.S. soldiers described their experiences in Vietnam.
5. how the nation felt about the war in the mid-1960s.

One of the first things Lyndon Johnson did upon becoming president on November 22, 1963, was to discuss the situation in Vietnam with the men who had advised Kennedy—Secretary of Defense Robert McNamara and National Security Adviser McGeorge Bundy. Johnson immediately committed himself to continuing what they assured him were the late president's policies. Strongly anticommunist himself, Johnson was already inclined to sustain the American commitment in Indochina. As the untested successor to a revered and martyred president, moreover, he felt obligated to carry on Kennedy's work. Most important, however, a continued American commitment to South Vietnam was fully consistent with the basic outlines of the foreign policy both Republicans and Democrats had embraced for nearly 20 years. The containment doctrine, as it was put into practice in the late 1940s, committed the United States to opposing communist expansion anywhere in the world. Johnson, like Eisenhower and Kennedy before him, believed in the domino theory. If Vietnam fell to communism, he warned, other nations in the region would soon follow.

American presence in Vietnam grew after the Gulf of Tonkin incident.

During his first months in office, President Johnson sent only 5,000 additional American military advisers to Vietnam and made plans to send only 5,000 more. Still, Johnson was uneasy about the situation in Vietnam and eager for congressional authorization to provide additional support to South Vietnam if that became necessary. Late in the summer, he got his authorization.

The Administration announced in August that an American destroyer on patrol in international waters in the **Gulf of Tonkin** had been attacked by North Vietnamese torpedo boats. (As you can see on the map on page 823, the Gulf of Tonkin borders southern China and southern North Vietnam.) Information later became public that raised doubts about whether the attack had been as "unprovoked," as the Administration maintained, and even whether it had occurred at all. At the time, however, few doubted the authenticity of what became known as the Gulf of Tonkin incident. Johnson asked Congress for a resolution of support. The House of Representatives unanimously approved a measure—known as the **Gulf of Tonkin Resolution**—authorizing the president to "take all necessary measures" to protect American forces and "prevent further aggression" in Vietnam. The Senate then approved it by a vote of 88 to 2. Johnson considered the resolution a legal authorization to continue and, if necessary, expand the war.

Johnson escalated the war after the 1964 election.

Johnson managed to postpone any further major decisions until after his victory in the 1964 election. He attacked his Republican opponent, **Barry Goldwater**, for advocating escalation in Vietnam and promised that he was "not going to send American boys nine or ten thousand miles away from home to do what Asian boys ought to be doing for themselves." By early

map study

LOGISTICS IN A GUERRILLA WAR

Movement Logistics in military terms means the planning and carrying out of a large-scale operation for movement of troops and supplies. The Vietnam War was a logistical nightmare for the United States. The war was fought 9,000 miles from America's shores and required tons of supplies daily. As the map at right shows, the United States had to ship all supplies first to bases in the Pacific and then to fortified positions along the Vietnam coast. Once the supplies were in Vietnam, they had to be protected from Viet Cong guerrillas who easily blended into the civilian population and even obtained jobs on U.S. military bases. Thus, although American forces established defenses around U.S. bases, the areas were never totally secure. Bombs planted by the enemy sometimes shattered base movie theaters and mess halls as haunting reminders of the unpredictability of guerrilla warfare.

North Vietnam sent many of its supplies south along the Ho Chi Minh Trail, shown in red on the map. The trail, following traditional paths through mountainous jungles in Laos and Cambodia to empty into South Vietnam, was gradually widened into a road capable of handling heavy trucks and thousands of troops. Along the trail, support facilities, often built underground to escape American detection and air strikes, included hospitals, fuel storage tanks, and storage caches, or hiding places. Throughout the war, United States forces tried but failed to effectively disrupt the flow of supplies and soldiers south.

The Viet Cong tunnel complex created almost insurmountable problems for American troops. Tunnel systems allowed the Viet Cong to appear and disappear almost by magic. The map illustrates the most famous tunnel complex located under Cu Chi about 25 miles north of Saigon. Note the conference rooms, sleeping chambers, storage halls, and kitchens built into this complex. American forces bombed, gassed, and cleared the jungle around Cu Chi but failed to destroy the tunnels. "Tunnel rats"—South Vietnamese soldiers and short, wiry U.S. combat engineer SWAT teams—fought heroically in the tunnels, but they too were unable to destroy the complexes. Study the tunnel diagram. What kinds of rooms were part of the tunnels?

Critical Thinking Describe the protective and safety devices built into the tunnel system. Why were these devices necessary?

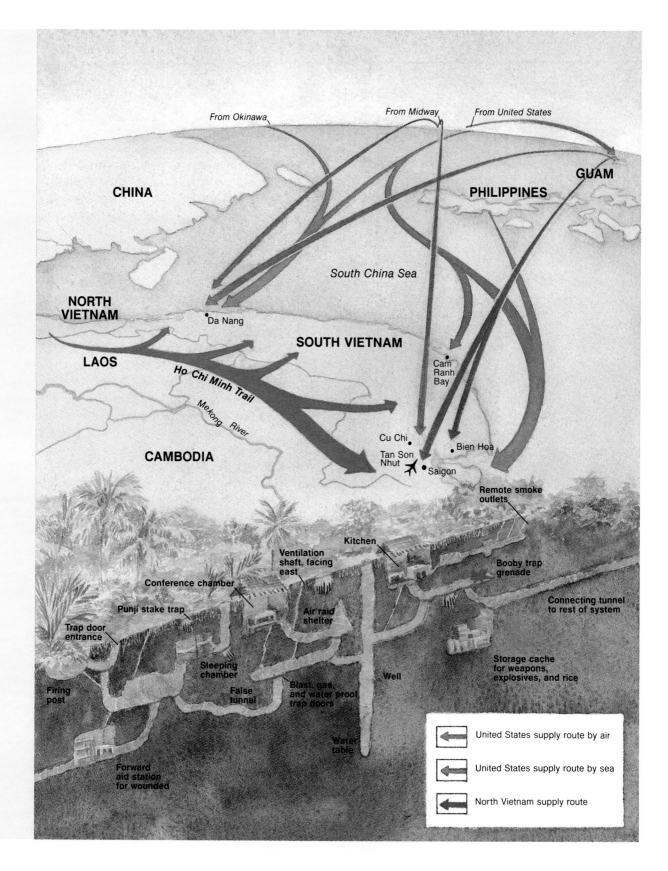

From Okinawa   From Midway   From United States

CHINA

GUAM

PHILIPPINES

South China Sea

NORTH
VIETNAM

• Da Nang

SOUTH VIETNAM

LAOS

Ho Chi Minh Trail

Cam
Ranh
Bay

Mekong River

CAMBODIA

Cu Chi

Tan Son
Nhut

✈
• Saigon

• Bien Hoa

Remote smoke
outlets

Kitchen

Ventilation
shaft, facing
east

Conference chamber

Booby trap
grenade

Punji stake trap

Air raid
shelter

Connecting tunnel
to rest of system

Trap door
entrance

Sleeping
chamber

Well

Storage cache
for weapons,
explosives, and rice

Firing
post

False
tunnel

Blast, gas,
and water proof
trap doors

Water
table

Forward
aid station
for wounded

←	United States supply route by air
←	United States supply route by sea
←	North Vietnam supply route

He continued to insist that Americans would not be actively engaged in combat. The marines, he said, were there to protect American bases. However, the United States now had more than 100,000 troops in South Vietnam. Contrary to popular belief, many of them were actively engaged in combat.

In July 1965 Johnson finally admitted that the American role in Vietnam had changed. United States troops, he announced, would now openly engage the enemy. They would do what Americans had not done since Korea: they would fight a ground war in Asia. By the end of 1965, about 180,000 American troops were in Vietnam. That number grew to nearly 400,000 a year later and to more than 500,000 by the end of 1967. Casualties also increased. At the end of 1963, less than 500 Americans had died in Vietnam. By the spring of 1966, more than 4,000 had been killed.

The infusion of American combat troops prevented the collapse of South Vietnam. The United States also succeeded in 1965 in installing a reasonably stable government in the south under General Nguyen Van Thieu. The war was far from being won, however. Although the Thieu regime managed to survive longer than most of its predecessors, it was unable to establish control over the countryside. The Viet Cong, not the Thieu regime, controlled a majority of South Vietnam's hamlets and villages.

Tough North Vietnamese resistance created a stalemate.

For the next seven years, American and South Vietnamese forces struggled to bring the war to a close. Although American officials spoke optimistically about progress, little evidence of it existed. The war had become a stalemate. The United States was preventing the communists from winning the war, but it was not defeating them.

Increased bombing. The bombing that the United States had begun in 1964 increased in succeeding years. Johnson correctly believed that the war in the south was being sustained by supplies from the north, and he concluded that the hostilities would stop only

Weighted down by heavy equipment, U.S. Marines conduct a search-and-destroy mission near the demilitarized zone. Although such missions often resulted in no enemy encounters, the ever-present danger of being fired upon by a camouflaged sniper or stepping on a branch-covered mine produced relentless stress.

1965, however, the military situation had grown so perilous to the South Vietnamese government that the United States faced a choice between escalation and defeat. Johnson chose escalation.

With the South Vietnamese government in complete disarray, the United States gradually assumed the major responsibility for fighting the war. In February 1965 Viet Cong forces attacked an American military base in South Vietnam, killing seven marines. Johnson retaliated by ordering American planes to bomb targets in North Vietnam. He hoped to destroy important transportation lines that supplied the Viet Cong's war needs. The bombing, once begun, continued off and on for seven years.

In March 1965 Johnson sent two battalions of marines to **Da Nang**, which, as the map on page 823 shows, is in northern South Vietnam.

if the North Vietnamese themselves felt the pressure. In March 1965 he launched Operation Rolling Thunder, a massive bombing of the north that turned large areas of the countryside into crater-pitted moonscapes. The North Vietnamese people suffered greatly from the bombing, but the attacks had no apparent effect on their willingness or ability to continue the war. If anything, many historians eventually concluded, the bombing strengthened their will to resist what they considered American aggression and imperialism.

Although the U.S. bombing claimed many lives, it failed to destroy the nation's munitions factories, which were scattered throughout North Vietnam and often hidden underground. The bombing also failed to seriously reduce the flow of North Vietnamese soldiers into the South, where they joined the Viet Cong forces and ultimately took over the war almost entirely from them. The United States tried to identify and bomb the jungle supply route the North Vietnamese troops used in their journey south, a route known as the **Ho Chi Minh Trail**. (You can follow this trail on the map on page 827.) However, much of that route ran through neighboring Laos, which for a time the United States was reluctant to attack. In any case, the North Vietnamese usually were able to alter their path on short notice in the face of an air attack.

Americans experienced similar frustrations on the ground. The United States possessed a much larger, better equipped, and more technologically sophisticated army than did its adversaries. Consequently, whenever Americans engaged the Viet Cong or the North Vietnamese in a conventional battle, the Americans won. However, not until very late in the conflict, after the Americans had largely departed, did Vietnam become primarily a conventional war. In the late 1960s, it was a guerrilla war, a type of war American soldiers were unaccustomed to fighting.

Geographical link to the stalemate.

Vietnam's geography played a very important part in undermining the American war effort. Much of the country was covered with jungles and rice paddies, making troop movement extremely difficult. The dense foliage provided the communists with natural cover from which to launch sneak attacks and ambushes, the key strategies used in guerrilla warfare. The vegetation also provided ideal hiding places for booby traps and mines.

With the aid of the natural environment, the Viet Cong and the North Vietnamese infiltrated hamlets, villages, and towns throughout South Vietnam. The enemy, which included significant numbers of women and children, often was indistinguishable from the rest of the population. Many enemy soldiers wore no uniforms. They worked in small groups and were thus able to move about inconspicuously. Because of the area's geography, American soldiers spent much of their time on patrols known as search-and-destroy missions, or "S and Ds," as the soldiers called them, looking for the enemy but never certain where or when they would appear.

America tried to compensate for the disadvantages produced by the environment by using its technological superiority. American planes and helicopters dropped **napalm**, a highly flammable kind of jellied gasoline on large areas to kill the thick jungle vegetation that helped the Viet Cong hide. Many innocent civilians were killed or horribly burned in the process, and crops and livestock were destroyed. At the same time, American forces, in the course of their search-and-destroy missions, used bulldozers and flame throwers to flatten or burn villages they considered communist sanctuaries. They also sprayed Agent Orange, a highly toxic defoliant, on thousands of acres of land. Many American soldiers as well as civilians were later afflicted with a wide variety of ailments and genetic disorders thought to be caused by Agent Orange.

In Washington the government issued falsely optimistic reports about supposed progress in Vietnam. It emphasized the large number of enemy casualties and suggested, as Robert McNamara said, that it was possible to "see the light at the end of the tunnel." Few of those who understood the war or who were fighting in it could see that light.

"Puff the Magic Dragon," the name given to the air force AC-47 gunship, provided cover to trapped ground troops throughout the war. The Dragon's Gatling guns fired their ammunition so fast—about 6,000 rounds per minute—that a constant stream of fire appeared to be shooting from their barrels.

By 1967 the American commander in South Vietnam, General **William Westmoreland**, was committed to an ambitious **pacification** program. Its purpose was to rout the Viet Cong from important areas not just by defeating them militarily, but by winning the "hearts and minds" of the local population. The program enjoyed limited success. American troops had difficulty establishing the same kind of rapport with provincial Vietnamese that the native forces of the Viet Cong were able to create. Even when they did, however, the American troops were often unable to counter the techniques of terror and intimidation the communists used to discourage local people from cooperating with the Americans.

The principal effect of the American strategies on the people of the south was to uproot them. The bombing, the search-and-destroy missions, the free-fire zones, and other tactics destroyed homes and sent villagers fleeing into cities or camps. By the end of 1967, South Vietnam had more than three million refugees.

As the war continued with no victory in sight, some American officers and officials tried to persuade Johnson to expand the fighting. Some called for more bombing, some for a much larger commitment of troops, some for attacking communist enclaves in neighboring countries. Johnson resisted such requests. Although Johnson was unwilling to abandon Vietnam, afraid that failing to meet a commitment would destroy America's "credibility" in the world, he was also reluctant to risk provoking communist China or the Soviet Union into intervening directly in the war.

U.S. soldiers found Vietnam an intensely frustrating experience.

Nearly three million American men and women served in the Vietnam War before it was over. Early in the war, most U.S. troops were trained professional soldiers, many of them members of the Special Forces. As time went on and the American presence grew, however, more and more of the soldiers sent to Vietnam were young draftees with no previous military experience. Because the draft laws offered exemptions to college students and to members of some professions, and because many formally educated people found ways to avoid going to the war, the American army in Vietnam over time came to consist of a disproportionate number of young men from the lower rungs of the socio-economic ladder.

American soldiers in Vietnam had diverse opinions about the war. Some believed in the cause for which they were fighting. Some were totally against the war. Some disagreed with the way in which the war was being fought—they wanted the United States to wage an all-out war. Some did not understand the cause for which they were fighting. Some were eager to fight regardless of the cause because they believed it was their patriotic duty to do so. Still others had mixed feelings about the war and their part in it.

Personal feelings aside, virtually all soldiers found the Vietnam War a difficult and frustrating experience. Draftees, in particular, found it hard to develop a commitment to anything beyond staying alive. Combat service in Vietnam was generally restricted to one year, and many young soldiers spent much of their time simply counting the days until their release. As the end grew nearer, they became more and more reluctant to take risks.

Robert Rawls was one of the many African Americans to serve in the war. Rawls had been working for the electric company in Cleveland, Ohio, when he received his draft notice in 1968. Like many other young men, Rawls did everything he could to avoid being drafted. He tried to return to school and join the National Guard. He even got married a few months be-fore his induction, hoping this would influence his local draft board. None of these tactics worked, however. Early in 1969 he arrived in South Vietnam.

After about a week of training, Rawls was assigned as a rifleman to the 1st Cavalry Division in Tay Ninh Province, west of Saigon. He recalled: "The first night they sent me on OP [observation] and I was as scared as I've ever been in my life. I just said, 'How could I do a year over here?'" Over the next few months, his unit conducted search-and-destroy missions, and Rawls began seeing fellow soldiers die all around him:

We got fire fights after fire fights. My first taste of death. **AN AMERICAN ★ SPEAKS** After fire fights you could smell it. They brought the [dead men] back wrapped in ponchos . . . they just threw them up on the helicopter and [piled empty, reusable supply cases] on top of them. You could see the guys' feet hanging out. . . . I had nightmares. . . . I can still see those guys.

On May 19 Rawls was wounded himself. Medics sent him to a medical facility where he said they "just patched me up." Then they sent him back to his unit. He said, "By that time my mind had just snapped. . . . I had a feeling that I wasn't coming back." Once he watched another GI shoot himself in the foot in order to get out of Vietnam. "I thought about doing that to get back home," he recalled.

In the field, Rawls became close friends with white soldiers. He remembered:

Out in the bush everybody was the same. You can't find no racism in the bush. We slept together, ate together, fought together.

In the towns, however, blacks and whites went their separate ways. At one point, when Rawls returned to Vietnam from a short leave in Hong Kong, he stayed in Saigon in an area called "Soul Kitchen," where black GIs clustered after going absent without leave (AWOL). He was found there by MPs and sent back to his unit with an official reprimand.

Rawls' experiences were not unusual. Life was difficult for most Americans in Vietnam.

The culture, the language, the food, and the landscape were all strange to them. Much of the population was suspicious and hostile. No place was safe. The difficulty in identifying the enemy created a temptation to assume that everyone was hostile. Occasionally American troops succumbed to that temptation with terrible results.

In March 1968 a unit of American troops, which had recently suffered severe casualties, entered the village of **My Lai** having received information that it was a Viet Cong stronghold. (My Lai, as you can see on the map on page 823, is on the east coast of northern South Vietnam.) Although the troops found no evidence of enemy activity there, they rounded up the residents of the hamlet, mostly women and children, and began firing on them. More than 200 civilians died. The American public did not learn about the **My Lai massacre** until nearly two years later, at which time the commander of the operation, Lt. **William Calley**, was tried and convicted for the atrocities. Calley's superiors, whom many believed were equally responsible for the massacre, were not charged with any crimes.

The My Lai massacre was not typical of American behavior in Vietnam. American ser-

vice organizations and the soldiers themselves did much to help the Vietnamese cope with the hardships of war. For example, 40,000 Vietnamese teachers were trained and 30,000 new classrooms were built. Programs to increase food production and improve health and sanitary conditions also helped citizens get through the terribly difficult times.

Life among the American soldiers themselves was also often difficult. Racial conflicts between white and black soldiers reflected the racial tensions that were gripping the United States itself at the same time. Widespread drug use to relieve the intense stress of warfare was another problem.

The lack of discernible progress in the war took a great toll on troop morale. In the 1970s in particular, a growing number of soldiers deserted. Some of them simply abandoned their units in Vietnam. Others failed to return after leaves abroad. Many of the troops remaining were by the early 1970s reluctant to put themselves at risk and refused to take assignments they considered too dangerous. Incidents of soldiers killing their own officers, a practice known as fragging, also occurred.

Indeed, fighting in Vietnam was such a terrible experience for many soldiers that the war

A wounded marine reaches out to comfort a more seriously injured buddy moments after enemy soldiers had lobbed grenades into their camp on Hill 484 near the demilitarized zone. Twenty marines lost their lives in the successful defense of the hill.

THE VIETNAM WAR
Skill: Distinguishing False from Accurate Images

Introducing the Skill. The story you have read of Robert Rawls' return home from Vietnam is typical of many Vietnam veterans. Their return served as a painful reminder to many Americans of the war's long and complicated history. Since the 1980s Hollywood has seized hold of the war, recreating on film much of the drama and horror of the Vietnam experience. *The Deer Hunter, Apocalypse Now, Rambo, Hamburger Hill, Platoon, In Country, Casualties of War, Born on the Fourth of July*—how does one know, however, short of having been there, whether these film images are accurate?

Learning the Skill. To find out whether a movie is presenting accurate images, one must learn to **distinguish false from accurate images**. This involves two main steps—first determining the credibility of the source and then detecting bias.

In the case of a movie, the matter of testing credibility involves the producer, director, or scriptwriter. First, check the qualifications of the movie's makers—do they have any particular experience or expertise in the area of the Vietnam War? Second, check their reputations—do they have records of making accurate statements, on or off the camera? Third, does this portrayal of a war experience agree with sources known to be credible?

To recognize bias, use the skills that you learned earlier. First look for these clues to bias: does the filmmaker repeatedly use emotionally charged words or visual images? Frequently use exaggeration? Present only one side of an issue? Then, consider whether there is a pattern among the clues found that suggests a bias.

In addition, ask yourself some basic questions about the action taking place on film. From whose point of view is the story being told? Is anyone's story neglected? Who is the sympathetic character or hero? Are the characters based on eyewitness accounts? Is the plot based on facts that can be verified or is it based on the writer's imagination?

Applying the Skill. Consider any two films on the Vietnam War experience that were produced in the 1980s or 1990s. Most should be available on videotape. Write a short summary of each film. Then apply the steps described above to determine whether the images being presented in each film are false or accurate. Be sure to provide evidence for your findings. Keep in mind that all filmmakers are not perfect historians and that some may adapt the truth to make it more dramatic or exciting. It may be that some images within a film are accurate and others false.

haunted them even on their return to the United States. Robert Rawls, for example, returned home after his year in Asia and found that life was not the same. He had nightmares and panic attacks. His marriage broke up. Even years later, he dreamed about the war.

The vast majority of Vietnam veterans returned to the United States and resumed normal lives. However, a significant minority—some who had suffered crippling physical injuries, others who came home with psychological scars—found the readjustment difficult, even impossible. The government did not make the soldiers' transition to civilian life any easier. It provided no job programs for them. Thus, many veterans were unable to find employment. In addition, veterans of other wars refused to accept the Vietnam soldiers into their veterans' associations and groups. As a result, Vietnam veterans were forced to form their own organizations and support groups.

Antiwar sentiment spread throughout the United States.

Not very many Americans questioned the government's policies in Vietnam as the nation moved toward full involvement in the war in the early 1960s. Gradually, however, opposition to the U.S. commitment grew and became the basis of an immense popular movement.

Opposition was growing in Congress, too. Early in 1966 Senator J. William Fulbright, chairman of the Senate Foreign Relations Committee, turned against the war. He held a series of hearings, some of them nationally televised, in which respected public figures such as George Kennan, the foreign policy expert who initiated the nation's containment policy under the Truman Administration, criticized the American effort in Vietnam. Other influential members of Congress gradually opposed the war as well, including, in 1967, **Robert F. Kennedy**, the brother of the late president and a senator from New York.

Even within the Administration, the consensus on the war seemed to be crumbling. Al-
though Secretary of State Dean Rusk never wavered in his commitment, Secretary of Defense Robert McNamara and National Security Adviser McGeorge Bundy both developed doubts about the war they had done so much to promote. Both quietly left the government. McNamara's successor, Clark Clifford, was openly skeptical about the war and worked to scale down the commitment.

Other factors, too, undermined popular support for the war. Military spending was increasing at the same time that the government was launching Johnson's ambitious Great Society programs. Inflation began to increase, and in August 1967, the president was forced to ask Congress for a tax increase. In return, conservatives demanded that Johnson scale back his Great Society programs. The war had become a threat not just to American soldiers, but to liberal social programs at home.

Like many of their peers, Jimi Hendrix, above, and Bob Dylan and Joan Baez, far right, used their musical artistry to help promote social change in the turbulent 1960s.

Vietnam-era Protest Music

How many times must a man look up before he can see the sky?
Yes, 'n' how many ears must one man have before he can hear people cry?
Yes, 'n' how many deaths will it take till he knows that too many people have died?

The answer, my friend, is blowin' in the wind,
The answer is blowin' in the wind."

"Blowin' in the Wind," penned by Bob Dylan and popularized by Peter, Paul, and Mary in 1963, was the classic statement of non-
violent protest against the Vietnam War and racism. This song, along with others by such artists as Pete Seeger, Joan Baez, Barry McGuire, and Paul Simon, marked the 1960s as an era in which music was the artistic medium for a generation concerned with war and social change.

Beginning in the mid-1960s, the Byrds brought the social statements of folk music to the driving beat of rock and roll. The Rolling Stones, the Doors, the Who, and Crosby, Stills, Nash, and Young all sang songs protesting a variety of social ills. African American artists such as Sly Stone and Jimi Hendrix brought a critical edge to the rhythm and blues tradition, Hendrix with a unique guitar style every bit as radical as his lyrics.

Highlights of American Life

The most powerful opposition to the war, however, came from outside the government. It emerged first on college and university campuses. Asian scholars and others raised questions about the assumptions that had led America to intervene in Vietnam and claimed that the government did not understand the nature of the conflict there. At the University of Michigan in 1965, members of the faculty staged a highly publicized teach-in, the beginning of a national debate about the wisdom and morality of the war.

By late 1967 antiwar sentiment was spreading on campuses throughout the country. The organizations of the New Left, most notably the Students for a Democratic Society (SDS), were making opposition to the war one of their principal public positions. Antiwar rallies and demonstrations were becoming staples of university life. Even in 1965, when most Americans still supported the Administration's policies, antiwar activists had managed to stage large public demonstrations—including a march on the White House that mobilized 25,000 people. Two years later, in October 1967, more than 100,000 protesters joined a march on the Pentagon to denounce the war.

SECTION **2** REVIEW

Identify Key People and Terms
Write a sentence to identify: Gulf of Tonkin Resolution, Barry Goldwater, napalm, William Westmoreland, pacification, My Lai massacre, William Calley, Robert F. Kennedy

Locate Key Places
1. What body of water lies south of China and North Vietnam?
2. In what part of South Vietnam is the city of Da Nang?
3. Through which nation does the Ho Chi Minh Trail mainly run?
4. Describe the geographical location of the village of My Lai.

Master the Main Ideas
1. **Analyzing U.S. involvement in foreign affairs:** What did the Gulf of Tonkin Resolution give President Johnson the authorization to do?
2. **Studying political leaders:** Why did President Johnson decide to escalate the war in Vietnam?
3. **Perceiving cause/effect relationships:** Why was Johnson's Operation Rolling Thunder considered a failure?
4. **Respecting the beliefs of others:** What were some of the feelings and experiences that made Vietnam a frustrating experience for many American soldiers?
5. **Supporting basic civic values of American society:** Why did so many Americans begin to speak out against American involvement in the war?

Apply Critical Thinking Skills: Making Comparisons
Compare the treatment of returning Vietnam veterans to the treatment of veterans who were returning home after World War II. What similarities were there? What differences?

By the late 1960s, artists generally turned away from topical protest songs in favor of more general, and more poetic, commentaries on the human condition. These new songs affirmed a new set of values and lifestyles often called the counterculture. This youth movement reached its peak with the Woodstock Music Festival, held in 1969 in rural New York. Here, half a million young people gathered to celebrate themselves and their music.

1968, he quickly won enough commitments from local party organizations to make him the frontrunner for the nomination. Kennedy and McCarthy, despite success in the primaries, were struggling to catch up.

King and Kennedy were assassinated.

So far, the war had been the dominant issue in the politics of 1968. In the midst of this bitter presidential campaign, however, racial tensions suddenly rose to the fore as a result of the tragic death of the Rev. Dr. Martin Luther King, Jr. The civil rights leader was shot and killed in Memphis, Tennessee, where he was lending his support to a garbage workers' strike. His white assassin was later captured, but his motives were never determined. King's death sparked the greatest outbreak of racial violence in American history. Rebellions and riots raged in more than 100 cities, leaving 43 people dead and more than 3,000 injured.

The events of April deepened the sense of crisis that was gripping the nation. Two months later, another tragedy deepened it further. On June 6 Robert Kennedy won the California presidential primary and appeared before supporters at the Ambassador Hotel in Los Angeles to acknowledge his victory. He told the enthusiastic crowd that his primary victories proved conclusively that:

The violence, the disenchantment with our society; the divisions, whether it's between blacks and whites, between the poor and the more affluent, or between age groups or the war in Vietnam [could be overcome].

AN AMERICAN ★ SPEAKS

As the young senator left the ballroom, a disturbed man emerged from the crowd and shot him in the head. Twenty-five hours later Kennedy died. His assassin was a Palestinian Arab who had apparently been angered by Kennedy's strong support of Israel.

By the time of his death, Robert Kennedy had emerged as a symbol to many Americans of the liberal commitment to helping the dispossessed. He had strong support among the young, blacks, Indians, Hispanics, and the poor. His public appearances produced passionate enthusiasm. His assassination, like that of Dr. King, removed from public life a remarkably popular leader. The combined effect of the two murders was to leave the nation in a state of numbness.

Jack Newfield, a speechwriter for Robert Kennedy, expressed the despair felt by millions of Americans after the deaths of King and Kennedy. Most of them, including Newfield, had yet to fully recover from the assassination of John F. Kennedy a little less than five years earlier:

Things were not really getting better . . . we shall not overcome. . . . We had already glimpsed the most compassionate leaders our nation could produce [King and the two Kennedys], and they had all been assassinated. And from this time forward, things would get worse: Our best political leaders were part of memory now, not hope.

AN AMERICAN ★ SPEAKS

Two months after Kennedy's death, Democrats gathered in Chicago for their party's national convention. It was now virtually inevitable that Hubert Humphrey would be the presidential nominee. Opposition to his candidacy was intense, however, because Humphrey supported Johnson's Vietnam policies. Inside the convention hall, delegates engaged in a long and bitter debate over the party platform and at times came into conflict with each other and with the security forces placed there by Chicago Mayor **Richard J. Daley**. A few miles away, in downtown Chicago, young antiwar protesters were staging a series of demonstrations. On the third night of the convention, as the delegates prepared to cast their ballots, the protesters provoked a confrontation with the Chicago police, who were under orders to keep them far away from the convention hall. The result was a bloody riot during which some policemen savagely beat the unarmed demonstrators with billy clubs and sprayed the crowd with tear gas. Aware that television cameras were recording the event, the demonstrators began to chant: "The whole world is watching."

Meanwhile, delegates inside the convention hall were outraged by the tactics Mayor Daley used to disperse the crowds outside. "Is there

Nixon won a narrow victory in 1968.

any way to get Mayor Daley to suspend the police-state tactics that are being perpetrated at this very moment?" an irate Colorado delegate shouted. Senator Abraham Ribicoff of Connecticut chastised Daley for his "Gestapo tactics." Some even called for the convention to be halted and moved to another city.

Despite the tremendous distractions, the convention managed to select Hubert Humphrey as the Democratic party's presidential nominee. His prospects were bleak, however. He presided over a sharply divided party. More importantly, he faced a powerful challenge from conservative Republicans. For Humphrey, the victory was somewhat bittersweet. After his nomination he told reporters:

I felt when we left that convention we were in an impossible situation. Chicago was a catastrophe. My wife and I went home heartbroken, battered and beaten. I told her I felt just like we had been in a shipwreck.

AN AMERICAN
★ SPEAKS

The turbulent events of 1968, and the sense of crisis they produced, convinced some Americans that radical changes in society and government would soon occur. Nonetheless, the election of 1968 finally made it clear that the majority's response to the turmoil was a conservative yearning for stability and order.

One sign of the call for conservatism was the independent presidential candidacy of Governor **George C. Wallace** of Alabama, and the surprising support it received. Wallace was one of the best known defenders of segregation in the South. He gained notoriety for his attempt to stop the court-ordered admission of African American students to the University of Alabama in 1963. He then expanded his complaints about liberalism to include attacks on intellectuals, government bureaucrats, welfare recipients, and radical students.

In 1968 Wallace became a candidate for president as the nominee of a new third party he created: the American party. His running

Club-wielding Chicago police attack antiwar demonstrators at Grant Park on the afternoon of August 28, 1968. Although most people were shocked by the strongarm tactics used by the police, hundreds of letters commending the police poured into Mayor Richard J. Daley's office.

mate was a retired air force general, Curtis LeMay, who advocated expanding the war in Vietnam. Wallace denounced the forced busing of students to achieve integration, the permissiveness of authorities toward race riots and antiwar demonstrations, and the growth of federal social programs. Although he was never a threat to win the presidency, polls showed that Wallace attracted support from as much as 20 percent of the public. His popularity was evidence of the strength of the conservative reaction to the turmoil of the time.

In the meantime, the Republican party in 1968 was uniting behind Richard Nixon. Nixon had already been at the center of national politics for nearly 20 years and had staged a remarkable comeback from what most people had considered political oblivion a few years earlier. Nixon was not as strident as Wallace, and his campaign addressed many issues beyond the essentially social concerns Wallace had raised. However, the heart of Nixon's appeal was similar to that of Wallace. He targeted his campaign toward what some called Middle America and what Nixon later called the **Silent Majority**: middle-class people who were, Nixon sensed, tired of hearing about their obligations to the poor, tired of the demands of minorities, tired of judicial decisions that seemed to favor criminals. Nixon promised "law and order" and less government. He also promised "peace with honor" in Vietnam, although he was vague about what that meant and how he intended to achieve it.

In the aftermath of the divisive and violent Democratic convention, Nixon and his running mate, Governor **Spiro Agnew** of Maryland, enjoyed a wide lead in the public opinion polls. That lead began to shrink, however, as the campaign continued and as Humphrey succeeded in distancing himself slightly from President Johnson's policies in Vietnam. Nixon was hurt, too, by George Wallace, who probably drew more votes from him than he did from Humphrey.

Although Wallace took many votes away from Nixon, he probably could have done even more damage to his campaign had it not been for the indiscretions of his running mate, Curtis LeMay. LeMay made some shockingly callous statements to the press concerning his desire to use whatever force was necessary to win the Vietnam War. In October, only a month before the election, LeMay told reporters that the nation should "bomb the North Vietnam-

Although antiwar sentiment grew tremendously following the Tet Offensive in 1968, many Americans still supported government policies in Vietnam. Among the most active supporters of the war were construction workers such as those shown below during a demonstration in New York City in May 1970.

ese back into the Stone Age." He then drove the nail into the coffin by saying, without the approval or knowledge of Wallace: "I think there are many times when it would be most efficient to use nuclear weapons."

In the end, Nixon prevailed. He defeated Humphrey by a very narrow margin, receiving 43.4 percent of the popular vote to Humphrey's 42.7 percent. The margin of victory was a slim 500,000 votes. His electoral margin was 301 to 191. Despite LeMay, George Wallace won 13.5 percent of the popular vote, an impressive showing for a third-party candidate, and carried five southern states with a total of 46 electoral ballots.

Nixon's victory was a narrow one. The electorate, by casting nearly 57 percent of its votes for two conservative candidates, had made it clear that it was more interested in stability than in change.

SECTION **3** REVIEW

Identify Key People and Terms
Write a sentence to identify: Tet Offensive, Eugene McCarthy, Hubert Humphrey, Richard J. Daley, George C. Wallace, Silent Majority, Spiro Agnew

Locate Key Places
Where is the city of Hue in relation to the demilitarized zone?

Master the Main Ideas
1. **Analyzing information:** Why were Americans shocked to hear about the Tet Offensive?
2. **Studying political issues and leaders:** Why did Robert Kennedy and Eugene McCarthy pose a threat to President Johnson?
3. **Studying reform leaders:** What effect did the assassinations of the Rev. Dr. Martin Luther King, Jr., and Senator Robert F. Kennedy have on the nation?
4. **Analyzing political elections:** What factors enabled Nixon to claim the presidency in 1968?

Apply Critical Thinking Skills: Making Comparisons
How were Nixon and Wallace similar? How were they different?

SECTION 4

The war ended in 1975.

Key Terms: lottery system, Vietnamization, Pentagon Papers, plumbers, Khmer Rouge

Reading Preview
As you read this section, you will learn:
1. how Nixon attempted to appease Americans who were opposed to the war.
2. what Nixon did when negotiations to halt the war became deadlocked.
3. how the Cambodian invasion affected the war.
4. what followed the Christmas bombing.
5. what happened when the North Vietnamese launched an offensive in the spring of 1975.

Once in office, President Richard Nixon chose **Henry A. Kissinger** as his national security adviser. A professor of government at Harvard, Kissinger soon exercised more control over American foreign policy than anyone but the president himself. Together, Nixon and Kissinger began tackling the problem of the war.

Nixon introduced a draft lottery and Vietnamization.

Nixon believed that popular opposition to the war had convinced the North Vietnamese that they did not need to make concessions to the United States. He wanted to convince Ho Chi Minh that the United States was prepared to "stay the course." Two things that contributed to popular dissatisfaction with the war were the military draft at home and the high level of American casualties in Vietnam. Nixon set out to limit both.

For the draft, the Administration introduced a new **lottery system** for 18-year-olds in 1969. Under the system, the 366 possible days of the

A young woman kneels beside the body of Jeffrey Miller, one of four students killed by guardsmen at Kent State University in 1970. The tragedy helped spark an unprecedented rash of student demonstrations across the country. According to one higher education official, Kent State and the Cambodian invasion ignited "the most massive expression ever of American college student discontent."

year (Leap Year included) were put on cards and placed into a cylinder. The cards were then randomly selected until all the cards were chosen. Men whose birthdays were selected first from the cylinder were selected for the draft first. Those who received numbers above a certain cutoff were not called for the draft but were still considered eligible for a year.

The new lottery system also called for the elimination of college deferments. Thus, virtually all potential draftees would be 19-year-olds. Although the system drew criticism from those who drew low numbers, it was generally considered better than the old system because it greatly reduced the number of people threatened with the draft. It also eliminated economics as a factor in determining who would be drafted—now everyone was eligible for the draft, rich and poor alike.

More fundamental than the lottery system was the policy of **Vietnamization**. Nixon announced early in his Administration that he would soon begin withdrawing U.S. troops from Vietnam while training and equipping the South Vietnamese to take more responsibility

for their own defense. He withdrew 60,000 troops in the fall of 1969 and continued to reduce the number over the next three years.

In the meantime, Nixon and Kissinger launched a diplomatic effort to end the war. Johnson had started peace talks with the North Vietnamese in 1968, but so far there had been no results. Nixon tried to break the stalemate with a series of new concessions to the communists. The North Vietnamese, however, were not willing to compromise on their main demand: that Vietnam be reunified under their control. The diplomatic deadlock continued.

Nixon ordered an invasion of Cambodia.

Discouraged by the lack of diplomatic progress, Nixon and Kissinger began considering military action to pressure the North Vietnamese to reduce their demands. The most effective way to apply pressure, they believed, was to attack the staging areas in **Cambodia** and **Laos** from which the North Vietnamese were supplying their troops and launching their attacks on South Vietnam. (As you can see on the map on page 823, these two nations share long, difficult-to-patrol borders with Vietnam.) In 1969 Nixon ordered American planes to begin bombing Cambodian territory in an effort to destroy the supposed communist sanctuaries there. He did not inform the public or Congress of these raids. It soon became clear, however, that bombing alone would not be enough. President Nixon began considering other ways of attacking the communist bases in Cambodia.

In early 1970 conservative military leaders overthrew the longtime neutral government of Cambodia. The new Cambodian government sided with the United States and gave it permission to attack communist positions within its borders.

On April 30, 1970, Nixon ordered American ground troops to cross into Cambodia and "clean out" the bases the communists had been using for their "increased military aggression." Nixon explained his decision to a national television audience, insisting that this was a limited operation. The troops would be withdrawn within weeks. The speech shocked the American public, however, and helped reignite the antiwar movement that had begun to smolder slightly during the first months of 1970. The invasion itself ended after a few weeks, as Nixon had promised. American troops, however, never found the supposed communist sanctuaries in Cambodia.

Hundreds of thousands of protesters traveled to Washington to rally against the decision to invade Cambodia. Millions participated in smaller demonstrations on college and university campuses across the country. Nixon made matters worse by referring to the student protesters as "bums." The crisis reached a peak on May 4, when members of the National Guard, who had been summoned to the campus of **Kent State University** in Ohio to maintain order, opened fire on a group of demonstrators, killing four of them. Ten days later local police killed two black students at **Jackson State University** in Mississippi during a demonstration there. These incidents deepened the disillusionment many young Americans felt toward their government.

VOICES FROM THE PAST

A Vietnam Veteran

The American men and women who fought in Vietnam described the war in letters home and in other personal accounts. One of the most powerful descriptions is the oral history Nam: The Vietnam War in the Words of the Men and Women Who Fought There, *by Mark Baker. In the following excerpt, how does one veteran learn to understand the language of the Vietnamese?*

I didn't really speak the language. I could understand a few phrases, though. One day during a fire fight, for the first time in my life, I heard the cries of the Vietnamese wounded; and I understood them. When somebody gets wounded, they call out for their mothers, their wives, their girl friends. There I was listening to the VC [Viet Cong, the communist guerrilla force in South Vietnam] cry for the same things. That's when the futility of the war really dawned on me. I thought, ". . . what a . . . waste this whole thing is."

The war dragged on.

The Cambodian invasion in 1970 failed to break the stalemate in the negotiations. As a result, the war continued to drag on.

Early in 1971 Nixon ordered the U.S. Air Force to assist the South Vietnamese army in an invasion of Laos. This was yet another effort to clean out enemy bases and cut off supplies on the Ho Chi Minh Trail. It was also a test of Vietnamization because no American ground troops participated in the operation. Although the Administration claimed the South Vietnamese army had performed well, many critics of the war disagreed. In any case, the Laos invasion, like the Cambodia invasion before it, produced few lasting military gains.

The Pentagon Papers. At about the same time as the Laos invasion, a former employee of the Defense Department, **Daniel Ellsberg**, delivered to the *New York Times* a set of secret documents that he had photocopied from classified files in the Pentagon. They contained an

Point	Counterpoint
Freedom of the Press	**National Security**
■ The First Amendment guarantees freedom of the press. ■ The American people have a right to know the truth about American involvement in Vietnam.	■ First Amendment rights do not apply in situations in which national security is jeopardized. ■ The printing of the Pentagon Papers would cause "irreparable injury" to our national defense.

internal history of American involvement in the war, written by officials of the Johnson Administration. Known as the **Pentagon Papers**, they attracted wide attention. Millions of readers were shocked by what these documents revealed about the way the United States had entered the war. The Nixon Administration, outraged at what it considered a major breach of security, tried unsuccessfully to convict Daniel Ellsberg of criminal behavior. It also tried to prevent the *New York Times* from publishing these papers. The Supreme Court, however, ruled in favor of the newspaper. In addition, the Administration began exploring ways to increase its ability to prevent leaks and discredit its enemies. As a result, a new White House unit, known as the **plumbers**, was established. Among its covert missions was a break-in at the offices of Ellsberg's psychiatrist in 1971. The purpose of the break-in was to find material the Administration could use to discredit Ellsberg.

Major communist offensive. Late in 1971 the North Vietnamese broke off negotiations with the United States. In March 1972 they began the Easter Offensive, the biggest communist offensive in South Vietnam since 1968. The offensive marked the first time regular units of the North Vietnamese army had openly entered the war. After learning that the South Vietnamese military was suffering heavy casualties, the Nixon Administration responded by ordering the bombing of **Haiphong** and Hanoi. (As the map on page 823 shows, Haiphong is on the Gulf of Tonkin.) It also ordered the U.S. Navy to set up mines in seven North Vietnamese harbors in an attempt to stop the shipment of supplies from communist China and the Soviet Union.

Even though the South Vietnamese army was having little success in turning back the North Vietnamese invasion in the spring of 1972, the withdrawal of American troops continued. By the end of the year, only 24,000 American troops remained. Four years earlier, there had been 540,000 troops.

A cease-fire was signed after the Christmas bombing.

The approach of the 1972 U.S. presidential election and the steadily deteriorating military situation in South Vietnam persuaded the Nixon Administration to alter its terms for peace. The North Vietnamese, who must also have realized that the months before the election were a good time to win concessions, became more open to negotiations, too.

In April Nixon dropped his longtime insistence on the removal of North Vietnamese troops from the South as a condition of American withdrawal. At about the same time, the North Vietnamese dropped their demand that Thieu be removed from power in the South before any settlement could be reached. Henry Kissinger then began a round of secret talks with the chief North Vietnamese negotiator, Le Duc Tho, in Paris. In mid-October they reached an agreement on a ceasefire and Kissinger held a press conference to announce that "peace is at hand." The South Vietnamese government balked at the terms, however. They were especially displeased with the provision that North Vietnamese troops be allowed to remain in the country.

Kissinger went back to Le Duc Tho to try to win some additional concessions that would meet the South Vietnamese objections. The North Vietnamese responded by making new demands of their own. On December 16 the talks broke off. Almost immediately, the Nixon administration began the heaviest and most destructive bombing raids on North Vietnam of the entire war. The raids, known as the Christmas bombing, continued for 12 days. Hanoi and Haiphong were particularly hard hit, and many civilians were killed. News of the event revived antiwar sentiment in the United States once more.

Soon after Nixon ended the bombing, the North Vietnamese returned to the bargaining table and the movement toward a settlement accelerated. On January 27, 1973, a cease-fire agreement was signed. It stopped all hostilities in Vietnam, after which all American forces would withdraw. It called for an exchange of prisoners. It set up a series of vague procedures for resolving the remaining differences between North and South Vietnam peacefully. It also permitted the North Vietnamese to leave their troops in the South. The agreement was, in other words, almost identical to the one Kissinger and Tho had constructed in October.

Although Nixon liked to claim that the Christmas bombing had produced the breakthrough, it is at least as likely that what really changed was not the position of Hanoi, but the position of Saigon. Under heavy American pressure, the South Vietnamese reluctantly accepted the new conditions.

South Vietnam fell to the communists.

Shortly after the American forces left Vietnam, the cease-fire broke down. Fighting continued throughout 1973 and 1974, with heavy casualties on both sides and steady gains by the communists. In the spring of 1975, the North Vietnamese launched their final great offensive. The South Vietnamese army was now hopelessly weakened, and the government in Saigon appealed desperately to the United States for military assistance.

Gerald Ford, who had assumed the presidency when Nixon resigned the post in 1974, (You will read about the resignation in the next chapter.) asked Congress to authorize funds for additional military aid. Congress refused, however. Many members believed that nothing could save South Vietnam short of another major American intervention—something few Americans, least of all the new president, were now willing to contemplate.

In late April 1975, sooner than any American

officials had predicted, communist forces marched into Saigon. In the last days before their arrival, there was near panic in the capital. Officials of the Thieu regime and many others struggled desperately to get out of the country. The United States, in the meantime, was trying to evacuate its remaining diplomatic and military personnel. As helicopters took off from the roof of the American embassy, frantic

Panic spread throughout Saigon during the last week of April 1975 as the United States began evacuating U.S. citizens from its embassy. Thousands of South Vietnamese scaled the walls of the embassy seeking to board one of the helicopters.

chart study

The Vietnam War was not only the nation's longest war, it was one of the costliest. The chart shows comparative costs for all major conflicts involving the United States. Which was the nation's costliest war in terms of estimated total costs?

Critical Thinking
What conclusions can you draw from this chart?

COSTS OF U.S. WARS, 1775–1985 (in millions of current dollars)			
	Wartime costs	Veterans' Benefit Costs	Interest on War Loans	Estimated Total Costs
American Revolution	100	70	20	190
War of 1812	93	49	16	158
Mexican War	73	64	10	147
Civil War (Union only)	3,200	8,580	1,172	12,952
Spanish-American War	400	6,000	60	6,460
World War I	26,000	75,000	11,000	112,000
World War II	288,000	290,000	86,000	664,000
Korean Conflict	54,000	99,000	11,000	164,000
Vietnam Conflict	140,600	13,173	unknown	153,800

On Veterans Day weekend in 1982 hundreds of thousands of Vietnam veterans and their families gathered for the dedication of the Vietnam Veterans Memorial in Washington, D.C. It was a time for many emotional reunions and camaraderie. It was also a time for spiritual healing. "The memorial was the beginning of the healing process over Vietnam," explained veteran Jan Scruggs. Max Cleland, also a veteran, agreed with Scruggs. "Within the soul of each Vietnam veteran there is probably something that says 'Bad war, good soldiers.' Now they can separate the war from the warrior."

South Vietnamese struggled to get in. Americans often had to beat them off.

This humiliating spectacle marked the end of the 20-year American commitment to the government of South Vietnam. It had been the longest war in American history, and it was now the only conflict the United States had ever clearly lost.

The cost of the conflict to Vietnam had been enormous. More than one million Vietnamese soldiers had died in the war, along with uncounted civilians. With its economy in shambles, Vietnam now fell under the control of an authoritarian communist regime closely tied to the Soviet Union.

Vietnam's neighbors also suffered. Cambodia and Laos, the other two nations of Indochina, fell under communist control. In Cambodia, which changed its name to Kampuchea, the **Khmer Rouge** established one of the most murderous governments in history. Its policies resulted in the deaths of more than a third of Kampuchea's [kam'pü chē'ə] entire population.

The United States also paid heavily for its role in Vietnam. The war cost the United States more than $150 billion. It damaged the nation's prestige in the world, and it eroded its self-confidence at home. Most importantly, it took the lives of about 58,000 Americans and injured 300,000 more.

For several years after the fall of South Vietnam, the American people seemed unwilling to talk about the conflict. Gradually, however, interest in the war revived. Filmmakers began releasing powerful movies about Vietnam. Veterans and former officials began publishing

memoirs and reflections. Historians began writing and teaching courses about the war. By the mid-1980s, Vietnam had returned to the center of public discussion.

Disagreement continued about the meaning of the war, and there were sometimes bitter arguments between those who considered the

war morally wrong and those who believed it to have been a "noble cause." Many people denounced what they called the "Vietnam syndrome," which they claimed was causing Americans to shrink from any further international commitments. Others noted that the collapse of Indochina, while a disaster for the people of the region, had not created a serious threat to the United States or its interests. The domino theory had been disproved. The only "dominoes" that had fallen had been Vietnam, Cambodia, and Laos, the three nations involved in the war itself.

Most Americans, however, gradually came to accept that Vietnam had been a mistake. Many believed that it had taught the United States that there were limits to what it could hope to accomplish in the world. Some of the bitterness that had poisoned American life while the

war was in progress slowly receded. Instead, there were widespread efforts to come to terms with the meaning of the war and promote healing and reconciliation. A symbol of that was the construction in 1982 of a simple yet eloquent memorial to the Americans who had died in Vietnam on the Mall in Washington, D.C.—a stark black granite wall, sunk into the ground, with the names of the 58,000 dead carved on its surface. The memorial, designed by Maya Lin, a young Chinese American, is visited by hundreds of thousands of Americans each year.

SECTION 4 REVIEW

Identify Key People and Terms
Write a sentence to identify: Henry A. Kissinger, lottery system, Vietnamization, Daniel Ellsberg, Pentagon Papers, plumbers, Khmer Rouge

Locate Key Places

1. Where are Cambodia and Laos in relation to North and South Vietnam?
2. In which states are Kent State University and Jackson State University located?
3. Which North Vietnamese city is located on the Gulf of Tonkin?

Master the Main Ideas

1. **Analyzing political decisions:** Why did Nixon institute a lottery and formulate the policy of Vietnamization?
2. **Perceiving cause/effect relationships:** Why did Nixon decide to bomb Cambodia?
3. **Analyzing information:** Why did the war continue to drag on after the invasion of Cambodia?
4. **Perceiving cause/effect relationships:** What led to the signing of the cease-fire agreement?
5. **Analyzing the effects of international conflicts:** After the war, what types of disagreements surfaced about the meaning of the conflict?

Apply Critical Thinking Skills: Drawing Conclusions
To what extent do you think a democratic government should be expected to inform its citizens during wartime? Why?

TOURING
THE PAST

*V*ietnam
Veterans
Memorial

Honoring the Americans lost in the longest war in U.S. history, the two long, polished, horizontal black wings of the Vietnam Veterans Memorial in Washington, D.C., emerge from the earth near the Lincoln Memorial and then recede. The two sides of the memorial are each about 250 feet long and come together at a 130° angle. The back of the memorial remains level with the surrounding grass of the Mall, and the front slopes gently downward to a depth of about ten feet where the sides of the memorial meet at the center. As visitors approach, they must descend to view the wall.

The east side points toward the Washington Monument at the eastern edge of the park. The west side points toward the Lincoln Memorial, 800 feet away.

Carved into the reflective, mirror-like black granite are more than 58,000 names—the names of the known dead and missing in the Vietnam War—in the order of date of death or date declared missing. The roll begins at the center of the memorial, starting on the east side, or wing, with the name of the first American killed in Vietnam, in 1961. The list continues to the end of the east side and begins again at the west side, ending at the

The war that divided America finds its memorial in a wall that has become a symbol of reconciliation and the healing of this division.

center of the memorial, near the bottom, with the name of the last person killed, in 1975. Thus, the names of the first and last persons to die meet at the center.

The memorial was the dream of Jan Scruggs, who went to Vietnam in 1969 when he was 19 years old and served in the infantry there for a little more than a year. Nine years later, after seeing the film *The Deer Hunter*, Scruggs started the Vietnam Veterans Memorial Fund and persuaded Congress to assign two acres on the Mall for the memorial. Private donations paid all other costs.

Scruggs insisted that the memorial show the names of all the men and women of the U.S. Armed Forces listed as killed or missing in Vietnam. The Vietnam Veterans Memorial Fund launched a nationwide competition to select a design, which was won by Maya Lin, then an architectural student at Yale University.

The fund specified that the design must maintain "visual harmony" with its site, including the Lincoln Memorial and the Washington Monument. This rule seemed to suggest a low, horizontal memorial, and the simplicity, nobility, and beauty of Lin's design satisfied this demand superbly. Yet some critics objected that the design was too abstract, somber, and remote. At one point controversy over the design stirred passions that echoed the war it commemorated. The work went ahead anyway, and the memorial reached completion in time for dedication at the first national gathering of Vietnam veterans in November 1982.

Millions of visitors come to the Vietnam Veterans Memorial each year. Many people run their hands over the carved letters of a familiar name. The design specified that the names be listed in chronological order of death—also a point of controversy. Alphabetical directories on either side of the memorial help visitors find names.

Perhaps to offset the austerity of the wall, people often leave private memorials— flowers, tiny flags, brief messages, photographs, medals, and other mementos. Objects left at the site are kept by the National Park Service.

MAYA LIN

Maya Lin describes her design inspirations:

Maya Lin, from Athens, Ohio, entered the competition to design the Vietnam Veterans Memorial at the urging of one of her professors at Yale University. Lin and a classmate decided first to visit the site. How did her appreciation of the park influence her design?

It was while I was at the site that I designed it. I just sort of visualized it. It just popped into my head. Some people were playing Frisbee. It was a beautiful park. I didn't want to destroy a living park. You use the landscape. You don't fight it. You absorb the landscape . . . When I looked at the site I just knew I wanted something horizontal that took you in, that made you feel safe within the park, yet at the same time reminding you of the dead. So I just imagined opening up the earth.

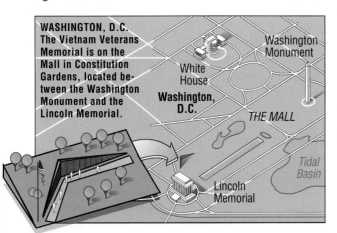

WASHINGTON, D.C. The Vietnam Veterans Memorial is on the Mall in Constitution Gardens, located between the Washington Monument and the Lincoln Memorial.

Washington Monument

White House

Washington, D.C.

THE MALL

Tidal Basin

Lincoln Memorial

Philip Caputo Encounters a Different Kind of War

21A

TIME FRAME
1965

GEOGRAPHIC SETTING
South Vietnam

By 1965 the Viet Cong and their North Vietnamese allies clearly were defeating the American-equipped and -advised South Vietnamese army. President Lyndon Johnson responded by increasing American involvement in the war. In early March the first American marines landed at Da Nang in northern South Vietnam. Novelist and journalist Philip Caputo (1941–   ) was a marine lieutenant with one of these combat units. In the following excerpt from his Vietnam memoir, *A Rumor of War,* (1977), Caputo reflected on how the experience of American troops fighting in Vietnam differed from combat in our previous wars.

After one of the wounded comrades he had rescued died, the exhausted and grief-stricken marine in the photograph on the facing page broke down. Larry Burrows, the English photographer who took this picture at the Marine base at Da Nang, South Vietnam, in the spring of 1965, was himself killed early in 1971 when the helicopter carrying him to cover the South Vietnamese invasion of Laos was shot down.

For Americans who did not come of age in the early sixties, it may be hard to grasp what those years were like—the pride and overpowering self-assurance that prevailed. Most of the thirty-five hundred men in our brigade, born during or immediately after World War II, were shaped by that era, the age of Kennedy's Camelot. We went overseas full of illusions, for which the intoxicating atmosphere of those years was as much to blame as our youth.

War is always attractive to young men who know nothing about it, but we had also been seduced into uniform by Kennedy's challenge to "ask what you can do for your country" and by the missionary idealism he had awakened in us. America seemed omnipotent then: the country could still claim it had never lost a war, and we believed we were ordained to play cop to the Communists' robber and spread our own political faith around the world. Like the French soldiers of the late eighteenth century, we saw ourselves as the champions of "a cause that was destined to triumph." So, when we marched into the rice paddies on that damp March afternoon, we carried, along with our packs and rifles, the implicit convictions that the Viet Cong would be quickly beaten and that we were doing something altogether noble and good. We kept the packs and rifles; the convictions, we lost.

The discovery that the men we had scorned as peasant guerillas were, in fact, a lethal, determined enemy and the casualty lists that lengthened each week with nothing to show for the blood being spilled broke our early confidence. By autumn, what had begun as an adventurous expedition had turned into an exhausting, indecisive war of attrition in which we fought for no cause other than our own survival.

Writing about this kind of warfare is not a simple task. Repeatedly, I have found myself wishing that I had been the veteran of a conventional war, with dramatic campaigns and historic battles for subject matter instead of a monotonous succession of ambushes and fire-fights. But there were no Normandies or Gettysburgs for us, no epic clashes that decided the fates of armies or nations. The war was mostly a matter of enduring weeks of expectant waiting and, at random intervals, of conducting vicious manhunts through jungles and swamps where snipers harassed us constantly and booby traps cut us down one by one.

The tedium was occasionally relieved by a large-scale search-and-destroy operation, but the exhilaration of riding the lead helicopter into a landing zone was usually followed by more of the same hot walking, with the mud sucking at our boots and the sun thudding against our helmets while an invisible enemy shot at us from distant tree lines. The rare instances when the VC [Viet Cong] chose to

fight a set-piece battle provided the only excitement; not ordinary excitement, but the manic ecstasy of contact. Weeks of bottled-up tensions would be released in a few minutes of orgiastic violence, men screaming and shouting obscenities above the explosions of grenades and the rapid, rippling bursts of automatic rifles.

Beyond adding a few more corpses to the weekly body count, none of these encounters achieved anything; none will ever appear in military histories or be studied by cadets at West Point. Still, they changed us and taught us, the men who fought in them; in those obscure skirmishes we learned the old lessons about fear, cowardice, courage, suffering, cruelty, and comradeship. Most of all, we learned about death at an age when it is common to think of oneself as immortal. Everyone loses that illusion eventually, but in civilian life it is lost in installments over the years. We lost it all at once and, in the span of months, passed from boyhood through manhood to a premature middle age. The knowledge of death, of the implacable limits placed on a man's existence, severed us from our youth as irrevocably as a surgeon's scissors had once severed us from the womb. And yet, few of us were past twenty-five. We left Vietnam peculiar creatures, with young shoulders that bore rather old heads.

Discussing the Reading

1. What factors did Caputo feel contributed to the initial enthusiasm of young Americans for the war in Vietnam?

2. What changed their view of the war?

CRITICAL THINKING
Identifying Central Issues

How did the Vietnam War differ from earlier American wars?

William Ehrhart Has Trouble Identifying the Enemy

21B

TIME FRAME
1967–1968

GEOGRAPHIC SETTING
South Vietnam and
the United States

The Viet Cong, not the American-backed Saigon regime, controlled most of South Vietnam's hamlets and villages. In an attempt to root out the enemy guerrillas, who blended easily into the local population, "free-fire" zones were designated, in which American soldiers were free to fire at all moving objects. These sometimes included innocent civilians. Born in Pennsylvania, poet William Ehrhart (1948–   ) served as a marine sergeant in Vietnam in 1967 and 1968. In the first of the following two poems, "Guerilla War," he described the difficulty of identifying Viet Cong guerillas from other South Vietnamese peasants. When they returned home from America's longest and least popular war, Vietnam vets often encountered indifference or even hostility. In his second poem, "Coming Home," Ehrhart described his arrival in the United States at the end of his tour of duty in 1968.

Guerilla War

It's practically impossible
to tell civilians
from the Vietcong.

Nobody wears uniforms.
5 They all talk
the same language
(and you couldn't understand them
even if they didn't).

They tape grenades
10 inside their clothes,
and carry satchel charges
in their market baskets.

Even their women fight;
and young boys,
15 and girls.

It's practically impossible
to tell civilians
from the Vietcong;

after awhile,
20 you quit trying.

Coming Home

San Francisco airport—

no more corpsmen stuffing ruptured
   chests
with cotton balls and not enough heat tabs
5 to eat a decent meal.

I asked some girl to sit
and have a Coke with me.
She thought I was crazy;
I thought she was going to call a cop.

10 I bought a ticket for Philadelphia.
At the loading gate, they told me:
"Thank you for flying TWA;
we hope you will enjoy your flight."

No brass bands;
15 no flags,
no girls,
no cameramen.

Only a small boy who asked me
what the ribbons on my jacket meant.

Running from the threat of a U.S. airstrike against Viet Cong snipers in Saigon, a boy heads for a slaughter house where the concrete pens may protect him from the bombs. This picture, taken in 1968, is typical in its depiction of civilians fleeing for safety while soldiers watch, apparently unconcerned.

Discussing the Reading

1. In "Guerilla War," what is the implication of the poem's last two lines?

2. What did Ehrhart's poem "Coming Home" suggest a soldier returning to his homeland from a war might expect?

3. What did Ehrhart actually encounter on his return from Vietnam?

CRITICAL THINKING
Checking Consistency

Would someone who opposed American involvement in Vietnam have been justified in not giving Vietnam vets the welcome traditionally accorded to American service personnel returning from active duty? Why or why not?

"Sometimes It Takes Tragedy to Bring People Together"

TIME FRAME
1968–1969

GEOGRAPHIC SETTING
Vietnam

Because draft deferments for college students allowed many young men from affluent families to escape military service, the burden of the Vietnam War fell heavily on working-class Americans. African Americans had a particularly heavy share of the combat—and the resulting casualties—in Vietnam. "Not since the Civil War," observed Vietnam War archivist Clark Smith, "when inductees with money were allowed to buy their exemptions from the national draft, has the burden of military service so directly fallen on a single group of Americans." One of these African Americans who fought in Vietnam was Robert Sanders, who arrived there in early July 1968. In the following excerpt from the oral history *Brothers: Black Soldiers in the Nam,* Sanders described how white and African American servicemen interacted in combat zones.

We never had peace of mind, never had time to relax. If it wasn't one thing, it was another. It was a nightmare. We had a saying about when we relaxed and started half-stepping: "When you half-step, it may be your last step." The enemy never fought us until he was ready to deal with us. That was what was so scary about it. He knew exactly where we were at all times. He was such a master of camouflage that he could be ten feet away from us and we'd never know it. He used all types of diversion and tricks. He would dig what we called spider holes. We'd be walking right on top of the enemy. As soon as he felt the last guy come through, or if the brush was so thick that the guy in back of you couldn't tell what was happening, within a split second he'd raise right out of the ground and just bust you in the back of the head with a single shot weapon. Then he'd be right back down in the ground, and you didn't even know where the shot came from. You'd be looking in the trees or in the bush next to you, and he'd be back down in the ground, maybe moving to a different location. He was good. "Sir Charlie," that was what we called him.

We respected Charlie. And we had some self-respect, too. Half the guys didn't want to be there in the first place; the other half didn't know what the hell was going on. But since we were all there, we didn't just want to give up the ghost, man. It got to be a challenge. Not a gung ho type of thing, but it got to the point that if they wanted to try and [knock us around], we'd deal with it. We believed we could beat anybody. . . .

For the first time in my life, I saw total unity and harmony. In the states, even in the rear in Nam, blacks and whites fought each other. But in the Nam, man, out in the field we were just a force of unity and harmony. We became just one person. When I first got to the Nam, I saw a lot of prejudice. . . . But Charlie had a tendency to make you unify in a hurry. After he started [knocking us around], your anger and your common sense told you that you needed everybody. I mean EVERYONE. That was because a few people could get the whole company killed in just a matter of seconds if they were not doing their job, if they were not sharing in trying to counter Charlie when he attacked. This was something you learned. The army couldn't make you understand. Naturally they told you, "You're a fighting team." You became a machine. You stuck together and you did everything together. You didn't have time for philosophizing. After a while, you saw it; you felt it; you became a part of it.

Sometimes it takes tragedy to bring

Smoke rises from the Citadel outside the ancient Vietnamese capital of Hue [hwā] in February, 1968. American soldiers settle near a wall of the fortress after its recapture from North Vietnamese forces, which attacked Hue and twenty-six other South Vietnamese cities during the Tet offensive.

people together. It really does. And I can't think of anything more tragic than that situation at that time. Little things happened. Guys ran out of cigarettes; they shared. We ran out of food during the monsoon up in the mountains. Whoever had any salt left or a little cocoa, maybe a package of coffee, shared it. That one little package of coffee went around to four or five guys. By the time it got to you, the coffee looked like tinted water, but it was something liquid. Being in a hell hole just automatically brought every guy together as one. It was a good feeling. That was the only thing that was good about Vietnam, as far as I'm concerned. For the first time in my life, I saw people as people. We was just us, you know, man, it was US.

The Vietnamese constantly appealed to blacks to get out of the war. They would leave leaflets laying all over the jungle. In perfectly good English, the leaflet would say, "Blacks get out, it's not your fight." . . . In some ways those leaflets affected morale. It would make us wonder why we were there. Most of the people were like me; they were naive. We didn't know what the hell was really going on. We knew that Communists were supposed to be bad, and that they were trying to take the South Vietnamese's rice away from them, and that we were out there to stop them. But at the same time, the Black Panther organization, the Muslims, the Kings didn't feel that we should be out there participating in it. We didn't have nothing to gain from being there. We felt that if we were drafted we had a duty to go to war because we were Americans. But coming home reminded us that going was no benefit to us. . . .

When I was in the Nam, Mohammed Ali was refusing to take the oath. Our reaction was that we shouldn't have taken it either. We felt that the American Dream didn't really serve us. What we experienced was the American Nightmare. Black people were fighting with honor in

115 Vietnam just like they did in other American wars. They never ran; they fought to the death. We felt that they put us on the front lines abroad and in the back lines at home. Most of the brothers felt the same,
120 even though we fought right along. We wouldn't give up. We did our best to keep trucking out there and in the woods, but we would always think about this. We used to sit down and have talks over it. . . .
125 We felt that blacks should not have had to fight in Vietnam if, when they got home, they couldn't even get a job. We had unity and harmony because we wanted to live. But we just wanted no part of the war. I
130 know I didn't. The benefits were just not there for us. Martin Luther King was saying this stuff when he got killed. We talked about King and Malcolm. King was a preacher, and he said, "If they kill a
135 preacher, what are they going to do to us, even though we're over here fighting for them?" It was the hypocritical part of all the talk of the war that bothered me.

Discussing the Reading

1. What attitude did Robert Sanders express toward the enemy in Vietnam?

2. What factors contributed to the "unity and harmony" between white and African American servicemen that Sanders noted?

CRITICAL THINKING
Expressing Problems

Starting in 1966, civil rights leader Martin Luther King, Jr., began to speak out against the Vietnam War. He felt that government resources needed to combat the problems of African Americans were being wasted on military spending. Many people criticized this move by King, arguing that he should confine his efforts to the civil rights movement. Had you been present, what would your position have been?

Richard Van de Geer Describes the Fall of Saigon

21D

TIME FRAME
1975

GEOGRAPHIC SETTING
South Vietnam

In the early months of 1975, the South Vietnamese army collapsed. The communist North Vietnamese and Viet Cong troops rapidly encircled Saigon. This account of the final evacuation of the city at the end of April, 1975, is from a tape recording sent by Air Force Second Lieutenant Richard Van de Geer to a close friend. Van de Geer was a helicopter pilot stationed in Cambodia. He was killed during the *Mayaguez* rescue mission a few weeks after the events described here. Tan Son Nhut was Saigon's principal airport; VC are the Viet Cong; Hueys are helicopters.

I made four sorties into Saigon. The situation with 150,000 [enemy troops] around the city, of course, was not the most salubrious [healthy] situation in
5 which to take a big, lumbering aircraft with nothing but defensive weapons to take people out.

And of course, Tan Son Nhut was closed.
10 I could tell you about how real the fear was that I felt, since from the time we crossed the Delta and made the run into Saigon we were over enemy territory. We were being fired upon by anti-aircraft
15 guns. The VC had commandeered Air America Hueys and they were flying them around, which simply made for a very interesting chess game.

I mean, it was bad. We thought that they
20 were going to call off the operation when

An American official punches a man trying to board a plane already overloaded with refugees during the evacuation of the city of Nha Trang, South Vietnam, early in April 1975. Shortly after this plane left, communist troops overran Nha Trang.

it became dark, because we never expected them to send us into such a bad situation to begin with, even if it was daytime. But, as you probably know, they
25 continued the mission until nearly 5 o'clock in the morning. The night sorties were the worst, because we flew lights out. The tracers kept everybody on edge. To see a city burning gives one a strange feel-
30 ing of insecurity.

Tan Son Nhut was being constantly shelled, and when I see you I will show you some pictures of where I was going in relationship to what was happening. And
35 you can judge for yourself that it wasn't the best of all situations. . . .

Let me throw a couple of facts your way, which may conflict with what you have been reading in the papers. I call
40 them facts in that I saw them happen. I will throw them out for whatever they are worth. Number One: At approximately 9 o'clock on the morning of the 29th [of April, 1975], which was the day that the
45 mission was executed, a Vietnamese Huey flew out towards [the] sea, and found a carrier.

It was nearly out of gas. It made an emergency landing on the carrier. [At that
50 time,] anybody who had an ability to fly anything commandeered aircraft from whatever source [out of Vietnam]. They flew out their families and their children and in some cases select individuals.

55 This aircraft that landed—landed about 50 feet away from mine—and the man who got out of this aircraft [had been] quoted approximately a week earlier as saying that any South Vietnamese who left
60 the country [was a] coward and that everybody should remain in South Vietnam and fight to the bitter end. This very same man was the first person to arrive on the U.S.S. *Midway* and, to my knowledge, the
65 first to be recovered by the 7th Fleet. This man was General [Nguyen Cao] Ky [vice-president of the Republic of South Vietnam]. Now I really don't have any personal feelings about the war over here. I really
70 don't care one way or the other in regard to who is right and who is wrong, because that's a waste of time, a waste of thinking. But I did find myself feeling that I wish he had been shot down. . . .

75 We pulled out close to 2,000 people. We couldn't pull out any more because it was beyond human endurance to go any more. . . .

I am back now. I got back today. I am in
80 bits and pieces, fairly incoherent only

because it's been such a fast pace. I assure [you] that I am in one piece. It could have been a different story. But I may have told you before that I am somewhat fatalistic
85 about believing that I shall never come to serious harm in the military. . . .

I can envision a small cottage someplace, with a lot of writing paper, and a dog, and a fireplace, and maybe enough
90 money to give myself some Irish coffee now and then and entertain my two friends. . . .

I don't think it will be too terribly long before we are together again.
95 I wish you peace, and I have a great deal of faith that the future has to be ours.

Adios, my friend.

Discussing the Reading

1. What factors did Richard Van de Geer say contributed to the difficulty of the evacuation?

2. Why did Van de Geer resent General Ky?

CRITICAL THINKING
Recognizing Bias

Richard Van de Geer claimed (lines 68–69) not to have "any personal feelings about the war over here." Is there any evidence in this account to suggest this estimate might not have been entirely true? Explain.

Eleanor Wimbish Writes to Her Son

21E

TIME FRAME
1984

GEOGRAPHIC SETTING
Washington, D.C.

In November 1982 the Vietnam Veterans Memorial, a simple V of black granite bearing the names of the nearly 58,000 American service personnel who died in Vietnam, was dedicated in Washington, D.C. Thousands of visitors came to see and touch the names of family members and friends. Many left mementoes. Eleanor Wimbish began leaving letters to her dead son under his name on the Memorial.

Dear Bill,
Today is February 13, 1984. I came to this black wall again to see and touch your name, and as I do I wonder if anyone
5 ever stops to realize that next to your name, on this black wall, is your mother's heart. A heart broken 15 years ago today, when you lost your life in Vietnam.

And as I look at your name, William R.
10 Stocks, I think of how many, many times I used to wonder how scared and homesick you must have been in that strange country called Vietnam. And if and how it might have changed you, for you were the
15 most happy-go-lucky kid in the world, hardly ever sad or unhappy. And until the day I die, I will see you as you laughed at me, even when I was very mad at you, and the next thing I knew, we were laughing
20 together.

But on this past New Year's Day, I had my answer. I talked by phone to a friend of yours from Michigan, who spent your last Christmas and the last four months of
25 your life with you. Jim told me how you died, for he was there and saw the helicopter crash. He told me how you had flown your quota and had not been scheduled to fly that day. How the regular pilot
30 was unable to fly, and had been replaced by someone with less experience. How they did not know the exact cause of the crash. How it was either hit by enemy fire, or they hit a pole or something unknown.
35 How the blades went through the chopper and hit you. How you lived about a half hour, but were unconscious and therefore did not suffer.

He said how your jobs were like sitting

40 ducks. They would send you men out to draw the enemy into the open and *then* they would send in the big guns and planes to take over. Meantime, death came to so many of you.

45 He told me how, after a while over there, instead of a yellow streak, the men got a mean streak down their backs. Each day the streak got bigger and the men became meaner. Everyone but *you,* Bill. He 50 said how you stayed the same, happy-go-lucky guy that you were when you arrived in Vietnam. How your warmth and friendliness drew the guys to you. How your [lieutenant] gave you the nickname of 55 "Spanky," and soon your group, Jim included, were all known as "Spanky's gang." How when you died it made it so much harder on them for you were their moral support. And he said how you of all 60 people should never have been the one to die.

Oh, God, how it hurts to write this. But I must face it and then put it to rest. I know that after Jim talked to me, he must have 65 relived it all over again and suffered so. Before I hung up the phone I told Jim I loved him. Loved him for just being your close friend, and for sharing the last days of your life with you, and for being there 70 with you when you died. How lucky you

were to have him for a friend, and how lucky he was to have had you.

They tell me the letters I write to you and leave here at this memorial are wak-75 ing others up to the fact that there is still much pain left, after all these years, from the Vietnam War.

But this I know. I would rather to have had you for 21 years, and all the pain that 80 goes with losing you, than never to have had you at all.

Mom

A letter and two roses are among the thousands of mementoes left by visitors to Washington's Vietnam Veterans Memorial, which attracts between three and four million visitors annually.

Discussing the Reading

1. What "answer" did Eleanor Wimbish feel she received in talking to her dead son's friend?

2. What final consolation did she find?

CRITICAL THINKING
Making Comparisons

Compare Eugene Sledge's feelings about his marine comrades killed on Okinawa (Source Reading 16B) with Eleanor Wimbish's toward her son. Which of the two would have liked to forget these feelings? For which did these feelings serve to educate others about the pain caused by war?

LBUTTS · RAY G DAVIS · THOMAS M FELTON · CHARLES D BRASIER · ERNEST D BURNS · ROBERT E WORRELL
ARNOLD FALCON GARCIA · JAMES H SMITH · WARREN C DEYERMOND · DUANE N S
HUGHES · MICHAEL D HUGHES · BRUCE E INGMAN · LEONARD M GOMOLICKE
DEZ Sr · JOHN V MORASCINI · GEORGE J PASCALE · EDWARD L KIM GREY · JEFFERSON S D
IOS · ELDON L REYNOLDS · JOE I RODRIGUEZ · GREGORY J · BRUCE E KA
DAN · WILLIAM D GILLINGHAM · LARRY L TECHMEIR · RICHARD J SCHO · MICHAEL S SP
L J TROYAN Jr · RALPH A WELLINGHOFF · ROY S WILLS · RONALD · ALBERTO TO
WAITE · STEPHEN J BRENNAN · JOHN E BLINER · TIMOTHY G CA · WI
Z · WILLIAM F ERICSON II · HAMPTON A ETHERIDGE III · ADOLPHUS CHRISTO · JAMES C HARM
LE GODBEY · JOHN C HANSEN · THOMAS E HEMPEL · JOHNNY N EUT ER · PETER F KRIST
MICHAEL A LACKNER · BRIAN E WOLFE
W 21 · CHARLE
· LINDSAY C T

Chapter Summary

Write supporting details under each of the following main ideas as you review the chapter.

Section 1
1. Ho Chi Minh sought Vietnamese independence.
2. South Vietnam established a pro-American government.
3. Diem asked for American aid.

Section 2
1. American presence in Vietnam grew after the Gulf of Tonkin incident.
2. Johnson escalated the war after the 1964 election.
3. Tough North Vietnamese resistance created a stalemate.
4. U.S. soldiers found Vietnam an intensely frustrating experience.
5. Antiwar sentiment spread throughout the United States.

Section 3
1. The Tet Offensive alarmed Americans.
2. McCarthy and Kennedy challenged President Johnson.
3. King and Kennedy were assassinated.
4. Nixon won a narrow victory in 1968.

Section 4
1. Nixon introduced a draft lottery and Vietnamization.
2. Nixon ordered an invasion of Cambodia.
3. The war dragged on.
4. A cease-fire was signed after the Christmas bombing.
5. South Vietnam fell to the communists.

Chapter Themes

1. **Relations with other nations:** After World War II, American foreign policy was based on the containment of communism. One of the places where Americans militarily challenged the communists was in South Vietnam, believing that if this nation fell to the communists, the rest of southeast Asia would follow.
2. **Conflict and cooperation:** The United States fought against the Viet Cong and the North Vietnamese and cooperated with the pro-West government of South Vietnam.

Chapter Study Guide

Identifying Key People and Terms

Name the key person or key term that describes the:
1. idea that once South Vietnam fell to the communists, other nations of southeast Asia would also fall
2. legislative act giving the American president authority to "take all necessary measures" to protect American forces and prevent further aggression in Vietnam
3. president who led South Vietnam after 1965
4. communist supply line from North Vietnam to South Vietnam
5. series of 1968 communist attacks that shook American confidence at home

Locating Key Places

1. At what parallel was the boundary between North and South Vietnam fixed by the Geneva Accords?
2. What cities were the capitals of North and South Vietnam?
3. In which American city did antiwar protesters demonstrate during the Democratic convention of 1968?

Mastering the Main Ideas

1. Why did Ho Chi Minh and his followers fight for so long in Vietnam, first against the French and then against the Americans?
2. Why did the United States government take on the fight against Ho Chi Minh and his followers after the defeat of the French?
3. How did the North Vietnamese and the Viet Cong achieve a victory over the technologically superior forces of the United States?
4. What was the "pacification program?" Did it work? Why or why not?

Applying Critical Thinking Skills

1. **Recognizing values:** What traditional American values did those who supported the war in Vietnam display? What traditional values did antiwar Americans demonstrate?
2. **Distinguishing false from accurate images:** Many Americans believed the domino theory to be an accurate image to describe the effects of losing a war in Vietnam. Do you think the image was an accurate one? Point out the postwar evidence to support your answer.

1954
Geneva Accords

1964
Gulf of Tonkin
Resolution

1968
My Lai
Massacre

1975
Vietnam War ends

1982
Vietnam
Veterans
Memorial

1970
Kent State/Jackson State tragedies

1972
Nixon visits China

1971
26th Amendment

3. Identifying alternatives: In the 1950s what choices regarding southeast Asia did the U.S. government have?

4. Testing conclusions: Many observers have said of the Vietnam War, "The Americans won all the battles, but lost the war." What evidence supports this conclusion about the American involvement in Vietnam? If you decide this conclusion is accurate, why do you think the Americans lost the war?

Chapter Activities

Learning Geography Through History

1. What geographical factors helped undermine the American war effort in South Vietnam?

2. In what conservative state did Senator Eugene McCarthy heavily defeat President Johnson in a presidential primary, causing Johnson to withdraw from the race for president in 1968?

Relating the United States to the World

1. What worldwide considerations prevented the United States from waging a total war against the Viet Cong and North Vietnamese?

2. North and South Vietnam were not the only sites of the Vietnam War. In what other nations of Southeast Asia did war action occur?

Linking Past to Present

1. For a long time, the American people had trouble honoring the veterans of the Vietnam War. Now, however, the veterans

have been remembered and continue to be honored. In what ways have Americans honored the veterans of the Vietnam War?

2. What is the "Vietnam syndrome"? Does it affect American foreign policy today?

Using the Time Line

1. When did the Vietnam War end?

2. Which settlement divided Vietnam along the 17th parallel?

3. What world event might lead observers to conclude that Richard Nixon wanted the war to end for bigger reasons than the truth or falsehood of the "domino theory"? Explain your answer.

Practicing Critical Thinking Strategies

Distinguishing False from Accurate Images

The American people were told by their leaders that the nation was winning the Vietnam War and that there was light at the end of the tunnel. This was clearly a false image of the war. Why do you think this image was presented to the American people? Do you think this was the correct thing to do? Why or why not?

Learning More About the Vietnam War and Its Aftermath

1. Using Source Readings: Read the Source Readings for this chapter and answer the questions.

2. Using Literature: Read the excerpt from Michael Herr's Vietnam War memoir, *Dispatches,* on pages 898–899, which gives an account of the siege of the U.S. Marine base at Khe Sanh.

Linking Past to Present

The rise and fall of Richard Nixon is illustrated clearly by these two photographs. In 1968 supporters at the Republican National Convention, inset, cheered his nomination and then voted him into office. In 1972 they overwhelmingly helped him win a second term. Less than two years later, these same supporters would shake their heads in disbelief as they read newspapers detailing the resignation of the president.

An Era of Turmoil

1 9 6 8 – 1 9 7 4

22

CHAPTER PREVIEW

In this chapter you will learn why the Nixon years were characterized by foreign and domestic turmoil.

The scene repeated itself again and again in the first months of 1973. A military plane taxied to a stop on a runway surrounded by spectators and television cameras. A band played. A "welcome home" mat lay on the tarmac. One by one, weary uniformed men emerged from the plane and rushed into the arms of family members. The American prisoners of war were coming home from Vietnam.

Americans had long expected the end of the frustrating and divisive Vietnam War to permit a time of national healing. Political passions would subside. Military spending would decline and permit more serious attention to domestic problems.

The return of the Vietnam veterans brought little calm to America, however. President Richard Nixon was deeply embroiled in the greatest political scandal in American history. The nation was also feeling the first shocks of a major transformation of its economy. The era of booming economic growth that had begun in 1945 was sputtering to a close. The American people, staggered by nearly a decade of social, political, and economic crises, seemed to be losing faith in their leaders, their government, and some believed, in themselves. The "age of limits" had begun.

What happened in the 1970s to cause such widespread popular cynicism and uncertainty? What steps did the nation take to mend itself?

1960	1965	1970	1975	1980

1969
U.S. astronauts land on moon

1971
Nixon combats inflation with wage and price controls

1974
Nixon resigns presidency; Ford becomes president; Ford pardons Nixon

1972
Nixon visits China and the Soviet Union

1973
Arab oil embargo begins; military junta ousts Chilean leader Salvador Allende; Spiro Agnew resigns as vice president

Americans hoped Nixon would restore stability.

Key Terms: New Federalism, Family Assistance Plan, revenue sharing, *Roe v. Wade*

Reading Preview
As you read this section, you will learn:

1. what Nixon did in response to the complaint that the federal government intruded too far into the lives of Americans.
2. how the Supreme Court was characterized during the 1970s.
3. what methods Nixon used to achieve his own domestic and international goals.
4. who won the election of 1972.

Americans who voted for Richard Nixon in 1968 believed that he was the person who could restore order and stability in their lives. They found in Nixon a man who matched their mood. Born in a small town in California to a lower-middle-class family, he had worked hard all his life and had overcome great odds to reach the pinnacle of political power. His natural constituency, he realized, was the great mass of struggling middle-class men and women who, like him, believed they had risen in the world as a result of their own efforts. Nixon called them the Silent Majority, and he played skillfully to their hopes and fears.

President Nixon reduced federal responsibilities.

Nixon had only limited interest in domestic policy. He considered himself a world statesman, and when he had to deal with problems at home he thought of them largely in political terms. What would most effectively secure his own political base? What would do the most to give him the freedom to pursue his great international objectives? Nonetheless, Nixon's government, like every other government, had to deal with domestic issues every day. Despite the president's own relative lack of interest, his Administration developed policies that left a lasting mark on American domestic life.

The Nixon Administration's stated domestic goals were consistent with the president's complaint that government had intruded too far into the lives of the people. It was necessary, the president claimed, to reduce some of the powers of the federal government. That reduction would come in part from a repudiation of certain responsibilities Washington had accepted in the 1960s. It would also come from transferring some powers back to state and local governments. President Nixon called his domestic initiatives the **New Federalism**.

Some of Nixon's domestic efforts bore little fruit. He tried to slow down forced integration of public schools, but neither Congress nor the courts obliged him. He attempted to reform the bureaucratically tangled national welfare system through the **Family Assistance Plan**. The plan, developed by Nixon's urban affairs adviser, Daniel Patrick Moynihan, called for guaranteed annual payments of $1,600 to all poor families. Democrats, however, quickly criticized Moynihan's plan for the low level of payments and a provision requiring heads of poor households, mainly women, to register for employment as a condition for receiving payments. Despite its many attractive features, including substantial aid to the working poor, the Family Assistance Plan failed to win congressional approval.

In other areas, however, the Administration enjoyed considerable success in achieving its goals. Nixon reduced funding for many of the Great Society programs of the Johnson Administration, some of which had already lost much of their budgets to the war in Vietnam. Some agencies he dismantled entirely. The Office of Economic Opportunity (OEO), for example, was dismantled in 1973. The OEO had been the centerpiece of the War on Poverty.

Nixon also launched a program he called **revenue sharing**. Under this program, which is still operating today, the federal government returns a portion of its tax receipts to state and local governments to meet local needs.

The Supreme Court practiced moderation.

Perhaps even more important on the domestic scene was Nixon's effort to redefine the Supreme Court. Presidents can influence the Court because Supreme Court justices, like all other federal judges, are nominated by the president and then confirmed or rejected by the Senate. For more than a decade, the Court, under the leadership of Chief Justice Earl Warren, had greatly expanded the role of government in protecting individual rights. Many Americans believed it had gone too far. For example, conservatives particularly resented the Court's decision in 1962 to prevent public schools from requiring the recitation of prayers (*Engle* v. *Vitale*). The Court said the prayer requirement violated the establishment of religion clause in the First Amendment. The amendment reads "Congress shall make no law respecting an establishment of religion."

Nixon's first opportunity to change the Court came almost immediately. Chief Justice Warren had announced his resignation in the last months of the Johnson Administration, but Congress had refused to confirm the appointment of liberal Associate Justice Abe Fortas to succeed him. Consequently, one of Nixon's first duties was to nominate a new chief justice. He selected **Warren Burger**, a federal appeals court judge who was known to favor judicial restraint.

A few months later, Fortas resigned as associate justice after accusations of financial impropriety. Although President Nixon tried twice to replace him with conservative judges, he was rebuffed by Congress. His first choice, Clement Haynsworth, was a respected jurist. Haynsworth, however, ran afoul of liberals, African American organizations, and others for his conservative decisions on civil rights. Nixon's second choice, G. Harold Carswell, was so undistinguished that even his defenders found it difficult to justify the appointment. One conservative senator admitted that Carswell was a "mediocre" judge but argued that mediocre people deserved representation on the Supreme Court too.

MEET THE PRESIDENT

RICHARD M. NIXON

Born: January 9, 1913
In office: 1969–1974

"Won some; lost some; all interesting." In six terse words Richard Nixon once summed up a political career dramatic in its triumphs and defeats—and historic in its conclusion. In August 1974 Nixon became the first president to resign from office.

At 40 Nixon became America's second-youngest vice president. At 49 he bitterly announced his own political extinction, yet only six years later he became president.

Nixon was a man who always played "hardball"—a tough, aggressive, confrontational style of politics. During Nixon's 1972 reelection campaign, hardball politics curved deep into foul territory. The "Watergate scandal" would take two years to unravel, obscuring the notable diplomatic achievements of the Nixon presidency and ending it in disgrace.

Madalyn Murray stands on the steps of the U.S. Supreme Court in 1963 with her two sons. Murray, who raised her sons as atheists, appealed a Maryland court ruling that upheld the reading of the Lord's Prayer and of the Bible in Baltimore public schools. The U.S. Supreme Court overturned the Maryland ruling, arguing that such a practice violated the rights of the Murrays. The ruling came only months after the Court ruled that public schools cannot require students to pray in school (*Engle* v. *Vitale*).

Frustrated by his failure to get Haynsworth and Carswell appointed to the Court, Nixon softened his approach somewhat by nominating less conservative candidates. This tactic helped gain Supreme Court seats for his next two appointments— Harry Blackmun and Lewis Powell. Both of these men were moderates whose decisions generally preserved the rights the Court had already established but slowed the expansion of rights into new areas. Although Nixon managed to get one more conservative appointed to the Court— William Rehnquist—the Court as a whole was notable for its moderation in the 1970s.

Three major decisions of the early 1970s, however, were as influential and controversial as any of the Warren Court. In 1971 the Court ruled (in *Swann* v. *Charlotte-Mecklenburg Board of Education*) that communities that have schools that are segregated because of residential patterns must employ forced busing to achieve integration. A year later it overturned existing capital punishment statutes (*Furman* v. *Georgia*). The new guidelines established by the Court were so strict that executions stopped throughout the nation for several years. In 1973 the Supreme Court made one of the most controversial decisions in its history. In **Roe v. Wade** the Court invalidated state laws that had forbidden women to have abortions. This decision was hotly debated between "pro-life" and "pro-choice" advocates throughout the 1980s and into the 1990s.

In other decisions, however, the Court made it clear that there were limits to the rights it would protect and the tools it would approve. In *Milliken* v. *Bradley* (1974), it rejected a plan to transfer students across district lines (in this case between Detroit and its suburbs) to achieve racial balance. Several years later, the Court established new and more restrictive guidelines for affirmative action programs in *Bakke* v. *Board of Regents of California* (1978). In this controversial case Allen Bakke, a white applicant to the University of California medical school at Davis, claimed that his rights had been violated when his application was rejected in favor of applications from less qualified minority students. The Court decided in Bakke's favor, saying that affirmative action denied him equal protection under the 14th Amendment. The decision was buffered, however. In another ruling the Court upheld the principle of affirmative action by saying that universities could make race "simply one element" in their selection of medical students.

Nixon tried to discredit liberals.

One of the keys to Nixon's victory in the 1968 election was the growing popular anger at protesters and dissenters. Nixon entered the White House aware that undermining dissent could pay political dividends. He also considered it essential to discredit and weaken the left before he could achieve his own domestic and international goals.

At first, Nixon's war on the dissenters was largely rhetorical. He instructed his vice

KENT STATE
Skill: Demonstrating Reasoned Judgment

Introducing the Skill.
What began as a peaceful assembly protesting the invasion of Cambodia on May 4, 1970, soon became a controversial national tragedy. Four students were killed by National Guardsmen called in to restore peace and order to the campus. What circumstances led the National Guardsmen to fire upon the students? Was the decision to use their rifles to quell the disturbance well reasoned? Why or why not?

Learning the Skill.
To judge whether the person who ordered the guardsmen to fire into the crowd was **demonstrating reasoned judgment**, you must examine the way in which the decision was reached. Did the person gather and use all available evidence? Did the person consider different perspectives or viewpoints? Did he or she reach a conclusion by following a logical and extended line of careful reasoning?

Applying the Skill.
Read the following excerpt from a report of a commission appointed by President Nixon shortly after the Kent State tragedy. Then answer the questions below.

The May 4 rally began as a peaceful assembly on the Commons—the traditional site of student assemblies. Even if the Guard had authority to prohibit a peaceful gathering—a question that is at least debatable—the decision to disperse the noon rally was a serious error. The timing and manner of the dispersal was disastrous. Many students were legitimately in the area as they went to and from class. The rally was held during the crowded noontime lunch period. The rally was peaceful, and there was no apparent impending violence. Only when the Guard attempted to disperse the rally did some students react violently. . . .

The actions of some students were violent and criminal and those of some others were dangerous, reckless, and irresponsible. The indiscriminate firing of rifles into a crowd of students and the deaths that followed were unnecessary, unwarranted, and inexcusable. . . .

Even if the guardsmen faced danger, it was not a danger that called for lethal force.

1. What judgment did the president's commission reach concerning the events at Kent State?
2. What evidence did the commission use to support its judgment?
3. What other possible solutions might the National Guard or the university have considered to end the demonstration?

president, Spiro Agnew, to make a series of strident speeches denouncing student protesters and the liberal figures in the media who seemed to support them. Nixon himself frequently spoke contemptuously of protesting students—most notably in the spring of 1970 when university campuses erupted after the American invasion of Cambodia. Nixon denounced the protesters as "bums." Then, when four students were killed by National Guardsmen at Kent State University in Ohio, he said that the students themselves were to blame for the tragedy. Later in 1970, as the president campaigned for Republican congressional candidates, he stood on top of his limousine and brazenly taunted student demonstrators gathered across the street from him.

The Nixon Administration also used covert, or secret, actions in an attempt to discredit liberal adversaries. Nixon's "plumbers," as you will recall reading earlier, illegally broke into Daniel Ellsberg's psychiatrist's office in an

The Arab oil embargo created lines of 50 cars or more at gas pumps across the nation.

In 1973, in the midst of a war between Israel and several Arab nations, OPEC announced that its members would ship no oil to nations supporting Israel. This action, known as the **Arab oil embargo**, included the United States and most of Western Europe. At about the same time, OPEC nations agreed to quadruple their prices.

These decisions sent shock waves through the United States. Americans experienced their first fuel shortage since early in World War II. Motorists had to wait in long lines at gas stations. Schools and offices closed down to save on heating costs. Factories cut production and laid off workers because they could not buy enough fuel to keep operating. After a few months, OPEC lifted the embargo. High oil prices remained, however. In addition, because virtually every major economic activity in America depended either directly or indirectly on oil, the higher cost of fuel led to higher costs for everything else. Inflation soared.

The Nixon Administration was uncertain about how to respond to the energy crisis that had developed. The government encouraged energy conservation, and the president spoke about the importance of achieving "energy independence." In fact, the United States had no viable plan that could quickly solve the energy problem. It was critically dependent on oil, and it did not produce enough itself to satisfy its demands. A dramatic increase in the price of fuel meant that economic problems were inevitable. Only a major change in the American way of life, a change few Americans seemed disposed to make, could have reduced the demand for energy enough to counteract the effects of the price increases.

American industry experienced severe problems.

The problems of inflation and energy hit the United States particularly hard because they came at a time when American industry was experiencing tremendous difficulties. In the first years after World War II, the United States had faced very little competition from abroad and had maintained industrial preeminence. As other nations recovered from wartime

raw materials from abroad. Now, however, other industrial nations—most notably Japan and the countries of Western Europe—were experiencing impressive industrial growth and were also bidding for raw materials. Competition for raw materials such as iron ore and petroleum began to drive the prices up.

Equally important, some of the suppliers of raw materials were beginning to realize that they could get higher prices for their goods if they worked in groups rather than individually. One of these groups was the **Organization of Petroleum Exporting Countries (OPEC)**. This organization has 13 members in the Middle East, Africa, South America, and Asia.

When OPEC was formed in 1960 it had only five members and had little power. In the early 1970s, however, it added new members and began to develop significant strength. As the demand for Middle Eastern oil grew, the OPEC nations became less and less willing to do what the major American and European oil companies demanded. Gradually, OPEC also began to see that its control of the oil supply could be a political weapon, which it could use in its struggle against Israel.

destruction and rebuilt their industrial plants, however, they began to compete with American companies. One result was that the United States experienced a significant decline in foreign markets for its goods. More importantly, however, American companies began to encounter foreign competition in their own domestic markets. Many Americans began buying European and Japanese industrial goods instead of similar but more expensive products made in the United States.

Both then and later, many American manufacturers complained that their foreign competitors engaged in unfair trade practices. In reality, however, the most important reasons for the declining competitiveness of American goods were cost and quality. Wages for industrial workers had risen dramatically after World War II, and the cost of those wages was reflected in the cost of American products. Perhaps more importantly, American factories had not modernized as fast as those of many other countries. These nations had been forced to rebuild industrial plants destroyed in the war. Europe and Japan thus had newer and more efficient plants than did the United States. Many American factories were 50 years old. Even when foreign competitors paid their workers wages comparable to those of American laborers, their modern facilities enabled them to employ fewer people to do comparable work at a higher quality.

Many American businesses responded to these problems with harsh new labor policies that often made the situation worse. Major industrial corporations tried to increase their control over their employees and to force them to work faster and more efficiently. In response, many workers became alienated from their jobs. Absenteeism and drug use increased. In addition, workers in some large corporations began viewing their employers as cold and impersonal. Consequently, they found it difficult to identify with their companies or with the products they were making. Such feelings often contributed to a decline in product quality and productivity in general.

The decreasing competitiveness of American manufacturing became particularly evident in the steel and automobile industries, which for the first time experienced substantial competition from abroad. Japanese and European cars and steel seized a growing proportion of the American market. Consequently, American companies cut back production and laid off workers. For more than a decade beginning in 1973, the incomes of industrial workers declined steadily while inflation continued. Union membership dropped to its lowest point since before World War II. Some American workers began to lose hope in the future. One of the most visible results of these challenges to American industry was the growing wave of plant closings throughout the industrial Northeast and Midwest.

Plant closings throughout the Northeast and Midwest devastated communities dependent upon the success of those factories. The region, once boasted as the nation's steel belt, was soon referred to as the rust belt.

Deindustrialization produced economic hardship.

Plant closings devastated many communities. This was especially true when, as was often the case, the closed factories were the major employers. An example of a community particularly hard-hit by plant closings was **Cortland County** in upstate New York. In the mid-1970s three major factories closed in the county. Plants owned by Westinghouse, GAF, and Brockway Motors all shut down during a single nine-month period. Forty percent of the workers in those plants were unemployed for ten months or more. Ten percent were without jobs for more than two years.

The effects of the closings on Cortland County went well beyond the hardship of the workers who were laid off, however. The impact of the closings rippled through the entire community. With their incomes greatly reduced, unemployed workers naturally also spent less money. That meant that merchants in Cortland County sold fewer goods and saw their own incomes reduced. They in turn laid off workers and closed stores, further reducing the community's income. Demand for housing declined, which caused a reduction in property values and a slowing of housing construction.

Many unemployed workers found themselves forced to rely on public assistance for the first time in their lives. Demand for food stamps rose sharply in the county in the months after the plant closings. As unemployment benefits ran out, many workers were forced to apply for welfare. Many of these people had been financially secure only months before. Having to turn to welfare to support themselves and their families was usually very humiliating. Their sentiments were probably best summed up by Arlo Guthrie, a popular folk singer of the time, whose song "Hard Times" contained these lyrics:

I ain't got a nickel to call mine . . . we ain't even got a lousy dime.

The plant closings also had a profound psychological effect on the area. According to one psychologist:

AN AMERICAN ★ SPEAKS

Unemployment can become a psychological illness with symptoms as clearly defined as a disease like measles. Tragically, too many of the unemployed face the trauma alone, feeling rejected even by those who love them.

Even people who remained employed sensed that their community was in decline. Some families left Cortland County and moved to other parts of the country where they believed work would be easier to find.

Other people such as 55-year-old Norman Sanders, an unemployed electrician, took odd jobs to make ends meet. He also found a creative way to cut living expenses. According to Sanders:

Americans on the Moon

Worn by the turmoil of the 1960s, Americans could find relief by gazing with awe and pride at the night sky.

It was a totally different moon than I had ever seen before. The moon that I knew from old was a flat yellow disc, and this was a huge three-dimensional sphere, almost a ghostly

view, tinged sort of pale white. It was very, very large and stationary in our window, utterly silent, of course, and it gave one a feeling of foreboding. It didn't seem like a very friendly or welcoming place. It made one wonder whether we should be invading its domain or not.

So astronaut Michael Collins described his first view of the moon as the Apollo 11 spacecraft swung in toward the crater-pocked surface. Although Collins had a sense of foreboding, Apollo 11 was a brilliant

success. On July 20, 1969, Neil Armstrong and Edwin Aldrin became the first people to set foot on the moon. The astronauts from Apollo 11 and from five subsequent Apollo voyages made the moon landings a uniquely American adventure. Video cameras captured them behaving like

Highlights of American Life

My two married sons and I set up a commune. We share **AN AMERICAN ★ SPEAKS** taxes, food bills and household expenses. We all get along real good.

After the Brockway Motors factory shut down, bumper stickers began to appear in the county: "The last person to leave Cortland please shut out the lights." Soon after the Brockway closing, a Montgomery Ward store and other large retail establishments closed in the town of Cortland, the county seat. These closings contributed further to what one group of scholars studying the community called a depression psychology, a widespread feeling of despair and pessimism about the future. The few people who managed to find new jobs in the community often had to accept drastically reduced wages. Haywood Willis, who earned $6 an hour as an auto worker, had to take a job unloading boxcars for $2.50 an hour.

You're mad at first, but that **AN AMERICAN ★ SPEAKS** don't change nothin'. I don't know if I'll be called back for a long time. Probably not until well after my money runs out.

space-suited tourists: posing for photographs, collecting souvenir rocks, and cruising around in their two-million-dollar convertible. Alan Shephard smuggled a golf club into space and, in the weak lunar gravity, hit a one-handed shot that made earthbound golfers gasp with admiration.

Bounding around on the moon, the Apollo astronauts made moon walking look like light-hearted fun. In fact, the missions involved considerable risk. America's six successful moon landings, between 1969 and 1972, are a testament to the bravery of the astronauts and to the reliability of American technology.

The problems of Cortland County were repeated in communities throughout the industrial regions of the United States in the 1970s and 1980s. Once-vibrant cities and towns grew suddenly quiet and desolate as their major employers shut their gates. Large numbers of people deserted their communities and moved south or west in search of better opportunities. Some industrial areas gradually revived by developing new and more profitable economic sectors, but seldom did the revival produce very many jobs for unskilled or semiskilled people. The United States, for decades the greatest manufacturing nation in the world, was deindustrializing and moving toward a service-oriented economy.

SECTION **2** REVIEW

Identify Key People and Terms
Write a sentence to identify: Federal Reserve System, recession, Organization of Petroleum Exporting Countries (OPEC), Arab oil embargo

Locate Key Places
Cortland County is located within which state?

Master the Main Ideas

1. **Analyzing the impact of inflation:** What were two methods used by Nixon to try to control inflation?
2. **Understanding the importance of civic participation:** What could individual Americans have done to reduce the demand for energy during the energy crisis?
3. **Supporting the freedom of consumers:** Why did many Americans decide to begin buying foreign industrial goods?
4. **Analyzing the impact of inflation:** How did plant closings affect people psychologically?

Apply Critical Thinking Skills: Drawing Conclusions
Do you think that it is right for a president to impose a freeze on wages and prices in a mixed free-enterprise economy? Why or why not? (In a mixed free-enterprise economy most economic decisions are made by individuals.)

GEOGRAPHY IN AMERICAN HISTORY

Sunbelt Migration

The nonmetallic element silicon is used in the making of computer chips, right. Manufacturers of high-tech products dominate California's Silicon Valley, which extends from Palo Alto to San Jose, far right.

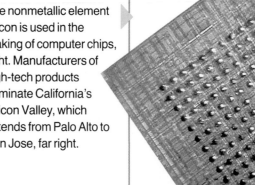

United States Population Shifts, 1970-1981

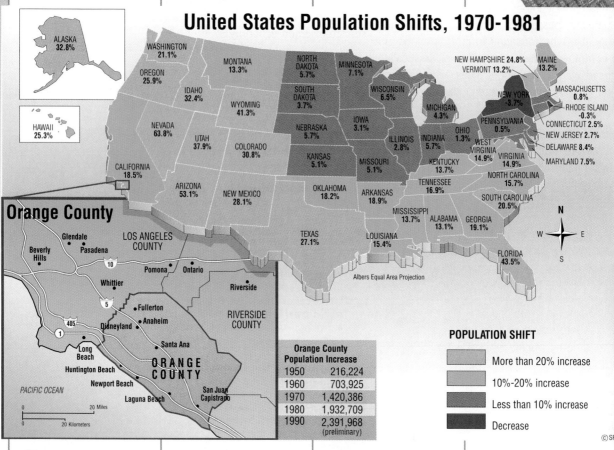

ALASKA 32.8%

HAWAII 25.3%

WASHINGTON 21.1%
OREGON 25.9%
MONTANA 13.3%
NORTH DAKOTA 5.7%
MINNESOTA 7.1%
NEW HAMPSHIRE 24.8%
VERMONT 13.2%
MAINE 13.2%
IDAHO 32.4%
WYOMING 41.3%
SOUTH DAKOTA 3.7%
WISCONSIN 6.5%
MICHIGAN 4.3%
NEW YORK -3.7%
MASSACHUSETTS 0.8%
RHODE ISLAND -0.3%
NEVADA 63.8%
UTAH 37.9%
COLORADO 30.8%
NEBRASKA 5.7%
IOWA 3.1%
ILLINOIS 2.8%
INDIANA 5.7%
OHIO 1.3%
PENNSYLVANIA 0.5%
WEST VIRGINIA 14.9%
CONNECTICUT 2.5%
NEW JERSEY 2.7%
DELAWARE 8.4%
MARYLAND 7.5%
CALIFORNIA 18.5%
KANSAS 5.1%
MISSOURI 5.1%
KENTUCKY 13.7%
VIRGINIA 14.9%
ARIZONA 53.1%
NEW MEXICO 28.1%
OKLAHOMA 18.2%
ARKANSAS 18.9%
TENNESSEE 16.9%
NORTH CAROLINA 15.7%
SOUTH CAROLINA 20.5%
MISSISSIPPI 13.7%
ALABAMA 13.1%
GEORGIA 19.1%
TEXAS 27.1%
LOUISIANA 15.4%
FLORIDA 43.5%

Albers Equal Area Projection

Orange County

Glendale, Beverly Hills, Pasadena, LOS ANGELES COUNTY, Pomona, Ontario, Whittier, Riverside, Fullerton, Anaheim, Disneyland, RIVERSIDE COUNTY, Santa Ana, Long Beach, ORANGE COUNTY, Huntington Beach, Newport Beach, San Juan Capistrano, Laguna Beach, PACIFIC OCEAN

0 20 Miles
0 20 Kilometers

Orange County Population Increase	
1950	216,224
1960	703,925
1970	1,420,386
1980	1,932,709
1990	2,391,968 (preliminary)

POPULATION SHIFT

- More than 20% increase
- 10%-20% increase
- Less than 10% increase
- Decrease

©SF

Movement The term *sunbelt* usually refers to the area extending from the southern Atlantic coast to California. However, note that western states north of the Sunbelt also gained population. Which two states had the greatest percent increase in population in the 1970s?

Critical Thinking What factors might have caused people to move south and west?

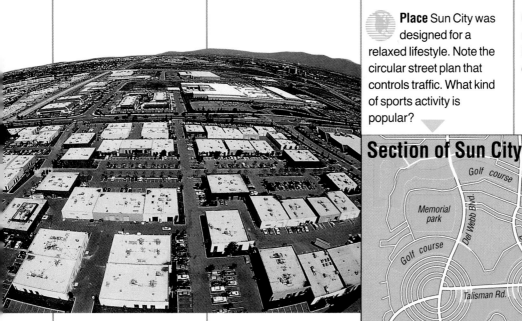

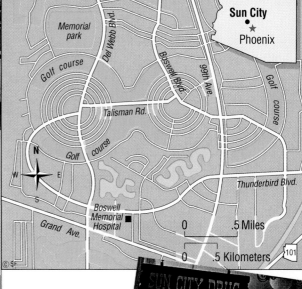

Place Sun City was designed for a relaxed lifestyle. Note the circular street plan that controls traffic. What kind of sports activity is popular?

Critical Thinking Why might people choose to live in a retirement community?

Section of Sun City

Golf course

Memorial park

Del Webb Blvd.

Golf course

Talisman Rd.

Boswell Blvd.

99th Ave.

Golf course

Golf course

Grand Ave.

Boswell Memorial Hospital

Thunderbird Blvd.

0   .5 Miles

0   .5 Kilometers

101

N
W   E
S

AZ

Sun City
★
Phoenix

One of the Sunbelt's attractions is its warm climate. Residents of southern California can enjoy a day at Laguna Beach year round.

Sun City, Arizona, a retirement community outside of Phoenix, protects itself with a 400-member posse of volunteers.

SUN CITY DRUG

875

SECTION 3

Nixon and Kissinger tackled problems in foreign affairs.

Key Terms: trilateralism, SALT I, détente, SALT II, Nixon Doctrine

Reading Preview
As you read this section, you will learn:
1. what Nixon and Kissinger accomplished in communist China.
2. the results of the meetings between Soviet and American officials between 1969 and 1973.
3. what plan Nixon devised to solve conflicts in the Third World.
4. what role the United States played in the October 1973 war.

The war in Vietnam proved in many ways just as damaging and preoccupying to the Nixon Administration as it had to the Johnson Administration. Nixon and his powerful national security adviser, Henry Kissinger, had spent four full years struggling to bring U.S. involvement in the war to a close in 1973.

Despite the toll the war had taken on Nixon, he still managed to pursue other foreign policy goals. His mission, as he saw it, was to build a new international order, a "structure of peace" that would change the way the great powers dealt with each other.

Henry Kissinger, the principal architect of détente, believed that the Cold War was to be managed and controlled, not won.

Nixon recognized that the world now had more than two great powers. Japan, Western Europe, and China were all emerging as major forces in world affairs. Both the communist and noncommunist alliances were becoming more diverse. No longer did America clearly dominate its NATO allies. Likewise, the Soviet Union did not have the same control over the Warsaw Pact nations as it once had.

Nixon and Kissinger believed that the emergence of Western Europe, Japan, and China meant that it would be necessary to encourage a new, "multi-polar" structure of international affairs, replacing the old "bi-polar" one that the Soviet Union and the United States had run since the end of World War II. This system would be based vaguely on the old European concept of a balance of powers. President Nixon said:

> It will be a safer world and a better world if we have a strong, healthy United States, Europe, Soviet Union, China, Japan—each balancing the other, not playing one against the other. . . .

AN AMERICAN ★ SPEAKS

To achieve this goal, Nixon and Kissinger believed that the United States would need to do three things. First, it would have to recognize that the noncommunist world was no longer a single bloc dominated by the United States. It now had three major power centers—America, Western Europe, and Japan. This idea became known as **trilateralism**. Second, America would have to work to bring China out of its isolation so that it could play a role as a major force in the communist world, counterbalancing the power of the Soviet Union. Third, the United States would need to improve relations with the Soviet Union.

Nixon and Kissinger forged new ties with communist China.

America had had no relations with China since the leaders of the communist revolution seized control of the nation in 1949. The United States continued during those years to recognize a weak exile regime on the island of Taiwan as the official government of China, despite the fact that the regime never had any real chance of ever regaining control of the mainland. Communist China, in the meantime, had cut itself off from almost all contact with the western world as its leaders had attempted to consolidate the revolution through the use of harsh and brutal methods. Millions of people who resisted the communist regime were imprisoned or executed.

迫 民 族 联 合

As part of his highly publicized visit to the People's Republic of China, President Nixon reviews Chinese troops with former Premier Zhou Enlai.

Nixon and Kissinger were nonetheless eager to begin a new relationship with communist China. They knew it was an important nation because of its enormous size and tremendous economic and military potential. They also hoped that new ties with China would give the United States greater leverage with the Soviet Union; the Soviets would be eager to prevent an American-Chinese alliance against them and would thus be more likely to make concessions to the West to prevent that.

The Chinese had reasons of their own to want a new relationship with the United States. They were at least as hostile to the Soviet Union as they were to the West. By developing ties to the United States, they would be strengthening themselves against possible Soviet aggression. They were also eager for access to western markets to help their struggling economy. Improved relations with the United States would pave the way for better trade relations with the entire noncommunist world.

Point

In favor of establishing relations with communist China

■ Communist China poses a potential threat to the United States because of its enormous size and military potential.
■ Improved relations with China will give the United States additional leverage in dealing with the Soviet Union.

Counterpoint

Against establishing relations with communist China

■ Communist China uses harsh and brutal methods to promote communism.
■ The United States recognizes the Taiwan-based government.

In the summer of 1971, Henry Kissinger made a secret trip to **Beijing**, the capital of the People's Republic of China. (The city of Beijing is in northeastern China.) Kissinger returned to Washington with an invitation from the Chinese leadership to President Nixon to visit China himself. Consequently, in February 1972 Nixon became the first U.S. president to visit China. Although President Nixon's historic visit with Premier **Zhou Enlai** and Chairman Mao Zedong produced no major agreements immediately, it helped erase decades of bitterness and paved the way for the restoration of formal diplomatic ties in 1979 and the development of new trade ties.

American-Soviet relations improved between 1969 and 1973.

While the Nixon Administration improved relations with China, it also attempted to ease tensions between the United States and the Soviet Union. In 1969 the American and Soviet governments began formal arms control negotiations in **Helsinki**, the capital of Finland. Nearly three years later, in the spring of 1972, the two countries agreed to a strategic arms limitation treaty, known as **SALT I**, which limited the number of intercontinental ballistic missiles on both sides. The Senate ratified the treaty later the same year.

Nixon also became the first American president to visit **Moscow**, the capital of the Soviet Union. During his cordial May 1972 visit,

Nixon made an unprecedented television address to the Soviet people. In his address the president talked about the need for friendship between the two nations and for further progress toward **détente**—a relaxation of tensions. In meetings with Soviet Premier Leonid Brezhnev, he agreed to sell the Soviets nearly a quarter of the American grain supply. This so-called "wheat deal" became highly controversial because the Soviets paid much less than market price for the grain.

Nevertheless, the search for détente between the two nations continued. In June 1973 Brezhnev visited Washington. The friendly meeting produced several agreements, including an informal one to speed up progress toward a second arms control treaty, **SALT II**.

The president established the Nixon Doctrine.

Nixon and Kissinger believed that a stable international order depended above all on good relations among the great powers. They also recognized, however, that many of the most difficult international problems involved the countries of the Third World—the nonindustrial, developing nations of Asia, Africa, and Latin America. Most of these nations were not firmly aligned with the United States or the Soviet Union.

Early in his presidency, Nixon tried to establish a new set of guidelines for dealing with

conflicts in the Third World. He wanted to prevent another frustrating American commitment like the one in Vietnam. The president's new guidelines became known as the **Nixon Doctrine**.

In theory the Nixon Doctrine stated that the United States would agree to help "allies and friends" resist aggression and communist subversion. However, it would leave the "basic responsibility" to the allies and friends themselves. The United States would give financial support and some military assistance, but it would not become too deeply involved in any conflict.

In practice, however, the Nixon Doctrine did little to improve American relations with the Third World. Rather than attempting to promote democracy and economic development in nonaligned nations, the United States sought simply to support pro-American governments, no matter how corrupt and unpopular they might be, and build them up militarily to allow them to play a role in defending the West against possible Soviet aggression. In reality, nonmilitary foreign aid actually declined under the Nixon Doctrine. In addition, Third World leaders sometimes used the military assistance the United States provided to suppress opposition within their own societies.

Misdirected military assistance did not seem to trouble the Nixon Administration, which was particularly eager to help friendly regimes

General Augusto Pinochet ousted Chilean president Salvador Allende in a 1973 coup. Pinochet's militant anti-communism received support from the United States. Under his regime, Pinochet jailed, tortured, and killed political opponents, suspended civil liberties, and banned all political parties.

withstand "radical" challenges from within. In 1970 the Central Intelligence Agency (CIA) intervened directly in an election in Chile to prevent a victory by **Salvador Allende**, the communist candidate. Although Allende won despite the CIA interference, the United States continued funding Allende's opponents after the election. In 1973 a military junta ousted Allende and installed a harsh right-wing regime that remained in power for the next 17 years. Although few people knew the exact extent of U.S. involvement in the coup, the Nixon Administration clearly welcomed the result.

The United States helped bring an end to the October 1973 war.

The most volatile area of the world in the 1970s was the Middle East, where the long-simmering conflict between **Israel** and the Arab nations was the source of constant danger. Arab hostility toward Israel had increased after the humiliating Arab defeat in the Six-Day War in 1967. In that war, as the map on page 880 shows, Israel occupied substantial new territory

President Nixon celebrates his triumphant visit to Moscow in which he and Soviet leader Leonid Brezhnev, left, signed two important arms reduction agreements.

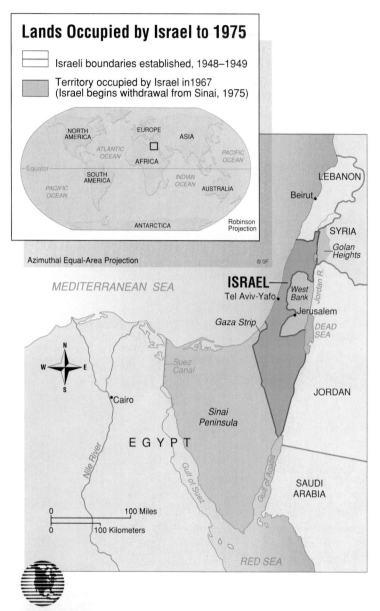

Lands Occupied by Israel to 1975

☐ Israeli boundaries established, 1948–1949

▨ Territory occupied by Israel in1967
(Israel begins withdrawal from Sinai, 1975)

Robinson Projection

Azimuthal Equal-Area Projection

© SF

NORTH AMERICA
EUROPE
ASIA
ATLANTIC OCEAN
AFRICA
PACIFIC OCEAN
Equator
SOUTH AMERICA
INDIAN OCEAN
AUSTRALIA
PACIFIC OCEAN
ANTARCTICA

MEDITERRANEAN SEA

LEBANON

Beirut

SYRIA

Golan Heights

ISRAEL

Tel Aviv-Yafo

West Bank

Jordan R.

Jerusalem

Gaza Strip

DEAD SEA

Suez Canal

JORDAN

Cairo

Sinai Peninsula

EGYPT

Nile River

Gulf of Suez

Gulf of Aqaba

SAUDI ARABIA

0   100 Miles
0   100 Kilometers

RED SEA

N W E S

map study

Location Israel, a Jewish nation located in the Middle East, is bordered by Arab countries. Name those countries.

Critical Thinking Why would Israel be interested in occupying the lands shown on the map?

formerly under Arab control. It refused to return it once the conflict ended.

Perhaps the most troubling problem in the region was the Palestinian question. Palestinian Arabs claimed that the land Israel occupied—both the territory within Israel's original boundaries and the territory Israel seized in 1967—was **Palestine**, their ancestral homeland. Many Palestinians had been refugees since the creation of Israel in 1948. Many more became refugees in the aftermath of the Six-Day War.

For a time, many Palestinians lived in camps in **Jordan**, which the map at left shows is directly east of Israel. **King Hussein**, Jordan's ruler, expelled them in 1970, however, because he feared that they threatened the stability of

his government. Thousands of Palestinians then moved to **Lebanon**, which the map shows is directly north of Israel.

Partly because of the Palestinian problem and partly because they wanted to avenge their defeat in 1967, Egypt and Syria attacked Israel in October 1973 on the day of the highest Jewish holy day, Yom Kippur. Israel was taken by surprise, and for more than a week the outcome remained uncertain. The outcome of the war remained further in doubt because the Nixon Administration seemed at first reluctant to send additional military aid to the Israelis. Finally, however, an effective Israeli offensive and new aid from the United States turned the tide. The Arab offensive was reversed. The American government then pressured Israel to accept a cease-fire and to end its own offensive.

The October war marked a turning point in American policy in the Middle East. The United States remained committed to the existence of Israel. However, it was now also concerned about its relations with the Arab nations. The new concern surfaced largely because of America's need for Middle Eastern oil, a need that was made clearly evident by the Arab oil boycott.

SECTION **3** REVIEW

Identify Key People and Terms
Write a sentence to identify: trilateralism, Zhou Enlai, SALT I, détente, SALT II, Nixon Doctrine, Salvador Allende, King Hussein

Locate Key Places
1. What are the capitals of the following countries: People's Republic of China, Finland, Soviet Union?
2. Which Middle Eastern nation was attacked on Yom Kippur?
3. What is the ancestral homeland of Palestinian Arabs?
4. Where are Jordan and Lebanon in relation to Israel?

Master the Main Ideas
1. **Analyzing causes/effects of American involvement in foreign affairs:** Why did Nixon and Kissinger feel it was important to forge new ties with communist China?
2. **Analyzing international cooperative efforts:** How did Nixon help ease tensions between the United States and the Soviet Union?
3. **Analyzing the impact of American foreign policies:** How successful was the Nixon Doctrine?
4. **Analyzing the impact of American foreign policies:** Why did the October 1973 war mark a turning point in American policy in the Middle East?

Apply Critical Thinking Skills: Checking Consistency
How was the Nixon Doctrine consistent with the Truman Doctrine? How did the Nixon Doctrine differ from the Truman Doctrine?

Israeli soldiers stand guard during the October 1973 war. Israel requires all of its non-Arab citizens, including unmarried women such as those shown in the inset photograph, to serve in the military after reaching age 18. Men are drafted for three years of service, and women for two. Men (up to age 49) and women (up to age 34) are required to receive yearly training in the reserves.

881

Watergate caused Nixon's downfall.

Key Terms: cover-up, Palace Guard, dirty tricks, hush money, executive privilege

Reading Preview
As you read this section, you will learn:

1. what Nixon hoped to gain by obstructing the FBI.
2. who was responsible for directing the Watergate cover-up.
3. what the press, Congress, and the courts discovered when they began to closely investigate the Nixon presidency.
4. how Nixon reacted to the threat of impeachment.

The arrest on June 17, 1972 of five burglars in the headquarters of the Democratic National Committee at the Watergate Office Building in Washington did not seem like a major political event at the time. When reporters Bob Woodward and Carl Bernstein of the *Washington Post* began to investigate the crime, however, they revealed that the burglars appeared to be connected to the president's reelection committee and even with the White House itself. The judge in charge of the trials of the Watergate burglars, **John J. Sirica**, soon pressed the defendants to talk about the "higher ups" for whom they had been working. The White House effort to dismiss the episode as a "third-rate burglary" seemed to be failing.

Nixon tried to cover up the burglary.

In fact, the burglary had been planned, authorized, and financed by high officials in the Nixon campaign, among them former Attorney General **John Mitchell**, the president's campaign manager. The Watergate burglars themselves had been in direct contact with **G. Gordon Liddy**, a member of the White House staff. They had been paid in cash out of

funds kept in a safe at the Nixon campaign headquarters.

The Watergate break-in was, moreover, only one of a series of illegal covert activities being conducted on behalf of the president's reelection. Within days of the burglary, the president was informed of the involvement of his campaign workers and was told that an FBI investigation was beginning to uncover that involvement. Almost immediately, he ordered his aides to obstruct the FBI investigation by telling the agency that they were intruding into national security matters involving the CIA. Nixon told John Mitchell:

I want you all to stonewall it, let them plead the Fifth Amendment, cover-up, or anything else. . . .

AN AMERICAN
★ SPEAKS

The president's order marked the beginning of what became known as the **cover-up**, the effort to keep the truth about Watergate from coming out.

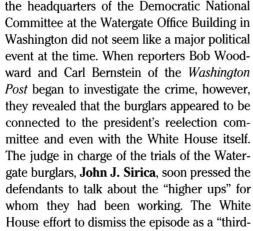

Nixon's Palace Guard: clockwise, top right, John Ehrlichman, John Dean, H. R. Haldeman, and John Mitchell engineered the Watergate cover-up. Former Nixon aide Jeb Magruder later recalled that "the cover-up, thus, was immediate and automatic. No one ever considered that there would not be a cover-up."

The Palace Guard directed the Watergate cover-up.

The Watergate crisis was a result in part of the nature of the Nixon White House and of the people who worked there. The president himself was secretive by nature. He viewed politics as a continual battle and encouraged a combative spirit among those who worked for him. He was convinced—not entirely without reason—that he had powerful enemies who were determined to discredit him. The president seemed to believe it was up to him to discredit his enemies first.

Nixon surrounded himself in the White House with a small circle of trusted advisers and allowed almost no one else regular access to him. Henry Kissinger, who became secretary of state as well as national security adviser in 1973, saw the president constantly on foreign policy matters. John Mitchell was an old and trusted friend. However, the most important leaders of what critics often called the White House **Palace Guard** were **H. R. Haldeman**, the president's chief of staff, and **John Ehrlichman**, his chief domestic adviser. Haldeman was the one who had informed Nixon in June 1972 of the FBI investigation of Watergate and who suggested obstructing that investigation by warning the Bureau of CIA involvement. Haldeman and Ehrlichman continued to direct the cover-up for months. Then Nixon passed the dubious honor to his young White House counsel, **John Dean**.

Cut off from friends and critics alike, Nixon was a solitary, often brooding figure. His isolation allowed his hatreds and resentments to grow. It also insulated him from people who might have warned him of his difficulties, therefore preventing him from becoming more reckless in his use of presidential power.

The press, Congress, and the courts uncovered new scandals.

The Watergate break-in helped prompt a broad inquiry into the nature of the Nixon presidency by the press, by Congress, and by the courts. Over the next two years, the president became the target of many different accusations.

Dirty tricks. One group of accusations involved what critics saw as a broad pattern of abuses of power by the White House. A series of illegal, covert activities by people employed by the Administration gradually came to light, including the break-in at the office of Daniel Ellsberg's psychiatrist. So did the collection of illegal campaign contributions by the president's reelection committee and the laundering, or concealment, of that money through accounts in Mexico to provide large stashes of cash to the campaign. Some of that cash was spent to sabotage the Democratic campaign through **dirty tricks**. For example, fake letters were sent to voters accusing Democratic candidates of misbehavior. The president himself was accused of engaging in real-estate and tax-avoidance schemes of dubious legality. These accusations eventually prompted President Nixon to declare to the American public: "I am not a crook!"

The principal scandal, however, always involved the Watergate break-in itself and the events it set in motion. Although no conclusive evidence showed that the president had planned, approved, or even known about the burglary in advance, considerable evidence suggested that he had been involved in the illegal efforts to obstruct investigations of it.

In the course of 1973, public interest in the Watergate affair steadily grew. Under prompting from Judge Sirica, James McCord, one of the convicted Watergate burglars, began cooperating with the prosecutors and telling of his connections with Liddy and other figures in the Administration and the campaign. Evidence began to emerge about cash payments to the burglars to buy their silence. Aggressive reporters found sources inside the government who implicated high White House officials.

A special Senate investigating committee, chaired by veteran Senator **Sam Ervin** of **North Carolina**, opened hearings into the matter that summer in an effort to determine how deeply involved the Administration, and the president himself, had been in the scandal. Particularly damaging testimony came from John Dean, whom the president had fired as White House counsel after Dean began coop-

Senator Sam Ervin chaired the Senate committee investigating the Watergate scandal.

Archibald Cox is sworn in as special prosecutor in charge of investigating the Watergate scandal. When Nixon discovered that he could not manipulate Cox, he promptly told Attorney General Elliot Richardson to fire him. Richardson refused and quit instead.

erating with the prosecutors. Dean stated that the president himself had known of and approved the cover-up and the payment of bribes called **hush money** to the suspects. He claimed that he had urged the president to end the cover-up and limit the damage it was doing to his Administration, but that the president had refused. That refusal was what had convinced Dean to go to the prosecutors, he said.

Nixon continued to deny personal involvement in or knowledge of any wrongdoing. He and his aides insisted that Dean was lying to protect himself. Because no other witnesses could be found who were willing to implicate the president directly, it seemed to be Dean's word against the president's. For a while, no evidence could be found to determine who was telling the truth.

Then another witness gave the Senate investigating committee some shocking information. Alexander Butterfield, a lower-level member of the White House staff, revealed that Nixon had installed a taping system in his various offices to record conversations for his memoirs. This meant that virtually all of the

conversations about which Dean and others had spoken had been recorded.

A special prosecutor, **Archibald Cox**, had been appointed by the president to investigate the Watergate scandals. This was done because critics had charged that letting the Justice Department and FBI handle the investigation was the same as allowing the president to investigate himself. They maintained that an independent prosecutor such as Cox would be able to operate without political interference from the White House.

Cox was a Harvard Law School professor and a Democrat, whom the president and his aides mistrusted from the beginning. As soon as the existence of the tapes was revealed, Cox subpoenaed the recordings of nine Watergate-related conversations and asked the courts to order the White House to immediately hand them over to him.

The president insisted that the tapes were protected by **executive privilege**—the right of the executive branch to maintain the privacy of its records against the claims of other branches of government. He insisted that Cox abandon his efforts to get the tapes. When Cox refused to withdraw his subpoena, Nixon ordered Attorney General **Elliot Richardson** to fire him.

The Saturday Night Massacre. Richardson had chosen Cox as special prosecutor and had promised him complete independence. Firing him, he claimed, would be a breach of that promise. Richardson resigned his office rather than comply. So did the deputy attorney general. However, the Justice Department's third-ranking officer, Robert Bork, carried out the president's order. These events were announced on a weekend and quickly became known as the "Saturday Night Massacre."

The episode made the president's predicament considerably worse. Public reaction was overwhelmingly negative. Members of Congress began considering impeachment motions. Consequently, Nixon soon was forced to back down and appoint a new special prosecutor, **Leon Jaworski**, who succeeded in getting Nixon to turn over some of the tapes. However, two crucial conversations were missing and one tape had an unexplained gap of more than 18 minutes. Even in its attempt to comply with the law, the White House created suspicions of its honesty.

The Agnew resignation. At the end of 1973 another unrelated scandal shook the Administration. Vice President Spiro Agnew found himself embroiled in troubles of his own. He was charged with having accepted bribes and kickbacks while serving as governor of **Maryland** in the 1960s and of having accepted illegal payments while serving as vice president. Agnew made a deal with the Justice Department. He pleaded "no contest" to a charge of income-tax evasion and resigned his office. In return for Agnew's plea, the government agreed to drop the remaining charges and to not imprison the vice president.

Nixon appointed **Gerald R. Ford**, a

Leon Jaworski, Cox's successor as Watergate special prosecutor, was equally aggressive in pressuring Nixon to turn over the tapes.

Republican congressman from **Michigan** and minority leader of the House, to replace Agnew. In doing so, he unintentionally encouraged those who hoped to remove him from office. Most Democrats would have found the highly partisan Agnew an unattractive alternative to Nixon. On the other hand, Ford was popular, unthreatening, and moderate —a much more appealing choice.

President Nixon's troubles during his second term were not limited to Watergate. In October 1973, after months of insisting upon his innocence, Vice President Spiro Agnew resigned from office, admitting to tax evasion.

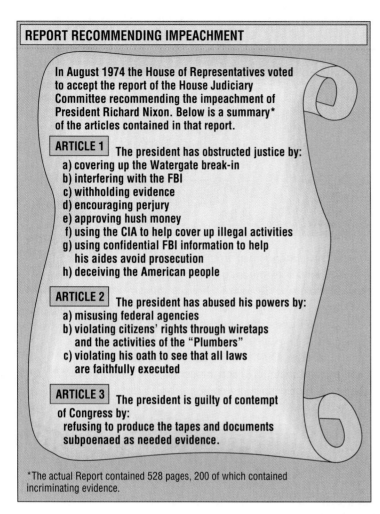

REPORT RECOMMENDING IMPEACHMENT

In August 1974 the House of Representatives voted to accept the report of the House Judiciary Committee recommending the impeachment of President Richard Nixon. Below is a summary* of the articles contained in that report.

ARTICLE 1 The president has obstructed justice by:
a) covering up the Watergate break-in
b) interfering with the FBI
c) withholding evidence
d) encouraging perjury
e) approving hush money
f) using the CIA to help cover up illegal activities
g) using confidential FBI information to help his aides avoid prosecution
h) deceiving the American people

ARTICLE 2 The president has abused his powers by:
a) misusing federal agencies
b) violating citizens' rights through wiretaps and the activities of the "Plumbers"
c) violating his oath to see that all laws are faithfully executed

ARTICLE 3 The president is guilty of contempt of Congress by:
refusing to produce the tapes and documents subpoenaed as needed evidence.

*The actual Report contained 528 pages, 200 of which contained incriminating evidence.

conversations. The president claimed the transcripts proved his innocence, and it was true that there was nothing clearly incriminating in the material he released. However, the public reaction to the transcripts was highly negative. Nixon's dialogue, laced with bitterness and vindictiveness, revealed a president who was willing to take extraordinary steps to, as Nixon put it, "get" his enemies.

By now Watergate had become a national obsession. The press and politicians talked of almost nothing else. Ordinary citizens who had never taken much interest in political news before found themselves riveted to television broadcasts and newspapers as the story unraveled. A paperback edition of the transcripts Nixon released in April became an overnight bestseller. The president himself found that he could not appear in public without being hounded about Watergate.

In the meantime, the legal machinery continued to move, increasing the pressure on the White House. Both the special prosecutor and the House Judiciary Committee, which was beginning to consider impeachment resolutions, insisted that the edited transcripts were unacceptable substitutes for the tapes themselves.

On July 24 the Supreme Court ruled unanimously that Nixon must turn over the subpoenaed tapes. Shortly afterward, the 38 emotionally drained members of the House Judiciary Committee reluctantly but dutifully approved a report recommending impeachment containing three major articles. The articles,

President Nixon reluctantly resigned his office.

In the meantime, the battle for the tapes continued as the Senate Watergate Committee, the House Judiciary Committee, and the special prosecutor all demanded access to more recordings. In April 1974, in an effort to head off further subpoenas, the White House released edited transcripts of a number of Watergate-related

This cartoon captioned "Hey guys, do you really think we need that clause about impeachment in there?" mocks Nixon's predicament.

Faced with the release of his secret tapes and pending impeachment proceedings, Richard Nixon resigned the office of president. Nixon gives a farewell ''thumbs-up'' to reporters as his wife Pat, daughter Tricia Nixon Cox, and son-in-law Edward Cox provide support.

shown on the chart on page 886, were passed by margins of 27-11, 28-10, and 21-17. Most of the committee members had concluded that the failure to impeach would do far greater harm to the nation than would the trauma of an impeachment trial.

Although sadness prevailed throughout the nationally televised House Judiciary Committee meetings, most of its members were satisfied that they had done the right thing in recommending impeachment. New Jersey Democrat Peter Rodino, chairman of the Committee, said that:

[was guided by a] simple principle, the principle that the law must deal fairly with every man. For me, this is the oldest principle of democracy. It is this simple but great principle which enables man to live justly and in decency in a free society. . . .

Even staunch Republicans knew impeachment was called for. Virginia's M. Caldwell Butler, a longtime supporter of Nixon, said:

If we fail to impeach, we will have condoned and left unpunished a course of conduct totally inconsistent with the reasonable expectations of the American people . . .

New York Democrat Charles Rangel believed that the dark cloud of impeachment had a silver lining:

Some say that this is a sad day in America's history. I think it could perhaps be one of our brightest days. It could be really a test of the strength of our Constitution, because what I think it means to most Americans is that when this or any other president violates his sacred oath of office, the people are not left helpless.

Before the full House was able to act on the impeachment report, the president released the tapes. One of them contained the conversation of a few days after the break-in in which Nixon and Haldeman had decided to try to ob-

Constitutional Faith

The Watergate scandal is remembered as a dark, divisive time that pitted the president against Congress in historic combat. For many Americans, however, the crisis produced new respect and affirmation for the United States Constitution. As a member of the House Judiciary Committee in 1974, Barbara Jordan gave vivid expression to the democratic values at stake in the impeachment proceedings. Why might the expression "We the People" be significant for an African American woman?

Earlier today we heard the beginning of the Preamble to the Constitution of the United States. "We the people . . ." It is a very eloquent beginning. But when that document was completed on the seventeenth of September in 1787 I was not included in that, "We, the people." I felt somehow for many years that George Washington and Alexander Hamilton just left me out by mistake. But through the process of amendment, interpretation, and court decision I have finally been included in "We, the people." Today, I am an inquisitor. My faith in the Constitution is whole, it is complete, it is total. I am not going to sit here and be an idle spectator to the diminution, the subversion, the destruction of the Constitution.

CRP's finances. As treasurer of Nixon's reelection campaign in 1972, he raised more than $52 million. Some of this money came from wealthy contributors, of whom a mere 283 gave close to $5 million. Some of these big contributors were individuals under investigation by the government. For example, Robert Vesco, a **Chicago** financier under investigation by the Securities and Exchange Commission (SEC), gave $200,000 to the campaign.

Large corporations also donated hundreds of thousands of dollars to President Nixon's 1972 reelection campaign despite the fact that federal election laws prohibit corporations from contributing directly to political campaigns. Some observers believe that the donations were accepted in return for political favors. For example, it was charged that the president personally intervened in a complex antitrust case after the company involved pledged $400,000 to help finance the 1972 Republican National Convention.

A third source of campaign funds was special interest groups and lobbies. In 1970, for example, the dairy industry pledged $2 million to help finance Nixon's reelection campaign, apparently in return for an increase in the federal price support for milk.

Stans' finance committee performed almost too well. CRP was awash with money, enough to finance the most outlandish schemes, plans that would surely have been vetoed had less

Texas Congresswoman Barbara Jordan eloquently presented her views when she served on the House Judiciary Committee that recommended the impeachment of Richard Nixon.

money been available. The money was there, however. The illegal break-in at Democratic National Committee headquarters at Watergate was just one of the many "dirty tricks" played by members of the Administration.

Watergate produced a number of important political reforms.

The Watergate scandal shocked the American people. As the story unfolded and eventually involved the president, questions were raised about the uncontrolled growth of presidential power. In the words of one historian, the nation's highest office had mutated into an "imperial presidency." Of course, this problem did not begin with Nixon. Previous presidents had employed "dirty tricks" against their political opponents. They had also made tapes of their conversations in the White House. The problem of candidates accepting large contributions from wealthy individuals, corporations, and special interest groups was also not new. What distinguished Watergate from all previous cases was the extent of the abuses revealed by the investigations.

As a result of these abuses, Congress showed a heightened interest in restricting the president's power and increasing its own. A series of new laws designed to increase the president's accountability to Congress were passed. In 1974 Congress approved a law limiting the president's control over the budget. The Nixon Administration had routinely refused to spend money appropriated by Congress for projects the president did not favor; the new law was designed to prevent that practice from continuing. Also in 1974 Congress passed the **Presidential Election Campaign Fund**, which established federal financing of presidential campaigns. It was designed to limit the role of private contributions, which had done so much to corrupt the Nixon campaign. The following year, revelations of abuses of power by the CIA prompted a new round of investigations and a new set of laws restricting the autonomy of that agency.

Gerald Ford told the American people as he took office in 1974 that "Our long national nightmare is over." The Watergate scandal did not disappear as quickly as he suggested. However, Nixon's resignation was testimony above all to the strong belief of Americans in the sanctity of the Constitution and the rule of law. The American people had not turned against Richard Nixon because they disliked his policies. They had reelected him by a record majority only two years before. They turned against him because they believed he had abused his office and broken the law. Indeed, Watergate had taught the nation a number of important lessons. Although these lessons were difficult to learn, the nation and its belief in constitutional government were strengthened as a result.

Gerald Ford became president without having been elected to either the presidency or the vice-presidency. This was a "first" in American history.

SECTION **5** REVIEW

Identify Key People and Terms
Write a sentence to identify: CRP, Maurice Stans, Presidential Election Campaign Fund

Locate Key Places
Robert Vesco was a financier in which American city?

Master the Main Ideas

1. **Analyzing political leaders:** What is meant by the phrase "Nixon believed that ends justify the means"?
2. **Understanding special interest groups:** What role did CRP play in the Watergate scandal?
3. **Studying the growth and development of government:** What were two reforms that were enacted as a result of Watergate?

Apply Critical Thinking Skills: Drawing Conclusions
Do you think the reforms enacted as a result of the Watergate scandal were sufficient to prevent the occurrence of future Watergates? Why or why not?

Richard Nixon Goes to China

22A

TIME FRAME
1972

GEOGRAPHIC SETTING
Beijing, China

In July of 1971 President Richard Nixon (1913–   ), who had made his political reputation by taking a hard line against communism, stunned the world by accepting an invitation from the communist government of China. In February 1972 Nixon visited the Chinese capital, Peking, now known as Beijing [bā′jing′]. A new era in American diplomatic relations was underway. In the following excerpt from his memoirs, published in 1978, Nixon described meetings with Prime Minister Zhou En-lai [jō en lī] and Communist Party Chairman Mao Zedong [mä′ō dsu′důng], previously known as Mao Tse-tung.

S everal Chinese photographers had rushed in ahead of us in order to record [Mao's and my] first meeting. We all sat in overstuffed armchairs set in a semi-
5 circle at the end of the long room. While the photographers continued to bustle around, we exchanged bantering small talk. Kissinger remarked that he had assigned Mao's writings to his classes at

10 Harvard. Indulging in characteristic self-deprecation, Mao said, "These writings of mine aren't anything. There is nothing instructive in what I wrote." I said, "The Chairman's writings moved a nation and
15 have changed the world." Mao, however, replied, "I haven't been able to change it. I've only been able to change a few places in the vicinity of Peking." . . .

"Mr. Chairman," I said, "I am aware of
20 the fact that over a period of years my position with regard to the People's Republic was one that the Chairman and the Prime Minister totally disagreed with. What brings us together is a recognition of a
25 new situation in the world and a recognition on our part that what is important is not a nation's internal political philosophy. What is important is its policy toward the rest of the world and toward us."

30 Although the meeting with Mao dealt mainly with what he called the "philosophy" of our new and potential relationship, I raised in general terms the ma-

jor substantive questions we would be discussing. I said that we should examine our policies and determine how they should develop in order to deal with the entire world as well as the immediate problems of Korea, Vietnam, and Taiwan.

I went on, "We, for example, must ask ourselves—again in the confines of this room—why the Soviets have more forces on the border facing you than they do on the border facing Western Europe? We must ask ourselves, What is the future of Japan? Is it better—and here I know we have disagreements—from China's standpoint for Japan to be neutral and totally defenseless, or is it better for Japan to have some mutual defense relations with the United States? One thing is sure—we can leave no vacuums, because they can be filled. The Prime Minister, for example, has pointed out that the United States 'reaches out its hands' and that the Soviet Union 'reaches out its hands.' The question is, which danger does the People's Republic of China face? Is it the danger of American aggression—or of Soviet aggression? These are hard questions, but we have to discuss them." . . .

As I look back on that week in China, [one] vivid memory of the trip is the unique personality of Chou En-lai. My meeting with Mao Tse-tung was too brief and too formal to have given me much more than a superficial personal impression. But many hours of formal talks and social conversation with Chou made me appreciate his brilliance and dynamism.

Unlike many world leaders and statesmen who are completely absorbed in one particular cause or issue, Chou En-lai was able to talk in broad terms about men and history. Even though his perspective was badly distorted by his rigid ideological frame of reference the extent of his knowledge was impressive. . . .

During our last long session together in the guesthouse in Peking, Chou said, "In your dining room upstairs we have a poem by Chairman Mao in his calligraphy [handwriting] about Lushan mountain. The last sentence reads, 'The beauty lies at the top of the mountain.' You have risked something to come to China. But there is another Chinese poem which reads, 'On perilous peaks dwell beauty in its infinite variety.' "

"We are at the top of the mountain now," I said.

"That's one poem," he continued. "Another one which I would have liked to have put up, but I couldn't find an appropriate place, is 'Ode to a Plum Blossom.' In that poem the Chairman meant that one who makes an initiative may not always be one who stretches out his or her hand. By the time the blossoms are fullblown, that is the time they are about to disappear." He took a small book from his pocket and read the poem.

"Spring disappears with rain and winds
    and comes with flying snow.
Ice hangs on a thousand feet of cliff
    yet at the tip of the topmost branch
    the plum blooms.
The plum is not a delicious girl showing off
    yet she heralds spring.
When mountain flowers are in wild bloom
    she giggles in all the color."

Seated amidst a lavish display of traditional Chinese cuisine, President Richard Nixon dines with Chinese Prime Minister Chou En-lai (on Nixon's right) during the president's visit in 1972.

Discussing the Reading

1. According to Richard Nixon's statement here, what was his purpose in visiting China?

2. Why was he so impressed with Chou En-lai?

CRITICAL THINKING
Identifying Alternatives

Why might it be easier for a professed anticommunist such as Richard Nixon to be able to change American foreign policy toward the communist world than it would be for a politician with more liberal views?

TIME FRAME
1973

GEOGRAPHIC SETTING
Washington, D.C.

Dismissed by President Nixon at the time as "a third-rate burglary," by the spring of 1973 the Watergate affair had become a major political scandal, leading to a Senate investigation into White House involvement in the burglary and related crimes. As the Watergate scandals unraveled, two reporters were credited with exposing the involvement of President Nixon and his staff. The reporters were Bob Woodward and Carl Bernstein, both then working for the *Washington Post.* In the following selection from their book *The Final Days,* Woodward and Bernstein describe one of the key incidents in the investigation—the disclosure by Alexander P. Butterfield, former assistant to White House Chief of Staff H. R. Haldeman, of the existence of the White House taping system. The disclosure took place July 13, 1973, before the staff of the Senate Watergate Committee. The existence of the Watergate tapes was critical, because evidence was needed to support or refute presidential counsel John Dean's assertions that the President had participated directly in the cover-up.

The temperature was in the nineties in Washington on Friday, July 13, the day witness Alexander Butterfield was to be interviewed by the Watergate Committee's staff. Room G-334 in the New Senate Office Building had only one small air-conditioning vent, and it was oppressively hot. A haze of tobacco smoke obscured the pale-yellow walls. The chairs were stained with grease from fast-food meals. Wastebaskets spilled over with cigarette butts and packages and sandwich wrappings. The faded green carpet was filthy. No janitors had been allowed in for fear that someone might plant an eavesdropping device.

Both Butterfield's manner and his memory impressed the committee's junior staff. With his hands folded in front of him, he considered carefully each question that was posed to him. He looked directly at his interrogator; he spoke in calm and even tones. . . .

"Did you see or hear anything which indicated to you that the President was involved in the alleged effort to keep the facts from the public?" Butterfield was asked.

"No, but the way the White House operated it could have happened certainly." The witness paused to reflect. " . . . The series of meetings in question [with Dean] didn't begin until February 1973. I was phasing out of my job and getting ready to leave for the FAA [Federal Aviation Agency]. I can't document anything or prove anything. I don't remember Watergate being anything."

The staff, trying to make the most of the situation, turned back to Butterfield's expertise on the President's office routine. The minute detail of material submitted to the committee from [special White House counsel J. Fred] Buzhardt was puzzling: one memorandum listed the times, dates, locations and participants for all the Dean-Nixon conversations; another described the substance of Dean's calls and meetings with the President. . . .

Pulling out a typed transcript of . . . the President's version of his conversations with Dean, an investigator asked Butterfield where such an account might have originated. Could it have been from someone's notes of the meetings?

Butterfield glanced over the document. He paused several times to remark on how detailed the account was. He appeared to be fascinated by that. He lingered over it. . . .

"Where did you get this?" Butterfield inquired.

"Mr. Buzhardt provided it to the committee. Could it have come from someone's notes of a meeting?" he was asked.

"No, it seems too detailed," Butterfield replied.

"Where else could this have come from?"

Butterfield stared down at the document. Slowly, he lifted it an inch off the table. "I don't know. Well, let me think about that awhile." He pushed the document toward the center of the green-felt-covered table.

The questioning moved into other areas. . . .

Don Sanders, the deputy counsel to the Republican minority, thought there might be some way to document the President's innocence. He led to his question cautiously. "Dean indicated that there might be some facility for taping. He said that on April 15 in the President's EOB [Executive Office Building] office he had the impression he was being taped, and that at the end of the meeting the President walked to a corner of the room and lowered his voice as if he was trying to stay off the tape himself while he discussed his earlier conversation with [his special counsel Charles] Colson about executive clemency [willingness to forgive wrongdoing]. Is it possible Dean knew what he was talking about?"

Butterfield thought for a moment, trying to frame a response to the complicated question. Then he leaned over to the center of the table and picked up the Buzhardt account of the Dean-Nixon meetings. "No, Dean didn't know about it," he said at last. "But that is where this must have come from. There is tape in each of the President's offices. It is kept by the Secret Service, and only four other men know about it. Dean had no way of knowing about it. He was just guessing."

Then, for 45 minutes, Butterfield described the taping system in detail. . . .

The next Monday, Butterfield testified publicly. He concluded his televised testimony by noting, "This matter which we have discussed here today, I think, is precisely the substance on which the President plans to present his defense. I believe, of course, that the President is innocent of any crime or wrongdoing, that he is innocent likewise of any complicity."

On the witness stand, former White House aide Alexander P. Butterfield guardedly answers questions from the Senate Watergate Committee in July of 1973. Butterfield's calm and measured responses during the hearings reflected his background as an Air Force colonel and fighter pilot. He was named head of the Federal Aviation Administration in April of 1973.

Discussing the Reading

1. What atmosphere is created by the physical details of the meeting room that were given in this account by Bob Woodward and Carl Bernstein?

2. What sort of person did they present Alexander Butterfield to be? What might explain his initial reluctance to admit the existence of the White House taping system? What might explain his final willingness to describe it in detail?

CRITICAL THINKING
Demonstrating Reasoned Judgment

Subsequent to the Watergate hearings, it was revealed that conversations in the White House had been taped by other administrations, for example, that of President Franklin Roosevelt. Does the president have the right to keep such a record? Why or why not?

Chapter Summary

Write supporting details under each of the following main ideas as you review the chapter.

Section 1
1. Nixon reduced federal responsibilities.
2. The Supreme Court practiced moderation.
3. Nixon tried to discredit liberals.
4. Nixon won by a landslide in 1972.

Section 2
1. Nixon failed to control inflation.
2. The nation experienced an energy crisis.
3. American industry experienced severe problems.
4. Deindustrialization produced economic hardship.

Section 3
1. Nixon and Kissinger forged new ties with communist China.
2. American-Soviet relations improved between 1969 and 1973.
3. The president established the Nixon Doctrine.
4. The United States helped bring an end to the October 1973 war.

Section 4
1. Nixon tried to cover up the Watergate burglary.
2. The Palace Guard directed the Watergate cover-up.
3. The press, Congress, and the courts uncovered new scandals.
4. President Nixon reluctantly resigned his office.

Section 5
1. Nixon believed that the ends justified the means.
2. Flaws in the election process also helped bring about Watergate.
3. Watergate produced a number of important political reforms.

Chapter Themes

1. **National destiny:** Recognizing that America's future might be threatened by volatile situations abroad, President Nixon, aided by Secretary of State Henry Kissinger, forged new relations with China and the Soviet Union, helped negotiate the end of the Vietnam War, and committed the United States to maintaining peace and stability in the Middle East.

2. **Constitutional and representative government:** The Watergate scandal demonstrated that the United States was a nation of law, not one run by the desires of a few people. The courts and Congress checked the power of the president, and he resigned rather than face certain impeachment. He was replaced by the vice president—as provided by the Constitution.

Chapter Study Guide

Identifying Key People and Terms

Name the key term that describes the:
1. New Federalism plan in which the states receive a rebate on some federal tax money
2. a short period of reduced economic income, output, and employment
3. 1972 treaty that limited intercontinental missiles in the United States and Soviet Union.
4. right of the president to maintain private records

Locating Key Places

1. Where are most OPEC nations located?
2. Where were the first SALT talks held?
3. In what two capital cities did Nixon meet with Mao Zedong and Leonid Brezhnev?

Mastering the Main Ideas

1. Why did Nixon win the 1972 election so overwhelmingly?
2. Explain how plant closings had a ripple effect in a community and its surrounding areas.
3. What major foreign policy decisions did Nixon make regarding China, the Soviet Union, Chile, and the Middle East?
4. Explain what Congressman Charles Rangel meant when he said that during the Watergate inquiry, "the people [were] not left helpless."
5. What were some of the positive results of the Watergate scandal?

Applying Critical Thinking Skills

1. **Making comparisons:** Choose one case that typified the Burger Court. Choose one case that typified the Warren Court. Based on these decisions, how would you characterize each court?
2. **Analyzing cause and effect:** How did the oil embargo affect the U.S. economy?

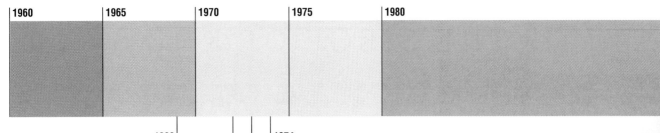

1960	1965	1970	1975	1980

1969
The Making of the President 1968
(White); moon landing

1974
Nixon resigns;
All the President's Men
(Woodward and Bernstein)

1972
Nixon visits China and the Soviet Union;
Watergate burglars arrested; SALT I

1973
Roe v. *Wade*;
Arab oil embargo; Agnew resigns

3. Demonstrating reasoned judgment: Explain how national self-interest motivated both the United States and China and led to Nixon's Beijing visit.

4. Identifying alternatives: Should Ford have pardoned Nixon or should he have been made to stand trial? Why?

5. Analyzing cause and effect: Why was it necessary to pass laws limiting presidential powers in 1974 and 1975?

Chapter Activities

Learning Geography Through History

1. What two major factors made the Middle East a world "hotspot"?
2. Where were the newer, more efficient industrial plants that were putting American industry out of business in the 1970s?

Relating the United States to the World

1. What three areas did Kissinger believe would become the major power centers of the noncommunist world? Why?
2. Explain how and why a multipolar structure would replace the bipolar arrangement that had persisted between the Soviet Union and the United States since World War II.

Linking Past to Present

1. One legacy of Watergate is the continuing public distrust of politicians. Cite any recent examples of politicians who have been investigated by Congress or the media.
2. How did Nixon's view of the presidency differ from other presidents' views?

Using the Time Line

1. What event showed the world that the United States was still the leader in scientific innovation?
2. What event signified the beginning of Richard Nixon's downfall?
3. When did Nixon visit China?

Practicing Critical Thinking Strategies

Demonstrating Reasoned Judgment
Read the material on page 871 regarding the American business response to foreign competition. Did American business leaders use reasoned judgment when they demanded that the federal government use protectionist methods to protect American merchants? What are the arguments for and against U.S. protectionist policies?

Learning More About an Era of Turmoil

1. **Using Source Readings:** Read the Source Readings for this chapter and answer the questions.
2. **Exploring Sources:** Read Woodward and Bernstein's Pulitzer Prize-winning account of their investigation into the Watergate affair in *All The President's Men*. The gripping behind-the-scenes report reads like a detective novel but is all true. Prepare a report for the class.
3. **Researching Legal Cases:** Use your library to read about *Webster* v. *Reproductive Health Services*, a 1989 Supreme Court case. Write a summary of how this Court ruling changed the *Roe* v. *Wade* ruling of the Nixon years.

THE SIEGE OF KHE SANH

In January 1968, during the Vietnamese New Year season called Tet, the Viet Cong and North Vietnamese forces launched a huge offensive that overran most of the major South Vietnamese cities. As part of the Tet Offensive, the Marine base at Khe Sanh [kä sän'] was besieged by North Vietnamese Army (NVA) troops from January until April. The Marines held out, but Khe Sanh was abandoned a short time later. American journalist Michael Herr (1940?–) reported the Vietnam War in 1967 and 1968 on assignment for *Esquire* magazine. His book *Dispatches* (1968), from which the following account of the siege of Khe Sanh is excerpted, has become one of the classics of the literature of the Vietnam War.

Sometimes you'd step from the bunker, all sense of time passing having left you, and find it dark out. The far side of the hills around the bowl of the base glimmering, but you could never see the source of the light, and it had the look of a city at night approached from a great distance. Flares were dropping everywhere around the fringes of the perimeter, laying a dead white light on the high ground rising from the piedmont [area at the foot of a mountain range]. There would be dozens of them at once sometimes, trailing an intense smoke, dropping white-hot sparks, and it seemed as though anything caught in their range would be made still, like figures in a game of living statues. There would be the muted rush of illumination rounds, fired from 60-mm. mortars inside the wire, dropping magnesium-brilliant above the NVA trenches for a few seconds, outlining the gaunt, flat spread of the mahogany trees, giving the landscape a ghastly clarity and dying out. You could watch mortar bursts, orange and gray-smoking, over the tops of trees three and four kilometers away, and the heavier shelling from support bases farther east along the DMZ [the Demilitarized Zone, the border between North and South Vietnam], from Camp Carrol and the Rockpile, directed against suspected troop movements or NVA

> Even the incoming was beautiful at night, beautiful and deeply dreadful.

rocket and mortar positions. Once in a while—I guess I saw it happen three or four times in all—there would be a secondary explosion, a direct hit on a supply of NVA ammunition. And at night it was beautiful. Even the incoming [enemy shellfire] was beautiful at night, beautiful and deeply dreadful.

I remembered the way a Phantom pilot had talked about how beautiful the surface-to-air missiles looked as they drifted up toward his plane to kill him, and remembered myself how lovely .50-caliber tracers could be, coming at you as you flew at night in a helicopter, how slow and graceful, arching up easily, a dream, so remote from anything that could harm you. It could make you feel a total serenity, an elevation that put you above death, but that never lasted very long. One hit anywhere in the chopper would bring you back, bitten lips, white knuckles and all, and then you knew where you were. It was different with the incoming at Khe Sanh. You didn't get to watch the shells very often. You knew if you heard one, the first one, that you were safe, or at least saved. If you were still standing up and looking after that, you deserved anything that happened to you.

Nights were when the air and artillery strikes were heaviest, because that was when we knew that the NVA was above ground and moving. At night you could lie out on some sandbags and watch the C-47's mounted with Vulcans doing their work. The C-47 was a standard prop flareship, but many of them carried 20- and 7.62-mm. guns on their doors, Mike-Mikes that could fire out 300 rounds per second, Gatling style, "a round in every square inch of a football field in less than a minute," as the handouts said. They used to call it Puff the

An excerpt from
DISPATCHES
by Michael Herr

Magic Dragon, but the Marines knew better: they named it Spooky. Every fifth round fired was a tracer, and when Spooky was working, everything stopped while that solid stream of violent red poured down out of the black sky. If you watched from a great distance, the stream would seem to dry up between bursts, vanishing slowly from air to ground like a comet tail, the sound of the guns disappearing too, a few seconds later. If you watched at a close range, you couldn't believe that anyone would have the courage to deal with that night after night, week after week, and you cultivated a respect for the Viet Cong and the NVA who had crouched under it every night now for months. It was awesome, worse than anything the Lord had ever put down on Egypt, and at night, you'd hear the Marines talking, watching it, yelling, "Get some!" until they grew quiet and someone would say, "Spooky understands." The nights were very beautiful. Night was when you really had the least to fear and feared the most. You could go through some very bad numbers at night.

Because, really, what a choice there was; what a prodigy of things to be afraid of! The moment that you understood this, really understood it, you lost your anxiety instantly. Anxiety was a luxury, a joke you had no room for once you knew the variety of deaths and mutilations the war offered. . . .

There were choices everywhere, but they were never choices that you could hope to make. There was even some small chance for personal style in your recognition of the one thing you feared more than any other. You could die in a sudden blood-burning crunch as your chopper hit the ground like dead weight, you could fly apart so that your pieces would never be gathered, you could take one neat round in the lung and go out hearing only the bubble of the last few breaths, you could die in the last stage of malaria with that faint tapping in your ears, and that could happen to you after months of firefights and rockets and machine guns. Enough, too many, were saved for that, and you always hoped that no irony would attend your passing. You could end in a pit somewhere with a spike through you, everything stopped forever except for the one or two motions, purely involuntary, as though you could kick it all away and come back. You could fall down dead so that the medics would have to spend half an hour looking for the hole that killed you, getting more and more spooked as the search went on. You could be shot, mined, grenaded, rocketed, mortared, sniped at, blown up and away so that your leavings had to be dropped into a sagging poncho and carried to Graves Registration, that's all she wrote. It was almost marvelous.

And at night, all of it seemed more possible. At night in Khe Sanh, waiting there, thinking about all of them (40,000, some said), thinking that they might really try it, could keep you up. If they did, when they did, it might not matter that you were in the best bunker in the DMZ, wouldn't matter that you were young and had plans, that you were loved, that you were a noncombatant, an observer. Because if it came, it would be in a bloodswarm of killing, and credentials would not be examined. (The only Vietnamese many of us knew was the words "Bao Chi! Bao Chi!"—Journalist! Journalist! or even "Bao Chi Fap!"—French journalist!, which was the same as crying, Don't shoot! Don't shoot!)

> You could go through some very bad numbers at night.

CRITICAL THINKING
Identifying Central Issues
Since warfare is a complex human activity, someone observing combat may see a variety of characteristics displayed—including courage, comradeship, fear, beauty, horror, humor, mystery, and many others. Select the two characteristics that you think are most notably displayed in Michael Herr's account of the siege of Khe Sanh and give evidence from the excerpt in support of your choices.

THE SETTING OUT

The poet and novelist N. Scott Momaday (1934–) is a Native American, a member of the Kiowa tribe of Oklahoma. In *The Way to Rainy Mountain* (1969), he collected and meditated on Kiowa traditions concerning their migration from western Montana to the southern Great Plains several centuries ago. Each episode in his account of this journey is narrated in three "voices," which Momaday described as "the mythical, the historical, and the personal." (In each of the following three sections from *The Way to Rainy Mountain*, the first passage expresses the mythological voice, the second the historical voice, and the third the personal voice.) Momaday felt that by proceeding in this way from the prehistoric to the contemporary, it was possible "to suggest an evolution of storytelling and to illustrate the relationship between the oral and written traditions."

You know, everything had to begin, and this is how it was: the Kiowas came one by one into the world through a hollow log. They were many more than now, but not all of them got out. There was a woman whose body was swollen up with child, and she got stuck in the log. After that, no one could get through, and that is why the Kiowas are a small tribe in number. They looked all around and saw the world. It made them glad to see so many things. They called themselves *Kwuda*, "coming out."

They called themselves Kwuda and later Tepda, both of which mean "coming out." And later still they took the name Gaigwu, a name which can be taken to indicate something of which the two halves differ from each other in appearance. It was once a custom among Kiowa warriors that they cut their hair on the right side of the head only and on a line level with the lobe of the ear, while on the left they let the hair grow long and wore it in a thick braid wrapped in otter skin. "Kiowa" is indicated in sign language by holding the hand palm up and slightly cupped to the right side side of the head and rotating it back and forth from the wrist. "Kiowa" is thought to derive from the softened Comanche form of Gaigwu.

I remember coming out upon the northern Great Plains in the late spring. There were meadows of blue and yellow wildflowers on the slopes, and I could see the still, sunlit plain below, reaching away out of sight. At first there is no discrimination in the eye, nothing but the land itself, whole and impenetrable. But then smallest things begin to stand out of the depths—herds and rivers and groves—and each of these has perfect being in terms of distance and of silence and of age. Yes, I thought, now I see the earth as it really is; never again will I see things as I saw them yesterday or the day before.

> Everything had to begin, and this is how it was.

Two

They were going along, and some were hunting. An antelope was killed and quartered in the meadow. Well, one of the big chiefs came up and took the udders of that animal for himself, but another big chief wanted those udders also, and there was a great quarrel between them. Then, in anger, one of these chiefs gathered all of his followers together and went away. They are called *Azatanhop*, "the udder-angry travelers off." No one knows where they went or what happened to them.

This is one of the oldest memories of the tribe. There have been reports of a people in the Northwest who speak a language that is similiar to Kiowa.

In the winter of 1848–49, the buffalo ranged away from easy reach, and food was scarce. There was an antelope drive in the vicinity of Bent's Fort, Colorado. According to ancient custom, antelope medicine [magic to attract game] was made, and the Kiowas set out on foot and on horseback—men, women, and children—after game. They formed a great circle, enclosing a large area of the plain, and began to converge upon the center. By this means antelope and

An excerpt from
THE WAY TO RAINY MOUNTAIN
by N. Scott Momaday

other animals were trapped and killed, often with clubs and even with the bare hands. By necessity were the Kiowas reminded of their ancient ways.

One morning on the high plains of Wyoming I saw several pronghorns [antelopes] in the distance. They were moving very slowly at an angle away from me, and they were almost invisible in the tall brown and yellow grass. They ambled along in their own wilderness dimension of time, as if no notion of flight could ever come upon them. But I remembered once having seen a frightened buck on the run, how the white rosette of its rump seemed to hang for the smallest fraction of time at the top of each frantic bound— like a succession of sunbursts against the purple hills.

Three

Before there were horses the Kiowas had need of dogs. That was a long time ago, when dogs could talk. There was a man who lived alone; he had been thrown away, and he made his camp here and there on the high ground. Now it was dangerous to be alone, for there were enemies all around. The man spent his arrows hunting food. He had one arrow left, and he shot a bear; but the bear was only wounded and it ran away. The man wondered what to do. Then a dog came up to him and said that many enemies were coming; they were close by and all around. The man could think of no way to save himself. But the dog said: "You know, I have puppies. They are young and weak and they have nothing to eat. If you will take care of my puppies, I will show you how to get away." The dog led the man here and there, around and around, and they came to safety.

A hundred years ago the Comanche Ten Bears

> The man could think of no way to save himself.

remarked upon the great number of horses which the Kiowas owned. "When we first knew you," he said, "you had nothing but dogs and sleds." It was so; the dog is primordial [existing at the very beginning]. Perhaps it was dreamed into being.

The principal warrior society of the Kiowas was the Ka-itsenko, "Real Dogs," and it was made up of ten men only, the ten most brave. Each of these men wore a long ceremonial sash and carried a sacred arrow. In time of battle he must by means of this arrow impale the end of his sash to the earth and stand his ground to the death. Tradition has it that the founder of the Ka-itsenko had a dream in which he saw a band of warriors, outfitted after the fashion of the society, being led by a dog. The dog sang the song of the Ka-itsenko, then said to the dreamer: "You are a dog; make a noise like a dog and sing a dog song."

There were always dogs about my grandmother's house. Some of them were nameless and lived a life of their own. They belonged there in a sense that the word "ownership" does not include. The old people paid them scarcely any attention, but they should have been sad, I think, to see them go.

CRITICAL THINKING
Identifying Assumptions
Indicate some of the ways in which the "mythical voice" in N. Scott Momaday's account of Kiowa tradition differs from the "historical voice." For example, what is presented as possible in the mythical sections that would be inappropriate in the historical sections? What kinds of authorities do the historical sections offer for their version of the past? Are the mythical sections backed by any such references to authorities?

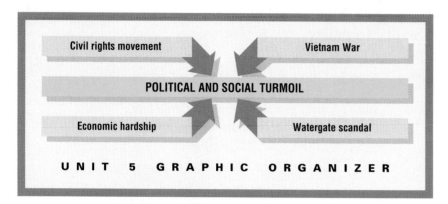

Civil rights movement → POLITICAL AND SOCIAL TURMOIL ← Vietnam War

Economic hardship → POLITICAL AND SOCIAL TURMOIL ← Watergate scandal

UNIT 5 GRAPHIC ORGANIZER

uphold the separate but equal doctrine of race relations voiced in *Plessy* v. *Ferguson* in 1896. Then in 1954, in a historic decision, *Brown* v. *Board of Education of Topeka,* the Supreme Court ruled against segregation in public schools. This was the first major victory in a popular movement that extended civil rights guarantees to all citizens.

A new leader emerged during the yearlong boycott that challenged racial segregation on city bus lines in Montgomery, Alabama, in 1955. The Reverend Dr. Martin Luther King, Jr., urged both militancy and nonviolence.

CHAPTER
SURVEY

19

The Struggle for Civil Rights
1954–1968

Nonviolent protests helped bring equality in American life. Since the 1880s, discrimination had deprived African Americans of their civil rights. The courts continued to

Some protesters favored direct action tactics. Other groups joined in the fight for civil rights with King's Southern Christian Leadership Conference (SCLC). African American

students formed the Student Nonviolent Coordinating Committee (SNCC). Some students staged sit-ins at segregated lunch counters. Others, calling themselves Freedom Riders, traveled on buses into the South. The students submitted to jail sentences as they challenged segregation laws through nonviolent actions.

Mass protests prompted a fight for civil rights. As the civil rights movement gained strength in the early 1960s, television coverage set off a wave of sympathy across America. Mass protests took place in Birmingham, Alabama. In August 1963 Martin Luther King, Jr., led a quarter of a million demonstrators in a march on Washington, D.C. King, a spellbinding speaker, appealed for jobs and an end to segregation and racial intolerance. Congress reflected the public mood by passing the Civil Rights Act of 1964, which barred discrimination in public places and employment. The Voting Rights Act of 1965 banned literacy tests, which had been used to keep African Americans from voting.

King's assassination weakened the freedom struggle. Even as Congress acted to end discrimination, many African Americans remained mired in poverty. In 1964 riots broke out in slum areas of several large cities. Tragically, the most effective voice against violence was soon silenced. Martin Luther King, Jr., was assassinated by a white sniper in April 1968. King's death left the civil rights movement much weakened. Nevertheless, the tactics King had developed helped end segregation, and African American voters held increased political power throughout the nation.

The Turbulent Sixties
1960–1968

The Sixties began optimistically. President John F. Kennedy, the youngest person ever elected to the country's highest office and its first Roman Catholic president, promised bold, new leadership for America. Kennedy proposed ambitious social and economic goals, calling his program the New Frontier. Although the president stirred Americans with his call for action, he was unable to gain support for his program in Congress. Accordingly, Kennedy's record of accomplishment was limited when he was cut down by an assassin's bullet in 1963.

An unfinished New Frontier became the Great Society. President Kennedy's successor, Lyndon B. Johnson, broadened New Frontier goals. A master politician, Johnson won congressional approval for much of his program, called the Great Society. New laws provided health care to the aged, educational programs, and aid to urban areas. His most ambitious plans called for education and job training to wipe out poverty. As Great Society programs multiplied, they began to compete with the costly Vietnam War. The performance of the social welfare programs also fell short of expectations. As a result, people began to question government's ability to solve social problems.

American leaders confronted communist threats abroad. President Kennedy had promised that America would help its friends and oppose the enemies of freedom throughout the world. His Alliance for Progress pumped economic aid into Latin America in an effort to head off the threat of communism there. He also inspired Americans with his plans for a Peace Corps, which sent American volunteers to work in poverty-stricken countries.

Opposition to communism also led to a threatened war with the Soviet Union over Cuba in 1962. After U.S. planes discovered Soviet missiles on Cuban soil, American warships blockaded that island. The crisis ended when the Soviets agreed to dismantle the missiles. Other points of tension were the erection of the Berlin Wall in 1961 to prevent East Germans from fleeing dictatorship and the shooting down of an American U-2 over the Soviet Union in 1960.

Women and minorities tried to change the system. During the 1960s, turmoil and violence flared as women and minority-group Americans pushed for reforms. Some students joined New Left groups that sought to end racism and other social injustices. Inspired by the gains made by African Americans in the 1960s, feminist, Native American, and Hispanic groups began to apply the methods used by the civil rights movement to their own causes. Their demands became the source of major cultural changes in the 1970s and 1980s. Ethnic groups also celebrated their distinctive identities. These groups challenged traditional ideas of the American melting pot, seeing ethnic diversity not as an obstacle but as a positive force.

Ingenuity

Americans have always been considered an inventive people, a practical people. "Yankee ingenuity" has been a familiar phrase almost as long as there have been Yankees. In the 19th and 20th centuries, this association of the United States with technological creativity became even closer as a long series of inventive Americans developed new products and industrial processes that transformed the world. What kind of people were these ingenious Americans? What traits did they share? The following quotations from famous American inventors and scientists provide some clues to answering these questions.

1746

Being in Boston, I met there with a Dr. Spence, who was lately arrived from Scotland and showed me some electrical experiments. They were imperfectly performed, as he was not very expert; but being in a subject quite new to me, they equally surprised and pleased me. Soon after my return to Philadelphia our library company received from [a British scientist] a present of a glass tube, with some account of the use of it in making such experiments. I eagerly seized the opportunity of repeating what I had seen at Boston, and by much practice acquired great readiness in performing those [experiments] also of which we had an account from England, adding a number of new ones.

▲ **Benjamin Franklin,** *The Autobiography*

1791

I direct to you as a present a copy of an almanac which I have calculated for the succeeding year. . . .

This calculation, sir, is the production of my arduous study. . . .

▲ **Benjamin Banneker, letter to Thomas Jefferson**

1792

Many, many a silent solitary hour have I spent in the most unnerved study anxiously pondering how to make funds to support me till the fruits of my labors be sufficient to pay them.

▲ **Robert Fulton, letter to his mother**

1793

There are a number of very respectable Gentlemen at Mrs. Greene's who all agreed that if a machine could be invented which could clean the cotton with expedition [speed], it would be a great thing both to the Country and to the inventor.

▲ **Eli Whitney, letter to his father**

1848

It is wondrous to see the earth's motion made manifest by the seeming movement of the stars.

▲ **Astronomer Maria Mitchell, diary entry**

1887

My laboratory will soon be completed. . . . I will have the best and largest Laboratory extant, and the facilities incomparably superior to any other for rapid and cheap development of an invention, & working it up into Commercial shape with models, patterns & special machinery. In fact there is no similar institution in Existence. We do our own castings [and] forgings. Can build anything from a lady's watch to a Locomotive.

▲ **Thomas Alva Edison, letter**

1903

Success. Four flights Thursday morning. All against twenty-one-mile wind. Started from level with engine power alone. Average speed through air thirty-one miles. Longest fifty-nine seconds. Inform press. Home Christmas.

▲ **Orville and Wilbur Wright, telegram to their father**

1940

In these times of war when men die on many fronts, it becomes imperative to get either fresh blood to them or some substitute capable of sustaining fluid balance and circulation in the early hours of their injury. It is difficult with present methods to supply whole blood for soldiers removed from civilian population centers. . . . Plasma, however, may be kept for long periods of time without marked changes . . . The pressing needs for further knowledge of its properties and shortcomings is sufficient justification for the studies just begun in that direction.

▲ **Charles Drew, study of blood preservation**

1969

Thinking is a momentary dismissal of irrelevancies.

▲ **Buckminster Fuller, *Utopia or Oblivion***

Define and Explain

Thomas Alva Edison, an American celebrated for his ingenuity, defined *genius* as "one percent inspiration and ninety-nine percent perspiration." What do you think Edison was trying to point out about the nature of creativity?

Assignment: Using the quotations from American scientists and inventors on these two pages as evidence, write an essay of no more than five paragraphs in which you define *ingenuity* in terms of several of the dominant characteristics shared by these creative people. (You may, of course, go beyond the sampling of material here and do some further biographical research.)

Gather and organize information. Read over these quotations and make a list of the personal characteristics they indicate. (Your list might include such traits as curiosity, persistence, solitariness, desire for fame, a sense of wonder, practicality, and so on.) Go over your list and select the two or three characteristics that seem to you to define *ingenuity*.

State your definition as a thesis sentence. Look at the characteristics you have selected and write a topic sentence that defines *ingenuity* in terms of these traits. For example, if you chose curiosity, practicality, and solitariness as your characteristics, your topic sentence might read,

"The ingenious American is often a loner who combines above-average curiosity and a hardheaded practicality."

Plan the essay. Return to the quotations (or other biographical evidence you have gathered) and decide which passages you want to cite as evidence. Decide on the order in which you will present the characteristics you have selected and your supporting evidence. Organize these characteristics and your evidence in a written plan or outline. Each of the characteristics should be discussed in a separate paragraph.

Write a draft of the essay. Write out an introductory paragraph presenting a thesis sentence and a guide sentence. Then write the two or three body paragraphs that present the defining characteristics and supporting quotations. Use appropriate transitional words and phrases to connect your pieces of evidence. Finally, write a brief concluding paragraph that summarizes your points.

Revise the draft. Re-examine the organization and development of your essay. Should the order of the paragraphs or supporting evidence be rearranged? Does the evidence support the topic sentences?

Proofread the essay and make a final copy. Correct errors in grammar, punctuation, and spelling.

Unit 6

You Are There

The American kids don't always know that I'm a foreigner. They tease less. I found out that if you act the way they do, say the things they say, do the things they do, they will be calm. So I try not to act strange to them. I wear T-shirts and stone-washed jeans and aviator glasses. My hair looks like their hair. I'm about five feet ten inches. Clint Eastwood and Charles Bronson are my heroes. After school I watch TV—"Three's Company" and "Different Strokes"—to help me know what's going on in American families, what they do.
—*Abdul, a 17-year-old Afghan immigrant, 1989*

This group of teenagers exemplifies America's multicultural nature.

America and Its Future

Unit Outline

Unit Themes

In this unit you will analyze the following themes of U.S. history:

▶ The American belief in a unique national destiny influences its relations with other nations.

▶ Encouraging technological and scientific innovation has helped American society.

▶ Americans have made choices based on geography as they interacted with the environment.

1978	1980	1982	1984	1986	1988	1990	1992

1979
Camp David Accords ease hostilities between Egypt and Israel; U.S. embassy in Tehran seized, 52 hostages taken

1980
Ronald Reagan elected president

1981
AIDS identified; Sandra Day O'Connor first woman named to U.S. Supreme Court

1982
E.T.: The Extra-Terrestrial becomes most successful movie ever

1985
Mikhail Gorbachev becomes Soviet leader

1988
George Bush elected president

1989
Berlin Wall crumbles

1991
Breakup of the Soviet Union; Iraq driven from Kuwait

1992
William Jefferson Clinton elected president

Linking Past to Present

Although the Secret Service had strongly recommended against it, Jimmy Carter, along with first lady Rosalyn, walked in his own inaugural parade in January 1977. In an era of political assassinations, the gesture was a bold one. Like Thomas Jefferson, inset, who often greeted visitors to the Executive Mansion in a torn dressing gown and carpet slippers, Carter wanted to be a president ordinary people could be comfortable with—one who would always be there to listen to their problems.

The Triumph of Conservatism

1 9 7 4 – 1 9 8 8

23

CHAPTER PREVIEW

In this chapter you will learn how three presidents tried to restore a sense of pride and confidence in America.

SECTIONS IN THIS CHAPTER:
1. Ford tried to restore national confidence in government.
2. Carter inherited enormously complex problems.
3. Reagan sparked social and economic improvements.
4. Reagan tried to reestablish American prestige.

Jimmy Carter, holding hands with his wife Rosalyn, walked in his own inaugural parade in January 1977. Not since Thomas Jefferson had a president chosen to walk instead of ride the route from the Capitol to the White House. Carter's walk was a symbolic gesture to the American people. Like Jefferson, who interpreted his election in 1800 as a rejection of privileged and aristocratic government, Carter considered his own triumph in 1976 a verdict on the "imperial presidency" of the 1960s and 1970s. Like Jefferson, he proposed to make government an expression of the ideals of ordinary Americans.

In the months that followed, Carter did other things that he hoped would symbolize the new era his Administration would represent. He visited small communities, attended town meetings, and spent the night in the homes of ordinary citizens.

The new president's gestures were more than a political gimmick. They were a reflection of the disillusionment that a decade of crises—the Vietnam War, domestic violence, Watergate, and others—had produced. Like his predecessor, Gerald Ford, and the man that followed him, Ronald Reagan, Carter, a conservative Democrat, had his work cut out for him in helping Americans rebuild a shaken faith in their nation's future. Would he or the other two chief executives be up to the task?

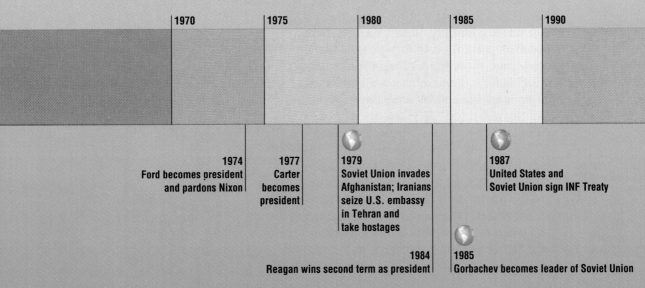

1970   1975   1980   1985   1990

1974 Ford becomes president and pardons Nixon

1977 Carter becomes president

1979 Soviet Union invades Afghanistan; Iranians seize U.S. embassy in Tehran and take hostages

1987 United States and Soviet Union sign INF Treaty

1984 Reagan wins second term as president

1985 Gorbachev becomes leader of Soviet Union

Ford tried to restore national confidence in government.

Key Term: rapprochement

Reading Preview
As you read this section, you will learn:
1. what major commitment President Ford made at the beginning of his term.
2. how successful Ford was in dealing with economic and energy problems.
3. how Ford dealt with the Soviet Union and China.
4. who won the 1976 presidential election.

Gerald Ford was the first president to face the challenge of restoring the popular confidence in government that Vietnam and Watergate had shattered. He was also the first chief executive in American history who had never been elected either vice president or president. Like Richard Nixon before him and Jimmy Carter after, he found popular disillusionment a difficult thing to overcome.

Ford committed himself to an open, honest government.

In his long career as a member of Congress from Michigan, Ford had seldom displayed unusual brilliance or exceptional leadership skills. Nor did he demonstrate them during the two years of his presidency. He did, however, have important political assets. He was amiable and unpretentious, popular with members of Congress, and committed to an open and honest government. For a while, Americans felt comfortable with Ford. They thought that they could finally forget the Watergate nightmare.

Only a month after assuming office, however, Ford did lasting damage to his reputation by granting Richard Nixon a "full, free and absolute" pardon for "all offenses against the United States." The pardon, Ford explained, was an act of compassion—for Nixon himself, who had already suffered enough, and for the American people, whom he wanted to spare the agony of watching a former president stand trial. The decision was profoundly unpopular, however. Most Americans considered the pardon a mistake. Some believed it was the result of a secret deal with the former president. Ford's standing with the public was never the same again.

Ford failed to solve economic and energy problems.

More damaging to the president's popularity, however, was his inability to deal with the economic problems he had inherited. Inflation continued to increase, rising above ten percent in 1975. Ford's efforts to control steadily rising prices through voluntary public efforts had no impact. Somewhat more effective were the monetary policies of the Federal Reserve Board, which raised interest rates and reduced the money supply. Ford, in the meantime, vetoed dozens of bills in an effort to hold down federal spending. These policies, in conjunction with the slogan WIN (Whip Inflation Now), succeeded in bringing inflation down below five percent briefly. However, they also helped produce the severest recession since the 1930s. Unemployment soared to nearly nine percent of the labor force.

Ford was also unable to find workable solutions to the continuing energy crisis. America was growing increasingly dependent on oil imported from the Middle East. The Organization of Petroleum Exporting Countries (OPEC) rec-

President Ford, with a WIN (Whip Inflation Now) button on his lapel, fields questions from reporters in 1974. Ford's attempts to "whip" inflation helped produce a severe recession.

ognized this and continued to raise its prices. In 1975 alone it raised prices by 400 percent.

Rapidly rising oil prices became one of the driving forces behind inflation. Although Ford called for energy conservation and tried to encourage increased domestic production, these efforts produced few results.

Ford continued Nixon's Soviet Union and China policies.

Ford fared somewhat better in international affairs. He retained Henry Kissinger as secretary of state and continued détente with the Soviet Union and **rapprochement**, or the establishment of friendly relations, with China. Late in 1974 Ford met with Soviet leader Leonid Brezhnev at **Vladivostok** in Siberia. There, the two leaders forged a new arms control agreement that became the basis for the second Strategic Arms Limitation Treaty, SALT II. The two superpowers also finalized another agreement the following summer, in **Helsinki**, Finland, that included a Soviet pledge to respect human rights. In the meantime, Henry Kissinger helped negotiate an agreement in the trou-

"IT GETS INTO EVERYTHING"

MEET THE PRESIDENT

GERALD FORD

Born: July 14, 1913
In office: 1974–1977

Gerald Ford produced a fistful of footnotes in his brief tenure in the executive branch. Ford was the first person to be appointed to a vice-presidential vacancy, the first to succeed a resigning president, and the only man ever to serve as vice president and president without being elected.

Ford starred on an undefeated football team at the University of Michigan and earned rapid promotion in the Navy during World War II. He won 13 consecutive terms to the House of Representatives and became minority leader in 1965.

In his brief presidency Ford had little chance to resolve the country's economic problems and international challenges. His single most decisive action—the pardon of Richard Nixon in 1974—was probably fatal to his reelection hopes. The title of his autobiography provides a useful description of his term: *A Time to Heal.*

bled Middle East by which Israel returned to Egypt some of the lands in the **Sinai Peninsula** that it had captured in the 1967 war. As the map on page 919 shows, the Sinai Peninsula separates the Mediterranean and Red seas.

Despite these successes, however, Ford could not escape the unhappy legacy of Vietnam, even though American involvement in the war had largely ended before he became president. The collapse of South Vietnam, Cambodia, and Laos in the spring of 1975 was a humiliating reminder of America's failure in southeast Asia. When the Khmer Rouge government of Cambodia seized an unarmed American merchant ship, the *Mayaguez*, in May 1975, Ford saw an opportunity to demonstrate American resolve. The president ordered 2,000 marines to attack Cambodia from

Political cartoonist Herbert Block mocked the way oil dictated U.S. foreign and domestic policy beginning in the mid-1970s.

JAMES E. CARTER

Born: October 1, 1924
In office: 1977–1981

His remarkable campaign began with a question, "Jimmy who?" and ended with the triumphant answer: "President Carter." Jimmy Carter's status as an unknown outsider had made him an appealing candidate; however, it would make him an ineffective president.

A graduate of the Naval Academy, Carter resigned from the Navy after the death of his father. He prospered as a farmer and businessman and was elected governor of Georgia in 1970.

Carter committed his presidency to issues of peace and human rights. Though he achieved some success in these areas, Americans developed little appreciation for Carter's style of moral leadership. International setbacks, Democratic disunity, and a feverish economy combined to end Carter's administration at one term—and to launch him on a new career as a notably energetic and admired ex-president.

Rosalyn Carter, the wife of Jimmy Carter, campaigned vigorously for her husband during the 1976 presidential election campaign.

of national pride and told the world that America was still a power to be reckoned with.

Jimmy Carter won the presidency in 1976.

Ford entered the 1976 campaign with several serious weaknesses. He had enjoyed few major policy successes during his short time in office, and he had presided over a period of great economic difficulty. He faced a strong challenge from the conservative wing of the Republican party, led by former governor **Ronald Reagan** of **California**, and only barely survived it to win the nomination.

The Democrats, however, were having problems of their own. Still reeling from the disastrous 1972 candidacy of George McGovern, the party seemed adrift, with no strong leaders available to take the helm. Out of the confusion of the primary season emerged a candidate who was virtually an unknown to the public: **Jimmy Carter**, a peanut farmer and former governor of **Georgia**.

Carter campaigned vigorously and appealed to voters by presenting himself as an "outsider" and a common man eager to restore honesty and decency to government. Again and again he promised audiences: "I'll never lie to you." By the end of the primary season, Carter had

neighboring Thailand and rescue the crew. Although the crew was released before the marines arrived, fighting ensued and 40 Americans lost their lives. Despite the deaths, many Americans believed Ford's actions had been appropriate. The show of force in Cambodia helped restore a sense

This colorfully dressed fellow exhibits his enthusiasm for Jimmy Carter's candidacy at the 1976 Democratic National Convention.

accumulated enough delegates to guarantee his nomination. By this time, however, many Americans had already begun to develop doubts about him because of his inexperience in national government.

The fragility of Carter's popularity became clear in the fall campaign. He left the Democratic convention with a large lead over Ford in public opinion polls. By election day, his advantage had dwindled to almost nothing. He won with only 50 percent of the vote, to Ford's 48, and only 297 electoral votes to Ford's 240.

SECTION 1 REVIEW

Identify Key People and Terms
Write a sentence to identify: rapprochement, Ronald Reagan, Jimmy Carter

Locate Key Places
1. In which countries are these cities located: Vladivostok, Helsinki?
2. The Sinai Peninsula separates which two bodies of water?
3. What are the home states of Ronald Reagan and Jimmy Carter?

Master the Main Ideas

1. **Studying political leaders:** Why did President Ford believe he had to make a commitment toward developing an open, honest government?
2. **Analyzing the economic role of government: (a)** What happened when Ford tried to hold down federal spending by vetoing dozens of bills? **(b)** What did Ford do in an attempt to solve the energy crisis?
3. **Studying American foreign policy: (a)** What did Ford do to improve Soviet-American relations in 1974? **(b)** What was Ford's China policy?
4. **Analyzing political elections:** Why do you think Jimmy Carter was able to capture the presidency in 1976?

Apply Critical Thinking Skills: Formulating Appropriate Questions
If you could have asked each of the presidential candidates in 1976 one question, what would that question have been? Why did you choose this particular question?

Carter inherited enormously complex problems.

Key Terms: stagflation, Camp David Accords, PLO

Reading Preview
As you read this section, you will learn:

1. how successful Carter was in dealing with stagflation.
2. what was the cornerstone of Carter's foreign policy.
3. who won the 1980 presidential election.

Carter became president at a moment when the nation faced problems of enormous complexity, for which no solutions were clear. In all likelihood, no leader could have succeeded under such dire circumstances. Carter, however, seemed to combine the problems he inherited with problems he created.

Although he had no experience at all in national government when he became president, he spurned assistance from Washington "insiders" and surrounded himself with a group of close-knit associates from Georgia. With few friends in Congress, few allies in the bureaucracy, and few clearly developed policy commitments, he seemed at times to be governing almost entirely through the use of symbols. He was a highly intelligent man who could analyze problems clearly and quickly. Yet critics complained that he had no larger vision capable of mobilizing the public behind him, and no political skills capable of moving the government in the direction he wanted.

Carter failed to halt stagflation.

Like Nixon and Ford before him, Carter spent much of his time dealing with the problems of inflation and energy. He entered office in the midst of a recession and tried to fight it by cutting taxes and increasing government spending. The recession abated, but inflation quickly resumed. By 1978 it had risen again to nearly ten percent. During Carter's last two years in office, it rose still further, at one point to 18 percent—the highest figure since the aftermath of World War II.

Ultimately, President Carter found himself presiding over a new economic phenomenon: **stagflation**. Economists define stagflation as a period during which high unemployment and economic stagnation is accompanied by high inflation. No conventional strategy seemed suitable for this problem. An attack on inflation would simply slow the already sluggish economy further, causing higher unemployment. An effort to stimulate growth and employment would increase inflation.

Caught between these difficulties, Carter tried to find a solution. He implemented a system of voluntary wage and price controls, with its effectiveness dependent upon the goodwill of companies and labor unions. He created some public works projects designed to aid the unemployed. However, both actions were half-measures that left his critics and his supporters unsatisfied. More importantly, neither measure had much impact on stagflation.

Carter had no more success in dealing with the energy crisis than Ford or Nixon had enjoyed. He proposed a series of "comprehensive

energy programs" to deal with the problem and called for voluntary conservation efforts. Congress, however, weakened his legislative proposals. In the summer of 1979, the United States experienced a second major fuel shortage, forcing motorists to wait once again in long lines to buy gasoline and causing many factories and businesses to curtail operations. In the midst of the crisis, OPEC announced another major price increase.

The fuel crisis and its economic repercussions, combined with Carter's inability to effectively work with Congress, seriously affected the president's credibility with the American public. In 1979 his popularity rating plummeted to a staggeringly low 26 percent. The only thing that prevented his popularity from dipping even lower was a number of very important foreign policy successes.

Human rights was the cornerstone of Carter's foreign policy.

Although Carter never managed to display any consistent vision of his domestic policies, he did for a time seem to have a coherent view of world affairs. A deeply religious man, he rejected what he considered the amoral character of the Nixon-Kissinger foreign policy. Carter attempted to introduce moral principles to the conduct of world affairs and above all to make respect for human rights the cornerstone of American policy. He declared: "Our commitment to human rights must be absolute."

The human rights policy of the Carter Administration was not, as some critics charged, mere rhetoric. The United States became much more outspoken than it had been under Nixon and Ford in denouncing political repression, imprisonment without trial, torture, and official murder throughout the world. Carter cut off military aid to Brazil and Argentina, South American countries generally friendly to the United States, to protest their governments' violent repression of their own people.

Carter's human rights policy helped the United States regain some of the moral stature it had lost as a result of the Vietnam War. However, it also created problems. European allies complained that Carter was introducing a

Creating the image of an "ordinary" citizen, President Carter, wearing a cardigan sweater, relaxes in the White House library as he prepares to deliver a fireside chat to the nation.

HUMAN RIGHTS

Skill: Identifying Alternatives

Introducing the Skill. President Carter, a deeply religious man, wanted to set a moral standard for the world. He said:

I feel very deeply that when people are put in prison without trial and tortured and deprived of basic human rights that the President of the United States ought to have a right to express displeasure and do something about it.

What Carter wanted to do was clearly humane, but was it effective foreign policy? A primary rule of foreign policy is that you don't interfere in the internal affairs of another country. What alternatives might President Carter have considered that would constitute effective foreign policy?

Learning the Skill. In determining foreign policy, leaders often begin by **identifying alternatives**, that is, listing a number of possible plans or solutions. Since complex problems often have no one right answer, determining a solution frequently involves evaluating several options and making compromises.

Applying the Skill. Consider the following alternatives used by President Carter in furthering his foreign policy goals in the area of human rights. Then answer the questions below.

a. granting financial aid or other assistance to nations that improve their human rights record

b. withholding support from nations with serious human rights violations

c. sending U.S. observers to monitor activities in areas of repression

d. using "quiet diplomacy," such as privately informing abusive governments of American concern and warning them of possible consequences of continuing human rights violations

e. imposing economic sanctions such as trade restrictions, boycotts, or embargoes

f. making dramatic gestures that focus world attention on human rights violations

1. Study your text to identify which two of the listed alternatives President Carter took in response to the Soviet invasion of Afghanistan.

2. Do you think Carter's response to the Soviet invasion of Afghanistan was effective foreign policy? Why or why not?

---

self-righteous tone to American policy. Advocates of détente worried that the emphasis on human rights would work against forging an improved relationship with the Soviet Union and China. To some degree, Carter solved these problems by using the human rights approach only selectively. According to one official, Carter's human rights policy was "absolute in principle but flexible in application."

Panama Canal treaties. Carter's first major diplomatic accomplishment was the completion of the Panama Canal treaties, two agreements that spelled out the terms by which the United States would restore sovereignty to Panama in the 500-square-mile **Canal Zone**. (As the map on page 930 shows, the Panama Canal Zone is in central Panama. The zone encompasses the Panama Canal and extends from the Caribbean Sea to the Pacific Ocean.)

Although domestic opposition to the treaties was intense, Carter argued that retaining control of the Canal, which the United States built and had run since 1914, would produce violence and instability in Latin America. The treaties, he insisted, safeguarded American interests and promoted better relations with America's neighbors. After a bitter debate, the Senate ratified the treaties in 1978 by a vote of 68 to 32, only one vote more than the necessary two-thirds.

In the meantime, Carter tried to continue the Nixon-Ford policies of improving relations with China and the Soviet Union. Late in 1978 Carter announced the restoration of formal diplomatic relations with China and sent the first American ambassador since 1949 to Beijing. Months later, he traveled to Vienna to meet with the aging Leonid Brezhnev. There they hammered out the final provisions of the SALT II arms control agreement, which set limits on the numbers of long-range missiles, bombers, and nuclear warheads on both sides. Conservatives in the Senate, including a number of prominent Democrats, were harshly critical of the treaty, insisting that it gave the Soviets a strategic advantage. Those criticisms reflected a deep distrust of the Soviet Union and a revulsion at its human rights policies at home and its interventionism overseas. Despite these criticisms, however, support for SALT II seemed strong enough to pass the treaty in the Senate. As you will learn later in this chapter, however, events in Afghanistan would delay its passage.

The Camp David Accords.   Carter's biggest diplomatic achievement came in the Middle East. Efforts to bring peace to that troubled region seemed hopelessly stalled when a dramatic event occurred in November 1977. The president of Egypt, **Anwar Sadat**, accepted an invitation from the prime minister of Israel, **Menachem Begin**, to visit Begin's country. Sadat had earlier expelled all Soviet advisers from his country and had begun efforts to create stronger ties with the West, particularly the United States. He had also survived efforts by **Muammar el-Qaddafi** [kä dä′fē], the radical leader of Libya, to overthrow and assassinate him. The Israeli secret service, the Mossad, had saved Sadat from one such assassination attempt. The Egyptian leader was disposed, therefore, to improve relations with Israel. On Sadat's arrival in

President Carter demonstrated his diplomatic acumen when he helped Israeli leader Menachem Begin, left, and Egyptian leader Anwar Sadat, right, agree to the Camp David Accords.

Tel Aviv, a seaport in western Israel, he announced that he was willing to recognize the right of Israel to exist as a state. Egypt thus became the first Arab nation to extend such recognition.

Although Egypt and Israel conducted talks that would have formalized Sadat's pledge to recognize Israel, they broke down in the summer of 1978 in the midst of criticism from other Arab leaders. At that point, Jimmy Carter intervened.

In September 1978 President Carter invited Sadat and Begin to visit Camp David, the presidential retreat in the mountains of western Maryland, for a prolonged negotiating session over which Carter would preside. For two weeks the president and Secretary of State **Cyrus Vance** worked to resolve the disputes between the two nations. Then Carter brought Sadat and Begin to the White House to announce an agreement on a "framework" for an Egyptian-Israeli peace treaty. This framework for peace, known as the **Camp David Accords**, was rather ambiguous, however. Consequently, six more months passed before the two countries were able to complete a mutually acceptable treaty. Finally, in March 1979, Sadat and Begin returned to the White House to sign a peace treaty in the presence of Jimmy Carter.

The treaty, which provided for the gradual return of the entire Sinai Peninsula to Egypt and the recognition of Israel's existence, was a tremendous accomplishment for President Carter. It was perhaps his finest moment. However, the treaty left the fate of the Palestine Arabs vague and unsettled. The **Palestine Liberation Organization (PLO)**, an organization formed for the purpose of getting the international community to accept the legitimacy of a homeland for Palestine, was excluded from the talks. Also absent from the talks were representatives of the Soviet Union. By not inviting either of these two parties to participate in the treaty negotiations, the United States effectively alienated Egypt from the other Arab nations and drove the more radical Arab states closer to the Soviet Union. Some Egyptians also disagreed with their nation's new relationship with Israel. In 1981 an

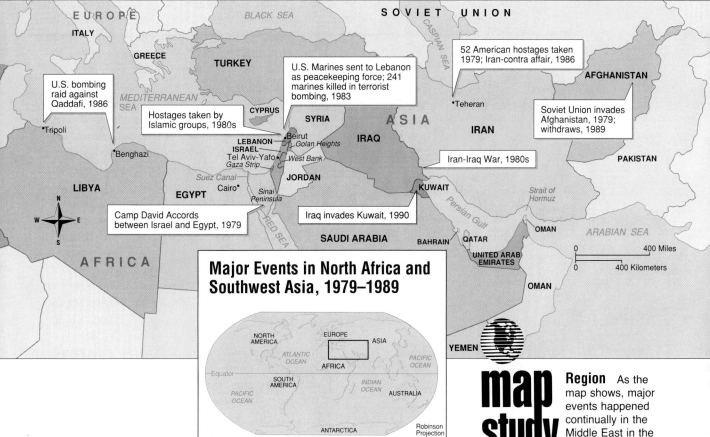

Major Events in North Africa and Southwest Asia, 1979–1989

U.S. bombing raid against Qaddafi, 1986

Hostages taken by Islamic groups, 1980s

U.S. Marines sent to Lebanon as peacekeeping force; 241 marines killed in terrorist bombing, 1983

52 American hostages taken 1979; Iran-contra affair, 1986

Soviet Union invades Afghanistan, 1979; withdraws, 1989

Iran-Iraq War, 1980s

Camp David Accords between Israel and Egypt, 1979

Iraq invades Kuwait, 1990

Azimuthal Equal-Area Projection

Robinson Projection

map study

Region As the map shows, major events happened continually in the Middle East in the 1980s. Note the many nations that exist in this relatively small region. Each nation has special interests and, in some cases, different religions and cultures. What two nations were at war in the 1980s?

Critical Thinking Analyze the map captions. How would you describe most of the events that took place? Is there any event that seems different from the others?

anti-Israeli Egyptian soldier protested this relationship by assassinating Anwar Sadat.

The year of the hostages. The Middle East was not only the source of Carter's greatest triumph. It was also the source of Carter's greatest crisis.

As you read before, the Central Intelligence Agency (CIA) had helped Muhammad Reza Pahlavi, the shah of Iran, regain his throne in 1953. Since that time, America had given the shah political support and, more recently, military assistance in an effort to make Iran a bulwark against Soviet expansion in the region. However, Pahlavi was developing serious problems with his own people in the late 1970s.

Iranians resented the shah's enormous wealth, estimated to be as as high as $100 million, and the corruption among members of his family. They hated the brutal and repressive policies of his autocratic government. Even members of the new middle class that was emerging as a result of the shah's commitment to economic development and modernization tended to oppose the government.

At the same time, the shah faced an even greater threat from the millions of Islamic fundamentalists among the Iranian people. Led by an angry clergy who considered the shah's westernization policies a threat to religious values, they rallied behind efforts to expel western

justice, was enraged when the United States permitted the shah to enter its borders for treatment. In retaliation, on November 4 an armed group of Islamic militants seized the American embassy in **Tehran**, the Iranian capital, and held 52 American diplomats, marine guards, and others as hostages.

The American public was outraged when they learned of the hostage situation. Helplessly, they sat back in front of their television sets and watched newscasts that showed angry Iranian mobs chanting "death to America." They were mortified as they watched the blindfolded hostages being paraded in front of thousands of cheering Iranians. Although a feeling of helplessness prevailed, many Americans began looking to the president to take drastic actions to get the hostages back and to recapture American pride. Some of them cried for the president to "nuke 'em into oblivion." As the crisis continued from day to day and from week to week, American anger grew steadily more intense.

The invasion of Afghanistan. A few weeks after the hostage seizure, on December 27, 1979, Soviet troops invaded **Afghanistan**, a nation of 16 million people east of Iran and south of the Soviet Union. Because Afghanistan had been largely under Soviet control since 1978, some Americans believed the invasion was simply an effort by the Kremlin to maintain its position there. To the Carter Administration and many Americans however, the action was a sign of larger Soviet aims. The president cautioned:

The [invasion is a] stepping stone to their possible control **AN AMERICAN ★ SPEAKS** over much of the world's oil supplies [and] the greatest threat to world peace since World War II.

The policies of détente, which Nixon, Ford, and Carter had all worked to advance, now collapsed. The president withdrew the SALT II treaty from consideration by the Senate. He imposed economic sanctions, including a grain embargo that proved unpopular with American farmers, on the Soviet Union. He also canceled American participation in the 1980 Olympic games in Moscow.

Above, one of the 52 American hostages captured by Islamic militants in Tehran in 1979 is paraded in front of cheering Iranians. Top, America's frustration with the hostage situation deepened in April 1980 when a desperate attempt to rescue the hostages was aborted when several helicopters broke down in the Iranian desert. During the pullout, an accident involving a helicopter and a C-130 Hercules transport plane took the lives of eight men and injured five others.

influences and restore traditional ways.

The combination of resentments finally produced a popular revolutionary movement. In January 1979 the shah fled the country. Soon after, members of the clergy—led by the zealously antiwestern **Ayatollah Ruhollah Khomeini**—seized power in Iran. The new regime was hostile to the West in general and to the United States in particular, which its leaders liked to refer to as a "stubborn, spoiled child" and the "Great Satan."

The Carter Administration tried in the months after the shah's departure to establish cordial relations with the new leaders of Iran. Anti-American sentiment frustrated most of those efforts, however. Then, in October 1979, the exiled shah entered the United States and checked into a hospital in New York for treatment of cancer, which within several months proved fatal. Iran, which wanted the shah returned so that it could execute its form of

Ronald Reagan won the presidency in 1980.

Events in Iran and Afghanistan played an important role in the 1980 presidential election. Jimmy Carter, running for reelection, entered the campaign with very little support even within his own party. Senator **Edward Kennedy** of Massachusetts, younger brother of former President John F. Kennedy, announced that he would challenge the president in the primaries. Public opinion polls taken during the early months of 1980 suggested that Carter would lose them all.

However, Americans generally rally to their leaders in times of crisis. After the seizure of the hostages, Carter rode on the wave of patriotism that was sweeping the nation and regained some of the popularity he had steadily lost during his term. Promising that he would balance the federal budget by stimulating productivity and investment and making the nation "strong and second to none in military power," Carter won most of the Democratic primaries and seemed on his way to renomination. His troubles, however, were not yet over. In April 1980 he approved a secret commando mission to rescue the American hostages from Tehran. The mission failed when several helicopters broke down in the desert. (See the photograph on page 920.) Secretary of State Cyrus Vance, who had opposed the poorly planned mission, resigned in protest. Kennedy, in the meantime, revived his campaign and began winning some important primary victories. His surge was too late, however, and Carter managed to hang on to win his party's nomination.

The Republican party, in the meantime, had united behind one of their most conservative and magnetic leaders: Ronald Reagan, a former movie actor and two-term governor of California. Reagan was a more powerful orator and more effective campaigner than Carter. He based his campaign on what his advisers concluded was the public's impatience with the "decline" of American power and prestige. He promised to cut back federal spending, reduce taxes, restore American greatness, and maintain peace. Reagan believed that peace could

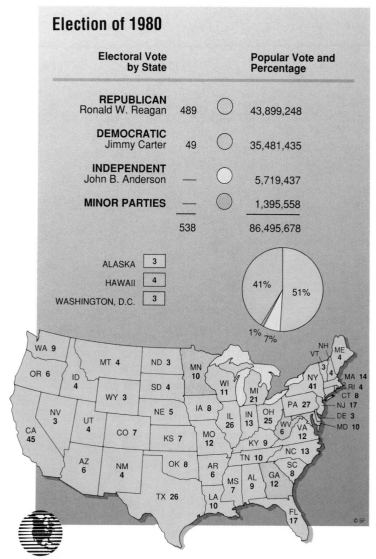

Election of 1980

	Electoral Vote by State		Popular Vote and Percentage
REPUBLICAN Ronald W. Reagan	489	○	43,899,248
DEMOCRATIC Jimmy Carter	49	○	35,481,435
INDEPENDENT John B. Anderson	—	○	5,719,437
MINOR PARTIES	—	○	1,395,558
	538		86,495,678

ALASKA 3
HAWAII 4
WASHINGTON, D.C. 3

41% 51% 1% 7%

© SF

map study

Region The electoral votes in this election indicate a Republican landslide. Which candidate took votes away from both parties?

Critical Thinking In many presidential elections there are regional patterns to the voting. Why was this not the case in the 1980 election?

Ronald Reagan gives a "thumbs-up" to his supporters after his victory in the 1980 presidential election.

RONALD REAGAN

Born: February 6, 1911
In office: 1981–1989

Thirty years of show business prepared Ronald Reagan for his greatest role. At 69 he became the oldest elected president and one of the most well liked.

Reagan appeared in more than 50 movies before serving two terms as governor of California. He won the Republican nomination for president in 1980 on his third try.

For his natural ease in addressing Americans, Reagan was called "the Great Communicator." His election marked a strong conservative shift in American life, and his two terms brought a revived economy, a costly military buildup, and a confident, active role for the United States in world affairs.

Reagan's lack of involve- ment in the details of his Administration contributed to steady eruptions of scandal. These did little damage to Reagan personally until the Iran-contra affair raised tardy questions about who really had been directing Reagan's White House epic.

electoral votes to Carter's 49. Equally striking were Republican successes in the congressional races. For the first time since 1952, Republicans took control of the Senate. Republicans also made enough gains in the House to put that chamber largely under the control of conservatives.

On the day of Reagan's inauguration, the 52 American hostages were released from Iran, the result of hard negotiating by the Carter Administration in its last days in office. Their return to the United States after 444 days in captivity produced frenzied celebrations and launched the Reagan Administration in an air of triumph.

SECTION 2 REVIEW

Identify Key People and Terms
Write a sentence to identify: stagflation, Anwar Sadat, Menachem Begin, Muammar el-Qaddafi, Cyrus Vance, Camp David Accords, PLO, Ayatollah Ruhollah Khomeini, Edward Kennedy, John Anderson

Locate Key Places
1. Which two bodies of water does the Panama Canal Zone link?
2. Tel Aviv and Tehran are located in which countries?
3. Name the country that was invaded by the Soviet Union in 1979.

Master the Main Ideas
1. **Analyzing the impact of inflation:** Why was Carter unable to do anything about stagflation?
2. **Analyzing U.S. foreign policy:** What were two human rights actions taken by Carter?
3. **Studying political campaigns:** What did Ronald Reagan promise the American public during the 1980 election campaign?

Apply Critical Thinking Skills: Recognizing Bias
Presidential candidates often use glittering generalities in their campaigns. These are broad statements that almost no one would disagree with. Did any of the 1980 presidential candidates use glittering generalities in his election campaign? If so, what were they?

only be maintained if the United States was strong militarily:

> **M**aintaining peace means that we build up our defen-sive strength to the point that no other nation is going to dare challenge us.

AN AMERICAN ★ SPEAKS

Many Americans were unhappy with both major party candidates, and some rallied behind the independent campaign of Representative **John Anderson** of Illinois, a Republican moderate. He believed that America's first defense priority should be to strengthen the economy and then to "restore and strengthen historic alliances." Although Carter and Reagan were neck and neck one week before the election, Reagan scored an impressive victory. He received 51 percent of the popular vote to Carter's 41 and Anderson's 7. He won 489

SECTION 3

Reagan sparked social and economic improvements.

Key Terms: supply-side economics, Equal Rights Amendment of 1972

Reading Preview
As you read this section, you will learn:

1. what characteristic of Ronald Reagan enabled him to win the hearts of many Americans.
2. what happened to the economy during Reagan's first term.
3. who won the election of 1984.
4. what stand Reagan took on social issues.

Ronald Reagan was a month shy of his 70th birthday when he took the oath of office as president. He was almost as old at the beginning of his term of office as any president but Eisenhower had been at the end of his. Like Jimmy Carter, he had no prior experience in Washington and few allies in Congress. Yet for much of his eight years in office, he was a brilliant political success.

Reagan's personality won him the hearts of many Americans.

Part of Reagan's appeal rested on his engaging public personality. He seemed much younger than his years, with his full head of dark hair (which he insisted he had never dyed), his ruddy cheeks, his jaunty gait, and his fondness for such vigorous outdoor activities as riding horses and chopping wood on his California ranch. He was seriously wounded in an assassination attempt in 1981, but he appeared to recover both his health and his good humor quickly. Four years later, he rebounded from cancer surgery with similar apparent ease.

As a former actor, he was a gifted television performer and a talented public speaker. He had a dazzling smile and an easy bearing that suggested great personal warmth. To some

people, Reagan was the quintessential grandfather figure. Above all, perhaps, he seemed entirely comfortable with himself and confident of his positions. The public responded by treating Reagan with rare affection. Even those who disagreed with his policies tended not to blame the president himself for them. When things went wrong, most people criticized his aides, the Congress, and anyone but Reagan himself. Some Democrats began referring to his administration as the "Teflon Presidency," a presidency to which no charges ever stuck. Whatever the reasons, Reagan maintained a very high popularity through most of his eight years in the White House.

Despite his vigorous public image, Reagan was one of the least active presidents ever to serve in office. Almost all his former associates who wrote or talked about their experiences in the White House described him as a detached, generally passive president who set a general ideological tone for his Administration but involved himself in few of its actual operations. Instead, he surrounded himself with energetic administrators and seldom second-guessed their decisions. At times, Reagan displayed astonishing ignorance of the actions of his subordinates—sometimes, perhaps, as a way to distance himself from failed policies, but often, it seemed clear, because he truly did not know or understand what his aides had done.

Whatever Reagan's personal role in the Administration, his presidency was a significant one for several reasons. It restored to the office of the presidency some of its former strength, prestige, and popularity. It helped revive some of the patriotism and national pride that the Vietnam War, Watergate, and other crises had challenged in the 1970s. Most of all perhaps, it produced the most important change in the direction of federal economic and social policy since the Great Society of the 1960s.

The economy revived during Reagan's first term in office.

The first major goal of the Reagan Administration was to revive the economy, which continued to suffer from stagflation. The president's solution was a program newly popular among some conservatives and known as **supply-side economics**, or Reaganomics. Many of the problems of the economy, supply-side theorists claimed, were a result of excessively high taxes. High taxes, in turn, prevented people from investing money in productive enterprises such as factories, equipment, and research. Accordingly, Reagan proposed a major tax reduction, offering particularly large savings to corporations and wealthy individuals—the people presumed to be the most likely to invest their savings in productive enterprises.

The tax cut, he predicted, would stimulate the nation's economic growth.

Cutting taxes was only one part of the supply-side program. Reagan also proposed a major reduction in federal spending. Reagan's economic advisers believed that less federal spending would reduce inflation, eliminate many useless and even destructive government programs, and bring the federal budget into balance. Within a few months of entering office, Reagan had won congressional approval of most of his economic program: the biggest

Stand and Deliver: Jaime Escalante

Students respond enthusiastically to Escalante's methods of teaching calculus.

In a famous 1983 report, a special commission declared that the troubled system of American public education put the nation "at risk." Garfield High School in East Los Angeles was once a classic inner-city example of what was wrong. Located in the heart of the Mexican American community, Garfield was afflicted by gangs and graffiti, drugs and dropping out. In the 1970s the school was in danger of losing its accreditation. Today Garfield is a showcase of a different kind—a symbol of what strong administrators, inspired teachers, and challenged students can accomplish.

A key figure in the turnaround at Garfield was a dynamic math teacher, Jaime Escalante. Half showman, half preacher—but all teacher—Escalante used a grab bag of techniques to interest, motivate, and drive his students to achieve. He chopped apples with a meat cleaver to demonstrate percentages. He appealed to their pride as Mexican Americans: "The Mayans were way ahead of everybody on the concept of zero, Johnny. You *burros* have math in your blood." Not content that his students were mastering basic math, Escalante began to teach calculus. In 1979 he started with five students, preparing them to take the Advanced Placement test for college credit. Four of them passed. By 1987 Garfield ranked fourth in the nation in the number of students taking the grueling AP calculus exam. Twenty-six percent of all Mexican American students in the entire country who passed the test were from Garfield High. These achievements won national attention and were celebrated in a Hollywood motion picture, *Stand and Deliver* (1988).

Problems remain at Garfield High; the dropout rate is still a major concern. However, possibilities are even more abundant. The work of Escalante and dozens of other teachers at Garfield have revived an old ideal that public schools in America can be staircases to success, and that teachers can be heroes.

Highlights of American Life

tax cut since 1964 and a $140 billion reduction over two years in domestic spending.

Americans soon discovered, however, that the supply-side program was not exactly what Reagan claimed it to be. The income tax cuts were real enough, but they were soon accompanied by significant increases in other taxes—most notably Social Security—that actually made the total tax burden higher for most individuals. In addition, while Reagan was reducing some domestic spending, he was both unable and unwilling to cut the biggest items in the budget: the so-called "entitlement" programs, the largest of which were Medicare and Social Security. The cost of those programs continued to rise and more than made up for the cuts Reagan was making in other areas.

The Administration also radically increased the defense budget to make up for what it claimed were years of neglect of the military during the Carter Administration. So instead of balancing the budget as he had promised, Reagan produced historic deficits. Before the 1980s the highest one-year deficit in American history had been $66 billion. Under Reagan the deficit was never less than $100 billion a year. In 1986 the deficit soared to $221 billion. The government accumulated twice as much debt during Reagan's eight years in office as it had in its entire previous history. Indeed, one of the most important legacies of the Reagan years was the creation of a political climate in which concern about deficits seemed to override all other domestic concerns. Throughout the 1980s officials were reluctant to support any proposal that involved major new costs.

In the short term, at least, the supply-side program seemed not to contribute to a revival of economic growth either. By early 1982, the nation was entering the worst recession since the 1930s. Unemployment approached 11 percent. Some parts of the country, particularly the industrial Midwest, were experiencing a genuine recession. By the middle of 1983, however, the economy was recovering rapidly and impressively. Unemployment was slowly declining, and the gross national product was growing significantly. At least as important, inflation seemed finally to be under control. The

national economy continued to grow and inflation remained reasonably low for the rest of the decade.

Many believed that the principal cause of the "Reagan recovery," as the Administration liked to call it, was the tight-money policy of the Federal Reserve Board under the leadership of Paul Volcker. Others argued it was a result of the worldwide glut in oil production and the rapidly falling energy prices that resulted. Still others claimed that it was a result of the enormous federal budget deficits, which pumped money into the depressed economy and started it moving again. Whatever the reason, the Reagan Administration received enormous political benefits from the health of the economy.

Called "voodoo economics" by its critics, Reaganomics, or supply-side economics, baffled many economists as well as the general public.

Reagan captured a second term as president in 1984.

The extent of the benefits gained by the Administration as a result of a healthy economy became clear in the election of 1984. Reagan entered the campaign at the head of a united party completely committed to his candidacy. The Democrats once again were divided. **Walter Mondale**, who was vice president under Jimmy Carter, was the early front-runner. However, he barely survived a powerful challenge from Senator **Gary Hart** of **Colorado** to receive his party's nomination.

Mondale produced momentary excitement at the Democratic convention when he selected Representative **Geraldine Ferraro** of **New York** as his running mate. She was the

Walter Mondale and Geraldine Ferraro greet supporters during the 1984 campaign. Reagan's popularity was too great an obstacle for the Democrats to overcome.

first woman ever to be named to a national party ticket. Despite Ferraro's excellent credentials, however, questions about the finances of Ferraro's family emerged and were vigorously pursued by the media. These allegations seriously deflected attention from the issues and provided the straw that finally broke the back of the Mondale campaign.

Reagan's victory in 1984 was one of the biggest in American history. He received 59 percent of the popular vote to Mondale's 41 percent. The Democrats won electoral votes only in Mondale's home state of **Minnesota** and in the District of Columbia. Republicans did not fare as well in the congressional elections, however. The Democrats gained a seat in the Senate and lost only a little ground in the House. Two years later the Democrats would regain control of the Senate.

Reagan took a conservative stand on social issues.

One of the keys to Reagan's victory in 1984 was his ability to hold together a large coalition of people of many diverse views. In particular he had to hold together his own political base of Republican conservatives.

Reagan was a self-proclaimed conservative. Conservatism, like liberalism, can mean many different things, however. Reagan Administration staffers subscribed to a wide variety of conservatism: people who wanted public poli-

cies more favorable to business; people who wanted America to deal more harshly with the Soviet Union; people who feared that "permissiveness" had crept into American life.

One group in the conservative camp gained the label "movement conservatives"—people to whom conservatism was a powerful ideology, not a pragmatic stance. To many of them, the most important issues were not economic or diplomatic, but social. In deference to the movement conservatives, Reagan took strong public positions on a wide range of controversial issues that many of his predecessors had tried to avoid.

Like most Republicans, the president opposed court-ordered busing of students to achieve school integration. He also opposed most forms of affirmative action—the policy of giving preference to minorities and women in

Many Americans rallied to express their divergent opinions of the Equal Rights Amendment (ERA).

hiring and school admissions to make up for past discrimination. For a time, he opposed renewing the Voting Rights Act of 1965, which empowered the federal government to supervise voter registration practices in the South to protect African American rights. He refused to support the **Equal Rights Amendment (ERA) of 1972** to the Constitution, which was intended to protect women from discrimination on the basis of their sex. Despite widespread popular support for the amendment, it finally died in 1982, when it failed to pass in the required three-fourths of the states. Only three other states would have been needed to make the amendment a part of the Constitution.

Reagan was also outspoken in opposing the right of women to have an abortion, in calling for a reintroduction of prayer into public schools, in opposing gun control, and in supporting the death penalty and other harsh measures for dealing with crime. Controversial as these positions were, they had little effect on most of what the Reagan Administration actually did. Few of these social issues were matters over which the president had any authority. Even the things Reagan could influence, such as enforcement of affirmative action, he generally acted on cautiously. He called repeatedly for legislation or a constitutional amendment banning abortion, but he took no active steps to achieve those controversial social goals.

Despite his inaction on some crucial social issues, the president still had a significant impact on the future of social issues through his judicial appointments. At every level of the judiciary, Reagan appointed conservative judges with a narrower view of the rights guaranteed by the Constitution than that of the judges who had dominated the more liberal courts of the 1960s and 1970s. He made three appointments to the Supreme Court: **Sandra Day O'Connor**, the first woman justice, Anthony Kennedy, and Antonin Scalia. They tipped the balance among the justices in a decidedly conservative direction. In addition, Reagan elevated the most conservative member of the Court, William Rehnquist, a Nixon appointee, to chief justice. By the end of the 1980s, the new Court was narrowing and even reversing some of the most important liberal decisions of courts of the 1960s and 1970s.

By nominating Sandra Day O'Connor to the Supreme Court, Ronald Reagan, who opposed ERA, fulfilled a campaign pledge to fill one of the first Supreme Court vacancies with "the most qualified woman" he could find. O'Connor is shown shaking hands with Elie Wiesel in 1986 after swearing him in to a second term as chairman of the United States Holocaust Memorial Council. Wiesel's wife, Marion, holds the Bible.

SECTION **3** REVIEW

Identify Key People and Terms:
Write a sentence to identify: supply-side economics, Walter Mondale, Gary Hart, Geraldine Ferraro, Equal Rights Amendment of 1972, Sandra Day O'Connor

Locate Key Places
Name the home states of the following political leaders: Gary Hart, Geraldine Ferraro, Walter Mondale

Master the Main Ideas

1. **Studying political leaders:** Why was President Reagan so popular with the American public?
2. **Studying the economic role of government:** What were two possible explanations for the "Reagan recovery"?
3. **Analyzing political elections:** Why was Reagan's victory in 1984 such a landslide?
4. **Analyzing social developments:** Provide an example of how Reagan's conservatism affected social issues.

Apply Critical Thinking Skills: Making Comparisons
Compare the personalities of Ronald Reagan and John F. Kennedy. What traits did these two leaders share? How was each person unique?

Reagan tried to reestablish American prestige.

Key Terms: Solidarity, SDI, Sandinistas, contras, Iran-contra affair, *glasnost*, *perestroika*, INF Treaty

Reading Preview
As you read this section, you will learn:

1. what was the status of U.S.–Soviet relations during Reagan's first term in office.
2. how Reagan reacted to the threat of communist takeovers in various parts of the world.
3. how Reagan responded to the problem of terrorism.
4. what event caused short-term damage to Reagan's public image.
5. what types of changes in world politics occurred in the late 1980s.

Reagan entered office determined to reverse what he felt were dangerous trends in American life. He wanted to reverse what he considered an alarming economic decline. He wanted to end the drift toward ever-bigger government. He wanted to stop the erosion of American military strength. He also wanted to rebuild American power and prestige in the world. To most members of his Administration, that meant seeing America play a more active role in the struggle against communism.

U.S.-Soviet relations continued to deteriorate.

American–Soviet relations had been deteriorating for at least two years when Reagan took office. They had declined especially rapidly in the year following the Soviet invasion of Afghanistan. In the first two years of the new Administration, those relations grew even chillier. The president and his first secretary of state, **Alexander Haig**, reverted to language, and at times to policies, that reminded many people of the early years of the Cold War in the 1950s. Reagan at various times called the Soviet Union an "evil empire" and the "focus of evil in the world." Much of the massive arms buildup of the Reagan years was clearly designed to strengthen America's position in a possible war with the Soviet Union.

Relations with the Soviets grew especially cold when the government of **Poland**, under strong pressure from Moscow, imposed martial law in late 1981. It was acting because of the growing strength of the independent labor union, **Solidarity**, which threatened the communist party's monopoly on power. America denounced the crackdown in Poland, blamed it on the Kremlin, and imposed economic sanctions on the Polish government. Reagan did not, however, consider military action.

In the meantime, the Reagan Administration seemed resistant to any further arms control agreements with the Soviets. The president ignored the demands of a growing antinuclear movement in both Europe and the United States, and proceeded with plans to station new intermediate-range nuclear missiles in Europe. At about the same time, he proposed a new antiballistic missile program to protect the United States from a nuclear attack. Several scientists and other advisers had persuaded the president that it was possible to use lasers and satellites to create an effective defense against incoming missiles. Subsequently, Reagan won appropriations from Congress to begin

This artist's rendering illustrates how Strategic Defense Initiative (SDI) lasers would destroy enemy missiles launched against the United States.

research into the system, which even its defenders conceded would cost hundreds of billions of dollars to deploy. The president called the new program the **Strategic Defense Initiative (SDI)**. Most Americans knew it as "Star Wars," a nickname derived from the popular science-fiction movie of the same name.

The Soviet Union considered SDI a major provocation and for nearly four years insisted that any arms control agreement begin with an American promise to abandon the program. The president consistently refused to consider that, and arms control remained stalled.

Reagan pledged to support opponents of communism around the world.

The Reagan Administration also attempted to revive American activism in those areas of the world where communists were threatening existing governments. The president announced that it would be the policy of the United States to support opponents of communism anywhere in the world, whether or not the conflicts involved the Soviet Union directly. This policy became known as the Reagan doctrine. In reality, however, the doctrine was little more than a restatement of earlier, pre-Vietnam Cold War policies that emphasized containment.

The Reagan doctrine had its biggest impact in Latin America. In October 1983 American forces came to the aid of anticommunists on the Caribbean island of **Grenada** [grənā′də] and ousted a government that the Administration believed was forging a relationship with the Soviet Union. As the map on page 930 shows, Grenada is one of the Windward Islands just north of the South American coastline.

Although 18 Americans died during the fighting, most Americans wholeheartedly supported the military action. Patriotism ran high and, at least momentarily, Americans seemed to regain their sense of status and safety as citizens of a world power. This support was not shared, however, by many governments. Most of America's European allies, including Britain, totally disapproved of the American military intervention in Grenada.

Reagan also increased American aid to the government of **El Salvador**, which the map on

Sincerely, Samantha Smith

Worried about the troubled relations between the United States and the Soviet Union, ten-year-old Samantha Smith wrote a letter to the new Soviet leader, Yuri Andropov. In April 1983 Andropov replied to her letter and later invited her to visit. Samantha's letter created an "international incident" of undeniable charm and goodwill. In your view, what is the key issue in Samantha's letter?

Dear Mr. Andropov,
My name is Samantha Smith. I am ten years old. Congratulations on your new job. I have been worrying about Russia and the United States getting into a nuclear war. Are you going to vote to have a war or not? If you aren't please tell me how you are going to help to not have a war. This question you do not have to answer, but I would like to know why you want to conquer the world or at least our country. God made the world for us to live together in peace and not to fight.

Sincerely,
Samantha Smith

page 930 shows is the smallest nation in Central America. El Salvador was in the midst of a civil war between its right-wing government and left-wing rebels who the American government claimed were receiving aid from Cuba and the Soviet Union. As it did during the Grenada military action, the Administration justified its actions in El Salvador by insisting that a rebel victory would give the Soviet Union an additional foothold in the Western Hemisphere. Critics, however, noted that the American-supported Salvadoran government was one of the most repressive and murderous in the world in dealing with its opponents. Although the election of the moderate **José Napoleon Duarte** [dü ar′tā] as president in 1984 allowed the Reagan Administration to argue that El Salvador was now a democracy, critics continued to argue that the new govern-

Major Events in Central America and the Caribbean, 1978–1992

UNITED STATES

Gulf of Mexico

MEXICO

BAHAMAS

ATLANTIC OCEAN

Azimuthal Equal-Area Projection   © SF

0   250   500 Miles

0   250   500 Kilometers

N
W   E
S

CUBA

Leftist guerrillas engage U.S.-backed government in civil war, 1980–1990; formal peace agreement, 1992

BELIZE

GUATEMALA

HONDURAS

EL SALVADOR

NICARAGUA

PACIFIC OCEAN

Sandinistas come to power, 1979; U.S.-backed contra rebels and Sandinistas fight civil war, 1979–1989; Sandinista rule and civil war end, 1990.

COSTA RICA

PANAMA

Panama Canal

CANAL ZONE

JAMAICA

HAITI

DOMINICAN REPUBLIC

Puerto Rico (U.S.)

ST. KITTS AND NEVIS

DOMINICA

ST. LUCIA

BARBADOS

ST. VINCENT AND THE GRENADINES

GRENADA

ANTIGUA AND BARBUDA

Pro-Castro regime takes power, March 1979; U.S. forces land, Oct. 1983; elections held, Dec. 1984

CARIBBEAN SEA

TRINIDAD AND TOBAGO

SOUTH AMERICA

U.S. and Panama negotiate Panama Canal treaties, 1978; U.S. invades Panama, arresting dictator Noriega on drug trafficking charges,1989

In this award-winning photograph, "Deeds of War," Salvadoran children shield their eyes from dust kicked up by helicopters during El Salvador's civil war.

ment was still dominated by a few wealthy interests. Therefore, the critics said, it was inappropriate for the United States to provide it aid. Despite American aid, the civil war continued inconclusively through the 1980s.

The Reagan Administration's biggest commitment in Latin America was in **Nicaragua**.

(The map above shows that Nicaragua is in central Central America.) In 1979 the corrupt dictator **Anastasio Somoza**—a longtime ally of the United States—was overthrown by a popular revolutionary movement that called itself the **Sandinistas**. The Carter Administration had attempted to forge a friendly relationship with the new government. By 1981, however, the Sandinistas were moving further to the left and becoming increasingly anti-American. The Reagan Administration ended the economic assistance Carter had begun. It also began to give covert support to an anti-Sandinista movement whose members were known as **contras**, meaning "those against" in Spanish. Money and arms flowed through the CIA and other channels to guerrilla organizations in remote bases in neighboring Costa Rica and Honduras. The contras then launched attacks in Nicaragua.

The contra war, as it came to be known, was one of the most controversial events of the Reagan Administration. President Reagan

map study

Location Which event involved a former U.S. territory?

Critical Thinking
Analyze the map captions. What similarity is there among the events described?

Marines clear rubble after the 1983 terrorist attack on the U.S. Marine headquarters in Beirut. The attack led Congress and the American public to question the Administration's policy and goals in Lebanon. In February 1984 Reagan withdrew the marines from Beirut, redeploying them on naval vessels in the Mediterranean.

appeared to have a deep, emotional attachment to the contras. He called them "freedom fighters" and the "moral equivalent of the founding fathers." Critics in Congress and the public argued that the contras had no popular support; that their leaders were drawn from the discredited Somoza regime; and that they had virtually no chance of prevailing without direct American military intervention on their behalf. On several occasions, Congress refused to appropriate any further funds for aid to the contras. In response to that, as you will learn later, the Administration began looking for other ways to assist the contras.

Reagan had few answers to the problem of terrorism.

Revolutionary groups have occasionally used forms of terrorism throughout history. It is a tactic that usually appeals to groups or countries too small or weak to exercise power in more conventional ways. In the late years of the 20th century, however, an unusually high number of terrorist acts occurred in many parts of the world. Terrorism produced an enormous challenge to the governments of the West, particularly the U.S. government.

Much of the terrorism was the work of militant Islamic sects in the Middle East, many of them inspired to fight for their goals by the Iranian revolution. In 1982 the Reagan Administration dispatched marines to **Beirut**, the capital of Lebanon. Lebanon had been in turmoil for some time because of rivalry among religious and political factions. Earlier that year, its problems grew worse because of an invasion by the Israeli army, which was trying to expel forces of the Palestine Liberation Organization (PLO) from the country. The American troops had been sent as a peacekeeping force. They were to allow the PLO to leave the country peaceably. Once there, however, the marines became identified with one of the factions in the civil war. In the fall of 1983, terrorists rammed a truck loaded with explosives into marine barracks near the Beirut airport. The tremendously powerful explosion, which killed 241 marines, angered the American public and the Reagan Administration.

Subsequent terrorist acts increased the anger in the United States. Several American passenger planes were bombed by terrorists, including a flight from London in December 1988 that killed several hundred Americans. That bombing was, some speculated, in retaliation for the accidental downing of an Iranian passenger plane by American forces patrolling the Persian Gulf a year earlier. Other terrorist attacks occurred on cruise ships and on commercial and diplomatic installations in Europe.

In the meantime, Islamic groups seized hostages from among the few Americans who remained in Lebanon.

One of those hostages was **Frank Reed**, an American schoolteacher who was kidnapped by a shadowy terrorist group known as the Islamic Dawn in September 1986 as he was on his way to play golf at a course near Beirut. He was finally released three-and-a-half years later, in late April 1990.

Born in 1934, Reed grew up in New England and graduated from the University of Maine. For several years he taught school in small towns in Maine and New Hampshire. However, he was naturally drawn to adventure. In 1967 he signed up for a trip to retrace the travels of the explorer, Admiral Byrd. His journeys took him to the South Pole, Australia, and eventually Lebanon.

Joined by his wife and son, freed hostage Frank Reed addresses the press from the balcony of the U.S. Air Force hospital in Wiesbaden, West Germany.

Reed liked Lebanon, and in 1978 he moved there. At the time of his abduction, he was the director of the Lebanon International School in West Beirut. He had married a Syrian woman, Fahima, with whom he had a child, and then converted to Islam. Fahima, fully aware of the volatile conditions in her country, pleaded with her husband to take the family out of Lebanon. Reed liked his life there, however, and strongly believed that his Islamic faith would protect him from terrorists bent on kidnapping Americans. He was wrong.

During Frank Reed's excruciatingly long period of captivity, he spent much of his time blindfolded and in solitary confinement. "It was lonely. It was boring," Reed told the press. The blindfold was removed for 90 minutes each night, during which time he was permitted to read or watch television. Reed refused to do so, however, explaining that it was "simply because I did not want to be entertained while I had lost my freedom."

Twice in the early months of his imprisonment, he tried to escape only to be savagely beaten upon his capture. When he was finally released, he expressed great bitterness, not just toward his kidnappers, but toward the United States government. He could not understand why it had not done more to secure his freedom and that of his fellow captives. When questioned by the press after his release, Reed was shocked that several Americans who he had spent some time in captivity with, were still prisoners:

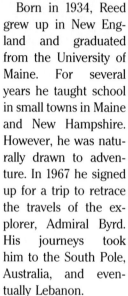

For God's sake, it's in the sixth year for these men. I'm absolutely embarrassed that I'm out before they are.

AN AMERICAN ★ SPEAKS

The Reagan Administration was just as frustrated and incensed by the acts of terrorism as most Americans. In 1986 a terrorist group bombed a German discotheque, killing an American soldier. The president became so enraged that he ordered American bombers to attack the desert headquarters of Muammar el-Qaddafi in **Tripoli**, Libya. Qaddafi was widely believed to be responsible for engineering this particular terrorist attack as well as others around the world. Although the American bombers hit their mark, the Libyan leader escaped injury. His daughter, however, reportedly was killed. After the attack, Qaddafi pledged revenge against the United States and warned President Reagan that his actions would mean war with Libya. His threats, however, were hollow ones.

For the most part, terrorist groups were almost impossible to identify or locate. Even so, the president was stung by the criticisms leveled at him by the families of hostages and others who, like Reed, could not understand the government's reluctance to make deals with terrorists. Partly as a result, the president began to explore new avenues to win the hostages' release—efforts that contributed to the greatest political crisis of his career.

The Iran-contra affair tarnished Reagan's public image.

Almost from the beginning, the Reagan Administration was troubled by scandals—so many of them, in fact, that critics began to talk about the "sleaze factor." Important officials resigned from the Defense Department, the CIA, the Environmental Protection Agency, and elsewhere because of charges of illegal or unethical behavior. Two cabinet officers—Secretary of Labor Ray Donovan and Attorney General Edwin Meese—were forced to resign because of personal scandals (although neither was convicted of any crime).

Most of these episodes had only a minor effect on Reagan's own popularity. In 1986, however, a scandal broke that the president could not evade.

In November the White House responded to reports in several newspapers by admitting that it had made a secret deal to sell weapons to the revolutionary government of Iran. The deal was part of an effort to strengthen "moderate elements" in the Iranian government, the Administration claimed. However, the media convinced many Americans that the deal was really designed to persuade the Iranians to assist in winning the release of Americans being held hostage in Lebanon. This revelation provoked public outrage because it contradicted Reagan's frequent promise that he would "never negotiate with terrorists."

Much more troubling to the public, however, was a second revelation that came a few days after the first. Some of the money from the sale of arms to Iran had been diverted secretly into a fund to aid the contras in Nicaragua. Because Congress had placed restrictions on the use of funds for the contras, the diversion of this money seemed to many people clearly illegal.

For months after the exposure of what became known as the **Iran-contra affair**, the White House found itself under official and unofficial investigation. The media displayed an aggressiveness it had not shown since Watergate in trying to uncover the truth about the affair. A special commission, headed by former Senator **John Tower**, issued a report sharply critical of the president. In addition, a congressional committee held public hearings and interrogated several important figures in the national security bureaucracy.

What emerged from the investigations was a picture of an independent "secret government" hidden in the Reagan White House. Its activities were hidden not only from Congress, but also from the rest of the Administration: from the State Department, the Defense Department, perhaps even the Central Intelligence Agency. Its purpose was to advance the Administration's foreign policy goals in ways that more conventional organs of government could not. Its methods, it appeared, were at times illegal.

The principal figure in this covert world seemed to be an obscure lieutenant colonel in the marines, **Oliver North**—a hard-working, ideologically driven man with a magnetic personality. North's appearance before the congressional committee investigating the Iran-contra affair created a sensation and made him, in the eyes of many Americans, a folk hero. Although North was found guilty of illegally supplying the contras with arms, many Americans believed that he was innocent because he had only carried out the orders of his superior, **John Poindexter**, the president's national security adviser. A soldier, they reasoned, is expected to follow orders without question. Besides, many Americans be-

Iran-contra Scandal

Point

North is a hero

- He only followed orders.
- It was a righteous cause.
- The hostages deserved freedom.

Counterpoint

North is a criminal

- He knowingly broke the law.
- He concealed evidence.
- He obstructed justice.

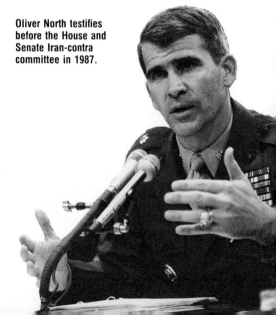

Oliver North testifies before the House and Senate Iran-contra committee in 1987.

lieved that the illegal funding had been carried out for a patriotic, righteous cause.

Although the scandal made Oliver North a hero—thousands of people bought North dolls, T-shirts, and other assorted memorabilia—it also exposed the degree to which the Reagan Administration had deceived Congress and the public. In this regard, the Iran-contra affair disturbed many Americans. Even though the investigations were never able to tie the president himself directly to any illegal activities, the episode did significant short-term damage to his popularity. Despite recovering a great deal of public affection by the end of his term, the affair convinced many Americans that Reagan was an absentee president, not sufficiently involved in the affairs of his own government.

Poindexter, North, and others were convicted for their roles in the Iran-contra affair.

In July 1990, however, a U.S. Court of Appeals suspended two of North's felony convictions and overturned one outright. Poindexter received a six-month jail term.

Dramatic changes in world politics began in the late 1980s.

During the last years of the Reagan Administration a dramatic, indeed revolutionary, change in international relations and the structure of world politics occurred. The change was precipitated by a variety of factors. Among these factors were the upheavals in Poland in 1981, which suggested the restiveness of the Soviet Union's Eastern European satellites, and the stalemated Soviet war in Afghanistan, which showed an erosion of Soviet military strength. In addition, the disastrous deterioration of the economies of the socialist nations played a part in the change. These nations,

President Reagan and Soviet leader Gorbachev greet each other at the 1985 summit meeting in Geneva. It was the first of five meetings between the two leaders.

which were nearing complete collapse in the mid-1980s, were falling further and further behind the capitalist nations of Western Europe and the United States.

However, most people attributed this change to the actions of a single man: **Mikhail Gorbachev** [gôr′bə chôf′], who became the leader of the Soviet Union in March 1985. Gorbachev, who was 54 when he first assumed office, was the youngest Soviet leader in many years. He recognized the serious problems facing the Soviet Union and the communist world and moved quickly to introduce positive changes. His new policies were described by two Russian words, *glasnost* [glas′nōst] and *perestroika* [pär əstroi′kə].

Glasnost means "openness," and the opening up of Soviet society under Gorbachev was surely one of the most surprising and remarkable developments of the late 1980s. Quickly, the Kremlin dismantled many of the repressive institutions that had been a cornerstone of the communist world for at least 50 years. Soviet citizens became more free to express dissent, to move without restriction around their country, to travel abroad, and even to emigrate to other lands.

Perestroika means "restructuring," and Gorbachev insisted that for the Soviet Union to prosper it must restructure its economic system to make it more efficient and productive. *Perestroika* moved more slowly than *glasnost*, but Gorbachev began efforts to decentralize control of the economy and to introduce at least some elements of capitalism.

The new Soviet regime also shifted its position on many of the international issues that had so long divided it from the West. At a summit meeting with Reagan in Iceland in 1986, Gorbachev made a dramatic proposal to reduce the nuclear arsenals of both sides by 50 percent or more. Disagreement about the future of the American SDI program prevented an agreement. However, 14 months later, after Gorbachev visited Washington and Reagan visited Moscow, the two nations agreed to a treaty eliminating American and Soviet intermediate-range nuclear missiles from Europe. The **INF Treaty**, as it was called, was the most significant arms control accord since the beginning of the nuclear age.

Reagan left office, therefore, at a moment when the nature of the Soviet empire and its relationship with the United States seemed in the midst of a dramatic change. Even in January 1989, however, few people could predict the extraordinary transformations that would reshape the world by the end of the year.

SECTION 4 REVIEW

Identify Key People and Terms
Write a sentence to identify: Alexander Haig, Solidarity, SDI, José Napoleon Duarte, Anastasio Somoza, Sandinistas, contras, Frank Reed, Iran-contra affair, John Tower, Oliver North, John Poindexter, Mikhail Gorbachev, *glasnost, perestroika*, INF Treaty

Locate Key Places
1. Which nation is the home of Solidarity?
2. Which of the following countries or cities—Grenada, El Salvador, Nicaragua, Beirut, Tripoli—are in Central America? The Middle East? The West Indies? Africa?

Master the Main Ideas

1. Studying U.S. foreign policy: What Soviet action in 1981 cooled relations between the United States and the Soviet Union?
2. Studying U.S. foreign policy: Provide two examples of interventionism under the Reagan doctrine.
3. Analyzing causes and effects of U.S. involvement in foreign affairs: What did Reagan do to try to stop the terrorist activities of Muammar el-Qaddafi?
4. Studying political leaders: What did the Iran-contra affair reveal about Reagan?
5. Studying international cooperative efforts: Why did U.S.–Soviet relations begin to improve in the late 1980s?

Apply Critical Thinking Skills: Recognizing Values
How did the policies of *glasnost* and *perestroika* show that the Soviet Union was reevaluating its values in the late 1980s and early 1990s?

An Afghan Teenager Comes to America

23A

TIME FRAME
Late 1980s

GEOGRAPHIC SETTING
Brooklyn, New York

In late December 1979, Soviet troops invaded Afghanistan, a mountainous country bordered by the Soviet Union, Pakistan, Iran, and China. Before the Soviets withdrew ten years later, three million of Afghanistan's 16 million people had fled the country. Among these refugees were six-year-old Abdul and his family. After a long stay in Iran and a short one in Pakistan, the family settled in Brooklyn, New York. Abdul was interviewed by Janet Bode for her book *New Kids on the Block: Oral Histories of Immigrant Teens* (1989). In the following excerpt from the interview, Abdul talks about the process of adjusting to his new life in America. Like most Afghans, Abdul and his family are Muslims, followers of Islam, the religion established by the Arab prophet Muhammad (A.D. 570?–632).

I was fourteen [when I came to America]. Within a month of arriving, I enrolled in a big public high school. I remember I was happy that I was coming to school again
5 to learn something, to become someone. But I was scared, too. The school counselor just looked at me and said, "If you're fourteen, you're in the eighth grade." Getting used to studying after six years was
10 hard. I had to learn English because my family didn't speak it and we couldn't talk to anyone.

One period a day they put me in ESL, English as a Second Language. The words
15 began to become a little familiar to my ears. But the American kids gave me a hard time. They made fun of me. And the curse words! All day. Every day. If the teacher asked me a question and I knew
20 the answer, when I said it, because I couldn't pronounce it well and I had the wrong accent, they laughed at me. I felt very bad.

I couldn't do anything about it. Even if I
25 had wanted to get physical, fight with them, it wasn't good. I'm not an animal. I'm a human being. I have a brain. I can talk. Why fight? Being peaceful, I think, is the best way. Some teachers knew what
30 was going on, but they didn't care. I was a problem they didn't need.

I wanted to go back to Afghanistan. I hated this place. I didn't have any friends.

I didn't have anyone to talk to. I still don't have a lot of friends, good friends, like best friends. My sister and brothers went to a different school. I was lonely, but I had to deal with it. I went through it. I went to school. I came home. And I had to study hard to learn English. Like in social studies I had to read, then I'd find a word where I didn't know the meaning and I had to look it up in the dictionary. It would take me a long time to do just one page.

Now I'm seventeen and the American kids don't always know that I'm a foreigner. They tease less. I found out that if you act the way they do, say the things they say, do the things they do, they will be calm. So I try not to act strange to them. I wear T-shirts and stone-washed jeans and aviator glasses. My hair looks like their hair. I'm about five feet ten inches. Clint Eastwood and Charles Bronson are my heroes. After school I watch TV—"Three's Company" and "Different Strokes"—to help me know what's going on in American families, what they do.

There are no others from Afghanistan in my school. Afghan people are spread all around. You can't find them too much. In each city you can find one or two. That's it. Sometimes I tell people where I'm from and I'm very surprised that they don't know Afghanistan. They are very weak in geography. They say, "Where's Afghanistan? Is it a town? Do they have cars? Do they have school?"

I always think about my country, going there one day, seeing it, practicing my religion with no problem. Religion is very important in my life. I am Muslim. We have a small mosque [a Muslim house of worship] where we go on Saturdays. From eleven to three I go to religious school. I study Dari and Pashto, the two languages of my country. Then from eight to midnight, I go to mosque. I believe in Allah and his Prophet Muhammed. The Qur'an [kúr än', or Koran] is the holy book.

A young Kuchi nomad boy poses for his photograph near Bamyian, Afghanistan. The turban, traditionally worn by Afghani males, covers a skull cap.

There are rules, the Islamic rules, for everything, for daily life. But here I can't practice my religion when I should. Five times a day I should pray, the first time before sunrise. I can do that with my family, but at school I can't say to my teacher, "Please, teacher, I need to leave because I must pray." Also the food in school is a problem. I'm not allowed to eat all kinds of food; pork, for example. I just eat pizza because of the cheese, that's all right. Other things I don't eat, because I don't know how they make it. Or it's not right, the way it should be for a Muslim. So I do without.

I don't date. My religion forbids it. My marriage will be arranged. For a Muslim, your parents have to decide who you should marry. For me, my mother and my uncle will discuss it and decide. Then they will say, "This girl is good for this son." That's fine with me. In fact, I think it's perfect. I know my mother; she went through it herself and she knows. I don't have to think about disease. I know I'm going to marry someday, so why should I date girls? I listen to my mother. I don't want to change my culture and forget my language.

Discussing the Reading

1. What kinds of difficulties did Abdul have in adjusting to his new life in America?

2. What strategy finally helped him overcome some of these difficulties?

CRITICAL THINKING
Recognizing Values

How important was his Muslim religion in Abdul's life? What role did Islam play in Abdul's adjustment to American life?

Chapter Summary

Write supporting details under each of the following main ideas as you review the chapter.

Section 1
1. Ford committed himself to an open, honest government.
2. Ford failed to solve economic and energy problems.
3. Ford continued Nixon's Soviet Union and China policies.
4. Jimmy Carter won the presidency in 1976.

Section 2
1. Carter failed to halt stagflation.
2. Human rights was the cornerstone of Carter's foreign policy.
3. Ronald Reagan won the presidency in 1980.

Section 3
1. Reagan's personality won him the hearts of many Americans.
2. The economy revived during Reagan's first term in office.
3. Reagan captured a second term as president.
4. Reagan took a conservative stand on social issues.

Section 4
1. U.S.–Soviet relations continued to deteriorate.
2. Reagan pledged to support opponents of communism around the world.
3. Reagan had few answers to the problem of terrorism.
4. The Iran-contra affair tarnished Reagan's public image.
5. Dramatic changes in world politics began in the late 1980s.

Chapter Themes

1. **Relations with other nations:** As conflicts escalated in the Middle East in the 1980s, the United States found itself in several different roles. For instance, Carter helped negotiate a settlement between Israel and Egypt. Under Reagan, terrorists killed 241 U.S. Marines who were serving as peacekeepers in Lebanon. Individual Americans were held hostage by terrorists in Iran and Lebanon. Carter and Reagan both took retaliatory actions against groups who had injured Americans. Finally, advisers in the Reagan Administration made arms deals with Iran to try to gain release of hostages.

2. **Conflict and cooperation:** Instances of conflict were easy to find in the 1970s and 1980s. Ford's pardon of Nixon was controversial and may have persuaded many to vote for Jimmy Carter, who appeared free of Washington's tarnished image. Conflict also arose when Carter canceled U.S. involvement in the 1980 Olympics after the Soviets invaded Afghanistan. The scandals of the Reagan years, especially the Iran-contra affair, produced outrage among Americans.

Chapter Study Guide

Identifying Key People and Terms

Name the key person or key term that describes the:
1. establishment of friendly relations with China
2. group dedicated to persuading the world that Palestinians deserve their own homeland
3. name for Reagan's economic plan
4. powerful independent Polish labor union

Locating Key Places

1. Where was the human rights pledge signed?
2. With which Latin American country did the United States sign treaties that will restore sovereignty over land now held by the United States?
3. In what Middle Eastern nation were 52 Americans held hostage by Islamic militants?

Mastering the Main Ideas

1. Why did the American public become disillusioned with President Gerald Ford?
2. (a) What is the difference between inflation and stagflation? (b) Did Carter try to deal with stagflation by "tightening the government's belt" or by some other method? Explain.
3. What factors enabled Reagan to win a second term as president?
4. How was the Reagan doctrine applied in Latin America?

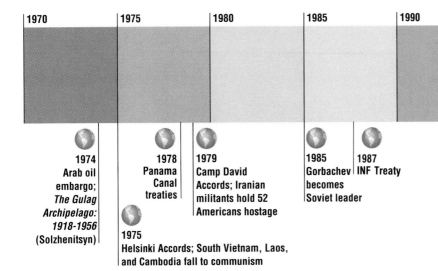

1970	1975	1980	1985	1990

1974
Arab oil embargo;
The Gulag Archipelago: 1918-1956 (Solzhenitsyn)

1978
Panama Canal treaties

1979
Camp David Accords; Iranian militants hold 52 Americans hostage

1985
Gorbachev becomes Soviet leader

1987
INF Treaty

1975
Helsinki Accords; South Vietnam, Laos, and Cambodia fall to communism

1. **Identifying central issues:** Despite Ford's foreign policy successes, Carter won the presidency. What may have been one reason?
2. **Identifying assumptions: (a)** How did Carter's foreign policy differ from Nixon's and Ford's? **(b)** Was Carter's policy effective? Explain.
3. **Making comparisons:** Based on your knowledge of presidential politics of the 1970s and 1980s, what would you say was the difference between a Republican and a Democrat at that time?
4. **Analyzing cause and effect: (a)** How did the relations between the United States and the Soviet Union change during the Reagan Administration? **(b)** What caused this change?

Chapter Activities

Learning Geography Through History

1. Name the three southeast Asian countries that were at war in the area where the *Mayaguez* incident took place.
2. What two Central American countries waged civil wars in the 1980s?

Relating the United States to the World

1. How did OPEC policies affect Americans?
2. In what area of the world have most terrorist acts taken place?

Using the Time Line

1. In what year did Iran seize the hostages?
2. Which countries fell to communism in the mid-1970s?

Linking Past to Present

1. In the late 1980s and the early 1990s, Jimmy Carter gained respect for his help in negotiating difficult disputes in Africa and his diligence in demanding human rights abroad. What similar experiences did he have while president?
2. In what way was Ronald Reagan's Administration like Warren G. Harding's?

Practicing Critical Thinking Strategies

Identifying Alternatives
President Reagan used military retaliation as one way of dealing with terrorism. What are some other alternatives that he might have also considered?

Learning More About the Triumph of Conservatism

1. **Using Source Readings:** Read the Source Readings for this chapter and answer the questions.
2. **Holding a debate:** Research the arguments for and against the ERA. Take a stand on either side and debate the issue with a partner who has taken the opposite stand.
3. **Writing letters to the editor:** Pretend that you just heard President Ford announce his pardon of Richard Nixon. Express your opinion about the pardon in a well-reasoned, persuasive letter that uses facts as well as emotional language.

TRUC ORIENT EXPRESS

Grand Opning

Linking Past to Present

The proud Vietnamese family shown in front of their new restaurant in Springfield, Massachusetts, is among a growing group of Asian immigrants to achieve success in America, a place many of them have called "the mountain of gold."

The "mountain of gold" was not always accessible to Asians. Before the mid-1960s, quota systems and exclusion laws virtually barred Asian immigrants from the country. The immigrants at the Angel Island internment center, inset, were refused entrance to America in the late 1920s and were forced to return to their homes in Japan and China.

Opportunities and Challenges

1 9 8 8 – P r e s e n t

24

CHAPTER PREVIEW

In this chapter you will learn about the challenges experienced by Americans during the Bush Administration and early Clinton Administration.

SECTIONS IN THIS CHAPTER:
1. **The Republicans remained in power.**
2. **The Cold War ended but Middle East tensions mounted.**
3. **Population characteristics changed rapidly.**
4. **Cities produced problems and opportunities.**
5. **Theme Essay: America examined its priorities.**

SPECIAL FEATURE:
A new president took office, William Jefferson Clinton.

Americans long have been known for meeting difficult challenges and seizing opportunities. The immigrants who first settled our nation overcame tremendous adversity and brought to life their most passionate dreams through ingenuity and hard work. Today's new immigrants, many of whom are Latino or Asian, are no different in character. They too are striving for many of the same dreams.

What is it about Americans that make them so determined to succeed at whatever they do? Anthropologist Margaret Mead once noted that Americans are successful because they never dwell on the past: "They are committed to the future . . . to experiments, to adventures, to new ways of life. . . ."

In the 1990s future-minded Americans, new and old, will be called upon to meet the many challenges presented by the modern world, a world that is experiencing revolutionary changes. What are some of these changes and how will the nation and its leaders respond to them? Will the world of the near future be a better place in which to live as a result of their actions?

1987	1988	1989	1990	1991	1992

1988
Bush wins presidential election

1989
The Berlin Wall crumbles;
Bush orders an invasion of Panama;
China crushes democracy movement in Beijing

1990
South African government frees Nelson Mandela; environmentalists hold second Earth Day

1991
Breakup of the Soviet Union; former Yugoslavia erupts into war; Iraq driven from Kuwait

1992
Clinton wins presidential election

The Republicans remained in power.

Key Term: Social Security trust fund

Reading Preview
As you read this section, you will learn:

1. who won the 1988 presidential election.
2. what course of action Bush and Congress took to decrease the nation's budget deficit.
3. what President Bush did to solve the Panamanian problem.

The problems of the Reagan Administration in its last two years, and the Democratic triumphs in the 1986 congressional elections, inspired many Democrats to hope for a presidential victory in 1988. However, the election produced another Republican victory. The Democrats' presidential drought continued.

George Bush captured the 1988 presidential election.

Although several of the most popular Democratic figures, including New York Governor Mario Cuomo, and U.S. senators Bill Bradley and Edward Kennedy, all refused to run, a variety of Democratic candidates surfaced before the 1988 primaries. Senator Gary Hart of Colorado was the favorite candidate of many Democrats. However, he was forced to withdraw from the race after newspapers published stories about an alleged extramarital relationship with a young woman. Most of the remaining Democratic candidates were relatively unknown nationally, with the significant exception of **Jesse Jackson**.

Jackson, an African American who had run for the Democratic presidential nomination in 1984, had widespread support from African Americans as well as a small but growing number of white liberals. During the Democratic primaries and caucuses he placed first in 8 contests. Jackson was perhaps the most gifted orator of all the candidates who vied for the presidency in 1988.

Right, Jesse Jackson speaks to members of the Democratic National Convention in 1988. Despite strong support in the primaries, Jackson was unable to capture the Democratic presidential nomination. Far right, the Republican nominee, George Bush, used this ad to portray Democratic candidate Michael Dukakis as weak and inexperienced on defense. Bush also used a variety of other negative campaign techniques.

America can't afford that risk.

Paid for by Bush Quayle 88

The eventual nominee, however, was **Michael Dukakis**, the three-term governor of Massachusetts. Dukakis emerged from the pack by capitalizing on his reputation as a good administrator and by claiming credit for the striking economic revival Massachusetts had enjoyed during his governorship. Dukakis was not an exciting campaigner, but Democrats remained optimistic through the summer. That was in large part because of their Republican opponent, Vice President **George Bush**.

Bush had been in public life for nearly 30 years. A native of Connecticut and the son of a United States senator, he had moved to Texas as a young man and had served two terms in the U.S. House of Representatives. Later he became ambassador to the UN, director of the CIA, chairman of the Republican National Committee, and finally—in 1981—vice president. In all those years, Bush had never become closely identified with a major issue. No one could point to any major accomplishments for which he could take credit. Bush had been a poor campaigner in 1980 when he tried to capture the Republican nomination for president. Ronald Reagan easily defeated him. In addition, Bush was widely ridiculed for his performance in the 1984 campaign, when he ran for reelection as vice president.

Despite these negative factors, Bush captured the Republican nomination fairly easily, fending off a challenge from Senator **Robert Dole** of Kansas in the early primaries. However, as the summer drew to a close, he was running far behind Dukakis in the polls.

Bush drew considerable criticism for his choice of a vice presidential running mate—Senator **J. Danforth Quayle** of Indiana—whom many people considered too young and inexperienced. However, he pushed his campaign into high gear in the last two months before the election. Bush survived the perceived liabilities created by his choice of Quayle by running one of the most negative campaigns of the 20th century. For three months Bush attacked Dukakis almost ceaselessly. He questioned the Democrat's patriotism. He attacked his record as governor of Massachusetts. He called him "soft" on crime.

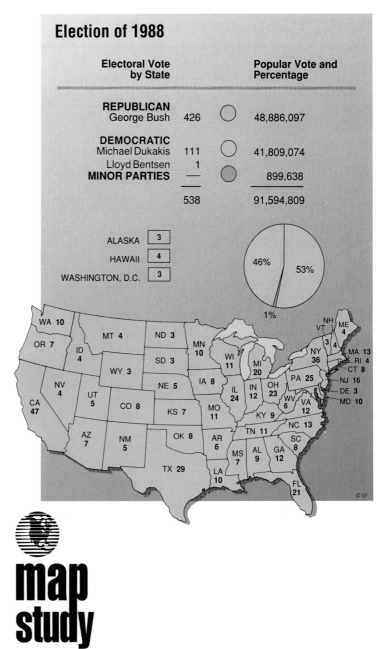

map study

Regions The map shows that regional voting patterns were relatively weak in the 1988 election. Although states in various parts of the country voted Democratic, the great majority of states voted Republican for George Bush. Did any state in the South vote Democratic?

Critical Thinking Note that the difference between Bush and Dukakis in the popular vote was only seven percent. In spite of this fairly close popular vote, why did Dukakis lose the election?

MEET THE PRESIDENT

GEORGE BUSH

Born: June 12, 1924
In office: 1989–1993

In 1988 George Bush became the first incumbent vice president since Martin Van Buren to be elected president. Heir of Ronald Reagan's political good-will, Bush also inherited some unwelcome problems, including a massive federal deficit and a costly scandal in the savings and loan industry.

A combat pilot in World War II, Bush prospered in the oil business before entering politics. The former Yale University first baseman proved to be a loyal team player, serving quietly in several key posts for Republican administrations before achieving two terms as Reagan's vice president.

The apparent end of the Cold War in Europe and the

Iraqi occupation of Kuwait were issues that challenged Bush in the early years of his term. He responded to both with his customary deliberation and prudence, but his lack of attention to a sinking domestic economy led to his loss in the 1992 election.

bold leadership style of Ronald Reagan and chose instead to follow a moderate course. The leading figures in his government were moderates, without the strong ideological convictions that so many Reagan Administration officials had embraced. Thus, the Bush Administration moved slowly to deal with the problems it confronted.

President Bush began his term of office committed to not raising taxes. Yet by the beginning of 1990, he began to realize that new taxes would have to be levied if the nation was going to even come close to balancing the federal budget. He also realized that spending for domestic programs would have to be cut. Although the government had reported declining budget deficits in the late 1980s, the declines were for the most part illusions. The deficit had declined because the federal government had counted as revenue the large surplus in the **Social Security trust fund**. That money is, in effect, already spent before it is collected because it is committed to funding future Social Security pensions. By using the trust fund to reduce the deficit in the late 1980s, the government was actually contributing to even greater future deficits.

The deficit was also declining because the Administration and Congress agreed not to count the enormous cost of the rescue of the savings and loan industry in the budget. That would have added billions of dollars more to the total of government expenditures. The savings and loan industry, long plagued by gross mismanagement, would have collapsed had the government not stepped in to bail it out.

In the fall of 1990 Congress took a major step toward balancing the budget by passing a comprehensive $500 billion deficit-reduction plan. The compromise plan, which was hotly debated for several months before its passage, called for large tax increases and funding reductions for domestic programs such as agriculture and Medicare. Although some economists feared the higher taxes would push the economy toward a recession because of reduced spending power, most agreed that the reduction of government debt would be beneficial in the long run.

By late September Bush had managed to create so many doubts about Dukakis that the Democrat's early lead in the polls had vanished. In the end, Bush's campaign promise, "Read my lips: no new taxes," and his particularly negative campaign tactics, helped him handily defeat Dukakis. Congress, however, remained solidly in Democratic hands.

The federal government increased taxes and cut expenses.

George Bush's first 18 months in the White House were notable for several things. First was the new president's broad popularity in the polls, which rose steadily throughout the first year and reached record levels early in 1990. Second was the lack of important initiatives or achievements by the Administration. The new president was a cautious man who rejected the

Bush ordered an invasion of Panama.

Although the fiscal dilemma was the number one domestic problem during Bush's first two years in office, happenings in other parts of the world often overshadowed it. Tensions in **Panama**, the Central American nation that the United States had, in effect, created early in the century, presented Bush with his first major foreign policy decision.

For several years before Bush became president, the United States had been locked in a struggle with **Manuel Noriega**, the military dictator of Panama. Although Noriega had long been an ally of the United States and had worked at times for the CIA, American criminal justice officials indicted him for drug trafficking. Americans were particularly concerned about the amount of drugs being shipped into the United States from countries such as Panama. In response to these concerns, President Reagan spent much of his last few years in office devising ways to overthrow the dictator.

Manuel Noriega displays his prisoner number after being charged in Miami for drug trafficking while he served as the leader of Panama.

Finally, after a minor incident late in 1989 involving the harassment of Americans by Panamanian troops, President Bush ordered American forces into Panama to capture Noriega. After several days of sanctuary in the Vatican embassy in Panama, Noriega surrendered to American military leaders. Subsequently, he was then taken to Miami, Florida, to stand trial on the drug charges. The government that had won election a year earlier but had never been allowed to take office was then installed.

The Panama situation represented a foreign policy challenge to the Bush Administration. Yet events in the Soviet Union, Europe, and particularly the Middle East would present it with far greater challenges. In these areas momentous changes were taking place—changes that made the years 1989 and 1990 among the most important in modern world history.

SECTION **1** REVIEW

Identify Key People and Terms
Write a sentence to identify: Jesse Jackson, Michael Dukakis, George Bush, Robert Dole, J. Danforth Quayle, Social Security trust fund, Manuel Noriega

Locate Key Places
Panama is located in which world region?

Master the Main Ideas
1. **Studying major political elections:** What major campaign promise did George Bush make in the 1988 presidential election?
2. **Analyzing political leaders:** Why were declining budget deficits in the late 1980s considered illusions?
3. **Analyzing the effects of U.S. involvement in foreign affairs:** What were two positive results of the U.S. invasion of Panama?

Apply Critical Thinking Skills: Recognizing Bias
Negative political campaigning has long been a tactic utilized by candidates for public office. Does the phrase "all's fair in love and war" apply to political campaigns, or should there be limits to what can be said about an opponent? Why or why not?

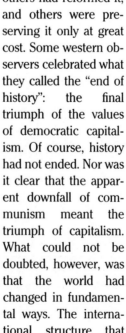
The Cold War ended but Middle East tensions mounted.

Key Terms: apartheid, African National Congress

Reading Preview
As you read this section, you will learn:

1. what political step was taken by many Eastern European nations in 1989 and 1990.
2. what resulted from widespread dissatisfaction with Soviet leadership.
3. what the South African government did to move closer to majority rule.
4. how President Bush responded to the changes in the communist world.
5. how the United States and the United Nations reacted to the Iraqi invasion of Kuwait.

A Czech youth demonstrates during a November 1989 general strike. The actions of the protesters led to the fall of the communist regime in Czechoslovakia.

By the end of 1989, virtually the entire communist world had experienced fundamental upheavals. By the middle of 1990, many of those nations had repudiated communism, others had reformed it, and others were preserving it only at great cost. Some western observers celebrated what they called the "end of history": the final triumph of the values of democratic capitalism. Of course, history had not ended. Nor was it clear that the apparent downfall of communism meant the triumph of capitalism. What could not be doubted, however, was that the world had changed in fundamental ways. The international structure that had survived with only relatively minor alterations since the 1940s would never again be the same.

Many Eastern European nations challenged communism.

By the end of 1989, virtually every nation in the Soviet bloc in Eastern Europe had either overthrown its communist government or forced its government to transform itself into a more democratic, less communistic system.

The Eastern European challenge. Many Eastern European nations were tired of the economic hardships and political repression that communism had brought them. They no longer wanted to be observers in the governmental process; they wanted to be an integral part of it. No longer did they want to suffer the economic hardships synonymous with the communist economic system.

In **Poland**, the once-outlawed labor organization, Solidarity, claimed overwhelming victories over communist candidates in national elections in 1989 and 1990. In late 1990 **Lech Walesa**, the founder of Solidarity, won a landslide victory in Poland's first direct presidential election. In Gdansk, where Solidarity was born in 1980, Walesa told cheering supporters that "The dreams of generations have been fulfilled before our very eyes."

In **Hungary**, the ruling party itself voted to repudiate communism and change both its doctrine and its name. In **Czechoslovakia**, a massive public demonstration forced the collapse of the communist regime. In **Romania**, in late December 1989, the attempt by longtime communist dictator **Nicolae Ceausescu** to crush a disident movement produced a popular revolution that drove him from power. Then, after several days of bloody street fighting, a noncommunist regime secured control of the country.

In **East Germany**, demonstrations in 1989 led to the collapse of the communist regime and the toppling of the Berlin Wall that had served as a barrier to freedom since 1961. On October 3, 1990, more quickly than anyone had thought possible, hundreds of thousands of Germans celebrated the reunification of East and West Germany.

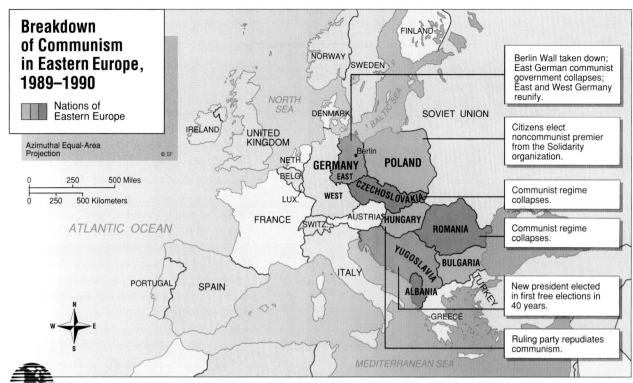

Breakdown of Communism in Eastern Europe, 1989–1990

Nations of Eastern Europe

Azimuthal Equal-Area Projection

© SF

0   250   500 Miles
0   250   500 Kilometers

ATLANTIC OCEAN

Berlin Wall taken down; East German communist government collapses; East and West Germany reunify.

Citizens elect noncommunist premier from the Solidarity organization.

Communist regime collapses.

Communist regime collapses.

New president elected in first free elections in 40 years.

Ruling party repudiates communism.

map study

Regions In late 1989 and 1990, Eastern European nations began to change their communistic political systems into more democratic ones. Which of these nations was reunified with a Western European nation?

Critical Thinking Political change occurred in six of the eight Eastern European nations in 1989–1990. Why might changes have taken place at the same time in so many countries in the region?

The Chinese challenge. In contrast, a challenge to communism outside of Eastern Europe failed. In China students began demonstrating in May 1989 for democratic reforms. Although the government had repeatedly promised such reforms in the past, the students now demanded that the nation's leaders keep those promises. By early June the demonstrations had spread to other cities and attracted the support of many other groups in the population. It seemed possible that the communist government of China might topple. Instead,

hardline communist leaders prevailed and ordered military forces into Beijing to suppress the uprising.

On June 3 troops equipped with tanks and heavy artillery moved into **Tiananmen Square** in central Beijing, scene of the principal dem-

A Romanian soldier and his companion snowman give a peace sign as they celebrate the overthrow of Nicolae Ceausescu's tyrannical regime in late 1989.

951

A Chinese student demonstrates for greater democracy in Beijing's Tiananmen Square.

Nationalist movements emerged throughout the Soviet Union.

China proved to be the only communist nation to survive a popular uprising in 1989 without major changes in its government. Even the Soviet Union was experiencing dramatic internal changes. Nationalist movements were emerging throughout the Soviet Union, and early in 1990 **Lithuania** became the first Soviet republic to declare its independence.

The biggest challenge to the Soviet central government came in Russia, the Soviet Union's largest and most populous republic. Elections in June 1990 elevated **Boris Yeltsin** to the presidency of the Russian republic. Yeltsin, who resigned from the communist party, was a harsh critic of Gorbachev, accusing him of moving too slowly toward reform. Almost immediately, Yeltsin began taking steps toward declaring Russian independence.

Gorbachev, fearing the complete breakup of the Soviet Union, proposed a new union treaty that would give real sovereignty to the republics. Hardliners, however, opposed the new treaty and tried to seize power through a coup. The coup failed, largely because the plotters did not have the full support of the military and because Boris Yeltsin's popularity enabled him to defy their orders.

With conservative forces defeated, changes came with breathtaking speed. In November 1991 Estonia, Latvia, and Lithuania achieved complete independence. The following month, Russia, Ukraine, and Byelarus (formerly Byelorussia) declared the Soviet Union dead and formed a new Commonwealth of Independent States. They were joined by the remaining republics, except Georgia. Shortly after, Gorbachev resigned as president of the now shattered Soviet Union.

The Soviet Union was not the only nation to break apart as a result of strong nationalist move-

Below, Azeris protest under a statue of Lenin in Baku, Azerbaijan. Below right, children join a political rally in Estonia.

onstration, and began a massacre in which hundreds, perhaps thousands, of student demonstrators and others died. The assault crushed the democracy movement and preserved the hardliners in power. It also marked the beginning of a period of harsh repression, economic hardship, and international criticism.

ments. In 1991 Yugoslavia fell apart as ethnic hatreds erupted into a brutal civil war. In 1993 Czechoslovakia peacefully split into two republics, Slovakia and the Czech Republic.

South Africa softened its position on apartheid.

The forces of democracy seemed to be making strides even in areas far from the European cradle of communism. **South Africa**, a militarily and economically strong nation in southern Africa, had been the object of international scorn for years because of its racist policy of **apartheid**: the rigid, legalized separation of the races. White South Africans, who represent only 16 percent of the nation's population, believed that only through apartheid could they maintain their dominance over the black South African majority. Black South Africans make up 71 percent of the population.

In the United States, opposition to apartheid had sparked a growing popular movement—which included efforts by students to force colleges and universities to divest themselves of stock in companies doing business in South Africa. Early in 1990 a new government in South Africa, led by President F. W. de Klerk, began softening its position on apartheid in significant ways. It lifted a longtime ban on the **African National Congress (ANC)**, the principal black opposition organization. Most dramatic of all, the government released the leader of the ANC, **Nelson Mandela**, who had been imprisoned by the government for 27 years because of his political views. He immediately emerged as the leader of a growing world movement committed to ending all vestiges of apartheid and creating majority rule.

Bush responded cautiously to the changes in the communist world.

Ever since the end of World War II, American foreign policy had been based on the belief that containing communism was the nation's principal task. However, the events in Europe and the Soviet Union suggested that the containment approach would soon become obsolete.

President Bush responded cautiously to the changes. Although he voiced his approval of

the collapse of communism in Eastern Europe and his support of the concept of German reunification—the rejoining of the two Germanies that had been separated since the end of World War II—he believed that certain conditions needed to be met before the nation abandoned containment. One of these conditions was that a reunified Germany must remain a part of the North Atlantic Treaty Organization (NATO). Although the Soviet Union originally opposed this condition, Mikhail Gorbachev announced in July 1990 that the new Germany could belong to NATO. This announcement removed the last major barrier to German reunification and helped Gorbachev win the Nobel Peace Prize in 1990.

President Bush also supported the domestic reforms Gorbachev was undertaking in the Soviet Union and expressed his hope that the Soviet leader would survive the political difficulties he was encountering at home. At two summit meetings with Gorbachev—one on the island of Malta in 1989 and another in Washington in 1990—Bush and Gorbachev emphasized their good personal relationship with one another and spoke optimistically of future agreements that would solidify relations between the two superpowers. Once the breakup of the Soviet Union occurred, Bush worked to develop a similar relationship with Boris Yeltsin and to support efforts to ease tensions.

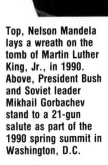

Top, Nelson Mandela lays a wreath on the tomb of Martin Luther King, Jr., in 1990. Above, President Bush and Soviet leader Mikhail Gorbachev stand to a 21-gun salute as part of the 1990 spring summit in Washington, D.C.

The United States sent hundreds of thousands of troops to Saudi Arabia in the wake of Iraq's invasion of Kuwait. The U.S. military made up the largest part of the multinational force deployed to defend against further Iraqi aggression.

The Bush Administration was less receptive to upheavals elsewhere in the communist world. Only weeks after the Chinese government massacred students in Beijing, two high officials of the Bush Administration visited China in an effort to sustain good relations between the communist government and the United States. Republicans and Democrats alike were harshly critical of that decision, charging that it sanctioned the brutal and repressive policies of the Chinese regime.

Americans were concerned about unfolding events in China and the disintegrating Soviet Union. Yet their attention abruptly turned to the Middle East in August 1990 when Iraq invaded the small, oil-rich nation of Kuwait.

America and its allies reacted swiftly when Iraq invaded Kuwait.

The Bush Administration faced a first, major test of its capacity to cope with the post-Cold War world beginning in August 1990, when it found itself embroiled in the most serious crisis in the Middle East in decades.

Operation Desert Shield. On August 2 **Saddam Hussein,** the ruthless dictator of Iraq, stunned the world when he invaded Kuwait, a small oil-rich nation directly south of Iraq. Hussein, who had been the uncontested ruler of his nation since 1979, quickly defeated Kuwait's small army and announced that Iraq had annexed Kuwait.

President Bush quickly reacted to the invasion. On August 7 he announced to the American people that he had launched Operation Desert Shield, a plan involving the deployment of a significant number of U.S. troops in Saudi Arabia. The president said that American forces were needed to defend Saudi Arabia, Iraq's southern neighbor, from a possible Iraqi invasion, and to make it possible to expel the Iraqis from Kuwait if necessary. At the same time, the president rapidly mobilized an impressive international coalition opposed to Iraq. Among this group were 28 nations, including Britain, France, and the Arab nations of Saudi Arabia, Egypt, and Syria, that pledged troops.

During the next five months, members of the coalition worked frantically to find a diplomatic solution to the crisis. They quickly approved economic sanctions against Iraq, hoping that an embargo would weaken Hussein's resolve. Neither diplomacy nor economic sanctions worked however.

In December the United Nations, spurred by reports of widespread atrocities against Kuwaiti citizens by Iraqi troops, passed a resolution approving the use of force against Iraq if it did not withdraw from Kuwait by January 15, 1991.

Apparently unable to comprehend the gravity of the situation, Hussein brushed aside last-minute UN peace proposals. The deadline passed and the world braced for war.

Operation Desert Storm. At 2:30 AM Baghdad time, January 17, the skies of the Iraqi capital lit up from a barrage of anti-aircraft fire aimed at streaking U.S. Air Force F15E fighter jets. With deadly precision, the jets hit their strategic targets. Within hours President Bush announced to the nation that Operation Desert Storm, the code name for the allied plan to liberate Kuwait, had begun. The president declared: "The world could wait no longer. . . . Now, the 28 countries with forces in the Gulf area have exhausted all reasonable efforts to reach a peaceful resolution, [and] have no choice but to drive Saddam from Kuwait by force. We will not fail."

The war that Hussein claimed would be the "mother of all battles" never materialized. Despite Hussein's million-man army and large air force, the allied forces claimed superiority from the start. In the air, coalition forces incessantly pounded strategic targets in Iraq and Kuwait between January 17 and February 23. Surprisingly Iraq's air force never challenged the allies. Hussein's lone strategy, it became clear, was the dropping of SCUD missiles on Israel in hopes of drawing it into the war. Israeli involvement, Hussein believed, would have split apart the coalition and pressured some Arab nations into joining him in a show of Arab unity. His strategy failed however. Israel showed restraint despite getting hit by several missiles, and U.S. Patriot missiles destroyed most of the SCUDs before they could reach their intended targets.

On February 24, in the wake of failed peace proposals initiated by the Soviet Union, the allied forces began their long-anticipated ground offensive. Under the command of General Norman "Stormin' Norman" Schwarzkopf, coalition forces swept into Iraq and Kuwait in a brilliant flanking maneuver that totally caught Iraq off guard. The result was a devastating defeat for Hussein's demoralized troops.

On February 27

(text continues
on page 958)

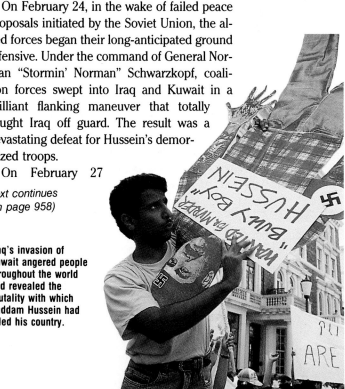

Iraq's invasion of Kuwait angered people throughout the world and revealed the brutality with which Saddam Hussein had ruled his country.

◀ **Persian Gulf Crisis** ▶

Point

Send American forces to Saudi Arabia

■ History clearly shows the effects of unchecked aggression.
■ America has a duty to protect its citizens in Iraq and Kuwait.
■ America and the world community depend on oil from the Middle East.

Counterpoint

Do not send American forces to Saudi Arabia

■ Middle Eastern problems should be solved by Middle Eastern countries.
■ American involvement could lead to a costly war.
■ Oil is not worth the cost in American lives.

GEOGRAPHY IN AMERICAN HISTORY

Persian Gulf Crisis

Persian Gulf Crisis: Operation Desert Shield

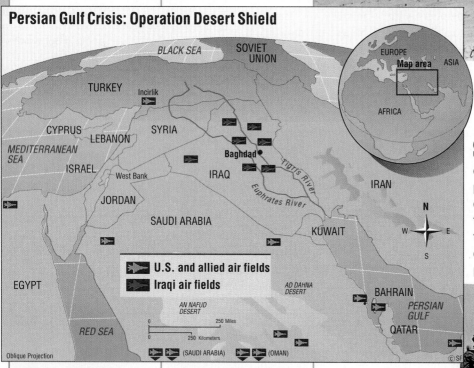

U.S. and allied air fields
Iraqi air fields

0 250 Miles
0 250 Kilometers

Oblique Projection

(SAUDI ARABIA) (OMAN)

© SF

Saudi Arabia's hot and dry climate presented problems for U.S. troops during the summer and fall of 1990. A soldier had to drink a minimum of a quart of water an hour to prevent dehydration.

Location Most U.S. and allied air fields are located in Saudi Arabia. The flat land provides advantages for air combat, although frequent sandstorms can damage equipment and reduce visibility. What nations border Iraq?

Critical Thinking What military forces besides air and ground troops were important in the Persian Gulf region? Why?

The desert terrain in Saudi Arabia was unfamiliar to American troops. Critics had speculated that American military equipment, designed to fight a potential war with the Soviet Union, was improper for desert operations. The critics were wrong, however. U.S. equipment performed nearly flawlessly during the conflict.

Persian Gulf Crisis: Operation Desert Storm

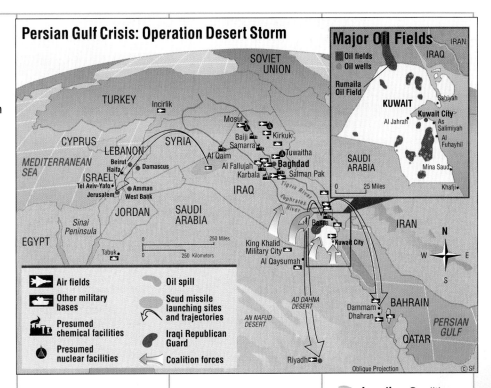

Major Oil Fields

- ■ Oil fields
- ▪ Oil wells

Legend:
- ✈ Air fields
- ⛴ Other military bases
- 🏭 Presumed chemical facilities
- ▲ Presumed nuclear facilities
- Oil spill
- Scud missile launching sites and trajectories
- Iraqi Republican Guard
- Coalition forces

Oblique Projection © SF

CHEMICAL WARFARE

Although Iraq never fired a single chemical weapon during the war, the allies were ready for such an attack. Gases and vapors released from chemical bombs burn and blister the skin and can kill by destroying a victim's nervous and respiratory systems.

PROTECTIVE GEAR

Boots and Gloves
Each soldier wore boots and gloves made of chemical resistant rubber.

Special Clothing
Multi-layer garments were designed to prevent the permeation of chemicals.

Face Mask
A soldier's head gear was equipped with a respirator.

First Aid Kit
Soldiers carried kits containing an antidote to be given to those contaminated by poison gas.

PROBLEMS WITH PROTECTIVE GEAR

- gear is hot and heavy, especially when worn in the desert
- inhibits a soldier's mobility
- reduces a soldier's visibility, especially one's peripheral vision
- makes the handling of heavy equipment difficult

Location Coalition forces located along Saudi Arabia's northern border swiftly broke through Iraqi fortifications in southern Iraq and Kuwait on February 24, 1991. Once through the Iraqi barrier, in which direction did most of the coalition forces proceed?

Critical Thinking Based on the coalition troop movements shown, what do you think was the primary goal of the allied commanders?

President Bush triumphantly announced to the world that "Kuwait is liberated. The Iraqi army is defeated."

With the liberation of Kuwait, President Bush achieved a record-breaking 89 percent approval rating from the American people. He also succeeded in vanquishing the "Vietnam Syndrome" that had hung over the nation for so long. Still unsettled, however, were issues about Palestine, internal affairs in Iraq, and the future U.S. role in the Middle East.

SECTION 2 REVIEW

Identify Key People and Terms
Write a sentence to identify: Lech Walesa, Nicolae Ceausescu, Boris Yeltsin, apartheid, African National Congress, Nelson Mandela, Saddam Hussein

Locate Key Places
1. Name five Eastern European nations that turned away from communism in the late 1980s.
2. What was the first Soviet republic to declare its independence?
3. In which city is Tiananmen Square located?
4. Where is apartheid practiced?

Master the Main Ideas
1. **Perceiving cause/effect relationships:** What two factors help explain why so many Eastern European nations began to challenge communism?
2. **Evaluating information:** What was the significance of the election of Boris Yeltsin to the presidency of Russia?
3. **Supporting constitutional principles:** Why do you think a popular movement condemning apartheid developed in the United States?
4. **Analyzing U.S. foreign policies:** What condition did President Bush insist upon before approving German reunification?
5. **Evaluating information:** What was the significance of the support given by the Soviet Union in the Persian Gulf?

Apply Critical Thinking Skills: Drawing Conclusions
Why did Israel "show restraint" during the war in the Persian Gulf?

SECTION 3

U.S. population changed rapidly.

Key Terms: demographers, boat people

Reading Preview
As you read this section, you will learn:

1. what happened as a result of a declining birth rate and increased life expectancy in the United States.
2. what happened as a result of the Immigration Reform Act of 1965.
3. which group of Americans experienced tremendous population increases in the 1980s.
4. which group of new immigrants came to America in the largest numbers.

World politics was not the only thing that was changing rapidly as the nation entered the 1990s. American society was also undergoing a revolutionary transformation. Profound changes in the nature of the American population, the distribution of wealth, and the character of the nation's culture suggested that the United States of the 21st century was likely to be a very different place from the United States of the 20th century.

The average age of the American population increased.

Among other things, the American people were growing older. The nation's birth rate, which had been increasing steadily ever since the 1940s, began to decline in the 1970s and remained low into the beginning of the 1990s. In 1970 the birth rate had been 18.4 births for every 1,000 people. Throughout the 1980s it remained below 16.

Why did the birth rate decline? Men and women were tending to marry later and were having fewer children, partly because so many women were pursuing professional careers and partly because housing costs and other expenses directly related to family size were increasing dramatically. The wider availability of contraceptive and sterilization procedures also contributed to the declining birth rate. So did the legalization of abortions. By the 1980s abortion had become the most commonly performed surgical procedure in the country. The declining birth rate, combined with increased life expectancy, meant that the average age of the American population was increasing. More than 12 percent of all Americans were over 65 at the end of the 1980s, a figure that was projected to rise to 20 percent by the end of the century. Only 8 percent had been that old in 1970. The "graying of America," the phrase often used to describe the increase in the percentage of people over 65, was partly responsible for the rapidly growing costs of Medicare and other social programs for the elderly.

A wave of non-European immigrants came to America.

An even more dramatic change in the American population came as a result of massive new immigration into the country in the 1970s and 1980s. This new immigration was spurred by the passage of the Immigration Reform Act of 1965, which eliminated provisions in early immigration laws establishing quotas on the basis of national origins. Before 1965 American immigration policy had favored immigrants from northern Europe. After 1965, although the law continued to limit the total number of immigrants, people from all nations could compete for the available spaces on a first-come, first-serve basis. It was as easy to immigrate legally from Asia or Latin America as it was to immigrate from Italy or Ireland. The result was a dramatic change in the sources of immigration.

In 1965 about 90 percent of the immigrants to the United States came from Europe. Twenty years later, only 10 percent of the new arrivals were Europeans. At the same time, the numbers of new arrivals in the United States increased dramatically, as quotas were expanded to admit refugees from southeast Asia and other areas of the world troubled by political unrest. In the 1970s more than four million

legal immigrants entered the United States. In the 1980s six million more newcomers arrived. In addition, many immigrants entered the country illegally, perhaps as many as came legally. The immigration of the 1970s and 1980s was the largest of the 20th century.

The new immigration was producing a dramatic change in the character of the American population. People of white European background had made up more than 90 percent of the American population in the 1920s. In the 1980s they made up under 80 percent. By the mid-21st century, many predicted, white Americans of European background would make up less than 50 percent of the population.

Time magazine ran a cover story in 1990 entitled "America's Changing Colors." It was an indication of how important a presence new immigrant groups from all parts of the world were becoming to American life. Two groups, Latinos and Asians, dominated the new immigrant population.

The Latino population grew enormously in the 1980s.

After 1965, more than a third of the legal immigrants to the United States were "Hispanic," as termed by the U.S. government, or "Latino" (feminine, "Latina") as many preferred to call

Under the revised immigration laws of 1986, illegal aliens who could prove that they had come to the United States before 1982 could receive amnesty by filing for citizenship. Below, applicants in New York City rush to meet the May 4, 1988, amnesty deadline.

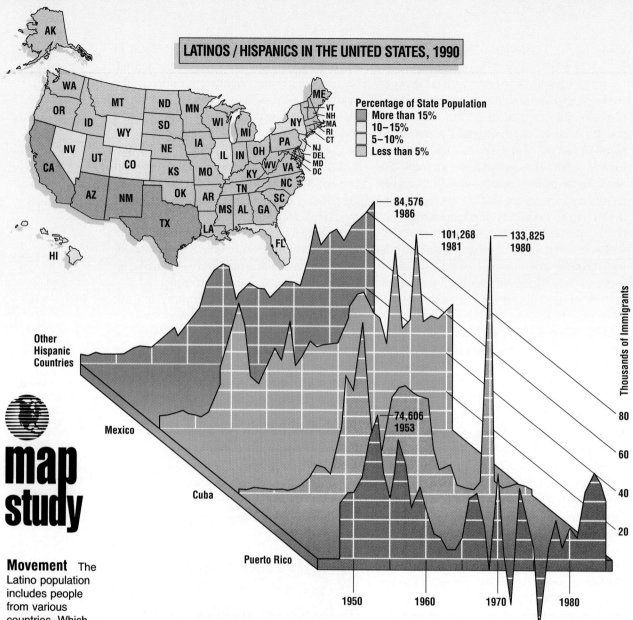

LATINOS / HISPANICS IN THE UNITED STATES, 1990

Percentage of State Population
- More than 15%
- 10–15%
- 5–10%
- Less than 5%

Other Hispanic Countries

Mexico

Cuba

Puerto Rico

Thousands of Immigrants

84,576
1986

101,268
1981

133,825
1980

74,606
1953

80

60

40

20

1950   1960   1970   1980

map study

Movement The Latino population includes people from various countries. Which nationalities are shown on the graph? Which nationality lost population in some years since 1965?

Critical Thinking Why might numbers of Latinos be greater in the Southwest than in other regions? Why might numbers of immigrants increase or decrease year by year?

themselves. By the beginning of the 1990s, Latinos formed more than a third of the population of New Mexico, about a quarter of the population of Texas, and more than 15 percent of the populations of California and Arizona. Many Latinos also lived in Colorado, New York, Florida, Nevada, New Jersey, and Illinois.

The Census Bureau estimated that the Hispanic population, about 24 million in 1992, would more than double by 2020 to 49 million. This rapid growth of the Latino population was the result of two factors, immigration and child-bearing.

Latino communities were the youngest population group in the United States. More than half were under the age of 26, and more than one-third were under 18.

The 1980 census had listed six percent of the population as being of "Hispanic" origin. The 1990 census showed a higher figure, nine percent. **Demographers**—people who study changes in population—say that Latinos will become the largest minority in the United States by the year 2013, passing African Americans.

As you read earlier, Latinos responded to the turbulent climate of the late 1960s by developing a sense of ethnic identity and organizing for increased political power. How well has this diverse group of Americans done in these endeavors?

Increased political power. By the early 1990s, Latinos had been elected or appointed to many important political positions. In 1988 President Ronald Reagan appointed a Mexican American, **Lauro F. Cavazos**, as Secretary of Education. Thus, Cavazos became the first Latino to be named to a president's cabinet. In 1989 President George Bush reaffirmed Reagan's confidence in Cavazos by keeping the Texan in his cabinet. Cavazos, the former president of Texas State Technical Institute, maintained that his most important mission would be to help reduce the nation's 25 percent high school dropout rate. He continually urged, "Please, children, do not leave school." He also pledged to make education more accessible to disadvantaged students. Cavazos resigned his post in late 1990.

In 1990 the U.S. Senate confirmed President Bush's appointment of Dr. **Antonia Coello Novello**, a 46-year-old native of Puerto Rico, as surgeon general. A pediatrician and former head of the National Institute of Child Health and Human Development, Novello became the first woman and the first Latina to hold the important post.

Before becoming surgeon general, she headed a national task force investigating the special problems of children with AIDS. Novello said that finding solutions to the AIDS problem should be one of the nation's top priorities in the coming years.

Increased voter registration. In addition to Cavazos and Novello, many other Latinos achieved success in national, state, and local politics. Much of their success can be attributed to a greater awareness within Latinos groups of the importance of voting. Groups such as the Southwest Voter Registration Project, organized in 1974 by **Willie Velásquez**, a Mexican American, were very successful in adding Latinos to the voting rolls. Between 1974 and 1988, Velásquez organized nearly 1,000 voter registration drives, resulting in the addition of more than one million voters.

Asians were the largest group of newcomers to America.

By the 1980s Asian immigrants were arriving in even greater numbers than Latinos. They made up more than 40 percent of the total of legal newcomers. Vietnam, Thailand, Cambodia, Laos, the Philippines, Korea, and India were the main sources of Asian immigration.

In 1990 the United States had nearly seven million Asian Americans. They lived mainly in large cities and in the West. Some of the new Asian immigrants were refugees, including many Vietnamese driven from their homes at the end of the Vietnam War. Large numbers of

Top, in 1990 Texas high school students Mary Torres and Nora Morales, at the far right, organized an effort to assist pupils in Mexico by bringing them much needed school supplies. Lauro Cavazos, above left, and Dr. Antonia Novello, above right, were two top Latino members of the Bush Administration.

VOICES FROM THE PAST

Making History in America

The arrival of immigrants from Asia in the 1970s and 1980s caused some Americans to quip that the Statue of Liberty might be facing the wrong direction. Historian Ronald Takaki was prompted to tell the story of Asian immigrants in American history. How does Takaki suggest the broad range of Asian involvement in American history?

In America, Asian immigrants and their offspring have been actors in history—the first Chinese working on the plantations of Hawaii and in the gold fields of California, the early Japanese immigrants transforming the brown San Joaquin Valley into verdant farmlands, the Korean immigrants struggling to free their homeland from Japanese colonialism, the Filipino farm workers and busboys seeking the America in their hearts . . . . Their dreams and hopes unfurled here before the wind, all of them—from the first Chinese miners sailing through the Golden Gate to the last Vietnamese boat people flying into Los Angeles International Airport—have been making history in America. And they have been telling us about it all along.

boat people—Vietnamese refugees who put to sea in crowded vessels without any clear destination—ultimately found their way to America. They suffered terrible dangers and hardships during their long and arduous journey.

Many Asian immigrants were highly educated professionals seeking greater opportunities in the United States. As with most new immigrant groups, Asian Americans found adjustment to the very different culture of the United States extremely difficult. An example was Ba That, an elderly Vietnamese woman who came to America in 1975 after the fall of Saigon. Born in a farming village in South Vietnam in 1914 and raised in a traditional Vietnamese family, she had relatives killed fighting for both sides in the long struggle to determine Vietnam's future. By the 1950s Ba That and her husband had moved to Saigon. As a result, she later recalled:

AN AMERICAN ★ SPEAKS

We automatically were associated with the French [and later with the Americans]. Because of this, all of our relatives who remained in the villages hated us as the enemy. The war separated everyone.

Ba That had two sons in the South Vietnamese military. Toward the end of the war, she began to worry what would happen to her sons and the rest of her family if the communists seized control of Saigon. She emptied her bank accounts, sold much of her property, and used the proceeds to buy a small boat. Just before the city fell, Ba That, her husband, and several of her children boarded the boat and sailed down the **Saigon River** to the sea. (The Saigon River is a small river that drains into the South China Sea just northeast of the Mekong Delta. This delta can be located on the map on page 823.) There they were taken on board a ship of the South Vietnamese navy and later transferred to an American ship. Weeks later, they arrived at a United States refugee camp in **Guam**, an island east of the Philippines.

Ba That was very sad when she left Vietnam. However, she recalled:

When I boarded the American ship I was happy because I knew we had left and were not going to die. . . . After waiting night after night [in Guam], our names were finally called, and all of our family who were in the camp went to the United States together.

On arriving in America, Ba That and her family were handed over to a sponsor who took them into his home in a small town in a southern state. Later, they rented a small townhouse nearby, which local church groups helped them furnish. For two years they lived on a combination of charity and the small earnings her children made from mowing lawns, gardening, and working in a shoe factory. Ba That looked back on this later as a happy time, when the family remained closely knit and the community seemed to welcome them. However, her children wanted better schools than were available in the town, and so finally, at their urging, Ba That agreed to move west.

Living in a city on the West Coast, far from the sponsors and church members who had eased their first years in America, Ba That felt isolated and afraid. "I regret that we moved. I prefer to live in the countryside, as we first did when we came to America," she said. Instead, she found herself completely dependent on her children. Because she found it difficult to learn English, she had difficulty getting around the city, shopping, even answering the telephone. She considered herself a stranger in a foreign land: "Here in America, I just remain. I don't change my traditional ways; I still keep them."

At the same time, however, her relationship with her children was changing. They were adapting to the new country more rapidly than she was, and they treated her, she felt, with less and less respect. She said, "I see that children do not obey me as much as when they were in Vietnam. Here we need them more; they don't need us."

Asian immigrants such as Ba That suffered not only from the problems of disorientation and adaptation. They also were victimized by discrimination. Asian Americans were resented in part because other Americans viewed them as successful. True, statistics showed that Asians as a group tended to excel academically and had higher-than-average family incomes. However, these statistics were somewhat mis-

leading. Most Asian Americans live in urban areas, places where incomes are higher for everyone. A wider dispersal of the population would probably give Asian Americans lower average incomes. In addition, several members of the family usually contribute to the family income, further distorting the picture. According to Robert O. Oxnam, president of the Asia Society, the stereotyping of Asian Americans as successful is a disturbing phenomenon:

The most pervasive worry among Asian Americans is **AN AMERICAN ★ SPEAKS** that they have been typecast as superstars who achieve wonders in a few limited fields, particularly science and mathematics. "When I was in high school," says Richard Mel, Jr., an assistant to New York's Mayor Koch, "I once got a 65 on a math quiz. The teacher scolded me, 'You're Chinese! You're supposed to be good in math.'"

Left, crammed into small boats, Vietnamese refugees seek permission to enter Hong Kong in 1990. Above, Asian American engineering students perform a test at the Massachusetts Institute of Technology (MIT).

AIDS struck first and most severely among male homosexuals, or gays, and in the early 1990s they remained the most numerous victims of the disease. However, as gay men began to recognize the danger and to take precautions against it, the most rapid increase in infection moved to intravenous drug users. Drug users spread the disease by sharing dirty hypodermic needles used to inject themselves with drugs. By the beginning of the 1990s, more than 90,000 cases of AIDS had been reported in the United States and more than 300,000 worldwide. That number seemed certain to increase despite efforts to educate people about the seriousness of the disease. In the early 1990s, scientists worked feverishly to find a vaccine and a cure for AIDS.

The rise of AIDS created fear among most Americans. Some of that fear took rational and healthy forms. Some Americans responded to AIDS by changing their sexual habits: by abstaining from sex, by being more careful in their choice of sexual partners, and by using condoms and other methods to prevent possible infection. Some drug addicts learned not to use dirty needles. In addition, hospitals and other institutions learned to screen their blood supplies more effectively.

However, some people reacted less sensibly to the fear of AIDS. Some people believed, incorrectly, that AIDS was contagious in the way a cold or the flu might be contagious; that simply being around an infected person put others at risk. This misconception led to widespread discrimination against people with AIDS.

The nation's courts made important rulings regarding AIDS in the late 1980s and early 1990s. On several occasions courts ruled that schools may not ban students from school because they have been infected with AIDS. Children sometimes received AIDS from blood transfusions. Sometimes children inherited the disease from their parents. The courts recognized that AIDS, dangerous as it is, cannot be spread through casual contact. However, discrimination against AIDS sufferers continued. The largest job still left undone was educating the public about the true nature of the disease.

The decline of affordable housing caused the homeless crisis.

Another striking phenomenon of American life in the 1980s and early 1990s was the rapidly growing population of homeless people in the United States. In the late 1980s, demographers estimated that as many as three million

AIDS victims such as the man in the wheelchair benefit from fund-raising events such as the AIDS Quilt exposition in Chicago, shown below. This quilt was made, patch by patch, by AIDS victims and their families and friends. The names of some of these people can be seen in the photograph.

Americans were homeless. Some people believed that the 1990 census would show that even more homeless people existed. The 1990 census marked the first time that the Bureau of the Census attempted to count America's homeless.

Numbers aside, anyone working or living in a major city was aware of the gravity of the problem. Thousands of men, women, and children—usually alone, but sometimes in family groups—were sleeping on streets, in parks or subway stations, or in municipal shelters. On virtually every city corner, people could be found begging for money or food. Every winter people could be discovered huddled under newspapers or in discarded refrigerator boxes. Those who couldn't find a warm nook or cranny above ground found refuge in the sewer systems. Countless people unable to find enough warmth died from exposure each year. What misfortunes had forced so many people into the streets?

Many people believed that homelessness was a result of a policy adopted in the early 1970s for treating the mentally ill, a policy known as **deinstitutionalization**. Mental health experts during the 1970s decided that many mentally ill people would do better living outside institutions, as part of the larger community. As a result, thousands of mental patients were released from hospitals. Many of them, unequipped to handle economic realities, became the homeless of the 1980s.

However, deinstitutionalization was not by itself an explanation for the homeless problem. Some experts attributed the homeless problem to the breakdown of families. Some homeless people were children rejected by or fleeing from their parents. Others were older people with no one to care for them. Families had always been a "safety net" for people in distress. As family ties grew weaker, that protection weakened too.

Although all of the above factors may have contributed to homelessness, the decline in affordable housing was perhaps the largest single reason for the problem. Gentrification was one reason for the severe decline of low-cost housing. Another reason was that the federal gov-

ernment, as well as many local and state governments, reduced their support of public housing projects because few neighborhoods wanted them nearby. Reductions in welfare assistance and the disappearance of industrial jobs also left many people who might otherwise have been able to afford housing without the resources to rent or buy a home.

Homelessness seemed to have a reasonably straightforward solution: building new housing that poor people could afford. However, in an age of budget cuts to help reduce the deficit, that was not a solution many politicians were willing or able to endorse.

A homeless man lies on a bench in Lafayette Square, across the street from the White House. His blankets—plastic and newspapers—provide his only protection from winter's wrath.

African American leaders cited education as the key to progress.

Like the homeless, many African Americans in the early 1990s had reason to doubt that the American dream would ever be within their grasp. Yet economic and political progress in the 1970s and 1980s, and the prospects for continued improvements, led many African American leaders to be optimistic about the future. Their optimism was based, in part, on the solid premise that education would go a long way toward solving problems within the black community. Education, they maintained, had already been responsible for a host of success stories and improvements for African Americans.

success of the civil rights movement in opening up other neighborhoods to African Americans. Many who could afford to move out of the inner city did so, leaving only the poor behind.

The drug epidemic further debilitated inner-city neighborhoods, as did the decline of the public school systems. As government funds became more scarce, programs to help alleviate inner-city poverty diminished. At the same time, many whites, and even some blacks, became increasingly hostile to affirmative action programs. Throughout the 1980s the federal government became notably less aggressive in implementing them. The courts in some cases overturned affirmative action programs in reverse discrimination suits.

Whatever the reasons, the decay of inner-city neighborhoods, and the degradation of their residents, was one of the most alarming features of American life in the 1980s. The family structure in these poor African American communities was much looser than its counterparts in white or middle-class black neighborhoods. A very high number of households were headed by single mothers. By 1990 more than half of all black children were born into single-parent homes. Thirty years earlier, only 20 percent of all black children had been born into single-parent homes. Many observers believed the absence of a stronger family structure made it especially difficult for these Americans to escape poverty.

African American leaders worked to find solutions to the problems confronting poor, urban African Americans. Everyone realized that innovative solutions would be needed. According to **John Jacob**, president of the National Urban League, young African Americans need to be given every opportunity to achieve their full potential:

In 1990 National Urban League president John Jacob stressed the importance of education for African American students.

We [the National Urban League] are heavily focused AN AMERICAN ★ SPEAKS on removing barriers that preclude young people from achieving their full potential in our society by becoming mainstream, by becoming better employed, by becoming better educated or by becoming better positioned in a whole economic and business development framework.

Jesse Jackson also believed that education was one of the major keys to improvement. He said:

We must encourage this generation to pursue mind development with the same passion that it has for AN AMERICAN ★ SPEAKS athletic development. We demand to be the very best at that, and we are. But in the final analysis, it is the one with the best mind and the most commitment to a dream who will prevail. . . . Our young people must not surrender to despair and hopelessness. With our vision and our collective strength, we can change the economic and moral landscape of America and the world.

SECTION **4** REVIEW

Identify Key People and Terms
Write a sentence to identify: gentrification, AIDS, deinstitutionalization, John Jacob

Locate Key Places
In which part of South America is Colombia?

Master the Main Ideas
1. **Studying the causes and effects of urbanization:** How was gentrification both positive and negative?
2. **Analyzing the significance of government land policies:** What government policy helped to bring about the homeless crisis?
3. **Studying the results of reform movements: (a)** How have African Americans improved their lives in the years since the civil rights movement? **(b)** What do African American leaders believe will be the key to continued success?

Applying Critical Thinking Skills: Determining Relevant Information
All of the following are reasonable explanations of why the homeless crisis developed except:

a. The federal government developed the policy of deinstitutionalization.
b. Family ties were not as strong as they used to be.
c. The government reduced welfare assistance.
d. Suburban housing costs increased tremendously.
Why did you choose your answer?

Theme Essay: America examined its priorities.

Key Terms: born-again Christians, Moral Majority, new right, pro-life movement, pro-choice movement, Earth Day, ecology, ozone layer, chlorofluorocarbons, global warming

Reading Preview
As you read this section, you will learn:

1. what many Americans did to restore traditional values.
2. what members of the new right tried to achieve.
3. what the environmental movement attempted to do.
4. what Americans thought about the future of the nation.

The rapid and profound changes in the character of American society in the late 20th century had important effects on American culture. Many Americans became fascinated with the startling new advances in technology that were transforming everyday life: computers, video technology, cable television, facsimile (FAX) machines, microwave ovens, automated banking machines, and many other innovations. Others yearned for a more natural world and expressed fears about the costs of technological progress.

Still others looked with alarm at the changing morals of their society and launched an effort to restore traditional values. The result was a series of heated conflicts about the nature of American culture.

Many Americans turned toward religion in the 1970s and 1980s.

Although many Americans expressed concern in the 1950s and 1960s about the decline of religion in the United States, the 1970s and 1980s saw the greatest revival of religious energy since the early 19th century. The religious awakening of the 1970s occurred mainly among evangelical Christians. By the end of the decade, more than 70 million Americans called themselves **born-again Christians**—people who had experienced a conversion and formed what they called a "direct personal relationship with Jesus Christ."

Much of the credit for the religious awakening of the 1970s can be given to evangelist Billy Graham, a North Carolina native who, beginning in the late 1940s, spread his Christian messages to millions of people through radio and television programs. Graham's emotional brand of evangelism won him a wide following, allowing him to build a powerful, heavily funded organization that supported humanitarian causes around the world. His success with gaining converts by way of TV and radio was unprecedented for the time. In the 1970s and 1980s, evangelists adopted many of Graham's successful techniques and employed them on their own TV and radio programs.

Before Billy Graham's rise in popularity, evangelicals had often been on the fringes of American life. Now they were moving toward its center. Evangelicals established their own churches and denominations. Equally striking, they created their own newspapers, magazines, radio stations, and television networks. They ran schools and universities. Born-again Christians occupied positions of influence in all areas of American life. One of them—Jimmy Carter—was elected president of the United States. Some evangelical Christians (including Carter) used their faith to justify commitments to social justice and peace. Others drew a different political message from their religion.

By the beginning of the 1980s, much Christian revivalism had become tied to a strong social and cultural conservatism; and many evangelical leaders were becoming active in political as well as religious matters. In fact, it was this political activism that helped elect Ronald Reagan president.

Jerry Falwell, a Baptist fundamentalist minister in Virginia, attracted wide publicity by forming a political organization he called the **Moral Majority**. The Moral Majority as well as other evangelical organizations promoted conservative causes such as the restoration of

Jerry Falwell, standing behind President Reagan, used his television talk show to promote a variety of conservative causes. During his two election campaigns, Reagan vigorously sought the support of Falwell's followers.

The new right attempted to achieve conservative goals.

Alongside the new evangelicals and the members of the Moral Majority, and often overlapping with them, was an important conservative movement known as the **new right**. It was militantly anticommunist and hostile to government activism, just as much as the right had always been. Its tactics, however, were very new: mass mailing campaigns, successful fund raising, elaborate political organizing, and the development of conservative publications.

Members of the new right were not, on the whole, like traditional conservatives—people closely tied to the corporate world and committed to the defense of elites. Elites refer to people in power such as government officials or the wealthy. People of the new right tended to be middle and lower-middle-class people whose political demands were generally more cultural and social than economic. A populist element to the new right's outlook existed—a resentment of elites and a call for a return of power to ordinary people. They defined ordinary people as people like themselves. This populist element was an important part of the coalition that elected and reelected Ronald Reagan. In the 1988 presidential election, George Bush also courted the votes of the people of the new right. He realized that they had become a powerful political force that could not be ignored.

The pro-life movement. The new right was a particularly important force in reviving the battle over a woman's right to an abortion. The 1973 Supreme Court decision in *Roe* v. *Wade*, which struck down laws banning abortions as unconstitutional, produced a powerful protest movement that grew through the late 1970s and by the mid-1980s had become a formidable political force. It called itself the right-to-life movement, or **pro-life movement**, claiming that unborn children had the same "right to life" as those who had been born. Much of its support came from the Roman Catholic church, whose clergy was generally adamant in its opposition to abortion. However, much support also came from evangelical Christians and other conservative Americans.

prayer to public schools, an end to federal interference in local affairs, restoration of bans on abortion, and a strong American military. They also called for the banning of certain books, films, and television programs they perceived to be immoral, and revived old demands for the teaching of scientific creationism in schools. Scientific creationism is the belief that the literal Biblical account of creation is as scientifically valid as the theory of evolution.

Pro-life activists across the country demonstrated to rally support for overturning the Roe decision.

They saw abortion as a threat to morality and to the sanctity of the family.

Abortion-related court rulings. Many opponents of abortion were also hostile to feminism in general. They saw abortion as a particularly offensive example of the way feminism was undermining traditional women's roles. In 1976 Representative Henry Hyde of Illinois won congressional approval of an amendment barring the use of Medicaid funds to pay for abortions. The Supreme Court later upheld the law. In the 1980s, the Reagan Administration imposed further limits on funding abortions. In addition, the Court, more conservative by the late 1980s because of the appointment of new justices by Reagan, began gradually to retreat from the Roe decision.

In *Webster* v. *Reproductive Health Services* (1989), the Court upheld a Missouri law barring state funds from any institution that performed abortions, even if the abortions themselves were not financed with public money. In 1990 the Court approved laws requiring minors to receive parental consent, or permission from a judge, before having abortions.

The pro-choice movement. The changing judicial climate mobilized defenders of abortion in the late 1980s. By the end of the decade they too had created a powerful political force—which they called the **pro-choice movement**—that fought to preserve a woman's right to choose how best to respond to a pregnancy. It soon became clear that in many parts of the country the pro-choice movement was more powerful than the pro-life movement. Battles over abortion, which one politician called the most divisive issue since slavery, seemed likely to continue for years.

The environmental movement warned the public of ecological threats.

Senator **Gaylord Nelson** of Wisconsin was one of the first national politicians in the postwar era to emphasize protection of the environment as a major public issue. In the spring of 1970, he called on those concerned about the environment to stage what became known as **Earth Day**, a nationwide demonstration of concern about the dangers to the natural world. Earth Day attracted millions of participants and was, many people believed, the beginning of the modern environmental movement.

The modern movement was different from the old "conservation" and "preservation" movements that sought to manage human use of the natural world or to preserve the wilderness intact. The new movement drew instead from **ecology**: the idea that all elements of the natural world are linked together in a complex and delicate web. A threat to any part of the web was a threat to the whole. Thus, air and water pollution, toxic wastes, oil spills, and other environmental events were not separate problems. They were part of a broad threat to the natural world.

The environmental movement gained new urgency in the late 1980s as scientists began warning of new and particularly alarming problems. One was the depletion of the **ozone layer**, the part of the earth's atmosphere that protects the globe from the harmful rays of the sun. The use of **chlorofluorocarbons**, chemicals used in aerosol sprays, refrigeration, and many kinds of plastic and Styrofoam products, was, scientists claimed, responsible for the ozone damage. Environmentalists were also concerned that various plastic items, such as disposable diapers and containers used by fast-food restaurants, posed risks to the environment because they were not biodegradable. That is, certain plastics are not broken down by organisms when buried in landfills.

Environmentalists succeeded in gaining restrictions on the manufacture of chlorofluorocarbons in the late 1980s. In 1990 they also achieved successes in several local communities, notably **Berkeley, California**, by helping pass laws outlawing the use of Styrofoam con-

Norma McCorvey, the "Jane Roe" whose case led to the 1973 Supreme Court ruling legalizing abortion, joins a pro-choice rally in Los Angeles in 1989.

ENVIRONMENTAL ACTION
Skill: Predicting Consequences

Introducing the Skill. Since the late 1980s, the United States has joined with other nations in an effort to protect the earth's atmosphere. As you read in your text, one of the first steps was a move to decrease the production of chlorofluorocarbons (CFCs), chemicals known to damage the earth's protective ozone layer. Representatives from several countries met to discuss cooperative solutions to shared environmental problems such as damage to the ozone layer. Already a hole has been detected in the ozone layer above Antarctica, prompting Carl Sagan, a prominent astronomer, to write:

The hole in the ozone layer is a kind of skywriting. Does it spell out a newly evolving ability to work together on behalf of our species, or our continuing complacency before a witch's brew of deadly perils?

Sagan set forth two possible scenarios, one of cooperative action and one of inaction. What benefits or problems might arise from each?

Learning the Skill. To evaluate each scenario, you might begin by **predicting consequences** of each, that is, using information and theories to project what effects a certain action or inaction might have. For example, scientists have predicted that if CFC production is not stopped, serious health problems will result—such as increased risk of skin cancer and cataracts.

Applying the Skill.
1. If a ban on chlorofluorocarbons were to go into effect today, what negative consequences might develop?
2. Use your text to predict the consequences of another environmental concern, global warming.

Oil spills, which have tragic effects on wildlife, were one of many environmental concerns raised by Americans at the 1990 Earth Day demonstrations. At right a bird is cleaned off after being drenched by oil in the Alaskan oil spill in 1988.

tainers. Other environmentally concerned communities promised to follow suit with similar ordinances.

Environmentalists warned too about the problem of **global warming**, a gradual increase in the world's temperature resulting from the widespread burning of oil and coal. Although no hard scientific evidence exists that shows that a global warming process is taking place, environmentalists believe that such a trend is likely if we continue to burn significant amounts of fossil fuels. A continued practice of burning oil and coal would alter the climate, environmentalists say, causing potentially catastrophic results. Among the effects would be an increase in droughts and a rise in both the temperature and level of the oceans. Long droughts would seriously affect world food production, which in turn would cause worldwide physical and economic hardship. Increases in the level of the oceans, caused by the melting of the polar ice caps, would endanger coastal communities.

Twenty years after the first Earth Day, on April 22, 1990, environmentalists and their supporters gathered in places all over the United States for a second Earth Day. In doing so, they demonstrated broad support for a movement that was becoming one of the most important of the late 20th century.

Americans held both pessimistic and optimistic views of the future.

As America neared the end of the 20th century, it was clear that its place in the world was very different from what it had been 50 or 100 years earlier. For most of the century, the United States had been unquestionably the wealthiest and most powerful nation in the world. Now it faced a future in which other parts of the world—most notably Japan and Western Europe—were catching up and even surpassing it in economic performance. In addition, with the apparent end of the Cold War, America's military strength was beginning to seem less important than it had once been.

Much talk in the United States in the 1980s and early 1990s concerned the prospect of national "decline." Those who predicted decline pointed not only to the strength of America's economic rivals, but to the serious internal problems that made it difficult for the nation to compete effectively. They cited the weaknesses of America's educational system, the lack of sufficient investment in research and development, the crumbling infrastructure, and the crippling fiscal crisis of the federal government. America, they predicted, could look forward to a future in which it became a less important force in world affairs, and a less and less prosperous nation relative to other nations.

Others took a more optimistic view of the nation's future. America might never again be as preeminent in the world as it had been through most of the 20th century. However, its size, its resources, and its resilient political system suggested that it would remain one of the world's leading nations. In a world filled with bold new possibilities, a world in which many of the principles the United States had long defended seemed to be emerging triumphant, Americans faced the challenge of sustaining their great experiment in creating a democratic society and invigorating the effort to produce a just and prosperous nation.

S E C T I O N **5** R E V I E W

Identify Key People and Terms
Write a sentence to identify: born-again Christians, Moral Majority, new right, pro-life movement, pro-choice movement, Gaylord Nelson, Earth Day, ecology, ozone layer, chlorofluorocarbons, global warming

Locate Key Places
What California city banned the use of Styrofoam containers in 1990?

Master the Main Ideas

1. **Analyzing religious movements:** How did evangelical Christian leaders spread the word about their faith?
2. **Studying social reform movements:** How did many members of the pro-life movement feel about feminism?
3. **Learning about the abuses of the natural environment:** What are the problems associated with the manufacture and disposal of products containing chlorofluorocarbons?
4. **Analyzing information:** Which futuristic viewpoint, pessimistic or optimistic, do you subscribe to? Why?

Applying Critical Thinking Skills: Recognizing values
What values do you think were held by the people in the pro-life movement? The pro-choice movement?

SPECIAL FEATURE:

A NEW PRESIDENT TOOK OFFICE

William Jefferson Clinton

William Jefferson Clinton takes the oath of office flanked by his daughter, Chelsea, left, and his wife, Hillary Rodham Clinton.

The 1992 presidential race returned the Democrats to power. Bill Clinton, the Democratic governor of Arkansas, defeated George Bush, who was seeking reelection. In a race with Bush and independent businessman Ross Perot, Clinton won 370 electoral votes to Bush's 168. In the popular vote, Clinton received 43 percent, Bush 38, and Perot 19.

The campaign was a three-way race. In early 1992 most political analysts believed President Bush would win the fall election easily. As a result of his leadership in the Gulf War, Bush was riding high in the opinion polls. Although the odds of a Democrat winning in November against so popular a president seemed long if not impossible, sev-

eral Democrat contenders sought their party's nomination. Among those entering the primaries were former senator Paul Tsongas of Massachusetts, Governor Douglas Wilder of Virginia, Senator Bob Kerrey of Nebraska, Senator Tom Harkin of Iowa, former governor Jerry Brown of California, and Governor Bill Clinton of Arkansas. Just as in 1988, a number of prominent Democrats, including Governor Mario Cuomo of New York, decided not to run.

On the Republic side, conservative columnist Pat Buchanan challenged President Bush. Although Buchanan's attacks on some of Bush's economic policies weakened the president, by early May Bush had garnered enough delegates to win nomination.

Meanwhile, a wholly unexpected event occurred. What appeared to be shaping up as a probable two-man race between Bush and a Democratic challenger changed dramatically when Texas billionaire Ross Perot hinted that he might enter the presidential race. He would run, he said, if volunteers collected enough signatures to put him on the ballot in all 50 states. Volunteers did just that. In July, however, Perot shocked his followers by announcing that he was putting his candidacy on hold.

Clinton then won the Democratic nomination at his party's convention in July. As his running mate, Clinton chose Senator Al Gore of Tennessee.

Perot's supporters nonetheless continued to organize, keeping him in effect a viable candidate until October when he formally reentered the race. If the voters sent him to Washington, Perot promised to take drastic action to end gridlock, balance the federal budget, and reduce the $4 trillion national debt. Large numbers of Democrats and Republicans, fed up with the legislative stalemate in Washington, flocked to the Perot banner.

In August, the Republican National Convention nominated George Bush and Dan Quayle for a second term. With the Republican right wing in control at the Convention, the party's platform emphasized family values and called for constitutional amendments banning abortion and requiring a balanced budget.

The campaign that followed was one of the ugliest in recent history. Bush denounced Clinton as another "tax-and-spend" Democrat and attacked his character and fitness to be president. His charge that Clinton had "waffled" on the issues brought a counter retort that Bush had reversed himself on economic policy, taxes, on abortion, and on U.S. policy toward Iraq. Clinton stressed economic issues, blaming Bush and Reagan for tax policies that favored the rich and contributed to the massive national debt, policies which he charged had failed to pull the nation out of the recession. He was, he said, "a new kind of Democrat" who could be trusted to take a responsible middle road in attacking the nation's mounting economic and social problems.

Perot waged his campaign largely through television ads and so-called "infomercials," spending millions of his own money. In the end, Clinton was able to win by sticking to his economic message and to his call for change.

Clinton chose a strong cabinet. Taking office January 20, 1993, as the nation's 42nd president, Clinton won widespread praise by choosing a cabinet of experienced and competent men and women. As Secretary of State, he chose Warren Christopher, a seasoned diplomat with many years of distinguished service. For Secretary of Defence, he chose Les Aspin, a congressional Democrat with extensive experience as chairman of the House Armed Services Committee. Senator Lloyd Bentsen, a trusted public servant and 1988 vice-presidential candidate, became Secretary of the Treasury. For the important and powerful Secretary of Health and Human Services, Clinton chose Donna Shalala, a university president. Henry Cisneros, the highly regarded former mayor of San Antonio, became the Secretary of Housing and Urban Development. For the post of Sec-

President Clinton chose a cabinet that included Henry Cisneros, above, and Janet Reno, top. To replace retiring Supreme Court Justice Byron R. White, Clinton nominated Ruth Bader Ginsburg, top left.

First Lady Hillary Rodham Clinton, center, met with a number of U.S. senators about health care including Carol Moseley-Braun, far left, Barbara Boxer, near left, Barbara Mikulski, right foreground, Diane Feinstein, right background, and Patty Murray, far right.

General Colin Powell, chairman of the Joint Chiefs of Staff, is warmly welcomed by U.S. troops engaged in Operation Restore Hope in Somalia in May 1993.

retary of the Interior, Clinton chose Bruce Babbitt, former governor of Arizona. These and other key appointments gave the president a competent experienced team to handle the nation's foreign and domestic affairs.

The only major cabinet post that proved hard to fill was that of Attorney General. Clinton first chose a skilled corporate lawyer, Zoe Baird, for the office. When she volunteered that she had once employed an illegal alien as a baby sitter in violation of federal law and had

not until later paid Social Security tax for the employee, she was forced to withdraw. Clinton then turned to Judge Kimba Wood who also withdrew because of what some of the president's staff thought was a similar problem. Republican critics gleefully referred to the President's failed attempts to find an Attorney General as "nannygate."

For a third try, Clinton chose Janet Reno, a Dade County prosecutor, highly regarded for her work in Florida. Her forthright response to issues quickly won her respect and admiration from the media and the general public.

The new president showed confidence in the abilities of his wife, Hillary Rodham Clinton, by placing her in charge of a special task force to devise a national health care plan. Candidate Clinton had promised to make universal health care a leading goal of his presidency. The First Lady quickly demonstrated her ability to tackle the problem.

The cost of health care had skyrocketed in recent years, seriously affecting the nation's economy. The public was aware that increasing costs to the private sector and to the government were contributing significantly to the mounting annual federal deficit. Although many applauded the Administration's determination to push for a solution, agreement on how it should be done brought bitter debate in and out of Congress.

Clinton's programs faced hurdles. President Clinton faced serious obstacles in achieving legislative success for his domestic agenda. Elected by only 43 percent of the vote, he could not claim a mandate for any particular proposal. He may also have hurt his chances for quick action on his economic and social program by taking a forceful stand on divisive social issues such as permitting gays in the military and federally funded abortions.

The president's attempt during the first hundred days to pass an economic stimulus package, which he deemed necessary to get the economy moving again, were defeated by a Senate filibuster led by Senator Robert Dole, the Republican minority leader. Clinton's budget fared better, narrowly winning support in both houses of Congress.

MEET THE PRESIDENT

Bill Clinton ushered in a new generation of political leadership when he took office in 1993 as the first Democrat elected president after 12 years of Republican dominance. Clinton promised an era of "change," a focus on solving America's pressing domestic issues—the loss of jobs in a restructuring economy, a worsening trade imbalance, a growing health-care crisis, and an ever-burgeoning national debt.

Born in Hope, Arkansas, Clinton had a stellar academic career—Georgetown, Oxford, Yale law school—and an even more meteoric political one, winning election to five terms as Arkansas' gov-

WILLIAM JEFFERSON CLINTON

Born: August 19, 1946
In office: 1993–

ernor. Though Clinton's first months as president were disappointing, Americans seemed willing to suspend their judgment and wait and see if the man from Hope could accomplish what he set out to do.

Foreign policy problems proved difficult.
President Clinton took office at a time when the international community was still reacting to the collapse of the Soviet Union and the end of the Cold War. George Bush had talked about "a new world order" and, by his active leadership in the Gulf War, had placed the United States in a special leadership role as the sole remaining superpower. This was dramatically illustrated when Bush, in the closing days of his Administration, dispatched American troops to war-ravaged Somalia. The U.S. mission, which had United Nations approval, was limited to reestablishing order in the countryside and delivering food and medical supplies to the starving Somalis.

In relations with Russia, Clinton got off to a good start by supporting Boris Yeltsin, the new Russian leader who was attempting the difficult task of introducing sweeping economic reforms. Clinton met with Yeltsin at a summit at Vancouver, B.C.

Clinton also gave his conditional support to NAFTA, the North American Free Trade Agreement negotiated in the Bush Administration that would link the United States, Canada, and Mexico in a single trading bloc. Many Americans feared that once ratified the agreement would mean a wholesale loss of American jobs as U.S. factories moved to Mexico. Clinton sought to allay these fears by supporting side agreements with Mexico.

The most persistent foreign policy headache continued to be the war in Bosnia. Clinton soon discovered, as George Bush had before him, that the break up of the former Yugoslavia had unleashed age-old hatreds among ethnic and religious groups that could not be contained. With the European powers unwilling to shoulder responsibility and use force to bring peace between Serbs and Bosnians, there appeared little the United States could do short of unilateral military action. With memories of the Vietnam quagmire still fresh in the minds of the American public, the option of U.S. ground intervention was ruled out. Working with the United Nations and NATO, the Clinton Administration tried various diplomatic initiatives, all of which were rejected by the Serbs.

With an international arms embargo in effect against them, the Bosnians remained in a losing battle. The Serbs continued their policy of "ethnic cleansing," which consisted of systematic massacre, rape, concentration camps, and forced relocation of the Muslim minority. Finally, Serbian forces occupied most of Bosnia. A substantial minority of Americans in and out of government believed the United States should use force, either air strikes or ground troops, in an effort to stop the ethnic cleansing so reminiscent of Nazi Germany's campaign of genocide against the Jews in World War II. Without a majority of Congressional and public support behind him, however, Clinton was unwilling to act.

Instead, Clinton focused the nation's attention on his domestic agenda. He campaigned hard across the country to win support for his economic program and health care reform.

An historic moment occurs as Yitzhak Rabin, Prime Minister of Israel, and Yasser Arafat, the Chairman of the Palestine Liberation Organization, shake hands in a White House ceremony with President Clinton September 13, 1993, after agreeing to a framework for peace negotiations ending decades of war between Israelis and Palestinians.

Discussing the Feature

1. Ultimately, what one issue seemed to be most important to voters in the 1992 presidential election?
2. What could Clinton point to as accomplishments in his first 100 days? What were his failures?

CRITICAL THINKING
Identifying Assumptions

Some Americans viewed the war in Bosnia as a holocaust in which the United States should intervene. Others feared intervention would lead to another Vietnam. Which view is most persuasive to you? Why?

Connie Kang Defends Korean Values

24B

TIME FRAME
1990

GEOGRAPHIC SETTING
Brooklyn, New York

Early in 1990, several African American groups began a boycott of a grocery store owned by Korean immigrants in the Flatbush section of Brooklyn. The African Americans charged that an incident in which a Haitian woman had allegedly been mistreated by one of the store's owners reflected the general lack of respect with which the Koreans treated their black customers. Later in 1990, African Americans began another boycott of a Korean-owned grocery. The second protest soon ended, but the original dispute was still unsettled when the following editorial, by K. Connie Kang, an Asian American journalist, appeared in the *New York Times* on September 8, 1990. The "Confucian culture" mentioned by Kang is the code of social conduct based on the writings of the Chinese philosopher Confucius (551–479 B.C.). Emphasizing familial duty and respect for tradition, Confucianism has had an enormous impact on Asian civilization.

O ne of the two black-led boycotts of Korean grocers in Brooklyn ended last week, but the original, eight-month boycott continues. It is no longer a commu-
5 nity affair, but a national concern.

As an Asian-American, I was jolted at the beginning of the boycott, which allegedly began with an assault on a customer by a store employee, by a comment from
10 a black resident: "The Koreans are a very rude people. They don't understand you have to smile."

Would she have reacted differently had she known smiling at strangers just isn't
15 part of the Korean culture? Would it have made a difference had she known Koreans are just as "unfriendly" to their own because they equate being solicitous to being insincere? The Korean demeanor is
20 the absence of a demeanor. Koreans have a name for it: *mu-pyo-jung*. It means "lack of expression."

Koreans who travel or live abroad are often concerned that this trait causes
25 misunderstanding. Before the 1988 Seoul Olympics, South Korean officials launched a television and radio campaign urging citizens to greet visitors with a friendly smile. Some tried but found it dif-
30 ficult. As one housewife told me: "It's hard to smile at strangers when you're not used to it. It seems so phony."

Though it may be difficult for most Americans to tell Koreans apart from Jap-
35 anese and Chinese, who have been in this country much longer, the contrast between Koreans and their Asian neighbors is striking. Having suffered invasions and a long period of colonization by Japan in
40 this century, Koreans have had to fight for their lives to retain their language and culture. Koreans are feisty. They certainly don't fit the subservient or docile Asian stereotype.
45 And Koreans live by *cheong*—a concept that has no Western translation. *Cheong* is love, respect, affinity and loyalty rolled into one. Cheong comes only with

time, and only betrayal can end it. For a people who live by this ethos [the characteristic attitudes of a group], a mechanical smile is hard to produce.

In America's inner cities, newcomers from Korea do business where no one else will, and where frustration levels are high. . . . Culturally and socially, the newcomers are ill equipped to run businesses in America's inner cities. But because they, like other Asian immigrants, are denied mainstream jobs, they pool their resources and start mom-and-pop stores.

Inner-city African-Americans wonder how these newcomers, who can hardly speak English, have the money to run their own businesses when they themselves can't even get a small loan from a bank. They have little hope of escaping the poverty cycle, yet they see new arrivals living in better neighborhoods and driving better cars.

What they don't see are the 16-hour days and the deep sacrifices made for their children. They don't see the contributions of family and friends, and the informal money-lending system called *kye* that Koreans use instead of banks.

All immigrants go through an "American passage" that requires cultural insight on both sides. Koreans, like other Asians who live in the U.S. mustn't forget that they are indebted to blacks for the social gains won by their civil rights struggle.

Asian-Americans must also remember that while the Confucian culture has taught us how to be good parents, sons and daughters and how to behave with people we know, it has not prepared us for living in a democracy. The Confucian ethos lacks the social conscience that makes democracy work. It isn't enough that we educate our children; we need to think of other people's children too.

One of the boycotted grocers told me this had been a painful but valuable experience: "We Koreans must learn to participate in this society," he said. "When this is over, I'm going to reach out. I want to give part-time work to black youths."

By working together, maybe we can do privately what institutions can't. With Asian-American drive and African-American political experience, we can make it work not only in New York but in Los Angeles, San Francisco, Oakland and Chicago.

A crowd gathers on a Brooklyn street, listening to an African American speak out on the boycott of Korean businesses.

Discussing the Reading

1. What did Connie Kang say is meant by *mu-pyo-jung*?

2. What debt did Kang feel that all Asian Americans owed to African Americans?

CRITICAL THINKING
Recognizing Values

According to Connie Kang, what values are emphasized by Confucian culture? What values are emphasized by democracy? Do you agree with Kang that Confucianism might not be a good value system for people living in a democracy? If you disagree, explain how the values of Confucianism and democracy harmonize.

TIME FRAME
1990

GEOGRAPHIC SETTING
New York City

In 1892, when the federal government assumed responsibility for processing immigrants to the United States, it opened Ellis Island as a reception center for these newcomers to America. A 27½-acre site in the upper part of New York Harbor, Ellis Island processed more than 70 percent of the 24 million immigrants who entered the United States between 1892 and 1954, the year the center was closed. Abandoned during the succeeding decades, the buildings on Ellis Island were badly deteriorated when a $156 million renovation program was begun in the mid-1980s. On Sunday, September 9, 1990, the renovated Ellis Island Immigration Museum was dedicated by Vice-President Dan Quayle. The following excerpts are from an article on the museum's dedication that appeared the following day in the *New York Times*.

Ellis Island, the imposing and often difficult door to America for millions of the country's immigrants, reopened today as a tourist attraction, the Ellis Island Immigration Museum. . . .

Greta Ugbogbo, one of 46 new citizens sworn in at the ceremony by Associate Justice Antonin Scalia of the Supreme Court of the United States, sat brimming with newly American smiles until someone asked her feelings about the Beaux-

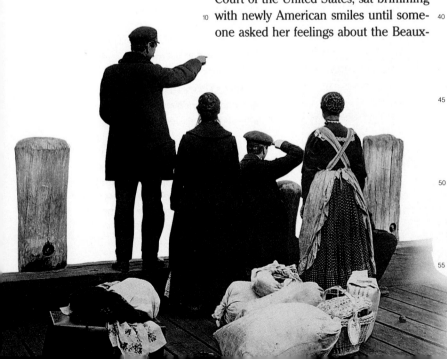

Arts [bō zär', an ornate late-19th century style of architecture] building in front of her. . . . Miss Ugbogbo said that her grandfather had been detained inside when he left their native Grenada and sought entry into the United States in the early 1940's. He was held on the island because no family members had come to pick him up, she said.

While on the island, her grandfather contracted tuberculosis, which he passed on to his eldest daughter upon his return to Grenada, Miss Ugbogbo said. Both died of the disease.

"It's sad thinking about the grandfather I never knew," said Miss Ugbogbo, who left Grenada [in 1981]. "And then it's very happy to be not just a part of America, but a part of this ceremony."

Louis Villamarin, an 86-year-old retired plumber, . . . recalled what had followed the last time he had entered the building, as a 19-year-old Spaniard: On doctors' orders, he had been stripped, poked, prodded and questioned, for what seemed like hours.

But that day, he said, his sense of discomfort had been overwhelmed by the thought of what awaited him off the island. . . .

"It wasn't too bad then," Mr. Villamarin said, and then he corrected himself: "It was beautiful. It is beautiful."

Inside the main building's old baggage room, Clara Larsen sat in her wheelchair recalling all the people who had been there on her last visit. That was in 1911, when concessionaires were not above trying to separate 12-year-olds from their worldly goods. Today, a still wary Mrs. Larsen, now 92, said she viewed the island's overhaul with skepticism.

Named as one of six Immigrant Guests of Honor, Mrs. Larsen, who was born in

On a pier at Ellis Island, the immigrant family (on the facing page) pauses to catch their first glimpse of New York City, about 1912. On the right is Ellis Island as it appears today. Although today the "Great Hall" is as hushed as the gallery of a museum, some people remember their experiences in what was once a "Tower of Babel" as hundreds of new arrivals to America spoke excitedly in dozens of languages.

the Russian Ukraine and fled the czarist pogroms against Jews, was seated on a dais with dignitaries representing all those who passed through the island.

60 But two grandnieces recounted her day in the spotlight: she was nearly elbowed out of line for the ferry by executives from A.T. & T. [one of the renovation's corporate sponsors], fought a Secret Service man 65 for access to an elevator, spent an hour waiting in line for food, and then was spirited to a special table just in time to miss the V.I.P. brunch entirely.

"The interior's different," Mrs. Larsen 70 said, "but the bureaucracy is the same." . . .

On the museum's front lawn were some who represented the newer hopes and troubles of immigration.

75 Herbert, a 20-year-old Salvadoran who declined to give his last name for fear of being deported, paused from his grass-trimming chores to say that from the looks of the great hall, he surmised that earlier 80 generations of immigrants must have had it better.

"It's much different now," said Herbert, a deserter from the United States-backed Salvadoran Armed Forces. "Now when 85 you come in, you come through Mexico."

His Nicaraguan co-worker Henry, who fought United States-backed contra rebels as a Sandinista soldier, said he, too, had found a hole in the fence separating Ti-

90 juana, Mexico, from Southern California. And they agreed that while the gateway had changed, the United States still beckoned immigrants with incentives that were magical as well as monetary.

95 For instance, they said, even as illegal aliens they were able to work on the Ellis Island Immigration Museum.

Discussing the Reading

1. What was similar about the recollections of Louis Villamarin and Clara Larsen of their experiences as young immigrants passing through Ellis Island?

2. What impressions of the experiences of earlier immigrants was drawn by the Salvadoran immigrant Herbert from the appearance of the buildings on Ellis Island? Do you think his inference was valid?

CRITICAL THINKING
Formulating Appropriate Questions

Henry, the former Sandinista soldier, had presumably been opposed to American intervention in the affairs of his country, yet still chose to come to the United States. Formulate a series of questions that you might ask him to elicit his reasons for choosing to live in the country that was funding his former enemies, the contras.

Chapter Summary

Write supporting details under each of the following main ideas as you review the chapter.

Section 1

1. George Bush captured the 1988 presidential election.
2. The federal government increased taxes and cut expenses.
3. Bush ordered an invasion of Panama.

Section 2

1. Many Eastern European nations challenged communism.
2. Nationalist movements emerged throughout the Soviet Union.
3. South Africa softened its position on apartheid.
4. Bush responded cautiously to the changes in the communist world.
5. America and the UN reacted swiftly when Iraq invaded Kuwait.

Section 3

1. The average age of the American population increased.
2. A wave of non-European immigrants came to America.
3. The Latino population grew enormously in the 1980s.
4. Asians were the largest group of newcomers to America.

Section 4

1. American cities exhibited both wealth and poverty.
2. The decline of affordable housing caused the homeless crisis.
3. African American leaders cited education as the key to progress.

Section 5

1. Many Americans turned toward religion in the 1970s and 1980s.
2. The new right attempted to achieve conservative goals.
3. The environmental movement warned the public of ecological threats.
4. Americans held both pessimistic and optimistic views of the future.

Special Feature: President Clinton

1. The campaign was a three-way race.
2. Clinton chose a strong cabinet.
3. Clinton's programs faced hurdles.
4. Foreign policy problems proved difficult.

Chapter Themes

1. **Conflict and cooperation:** The crumbling of the Berlin Wall, Soviet reforms, and the waning importance of communism in Eastern Europe sparked the beginning of a new era of cooperation between the United States and the Soviet Union and the end of the Cold War. In the meantime, the United States continued its policy of using armed force or the threat of armed force to thwart aggressive government leaders whose actions threatened world peace or the global economy.
2. **Racial, ethnic, and religious diversity:** In the last decades of the 20th century, Americans grappled with thorny social and ethical issues, such as homelessness, poverty, illegal drugs, AIDS, abortion, environmental protection, and religion in politics.

Chapter Study Guide

Identifying Key People and Terms

Name the key person or key term that describes the:
1. African American leader who made serious runs for the presidency of the United States
2. South African policy of separation of the races
3. deadly disease whose virus is transmitted between people through the exchange of bodily fluids

Locating Key Places

1. What nation was ruled by Manuel Noriega in the 1980s?
2. What geographical world region first benefited from Gorbachev's proposed restructuring of the Soviet economy?
3. In what city did the Chinese government massacre hundreds of pro-democracy student demonstrators?

Mastering the Main Ideas

1. Name two major international political problems Americans face in the 1990s.
2. What are some major economic problems Americans face in the 1990s?
3. What is global warming, and how could it endanger the people of the world?
4. How have minority groups improved themselves politically and economically in the 1980s and 1990s?
5. What are some problems Americans who live in cities must try to solve in the 1990s?

1987	1988	1989	1990	1991	1992

1988
Bush wins presidential election

1989
Massacre at
Tiananmen Square;
Berlin Wall crumbles;
U.S. invades Panama;
many Eastern European nations reject communism

1990
Second Earth Day;
Mandela freed; Iraq
invades Kuwait;
German
reunification

1991
Breakup of the
Soviet Union;
breakup of
Yugoslavia erupts
into war; Iraq
driven from Kuwait

1992
Clinton wins
presidential
election

Applying Critical Thinking Skills

1. **Distinguishing false from accurate images:** The image most people have of American society is that it is white, Anglo-Saxon, and Protestant. What developments of the 1980s and 1990s show this to be a false image?
2. **Recognizing values:** Problems such as the AIDS epidemic, abortion, and the plight of the homeless are not simply economic issues. How do they challenge the values held by millions of Americans?
3. **Identifying alternatives:** What are a few alternatives the American people face when they make decisions about how to protect the earth's environment?

Chapter Activities

Learning Geography Through History

1. What region of the world seems to you to be of most concern when you contemplate life in the year 2000?
2. How is the urban geographical process of gentrification both an opportunity and a problem for Americans in the 1990s?

Relating the United States to the World

1. Why is the United States depending on the Colombian government to help solve the American drug problem?
2. Why is it that Americans feel obligated to help nations that are in need?

Linking Past to Present

1. What are some epidemics of the past that seemed as horrifying as AIDS is today?

2. Compare the relationship between the U.S.S.R. and the United States in the 1950s with Russia and the United States today. How are the two periods different?

Using the Time Line

1. What military action did the United States take in 1989?
2. In what year did the world celebrate an environmental "holiday"?

Practicing Critical Thinking Strategies

Predicting Consequences
A strong political alliance between Russia and the United States is a possibility considering recent improvements between the two nations. What possible consequences would result from such an alliance?

Learning More About Opportunities and Challenges

1. **Using Source Readings:** Read the Source Readings for the chapter and answer the questions.
2. **Using Literature:** Read the excerpt from Amy Tan's recent novel *The Joy Luck Club*, which deals with lives of postwar Chinese immigrants to the United States and their American-born children, on pages 992–993.
3. **Making a Time Capsule:** Write down ten sentences describing what you think will be important developments in the next ten years. Make sure to include significant scientific and technological discoveries; social, economic, and political developments; and changes in values. Put the list in a safe place and then ten years from today, examine the list to see how accurate you were.

987

Epilogue

In the course of reading *American Voices,* you have been witness to the life of our nation from the earliest days of exploration to the dawn of the 21st century. You have seen how an infant republic became a mighty nation, how a few English immigrants were later joined by countless thousands from all parts of the world to form one people with a unique destiny. We have tried to tell the story as it happened, without resorting to sentimentality or romanticization. We have not neglected to recount deeds of valor or to tell of lives touched with greatness. Nor have we omitted from the story reference to actions that were less than noble. We have told of national shortcomings, some of which are only belatedly being corrected. There are chapters in the story in which no one can take pride — the sinfulness of slavery, the ruthless genocide of the Native American, and the destruction of much of our natural environment.

In the Prologue to *American Voices,* we set forth the major themes that define the American character. These themes have served both as ideals and goals. They are not carved in stone but are as enduring as America itself.

They all have one thing in common. They are varying expressions of the overriding idea of freedom, the principle that gave birth to America as a nation and has sustained it ever since against all enemies within and without.

Today we justifiably regard our ethnic and cultural diversity as a major strength. The path by which we reached this happy state was not always strewn with roses. The 17th, 18th, and early 19th centuries brought bitter strife between old and new immigrants — between the Native Americans and land-hungry pioneers. The ruthless extermination of a proud people by the relentless westward sweep of the pioneer is part of that past. We know what happened and why. The results, wholly justified in the eyes of the white settlers of the time, take on a different light when placed against the human rights standards of today. Nor was the picture much prettier as new waves of immigrants, seeking the same goals as the first settlers, often had to endure discrimination, intolerance, and economic privation — the Irish newcomers to eastern cities, southern and eastern Europeans as part of the "new" immigration, and more recently the influx of Hispanics and

Asians to our shores. The extent to which these handicaps could be and were overcome is indisputable evidence that the idea of freedom in the land of opportunity was genuine and enduring. None would dispute that the strength of America today as a society and as a culture is the direct result of its rich ethnic and cultural mix.

In no section of American life has liberty and freedom played a more significant role than in our commitment to free enterprise and private property. The overwhelming majority of those who came to this country came because it afforded opportunities available

element of free enterprise, steps were taken from time to time to limit greed and exploitation. The degree to which this should be done has been a running debate in our political life that continues today. To ensure smooth and equitable operation of the system, the American people through their representatives in Congress have increasingly sought to guarantee every American the right to compete unfettered in the market place. Competition is as much a part of American life today as it has ever been. Our national mania for competitive sports is dramatic testimony of our belief in the idea that talent, hard work, and playing by

nowhere else. Drawing inspiration from religious teachings that stressed the nobility of work and the rewards both on earth and in heaven of a job well done, unhindered by restrictive laws, and given an environment where opportunity abounded, early Americans created a system of free enterprise that in its essential characteristics has remained unchanged throughout our history. The American Revolution was as much a struggle for economic freedom as it was for political independence. With the adoption of the U.S. Constitution in 1788, key elements were in place for untrammeled economic growth. It was not, however, until after the Emancipation Proclamation in 1863 that African Americans could even begin to share in the economic plenty which the system encouraged and which white Americans already enjoyed. Their as yet incomplete struggle for equality of opportunity, along with that of other minorities, fills many pages in the nation's history.

In a dynamic society, change is the norm of life. Consequently, the American economic system has undergone vast changes in 200 years. To preserve for all the equal opportunity

the rules are the ingredients of success.

The American political system is defined by a reliance on constitutional government and a commitment to the rule of law. From the days of the Mayflower Compact to the latest Supreme Court decision, Americans have sought ways of protecting citizens against the tendency of government to act arbitrarily. Their old world heritage taught them that "power corrupts and absolute power corrupts absolutely," and that only a written document — a constitution — could afford protection against tyranny. They further realized that however benign a constitutional government might be, the written document from which it derives its authority must include a bill of rights that protects the civil liberties of all its citizens. Hence they quickly added the first ten amendments to the basic document.

To prevent the government from becoming the sole judge of its actions, an elaborate judicial system has evolved. It serves as a powerful check on a potential abuse of power by the executive and legislative branches of government. Time and again the courts have affirmed that ours is a government of laws, not of men, and that no one, no matter how powerful, is above the law. This important principle has acted as a self-correcting mechanism. When powerful economic groups, whether captains of industry or labor czars, have become oppressive, the law and the courts have stepped in to regulate. In the 20th century, the courts have provided protection for the civil rights of minorities in cases where the government and the society in general have been laggard in providing equal justice for all. Such is the success of our constitutional government that it has been copied by many nations, particularly by the new nations of Africa and Asia.

and then at an alarming pace, upset the balance of nature and transformed the land. On the positive side, American entrepreneurial spirit encouraged by free enterprise and an open society, used the resources of nature to build a great industrial nation that provided its citizens with unprecedented wealth and power. There was, however, a price to be paid. After 200 years Americans began to realize that the environment was suffering perhaps irretrievable damage from wasteful and irresponsible agricultural and industrial practices. Environmentalists warned that air pollution, water contamination, soil erosion, depletion

An important theme in American history has been the constant interplay of conflict and cooperation. Our free institutions encourage the clash of ideas, the compromising of differences, and civic cooperation. Thirteen quarreling colonies set aside their differences and cooperated in winning independence. Clashing views on how a national government should be organized were compromised and the resulting cooperation produced the Constitution and the Bill of Rights. When cooperation broke down in the mid-19th century over a moral issue that precluded compromise, a tragic conflict ensued. From the terrible consequences of that bitter struggle a new and stronger nation emerged, rededicated to the principle that no matter how great our disagreements on issues and policies, compromise and cooperation best serve the common good.

From the time the first immigrants reached Alaska from Siberia, geography has played a significant role in the development of American life and culture. For thousands of years before Columbus, Native Americans lived in harmony with the environment. The changes introduced by European settlers, at first slowly

of natural resources, and global warming were threatening the health of Planet Earth. Today Americans are engaged in a determined effort to reverse the trend and to restore the balance of nature. There is a growing awareness that only if intelligently managed will our geographic resources continue to support our people and keep our nation strong.

American public and private morality is defined by religious and ethical principles. Foreign observers of American society have frequently remarked on the strong religious influences in our culture. In a land of religious liberty such influences take many forms. Strict adherence to the ideal of separation of church and state means that these influences are always "unofficial." The Judeo-Christian tradition with its emphasis on moral and ethical behavior has been predominant. It has not, however, prevented other influences from the other great world religions from being strongly felt. It need only be remembered that many of our forbears came here seeking the freedom to worship God in their own way. The varieties of religious affiliation made religious tolerance a necessity. All forms of belief and unbelief have flourished under the banner of toleration.

Americans maintain a belief in a unique national destiny. The first settlements in New England were made by men and women who had a vision of a new society that would be as a city on a hill, a beacon to all the world. Every succeeding group of immigrants has shared this vision. As the population grew and the nation expanded, Americans continued to see themselves as destined by providence for a special role in history. It was this sense of mission that took hardy pioneers westward across the Appalachians and still later across the tree-

American shield and nourished with massive economic aid, their economies prospered and their democracies flourished. The collapse of communism and the end of the Cold War — both to a large extent the result of American resolve — gave the world a new birth of freedom. The price we paid can be viewed as significant, given the presence of both a menacing and growing national debt and of the many unmet needs in our own society. Faced today with new foreign challenges, both economic and military, the American people are united in the firm resolve that their collective efforts will lead the United States and people

less plains to the Continental Divide and on to the Pacific Ocean. Along the way, they triumphed over nature and pushed aside the native inhabitants and the foreign powers that stood in their way.

The technological revolution that began in the early 19th century and which continues today made the United States the world's leading industrial nation. The ingenuity of American inventors such as Thomas Edison fed the free enterprise system with a constant stream of technological breakthroughs. American means of production and distribution were perfected and adopted worldwide. The 20th century became the American century. While remaining true to their principles of freedom, equality, and justice, the American people sought to give universal application to the themes that made the nation great. American generosity following the devastation of World War II had no parallel in history. Never had a victor been so generous to the vanquished. American wealth and technology transformed Western Europe and brought democratic institutions to Korea and Japan. Protected by the

in other nations to a better world.

Americans of the 1990s live in a country which remains, for all its problems, the envy of the world. We are the heirs to a proven system of government that guarantees its citizens political and religious freedom and encourages individual enterprise through a free market system. The advantages and freedoms we enjoy are our legacy from the men and women who built this nation and who sustained it through the periods of trial and crisis that form a part of our past. Busy with our everyday affairs, we do not pause as often as we should to honor those whose sacrifices made possible the realization of the American dream. Throughout our land and at countless sites in Europe and the Pacific are crosses and gravestones marking the final resting place of American youth who gave their all that we might remain free. We think of them, their youthful dreams and hopes unfullfilled, on the Fourth of July and on Veterans Day. They should never be far from our thoughts because the pride we take in America is their priceless gift to us. These are the *American Voices.*

JING-MEI AND HER PIANO

"My mother believed you could be anything you wanted to be in America," observes Jing-mei Woo, one of the narrators of *The Joy Luck Club* (1989), the first novel by Chinese American writer Amy Tan (1952–   ). Tan's novel presents the experiences of four women, post-World War II refugees from China living in San Francisco, and their American-born daughters. In the following excerpt, Jing-mei recalls the aftermath of her mother's failed attempt to turn her into a prodigy on the piano. Jing-mei's first public performance, at a local talent show, has been a disaster.

After the show, the Hsus, the Jongs, and the St. Clairs from the Joy Luck Club came up to my mother and father.

"Lots of talented kids," Auntie Lindo said vaguely, smiling broadly.

"That was somethin' else," said my father, and I wondered if he was referring to me in a humorous way, or whether he even remembered what I had done.

Waverly looked at me and shrugged her shoulders. "You aren't a genius like me," she said matter-of-factly. And if I hadn't felt so bad, I would have pulled her braids and punched her stomach.

But my mother's expression was what devastated me: a quiet, blank look that said she had lost everything. I felt the same way, and it seemed as if everybody were now coming up, like gawkers at the scene of an accident, to see what parts were actually missing. When we got on the bus to go home, my father was humming the busy-bee tune [the piece played by one of the children at the recital] and my mother was silent. I kept thinking she wanted to wait until we got home before shouting at me. But when my father unlocked the door to our apartment, my mother walked in and then went to the back, into the bedroom. No accusations. No blame. And in a way, I felt disappointed. I had been waiting for her to start shouting, so I could shout back and cry and blame her for all my misery.

I assumed my talent-show fiasco meant I never had to play the piano again. But two days later, after school, my mother came out of the kitchen and saw me watching TV.

"Four clock," she reminded me as if it were any other day. I was stunned, as though she were asking me to go through the talent-show torture again. I wedged myself more tightly in front of the TV.

"Turn off TV," she called from the kitchen five minutes later.

I didn't budge. And then I decided. I didn't have to do what my mother said anymore. I wasn't her slave. This wasn't China. I had listened to her before and look what happened. She was the stupid one.

She came out from the kitchen and stood in the arched entryway of the living room. "Four clock," she said once again, louder.

"I'm not going to play anymore," I said nonchalantly. "Why should I? I'm not a genius."

She walked over and stood in front of the TV. I saw her chest was heaving up and down in an angry way.

"No!" I said, and I now felt stronger, as if my true self had finally emerged. So this was what had been inside me all along.

"No! I won't!" I screamed.

She yanked me by the arm, pulled me off the floor, snapped off the TV. She was frighteningly strong, half pulling, half carrying me toward the piano as I kicked the throw rugs under my feet. She lifted me up and onto the hard bench. I was sobbing by now, looking at her bitterly. Her chest was heaving even more and her mouth was open, smiling crazily as if she were pleased I was crying.

"You want me to be someone that I'm not!" I sobbed. "I'll never be the kind of daughter you want me to be!"

"Only two kinds of daughters," she shouted in Chinese. "Those who are obedient and those

> Only one kind of daughter can live in this house. Obedient daughter!

An excerpt from
THE JOY LUCK CLUB
by Amy Tan

who follow their own mind! Only one kind of daughter can live in this house. Obedient daughter!"

"Then I wish I wasn't your daughter. I wish you weren't my mother," I shouted. As I said these things I got scared. It felt like worms and toads and slimy things crawling out of my chest, but it also felt good, as if this awful side of me had surfaced, at last.

"Too late change this," said my mother shrilly.

And I could sense her anger rising to its breaking point. I wanted to see it spill over. And that's when I remembered the babies she had lost in China, the ones we never talked about. "Then I wish I'd never been born!" I shouted. "I wish I were dead! Like them."

It was as if I had said the magic words. Alakazam!—and her face went blank, her mouth closed, her arms went slack, and she backed out of the room, stunned, as if she were blowing away like a small brown leaf, thin, brittle, lifeless.

It was not the only disappointment my mother felt in me. In the years that followed, I failed her so many times, each time asserting my own will, my right to fall short of expectations. I didn't get straight As. I didn't become class president. I didn't get into Stanford. I dropped out of college.

For unlike my mother, I did not believe I could be anything I wanted to be. I could only be me.

And for all those years, we never talked about the disaster at the recital or my terrible accusations afterward at the piano bench. All that remained unchecked, like a betrayal that was now unspeakable. So I never found a way to ask her why she had hoped for something so large that failure was inevitable.

And even worse, I never asked her what frightened me the most: Why had she given up hope?

For after our struggle at the piano, she never mentioned my playing again. The lessons stopped. The lid to the piano was closed, shutting out the dust, my misery, and her dreams.

So she surprised me. A few years ago, she offered to give me the piano, for my thirtieth birthday. I had not played in all those years. I saw the offer as a sign of forgiveness, a tremendous burden removed.

"Are you sure?" I asked shyly. "I mean, won't you and Dad miss it?"

"No, this your piano," she said firmly. "Always your piano. You only one can play."

> I saw the offer as a sign of forgiveness.

"Well, I probably can't play anymore," I said. "It's been years."

"You pick up fast," said my mother, as if she knew this was certain. "You have natural talent. You could been genius if you want to."

"No I couldn't."

"You just not trying," said my mother. And she was neither angry nor sad. She said it as if to announce a fact that could never be disproved. "Take it," she said.

But I didn't at first. It was enough that she had offered it to me. And after that, every time I saw it in my parents' living room, standing in front of the bay windows, it made me feel proud, as if it were a shiny trophy I had won back.

CRITICAL THINKING
Recognizing Values
What values cause the conflict between Jing-mei and her mother? Is this difference in values finally reconciled? Explain.

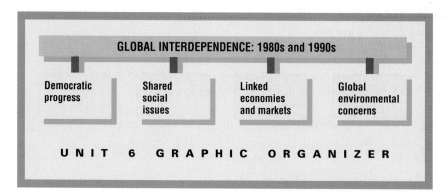

GLOBAL INTERDEPENDENCE: 1980s and 1990s

| Democratic progress | Shared social issues | Linked economies and markets | Global environmental concerns |

U N I T   6   G R A P H I C   O R G A N I Z E R

C H A P T E R
S U R V E Y

23

The Triumph of Conservatism
1974–1988

Gerald R. Ford tried to restore confidence in the presidency.

Vice President Ford was sworn into the office of president in August 1974. He became the first president in American history to assume the office without having been elected to either the presidency or the vice presidency. President Ford's pardon of Richard Nixon soon damaged his popularity. Even more damaging was the president's inability to improve the economy. Inflation continued to rise, as did oil prices. Ford's conduct of foreign affairs proved more successful. During the *Mayaguez* crisis in May 1975, he acted decisively, sending marines to free an American freighter seized by communist Cambodia.

President Carter changed U.S. Middle East policy.

Democratic president Jimmy Carter, elected in 1976, failed to turn around the sliding U.S. economy. The president's human rights policy, however, helped restore U.S. moral stature among other nations. President Carter's most remarkable victory was an agreement called the Camp David Accords reached in March 1979. The accords set up a framework for peace between Israel and Egypt. A major failure in the Middle East came with the toppling of a pro-U.S. Iranian government. Militants seized the U.S. embassy in Tehran, the Iranian capital, and held 52 Americans hostage for 444 days.

The hostage crisis and the nation's economic problems combined to doom Carter's re-election hopes.

Ronald Reagan won the presidency in 1980.

The new president seemed blessed with luck when Iran freed the hostages on inauguration day in 1981. President Reagan took office with firm plans to attack big government. To bolster the economy, he planned to reduce both taxes and government spending. The economy did revive. However, although the president cut some government spending, increases in the cost of other programs more than made up for these cuts. Nevertheless, the president's endless optimism kept his popularity high.

President Reagan moved to rebuild U.S. world prestige.

President Reagan hoped to reverse the decline of American power and prestige in the world. In keeping with this policy, his Administration took a hard line against communism. By 1985, though, Reagan began to soften his position. Soviet leader Mikhail Gorbachev introduced two policies, *glasnost* and *perestroika*, which set the stage for a new international order. The two nations reached a dramatic arms control agreement, the INF Treaty, in 1988. The treaty marked the most hopeful event in years for both superpowers.

CHAPTER SURVEY

24

Opportunities and Challenges
1988–Present

Changes at home and abroad challenged U.S. leadership.

George Bush, vice president under Reagan, won the presidential election in 1988. Bush took a slow, cautious approach to the nation's problems. His first concern was the federal debt, now harming the nation's economy. Early in his term, stunning world events occurred. The communist system in Europe fell apart. People yearning for freedom tore down the Berlin Wall. China was shaken by a movement toward democracy. A changing world required new ideas and actions from American government.

The United States encouraged freedom in a changing world.

In 1989 and 1990, almost every nation in the Soviet bloc overthrew its government or forced democratic reforms. These forces eventually led to the breakup of the Soviet Union as well as Yugoslavia, which plunged into a brutal civil war. Change also occurred in China, where a pro-democracy movement was crushed by communist leaders. In South Africa, the ruling white government softened its position on apartheid, freeing African National Congress leader Nelson Mandela.

The Bush Administration responded cautiously to these events, trying to encourage movement toward democracy as it adjusted to America's new role as the world's sole super-power. After Iraq invaded Kuwait, Bush took direct action, assembling an international military force to drive Iraq from Kuwait in 1991.

New forces shaped American society and culture.

The average age of the American population increased. New immigrants arrived in record numbers from Asia and Latin America. Ethnic minority groups became a major presence in American society and politics. Many African Americans and Latinos joined the middle class; many won elective office.

Americans pondered their values and their future.

The 1970s and 1980s brought a fresh awakening of religious belief. Many evangelists used television to share their message. A new, conservative mood influenced the way Americans felt about key social and moral issues. The issue of abortion sharply divided American society.

For many decades the United States had been a dominant military and economic power in the world. Some Americans faced the 1990s in fear that their nation would fall to a lesser place in a changing world. Would the United States be able to keep up with the rising economic power of other countries? Other Americans faced the future with opti-mism. Recent world events renewed their confidence in American princi-ples of democracy, justice, and free enterprise.

A new president was inaugurated.

Democrat Bill Clinton won the presidential election in 1992, ending 12 years of Republican leadership. Clinton called for change and focused attention on America's problems at home, including the state of the economy and the need for health care reform.

995

Religion

Religion has always been a primary influence in American life, shaping our outlook and our institutions. As a result of this influence, issues involving religion, such as freedom of worship and the conflict between faith and doubt, have also been debated throughout American history. The following quotations reflect both the persistent influence of religion in America and the continuing debate it generates.

1637

Take heed what ye go about to do unto me. You have power over my body, but the Lord Jesus hath power over my body and soul; neither can you do me any harm, for I am in the hands of the eternal Jehovah, my Savior.

▲ **Anne Hutchinson, testimony at her trial**

1649

And whereas the inforceing of the conscience in matters of Religion hath frequently fallen out to be of dangerous Consequence . . . And for the more quiett and peaceable government of the Province, and the better to preserve mutuall Love and amity [friendship]. . . . Be it therefore . . . enacted . . . that noe person or persons whatsoever within this Province . . . professing to believe in Jesus Christ, shall henceforth bee any waies troubled, Molested, or discountenanced for . . . his or her religion nor in the free exercise thereof . . .

▲ **Maryland Toleration Act (original spelling retained)**

1779

Amazing grace! How sweet the sound
That saved a wretch like me!
I once was lost, but now am found,
Was blind, but now I see.

▲ **Ex-slaver John Newton wrote this hymn, sung to an early American song of unknown origin**

1789

Congress shall make no law respecting establishment of religion, or prohibiting the exercise thereof.

▲ **1st Amendment of the Constitution of the United States**

1805

Brother, the Great Spirit has made us all; but he has made a great difference between his white and red children; he has given us a different complexion and different customs; to you he has given the arts [science and technology would have been included under this term]; to these he has not opened our eyes; we know these things to be true. Since he has made so great a difference between us in other things, why may we not conclude that he has given us a different religion according to our understanding; the Great Spirit does right; he knows what is best for his children; we are satisfied.

Brother, we do not wish to destroy your religion, or take it from you; we only wish to enjoy our own.

▲ **Red Jacket, speech to a Christian missionary**

1800s

Deep river, my home is over Jordan.
Deep river, Lord, I want to cross over into Campground.
Oh, children, oh, don't you want to go
To that gospel feast, that promised land,
That land where all is peace?

▲ **African American spiritual**

1872

infidel, *n.* In New York, one who does not believe in the Christian religion; in Constantinople, one who does.

religion, *n.* A daughter of Hope and Fear, explaining to Ignorance the nature of the Unknowable.

▲ **Ambrose Bierce, *The Devil's Dictionary***

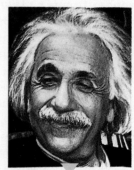

1921

The Lord God is subtle but malicious he is not.

▲ **Albert Einstein, remark later inscribed in Fine Hall at Princeton University**

1966

God Is Beside You on the Picketline.

▲ **Cesar Chavez, slogan used during grapeworkers' strike**

1974

The Buddha, the Godhead, resides quite as comfortably in the circuits of a digital computer or the gears of a cycle transmission as he does at the top of a mountain or the petals of a flower.

▲ **Robert Pirsig, *Zen and the Art of Motorcycle Maintenance***

1983

The real crisis we face today is a spiritual one; at root, it is a test of moral will and faith. . . .

For Marxism-Leninism is actually the second oldest faith, first proclaimed in the Garden of Eden with the words of temptation: "Ye shall be as gods." The Western world can answer this challenge, but only provided that its faith in God and the freedom He enjoins [requires] is as great as communism's faith in man.

▲ **Ronald Reagan, speech to Protestant evangelicals**

Analyze

After he became convinced that a national bill of rights was necessary, James Madison examined numerous individual proposals and the state bills of rights. Freedom of religion was at or near the top of many of these documents. Religious issues continue to be important to Americans today, both to those who profess a religion and to those who do not.

Assignment: Write an essay of three to five paragraphs in which you analyze the American tradition of religious freedom, isolating one or more elements that seem important to you. Use the following process.

Explore the idea of religious freedom. Begin by examining the quotations on these two pages. Isolate those which deal with freedom of religion, religious toleration, or religious diversity. Take notes, writing down a phrase or two indicating which of these three aspects of religious freedom each quotation reflects. (Anne Hutchinson, for example, asserted the total freedom of the individual conscience; Red Jacket made a plea for religious diversity, based on the cultural differences between Native Americans and whites; and so on.) Look over your notes and pick out one or more important aspects of religious freedom. Write a clear topic sentence that states your point or points about religious freedom. (For example, a topic sentence might be the following:

"The American tradition of religious freedom is based on the need for people of differing religious beliefs to live in harmony.")

Organize your essay. Decide how you are going to organize your essay. In writing an essay developing the topic sentence stated above, you might select several quotations that dealt with the religious diversity of American society. In the remainder of your first paragraph and in the succeeding paragraphs, you would explore what these quotations reveal about the tradition of religious freedom in the United States. (What, for example, do the Maryland Toleration Act or Red Jacket's speech assert about religious freedom? How broad is the religious freedom allowed by each of these statements?) Conclude your final paragraph with a clear, effective summary of the points you have made.

Write a draft of the essay. Following the plan of organization you have developed, write out a complete draft of the essay.

Revise the draft. Examine the organization and development of your essay, asking yourself the following questions: Is the topic sentence clearly stated? Does each quotation you have chosen help develop your topic?

Proofread the essay and make a final draft. Read the essay again. Correct any errors in grammar, punctuation, and spelling. Make a final copy of the essay.

Reference Section

Atlas

All maps in *American Voices* are based on the latest information available at the time of printing.

World: Political

United States

U.S. territories and areas of special sovereignty

Robinson Projection

ARCTIC OCEAN

80°N

140° West Longitude

Arctic Circle   Alaska (U.S.)

60°N

CANADA

Aleutian Islands

NORTH AMERICA

UNITED STATES

ATLANTIC OCEAN

40°North Latitude

PACIFIC OCEAN

Bermuda (U.K.)

Midway Islands

MEXICO   CUBA   BAHAMAS   Puerto Rico

DOMINICAN REPUBLIC   Virgin Is. (U.K.)   Virgin Is.

Tropic of Cancer   Hawaii (U.S.)

20°N

JAMAICA   HAITI   ST. KITTS AND NEVIS

BELIZE   ANTIGUA AND BARBUDA

Johnston Atoll

GUATEMALA   HONDURAS   Navassa I.   DOMINICA

EL SALVADOR   NICARAGUA   ST. LUCIA   ST. VINCENT AND THE GRENADINES

GRENADA   BARBADOS

Kingman Reef

COSTA RICA   TRINIDAD AND TOBAGO

Palmyra Atoll   VENEZUELA   GUYANA

Howland Island   KIRIBATI   PANAMA   SURINAME

Baker Island   Jarvis Island   0° Equator   COLOMBIA   FR. GUIANA (FRANCE)

Galapagos Islands (ECUADOR)   ECUADOR

P O L Y N E S I A

WESTERN SAMOA   American Samoa   PERU   SOUTH AMERICA

UNITED STATES   BRAZIL

TONGA

20°S   French   BOLIVIA

Tropic of Capricorn   Polynesia (FRANCE)   PARAGUAY

Easter Island (CHILE)   CHILE   URUGUAY

PACIFIC OCEAN   ARGENTINA

40°S

Pacific Rim

RUSSIA   CANADA

Alaska (U.S.)

CHINA   NORTH KOREA   UNITED STATES

JAPAN   MEXICO

SOUTH KOREA

TAIWAN   Hawaii (U.S.)

PHILIPPINES

SINGAPORE   PACIFIC OCEAN

Equator

INDONESIA   PAPUA NEW GUINEA

SOLOMON IS.   TUVALU

VANUATU   FIJI   TONGA

AUSTRALIA

NEW ZEALAND

60°S

Antarctic Circle

Falkland Islands (U.K.)

80°S   ANTARCTICA

180°   160°W   140°W   120°W   100°W   80°W   60°W

Central America and the West Indies

30°N

Gulf of California   110°W   100°W   90°W   80°W

UNITED STATES

Gulf of Mexico   ATLANTIC OCEAN

Tropic of Cancer   NORTH AMERICA   BAHAMAS

20°N   MEXICO   CUBA   Puerto Rico

DOMINICAN REPUBLIC   Virgin Is. (U.K.)   Virgin Is.

HAITI   ANTIGUA AND BARBUDA

JAMAICA   Guadeloupe (Fr.)

Navassa Island   ST. KITTS   DOMINICA

BELIZE   AND NEVIS   Martinique (Fr.)

West Indies   ST. LUCIA

GUATEMALA   HONDURAS   CARIBBEAN SEA   ST. VINCENT AND   BARBADOS

EL SALVADOR   THE GRENADINES

PACIFIC OCEAN   NICARAGUA   GRENADA

10°N   TRINIDAD AND TOBAGO

Central America

COSTA RICA   Panama Canal   VENEZUELA

0   500 Miles

0   500 Kilometers   PANAMA   COLOMBIA   SOUTH AMERICA   GUYANA   SURINAME

W   E   N   S

Albers Equal-Area Projection

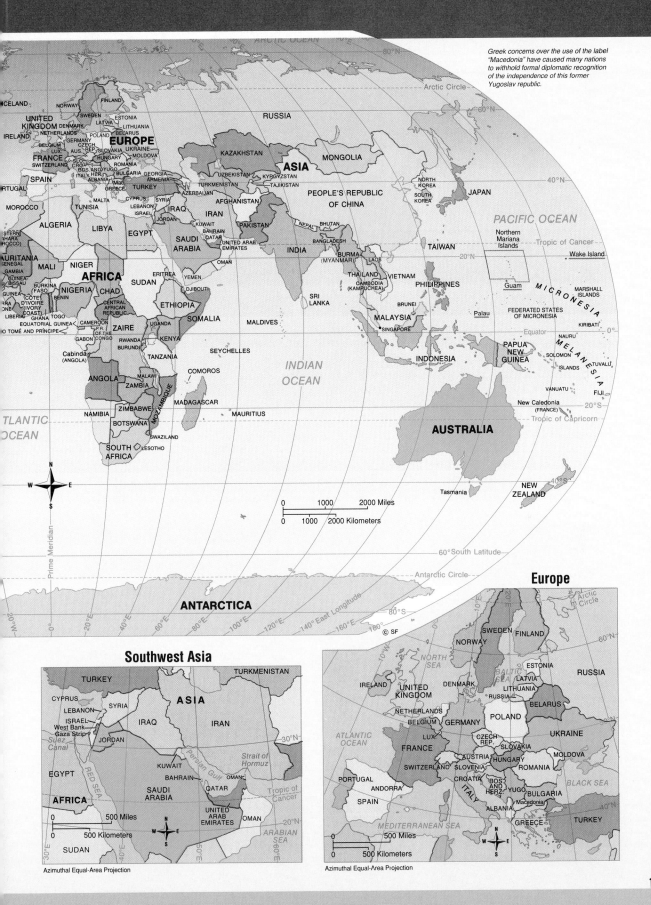

RUSSIA

ARCTIC OCEAN

ALASKA

Arctic Circle

CANADA

Fairbanks

Yukon River

Anchorage

0 ____ 500 Miles

0 ____ 500 Kilometers

BERING SEA

PACIFIC OCEAN

Gulf of Alaska

Juneau

CANADA

Puget Sound

Columbia River

Olympia
Seattle
Tacoma
Spokane

WASHINGTON

Portland
Columbia River
Salem
Eugene

OREGON

IDAHO

Snake River

Boise

Idaho Falls

Pocatello

Great Falls

Missouri River

Helena

MONTANA

Billings

WYOMING

Casper

Cheye

Laramie

United States: Political

	International boundaries
	State boundaries
⊛	National capital
★	State capitals
•	Other cities

Albers Equal-Area Projections   © SF

Sacramento

Sacramento River

Lake Tahoe

Reno

Carson City

NEVADA

Great Salt Lake

Salt Lake City

Ogden

Provo

UTAH

Green River

Colorado River

Denver

COLORA

Colorado Springs

Puebl

San Francisco
Oakland
San Jose

San Joaquin River

Fresno

CALIFORNIA

Bakersfield

Las Vegas

Los Angeles
Long Beach
Anaheim
Santa Ana

San Diego

Colorado River

ARIZONA

Albuquerque

Santa Fe

NEW MEXICO

Phoenix
Mesa

Tucson

Las Cruces

El Paso

PACIFIC OCEAN

160°W   155°W

22°N   22°N

Honolulu

PACIFIC

HAWAII

OCEAN

Hilo

19°N   19°N

0 ____ 50 Miles

0 ____ 50 Kilometers

160°W   155°W

Tropic of Cancer

MEXICO

0   250   500 Miles

0   250   500 Kilometers

CANADA

NORTH DAKOTA
Grand Forks
Bismarck ★   Fargo •

SOUTH DAKOTA
Rapid City •   ★ Pierre

NEBRASKA
Grand Island •   Omaha •
Lincoln ★

KANSAS
Topeka ★   Kansas City •
Wichita •

OKLAHOMA
Amarillo •   Oklahoma City ★   Tulsa •
Lawton •   Fort Smith

TEXAS
Lubbock •
Fort Worth •   Dallas •
Austin ★
Houston •
San Antonio •
Corpus Christi •

MINNESOTA
Duluth •
Minneapolis •   ★ St. Paul

WISCONSIN
Green Bay •
Madison ★   Milwaukee •

IOWA
Des Moines ★   Cedar Rapids •
Davenport •

ILLINOIS
Rockford •   Chicago •
Peoria •
Springfield ★

MISSOURI
Kansas City •
St. Louis •
Jefferson City ★
Springfield •

ARKANSAS
Little Rock ★
Pine Bluff •

LOUISIANA
Shreveport •
Baton Rouge ★   Biloxi •
New Orleans •

MICHIGAN
Lake Superior
Lake Michigan

Grand Rapids •   Lansing ★
Gary •   Detroit •

INDIANA
Fort Wayne •
Indianapolis ★
Louisville •   Frankfort ★
Lexington •

KENTUCKY

TENNESSEE
Nashville ★   Knoxville •
Memphis •   Huntsville •

MISSISSIPPI
Jackson ★
Meridian •

ALABAMA
Birmingham •
Montgomery ★   Columbus •

OHIO
Toledo •   Cleveland •
Akron •
Columbus ★
Cincinnati •
Huntington •
Charleston ★

WEST VIRGINIA
Wheeling •

GEORGIA
Atlanta ★
Macon •
Columbus •   Savannah •

FLORIDA
Tallahassee ★   Jacksonville •
Orlando •
Tampa •
St. Petersburg •   Fort Lauderdale •
Miami •

Rochester •   Buffalo •
Syracuse •
Albany ★

NEW YORK
PENNSYLVANIA
Harrisburg ★
Pittsburgh •   Philadelphia •

NEW HAMPSHIRE
Concord ★   Manchester •

MAINE
Augusta ★
Lewiston •
Portland •

VERMONT
Montpelier ★   Burlington •

MASSACHUSETTS
Worcester •   Boston ★

CONNECTICUT
Hartford ★   Providence ★
Bridgeport •

RHODE ISLAND

NEW JERSEY
Jersey City •   New York City
Newark •
Trenton ★

DELAWARE
Wilmington •
Dover ★

MARYLAND
Baltimore •
Annapolis ★
Washington, D.C.

VIRGINIA
Richmond ★
Norfolk •   Virginia Beach •

NORTH CAROLINA
Winston-Salem •   Greensboro •
Raleigh ★
Charlotte •

SOUTH CAROLINA
Greenville •
Columbia ★
Charleston •

ATLANTIC OCEAN

Gulf of Mexico

BAHAMAS

Tropic of Cancer

CUBA

Chesapeake Bay
Straits of Florida

Lake Ontario
Lake Erie
Lake Huron

St. Lawrence River
Bay of Fundy
Hudson River
James River
Ohio River
Mississippi River
Missouri River
Arkansas River
Platte River
Red River
Brazos River
Rio Grande
Tennessee River
Alabama River

55°N
75°W
70° West Longitude
65°W
50°N
45°N
40°N
35° North Latitude
30°N
25°N

100°W
95°W
90°W
85°W
80°W

ATLAS

ATLANTIC OCEAN

PUERTO RICO
(U.S.)   San Juan

20°N   65°W   20°N

65°W

0   100 Miles
0   100 Kilometers

N
W   E
S

1003

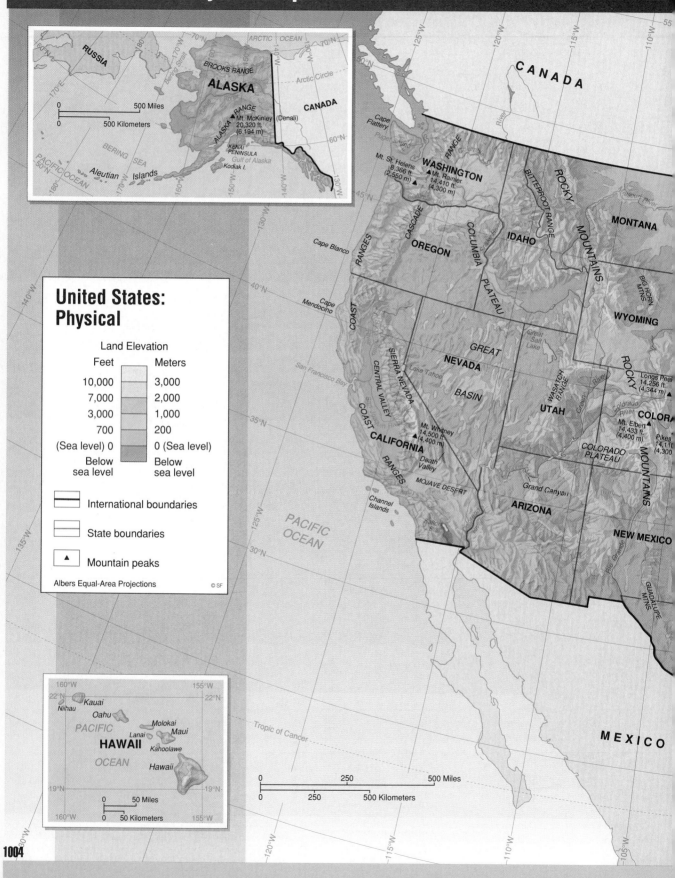

United States: Physical

Land Elevation

Feet	Meters
10,000	3,000
7,000	2,000
3,000	1,000
700	200
(Sea level) 0	0 (Sea level)
Below sea level	Below sea level

International boundaries

State boundaries

▲ Mountain peaks

Albers Equal-Area Projections

© SF

ALASKA

RUSSIA

BROOKS RANGE

ARCTIC OCEAN

Arctic Circle

CANADA

ALASKA RANGE

▲ Mt. McKinley (Denali)
20,320 ft.
(6,194 m)

KENAI PENINSULA

Gulf of Alaska

Kodiak I.

BERING SEA

PACIFIC OCEAN

Aleutian Islands

0 — 500 Miles
0 — 500 Kilometers

HAWAII

Kauai
Niihau
Oahu
PACIFIC
Lanai — Molokai
Maui
Kahoolawe
OCEAN
Hawaii

0 — 50 Miles
0 — 50 Kilometers

CANADA

WASHINGTON

Cape Flattery
Puget Sound
Mt. St. Helens
8,366 ft
(2,550 m)
▲ Mt. Rainier
14,410 ft
(4,300 m)

CASCADE RANGE

OREGON

COLUMBIA PLATEAU

IDAHO

ROCKY MOUNTAINS

BITTERROOT RANGE

MONTANA

BIG HORN MTNS.

WYOMING

Cape Blanco

Cape Mendocino

COAST RANGES

San Francisco Bay

CENTRAL VALLEY

SIERRA NEVADA

Lake Tahoe

GREAT BASIN

NEVADA

Great Salt Lake

WASATCH RANGE

UTAH

Green River

ROCKY

Longs Peak
14,256 ft
(4,344 m)

COLORADO

Mt. Elbert
14,433 ft
(4,400 m)

Colorado River

Pikes
14,11
(4,300

COLORADO PLATEAU

MOUNTAINS

CALIFORNIA

Mt. Whitney
14,500 ft
(4,400 m)

Death Valley

COAST RANGES

MOJAVE DESERT

Channel Islands

Salton

Grand Canyon

ARIZONA

NEW MEXICO

Rio Grande

GUADALUPE MTNS.

PACIFIC OCEAN

Tropic of Cancer

MEXICO

0 — 250 — 500 Miles
0 — 250 — 500 Kilometers

CANADA

NORTH DAKOTA

MINNESOTA

SOUTH DAKOTA

WISCONSIN

M I C H I G A N

NEBRASKA

IOWA

KANSAS

MISSOURI

OKLAHOMA

ARKANSAS

TEXAS

LOUISIANA

MISSISSIPPI

ALABAMA

GEORGIA

TENNESSEE

KENTUCKY

ILLINOIS

INDIANA

OHIO

PENNSYLVANIA

NEW
YORK

VERMONT

MAINE

NEW
HAMPSHIRE

MASSACHUSETTS

RHODE ISLAND

CONNECTICUT

NEW JERSEY

DELAWARE

MARYLAND

VIRGINIA

NORTH
CAROLINA

SOUTH
CAROLINA

FLORIDA

Washington,
D.C.

GREAT PLAINS

CENTRAL

PLAINS

OZARK PLATEAU

OUACHITA MTNS.

APPALACHIAN

BLUE RIDGE MTNS.

PIEDMONT

MOUNTAINS

ALLEGHENY MTNS.

ADIRONDACK
MTNS.

WHITE
MTNS.

CATSKILL
MTNS.

Mt. Mitchell
6,684 ft.
(2,030 m)

COASTAL PLAIN

COASTAL

PLAIN

Mississippi
Delta

FLORIDA
PENINSULA

DELMARVA
PENINSULA

Lake Superior

Lake Michigan

Lake Huron

Lake Erie

Lake
Ontario

St. Lawrence River

Bay of Fundy

Cape Cod

Long Island

Chesapeake Bay

Cape Hatteras

Cape Fear

Cape
Canaveral

Florida Keys

Straits of Florida

Mississippi River

Ohio River

Missouri River

Platte River

Platte River

Arkansas River

Red River

Illinois River

Gulf of
Mexico

ATLANTIC
OCEAN

BAHAMAS

CUBA

Tropic of Cancer

55°N

50°N

45°N

40°N

35°North Latitude

30°N

25°N

95°W

90°W

85°W

80°W

75°W

70° West Longitude

65°W

95°W

90°W

85°W

80°W

75°W

100°W

100°W

N
W   E
S

ATLANTIC OCEAN

PUERTO RICO
(U.S.)

20°N

20°N

65°W

65°W

0   100 Miles

0   100 Kilometers

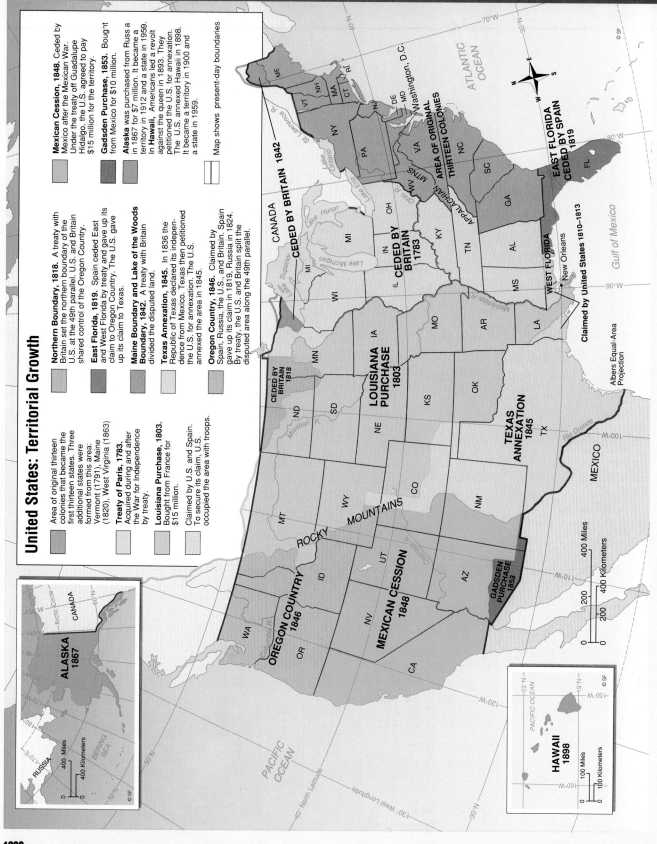

United States: Territorial Growth

Mexican Cession, 1848. Ceded by Mexico after the Mexican War. Under the treaty of Guadalupe Hidalgo, the U.S. agreed to pay $15 million for the territory.

Gadsden Purchase, 1853. Bought from Mexico for $10 million.

Alaska was purchased from Russia in 1867 for $7 million. It became a territory in 1912 and a state in 1959. In **Hawaii**, Americans led a revolt against the queen in 1893. They petitioned the U.S. for annexation. The U.S. annexed Hawaii in 1898. It became a territory in 1900 and a state in 1959.

Map shows present-day boundaries

Northern Boundary, 1818. A treaty with Britain set the northern boundary of the U.S. at the 49th parallel. U.S. and Britain shared control of the Oregon Country.

East Florida, 1819. Spain ceded East and West Florida by treaty and gave up its claim to Oregon Country. The U.S. gave up its claim to Texas.

Treaty of Paris, 1783. Acquired during and after the War for Independence by treaty.

Maine Boundary and Lake of the Woods Boundary, 1842. A treaty with Britain divided the disputed land.

Louisiana Purchase, 1803. Bought from France for $15 million.

Texas Annexation, 1845. In 1836 the Republic of Texas declared its independence from Mexico. Texas then petitioned the U.S. for annexation. The U.S. annexed the area in 1845.

Claimed by U.S. and Spain. To secure its claim, U.S. occupied the area with troops.

Oregon Country, 1846. Claimed by Spain, Russia, the U.S., and Britain. Spain gave up its claim in 1819, Russia in 1824. By treaty, the U.S. and Britain split the disputed area along the 49th parallel.

Area of original thirteen colonies that became the first thirteen states. Three additional states were formed from this area: Vermont (1791), Maine (1820), and West Virginia (1863).

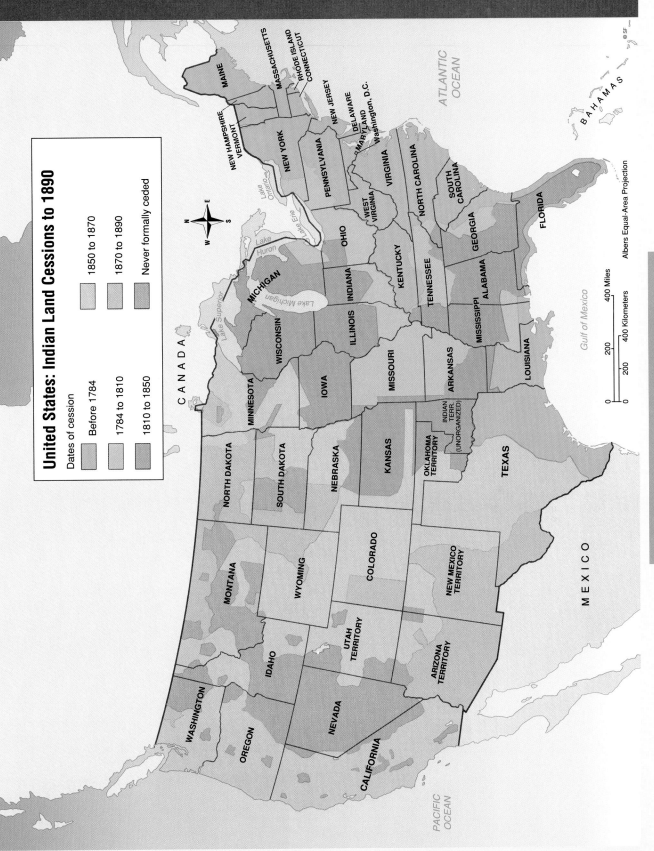

United States: Indian Land Cessions to 1890

Dates of cession

- Before 1784
- 1784 to 1810
- 1810 to 1850
- 1850 to 1870
- 1870 to 1890
- Never formally ceded

Albers Equal-Area Projection

0   200   400 Miles

0   200   400 Kilometers

ATLANTIC OCEAN

BAHAMAS

Gulf of Mexico

CANADA

MEXICO

PACIFIC OCEAN

Lake Ontario
Lake Erie
Lake Huron
Lake Superior
Lake Michigan

MAINE
NEW HAMPSHIRE
VERMONT
MASSACHUSETTS
RHODE ISLAND
CONNECTICUT
NEW YORK
NEW JERSEY
PENNSYLVANIA
DELAWARE
MARYLAND
Washington, D.C.
WEST VIRGINIA
VIRGINIA
NORTH CAROLINA
SOUTH CAROLINA
GEORGIA
FLORIDA
OHIO
KENTUCKY
TENNESSEE
ALABAMA
MISSISSIPPI
LOUISIANA
MICHIGAN
INDIANA
ILLINOIS
WISCONSIN
IOWA
MISSOURI
ARKANSAS
MINNESOTA
INDIAN TERR. (UNORGANIZED)
OKLAHOMA TERRITORY
TEXAS
NORTH DAKOTA
SOUTH DAKOTA
NEBRASKA
KANSAS
COLORADO
NEW MEXICO TERRITORY
MONTANA
WYOMING
UTAH TERRITORY
ARIZONA TERRITORY
IDAHO
NEVADA
CALIFORNIA
WASHINGTON
OREGON

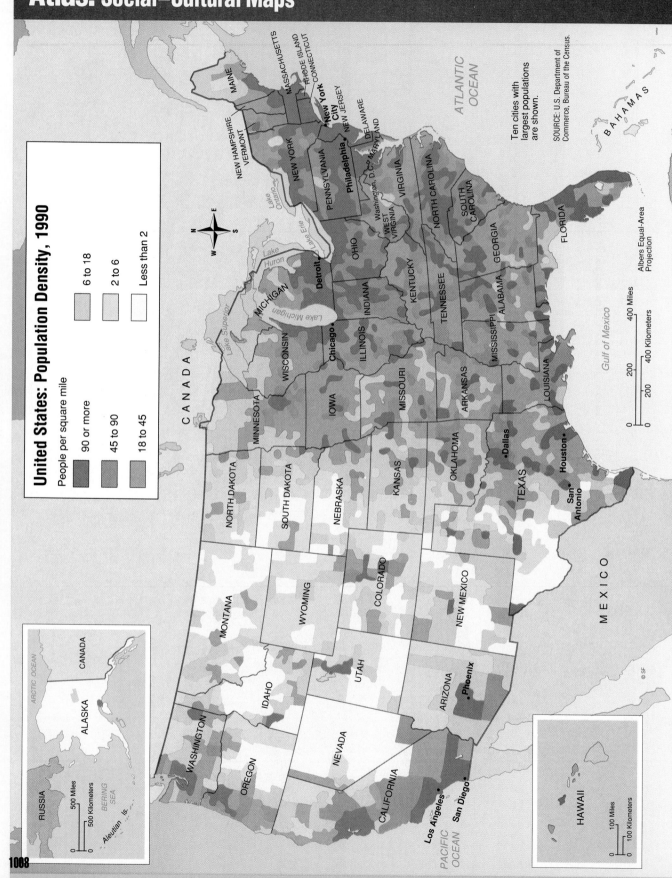

United States: Population Density, 1990

People per square mile

- 90 or more
- 45 to 90
- 18 to 45
- 6 to 18
- 2 to 6
- Less than 2

Ten cities with largest populations are shown.

SOURCE: U.S. Department of Commerce, Bureau of the Census.

Albers Equal-Area Projection

ATLANTIC OCEAN

BAHAMAS

Gulf of Mexico

MEXICO

PACIFIC OCEAN

CANADA

MAINE
MASSACHUSETTS
RHODE ISLAND
CONNECTICUT
NEW HAMPSHIRE
VERMONT
NEW YORK
New York City
NEW JERSEY
DELAWARE
PENNSYLVANIA
Philadelphia
MARYLAND
Washington, D.C.
WEST VIRGINIA
VIRGINIA
NORTH CAROLINA
SOUTH CAROLINA
GEORGIA
FLORIDA
OHIO
KENTUCKY
TENNESSEE
ALABAMA
MISSISSIPPI
INDIANA
ILLINOIS
Chicago
MICHIGAN
Detroit
WISCONSIN
IOWA
MISSOURI
ARKANSAS
LOUISIANA
MINNESOTA
NORTH DAKOTA
SOUTH DAKOTA
NEBRASKA
KANSAS
OKLAHOMA
TEXAS
Dallas
Houston
San Antonio
MONTANA
WYOMING
COLORADO
NEW MEXICO
IDAHO
UTAH
ARIZONA
Phoenix
WASHINGTON
OREGON
NEVADA
CALIFORNIA
Los Angeles
San Diego

Lake Ontario
Lake Erie
Lake Huron
Lake Michigan
Lake Superior

RUSSIA
CANADA
ALASKA
ARCTIC OCEAN
BERING SEA
Aleutian Is.

500 Miles
500 Kilometers

HAWAII

100 Miles
100 Kilometers

400 Miles
400 Kilometers
200
200

© SF

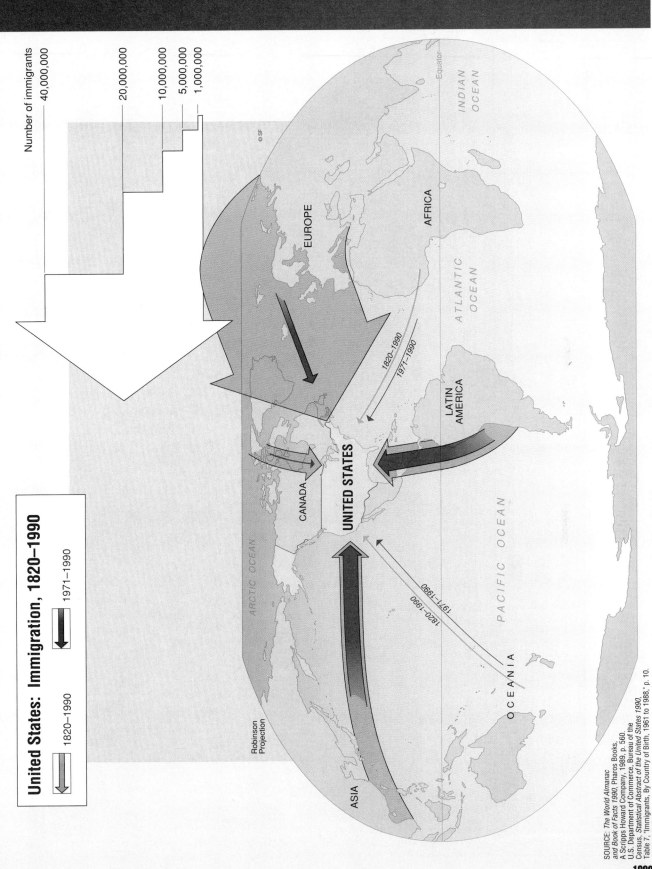

United States: Immigration, 1820–1990

1820–1990

1971–1990

Number of immigrants

40,000,000

20,000,000

10,000,000

5,000,000

1,000,000

© SF

EUROPE

AFRICA

INDIAN OCEAN

1820–1990

1971–1990

ATLANTIC OCEAN

Equator

LATIN AMERICA

CANADA

UNITED STATES

ARCTIC OCEAN

ASIA

OCEANIA

PACIFIC OCEAN

1820–1990

1971–1990

Robinson Projection

SOURCE: *The World Almanac and Book of Facts 1990*, Pharos Books, A Scripps Howard Company, 1989, p. 560. U.S. Department of Commerce, Bureau of the Census, *Statistical Abstract of the United States 1990*, Table 7, "Immigrants, By Country of Birth, 1961 to 1988," p. 10.

ATLAS

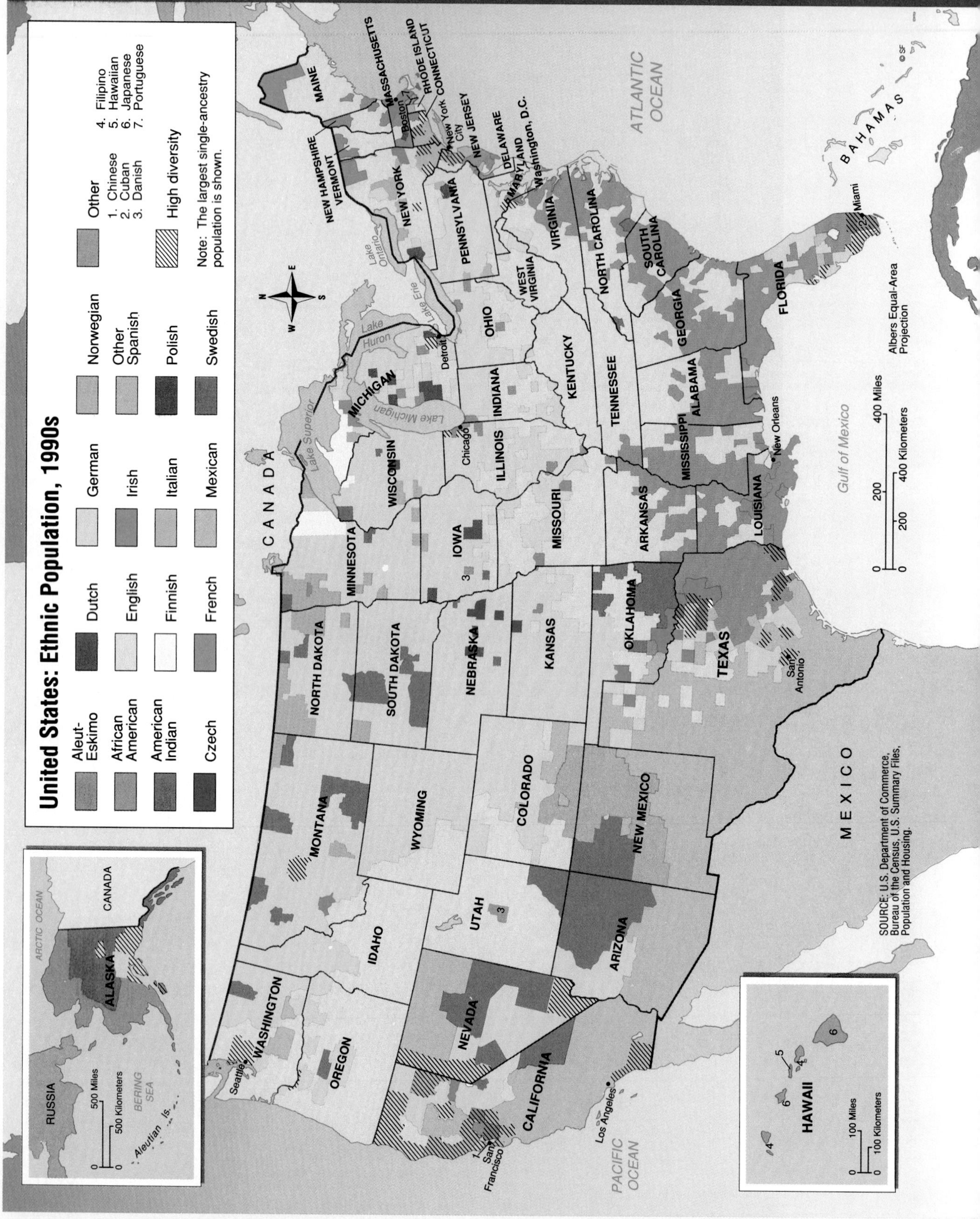

United States: Ethnic Population, 1990s

Legend:

- Aleut-Eskimo
- African American
- American Indian
- Czech
- Dutch
- English
- Finnish
- French
- German
- Irish
- Italian
- Mexican
- Norwegian
- Other Spanish
- Polish
- Swedish

Other
1. Chinese
2. Cuban
3. Danish
4. Filipino
5. Hawaiian
6. Japanese
7. Portuguese

High diversity

Note: The largest single-ancestry population is shown.

Labels on map:

CANADA

MAINE
NEW HAMPSHIRE
VERMONT
MASSACHUSETTS
Boston
RHODE ISLAND
CONNECTICUT
NEW YORK
New York City
NEW JERSEY
DELAWARE
MARYLAND
Washington, D.C.
PENNSYLVANIA
WEST VIRGINIA
VIRGINIA
NORTH CAROLINA
SOUTH CAROLINA
GEORGIA
FLORIDA
Miami
ALABAMA
MISSISSIPPI
LOUISIANA
New Orleans
TENNESSEE
KENTUCKY
OHIO
INDIANA
ILLINOIS
Chicago
MICHIGAN
Detroit
WISCONSIN
MINNESOTA
IOWA
MISSOURI
ARKANSAS
OKLAHOMA
TEXAS
San Antonio
NORTH DAKOTA
SOUTH DAKOTA
NEBRASKA
KANSAS
COLORADO
WYOMING
MONTANA
IDAHO
UTAH
NEVADA
ARIZONA
NEW MEXICO
CALIFORNIA
Los Angeles
San Francisco
SF
OREGON
WASHINGTON
Seattle

Lake Ontario
Lake Erie
Lake Huron
Lake Superior
Lake Michigan

ATLANTIC OCEAN
BAHAMAS
Gulf of Mexico
PACIFIC OCEAN
MEXICO

Albers Equal-Area Projection

400 Miles
400 Kilometers
200
200

Alaska inset:

ARCTIC OCEAN
RUSSIA
CANADA
ALASKA
BERING SEA
Aleutian Is.
500 Miles
500 Kilometers

Hawaii inset:

HAWAII
100 Miles
100 Kilometers

SOURCE: U.S. Department of Commerce, Bureau of the Census, U.S. Summary Files, Population and Housing.

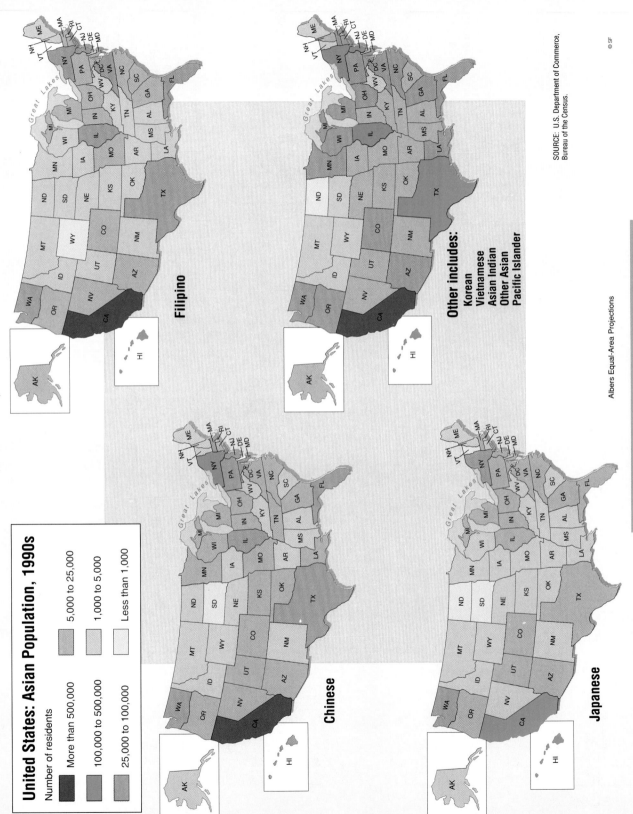

United States: Asian Population, 1990s

Number of residents

- More than 500,000
- 100,000 to 500,000
- 25,000 to 100,000
- 5,000 to 25,000
- 1,000 to 5,000
- Less than 1,000

Filipino

Chinese

Japanese

Other includes:
Korean
Vietnamese
Asian Indian
Other Asian
Pacific Islander

SOURCE: U.S. Department of Commerce, Bureau of the Census.

© SF

ATLAS

Albers Equal-Area Projections

United States: Membership in Christian Religions, 1990s

1. Roman Catholic Church — 57,020,000
2. Southern Baptist Convention — 14,908,000
3. United Methodist Church — 8,979,000
4. National Baptist Convention, U.S.A., Inc. — 5,500,000
5. Evangelical Lutheran — 5,239,000
6. Church of Jesus Christ of Latter-day Saints — 4,175,000
7. Church of God in Christ — 3,710,000
8. Presbyterian Church (U.S.A.) — 2,886,000
9. National Baptist Convention of America — 2,669,000
10. Lutheran Church—Missouri Synod — 2,609,000
11. Episcopal Church — 2,433,000
12. African Methodist Episcopal Church — 2,210,000
13. Assemblies of God — 2,138,000
14. Greek Orthodox Archdiocese of North and South America — 1,950,000
15. United Church of Christ — 1,626,000
16. Churches of Christ — 1,626,000
17. American Baptist Churches in the U.S.A. — 1,550,000
18. African Methodist Episcopal Zion Church — 1,220,260
19. Christian Church (Disciples of Christ) — 1,052,000
20. Christian Churches and Churches of Christ — 1,071,000
21. Orthodox Church in America — 1,000,000

United States: Membership in Non-Christian Religions, 1990s

1. Islam — 6,000,000
2. Judaism — 5,944,000
3. Bahai — 110,000
4. Buddhism — 19,000

United States: Religious Denominations, 1990s

Baptist
Catholic
Christian
Latter-day Saints
Lutheran
Methodist

Tint shows areas where a denomination includes at least 25% of reported church membership. When no denomination includes more than 25% of church membership, area is shown as white.

Albers Equal-Area Projections

SOURCE: *1991 Yearbook of American and Canadian Churches*

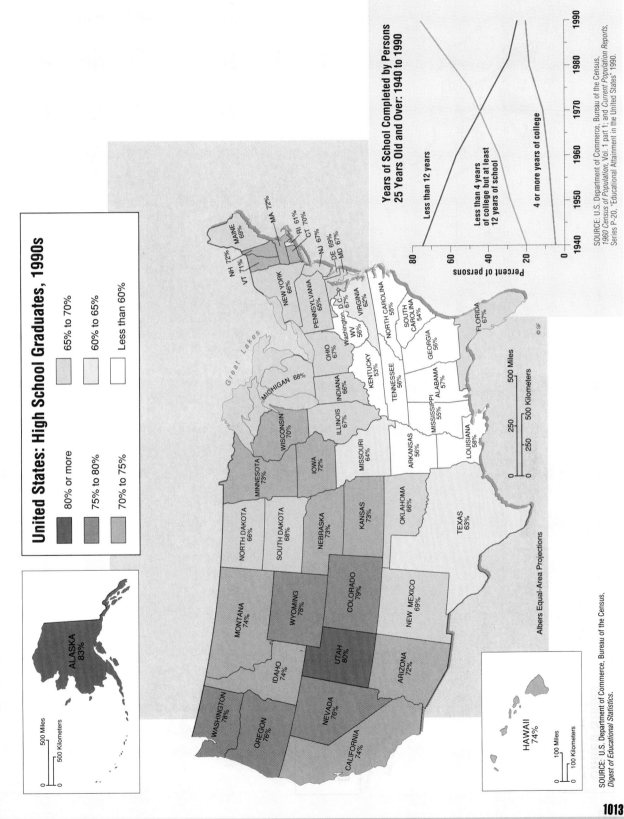

United States: High School Graduates, 1990s

- 80% or more
- 75% to 80%
- 70% to 75%
- 65% to 70%
- 60% to 65%
- Less than 60%

Years of School Completed by Persons 25 Years Old and Over: 1940 to 1990

Less than 12 years

Less than 4 years of college but at least 12 years of school

4 or more years of college

Percent of persons

1940 1950 1960 1970 1980 1990

SOURCE: U.S. Department of Commerce, Bureau of the Census, *1960 Census of Population*, Vol. 1 part 1; and *Current Population Reports*, Series P-20, "Educational Attainment in the United States" 1990.

ALASKA 83%

WASHINGTON 78%
OREGON 76%
CALIFORNIA 74%
NEVADA 76%
IDAHO 74%
MONTANA 74%
WYOMING 78%
UTAH 80%
ARIZONA 72%
COLORADO 79%
NEW MEXICO 69%
NORTH DAKOTA 66%
SOUTH DAKOTA 68%
NEBRASKA 73%
KANSAS 73%
OKLAHOMA 66%
TEXAS 63%
MINNESOTA 73%
IOWA 72%
WISCONSIN 70%
MICHIGAN 68%
ILLINOIS 67%
MISSOURI 64%
ARKANSAS 56%
LOUISIANA 58%
INDIANA 66%
KENTUCKY 53%
TENNESSEE 56%
MISSISSIPPI 55%
ALABAMA 57%
OHIO 67%
WV 56%
VIRGINIA 62%
NORTH CAROLINA 53%
SOUTH CAROLINA 54%
GEORGIA 56%
FLORIDA 67%
PENNSYLVANIA 65%
NEW YORK 66%
MAINE 69%
NH 72%
VT 71%
MA 72%
RI 61%
CT 70%
NJ 67%
DE 69%
MD 67%
Washington, D.C. 67%

Great Lakes

Albers Equal-Area Projections

© SF

0 250 500 Miles
0 250 500 Kilometers

HAWAII 74%

0 100 Miles
0 100 Kilometers

0 500 Miles
0 500 Kilometers

SOURCE: U.S. Department of Commerce, Bureau of the Census, *Digest of Educational Statistics*.

United States: World Trade, 1990

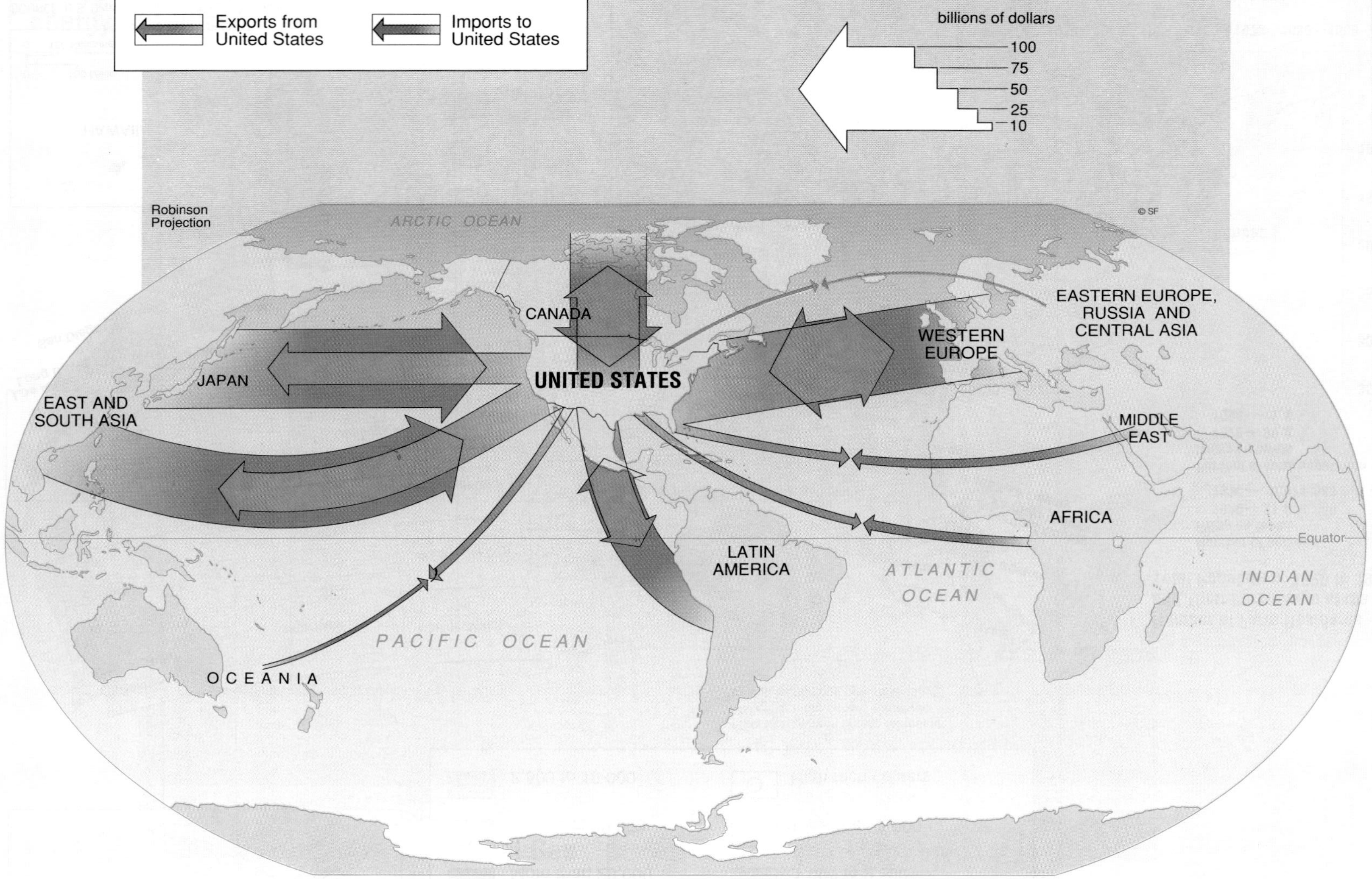

Exports from United States

Imports to United States

billions of dollars

100
75
50
25
10

Robinson Projection

© SF

ARCTIC OCEAN

EASTERN EUROPE, RUSSIA AND CENTRAL ASIA

WESTERN EUROPE

MIDDLE EAST

AFRICA

CANADA

UNITED STATES

LATIN AMERICA

ATLANTIC OCEAN

INDIAN OCEAN

Equator

PACIFIC OCEAN

JAPAN

EAST AND SOUTH ASIA

OCEANIA

SOURCE: U.S. Department of Commerce, Bureau of the Census, *Statistical Abstract of the United States.*

State	Origin of State Name	State Nickname	State Capital	Admitted to the Union	Population (1990)	Representatives in Congress (based on 1990 census)
❶ **Alabama**	tribe of the Creek confederacy	Yellowhammer State	Montgomery	1819	4,063,000	7
❷ **Alaska**	Russian version of Aleut word meaning "great land"	The Last Frontier	Juneau	1959	552,000	1
❸ **Arizona**	Spanish version of Pima word meaning "little spring place"	Grand Canyon State	Phoenix	1912	3,678,000	6
❹ **Arkansas**	French version of "Kansas," a Sioux word meaning "south wind people"	Land of Opportunity	Little Rock	1836	2,362,000	4
❺ **California**	mythical island paradise in Spanish literature	Golden State	Sacramento	1850	29,839,000	52
❻ **Colorado**	Spanish, "red"	Centennial State	Denver	1876	3,308,000	6
❼ **Connecticut**	Algonquin, "beside the long river"	Nutmeg State	Hartford	1788	3,296,000	6
❽ **Delaware**	honors Lord De La Warr, early governor of Virginia	Diamond State	Dover	1787	669,000	1
❾ **District of Columbia**	honors Columbus	—	—	—	610,000	1*
❿ **Florida**	Spanish, "feast of flowers"	Sunshine State	Tallahassee	1845	13,003,000	23
⓫ **Georgia**	honors King George II	Peach State	Atlanta	1788	6,508,000	11
⓬ **Hawaii**	Polynesian word for "homeland"	Aloha State	Honolulu	1959	1,115,000	2
⓭ **Idaho**	Shoshone, "salmon tribe" or "light on the mountains"	Gem State	Boise	1890	1,012,000	2
⓮ **Illinois**	Algonquin, "men" or "warriors"	Prairie State	Springfield	1818	11,467,000	20
⓯ **Indiana**	land of the Indians	Hoosier State	Indianapolis	1816	5,564,000	10
⓰ **Iowa**	Sioux, "beautiful land"	Hawkeye State	Des Moines	1846	2,787,000	5
⓱ **Kansas**	Sioux, "south wind people"	Sunflower State	Topeka	1861	2,486,000	4
⓲ **Kentucky**	Iroquois, "meadowland"	Bluegrass State	Frankfort	1792	3,699,000	6
⓳ **Louisiana**	honors Louis XIV of France	Pelican State	Baton Rouge	1812	4,238,000	7
⓴ **Maine**	after former French province of Mayne	Pine Tree State	Augusta	1820	1,233,000	2

*Committee voting only.

U.S. DATA BANK

Facts About the States

State	Origin of State Name	State Nickname	State Capital	Admitted to the Union	Population (1990)	Representatives in Congress (based on 1990 census)	
21 Maryland	honors Queen Henrietta Maria	Free State	Annapolis	1788	4,799,000	8	
22 Massachusetts	Algonquin, "large mountain place"	Bay State	Boston	1788	6,029,000	10	
23 Michigan	Chippewa, "great water"	Wolverine State	Lansing	1837	9,329,000	16	
24 Minnesota	Sioux, "sky-tinted water"	North Star State	St. Paul	1858	4,387,000	8	
25 Mississippi	Chippewa, "great river"	Magnolia State	Jackson	1817	2,586,000	5	
26 Missouri	tribe named after Missouri River, or "muddy water"	Show Me State	Jefferson City	1821	5,138,000	9	
27 Montana	Spanish, "mountainous"	Treasure State	Helena	1889	804,000	1	
28 Nebraska	Omaha name for Platte River, "broad river"	Cornhusker State	Lincoln	1867	1,585,000	3	
29 Nevada	Spanish "snow-clad"	Silver State	Carson City	1864	1,206,000	2	
30 New Hampshire	after English county of Hampshire	Granite State	Concord	1788	1,114,000	2	
31 New Jersey	after island of Jersey in English Channel	Garden State	Trenton	1787	7,749,000	13	
32 New Mexico	Aztec war god, "Mexitil"	Land of Enchantment	Santa Fe	1912	1,522,000	3	
33 New York	honors English Duke of York	Empire State	Albany	1788	18,045,000	31	
34 North Carolina	honors King Charles I	Tar Heel State	Raleigh	1789	6,658,000	12	
35 North Dakota	Sioux, "friend" or "ally"	Sioux State	Bismarck	1889	641,000	1	
36 Ohio	Iroquois, "beautiful river"	Buckeye State	Columbus	1803	10,887,000	19	
37 Oklahoma	Choctaw, "red people"	Sooner State	Oklahoma City	1907	3,158,000	6	
38 Oregon	Indian, "beautiful water"	Beaver State	Salem	1859	2,854,000	5	
39 Pennsylvania	honors Admiral William Penn, father of founder of colony	Keystone State	Harrisburg	1787	11,925,000	21	
40 Rhode Island	after Greek island of Rhodes	Ocean State	Providence	1790	1,006,000	2	
41 South Carolina	honors King Charles I	Palmetto State	Columbia	1788	3,506,000	6	
42 South Dakota	Sioux, "friend" or "ally"	Sunshine State	Pierre	1889	700,000	1	
43 Tennessee	name of Cherokee villages on the Little Tennessee River	Volunteer State	Nashville	1796	4,897,000	9	

State	Origin of State Name	State Nickname	State Capital	Admitted to the Union	Population (1990)	Representatives in Congress (based on 1990 census)
44 Texas	Caddo, "friendly tribe"	Lone Star State	Austin	1845	17,060,000	30
45 Utah	Navajo, "higher up," referring to the Utes	Beehive State	Salt Lake City	1896	1,728,000	3
46 Vermont	French, "green mountain"	Green Mountain State	Montpelier	1791	565,000	1
47 Virginia	honors "Virgin Queen" Elizabeth I	The Old Dominion	Richmond	1788	6,217,000	11
48 Washington	honors George Washington	Evergreen State	Olympia	1889	4,888,000	9
49 West Virginia	honors "Virgin Queen" Elizabeth I	Mountain State	Charleston	1863	1,802,000	3
50 Wisconsin	Chippewa, "grassy place"	Badger State	Madison	1848	4,907,000	9
51 Wyoming	Algonquin, "large prairie"; honors Wyoming Valley, Pennsylvania	Equality State	Cheyenne	1890	456,000	1

Rules for Displaying the American Flag

In a group of state and local flags.

With other flags on a halyard.

With another flag with crossed staffs.

1 The blue field (union) must always be at the top. The United States flag is always hoisted first and lowered last; no other flag should fly higher.

2 The flag should be on display on or near the main building of all public institutions. It should be displayed only from sunrise to sunset in good weather. An all-weather flag can be displayed in bad weather.

3 When the flag is raised or lowered during the national anthem, all present should face the flag and stand at attention with the right hand over the heart.

4 No disrespect should be shown the flag. It should not be dipped to honor any person or thing. It should never touch anything beneath it. Nothing should be placed on it, drawn on it, or attached to it.

Presidents of the United States

President	Party	State	Vice President	Term in Office
① George Washington Born: 1732 Died: 1799	None	Virginia	John Adams	1789–1797
② John Adams Born: 1735 Died: 1826	Federalist	Massachusetts	Thomas Jefferson	1797–1801
③ Thomas Jefferson Born: 1743 Died: 1826	Dem.–Rep.	Virginia	Aaron Burr George Clinton	1801–1809
④ James Madison Born: 1751 Died: 1836	Dem.–Rep.	Virginia	George Clinton Elbridge Gerry	1809–1817
⑤ James Monroe Born: 1758 Died: 1831	Dem.–Rep.	Virginia	Daniel D. Tompkins	1817–1825
⑥ John Quincy Adams Born: 1767 Died: 1848	Dem.–Rep.	Massachusetts	John C. Calhoun	1825–1829
⑦ Andrew Jackson Born: 1767 Died: 1845	Democrat	Tennessee (SC)*	John C. Calhoun Martin Van Buren	1829–1837
⑧ Martin Van Buren Born: 1782 Died: 1862	Democrat	New York	Richard M. Johnson	1837–1841
⑨ William Henry Harrison Born: 1773 Died: 1841	Whig	Ohio (VA)	John Tyler	1841
⑩ John Tyler Born: 1790 Died: 1862	Whig	Virginia		1841–1845
⑪ James K. Polk Born: 1795 Died: 1849	Democrat	Tennessee (NC)	George M. Dallas	1845–1849
⑫ Zachary Taylor Born: 1784 Died: 1850	Whig	Louisiana (VA)	Millard Fillmore	1849–1850
⑬ Millard Fillmore Born: 1800 Died: 1874	Whig	New York		1850–1853
⑭ Franklin Pierce Born: 1804 Died: 1869	Democrat	New Hampshire	William R. King	1853–1857
⑮ James Buchanan Born: 1791 Died: 1868	Democrat	Pennsylvania	John C. Breckinridge	1857–1861
⑯ Abraham Lincoln Born: 1809 Died: 1865	Republican	Illinois (KY)	Hannibal Hamlin Andrew Johnson	1861–1865
⑰ Andrew Johnson Born: 1808 Died: 1875	Democrat	Tennessee (NC)		1865–1869
⑱ Ulysses S. Grant Born: 1822 Died: 1885	Republican	Illinois (OH)	Schuyler Colfax Henry Wilson	1869–1877
⑲ Rutherford B. Hayes Born: 1822 Died: 1893	Republican	Ohio	William A. Wheeler	1877–1881
⑳ James A. Garfield Born: 1831 Died: 1881	Republican	Ohio	Chester A. Arthur	1881
㉑ Chester A. Arthur Born: 1829 Died: 1886	Republican	New York (VT)		1881–1885
㉒ Grover Cleveland Born: 1837 Died: 1908	Democrat	New York (NJ)	Thomas A. Hendricks	1885–1889

*State of residence at time of election. If state of birth is different, it is shown in parentheses.

	President	Party	State	Vice President	Term in Office	
㉓	**Benjamin Harrison** Born: 1833 Died: 1901	Republican	Indiana (OH)	Levi P. Morton	1889–1893	
㉔	**Grover Cleveland** Born: 1837 Died: 1908	Democrat	New York (NJ)	Adlai E. Stevenson	1893–1897	
㉕	**William McKinley** Born: 1843 Died: 1901	Republican	Ohio	Garret A. Hobart Theodore Roosevelt	1897–1901	
㉖	**Theodore Roosevelt** Born: 1858 Died: 1919	Republican	New York	Charles W. Fairbanks*	1901–1909	
㉗	**William H. Taft** Born: 1857 Died: 1930	Republican	Ohio	James S. Sherman	1909–1913	
㉘	**Woodrow Wilson** Born: 1856 Died: 1924	Democrat	New Jersey (VA)	Thomas R. Marshall	1913–1921	
㉙	**Warren G. Harding** Born: 1865 Died: 1923	Republican	Ohio	Calvin Coolidge	1921–1923	
㉚	**Calvin Coolidge** Born: 1872 Died: 1933	Republican	Massachusetts (VT)	Charles G. Dawes*	1923–1929	
㉛	**Herbert C. Hoover** Born: 1874 Died: 1964	Republican	California (IA)	Charles Curtis	1929–1933	
㉜	**Franklin D. Roosevelt** Born: 1882 Died: 1945	Democrat	New York	John Nance Garner Henry A. Wallace Harry S. Truman	1933–1945	
㉝	**Harry S. Truman** Born: 1884 Died: 1972	Democrat	Missouri	Alben W. Barkley*	1945–1953	
㉞	**Dwight D. Eisenhower** Born: 1890 Died: 1969	Republican	New York (TX)	Richard M. Nixon	1953–1961	
㉟	**John F. Kennedy** Born: 1917 Died: 1963	Democrat	Massachusetts	Lyndon B. Johnson	1961–1963	
㊱	**Lyndon B. Johnson** Born: 1908 Died: 1973	Democrat	Texas	Hubert Humphrey*	1963–1969	
㊲	**Richard M. Nixon** Born: 1913	Republican	New York (CA)	Spiro T. Agnew Gerald R. Ford	1969–1974	
㊳	**Gerald R. Ford** Born: 1913	Republican	Michigan (NE)	Nelson A. Rockefeller	1974–1977	
㊴	**James Carter** Born: 1924	Democrat	Georgia	Walter Mondale	1977–1981	
㊵	**Ronald Reagan** Born: 1911	Republican	California (IL)	George Bush	1981–1989	
㊶	**George Bush** Born: 1924	Republican	Texas (MA)	J. Danforth Quayle	**1989–1993**	
㊷	**William Jefferson Clinton** Born: 1946	Democrat	Arkansas	Albert Gore, Jr.	1993–	

*Served during second term only.

Charts, Graphs, Tables

IMPORTS/EXPORTS, 1790–1990

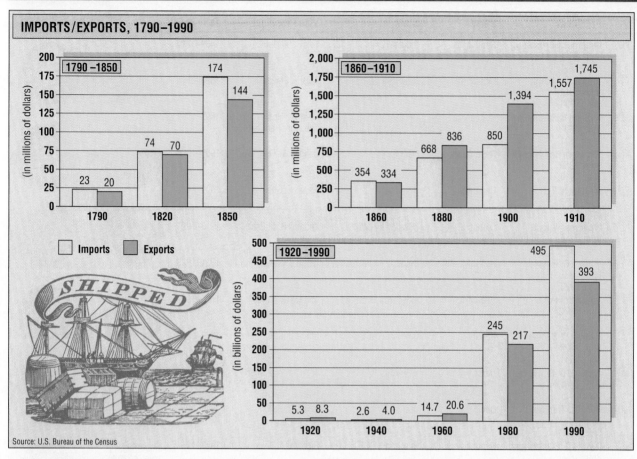

1790–1850 (in millions of dollars)

	1790	1820	1850
Imports	23	74	174
Exports	20	70	144

1860–1910 (in millions of dollars)

	1860	1880	1900	1910
Imports	354	668	850	1,557
Exports	334	836	1,394	1,745

Imports ☐   **Exports** ▨

1920–1990 (in billions of dollars)

	1920	1940	1960	1980	1990
Imports	5.3	2.6	14.7	245	495
Exports	8.3	4.0	20.6	217	393

Source: U.S. Bureau of the Census

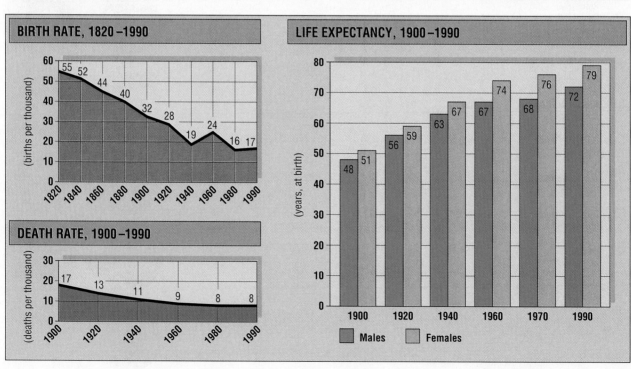

BIRTH RATE, 1820–1990

(births per thousand)

1820	1840	1860	1880	1900	1920	1940	1960	1980	1990
55	52	44	40	32	28	19	24	16	17

DEATH RATE, 1900–1990

(deaths per thousand)

1900	1920	1940	1960	1980	1990
17	13	11	9	8	8

LIFE EXPECTANCY, 1900–1990

(years, at birth)

	1900	1920	1940	1960	1970	1990
Males	48	56	63	67	68	72
Females	51	59	67	74	76	79

Males ▨   **Females** ▨

RETAIL PRICES OF SELECTED FOODS, 1890-1990

Year	Flour per lb.	Milk per gal.	Bread per lb.	Eggs per doz.	Steak per lb.	Potatoes per lb.	Sugar per lb.	Coffee per lb.
1990	$.25	$2.78	$.70	$1.00	$3.42	$.32	$.43	$2.94
1980		$2.10	$.51	$.84		$.18	$.35	
1970	$.12	$1.32	$.24	$.61	$1.30	$.09	$.13	$.91
1960	$.11	$1.04	$.20	$.57	$1.06	$.07	$.12	$.75
1950	$.10	$.84	$.14	$.60	$.94	$.05	$.10	$.79
1940	$.04	$.51	$.08	$.33	$.36	$.02	$.05	$.21
1930	$.05	$.56	$.07	$.45	$.43	$.04	$.06	$.40
1920	$.08	$.67	$.12	$.68	$.40	$.06	$.19	$.47
1910	$.04	$.34		$.34	$.17	$.02	$.06	
1900	$.03	$.27		$.21	$.13	$.01	$.06	
1890	$.03	$.27		$.21	$.12	$.02	$.07	

WHOLESALE PRICES OF SELECTED GOODS, 1800-1990

Year	Wool per lb.	Cotton fabric per yard	Nails per lb.	Bricks per 1,000	Coal per ton
1990	$.85				$22.00
1980	$.88				$26.29
1970	$1.03				$16.57
1960	$1.16	$.22	$.10		$13.95
1950	$1.98	$.26	$.06	$25.67	$12.58
1940	$.97	$.09	$.03	$12.13	$9.55
1930	$.76	$.11	$.02	$10.10	$12.72
1920	$1.60	$.29	$.04	$21.85	$9.50
1910	$.67	$.08	$.02	$5.72	$4.81
1900	$.66	$.06	$.03	$5.25	$3.92
1890	$.72	$.07	$.03	$6.56	$3.35
1880	$1.03	$.08	$.04	$6.94	$4.53
1870	$.90	$.14	$.04	$8.40	$4.39
1860	$1.03	$.08	$.03	$4.49	$3.40
1850	$.83	$.07	$.04	$4.85	$3.64
1840	$.39		$.06		$4.91
1830	$.39		$.06		$9.05
1820	$.75		$.10		
1810			$.10		
1800			$.11		

Source: U.S. Bureau of the Census

Highlights of American Culture

① Cotton's moral guide *Milk for Babes*, 1646

② A page from *Codex Mendoza* (Aztec)

Literature

- **Native American** oral tradition of poems and tales and songs
- **1100s–1500s** **Aztec and Maya codices** (folded manuscript pages protected by a cover) concerning religious ceremonies and astrology
- **1608** **John Smith**, *A True Relation* (first English book written in America)
- **1616** **John Smith**, *A Description of New England*
- **1640** **John Cotton, Richard Mather**, et al., *Bay Psalm Book* (first work printed in the colonies)
- **1650** **Anne Bradstreet**, *The Tenth Muse*
- **1656** **William Bradford**, *History of Plimmoth Plantation*
- **1693** **Cotton Mather**, *The Wonders of the Invisible World*

Music and the Stage

- **Native American** traditional music and dancing, with voices accompanied by drums and rattles
- **1500s–1800s** **African American** folk singing and ceremonial ecstatic dancing, mostly on plantations
- **1640** **John Cotton, Richard Mather**, et al., *Bay Psalm Book* (psalm verses to be used with pre-existing tunes of the day)

The Old Plantation depicts a banjo, an instrument of African American origin from the 1600s.

Visual Arts

- **100BC** **Olmec sculptor**, *Wrestler*
- **1400s** **Aztec sculptor** creates *Coatlicue* (goddess of Earth and Death),
- **1670** **The Mason Limner**, *The Mason Children*

① Olmec carved head, 1500-800 B.C.

② Detail from Maya wall mural, "Maya Lords," Bonampac, Mexico, A.D. 300-900

Architecture

- **1000s** **Maya architects** build the Temple of the Warriors, Chichen Itza, Yucatan
- **1100s** **Anasazi architects** build the Cliff Palace, Mesa Verde, Colorado
- **1500s** **Church of Santo Domingo** built in Oaxaca, Mexico
- **1683** **Parson Capen House,** Topsfield, Massachusetts

Cliff Palace, Mesa Verde, Colorado, 1100s

▶ **Pre-Columbian**

- 1733 **Benjamin Franklin**, *Poor Richard's Almanack* (first installment)
- 1738 **William Byrd II**, *History of the Dividing Line*
- 1741 **Jonathan Edwards**, *Sinners in the Hands of an Angry God*

Cover sheet of first edition of *Sinners in the Hands of an Angry God*

- 1771 **Benjamin Franklin**, *Autobiography* (begun)
- 1773 **Phillis Wheatley**, *Poems on Various Subjects, Religious and Moral*
- 1776 **Thomas Paine**, *Common Sense*
- 1776 **Thomas Jefferson**, et al., *The Declaration of Independence*
- 1788 **Alexander Hamilton, James Madison, and John Jay**, *The Federalist*
- 1794 **Thomas Paine**, *The Age of Reason*

- 1720s **Singing-schools** flourish in New England, and the first publication of sacred tunebooks occurs
- 1735 **The first opera** heard in America, *Flora, or Hob in the Well,* is staged in Charleston, South Carolina

- 1761 **Benjamin Franklin** invents an improved version of the armonica, an instrument making use of glass bowls
- 1767 **Anonymous**, "Yankee Doodle" (earliest known appearance of the song)
- 1790 English-born **Alexander Reinagle** writes four piano sonatas, the first piano pieces composed in America

Dancing and musical performance in the 1700s

- 1721 **Anonymous** *Anne Pollard*
- 1723 **Pieter Vanderlyn**, *Mrs. Petrus Vas*
- 1725 **Anonymous**, *Pau de Wandelaer*

Anonymous, *Anne Pollard*, 1721

- 1765 **Matthew Pratt**, *The American School*
- 1765 **John Singleton Copley**, *Henry Pelham (Boy with a Squirrel)*
- 1770 **Benjamin West**, *The Death of General Wolfe*
- 1793 **Gilbert Stuart**, *Mrs. Richard Yates*

John Singleton Copley, *Henry Pelham*, 1765

- 1720 **Governor's Palace**, Williamsburg, Virginia
- 1734 **Westover**, Charles City County, Virginia
- 1731-1753 **Edmund Woolley** and Andrew Hamilton, The State House (Independence Hall), Philadelphia
- 1750 **Royall House**, Medford, Massachusetts

- 1792 **James Hoban**, The White House, Washington, D.C.
- 1797 **San Xavier del Bac**, near Tucson, Arizona
- 1798 **Charles Bulfinch**, State House, Boston, Massachusetts

San Xavier del Bac, near Tucson. Arizona, 1797

▶ **1700**

▶ **1750**

Highlights of American Culture

Literature

- 1819 **Washington Irving,** *The Sketch Book*
- 1826 **James Fenimore Cooper,** *The Last of the Mohicans*
- 1836 **Oliver Wendell Holmes,** *Poems*
- 1841 **Ralph Waldo Emerson,** *Essays*
- 1845 **Frederick Douglass,** *Narrative of the Life of Frederick Douglass*
- 1845 **Edgar Allan Poe,** *The Raven and Other Poems*

  ① Frederick Douglass, circa 1845

  ② A caricature of Poe and his famous raven

① ②

Music and the Stage

- 1814 **Francis Scott Key,** "The Star Spangled Banner"
- 1817 Czech-born **Anthony Philip Heinrich** conducts, in Lexington, Kentucky, the first known performance in America of a Beethoven symphony
- 1820 **Heinrich** composes *The Dawning of Music in Kentucky*, a collection of songs and instrumental pieces, and becomes the first "professional" composer in America
- 1831 **Samuel Smith,** "America" (to an English melody)
- 1837 **James Sanderson** (music) and **Sir Walter Scott** (words), "Hail to the Chief"
- 1843 **Uncertain,** "Columbia, the Gem of the Ocean"
- 1848 **Stephen Foster,** "Oh, Susanna"

Visual Arts

- 1823 **Raphaelle Peale,** *After the Bath*
- 1830s **John James Audubon publishes** *The Birds of America*
- 1835 **Hiram Powers,** *Andrew Jackson,* sculpture
- 1845 **George Caleb Bingham,** *Fur Traders on the Missouri*

  ① John James Audubon, *Carolina Parroquet*, 1825

  ② George Caleb Bingham, *The Trappers' Return*, 1851

① ②

Architecture

- 1805 **Benjamin Latrobe,** Catholic Cathedral, Baltimore, Maryland
- 1817-1826 **Thomas Jefferson,** The University of Virginia, Charlottesville
- 1828 **James Bucklin and Russell Warren,** Providence Arcade, Providence, Rhode Island

  Thomas Jefferson, The University of Virginia, Charlottesville, 1817-1826

▶ **1800**

- 1850 **Nathaniel Hawthorne,** *The Scarlet Letter*
- 1851 **Herman Melville,** *Moby Dick*
- 1852 **Harriet Beecher Stowe,** *Uncle Tom's Cabin*
- 1854 **Henry David Thoreau,** *Walden*
- 1855 **Walt Whitman,** *Complete Poems and Prose*
- 1863 **Henry Wadsworth Longfellow,** *Tales of a Wayside Inn*
- 1868 **Louisa May Alcott,** *Little Women*
- 1877 **Henry James,** *The American*
- 1884 **Mark Twain,** *The Adventures of Huckleberry Finn*
- 1890 **Emily Dickinson,** *Poems*
- 1895 **Stephen Crane,** *The Red Badge of Courage*
- 1896 **Paul Laurence Dunbar,** *Lyrics of Lowly Life*

Harriet Beecher Stowe, circa 1852

Illustration from the first edition of *The Adventures of Huckleberry Finn*

- 1850 **Louis Moreau Gottschalk** writes several syncopated piano works that anticipate ragtime and jazz
- 1859 **Dan Emmett,** "Dixie"
- 1861 **Julia Ward Howe,** "The Battle Hymn of the Republic" (to a tune from an early hymn)
- 1863 **Patrick Gilmore,** "When Johnny Comes Marching Home"
- 1867 Publication of ***Slave Songs of the United States***
- 1870s The Jubilee Singers of Fisk University popularize **black spirituals**
- 1894 New Orleans cornetist **Buddy Bolden** forms his first musical group, and the dawn of jazz begins
- 1896 **John Philip Sousa,** "The Stars and Stripes Forever"
- 1899 **Scott Joplin,** "Maple Leaf Rag"
  The "Maple Leaf Rag" sold 400 copies in its first months of publication but 500,000 by 1909

- 1860 **Frederic E. Church,** *Twilight in the Wilderness*
- 1868 **Albert Bierstadt,** *Western Landscape with Lake and Mountains*
- 1875 **Thomas Eakins,** *The Gross Clinic*
- 1884-1896 **Augustus Saint-Gaudens,** *Robert Gould Shaw Memorial,* monument
- 1886 **Winslow Homer,** *Eight Bells*
- 1890 **Childe Hassam,** *Washington Arch, Spring,* 1890
- 1892 **Mary Cassatt,** *The Bath*
- 1893 **Henry Ossawa Tanner,** *The Banjo Lesson*

  ❶ Henry Ossawa Tanner, *The Banjo Lesson,* 1893

  ❷ Mary Cassatt, *The Bath,* 1892

  ❸ Thomas Eakins, *The Gross Clinic,* 1875

❶

❷

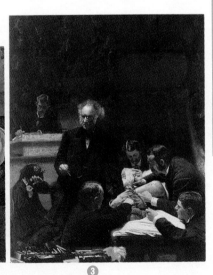
❸

- 1865 **P.B. Wight,** National Academy of Design, New York City
- 1887 **H.H. Richardson,** Allegheny County Courthouse and Gaol, Pittsburgh, Pennsylvania
- 1889 **Louis Sullivan,** Auditorium Building, Chicago, Illinois
- 1894 **Burnham and Root,** Reliance Building, Chicago, Illinois
  Louis Sullivan, Auditorium Building, Chicago, 1889

 1850

Highlights of American Culture

Literature

- 1903 **Jack London,** *The Call of the Wild*
- 1906 **Upton Sinclair,** *The Jungle*
- 1911 **Edith Wharton,** *Ethan Frome*
- 1916 **Carl Sandburg,** *Chicago Poems*
- 1925 **F. Scott Fitzgerald,** *The Great Gatsby*
- 1930 **Robert Frost,** *Collected Poems*
- 1931 **Pearl S. Buck,** *The Good Earth*
- 1938 **Thornton Wilder,** *Our Town*
- 1939 **John Steinbeck,** *The Grapes of Wrath*
- 1940 **Richard Wright,** *Native Son*
- 1945 **Tennessee Williams,** *The Glass Menagerie*
- 1949 **Arthur Miller,** *The Death of a Salesman*

Tennessee Williams, self-portrait, 1947

Music and the Stage

- 1906 **Charles Ives,** *The Unanswered Question* for Orchestra
- 1911 **Irving Berlin,** "Alexander's Ragtime Band"
- 1917 **George M. Cohan,** "Over There"
- 1920s **Gospel music** appears in African American churches
- 1922 **Louis Armstrong** joins King Oliver's jazz band
- 1924 **George Gershwin,** *Rhapsody in Blue* for Jazz Band
- 1927 **Jerome Kern,** *Show Boat* (musical)
- 1927 **Duke Ellington's** jazz band sets up in New York
- 1930 **William Grant Still,** *Afro-American Symphony*
- 1931 **Ferde Grofé,** *Grand Canyon Suite* for Orchestra
- 1935 **George Gershwin,** *Porgy and Bess* (opera)
- 1943 **Richard Rodgers,** *Oklahoma!* (musical)
- 1944 **Aaron Copland,** *Appalachian Spring* (ballet)
- 1948 **Cole Porter,** *Kiss Me, Kate* (musical)

❶ "Ko Ko" — a jazz bebop-style hit of 1945

❷ Berlin's 1921 hit song, "All By Myself"

Visual Arts

- 1902 **John Singer Sargent,** *William Merritt Chase*
- 1909 **George Bellows,** *Stag at Sharkey's*
- 1913 The **"Armory Show,"** New York City
- 1914 **Marsden Hartley,** *Portrait of a German Officer*
- 1915 **D.W. Griffith,** *The Birth of a Nation,* motion picture
- 1918 **Joseph Stella,** *Brooklyn Bridge*
- 1927 **Georgia O'Keeffe,** *Radiator Building—Night*
- 1930s **Dorothea Lange** photographs migrant families
- 1931 **Stuart Davis,** *Garage Lights*
- 1939 **Alexander Calder,** *Lobster Trap and Fish Tails,* mobile
- 1941 **Jacob Lawrence,** *Migration of the Negro*
- 1941 **Orson Welles,** *Citizen Kane,* motion picture
- 1942 **Edward Hopper,** *Nighthawks*

❶ Stuart Davis, *Garage Lights,* 1931

❷ Orson Welles in *Citizen Kane,* 1941

❸ Jacob Lawrence, *Migration of the Negro.* 1941

❹ Joseph Stella, *Brooklyn Bridge,* 1918

Architecture

- 1909 **Frank Lloyd Wright,** Robie House, Chicago, Illinois
- 1913 **Cass Gilbert,** Woolworth Building, New York City
- 1939 **Frank Lloyd Wright,** S.C. Johnson and Son Company Administration Building, Racine, Wisconsin

Frank Lloyd Wright, Robie House, 1909

1900

- 1951 **J.D. Salinger,** *The Catcher in the Rye*
- 1952 **Ralph Ellison,** *Invisible Man*
- 1952 **Ernest Hemingway,** *The Old Man and the Sea*
- 1953 **James Baldwin,** *Go Tell It on the Mountain*
- 1954 **E.E. Cummings,** *Poems: 1923-1954*
- 1955 **Frances Goodrich and Albert Hackett,** *The Diary of Anne Frank*
- 1957 **William Gibson,** *The Miracle Worker*
- 1959 **Langston Hughes,** *Selected Poems*
- 1959 **Lorraine Hansberry,** *A Raisin in the Sun*
- 1960 **Harper Lee,** *To Kill a Mockingbird*
- 1961 **Joseph Heller,** *Catch-22*
- 1966 **Truman Capote,** *In Cold Blood*

- 1968 **Gwendolyn Brooks,** *In the Mecca*
- 1969 **N. Scott Momaday,** *The Way to Rainy Mountain*
- 1969 **Kurt Vonnegut, Jr.,** *Slaughterhouse-Five*
- 1970 **Maya Angelou,** *I Know Why the Caged Bird Sings*
- 1971 **Ernest Gaines,** *The Autobiography of Miss Jane Pittman*
- 1976 **Alex Haley,** *Roots*
- 1980 **Eudora Welty,** *The Collected Stories*
- 1981 **Sylvia Plath,** *The Collected Poems* (posthumous)
- 1982 **Alice Walker,** *The Color Purple*
- 1989 **Amy Tan,** *The Joy Luck Club*
- 1990 **Gary Soto,** *Baseball in April and Other Stories*
- 1993 **Tony Kushner,** *Angels in America*

- 1952 Disc jockey **Alan Freed** claims to have coined the phase "rock-and-roll" on the air in Cleveland
- 1952 First public concert of electroacoustic music
- 1953 **Big Mama Thornton** introduces "Hound Dog," a song made popular by Elvis Presley three years later
- 1956 **Frederick Loewe,** *My Fair Lady* (musical)
- 1957 **Leonard Bernstein,** *West Side Story* (musical)
- 1963 **Bob Dylan,** "Blowin' in the Wind"
- 1964 **Jerry Herman,** *Hello, Dolly!* (musical)
- 1967 **Galt MacDermott,** *Hair* (musical)
- 1969 Jazz-rock evolves from trumpeter **Miles Davis'** experiments with electronic instruments
- 1969 Nearly half-a-million attend a three-day counter-culture **Woodstock Music and Arts Festival** in rural New York

- 1975 **Charlie Smalls,** *The Wiz* (musical)
- 1975 **Marvin Hamlisch,** *A Chorus Line* (musical)
- 1976 **Philip Glass,** *Einstein on the Beach* (opera)
- 1983 **Ellen Zwilich** first woman to win Pulitzer in music
- 1987 **John Adams,** *Nixon in China* (opera)
- 1990 **Grand Ole Opry** broadcasts 65th straight year
- 1992 **William Bolcom,** *McTeague* (opera)

- 1950 **Jackson Pollock,** *Autumn Rhythm*
- 1952 **Willem De Kooning,** *Woman I*
- 1958 **Jasper Johns,** *Three Flags*
- 1959 **Robert Rauschenberg,** *Monogram*
- 1963 **Louise Nevelson,** *Tide I Tide,* sculpture
- 1964 **David Smith,** *Cubi XXI,* sculpture
- 1965 **Andy Warhol,** *Four Campbell's Soup Cans*
- 1967 **Helen Frankenthaler,** *Flood*
- 1970 **Robert Smithson,** *Spiral Jetty*
- 1972 **Francis Ford Coppola,** *The Godfather,* motion picture
- 1975 **Frank Stella,** *Montenegro I,* construction
- 1992 **Clint Eastwood,** *Unforgiven,* motion picture

① David Smith, *The Letter,* 1950

② Andy Warhol, *Four Campbell's Soup Cans,* 1965

③ Marlon Brando in *The Godfather,* 1972

- 1958 **Mies van der Rohe and Philip Johnson,** Seagram Building, New York City
- 1959 **Frank Lloyd Wright,** Solomon R. Guggenheim Museum, New York City
- 1962 **Eero Saarinen,** Dulles International Airport, near Washington, D.C.
- 1978 **I.M. Pei,** National Gallery of Art Addition, Washington D.C.
- 1982 **Michael Graves,** Portland Building, Portland, Oregon
- 1982 **Philip Johnson and John Burgee,** A.T.&T. Building, New York City
- 1987 **Helmut Jahn,** United Airlines Terminal, Chicago

Michael Graves, Portland Building, Portland, Oregon

1950-Present

Biographical Dictionary

A

Abernathy, Ralph (1926-1990), African American civil rights leader and close associate of Reverend Dr. Martin Luther King, Jr., helped organize various civil rights protests. Headed the Southern Christian Leadership Conference after Dr. King's death. (p. 754)

Acheson, Dean (1893-1971), U.S. government official. Undersecretary of state (1945-1947); secretary of state (1949-1953). A major architect of U.S. foreign policy after World War II. Helped develop the Truman Doctrine (1947), the Marshall Plan (1948), and the North Atlantic Treaty Organization (NATO) in 1949. A strong anticommunist, Acheson advocated a policy of containment and the strengthening of the U.S. nuclear arsenal. (p. 679)

Adams, John Quincy (1767-1848), sixth U.S. president (1825-1829). Son of John Adams. Helped negotiate peace with Britain after War of 1812 (1814). Negotiated treaty with Spain which secured Florida (1819). Evolved principles of Monroe Doctrine (1823) and helped establish Smithsonian Institution. After his presidency he served in the House of Representatives (1831-1848). (p. 166)

Adams, Samuel (1722-1803), U.S. revolutionary leader who led protests against the Stamp Act and helped organize the Sons of Liberty, the Nonimportation Association, and the Massachusetts Committee of Correspondence. Led the Boston Tea Party and signed the Declaration of Independence. (p. 62)

Jane Addams

Addams, Jane (1860-1935), American social worker who founded Hull House settlement house in Chicago (1889). Named chairman of Woman's Peace party and president of International Congress of Women at The Hague (1915). Shared Nobel Peace Prize (1931). (p. 308)

Agnew, Spiro (1918-), U.S. vice president (1969-1973). Governor of Maryland (1967-1969). As governor and vice president, accepted bribes from contractors for helping them get state business in Maryland. Charged with income tax evasion and resigned from vice presidency (1973). (p. 840)

Aguinaldo [ä gē näl ´ dō], **Emilio** [ä mē ´ lyō] (1869-1964), leader of the Philippine independence movement against U.S. rule. After his capture in March 1901 he swore allegiance to the United States and helped pacify the Philippines. (p. 394)

Allende [ä yän ´ dā], **Salvador** (1908-1973), Chilean political leader elected to the presidency in 1970. An acknowledged Marxist, he was deposed in a right-wing military coup in 1973 during which he was either assassinated or committed suicide. (p. 879)

Anderson, John (1922-), U.S. political figure. Representative to Congress from Illinois. Ran as a moderate independent Republican candidate for president in the 1980 presidential election. Received 7 percent of popular vote. (p. 922)

Susan B. Anthony

Anthony, Susan B. (1820-1906), U.S. feminist. Major figure in women's rights movement between 1850 and 1906. Organized conventions and campaigns for petitions, raised money, organized National Woman Suffrage Association (1869) and served as its president. (p. 299)

Armstrong, Louis (1900?-1971), African American jazz musician called "Satchmo." Led his own jazz band in Chicago during the 1920s and later organized a "big band." Appeared in movies and on television. (p. 511)

Austin, Stephen F. (1793-1836), U.S. army officer. Founded American settlements in Texas (1821). Imprisoned in Mexico City (1833-1834) because he called for Texas independence. Secretary of state for Republic of Texas (1836). (p. 175)

B

Baker, Ella (1905-1986), U.S. civil rights activist. Leader in social reform movement from the 1930s. In 1960s she encouraged African American students to form their own organization, independent from that of Martin Luther King, Jr. Result was establishment of Student Nonviolent Coordinating Committee (SNCC) in April 1960. (p. 759)

Emilio Aguinaldo

Baraka [bä rä ´ kä], **Amiri** [ä mir ´ ē] (1934-), U.S. playwright. A leader of the Black Arts movement of 1960s and 1970s. He changed his name from LeRoi Jones as an expression of black pride. Wrote plays including *Slave Ship* (1969), a novel, *The Systems of Dante's Hell* (1965), and poems including *Selected Poetry of Amiri Baraka/LeRoi Jones* (1979). (p. 775)

Barton, Clara (1821-1912), U.S. army nurse. Organized medical supplies and hospitals during Civil War. Called the "Angel of the Battlefield." Founded American Red Cross (1881). (p. 231)

Baruch, Bernard (1870-1965), U.S. businessman and statesman. During World War I, headed War Industries Board, which greatly increased America's industrial production. Appointed U.S. representative to United Nations Atomic Energy Commission (1946). (p. 430)

Beauregard [bō ´ rə gärd], **P. G. T.** (1818-1893), U.S. Army and Confederate general who fired upon Fort Sumter, opening the Civil War. Also commanded at 1st Bull Run, Shiloh, and Petersburg. (p. 222)

Beecher, Lyman (1775-1863), U.S. clergyman. Father of writer Harriet Beecher Stowe (*Uncle Tom's Cabin*) and preacher Henry Ward Beecher. (p. 171)

Begin [bā ´ gin], **Menachem** [me nä ´ kem] (1913-1992), Israeli political leader. Prime minister of Israel (1977-1983). Signed Camp David Accords with Egypt, paving way for peace treaty between Egypt and Israel (1979). Shared Nobel Peace Prize for his efforts to end Arab-Israeli conflict (1978). (p. 918)

Mary McLeod Bethune

Bethune [bə thün ´], **Mary McLeod** (1875-1955), African American educator. President of Bethune-Cookman College. Founded National Council for Negro Women (1935). Appointed director of Division of Negro Affairs in National Youth Administration (1936), where she worked for better educational, recreational, and employment opportunities for African Americans. (p. 575)

Beveridge, Albert (1862-1927), Republican senator from Indiana (1899-1911) and leading progressive. Drafted Meat Inspection Act (1906), favored legislation against child labor, and supported conservation of natural resources. An expansionist, Beveridge argued in favor of an American empire and a strong, modern navy. (p. 391)

Blackwell, Elizabeth (1821-1910), U.S. physician. First U.S. woman to receive a medical degree. Established the New York Infirmary for Women and Children in 1857. Organized a training program for army nurses during the Civil War. Founded medical college for women at the New York Infirmary in 1868. (p. 231)

Blackwell, Henry (1825-1909), U.S. political activist. Founded American Woman Suffrage Association (1869) with his wife, Lucy Stone. Organization focused on goal of obtaining political rights for women. (p. 300)

Bonaparte, Napoleon (1769-1821), French military leader and emperor of France (1804). Led successful battles using huge armies and complicated military maneuvers. Dominated Europe by 1807. Finally defeated by British at Waterloo, Belgium, in 1815. Napoleon's rule changed the course of European history. Sold Louisiana to the United States (1803) and directed naval conflicts that led to War of 1812 between the United States and Britain. (p. 118)

Brezhnev [brezh ′ nef], **Leonid** [lā ô nyĕt ′] (1906-1982), Soviet political leader. General secretary of Soviet Communist party (1964 to 1982); president of Soviet Union (1977 to 1982). (p. 801)

Bruce, Blanche K. (1841-1898), U.S. politician. Former slave. First African American elected to U.S. Senate for a full term (1875-1881, from Mississippi). (p. 240)

Bryan, William Jennings (1860-1925), U.S. political leader. Democratic party leader (1896-1912). His "Cross of Gold" speech (1896) won him the presidential nomination in 1896, but Bryan lost the election to William McKinley. As secretary of state (1913-1915), followed policy of strict neutrality after outbreak of World War I. Prosecuted John T. Scopes, Tennessee teacher indicted for violating state law against teaching of evolution (1925). (p. 316)

Buchanan, James (1791-1868), 15th U.S. president (1857-1861). Supported Supreme Court's Dred Scott decision. Remembered chiefly as president in office when seven southern states seceded. Supported Union but did little to keep it together. (p. 188)

Burger, Warren (1907-), U.S. Supreme Court chief justice (1969-1986); appointed by Richard Nixon in attempt to steer the court in a more conservative direction. As chief justice, he generally favored rights of society over rights of individuals but took more liberal stand than expected with regard to civil rights. (p. 865)

Bush, George (1924-), 41st U.S. president (1989-1993). Served in U.S. House of Representatives (Texas, 1966-1970); ambassador to United Nations; director of the CIA; chairman of Republican National Committee. U.S. vice president (1981-1989). (p. 947)

C

Calhoun, John C. (1782-1850), U.S. political leader from South Carolina. Champion of slavery and states' rights; developed nullification doctrine. Vice president (1825-1832); resigned from office because of his dispute with President Jackson over nullification. (p. 167)

Calley, William (1943-), U.S. soldier. Commander of the operation that resulted in the My Lai massacre in Vietnam. Tried and convicted for committing atrocities. (p. 832)

Calvert, Cecilius (1605-1675), U.S. colonial leader. Son of George Calvert. Established colony of Maryland in 1632. Tried to provide refuge for Catholics, who were a minority in the colony.

Secured Maryland Toleration Act (1649), promoting religious toleration. (p. 54)

Calvin, John (1509-1564), French leader of the Protestant Reformation at Geneva. Became Protestant (1533) and leader of Geneva's Protestant Pastors (1538). Believed in separation of church and state. Wrote *Institutes of the Christian Religion* (1536). (p. 23)

Capone, Al (1899?-1947), U.S. gang leader. Led crime syndicate in Chicago during 1920s. Engineered St. Valentine's Day Massacre in Chicago (1929). Convicted of income tax evasion (1931) and imprisoned. (p. 472)

Carmichael, Stokely (1941-), U.S. civil rights activist and SNCC organizer. Helped Lowndes County, Alabama, African Americans create the Lowndes County Freedom Organization, a political organization that chose black panther as its symbol to reflect new sense of militancy among African Americans in 1964. (p. 769)

Carranza [kä rän ′ sä], **Venustiano** [vä nüs tyä ′ nō] (1859-1920), Mexican revolutionary and politician. Succeeded Huerta as leader of Mexico; dealt with revolts from Francisco Villa; allowed U.S. troops to chase Villa into Mexico; maintained Mexico's neutrality in World War I; murdered during a revolt against his government. (p. 403)

Carter, James Earl, Jr., "Jimmy" (1924-), 39th U.S. president (1977-1981). Governor of Georgia (1971-1975). Created U.S. departments of Health and Human Services and Energy. Ended U.S. control of Panama Canal (1977). Helped work out a peace treaty between Egypt and Israel (1978). During his Administration (1979), Iranian militants seized U.S. embassy in Iran and took 52 Americans hostage. Defeated for re-election by Ronald Reagan (1980). (p. 914)

Catt, Carrie Chapman (1859-1947), U.S. feminist. In 1900, took over leadership of the National American Woman Suffrage Association. Helped secure passage of 19th Amendment that guaranteed women the right to vote. (p. 349)

Cavazos [kä vä ′ sōs], **Lauro F.** [lou ′ rō] (1927-), U.S. educator. President of Texas Tech University. Appointed by Ronald Reagan as secretary of education, first Latino to be named to a president's cabinet. Continued under President Bush until late 1990. (p. 961)

Ceausescu [chou shes ′ kü], **Nicolae** [nē ′ kō lī ′] (1918-1989), Romanian political leader. Communist dictator of Romania, overthrown by popular revolution in December, 1989. He and his wife were captured and executed. (p. 950)

Chamberlain, Neville (1869-1940), British statesman. Prime minister of Britain (1937-1940). Known for failed policy of appeasement toward Nazi Germany. Participated in the Munich Conference (1938), which gave Hitler a large piece of Czechoslovakia; returning from the Conference, he proclaimed to the British people that he had achieved "peace in our time." (p. 609)

Champlain, Samuel de (1567-1635), French explorer. Founded Quebec (1608); discovered Lake Champlain; built trading post in Montreal (1611). (p. 35)

Chaplin, Charlie (1889-1977), British-born motion-picture comedian and producer. The most popular U.S. film star in 1920s; his films often criticized social order of the times. (p. 502)

Chavez [chä ′ vez], **Cesar** [sä ′ sär] (1927-1993), U.S. labor organizer. Organized the United Farm Workers Union (1966) to improve conditions for migrant workers, many of them Latinos. Led a successful strike and boycott of nonunion produce. (1970-1978). (p. 811)

Cesar Chavez

Chiang Kai-shek [chyäng ′ kī ′ shek ′] (1887-1975), Chinese general and Nationalist leader of China and later, Taiwan. Fought civil war against communists in China (1927-1936, 1946-1949). After defeat by Chinese communists, fled to the island of Taiwan (1949) and established a Chinese Nationalist government there. President of Taiwan (1950-1975). (p. 686)

Chief Joseph

Chief Joseph (1840?-1904), Chief of Nez Percé Indians, took followers on 1,600-mile trek to Canada to avoid capture by U.S. forces and resettlement on reservation (1877). Chief Joseph and followers were captured 30 miles from Canadian border and sent to reservation in Oklahoma (1878). (p. 270)

Churchill, Winston (1874-1965), British statesman and author. Prime minister of Britain (1940-1945, 1951-1955). Led Britain as member of the Allies during World War II. Inspired British to stand firm against Germany during Battle of Britain (1940). Wrote *While England Slept* (1938) and *The Second World War* (1948-1953). Won Nobel prize for literature (1953). (p. 609)

Clay, Henry (1777-1852), U.S. senator and representative from Kentucky; secretary of state (1825-1829). As spokesman for the West, supported federal programs for internal improvements. Called the "Great Compromiser"; played a major role in arranging the Missouri Compromise (1820), ending the nullification crisis (1833), and in promoting the Compromise of 1850. (p. 187)

Cleveland, Grover (1837-1908), 22nd and 24th U.S. president (1885-1889, 1893-1897). During first term, Interstate Commerce Act enacted (1887). During second term, nation's economy suffered a severe depression (1893-1897), which Cleveland was unable to combat successfully. (p. 298)

Clinton, William Jefferson (1946-), 42nd U.S. president (1993-). Served as governor of Arkansas (1979-1981; 1983-1992). Elected on mandate for change after 12 years of Republican presidential leadership. (p. 976)

Columbus, Christopher (1451-1506), a citizen of the Italian republic of Genoa, he is credited with opening the Americas to European contacts (October 12, 1492). He sailed under a contract with King Ferdinand and Queen Isabella (Spain) to find a short route to the Indies. With three ships, the *Niña*, the *Pinta*, and *Santa María*, Columbus and crew of 90 sailed westward and discovered the Bahamas, Cuba, and Hispaniola. On later voyages he discovered Dominica (1493), Jamaica (1494), Trinidad (1498), and Honduras (1502). His voyages brought the Americas into lasting contact with Europe, greatly stimulating Europe's wealth and expanding the world's knowledge. (p. 24)

Coolidge, Calvin (1872-1933), 30th U.S. president (1923-1929). Favored conservative business interests. U.S. economic prosperity marked the Coolidge years. (p. 477)

Cortés [kôr tez ′], **Hernán** [er nän ′] (1485-1547), Spanish conqueror of Mexico. Destroyed Aztec Empire (1521); built Mexico City on ruins of Tenochtitlán, the Aztec capital. Explored Lower California (1536). (p. 26)

Coughlin, Charles E. [käg ′ lən] (1891-1979), U.S. religious leader. Catholic priest from Royal Oak, Michigan; attracted large following through weekly national radio broadcast of his sermons. Extreme anti-Semitic views were listened to by some 30 million Americans. Eventually silenced by hierarchy of Catholic church. (p. 566)

Cox, Archibald (1912-   ), U.S. political figure. Harvard Law School professor. Special prosecutor appointed by President Richard Nixon to investigate Watergate scandal. When Cox subpoenaed nine Watergate-related tapes, Nixon ordered Attorney General Elliot Richardson to fire him. Richardson and deputy attorney general resigned instead. Cox then fired by Justice Department's third-ranking officer (Oct. 1973). Series of events was known as the "Saturday Night Massacre." (p. 884)

Crazy Horse (1849?-1877), American Indian leader of Sioux tribe who joined forces with Sitting Bull to defeat Custer in 1876 at Battle of the Little Bighorn. (p. 272)

Croly, Herbert (1869-1930), U.S. editor and author. Editor of *Architectural Record* (1900-1906); founder (1914) and editor (1914-1930) of *The New Republic*. Wrote influential book in 1909, *The Promise of American Life*. (p. 439)

D

Daley, Richard J. (1902-1976), U.S. political figure. Mayor of Chicago (1955-1976). Often considered last of the "bosses" of a large city. (p. 838)

Darrow, Clarence (1857-1938), U.S. trial lawyer. Known for defense of schoolteacher John Scopes charged with teaching evolution in 1925. Also defended Socialist leader Eugene V. Debs when he was indicted for conspiracy (1894), and Nathan Leopold and Richard Loeb when accused of killing Bobby Franks (1924). (p. 473)

Davis, Jefferson (1808-1889), U.S. political figure. President of Confederate States of America (Confederacy). Indicted for treason and imprisoned (1865-1867), but never brought to trial. Refused to seek a pardon and remained ineligible for later public office. (p. 193)

Dean, John (1938-   ), U.S. political figure. White House counsel during Nixon administration. Participated in Watergate cover-up. Later convicted and served time in prison for his involvement in crimes. (p. 883)

Eugene V. Debs

Debs, Eugene V. (1855-1926), U.S. socialist and labor leader. Helped organize American Railway Union (1893). Jailed during Pullman Strike (1894). Founded American Socialist party (1901). Candidate for president on socialist ticket (1900, 1904, 1908, 1912, 1920). (p. 313)

De Gaulle [də gōl ′], **Charles** (1890-1970), French general and political leader. President of France (1959-1969). During World War II, headed exiled Free French government in London. (p. 615)

Dewey, George (1837-1917), U.S. naval officer. Destroyed Spanish fleet at Manila Bay in Philippines during Spanish-American War (1898). Victory secured Philippines as a future American naval base. (p. 389)

Díaz [dē ′ äs], **Porfirio** [pôr fē ′ ryō] (1830-1915), Mexican general and political leader. President of Mexico (1877-1880, 1884-1911). Helped modernize Mexico's economy, but ordinary people gained little. Considered by many a dictator; ousted in a revolution in 1911. (p. 403)

John Dickinson

Dickinson, John (1732-1808), U.S. lawyer and statesman. Voted against Declaration of Independence, drafted Articles of Confederation, and helped secure adoption of the Constitution. (p. 70)

Dix, Dorothea (1802-1887), U.S. social reformer. Beginning in 1841 investigated conditions in insane asylums and brought about major reforms in Massachusetts and other states. Also helped reform prisons, schools for the blind, and almshouses. During the Civil War appointed and supervised women army nurses. (p. 173)

Dole, Robert (1923-   ), U.S. politician. World War II hero. Senator from Kansas (1969-   ). Chairman of Senate Finance Committee (1981-1987). Candidate for Republican nomination for president (1980 and 1988). (p. 947)

Douglas, Stephen A. (1813-1861), U.S. senator. Democrat from Illinois. Helped pass Compromise of 1850. Stirred controversy with Kansas-Nebraska Act (1854). 1858 debates with Lincoln made Lincoln nationally known. (p. 188)

Douglass, Frederick (1817?-1895), U.S. abolitionist lecturer and writer. Escaped from slavery in 1838. Founded and edited *North Star* (1847), an abolitionist paper. Also a strong supporter of women's suffrage. U.S. minister to Haiti (1889-1891). (p. 174)

Drake, Francis (1540-1596), English "sea dog" (pirate); led 2nd expedition around the world (1577-1580). Major figure in battle against Spanish Armada (1588), which helped England become a mighty sea power and opened the door to its colonization of eastern North America. (p. 33)

Duarte [dwär ′ tä], **José Napoleon** (1926-1990), elected president of El Salvador (1984). A moderate supported by the U.S. government; worked for a peaceful resolution of his country's civil war. (p. 929)

W. E. B. Du Bois

Du Bois [dü bois ′], **W. E. B.** (1868-1963), U.S. writer and reformer. Helped launch Niagara Movement for racial equality (1905). With progressives such as Jane Addams and others, created National Association for the Advancement of Colored People (NAACP) in 1909. Wrote *The Souls of Black Folk* (1903) and *Black Reconstruction* (1935). (p. 350)

Dukakis, Michael (1933-   ), U.S. politician. Governor of Massachusetts (1975-1979; 1983-1991). Democratic nominee for president in 1988. Lost election to George Bush. (p. 947)

Dulles [dul ′ əs], **John Foster** (1888-1959), U.S. political figure. Secretary of state (1953-1959) and major architect of U.S. foreign policy during Cold War. A staunch anticommunist, he advocated a policy of "brinkmanship" in dealing with the Soviet Union and the "liberation" of communist-controlled areas. Developed Eisenhower Doctrine (1957) to preserve peace in Middle East. (p. 714)

E

Eddy, Mary Baker (1821-1910), U.S. religious leader. Founder of Christian Science Church. In 1875, headed a group of Christian healers and wrote *Science and Health with Key to the Scriptures*, a statement of Christian Science beliefs. In 1879 organized First Church of Christ, Scientist, in Boston. Founded the *Christian Science Monitor* newspaper in 1908. (p. 300)

Ederle, Gertrude (1906-   ), U.S. sports figure. 1924 Olympic gold-medal winner. First woman to swim the English Channel (1926). Set a record time of 14 hours and 31 minutes for the 31-mile distance. (p. 499)

Edison, Thomas A. (1847-1931), U.S. inventor. Invented phonograph (1877) and incandescent light bulb (1879). His research laboratories invented or made improvements on a wide variety of products including storage battery, dictaphone, mimeograph, and electric locomotive. (p. 277)

Edwards, Jonathan (1703-1758), U.S. religious leader who participated in religious revival in 1730s that became known as the "Great Awakening." (p. 57)

Ehrlichman, John (1925-   ), U.S. political figure. Chief domestic adviser for Nixon administration. Active in cover-up of Watergate crimes; convicted and sentenced to prison for his part in the scandal. (p. 883)

Eisenhower, Dwight D. (1890-1969), 34th U.S. president (1953-1961). Served as Supreme Commander of the Allied Expeditionary Force in Western Europe during World War II and supreme commander of D-Day invasion of France (1944). During his presidential years, Korean War ended (1953), Army-McCarthy hearings were held in U.S. Senate (1953-1954), and Supreme Court ruled against segregated schools (1954). (p. 637)

Eliot, T.S. (1888-1965), British poet, born in the United States. His collection of poems, *The Waste Land* (1922), portrayed the loneliness and alienation of modern life. Awarded Nobel Prize for literature (1948). (p. 509)

Elizabeth I

Elizabeth I (1533-1603), Queen of England (1558 to 1603). During her reign, England became a first-rate sea power, commerce and industry prospered, and colonization began. The Elizabethan Age was an era of great English literature, most notably that of William Shakespeare. (p. 33)

Ellington, Duke (1899-1974), African American jazz musician and composer. Wrote thousands of pieces of music including "Sophisticated Lady" and "I Got It Bad." His jazz band performed in New York City and throughout the world. (p. 511)

Ellsberg, Daniel (1931-   ), U.S. Defense Department employee. Photocopied documents from classified Pentagon files detailing history of U.S. involvement in Vietnam War; gave documents, known as the Pentagon Papers, to *New York Times* for publication. Nixon administration tried unsuccessfully to convict him of criminal behavior and block publication of Papers. (p. 843)

Ervin, Sam (1896-1985), U.S. senator. Democrat from North Carolina. Chaired Senate committee that held televised hearings on Watergate burglary and related crimes (1973). Hearings revealed extensive evidence of wrongdoing by President Nixon and high-ranking members of his administration. (p. 883)

Evers, Medgar (1925-1963), U.S. civil rights activist. As Mississippi field secretary for NAACP, helped register African American voters and set up boycotts against discriminatory businesses. Fatally shot in Jackson, Mississippi. (p. 767)

F

Faulkner, William (1897-1962), U.S. writer. Works portray life in the South. Books include *The Sound and the Fury* (1929), *Absalom, Absalom!* (1936), and *A Fable* (1954), which won the Pulitzer Prize in 1955. Awarded the Nobel Prize for literature (1950). (p. 509)

Ferraro, Geraldine (1935-   ), U.S. political figure. Served in U.S. House of Representatives (1979-1984). Democratic nominee for U.S. vice president (1984), first woman chosen for such a position by a major American political party. (p. 925)

Fillmore, Millard (1800-1874), 13th U.S. president (1850-1853). Taking office after Zachary Taylor's death, Fillmore signed the Compromise of 1850. Defeated by Pierce in 1852. Ran unsuccessfully on "Know-Nothing" political party ticket (1856). (p. 187)

Finney, Charles G. (1792-1875), U.S. clergyman and educator. Conducted revival meetings in western New York (1823-1832). Founded tabernacle in New York City (1834). Taught at Oberlin College in Ohio (1835-1875); became president of Oberlin (1851-1866). (p. 171)

Fitzgerald, F. Scott (1896-1940), U.S. novelist and chronicler of the "lost generation." Books include *This Side of Paradise* (1920), *The Great Gatsby* (1925), and *Tender Is the Night* (1934). (p. 507)

Flesch, Rudolph (1911-1986), U.S. educator and writer. Author of best-selling book *Why Johnny Can't Read* (1955) in which he stated that "the teaching of reading was too important to be left to the educators." (p. 724)

Ford, Gerald R. (1913-   ), 38th U.S. president (1974-1977). Became president after Richard Nixon's resignation. As president, supported tax cuts, limits on social spending, and voluntary wage and price controls in an unsuccessful effort to control inflation. Granted Nixon an unconditional pardon (1974). (p. 885)

Ford, Henry (1863-1947), U.S. industrialist. Organized Ford Motor Company (1903), which produced Model T Ford (1908). By using techniques of mass production assembly line, made automobile affordable for average American. Established Ford Foundation (1936), which engages in educational and other philanthropy (using wealth to help people). (p. 493)

Franklin, Benjamin (1706-1790), U.S. statesman, author, scientist, printer, and inventor. Helped draft Declaration of Independence; helped negotiate peace treaty with Britain after Revolutionary War; delegate to Constitutional Convention. Made major discoveries in electricity, established first circulating library in America, and invented the Franklin stove. (p. 57)

Freud [froid], **Sigmund** (1856-1939), Austrian doctor who introduced idea of psychoanalysis (examining a person's mind to discover unconscious desires, fears, or anxieties that produce emotional disorder); theories became popular in the United States during 1920s. (p. 505)

Friedan, Betty (1921-   ), U.S. feminist writer and organizer. Wrote *The Feminine Mystique* (1963), an influential book in the women's movement. Helped found National Organization for Women (NOW) in 1966, an organization that seeks equality for women. Helped form National Women's Political Caucus (1971). (p. 806)

G

Gallaudet, Thomas Hopkins (1787-1851), educator. Started free school for hearing impaired (1817). Taught at New York University (1832-1833). (p. 173)

Bernardo de Gálvez

Gálvez, Bernardo de (1746-1786), Spanish colonial official. Governor of Louisiana; during Revolutionary War assisted the Patriots by capturing Baton Rouge and Natchez (1779), Mobile (1780), and Pensacola (1783). Helped Spain acquire Florida in peace settlement (1783). Captain general of Cuba (1784), and viceroy of New Spain (1784-1786). (p. 67)

Gandhi [gän ' dē, gan ' dē], **Mohandas K.** (1869-1948), Hindu political, social, and religious leader in India. Methods of nonviolent protest inspired Reverend Dr. Martin Luther King, Jr., during U.S. civil rights movement. (p. 754)

Garnet, Henry Highland (1815-1882), African American clergyman. Leader of abolition movement; advocated killing of masters by slaves. U.S. minister to Liberia (1881). (p. 174)

Garrison, William Lloyd (1805-1879), U.S. editor and abolitionist. Founded New England Anti-Slavery Society (1831) and called for emancipation in his newspaper, *The Liberator*. (p. 174)

Garvey, Marcus (1887-1940), Jamaican immigrant who organized Universal Negro Improvement Association (1914), founded Harlem branch in 1916. Goals were to instill black pride and acquire economic power for African Americans. Led "back to Africa" movement, which proved unsuccessful. (p. 469)

Barry Goldwater

Goldwater, Barry (1909-   ), U.S. politician. Senator from Arizona (1953-1964, 1969-1987). Republican candidate for president (1964); defeated by Lyndon Johnson. (p. 826)

Gompers, Samuel (1850-1924), U.S. labor leader. Formed American Federation of Labor (AFL) in 1886. As president of AFL, stressed practical goals for workers such as higher wages, fewer hours, and increased safety on the job. (p. 311)

Gorbachev [gôr′bə chôf′], **Mikhail** (1931-   ), Soviet statesman. General secretary of communist party and leader of the Soviet Union 1985-1991. Responsible for policies of *glasnost* (openness) and *perestroika* (reform). Set up INF arms control treaty with Ronald Reagan (1988). (p. 935)

Gore, Al (1948-   ), U.S. political figure. Born Albert Gore, Jr. U.S. congressman from Tennessee (1977-1985), U.S. senator (1985-1992). Vice president of the U.S. (1993-   ). (p. 977)

Gorgas, William C. (1854-1920), U.S. army officer and surgeon. Led campaign (1904-1913) to rid swamps and jungles of *Anopheles* mosquito, which transmits malaria, and *Aedes* mosquito, which transmits yellow fever, during building of Panama Canal. (p. 400)

Graham, Billy (1918-   ) U.S. religious leader. North Carolina evangelist; in late 1940s began spreading Christian messages to millions through radio and television. Emotional brand of evangelism won him a large following and allowed him to build a powerful, heavily-funded organization supporting various humanitarian causes. (p. 710)

Grant, Ulysses S. (1822-1885), 18th U.S. president (1869-1877). Led Union armies to victory in Civil War (1865). President during Reconstruction era. Administration was tainted by financial scandals. (p. 224)

Guthrie, Woody (1912-1967), U.S. musician, songwriter, and folksinger. Traveled widely during the Depression playing guitar and harmonica in support of labor unions and of those most affected by the Depression. Songs included "This Land Is Your Land," "Union Maid," "Hard Traveling," and "So Long (It's Been Good to Know Yuh)." (p. 534)

H

Haig, Alexander (1924-   ), U.S. political and military figure. West Point graduate (1947) and U.S. army four-star general; Nixon administration chief of staff (1973). NATO forces commander (1974-1979). First secretary of state for the Reagan Administration (1981-1982). Responsible for U.S. policies reminiscent of early cold war period. (p. 928)

Haldeman, H. R. (1926-   ), U.S. political figure. White House chief of staff during Nixon Administration. With John Ehrlichman, directed cover-up of the Watergate scandal. Convicted of obstruction of justice and served time in prison for his role in the scandal. (p. 883)

Hamer, Fannie Lou (1917-1977), U.S. voting rights activist. Arrested for trying to register to vote. As she became more active in the voting rights movement, she encountered violent attacks and could not find employment. In 1963 joined SNCC. Mississippi Freedom Democratic party delegate to Democratic convention (1964); delegation was refused seating in favor of the regular Mississippi Democratic delegation. (p. 768)

Alexander Hamilton

Hamilton, Alexander (1755-1804), U.S. statesman. Revolutionary aide to George Washington and key figure in adoption of U.S. Constitution. Wrote many Federalist papers, which won support for the Constitution. As first U.S. secretary of the treasury, established sound fiscal system and good public credit. Fatally wounded in duel with U.S. vice president Aaron Burr. (p. 73)

Harding, Warren G. (1865-1923), 29th U.S. president (1921-1923). Campaigned on pledge to return to "normalcy." During his Administration, limitation of naval armaments agreed upon at international conference held in Washington, D.C. (1921-1922). Became ill and died in office. After his death, Teapot Dome scandal and other corruption in his Administration exposed. (p. 474)

Hart, Gary (1936-   ), U.S. political figure. Senator from Colorado (1975-1987). Ran for Democratic party nomination in the 1984 presidential election; failed to gain party's recognition when it was reported that he had engaged in an extramarital affair. (p. 925)

Hay, John (1838-1905), U.S. political figure. Secretary of state (1898-1905) in McKinley and Theodore Roosevelt administrations. Proposed Open Door Policy in China. Negotiated Hay-Pauncefote Treaty with Great Britain (1901), in which Britain permitted the United States to construct and control a canal through Panama open to ships of all nations. (p. 386)

Hayden, Tom (1939-   ), U.S. political activist. Associated with New Left in 1960s; participated in civil rights Freedom Rides. With others founded the Students for a Democratic Society (SDS). (p. 802)

Hayes, Rutherford B. (1822-1893), 19th U.S. president (1877-1881). Declared president by special commission in disputed election. Ended era of Reconstruction by removing remaining federal troops from the South. (p. 244)

Hearst, William Randolph (1863-1951), U.S. editor and publisher of newspapers and magazines. Published the *Journal,* which competed with Joseph Pulitzer's *World* in New York City. Heated battle for readers led to exaggerated reporting called yellow journalism. (p. 387)

Ernest Hemingway

Hemingway, Ernest (1899-1961), U.S. writer and chronicler of the "lost generation." Books include *The Sun Also Rises* (1926), *A Farewell to Arms* (1929), and *The Old Man and the Sea* (1952), for which he won the Nobel Prize for literature (1954). (p. 508)

Hiss, Alger (1904-   ), U.S. State Department official. During red scare period following World War II, accused of being a Soviet spy. Convicted of perjury and sentenced to five years in prison. Later, evidence surfaced of his innocence. (p. 695)

Hitler, Adolf (1889-1945), German National Socialist leader. Dictator of Germany (1933-1945). Called the *führer* (leader). Helped found Nazi party (1919-1920). Started World War II by invading Poland (1939). Murdered about six million Jews and other persons in concentration camps. Committed suicide. (p. 602)

Hoar, George F. (1826-1904), U.S. political leader. Served in U.S. House of Representatives (1869-1877) and was U.S. senator from Massachusetts (1877-1904). Helped found Republican party. Urged civil service reform and opposed his party's policy of imperialism. (p. 392)

Hobby, Oveta Culp (1905-   ), U.S. editor and publisher of a Texas newspaper. During World War II, directed Women's Army Corps (WAC). First U.S. secretary of health, education, and welfare (1953-1955). (p. 653)

Oveta Culp Hobby

Ho Chi Minh [hō′chē′min′] (1890-1969), Communist ruler of North Vietnam (1954-1969). Educated in Paris and Moscow. Ousted French from Vietnam. During 1950s and 1960s, his government supplied and aided rebels in South Vietnam who were trying to overthrow the anticommunist government there. (p. 822)

Hoover, Herbert (1874-1964), 31st U.S. president (1929-1933). Headed Food Administration during World War I. During first year of his presidency, stock market crashed, and Great Depression began. Refused to extend role of the federal government in combating crisis but did create Reconstruction Finance Corporation (1932) to provide loans to banks and certain businesses. Depression grew steadily worse. (p. 430)

Hoover, J. Edgar (1895-1972), U.S. criminologist. As head of General Intelligence Division in Justice Department (1919-1924), collected information on suspected radicals, which was used in the Palmer Raids (raids on suspected radicals). Served as director of Federal Bureau of Investigation (FBI) from 1924 until his death in 1972. (p. 463)

Hopkins, Harry L. (1890-1946), U.S. political figure. During Great Depression headed Federal Emergency Relief Administration (FERA), which made federal money available to state and local governments for relief. Also headed two agencies that employed persons in public works projects — the Civil Works Administration (CWA) and the Works Progress Administration (WPA). (p. 563)

Hopper, Edward (1882-1967), U.S. artist. Expanded subject matter and art techniques during 1920s. Known for starkly lit scenes of lonely roads, vacant rooms, and women seated alone, lost in thought. His most famous work, *Nighthawks* (1942), shows the loneliness and feeling of isolation the artist saw in American big-city life. (p. 509)

Sam Houston

Houston, Sam (1793-1863), U.S. general and statesman. Commander-in-chief of Texas army. Defeated Mexicans at Battle of San Jacinto (1836), captured Mexican general, Santa Anna,

and won Texas independence (1836). President of Texas (1836-1838, 1841-1844). Governor of Texas (1859-1861); opposed secession of Texas from Union during Civil War and was forced to resign. (p. 176)

Howe, Samuel Gridley (1801-1876), educator and social reformer. Involved with education of handicapped, prison reform, and antislavery movement. Married Julia Ward (Howe). (p. 173)

Huerta, [wer′tă] **Victoriano** [bĕk tō ryä′nō] (1854-1916), Mexican soldier, revolutionary, and politician. Murdered Francisco Madero, successor to Porfirio Díaz, in 1913 and declared himself president of Mexico. U.S. president Woodrow Wilson failed to recognize Huerta's government which lasted only three months and collapsed with U.S. help. (p.403)

Hughes, Langston (1902-1967), U.S. author who was part of Harlem Renaissance of 1920s. Works expressed pride of African Americans in their own history and culture and include *Weary Blues* (1926), *Shakespeare in Harlem* (1942), and *Montage of a Dream Deferred* (1951). (p. 510)

Humphrey, Hubert H. (1911-1978), U.S. vice president (1965-1969) and Democratic presidential nominee in 1968, defeated by Richard Nixon. As senator from Minnesota (1949-1964, 1971-1978), supported civil rights, aid to education, and arms control. (p. 837)

Hussein I [hū sān′], **King** (1935-   ), king of Jordan (1952-   ). In 1970 expelled Palestinians living in Jordan because he feared they threatened stability of his government. (p. 880)

Hussein [hū sān′], **Saddam** [sä däm′] (1937-   ), dictator of Iraq (1979-   ); conducted war with Iran (1980-1988). Invasion of Kuwait in August 1990 precipitated Persian Gulf war. (p. 955)

Anne Hutchinson

Hutchinson, Anne (1591-1643), U.S. religious leader who preached individual, personal salvation with God's grace and love, without regard to church or minister. Excommunicated from Puritan church and banished from Massachusetts Bay Colony (1637). She and her family settled in Rhode Island (1638) and then New Netherland, where they were killed by Indians. (p. 52)

I

Isabella (of Castile), **Queen.** Spanish ruler. Also known as Isabel the Catholic. Her marriage to Ferdinand of Aragon led to unification in 1479 of Castile and Aragon, Spain's two largest kingdoms. Expelled all Jews and Muslims from Spain (1492). Supported Columbus in search for new route to Indies. (p. 24)

Andrew Jackson

J

Jackson, Andrew (1767-1845), 7th U.S. president (1829-1837). Defeated Creeks at Horseshoe Bend (1814). Hero of Battle of New Orleans (1815). As president, introduced spoils system, destroyed Second Bank of the United States, forcibly removed eastern Indians to the West, and engaged in nullification controversy with South Carolina. (p. 166)

Jackson, Jesse (1941-   ), U.S. Baptist minister and civil rights leader. Founded Operation PUSH, a civil rights organization, in Chicago (1971). Candidate for the 1984 and 1988 Democratic presidential nominations; first African American to run for president. (p. 946)

Jacob, John (1934-   ), U.S. social reformer. President of National Urban League (1982-present); instituted national education program for African American children and parents to actively pursue specific education goals. (p. 970)

Jaworski, Leon (1905-1982), U.S. lawyer. Second special prosecutor appointed by President Richard Nixon to investigate Watergate scandal. Succeeded in getting Nixon to turn over some of Watergate-related audio tapes believed to contain evidence that would incriminate government leaders. (p. 885)

Jay, John (1745-1829), U.S. statesman. Helped negotiate peace treaty with Britain in 1783 (Treaty of Paris). With Hamilton and Madison, wrote the Federalist papers, supporting the Constitution. First chief justice of Supreme Court (1789-1795). Negotiated unpopular treaty (Jay's Treaty, 1795) with Britain. (p. 73)

Jefferson, Thomas (1743-1826), 3rd U.S. president (1801-1809). Wrote Declaration of Independence. First U.S. secretary of state (1789-1793). As president, responsible for Louisiana Purchase (1803), war with Barbary Pirates (1801-1805), and Embargo Act (1807). (p. 64)

Johnson, Andrew (1808-1875), 17th U.S. president (1865-1869). Became president after assassination of Abraham Lincoln (1865). Fought with Congress over Reconstruction policies. Impeached but not convicted (1868). (p. 236)

Johnson, Lyndon B. (1908-1973), 36th U.S. president (1963-1969). Secured passage of wide range of social programs including Economic Opportunity Act (1964), Civil Rights Act (1964), Voting Rights Act (1965), and Medicare (1965). Escalated American military efforts in Vietnam. Decided not to seek re-election as result of declining popularity due to Vietnam War. (p. 790)

Jones, Mary Harris, "Mother Jones" (1830-1930), Irish immigrant. After deaths of her husband and four children in 1860s, she devoted herself to U.S. labor movement. Led demonstrations, fought child labor, and organized women to support strikes. (p. 311)

Joseph, Chief. See Chief Joseph.

Benito Juárez

Juárez [hwär ′ es], **Benito** [bä nē ′ tō] (1806-1872), president of Mexico (1858-1863 and 1867-1872). In 1867, with U.S. troops posted at border, led Mexican people in revolt against Mexico's puppet emperor, Maximilian of Austria, who was deposed and executed. (p. 383)

K

Kelley, Florence (1859-1932), U.S. reformer. Worked at Chicago's Hull House (1891-1899); helped create first Illinois factory inspection law and became the first Illinois factory inspector (1893-1897). Headed National Consumers' League, founded National Child Labor Committee, and helped found National Association for the Advancement of Colored People. Urged laws restricting women's work hours. (p. 349)

Kennan, George (1904-   ), U.S. diplomat and government official. After World War II, deputy to secretary of state, George Marshall; director of policy planning staff. Expert on Soviet Union; responsible for the Cold War strategy of containment confining communism to its current boundaries. (p. 679)

Kennedy, Edward (1932-   ), U.S. senator from Massachusetts since 1962 and brother of John and Robert Kennedy. Ran as candidate for 1980 Democratic presidential nomination, but lost nomination to Jimmy Carter. (p. 921)

Kennedy, John F. (1917-1963), 35th U.S. president (1961-1963). First Catholic and youngest man elected president. Supported unsuccessful invasion of Cuba (1961), forced Soviets to remove their missiles in Cuba (1962), and signed nuclear test ban treaty (1963). Assassinated in Dallas, Texas (1963). (p. 789)

Kennedy, Robert F. (1925-1968), U.S. political figure. Brother of John F. Kennedy. Served as his brother's closest adviser and U.S. attorney general (1961-1964). As attorney general, supported reforms in criminal justice system and fought to protect African Americans' civil rights. Elected senator from New York (1964). Antiwar candidate for 1968 Democratic presidential nomination; assassinated in Los Angeles after his victory in California primary. (p. 834)

Kerouac [ker ′ ü ak], **Jack** (1922-1969), U.S. writer. Drifted around U.S. and Mexico working at odd jobs. Set the tone for the beatnik ("beat") rebellion of the 1950s and 1960s in his novel *On the Road* (1957). (p. 723)

Keynes [kānz], **John Maynard** (1883-1946), British economist. Central to his teachings was idea that government deficit spending in recession could help economy recover, an idea that seemed at the time to be confirmed by Franklin D. Roosevelt's programs during Great Depression of 1930s. (p. 574)

Khomeini [hō mā ne ′], **Ayatollah Ruhollah** [rü hō ′ lə] (1900-1989), Iranian Islamic religious leader. Ruler of Iran (1979-1989). Overthrew shah of Iran (1979). Supported revolutionaries who took 52 Americans hostage at U.S. embassy in Iran (1979). Hostages released on the day Ronald Reagan was inaugurated president in 1981. (p. 920)

Martin Luther King, Jr.

King, Martin Luther, Jr., Reverend Dr. (1929-1968), African American Baptist minister. Key leader of African American civil rights movement, using nonviolent methods of protest, in 1950s and 1960s. Directed Montgomery bus boycott (1955-1956). Formed Southern Christian Leadership Conference (1957). Helped lead March on Washington (1963). Awarded Nobel Peace Prize (1964). Assassinated in Memphis, Tennessee (1968). (p. 753)

Kissinger, Henry A. (1923-   ), German-born U.S. government official. Appointed assistant to the president for national security affairs (1969-1975) and secretary of state (1973-1977); major architect of U.S. foreign policy during Nixon and Ford administrations. Helped negotiate opening of relations with mainland China (1972), promoted détente with Soviet Union, and negotiated peace treaty with Vietnam (1973). Shared Nobel Peace Prize (1973). (p. 841)

L

La Follette [lə fol ′ət], **Robert M.** (1855-1925), U.S. government official. Reform governor of Wisconsin (1901-1906) and U.S. senator (1906-1925). Program as governor served as model of progressive government; established direct primary system for nominating political candidates (1903), instituted tax reform, and supported laws against corruption. In U.S. Senate, opposed Wilson's foreign policy and U.S. participation in the League of Nations. (p. 352)

Robert M. La Follette

Lange [lang], **Dorothea** (1895-1965), U.S. photographer known for photographs of Depression era. Recorded Japanese American evacuation to internment camps during World War II; did many photo essays for *Life* magazine. Published some of her photographs in *An American Exodus* (1939). (p. 534)

Las Casas [läs kä ′ säs], **Bartolomé de** [bär tō ′ lō mā ′ ŦŦä] (1474-1566), Spanish missionary to America and first priest ordained there. Protested enslavement of Indians and won laws to protect them (1542). Wrote the *Brief Relation of the Destruction of the Indies* (1552). (p. 30)

Bartolomé de las Casas

Lawson, James (1928-   ), U.S. civil rights activist. As student at Vanderbilt Divinity School, headed workshop to teach students about Gandhian nonviolent protest tactics. (p. 758)

Lee, Robert E. (1807-1870), U.S. army general. Commander of Confederate Army of Northern Virginia during U.S. Civil War. Fought in Virginia, Maryland, and at Gettysburg. Surrendered to Grant at Appomattox Court House (1865). (p. 222)

Lewis, John (1940-   ), African American civil rights leader. SNCC chairperson. Participant in civil rights protest march from Selma, Alabama, to state capitol in Montgomery; suffered fractured skull when policeman attacked nonviolent marchers. (p. 770)

John L. Lewis

Lewis, John L. (1880-1969), U.S. reformer. President of United Mine Workers (UMW) Union from 1920 until retirement in 1960. Led successful strikes against soft-coal industry (1919, 1922). Helped form Congress of Industrial Organizations (CIO) in 1935, a union that organized workers along industrial lines. (p. 462)

Lewis, Sinclair (1885-1951), U.S. novelist and chronicler of confining and hypocritical small-town life of 1920s. Novels include *Main Street* (1920), *Babbitt* (1922), *Arrowsmith* (1925), and *Elmer Gantry* (1927). In 1930, became first American to receive Nobel Prize for literature. (p. 509)

Liddy, G. Gordon (1930-   ), U.S. political figure. White House staff member in Nixon Administration and counsel to Nixon's re-election campaign committee. Helped lead group that burglarized Democratic National Committee headquarters at Watergate complex (1972). Imprisoned for part in Watergate burglary. Autobiography, *Will* (1980), was best seller. (p. 882)

Liliuokalani [li lē ʹə wō kə lä ʹ nē] (1838-1917), queen of Hawaii (1891-1893). Led "Hawaii for the Hawaiians" movement in an attempt to end U.S. control of the islands; overthrown by American planters with help of U.S. Marines. President Cleveland opposed this and refused to annex Hawaii but was unable to restore the queen to her throne. (p. 384)

Liliuokalani

Lincoln, Abraham (1809-1865), 16th U.S. president (1861-1865). Election sparked secession of South Carolina and formation of Confederacy. As president, he was commander in chief of Union armies; issued Emancipation Proclamation (1863), beginning of the end of slavery in the United States. Assassinated in 1865, five days after Civil War ended. (p. 192)

Lindbergh, Charles (1902-1974), U.S. aviator. First person to make solo nonstop flight across Atlantic Ocean (1927). (p. 501)

Lippmann, Walter (1889-1974), U.S. journalist and author. Founded *New Republic* (1914), was editor of New York *World* (1929-1931), and wrote columns for New York *Herald Tribune* (1931-1967). Awarded Pulitzer Prize in 1958 and 1962. In *The Public Philosophy* (1955) questioned the ability of a democracy to conduct foreign affairs effectively. (p. 615)

John Locke

Locke, John (1632-1704), English philosopher whose social contract theory and views on government influenced Jefferson in writing the Declaration of Independence. (p. 57)

Lodge, Henry Cabot (1850-1924), U.S. statesman. Served in Congress (1887-1893) and U.S. Senate (1893-1924). Helped draft Sherman Antitrust Act (1890) and Pure Food and Drug Act (1906). Supported imperialist foreign policy and strong navy. Led fight against Treaty of Versailles and American membership in League of Nations (1919). (p. 391, 438)

Long, Huey P. (1893-1935), U.S. senator from Louisiana (1932-1935). Nicknamed the "Kingfish." Organized national "Share Our Wealth" program which promised every American family a minimum annual income (1935). Announcing his candidacy for the presidency, he was fatally wounded at the state capitol by political enemy (1935). Assassination ended threat to New Deal of a third party candidacy in 1936 election. (p. 567)

Love, Nat (1854-1921), Black cowboy and ex-slave from Tennessee who spent 20 years on cattle trails and was nicknamed Deadwood Dick. He wrote about his life in *The Life and Adventures of Nat Love* (1907). (p. 268)

Luther, Martin (1483-1546), leader of the Protestant Reformation in Germany. (p. 23)

M

MacArthur, Douglas (1880-1964), U.S. military leader. Ordered by President Hoover to clear Washington, D.C. of the Bonus Army (1932). Appointed commander of U.S. forces in Pacific during World War II. Named commander of United Nations forces in Korea (1950). Relieved of command in Korea after dispute with President Truman over strategy (1951). (p. 635)

Madison, James (1751-1836), Fourth U.S. president (1809-1817). Called the "Father of the Constitution," he played a major role in its drafting. Wrote the Federalist papers with Hamilton and Jay; drafted Virginia Resolutions (1789). President during War of 1812. (p. 71)

Mahan, Alfred Thayer [mə han ʹ], (1840-1914), U.S. naval officer whose book, *The Influence of Sea Power Upon History* (1890), had a major impact on American expansionists Theodore Roosevelt, Henry Cabot Lodge, and Albert Beveridge. Argued for a strong navy, naval bases, and colonial possessions. (p. 385)

Malcolm X (Malcolm Little) (1925-1965), U.S. Black Muslim minister and political leader. Leader of Black Muslims, a political and religious movement based on black separatism and black power. Assassinated in New York City (1965). *The Autobiography of Malcolm X* (1965) was published after his death. (p. 772)

Mandela, Nelson (1918-   ), South African antiapartheid leader. Leader of African National Congress (ANC). In 1990, after 27 years, released from prison by South African government. Emerged as leader of movement to end all vestiges of apartheid and create majority rule. (p. 953)

Horace Mann

Mann, Horace (1796-1859), U.S. educator. Reformed public schools of Massachusetts, providing model for other school systems. Head of Massachusetts Board of Education from 1837 to 1848. (p. 173)

Mao Zedong [mä′ō dzu′dùng′] (1893-1976), Communist leader in China (1949-1976). Defeated Chinese Nationalists and won control of China (1949) in a civil war. Helped North Korea during Korean War (1950-1953). (p. 686)

Marshall, George (1880-1959), U.S. soldier and statesman. Chairman of U.S. armed forces and principal Allied strategist during World War II. After the war, served as secretary of state (1947-1949); helped formulate Truman Doctrine and Marshall Plan (1947). Awarded Nobel Peace Prize (1953). (p. 636)

Marshall, John (1755-1835), U.S. judicial figure. Chief justice of the Supreme Court (1801-1835). His decisions were fundamental in strengthening federal government. In *Marbury* v. *Madison* (1803), he established the Court's power of judicial review. (p. 117)

Thurgood Marshall

Marshall, Thurgood (1908-1993), U.S. civil rights leader and jurist. First African American to serve on U.S. Supreme Court (1967-1991). Argued against segregation as NAACP counsel (1938-1961), resulting in Supreme Court decision ruling public school segregation unconstitutional. (p. 755)

Martí [mär tē′], **José** (1853-1895), Cuban revolutionary, poet, and journalist. Exiled twice by Spanish-controlled Cuban government for insurgent activity (1871 and 1878). During second exile, lived in United States where he gained support for Cuban independence. Returned to Cuba

José Martí

in 1895 to lead fight for independence and was killed in battle. (p. 386)

McCarthy, Eugene (1916-   ), U.S. political figure. Senator from Minnesota (1959-1971). As antiwar candidate, won surprise upset over incumbent President Lyndon Johnson in New Hampshire's Democratic primary (1968); victory helped persuade Johnson to deescalate Vietnam War and not run for re-election; McCarthy ran for president as independent (1976). (p. 837)

McCarthy, Joseph (1908-1957), U.S. political figure. Republican senator from Wisconsin (1947-1957). Charged in a speech delivered in Wheeling, West Virginia (1950), that over 200 communists were working in the U.S. State Department. His accusations were never proven. He was discredited during televised Senate hearings to examine his charges that the U.S. Army was a hotbed of communism (1954). Censured by the Senate in 1954. (p. 696)

McClellan, George (1826-1885), U.S. general in chief of Union armies. Directed Peninsular Campaign (May-July 1862), then removed from position. Reinstated but removed again after Antietam (Sept. 1862). (p. 223)

McGovern, George (1922-   ), U.S. senator from South Dakota (1963-1980). Helped reform Democratic party's rules (1970), which reduced power of party officials while increasing power of minorities, women, and young people. An opponent of the war in Vietnam; Democratic presidential nominee in 1972; defeated by Richard Nixon. He ran unsuccessfully for the Democratic presidential nomination in 1984. (p. 868)

McKinley, William (1843-1901), 25th U.S. president (1897-1901). During his Administration, the highest tariff in U.S. history was enacted (1897), the depression of the 1890s ended, Hawaii was annexed (1898), and the Philippines, Puerto Rico, and Guam were acquired (1898). Assassinated by anarchist (person who opposes all forms of government) in 1901. (p. 316)

Meade, George (1815-1872), Union general in Civil War. Commanded troops at Gettysburg (July, 1863). Commander of Army of the Potomac (1863-1865). (p. 227)

Meredith, James (1933-   ), U.S. Air Force veteran and African American refused admission to University of Mississippi, an all-white school at the time (1962). Gained admission after President John F. Kennedy sent federal marshalls to escort him onto the campus. (p. 767)

Mitchell, John (1913-1988), U.S. attorney general (1969-1972). Director of Richard Nixon's 1972 re-election campaign. Convicted of conspiracy, obstruction of justice, and perjury (lying under oath) in connection with Watergate scandal (1975). (p. 882)

Mondale, Walter (1928-   ), U.S. senator from Minnesota (1964-1976) and U.S. vice president under Jimmy Carter (1977-1981). As senator, supported civil rights, consumer protection, and aid to education. Democratic nominee for president (1984); defeated by Ronald Reagan. (p. 925)

Montesquieu [mon tə skyū′], **Baron de La Brède** [də lä bred′] (1689-1755), French philosopher and writer (real name Charles de Secondat). Writings influenced American political thought. (p. 57)

Morgan, J. Pierpont (1837-1913), U.S. investment banker. Established leading banking house (1877). Played important role in reorganization of American railroads (1885). Helped reorganize U.S. Steel Corporation (1901). (p. 276)

Mott, Lucretia (1793-1880), U.S. Quaker minister, orator, and abolitionist. With Elizabeth Cady Stanton, planned Seneca Falls Convention (1848), the first women's rights convention in American history. (p. 173)

Muhammad, Elijah (1897-1975), U.S. religious leader. Head of religiously inspired group called the Nation of Islam from 1934 until his death. He and his 100,000 Black Muslim followers believed in racial separation and black superiority. Demanded that African Americans receive their own territory. (p. 773)

Muir [myûr], **John** (1838-1914), U.S. naturalist and writer. Born in Scotland. Founded Sierra Club, urged establishment of Yosemite and Sequoia national parks, and advocated preservation of wilderness areas. (p. 359)

Mussolini [mùs′ə lē nē, mū′sə lē′nē], **Benito** [bā nē′tō] (1883-1945), Italian political figure. Called "Il Duce" (the leader). Organized Fascist party (1919) and ruled Italy as dictator (1922-1943). Signed pact with Hitler's Germany, forging the Axis powers. Allied with Germany during World War II. Shot by Italian political opponents (1945). (p. 600)

N

Nader, Ralph (1934-   ), U.S. consumer advocate. In his book, *Unsafe at Any Speed* (1965), charged that many American cars were safety hazards because American automobile manufacturers stressed profits and style over safety features. Also criticized many other products. As a result of his work, legislation was enacted to protect consumers. (p. 794)

Napoleon I. See Bonaparte, Napoleon.

Nelson, Gaylord (1916-   ), U.S. politician and environmentalist. Senator from Wisconsin. In spring of 1970, called on those concerned about environment to stage what became known as Earth Day. One of the first politicians to emphasize protection of environment as major public issue. (p. 973)

Ngo Dinh Diem [nō din zi em], (1901-1963), leader of South Vietnam (1954-1963). Obtained American aid in civil war with North Vietnam. Instituted harsh policies against majority Buddhist population, which led to military coup (1963) and his execution. (p. 823)

Nimitz, Chester (1885-1966), U.S. admiral. During World War II, commanded U.S. Pacific fleet (1941-1945). Was chief of naval operations (1945-1947). (p. 645)

Nixon, Richard M. (1913-   ), 37th U.S. president (1969-1974). Established détente with China and Soviet Union (1972) and ended U.S. participation in Vietnam War (1973). The Watergate scandal overshadowed his second term, resulting in his resignation (1974). (p. 864)

Nobel, Alfred (1833-1896), Swedish inventor of dynamite and manufacturer of explosives, left money to establish Nobel prizes. (p. 416)

Noriega, Manuel (1938-   ), Panamanian soldier. Military dictator of Panama (1983-1989). Originally a U.S. ally, Panama was invaded by American troops in 1989, and Noriega was taken to Miami, Florida, to stand trial on drug charges. (p. 949)

Norris, George W. (1861-1944), U.S. politician. Progressive Republican from Nebraska; served in U.S. Senate (1913-1943). Voted against President Wilson's declaration of war in April 1917. Active in creating Tennessee Valley Authority

(1933); TVA honored him by naming their first dam Norris Dam (1936). (p. 424)

North, Oliver (1943-   ), U.S. military and political figure. Lieutenant colonel in Marines. During Iran-contra affair, carried out orders of his superior, John Poindexter, President Reagan's national security adviser, and supplied contras with arms. Convicted, fined $150,000 and put on two years' probation. (p. 933)

Novello, Antonia Coello (1944-   ), U.S. pediatrician. Headed National Institute of Child Health and Human Development and a special national task force investigating problems of children with AIDS. In 1990 President George Bush appointed her U.S. surgeon general, the first woman and Latina to hold the post. (p. 961)

Sandra Day O'Connor

O

O'Connor, Sandra Day (1930-   ) U.S. jurist. Assistant attorney general in Arizona (1965-1969); state senator (1969-1974); Arizona Court of Appeals judge (1979-1981). First woman appointed to Supreme Court (1981) by President Ronald Reagan. (p. 927)

Oglethorpe, James (1696-1785), English philanthropist. Received charter from George II in 1732 to found colony of Georgia. Oglethorpe's goal was to help unemployed debtors begin a new life. (p. 54)

O'Keeffe, Georgia (1887-1986), U.S. artist. Expanded subject matter and techniques of art during Jazz Age. Known for desert scenes and paintings of huge, stylized flowers. Elected to American academies of Arts and Letters (1963) and Arts and Sciences (1969). (p. 509)

Owens, Jesse (1913-1980), U.S. athlete. Track star of 1936 Olympic games. Owens captured four gold medals during the games and earned title "the fastest man in the world." Owens' success, because he was an African American, embarrassed Adolf Hitler. (p. 605)

P

Pahlavi, Muhammed Reza. *See* Shah of Iran.

Paine, Thomas (1737-1809), U.S. political and religious writer. Published *Common Sense* in 1776; urged colonists to declare their independence from England. Also published *Crisis* (1776-

1783), which lifted morale of Patriot troops. (p. 63)

Palmer, A. Mitchell (1872-1936), U. S. attorney general (1919-1921). Authorized raids, called the Palmer Raids, in which thousands of suspected radicals were rounded up and jailed without regard for their constitutional rights. (p. 462)

Parks, Rosa (1913-   ), African American civil rights worker. Refused to give up her seat to a white passenger on a Montgomery, Alabama bus; sparked boycott of city's buses by African Americans (1955-1956). Boycott was first major challenge to racial segregation in the United States. (p. 753)

Patton, George (1885-1945), U.S. military leader. Commander of troops during World War II in Morocco, Tunisia, and Sicily. Led Third Army across France and Germany (1944-1945). One of the first militarists to make extensive use of tanks in wartime. (p. 639)

I. M. Pei

Pei, [pā], **I. M.** (1917-   ), Chinese American architect. Noted for designing urban architecture in unusual geometric forms. Projects include Mile High Center (1955) and John F. Kennedy Library (1979). (p. 964)

Penn, William (1644-1718), English Quaker who founded Pennsylvania, West Jersey, and Delaware. Penn's Holy Experiment in Pennsylvania was an attempt to follow Quaker principles of simplicity, truth, and pacifism. (p. 53)

William Penn

Perkins, Frances (1882-1965), U.S. social worker. First woman cabinet member; appointed secretary of labor by Franklin Roosevelt and served in that position from 1933 to 1945. (p. 577)

Pershing, John (1860-1948), U.S. army general. Led 6,000-man army expedition into Mexico to capture Mexican General Pancho Villa (1916). Commanded American Expeditionary Forces (1917-1918) in France during World War I.

Served as army chief of staff (1921-1924). Nicknamed "Black Jack." (p. 403)

Pinchot [pin shō ʾ], **Gifford** (1865-1946), U.S. conservationist and government official. First U.S. professional forester; Theodore Roosevelt's chief adviser on natural resources; professor at Yale University. Governor of Pennsylvania (1923-1927, 1931-1935). (p. 359)

Pitt, William (1708-1778), English politician. Became member of House of Commons (1735), paymaster general and privy councilor (1746), secretary of state and leader of House of Commons (1757). Given control of English war effort, was instrumental in ending French and Indian War, known as the Seven Years' War in Europe (1754-1763). Opposed attempts to tax American colonies. (p. 60)

Pizarro, Francisco (1471?-1541), Spanish conqueror of Peru (1532). Executed Atahualpa, Inca ruler; destroyed Inca Empire; founded Lima, capital of Peru. (p. 26)

Pocahontas

Pocahontas (1595?-1617), American Indian princess (real name Matoaka). At age of 12 (1607) she may have saved life of John Smith, leader of Jamestown colony. She reportedly persuaded her father, Powhatan, to give food to starving English settlers. (p. 38)

Poindexter, John (1936-   ), U.S. political figure. President Ronald Reagan's national security adviser during Iran-contra affair. Convicted of ordering arms sent to contras. As "decision-making head" of operation, received six-month jail term in June 1990. (p. 933)

Polk, James K. (1795-1849), 11th U.S. president (1845-1849). Pushed annexation of Texas (1845); settled Oregon boundary dispute with Britain (1846). Launched Mexican War (1846-1848); won California and New Mexico for the United States. (p. 178)

Pontiac (1720?-1769), American Indian chief of the Ottawa. Organized alliance of Ottawa, Delaware, Miami, Shawnee, and other tribes against frontier settlers (1763). After his defeat, British issued Proclamation of 1763 to keep Indians and settlers apart. (p. 61)

Powderly, Terence V. (1849-1924), U.S. labor reformer. Headed Knights of Labor (1879-1893), largest and most powerful labor union of its day. More interested in reform issues such as need for child labor laws and trust regulation than workplace issues such as wages, hours, and safety on the job. (p. 310)

Powers, Francis Gary (1929-1977), U.S. pilot. Flew U.S. U-2 spy plane that was shot down over Soviet Union in 1960. Incident broke up scheduled summit meeting between Khrushchev and Eisenhower, which was designed to resolve growing tensions over divided Berlin and limit nuclear weapons. (p. 718)

Pulitzer, Joseph (1847-1911), U.S. journalist and newspaper publisher, born in Hungary. In New York, published the *World*, which competed with William Randolph Hearst's *Journal* in an unscrupulous battle to gain readers. The exaggerated reporting practices of their newspapers became known as yellow journalism. (p. 387)

Q

Qaddafi, [kä dä ′ fē] **Muammar el-** [mū ′ ä mär ′ äl] (1942-   ), Libyan army officer and leader of the country since 1969. (p. 918)

Quayle, J. Danforth (Dan) (1947-   ), U.S. politician. U.S. representative (1977-1981) and senator from Indiana (1981-1989). Vice president of the U.S. **(1989-1993). (p. 947)**

Queen Isabella. *See* Isabella, Queen.

R

Rainey, Ma (1886-1939), African American singer. First great African American blues singer of Jazz Age. Her style influenced many blues singers who followed including Bessie Smith. (p. 512)

Randolph, A. Philip (1889-1979), U.S. labor and civil rights leader. Founded Brotherhood of Sleeping Car Porters (1925). Threatened Franklin Roosevelt with massive march on Washington to protest discrimination against African Americans in government defense industry. Threatened march led to establishment of Fair Employment Practices Committee (FEPC) in 1941. He was a principal organizer of March on Washington (1963). (p. 653)

Rankin, Jeannette (1880-1973), U.S. legislator, women's suffrage leader, and pacifist. First woman member of U.S. House of Representatives (1917-1919), from Montana; later served in 1941-1943; voted against presidential declarations of war in 1917 and in 1941; also opposed U.S. involvement in Vietnam. (p. 424)

Ronald Reagan

Reagan, Ronald (1911-   ), 40th U.S. president (1981-1989). Governor of California (1967-1975). His economic policy, called Reaganomics, resulted in tax cuts and wide reduction in federal spending for social programs. Administration greatly increased military spending. Met with Mikhail Gorbachev to discuss arms control (1985). (p. 914)

Reed, Frank (1934-   ), U.S. educator. While director of Lebanon International School in West Beirut, kidnapped by Islamic Dawn terrorist group (1986) and held hostage for 3½ years. Finally released in April 1990. (p. 932)

Revels, Hiram (1822-1901), U.S. clergyman, educator, and politician. First African American elected to U.S. Senate (1870-1871), from Mississippi. President of Alcorn University. (p. 240)

Rice, Joseph Mayer (1857-1934), U.S. pediatrician and education reformer. One of foremost critics of U.S. education in 1890s; wrote *The Public School System of the United States* (1893), which charged that inept teaching was widespread. Book led to new reform movement called progressive education. (p. 320)

Richardson, Elliot (1920-   ), U.S. attorney general. Secretary of health, education and welfare (1970-1973). Served as attorney general (May-October 1973). Resigned when President Nixon ordered him to fire special prosecutor Archibald Cox, who had subpoenaed Watergate-related audio tapes during the so-called Saturday Night Massacre; Secretary of Commerce (1976, 1977); ambassador at large (1977-1980). (p. 885)

Robeson, Paul (1898-1976), African American actor and singer. Former All-American football player; starred on Broadway in Eugene O'Neill's *All God's Chillun Got Wings* and the musical *Showboat*; gained worldwide fame in London production of Shakespeare's *Othello*. (p. 503)

Eleanor Roosevelt

Roosevelt, Eleanor (1884-1962), U.S. humanitarian and wife of Franklin Roosevelt. One of FDR's closest advisers; helped establish policies for New Deal programs such as CWA, WPA, and NYA. Traveled on fact-finding missions for her husband and championed cause of underprivileged and minority groups. U.S. delegate to UN General Assembly (1945, 1949-1952, 1961-1962). (p. 564)

Roosevelt, Franklin Delano (1882-1945), 32nd U.S. president (1933-1945). His New Deal programs used power of federal government to overcome Great Depression. As president, he was commander in chief of U.S. forces during World War II. His decisions at conferences with Allied leaders during the war helped shape postwar world. (p. 546)

Roosevelt, Theodore (1858-1919), 26th U.S. president (1901-1909). Helped conserve natural resources, regulated business trusts and monopolies, and supported passage of Pure Food and Drug Act (1906). Secured right to build and control Panama Canal (1903). Denied Republican presidential nomination in 1912, ran as nominee of Progressive "Bull Moose" party. Defeated by Woodrow Wilson. (p. 355)

Rosenberg, Ethel (1915-1953) and **Julius** (1918-1953), U.S. communists. Arrested and tried for conspiracy to transmit atomic secrets to Soviet Union; found guilty of treason in 1951. Protesting their innocence, they were executed on June 19, 1953. (p. 696)

Rousseau [rü sō ′], **Jean Jacques** [zhän zhäk] (1712-1778). French philosopher; wrote about government and education. (p. 57)

Ruth, George Herman, "Babe" (1895-1948), U.S. professional baseball player. Set many major league records and became first great home-run hitter in baseball. (p. 499)

S

Sadat [sä dät ′], **Anwar** [än ′ wär] (1918-1981), Egyptian political official. President of Egypt (1970-1981). Signed Camp David Accords with Israel, paving the way for peace treaty between Egypt and Israel (1978). Shared Nobel Peace Prize for his efforts to end Arab-Israeli conflict (1978). Assassinated in Cairo by political opponents (1981). (p. 918)

Santa Anna, Antonio López de (1795?-1876), Mexican general, president, and dictator. Also spelled "Santa Ana." Stormed the Alamo in San Antonio, Texas (1836), wiping out Texas troops. Later, at San Jacinto, Sam Houston defeated and captured him (1836). Commanded troops in Mexican War (1846-1848) but was defeated. (p. 176)

Antonio López de Santa Anna

Scott, Dred (1795-1858), slave who sued master for freedom because he had lived with master for five years in free territory; in *Dred Scott* v. *Sandford* (1857), Supreme Court ruled against Scott's freedom, making Missouri Compromise unconstitutional. (p. 189)

Scott, Winfield (1786-1866), U.S. army officer. Fought in War of 1812; general in chief of U.S.

army (1841-1861); commanded army during Mexican War (1846-1848); largely responsible for victory over Mexican army. Nicknamed "Old Fuss and Feathers." (p. 183)

Seward, William H. (1801-1872), U.S. political leader. U.S. secretary of state from 1861 to 1869. Ardent expansionist; succeeded in purchasing Alaska from Russia for $7.2 million (1867). Known as "Seward's Folly," this purchase added 586,000 square miles to the United States. (p. 383)

Shah of Iran (Muhammed Reza Pahlavi) (1919-1980), the Shah of Iran (1941-1979). Pro-American ruler of Iran; survived 1953 communist uprising against his government with American aid; tried to Westernize the basically Islamic culture of Iran. After a revolution in 1979, forced to flee his country. Entered the United States for medical treatment in 1979, an action that led Iranian revolutionaries to seize the U.S. embassy in Iran and take 52 hostages. (p. 717)

Sheen, Fulton J. (1895-1979), U.S. Catholic theologian. Professor at Catholic University of America. Director of Society for the Propagation of the Faith in the United States; bishop of Rochester, N.Y. (1966-1969). Noted for anticommunist writings, for radio program "The Catholic Hour," first broadcast in 1930, and for television program "Life is Worth Living" during 1950s. (p. 710)

Sherman, William Tecumseh (1820-1891), Union army general during Civil War. Remembered especially for his destructive march from Chattanooga to Savannah and through the Carolinas (1864-1865). (p. 229)

Shuttlesworth, Fred (1922-   ), U.S. minister and civil rights activist. During 1950s he formed Alabama Christian Movement for Human Rights. His church was bombed, and he was arrested for helping Freedom Riders. In 1963 he asked Reverend Dr. Martin Luther King, Jr., to come to Birmingham, Alabama, for a major campaign against racial segregation. (p. 762)

John J. Sirica

Sirica, John J. (1904-1992), U.S. chief judge of Washington's Federal District Court at time of Watergate scandal. Tried seven Watergate defendants who were convicted of breaking into Democratic National Committee headquarters in Washington, D.C. Pressured defendants to tell court who was really behind the break-in, thus helping unravel the cover-up. (p. 882)

Sitting Bull

Sitting Bull (1834?-1890), Sioux leader. Led Sioux Confederacy that defeated Custer in 1876 at Battle of the Little Bighorn. (p. 272)

Smith, Alfred E. (1873-1944), U.S. government official. Governor of New York (1919-1920, 1923-1928). First Roman Catholic nominee for president (1928). His religion and city background became major issues of campaign and led to his defeat by Herbert Hoover. (p. 479)

Smith, Bessie (1898?-1937), African American blues singer and songwriter. Noted for her intense performing style; recorded almost 200 songs with many famous instrumentalists of her time. (p. 512)

Smith, John (1580-1631), English explorer. Leader of Jamestown, Virginia, the first permanent English settlement in North America (1607). Also explored and named New England (1614). (p. 38)

Somoza, Anastasio (1925-1980), Nicaraguan political leader. Dictator of Nicaragua (1967-1972, 1974-1979) and longtime U.S. ally. In 1979 overthrown by leftist revolutionaries calling themselves Sandinistas. (p. 930)

Stalin [stä ′ lin], **Joseph** (1879-1953), name taken by Iosif Dzhugashvili [yô ′ syif jü ′ gä shvē ′ lē], Soviet political leader. Dictator of Soviet Union (1929-1953). Fought on side of Allies during World War II. His harsh policies helped transform Soviet Union into a major industrial and military power. After World War II, set up communist governments in Eastern Europe. (p. 600)

Stans, Maurice (1908-   ), U.S. political figure. Served as secretary of commerce during Nixon Administration. Appointed treasurer of Nixon's re-election campaign in 1972 and raised more than $52 million, some coming from wealthy contributors. (p. 889)

Stanton, Elizabeth Cady (1815-1902), U.S. feminist reformer. Women's rights leader between 1848 and 1902. Organized Seneca Falls Convention (1848). Worked closely with Susan B. Anthony for rest of century in various organizations and campaigns. A founder of National Woman Suffrage Association (1869). (p. 173, 299)

Elizabeth Cady Stanton

Steinbeck, John (1902-1968), U.S. novelist and chronicler of the Great Depression. Works include the classic novel, *The Grapes of Wrath*, for which he was awarded the 1940 Pulitzer Prize; *Of Mice and Men* (1937); *Cannery Row* (1945); *East of Eden* (1952); and *The Winter of Our Discontent* (1961). Given Nobel Prize for literature in 1962. (p. 530)

Stevens, Thaddeus (1792-1868), U.S. political leader and attorney. Pennsylvania member of U.S. House of Representatives (1849-1853, 1859-1868). Radical Republican favoring harsh treatment for South's reentry into Union. Helped draw up 14th Amendment and Reconstruction Acts of 1867; proposed impeachment of President Andrew Johnson (1868). (p. 233)

Adlai Stevenson

Stevenson, Adlai (1900-1965), U.S. political figure. Governor of Illinois (1949-1953). Ran as Democratic nominee for president (1952, 1956), but defeated both times by Dwight Eisenhower. Served as U.S. ambassador to UN from 1961 until his death. (p. 711)

Lucy Stone

Stone, Lucy (1818-1893), U.S. women's rights leader. Outstanding public speaker; won many supporters to cause of women's rights, including Susan B. Anthony. A founder of American Woman Suffrage Association (1869). (p. 299)

Strong, Josiah (1847-1916), U.S. Congregational minister. Wrote *Our Country* (1885) in which he urged spread of Protestant Christianity to Mexico, Central America, South America, Pacific islands, and Africa. (p. 384)

Sumner, Charles (1811-1874), U.S. politician. U.S. senator from Massachusetts (1851-1874). Staunch opponent of slavery in Senate; Radical Republican demanding harsh treatment of South after Civil War. Instrumental in Andrew Johnson's impeachment trial (1868). (p. 233)

T

Taft, William Howard (1857-1930), 27th U.S. president (1909-1913). Chief justice of U.S. Supreme Court (1921-1930). As president, vigorously enforced Sherman Antitrust Act. Foreign policy, often called dollar diplomacy, involved use of both diplomacy and investments to protect American interests in foreign countries, particularly in Latin America. (p. 360)

Taylor, Frederick W. (1856-1915), U.S. efficiency engineer. Developed concept of scientific management in which unneccessary steps in manufacturing process are eliminated and production and efficiency are increased. His principles helped American industry produce products more efficiently but often made work more repetitious and tiring for workers. (p. 492)

Zachary Taylor

Taylor, Zachary (1784-1850), 12th U.S. president (1849-1850). A hero of Mexican War; first president elected to office with no previous political experience. Crisis of 1850 occurred during his presidency. (p. 181)

Thomas, Norman (1884-1968), U.S. socialist reformer and politician. Joined Socialist party (1918). Thomas and others founded American Civil Liberties Union in 1920. He was Socialist party's presidential candidate in national elections from 1928 to 1948. After World War II, he became involved in world peace and nuclear disarmament efforts. (p. 535)

Thoreau [thə rō ′], **Henry David** (1817-1862), U.S. author and naturalist. A transcendentalist, he promoted individualism in *Civil Disobedience* (1849) and *Walden* (1854). (p. 183)

Tilden, Samuel J. (1814-1886). Politician. Lawyer and Free Soil movement leader. Governor of New York (1875-1876). Democratic presidential candidate (1876). Election irregularities gave presidency to Rutherford B. Hayes although Tilden led in both the popular and electoral votes. (p. 244)

Tojo [tō ′ jō], **Hideki** [hē de ′ kē] (1884-1948), general and prime minister of Japan (1941-1944). Led Japan into war with the United States (1941). Convicted as war criminal after Japanese surrender (1945). Hanged in 1948. (p. 633)

Tower, John (1925-1991), U.S. political figure and U.S. senator. Headed special commission to try to uncover truth about Iran-contra affair. Issued report sharply critical of President Reagan's actions in affair. (p. 933)

Townsend, Francis E. (1867-1960), U.S. physician and radical critic of New Deal. Proposed Townsend Plan, which called for monthly pensions of $200 to every American over 60 (1934). After presenting his plan in a local newspaper, he developed a national following estimated at five million. (p. 566) (p. 62)

Townshend, Charles (1725-1767), English politician. Entered Parliament (1747), lord of admiralty (1754-1755), secretary at war (1761-1762), paymaster general (1765-1766), chancellor of exchequer (1766), prime minister (1767). Added to the separation between England and American colonies by passing Townshend Acts which heavily taxed colonists. (p. 62)

Truman, Harry S. (1884-1972), 33rd U.S. president (1945-1953). Authorized use of atomic bomb against Japan (1945), ending World War II. Sponsored Fair Deal, civil rights legislation, and repeal of Taft-Hartley Act (1947). Proposed Truman Doctrine (1947), Marshall Plan (1947), and North Atlantic Treaty Organization (NATO) in 1949, to combat threat of communist aggression. Korean War (1950-1953) began during his second term. (p. 649)

Tyler, John (1790-1862), Tenth U.S. president (1841-1845). First vice president to become president upon death of chief executive (William Harrison). Signed bill approving statehood for Texas and Florida. Although he won by running on Whig ticket, later disagreements destroyed Whig programs. (p. 180)

U-V

Van Buren, Martin (1782-1862), Eighth U.S. president (1837-1841). Political organizer of Democratic machine that swept Andrew Jackson into office. As president, Van Buren suffered politically from effects of Panic of 1837. Lost elections of 1840 (as Democrat) and 1848 (as Free-Soiler). (p. 166)

Vance, Cyrus (1917-   ), U.S. political figure. Secretary of state during Carter Administration. Instrumental in resolving disputes between Israel and Egypt that resulted in Camp David Accords (a framework for peace in the Middle East) in 1979. (p. 918)

Velásquez, Willie U.S. voting rights activist. Organized Southwest Voter Registration Project (1974), which was successful in adding Hispanic Americans to voting rolls. Organized nearly a thousand voter registration drives between 1974 and 1988, adding more than one million new voters. (p. 961)

Villa [vē ′ yä], **Pancho** [pän ′ chō] (1877-1923), Mexican general. Raided Columbus, New Mexico, killing 17 Americans (1916). Successfully evaded capture by U.S. general John Pershing's 6,000-man army. Punitive expedition outraged public opinion in Mexico and in much of Central and South America. Eventually ambushed and shot by enemies (1923). (p. 403)

Pancho Villa

Von Braun [von brôn ′] **Wernher** [wėr ′ nər] (1912-1977), U.S. rocket engineer born in Germany. In Germany helped create V-2 missiles. Came to the United States in 1945; developed rockets for U.S. Army; deputy administrator for National Aeronautics and Space Administration (NASA) (1970 to 1972). Developed rockets used for Apollo space flights. (p. 727)

W

Wald, Lillian (1867-1940), U.S. social reformer. Founded New York's Henry Street Settlement House (1893). Suggested idea of National Children's Bureau to President Taft. Such a bureau was established as part of Department of Labor in 1912. (p. 308)

Wallace, George (1919-   ), U.S. political figure. Elected governor of Alabama (1962, 1970, 1974, 1982). As governor, attempted to block enrollment of African American students at University of Alabama (1963). Candidate for president (1968, 1972, 1976). Paralyzed in an assassination attempt while campaigning for 1972 Democratic presidential nomination. (p. 839)

Warren, Earl (1891-1974), U.S. political figure. 13th chief justice of U.S. Supreme Court (1953-1969). Important decisions during his tenure include the desegregation of public schools (1954) and extension of the 14th Amendment to guarantee an accused person the right to a lawyer (1966). Headed Warren Commission (1963-1964), which investigated assassination of John F. Kennedy. (p. 790)

Mercy Otis Warren

Warren, Mercy Otis (1728-1814), U.S. writer and historian of Revolutionary era. Wrote plays, political dramas, and historical works including three-volume work, *History of the Rise, Progress and Termination of the American Revolution* (1805). (p. 56)

Booker T. Washington

Washington, Booker T. (1856-1915), African American educator. In 1881 headed Tuskegee Normal and Industrial Institute, industrial and agricultural school for African Americans located in Tuskegee, Alabama. In 1895 delivered speech known as Atlanta Compromise in which he told African Americans that fulfillment of goals lay in self-improvement and stressed need for interracial cooperation. (p. 301)

George Washington

Washington, George (1732-1799), First U.S. president (1789-1797). Member of Continental Congress and head of Continental Army. Influenced many to support U.S. Constitution; established policies for new nation, giving it a solid beginning. Known as "Father of His Country." (p. 60)

Weaver, Robert (1907-   ), U.S. political figure. Franklin D. Roosevelt's adviser to Department of Interior during New Deal. Became nation's first African American cabinet officer, secretary of Department of Housing and Urban Development under Lyndon Johnson. (p. 794)

Daniel Webster

Webster, Daniel (1782-1852), U.S. statesman and lawyer. Member of House of Representatives from New Hampshire (1813-1817), from Massachusetts (1823-1827); U.S. senator (1827-1841, 1845-1850); U.S. secretary of state (1841-1843, 1850-1852). Known for oratory in Senate, especially on compromise and preserving union. Supported Compromise of 1850. (p. 168)

Westmoreland, William (1914-   ), U.S. military leader. General and commander in South Vietnam during U.S. involvement. Responsible for pacification program in South Vietnam. (p. 830)

Whitefield, George (1714-1770), English minister. With John and Charles Wesley, founded Methodism. A major figure in the religious revival of late colonial period known as the Great Awakening. (p. 58)

Whitney, Eli (1765-1825), U.S. inventor. Designed cotton gin (1793) and devised system of manufacturing based on interchangeable parts (1800). (p. 165)

Williams, Roger (1603?-1683), U.S. religious reformer. Minister and founder of Rhode Island (1636). Advocated complete religious freedom and political liberty as right of people. Contributed greatly to separation of church and state which became part of the U.S. democratic tradition. (p. 51)

Wilson, Woodrow (1856-1924), 28th U.S. president (1913-1921). During his first term, Federal Reserve System (1913), Federal Trade Commission (1914), and Clayton Antitrust Act (1914) were enacted. President during U.S. involvement in World War I (1917-1918). After World War I, helped create the League of Nations but was unable to bring the United States into this organization. (p. 363)

Woodrow Wilson

Winthrop, John (1588-1649), U.S. colonial leader, first governor of Massachusetts Bay Colony. Instrumental in founding that colony and in establishing Puritan rule of "saints" in Massachusetts Bay. (p. 51)

Woods, Robert A. (1865-1925), U.S. social worker and reformer. Founded South End House, settlement house in Boston (1892). (p. 308)

Richard Wright

Wright, Richard (1908-1960), African American novelist. Member of Communist party (1932-1944); felt it would overcome racial oppression but ultimately rejected this stand. His novels deal with problems of urban African Americans including racial prejudice and alienation from society. Among his novels are *Native Son* (1940) and *The Long Dream* (1958); nonfiction works include his autobiography, *Black Boy* (1945). (p. 535)

X-Y

Yeltsin, Boris (1931-   ), Soviet politician. Dissident who resigned from Communist party; harsh critic of Mikhail Gorbachev's attempts at reform. In June 1990 elected to presidency of Federation of Russia, the largest Soviet republic. (p. 952)

Young, Brigham (1801-1877), U.S. religious leader. Became Mormon in 1832 and head of the Mormon church in 1844. In 1848 moved his followers to Great Basin and Great Salt Lake area of Utah. Became governor of Territory of Utah (1850-1857). (p. 179)

Z

Zhou Enlai [jō′ en′ lī′] (1898-1976), Chinese political leader and revolutionary. Member of Chinese Communist Party; active in establishing communist government in China. Served as Chinese prime minister (1949-1976) and foreign minister (1949-1958). (p. 878)

Styrofoam products; some scientists claim these are responsible for damage to Earth's ozone layer. (p. 973)

Christianity   religion based on teachings of Jesus Christ as they appear in the Bible; Christian religion. (p. 22)

city-manager plan   a form of city government, first tried in Staunton, Virginia, in 1908; city council is elected to make laws and set policy; council in turn appoints manager trained in municipal government. (p. 352)

Civilian Conservation Corps (CCC)   a New Deal agency employing men between ages of 18 and 25 to replant forests, stock lakes and streams with fish, restore historic battlefields, build parks, and fight forest fires. (p. 564)

civil liberties   rights guaranteed to an individual by laws or constitution of a state or country; also the freedom to enjoy these rights without undue restraint by government. (p. 107)

Civil Rights Act of 1866   act passed by Congress that guaranteed citizenship to African Americans; gave federal government right to protect their civil rights; Andrew Johnson vetoed bill. (p. 238)

Civil Rights Act of 1964   act passed by Congress that barred discrimination in public places, gave attorney general authority to bring suits to desegregate schools or other public facilities, banned discrimination in employment on basis of race, color, sex, nationality, or religion. (p. 765)

Clayton Antitrust Act   an act of Congress (1914) that exempted unions from antitrust actions and outlawed interlocking directorates of companies. (p. 368)

Coercive Acts   series of orders issued by British government in 1774 that closed port of Boston, made changes in Massachusetts government structure, lodged British troops among the people, let British officials charged with murder have trials in England. (p. 62)

Cold War   rivalry between United States and Soviet Union that began after World War II; carried on by political and economic means instead of direct military action. (p. 674)

Commission on National Goals   commission appointed by President Dwight D. Eisenhower to give nation a new sense of purpose; report issued by commission called for increased military spending, broader educational opportunities, and more government support for the arts and sciences. (p. 727)

commission system   a form of city government invented by progressive reformers and initiated in Galveston, Texas, in 1901; lawmaking and executive functions are vested in a nonpartisan commission of three to five members, each of whom heads a major city function. (p. 351)

Common Sense   a pamphlet published by Thomas Paine in January 1776 arguing for the independence of the American colonies from England; 120,000 copies were sold in three months. (p. 63)

Compromise of 1850   a compromise in slavery debate which northerners and southerners accepted as alternative to dissolving the Union; California was admitted to Union as free state, New Mexico and Utah were organized as territories, and the question of slavery was left open to voters; Texas was paid $10 million; slave trade was abolished in Washington, D.C., and a harsher Fugitive Slave Law was passed. (p. 187)

Compromise of 1877   solution to dispute over electoral vote in election of 1876; Compromise gave Republican Rutherford B. Hayes the presidency and Democrats gained promise that all federal troops would be withdrawn from South. (p. 244)

concurrent powers   powers held in common by state and federal governments as established by the Constitution. (p. 97)

Congress of Industrial Organizations (CIO)   union established in 1938 by John L. Lewis to create industrial unions principally among the unskilled workers not represented by craft unions; originally established as a committee within the American Federation of Labor in 1935; became a direct rival of the AFL until the two reunited in 1955. (p. 571)

conquistadores   [kon kē ' stə dôr ez] Spanish conquerors in North and South America during 1500s. (p. 26)

conservation   official protection and care of forests, rivers, and other natural resources. (p. 359)

containment   [kən tān ' ment] United States policy toward Soviet Union in decades after World War II in which the United States committed itself to stopping spread of communism. (p. 679)

Continental Congress   meetings of colonial representatives in 1774 and 1775 to respond to Coercive Acts, plan for possible war against Britain, and finally (July 2, 1776) to approve Declaration of Independence. (p. 62)

contras   Nicaraguan rebel fighters who opposed leftist Sandinistas; backed by President Reagan; Spanish for "those against." (p. 930)

convoy   system originated by United States during World War I to use armed escort ships to protect merchant vessels as they crossed the Atlantic Ocean. (p. 427)

Copperheads   persons in the North who sympathized with the South during the Civil War. (p. 232)

Coral Sea, Battle of   during World War II, a strategic victory for the Americans in the Pacific that halted the Japanese advance on Australia in May 1942; battle proved the aircraft carrier had replaced battleship as most formidable naval weapon. (p. 644)

corporation   business organization owned by many investors rather than by single owner or small number of partners. (p. 280)

counterculture   a 1960s youth movement that rejected many of the established values and customs of modern society. (p. 804)

coureurs de bois   [kü rer ' də bwä] colonial French fur traders or trappers who lived among the Indians and adopted many Indian customs. (p. 35)

court-packing plan   President Franklin Roosevelt's plan to appoint members to the Supreme Court who would support certain of his New Deal programs. (p. 573)

covert   [kō ' vərt] kept from sight; concealed; secret; hidden. (p. 679)

cover-up   something that covers up or hides an evil or criminal act: legally, a cover-up of a crime is itself a crime. (p. 882)

Coxey's army   several hundred unemployed workers, led by Ohio businessman and Populist Jacob Coxey, who demonstrated in April 1894, in Washington, D.C., against Congress's failure to pass a bill creating federal jobs for the unemployed; marchers were ignored by Congress and beaten and dispersed by police. (p. 316)

Crédit Mobilier   [kred ' it mō bil yā '] a political scandal in 1872 in which Vice President Colfax and other high Republican officials were found to have received shares in the Crédit Mobilier construction company in return for helping the company avoid investigation of large stock swindles and fraudulent government contracts. (p. 299)

CRP (Committee for the Re-election of the President)   committee organized in 1971 to re-elect Richard Nixon; headed by former Attorney General John Mitchell. (p. 889)

Crop-lien system   a system in which a farm family would borrow money against next year's crop from a local merchant; higher than normal prices for items thus purchased served to keep farmers in debt. (p. 242)

Cuban Missile Crisis   a confrontation in 1962 between the United States and the Soviet Union involving placement of Soviet nuclear missiles in Cuba, only 90 miles from the United States; the United States demanded removal of missiles and naval blockade was set up to stop Soviet ships from bringing additional weapons to Cuba; Soviet ships turned back; the Soviet Union agreed to remove missiles as long as United States would not invade Cuba. (p. 800)

D

Dawes Act   a law passed in 1887, dissolved tribes, ended tribal ownership of land, allotted specific acreage to individual Indians, and forced Indians to accept values of white American culture. (p. 273)

D-Day   June 6, 1944, day that Allied invasion of France began during World War II. (p. 640)

Declaration of Independence   official document adopted by Second Continental Congress on July 4, 1776, in which American colonies declared themselves independent from England; written primarily by Thomas Jefferson. (p. 64)

Declaratory Act act passed by British Parliament in 1766 asserting that Parliament had the right and authority to make laws for the colonies in all cases; acts of colonial assemblies could be voided. (p. 62)

de facto segregation segregation that has developed by custom rather than law such as unfair or discriminatory practices in the sale or rental of housing. (p. 777)

deinstitutionalization mental health policy begun in 1970s in which mental health experts decided that many mentally ill people should live outside institutions as part of the larger community. (p. 967)

de jure segregation racial segregation that is supported by law. (p. 777)

De Lôme letter a letter written in 1898 by Enrique Dupuy de Lôme, Spanish minister to the United States, criticizing President McKinley; Cuban revolutionaries stole and made public the letter in effort to gain U.S. support in their fight for independence from Spain (p. 387)

Democratic party one of two main political parties in United States; in the 1800s, upheld doctrine of states' rights and represented agricultural interests. (p. 166)

Democratic-Republican party political party composed of supporters of Jefferson in 1790s; worked in opposition to Hamilton's Federalists. (p. 114)

demographer person who studies changes in population groupings. (p. 960)

Depression of 1893 severe depression with highest levels of business failure since Civil War; unemployment increased from 3 percent in 1892 to 18 percent in 1894; Cleveland Administration asked Congress to stop all silver coinage, to replenish federal gold reserves, to reduce tariffs; Cleveland opposed enactment of income tax. (p. 315)

détente [dā tänt′] relaxation of tensions between nations. (p. 878)

direct primary a primary election in which a party's candidates for elective office are chosen directly by voters instead of by party members at a convention. (p. 352)

dirty tricks term applied to methods used to sabotage the Democratic presidential campaign of 1972 by members of President Nixon's re-election committee. (p. 883)

disfranchisement taking away the right to vote or hold office from a group or individual; practice was enacted in most of the southern states during late 1800s and early 1900s in effort to deny African Americans their civil rights. (p. 301)

dividends a portion of a company's yearly profits which shareholders receive for investing their money in the company. (p. 280)

Dixiecrats the term used by press in 1948 for Southern Democrats who favored states' rights, wanted to protect southern white interests, and limit political and economic power of African Americans; Dixiecrats supported Governor Strom Thurmond of South Carolina in the national presidential election. (p. 694)

dollar diplomacy name given by President Taft's critics to policy that used both diplomacy and dollars to protect American interests in foreign countries, particularly in Latin America. (p. 403)

domino theory idea developed during the Eisenhower Administration that the fall of one nation to communism would lead to the fall of its neighbors; theory formed the basis of U.S. policy in Vietnam. (p. 822)

due process of law whole course of legal measures which, carried out according to established rules, serves to protect people and their interests. (p. 108)

dumbbell tenement a design in 1879 by James E. Ware that won a contest for cheap housing for the poor in New York City; floor plan resulted in dark, cramped apartments without private baths; by 1890, such tenements housed more than half the city's population. (p. 306)

E

Earth Day in spring of 1970, a nationwide demonstration of concern about dangers to natural world that was, many believe, the beginning of the modern environmental movement. (p. 973)

ecology idea that all elements of the natural world are linked together in a complex and delicate web; a threat to any part of the web is a threat to the whole. (p. 973)

Eighteenth Amendment an amendment to the U.S. Constitution (1919) that forbade the manufacture, sale, or transport of alcoholic beverages in the United States. (p. 471)

elastic clause a clause in the U.S. Constitution (Article 1, Section 8, clause 18) that gives Congress the power "to make all laws which shall be necessary and proper" to carry out its other powers; this clause allows Congress to respond to changing circumstances. (p. 105)

Emancipation Proclamation document issued by President Lincoln on September 22, 1862 (effective January 1, 1863), that freed slaves who were in areas still fighting against the Union. (p. 226)

embargo [em bär′ gō] a restriction on foreign trade. (p. 119)

enforcement acts acts passed by Congress in 1870 and 1871; outlawed terrorist societies and authorized use of army against them; acts aimed at stopping Ku Klux Klan that was terrorizing African Americans in the South. (p. 242)

Enlightenment a philosophical movement in Europe in 1700s; emphasized rationalism, intellectual freedom, and freedom from prejudice and superstition in social and political activity; occurred during Age of Reason. (p. 57)

equality before the law all citizens are equal in fundamental civil rights, such as right to fair trial. (p. 234)

Equal Rights Amendment (ERA) of 1972 proposed amendment to U.S. Constitution, intended to protect women from discrimination on the basis of their sex; ERA died in 1982 when it failed to pass in required three-fourths of the states. (p. 927)

executive privilege right of executive branch to maintain privacy of its records against claims of other branches of government; right was invoked by Richard Nixon during Watergate scandal to prevent investigators from obtaining his audio-tapes. (p. 884)

expansionists Americans in late 1800s who felt that the United States should seek new frontiers overseas to extend "American influence to outlying islands and adjoining countries." (p. 382)

ex post facto laws laws that impose punishment for acts that were not crimes at the time they were committed but were declared illegal later. (p. 107)

F

Fair Deal President Harry S. Truman's postwar proposals to extend the New Deal by expanding the Social Security system, increasing the minimum wage, mandating full employment, ending racial discrimination in housing, increasing the power of the Fair Employment Practices Commission, building new public housing, clearing slums, aiding education, and supporting national health insurance and scientific research. (p. 692)

Fair Labor Standards Act of 1938 a law passed by Congress providing for a minimum wage of 25 cents an hour, and a maximum work week of 44 hours, with overtime rates paid for work after 40 hours, and forbidding labor by children under 16. (p. 574)

Family Assistance Plan an effort by President Richard Nixon to reform the national welfare system; plan called for guaranteed annual payments of $1,600 to all poor families; plan failed to win Congressional approval. (p. 864)

Farmers' Alliance a combination of several agricultural organizations that merged in 1889; political organization similar to the Grange, the Alliance entered and ran candidates throughout the South and West. (p. 315)

federalism system of government in which power is shared by a central government (the federal government) and by state governments. (p. 96)

Federalist party political party of Alexander Hamilton and those who believed in his policies; Hamilton favored a strong banking/financial system and a strong central government. (p. 114)

Federalists the supporters of the Constitution during the ratification process; members of Federalist party. (p. 73)

Federal Reserve Act an act of Congress that established 12 Federal Reserve Districts, each with a Federal Reserve Bank; all national banks were required to belong to this system; federal government would also keep its money in Reserve banks and would issue paper money for public use. (p. 367)

Federal Reserve System the banking system for the United States; policy-making arm is the Federal Reserve Board; there are 12 Federal Reserve Districts in U.S., each with Federal Reserve Bank. Federal Reserve System controls nation's money supply. (p. 869)

Federal Trade Commission Act act of Congress in 1914 designed to eliminate unfair business competition in interstate commerce. (p. 368)

Fifteenth Amendment amendment to U.S. Constitution passed in 1870 that guaranteed the right of former slaves to vote. (p. 240)

fifth columnists agents living in a country who secretly aid its enemies by sabotage, espionage, and so on; used often by Nazi Germany during World War II. (p. 612)

Final Solution Hitler's plan to murder all Jews and other "racially inferior" peoples. (p. 642)

flapper a symbol of the 1920s, typically a short-haired, young woman who rejected traditional views of femininity and women's behavior. Smoking, drinking, and swearing were characteristic of the flapper, who also preferred short skirts, no corsets, and cosmetics. (p. 504)

flexible response a foreign policy established by the Kennedy Administration based on building up and maintaining both nuclear and conventional forces so that the United States would be able to choose either option in response to a communist threat anywhere in the world. (p. 798)

Foraker Act bill passed by Congress in 1900; gave island of Puerto Rico a civil government after a year and a half of U.S. army rule; Puerto Ricans were citizens of Puerto Rico, but not U.S.; they were permitted to elect a legislature but final authority lay with U.S.–appointed governor and council. (p. 393)

Forty-Niners the gold-seekers who rushed to California in 1849 after gold was discovered there. (p. 179)

Fourteen Points an outline of President Woodrow Wilson's concept of what he thought peace settlement should be following World War I, including no secret treaties, freedom of seas, reduction of armaments, and establishment of a league of nations to afford "mutual guarantees of political independence and territorial integrity to great and small states alike." (p. 434)

Fourteenth Amendment amendment to U.S. Constitution in 1868 that granted citizenship to former slaves, established equality before the law as fundamental right of American citizens, punished former Confederate officers, and canceled Confederate debts. (p. 238)

Freedmen's Bureau agency created in 1865, empowered to protect legal rights of former slaves, provide for their education and medical care, and feed and care for war refugees. (p. 234)

Freedom Riders African American and white civil rights protesters who, during the spring and summer of 1961, staged "freedom rides" by traveling by bus through the South and attempting to integrate segregated bus facilities. (p. 760)

freedom schools one aspect of 1964 Mississippi Summer Project organized to bring white volunteers to join African Americans in civil rights struggle in the South; schools developed new techniques to improve academic and political skills of African American children and some adults. (p. 768)

free inquiry the essential ingredient of scientific investigation and technological advance. (p. 247)

Freeport Doctrine during the Lincoln-Douglas debates in 1858, Douglas's opinion concerning Dred Scott decision that slavery could exist in a territory only if it was upheld by local regulations, regardless of what the Supreme Court had decided. (p. 192)

Free-Soil Party a political party that in 1848 came out against the extension of slavery in the territories. (p. 187)

Free Speech Movement group formed at University of California at Berkeley in 1964 to protest university's denial of a place to solicit volunteers and funds for off-campus causes; group caused turmoil on campus until administration backed down and the protesters won rights of free speech and association. (p. 804)

French and Indian War war between England and France for control of North America that began in colonies in 1754; known in Europe as Seven Years' War; in 1763 France was eliminated as rival in North America. (p. 60)

Fugitive Slave Law part of Compromise of 1850, allowing any slave owner to reclaim a runaway slave simply by swearing that the fugitive was his or her slave. (p. 187)

fundamentalism belief that the words of the Bible were inspired by God and should be taken literally and followed exactly; one who holds similar beliefs in any religion; originated in about 1910. (p. 472)

G

Gadsden Purchase purchase in 1853 of large tract of Mexican land south of the Gila River for $10 million, which rounded out the present southern boundary of the United States. (p. 184)

Geneva Accords a peace settlement for Indochina in 1954 that neutralized Laos and Cambodia and temporarily divided Vietnam along the 17th parallel between the Vietnamese leader Ho Chi Minh in the North and the French in the South, until 1956, when national elections would choose a government for all of Vietnam. (p. 823)

genocide [jen ′ə sīd] the systematic extermination of a whole cultural or racial group. (p. 603)

gentrification [jen ′ trə fə kā ′ shən] rehabilitation of run-down areas of a city for higher-income residents; involves forcing out lower-income people with rising property values. (p. 965)

Gettysburg, Battle of in early July 1863, site of Lee's final advance onto Northern soil, where, in a three-day battle, he could not overcome Meade's strongly entrenched forces, and once again retreated into Virginia. (p. 227)

ghetto [get ′ ō] a section of European towns and cities where Jews were once required to live; word now means section of city where impoverished minority groups are concentrated because they find it difficult to locate housing elsewhere. (p. 468)

glasnost [glas ′ nōst] Russian word meaning "openness"; used to describe opening up of Soviet society under Soviet leader Mikhail Gorbachev. (p. 935)

global warming gradual increase in world's temperature resulting from widespread burning of oil and coal. (p. 974)

Grand Ole Opry music hall in Nashville, Tennessee, where weekly broadcasts of country music groups have kept alive ballad tradition of English, Scottish, and Irish settlers in mountain regions of U.S. (p. 506)

Grange agrarian association founded in 1867 to assist farmers; served both as social club to improve cultural life and as political body that stressed cooperative business ventures, economic freedom, and reduction in railroad-freight fees. (p. 315)

Great Awakening series of religious revivals in American colonies during early 1700s. (p. 57)

Great Compromise agreement between small states and large states during Constitutional Convention that allowed for representation according to population in the House of Representatives and equal representation for all states in the Senate. (p. 72)

Great Depression a very severe economic downturn that lasted throughout 1930s; Depression began with stock market crash of October 1929. (p. 526)

Great Migration beginning in 1916, the first mass movement of African American southerners to northern and western cities to escape racial injustice and find employment and better educational opportunities. (p. 431)

Great Railroad Strike of 1877 strike by nation's railroad workers when depression of 1877 led railroad companies to cut wages; railway network in East and Midwest was paralyzed; violence broke out in Pittsburgh when strikers rioted and state militia killed ten people; President Rutherford Hayes sent federal troops to Pittsburgh to put down strike. (p. 312)

Great Society President Lyndon B. Johnson's program for using America's prosperity to help improve quality of life for all the nation's people. (p. 791)

greenbacks U.S. paper money, having the back printed in green; greenbacks were originally issued in 1862 without any gold or silver reserve behind them. (p. 230)

Green Berets special forces in 1960s trained in techniques of fighting a modern limited war; name came from their distinctive headgear. (p. 798)

Gulf of Tonkin Resolution almost unanimous resolution of both houses of Congress in 1964 that supported President Johnson in his intention to "take all necessary measures" to protect American forces and "prevent further aggression" in Vietnam, following alleged unprovoked attack in Gulf of Tonkin off coast of North Vietnam between North Vietnamese torpedo boats and U.S. warships. (p. 826)

H

Harlem Renaissance flowering in 1920s of artistic creativity by African American writers and artists living in New York City's Harlem; movement spread to other African American population centers by end of decade. (p. 510)

Hartford Convention meeting of 26 Federalist party antiwar delegates at which rights of states to reject national policies to which they objected was asserted. (p. 122)

Hay-Bunau-Varilla Treaty treaty between Panama and U.S. in 1903 giving U.S. complete control over Canal Zone for price of $10 million and annual rent of $250,000; effectively made Panama a protectorate of the U.S. (p. 400)

Haymarket riot violence following a labor rally on May 4, 1886, in Chicago's Haymarket Square, when a thrown bomb resulted in seven police fatalities; many people were wounded when police opened fire. (p. 312)

Hay-Pauncefote Treaty [hā′pôns′fūt] treaty negotiated in 1901 by John Hay; permitted U.S. to build and control canal across Panama on condition it would be open to ships of all nations and would remain neutral in wartime. (p. 400)

H-bomb hydrogen bomb that uses fusion of atoms to cause explosion of tremendous force; bomb is many times more powerful than atomic bomb. (p. 686)

headright system revised land policy of London Company, whereby company granted every male newcomer, who paid his own passage to America, 50 acres of land; system created thriving community at Jamestown by 1619. (p. 39)

Hepburn Act law passed by Congress in 1906 which gave the Interstate Commerce Commission power to set maximum railroad rates. (p. 356)

hippies youthful adherents of the counterculture in 1960s and 1970s, who rejected conventional standards of dress and behavior. (p. 805)

Holocaust the attempted extermination of all Jews in Europe by the Nazis during World War II, resulting in the mass murder of about 6 million Jews. (p. 642)

Homestead strike strike in 1892 against Carnegie Steel Company in Homestead, Pennsylvania; Carnegie refused to negotiate with union and company tried to end strike by bringing in non-union workers; striking workers barricaded themselves inside the plant and ten strikers were killed by Pinkerton guards; governor sent in 8,000 state troopers to restore order. (p. 312)

House of Burgesses first colonial assembly in New World, created by Virginia Company; convened at Jamestown in 1619 to meet with governor and his council; landowning colonists elected representatives to this assembly. (p. 39)

hush money money bribes paid to keep a person from telling something; accusation made during Watergate scandal that President Nixon approved payment of bribes to Watergate suspects. (p. 884)

I

impeachment accusation of wrongdoing against a public official. (p. 100)

imperialism policy of extending the rule of one country over other countries or colonies, usually for the purpose of controlling raw materials, markets, or military bases. (p. 385)

impressment seizing of property for public use or of people to serve in the armed forces; kidnapping of sailors from American ships by the British in the late 1700s. (p. 119)

Incas [ing′kəz] ancient people of South America who had highly developed culture and ruled a large empire in Peru and other parts of South America until it fell to the Spaniards in the 1500s. (p. 16)

indemnity payment for damage, loss, or hardship; money demanded by victorious nation at end of war as condition of peace. (p. 397)

indentured servants people bound by contract to serve or work for someone else; many colonists in the 1600s became indentured in exchange for passage to the American colonies. (p. 56)

Indian Removal Act act passed by Congress in 1830 that allowed the federal government to seize most Indian lands as long as some compensation was paid. (p. 170)

Industrial Revolution change from household industries to factory production using powered machinery; era in which such a change took place. (p. 165)

INF Treaty treaty in 1987 between the United States and the Soviet Union in which the two nations agreed to eliminate American and Soviet intermediate-range nuclear forces from Europe. (p. 935)

initiative a procedure that allows citizens to introduce bills on the ballot or in state legislatures by petition. (p. 353)

installment plan a plan permitting people to buy an item for a small down payment with balance to be paid in weekly or monthly payments. (p. 498)

Insular Cases cases before U.S. Supreme Court in 1901 concerning previously foreign islands, now U.S. possessions; Court found that constitutional guarantees did not apply to Puerto Rico and other U.S. possessions, and that "the Constitution does not follow the flag." (p. 394)

internment camps during World War II, U.S. camps in isolated parts of western and southwestern states to which Japanese Americans living on West Coast were shipped by War Relocation Authority due to fears of sabotage spread by anti-Asia groups and others; many Japanese Americans lost all their property and businesses and were subjected to poor living conditions during the war; in 1988, U.S. government apologized for this treatment and later began making special payments as token reimbursement for wartime mistreatment. (p. 655)

Interstate Commerce Commission (ICC) regulatory agency created by the Interstate Commerce Act in 1887 to regulate freight rates. (p. 303)

Iran-contra affair scandal in 1986 in Reagan Administration; government officials admitted to making secret deal to sell weapons to government of Iran; also revealed that some money from weapons sale had been illegally diverted secretly into a fund to aid contras in Nicaragua; special commission set up to investigate the affair found a "secret government" acting, often illegally, to advance certain Administration foreign policy goals. (p. 933)

Islam religion of the Muslims, based on teachings of Mohammed as they appear in the Koran; founded in 7th century; followers believe there is only one God, Allah, and that Mohammed is his prophet. (p. 20)

isolationism principle or policy of avoiding involvement in foreign affairs; term often used to describe U.S. diplomatic policy in years between World War I and World War II. (p. 441)

J

Jazz Singer, The   first sound motion picture, produced by Warner Brothers Studio in 1927. (p. 502)

Jim Crow laws   laws passed in South after Reconstruction (1880s) to segregate the races. (p. 752)

joint-stock company   a business organization formed to finance new settlements in America in which many individuals could invest small amounts of money and thereby share their resources as well as financial risks. (p. 37)

Judaism   religion of the Jews, based on teachings of Moses and prophets as found in Old Testament of Bible and on interpretations of rabbis; Judaism teaches belief in one God. (p. 22)

judicial review   the power of the courts to review laws and determine whether they are constitutional. (p. 118)

Judiciary Act of 1789   act of Congress creating federal court system; provided for a Supreme Court with six members — a chief justice and five associates to be appointed by the president with the consent of the Senate. (p. 111)

Jungle, The   most famous of the muckraking novels, published in 1906 by Upton Sinclair; described shocking working conditions and primitive health standards in Chicago stockyards and meat-packing plants. (p. 347)

K

Kentucky and Virginia Resolutions   resolutions drafted by Jefferson and Madison stating that Alien and Sedition Acts violated freedoms guaranteed by Bill of Rights. (p. 115)

Khmer Rouge   after fall of Vietnam, communist group that gained control of Cambodia, changed country's name to Kampuchea, and established cruel government. (p. 846)

Knights of Labor   American labor organization founded in 1869 that welcomed all members of the "producing classes;" fought for end to child labor, equal pay for women, eight-hour work day, safer workplaces, and nationalization of railroads and telegraph lines; flourished in 1880s. (p. 310)

Kristallnacht   the Night of Broken Glass in November 1938, in Nazi Germany; organized night of terror by Nazi gangs against Jews; Jewish homes were broken into, occupants were beaten, synagogues were burned, and Jewish businesses were looted. (p. 605)

Ku Klux Klan   an organization of white people formed in the South after Civil War and revived in 1920s to maintain white supremacy by suppressing certain minority groups, primarily African Americans. (p. 242)

L

Land Ordinance of 1785   law passed for the orderly sale and settlement of the Northwest Territory; created system of townships with one section of each township set aside for a public school. (p. 71)

League of Nations   an association of nations established in 1920 to protect political independence and territorial integrity of all nations; formally dissolved in April 1946; United Nations assumed some of its functions. (p. 436)

League of the Iroquois   most powerful of confederacies organized by the eastern Indians, consisting of five (later six) tribes; Iroquois controlled area that is now New York State, which made them a key factor in the early struggle between England and France for control of North America; their decision to side with the English helped drive the French from North America. (p. 35)

Lebensraum [lã ' bəns roum ']   German word meaning living space; in 1930s, Nazi theory that a country must have room for economic expansion; German nationalists proposed that Germany's eastern neighbors should provide living space for the nation in its efforts to build an empire. (p. 600)

Lend-Lease Act   act passed by Congress in March 1941 permitting president to "sell, transfer, exchange, lease, lend, or otherwise dispose of any defense article for "any country whose defense the president deems vital to the defense of the United States." (p. 622)

limited liability   a term that means the owners of a corporation cannot be held legally liable for the debts of the business; if the company fails, stockholders lose only the money they invested in shares of stock. (p. 280)

Little Bighorn, Battle of the   on June 25, 1876, the Sioux, led by Sitting Bull and Crazy Horse, defeated federal troops led by Lieutenant Colonel George A. Custer along the Little Bighorn River in Montana; also known as "Custer's Last Stand." (p. 272)

lottery system   a system introduced by the Nixon Administration in 1969, for military draft; cards with all the days of the year were randomly selected; men whose birthdays were drawn first were drafted first; those who received numbers above a certain cutoff were not called for the draft but were considered eligible for a year; system eliminated college deferments and economics as factors in draft. (p. 841)

Louisiana Purchase   purchase in 1803 of France's mainland American territories by the United States for $15 million. (p. 119)

Loyalists   in the late 1770s, those American colonists who remained loyal to England and actively opposed independence. (p. 65)

Luftwaffe [lúft ' vä ' fə]   the German air force, especially in World War II. (p. 612)

Lusitania   British passenger liner sunk by German U-boat on May 7, 1915, with great loss of life. (p. 422)

M

Maginot [mazh ' ə nō] **Line**   elaborate system of defensive structures built by France along border with Germany after World War I; the German army outflanked it in 1940. (p. 612)

Maine   U.S. battleship mysteriously destroyed by explosion in harbor of Havana, Cuba, in February 1898; U.S. yellow journalists blamed Spain and President McKinley began preparing for war. (p. 387)

mandate   after a war, a territory or colony taken from the defeated nations and placed under the control of one or more of the victors; term applied to former German colonies and Ottoman Empire lands administered by Allies on behalf of League of Nations after World War I. (p. 437)

Manhattan Project   a U.S. Army–administered scientific and technical program, begun in 1942, that set up atomic bomb research center in New Mexico to develop atomic bomb as a weapon; first device successfully detonated at Almagordo, New Mexico, July 16, 1945. (p. 649)

Manifest Destiny   belief in the 1840s of the inevitable expansion of the United States which was believed to have the right and duty to bring progress and democracy to the entire Western Hemisphere. (p. 175)

Marbury v. ***Madison***   in 1803, case brought before Supreme Court by William Marbury, appointed to a judicial post by outgoing President Adams in 1801 but not commissioned by Jefferson, the incoming president; Chief Justice Marshall found that Marbury deserved post according to Judiciary Act of 1789 but that part of the act itself was unconstitutional. (p. 118)

March on Washington for Jobs and Freedom   largest single demonstration of early 1960s, August 28, 1963; 250,000 people gathered at Lincoln Memorial in Washington, D.C., to show increasing public support for civil rights legislation; those attending included major civil rights groups, labor unions, and religious leaders; the Rev. Dr. Martin Luther King, Jr., delivered his famous "I Have a Dream" speech. (p. 764)

Marshall Plan   after World War II, a plan drawn up by Secretary of State George Marshall and others to provide aid for European countries still suffering the effects of the war. (p. 680)

massive retaliation   the idea of relying on nuclear weapons in case of war. (p. 715)

mass production   the making of goods in large quantities, especially by machinery. (p. 277)

matrilineal [mat′rə lin′ē əl]   having or maintaining relationship through female line of a family, tribe, and so on. (p. 18)

Maya [mī′ə, mä′yə]   ancient American Indian people with highly developed civilization, located on Yucatán peninsula; civilization at peak around 250–900 A.D. (p. 16)

Mayflower Compact   agreement signed by men aboard the *Mayflower* setting up a voluntary government for the Plymouth colony. (p. 51)

McCarthyism   the crusade against communism triggered by Senator Joseph McCarthy of Wisconsin in the early 1950s that relied on the use of unsubstantiated accusations of treason and support of communism. (p. 697)

McNary-Haugen bill   a bill supported by farmers and passed by Congress during Coolidge Administration; bill proposed to raise domestic prices of wheat, cotton, and corn and have a government board sell part of grain crop on world market; President Calvin Coolidge vetoed bill twice. (p. 483)

Meat Inspection Act   law passed by Congress in 1906 that required federal inspection of meat packing facilities. (p. 354)

Medicaid   part of the health care program established by President Lyndon B. Johnson that helped provide medical benefits for those who could not afford them. (p. 793)

Medicare   part of health care program established by President Lyndon B. Johnson that provided low-cost medical insurance for people over the age of 65. (p. 793)

Merrimac   steam-powered wooden ship revamped by Confederacy with four-inch armorplate; on first day of action in 1862, sank two Union ships and ran three more aground. (p. 223)

middle passage   ocean voyage taken by slaves from Africa to the Americas. (p. 54)

midnight judges   Federalist judges of circuit and lower courts in 1800 whose commissions were signed by President John Adams the day and evening of his last day in office so that Federalists might secure judicial branch for their party. (p. 117)

Midway, Battle of   during World War II, first defeat suffered by modern Japanese navy in June 1942; Japanese assembled more than 150 ships for major attack on Midway Island, planning to destroy last remnants of U.S. fleet; U.S. bombers tore apart four carriers and Japanese fleet retreated. (p. 645)

mission   group (and its buildings) sent by religious organization to spread its beliefs; religious center in Spanish America whose goal was to convert the Indians to Christianity. (p. 30)

Mississippi Freedom Democratic party (MFDP)   alternative to regular Democratic party in Mississippi organized in 1964 by civil rights workers; open to all races; sent delegation to Democratic convention of 1964 but was unable to unseat regular state delegation. (p. 769)

Mississippi Summer Project   a plan developed by African American civil rights workers in Mississippi in 1963 to recruit a large number of white volunteers to work in the state to attract national attention and perhaps restrain white violence; put into operation in 1964, Project's successes included freedom schools and political organization of civil rights advocates. (p. 768)

Missouri Compromise   compromise on February 19, 1820, by which Missouri would enter the Union as a slave state and Maine as a free one; banned slavery north of latitude 36°30′N except for Missouri. (p. 123)

Monitor   Northern ironclad ship battled by Confederate ironclad the *Merrimac* at mouth of James River in Virginia; neither ship damaged seriously. (p. 223)

monopoly   the exclusive control of a commodity or service. (p. 282)

Monroe Doctrine   policy set forth by President James Monroe in 1823, that American continents were not to be considered subjects for future colonization by European powers; in turn, United States would not interfere in Europe's internal affairs. (p. 123)

Moral Majority   a political organization formed in 1979 by Baptist fundamentalist minister Jerry Falwell to promote conservative causes such as the restoration of prayer in public schools, an end to federal interference in local affairs, restoration of bans on abortion, and a strong U.S. military. (p. 971)

Mountain Men   fur trappers and traders who worked in Rocky Mountain region in early 1800s. (p. 177)

muckrakers   writers of the Progressive Era who pioneered investigative journalism and exposed social and political corruption of the time. (p. 347)

Muller v. Oregon   Supreme Court case in 1908 upholding Oregon's ten-hour-a-day work law for women. (p. 349)

My Lai massacre   the destruction of a small Vietnamese hamlet in March 1968 and the killing of Vietnamese civilians by American combat troops. (p. 832)

N

napalm   thickened or jellied gasoline used for incendiary bombs and in flamethrowers; used in Vietnam to kill thick jungle vegetation that provides places for the Viet Cong to hide. (p. 829)

National Association for the Advancement of Colored People (NAACP)   organization formed in 1909 by W. E. B. DuBois and others to promote civil rights, equality in job opportunities and education, and an end to segregation for African Americans. (p. 350)

National Industrial Recovery Act (NIRA)   an act designed in 1933 to join the federal government with business and labor to fight the Depression so that wages might be increased, the jobless might be employed, and production might balance consumption; surpluses, which lowered prices, could be avoided. (p. 560)

nationalism   devotion to one's nation; doctrine that national interests and security are more important than international considerations; desire for national independence. (p. 417)

National Labor Relations Board (NLRB)   governmental board created by Wagner Act in 1935; board works to prevent unfair labor practices such as coercion of employees and dismissal of employee merely for belonging to a union; and to prevent the establishment of company unions that are dominated by management. (p. 571)

National Organization for Women (NOW)   an organization founded in 1966 by Betty Friedan and other feminist leaders to obtain legal, social, and economic equality for women. (p. 807)

National Recovery Administration (NRA)   government agency established by President Franklin D. Roosevelt to write, coordinate, and implement codes of fair competition set up by National Industrial Recovery Act (NIRA); codes were detailed and complicated; problems arose in their administration. (p. 560)

National Woman's party   remnant of women's suffrage movement of early 1920s which supported expansion of Civil Rights Act of 1964 to include discrimination against women; clause outlawing sexual discrimination was adopted in the act. (p. 766)

Nation of Islam   religiously inspired African American group whose followers were known as Black Muslims; followers believe in racial separation and black superiority. (p. 773)

nativism   prejudice against immigrants; anti-immigration attitude. (p. 284)

NATO   the North Atlantic Treaty Organization formed in 1949 as a military alliance among the United States, Canada, and ten European nations. (p. 680)

Nazi [nä′tsē] **party**   National Socialist German Workers' party of Adolf Hitler, German dictator; doctrines and practices included suppression of civil liberties, militarism, racism, anti-Semitism, and quest for world conquest by the German "master race." (p. 603)

Nazi-Soviet Nonagression Pact   pact signed on August 23, 1939, between Nazi Germany and the Soviet Union which secured Hitler's eastern front from Soviet attack and gave Stalin extra time to build up the Soviet Union's military strength. (p. 611)

Neutrality Acts   laws passed by U.S. Congress in 1935, 1936, and 1937 aimed to keep U.S. neutral in struggle beginning in Europe; Neutrality Acts banned transportation of war material to warring nations; required that raw material that could be used for war be sold for cash and carried by warring nation's own ships; no warring nation could borrow money from the U.S.; U.S. citizens could not travel on ships of warring nations. (p. 620)

New Federalism domestic program of President Richard Nixon; included reducing some powers of federal government and transferring some powers back to state and local governments. (p. 864)

New Frontier domestic political program of President John F. Kennedy, including Medicare for the elderly, federal aid to education, programs to fight unemployment, a new department for urban affairs, creation of a federal agency for water pollution control, and the lowering of tariffs between the United States and the European Common Market. (p. 789)

new right conservative movement of 1980s hostile to government activism and militantly anticommunist; supporters used new tactics such as mass mailing campaigns, successful fund raising, elaborate political organizing, creation of new "think tanks," and publications to promote beliefs. (p. 972)

Nineteenth Amendment an amendment to the Constitution in 1920 that guaranteed women the right to vote and granted Congress the power to enforce this guarantee. (p. 481)

Nixon Doctrine guidelines developed by President Richard Nixon and his adviser Henry Kissinger for dealing with conflicts in Third World; U.S. would help "allies and friends" resist aggression and communist subversion but would leave "basic responsibility" to allies and friends themselves; U.S. would provide financial support and some military assistance, but would not become deeply involved. (p. 879)

nominating convention technique for choosing political candidates developed in 1820s; party candidates selected by democratically elected delegates; more people thus included in decision-making process. (p. 165)

normal schools teacher-training academies for women established by states in 1800s to fill need for well-educated public school teachers. (p. 173)

North Atlantic Treaty Organization (NATO) military alliance between the United States and Western Europe formed to stop the spread of communism in Europe in 1949. (p. 680)

Northwest Ordinance of 1787 an act of Congress under Articles of Confederation providing for governing of Northwest Territory — land north and west of Ohio River — and providing for eventual admission to the Union of three to five states. (p. 71)

nullify make not binding; render void; cancel. (p. 168)

O

OPEC (Organization of Petroleum Exporting Countries) an organization of countries exporting petroleum that banded together to control oil prices. (p. 870)

Open Door Policy policy stated in 1899 by Secretary of State John Hay that the privilege of trading with China should remain open to all nations; nations that controlled spheres of influence were to keep ports, railroads, and trading privileges available. (p. 385)

Operation Overlord name given to the World War II Allied plan to invade France and, eventually, Germany; invasion was planned for Normandy Peninsula and began on June 6, 1944, under command of General Eisenhower; by August, Paris was under Allied control. (p. 640)

Operation Torch World War II invasion of North Africa by British and American troops; begun in November 1942, the American and British armies successfully drove out Germans by May 1943. (p. 637)

ozone layer the part of the earth's atmosphere that protects the globe from the harmful ultraviolet rays of the sun. (p. 973)

P

pacification General William Westmoreland's 1967 program to rout Viet Cong from important areas in Vietnam, not just by defeating them militarily but by winning "hearts and minds" of local population; program met with limited success. (p. 830)

pacifist a person opposed to war who favors settling all disputes between nations by peaceful means. (p. 416)

Palace Guard term applied by critics to President Nixon's small circle of White House advisers. (p. 883)

panzer divisions name given tank divisions of German army in World War II. (p. 611)

Patriots the American colonists who actively supported revolution and independence from England. (p. 65)

Peace Corps organization established by President John F. Kennedy made up of American volunteers who lived and worked in developing countries where they helped people battle hunger, disease, and lack of education. (p. 798)

Pendleton Act legislative act passed by Congress in 1883 that set up a system whereby many government jobs would be filled on basis of competitive examinations; act also prohibited collection of campaign funds from federal employees and created Civil Service Commission. (p. 299)

Pentagon Papers secret documents photocopied from classified files in the Pentagon and delivered to *The New York Times* by former Defense Department employee, Daniel Ellsberg; papers contained a history of American involvement in Vietnam War; Nixon Administration considered publication a security breach and tried unsuccessfully to convict Ellsberg of criminal behavior. (p. 844)

perestroika [păr ə stroi ′ kə] Russian word meaning "restructuring"; used to describe restructuring of Soviet economic system under Gorbachev. (p. 935)

Philippine insurrection term applied by American authorities in the late 19th and early 20th centuries to the Filipinos' struggle for independence against the U.S., which replaced Spain as Philippine colonial ruler. (p. 395)

Pilgrims a group of religious reformers who fled England to seek religious freedom first in Holland and later, in 1620, in the New World; established first permanent colony in New England at Plymouth in what is now Massachusetts. (p. 50)

Platt Amendment a rider attached to Army Appropriations Bill of 1901, introduced by Senator Orville H. Platt of Connecticut, severely limiting Cuba's political freedom; Cuban government agreed to not make treaties with foreign powers that might endanger its independence, agreed to let United States intervene in Cuban affairs to preserve independence and maintain order, and agreed to lease facilities for U.S. naval and coaling stations. (p. 393)

PLO (Palestine Liberation Organization) organization formed for the purpose of getting the international community to accept the legitimacy of a Palestinian homeland. (p. 918)

plumbers White House unit created by Nixon Administration after Pentagon Papers were leaked; purpose was to increase Administration's ability to prevent future leaks and discredit its enemies; various covert missions were carried out including break-in at Watergate building in Washington, D.C., that led to Nixon's resignation. (p. 844)

political machine political organization composed of politicians and political workers who owe allegiance to a political boss. (p. 307)

polytheistic [pol ′ ē thē is ťik] having to do with or characterized by belief in more than one god. (p. 18)

pool business arrangement used in 1870s and 1880s in which several companies agreed to divide available business in an area among themselves and prevent competition by controlling prices. (p. 280)

Poor People's Campaign a plan of the Rev. Dr. Martin Luther King, Jr.'s in 1967 to bring thousands of poor people to Washington in an effort to pressure President Lyndon Johnson into increasing funding for the "War on Poverty." (p. 775)

popular sovereignty prc–Civil War policy of letting the voters who lived in a newly organized territory decide whether to allow slavery there. (p. 188)

Populists members of the People's (or Populist) party created in 1892 by Farmers' Alliance members; Populist platform reflected needs of farmers but also addressed concerns of other reform groups. (p. 315)

Presidential Election Campaign Fund bill passed by Congress in 1974 that established federal financing of presidential campaigns; effort to limit role of private contributions. (p. 891)

presidio [pri sid′ē ō] a military post or fortified area of a settlement in colonial Spanish America. (p. 30)

pro-choice movement a powerful political force of the late 1980s working to preserve a woman's right to choose how best to respond to a pregnancy; this movement was in response to the changing judicial climate in the United States that seemed to be leaning away from individual choice about abortion. (p. 973)

progressive education an approach to instruction whose goal is to fit the course of study in schools to the needs and interests of the students rather than to force students into a given curriculum. (p. 320)

Progressive party a political party formed in August, 1912, by supporters of Theodore Roosevelt; also called the "Bull Moose" party. (p. 363)

progressivism a reform movement of the late 19th and early 20th centuries that worked to improve various aspects of American life such as city and state government, conservation, working conditions, poverty, and regulation of certain business practices. (p. 346)

Prohibition the period between 1920 and 1933 when the manufacture, sale, or transport of any alcoholic beverage in the United States was prohibited; Prohibition became law through the 18th Amendment, which was repealed by the 21st Amendment. (p. 471)

Project C plan prepared in 1963 by leaders of Southern Christian Leadership Conference to provoke confrontations with white officials in Birmingham, Alabama, in hope of causing federal intervention on behalf of civil rights reforms. The "C" represented confrontation. (p. 762)

pro-life movement powerful protest movement against abortion rights that began in late 1970s and became formidable political force by mid-1980s; also known as right-to-life movement. (p. 972)

Protestant Reformation religious movement in Europe in 1500s, led by Martin Luther and John Calvin, that aimed at reform within the Roman Catholic Church but led to establishment of new Protestant churches. (p. 22)

Public Works Administration (PWA) a New Deal agency established by Congress in June 1933 to administer spending of government funds for major public works such as bridges, municipal water and sewer systems, schools, parks, auditoriums, public swimming pools, and even two naval aircraft carriers. (p. 561)

Pullman strike in 1894, widespread railroad strike brought on when Eugene V. Debs' American Railway Union voted to boycott the Pullman Company; despite protest of Illinois governor, U.S. government argued that strikers were obstructing mails and sent troops to protect trains staffed by strikebreakers; four-day battle ensued in which 30 people were killed and many injured; injunction issued to end strike but union leaders refused and were jailed. (p. 312)

pump priming pouring small amount of water down pump shaft so pump washer will seal and bring water from the well; President Franklin D. Roosevelt applied idea to economy in 1933, when he hoped that a small amount of government spending would create additional spending in private industry. (p. 561)

Pure Food and Drug Act a law passed by Congress in 1906 that prohibited manufacture, sale, or shipment of impure or mislabeled food and drugs in interstate commerce. (p. 354)

Puritans members of Protestant group in Church of England during 1500s and 1600s who wanted simpler forms of worship and stricter morals. (p. 50)

Q

Quakers dissenting Protestant sect, formally known as Society of Friends, that fled persecution in England and found refuge in colony of New Jersey; later established Pennsylvania. (p. 53)

R

Radical Republicans during the Civil War, strongest supporters of the war, who believed that slavery should be abolished, African Americans should have civil rights, and the South should be treated harshly. (p. 233)

rapprochement renewal of friendly relations; Gerald Ford's reestablishment of friendly relations with China in the mid-1970s. (p. 913)

rationing practice of distributing something in limited amounts; during World War II, U.S. government issued coupons to limit the number of items a person could buy, thus reducing demand for scarce goods. (p. 655)

recall procedure that allows voters to remove an official from office before his or her term has expired. (p. 354)

recession a period of temporary decline in business activity, shorter and less extreme than a depression. (p. 869)

reclamation restoration to productivity of dry lands through irrigation; 1902 National Reclamation Act (Newlands Act) began federal reclamation to help farmers; promoted conservation. (p. 359)

reconcentración policy instituted by Spanish government in Cuba in 1896 under which civilian population was herded into fortified towns; those outside the towns were considered insurgents in the fight against Spanish control of Cuba and were subject to military action. (p. 387)

redistribution of income use of taxes and transfer payments to shift income from one group to provide financial help for another group. (p. 795)

red scare beginning in 1919, concern that formation of communist parties in the United States might lead to violent, radical change; arrest or deportation of many communists and socialists took place during this period. (p. 463)

referendum process that allows citizens to vote on a proposed law or, through petition, to submit an existing law to a vote. (p. 353)

Renaissance [ren′ə säns′] the great revival of art and learning in Europe between about 1250 and 1600. (p. 22)

reparations payments made by a defeated country for the damages it caused during a war. (p. 436)

reservations areas of land set aside by the U.S. government for Indian tribes; lands under federal jurisdiction. (p. 271)

reserved powers any right or power not specifically assigned or denied by the Constitution, reserved to the states or the people; concept later officially confirmed by 10th Amendment. (p. 97)

revenue sharing program launched by President Richard Nixon under which federal government returns portion of its tax receipts to state and local governments to meet local needs. (p. 864)

Roe* v. *Wade controversial decision by the Supreme Court in 1973 that invalidated state laws that had forbidden women to have abortions. (p. 866)

Roosevelt Corollary an addition to the Monroe Doctrine stating that the United States should take on duties of international police force in Western Hemisphere; issued by President Theodore Roosevelt in 1904. (p. 402)

Rough Riders a cavalry regiment headed by Theodore Roosevelt that participated in Spanish-American War of 1898. (p. 389)

Royal Air Force (RAF) the British air force. (p. 615)

royal colony a colony ruled directly by the Crown according to the laws of England. (p. 39)

Russo-Japanese War a war between Russia and Japan in 1904–1905 over Manchuria and Korea; Japan won and was given Korea and principal Russian holdings in Manchuria; U.S. President Theodore Roosevelt received Nobel Peace Prize for his part in mediating the peace process. (p. 399)

S

Sacco-Vanzetti case the arrest, trial, and subsequent execution of two Italian immigrants suspected of taking part in an armed robbery in Massachusetts in which two men were killed; though evidence was sketchy, both Sacco and Vanzetti were found guilty; many people felt they were actually innocent but as foreign-born radicals, they were symbols of political radicalism feared by conservatives. (p. 465)

SALT I first Strategic Arms Limitation Treaty (1972); placed limitations on number, type, and deployment of intercontinental ballistic missiles, antiballistic missiles, and missile-bearing submarines, as part of President Richard Nixon's détente with Soviet Union; ratified by Senate in 1972. (p. 878)

SALT II second Strategic Arms Limitation Treaty (1979); limited number, type, and deployment of intercontinental ballistic missiles; keystone of President Jimmy Carter's policy toward the Soviet Union; Soviet Union's invasion of Afghanistan (December 1979) and military assistance to revolutionary African regimes were among factors that caused Senate not to approve treaty. (p. 913)

Sandinistas left-wing Nicaraguan guerrillas who came to power in 1979; supported by President Jimmy Carter; President Reagan stopped all U.S. aid because he suspected Sandinistas were supporting other revolutionary movements in the region. (p. 930)

satellite countries nominally independent but actually controlled by a more powerful country, especially countries under control of the Soviet Union after World War II. (p. 677)

scalawags name given white Southerners who cooperated with Radical Republicans during Reconstruction and were denounced as traitors to their race and region. (p. 241)

scientific management business approach that focused on efficiency and speed, advocated by Frederick W. Taylor; using principles of scientific management, Taylor streamlined methods of mass production. (p. 492)

Scopes trial trial in 1925 in which a Tennessee school teacher was charged with breaking a Tennessee law that banned the teaching of evolution; became a test cast for ACLU to challenge fundamentalists of the time; Scopes defense team led by Clarence Darrow; prosecutor was William Jennings Bryan; Scopes convicted and fined $100 but Tennessee's Supreme Court set aside conviction; known as "Monkey Trial." (p. 474)

Scottsboro case case that symbolized race relations in Depression era; in March 1931, nine African American teenagers arrested in Scottsboro, Alabama, for rape of two white women; eight were convicted and sentenced to death by an all-white jury despite lack of real evidence; in 1932, Supreme Court overturned original convictions; new trials began in 1933, but defendants never were acquitted. (p. 539)

sea dogs English sailors who plundered Spanish ships in 16th century. (p. 33)

Securities and Exchange Commission (SEC) commission created by Congress in 1934 to administer Securities Act that required any company selling stock to fully inform investors of all company financial information, to regulate buying on margin, and to prevent unfair manipulation of stock exchanges throughout United States. (p. 562)

self-determination right of people of a country to choose their own leaders in free elections. (p. 435)

separation of powers in the United States, division of authority among executive, legislative, and judicial branches of government. (p. 100)

Separatists most radical of Puritan groups that separated themselves totally from Anglican Church in 16th century. (p. 50)

settlement house neighborhood community center set up to help the needy; in late 1800s functioned as center in city slums; established through settlement movement's new approach to urban reform. (p. 308)

Seventeenth Amendment amendment to Constitution proposed in 1912 and ratified in 1913, changing method of electing U.S. senators from election by state legislatures to direct election by voters of the state. (p. 362)

sharecropping after the Civil War, economic system that developed in the South; a farm family made a contract with a landowner, agreeing to pay for use of land with a share of crop. (p. 242)

Shays' Rebellion rebellion in 1786 of angry farmers in western Massachusetts led by Daniel Shays, former captain in Continental Army, against increased taxes imposed by state; rebellion crushed by militia. (p. 71)

Sherman Antitrust Act a law passed by Congress in 1890 that outlawed monopolies and banned "every contract, combination in the form of trust or otherwise, or conspiracy in restraint of trade." (p. 304)

Silent Majority group known also as Middle America, the middle-class people targeted by Richard Nixon in his 1968 campaign for the presidency. (p. 840)

sit-in protest demonstration tactic in 1960s in which African Americans and whites sat down at segregated lunch counters and refused to move until the African Americans were served. (p. 758)

Sixteenth Amendment amendment to the Constitution, proposed in 1909 and ratified in 1913, that permitted the federal government to collect income taxes. (p. 362)

social contract new theory of government in England in 1700s in which ruler protected property and lives of the people; in return, citizens were obliged to be loyal, pay taxes, and obey laws. (p. 57)

Social Darwinism philosopher Herbert Spencer's doctrine drawn from Charles Darwin's biological concepts; Spencer wrote that a process similar to Darwin's natural selection

in animal world was at work in society and that "survival of the fittest" preserved the strong and weeded out the weak. (p. 279)

Socialist Party of America U.S. political party formed in 1901 and led by Eugene Debs; believed in replacing capitalism with public ownership of means of production; believed that a change to this system could be accomplished through the ballot. (p. 348)

socialized medicine providing medical care and hospital services for all persons, either free or at nominal cost, especially through government subsidization. (p. 793)

Social Security Act of 1935 a law to provide old-age assistance to American workers in form of monthly pension for those over 65; to establish unemployment insurance system to help unemployed workers for a limited amount of time as they looked for jobs; to aid dependent children and the handicapped; programs funded by tax on worker salaries on payrolls of employers. (p. 568)

Social Security trust fund money committed to funding future Social Security pensions. (p. 948)

Solidarity Polish independent labor union that succeeded in breaking communist party's monopoly on power; Solidarity's founder, Lech Walesa, became president of Poland in 1990. (p. 928)

Southern Christian Leadership Conference (SCLC) organization formed by the Reverend Dr. Martin Luther King, Jr., and others in 1957, consisting mainly of southern churches, to campaign for civil rights for African American citizens in the United States. (p. 757)

Spanish Armada huge fleet of Spanish ships sent in 1588 by King Philip II to destroy the English fleet and invade England; harassed by Drake's lighter, more maneuverable ships and pounded by heavy storms, most of Spanish fleet was lost. (p. 34)

speakeasies secret places where alcoholic drinks were sold contrary to law during Prohibition. (p. 471)

spheres of influence areas of China divided among and economically and politically controlled by a number of European countries and Japan in late 1800s. (p. 395)

Spitfire fighter plane used extensively by Britain's Royal Air Force in Battle of Britain during World War II. (p. 618)

Sputnik [sput′nik] the first artificial earth satellite, launched by the Soviet Union in 1957. (p. 718)

stagflation economic situation combining business slowdown, or stagnation, plus inflation; steps taken to curb either tendency can worsen the other. (p. 916)

Stamp Act measure passed by English Parliament in 1765 that provided for a direct tax on ordinary goods and services used by the colonists. (p. 61)

Stimson Doctrine a doctrine denying diplomatic recognition to any territory taken over by force; response to Japan's invasion of Manchuria in 1931. (p. 601)

Strategic Defense Initiative (SDI) President Ronald Reagan's proposal for a protective laser shield in space that would prevent enemy nuclear missiles from reaching the United States; commonly called "Star Wars." (p. 929)

Student Nonviolent Coordinating Committee (SNCC) civil rights organization created by civil rights activist Ella Baker and others; provided "group-centered" leadership rather than "leader-centered" group such as Dr. King's SCLC. (p. 759)

Students for a Democratic Society (SDS) organization formed in 1962 by Tom Hayden and others, a group of young people disenchanted with society and concerned with racial injustice, threat of nuclear war, and decline in quality of human life; SDS was involved in protest movement of 1960s and early 1970s. (p. 803)

supply-side economics a theory of economics that advocates increasing nation's supply of goods and services by encouraging increased private investment, primarily through a large tax cut. (p. 924)

supremacy clause Article VI of U.S. Constitution which states that Constitution and national laws and treaties are "the supreme law of the land"; clause designates national government as ultimate authority. (p. 97)

Sussex pledge a pledge issued by the German government in May 1916, after sinking the French passenger ship *Sussex*, promising that no more passenger or merchant ships would be sunk without warning. (p. 422)

T

tabloid a newspaper, usually smaller and easier to hold than the ordinary size newspaper page, that has many pictures, short articles, and large, often sensational, headlines. (p. 500)

Taft-Hartley Act a law passed by Congress in 1947 over President Truman's veto that outlawed the closed shop, required unions to accept a 60-day "cooling-off period" before going on strike, and empowered the president to issue injunctions to prevent strikes that hurt the national safety. (p. 693)

Tammany Hall the Democractic political machine in New York City named for its headquarters building on Madison Avenue; established in the mid-1800s. (p. 307)

Tariff of Abominations name given to protective tariff in 1828 by angry southerners who favored free trade; priced certain imported raw materials out of American market; again brought up the subject of nullification. (p. 167)

Teapot Dome Scandal the secret, illegal leasing of oil-rich properties in Wyoming and California by Secretary of the Interior Albert

Fall, during President Warren G. Harding's Administration, to several private oil-company executives in return for large cash payments; Fall was found not guilty of defrauding the government. (p. 476)

Teller Amendment a resolution, introduced in Congress by Senator Henry M. Teller of Colorado in 1898, stating that the United States had no designs on Cuba and would withdraw troops sent there during Spanish-American War. (p. 388)

temperance movement movement against use of alcoholic beverages that started in early 1800s as effort to moderate drinking habits through persuasion and education; eventually led to national prohibition through 18th Amendment passed in 1919. (p. 172)

Tennessee Valley Authority public corporation created by Congress in 1933 to buy or build dams, generate electrical power, help establish flood control, and manufacture and sell fertilizer; TVA dams and electricity they produced brought cheap power and measure of prosperity to citizens living in Tennessee River Valley. (p. 557)

Tenure of Office Act act of Congress in 1867 that barred the president from removing officeholders without Senate approval. (p. 239)

Tet Offensive during Tet (the Vietnamese New Year) in January 1968, a massive offensive by North Vietnamese and Viet Cong overran many South Vietnamese cities and laid siege to U.S. embassy in Saigon; caused both military and political leaders in United States to question Vietnam policy. (p. 836)

Third Reich [rīk] totalitarian state in Germany (from 1933 to 1945) under Adolf Hitler. (p. 604)

Third World economically underdeveloped nations of the world, particularly those in Africa, Asia, and Latin America. (p. 797)

Thirteenth Amendment amendment to the Constitution abolishing slavery throughout the United States; passed in 1865. (p. 234)

38th parallel arbitrarily chosen to divide Korea in 1945; Soviets installed communist government in industrial area north of line; Syngman Rhee, conservative nationalist, emerged in agrarian south as American-sponsored ruler. (p. 687)

Three-fifths Compromise during Constitutional Convention in 1787, a compromise reached between northern and southern states in which for purposes of representation and taxation five slaves would be considered as three people. (p. 72)

Treaty of Guadalupe Hidalgo treaty signed on February 2, 1848, ending the war between the United States and Mexico; the United States gained title to Texas, New Mexico, and California, agreed to pay Mexico $15 million, and paid Mexican debt to American citizens. (p. 184)

Treaty of Paris of 1783 the treaty between the United States and England ending the

Revolutionary War; the United States gained recognition as a sovereign nation and received most of the lands between the Great Lakes, the Appalachian Mountains, and the Mississippi River; also gained right to continue fishing off Canadian coast. (p. 68)

trilateralism idea developed during Nixon Administration that noncommunist world was no longer dominated by U.S. but had three major power centers — America, Europe, and Japan. (p. 876)

Tripartite Pact defensive pact among Germany, Italy, and Japan signed in late 1940. (p. 633)

Triple Alliance one of the two great European alliances before World War I, made up of Germany, Austria-Hungary, Italy, and later, the Ottoman Empire. (p. 416)

Triple Entente one of the two great European alliances before World War I, made up of Britain, France, and Russia. (p. 416)

Truman Doctrine policy announced in 1947 by President Harry S. Truman that United States would support anticommunist regime in Greece and free peoples anywhere in the world who were resisting communism. (p. 680)

trunk lines major railroad lines. (p. 275)

trust a common type of business consolidation in the 1880s and early 1890s; could operate as one giant company, control the production and price of some commodity, and reduce competition. (p. 280)

trustbusting government's attempts to break up monopolies through antitrust suits, especially as carried out by President Theodore Roosevelt against the Northern Securities Company, which the Supreme Court ordered dissolved in 1904. (p. 355)

Tweed Ring a group of unscrupulous Democratic politicians led by William Tweed during 1860s and 1870s in New York City that collected bribes from companies bidding on contracts to perform city services; also juggled the city's financial accounts to steal millions of dollars. (p. 308)

U

Underwood Tariff bill passed by Congress in 1913 that lowered rates on many items, including cotton, woolen goods, steel, coal, and wood; first real reduction in rates since Civil War, permitting competition in industries that had been virtual monopolies for many years; provided for first tax on personal income. (p. 367)

United Farm Workers union of migrant farm workers organized by Cesar Chavez in the 1960s to improve wages and benefits; organized strikes and boycotts of lettuce and table grapes. (p. 811)

United Mine Workers (UMW) union formed in 1890 for protection of mine workers; 394,000 members struck soft-coal industry in 1919. (p. 311)

unwritten constitution political changes shaped by tradition or practical considerations and not provided for in the Constitution; includes party system, congressional standing committees, and seniority in congressional committees. (p. 106)

Urban League national group formed in 1910 to aid the adjustment of African Americans to cities. (p. 431)

V

veto right to reject bills passed by a lawmaking body; the right to prevent some action proposed by that body, as in the United Nations Security Council. (p. 100)

Viet Cong communist guerrilla forces in South Vietnam during Vietnam War; National Front for the Liberation of Vietnam (NLF); the group organized by communist forces in South Vietnam loyal to Ho Chi Minh in the North. (p. 823)

Vietminh a communist group formed by Ho Chi Minh and others in Vietnam during World War II to promote independence. (p. 822)

Vietnamization Nixon administration policy announced in 1972 of gradually withdrawing American troops from Vietnam while training South Vietnamese to take more responsibility for their own defense. (p. 842)

Volstead Act law used to enforce the 18th Amendment; defined any liquor containing ½ of 1% alcohol as illegal and gave enforcement powers to Bureau of Internal Revenue. (p. 471)

Voting Rights Act of 1965 act passed by Congress that banned literacy tests used for decades to prevent African American citizens from voting in the South; act empowered attorney general to send examiners into areas where there were charges of discrimination. (p. 771)

W

Wade-Davis Bill a bill passed in Congress in July 1864 that proposed harsh measures for the reconstruction of the southern states; Lincoln killed the bill with a pocket veto. (p. 234)

Wagner Act an act passed in 1935 after the National Industrial Recovery Act had been found unconstitutional by the Supreme Court; revived many pro-labor provisions of NIRA; also known as the National Labor Relations Act. (p. 571)

War Hawk group in Congress that felt war was only way to defend American honor in 1812; supported war with Britain. (p. 120)

War on Poverty President Lyndon B. Johnson's legislative program to combat unemployment and illiteracy, launched in 1964 with creation of Office of Economic Opportunity (OEO) to oversee antipoverty programs. (p. 794)

water rights rights to use certain bodies of water and the water table; especially important in arid West of the U.S.; subject to complex state laws and local customs during Western development. (p. 358)

welfare capitalism form of capitalism in which companies provide benefits for their workers in an effort to keep employees happy and productive. (p. 462)

Whig party party that took its name from the party in England that supported Parliament; formed in 1834. (p. 170)

white-collar workers people employed in clerical, professional, or office work, such as retail clerks, office workers, and bank tellers. (p. 721)

Wilmot Proviso amendment to a congressional bill in 1846 that sought to prohibit slavery in any territory purchased from Mexico. (p. 186)

workmen's compensation laws requiring an employer to pay a worker who is injured or contracts a disease as a result of his or her employment. (p. 366)

Works Progress Administration (WPA) government agency of the New Deal; put unemployed people to work building playgrounds, schools, hospitals, bridges, and repairing airports and highways; white-collar workers, including artists and writers, also found work with this agency which spent $11 billion on 250,000 projects and employed over two million people at most times. (p. 568)

writ of habeas corpus [hā ′bē əs kôr ′pəs] court order requiring that a prisoner be brought before a court to decide whether accused is being held lawfully. (p. 107)

X

xenophobia a hatred or fear of foreigners or strangers. (p. 284)

Y

Yalta Conference second of three World War II meetings of United States, Britain, and Soviet Union; decisions made to divide Germany into four occupation zones; to allow free postwar elections in Eastern Europe and to have Soviet Union enter war against Japan as soon as Germany was defeated, in return for concessions in Eastern Europe and Asia. (p. 641)

Z

Zimmermann note message from Arthur Zimmermann, the German foreign minister, to the German minister to Mexico directing him to offer Texas, New Mexico, and Arizona to Mexico in return for its entrance into World War I on the German side, against the United States. (p. 423)

hat, āge, fär; let, ēqual, tėrm;
it, īce; hot, ōpen, ôrder;
oil, out; cup, pút, rüle;
ch, child; ng, long; sh, she;
th, thin; ᴛʜ, then; zh, measure;

ə represents *a* in about, *e* in taken, *i* in
pencil, *o* in lemon, *u* in circus.

Pronunciations are from the *Scott,
Foresman Advanced Dictionary.*
Page numbers show where each term is
first discussed.

A

Afghanistan [af gan′ ə stan]   mountainous country in southwest Asia, between Pakistan and Iran. Capital: Kabul. (33°N/65°E) p. 920

Alamo [al′ ə mō]   a mission building in San Antonio, Texas, used as fort by a small rebel force of Texans fighting for independence from Mexico in 1836. p. 176

Alaska   Pacific state of the United States in the northwestern part of North America; territory purchased from Russia in 1867. Capital: Juneau. (65°N/153°W) p. 383

Alsace-Lorraine [al säs′ lə rän′]   region in northeast France, consisting of Alsace and Lorraine; German province 1871-1919 and 1940-1945. (49°N/8°E) p. 416

Appalachia [ap′ə lā′ chə]   region in eastern United States covering parts of 11 states from northern Pennsylvania to northern Alabama; population about 15 million. p. 796

Appomattox [ap′ə mat′ əks] **Court House,** Virginia, village in central Virginia where Lee surrendered to Grant on April 9, 1865. (37°N/79°W) p. 230

Ardennes [är den′] **Forest**   mountain and forest region in northeast France, southeast Belgium, and Luxembourg; location of Battle of the Bulge, last major German counteroffensive of World War II (1944). (50°N/5°E) p. 614

Atlanta, Georgia   city in northwest part of state, capital of Georgia; General William Sherman set out from here in November 1864 on 300-mile march to sea through Georgia to crush the South's will to fight. (33°N/84°W) p. 229

B

Balkan Peninsula [bôl′ kən]   peninsula in southeast Europe, extending south into the Mediterranean Sea; region in which national struggles led to 1914 assassination of Austro-Hungarian Archduke Franz Ferdinand and subsequent outbreak of World War I. (42°N/23°E) p. 417

Baltimore, Maryland   city at northern end of Chesapeake Bay; one of largest American cities of early 1800s. (39°N/77°W) p. 319

Bataan Peninsula [bə tan′]   peninsula near Manila in Philippines. During World War II, United States and Philippine troops retreated down peninsula under Japanese attack (1941–1942) and surrendered after siege on

island of Corregidor (1942). (15°N/121°E) p. 635

Beijing [bā′ jing′]   capital of China near northeast coast; formerly Peking. (40°N/116°E) p. 878

Beirut [bā rüt′]   capital and chief seaport of Lebanon, on the Mediterranean. (34°N/36°E) p. 931

Bering Strait [bir′ ing strāt]   narrow strait between the Bering Sea and the Arctic Ocean, lying between the continents of Asia and North America. The strait may once have been a land bridge. (66°N/170°W) p. 14

Berkeley, California   city in western California, near San Francisco; among environmentally concerned communities that restricted Styrofoam use in 1990. (38°N/122°W) p. 973

Birmingham, Alabama   city in central Alabama. Rev. Dr. Martin Luther King, Jr., led civil rights demonstrations here in 1963. (34°N/87°W) p. 760

C

California   Pacific state of the United States. Capital: Sacramento. (37°N/120°W) p. 187

Cambodia [kam bō′dē ə]   country in southeast Asia; also known as Kampuchea [kam′-pü chē′ ə]. Involved in Vietnam War fighting in 1970s. Capital: Phnom Penh. (13°N/105°E) p. 842

Cambridge, Massachusetts   city in eastern Massachusetts, near Boston, located on the Charles River. (42°N/71°W) p. 55

Canal Zone   Panama Canal and the land five miles on each side, governed by the United States from 1903 to 1979, and now governed by Panama. (9°N/80°W) p. 400

Chicago, Illinois   city on Lake Michigan in northeast Illinois where many of America's first skyscrapers were built. (42°N/88°W) p. 306

Colombia [kə lum′bē ə]   country in northwest South America. Capital: Bogotá. (4°N/72°W) p. 965

Colorado   western state of the United States, partly on the Great Plains and partly in the Rockies; explored by Zebulon Pike in 1806 and organized as a territory after the Pikes Peak gold rush of 1858. Capital: Denver. (40°N/106°W) p. 925

Concord, Massachusetts   town in northeast Massachusetts where the second battle of the

American Revolution was fought on April 19, 1775. (42°N/71°W) p. 63

Cortland County   region in upstate New York, hit hard by plant closings in the mid-1970s. (44°N/74°W) p. 871

Cuba   country on the largest island in the West Indies, south of Florida; involved in fighting during Spanish-American War (1898) and U.S.-Soviet missile crisis (1962). Capital: Havana. (22°N/80°W) p. 717

Czechoslovakia [chek′ə slō vä′kē ə]   country in Eastern Europe. Capital: Prague. (50°N/17°E) p. 677

D

Dallas, Texas   city in northeastern Texas in which President John F. Kennedy was assassinated in 1963. (33°N/97°W) p. 790

Da Nang [dä′ näng′]   seaport in central Vietnam, on the South China Sea. (16°N/108°E) p. 828

Dardanelles [därd′n elz′]   strait in northwest Turkey; connects the Sea of Marmara with the Aegean Sea; separates European from Asian Turkey; formerly called the Hellespont. (40°N/26°E) p. 680

Detroit, Michigan   city in southeastern Michigan; major industrial center; automobile manufacturing center; produced military equipment during World War II. (42°N/83°W) p. 494

Dien Bien Phu [dyen′ byen′ fü′]   town in northwest Vietnam taken by Vietminh troops in 1954 in a decisive battle that ended French power in Vietnam. (21°N/108°E) p. 823

District of Columbia   federal district in eastern United States between Maryland and Virginia, governed by Congress, area same as that of capital city, Washington; site chosen by George Washington in 1791. (39°N/77°W) p. 187

Dominican Republic   country on the eastern part of the island of Hispaniola, in the West Indies. Capital: Santo Domingo. (19°N/71°W) p. 800

Dunkirk [dun′ kərk]   seaport in northern France from which British forces crossed the English Channel to escape the German army in 1940. (51°N/2°E) p. 615

Dust Bowl   large area of western plains states affected in the mid-1930s by drought and dust storms that carried away much of the top soil. p. 530

E

East Germany country in central Europe, comprising much of the eastern part of pre-World War II Germany; reunified with West Germany in 1990. Former capital: East Berlin. (52°N/12°E) p. 950

East St. Louis, Illinois city in southwest Illinois, across the Mississippi River from St. Louis, Missouri. (39°N/90°W) p. 432

Ellis Island small island in New York harbor; from 1891 to 1954 immigrants were examined there before entering the United States. (41°N/74°W) p. 283

El Salvador [el sal′və dôr] country in western Central America; location of widespread unrest and protests during 1970s and 1980s. Capital: San Salvador. (14°N/89°W) p. 929

Erie Canal waterway in New York State between Buffalo and Albany, connecting Lake Erie with the Hudson River and the port of New York. Parts of the canal are now abandoned, but most of it is included in the New York State Barge Canal System. (43°N/76°W) p. 164

Ethiopia [ē′thē ō′ pē ə] country in eastern Africa; formerly called Abyssinia. Capital: Addis Ababa. (9°N/39°E) p. 608

Europe continent east of the North Atlantic Ocean and west of Asia. (50°N/20°E) p. 483

F

Fort Sumter fort in harbor of Charleston, South Carolina, where first engagement of the Civil War occurred when Confederates bombarded the Union-held position in 1861. (33°N/80°W) p. 220

France industrialized country in Western Europe. Capital: Paris. (47°N/3°E) p. 416

G

Georgia southeastern state of the United States; the last of the 13 American colonies founded by the English. Capital: Atlanta. (33°N/83°W) p. 914

Germany country in central Europe divided after World War II into West Germany and East Germany, with parts of its territory going to Poland and the Soviet Union; reunified in 1990. Capital: Berlin. (51°N/10°E) p. 575

Greensboro, North Carolina city in northern North Carolina in which black college students in 1960 staged the first sit-in to protest segregation in public facilities. (36°N/80°W) p. 758

Grenada [grə nä′də] Caribbean island country; location of 1983 incursion by U.S. troops to restore calm after assassination of Grenada's leader. Capital: St. George's. (12°N/62°W) p. 929

Guadalcanal [gwä′dl kə nal′] one of the Solomon Islands in the western Pacific Ocean; Japanese defeated there during World War II by United States forces (1942 and 1943). (10°S/160°E) p. 646

Guam [gwäm] island in the Pacific Ocean east of the Philippines; acquired by the United States from Spain after the Spanish-American War in 1898. Capital: Agana. (13°N/145°E) p. 962

Guantánamo [gwän tä′nä mō] **Bay** inlet of the Caribbean Sea in southeast Cuba, site of a United States naval base. (20°N/75°W) p. 393

H

Haight-Ashbury neighborhood of San Francisco, California; noted for its counterculture and hippy residents of the 1960s and 1970s. (38°N/122°W) p. 805

Haiphong [hi′fông′], Vietnam seaport in northern Vietnam near the Gulf of Tonkin and east of Hanoi; site bombed by United States in Vietnam War (1972). (21°N/107°E) p. 844

Hanoi [hă noi′] Vietnam capital of Vietnam, in the northern part of the country. (21°N/106°E) p. 823

Harlem northern section of Manhattan, bordering the Harlem and East rivers, in New York City, the Cultural Center of African Americans in the 1920s. (41°N/74°W) p. 468

Helsinki [hel′sing kē], Finland seaport and capital of Finland located in the southern part of the country. (60°N/25°E) p. 878

Hetch Hetchy Valley valley in northwestern Yosemite National Park in California; involved in a bitter dispute between preservationists and conservationists over the flooding of the valley for use as a water supply for San Francisco. (38°N/119°W) p. 360

Hiroshima [hir′ō shē′ mə], Japan seaport in western Japan; largely destroyed by the first military use of the atomic bomb on August 6, 1945. (34°N/132°E) p. 650

Ho Chi Minh Trail jungle supply route used by North Vietnamese troops to enter South Vietnam during the Vietnam War; route ran mainly through Laos. (14°N/107°E) p. 829

Hollywood, California Los Angeles district that became the center of the American motion picture and television industries. (34°N/118°W) p. 501

Hue [hwä], Vietnam seaport in central Vietnam; ancient capital of Vietnam. (16°N/108°E) p. 836

Hungary country in central Europe, formerly part of Austro-Hungarian empire; one of Eastern European countries in which communist party leaders were forced out of power in 1989 reforms. Capital: Budapest. (47°N/19°E) p. 950

I

Indian Territory land located west of the Mississippi River in the Great Plains region that now comprises most of Oklahoma; Cherokee Indians were forcibly moved there during Andrew Jackson's administration. (35°N/97°W) p. 169

Iran country in southwest Asia; formerly called Persia; under government of Ayatollah Ruhollah Khomeini, American embassy in Tehran was seized (1979) and 52 hostages were held until 1981. Capital: Tehran. (32°N/53°E) p. 717

Israel [iz′rē əl] country in southwest Asia on the Mediterranean Sea including the major part of Palestine; the ancient kingdom of the Jews. Capital: Jerusalem. (32°N/35°E) p. 879

J

Jackson, Mississippi Mississippi capital located in the central section of the state. (32°N/90°W) p. 760

Jackson State University, Mississippi university where police killed and wounded students during antiwar demonstrations (May 14, 1970). p. 843

Jamestown, Virginia town in southeastern Virginia; first permanent English colony established in North America (1607). (37°N/77°W) p. 37

Jordan [jôrd′n] country in southwest Asia, east of Israel. Capital: Amman. (31°N/36°E) p. 880

K

Kansas north-central state of the United States; in the region explored by Zebulon Pike in 1806. Capital: Topeka. (39°N/98°W) p. 572

Kent State University, Ohio site of anti-war demonstrations during which the National Guard killed four demonstrators (May 4, 1970). p. 843

L

Laos [lä′ōs] country in southeast Asia, west of Vietnam; SEATO country drawn into Vietnam War. Capital: Vientiane. (18°N/105°E) p. 842

Lebanon [leb′ə nən] country in southwest Asia at the eastern end of the Mediterranean Sea north of Israel. Capital: Beirut. (34°N/36°E) p. 881

Lexington, Massachusetts town in northeast Massachusetts where the first battle of the American Revolution was fought on April 19, 1775. (42°N/71°W) p. 63

Leyte Gulf [lā′tē] gulf near the east central Philippine island of Leyte; site of World War II Battle for Leyte Gulf (October 23-26, 1944) during which Japanese sea power was shattered. (11°N/125°E) p. 649

Lincoln Memorial, Washington, D.C. memorial honoring Abraham Lincoln, 16th president of the United States. p. 764

Lithuania [lith′ū ā′nē ə] constituent republic of the U.S.S.R. in the western part, on the Baltic Sea; declared independence in 1990. Capital: Vilnius. (56°N/24°E) p. 952

Louisiana southern state of the United States; the territory drained by the Mississippi River and its tributaries, claimed by French explorers in the late 1600s. Capital: Baton Rouge. (31°N/92°W) p. 567

M

Manchuria [man chùr′ē ə] region in northeast China, including several provinces of China; rich in coal and other resources; the seizure of this area in September, 1931, by Japan is considered by some to be the start of World War II. (42°N/125°E) p. 398

Manila Bay large bay at Manila in the Philippines; the American fleet under Admiral George Dewey defeated the Spanish fleet there in 1898. (15°N/121°E) p. 389

Mariana Islands group of 15 small islands in the Pacific Ocean, east of the Philippines; the largest island, Guam is a territory of the United States; the other islands are a self-governing commonwealth under the protection of the United States. (16°N/146°E) p. 646

Maryland southeastern state of the United States; one of the Chesapeake Bay colonies and one of the original 13 states. Capital: Annapolis. (39°N/77°W) p. 885

Massachusetts northeast New England state of the United States; originally the Massachusetts Bay Colony and the Plymouth Colony; one of the original 13 states. Capital: Boston. (42°N/72°W) p. 247

Massachusetts Bay Colony settlement of towns established by the Pilgrims in 1630 beside Boston Bay and along the Charles River. (42°N/71°W) p. 51

Mediterranean Sea [med ′ə tə rā ′nē ən] a large sea bordered by Europe, Asia, and Africa. (35°N/15°E) p. 20

Memphis, Tennessee city in southwest Tennessee on the Mississippi River; a busy river port during the steamboat era. (35°N/90°W) p. 775

Menlo Park, New Jersey community in central New Jersey; location of Thomas A. Edison's research laboratory established in 1876. (41°N/74°W) p. 277

Meuse-Argonne [myüz är ′gon] region in northeast France in the upper valley of the Meuse River, crossed by a wooded ridge, the Argonne Forest, where the last major offensive of World War I occurred. (49°N/5°E) p. 429

Michigan north-central state of the United States; one of the states formed in the Northwest Territory. Capital: Lansing. (44°N/85°W) p. 885

Midway Island an area made up of two islands in a group of small islands in the Pacific Ocean, belonging to the United States, halfway between the United States and the Philippines; the Japanese goal in the World War II Battle of Midway (June 1942). (28°N/177°W) p. 644

Minnesota a north-central state of the United States; made up of land partly from the Northwest Territory and partly from the Louisiana Territory. Capital: St. Paul. (46°N/94°W) p. 926

Mississippi a southern state of the United States; one of the states of the Confederacy during the Civil War. (33°N/90°W) p. 240

Montgomery Alabama capital, in the central part of the state; city in which African Americans, led by Rev. Dr. Martin Luther King, Jr., organized a successful bus boycott in 1955 to protest segregation. (32°N/86°W) p. 753

Moscow, Soviet Union capital of the Soviet Union and of the Russian Soviet Federated Socialist Republic in the western part of the Soviet Union. (56°N/38°E) p. 622

Muncie, Indiana city in east-central Indiana; used as basis for average medium-sized city in sociology study entitled *Middletown*. (40°N/85°W) p. 533

My Lai [mē ′ lī] Vietnam a village on the east coast of South Vietnam; site of massacre precipitated by American troops in March 1968. (14°N/108°E) p. 832

N

Nagasaki [nä ′ gə sä ′ kē] seaport in southwest Japan; target of the second atomic bomb to be used in war (August 9, 1945). (33°N/130°E) p. 651

Nashville, Tennessee Tennessee capital, in the central part of the state. (36°N/87°W) p. 506

New England the northeastern part of the United States, includes the states of Maine, New Hampshire, Vermont, Massachusetts, Rhode Island, and Connecticut; the English colonies in the northeastern part of the present-day United States. p. 707

New Jersey northeastern Atlantic coast state of the United States; one of the original 13 English colonies and one of the original 13 states. Capital: Trenton. (40°N/74°W) p. 366

New Netherland the Dutch colony that became New York after the English took it over. (43°N/76°W) p. 53

New Orleans, Louisiana seaport city in southeast Louisiana, important port near the mouth of the Mississippi River. (30°N/90°W) p. 118

New York Atlantic coast state of the United States; one of the 13 English colonies and one of the original 13 states; originally settled as the Dutch colony of New Netherland at the mouth of the Hudson River; renamed New York by the British. Capital: Albany. (43°N/75°W) p. 925

New York City seaport in southeastern New York State, at the mouth of the Hudson River; the largest city in the United States. (41°N/74°W) p. 111

Niagara Falls, Canada city in southeast Ontario, on the Niagara River at Niagara Falls; site of 1905 meeting of African American leaders who called for action to protest segregation and inequality. (43°N/79°W) p. 350

Nicaragua [nik ′ə rä ′ gwə] country in Central America, north of Costa Rica. Capital: Managua. (12°N/85°W) p. 930

Normandy Peninsula peninsula in northwest France, part of Normandy province; site of European invasion by Allies in World War II (June 6, 1944). (49°N/1°E) p. 640

North Carolina state in southeast United States; one of the 13 English colonies and one of the original 13 states. Capital: Raleigh. (35°N/80°W) p. 883

Northwest Territory early territory of the United States north of the Ohio River and east of the Mississippi, also bounded by the Great Lakes; organized by Congress in 1787; now forming the states of Ohio, Indiana, Illinois, Michigan, Wisconsin, and northeast Minnesota. p. 71

O

Ohio north-central state of the United States; the first state in the Northwest Territory; Capital: Columbus. (40°N/83°W) p. 474

Ohio Valley the region drained by the Ohio River and its tributaries, claimed in colonial times by both England and France. (38°N/86°W) p. 59

P

Palestine [pal ′ə stīn] region or country in southwest Asia between the Mediterranean Sea and the Jordan River, sometimes including various other lands; now divided chiefly between Israel and Jordan; area sometimes called the Holy Land. (32°N/35°E) p. 880

Panama Central American country on the Isthmus of Panama; location of Panama Canal. Capital: Panama City. (9°N/80°W) p. 949

Panama, Isthmus of narrow, mountainous land link between North and South America. (9°N/80°W) p. 399

Pearl Harbor, Hawaii United States naval base near Honolulu, on the south coast of Oahu; site of attack by Japanese bombers on December 7, 1941. (21°N/158°W) p. 634

Pennsylvania state in northeast United States; one of the original 13 colonies; founded in 1682 by William Penn. Capital: Harrisburg. (41°N/78°W) p. 356

Philadelphia, Pennsylvania city in southeast Pennsylvania, on the Delaware River; chief city of the Pennsylvania colony and the largest colonial city. (40°N/75°W) p. 71

Pigs, Bay of swampy, isolated region on the southern coast of Cuba; site of failed invasion of Cuba in 1961. (22°N/81°W) p. 798

Pittsburgh, Pennsylvania city in southwest Pennsylvania where Allegheny and Monongahela rivers meet; a center of the iron and steel industry. (40°N/80°W) p. 279

Plymouth, Massachusetts town in present-day southeast Massachusetts, first successful English colony founded by Puritans in 1620. (42°N/71°W) p. 51

Poland country in central Europe between Germany and the Soviet Union; one of the Eastern European countries swept by reform in 1989. Capital: Warsaw. (52°N/19°E) p. 928

Promontory [prom ′ən tôr ′ē] **Point,** Utah site near the Great Salt Lake where two rail lines were joined on May 10, 1869, linking the eastern and western United States. (41°N/112°W) p. 266

Providence, Rhode Island capital city in northeast Rhode Island; town founded by Roger Williams (1636) when he fled from Massachusetts. (42°N/71°W) p. 52

Pullman, Illinois town built and owned by the Pullman Company; site of violent strike activity in 1894; now a part of Chicago. (42°N/88°W) p. 312

Q

Quebec [kwi bek ′] Canada capital city of Quebec province in southeast Canada, located on the St. Lawrence River; first settlement in New France. (47°N/71°W) p. 35

R

Rhineland German region, west of Rhine River; region along the Rhine River bordering France, Germany and Belgium; invaded by Hitler in 1936. (47°N/7°E) p. 607

Richmond, Virginia   Virginia capital, located in the eastern part of the state; capital of the Confederate States of America during the Civil War. (38°N/77°W) p. 220

Romania [rō mā′nē ə]   country in southeastern Europe; one of the Eastern European countries swept by reform in 1989. Capital: Bucharest. (46°N/25°E) p. 950

S

Saar Valley [sär]   border region of southwest Germany along the Saar River which flows from northeast France through Germany into the Moselle River; region returned to Germany by League of Nations in 1935 that marked beginning of Hitler's expansion. (50°N/6°E) p. 437

Saigon [sī gon′], Vietnam   former name of Ho Chi Minh City; located in southern Vietnam; formerly the capital of South Vietnam. (11°N/107°E) p. 824

Saigon River   small river draining into the South China Sea just northeast of the Mekong Delta. (11°N/106°E) p. 962

Saint Augustine, Florida   town in northeast Florida; the oldest European town in the United States, founded by the Spanish in 1565. (30°N/81°W) p. 31

Saipan [sī pan′]   island in the west Pacific, one of the Mariana Islands; site of United States B-29 bomber raids on Japan during World War II (1944). (15°N/146°E) p. 646

San Antonio, Texas   city in south Texas, the site of the Alamo. (30°N/99°W) p. 176

San Francisco, California   major seaport located in California; founded as Spanish town and mission (1776). (38°N/122°W) p. 723

San Jacinto, Texas   town in eastern Texas; site of a battle during the Mexican War where the Mexican general Santa Anna was captured on April 21, 1836. (30°N/95°W) p. 176

San Salvador [san sal′ və dôr]   island in the central Bahamas chain, believed to be the first land in the New World seen by Columbus in 1492. (24°N/75°W) p. 25

Santiago [san′tyä′gō] Cuba   port city in southeast Cuba; American forces were concentrated there during the Spanish-American War in 1898. (20°N/76°W) p. 390

Saratoga, New York   county in northeast New York State near the site of significant battles of the Revolutionary War in October 1777. (43°N/75°W) p. 67

Scottsboro, Alabama   northeast Alabama city; small town that gave name to Scottsboro case in 1931; nine African American teenagers arrested and charged with roughing up white hobos and throwing them off freight train; two white women pulled off same train claimed young men had raped them; no evidence surfaced; eight of nine defendants sentenced to death in subsequent trial. (35°N/86°W) p. 539

Selma, Alabama   city in Alabama located in the central part of the state; the site of civil rights confrontations in 1965. (32°N/87°W) p. 770

Seneca Falls, New York   town in north-central New York State; Seneca Falls Convention to promote women's rights held there in 1848. (43°N/77°W) p. 173

Sicily [sis′ə lē]   island in the Mediterranean Sea, near the southwest tip of the Italian peninsula; largest island in the Mediterranean; part of Italy since 1860. (37°N/14°E) p. 639

Sinai Peninsula [sī′ nī]   triangular peninsula in northeast Egypt, between the Mediterranean Sea and the north end of the Red Sea; site of 1956 Israeli attack on Egyptian forces to keep Suez Canal open. (29°N/34°E) p. 913

South Africa   country in southern Africa; formerly Union of South Africa. Capitals: Pretoria, Cape Town, and Bloemfontein. (32°S/17°E) p. 953

Stalingrad [stä′lin grad] Soviet Union   former name of Volgograd; city in the southwest Soviet Union, on the Volga River; location of World War II battle that was the turning point of war in eastern Europe. (49°N/44°E) p. 638

Sudetenland [sü dāt′n land′]   mountainous region in northwest Czechoslovakia; region taken over by Hitler in 1938. (50°N/18°E) p. 609

Suez Canal   canal in Egypt across the Isthmus of Suez; connects the Mediterranean and Red seas. (30°N/33°E) p. 716

Switzerland   small country in central Europe, north of Italy; pledged to neutrality in European wars since the early 1500s. Capital: Bern. (46°N/8°E) p. 441

T

Tehran [te′ə ran′], Iran   capital of Iran, in the northern part of the country. (36°N/51°E) p. 920

Tel Aviv [tel′ ə vēv′], Israel   seaport in the western part of the country; includes the formerly separate city of Jaffa. (32°N/35°E) p. 918

Tennessee   south-central state of the United States; one of the first two states west of the Appalachian Mountains to enter the Union. Capital: Nashville. (36°N/86°W) p. 472

Tennessee Valley   region along the Tennessee River; consists of 40,000 square miles of land stretching into the states of Tennessee, Kentucky, Virginia, North Carolina, Georgia, Alabama, and Mississippi; site of the New Deal's Tennessee Valley Authority. (37°N/89°W) p. 557

38th parallel   line used by the United States and the Soviet Union to divide Korea after World War II; north of the line is North Korea; south of the line is South Korea. p. 687

Tiananmen Square   large square in central Beijing, China; location of pro-democracy demonstrations by Chinese students; demonstrations ended in a massacre by Chinese troops (June 3, 1989). (40°N/116°E) p. 951

Tonkin, Gulf of   arm of the South China Sea between Vietnam and Hainan Island. (20°N/108°E) p. 826

Trenton, New Jersey   site of Revolutionary War battle in which Washington defeated Hessian mercenaries and forced surrender of their British garrison on December 25, 1776. (40°N/75°W) p. 67

Tripoli [trip′ə lē], Libya   seaport and capital of Libya, in northwest part of country; attacked in 1986 by American bombers in effort to destroy headquarters of Muammar el-Qaddafi in retaliation for Libyan leader's involvement in terrorist attacks. (33°N/13°E) p. 932

V

Vera Cruz [ver′ə krüz′], Mexico   seaport in southeast Mexico, located about 250 miles directly east of Mexico City. Site of 1847 Mexican War battle that decided the war in favor of the United States. (19°N/95°W) p. 183

Vicksburg, Mississippi   a city in western Mississippi besieged by Grant until its surrender in 1863 led to Union control of entire Mississippi River. (32°N/91°W) p. 228

Vladivostok [vlad′ə vos′tok], Soviet Union   seaport on the Sea of Japan in the southeastern Soviet Union; location of British-Japanese intervention in 1918. (43°N/132°E) p. 913

W

Washington, D.C.   capital of the United States covering the entire District of Columbia; situated along the Potomac River between Maryland and Virginia. (39°N/77°W) p. 113

Watergate Office Building   building in Washington, D.C.; site of the infamous Watergate break-in (June 1972) which led to President Nixon's downfall. p. 868

Wisconsin   north-central state of the United States. One of the states formed in the Northwest Territory. Capital: Madison. (45°N/90°W) p. 353

Wounded Knee, South Dakota   site of battle between federal soldiers and a band of Sioux men, women, and children who had left their reservation in 1890; many Sioux were killed or wounded; now located on a Sioux reservation in southern South Dakota. (43°N/99°W) pp. 273, 809

Wyoming   western state of the United States; the first territory to adopt women's suffrage. Capital: Cheyenne. (43°N/108°W) p. 300

Y

Yalu River [yä′lü], Korea   river in eastern Asia between China and North Korea; line dividing Chinese and American troops during Korean War (1950-1953) (40°N/125°E) p. 688

Yorktown, Virginia   village in southeast Virginia, on the York River, where Lord Cornwallis surrendered to George Washington in 1781. (40°N/77°W) p. 68

Yucatán Peninsula [yü′kə tan′]   peninsula of southeast Mexico and northern Central America (the countries of Guatemala and Belize); the Maya culture developed there about 500 B.C. (20°N/89°W) p. 16

Yugoslavia [yü′gō slä′vē ə]   country in southeast Europe, on the Adriatic Sea; the one country in Eastern Europe that did not fall under Soviet control after World War II. Capital: Belgrade. (44°N/19°E) p. 951

I N D E X

I N D E X

Acknowledgments

Illustrations

Unless otherwise acknowledged, all photos are the property of Scott, Foresman. Page abbreviations are as follows: (t) top, (c) center, (b) bottom, (l) left, (r) right, (INS) inset.

v Copyright Yale University Art Gallery. **vi** (tl) Courtesy of the Trustees of the British Museum. (tr) The Ohio Historical Society. (cr) Pierpont Morgan Library. (bl) Anne S. K. Brown Military Collection, Brown University. (br) Guilford Courthouse National Military Park. **vii** (t) Pennsylvania State Capitol/Photo: Brian K. Foster. (b) Chicago Historical Society. **viii** (t) Gettysburg National Military Park, PA. National Park Service. (c) Anglo-American Museum. (b) Library of Congress. **ix** (c) Culver Pictures. (b) Sierra Club Library. **x** (l) Culver Pictures. (tr) Smithsonian Institution. (br) LA MITRAILLEUSE, 1915, Christopher Nevinson, Art Resource, NY Tate Gallery. **xi** (c) Culver Pictures. (b) OFFICE GIRLS, Raphael Soyer, 1936, From the collection of Whitney Museum of American Art. **xiii** (t) The National Archives. (b) UPI/Bettmann. **xiv** (b) Life Magazine Time Warner Inc. **xv** (t) Fred Ward/Black Star. (c) Leo Castelli Gallery. (b) Life Magazine Time Warner Inc. **xvi** (t) AP/Wide World. (b) Costa Manos/Magnum Photos. **xvii** (t) J. L. Atlan/Sygma. (b) UPI/Bettmann. **xxv** Universal Press Syndicate. Reprinted with permission. All Rights Reserved. **xxvii** Drawing by Arno: (c) 1931, 1959, The New Yorker Magazine, Inc.. **xxviii** (l) Library of Congress. (r) Drawing by Frank Williams in *The Detroit Free Press*. **xxx** NASA. **xxxi** James Blank/Stock Boston. **xxxii** (tl) John Lemker/Earth Scenes. (tr) Robert P. Carr/Bruce Coleman Inc. (b) GEOPIC (TM)/Earth Satellite Corp. **xxxiv** (t) Charles Feil/Stock Boston. (bl) Mike Andrews/Earth Scenes. (br) Keith Gunnar/Bruce Coleman Inc. **xxxv** (tl) Culver Pictures. (tr) Lee Foster/Bruce Coleman Inc. (bl) Nathan Benn/Stock Boston. (br) Bob Daemmrich/Stock Boston. **xxxviii** (tl) Robert P. Comport/Earth Scenes. (bl) Gordon Wiltsie/Peter Arnold, Inc. (r) Nicholas de Vore III/Bruce Coleman Inc. **xxxix** (tl) Jim Brandenburg/Bruce Coleman Inc. (bl) D. Cavagnaro/Peter Arnold, Inc. (tr) Clyde H. Smith/Peter Arnold, Inc. (br) E. R. Degginger/Earth Scenes. **xlii** (t) Metropolitan Museum of Art, Gift of Edgar William and Bernice Chrysler Garbisch, 1964. **xlii** (b) Amon Carter Museum of Art, Fort Worth, TX. **1** (t) Courtesy History Division, Los Angeles County Museum of Natural History. (c) David Frazier. (b) Randy Taylor/Sygma. **2** (t) Steve Schapiro/Gamma-Liaison. (cl) Oregon Historical Society. (cr) Library of Congress. (b) CHICAGO SUN TIMES, photo by Amanda Alcock. **3** (t) John Running. (cl) Courtesy of Sears and Roebuck. (cr) Brent Jones. (b) Bob Daemmrich. **4** (t) Witt/SIPA. (c) R. Maiman/Sygma. **4-5** (b) Bob Adelman/Magnum. **5** (t) The Bettmann Archive. (c) Paul F. Gero/Sygma. (b) Charpentier/SIPA. **6** (t) Thomas Gilcrease Institute of History and Art, Tulsa. (b) David Muench. **7** (tl) Susan Greenwood/Gamma-Liaison. (tr) Massachusetts Historical Society. (c) Sally Myers. (b) The Huntington Library, San Marino, CA. **8** (t) Private Collection (b) NASA. **9** (t) Brown Brothers. (c) Hank Morgan/Rainbow. (b) Dan McCoy/Rainbow. (ins) Courtesy Harrah's Automobile Collection. **10** TECUMSEH, Stanley Arthurs, Delaware Art Museum, Wilmington. **12** Santi Visaley/The Image Bank. (INS) Erich Lessing/Magnum Photos. **17** (l) Tony Linck. (r) The Ohio Historical Society. **18** S. J. Krasemann/Peter Arnold, Inc. **21** (l) Courtesy of the Trustees of the British Museum. (r) Werner Forman Archive. **23** Pierpont Morgan Library. (INS) Courtesy of The Adler Planetarium. **24** Smithsonian institution. **25** (t) New York Public Library, Astor, Lenox and Tilden Foundations. **30** Frank Lerner, from the Collection of Mr. and Mrs. Larry Frank. **34** LASALLE ERECTING A CROSS AND TAKING POSSESSION OF THE LAND. March 25, 1682, George CATLIN, National Gallery of Art, Washington, D.C. **35** Public Archives of Canada. **37** Jamestown National Historic Park. **40** Photograph granted and authorized by El Patrimonio Nacional, owner of same. **41** Bibliothèque Nationale. **43** The Granger Collection, New York. **44** Museum fur Volkerkunde, Vienna/Werner Forman Archive. **45** (t) National Portrait Gallery, Smithsonian Institution. (b) Courtesy of the Trustees of the British Museum. **48** TSW/Click Chicago. (INS) The New-York Historical Society, New York City. **50** Courtesy of the Pilgrim Society, Plymouth, MA. **51** (t) Courtesy of Archives of '76, Bay Village, OH. **51** (b) The New-York Historical Society, New York City. **53** (l) Courtesy, Museum of Fine Arts, Boston, Bequest of Maxim Karalik. (r) Hispanic Society of America, NY. **54** RICE FIELDS IN THE STATE OF ARKANSAS by Franz Holzlhuber, Courtesy of Glenbow Museum, Calgary, Alberta, Canada. **56** (t) Free Library of Philadelphia. (bl) The Granger Collection, New York. (br) Courtesy, Museum of Fine Arts, Boston. **58** (t) National Portrait Gallery, London. (br) Historical Society of Pennsylvania. **60** Copyright Yale University Art Gallery. **61** (t) The Granger Collection, New York. **62** (b) The Metropolitan Museum of Art, Gift of Mrs. Russell Sage, 1909. **63** Chicago Historical Society. **64** FREEDOM WRITES IN A BIG, BOLD HAND by John Clymer, John Hancock Mutual Life Insurance. **67** (t) Public Archives of Canada. (b) Culver Pictures. **68** (t) Virginia State Library and Archives. (bl) Courtesy, Virginia Historical Society, Richmond. (br) Gary Foreman. **71** Courtesy The Brooklyn Museum. **73** Independence National Historical Park Collection/Eastern National Parks and Monuments Association. **77** Collection of the Maine Historical Society. **79** Brown County Library. **80** Library of Congress. **81** Library of Congress. **82–83** Copyright Yale University Art Gallery, The Mabel Brady Garvan Collection. **84** Courtesy of the Pilgrim Society, Plymouth, MA. **85** National Gallery of Art, Washington, D.C. **86** The Bettmann Archive. **88–89** Collection of John B. Knox. **90** New York Public Library, Astor, Lenox and Tilden Foundations. **94** Everett C. Johnson. (INS) Courtesy U.S. Capitol Historical Society, National Geographic Photographer George F. Mobley. **98** The Metropolitan Museum of Art, Gift of Edgar William and Bernice Chrysler Garbisch, 1963. **99** Copyright Yale University Art Gallery, Mabel Brady Garvan Collection. **102** (t) Historical Pictures Service, Chicago. (b) Historical Society of York County, PA. **103** Collection of the Boatmen's National Bank of St. Louis. **105** Courtesy The Norman Rockwell Museum at Stockbridge, NY. **106** Harry Benson/Life Magazine, Time Warner Inc. **109** Smithsonian Institution. **111** Jointly owned by The National Portrait Gallery, Smithsonian Institution and the Museum of Fine Arts, Boston. **112** (l) The Metropolitan Museum of Art, Bequest of Susan W. Taylor, 1979. (r) New York Public Library, Astor, Lenox and Tilden Foundations. **113** (t) Library of Congress. (b) White House Historical Association. Photograph by National Geographic Society. **115** (t) Harvard University Portrait Collection, Gift of Andrew Carnegie, 1794. (b) White House Historical Association. Photography by National Geographic Society. **117** (both) Robert Llewellyn. **119** (t) Montana Historical Society. (b) The New-York Historical Society, New York City. **120** (t) National Gallery of Art, Washington, D.C., Alisa Mellon Bruce Fund. (b) Pennsylvania Academy of the Fine Arts. **121** The Granger Collection, New York. **122** (l) Pennsylvania Academy of the Fine Arts. (r) from Victor Collof, VOYAGE DANS L'AMERIQUE, 1826. **124–125** National Maritime Museum, Greenwich, England. **126** Supreme Court Historical Society. **127** (b) New York Public Library, Astor, Lenox and Tilden Foundations. **128** White House Historical Association/Smithsonian Institution. (INS) New York State Historical Association, Cooperstown. **132** (l) Library of Congress, (c) Philadelphia Museum of Art. **135** From *Nisei: The Quiet Americans*. **138** New York State Historical Association, Cooperstown. **141** (1) Philadelphia Museum of Art. (c) George Eastman House, International Museum of Photography, (r) Library of Congress. **142** Library of Congress. **143** Schomburg Collection, New York Public Library, Astor, Lenox & Tilden Foundations. **145** Solomon D. Butcher Collection, Nebraska State Historical Society. **149** Los Angeles Public Library. **155** Cook Collection, Valentine Museum. **156** The Brooklyn Museum, Dick S. Ramsay Fund. **158** NFB Photeque/Bud Glinz. **159** Library of Congress. **161** (t) Library of Congress. **162** Gary Braasch. (INS) From THE OLD WEST: THE PIONEERS, Time-Life Books, Inc. © 1974, Paulus Leeser Photography, Inc. **164** The New-York Historical Society, New York City. **165** Massachusetts Historical Society. **166** National Gallery of Art, Washington, D.C., Andrew W. Mellon Collection. **167** (t) Daughters of the American Revolution, Washington, D.C. (b) Library of Congress. **169** (t) William L. Clements Library, University of Michigan. **170** The Mattatuck Museum, Waterbury, CT. (INSET TOP & BOTTOM) The Cincinnati Historical Society. **172** (t) The New-York Historical Society, New York City. (b) Library of Congress. **173** The Bettmann Archive. (b) National Library of Medicine, Bethesda, MD. **174** (t) The New-York Historical Society, New York City. (bl) Culver Pictures. (br) Library of Congress. (tl) Texas State Capitol. **176** (tr) Russell Hamilton Fish III. **177** (t) Friends of the Governor's Mansion, Austin, TX. (b) Walters Art Gallery, Baltimore. **179** Union Pacific Railroad Museum Collection. (b) Courtesy, Levi Strauss & Company, San Francisco, CA. **183** Anne S. K. Brown Military Collection, Brown University. (INS) Courtesy West Point Museum Collection. **185** Putnam County Historical Society, NY. **186** Courtesy Jay P. Altmayer. (INS) Southern Historical Collection, University of North Carolina Library, Chapel Hill. **189** June 27, 1857/Frank Leslie's Illustrated Newspaper. **190** (tl) The Metropolitan Museum of Art, Gift of Mrs. Jacob H. Lazarus, 1893. (tr) In the Collection of the Corcoran Gallery of Art. (bl) National Portrait Gallery, Smithsonian Institution. (br) In the Collection of the Corcoran Gallery of Art. **191** (tl) In the Collection of the Corcoran Gallery of Art. (tr) National Portrait Gallery, Smithsonian Institution. (bl) National Portrait Gallery, Smithsonian Institution. (br) In the Collection of the Corcoran Gallery of Art. **192** (t) The Huntington Library and Art Gallery, San Marino, CA. (b) Library of Congress. **194** Field Museum of Natural History, Chicago. **196** Library of Congress. **197** The New-York Historical Society, New York City. **198** Courtesy Continental Insurance. **200** Idaho Historical Society. **203** In the Collection of the Corcoran Gallery of Art. **206** David Joel/TSW/Click Chicago. (INS) RIDE FOR LIBERTY, Eastman Johnson/Courtesy The Brooklyn Museum. **208** (tl) The Ohio Historical Society. (c) Fort Ward Museum, City of Alexandria, Virginia. Photographed by Henry Beville, and Courtesy Chris Nelson, Photographed by Michael Latil. (tr) Tennessee State Museum, Photographed by Bill LaFevor. (c) Library of Congress. (b) The Museum of the City of New York, Harry Peters Collection. **209** (t) In the Collection of the Corcoran Gallery of Art, Gift of William Wilson Corcoran. (c) Virginia Military Institute Museum. (bl) Frank & Marie-T. Wood Print Collections, Alexandria, VA. Photographed by Larry Sherer. (br) MALVERN HILL painting by Alfred Ward, Courtesy R. Gordon Barton, The Sporting Gallery, Inc. Middleburg, VA. **210** (tl) Library of Congress. **210–211** Chicago Historical Society. (c) Tennessee Historical Society. (b) City of Niles, Michigan/Fort St. Joseph Museum. **211** (t) Library of Congress. (b) United States Naval Academy Museum, Beverly R. Robinson Collection. **212** (tl) Library of Congress. (tr) Library of Congress. (c) Collection of Mrs. Nelson A. Rockefeller. **212–213** Collections of the State Museum of Pennsylvania, photographed by Henry Groskinsky. **213** (tl) The New-York Historical Society, New York City. (tr) Courtesy Ronn Palm. (cl) Courtesy Beverly Du Bose, photographed by Kevin Youngblood. (cr) Courtesy Troiani Collection, photographed by Al Fremi. (br) Kean Archives, Philadelphia, PA. **214** (tl) Collection of Lester S. Levy. (tr) Chicago Historical Society. (bl) Henry Beville/Courtesy Bill Turner. (br) Library of Congress. **215** (t) The Metropolitan Museum of Art, Harris Brisbane Dick Fund, 1929. (c) Collection of the Western Reserve Historical Society. (b) Library of Congress. **216** (tl) Old State House, Little Rock, AR. (tr) Sketch by Walton Taber, Tennessee State Museum, photographed by Bill LaFevor. **216–217** Painting by Thure de Thulstrup, Courtesy Seventh Regiment Fund, Inc., photographed by Al Freni. **217** (t) Library of Congress. (c) Acme/UPI/Bettmann. (b) Library of Congress. **218** (tl) Library of Congress. (tc) Library of Congress. (tr) Scala/Art Resource, NY. (bl) U.S. Signal Corps photo/The National Archives. **218–219** (c) Tom Lovell, The Greenwich Workshop Inc. © 1987, 30 Lindeman Dr., Trumbull, CT 06611. **219** (t) From BATTLES AND LEADERS OF THE CIVIL WAR, Vol. 4, published by the Century Co., New York, 1887, Valentine Museum, Richmond, VA. (b) Courtesy The Museum of the Confederacy, Richmond, VA. **220** William L. Clements Library, University of Michigan. **223** Chicago Historical Society. **224** Library of Congress. (b) Library of Congress. **225** Library of Congress. **226** The New-York Historical Society, New York City. (INS) Library of Congress. **227** Gettysburg National Military Park, PA. National Park Service. **228** Library of Congress. **230** (t) Courtesy, Virginia Historical Society, Richmond. (b) Boston Public Library. **231** Courtesy The American Red Cross. **232** (ALL) Library of Congress. **233** (t) The National Archives. (b) The Bettmann Archive. **235** (tl) National Museum of American Art, Smithsonian. (tc) From the Collections of Henry Ford Museum & Greenfield Villa. (tr) Ford's Theater/U. S. Dept. of the Interior, National Park Service. (b) Frank & Marie T. Wood Print Collections, Alexandria, VA. **236** (t) Courtesy William Gladstone Collection. (b) Rufus & S. Willard Saxton Papers/Yale University Library. **237** Tennessee Historical Society. **238–239** April 11, 1868/Harper's Weekly. **239** (t) Courtesy of the Newberry Library, Chicago. **240** (tl) Library of Congress. (tr) Culver Pictures. (b) Wood Art Gallery, Montpelier, VT. **241** (t) National Portrait Gallery, Smithsonian Institution. (b) Photography by National Geographic/White House Historical Association Society. **242** From the archives of the Rutherford B. Hayes Presidential Center, Fremont, OH. **245** (t) Mississippi State Historical Museum/Mississippi Department of Archives and History. (c) The Granger Collection, NY. **246** Courtesy of Hampton University Archives. **248** National Park Service/Gettysburg National Military Park, PA. National Park Service. **249** Gettysburg National Military Park, PA. National Park Service. **251** Currier & Ives/The Museum of the City of New York. **253** Courtesy West Point Museum Collection. **254–255** Photos courtesy David Finn. **256–257** Courtesy Thomas Publications. **258** Illinois State Historical Library. **259** Library of Congress. **262** Ken Akers/Visual Images West, Inc. (INS) ON THE ROAD Thomas Otter/Nelson Gallery of Art/Atkins Museum, Kansas City, MO. **264** Library of Congress. **267** (t) Library of Congress. (b) The Kansas State Historical Society, Topeka. **268** (t) Larry D. Hodge. (c) Multicultural Music and Art Foundation, Northridge, Mrs. Elisabeth Waldo Dentzel, Dentzel Center. (b) Baker Library, Harvard Business School. **269** Western History Collection, Denver Public Library. **272** From A PICTOGRAPHIC HISTORY OF THE OGLALA SIOUX by Amos Bad Heart Bull, text by Helen Blish. Published by the University of Nebraska Press. **273** Philadelphia Museum of Art Collection. **274** Harper's Weekly. **278** (tl) Free Library of Philadelphia. (tr) The Metropolitan Museum of Art, The Thomas J. Watson Library. (b) Bruce Wrighton, Courtesy of Herkimer County Historical Society, NY. **282** Puck. **284** (l) Metaform Inc. (r) Metaform Inc. **285** The Museum of the City of New York, Jacob A. Riis Collection. **286–287** Thomas Gilcrease Institute of American History & Art, Tulsa. **288** Union Pacific Railroad Museum. (INS) BUFFALO DREAM — Al Momaday. Photo courtesy Patricia Janis Broder from "American Indian Painting and Sculpture," Copyright © 1981 by Cross River Press, Ltd., Abbeville Press, Inc. NY. **289** The Kansas State Historical Society, Topeka. **290** The Museum of the City of New York, The Jacob A. Riis Collection. **291** Courtesy Hultz Photo Collection. **292** Courtesy Marshall Sumida, Photo: National Japanese American Historical Society. **293** Courtesy of Visual Communications, Asian-American Studies Central, Inc. **296** Oscar Abolafia/Gamma-Liaison. (INS) The New-York Historical Society, New York City. **298** Culver Pictures. **299** (t) October 20, 1877/Harper's Weekly. (b) Culver Pictures. **301** (l) Library of Congress. (r) Library of Congress. **303** Library of Congress. **304–305** A. Major, litho, 1883/The New-York Historical Society, New York City. **305** (r) The New-York Historical Society, New York City. **306** The Museum of the City of New York, Photograph by Byron. The Byron Collection. **307** The Museum of the City of New York, Photograph by Jacob A. Riis. The Jacob A. Riis Collection. **308** Nov. 11, 1871/Harper's Weekly. **309** H. J. Heinz Company. **311** (t) Library of Congress. (b) Culver Pictures. **312** (t) Carnegie Library of Pittsburgh. (b) Oct. 4, 1893/Puck. **313** Library of Congress. **316** In the Collection of the Corcoran Gallery of Art. **317** (l) The Bancroft Library, University of California, Berkeley. (r) University of Hartford Collection, Connecticut. **318** NEW ENGLAND COUNTRY SCHOOL, Winslow Homer, St. Louis Art Museum. **322** Sept. 23, 1871/Thomas Nast. **323** Sept. 16, 1871/Thomas Nast. **324** May 15, 1886/Harper's Weekly. **326, 327** 1859/Harper's Weekly. **332** (t) S. J. Krasemann/Peter Arnold, Inc. **333** (tl) The New-York Historical Society, New York City. (b) The Metropolitan Museum of Art, Gift of Mrs. Russell Sage, 1909. **334** (tl) Everett C. Johnson. (tr) Courtesy U.S. Capitol Historical Society, National Geographic Photographer: George F. Mobley. (b) The New-York Historical Society, New York City. **335** (l) The Granger Collection, New York. (c) From THE OLD WEST: THE PIONEERS, © 1974 Time-Life Books, Inc. Paulus Leeser Photography, Inc. (r) The New-York Historical Society, New York City. **336** (l) Union Pacific Railroad Museum Collection. (c) Courtesy The Brooklyn Museum. (r) Gettysburg National Military Park, PA. National Park Service. **337** (c) Courtesy William Gladstone Collection. (r) Rutherford B. Hayes Presidential Center, Fremont, OH. (t) Library of Congress. **338** (l) ON THE ROAD Thomas Otter/Nelson Gallery of Art/Atkins Museum, Kansas City, MO. (c) Library of Congress. (r) The Museum of the City of New York, Jacob A. Riis Collection. **339** (l) The New-York Historical Society, New York City. (c) Culver Pictures. (r) Library of Congress. **340** (l) The Bettmann Archive. (c) The Bettmann Archive. (tr) UPI/Bettmann. (br) Courtesy Virginia Polytechnic Institute and State University. **341** Cynthia Johnson/Gamma-Liaison. **342** Printed by permission of the Estate of Norman Rockwell, Christie's photo. **344** Stock Boston. (INS) The Museum of the City of New York, Photograph by Jacob A. Riis. **346** (ALL) Albin O. Kuhn Library & Gallery, University of Maryland, (Baltimore). **347** Culver Pictures. **348** Historical Pictures Service, Chicago. **349** Library of Congress. **350** Schomberg Collection, New York Public Library, Astor, Lenox & Tilden Foundation. **351** Library of Congress. **352** Galveston Library, Galveston, Texas. **353** (t) Chester

Brummel. (b) from LADIES HOME JOURNAL, Feb. 1901. **356** White House Historical Association, Photography by National Geographic Society. **357** Brown Brothers. **358** David Muench. **360** (r) Sierra Club Library. (r) TSW/Click/Chicago. **362** (t) White House Historical Association, Photography by National Geographic Society. (b) National Portrait Gallery, Smithsonian Institution. **366** Culver Pictures. **369** (l) Duchamp's NUDE DESCENDING A STAIRCASE/Philadelphia Museum of Art Collection. (r) MLLE. POGANY I, marble, Brancusi/Philadelphia Museum of Art Collection, Gift of Mrs. Rodolphe Meyer de Schavensee. **370** Henry Groskinsky. **371** Library of Congress. **373** By permission of the artist LOIS MAILOU JONES, in the collection of The Hirshhorn Museum, Washington, D.C. **375** Courtesy U.S. Postal Service. **380** Fred J. Maroon. (INS) United States Naval Academy Museum. **382** Chicago Historical Society. **383** (b) Instituto Nacional de Bellas Artes. **384** Culver Pictures. **385** The Bettmann Archive. **388** (r) Newspaper Collection/New York Public Library, Astor, Lenox and Tilden Foundations. **391** The Bettmann Archive. **393** The Bettmann Archive. **395** Library of Congress. (INS) Brown Brothers. **397** The Pearl S. Buck Foundation. **398** Catherine Ursillo/Photo Researchers. **400** Philatelic Collection/Smithsonian Institution. **401** Dr. Edward S. Ross. **405** Mariners' Museum. **406** Hawaii State Archives. **408** The Granger Collection, New York. **409** Harper's Weekly. **411** (t) El Paso Public Library. **414** Bruce Coleman Inc. (INS) Smithsonian Institution. **418** UPI/Bettmann. **419** LA MITRAILLEUSE by C. R. W. Nevinson 1915, Tate Gallery, Art Resource, NY. **423** The National Archives. **424** (t) The National Archives. (b) April 4, 1918/Life Magazine Time Warner Inc. **425** Brown Brothers. (INS) The National Archives. **426** The National Archives. **427** (t) OVER THE TOP—John Nash/Trustees of The Imperial War Museum, London. (b) The National Archives. **430** United States Military Academy/Courtesy West Point Museum Collection. **432** (t) The National Archives. (b) Copy courtesy Univ. of Texas, Institute of Texan Cultures. **433** Brown Brothers. **438** THE AVENUE IN THE RAIN, 1917, Childe Hassam, White House Historical Association. **439** AP/Wide World. **440** UPI/Bettmann. **442** (t) Arshile Gorky Estate. (b) From the collection of Whitney Museum of American Art. **443** NYT Pictures. **444** The National Archives. **445** Brown Brothers. **446** The National Archives. **453** (l) Schomberg Collection, New York Public Library, Astor, Lenox & Tilden Foundation. (r) Culver Pictures. **454** (tl) United States Naval Academy Museum. (tr) Instituto Nacional de Bellas Artes. **455** (tl) Smithsonian Institution. (tr) The National Archives. (b) Brown Brothers. (r) AP/Wide World. **456** (l) The Bettmann Archive. (tc) The Bettmann Archive. (bc) The Bettmann Archive. (tr) The Bettmann Archive. (cr) Chicago Historical Society. (br) The Bettmann Archive. **457** (t) UPI/Bettmann. (b) UPI/Bettmann. **460** R. Maiman/Sygma. (INS) Chicago Historical Society. **462** UPI/Bettmann. **463** J. T. McCutcheon, 1929/Chicago Historical Society. **464** (t) Mrs. Robert Rubio, Copy courtesy Institute of Texan Cultures Univ. of Texas. (b) from the collection of the Balzekas Museum of Lithuanian Culture, Chicago. **468** Photo by Otis C. Butler/Schomberg Collection, New York Public Library, Astor, Lenox & Tilden Foundation. **469** AP/Wide World. **471** (t) Brown Brothers. (b) California Historical Society. **472** Brown Brothers. **473** Acme/UPI/Bettmann. **475** National Portrait Gallery, Smithsonian Institution. **476** Union League Club, New York City. **477** Culver Pictures. **478** (b) The Ohio Historical Society. **479** BOOMTOWN, Thomas Hart Benton/Memorial Art Gallery of the University of Rochester, Marion Stratton Gould Fund. **480** (l) September 11, 1920/FRANK LESLIE'S ILLUSTRATED NEWSPAPER. (r) Brown Brothers. **482** The Bettmann Archive. **485** Courtesy Warner Brothers Pictures. **487** Photo: Arthur Rothstein. **490** Stacia Timonere. (INS) Culver Pictures. **493** University of Louisville Photographic Archives. **495** (t) VANITY FAIR. (b) Brown Brothers. **496** State Historical Society of Wisconsin. **497** at Davis Library/University of California. **499** (l) Brown Brothers. (r) DEMPSEY AND FIRPO by George Bellows/From the collection of Whitney Museum of American Art. **500** (l) Culver Pictures. (r) Culver Pictures. **501** Library of Congress. (INS) Lawrence Scripps Wilkinson Collection of Toys, Detroit. **502** The Museum of Modern Art, New York, Film Stills Archive. (INT) The Museum of Modern Art, New York, Film Stills Archive. **503** (INT) Culver Pictures. (INB) The Museum of the City of New York. **504** UPI/Bettmann. **505** Telephone Museum, San Francisco, CA. **507** from the F. Scott Fitzgerald papers, Princeton University Library. **508** Vanity Fair. **508** COW'S SKULL, RED, WHITE, AND BLUE, Georgia O'Keeffe, The Metropolitan Museum of Art, Alfred Stieglitz Collection. **510** (l) UPI/Bettmann. (r) Hampton University Museum. **511** (t) Culver Pictures. (b) The Bettmann Archive. **512** (l) The National Archives. **512–513** The Bettmann Archive. **514** © 1983 Ron Watts/West Light. **515** Craig Aurness/West Light. **516** (r) Culver Pictures. **520** UPI/Bettmann. **524** 1988 © Joseph Rodriguez/Black Star. (INS) New York Daily News Photo. **527** (t) Brown Brothers. **529** UPI/Bettmann. **531** AP/Wide World. (INS) Library of Congress. **532** Library of Congress. **533** Ball State University, Archives & Special Collections, Bracken Library. **534** (t) Library of Congress. (b) Collection of The Oakland Museum, Photo by Paul Taylor. **535** Dorothea Lange Collection/Collection of The Oakland Museum. **536** George C. Berticevich Collection. **537** (t) © 1972 Freelance, Lansdale, Pa. (b) The Kobal Collection. **538** (l) OFFICE GIRLS, 1936—Raphael Soyer. Photo by Whitney Sandak, Inc., CT. (r) UPI/Bettmann. **539** Brown Brothers. **540** AP/Wide World. **542** Dorothea Lange Collection/Collection of The Oakland Museum. **543** National Portrait Gallery, Smithsonian Institution. **544** Acme/UPI/Bettmann. **545** Drawing by Peter Arno © 1931, 1959; The New Yorker Magazine, Inc. **547** UPI/Bettmann. **548** Arthur Rothstein. **549** From the collection of Whitney Museum of American Art. **550** Library of Congress. **551** Dorothea Lange Collection/Collection of The Oakland Museum. **554** Photo courtesy of James Benton. (INS) New York Public Library, Astor, Lenox and Tilden Foundations. **556** Library of Congress. **557** White House Historical Association, photography by National Geographic Society. **561** (t) THE SAN ANTONIO LIGHT Collection, Courtesy Institute of Texan Cultures, University of Texas. (INT) Culver Pictures. **561** Library of Congress. **563** State Historical Society of Wisconsin. **564** (l) The Franklin D. Roosevelt Library. (r) AP/Wide World. **566** (l) UPI/Bettmann. (c) AP/Wide World. (r) AP/Wide World. **568** Library of Congress. **569** (t) U.S. Dept. of the Interior. (c) ARTISTS ON WPA—Moses Soyer, National Museum of American Art/Art Resource, NY. (b) Library of Congress. **570** D. R. Fitzpatrick, ST. LOUIS POST-DISPATCH, March 1937. **571** Library of Congress. **572** The Archives of Labor and Urban Affairs, Wayne State Univ. **574** Library of Congress. **575** (l) Frank Driggs. (r) Frank Driggs. **576** Library of Congress. (INS) National Portrait Gallery, Smithsonian Institution, Gift of the Harmon Foundation. **577** (t) THE SAN ANTONIO LIGHT Collection, Courtesy Institute of Texan Cultures, University of Texas. (c) Acme/UPI/Bettmann. (b) The Bettmann Archive. **580** From the Collection of The Detroit Institute of Art. **581** Pacific Stock Exchange, San Francisco. Photo: Dirk Bakker. **582–583** Bureau of Mines/U.S. Dept. of the Interior. **584–585** The National Archives. **590** (l) Chicago Historical Society. (c) UPI/Bettmann. (r) Memorial Art Gallery of the University of Rochester. **591** (l) Culver Pictures. (c) Hampton University Museum. **592** (tl) New York Daily News Photo. (tr) Dorothea Lange Collection/Collection of The Oakland Museum. (c) UPI/Bettmann. (b) AP/Wide World. **593** (tl) New York Public Library, Astor, Lenox and Tilden Foundations. (tr) Library of Congress. (c) The Archives of Labor and Urban Affairs, Wayne State Univ. (b) The Bettmann Archive. **594** (t) The Bettmann Archive. (b) The Bettmann Archive. **595** UPI/Bettmann. **596** UPI/Bettmann. **598** AP/Wide World. (INS) Hugo Jaeger/Life Magazine Time Warner Inc. **601** AP/Wide World. **602** Paul Dorsey, © 1938/Life Magazine Time Warner Inc. **603** (tl) UPI/Bettmann. (tr) Popperfoto. (b) UPI/Bettmann. **604** (t) Library of Congress. (b) E. Thaler/Pressefoto. **605** (t) UPI/Bettmann. (b) Photoworld/FPG. **606** The Bettmann Archive. **607** Ullstein Bilderdienst. **608** Prado. **609** UPI/Bettmann. **611** Ullstein Bilderdienst. **612** Clifford K. Berryman/Distributed by King Features Syndicate, Inc. **613** MARS. **614** WITHDRAWAL FROM DUNKIRK—Richard Eurich/National Maritime Museum, Greenwich, England. **615** AP/Wide World. **618–619** Trustees of The Imperial War Museum, London. **618** (b) Hulton/UPI/Bettmann. **619** (INS) Robert Capa/Magnum Photos. **621** © CBS Inc. **623** Acme/UPI/Bettmann. **625** Associated Newspapers, Ltd. **627** The Franklin D. Roosevelt Library. Photo courtesy PHILADELPHIA RECORD, August, 1941. **630** Journalism Services, all rights reserved. (INS) The National Archives. **632** UPI/Bettmann. **633** AP/Wide World. **634** UPI/Bettmann. (INS) San Francisco Chronicle. **635** Acme/UPI/Bettmann. **637** Trustees of The Imperial War Museum, London. (INS) Ullstein Bilderdienst. **639** (l) Library of Congress. (r) U.S. Army Photo. **640** (r) U.S. Army Photo. (l) SOVFOTO. **641** United States Coast Guard. **642** (t) From a painting by Zygmunt Menkes photographed by Robert Crandall Associates. (bl) U.S. Army Photo. (br) Margaret Bourke-White © 1945/Life Magazine Time Warner Inc. **643** Acme/UPI/Bettmann. **644** Official U.S. Navy Photograph. **645** KAMIKAZE ATTACKS ON CARRIER HORNET, U.S. Navy Combat Art Center. **646** Marine Corp Photo/U.S. Department of Defense. **647** Carl Mydans © 1945/Life Magazine Time Warner Inc. **651** (t) United States Air Force photo. (c) Yosuke Yamabata. (b) Hiroshima City Tourist Association. **653** (l) Library of Congress. (r) Library of Congress. **654** UPI/Bettmann. **655** Hansel Mieth/Life Magazine Time Warner Inc. **657** (l) The Franklin D. Roosevelt Library. (r) Library of Congress. **658** U.S. Dept. of Energy, Oak Ridge/Marlar and Associates. **659** U.S. Dept. of Energy, Oak Ridge/Marlar and Associates. **660** AP/Wide World. **663** U.S. Department of Defense. **664** AP/Wide World. **665** (t) Larnois/Black Star. **667** Schomberg Collection, New York Public Library. **669** (r) Ron Sachs/Uniphoto. (l) UPI/Bettmann. **672** J. Langevin/Sygma. (INS) UPI/Bettmann. **676** Harry S. Truman Library. **677** White House Historical Association, Photography by National Geographic Society. **678** George Skadding © 1946/Life Magazine Time Warner Inc. **679** Justus, The Minneapolis Star. **681** (t) Acme/UPI/Bettmann. (b) AP/Wide World. **682** (t) UPI/Bettmann. (b) The Bettmann Archive. **686** United States Air Force photo/Photo Courtesy Life Picture Service. **687** The Bettmann Archive. **689** (t) UPI/Bettmann. (b) UPI/Bettmann. **691** Margaret Bourke-White © 1943/Life Magazine Time Warner Inc. **692** UPI/Bettmann. **693** AP/Wide World. **695** UPI/Bettmann. **696** (t) UPI/Bettmann. (b) AP/Wide World. **699** Cartier-Bresson/Magnum Photos. **700** United States Coast Guard. **701** Leo Joseph Roche/Buffalo Courier Express. **704** Baron Wolman. **704** Culver Pictures. **707** (b) Bern Keating/Black Star. **708** Hank Walker/Life Magazine Time Warner Inc. **709** (ALL) Youman/Schulman Collection. **710** AP/Wide World. **711** Thomas E. Stephen/Courtesy West Point Museum Collection, U.S. Military Academy, West Point, New York, USA. **715** Life Magazine Time Warner Inc. **716–717** Henriques/Magnum Photos. **718–719** UPI/Bettmann. **720** The Bettmann Archive. **721** Robert A. Isaacs. **722** (tl) UPI/Bettmann. **722** (tr) Martha Holmes 1949/Life Magazine Time Warner Inc. **722** (b) Fred DeWitt/Time Warner Inc. **723** New York CONVERGENCE, 1952, Jackson Pollock, Albright-Knox Art Gallery, Buffalo Art Resource, NY. **725** (t) AP/Wide World. (b) SOVFOTO. **726** By Frank Williams in the DETROIT FREE PRESS/Time-Life Books, Inc. **728** Arnold/Magnum Photos. **730** Bob Verlin/Monkmeyer Press Photo Service. **741** (t) Clifford K. Berryman/Distributed by King Features Syndicate, Inc. (b) Paul Dorsey, © 1938/Life Magazine Time Warner Inc. **742** (l) WITHDRAWAL FROM DUNKIRK—Richard Eurich/National Maritime Museum, Greenwich, England. (c) The National Archives. (r) AP/Wide World. **743** (tl) U.S. Army Photo. (bl) U.S. Navy Combat Art Center. **745** (r) Robert A. Isaacs. **746** (l) Courtesy of Trustees of Amherst College/Amherst College Library. (tc) The Bettmann Archive. (bc) The Bettmann Archive. (r) The Bettmann Archive. **747** UPI/Bettmann. **748** Nik Wheeler/Black Star. **750** John O'Hagan. (INS) UPI/Bettmann. **752** Ed Clark/Life Magazine Time Warner Inc. **753** UPI/Bettmann. **755** AP/Wide World. **756** UPI/Bettmann. (INS) UPI/Bettmann. **758** Sarah Leen/Matrix. **759** (t) UPI/Bettmann. (br) Steve Schapiro/Black Star. (bl) Culver Pictures. **760–761** UPI/Bettmann. **763** (b) Charles Moore/Black Star. (t) AP/Wide World. **764** (l) Fred Ward/Black Star. (r) Leonard Freed/Magnum Photos. **767** AP/Wide World. **769** (t) Steve Schapiro/Black Star. (b) UPI/Bettmann. **770** James H. Karales © 1965 Look Magazine/Library of Congress. **773** Eve Arnold/Magnum Photos. **774** (bl) UPI/Bettmann. (c) UPI/Bettmann. (tr) Karen Kuehn/Matrix. (br) UPI/Bettmann. **775** UPI/Bettmann. **776** Mark Richards. **777** Jeffrey Scales. **778** UPI/Bettmann. **780** Bob Adelman/Magnum Photos. **783** UPI/Bettmann. **786** NASA. (INS) NASA. **789** (l) Paul Schutzer/Life Magazine Time Warner Inc. (r) John Fitzgerald Kennedy Library. **790** AP/Wide World. **791** UPI/Bettmann. **792** White House Historical Association, Photography by National Geographic Society. **794** (l) UPI/Bettmann. (r) UPI/Bettmann. **796** Jacques Chenet/Woodfin Camp & Associates. **798** (t) Kulik Photography. (b) Courtesy Peace Corps. **799** UPI/Bettmann. **800** UPI/Bettmann. **801** Life Magazine Time Warner Inc. **802** UPI/Bettmann. **803** UPI/Bettmann. (INS) UPI/Bettmann. **804** (t) Paul Fusco/Magnum Photos. (b) Wayne Miller/Magnum Photos. **805** (t) Arthur Tress/Magnum Photos. (b) AP/Wide World. **806** (t) Courtesy Leo Castelli Gallery. (b) MAP, 1961, Jasper Johns/The Museum of Modern Art, New York, Gift of Mr. and Mrs. Robert C. Scull. **808** AP/Wide World. **810** AP/Wide World. **811** Bob Fitch/Black Star. **812** Superstock/Shostal. **813** Nancy Ellison/Sygma. **815** Photo: Richard Erdoes. **817** Gerhard Gscheidle/Magnum Photos. **820** Peter Marlow/Magnum Photos. (INS) Robert Ellison/Empire News/Black Star. **822** H. Roger Viollet. **824** (t) Audrey K. Belknap/Cyr Color Photo Agency. (b) AP/Wide World. **828** Larry Burrows © 1966 Life Magazine, Time Warner Inc. **830** Larry Burrows © 1966 Life Magazine, Time Warner Inc. **832** Larry Burrows © 1966 Life Magazine, Time Warner Inc. **834** Baron Wolman. **835** (t) Collection of Barbara Frankel. (b) John Launois/Black Star. **836** AP/Wide World. **839** Jeffrey Blackfont/Jeroboam Inc. **840** Michael Abramson/Gamma-Liaison. **842** John P. Filo, Valley Daily News, Tarentum, Pa. **845** Nik Wheeler/Black Star. **846** Christopher Morris/Black Star. **848** Sal Lopes. **849** UPI/Bettmann. **851** Larry Burrows/Life Magazine Time Warner Inc. **852–853** P. J. Griffiths/Magnum Photos. **855** Donald McCullin/Magnum Photos. **857** UPI/Bettmann. **859** Nature by Nachel, Gail & Jim Nachel. **862** Alex Webb/Magnum Photos. (INS) UPI/Bettmann. **865** UPI/Bettmann. **865** (t) White House Historical Association, Photography by National Geographic Society. **866** UPI/Bettmann. **868** Dirk Halstead/Gamma-Liaison. **869** Mount Vernon Ladies Association. **870** AP/Wide World. (INS) Dennis Brack/Black Star. **871** Eugene Richards/Magnum Photos. **872** NASA. **876** J.P. Laffont/Sygma. **877** UPI/Bettmann. **878–879** Dennis Brack/Black Star. **879** General Augusto Pinochet. **880–881** Leonard Freed/Magnum Photos. **881** (INS) Leonard Freed/Magnum Photos. **882** (tl) Elliott Erwitt/Magnum Photos. (tr) J.P. Laffont/Sygma. (bl) J.P. Laffont/Sygma. (br) J.P. Laffont/Sygma. **883** Fred Ward/Black Star. **884** UPI/Bettmann. **885** (t) AP/Wide World. (b) UPI/Bettmann. **886** Rob Lawlor/Philadelphia Daily News. **888** Roland Freeman/Magnum Photos. **890** AP/Wide World. **891** J.P. Laffont/Sygma. **892** Magnum Photos. **895** AP/Wide World. **902** (t) UPI/Bettmann. (b) James H. Karales (c) 1965 LOOK Magazine/Library of Congress. **903** NASA. (c) UPI/Bettmann. (r) Arthur Tress/Magnum Photos. **904** (tl) Robert Ellison/Empire News/Black Star. (tr) H. Roger Viollet. (r) Christopher Morris/Black Star. (b) Michael Abramson/Gamma-Liaison. **905** (tl) UPI/Bettmann. (tr) Eugene Richards/Magnum Photos. (b) UPI/Bettmann. **906** (l) The Bettmann Archive. (tc) The Maryland Historical Society. (bc) The Bettmann Archive. (r) The Bettmann Archive. **908** Mary Kate Denny/Photo Edit. **910** The White House. (INS) The New-York Historical Society, New York City. **912** UPI/Bettmann. **913** (l) From HERBLOCK ON ALL FRONTS, New American Library, 1980 by Herblock in THE WASHINGTON POST. (r) White House Historical Association, Photography by National Geographic Society. **914** (b) Chie Nishio/Nancy Palmer Agency. (tl) White House Historical Association, Photography by National Geographic Society. (tr) Charles M. Rafshoon. **916** UPI/Bettmann. **918** Bill Fitz-Patrick/The White House. **920** (t) J.L. Atlan/Sygma. (b) Ledru/Sygma. **921** J.L. Atlan/Sygma. **922** UPI/Bettmann. **924** Stephen Ellison © 1988/People Weekly/Time Warner Inc. **925** 1981/Bob Zschiesche/Courtesy Our Folks. **926** (t) Arthur Grace/Sygma. (c) Owen Franken/Sygma. (b) Alon Reininger/Contact Press Images. **927** AP/Wide World. **928** Los Alamos National Laboratory. **930** James Nachtwey/Magnum Photos. **931** Stuart Franklin/Sygma. **932** Reuters/UPI/Bettmann. **933** UPI/Bettmann. **934** Larry Downing/Woodfin Camp & Associates. **936** Victor Englebert. **939** UPI/Bettmann. (INS) Milt & Joan Mann/Cameramann International, Ltd. **941** Ron Sachs/Sygma. **944** Bob Sacha. (INS) AP/Wide World. **946** UPI/Bettmann. (INS) Erich Hartmann/Magnum Photos. **948** David Valdez/The White House. **949** UPI/Bettmann. **950** Ian Berry/Magnum Photos. **951** Reuters/UPI/Bettmann. **952** (t) S. Franklin/Magnum Photos. (bl) Sygma. (br) F. Zecchin/Magnum Photos. **953** (t) UPI/Bettmann. (b) Reuters/UPI/Bettmann. **954** (l) Dennis Brack/Time Warner Inc. (r) Reuters/UPI/Bettmann. **955** Geoff Franklin/Sygma. **959** Eli Reed/Magnum Photos. **961** (t) Brad Doherty. (bl) Al Stephenson/Picture Group. (br) Reuters/UPI/Bettmann. **963** (t) Ira Wymann. (b) AP/Wide World. **965** Jose Azel/Contact Press Images. **966** (l) Bob Glaze/Artstreet. (r) Alon Reininger/Contact Press Images. **967** UPI/Bettmann. **968** (t) Martin A. Levick. (bl) Ken Regan/Camera 5. (br) Ken Regan/Camera 5. **970** UPI/Bettmann. **972** (t) John Bryson. (b) Les Stone/Sygma. (t) ohn Bryson/Sygma. **973** Paul F. Gero/Sygma. **974** (l) A. **Tannenbaum/Sygma, (r) Gerhard Gscheidle/Peter Arnold, Inc. 976 Reuters/Bettmann. (INS) Official White House photo. 977(clockwise from t) Chick Harrity/U.S. News & World Report. Diana Walker/Gamma-Liaison. Robert Trippett/SIDA. Reuters/Bettmann. 978 (t) David Hume Kennerly/Gamma. (b) Larry Downing/Sygma. 979 Reuters/Bettmann. 980–981 Painting by Tom Heflin. 982–983 AP/Wide World. 984 Library of Congress. 985 (c) Time-Life, Inc./Henry Groskinsky. 988 (d) Guadalupe Acosta Family. 991 (b) University of**

Oregon Library, (e) The Bancroft Library.   **994** (t) Bill Fitz-Patrick/The White House. (b) Larry Downing/Woodfin Camp & Associates.   **995** (l) AP/Wide World. (c) Ian Berry/Magnum Photos. (r) The Bettmann Archive.   **996** (l) The Bettman Archive. (r) The Bettmann Archive.   **997** UPI/Bettmann.   **1026** (tr) From the Codex Mendoza in Lord Kingsborough's ANTIQUITIES OF MEXICO, 1829.

The Bettman Archive.   **996** (l) The Bettman Archive. (r) The Bettman Archive.   **997** UPI/Bettmann.   **1026** (tr) From the Codex Mendoza in Lord Kingsborough's ANTIQUITIES OF MEXICO, 1829. (tc) Abby Aldrich Rockefeller Folk Art Center. (cc) Emil Muench. (cr) The Peabody Museum of Archaeology and Ethnology. (b) Museum of New Mexico.   **1027** (tr) Historical Society of York County, PA. (cl) Massachusetts Historical Society. (cr) Courtesy, Museum of Fine Arts, Boston. (b) Don and Pat Valenti.   **1028** (t) National Portrait Gallery, Smithsonian Institution. (tc) The New-York Historical Society, New York City. (bcl) The New-York Historical Society, New York City. (bcr) From the Collection of The Detroit Institute of Art. (b) University of Virginia Library/Engraved by Bohn. Printed by E. Sachse & Co.   **1029** (tl) The Schlesinger Library, Harvard University. (tr) from THE ADVENTURES OF HUCKLEBERRY FINN, 1885, Charles L. Webster & Co., NY. (tc) The Granger Collection, New York. (bcl) Hampton Institute. (bc) The Art Institute of Chicago. All Rights Reserved. (bcr) Photographed by Philadelphia Museum of Art Collection, Courtesy of The Jefferson Medical College of Philadelphia. (b) Office of Development, Roosevelt University.   **1030** (t) University of Texas at Austin/Harry Ransom Humanities Research Center. (CTL) Institute for Jazz Studies, Rutgers University. (tcr) The Granger Collection, New York. (ccr) Marion Stratton Gould Fund/Collection of the Memorial Art Gallery of the University of Rochester. (ccl) The Museum of Modern Art, New York, Film Stills Archive. (bcl) The Museum of Modern Art, New York, Gift of Mrs. David N. Levy. (bcr) Copyright Yale University Art Gallery, Gift of Collection Societe Anonyme. (cc) Courtesy Leo Castelli Gallery.   **1031** (cl) Munson-Williams Proctor Institute, Utica, NY (cr) Francis Ford Coppola — THE GODFATHER, © 1972 by Paramount Pictures Corp. (b) Peter Aaron/ESTO.   **1031** (b) Peter Aaron/ESTO.   **1032** (l) The University Library, Jane Addams Memorial Collection, University of Illinois at Chicago. (tr) Sophia Smith Collection, Woman's History Archives, Smith College. (bc) Brown Brothers. (r) Library of Congress.   **1033** (t) Paul Fusco/Magnum Photos. (b) Montana Historical Society.   **1034** (t) Tamiment Library, New York University. (cl) Historical Society of Pennsylvania. (cr) UPI/Bettmann.   **1035** (l) Folger Art Library. (r) Museo Nacional de Historia, Mexico City.   **1036** (tl) UPI/Bettmann. (c) E.M. Weil Photography. (r) UPI/Bettmann. (b) © 1953 Time Warner Inc..   **1037** (t) National Gallery of Art, Washington, D.C., Mellon Collection. (bl) The State Capitol, Austin, TX. (br) Culver Pictures.   **1038** (l) Museo Nacional de Historia, Mexico City. (c) Courtesy United States Postal Service. (bbr) The Hispanic Society of America.   **1039** (tl) UPI/Bettmann. (bl) Hawaii State Archives. (c) The Governing Body, Christ Church, Oxford. (r) American Antiquarian Society.   **1040** (t) Yoichi R. Okamoto/Photo Researchers. (b) Culver Pictures.   **1041** (t) Supreme Court Historical Society. (c) Phil Matt/Gamma-Liaison. (r) National Portrait Gallery, Smithsonian Institution. (b) Courtesy of the Pennsylvania Academy of Fine Arts.   **1042** (l) Bill Fitz-Patrick/The White House. (c) AP/Wide World. (r) Museum of History, Chapultepec Castle, Mexico.   **1043** (l) Dennis Brack/Black Star. (tc) Library of Congress. (bc) Picture Collection, New York Public Library, Astor, Lenox and Tilden Foundations. (tr) UPI/Bettmann. (br) Sophia Smith Collection, Woman's History Archives, Smith College.   **1044** (t) The White House Historical Society. (r) Museum of Fine Arts, Boston, Bequest of Winslow Warren. (b) Brown Brothers.   **1045** (tl) Library of Congress. (bl) National Gallery of Art, Washington, D.C., Gift of Edgar William and Bernice Chrysler Garbisch. (tc) UPI/Bettmann. (bc) Brown Brothers. (r) AP/Wide World.

Quoted Material

16 From *The Art of Nahuatl Speech: The Bancroft Dialogues*, edited by Frances Karttunen and James Lockhart. Copyright © 1987 by The Regents of the University of California. Reprinted by permission of University of California, Los Angeles.   **42** From *The Broken Spears* by Miguel Leon-Portilla. Copyright © 1962 by Beacon Press. Reprinted by permission of Beacon Press.   **199** From "Report" by Francisco Ruiz, translated in Amelia Williams', "A Critical Study of the Siege of the Alamo and the Personnel of its Defenders" in *Southwestern Historical Quarterly*, XXXVII (July 1933) pp. 39-40. Reprinted by permission of the Texas State Historical Association.   **200** From *Thousand Pieces of Gold* by Ruthanne Lum McCunn. Copyright © 1981 by Ruthanne Lum McCunn. Reprinted by permission of Beacon Press.   **202** Abridged from *Unwritten History of Slavery, Autobiographical Accounts of Negro Ex-Slaves*. Copyright © 1968 by Fisk University. Reprinted by permission of Fisk University Library Special Collections.   **288** Adaptation of excerpt on pp. 138-139 "The End of the World: The Buffalo Go — Kiowa" in *American Indian Mythology* by Alice Marriott and Carol K. Rachlin (Thomas Y. Crowell). Copyright © 1968 by Alice Marriott and Carol K. Rachlin. Reprinted by permission of Harper & Row, Publishers, Inc. and John Meyer.   **290** From "Growing Up on the Lower East Side" in *America's Immigrants* by Rhoda Hoff. Copyright © 1967 by Rhoda Hoff. Reprinted by permission of McIntosh and Otis, Inc.   **292** Bill Hosokawa, from *Nisei: The Quiet Americans*, William Morrow. Reprinted by permission.   **340** "The Funeral of Martin Luther King, Jr." from *Black Judgement* by Nikki Giovanni. Reprinted by permission.   **408** From "Flowers of Exile" in *Jose Martí: Major Poems*, pp. 162-163. Translated by Elinor Randall. Edited by Philip S. Foner (New York:

Holmes & Meier, 1982). Copyright © 1982 by Holmes & Meier Publishers, Inc. Reprinted by permission of the publisher.   **410** From *The Under Dogs* by Mariano Azuela. Reprinted by permission of Trinity University Press.   **445** Excerpt from *I Saw Them Die: The Diary and Recollections of Shirley Millard*, by Adele Comandini, reprinted by permission of Harcourt Brace Jovanovich, Inc.   **450** "The Shimerdas" from *My Ántonia* by Willa Cather. Copyright © 1918 by Willa Sibert Cather. Copyright © renewed 1946 by Willa Sibert Cather. Copyright © 1926 by Willa Sibert Cather. Copyright © renewed 1954 by Edith Lewis. Copyright © 1949 by Houghton Mifflin Co. Copyright © renewed 1977 by Bertha Handlan. Reprinted by permission of Houghton Mifflin Co.   **456** William Safire, from "Bleeding Hearts," from *Safire's Political Dictionary*, Random House. Reprinted by permission.   **484** Excerpt from *Babbitt*, copyright 1922 by Harcourt Brace Jovanovich, Inc. and renewed 1950 by Sinclair Lewis, reprinted by permission of the publisher.   **486, 529, 563, 656** From *Hard Times: An Oral History of the Great Depression* by Studs Terkel. Copyright © 1970 by Studs Terkel. Reprinted by permission of Pantheon Books, a Division of Random House Inc.   **506** Reprinted by permission of Greenwood Publishing Group, Inc. Westport, CT, from *A Documentary History of the Mexican Americans*, edited by Wayne Moquin and Charles Van Doren. Copyright © 1971 by Praeger Publishers, Inc. Emma Gelders Sterne, from *His was the Voice: The Life of W. E. B. DuBois*, Harper & Row. Reprinted by permission.   **510, 513** Excerpts from *The Big Sea* by Langston Hughes. Copyright © 1940 by Langston Hughes. Renewal copyright © 1968 by Arna Bontemps and George Houston Bass. Reprinted by permission of Hill and Wang, a division of Farrar, Straus and Giroux, Inc.   **517** "The Babe Slams No. 60" by James S. Carolan in *The New York Times*, October 1, 1927. Copyright © 1927 by The New York Times Company. Reprinted by permission.   **520** "Homesick Blues," "Bound No'th Blues," and "A Note on Blues." Copyright © 1927 by Alfred A. Knopf Inc. and renewed 1955 by Langston Hughes. Reprinted from *The Dream Keeper and Other Poems* by Langston Hughes, by permission of the publisher and Harold Ober Associates, Inc.   **530, 588** From *The Grapes of Wrath* by John Steinbeck. Copyright © 1939, renewed copyright © 1967 by John Steinbeck. Reprinted by permission of the publisher, Viking Penguin, a division of Penguin Books USA Inc.   **548** "Boy with His Hair Cut Short" from *The Collected Poems of Muriel Rukeyser*. Copyright © 1938, 1939, 1944, 1948, 1951, 1957, 1958, 1962, 1968, 1973, 1976, and 1978 by Muriel Rukeyser. Reprinted by permission of William L. Rukeyser.   **571** From "Evelyn Macon" in *First-Person America*, edited by Ann Banks. Copyright © 1980 by Ann Banks. Reprinted by permission of E. Markson Literary Agency.   **582** Florence Reece, Lyrics of "Which Side Are You On?" Storm King Music. Reprinted by permission.   **584** From *Down These Mean Streets* by Piri Thomas. Copyright © 1967 by Piri Thomas. Reprinted by permission of Alfred A. Knopf, Inc.   **594** From *The Time of Your Life* by William Saroyan. Reprinted by permission of the William Saroyan Foundation.   **595** "Harrison Bergeron" from *Welcome to the Monkey House* by Kurt Vonnegut, Jr. Used by permission of Delacorte Press/Seymour Lawrence, a division of Bantam, Doubleday, Dell Publishing Group, Inc.   **624** Edward R. Murrow, "October 10, 1940," from *This is London*, Random House. Reprinted by permission.   **626** Abridged from speech by Charles A. Lindbergh, Jr., in *The New York Times*, April 24, 1941. Copyright © 1941 by The New York Times Company. Reprinted by permission.   **640, 666, 692** Reprinted by permission of The Putnam Publishing Group from *The Homefront* by Mark J. Harris. Copyright © 1984 by Mark Jonathan Harris, Franklin D. Mitchell, and Steven J. Schechter.   **651** From "I Was Reborn at Hiroshima" by Yasuo Takeyama in *The New York Times*, August 6, 1989. Copyright © 1989 by The New York Times Company. Reprinted by permission.   **660** Excerpt from *Night* by Elie Wiesel. Copyright © 1960 by MacGibbon & Kee. Renewal copyright © 1988 by the Collins Publishing Group. Reprinted by permission of Hill and Wang, a division of Farrar, Straus and Giroux, Inc.   **662** From *With the Old Breed at Peleliu and Okinawa* by E.B. Sledge. Copyright © 1981 by Presidio Press. Reprinted with permission from Presidio Press, 31 Pamaron Way, Novato, CA 94949. Frank Conroy, from "My Generation," in *Esquire*, October, 1968. Conadio & Ashworth. Reprinted by permission.   **664** From *Memoirs of Harry S. Truman, Volume One: Year of Decisions*. Copyright © 1955 by Time Inc. Reprinted by permission of Stinson, Mag, & Fizzell for the Estate of Harry S. Truman.   **668** From the book *Journey to Washington* by Daniel K. Inouye with Lawrence Elliot. © 1967 by Prentice-Hall, Inc. Published by Prentice-Hall, Inc., Englewood Cliffs, NJ 07632.   **698** "Garden of My Childhood" by Kuangchi C. Chang, reprinted from *The American Scholar*, Volume 26, Number 3, Summer 1957. Copyright © 1957 by The Phi Beta Kappa Society.   **700** Reprinted by permission of The Putnam Berkley Group from *Plain Speaking: An Oral Biography of Harry Truman*. Copyright © 1973 by Merle Miller.   **720** From the song "Little Boxes," words and music by Malvina Reynolds. Copyright © 1962 by Schroder Music Co. (ASCAP) Renewed 1990 by Nancy Schimmel.   **721** From "My Generation" by Frank Conroy in *Esquire*, October 1968. Reprinted by permission of Donadio & Ashworth, Inc.   **730** From "Teener's Hero" in *Time*, May 14, 1956. Copyright 1956 by Time Warner Inc. Reprinted by permission.   **734** Excerpt from *The Mambo Kings Play Songs of Love* by Oscar Hijuelos. Copyright © 1989 by Oscar Hijuelos. Reprinted by permission of Farrar, Straus and Giroux, Inc.   **736** From *A Raisin in the Sun* by Lorraine Hansberry. Copyright © 1958 by Robert Nemiroff, as an unpublished work. Copyright © 1959, 1966, 1984 by Robert Nemiroff. Reprinted by permission of Random House

Inc.   **738** "The Portrait" from *And the Earth Did Not Devour Him* by Tomás Rivera. Copyright © 1987 by Consuelo Rivera. Reprinted by permission of Arte Público Press.   **746** From *Death of a Salesman* by Arthur Miller. Copyright © 1949, renewed copyright © 1977 by Arthur Miller. Reprinted by permission of the publisher Viking Penguin a division of Penguin Books USA Inc.   **747** "AC-CENT-TCHU-ATE THE POSITIVE" by Johnny Mercer and Harold Arlen. Copyright © 1944 by Harwin Music Co. Copyright renewed 1972 by Harwin Music Co. All rights reserved. Used by permission.   **765** "Dream Deferred" from *The Panther and the Lash* by Langston Hughes. Copyright 1951 by Langston Hughes. Reprinted by permission of Alfred A. Knopf, Inc. Excerpted from *I Have a Dream* by Martin Luther King, Jr. Copyright © 1963 by Martin Luther King, Jr. Reprinted by permission of Joan Daves. Nobel Prize Speech from *The Faulkner Reader* by William Faulkner, published by Random House, Inc., 1954.   **778** Reprinted by permission of The Putnam Publishing Group from *My Soul Is Rested* by Howell Raines. Copyright © 1977 by Howell Raines.   **780** From "We Shall Overcome" by Zilphia Horton, Frank Hamilton, Guy Carawan and Pete Seeger. Copyright © 1960 (renewed) and 1963 by Ludlow Music, Inc. New York, NY. Used by permission.   **781** "Keep Your Eyes on the Prize" Copyright © 1963 by Oak Publications, a division of Music Sales Corporation. International copyright secured. All rights reserved. Used by permission.   **782** From *Malcolm X Speaks* by Malcolm X. Copyright © 1965 by Betty Shabazz and Pathfinder Press. Reprinted by permission of Pathfinder Press.   **810** From *Mexican-Americans of South Texas*, by William Madsen. Copyright © 1964 by Holt, Rinehart and Winston, Inc. Reprinted by permission of the publisher.   **812** Reprinted from *The Feminine Mystique* by Betty Friedan, by permission of W. W. Norton & Company, Inc. Copyright © 1974 by Betty Friedan.   **814** From *Lakota Woman* by Mary Crow Dog. Copyright © 1990 by Mary Crow Dog and Richard Erdoes. Reprinted by permission of Grove Weidenfeld.   **816** Luis Valdez and Stan Steiner, "Peregrinacion, Penitencia, Revolucion" by Cesar Chavez in *Aztlan: An Anthology of Mexican-American Literature*, Random House. Reprinted by permission.   **834** "Blowin' in the Wind" by Bob Dylan. Copyright © 1962 by Warner Bros. Music; copyright renewed 1990 by Bob Dylan. This arrangement copyright © 1992 by Special Rider Music. All rights reserved. International copyright secured. Used by permission.   **848** Phil McCombs, from "Maya Lin," *The Washington Post*, January 3, 1982. Reprinted by permission.   **850** From *A Rumor of War* by Philip Caputo. Copyright © 1977 by Philip Caputo. Reprinted by permission of Henry Holt and Company, Inc.   **852** "Coming Home" and "Guerilla War" from *To Those Who Have Gone Home Tired: New and Selected Poems*, by W. D. Ehrhart. Copyright © 1984 by Thunder's Mouth Press. Used by permission of the publisher, Thunder's Mouth Press.   **854** From *Brothers: Black Soldiers in the Nam* by Stanley Goff, Robert Sanders, and Clark Smith. Copyright © 1982 by Presidio Press. Reprinted with permission from Presidio Press, 31 Pamaron Way, Novato, CA 94949.   **858, 860** From *Dear America: Letters Home From Vietnam*. Copyright © 1985 by the Vietnam Veterans Memorial Commission. Reprinted by permission. From *Nam: The Vietnam War in the Words of the Men and Women Who Fought There* by Mark Baker. Copyright © 1981 by Mark Baker. Reprinted by permission of William Morrow and Company.   **872** From "Hard Times" by Arlo Guthrie. Copyright © 1974 by Howard Beach Music, Inc. All rights reserved. Reprinted by permission.   **876** Reprinted from *American Tapestry: Eyewitness Accounts of the Twentieth Century* by Tom Tiede. Copyright © 1988 by Tom Tiede. Reprinted with the permission of Pharos Books, Inc.   **892** Reprinted by permission of Warner Books/New York from *RN: The Memoirs of Richard Nixon* by Richard Nixon. Copyright © 1978 by Richard Nixon.   **894** From *The Final Days* by Carl Bernstein and Bob Woodward. Copyright © 1976 by Carl Bernstein and Bob Woodward. Reprinted by permission of Simon & Schuster, Inc.   **898** From *Dispatches* by Michael Herr. Copyright © 1968, 1969, 1970, 1977 by Michael Herr. Reprinted by permission of Alfred A. Knopf, Inc.   **900** From *The Way to Rainy Mountain* by N. Scott Momaday. Copyright © 1969 by The University of New Mexico Press. Reprinted by permission.   **907** Emma Gelders Sterne, *Blood Brothers: Four Men of Science* Random House. Reprinted by permission.   **908, 936** From *New Kids on the Block: Oral Histories of Immigrant Teens* by Janet Bode. Copyright © 1989 by Janet Bode. Reprinted by permission.   **938** Excerpt abridged from *Free To Choose* by Milton and Rose Friedman. Copyright © 1980 by Milton and Rose Friedman. Reprinted by permission of Harcourt Brace Jovanovich, Inc.   **940** From "Pulled to the Top by His Bootstraps" by Richard Mackenzie in *Insight*, October 8, 1990. Copyright © 1990 by *Insight*. All rights reserved. Reprinted by permission from *Insight*.   **963** From "Why Asians Succeed Here" by Robert B. Oxnam in *The New York Times*, November 30, 1986. Copyright © 1986 by The New York Times Company. Reprinted by permission.   **978** "My Mother Pieced Quilts" by Teresa Palomo Acosta. Copyright © 1975 by Teresa Palomo Acosta. Reprinted by permission of the author.   **980** "Koreans Have a Reason Not to Smile" by K. Connie Kang in *The New York Times*, September 8, 1990. Copyright © 1990 by The New York Times Company. Reprinted by permission.   **982** "Ellis Island Doors Reopening, This Time as Haven to Tourists" by Tim Golden in *The New York Times*, September 10, 1990. Copyright © 1990 by The New York Times Company. Reprinted by permission.   **992** Reprinted by permission of The Putnam Publishing Group from *The Joy Luck Club* by Amy Tan. Copyright © 1989 by Amy Tan.   **1010** James Paul Allen and Eugene James Turner, Maps from *We the People: An Atlas of America's Ethnic Diversity*, Macmillan. Reprinted by permission.